Contents

S0-AQM-961

● ● ● ● ● ● ● ● ● ● ● ●

PART **1** THE BIRTH OF CIVILIZATION **2**

•••••••• ••••••

THE HERITAGE OF
WORLD CIVILIZATIONS

Volume One: To 1700

Making of the Modern World
Eleanor Roosevelt College
University of California San Diego

CRAIG • GRAHAM • KAGAN • OZMENT • TURNER

Taken from:

The Heritage of World Civilizations Volume One: To 1700, Seventh Edition
by Albert M. Craig, William A. Graham, Donald Kagan, Steven Ozment, and Frank M. Turner

PEARSON CUSTOM PUBLISHING
75 Arlington Street, Suite 300, Boston, MA 02116
A Pearson Education Company

Brief Contents

Africa: Early History to 1000 C.E. 147

Republican and Imperial Rome 171

China's First Empire 221 B.C.E.–589 C.E. 207

PART 3 CONSOLIDATION AND INTERACTION OF WORLD CIVILIZATIONS 224

Imperial China 589–1368 229

Japan Early History to 1467 257

CHAPTER 10

Iran and India Before Islam 285

CHAPTER 11

The Formation of Islamic Civilization, 622–945 301

CHAPTER 12

The Byzantine Empire and Western Europe to 1000 323

PART **4** THE WORLD IN TRANSITION **432**

CHAPTER **16**

Europe 1500–1650: Expansion, Reformation, and Religious Wars **437**

CHAPTER **17**

Africa ca. 1000–1800 **477**

CHAPTER **21**

The Last Great Islamic Empires 1500–1800 609

Global Perspective: The Last Great Islamic Empires 610

••••••••••••

PART 5 ENLIGHTENMENT AND REVOLUTION IN THE WEST 632

CHAPTER **22**

The Age of European Enlightenment 637

Global Perspective: The European Enlightenment 638

23

Revolutions in the Transatlantic World   665

24

Political Consolidation in Nineteenth-Century Europe and North America, 1815–1880   699

PART **7** GLOBAL CONFLICT AND CHANGE 866

CHAPTER **29**

CHAPTER **30**

CHAPTER **31**

CHAPTER **32**

The West Since World War II **959**

CHAPTER **33**

East Asia: The Recent Decades **993**

CHAPTER **34**

Postcolonialism and Beyond **1023**

Documents

Maps

Preface

The response of the United States to the events of September 11, 2001, including the war in Iraq and Afghanistan have brought upon the world a new awareness of human history in a global context. Prior to the attacks on New York and Washington and the subsequent U.S. intervention in the Middle East, readers in North America generally understood world history and globalism as academic concepts. They now understand them as realities shaping their daily lives and experience. The immediate pressures of the present and of the foreseeable future draw us to seek a more certain and extensive understanding of the past.

The idea of globalization is now a pressing reality on the lives of nations, affecting the domestic security of their citizens, the deployment of armed forces, their standard of living, and the environment. Whether, as Samuel Huntington, the distinguished Harvard political scientist, contends, we are witnessing a clash of civilizations, we have certainly entered a new era in which no active citizen or educated person can escape the necessity of understanding the past in global terms. Both the historical experience and the moral, political, and religious values of the different world civilizations now demand our attention and our understanding. It is our hope that in these new, challenging times *The Heritage of World Civilizations* will provide one path to such knowledge.

The Roots of Globalization

Globalization—that is, the increasing interaction and interdependency of the various regions of the world—has resulted from two major historical developments: the closing of the European era of world history and the rise of technology.

From approximately 1500 C.E. to the middle of the twentieth century, Europeans gradually came to dominate the world through colonization (most particularly in North and South America), state-building, economic productivity, and military power. That era of European dominance ended during the third quarter of the twentieth century after Europe had brought unprecedented destruction on itself during World War II and as the nations of Asia, the Near East, and Africa achieved new positions on the world scene. Their new political independence, their control over strategic natural resources, and the expansion of their economies (especially those of the nations of the Pacific rim of Asia), and in some cases their access to nuclear weapons have changed the shape of world affairs.

Further changing the world political and social situation has been a growing discrepancy in the economic development of different regions that is often portrayed as a problem between the northern and southern hemispheres. Beyond the emergence of this economic disparity has been the remarkable advance of radical political Islamism during the past forty years. In the midst of all these developments, as a result of the political collapse of the former Soviet Union, the United States has emerged as the single major world power.

The second historical development that continues to fuel the pace of globalization is the advance of technology, associated most importantly with transportation, military weapons, and electronic communication. The advances in transportation over the past two centuries including ships, railways, and airplanes have made more parts of the world and its resources accessible to more people in ever shorter spans of time. Over the past century and a half, military weapons of increasingly destructive power enabled Europeans and then later the United States to dominate other regions of the globe. Now, the spread of these weapons means that any nation with sophisticated military technology can threaten other nations, no matter how far away. Furthermore, technologies that originated in the West from the early twentieth century to the present have been turned against the West. More recently, the electronic revolution associated with computer technology and most particularly the internet has sparked unprecedented speed and complexity in global communications. It is astonishing to recall that personal computers have been generally available for less than twenty-five years and the rapid personal communication associated with them has existed for less than fifteen years.

Why not, then, focus only on new factors in the modern world, such as the impact of technology and the end of the European era? To do so would ignore the very deep roots that these developments have in the past. More important, the events of recent years demonstrate, as the authors of this book have long contended, that the major religious traditions continue to shape and drive the modern world as well as the world of the past. The religious traditions link today's civilizations to their most ancient roots. We believe this emphasis on the great religious traditions recognizes not only a factor that has shaped the past, but one that is profoundly and dynamically alive in our world today.

Strengths of the Text

Balanced and Flexible Presentation   In this edition, as in past editions, we have sought to present world history fairly, accurately, and in a way that does justice to its great variety. History has many facets, no one of which can account for the others. Any attempt to tell the story of civilization from a single perspective, no matter how timely, is bound to neglect or suppress some important part of that story.

Historians have recently brought a vast array of new tools and concepts to bear on the study of history. Our coverage introduces students to various aspects of social and intellectual history as well as to the more traditional political, diplomatic, and military coverage. We firmly believe that only through an appreciation of all pathways to understanding of the past can the real heritage of world civilizations be claimed.

The Heritage of World Civilizations, Seventh Edition, is designed to accommodate a variety of approaches to a course in world history, allowing teachers to stress what is most important to them. Some teachers will ask students to read all the chapters. Others will select among them to reinforce assigned readings and lectures.

Clarity and Accessibility Good narrative history requires clear, vigorous prose. Our goal has been to make our presentation fully accessible to students without compromising on vocabulary or conceptual level. We hope this effort will benefit both teachers and students.

Current Scholarship As in previous editions, changes in this edition reflect our determination to incorporate the most recent developments in historical scholarship and the expanding concerns of professional historians. To better highlight the dynamic processes of world history, significant new coverage of the Silk Road, Byzantium, the Crusades, Southeast Asia, women in Islam, nineteenth-century European science, the homefront during World War II, student protest and popular music, and recent events in the Middle East has been added to the Seventh Edition.

Content and Organization

The many changes in content and organization in this edition of *The Heritage of World Civilizations* reflect our ongoing effort to present a truly global survey of world civilizations that at the same time gives a rich picture of the history of individual regions:

◆ **Strengthened Global Approach.** The Seventh Edition more explicitly highlights the connections and parallels in global history among regions of the world. Greater emphasis is now placed on cultural exchange, trade, encounter, and the diffusion of ideas. Each chapter now begins with a "Global Perspective" section that succinctly places in a wider, global framework the regions and topics that are to be discussed. In addition, each of the seven parts opens with a two-page global map that visually depicts the key themes in the chapters that follow.

◆ **Expanded and Improved Map Program.** The entire map program for the Seventh Edition has been completely clarified and expanded. Twenty-one maps are new to the Sev-

enth Edition and graphically illustrate key global developments such as trade in the classical world, the spread of Buddhism, the Islamicization of Southeast Asia, the Columbian exchange, world slavery, European global conflicts in the eighteenth century, global migration, the Holocaust, and the so-called "clash of civilizations." Every single map in the text has been redesigned for greater visual appeal and accuracy. All maps are now referenced in the narrative. A listing of all the maps in the text can be found on p. xxiii–xxiv.

◆ **Improved, Streamlined Organization.** To better accommodate typical teaching sequences, the number of chapters has been reduced to 34, with coverage of European society and state-building in the seventeenth and eighteenth centuries now treated in a single chapter. In addition, coverage of Han China (chapter 7) now immediately succeeds coverage of the Rome (chapter 6) making it easier to draw connections and parallels between these two empires. The final chapter has been exensively reorganized to better examine important recent events in the Middle East.

◆ **New Design and Photo Program.** The entire text has been set in a lively and engaging new design. Each of the 34 chapters includes photos never before included in previous editions of the text and the number of illustrations has been increased. Seven new graphs and tables have also been added to the text to help students visualize important data.

Pedagogical Features

This edition retains many of the pedagogical features of previous editions, while providing increased assessment opportunities.

NEW ◆ **Two-page Global Maps** open each of the seven parts of the book. These provide a visual and geographical overview of the key themes presented in the chapters that follow. Introduction and questions help students make connections across time and space.

◆ **Part Timelines** show chronologically the major events in five regions—Europe, the Near East and India, East Asia, Africa, and the Americas—side by side. Appropriate photographs enrich each timeline.

◆ **Religions of the World** essays examine the historical impact of each of the world's great religious traditions: Judaism, Christianity, Islam, Buddhism, and Hinduism.

◆ **Chapter Outlines** open each chapter and help students access important topics for study and review.

NEW ◆ **Global Perspective Essays** introduce the key problems of each chapter and place them in a global and historical context. Questions prompt student to consider the causes, connections, and consequences of the topics they will encounter in the main narrative.

◆ **Overview Tables** summarize key concepts and reinforce material presented in the main narrative.

◆ **Chronologies** within each chapter help students situate key events in time.

◆ **Documents,** including selections from sacred books, poems, philosophical tracts, political manifestos, letters, and travel accounts, expose students to the raw material of history, providing an intimate contact with peoples of the past. Questions accompanying the source documents direct students toward important, thought-provoking issues and help them relate the documents to the main narrative.

◆ **Key Terms** are boldfaced in the text, listed (with page reference) at the end of each chapter, and defined in the book's glossary.

◆ **Interactive Maps,** usually one per chapter, prompt students to explore the relationship between geography and history in a dynamic fashion.

◆ **Chapter Summaries** conclude each chapter, organized by subtopic, and recap important points.

◆ **Chapter Review Questions** help students interpret the broad themes of each chapter. These questions can be used for class discussion and essay topics.

◆ **Documents CD-ROM,** containing over 200 documents in world history, is bound with all new copies of the text. A list of relevant documents found on the CD-ROM is found at the end of each chapter.

A Note on Dates and Transliteration We have used B.C.E. (before the common era) and C.E. (common era) instead of B.C. (before Christ) and A.D. (anno domini, the year of our Lord) to designate dates.

Until recently, most scholarship on China used the Wade-Giles system of romanization for Chinese names and terms. China, today, however, uses another system known as pinyin. Virtually all Western newspapers have adopted it. In order that students may move easily from the present text to the existing body of advanced scholarship on Chinese history, we now use the pinyin system throughout the text.

Also, we have followed the currently accepted English transliterations of Arabic words. For example, today Koran is being replaced by the more accurate Qur'an; similarly Muhammad is preferable to Mohammed and Muslim to Moslem. We have not tried to distinguish the letters 'ayn and hamza; both are rendered by a simple apostrophe (') as in shi'ite.

With regard to Sanskritic transliteration, we have not distinguished linguals and dentals, and both palatal and lingual s are rendered sh, as in Shiva and Upanishad.

Ancillary Instructional Materials

The Heritage of World Civilizations, Seventh Edition, comes with an extensive package of ancillary materials.

For the Instructor

◆ The *Instructor's Manual/Test-Item File* includes chapter outlines, overviews, key concepts, discussion questions, suggestions for useful audiovisual resources, and approximately 1500 test items (essay, multiple choice, true/false, and matching).

◆ The *Instructor Resource CDROM*, compatible with both Windows and Macintosh environments, provides instructors with such essential teaching tools as hundreds of digitized images and maps for classroom presentations, PowerPoint lectures, and other Instructional material. The assets on the IRCDROM can be easily exported into online courses, such as WebCT and Blackboard.

◆ *Test Manager* is a computerized test management program for Windows and Macintosh environments. The program allows instructors to select items from the test-item file to create tests. It also allows online testing.

◆ The *Transparency Package* provides instructors with full color transparency acetates of all the maps, charts, and graphs in the text for use in the classroom.

For the Student

◆ *History Notes* (Volumes I and II) provides practice tests, essay questions, and map exercise to help reinforce key concepts.

◆ *Documents in World History* (Volumes I and II) is a collection of 200 primary source documents in global history. Questions accompanying the documents can be used for discussion or as writing assignments.

◆ Produced in collaboration with Dorling Kindersley, the world's most respected cartography publisher, *The Prentice Hall Atlas of World History* includes approximately 100 maps fundamental to the study of world history—from early hominids to the twenty-first century.

◆ *Reading Critically About History* is a brief guide to reading effectively that provides students with helpful strategies for reading a history textbook.

◆ *Understanding and Answering Essay Questions* suggest helpful analytical tools for understanding different types of essay questions, and provides precise guidelines for preparing well-carfted essay answers.

◆ Prentice Hall is pleased to provide adopters of *The Heritage of World Civilizations* with an opportunity to receive significant discounts when copies of the text are bundled with Penguin Classics titles in world history. Contact your local Prentice Hall representative for details.

Media Resources

Key ◆ Prentice Hall's New Online Resource **OneKey** lets instructors and students in to the best teaching and learning resources–all in one place. This all-inclusive online resource is designed to help you minimize class preparation and maximize teaching time. Conveniently organized by chapter, OneKey for *The Heritage of World Civilizations*, Seventh Edition, reinforces what students have learned in class and from the text. Among the student resources available for each chapter are: a complete, media-rich e-book version of *The Heritage of World Civilizations* Seventh Edition; quizzes organized by the main subtopics of each chapter; over 200 primary-source documents; and interactive map quizzes.

For instructors, OneKey includes images and maps from *The Heritage of World Civilizations* Seventh Edition; instructional material; hundreds of primary-source documents; and PowerPoint presentations.

◆ *Prentice Hall One Search with Research Navigator: History 2005* This brief guide focuses on developing critical-thinking skills necessary for evaluating and using online sources. It provides a brief introduction to navigating the Internet with specific references to History web sites. It also provides an access code and instruction on using Research Navigator, a powerful research tool that provides access to three exclusive databases of reliable source material: ContentSelect Academic Journal Database, the New York Times Search by Subject Archive, and Link Library.

◆ The *Companion Website*™ (*www.prenhall.com/craig*) works in tandem with the text and features objectives, study questions, web links to related Internet resources, document exercises, interactive maps, and map labelling exercises.

◆ *World History Document CD-ROM* Bound into every new copy of this textbook is a free World History Documents CD-ROM. This is a powerful resource for research and additional reading that contains more than 200 primary source documents central to World History. Each document provides essay questions that are linked directly to a website where short-essay answers can be submitted oline or printed out. A complete list of documents on the CD-ROM is found at the end of the text.

Pearson Prentice Hall is pleased to serve as a sponsor of the **The World History Association Teaching Prize** and **The World History Association and Phi Alpha Theta Student Paper Prize** (undergraduate and graduate divisions). Both of these prizes are awarded annually. For more information, contact *thewha@hawaii.edu*

Acknowledgments

We are grateful to the many scholars and teachers whose thoughtful and often detailed comments helped shape this as well as previous editions of *The Heritage of World Civilizations*. The Advice and guidance provided by Magnus T. Bernhardsson of Williams College in the revision of the coverage of Islam is especially appreciated. We also thank Tianyuan Tan of Harvard University, who helped with conversion of Chinese words to the pinyin system and Gayle K. Brunelle, California State University (Fullerton), who provided invaluable input on strengthening the book's global approach.

Wayne Ackerson, *Salisbury State University*

Jack Martin Balcer, *Ohio State University*

Charmarie J. Blaisdell, *Northeastern University*

Deborah Buffton, *University of Wisconsin at La Crosse*

Loretta Burns, *Mankato State University*

Gayle K. Brunelle, *California State University, Fullerton*

Chun-shu Chang, *University of Michigan, Ann Arbor*

Mark Chavalas, *University of Wisconsin at La Crosse*

Anthony Cheeseboro, *Southern Illinois University at Edwardsville*

William J. Courteney, *University of Wisconsin*

Samuel Willard Crompton, *Holyoke Community College*

James B. Crowley, *Yale University*

Bruce Cummings, *The University of Chicago*

Stephen F. Dale, *Ohio State University, Columbus*

Clarence B. Davis, *Marian College*

Raymond Van Dam, *University of Michigan, Ann Arbor*

Bill Donovan, *Loyola University of Maryland*

Wayne Farris, *University of Tennessee*

Anita Fisher, *Clark College*

Suzanne Gay, *Oberlin College*

Katrina A. Glass, *United States Military Academy*

Robert Gerlich, *Loyola University*

Samuel Robert Goldberger, *Capital Community-Technical College*

Andrew Gow, *University of Alberta*

Katheryn L. Green, *University of Wisconsin, Madison*

David Griffiths, *University of North Carolina, Chapel Hill*

Louis Haas, *Duquesne University*

Joseph T. Hapak, *Moraine Valley Community College*

Hue-Tam Ho Tai, *Harvard University*

David Kieft, *University of Minnesota*

Frederick Krome, *Northern Kentucky University*

Lisa M. Lane, *Mira Costa College*

Richard Law, *Washington State University*

David Lelyveld, *Columbia University*

Jan Lewis, *Rutgers University, Newark*

James C. Livingston, *College of William and Mary*

Richard L. Moore Jr., *St. Augustine's College*

Beth Nachison, *Southern Connecticut State University*

Robin S. Oggins, *Binghamton University*

Louis A. Perez Jr., *University of South Florida*

Jonathan Perry, *University of Central Florida*

Cora Ann Presley, *Tulane University*

Norman Raiford, *Greenville Technical College*

Norman Ravitch, *University of California, Riverside*

Thomas M. Ricks, *University of Pennsylvania*

Philip F. Riley, *James Madison University*

Thomas Robisheaux, *Duke University*

William S. Rodner, *Tidewater Community College*

David Ruffley, *United States Air Force Academy*

Dankwart A. Rustow, *The City University of New York*

James J. Sack, *University of Illinois at Chicago*

William Schell, *Murray State University*

Marvin Slind, *Washington State University*

Daniel Scavone, *University of Southern Indiana*

Roger Schlesinger, *Washington State University*

Charles C. Stewart, *University of Illinois*

Nancy L. Stockdale, *University of Central Florida*

Carson Tavenner, *United States Air Force Academy*

Truong-buu Lam, *University of Hawaii*

Harry L. Watson, *Loyola College of Maryland*

William B. Whisenhunt, *College of DuPage*

Paul Varley, *Columbia University*

Finally, we would like to thank the dedicated people who helped produce this revision: our acquisitions editor, Charles Cavaliere; our development editor, Barbara Muller; Laura Gardner who created the handsome new design for this edition; Kathleen Sleys, our production editor; and Ben Smith our manufacturing buyer.

A.M.C.
W.A.G.
D.K.
S.O.
F.M.T.

About the Authors

Albert M. Craig is the Harvard-Yenching Research Professor of History at Harvard University, where he has taught since 1959. A graduate of Northwestern University, he took his Ph.D. at Harvard University. He has studied at Strasbourg University and at Kyoto, Keio, and Tokyo universities in Japan. He is the author of *Choshu in the Meiji Restoration* (1961), *The Heritage of Chinese Civilization* (2001), and, with others, of *East Asia, Tradition and Transformation* (1989). He is the editor of *Japan, A Comparative View* (1973) and co-editor of *Personality in Japanese History* (1970). At present he is engaged in research on the thought of Fukuzawa Yukichi. For eleven years (1976–1987) he was the director of the Harvard-Yenching Institute. He has also been a visiting professor at Kyoto and Tokyo Universities. He has received Guggenheim, Fulbright, and Japan Foundation Fellowships. In 1988 he was awarded the Order of the Rising Sun by the Japanese government.

William A. Graham is Albertson Professor of Middle Eastern Studies and Professor of the History of Religion at Harvard University, and Master of Currier House at Harvard University. From 1990–1996 he directed Harvard's Center for Middle Eastern Studies. He has taught for twenty-six years at Harvard, where he received the A.M. and Ph.D. degrees. He also studied in Göttingen, Tübingen, and Lebanon. He is the author of *Divine World and Prophetic World in Early Islam* (1977), awarded the American Council of Learned Societies History of Religions book prize in 1978, and of *Beyond the Written Word: Oral Aspects of Scripture in the History of Religion* (1987). He has published a variety of articles in both Islamic studies and the general history of religion and is one of the editors of the *Encyclopedia of the Qur'an.* He serves currently on the editorial board of several journals and has held John Simon Guggenheim and Alexander von Humboldt research fellowships. *Three Faiths, One God*, co-authored with Jacob Neusner and Bruce Chilton, published in January 2003.

Donald Kagan is Sterling Professor of History and Classics at Yale University, where he has taught since 1969. He received the A.B. degree in history from Brooklyn College, the M.A. in classics from Brown University, and the Ph.D. in history from Ohio State University. During 1958–1959 he studied at the American School of Classical Studies as a Fulbright Scholar. He has received three awards for undergraduate teaching at Cornell and Yale. He is the author of a history of Greek political thought, *The Great Dialogue* (1965); a four-volume history of the Peloponnesian war, *The Origins of the Peloponnesian War* (1969); *The Archidamian War* (1974); *The Peace of Nicias and the Sicilian Expedition* (1981); *The Fall of the Athenian Empire* (1987); and a biography of Pericles, *Pericles of Athens and the Birth of Democracy* (1991); *On the Origins of War* (1995), and *The Peloponnesian War* (2003). He is coauthor, with Frederick W. Kagan of *While America Sleeps* (2000). With Brian Tierney and L. Pearce Williams, he is the editor of *Great Issues in Western Civilization*, a collection of readings. He was awarded the National Humanities Medal for 2002.

Steven Ozment is McLean Professor of Ancient and Modern History at Harvard University. He has taught Western Civilization at Yale, Stanford, and Harvard. He is the author of eleven books. *The Age of Reform, 1250–1550* (1980) won the Schaff Prize and was nominated for the 1981 National Book Award. Five of his books have been selections of the History Book Club: *Magdalena and Balthasar: An Intimate Portrait of Life in Sixteenth Century Europe* (1986), *Three Behaim Boys: Growing Up in Early Modern Germany* (1990), *Protestants: The Birth of A Revolution* (1992), *The Burgermeister's Daughter: Scandal in a Sixteenth Century German Town* (1996), and *Flesh and Spirit: Private Life in Early Modern Germany* (1999). His most recent publications are *Ancestors: The Loving Family of Old Europe* (2001), *A Mighty Fortress: A New History of the German People* (2004), and "Why We Study Western Civ," *The Public Interest* 158 (2005).

Steven Ozment is McLean Professor of Ancient and Modern History at Harvard University. He has taught Western Civilization at Yale, Stanford, and Harvard. He is the author of nine books. *The Age of Reform, 1250–1550* (1980) won the Schaff Prize and was nominated for the 1981 National Book Award. Five of his books have been selections of the History Book Club: *Magdalena and Balthasar: An Intimate Portrait of Life in Sixteenth Century Europe* (1986), *Three Behaim Boys: Growing Up in Early Modern Germany* (1990), *Protestants: The Birth of A Revolution* (1992), *The Burgermeister's Daughter: Scandal in a Sixteenth Century German Town* (1996), and *Flesh and Spirit: Private Life in Early Modern Germany* (1999). His most recent book is *Ancestors: The Loving Family of Old Europe* (2001). A history of Germany, *A Mighty Fortress: A New History of the German People*, published in January 2004.

Frank M. Turner is John Hay Whitney Professor of History at Yale University and Director of the Beinecke Rare Book and Manuscript Library at Yale University, where he served as University Provost from 1988 to 1992. He received his B.A. degree at the College of William and Mary and his Ph.D. from Yale. He has received the Yale College Award for Distinguished Undergraduate Teaching. He has directed a National Endowment for the Humanities Summer Institute. His scholarly research has received the support of fellowships from the National Endowment for the Humanities and the Guggenheim Foundation and the Woodrow Wilson Center. He is the author of *Between Science and Religion: The Reaction to Scientific Naturalism in Late Victorian England* (1974), *The Greek Heritage in Victorian Britain* (1981), which received the British Council Prize of the Conference on British Studies and the Yale Press Governors Award, *Contesting Cultural Authority: Essays in Victorian Intellectual Life* (1993), and *John Henry Newman: The Challenge to Evangelical Religion* (2002). He has also contributed numerous articles to journals and has served on the editorial advisory boards of *The Journal of Modern History, Isis,* and *Victorian Studies.* He edited *The Idea of a University*, by John Henry Newman (1996) and *Reflections on the Revolution in France* by Edmund Burke (2003). Since 1996 he has served as a Trustee of Connecticut College. In 2003, Professor Turner was appointed Director of the Beinecke Rare Book and Manuscript Library at Yale University..

THE HERITAGE OF
WORLD CIVILIZATIONS

Homo sapiens—modern humans—first appeared about one hundred thousand years ago. Since then the pace of human control over the environment has constantly accelerated. It took us tens of thousands of years to domesticate animals and to master the rudiments of agriculture. It took us another seven thousand years to nine thousand years to develop cites, systems of writing, then bronze and iron. Several hundred years later the great religious and philosophical revolutions of the ancient world occurred, followed by the empires of China, Iran, and Rome.

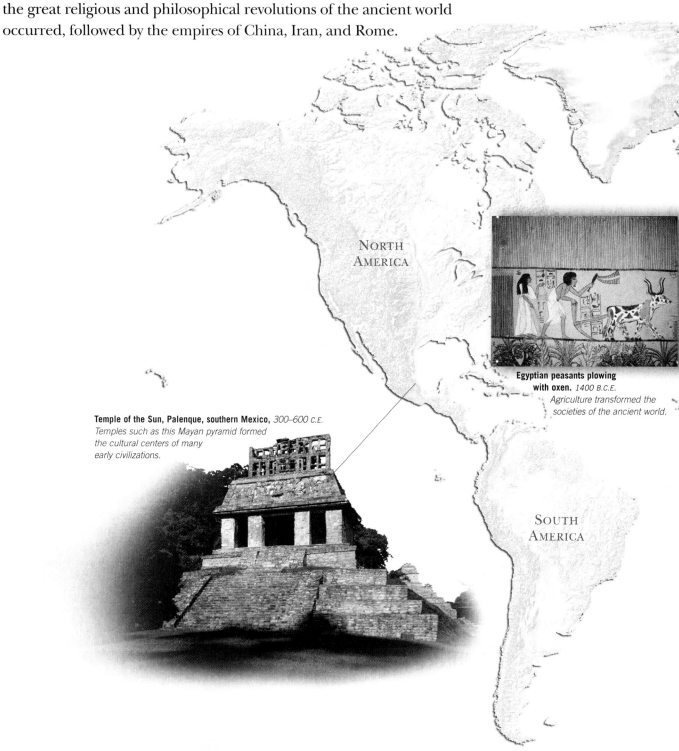

NORTH
AMERICA

Egyptian peasants plowing with oxen. *1400 B.C.E. Agriculture transformed the societies of the ancient world.*

Temple of the Sun, Palenque, southern Mexico, *300–600 C.E. Temples such as this Mayan pyramid formed the cultural centers of many early civilizations.*

SOUTH
AMERICA

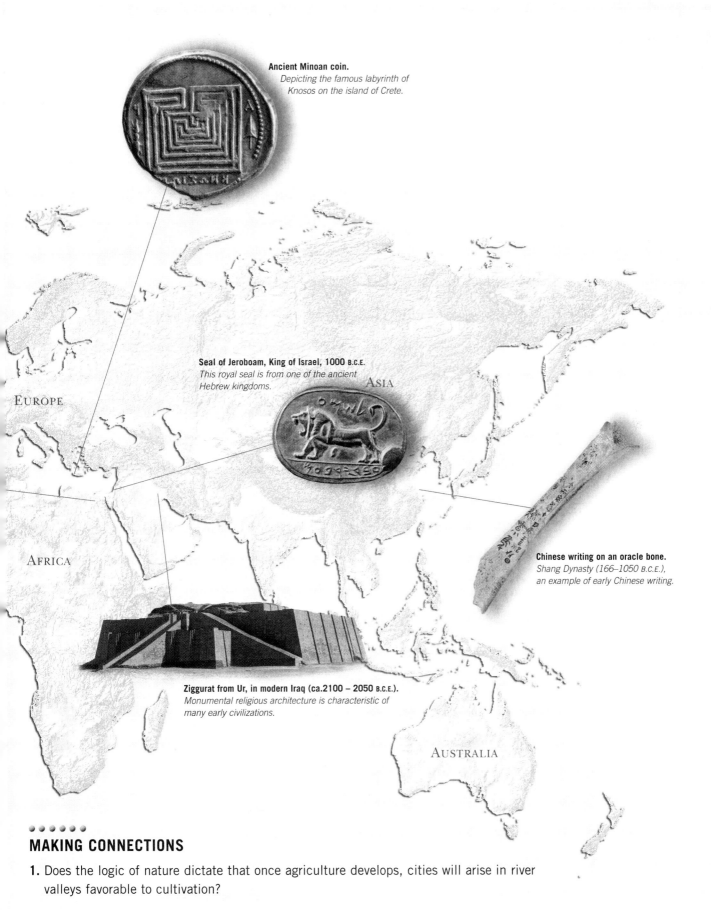

Ancient Minoan coin.
Depicting the famous labyrinth of Knosos on the island of Crete.

Seal of Jeroboam, King of Israel, 1000 B.C.E.
This royal seal is from one of the ancient Hebrew kingdoms.

EUROPE

ASIA

AFRICA

Chinese writing on an oracle bone.
Shang Dynasty (166–1050 B.C.E.), an example of early Chinese writing.

Ziggurat from Ur, in modern Iraq (ca.2100 – 2050 B.C.E.).
Monumental religious architecture is characteristic of many early civilizations.

AUSTRALIA

MAKING CONNECTIONS

1. Does the logic of nature dictate that once agriculture develops, cities will arise in river valleys favorable to cultivation?

2. Is it conceivable that contacts between early civilizations were more numerous than we now imagine?

THE COMING OF CIVILIZATION

EUROPE

The victory stele ▶
of Naram-Sin
c.a. 2230 b.c.e.

◀ Paleolithic sculpture

NEAR EAST/ INDIA

ca. 8000   Neolithic Revolution, Mesopotamia

ca. 3500	Development of Sumerian Cities
ca. 3000	Development of Writing in Mesopotamia
ca. 2800–2370	Early Dynastic period of Sumerian city–states
ca. 2370	Sargon establishes Akkadian dynasty and empire
ca. 2250–1750	Indus(Harappan) civilization; writing first appears in India
ca. 2125–2027	Third dynasty of Ur
ca. 2000–1800	Establishment of Amorites in Mesopotamia
ca. 1800–1500	Aryan peoples invade northwestern India
ca. 1792–1750	Reign of Hammurabi
ca. 1550	Establishment of Kassite dynasty at Babylon

▲ Burial Urn from China, Neolithic period

EAST ASIA

2205–1766	Traditional dates of Xia dynasty
1766	Bronze Age city–states, aristocratic charioteers, pictographic writing
1766–1050	Traditional dates of Shang dynasty; writing first appears in China

4000 B.C.E.   Neolithic Revolution

Ceremonial food vessel, ▶
Shang dynasty

AFRICA

3100–2700	Early Dynastic period (I–II), Egypt
ca. 3000	Writing first appears in Egypt
2700–2200	Old Kingdom (III–VI)
2200–2025	First Intermediate period (VII–XI)
2025–1630	Middle Kingdom (XII–XIII)
1630–1550	Second Intermediate period (XIV–XVII)
1550–1075	New Kindom (XVIII–XX)

Neolithic statues from ▶
Ain Ghazal, Jordan

Seated Egyptian scribe ▶
from the Fifth Dynasty

THE AMERICAS

ca. 4000   Neolithic revolution in Mexico

ca. 2750   Monumental architecture at Aspero

624–545	Thales of Miletus
ca. 611–546	Anaximander
ca. 546	Anaximenes

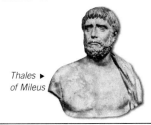

Thales ▶
of Mileus

469–399	Socrates
429–347	Plato
384–322	Aristotle
435–404	Great Peloponnesian War
ca. 460–400	Thucydides
ca. 400	Hippocrates of Cos
384–322	Demosthenes

▲ Poseidon, Athena, Apollo
and Artemis,
5th century b.c.e.

1500–1000	Rig-Vedic period, India
1400–1200	Hittite Empire
ca. 1100	Rise of Assyrian Power

ca. 1000–961	Reign of King David
ca. 961–922	Reign of King Solomon
ca. 1000–500	Late Vedic period, India
ca. 1000–800/600	Composition of Brahmanas
ca. 800–500	Composition of major Upanishads
ca. 700–500	Probable reintroduction of writing
732–722	Assyrian conquest of Syria-Palestine
722	Assyrian conquest of Israel (Northern Kingdom)
612	Destruction of Assyrian capital at Nineveh
612–539	Neo-Babylonian (Chaldean) Empire
586	Destruction of Jerusalem fall of Judah (southern kingdom); Babylonian captivity
539	Restoration of Temple; return of exiles
540–ca. 468	Mahavira, the Jina/Vardamana
ca. 566–ca. 486	Siddhartha Gautama, the Buddha

| ca. 400 B.C.E.–200 C.E. | Composition of great epics, the *Mahabharata* and *Ramayana* |

Indus stone ▶
stamp seal

◀ Ishtar Gate
in Babylon

| 1150–256 | Traditional dates of Zhou dynasty |

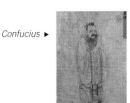

Confucius ▶

500	Age of philosophers
370–290	Mencius
Fourth century	Laozi
221	China is unified under the Qin

Laozi ▶

| 771 | Iron Age territorial states |
| 551–479 | Confucius |

| 671 | Assyrian conquest of Egypt |

◀ Babylonian map
of the world,
612–539 b.c.e.

| 1500–400 | The Olmec |

| 800 B.C.E.–200 C.E. | Chavin (Early) Horizon |

| 200 B.C.E.–750 C.E. | The Classic period in central Mexico |
| 150 B.C.E.–900 C.E. | The Classic period of Mayan civilization in the Yucatán and Guatemala |

◀ Olmec head

Aztec calendar ▶

The Birth of Civilization

- Early Humans and Their Culture

- Early Civilizations to About 1000 B.C.E.

- Ancient Near Eastern Empires

- Early Indian Civilization

- Early Chinese Civilization

- The Rise of Civilization in the Americas

◄ The city of Ur was the capital of a south Mesopotamian empire toward the end of the third millenium. The Royal Standard of Ur, from the Royal Graves, depicts the Sumerian ruler at war and in peacetime. The panels are crafted in lapis lazuli and shell from as far away as Afghanistan.
The British Museum.

GLOBAL PERSPECTIVE

Civilizations

The way of life of prehistoric cave dwellers differed immensely from that of today's civilized world. Yet the few millennia in which we have been civilized are but a tiny fraction of the long span of human existence. Especially during the recent millennia, changes in our culture/way of life have far outpaced changes in our bodies. We retain the emotional makeup and motor reflexes of prehistoric men and women while living highly organized and often sedentary lives.

We might best view the early civilizations by asking how they fit into the sweep of history. One notable feature of human history is the acceleration in the pace of change. From the time that modern humans first appeared 100,000 years ago until 7000 B.C.E., few changes occurred. Humans migrated from Africa to other parts of the world and adapted to new climes. All lived by hunting, fishing, and gathering. The chief advance in technology during this longest span of human existence was from rough to smooth stone weapons and tools.

Then, from about 7000 B.C.E., innovations began. Humans learned to till the soil, domesticate animals, and make pots for the storage of food. A few millennia later, bronze was discovered and the so-called river valley civilizations formed along the Nile, the Tigris-Euphrates, the Indus, and the Yellow River. Cities rose. Writing was invented. Societies divided into classes or castes: most members engaged in farming, a few traded, and others assumed military, priestly, or governmental roles. As these civilizations expanded, they became richer, more populous, and more powerful.

The last millennium B.C.E. witnessed two major developments. One was the emergence, during 600-300 B.C.E., of the religious and philosophical revolutions that would indelibly mark their respective civilizations: monotheistic Judaism from which would later develop the world religions of Christianity and Islam; Hinduism and Buddhism in southern Asia; the philosophies of Greece and China. The second development was the rise of the iron-age empires—the Roman, the Mauryan along the Ganges, the Han in China—during the centuries straddling the end of the millennium.

After the fall of these early empires, swift changes occurred. For a millenium, Europe and Byzantium fell behind, while China and the Middle East led in technology and the arts of government. But by 1500 Europe had cought up, and after 1700, it led. India had invented Arabic numerals and Arab

thinkers inspired the Renaissance, but it was Europe that produced Copernicus and Newton.

The nineteenth century saw the invention of the steam engine, the steamship, the locomotive, the telegraph and telephone, and the automobile. After that came electric lights, the radio, and, in the century that followed, the airplane.

In the twentieth century, invention and scientific discovery became institutionalized in university, corporate, and government laboratories. Ever larger amounts of resources were committed to research. By the beginning of the twenty-first century man had walked on the moon, deciphered the human genome, and unlocked the power of the atom. Today, as discoveries occur ever more rapidly, we cannot imagine the science of a hundred years into the future.

If this process of accelerating change had its origins in 7000 B.C.E., what was the original impetus? Does the logic of nature dictate that once agriculture develops, cities will rise in alluvial valleys favorable to cultivation? Was it inevitable that the firing of clay to produce pots would produce metals from metallic oxides and lead to the discovery of smelting? Did the formation of aristocratic and priestly classes automatically lead to record keeping and writing? If so, it is not at all surprising that parallel and independent developments should have occurred in regions as widely separated as China and the Middle East.

Or was the almost simultaneous rise of the ancient Eurasian civilizations the result of diffusion? Did migrating peoples carry seeds, new tools, and metals over long distances? The available evidence provides no definitive answer. Understanding the origins of the early civilizations and the lives of the men and women who lived in them from what is left of their material culture is like reconstructing a dinosaur from a broken tooth and a fragment of jawbone.

THINK AHEAD

◆ Are our prehistoric bodies fit for today's civilization?
◆ What were the processes behind the creation of early civilizations?
◆ How do early civilizations fit in with the sweep of history?

SCIENTISTS ESTIMATE THAT THE EARTH MAY BE AS many as six billion years old and that the first humanlike creatures appeared in Africa perhaps 3 to 5 million years ago. Some 1 to 2 million years ago, erect and tool-using early humans spread over much of Africa, Europe, and Asia. Our own species, *Homo sapiens*, probably emerged some 200,000 years ago, and the earliest remains of fully modern humans date to about 100,000 years ago.

The earliest humans lived by hunting, fishing, and collecting wild plants. Only some 10,000 years ago did they learn to cultivate plants, herd animals, and make airtight pottery for storage. These discoveries transformed them from gatherers to producers and allowed ▨ and to lead a settled life. Beginning a▨ far more complex way of life began to app▨ the world. In these places humans learned ▨ harvests through irrigation and other meth▨ possible much larger populations. They came t▨ towns, cities, and other centers, where they erected imp▨ structures and where industry and commerce flourish▨ They developed writing, enabling them to keep inventories o▨ food and other resources. Specialized occupations emerged, complex religions took form, and social divisions increased. These changes marked the birth of civilization.

Early Humans and their Culture

Humans, unlike other animals, are cultural beings. **Culture is the sum total of the ways of living built up by a group and passed on from one generation to another.** Culture includes behavior such as courtship or child-rearing practices; material things such as tools, clothing, and shelter; and ideas, institutions, and beliefs. Language, apparently a uniquely human trait, lies behind our ability to create ideas and institutions and to transmit culture from one generation to another. Our flexible and dexterous hands enable us to hold and make tools and so to create the material artifacts of culture. Because culture is learned and not inherited, it permits rapid adaptation to changing conditions, making possible the spread of humanity to almost all the lands of the globe.

THE PALEOLITHIC AGE

Anthropologists designate early human cultures by their tools. The earliest period—the **Paleolithic Age** (from the Greek, "old stone")—dates from the earliest use of stone tools some 1 million years ago to about 10,000 B.C.E. During this immensely long period, people were hunters, fishers, and gatherers, but not producers, of food. They learned to make and use increasingly sophisticated tools of stone and perishable materials like wood; they learned to make and control fire; and they acquired language and the ability to use it to pass on what they had learned.

These early humans, dependent on nature for food and vulnerable to wild beasts and natural disasters, may have developed responses to the world rooted in fear of the unknown—of the uncertainties of human life or the overpowering forces of nature. Religious and magical beliefs and practices may have emerged in an effort to propitiate or coerce the superhuman forces thought to animate or direct the natural world.

Evidence of religious faith and practice, as well as of magic, goes as far back as archaeology can take us. Fear or awe, exultation, gratitude, and empathy with the natural world must all have figured in the cave art and in the ritual practices, such as burial, that we find evidenced at Paleolithic sites around the globe. The sense that there is more to the world than meets

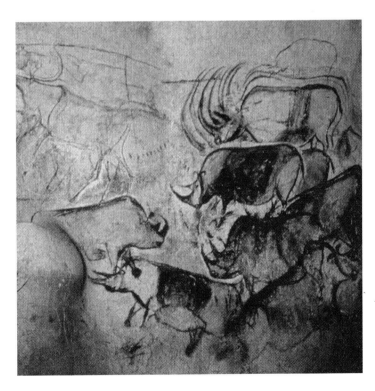

⋀ **Paleolithic Cave Drawings.** Approximately 30,000 years ago, in a Chauvet cave, near Avignon, France, Paleolithic artists decorated the walls with exquisite drawings of animals.
Jean Clottes/Corbis Sygma Photo News.

response to the
...nd.

...likely relatively
...ursuing game,
...of the Bering
...he American
...imately sepa-
...man groups
...ir isolation,
...ericas expe-
...to those of ...

riencea cuitures
Eurasia and Africa.

The style of life and the level of technology of the Paleolithic period could support only a sparsely settled society. If hunters were too numerous, game would not suffice. In Paleolithic times people were subject to the same natural and ecological constraints that today mantain a balance between wolves and deer in Alaska.

Paleolithic society, was probably characterized by a division of labor by sex. Men most likely hunted, fished, and fought other families, clans, and tribes. Women, less mobile because of childbearing, most likely gathered nuts, berries, and wild grains, wove baskets, and made clothing. Women gathering food probably discovered how to plant and care for seeds, knowledge that eventually led to agriculture and the Neolithic revolution.

THE NEOLITHIC AGE

Only a few Paleolithic societies made the initial shift from hunting and gathering to agriculture. Anthropologists and archaeologists disagree as to why, but however it happened, some 10,000 years ago parts of what we now call the Near East began to change from a nomadic hunter-gatherer culture to a more settled agricultural one. Because the shift to agriculture coincided with advances in stone tool technology—the development of greater precision, for example, in chipping and grinding—this period is called the Neolithic Age (from the Greek, "new stone"). Productive animals, such as sheep and goats, and food crops, such as wheat and barley, were first domesticated in the mountain foothills where they already lived or grew in the wild. Once they had domesticated these plants and animals, people could move to areas where these plants and animals did not occur naturally, such as the river valleys of the region. The invention of pottery during the Neolithic Age enabled people to store surplus foods and liquids and to transport them, as well as to cook agricultural products that were difficult to eat or digest raw. They made cloth from flax and wool. Crops required constant care from planting to harvest, so Neolithic farmers built permanent dwellings. The earliest of these tended to be circular huts, large enough to house only one or two people and clus-

This famous statuette found near Willendorf, Austria, in 1908, may be 25,000 years old. It is only 4 and one-half inches tall.
Erich Lessing/Art Resource.

tered in groups around a central storage place. Later people built square and rectangular family-sized houses with individual storage places and enclosures to house livestock. Houses in a Neolithic village were normally all the same size and were built on the same plan, suggesting that most Neolithic villagers had about the same level of wealth and social status. A few items, such as stones and shells, were traded long distance, but Neolithic villages tended to be self-sufficient.

Two larger Neolithic settlements do not fit this village pattern. One was found at Çatal Hüyük, in a fertile agricultural region about 150 miles south of Ankara, the capital of present-day Turkey. This was a large town covering over fifteen acres, with a population probably well over six thousand people. The houses were clustered so closely that they had no doors but were entered by ladders from the roofs. Many were decorated inside with sculptures of animal heads and horns, as well as paintings that were apparently redone regularly. Some appear to depict ritual or festive occasions involving men and women. One is the world's oldest landscape picture, showing a nearby volcano exploding. The agriculture, arts, and crafts of this town were astonishingly diversified and at a much higher level of attainment than in other, smaller settlements of the period. The site of Jericho, an oasis around a spring near the Dead Sea, was occupied as early as 12,000 B.C.E. Around 8000 B.C.E. a town of eight to ten acres grew up, surrounded by a massive stone wall with at least one tower against the inner face. Although this wall may have been for defense, scholars dispute its use because no other Neolithic settlement has been found with fortifications. The inhabitants of Neolithic Jericho had a mixed agricultural, herding, and hunting economy and may have traded salt. They had no pottery but plastered the skulls of their dead to make realistic memorial portraits of them. These two sites show that the economy and the settlement patterns of the Neolithic period may be more complicated than many scholars have thought.

Throughout the Paleolithic Age, the human population had been small and relatively stable. The shift from food gathering to food production may not have been associated with an immediate change in population, but over time in the regions where agriculture and animal husbandry appeared, the number of human beings grew at an unprecedented rate. One reason for this is that farmers usually had larger families than hunters. Their children began to work and matured at a younger age than the children of hunters. When animals and plants were

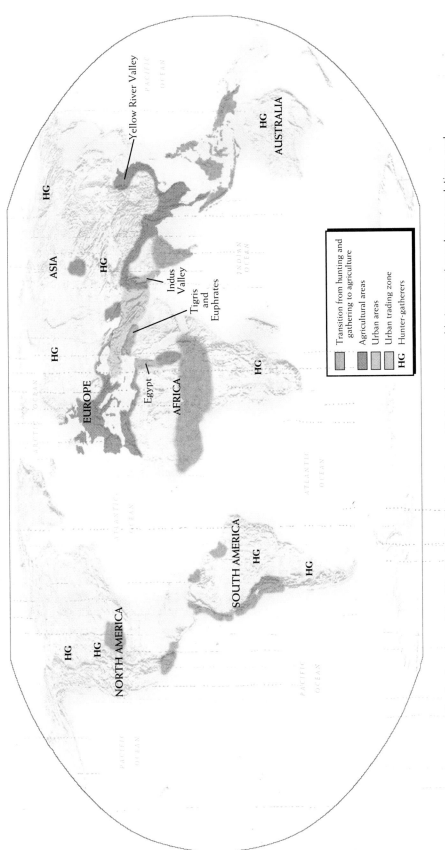

MAP 1–1 The World in 5000 B.C.E. The fertile valleys of the Nile, Tigris, Euphrates, Indus, and Yellow rivers were able to support very large populations, and it was here that the great urban civilization of the ancient world emerged.

domesticated and brought to the river valleys, the relationship between human beings and nature was changed forever. People had learned to control nature, a vital prerequisite for the emergence of civilization. But farmers had to work harder and longer than hunters did, and they had to stay in one place. Herders, on the other hand, often moved from place to place in search of pasture and water, returning to their villages in the spring. Some scholars refer to the dramatic changes in subsistence, settlement, technology, and population of this time as the **Neolithic Revolution**. The earliest Neolithic societies appeared in the Middle East about 8000 B.C.E., in China about 4000 B.C.E., and in India about 3600 B.C.E. Neolithic agriculture was based on wheat and barley in the Middle East, on millet and rice in China, and on corn in Mesoamerica, several millennia later.

THE BRONZE AGE AND THE BIRTH OF CIVILIZATION

Neolithic agricultural villages and herding cultures gradually replaced Paleolithic culture in much of the world. Then another major shift occurred, first in the plains along the Tigris and Euphrates Rivers in the region the Greeks and Romans called **Mesopotamia** (modern Iraq), later in the valley of the Nile River in Egypt, and somewhat later in India and the Yellow River basin in China. This shift was initially associated with the growth of towns alongside villages, creating a hierarchy of larger and smaller settlements in the same region. Some towns then grew into much larger urban centers and often drew populations into them, so that nearby villages and towns declined. The urban centers, or cities, usually had monumental buildings, such as temples and fortifications. These were vastly larger than individual houses and could be built only by the sustained effort of hundreds and even thousands of people over many years. Elaborate representational artwork appeared, sometimes made of rare and imported materials. New technologies, such as smelting and the manufacture of metal tools and weapons, were characteristic of urban life. Commodities like pottery and textiles that had been made in individual houses in villages were mass produced in cities, which also were characterized by social stratification—that is, different classes of people based on factors such as control of resources, family, religious or political authority, and personal wealth. The earliest writing is also associated with the growth of cities. Writing, like representational art, was a powerful means of communicating over space and time and was probably invented to deal with urban problems of management and record keeping. These attributes—urbanism; technological, industrial, and social

◀ **Neolithic Clay Statues.** At Ain Ghazal, a Neolithic site in Jordan, several pits contained male and female statues made of clay modeled over a reed framework. Similar figures have been found at Jericho and other sites, all from the same period, ca. 8500–7000 B.C.E. They were probably used in religious rituals, perhaps connected with ancestor worship, as were plastered skulls, masks, carved heads, and other artifacts. Archeological Museum, Amman, Jordan/Art Resource. © Photograph by Erich Lessing.

change; long-distance trade; and new methods of symbolic communication—are defining characteristics of the form of human culture called **civilization**. At about the time the earliest civilizations were emerging, someone discovered how to combine tin and copper to make a stronger and more useful material— bronze. Archaeologists coined the term **Bronze Age** to refer to the period 3100–1200 B.C.E. in the Near East and eastern Mediterranean.

Early Civilizations to About 1000 B.C.E.

By 4000 B.C.E., people had settled in large numbers in the river-watered lowlands of Mesopotamia and Egypt. By about 3000 B.C.E., when the invention of writing gave birth to history, urban life and the organization of society into centralized states were well established in the valleys of the Tigris and Euphrates Rivers in Mesopotamia and the Nile River in Egypt.

Much of the urban population consists of people who do not grow their own food, so urban life is possible only where farmers and stockbreeders can be made to produce a substantial surplus beyond their own needs. Also, some process has to be in place so that this surplus can be collected and redeployed to sustain city dwellers. Moreover, efficient farming of plains alongside rivers requires intelligent management of water resources for irrigation. In Mesopotamia, irrigation was essential, because in the south (Babylonia), rainfall was insufficient to sustain crops. Furthermore, the rivers, fed by melting snows in Armenia, rose to flood the fields in the spring, about the time for harvest, when water was not needed. When water was needed for the autumn planting, less was available. This meant that people had to build dikes to keep the rivers from flooding the fields in the spring and had to devise means to store water for use in the autumn. The Mesopotamians became skilled at that activity early on. In Egypt, on the other hand, the Nile River flooded at the right moment for cultivation, so irrigation was simply a matter of directing the water to the fields. In Mesopotamia, villages, towns, and cities tended to be strung along natural watercourses and, eventually, man-made canal systems. Thus, control of water could be important in warfare; an enemy could cut off water upstream of a city to force it to submit. Because the Mesopotamian plain was flat, branches of the rivers often changed their courses, and people would have to abandon their cities and move to new locations. Archaeologists once believed that urban life and centralized government arose in response to the need to regulate irrigation. This theory supposed that only a strong central authority could construct and maintain the necessary waterworks. More recently, archaeologists have shown that large-scale irrigation appeared only long after urban civilization had already developed, so major waterworks were a consequence of urbanism, not a cause of it.

MESOPOTAMIAN CIVILIZATION

The first civilization appears to have arisen in Mesopotamia. The region is divided into two ecological zones, roughly north and south of modern Baghdad. In the south (Babylonia), as noted,

irrigation is vital; in the north (Assyria), agriculture is possible with rainfall and wells. The south has high yields from irrigated lands, while the north has lower yields, but much more land under cultivation, so it can produce more than the south. The oldest Mesopotamian cities seem to have been founded by a people called the Sumerians during the fourth millennium B.C.E., in the land of Sumer, which is the southern half of Babylonia. By 3000 B.C.E., the Sumerian city of Uruk was the largest city in the world (see Map 1–2). Colonies of people from Uruk built cities and outposts in northern Syria and southern Anatolia. One of these, at Habubah Kabirah on the Euphrates River in Syria, was built on a regular plain on virgin ground, with strong defensive walls, but was abandoned after a few generations and never inhabited again. No one knows how the Sumerians were able to establish colonies so far from their homeland or even what their purpose was. They may have been trading centers.

From about 2800 to 2370 B.C.E., in what is called the Early Dynastic period, several Sumerian city-states existed in southern Mesopotamia, arranged in north–south lines along the major

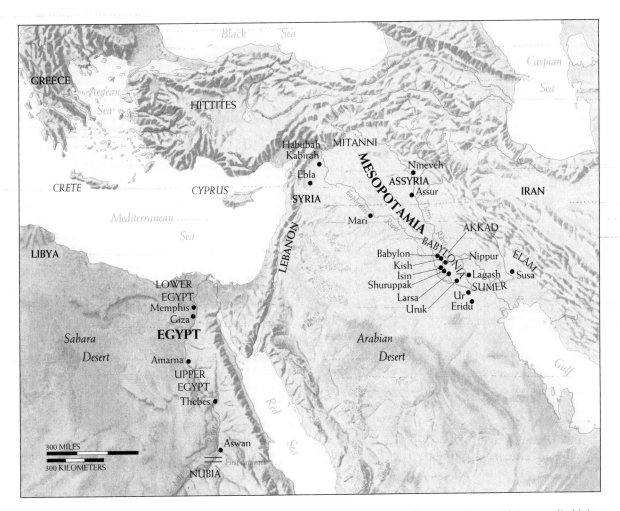

MAP 1–2 The Ancient Near East.   Two river valley civilizations thrived in the Ancient Near East: Egypt, which was united into a single state, and Mesopotamia, which was long divided into a number of city-states.

watercourses. Among these cities were Uruk, Ur, Nippur, Shuruppak, and Lagash. Some of the city-states formed leagues among themselves that apparently had both political and religious significance. Quarrels over water and agricultural land led to incessant warfare, and in time, stronger towns and leagues conquered weaker ones and expanded to form kingdoms ruling several city-states.

Unlike the Sumerians, the people who occupied northern Mesopotamia and Syria spoke mostly Semitic languages (that is, languages in the same family as Arabic and Hebrew). The Sumerian language is not related to any language known today. Many of these Semitic peoples absorbed aspects of Sumerian culture, especially writing. At the western end of this broad territory, at Ebla in northern Syria, scribes kept records using Sumerian writing and studied Sumerian word lists. In northern Babylonia, the Mesopotamians believed that the large city of Kish had history's first kings. In the far east of this territory, not far from modern Baghdad, a people known as the Akkadians established their own kingdom at a capital city called Akkade, under their first king, Sargon, who had been a servant of the king of Kish.

The Akkadians conquered all the Sumerian city-states and invaded southwestern Iran and northern Syria. This was history's first empire, having a heartland, provinces, and an absolute ruler. It included numerous peoples, cities, languages, and cultures, as well as different ecological zones, under one rule. Sargon's name became legendary as the first great conqueror of history. His grandson, Naram-Sin, ruled from the Persian Gulf to the Mediterranean Sea, with a standardized administration, vast wealth and power, and a grand style that to later Mesopotamians was a high point of their history. Naram-Sin even declared himself a god and had temples built to himself, something no Sumerian ruler had ever done. External attack and internal weakness destroyed the Akkadian Empire, but several smaller states flourished independently, notably Lagash in Sumer, under its ruler Gudea.

About 2125 B.C.E. the Sumerian city of Ur rose to dominance, and the rulers of the Third Dynasty of Ur established an empire built on the foundation of the Akkadian Empire, but far smaller. In this period, Sumerian culture and literature flourished. Epic poems were composed, glorifying the deeds of the ancestors of the kings of Ur. A highly centralized administration kept detailed records of agriculture, animal husbandry,

Akkadian Victory Stele. The victory stele of Naram-Sin, King of Akkad, over the mountain-dwelling Lullubi, Mesopotamian, Akkadian period, ca. 2230 B.C.E. (pink sandstone). The king wearing the horned helmet denoting divine power, strides forward at the head of his army. This is one of the finest sculptures to survive from the Akkadian period.

Louvre, Paris, France. The Bridgeman Art Library International Ltd.

commerce, and other matters. Over a hundred thousand of these documents have been found in the ruins of Sumerian cities. After little more than a century of prominence, the kingdom of Ur disintegrated in the face of famine and invasion. From the east, the Elamites attacked the city of Ur and captured the king. From the north and west, a Semitic-speaking people, the Amorites, invaded Mesopotamia in large numbers, settling around the Sumerian cities and eventually founding their own dynasties in some of them, such as at Uruk, Babylon, Isin, and Larsa.

The fall of the Third Dynasty of Ur ended Sumerian rule, and the Sumerians gradually disappeared as an identifiable group. The Sumerian language survived only in writing as the learned language of Babylonia taught in schools and used by priests and scholars. So great was the respect for Sumerian that seventeen centuries after the fall of Ur, when Alexander the Great arrived in Babylon, Sumerian was still used there as a scholarly and religious language.

For some time after the fall of Ur, there was relative peace in Babylonia under the Amorite kings of Isin, who used Sumerian at their court and considered themselves the successors of the kings of Ur. Eventually, another Amorite dynasty at the city of Larsa contested control of Babylonia, and a period of warfare began, mostly centering around attacks on strategic points on waterways. A powerful new dynasty at Babylon defeated Isin, Larsa, and other rivals and dominated Mesopotamia for nearly three hundred years. Its high point was the reign of its most famous king, Hammurabi (r. ca. 1792–1750 B.C.E.), best known today for the collection of laws that bears his name. (See Document, "The Code of Hammurabi.") Hammurabi destroyed the great city of Mari on the Euphrates and created a kingdom embracing most of Mesopotamia.

Writing and Mathematics   Government, business, and scholarship required an effective writing system. The Sumerians invented the writing system now known as **cuneiform** (from the

The Code of Hammurabi (r. 1792–1750 B.C.E.) was only one of many law codes that Mesopotamian societies produced, probably because in this culture rulers were not considered divine. As a result, civil law codes, separate from religious regulations, were necessary to govern human behavior. From a modern perspective, Mesopotamian law codes such as that of Hammurabi seem unjust, in that they prescribed different rights, responsibilities, and punishments, depending on gender, class, and whether a person was enslaved or free. But they represent an enormous advance in legal thought because they codified and standardized laws and punishments, which made the legal process less dependent on the whims or favoritism of rulers or judges. They also offer invaluable evidence to historians about the social structures and culture of the society that produced them.

♦ What do the passages suggest about the way Mesopotamians viewed the role of marriage in society, and the role of women in marriage? If you formed your judgment about the roles women played in Babylonian society from passages 129, 137, and 138 alone, you might assume that women primarily reared children and were confined to the home. What do the other passages here reveal about other roles that women played in this culture? What does this difference suggest about the importance of evidence and the accidents of its survival in understanding the lives of women in history?

109. If rebels meet in the house of a wineseller and she does not seize them and take them to the palace, that wineseller shall be slain.

110. If a priestess who has not remained in the temple, shall open a wine-shop, or enter a wine-shop for a drink, that woman shall be burned.

117. If a man has contracted a debt, and has given his wife, his son, his daughter for silver or for labor, three years shall they serve in the house of their purchaser or bondsmaster; in the fourth year they shall regain their original condition.

129. If the wife of a man is found lying with another male, they shall be bound and thrown into the water. If the husband lets his wife live, then the king shall let his servant live …

137. If a man had decided to divorce … a wife who has presented him with children, then he shall give back to that woman her dowry, and he shall give her the use of field, garden, and property, and she shall bring up her children. After she has brought up her children, she shall take a son's portion of all that is given to her children, and she marry the husband of her heart.

138. If a man divorces his spouse who has not borne him children, he shall give to her all the silver of the bride-price, and restore to her the dowry which she brought from the house of her father, and so he shall divorce her.

Source: *The Human Record*, vol. I, Afred J. Andrea, James H. Overfield, eds., pp. 14–15. Their source is Chilperic Edwards, *The Hammurabi Code* (1904), pp. 23–80.

Latin *cuneus,* "wedge") because of the wedge-shaped marks they made by writing on clay tablets with a cut-reed stylus. At first the writing system was sketchy, giving only a few elements of a sentence to help a reader remember something that he probably already knew. Later, people thought to write whole sentences in the order in which they were to be spoken, so writing could communicate new information to a reader. The Sumerian writing system used several thousand characters, some of which stood for words and some for sounds. Some characters stood for many different sounds or words, and some sounds could be written using a choice of many different characters. The result was a writing system that was difficult to learn. Sumerian students were fond of complaining about their unfair teachers, the difficulty of their schoolwork, and their too-short vacations. Sumerian and Babylonian schools emphasized language and literature, accounting, legal practice, and mathematics, espe-

cially geometry, along with memorization of much abstract knowledge that had no relevance to everyday life. The ability to read and write was restricted to an elite who could afford to go to school. Success in school and factors such as good family connections meant that a literate Sumerian could find employment as a clerk, surveyor, teacher, diplomat, or administrator.

The Sumerians also began the development of mathematics. The earliest Sumerian records suggest that before 3000 B.C.E. people had not yet conceptualized the idea of numbers independently of counting specific things. Therefore, the earliest writing used different numerals for counting different things, and the numerals had no independent value. (For example, the same sign could be 10 or 18, depending on what was counted.) Once an independent concept of number was established, mathematics developed rapidly. The Sumerian system was based on the number 60 (sexagesimal), rather than the number 10 (decimal), the system in general use today. Sumerian counting survives in the modern 60-minute hour and the circle of 360 degrees. By the time of Hammurabi, the Mesopotamians were expert in many types of mathematics, including mathematical astronomy. The calendar the Mesopotamians used had twelve lunar months of thirty days each. To keep it in accordance with the solar year and the seasons, the Mesopotamians occasionally introduced a thirteenth month.

Religion   The Sumerians and their successors worshiped many gods and goddesses. They visualized these in human form, with human needs and weaknesses. Most of the gods were identified with some natural phenomenon such as the sky, fresh water, or storms. They differed from humans in their greater power, sublime position in the universe, and immortality. The Mesopotamians believed that the human race was created to serve the gods and to relieve the gods of the necessity of providing for themselves. The gods were considered universal, but also as residing in specific places, usually one important god or goddess in each city. Mesopotamian temples were run like great households where the gods were fed lavish meals, entertained with music, and honored with devotion and ritual. There were gardens for their pleasure and bedrooms to retire to at night. The images of the gods were dressed and adorned with the finest materials. Theologians organized the gods into families and generations. Human social institutions, such as kingship, or crafts, such as carpentry, were associated with specific gods, so the boundaries between human and divine society were not always clearly drawn. Since the great gods were visualized like human rulers, remote from the common people and their concerns, the Mesopotamians imagined another, more personal intercessor god who was supposed to look after a person, rather like a guardian spirit. The public festivals of the gods were important holidays, with parades, ceremonies, and special foods. People wore their best clothes and celebrated their city and its gods. The Mesopotamians were religiously tolerant and readily accepted the possibility that different people might have different gods.

The Mesopotamians had a vague and gloomy picture of the afterworld. The winged spirits of the dead were recognizable as individuals. They were confined to a dusty, dark netherworld, doomed to perpetual hunger and thirst unless someone offered them food and drink. Some spirits escaped to haunt human beings. There was no preferential treatment in the afterlife for those who had led religious or virtuous lives—everyone was in equal misery. Mesopotamian families often had a ceremony to remember and honor their dead. People were usually buried together with goods such as pottery and ornaments. In the Early Dynastic period, certain kings were buried with a large retinue of attendants, includ-

ing soldiers and musicians, who apparently took poison during the funeral ceremony and were buried where they fell. But this practice soon disappeared. Children were sometimes buried under the floors of houses. Some families used burial vaults, others large cemeteries. No tombstones or inscriptions identified the deceased. Mesopotamian religion focused on problems of this world and how to lead a good life before dying.

The Mesopotamian peoples who came after the Sumerians believed that the gods revealed a person's destiny to those who could understand the omens, or indications of what was going to happen. The Babylonians therefore developed an elaborate science of divination based on chance observations, such as a cat walking in the street, and on ritual procedures, such as asking a question of the gods and then slaughtering a sheep to examine its liver and entrails for certain marks and features. Some omens, such as monstrous births or eclipses, were thought to apply to the government, while others, such as birds flying over a person's house, were thought to apply to the individual. Thousands of omens, including both the observation and the outcome thereof, were compiled into huge encyclopedias that scholars could consult. Divination was often done before making major decisions and to discover the causes of illness, unhappiness, and failure. The hope was to avert unfavorable future events by discovering them in time and carrying out rituals or avoiding certain actions. Diviners were paid professionals, not priests. Witchcraft was also widely feared and blamed for illnesses and harm to people. There were many rituals against witchcraft, such as making a figurine of a witch and burning it, thereby burning up the witchcraft.

Religion played a large part in the literature and art of Mesopotamia. Epic poems told of the deeds of the gods, such as how the world was created and organized, of a great flood the gods sent to wipe out the human race, and of the hero-king Gilgamesh, who tried to escape death by going on a fantastic journey to find the sole survivor of the great flood. (See Document, "The Babylonian Story of the Flood.") The presence of many literary and artistic works that were not religious in character suggests that religion did not dominate all aspects of the Mesopotamians' lives. Religious architecture took the form of great temple complexes in the major cities. The most imposing religious structure was the *ziggurat*, a tower in stages, sometimes with a small chamber on top. The terraces may have been planted with trees to resemble a mountain. Poetry about ziggurats often compares them to mountains, with their peaks in the sky and their roots in the netherworld, linking heaven to earth, but their precise purpose is not known. Eroded remains of many of these monumental structures still dot the Iraqi landscape. Through the Bible, they have entered Western tradition as the Tower of Babel.

Society   Hundreds of thousands of cuneiform texts from the early third millennium B.C.E. until the third century B.C.E. reveal a full and detailed picture of how peoples in ancient Mesopotamia conducted their lives and of the social conditions in which they lived. From the time of Hammurabi, for example, there are many royal letters to and from the various rulers of the age, letters from the king to his subordinates, administrative records from many different cities, and numerous letters and documents belonging to private families.

Categorizing the laws of Hammurabi according to the aspects of life with which they deal reveals much about Babylonian life in his time. The third largest category of laws deals with commerce, relating to such issues as contracts, debts, rates of interest, security, and default. Business documents of Hammurabi's time show how people invested their money in land, moneylending, government contracts, and international trade. Some of these laws regulate professionals, such as builders, judges, and surgeons. The second largest category of laws deals with land tenure, especially land given by the king to soldiers and marines in return for their service. The letters of Hammurabi that deal with land tenure show that he was concerned to uphold individual rights of landholders against powerful officials who tried to take their land from them. The largest category of laws relates to the family and its maintenance and protection, including marriage, inheritance, and adoption.

Parents usually arranged marriages, and betrothal was followed by the signing of a marriage contract. The bride usually left her own family to join her husband's. The husband-to-be could make a bridal payment, and the father of the bride-to-be provided a dowry for his daughter in money, land, or objects. A marriage started out monogamous, but a husband whose wife was childless or sickly could take a second wife. Sometimes husbands also sired children from domestic slave women. Women could own their own property and do business on their own. Women divorced by their husbands without good cause could get back their dowry. A woman seeking divorce could also recover her dowry if her husband could not convict her of wrongdoing. A married woman's place was thought to be in the home, but hundreds of letters between wives and husbands show them as equal partners in the ventures of life. Single women who were not part of families could establish a business on their own, often as tavern owners or moneylenders, or could be associated with temples, sometimes working as midwives and wet nurses, or taking care of orphaned children.

Slavery: Chattel Slaves and Debt Slaves   There were two main types of slavery in Mesopotamia: chattel and debt slavery. Chattel slaves were bought like any other piece of property and had no legal rights. They had to wear their hair in a certain way and were sometimes branded or tattooed on their hands. They

Babylonian World Map. This clay tablet from the Neo-Babylonian period (612–539 B.C.E.) shows a map of the world as seen by the Babylonians. The "Salt Sea" is shown as a circle. An arc inside it is labeled "Mountains." Below it is a rectangular box marked "Babylon," and to the right of the box is a small circle marked "Assyria."
Courtesy of the Trustees of the British Museum. © The British Museum

were often non-Mesopotamians bought from slave merchants. Prisoners of war could also be enslaved. Chattel slaves were expensive luxuries during most of Mesopotamian history. They were used in domestic service rather than in production, such as field work. A wealthy household might have five or six slaves, male and female.

Debt slavery was more common than chattel slavery. Rates of interest were high, as much as $33\frac{1}{3}$ percent, so people often defaulted on loans. One reason the interest rates were so high was that the government periodically canceled certain types of debts, debt slavery, and obligations, so lenders ran the risk of losing their money. If debtors had pledged themselves or members of their families as surety for a loan, they became the slave of the creditor; their labor went to pay the interest on the loan. Debt slaves could not be sold but could redeem their freedom by paying off the loan. True chattel slavery did not become common until the Neo-Babylonian period (612–539 B.C.E.).

The Babylonian Story of the Flood

The passage that follows is part of the Babylonian Epic of Gilgamesh. *It did not form a part of the original epic but was added at some point from an earlier independent Babylonian Story of the Flood, which suggested that the gods sent a flood as a drastic effort at population control because there were too many people on the earth. The gods realized their mistake when there were no more people to provide for them, so they made sure that everyone would die sooner or later, and they restricted childbirth through various social and medical means. A version of this story was later combined with the* Epic of Gilgamesh. *Gilgamesh was a legendary king who became terrified of death when his best friend and companion died. He resolved to locate Utanapishtim, who, with his wife, was the only survivor of the great flood, in order to ask him how he, too, could escape death. After many adventures, Gilgamesh crossed the distant ocean and the "waters of death" to ask Utanapishtim the secret of eternal life. In response, Utanapishtim narrated the story of the great flood, to show that his own immortality derived from a one-time event in the past, so that Gilgamesh could not share his destiny. Note the similarities and the differences between this and the biblical story of Noah.*

♦ How is this tale similar to the story of Noah in the Book of Genesis in the Hebrew Bible? How is it different?

Six days and seven nights
The wind continued, the deluge and windstorm levelled
  the land.
When the seventh day arrived,
The windstorm and deluge left off their battle,
Which had struggled, like a woman in labor.

The sea grew calm, the tempest stilled, the deluge
  ceased,
I looked at the weather, stillness reigned,
And the whole human race had turned into clay.
The landscape was flat as a rooftop.
I opened the hatch, sunlight fell upon my face.
Falling to my knees, I sat down weeping,
Tears running down my face.
I looked at the edges of the world, the borders of the
  sea,
At twelve times sixty double leagues the periphery
  emerged.
The boat had come to rest on Mount Nimush,
Mount Nimush held the boat fast, not letting it move.
One day, a second day Mount Nimush held the boat
  fast, not letting it move.
A third day, a fourth day Mount Nimush held the boat
  fast, not letting it move.
A fifth day, a sixth day Mount Nimush held the boat fast,
  not letting it move.
When the seventh day arrived,
I brought out a dove and set it free.
The dove went off and returned,
No landing place came to its view, so it turned back.
I brought out a swallow and set it free,
The swallow went off and returned,
No landing space came to its view, so it turned back.
I brought out a raven and set it free.
The raven went off and saw the ebbing of the waters.
It ate, preened, left droppings, did not turn back.
I released all to the four directions,

Although laws against fugitive slaves or slaves who denied their masters were harsh—the Code of Hammurabi permits the death penalty for anyone who sheltered or helped a runaway slave to escape—Mesopotamian slavery appears enlightened compared with other slave systems in history. Slaves were generally of the same people as their masters. They had been enslaved because of misfortune from which their masters were not immune, and they generally labored alongside them. Slaves could engage in business and, with certain restrictions, hold property. They could marry free men or women, and the resulting children would normally be free. A slave who acquired the means could buy his or her freedom. Children of a slave by a master might be allowed to share his property after his death. Notwithstanding these policies, slaves were property, subject to an owner's will and had little legal protection.

EGYPTIAN CIVILIZATION

As Mesopotamian civilization arose in the valley of the Tigris and Euphrates, another great civilization emerged in Egypt, centered on the Nile River. From its sources in Lake Victoria and the Ethiopian highlands, the Nile flows north some four

CHRONOLOGY

Key Events and People in Mesopotamian History

ca. 3500 B.C.E.	Development of Sumerian cities, especially Uruk
ca. 2800–2370 B.C.E.	Early Dynastic period of Sumerian city-states
ca. 2370 B.C.E.	Sargon establishes Akkadian dynasty and empire
ca. 2125–2027 B.C.E.	Third Dynasty of Ur
ca. 2000–1800 B.C.E.	Establishment of Amorites in Mesopotamia
ca. 1792–1750 B.C.E.	Reign of Hammurabi
ca. 1550 B.C.E.	Establishment of Kassite dynasty at Babylon

I brought out an offering and offered it to the four
  directions.
I set up an incense burner on the summit of the
  mountain,
I arranged seven and seven cult vessels,
I heaped reeds, cedar, and myrtle in their bowls.
The gods smelled the savor,
The gods smelled the sweet savor,
The gods crowded round the sacrificer like flies.
As soon as the Belet-ili arrived,
She held up the great fly-ornaments that Anu had made
  in his ardor:
'O ye gods, as surely as I shall not forget these lapis
  pendants on my neck,
'I shall be mindful of these days and not forget, not
  ever!
'The gods should come to the incense burner,
'But Enlil should not come to the incense burner,
'For he, irrationally, brought on the flood,
'And marked my people for destruction!'
As soon as Enlil arrived,
He saw the boat, Enlil flew into a rage,
He was filled with fury at the gods:
'Who came through alive? No man was to survive
  destruction!'
Ninurta made ready to speak,
Said to the valiant Enlil:
'Who but Ea could contrive such a thing?
'For Ea alone knows every artifice.'
Ea made ready to speak,
Said to the valiant Enlil:

'You, O valiant one, are the wisest of the gods,
'How could you, irrationally, have brought on the flood?
'Punish the wrong-doer for his wrong-doing,
'Punish the transgressor for his transgression,
'But be lenient, lest he be cut off,
'Bear with him, lest he ....
'Instead of your bringing on a flood,
'Let the lion rise up to diminish the human race!
'Instead of your bringing on a flood,
'Let the wolf rise up to diminish the human race!
'Instead of your bringing on a flood,
'Let famine rise up to wreak havoc in the land!
'Instead of your bringing on a flood,
'Let pestilence rise up to wreak havoc in the land!
'It was not I who disclosed the secret of the great gods,
'I made Atrahasis have a dream and so he heard the
  secret of the gods.
'Now then, make some plan for him.'
Then Enlil came up into the boat,
Leading me by the hand, he brought me up too.
He brought my wife up and had her kneel beside me.
He touched our brows, stood between us to bless us:
'Hitherto Utanapishtim has been a human being,
'Now Utanapishtim and his wife shall become like us
  gods.
'Utanapishtim shall dwell far distant at the source of the
  rivers.'

"The Babylonian Story of the Flood" from Babylonian *Epic of Gilgamesh*,
trans. by Benjamin R. Foster, from *The Epic of Gilgamesh*
© 2001 W. W. Norton & Co. Used by permission of Norton & Co., Inc.

thousand miles to the Mediterranean. Ancient Egypt included the 750-mile stretch of smooth, navigable river from Aswan to the sea. South of Aswan the river's course is interrupted by several cataracts—rocky areas of rapids and whirlpools.

The Egyptians recognized two sets of geographical divisions in their country. Upper (southern) Egypt consisted of the narrow valley of the Nile. Lower (northern) Egypt referred to the broad triangular area, named by the Greeks after their letter *delta*, formed by the Nile as it branches out to empty into the Mediterranean (see Map 1–3). They also made a distinction between what they termed the "black land," the dark fertile fields along the Nile, and the "red land," the desert cliffs and plateaus bordering the valley.

The Nile alone made agriculture possible in Egypt's desert environment. Each year the rains of central Africa caused the river to rise over its floodplain, cresting in September and October. In places the plain extends several miles on either side; elsewhere the cliffs slope down to the water's edge.

When the floodwaters receded, they left a rich layer of organically fertile silt. The construction and maintenance of canals, dams, and irrigation ditches to control the river's water, together with careful planning and organization of planting and harvesting, produced agricultural prosperity unmatched in the ancient world.

The Nile served as the major highway connecting Upper and Lower Egypt. There was also a network of desert roads running north and south, as well as routes across the eastern desert to the Sinai and the Red Sea. Other tracks led to oases in the western desert. Thanks to geography and climate, Egypt was more isolated and enjoyed far more security than Mesopotamia. This security, along with the predictable flood calendar, gave Egyptian civilization a more optimistic outlook than the civilizations of the Tigris and Euphrates, which were more prone to storms, flash floods, and invasions.

The three thousand year span of ancient Egyptian history is traditionally divided into thirty-one royal dynasties, from

MAP ● EXPLORATION

Interactive map: To explore this map further, go to http://www.prenhall.com/craig3/map1.3

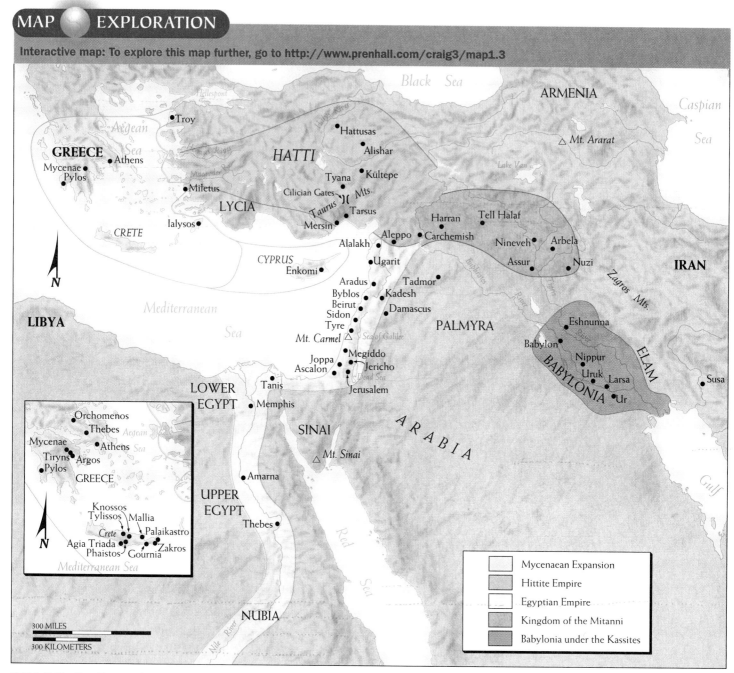

MAP 1–3 The Near East and Greece ca. 1400 B.C.E.
About 1400 B.C.E., the Near East was divided among four empires. Egypt extended south to Nubia and north through Palestine and Phoenicia. Kassites ruled in Mesopotamia, Hittites in Asia Minor, and the Mitannians in Assyrian lands. In the Aegean, the Mycenaean kingdoms were at their height.

the first, said to have been founded by Menes, the king who originally united Upper and Lower Egypt, to the last, conquered by Alexander the Great in 332 B.C.E. (as we shall see in Chapter 3). Ptolemy, one of Alexander's generals, founded the Ptolemaic Dynasty, whose last ruler was Cleopatra. In 30 B.C.E. the Romans defeated Egypt, effectively end-

ing the independent existence of a civilization that had lasted three millennia.

The unification of Upper and Lower Egypt was vital, for it meant that the entire river valley could benefit from an unimpeded distribution of resources. Three times in its history, Egypt experienced a century or more of political and social

DOCUMENT | An Assyrian Woman Writes to Her Husband, ca. 1800 B.C.E.

The wives of early Assyrian businessmen were often active in their husbands' business affairs. They made extra money for themselves by having slave girls weave textiles that the husbands then sold on business trips. Their letters are among the largest groups of women's records from the ancient world. The woman writing this letter, Taram-Kubi, complains of her husband's selfishness and points out all the matters she has worked on during his absence on business.

◆ What functions did this woman perform on behalf of the family? How do you judge her real power in regard to her husband? On what evidence do you base that judgment? What does this document reveal about the place of women in Assyrian society?

You wrote to me saying, "You'll need to safeguard the bracelets and rings which are there so they'll be available [to buy] food." In fact you sent [the man] Ilumbani a half pound of gold! Which are the bracelets you left me? When you left, you didn't leave me an ounce of silver, you picked the house clean and took away everything! After you left, there was a severe famine in the city. Not so much as a quart of grain did you leave me, I always had to buy grain for our food. Besides that, I paid the assessment for the divine icon(?); in fact, I paid for my part in full. Besides that, I paid over to the Town Hall the grain owed [the man] Atata. What is the extravagance you keep writing to me about? There is nothing for us to eat—we're the ones being extravagant? I picked up whatever I had to hand and sent it to you—today I'm living in an empty house. It's high time you sent me the money realized on my weavings, in silver, from what you have to hand, so I can buy ten quarts of grain!

Trans. by Benjamin R. Foster, 1999.

---

disintegration, known as Intermediate periods. During these eras, rival dynasties often set up separate power bases in Upper and Lower Egypt until a strong leader reunified the land.

The Old Kingdom (2700–2200 B.C.E.)

The Old Kingdom represents the culmination of the cultural and historical developments of the Early Dynastic period. For over four hundred years, Egypt enjoyed internal stability and great prosperity. During this period, the **pharaoh** was a king who was also a god (the term comes from the Egyptian for "great house," much as we use "White House" to refer to the president). From his capital at Memphis, the god-king administered Egypt according to set principles—prime among them was *maat*, an ideal of order, justice, and truth. In return for the king's building and maintaining temples, the gods preserved the equilibrium of the state and ensured the king's continuing power, which was absolute. Because the king was obligated to act infallibly in a benign and beneficent manner, the welfare of the people of Egypt was automatically guaranteed and safeguarded.

Nothing better illustrates the nature of Old Kingdom royal power than the pyramids built as pharaonic tombs. Beginning in the Early Dynastic period, kings constructed increasingly elaborate burial complexes in Upper Egypt. Djoser, a Third Dynasty king, was the first to erect a monumental six-step pyramid of hard stone. Subsequent pharaohs built other stepped pyramids until Snefru, the founder of the Fourth Dynasty, converted a stepped pyramid to a true pyramid over the course of putting up three monuments.

Djoser's son Khufu (Cheops in the Greek version of his name) chose the desert plateau of Giza, south of Memphis, as the site for the largest pyramid ever constructed. Its dimensions are prodigious: 481 feet high, 756 feet long on each side, and its base covering 13.1 acres. The pyramid is made of 2.3 million stone blocks averaging 2.5 tons each. It is also a geometrical wonder, deviating from absolutely level and square only by the most minute measurements using the latest modern devices. Khufu's successors, Khafre (Chephren) and Menkaure (Mycerinus), built equally perfect pyramids at Giza, and together the three constitute one of the most extraordinary achievements in human history. Khafre also built the huge composite creature, part lion and part human, which the Greeks named the Sphinx. Recent research has shown that the Sphinx played a crucial role in the solar cult aspects of the pyramid complex.

The pyramids are remarkable not only for the great technical skill they demonstrate, but also for the concentration of resources they represent. They are evidence that the pharaohs controlled vast wealth and had the power to focus and organize enormous human effort over the years it took to build each pyramid. They also provide a visible indication of the nature of the Egyptian state: The pyramids, like the pharaohs, tower above the land, while the low tombs at their base, like the officials buried there, seem to huddle in relative unimportance.

Originally, the pyramids and their associated cult buildings contained statuary, offerings, and all that the pharaoh needed for the afterlife. Despite great precautions and ingenious concealment methods, tomb robbers took nearly everything, leaving little for modern archaeologists to recover. Several full-size wooden boats have been found, however, still in their own graves at the base of the pyramids, ready for the pharaoh's journeys in the next world. Recent excavations have uncovered remains of the large town built to house the thousands of pyramid builders, including the farmers who worked at Giza during the annual flooding of their fields.

Numerous officials, both members of the royal family and nonroyal men of ability, aided the god-kings. The highest office was the *vizier* (a modern term from Arabic). Central offices dealing with granaries, surveys, assessments, taxes, and salaries administered the land. Water management was local rather than on a national level. Upper and Lower Egypt were divided into *nomes*, or districts, each governed by a *nomarch*, or governor, and his local officials. The kings could also appoint royal officials to oversee groups of nomes or to supervise pharaonic landholdings throughout Egypt.

The First Intermediate Period and Middle Kingdom (2200–1630 B.C.E.)

Toward the end of the Old Kingdom, for a combination of political and economic reasons, absolute pharaonic power waned as the nomarchs and other officials became more independent and influential. About 2200 B.C.E. the Old Kingdom collapsed and gave way to the decentralization and disorder of the First Intermediate period, which lasted until about 2025 B.C.E. Eventually, the kings of Dynasty 11, based in Thebes in Upper Egypt, defeated the rival Dynasty 10, based in a city south of Giza.

Amunemhet I, the founder of Dynasty 12 and the Middle Kingdom, probably began his career as a successful vizier under an Eleventh Dynasty king. After reuniting Upper and Lower Egypt, he turned his attention to making three important and long-lasting administrative changes. First, he moved his royal residence from Thebes to a brand-new town, just south of the old capital at Memphis, signaling a fresh start rooted in past glories. Second, he reorganized the nome structure by more clearly defining the nomarchs' duties to the state, granting them some local autonomy within the royal structure. Third, he established a co-regency system to smooth transitions from one reign to another.

Amunemhet I and the other Middle Kingdom pharaohs sought to evoke the past by building pyramid complexes like those of the later Old Kingdom rulers. Yet the events of the First Intermediate period had irrevocably changed the nature of Egyptian kingship. Gone was the absolute, distant god-king; the king was now more directly concerned with his people. In art, instead of the supremely confident faces of the Old Kingdom pharaohs, the Middle Kingdom rulers seem thoughtful, careworn, and brooding.

Egypt's relations with its neighbors became more aggressive during the Middle Kingdom. To the south, royal fortresses were built to control Nubia and the growing trade in African resources. To the north and east, Syria and Palestine increasingly came under Egyptian influence, even as fortifications sought to prevent settlers from the Levant from moving into the Delta.

The Second Intermediate Period and the New Kingdom (1630–1075 B.C.E.)

For some unknown reason, during Dynasty 13, the kingship changed hands rapidly and the western Delta established itself as an independent Dynasty 14, ushering in the Second Intermediate period. The eastern Delta, with its expanding Asiatic populations, came under the control of the Hyksos (Dynasty 15) and minor Asiatic kings (Dynasty 16). Meanwhile, the

Pyramids at Giza. The three largest pyramids of Egypt, located at Giza, near Cairo, are the colossal tombs of pharaohs of the Fourth Dynasty (ca. 2640–2510 B.C.E.): Khufu (right), Chafre (center), and Menkaure (left). The small pyramids and tombs at their bases were those of the pharaohs' queens and officials.
Pictor/Uniphoto Picture Agency.

Dynasty 13 kings left their northern capital and regrouped in Thebes (Dynasty 17).

Though much later sources describe the Hyksos ("chief of foreign lands" in Egyptian) as ruthless invaders from parts unknown, they were almost certainly Amorites from the Levant, part of the gradual infiltration of the Delta during the Middle Kingdom. Ongoing excavations at the Hyksos capital of Avaris in the eastern Delta have revealed architecture, pottery, and other goods consistent with that cultural background. After nearly a century of rule, the Hyksos were expelled, a process begun by Kamose, the last king of Dynasty 17, and completed by his brother Ahmose, the first king of the Eighteenth Dynasty and the founder of the New Kingdom.

During the Eighteenth Dynasty, Egypt pursued foreign expansion with renewed vigor. Military expeditions reached as far north as the Euphrates in Syria, with frequent campaigns in the Levant. To the south, major Egyptian temples were built in the Sudan, almost thirteen hundred miles from Memphis. Egypt's economic and political power was at its height.

Egypt's position was reflected in the unprecedented luxury and cosmopolitanism of the royal court and in the ambitious palace and temple projects undertaken throughout the country. Perhaps to foil tomb robbers, the Eighteenth Dynasty pharaohs were the first to cut their tombs deep into the rock cliffs of a desolate valley in Thebes, known today as the Valley of the Kings. To date, only one intact royal tomb has been discovered there, that of the young Eighteenth Dynasty king Tutankhamun, and even it had been disturbed shortly after his death. The thousands of goods buried with him, many of them marvels of craftsmanship, give a glimpse of Egypt's material wealth during this period.

Following the premature death of Tutankhamun in 1323 B.C.E., a military commander named Horemheb assumed the kingship, which passed in turn to his own army commander, Ramses I. The Ramessides of Dynasty 19 undertook numerous monumental projects, among them Ramses II's rock-cut temples at Abu Simbel, south of the First Cataract, which had to be moved to a higher location when the Aswan High Dam was built in the 1960s. There and elsewhere, Ramses II left textual and pictorial accounts of his battle in 1285 B.C.E. against the Hittites at Kadesh on the Orontes in Syria. Sixteen years later, the Egyptians and Hittites signed a formal peace treaty, forging an alliance against an increasingly volatile political situation in the Middle East and the eastern Mediterranean during the thirteenth century B.C.E.

Merneptah, one of the hundred offspring of Ramses II, held off a hostile Libyan attack, as well as incursions by the Sea Peoples, a loose coalition of Mediterranean raiders who seem to have provoked and taken advantage of unsettled conditions. One of Merneptah's inscriptions commemorating his military triumphs contains the first known mention of Israel.

Despite Merneptah's efforts, by the end of the Twentieth Dynasty, Egypt's period of imperial glory had passed. The next thousand years witnessed a Third Intermediate period, a Saite renaissance, Persian domination, conquest by Alexander the Great, the Ptolemaic period, and finally, defeat at the hands of the Roman emperor Octavian in 30 B.C.E.

Language and Literature   Writing first appears in Egypt about 3000 B.C.E. While the impetus for the first Egyptian writing probably came from Mesopotamia, the Egyptians may have invented it on their own. The writing system, dubbed **hieroglyphs** ("sacred carvings") by the Greeks, was highly sophisticated, involving hundreds of picture signs that remained relatively constant in the way they were rendered for over three thousand years. Many of them formed a syllabary of one, two, or three consonantal sounds, while some conveyed a word's meaning or category, either independently or added to the end of the word. Texts were usually written horizontally from right to left but could be written from left to right, as well as vertically from top to bottom in both horizontal directions. A cursive version of hieroglyphs was used for business documents and literary texts, which were penned rapidly in black and red ink. The Egyptian language, part of the Afro-Asiatic (or Hamito-Semitic) family, evolved through several stages— Old Middle, and Late Egyptian, Demotic, and Coptic—thus giving it a history of continuous recorded use well into the medieval period.

Egyptian literature includes narratives, myths, books of instruction in wisdom, letters, religious texts, and poetry, written on papyri, limestone flakes, and postherds. (See Document, "Love Poems from the New Kingdom.") Unfortunately, only a small fraction of this enormous literature has survived, and many texts are incomplete. Though they surely existed, we have no epics or dramas from ancient Egypt. Such nonliterary documents as lists of kings, autobiographies in tombs, wine jar labels, judicial records, astronomical observations, and medical and other scientific texts are invaluable for our understanding of Egyptian history and civilization.

Religion: Gods and Temples Egyptian religion encompasses a multitude of concepts that often seem mutually contradictory to us. Three separate explanations for the origin of the universe were formulated, each based in the philosophical traditions of a venerable Egyptian city. The cosmogony of Heliopolis, north of Memphis, held that the creator–sun god Atum (also identified as Re) emerged from the darkness of a vast sea to stand upon a primeval mound, containing within himself the life force of the gods he was to create. At Memphis, it was the god Ptah who created the other gods by uttering their names. Further south, at Hermopolis, eight male and female entities within a primordial slime suddenly exploded, and the energy that resulted created the sun and Atum, from which the rest came.

The Egyptian gods, or pantheon, defy neat catego-

rization, in part because of the common tendency to combine the character and function of one or more gods. Amun, one of the eight entities in the Hermopolitan cosmogony, provides a good example. Thebes, Amun's cult center, rose to prominence in the Middle Kingdom. In the New Kingdom, Amun was elevated above his seven cohorts and took on aspects of the sun god Re to become Amun-Re.

Not surprisingly in a nearly rainless land, solar cults and mythologies were highly developed. Much thought was devoted to conceptualizing what happened as the sun god made his perilous way through the underworld in the night hours between sunset and sunrise. Three long texts trace Re's journey as he vanquishes immense snakes and other foes.

The Eighteenth Dynasty was one of several periods during which solar cults were in ascendancy. Early in his reign, Amunhotep IV promoted a single, previously minor aspect of the sun, the Aten ("disc") above Re himself and the rest of the gods. He declared that the Aten was the creator god who brought life to mankind and all living beings, with himself and his queen Nefertiti the sole mediators between the Aten and the people. For religious and political reasons still imperfectly understood, he went further, changing his name to Akhenaten ("the effective spirit of the Aten"), building a new capital called Akhetaten ("the horizon of the Aten") near Amarna north of Thebes and chiseling out the name of Amun from inscriptions everywhere. Shortly after his death, Amarna was abandoned and partially razed. A large diplomatic archive of tablets written in Akkadian was left at the site, which give us a vivid, if one-sided, picture of the political correspondence of the day. During the reigns of Akhenaten's successors, Tutankhamun (born Tutankhaten) and Horemheb, Amun was restored to his former position, and Akhenaten's monuments were defaced and even demolished.

In representations, Egyptian gods have human bodies, possess human or animal heads, and wear crowns, celestial discs, or thorns. The lone exception is the Aten,

◀ **Seated Egyptian Scribe.** One of the hallmarks of the early river valley civilizations was the development of writing. Ancient Egyptian scribes had to undergo rigorous training but were rewarded with a position of respect and privilege. This statue from the Fifth Dynasty (ca. 2510–2460 B.C.E.) is of painted limestone and measures 21 inches (53 cm) in height. Musèe de Louvre, Paris, © Giraudon/Art Resource, N.Y.

DOCUMENT   Love Poems from the New Kingdom

Numerous love poems from ancient Egypt reveal the Egyptians' love of life through their frank sensuality.

◆ How does the girl in the first poem propose to escape the supervision of her parents? What ails the young man in the second poem?

SHE: Love, how I'd love to slip down to the pond, bathe with you close by on the bank.
Just for you I'd wear my new Memphis swimsuit, made of sheer linen, fit for a queen—Come see how it looks in the water!
Couldn't I coax you to wade in with me? Let the cool creep slowly around us?
Then I'd dive deep down and come up for you dripping,
Let you fill your eyes with the little red fish that I'd catch.

And I'd say, standing there tall in the shallows:
Look at my fish, love, how it lies in my hand,
How my fingers caress it, slip down its sides …
But then I'd say softer, eyes bright with your seeing:
A gift, love. No words.
Come closer and look, it's all me.

HE: I think I'll go home and lie very still, feigning terminal illness.
Then the neighbors will all troop over to stare, my love, perhaps, among them.
How she'll smile while the specialists snarl in their teeth!—she perfectly well knows what ails me.

From *Love Songs of the New Kingdom*, trans. from the Ancient Egyptian by John L. Foster, copyright © 1969, 1970, 1971, 1972, 1973, and 1974 by John L. Foster, pp. 20 and 72. Reprinted by permission of the University of Texas Press.

made nearly abstract by Akhenaten, who altered its image to a plain disc with solar rays ending in small hands holding the hieroglyphic sign for life to the nostrils of Akhenaten and Nefertiti. The gods were thought to reside in their cult centers, where, from the New Kingdom on, increasingly ostentatious temples were built, staffed by full-time priests. At Thebes, for instance, for over two thousand years successive kings enlarged the great Karnak temple complex dedicated to Amun. Though the ordinary person could not enter a temple precinct, great festivals took place for all to see. During Amun's major festival of Opet, the statue of the god traveled in a divine boat along the Nile, whose banks were thronged with spectators.

Worship and the Afterlife Most Egyptians worshiped at small local shrines. They left offerings to the chosen gods, as well as votive inscriptions with simple prayers. Private houses often had niches containing busts for ancestor worship and statues of household deities. The Egyptians strongly believed in the power of magic, dreams, and oracles, and they possessed a wide variety of amulets to ward off evil.

Scene from *Book of the Dead*. The Egyptians believed in the possibility of life after death through the god Osiris. Before the person could be presented to Osiris, forty-two assessor-gods tested aspects of the person's life. In this scene from a papyrus manuscript of the *Book of the Dead*, the deceased and his wife (on the left) watch the scales of justice weighing his heart (on the left side of the scales) against the feather of truth. The jackal-headed god Anubis also watches the scales, while the ibis-headed god Thoth keeps the record.
British Museum, London/The Bridgeman Art Library International Ltd.

The Egyptians thought that the afterlife was full of dangers, which could be overcome by magical means, among them the spells in the *Book of the Dead.* The goals were to join and be identified with the gods, especially Osiris, or to sail in the "boat of millions." Originally only the king could hope to enjoy immortality with the gods, but gradually this became available to all. Since the Egyptians believed that the preservation of the body was essential for continued existence in the afterlife, early on they developed mummification, a process that by the New Kingdom took seventy days. How lavishly tombs were prepared and decorated varied over the course of Egyptian history and in accordance with the wealth of a family. A high-ranking Dynasty 18 official, for example, typically had a Theban rock-cut tomb of several rooms embellished with scenes from daily life and funerary texts, as well as provisions and equipment for the afterlife, statuettes of workers, and a place for descendants to leave offerings.

Women in Egyptian Society   It is difficult to assess the position of women in Egyptian society, because our pictorial and textual evidence comes almost entirely from male sources. Women's prime roles were connected with the management of the household. They could not hold office, go to scribal schools, or become artisans. Nevertheless, women could own

⚑ **Hunting Trip.** This painting from the Theban tomb of a high-ranking 18th Dynasty official shows him, accompanied by his wife and daughter, on a hunting trip through the papyrus marshes, an activity the family enjoyed during their lives on earth and would continue in the afterlife.
Courtesy of the Trustees of the British Museum.
Copyright The British Museum.

and control property, sue for divorce, and, at least in theory, enjoy equal legal protection.

Royal women often wielded considerable influence, particularly in the Eighteenth Dynasty. The most remarkable was Hatshepsut, daughter of Thutmosis I and widow of Thutmosis II, who ruled as pharaoh for nearly twenty years. Many Egyptian queens held the title "god's wife of Amun," a power base of great importance.

In art, royal and nonroyal women are conventionally shown smaller than their husbands or sons, yet it is probably of greater significance that they are so frequently depicted in such a wide variety of contexts. Much care was lavished on details of their gestures, clothing, and hairstyles. With their husbands, they attend banquets, boat in the papyrus marshes, make and receive offerings, and supervise the myriad affairs of daily life.

Slaves   Slaves did not become numerous in Egypt until the growth of Egyptian imperial power in the Middle Kingdom (2052–1786 B.C.E.). During that period, black Africans from Nubia to the south and Asians from the east were captured in war and brought back to Egypt as slaves. The great period of Egyptian imperial expansion, the New Kingdom (1550–1075 B.C.E.), vastly increased the number of slaves and captives in Egypt. Sometimes an entire people were enslaved, as the Hebrews were, according to the Bible.

Slaves in Egypt performed many tasks. They labored in the fields with the peasants, in the shops of artisans, and as domestic servants. Others worked as policemen and soldiers. Many slaves labored to erect the great temples, obelisks, and other huge monuments of Egypt's imperial age. As in Mesopotamia, slaves were branded for identification and to help prevent their escape. Egyptian slaves could be freed, although manumission seems to have been rare. Nonetheless, former slaves were not set apart and could expect to be assimilated into the mass of the population.

Ancient Near Eastern Empires

In the time of the Eighteenth Dynasty in Egypt, new groups of peoples had established themselves in the Near East: the Kassites in Babylonia, the Hittites in Asia Minor, and the Mitannians in northern Syria and Mesopotamia (see Map 1–2). The Kassites and Mitannians were warrior peoples who ruled as a minority over more civilized folk and absorbed their culture. The Hittites established a kingdom of their own and forged an empire that lasted some two hundred years.

THE HITTITES

The Hittites were an Indo-European people, speaking a language related to Greek and Sanskrit. By about 1500 B.C.E., they established a strong, centralized government with a capital at

Hattusas (near Ankara, the capital of modern Turkey). Between 1400 and 1200 B.C.E., they emerged as a leading military power in the Middle East and contested Egypt's ambitions to control Palestine and Syria. This struggle culminated in a great battle between the Egyptian and Hittite armies at Kadesh in northern Syria (1285 B.C.E.) and ended as a standoff. The Hittites also broke the power of the Mitannian state in northern Syria. The Hittites adopted Mesopotamian writing and many aspects of Mesopotamian culture, especially through the Hurrian peoples of northern Syria and southern Anatolia. Their extensive historical records are the first to mention the Greeks, whom the Hittites called Ahhiyawa (the Achaeans of Homer). By 1200 B.C.E., the Hittite kingdom disappeared, swept away in the general invasions and collapse of the Middle Eastern nation-states at that time. Successors to the empire, called the Neo-Hittite states, flourished in southern Asia Minor and northern Syria until the Assyrians destroyed them in the first millennium B.C.E.

The government of the Hittites was different from that of Mesopotamia in that Hittite kings did not claim to be divine or even to be the chosen representatives of the gods. In the early period, a council of nobles limited the king's power, and the assembled army had to ratify his succession to the throne.

The Discovery of Iron   An important technological change took place in northern Anatolia, somewhat earlier than the creation of the Hittite Kingdom, but perhaps within its region. This was the discovery of how to smelt iron and the decision to use it rather than copper or bronze to manufacture weapons and tools. Archaeologists refer to the period after 1100 B.C.E. as the Iron Age.

THE KASSITES

The Kassites were a people of unknown origin who spoke their own Kassite language and who established at Babylon a dynasty that ruled for nearly five hundred years. The Kassites were organized into large tribal families and carved out great domains for themselves in Babylonia. They promoted Babylonian culture, and many of the most important works of Babylonian literature were written during their rule. Under the Kassites, Babylonia became one of the great nation-states of the late Bronze Age, along with Mitanni on the upper Euphrates, Assyria, Egypt, and the empire of the Hittites in Anatolia. The kings of these states frequently wrote to each other and exchanged lavish gifts. They supported a military aristocracy based on horses and chariots, the prestige weaponry of the age. Though equally matched in power, the kings of this time conspired against each other, with Egypt and the Hittites hoping to control Syria and Palestine, and Babylonia and Assyria testing each other's borders. Their wars were often inconclusive.

THE MITANNIANS

The Mitannians belonged to a large group of people called the Hurrians, some of whom had been living in Mesopotamia and Syria in the time of the kings of Akkad and Ur. Their language is imperfectly understood, and the location of their capital city, Washukanni, is uncertain. The Hurrians were important mediators of Mesopotamian culture to Syria and Anatolia. They developed the art of chariot warfare and horse training to a high degree and created a large state that reached from the Euphrates to the foothills of Iran. The Hittites destroyed their kingdom, and the Assyrian empire eventually incorporated what was left of it.

THE ASSYRIANS

The Assyrians were originally a people living in Assur, a city in northern Mesopotamia on the Tigris River. They spoke a Semitic language closely related to Babylonian. They had a proud, independent culture heavily influenced by Babylonia. Assur had been an early center for trade but emerged as a political power during the fourteenth century B.C.E., after the decline of Mitanni. The first Assyrian Empire spread north and west against the neo-Hittite states but was brought to an end in the general collapse of Near Eastern states at the end of the second millennium. A people called the Arameans, a Semitic nomadic and agricultural people originally from northern Syria who spoke a language called Aramaic, invaded Assyria. Aramaic is still used in parts of the Near East and is one of the languages of medieval Jewish and Middle Eastern Christian culture.

THE SECOND ASSYRIAN EMPIRE

After 1000 B.C.E., the Assyrians began a second period of expansion, and by 665 B.C.E. they controlled all of Mesopotamia, much of southern Asia Minor, Syria, Palestine, and Egypt to its southern frontier. They succeeded thanks to a large, well-disciplined army and a society that valued military skills. Some Assyrian kings boasted of their atrocities, so that their names inspired terror

CHRONOLOGY

Major Periods in Ancient Egyptian History (Dynasties in Roman Numerals)

3100–2700 B.C.E.	Early Dynastic period (I–II)
2700–2200 B.C.E.	Old Kingdom (III–VI)
2200–2025 B.C.E.	First Intermediate period (VII–XI)
2025–1630 B.C.E.	Middle Kingdom (XII–XIII)
1630–1550 B.C.E.	Second Intermediate period (XIV–XVII)
1550–1075 B.C.E.	New Kingdom (XVIII–XX)

throughout the Near East. They constructed magnificent palaces at Nineveh and Nimrud (near modern Mosul, Iraq), surrounded by parks and gardens. The walls of the reception rooms and hallways were decorated with stone reliefs and inscriptions proclaiming the power and conquests of the king. (See Document, "An Assyrian Woman Writes to Her Husband, ca. 1800 B.C.E.")

The Assyrians organized their empire into provinces with governors, military garrisons, and administration for taxation, communications, and intelligence. Important officers were assigned large areas of land throughout the empire, and agricultural colonies were set up in key regions to store up supplies for military actions beyond the frontiers. Vassal kings had to send tribute and delegations to the Assyrian capital every year. Tens of thousands of people were forcibly displaced from their homes and resettled in other areas of the empire, partly to populate sparsely inhabited regions, partly to diminish resistance to Assyrian rule. Among those resettled were the people of the kingdom of Israel, which the Assyrians invaded and destroyed.

The empire became too large to govern efficiently. The last years of Assyria are obscure, but civil war apparently divided the country. The Medes, a powerful people from western and central Iran, had been expanding across the Iranian plateau. They were feared for their cavalry and archers, against which traditional Middle Eastern armies were ineffective. The Medes attacked Assyria and were joined by the Babylonians, who had always been restive under Assyrian rule, under the leadership of a general named Nebuchadnezzar. In 612 B.C.E., they so thoroughly destroyed the Assyrian cities, including Nineveh that Assyria never recovered. The ruins of the great Assyrian palaces lay untouched until archaeologists began to explore them in the nineteenth century.

THE NEO-BABYLONIANS

The Medes did not follow up on their conquests, so Nebuchadnezzar took over much of the Assyrian Empire. Under him and his successors, Babylon grew into one of the greatest cities of the world. The Greek traveler Herodotus described its wonders, including its great temples, fortification walls, boulevards, parks, and palaces, to a Greek readership that had never seen the like. Babylon prospered as a center of world trade, linking

◄ **Assyrian Palace Relief.** This eighth-century B.C.E. relief of a hero gripping a lion formed part of the decoration of an Assyrian palace. The immense size of the figure and his powerful limbs and muscles may well have suggested the might of the Assyrian king.
Giraudon/Art Resource, N.Y.

Egypt, India, Iran, and Syria-Palestine by land and sea routes. For centuries, an astronomical center at Babylon kept detailed records of observations that were the longest running chronicle of the ancient world. Nebuchadnezzar's dynasty did not last long, and the government passed to various men in rapid succession. The last independent king of Babylon set up a second capital in the Arabian desert and tried to force the Babylonians to honor the moon god above all other gods. He allowed dishonest or incompetent speculators to lease huge areas of temple land for their personal profit. These policies proved unpopular—some said that the king was insane—and many Babylonians may have welcomed the Persian conquest that came in 539 B.C.E. After that, Babylonia began another, even more prosperous phase of its history as one of the most important provinces of another great Eastern empire, that of the Persians. We shall return to the Persians in Chapter 4.

Early Indian Civilization

To the east of Mesopotamia, beyond the Iranian plateau and the mountains of Baluchistan, the Asian continent bends sharply southward below the Himalayan mountain barrier to

CHRONOLOGY

Key Events in the History of Ancient Near Eastern Empires

ca. 1400–1200 B.C.E.	Hittite Empire
ca. 1100 B.C.E.	Rise of Assyrian power
732–722 B.C.E.	Assyrian conquest of Syria-Palestine
671 B.C.E.	Assyrian conquest of Egypt
612 B.C.E.	Destruction of Assyrian capital at Nineveh
612–539 B.C.E.	Neo-Babylonian (Chaldean) Empire

form the Indian subcontinent (see Map 1–4). Several sizable rivers flow west and south out of the Himalayas in Kashmir and the Punjab (*Panjab*, "five rivers"), merging into the single stream of the Indus River in Sind before emptying into the Indian Ocean. The headwaters of south Asia's other great river system—the Ganges and its tributaries—are also in the Himalayas but flow south and east to the Bay of Bengal on the opposite side of the subcontinent.

The earliest evidence of a settled, neolithic way of life on the subcontinent comes from the foothills of Sind and Baluchistan and dates to about 5500 B.C.E. with evidence of barley and wheat cultivation, baked brick dwellings, and, later, domestication of animals such as goats, sheep, and cows, and, after about 4000 B.C.E., metalworking. The subcontinent's earliest literate, urban civilization arose in the valley of the Indus River sometime after 2600, and by about 2300 B.C.E. was trading with Mesopotamia. Known as the Indus Valley culture (or the **Harappan** civilization, after the archaeological site at which it was first recognized), it lasted only a few centuries and left many unanswered questions about its history and culture. The region's second identifiable civilization was of a different character. Dating to about 1500 B.C.E., it is known as the Vedic Aryan civilization—after the nomadic Indo-European immigrant people, or **Aryans**, who founded it, and their holy texts, or **Vedas**. This civilization endured for nearly a thousand years without cities or writing, but its religious and social traditions commingled with older traditions in the subcontinent—notably that of the Indus culture—to form the Indian civilization as it has developed in the past 2500 years.

MAP 1–4 Indus and Vedic Aryan Cultures. Indus culture likely influenced the Vedic Aryans, although the influence cannot be proved. Some scholars surmise, for example, that the fortified Aryan city of Hariyupiya, mentioned in later texts, may have been the same site as the older Indus city of Harappa.

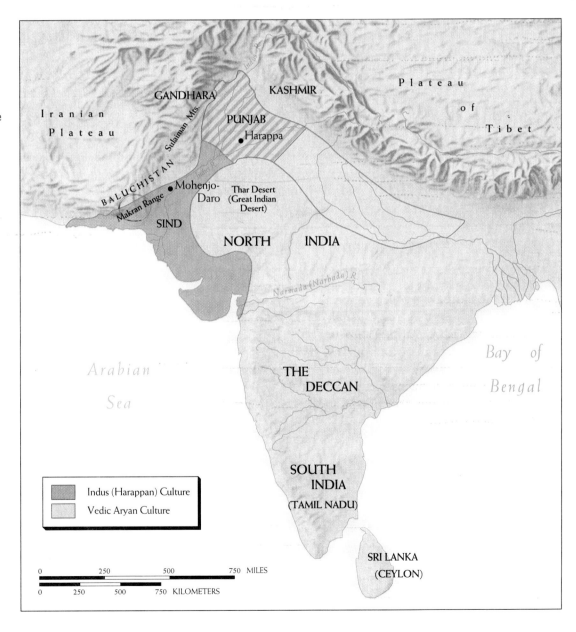

THE INDUS CIVILIZATION

Archaeologists discovered the existence of the Indus culture at the site of Harappa in the 1920s. Since then, some seventy cities, the largest being Harappa and Mohenjo-Daro, have been identified over a vast area from the Himalayan foothills west and south on the coasts of the Arabian Sea. This urban civilization had bronze tools, writing, covered drainage systems, and a diversified social and economic organization. Because it disappeared before 1500 B.C.E. and its writing is still undeciphered, it remains the least understood of the early river valley civilizations. Archaeological evidence and inferences from later Indian life, however, allow us to reconstruct something of its high and once thriving culture.

General Character   The Indus culture covered an area many times larger than either Middle Kingdom Egypt or Third Dynasty Ur, yet the archaeological finds show it to have been remarkably homogeneous. City layouts, building construction, weights and measures, seal inscriptions, patterned pottery and figurines, and even the burnt brick used for buildings and flood walls are unusually uniform in all Indus towns, suggesting an integrated economic system and good internal communications.

Indus culture was also remarkably constant over time. Because the main cities and towns lay in river lowlands subject to flooding, they were rebuilt often, with each reconstruction closely following the previous pattern. Similarly, the Indus script, known from more than two thousand stamp seals and apparently using both pictographic and phonetic symbols, shows no evidence of change over time. This evidence of stability, regularity, and traditionalism has led scholars to speculate that a centralized government, perhaps a conservative (priestly) theocracy rather than a more unstable royal dynasty and court, controlled this far-flung society.

Cities   Harappa and Mohenjo-Daro both apparently had populations of more than thirty-five thousand and were meticulously designed on a similar plan. To the west of each stood a large, walled citadel on a raised rectangular platform about eight hundred by fourteen hundred feet in size. East of this the town proper was laid out on a north–south, east–west grid of main avenues, some as wide as thirty feet. The citadel apparently contained the main public buildings. A large bath, with a brick-lined pool, a subterranean furnace, and columned porticoes have been excavated at Mohenjo-Daro. Both Harappa and Mohenjo-Daro have buildings tentatively identified as temples.

The periphery of each city had a cemetery and a large granary for food storage. The town "blocks" formed by the main avenues were crisscrossed by small, less rigidly planned lanes, off of which opened private houses, sometimes of more than one story. The typical house was built around a central courtyard and presented only blank walls to the lanes or streets outside, an arrangement still common in many Near Eastern and south Asian cities.

Perhaps the most striking feature of these cities was a complex system of covered drains and sewers. Private houses were

---

OVERVIEW   The First Civilizations

Civilization is a form of human culture marked by the development of cities, the ability to make and use metal tools and instruments, and the invention of a system of writing. The first civilizations appeared in the Near East between 4000 and 3000 B.C.E. By the second millennium B.C.E., there were civilized societies in Eurasia, China, and the Americas.

Mesopotamia	Sumerians arrive in the Tigris-Euphrates river valley, ca. 3500 B.C.E. and establish the first city-states ca. 2800 B.C.E.
Egypt	Egyptian civilization develops along the Nile River, ca. 3100 B.C.E. Egypt becomes a unified state ca. 2700 B.C.E.
Indus Valley	Flourishing urban civilization develops in northern India along the Indus River, ca. 2250 B.C.E.
China	City-states appear in the Yellow River basin ca. 1766 B.C.E.
Americas	Agricultural surplus gives rise to the first cities in Mesoamerica, ca. 1500 B.C.E. and to the first Andean civilization in South America, ca. 2750 B.C.E.

serviced by wells, bathrooms, and latrines, and the great bath at Mohenjo-Daro was filled from its own large well. The drainage system that served these facilities was an engineering feat unrivaled until the time of the Romans, nearly two thousand years later.

Economic Life   The economy of the Indus state or states was based on agriculture. Wheat and barley were the main crops; rice, peas, lentils, sesame, dates, and cotton were also important. Cattle, dogs, cats, goats, sheep, and fowl were raised, and elephants and water buffalo were likely used as beasts of burden. The Indus Valley people wove cloth from cotton, made metal tools, and used the potter's wheel.

Evidence points to trade between the Indus culture and Mesopotamia. Indus stone stamp seals have been found in Mesopotamia, and Akkadian texts mention a "Melukka" region, perhaps the Indus basin, as a source of ivory, precious stones, and other wares. The island of Bahrain in the Persian Gulf may have been a staging point for Indus-Mesopotamian sea trade. Metals and semiprecious stones were apparently imported into the Indus region from present-day Iran and Afghanistan, as well as from central Asia, from farther south on the Indian peninsula, and perhaps from Arabia. Similarities in artistic styles suggest that trade contacts resulted in cultural borrowings.

Material Culture   Among the most striking accomplishments of the Indus culture are fine bronze and stone sculptures. Other evidence of the skill of Indus artisans includes copper and bronze tools and vessels, black-on-red painted pottery, dressed stonework, stone and terra-cotta figurines and toys, silver vessels and ornaments, gold jewelry, and dyed woven fabric. Indus stamp seals, which provide the only examples of the still undeciphered Indus script, also bear representations of animals, humans, and what are thought to be divine or semidivine beings. Similar figures are also found on painted pottery and engraved copper tablets. Compared with the art of of Egypt or Mesopotamia, this art seems limited, however. Except for some decorative brickwork, no monumental friezes, mosaics, or sculpture have been found.

Religion   The Indus remains reveal somewhat more regarding the religious realm. The elaborate bath facilities suggest that ritual bathing and water purification rites were important, as they still are in India today. The stone images from the so-called temples of Mohenjo-Daro and the more common terra-cotta figurines from other sites also suggest links to later Indian religious practices and symbols. The many images of male animals such as the humped bull might be symbols of power and fertility or might indicate animal worship. A recurring image of a male figure with leafy headdress and horns, often seated in a posture associated later in India with yogic medita-

▲ **Ancient Mohenjo-Daro.** Like most cities of the Indus Valley civilization, Mohenjo-Daro was built principally of mud brick. The structures are laid on straight lines; streets cross each other at right angles. The impression is one of order, prosperity, and civic discipline.
Borromeo/Art Resource, N.Y.

tion, has been likened to the Vedic Aryan "Lord of All Creatures." He has features in common with the Hindu god Shiva, especially where he is depicted with three faces and an erect phallus. Also found in Indus artifacts are the pipal tree and the left-handed swastika, both symbols later important to Hindus.

Terra-cotta figurines of females, often pregnant or carrying a child, are similar to female images in several prehistoric cultures. As possible precursors of Shiva's consort (known as Devi, Durga, and other names), they too may represent an element of pre-Aryan religion that reemerged later to figure in "Hindu" culture. Yet other aspects of Indus religion—burial customs, for example—are not clearly related to later Indian practices. They remind us, however, that the Indus peoples, like all others, had their own ways of coming to terms with the mysteries of birth, life, and death.

The Passing of Indus Civilization   Sometime in the period from about 1800 to 1700 B.C.E., Indus civilization disappeared. It is not clear whether its demise was related to the warlike Aryan invaders who may first have appeared in the upper Indus about 1800 B.C.E. and later used their horse-drawn chariots to subdue indigenous peoples and move across the north Indian plains. Some scholars think it was destroyed by abnormal flooding (perhaps from careless damming of the Indus), changes in the course of the Indus, collapse of military power, or a long period of dessication even before the Aryans arrived. Regardless of cause, the Indus culture disappeared by about 1700 and remains too shadowy for us to measure its proper influence. Nonetheless, these predecessors of the Aryans likely made significant contributions to later life in the subcontinent in ways that we have yet to discover.

◁ **Indus Stamp Seal.** Note the familiar humped bull of India on this stone stamp seal.
© Scala/Art Resource, N.Y.

THE VEDIC ARYAN CIVILIZATION

We know more about the Aryan culture that effectively "refounded" Indian civilization around 1500 B.C.E. Yet unlike Indus civilization, it was not urban and left neither city ruins nor substantial artifacts beyond tools, weapons, and pottery. Virtually our only source of knowledge about ancient Aryan life are the words of the Vedas, the Aryan sacred texts—hence we know the culture as "Vedic." Although the latest Vedic texts date from perhaps 500 B.C.E., the earliest may go back to 1700 B.C.E. Transmitted orally through the centuries, the Vedas were not written down until writing was reintroduced to India sometime after 700 B.C.E. (Indeed, until recently, writing down the Vedas at all was shunned in favor of memorization and recitation among the Brahmans.) The Vedas are ritual, priestly, and speculative, not historical works. They reveal little about events but do offer insight into the religion, society, values, and thought of early Aryan India.

Veda, which means "knowledge," is the collective term for the texts still recognized today by most Indians as the holiest sources of their tradition. For Hindus, Veda is the eternal wisdom of primordial seers preserved for thousands of years in an unbroken oral tradition. The Vedas are the four major compilations of Vedic ritual, explanatory, and speculative texts. The collection of 1,028 religious hymns known as the Rig-Veda represents the oldest materials of the Vedas. The latest of these hymns date from about 1000 B.C.E., the oldest from perhaps 1700–1200 B.C.E., when the Aryans spread across the northern plains to the upper reaches of the Ganges.

Aryan is a different kind of term. The second-millennium invaders of northern India called themselves *Aryas* as opposed to the peoples whom they conquered. Vedic Sanskrit, the language of the invaders, gave this word to later Sanskrit as a term for "noble" or "free-born" (*arya*). The word is found also in old

Iranian, or Persian, texts, and even the term *Iran* is derived from the Old Persian equivalent of *arya*. It was apparently the original name of peoples who migrated out of the steppeland between Eastern Europe and Central Asia into Europe, Greece, Anatolia, the Iranian plateau, and India during the second and first millennia B.C.E. Those who came to India are thus more precisely designated Indo-Aryans, or Vedic Aryans.

In the nineteenth century, *Aryan* was the term applied to the widespread language group known more commonly today as **Indo-European**. To this widely distributed family belong Greek, Latin, the Romance and Germanic languages, the Slavic tongues, and the Indo-Iranian languages, including Persian and Sanskrit and their derivatives. The Nazis perversely misused "Aryan" to refer to a white "master race." Today most scholars use *Aryan* only to identify the Indo-European speakers who invaded India and the Iranian plateau in the second millennium B.C.E. and the Indo-Iranian languages.

"Aryanizing" of North India   The Vedic Aryans were seminomadic warriors who reached India in small tribal groups through the mountain passes of the Hindu Kush. They were horsemen and cattle herders rather than farmers and city builders. They left their mark not in material culture, but in the changes that their conquests brought to the regions they overran: a new language, social organization, techniques of warfare, and religious forms and ideas.

The early Aryans penetrated first into the Punjab and the Indus valley around 1800–1500 B.C.E., presumably in search of grazing lands for their livestock. Their horses, chariots, and copper-bronze weapons likely gave them military superiority over the Indus peoples or their successors. Rig-Vedic hymns echo these early conflicts. The god Indra, for example, is hailed as the warrior who smashes the fortifications of enemies (Indus citadels?) and slays the great serpent who had blocked the rivers (referring to the destruction of the dams that controlled the Indus waters?). The references to human rather than divine warriors in some later Rig-Vedic hymns may reflect actual historical events. One late hymn praises the king of the

Bharatas, giving us the Indian name for modern India, *Bharat*, "land of the Bharatas."

During the Rig-Vedic age (ca. 1700–1000 B.C.E.), the newcomers settled in the Punjab and beyond, where they took up agriculture and stockbreeding. How far they penetrated before 1000 B.C.E. is not clear, but their main locus remained the Punjab and the plains west of the Yamuna River. Then, between about 1000 and 500 B.C.E., the *late Vedic age*, these Aryan Indians spread across the plain between the Yamuna and the Ganges and eastward. They cleared (probably by burning) the heavy forests that covered this region and then settled there. They also moved farther northeast to the Himalayan foothills and southeast along the Ganges, in what was to be the cradle of subsequent Indian civilization. During this age the importance of the Punjab receded.

The late Vedic period is also called the Brahmanic age because it was dominated by the priestly religion of the Brahman class, as evidenced in commentaries called the *Brahmanas* (ca. 1000–800 or 600 B.C.E.). It is also sometimes called the epic age because it provided the setting for India's two classical epics, the *Mahabharata* and the *Ramayana*. Both were composed much later, probably between 400 B.C.E. and 200 C.E., but contain older material and refer to older events. The *Mahabharata*, the world's longest epic poem, centers on the rivalry of two Aryan clans in the region northwest of modern Delhi, perhaps around 900 B.C.E. The *Ramayana* tells of the legendary, dramatic adventures of King Rama. Both epics reflect the complex cultural and social mixing of Aryan and other earlier subcontinent peoples.

By about 200 C.E., this mixing produced a distinctive new "Indian" civilization over most of the subcontinent. Its basis was clearly Aryan, but its language, society, and religion incorporated many non-Aryan elements. Harappan culture vanished, but both it and other regional cultures contributed to the formation of Indian culture as we know it.

Vedic Aryan Society   Aryan society was apparently patrilineal—with succession and inheritance in the male line—and its gods were likewise predominantly male. Marriage appears to have been monogamous, and widows could remarry. Related families formed larger kin groups. The largest social grouping was the tribe, ruled by a chieftain or *raja* ("king" in Sanskrit), who shared power with a tribal council. In early Vedic days the ruler was chosen for his prowess; his chief responsibility was to lead in battle, and he had no priestly function or sacred authority. A chief priest looked after the sacrifices on which religious life centered. By the Brahmanic age the king, with the help of priests, had assumed the role of judge in legal matters and become a hereditary ruler claiming divine qualities. The power of the priestly class had also increased.

Although there were probably subgroups of warriors and priests, Aryan society seems originally to have had only two

basic divisions: noble and common. The Dasas—the darker, conquered peoples—came to form a third group (together with those who intermarried with them) of the socially excluded. Over time, a more rigid scheme of four social classes (excluding the non-Aryan Dasas) evolved. By the late Rig-Vedic period, religious theory explicitly sanctioned these four divisions, or *varnas*—the priestly (Brahman), the warrior/noble (Kshatriya), the peasant/tradesman (Vaishya), and the servant (*Shudra*). Only the members of the three upper classes participated fully in social, political, and religious life. This scheme underlies the rigid caste system that later became fundamental to Indian society.

Material Culture   The early, seminomadic Aryans lived simply in wood-and-thatch or, later, mud-walled dwellings. They measured wealth in cattle and were accomplished at carpentry and bronze working (iron probably was not known in India before 1000 B.C.E.). They used gold for ornamentation and produced woolen textiles. They also cultivated some crops, especially grains, and were familiar with intoxicating drinks, including soma, used in religious rites, and a kind of mead.

References to singing, dancing, and musical instruments suggest that music was a favored pastime in the Vedic period. Gambling, especially dicing, appears to have been popular One of the few secular pieces among the Vedic hymns is a "Gambler's Lament," which closes with a plea to the dice: "Take pity on us. Do not bewitch us with your fierce magic. Let no one be trapped by the brown dice!"

The Brahmanic age left few material remains. Urban culture remained undeveloped, although mud-brick towns appeared as new lands were cleared for cultivation. Established kingdoms with fixed capitals now existed. Trade grew, especially along the Ganges, although there is no evidence of a coinage system. Later texts mention specialized artisans, including goldsmiths, basket makers, weavers, potters, and entertainers. Writing had been reintroduced to India around 700 B.C.E., perhaps from Mesopotamia along with traded goods.

Religion   Vedic India's main identifiable contributions to later history were religious. The Vedas reflect the broad development of Vedic Brahmanic religion in the millennium after the coming of the first Aryans. They tell us primarily about the public cult and domestic rituals of the Aryan upper classes. Among the rest of the population, non-Aryan practices and ideas likely continued to flourish. Apparently non-Aryan elements are visible occasionally even in the Vedic texts themselves, especially later ones. The Upanishads (after ca. 800 B.C.E.) thus refers to fertility and female deities, ritual pollution and ablutions, and the transmigration of the soul after death.

The central Vedic cult—controlled by priests serving a military aristocracy—remained dominant until the middle of the

DOCUMENT | Hymn to Indra

This hymn celebrates the greatest deed ascribed to Indra, the slaying of the dragon Vritra to release the waters needed by people and livestock (which is also heralded at one point in the hymn as the act of creation itself). These waters are apparently those of the dammed-up rivers, but possibly also the rains as well. This victory also symbolizes the victory of the Aryans over the dark-skinned Dasas. Note the sexual as well as water imagery. The kadrukas *may be the bowls used for soma in the sacrifice. The vajra is Indra's thunderbolt; the name* Dasa *for the lord of the waters is also that used for the peoples defeated by the Aryans and for all enemies of Indra, of whom the* Pani *tribe is one.*

> ◆ What are the main kinds of imagery used for Indra and his actions in the hymn? What divine acts does the hymn ascribe to Indra?

Indra's heroic deeds, indeed, will I proclaim, the first ones which the wielder of the vajra accomplished. He killed the dragon, released the waters, and split open the sides of the mountains.

He killed the dragon lying spread out on the mountain; for him Tvashtar fashioned the roaring vajra. Like bellowing cows, the waters, gliding, have gone down straightway to the ocean.

Showing off his virile power he chose soma; from the three kadrukas he drank of the extracted soma. The bounteous god took up the missile, the vajra; he killed the first-born among the dragons.

When you, O Indra, killed the first-born among the dragons and further overpowered the wily tricks (maya) of the trick-sters, bringing forth, at that very moment, the sun, the heaven and the dawn—since then, indeed, have you not come across another enemy. Indra killed Vritra, the greater enemy, the shoulderless one, with his mighty and fatal weapon, the vajra. Like branches of a tree lopped off with an axe, the dragon lies prostrate upon the earth. …

Over him, who lay in that manner like a shattered reed flowed the waters for the sake of man. At the feet of the very waters, which Vritra had [once] enclosed with his might, the dragon [now] lay [prostrate]. …

With the Dasa as their lord and with the dragon as their warder, the waters remained imprisoned, like cows held by the Pani. Having killed Vritra, [Indra] threw open the cleft of waters which had been closed.

You became the hair of a horse's tail, O Indra, when he [Vritra] struck at your sharp-pointed vajra—the one god [eka deva] though you were. You won the cows, O brave one, you won soma; you released the seven rivers, so that they should flow. …

Indra, who wields the vajra in his hand, is the lord of what moves and what remains rested, of what is peaceful and what is horned. He alone rules over the tribes as their king; he encloses them as does a rim the spokes.

—Rig-Veda *1.32*

first millennium B.C.E. By that time other, perhaps older, religious forms were evidently asserting themselves among the populace. The increasing ritual formalism of Brahmanic religion provoked challenges both in popular practice and in religious thought that culminated in Buddhist, Jain, and Hindu traditions of piety and practice (see Chapter 2).

The earliest Indo-Aryans seem to have worshiped numerous gods, most of whom embodied or were associated with powers of nature. The Rig-Vedic hymns are addressed to anthropomorphic deities linked to natural phenomena such as the sky, the clouds, and the sun. These gods are comparable to those of ancient Greece (see Chapter 3) and are apparently distantly related to them through the Indo-European heritage the Greeks and Aryans shared. The name of the Aryan father-god Dyaus, for example, is linguistically related to the Greek Zeus. In Vedic India, however, unlike Greece, the father-god had become less important than his children, especially Indra, god of war and the storm, who led his heavenly warriors across the sky to slay dragons or other enemies with his thunderbolt. (See Document, "Hymn to Indra.")

Also of major importance was Varuna, who may have had connections with the later Iranian god Ahura Mazda (see Chapter 4) and the Greek god of the heavens, Uranos. Varuna was more remote from human affairs than Indra. Depicted as a regal figure seated on his heavenly throne, he guarded the cosmic order, *Rta*, which was both the law of nature and the universal moral law or truth. As the god who commanded awe and demanded righteous behavior, Varuna had characteristics of a supreme, omnipresent divinity.

Another prominent Vedic god was Agni, the god of fire (his name, which is the Sanskrit word for fire, is related to Latin *ignis*, "fire," and thus to English *ignite*). He mediated between heaven and earth through the fire sacrifice, and was thus the god of sacrifice and the priests. He was also god of the hearth, and thus of the home. Like flame itself, he was a mysterious deity.

Other Vedic gods include Soma, the god of the hallucinogenic soma plant and the drink made from it; Ushas, goddess of dawn (one of few female deities); Yama, god of the dead; Rudra, the archer and storm god; Vishnu, a solar deity; and the sun god, Surya. The Vedic hymns praise each god they address as possessing almost all powers, including those associated with other gods.

Ritual sacrifice was the central focus of Vedic religion, its goal apparently to invoke the presence of the gods to whom an offering was made rather than to expiate sins or express thanksgiving. Drinking soma juice was part of the ritual. A recurring theme of the Vedic hymns that accompanied the rituals is the desire for prosperity, health, and victory. Fire sacrifices were particularly important.

The late Vedic texts emphasize magical and cosmic aspects of ritual and sacrifice. Indeed, some of the *Brahmanas* maintain that only exacting performance of the sacrifice can maintain the world order.

The word *Brahman*, originally used to designate the ritual utterance or word of power, came to refer also to the generalized divine power present in the sacrifice. In the **Upanishads**, some of the latest Vedic texts and the ones most concerned with speculation about the universe, *Brahman* was extended to refer to the Absolute, the transcendent principle of reality. As the guardian of ritual and the master of the sacred word, the priest was known throughout the Vedic Aryan period by a related word, *Brahmana*, for which the English is *Brahman*. Echoes of these associations were to lend force in later Hindu tradition to the special status of the Brahman caste groups as the highest social class (see Chapter 4).

CHRONOLOGY

Ancient India

ca. 2250–1750 (2500–1500?) B.C.E.	Indus (Harappan) civilization (written script still undeciphered)
ca. 1800–1500 B.C.E.	Aryan peoples invade northwestern India
ca. 1500–1000 B.C.E.	Rig-Vedic period: composition of Rig-Vedic hymns; Punjab as center of Indo-Aryan civilization
ca. 1000–500 B.C.E.	Late Vedic period: Doab as center of Indo-Aryan civilization
ca. 1000–800/600 B.C.E.	Composition of Brahmanas and other Vedic texts
ca. 800–500 B.C.E.	Composition of major Upanishads
ca. 700–500 B.C.E.	Probable reintroduction of writing
ca. 400 B.C.E.–200 C.E.	Composition of great epics, the *Mahabharata* and *Ramayana*

Early Chinese Civilization

NEOLITHIC ORIGINS IN THE YELLOW RIVER VALLEY

Agriculture began in China about 4000 B.C.E. in the basin of the southern bend of the Yellow River. This is the northernmost of east Asia's four great river systems. The others are the Yangtze in central China, the West River in southern China, and the Red River in what is today northern Vietnam (see Map 1–5). All drain eastward into the Pacific Ocean. In recent millennia, the Yellow River has flowed through a deforested plain, cold in winter and subject to periodic droughts. But in 4000 B.C.E., its climate was warmer, with forested highlands in the west and swampy marshes to the east. The bamboo rat that today can be found only in semitropical Southeast Asia lived along the Yellow River.

The chief crop of China's agricultural revolution was millet. A second agricultural development focusing on rice may have occurred on the Huai River between the Yellow River and the Yangtze near the coast. In time, wheat entered China from the west. The early Chinese cleared land and burned its cover to plant millet and cabbage and, later, rice and soybeans. When the soil became exhausted, fields were abandoned, and sometimes early villages were abandoned, too. Tools were of stone: axes, hoes, spades, and sickle-shaped knives. The early Chinese domesticated pigs, sheep, cattle, dogs, and chickens. Game was also plentiful, and hunting continued to be important to the village economy. In excavated village garbage heaps of ancient China are found the bones of deer, wild cattle, antelopes, rhinoceros, hares, and marmots. Grain was stored in pottery painted in bold, geometric designs of red and black. This pottery gave way to a harder, thin black pottery, made on a potter's wheel, whose use spread west along the Yellow River and south to the Yangtze. The tripodal shapes of Neolithic pots prefigure later Chinese bronzes.

The earliest cultivators lived in wattle-and-daub pit dwellings with wooden support posts and sunken, plastered floors. Their villages were located in isolated clearings along slopes of river valleys. Archaeological finds of weapons and remains of earthen walls suggest tribal warfare between villages. Little is known of the religion of these people, although some evidence indicates the worship of ancestral spirits. They practiced divination by applying heat to a hole drilled in the shoulder bone of a steer or the undershell of a tortoise and then interpreting the resulting cracks in the bone. They buried their dead in cemeteries with jars of food. Tribal leaders wore rings and beads of jade.

EARLY BRONZE AGE: THE SHANG

The traditional history of China tells of three ancient dynasties: Xia (2205–1766 B.C.E.), Shang (1766–1050 B.C.E.), and Zhou (1050–256 B.C.E.). Until early in this century, historians thought the first two were legendary. Then, in the 1920s, archaeological

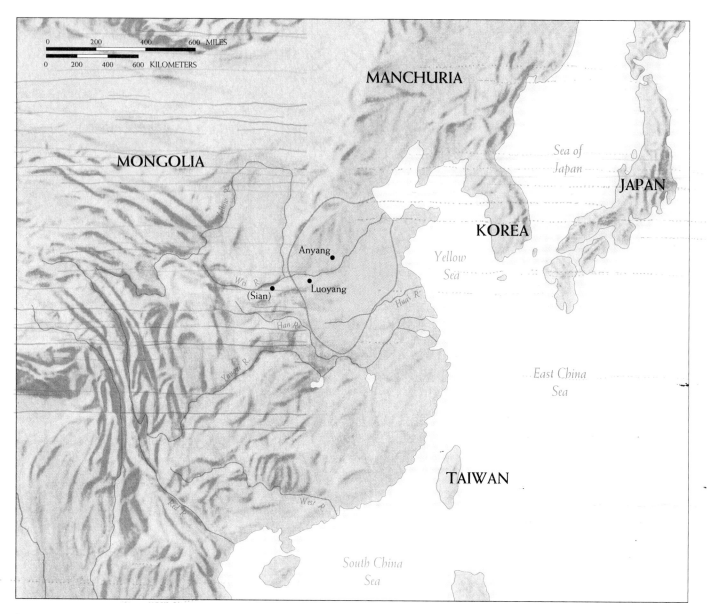

MAP 1–5 Bronze Age China During the Shang Dynasty, 1766–1050 B.C.E.
Anyang was a late Shang dynasty capital. Sian and Luoyang were the capitals of the Western and Eastern Zhou.

excavations at "the wastes of Yin" near present-day Anyang uncovered the ruins of a walled city that had been a late Shang capital (see Map 1–5). Other Shang cities have been discovered more recently. The ruins contained the archives of the department of divination of the Shang court, with thousands on thousands of "oracle bones" incised with archaic Chinese writing. The names of kings on the bones fit almost perfectly those of the traditional historical record. This evidence that the Shang actually existed has led historians to suggest that the Xia may also have been an actual dynasty. Perhaps the Xia was a late Neolithic black-pottery kingdom; perhaps it already had bronze and was responsible for the earliest, still missing stage of Chinese writing.

The characteristic political institution of Bronze Age China was the city-state. The largest was the Shang capital, which, frequently moved, lacked the monumental architecture of Egypt or Mesopotamia. The walled city contained public buildings, altars, and the residences of the aristocracy; it was surrounded by a sea of Neolithic tribal villages. By late Shang times, several such cities were spotted across the north China plain. The Shang kings possessed political, economic, social, and religious authority. When they died, they were sometimes succeeded by younger brothers and sometimes by sons. The rulers of other city-states acknowledged their authority.

The military aristocracy went to war in chariots, supported by levies of foot soldiers. Their weapons were spears and powerful compound bows. Accounts tell of armies of three or four thousand troops and of a battle involving thirteen thousand. The Shang fought against barbarian tribes and, occasionally, against other city-states in rebellion against Shang rule. Captured prisoners were enslaved.

The three most notable features of Shang China were writing, bronzes, and the appearance of social classes. (See Language, "Chinese Writing"; also Language: "Languages of East Asia.") Scribes at the Shang court kept records on strips of bamboo, but these have not survived. What have survived are inscriptions on bronze artifacts and the oracle bones. Some bones contain the question put to the oracle, the answer, and the outcome of the matter. Representative questions were: Which ancestor is causing the king's earache? If the king goes hunting at Ch'i, will there be a disaster? Will the king's child be a son? If the king sends his army to attack an enemy, will the deity help him? Was a sacrifice acceptable to ancestral deities?

What we know of Shang religion is based on the bones. The Shang believed in a supreme "Deity Above," who had authority over the human world. Also serving at the court of the Deity Above were lesser natural deities—the sun, moon, earth, rain, wind, and the six clouds. Even the Shang king sacrificed not to the Deity Above but to his ancestors, who interceded with the Deity Above on the king's behalf. Kings, while alive at least, were not considered divine but were the high priests of the state.

In Shang times, as later, religion in China was closely associated with cosmology. The Shang people observed the movements of the planets and stars and reported eclipses. Celestial happenings were seen as omens from the gods. The chief cosmologists also recorded events at the court. The Shang calendar had a month of 30 days and a year of 360 days. Adjustments were made periodically by adding an extra month. The calendar was used by the king to tell his people when to sow and when to reap.

Bronze appeared in China about 2000 B.C.E., a thousand years later than in Mesopotamia and five hundred years later than in India. The Shang likely developed bronze technology independently, however, because Shang methods of casting were more advanced than those of Mesopotamia, and because the designs on its bronzes emerged directly from those of the preceding black-pottery culture. Bronze was used for weapons, armor, and chariot fittings, and for a variety of ceremonial vessels of amazing fineness and beauty.

Among the Shang, as with other early river valley civilizations, the increasing control of nature through agriculture and metallurgy was accompanied by the emergence of a rigidly stratified society in which the many were compelled to serve the few. A monopoly of bronze weapons enabled aristo-

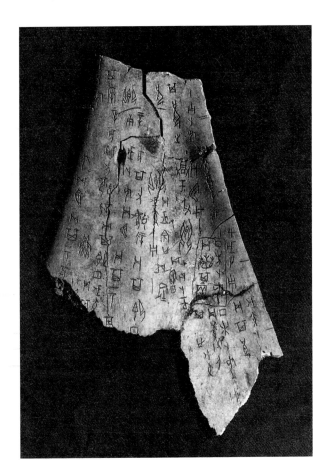

⚑ **Oracle Bone.** Inscribed oracle bone from the Shang dynasty city of Anyang.
From the collection of the C.V. Starr East Asian Library, Columbia University.

crats to exploit other groups. A hierarchy of class defined life in the Chinese city-state. The king and the officials of his court lived within the walled city. Their houses were spacious, built above the ground with roofs supported by rows of wooden pillars, resting on foundation stones. Their lifestyle was opulent for ancient times. They wore fine clothes, feasted at banquets, and drank wine from bronze vessels. In contrast, a far larger population of agricultural workers lived outside the city in cramped pit dwellings. Their life was meager and hard. Archaeological excavations of their underground hovels have uncovered only clay pots.

Nowhere was the gulf between the royal lineage and the baseborn more apparent than it was in the Shang institution of human sacrifice. One Shang tomb thirty-nine feet long, twenty-six feet wide, and twenty-six feet deep contained the decapitated bodies of humans, horses, and dogs, as well as ornaments of bone, stone, and jade. When a king died, hundreds of slaves or prisoners of war, sometimes together with those who had served the king during his lifetime, might be buried with him. Sacrifices also were made when a palace or an altar was built.

LANGUAGE Chinese Writing

The Chinese system of writing dates back at least to the Shang dynasty (1766–1050 B.C.E.), when animal bones and tortoise shells (the so-called oracle bones) were incised for the purpose of divination. About half of the three thousand characters used in Shang times have been deciphered. They evolved over the centuries into the fifty thousand characters found in the largest dictionaries. But even today only about three or four thousand are in common use. A scholar may know twice that number.

Characters developed from little pictures. Note the progressive stylization. By 200 B.C.E., the writing had become standardized and close to the modern form of the printed character.

	Shang (1400 B.C.E.)	Zhou (600 B.C.E.)	Seal Script (200 B.C.E.)	Modern
Sun				
Moon				
Tree				
Bird				
Mouth				
Horse				

Other characters combined two pictures to express an idea. The following examples use modern characters:

Sun	日	+ moon	月	= bright	明	
Mouth	口	+ bird	鳥	= to chirp	鳴	
Woman	女	+ child	子	= good	好	
Tree	木	+ sun	日	= east	東	

It was a matter of convention that the sun behind a tree meant the rising sun in the east and not the setting sun in the west.

Characters were formed several other ways. In one, a sound element was combined with a meaning element. Chinese has many homonyms, or words with the same sound. The character 台, for example, is read *tai* and means "elevation" or "to raise up." But in spoken Chinese, there are other words with the same sound that mean "moss," "trample," "a nag," and "idle." Thus,

Tai	台	+ grass	艹	= moss	苔	
Tai	台	+ foot	足	= trample	跆	
Tai	台	+ horse	馬	= a nag	駘	
Tai	台	+ heart	心	= idle	怠	

In each case the sound comes from the 台, and the meaning from the other element. Note that the 台 may be at the bottom, the top, or the right. This positioning, too, is a matter of convention.

Tables by A. Craig; calligraphy by Teruko Craig.

LATE BRONZE AGE: THE WESTERN ZHOU

To the west of the area of Shang rule, in the valley of the Wei River, a tributary of the Yellow River, lived the Zhou people. Culturally closer to the Neolithic black-pottery people, they were less civilized and more warlike than the Shang. References to the Zhou in the Shang oracle bones indicate that the Shang had relations with them—sometimes friendly, sometimes hostile. According to the traditional historical record, the last Shang kings were weak, cruel, and tyrannical. By 1050 B.C.E., they had been debilitated by campaigns against nomads in the north and rebellious tribes in the east. Taking advantage of this opportunity, the Zhou made alliances with disaffected city-states and swept in, conquering the Shang.

In most respects, the Zhou continued the Shang pattern of life and rule. The agrarian-based city-state continued to be the basic unit of society, and it is estimated that there were about two hundred of them in the eighth century B.C.E. The Zhou social hierarchy was not unlike that of the Shang, with kings and lords at the top, officials and warriors below them, and peasants and slaves at the bottom. Slaves served primarily as domestic servants. The Zhou assimilated Shang culture, continuing without interruption the development of China's ideographic writing. The Zhou also maintained the practice of casting bronze ceremonial vessels, but their vessels lack the fineness that set the Shang above the rest of the Bronze Age world.

The Zhou kept their capital in the west but set up a secondary capital at Luoyang, along the southern bend of the Yellow River (see Map 1–5). They appointed their kinsmen or other aristocratic allies to rule in other city-states. Blood or lineage ties were essential to the Zhou pattern of rule. The Zhou king was the head of the senior branch of the family. He per-

LANGUAGE   Languages of East Asia

The two main language families in present-day east Asia are the Sinitic and the Ural-Altaic. They are as different from each other as they are from European tongues. The Sinitic languages are Chinese, Vietnamese, Thai, Burmese, and Tibetan. Within Chinese are several mutually unintelligible dialects. Standard Chinese, based on the Beijing dialect, is further from Cantonese than Spanish is from French. Ural-Altaic languages are spoken to the east, north, and west of China. They include Japanese, Korean, Manchurian, Mongolian, the Turkic languages, and, in Europe, Finnish and Hungarian.

---

formed the sacrifices to the Deity Above for the entire family. The rankings of the lords of other princely states reflected their degree of closeness to the senior line of Zhou kings.

One difference between the Shang and the Zhou was in the nature of the political legitimacy each claimed. The Shang kings, descended from shamanistic (priestly) rulers, had a built-in religious authority and needed no theory to justify their rule. But the Zhou, having conquered the Shang, needed a rationale for why they, and not the Shang, were now the rightful rulers. Their argument was that Heaven (the name for the supreme being that gradually replaced the Deity Above during the early Zhou), appalled by the wickedness of the last Shang king, had withdrawn its mandate to rule from the Shang, awarding it instead to the Zhou. This concept of the **Mandate of Heaven** was subsequently invoked by every dynasty in China down to the twenty-first century. The ideograph for Heaven is related to that for man, and the concept initially had human, or anthropomorphic, attributes. In the later Zhou, however, although it continued to be viewed as having a moral will, Heaven became less anthropomorphic and more of an abstract metaphysical force.

IRON AGE: THE EASTERN ZHOU

In 771 B.C.E. the Wei valley capital of the Western Zhou was overrun by barbarians. The explanation of the event in Chinese tradition calls to mind the story of "the boy who cried wolf." The last Western Zhou king was so infatuated with a favorite concubine that he repeatedly lit bonfires signaling a barbarian attack. His concubine would clap her hands in delight at the sight of the army assembled in martial splendor. But the army tired of the charade, and when invaders actually came, the king's beacons were ignored. The king was killed and the Zhou capital sacked. The heir to the throne, with some members of the court, escaped to the secondary capital at Luoyang, two hundred miles to the east and just south of the bend in the Yellow River, beginning the Eastern Zhou period.

The first phase of the Eastern Zhou, sometimes called the Spring and Autumn period after a classic history by that name, lasted until 481 B.C.E. After their flight to Luoyang, the Zhou kings were never able to reestablish their old authority. By the early seventh century B.C.E., Luoyang's political power was nominal, although it remained a center of culture and ritual observances. (See Document, "Human Sacrifice in Early China.") Kinship and religious ties to the Zhou house had worn thin, and it no longer had the military strength to reimpose its rule. During the seventh and sixth centuries B.C.E. the political configuration was an equilibrium of many small principalities on the north-central plain surrounded by larger, wholly autonomous territorial states along the borders of the plain (see Map 1–6). The larger states consolidated the areas within their borders, absorbed tribal peoples, and expanded, conquering states on their periphery.

To defend themselves against the more aggressive territorial states, and in the absence of effective Zhou authority, smaller states entered defensive alliances. The earliest alliance, of 681 B.C.E., was directed against the half-barbarian state of Chu, which straddled the Yangzi in the south. Princes and lords of smaller states elected as their *hegemon* (or military overlord) the lord of a northern territorial state and pledged him their support. At the formal ceremony that established the alliance, a bull was sacrificed. The hegemon and other lords smeared its blood on their mouths and swore oaths to the gods to uphold the alliance. That the oaths were not always upheld can be surmised from the Chinese expression, "to break an oath while the blood is still wet on one's lips."

During the next two centuries, alliances shifted and hegemons changed. At best, alliances only slowed down the pace of military aggrandizement.

The second phase of the Eastern Zhou is known as the Warring States period after a chronicle of the same name treating the years from 401 to 256 B.C.E. By the fifth century B.C.E., all defensive alliances had collapsed. Strong states swallowed their weaker neighbors. The border states grew in size and power. Interstate stability disappeared. By the fourth century B.C.E., only eight or nine great territorial states remained as contenders. The only question was which one would defeat the others and go on to unify China.

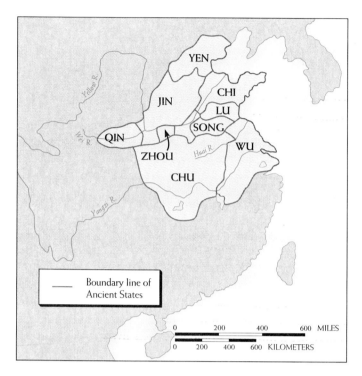

MAP 1–6 Early Iron Age Territorial States in China During the Sixth Century B.C.E. After the fall of the Western Zhou in China in 771 B.C.E., large territorial states formed that became increasingly independent of the later Zhou kings.

Three basic changes in Chinese society contributed to the rise of large territorial states. One was the expansion of population and agricultural lands. The walled cities of the Shang and Western Zhou had been like oases in the wilds, bounded by plains, marshes, and forests. Game was plentiful; thus, hunting, along with sheep and cattle breeding, supplemented agriculture. But in the Eastern Zhou, as population grew, wilds began to disappear, the economy became almost entirely agricultural, and hunting became an aristocratic pastime. Friction arose over boundaries as states began to abut. These changes accelerated in the late sixth century B.C.E. after the start of the Iron Age. With iron tools, farmers cleared new lands and plowed deeper, raising yields and increasing agricultural surpluses. Irrigation and drainage canals became important for the first time. Serfs gave way to independent farmers, who bought and sold land. By the third century B.C.E., China had about 20 million people, making it the most populous country in the world, a distinction it has never lost.

A second development was the rise of commerce. Roads built for war were used by merchants. Goods were transported by horses, oxcarts, riverboats, and the camel, which entered China in the third century B.C.E. The products of one region were traded for those of another. Copper coins joined bolts of silk and precious metals as media of exchange. Rich merchants rivaled in lifestyle the landowning lower nobility. New outer walls were added to cities to provide for expanded merchant quarters. Bronze bells and mirrors, clay figurines, lacquer boxes, and musical instruments found in late Zhou tombs give ample evidence that the material and artistic culture of China leaped ahead during this period, despite its endemic wars.

A third change that doomed the city-state was the rise of a new kind of army. The war chariots of the old aristocracy, practical only on level terrain, gave way to cavalry armed with crossbows. Most of the fighting was done by conscript foot soldiers. Armies of the territorial states numbered in the hundreds of thousands. The old nobility gave way to professional commanders. The old aristocratic etiquette, which governed behavior even in battle, gave way to military tactics that were bloody and ruthless. Prisoners were often massacred.

Change also affected government. Lords of the new territorial states began to style themselves as kings, taking the title that previously only Zhou royalty had enjoyed. At some courts, the hereditary nobility began to decline, supplanted by ministers appointed for their knowledge of statecraft. To survive, new states had to transform their agricultural and commercial wealth into military strength. To collect taxes conscript soldiers, and administer the affairs of state required records and literate officials. Academies were established to fill the need. Beneath the ministers, a literate bureaucracy developed. Its

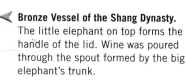

◀ **Bronze Vessel of the Shang Dynasty.** The little elephant on top forms the handle of the lid. Wine was poured through the spout formed by the big elephant's trunk.
The Freer Gallery of Art, Smithsonian Institution, Washington, D.C.

DOCUMENT | Human Sacrifice in Early China

By the seventh century B.C.E. human sacrifice was less frequent in China but still happened. This poem was composed when Duke Mu of the state of Qin died in 631 B.C.E.(For want of better terms, Chinese titles are usually translated into roughly equivalent titles among the English nobility.) Were human feelings different, as Professor K. C. Chang has asked, a thousand years earlier during the Shang? The poem suggests that despite religious belief and the honor accorded the victims, they may not have gone gladly to the grave. Note the identification of Heaven with "that blue one," the sky.

◆ We believe today that it is honorable to die in war for one's nation. How is that different from dying to serve one's lord in the afterlife?

"Kio" sings the oriole
As it lights on the thorn-bush.
Who went with Duke Mu to the grave?
Yen-hsi of the clan Tsu-chu.
Now this Yen-hsi
Was the pick of all our men;

But as he drew near the tomb-hole
His limbs shook with dread.
That blue one, Heaven,
Takes all our good men.
Could we but ransom him
There are a hundred would give their lives.
"Kio" sings the oriole
As it lights on the mulberry-tree.
Who went with Duke Mu to the grave?
Chung-hang of the clan Tsu-chu.
Now this Chung-hang
Was the sturdiest of all our men;
But as he drew near the tomb-hole
His limbs shook with dread.
That blue one, Heaven,
Takes all our good men.
Could we but ransom him
There are a hundred would give their lives.

From *The Book of Songs*, trans. by Arthur Waley (New York: Grove Press, 1960), p. 311.

members were referred to as *shi*, a term that had once meant "warrior" but gradually came to mean "scholar-bureaucrat." The *shi* were of mixed social origins, including petty nobility, literate members of the old warrior class, landlords, merchants, and rising commoners. From this class, as we will see in Chapter 2, came the philosophers who created the "one hundred schools" and transformed the culture of China.

The Rise of Civilization in the Americas

During the last ice age the Bering region between Siberia and Alaska was dry land. Sometime before twelve thousand years ago, and perhaps as early as thirty thousand years ago, humans crossed this land bridge, probably in several migrations. Over many centuries these Asian immigrants moved south and east until they eventually crossed the more than eleven-thousand miles to the tip of South America and the more than four thousand miles to the eastern regions of North America. In light of the vast distances and imposing geographic barriers involved, these ancient migrations must have been as heroic as any in human history. From them a wide variety of original American cultures and many hundreds of languages arose.

The earliest immigrants to the Americas, like all other Paleolithic peoples, lived by hunting, fishing, and gathering. At the time of the initial migrations, herds of large game animals such as mammoths were plentiful. By the end of the ice age, however, mammoths and many other forms of game had become extinct in the Americas. Compared to Africa and Eurasia, many parts of North and South America were poor in animal resources and the rich source of protein they provide. Neither horses nor cattle populated the American continents. Where fishing or small game were not sufficiently plentiful, people had to rely on protein from vegetable sources. One result was the remarkable manner in which the original Americans participated in the Neolithic revolution. American production of plants providing protein far outpaced that of European agriculture. In this regard one of the most important early developments was the cultivation of

CHRONOLOGY

Early China

4000 B.C.E.	Neolithic agricultural villages
1766 B.C.E.	Bronze Age city-states, aristocratic charioteers, pictographic writing
771 B.C.E.	Iron Age territorial states
500 B.C.E.	Age of philosophers
221 B.C.E.	China is unified

maize (corn). Wherever maize could be extensively grown, a major ingredient in the food supply was secured. The cultivation of maize appears to have been in place in Mexico by approximately 4000 B.C.E. and to have developed farther south somewhat later. Other important foods were potatoes (developed in the Andes), manioc, squash, beans, peppers, and tomatoes. Many of these foods entered the diet of Europeans, Asians, and other peoples after the European conquest of the Americas in the sixteenth century C.E.

Eventually four areas of relatively dense settlement emerged in the Americas. One of these, in the Pacific Northwest in the area around Puget Sound, depended on the region's extraordinary abundance of fish rather than on agriculture; this area did not develop urbanized states. Another was the Mississippi valley, where, based on maize agriculture, the inhabitants developed a high level of social and political integration that had collapsed several centuries before European contact. The other two, Mesoamerica and the Andean region of South America, saw the emergence of strong, long-lasting states. In other regions with maize agriculture and settled village life—notably the North American Southwest—food supplies might have been too insecure to support the development of states.

Chapter 15 examines Mesoamerican and Andean civilization in detail. Here we give only a brief overview of their development. **Mesoamerica**, which extends from the central part of modern Mexico into Central America, is a region of great geographical diversity, ranging from tropical rain forest to semiarid mountains (see Map 1–7). Archaeologists traditionally divide its preconquest history into three broad periods: Pre-Classic or Formative (2000 B.C.E.–150 C.E.), Classic (150–900 C.E.), and Post-Classic (900–1521). The earliest Mesoamerican civilization, that of the Olmecs, arose during the Pre-Classic on the Gulf coast beginning approximately 1500 B.C.E. The Olmec centers at San Lorenzo (c. 1200–c. 900 B.C.E.) and La Venta (c. 900–c. 400 B.C.E.) exhibit many of the characteristics of later Mesoamerican cities, including the symmetrical arrangement of large platforms, plazas, and

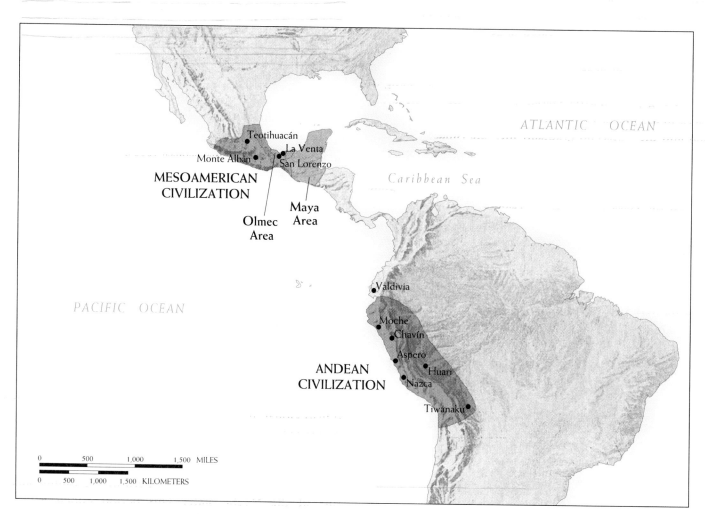

MAP 1–7 Civilization in Mesoamerica and the Andean Region. Both Mesoamerica and the Andean region of South America saw the development of a series of civilizations beginning between 1500 and 1000 B.C.E.

CHRONOLOGY

Early Civilizations of Mesoamerica

1500–400 B.C.E.	The Olmec
200–750 C.E.	The Classic period in central Mexico. Dominance of Teotihuacán in the Valley of Mexico and Monte Alban in the Valley of Oaxaca
150–900 C.E.	The Classic period of Mayan civilization in the Yucatán and Guatemala

other monumental structures along a central axis and possibly courts for the ritual ball game played throughout Mesoamerica at the time of the Spanish conquest. Writing developed in Mesoamerica during the Late Formative period. As we will see in Chapter 15, succeeding civilizations—including the Classic period civilization of Teotihuacán, the Post-Classic civilizations of the Toltecs and Aztecs, and the Classic and Post-Classic civilization of the Mayas—created large cities, developed sophisticated calendar systems, and were organized in complex social and political structures.

The Andean region is one of dramatic contrasts. Along its western edge, the narrow coastal plain is one of the driest deserts in the world. The Andes rise abruptly from the coastal plain and then descend gradually into the Amazon basin to the east. Agriculture is possible on the coast only in the valleys of the many rivers that flow from the Andes into the Pacific. The earliest monumental architecture in the Andean region, built on the coast at the site of Aspero by people who depended on a combination of agriculture and the Pacific's rich marine resources, dates to about 2750 B.C.E., contemporary with the Great Pyramids of Egypt's Old Kingdom.

From 800 to 200 B.C.E. a civilization associated with the site of Chavín de Huantar in the highlands of Peru exerted great influence in the Andes. Artifacts in the distinctive Chavín style can be found over a large area dating to this pe-

▲ Olmec Head. This colossal Olmec head, now in the Museo Nacional de Antropologia in Mexico City, was excavated at San Lorenzo. Carved of basalt, it may be a portrait of an Olmec ruler. Olmec civilization thrived between 1500 and 800 B.C.E.
Josephus Daniels/Photo Researchers, Inc.

riod, which archaeologists call the Early Horizon. In many areas, this was a time of technical innovation, including pottery, textiles, and metallurgy. Whether the spread of the Chavín style represents actual political integration or the influence of a strong religious center is not known. The period following the decline of Chavín, which archaeologists call the Early Intermediate period, saw the development of distinctive cultures in several regions. Notable among these are the Moche culture on the northern coast of Peru and the Nazca culture on the southern coast. A second period of transregional integration—called the Middle Horizon—occurred around 600 C.E., this time probably associated with empires centered on the highland sites of Huari and Tiahuanaco. The succeeding Late Intermediate period was dominated on the northern coast of Peru by the Chimu successors of the Moche state. This period ended with the founding of the vast, tightly controlled empire of the Incas in the fourteenth and fifteenth centuries C.E.

CHRONOLOGY

Early Civilization of the Andes

ca. 2750 B.C.E.?	Monumental architecture at Aspero
800–200 B.C.E.	Chavín (Early) Horizon
200 B.C.E.–600 C.E.	Early Intermediate period (Moche on the northern coast of Peru, Nazca on the southern coast)

Indus Stamp Seal.

Summary

The Emergence of Civilization Beginning in 10,000 B.C.E. human beings shifted from a hunter-gather way of life to one marked by settled agriculture and the domestication of animals—a shift known as the "Neolithic Revolution." Between 4000 and 3000 B.C.E., civilization began to appear in the Tigris and Euphrates valleys in Mesopotamia, then along the Nile River in Egypt, and somewhat later in the Indus valley in India and the Yellow River basin in China. Each of these early civilizations developed urban centers, monumental architecture, a hierarchical society, and a system of writing. The period is known as the Bronze Age because it coincided with the discovery of the technique for making bronze tools and weapons.

Mesopotamia The Sumerians founded the oldest Mesopotamian cities around 3000 B.C.E. Beginning around 2370 B.C.E., the Sumerian city-states were conquered and absorbed in turn by the Akkadian, Babylonian, and Assyrian Empires. The Sumerians passed much of their civilization down to their successors: a system of writing on clay tablets called *cuneiform*, the worship of gods based on natural forces, semidivine kings, and a highly developed bureaucracy.

Egypt Watered by the Nile River and protected by deserts and the sea, Egyptian civilization was more secure and peaceful than that of Mesopotamia. Egypt became a unified kingdom around 2700 B.C.E. Religion dominated Egyptian life. The kings, or pharaohs, were considered gods on whom the lives and prosperity of their people depended. Egyptian history is divided into three main periods: Old Kingdom (2700–2200 B.C.E.), Middle Kingdom (2052–1786 B.C.E.), and New Kingdom (1575–1087 B.C.E.). Under the New Kingdom, Egypt contended for mastery of the Near East with the Hittite Empire.

Indus Civilization By 2300 B.C.E. at least 70 Indus cities, the largest being Harappa and Mohenjo-Daro, had developed a sophisticated urban culture. Between 1800 and 1700 B.C.E., Indus civilization disappeared for unknown reasons. In its place, Indo-European (or Aryan) invaders established the "Vedic" culture, named after the ritual writings known as the Vedas. In turn, Vedic culture evolved into a "new" Indian civilization that spread over the whole subcontinent.

China The Shang dynasty (1766–1050 B.C.E.) founded the earliest known Bronze Age civilization in China. The Shang and their successors, the Zhou (1050–256 B.C.E.), ruled as warrior aristocrats from city-states that fought outsiders and each other. By the fourth century B.C.E., as population and commerce expanded, rulers needed bigger armies to defend their states and trained bureaucrats to administer them. The result was the consolidation of many petty states into a few large territorial units.

The Americas The first civilizations in the Americas arose in places that produced an agricultural surplus. In Mesoamerica (central Mexico and Central America) this was based on the cultivation of maize (corn). In the Andes valleys, it was based on a combination of agriculture and the rich marine resources of the Pacific. The Olmecs (1500–400 B.C.E.) established the first civilization in Mesoamerica, whereas the first monumental architecture appeared in the Andes region around 2750 B.C.E..

Review Questions

1. How was life during the Paleolithic Age different from that in the Neolithic Age? What advances in agriculture and human development had taken place by the end of the Neolithic era? Is it valid to speak of a "Neolithic Revolution"?

2. What defines civilization? What are the similarities and differences among the world's earliest civilizations?

3. What general conclusions can you draw about the differences in the political and intellectual outlooks of the civilizations of Egypt and Mesopotamia? Compare especially Egyptian and Mesopotamian religious views. In what ways did the regional geography influence the religious outlooks of these two civilizations?

4. Why were the Assyrians so successful in establishing their Near Eastern Empire? How did their empire differ from that of the Hittites or Egyptians? In what ways did this empire benefit the civilized Middle East? Why did the Assyrian Empire ultimately fail to survive?

5. How does the early history of Indian civilization differ from that of the river valley civilizations of China, Mesopotamia, and Egypt? What does the evidence suggest were the social, economic, and political differences between the Indus civilization and the Vedic Aryan civilization?

6. What were the stages of early Chinese history? What led each to evolve toward the next?

7. From the appearance of civilization in the Americas, what can you conclude about the factors that give rise to it?

Key Terms

Aryans   (p. 29)

Bronze Age   (p. 12)

civilization   (p. 12)

culture   (p. 9)

cuneiform   (p. 15)

diffusion   (p. 8)

Harappan   (p. 29)

hieroglyphs   (p. 23)

Indo-European   (p. 32)

Mahabharata **and** *Ramayana*   (p. 33)

Mandate of Heaven   (p. 39)

Mesoamerica   (p. 42)

Mesopotamia   (p. 12)

Neolithic Revolution   (p. 12)

Paleolithic Age   (p. 9)

pharaoh   (p. 21)

raja   (p. 33)

Upanishads   (p. 35)

Vedas   (p. 29)

Documents CD-ROM

The Fertile Crescent
   1.1   Lugal Sulgi: Role Model for Mesopotamian Royalty
   1.2   The Nippur Murder Trial and the "Silent Wife"
   1.3   The Reign of Sargon
   1.4   The Epic of Gilgamesh
   1.5   The Code of Hammurabi
   1.6   Daily Life in Egypt
1.7 A Humble Farmer Pleads His Own Case: The Workings of Ma'at
   1.8   Some Common-sense Advice from the Scribe Any to His Son

1.10 Assyrian War Tactics

Early Civilization in East Asia
   2.1   Might makes Right: the "Shu ching" Sets Forth the Mandate of Heaven
   2.2   The Spirit World
   2.3   Ch'u Yuan and Sung Yu: Individual Voices in a Chaotic Era

Early Civilization in South Asia
   3.1   Rig Veda

NOTE: *To learn more about the topics in this chapter, see the Suggested Readings at the end of the book.*

2

Four Great Revolutions in Thought and Religion

◄ **CONFUCIUS.** Confucius, depicted wearing the robes of a scholar of a later age.

Collection of the National Palace Museum, Taipei, Taiwan, Republic of China

Philosophy and Religion

Between 800 and 300 B.C.E., four philosophical or religious revolutions shaped the subsequent history of the world. The names of many involved in these revolutions are world-famous—Socrates, Plato, Aristotle, the Buddha, Isaiah, and Confucius. All the revolutions occurred in or near the four heartland areas in which the river valley civilizations (described in Chapter 1) had appeared fifteen hundred or more years earlier. The transition from the early river valley civilizations to the intellectual and spiritual breakthroughs of the middle of the first millennium B.C.E. is schematized in the chart on page 49.

Before considering each of the original breakthroughs that occurred between 800 and 300 B.C.E., we might ask whether they have anything in common. Five points are worth noting.

1. All the philosophical or religious revolutions occurred in or near the original river valley civilizations. These areas contained the most advanced cultures of the ancient world. They had sophisticated agriculture, cities with many literate inhabitants, and specialized trades and professions. In short, they had the material preconditions for breakthroughs in religion and thought.

2. Each of the revolutions in thought and ethos was born of a crisis in the ancient world. The appearance of iron meant better tools and weapons and, by extension, greater riches and more powerful armies. Old societies began to change and then to disintegrate. Old aristocratic and priestly codes of behavior broke down, producing a demand for more universalized rules of behavior, in other words, for ethics. The very relation of humans to nature or to the universe seemed to be changing. This predicament led to new visions of social and political order. The similarity between the Jewish Messiah, the Chinese sage-king, and Plato's philosopher-king is more than accidental. Each was a response to a crisis in a society of the ancient world. Each would reconnect ethics to history and restore order to a troubled society.

3. The number of philosophical and religious revolutions can be counted on the fingers of one hand. The reason is

not that humans' creativity dried up after 300 B.C.E., but that subsequent breakthroughs and advances tended to occur within the original traditions, which, absorbing new energies, continued to evolve.

4. After the first- and second-stage transformations, much of the cultural history of the world involves the spread of cultures derived from these original heartlands to ever wider spheres. Christianity spread to northern and eastern Europe, the Americas, and parts of Asia and Africa; Buddhism to central, southeastern, and eastern Asia; Confucianism to Korea, Vietnam, and Japan; and Islam to Africa, southeastern Europe, and southern, central, and southeastern Asia. Sometimes the spread was the result of movements of people; other areas were like dry grasslands needing only the spark of the new ideas to be ignited. Typically, the process spread out over centuries.

5. Once a cultural pattern was set, it usually endured. Each major culture was resistant to the others and was only rarely displaced. Even in modern times, although the culture of modern science, and the learning associated with it, has penetrated every cultural zone, it has reshaped—and is reshaping, not displacing—the major cultures. Only Confucianism, the most secular of the traditional cultures, crumbled at the touch of science, and even its ethos remains a potent force in east Asian societies. These major cultures endured because they were not only responses to particular crises, but also attempts to answer universal questions concerning the human condition: What are human beings? What is our relation to the universe? How should we relate to others?

THINK AHEAD
♦ Why do you think so many revolutionary philosophical and religious ideas emerged at about the same time in many different regions? Do these ideas share any fundamental concerns?

A LL HUMAN CULTURES DEVELOP RELIGIOUS OR philosophical systems. Some scientists have even debated whether humans are somehow "hard-wired" biologically to tend toward religious beliefs. Regardless of the outcome of that debate, clearly religion and philosophy meet profound human psychological needs. They offer people explanations of where they and their societies came from, why they exist, and what the future holds for them, in this life and beyond.

Comparing the Four Great Revolutions

The most straightforward case is that of China. Both geographically and culturally, its philosophical breakthrough grew directly out of the earlier river valley civilization. No such continuity existed elsewhere in the world. The natural barriers of the Central Asian steppes, mountain ranges, and deserts allowed China to develop its own unique culture relatively undisturbed and uninfluenced by outside forces.

The sharpest contrast with China is the Indian subcontinent, which lacked geographic and cultural continuity. By the middle of the second millennium B.C.E., the Indus civilization had collapsed. It was replaced by the culture of the Indo-Aryan warriors who swept in from the northwest. Absorbing many particulars from the earlier tradition, they built a new civilization on the plains farther east along the mighty Ganges River. The great tradition of Indian thought and religion emerged after 600 B.C.E. from this Ganges civilization.

In southwest Asia and along the shores of the Mediterranean, the transition was more complex than that in either China or India. No direct line of development can be traced from the Nile civilization of ancient Egypt or the civilization of the Tigris-Euphrates river valley to Greek philosophy or to Judaic monotheism. Rather, the ancient river valley civilizations evolved into a complex amalgam that we call ancient Near Eastern civilization. This cosmopolitan culture included diverse older religious, mythical, and cosmological traditions, as well as newer mystery cults. The Greeks and the ancient Hebrews were two among many outside peoples who invaded this region, settled down, and both absorbed and contributed to the composite civilization.

Judaic monotheism and Greek philosophy—representing different outgrowths of this amalgam—were each important in their own right. They have continued as vital elements in Western and Near Eastern civilizations. But their greatest influence occurred centuries later when they helped shape first Chris-

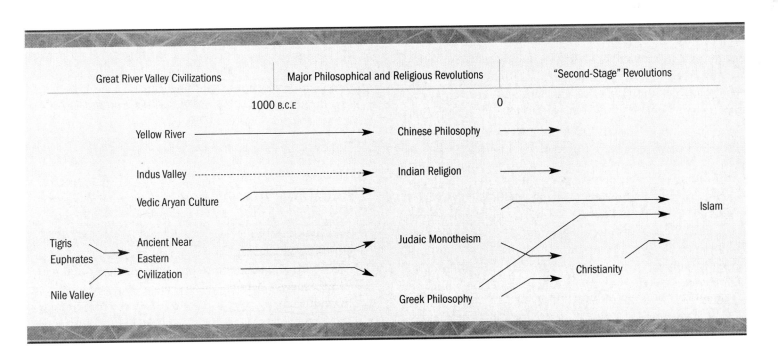

Great River Valley Civilizations	Major Philosophical and Religious Revolutions	"Second-Stage" Revolutions
1000 B.C.E	0	
Yellow River	Chinese Philosophy	
Indus Valley	Indian Religion	
Vedic Aryan Culture		Islam
Tigris Euphrates / Nile Valley → Ancient Near Eastern Civilization	Judaic Monotheism	Christianity
	Greek Philosophy	

tianity and then Islam. The major cultural zones in world history since the mid–first millennium C.E. are the Chinese, the Indian, the Western Christian, and the Islamic. But the latter two were formed much later than the Chinese and the Indian. They represent a second-stage formation of which the first stage comprised the Judaic and the Greek.

Philosophy in China

The beauty of ancient Shang bronzes is breathtaking, but they also have an archaic strangeness. Like Olmec stone sculpture of prehistoric America, they are products of a culture so far removed from our own as to be almost incomprehensible. By contrast, the humanism of the Confucian writings and the poetry of the Eastern Zhou (771–256 B.C.E.) speak to us directly. However much the philosophies of these centuries grew out of the earlier matrix of archaic culture, they mark a break with it and the beginning of what we think of today as the Chinese tradition.

The background of the philosophical revolution in China was the disintegration of the old Zhou society (see Chapter 1 for details). New territorial states replaced the many Zhou city-states. Ruthless, upstart, peasant armies, augmented by an Early Iron Age cavalry armed with crossbows, began to replace the old nobility, who had gone to war in chariots. A rising merchant class disrupted the formerly stable agricultural economy. As the old etiquette crumbled and old rituals lost their force, a search began for new principles by which to re-create a peaceful society and new rules by which to live.

Of the four great revolutions in thought of the first millennium B.C.E., the Chinese was more akin, perhaps, to the Greek than to the Indian religious transformations or to Judaic monotheism. Just as Greece had a gamut of philosophies, so in China there were the "one hundred schools." (When Mao Tsetung said in 1956, "Let the one hundred flowers bloom"—encouraging a momentary easing of intellectual repression—he was referring to the creative era of Zhou philosophy.) Whereas Greek thought was speculative and more concerned with the world of nature, Chinese thought was sociopolitical and more practical. Even the Daoist sages, who were inherently apolitical, found it necessary to offer a political philosophy. Chinese thought also had far greater staying power than Greek thought, which only a few centuries after the glory of Athens was submerged by Christianity. It became the handmaiden of theology and did not re-emerge as an independent force until the Renaissance. In contrast, Chinese philosophy, although challenged by Buddhism, remained dominant until the early twentieth century. How were these early philosophies able to maintain such a grip on China when the cultures of every other part of the world fell under the sway of religions?

Part of the answer is that most Chinese philosophy had a religious dimension. But it was another kind of religion, with assumptions different from those derived from Judaic roots. In the Christian or Islamic worldview, there is a God who, however concerned with humankind, is not of this world. This worldview leads to dualism, the distinction between an otherworld, which is supernatural, and this world, which is natural.

In the Chinese worldview, the two spheres are not separate: The cosmos is single, continuous, and nondualistic. It includes heaven, earth, and man. Heaven is above. Earth is below. Man, ideally guided by a wise and virtuous ruler, stands in between and regulates or harmonizes the cosmological forces of heaven and earth by the power of his virtue and by performing the sacrifices. The forms that this cosmology took under the last Manchu dynasty (1644–1912) can be seen today in the city of Beijing: The Temple of Heaven is in the south; the Temple of Earth is in the northeast; and the Imperial Palace is—symbolically, at least—in between. To say that the emperor's sacrifices at the Temple of Heaven were secular (and, therefore, not religious) or religious (and not secular) misses the point. It projects our own dualistic assumptions onto China. Similarly, when we speak of the Daoist sage becoming one with nature, it is not the nature of a twenty-first-century natural scientist; it is a nature that contains metaphysical and cosmological forces that our worldview might label as religious.

Most of the one hundred schools—if, in fact, there were that many—are unknown today. Many works disappeared in the book burning of the Qin dynasty (256–221 B.C.E.). But apart from the three major schools of Confucianism, Daoism, and Legalism, texts of enough other schools have survived to convey a sense of the range and vitality of Zhou thought:

1. *Rhetoricians.* This school taught the arts of persuasion to be used in diplomatic negotiations. Its principal work instructed the rulers of territorial states by using historical anecdote. A practical work, it was popular for its humor and lively style.

2. *Logicians.* This school taught logic and relativity. For example, one proposition was "The south has no limit and has a limit." Another was "A white horse is not a horse": The concept of *horse* is not the same as the concept of *white horse.*

3. *Strategists.* *The Art of War* by Sunzi became the classic of military science in China and is studied today by guerrillas and in military academies around the world. It praises the general who wins victories without battles but also talks of organizing states for war, of supply, of spies, and of propaganda.

4. *Cosmologists.* This school described the functions of the cosmos in terms of *yin* and *yang*, the complementary negative and positive forces of nature, and in terms of the five elements (metal, wood, earth, fire, and water). Its ideas were later absorbed by other schools.

5. *Mohists.* Mozi (470–391 B.C.E.) was an early critic of Confucius. His goals were peace, wealth, and the increase of population. He taught an ethic of universal love—to overcome a selfish human nature. He preached discipline and austerity and was critical of whatever lacked utility, including music and the other arts, elaborate funerals, wasteful rites, and, above all, war. To achieve his goals, Mozi argued for a strong state: Subjects must obey their rulers, who in turn must obey Heaven. Heaven would punish evil and reward good. To promote peace, Mozi organized his followers into military units to aid states that were attacked.

CONFUCIANISM

Confucius was born in 551 B.C.E. in a minor state in northeastern China. He probably belonged to the lower nobility or the knightly class, because he received an education in writing, music, and rituals. His father died when Confucius was young, so he may have known privation. He made his living by teaching. He traveled with his disciples from state to state, seeking a ruler who would put his ideas into practice. Although he may once have held a minor position, his ideas were rejected as impractical. He died in 479 B.C.E., honored as a teacher and scholar but having failed to find a ruler to advise. The name *Confucius* is the Latinized form of *Kong Fuzi*, or *Master Kong*, as he is known in China.

We know of Confucius only through the *Analects*, his sayings collected by his disciples, or perhaps by their disciples. They are mostly in the form of "The Master said," followed by his words. (See Document, "Confucius Defines the Gentleman.") The picture that emerges is of a man of moderation, propriety, optimism, good sense, and wisdom. In an age of cruelty and superstition, he was humane, rational, and upright, demanding much of others and more of himself. Asked about death, he replied, "You do not understand even life. How can you understand death?"[1] Asked about how to serve the spirits and the gods, in which he did not disbelieve, he answered, "You are not able even to serve man. How can you serve the spirits?"

Confucius described himself as a transmitter and a conservator of tradition, not an innovator. He idealized the early Shang and Zhou kings as paragons of virtue and particularly saw early Zhou society as a golden age. He sought the secrets of this golden age in its writings. Some of these writings, along with later texts, became the Confucian classics, which through most of Chinese history had an authority not unlike Scripture in the West. Five of the thirteen classics were the following:

1. *The Book of Changes* (also known as the *Classic of Divination*). A handbook for diviners, this book was later seen as containing metaphysical truths about the universe.

2. *The Book of History.* This book contains documents and speeches from the early Zhou, some authentic. Chinese tradition holds that it was edited by Confucius. It was interpreted as the record of sage-kings.

3. *The Book of Poetry.* This book contains some three hundred poems from the early Zhou. Representing a sophisticated literary tradition, it includes love songs as well as poems of friendship, ritual, and politics. Many were given political and moral interpretations in later times.

4. *The Book of Rites.* This book includes both rituals and rules of etiquette. Rites were important to Confucians, both as a support for proper behavior and because they were seen as corresponding to the forces of nature.

5. *The Spring and Autumn Annals.* A brief record of the major occurrences from 722 to 481 B.C.E. in the state where Confucius was born, this book, according to Chinese tradition, was edited by Confucius and reflected his moral judgments on past historical figures.

Basing his teachings on these writings, Confucius proposed to resolve the turmoil of his own age by a return to the good old ways of the early Zhou. When asked about government, he said, "Let the ruler be a ruler, the subject a subject, the father a father, the son a son." (The five Confucian relationships were ruler-subject, father-son, husband-wife, older brother-younger brother, and friend-friend.) If everyone fulfilled the duties of his or her status, then harmony would prevail. Confucius understood the fundamental truth that the well-being of a society depends on the morality of its members. His vision was of an unbroken social harmony extending from the individual family member to the monarch.

But a return to the early Zhou was impossible. China was undergoing a dynamic transition from hundreds of small city-states to a few large territorial states. Specialized classes were appearing.

◀ **A Zhou Dynasty Bronze Bell.** While pre-Confucian, the incised text along the bell's sides contains elements that were later incorporated into Chinese philosophy: an appeal to the Lord of Heaven, a reference to border peoples as "barbarians," and a sense of family stretching from "our illustrious ancestors" residing in Heaven to the monarch and his descendants.
National Palace Museum, Taiwan, R.O.C.

---

[1] This quotation and all quotations from Confucius in this passage are from Confucius, *The Analects*, trans. by D. C. Lau (Penguin Books, 1979).

DOCUMENT   Confucius Defines the Gentleman

For more than two thousand years in China, the cultural ideal was the gentleman, who combined knowledge of the ancient sages with an inner morality and outer propriety.

◆ How does the injunction "to repay an injury with straightness" compare to the Christian injunction to turn the other cheek? Which do you think is more appropriate?

The Master said, "I never enlighten anyone who has not been driven to distraction by trying to understand a difficulty or who has not got into a frenzy trying to put his ideas into words.

"When I have pointed out one corner of a square to anyone and he does not come back with the other three, I will not point it out to him a second time."

The Master said, "Yu, shall I tell you what it is to know? To say you know when you know, and to say you do not when you do not, that is knowledge."

The Master said, "Is it not a pleasure, having learned something, to try it out at due intervals? Is it not a joy to have friends come from afar? Is it not gentlemanly not to take offence when others fail to appreciate your abilities?"

Someone said, "Repay an injury with a good turn. What do you think of this saying?" The Master said, "What, then, do you repay a good turn with? You repay an injury with straightness, but you repay a good turn with a good turn."

Lin Fang asked about the basis of the rites. The Master said, "A noble question indeed! With the rites, it is better to err on the side of frugality than on the side of extravagance; in mourning, it is better to err on the side of grief than on the side of formality."

The Master said, "I suppose I should give up hope. I have yet to meet the man who is as fond of virtue as he is of beauty in women."

The Master said, "The gentleman agrees with others without being an echo. The small man echoes without being in agreement."

The Master said, "The gentleman is at ease without being arrogant; the small man is arrogant without being at ease."

The Master said, "There is no point in seeking the views of a gentleman who, though he sets his heart on the Way, is ashamed of poor food and poor clothes."

Confucius, *The Analects*, trans. by D. C. Lau (New York: Penguin Classics, 1979), © D. C. Lau, 1979.

Old rituals no longer worked. It was thus not enough to stress basic human relationships. The genius of Confucius was to transform the old aristocratic code into a new ethic that any educated Chinese could practice. His reinterpretation of the early Chou tradition can be seen in the concept of the *junzi*. This term literally meant "the son of the ruler" (or the aristocrat). Confucius redefined it to mean one of noble behavior, a person with the inner virtues of humanity, integrity, righteousness, altruism, and loyalty, and an outward demeanor and propriety to match.

This redefinition was not unlike the change in the meaning of *gentleman* in England, from "one who is gentle-born" to "one who is gentle-behaved." But whereas *gentleman* remained a fairly superficial category in the West, in China *junzi* went deeper. Confucius saw ethics as grounded in nature. The true gentleman was in touch with his own basic nature, which in turn was a part of the cosmic order. Confucius expressed this saying: "Heaven is the author of the virtue that is in me." Confucius's description of his own passage through life goes far beyond good manners: "At fifteen I set my heart on learning; at thirty I took my stand; at forty I came to be free from doubts; at fifty I understood the Decree of Heaven; at sixty my ear was attuned; at seventy I followed my heart's desire without overstepping the line."

Confucius often contrasted the gentleman with the small or common person. The gentleman, educated in the classics and cultivating the Way, understands moral action. The common people, in contrast, "can be made to follow a path but not to understand it." Good government for Confucius depended on the appointment to office of good men, who would serve as examples for the multitude: "Just desire the good yourself and the common people will be good. The virtue of the gentleman is like wind; the virtue of the small man is like grass. Let the wind blow over the grass and it is sure to bend." Beyond the gentleman was the sage-king, who possessed an almost mystical virtue and power. For Confucius, the early Zhou kings were clearly sages. But he wrote, "I have no hopes of meeting a sage. I would be content if I met someone who is a gentleman."

Confucianism was not adopted as the official philosophy of China until the second century B.C.E., during the Han dynasty (202 B.C.E.–9 C.E., see Chapter 7). But two other important Confucian philosophers had appeared in the meantime. Mencius (370–290 B.C.E.) represents the idealistic extension of Confucius's thought. His interpretation was accepted during most of history. He is famous for his argument that humans tend toward the good just as water runs downward. The role

China

551–479 B.C.E.	Confucius
370–290 B.C.E.	Mencius
Fourth century B.C.E.	Laozi
221 B.C.E.	Qin unifies China

of education, therefore, is to uncover and cultivate that innate goodness. Moreover, just as humans tend toward the good, so does Heaven possess a moral will. The will of Heaven is that a government should see to the education and well-being of its people. The rebellion of people against a government is the primary evidence that Heaven has withdrawn its mandate. At times in Chinese history, only lip service was paid to a concern for the people. In fact, rebellions occurred more often against weak governments than against harsh ones. But the idea that government ought to care for the people became a permanent part of the Confucian tradition.

The other influential Confucian philosopher was Xunzi (300–237 B.C.E.), who represents a tough-minded extension of Confucius's thought. Xunzi felt Heaven was amoral, indifferent to whether China was ruled by a tyrant or a sage. He believed human nature was bad or at least that desires and emotions, if unchecked and unrefined, led to social conflict. So he emphasized etiquette and education as restraints on an unruly human nature, and good institutions, including punishments and rewards, as a means for shaping behavior. These ideas influenced the thinkers of the Legalist school.

DAOISM

It is often said that the Chinese have been Confucian while in office and Daoist in their private lives. **Daoism** offered a refuge from the burden of social responsibilities. The classics of the school are the *Laozi*, dating from the fourth century B.C.E., and the *Zhuangzi*, dating from about a century later.

The central concept of Daoism is the *Dao*, or Way. It is mysterious, ineffable, and cannot be named. It is the creator of the universe, the sustainer of the universe, and the process or flux of the universe. The *Dao* functions on a cosmic, not a human, scale. As the *Laozi* put it, "Heaven and Earth are ruthless, and treat the myriad creatures as straw dogs; the sage (in accord with the *Dao*) is ruthless, and treats the people as straw dogs."[2]

What does it mean to be a sage? How does a human join the rhythms of nature? The answer given by the *Laozi* is by regain-

ing or returning to an original simplicity. Various similes describe this state: "to return to the infinite," "to return to being a babe," or "to return to being the uncarved block." To attain this state, one must "learn to be without learning." Knowledge is bad because it creates distinctions, and because it leads to the succession of ideas and images that interfere with participation in the *Dao*. One must also learn to be without desires beyond the immediate and simple needs of nature: "The nameless uncarved block is but freedom from desire."

If the sage treats the people as straw dogs, it would appear that he is beyond good and evil. But elsewhere in the *Laozi*, the sage is described as one who "excels in saving people." If not a contradiction, this is at least a paradox. The resolution is that the sage is clearly beyond morality but is not immoral or even amoral. On the contrary, by being in harmony with the *Dao*, the sage is impeccably moral—as one who clings to the forms of morality or makes morality a goal could never be. So in the *Laozi* it is written, "Exterminate benevolence, discard rectitude, and the people will again be filial; exterminate ingenuity, discard profit, and there will be no more thieves and bandits." In this formulation we also see the basis for the political philosophy of Daoism, which can be summed up as "not doing" (*wuwei*). This means something between "doing nothing" and "being, but not acting." In this concept, there is some overlap with Confucianism. The Confucian sage-king exerts a moral force by dint of his internal accord with nature. A perfect Confucian sage could rule without doing. Confucius said,

▲ **Laozi.** Laozi, the founder of Daoism, as imagined by a later artist.
Courtesy of the Freer Gallery of Art, Smithsonian Institution, Washington, D.C. (72.1).

---

[2]All quotations from the Laozi are from *Tao Te Ching*, trans. by D. C. Lau (Penguin Books, 1963).

DOCUMENT | Daoism

Can inner, transformative, religious experience take people beyond every-day worldly concerns and imbue them with moral charisma or moral authority? What other religions might call "supernatural," Daoism sees as truly natural.

◆ How does the Way in Daoism compare with Confucius's use of the same term?

Laozi Tells of the Way of the Sage

The way that can be spoken of
Is not the constant way;
The name that can be named
Is not the constant name.
The nameless was the beginning of heaven and earth;
The named was the mother of the myriad creatures.
The spirit of the valley never dies
This is called the mysterious female.
The gateway of the mysterious female
Is called the root of heaven and earth.
Dimly visible, it seems as if it were there,
Yet use will never drain it.
There is a thing confusedly formed,
Born before heaven and earth.
Silent and void
It stands alone and does not change,
Goes round and does not weary.
It is capable of being the mother of the world.
I know not its name
So I style it "the way."
When the way prevails in the empire, fleetfooted horses
　are relegated to ploughing the fields; when the way

does not prevail in the empire, war-horses breed on the border.
One who knows does not speak; one who speaks does not know.
Therefore the sage puts his person last and it comes first,
Treats it as extraneous to himself and it is preserved.
Is it not because he is without thought of self that he is able to accomplish his private ends?

Zhuangzi Compares Governmental Office to a Dead Rat

When Hui Tzu was prime minister of Liang, Zhuangzi set off to visit him. Someone said to Xunzi, "Zhuangzi is coming because he wants to replace you as prime minister!" With this Xunzi was filled with alarm and searched all over the state for three days and three nights trying to find Zhuangzi. Zhuangzi then came to see him and said, "In the south there is a bird called the Yuan-ch'u—I wonder if you've ever heard of it? The Yuan-ch'u rises up from the South Sea and flies to the North Sea, and it will rest on nothing but the Wu-t'ung tree, eat nothing but the fruit of the Lien, and drink only from springs of sweet water. Once there was an owl who had gotten hold of a half-rotten old rat, and as the Yuan-ch'u passed by, it raised its head, looked up at the Yuan-ch'u, and said, 'Shoo!' Now that you have this Liang state of yours, are you trying to shoo me?"

Laozi selection from *Laozi, Tao Te Ching*, trans. by D. C. Lau (New York: Penguin Classics, 1963). © D. C. Lau. Zhuangzi selection from *The Complete Works of Chuang-tzu*, trans. by Burton Watson. © 1968 by Columbia University Press. Reprinted by permission of the publisher.

"If there was a ruler who achieved order without taking any action, it was, perhaps, Shun [the sage-emperor]. There was nothing for him to do but to hold himself in a respectful posture and to face due south." In Daoism, all true sages had this Shun-like power to rule without action: "The Way never acts yet nothing is left undone. Should lords and princes be able to hold fast to it, the myriad creatures will be transformed of their own accord." Or, says the *Laozi*, "I am free from desire and the people of themselves become simple like the uncarved block." The sage acts without acting, and "when his task is accomplished and his work is done, the people will say, 'It happened to us naturally.'" (See Document, "Daoism.")

Along with the basic Daoist prescription of becoming one with the *Dao* are two other assumptions or principles. One is that any action pushed to an extreme will initiate a countervailing reaction in the direction of the opposite extreme. The other is that

too much government, even good government, can become oppressive by its very weight. As the *Laozi* put it, "The people are hungry; it is because those in authority eat up too much in taxes that the people are hungry. The people are difficult to govern; it is because those in authority are too fond of action that the people are difficult to govern." Elsewhere, the same idea was expressed in even homelier terms: "Govern a large state as you would cook small fish," that is, without too much stirring.

LEGALISM

A third great current in classical Chinese thought, and by far the most influential in its own age, was **Legalism**. Like the philosophers of other schools, the Legalists were concerned with ending the wars that plagued China. True peace, they believed, required a united country and a strong state. They favored conscription and considered war a means of extending state power.

DOCUMENT | Legalism

According to Legalism, the state can only regulate behavior, it cannot affect the inner dimensions of human life. Rewards and punishments, furthermore, are far more efficient in controlling behavior than moral appeals.

◆ Do the tenets of Legalism have any modern parallels? What do you think of Legalism as a philosophy of government? As an approach to the problem of crime? How does Legalism compare with other approaches to law, leadership, and government? [See, for example, "Athenian Democracy: An Unfriendly View" (Chapter 3), "The Edicts of Ashoka" (Chapter 4), and "Machiavelli Discusses the Most Important Trait for a Ruler" (Chapter 16).

Han Feizi Argues for the Efficacy of Punishments

Now take a young fellow who is a bad character. His parents may get angry at him, but he never makes any change. The villagers may reprove him, but he is not moved. His teachers and elders may admonish him but he never reforms. The love of his parents, the efforts of the villagers, and the wisdom of his teachers and elders—all the three excellent disciplines are applied to him, and yet not even a hair on his shins is altered. It is only after the district magistrate sends out his soldiers and in the name of the law searches for wicked individuals that the young man becomes afraid and changes his ways and alters his deeds. So while the love of parents is not sufficient to discipline the children, the severe penalties of the district magistrate are. This is because men became naturally spoiled by love, but are submissive to authority. …

That being so, rewards should be rich and certain so that the people will be attracted by them; punishments should be severe and definite so that the people will fear them; and laws should be uniform and steadfast so that the people will be familiar with them. Consequently, the sovereign should show no wavering in bestowing rewards and grant no pardon in administering punishments, and he should add honor to rewards and disgrace to punishments—when this is done, then both the worthy and the unworthy will want to exert themselves. …

Han Feizi Attacks Confucianism

There was once a man of Sung who tilled his field. In the midst of his field stood the stump of a tree, and one day a hare, running at full speed, bumped into the stump, broke its neck, and died. Thereupon the man left his plow and kept watch at the stump, hoping that he would get another hare. But he never caught another hare, and was only ridiculed by the people of Sung. Now those who try to rule the people of the present age with the conduct of government of the early kings are all doing exactly the same thing as that fellow who kept watch by the stump. …

Those who are ignorant about government insistently say: "Win the hearts of the people." If order could be procured by winning the hearts of the people, then even the wise ministers Yi Yin and Kuan Chung would be of no use. For all that the ruler would need to do would be just to listen to the people. Actually, the intelligence of the people is not to be relied upon any more than the mind of a baby. If the baby does not have his head shaved, his sores will recur; if he does not have his boil cut open, his illness will go from bad to worse. However, in order to shave his head or open the boil someone has to hold the baby while the affectionate mother is performing the work, and yet he keeps crying and yelling incessantly. The baby does not understand that suffering a small pain is the way to obtain a great benefit.

Now, the sovereign urges the tillage of land and the cultivation of pastures for the purpose of increasing production for the people, but they think the sovereign is cruel. The sovereign regulates penalties and increases punishments for the purpose of repressing the wicked, but the people think the sovereign is severe. Again he levies taxes in cash and in grain to fill up the granaries and treasuries in order to relieve famine and provide for the army, but they think the sovereign is greedy. Finally, he insists upon universal military training without personal favoritism, and urges his forces to fight hard in order to take the enemy captive, but the people think the sovereign is violent. These four measures are methods for attaining order and maintaining peace, but the people are too ignorant to appreciate them.

From *Sources of Chinese Tradition*, trans. by William Theodore de Bary. © 1960 by Columbia University Press. Reprinted by permission of the publisher.

The Legalists did not seek a model in the distant past. In ancient times, said one, there were fewer people and more food, so it was easier to rule; different conditions require new principles of government. Nor did the Legalists model their state on a heavenly order of values. Human nature is selfish, argued both of the leading Legalists, Han Feizi (d. 233 B.C.E.) and Li Si (d. 208 B.C.E.). It is human to like rewards or pleasure and to dislike punishments or pain. If laws are severe and impartial, if what strengthens the state is rewarded and what weakens the state is punished, then a strong state and a good society will ensue. (See Document, "Legalism.")

Laws, therefore, should contain incentives for loyalty and bravery in battle, and for obedience, diligence, and frugality in everyday life. The Legalists despised merchants as parasites and approved of productive farmers. They particularly despised purveyors of doctrines different from their own and were critical of rulers who honored philosophers while ignoring their philosophies.

Legalism was the philosophy of the state of Qin, which destroyed the Zhou in 256 B.C.E. and unified China in 221 B.C.E. Because Qin laws were cruel and severe, and because Legalism put human laws above an ethic modeled on Heaven, later generations of Chinese have denounced its doctrines. They saw it, not without justification, as a philosophy that consumed its founders: Han Feizi became an official of the Qin state but was eventually poisoned in a prison cell by Li Si, who was jealous of his growing influence. Li Si, although he became prime minister of Qin, was killed in 208 B.C.E. in a political struggle with a court eunuch. Yet for all the abuse heaped on Legalist doctrines, its legacy of administrative and criminal laws became a vital part of subsequent dynastic China. Even Confucian statesmen could not do without them.

Religion in India

By 400 B.C.E., new social and religious forms took shape on the Indian subcontinent that drew both on the older traditions of the Aryan noble and priestly elites, and on non-Aryan ideas and practices. This tradition took its classical "Indian" shape in the early first millennium C.E. Its fundamental institutions and ideas came to prevail virtually throughout the subcontinent. Despite staggering internal diversity and divisions, and long periods of foreign rule, this Indian culture has survived for over two thousand years as a coherent tradition of cultural heritage, social organization, and religious worldview.

"HINDU" AND "INDIAN"

Indian culture and tradition include more than the word **Hindu** commonly implies today. Earlier, *Hindu* simply meant "Indian." Taken from the Indo-Iranian name for the Indus, it was the term outsiders, like the Persians and the Greeks, used for the people or land of the subcontinent. Later, first invading Muslims, then Europeans used Hindu to characterize the most prominent religious and social institutions of India as a whole. Heading the list of such "Hindu" institutions were the concept of transmigration, the sacredness of the Vedas and the cow, worship of Shiva and Vishnu, and caste distinctions. Most Indians in the past twenty-five hundred years have accepted these institutions, but Indian Buddhists, Jains, Muslims, Sikhs, and Christians have rejected some or all of them.

Hindu is not a term for any single or uniform religious community. "Hindu" religion and culture lumps together an immense diversity of social, racial, linguistic, and religious groups.

Indian, on the other hand, commonly refers today to all native inhabitants of the subcontinent, whatever their beliefs. In this book we shall generally use the term *Indian* in this inclusive sense when referring to the subcontinent or its peoples. However, for the period before the arrival of Muslim culture (ca. 1000 C.E.), we will use *Indian* to refer to the distinctively In-dian tradition of thought and culture that began around the middle of the first millennium B.C.E. and achieved its classical formulation in the Hindu society and religion of the first millennium C.E.

HISTORICAL BACKGROUND

We saw in Chapter 1 how, in the late Vedic or Brahmanic period, a priest-centered cult dominated the upper classes of Aryanized northern Indian society. By the sixth century B.C.E., this had become an elite, esoteric cult to which most people had little or no access. Elaborate animal sacrifices on behalf of Aryan rulers were an economic burden on the peasants, whose livestock provided the victims. Such sacrifices were also largely irrelevant to the religious concerns of both peasants and town dwellers. New, ascetic tendencies questioned the basic values and practices of the older Aryan religion. During the seventh and sixth centuries B.C.E., skepticism in religious matters accompanied social and political upheavals.

The latest Vedic texts themselves reflected a reaction against excessive emphasis on the power of sacrifice and ritual, accumulation of worldly wealth and power, and hope for an afterlife in a paradise. The treatises of the **Brahmanas** (ca. 1000–800 B.C.E.) dealt with the ritual application of the old Vedic texts, the explanation of Vedic rites and mythology, and the theory of the sacrifice. Early on they focused on controlling the sacred power (*Brahman*) of the sacrificial ritual, but they gradually stressed acquiring this power through knowledge instead of ritual.

This tendency became central in the Upanishads (ca. 800–500 B.C.E.). The Upanishadic sages and the early Jains and Buddhists (fifth century B.C.E.) shared certain revolutionary ideas and concerns. Their thinking and piety influenced not only all later Indian intellectual thought but also, through the spread of the Buddhist tradition, much of the intellectual and religious life of east and southeast Asia as well. Thus, the middle centuries of the first millennium B.C.E. in India began a religious and philosophical revolution that ranks alongside those of Chinese philosophy and religion, Judaic monotheism, and Greek philosophy as a turning point in the history of civilization.

THE UPANISHADIC WORLDVIEW

In the Upanishads two new emphases emerge: knowledge over ritual and immortality in terms of escape from existence itself. These were already evident in two sentences from the prayer of an early Upanishadic thinker who said, "From the unreal lead me to the Real. … From death lead me to immortality." The first sentence points to the Upanishadic focus on speculation about the nature of things, the quest for ultimate truth. Here knowledge, not the sacred word or act, has become the ultimate source of power. The second sentence reflects a new concern with life after death. The old Vedic ideal of living a full and upright life so

DOCUMENT	The "Turning of the Wheel of the Dharma": Basic Teachings of the Buddha

Following are selections from the sermon said to have been the first preached by the Buddha. It was directed at five former companions with whom he had practiced extreme austerities. When he abandoned asceticism to meditate under the Bodh tree, they had left him. This sermon is said to have made them the first to follow him. Because it set in motion the Buddha's teaching, or Dharma, *on earth, it is usually described as "setting in motion the wheel of Dharma." The text is from the* Dhammacakkappavattanasutta.

◆ What extremes does the Middle Path try to avoid? What emotion drives the chain of suffering? How does the "knowledge" that brings salvation compare to the knowledge sought in the Hindu tradition?

Thus have I heard. The Blessed One was once living in the Deer Park at Isipatana (the Resort of Seers) near Baranasi (Benares). There he addressed the group of five bhikkhus.

"Bhikkhus, these two extremes ought not to be practiced by one who has gone forth from the household life. What are the two? There is devotion to the indulgence of sense-pleasures, which is low, common, the way of ordinary people, unworthy and unprofitable; and there is devotion to self-mortification, which is painful, unworthy and unprofitable.

"Avoiding both these extremes, the Tathagata has realized the Middle Path: it gives vision, it gives knowledge, and it leads to calm, to insight, to enlightenment, to Nibbana. And what is that Middle Path? It is simply the Noble Eightfold Path, namely, right view, right thought, right speech, right action, right livelihood, right effort, right mindfulness, right concentration. This is the Middle Path realized by the Tathagata, which gives vision, which gives knowledge, and which leads to calm, to insight, to enlightenment, to Nibbana. …

"The Noble Truth of suffering (*Dukkha*) is this: Birth is suffering; aging is suffering; sickness is suffering; death is suffering; sorrow and lamentation, pain, grief and despair are suffering; association with the unpleasant is suffering; dissociation from the pleasant is suffering; not to get what one wants is suffering—in brief, the five aggregates of attachment are suffering.

"The Noble Truth of the origin of suffering is this: It is this thirst (craving) which produces re-existence and re-becoming, bound up with passionate greed. It finds fresh delight now here and now there, namely, thirst for nonexistence (self-annihilation).

"The Noble Truth of the Cessation of suffering is this: It is the complete cessation of that very thirst, giving it up, renouncing it, emancipating oneself from it, detaching oneself from it.

"The Noble Truth of the Path leading to the Cessation of suffering is this: It is simply the Noble Eightfold Path. …

"'This is the Noble Truth of Suffering (*Dukkha*)': such was the vision, the knowledge, the wisdom, the science, the light, that arose in me with regard to things not heard before. 'This suffering, as a noble truth, should be fully understood.'

"'This is the Noble Truth of the Cessation of suffering': such was the vision 'This Cessation of suffering, as a noble truth, should be realized.'

"'This is the Noble Truth of the Path leading to the Cessation of suffering': such was the vision, 'This Path leading to the Cessation of suffering, as a noble truth, has been followed (cultivated).'

"As long as my vision of true knowledge was not fully clear regarding the Four Noble Truths, I did not claim to have realized the perfect Enlightenment that is supreme in the world with its gods, in this world with its recluses and brahmanas, with its princes and men. But when my vision of true knowledge was fully clear regarding the Four Noble Truths, then I claimed to have realized the perfect Enlightenment that is supreme in the world with its gods, in this world with its recluses and brahmanas, with its princes and men. And a vision of true knowledge arose in me thus: My heart's deliverance is unassailable. This is the last birth. Now there is no more re-becoming (rebirth)."

This the Blessed One said. The group of five bhikkhus was glad, and they rejoiced at his words.

—*Samyutta-nikaya, LVI, II*

From *What the Buddha Taught* by Walpola Rahula. Copyright © 1974 by W. Rahula, pp. 92–94. Used by permission of Grove Atlantic Inc.

as to attain an afterlife among the gods no longer appears adequate. Immortality is now interpreted in terms of escape from existence in any form. These two Upanishadic emphases gave birth to ideas that were to change the shape of Indian thought forever. They also provide the key to its basic worldview.

The Nature of Reality   The quest for knowledge by the Upanishadic sages focused on the nature of the individual self (*atman*) and its relation to ultimate reality (*Brahman*). The gods are now merely part of the total scheme of things, subject to the laws of existence, and not to be put on the same plane with the transcendent Absolute. Prayer and sacrifice to particular gods for their help continue; but the higher goal is realization of *Brahman* through mental action alone not ritual,

The culmination of Upanishadic speculation is the recognition that the way to the Absolute is through the self. Through contemplation, *atman-Brahman* is recognized not as a deity, but as the principle of reality itself: the unborn, unmade, unchanging infinite.

DOCUMENT | Discussions of Brahman and Atman from the Upanishads

Much of the Upanishads is couched in the form of teacher-student dialogue. The following two selections are responses of teachers to the questions of their disciples.

> ◆ Does either of these passages provide a guide to salvation? If so, why, and what is the suggested path to salvation? In what sense and degree are the passages concerned with ignorance and enlightenment?

A Report of the Sage Sandilya's Statement About the Identity of Atman and Brahman

Verily, this whole world is Brahman. Tranquil, let one worship it as that from which he came forth, as that into which he will be dissolved, as that in which he breathes. Now, verily, a person consists of purpose. According to the purpose which a person has in this world, thus does he become on departing hence. So let him form for himself a purpose. He who consists of mind, whose body is life, whose form is light, whose conception is truth, whose soul [*atman*] is space, containing all odors, containing all tastes, encompassing this whole world, the unspeaking, the unconcerned—this Soul of mine within the heart is smaller than a grain of rice, or a barley-corn, or a mustard-seed, or a grain of millet; or the kernel of a grain of millet; this Soul of mine within the heart is greater than the earth, greater than the atmosphere, greater than the sky, greater than these worlds. Containing all works, containing all desires, containing all odors, containing all tastes, encompassing this whole world, the unspeaking, the unconcerned—this Soul of mine within the heart, this is Brahman. Into him I shall enter on departing hence. If one would believe this, he would have no more doubt."—Thus used Sandilya to say. …

—*Chandogya Upanishad 3.14*

The Young Brahman, Shvetaketu, Is Instructed in the Identity of Atman and Brahman by His Father

"These rivers, my dear, flow, the eastern toward the east, the western toward the west. They go just from the ocean to the ocean. They become the ocean itself. As there they know not 'I am this one,' 'I am that one'—even so, indeed, my dear, all creatures here, though they have come forth from Being, know not 'We have come forth from Being.' Whatever they are in this world, whether tiger, or lion, or wolf, or boar, or worm, or fly, or gnat, or mosquito, that they become. That which is the finest essence—this whole world has that as its soul. That is Reality. That is *Atman.* That art thou, Shvetaketu."

—*Chandogya Upanishad 6.10*

Of this reality, all that can be said is that it is "neither this nor that," because the ultimate cannot be conceptualized or described in finite terms. Beneath the impermanence of ordinary reality is the changeless *Brahman*, to which every being's immortal self belongs. The difficulty is recognizing this self, and with it the Absolute, while one is enmeshed in mortal existence. (See Document, "Discussions of Brahman and Atman from the Upanishads.")

A second, related focus of Upanishadic inquiry was the nature of "normal" existence. The realm of life is seen to be ultimately impermanent, ever changing. What seem to be "solid" things—the physical world, our bodies and personalities, worldly success—are revealed in the Upanishads as insubstantial, impermanent. Even happiness is transient. Existence is neither satisfying nor lasting. Only *Brahman* is eternal, unchanging. This perception already shows a marked tendency toward the Buddhist emphasis on impermanence and suffering as the fundamental facts of existence.

Life After Death The new understanding of immortality that emerges in the Upanishads is related to these basic perceptions about the self, the Absolute, and the world of existence. The Up-

anishadic sages conceived of existence as a ceaseless cycle, a never-ending alternation between life and death. This idea became the basic assumption of all Indian thought and religious life.

The idea of the endless cycle of existence, or **samsara**, is only superficially similar to our idea of "transmigration" of souls. For Indians, it is the key to understanding reality. Furthermore, it is not liberating, but burdensome: the terrifying prospect of endless "redeath" as the normal lot of all beings in this world, whether animals, plants, humans, or gods. This is the fundamental problem for all later Indian thought.

Karma The key to resolving the dilemma of *samsara* lies in the concept of *karma*, which in Sanskrit literally means "work" or "action." At base, it is the concept that every action has its inevitable effects, sooner or later; as long as there is action of mind or body, there is continued effect and hence continued existence. Good deeds bring good results, perhaps even rebirth in a heaven or as a god, and evil ones bring evil consequences, whether in this life or by rebirth in the next, whether in the everyday world or in the lower worlds of hell. Because of the fundamental impermanence of everything in existence (heavens and hells included), good as well as evil is temporary. The flux of existence knows only movement, change, endless cause and effect far transcending a mere human life-span, or even a mere world eon.

Solutions   The Indian tradition developed two kinds of solutions to the problem of *samsara*. The first involves a strategy of maximizing good actions and minimizing bad actions to achieve the best possible rebirth in one's next round of existence. The second, and more radical, solution seeks "liberation" (*moksha*) from existence: escaping all karmic effects by escaping action itself.

The first strategy has been followed by the great masses of Hindus, Buddhists, and Jains over the centuries. It has been characterized by Franklin Edgerton as the "ordinary norm," as opposed to the "extraordinary norm," the path of only the select elite, the greatest seekers of Upanishadic truth, Jain asceticism, or the Buddhist Middle Path. Essentially, the ordinary norm aims at living according to a code of social and moral responsibility. The most significant such codes in Indian history are those of the masses of Hindus, Buddhists, and Jains over the centuries. On the other hand, the seekers of the extraordinary norm usually follow an ascetic discipline aimed at withdrawal from the karmic cycle altogether and the consequent release (*moksha*) from cause and effect, good and evil, birth and rebirth. These two characteristic Indian responses to the problem posed by *samsara* underlie the fundamental forms of Indian thought and piety that took shape in the mid- to late first millennium B.C.E.

Social Responsibility: *Dharma* as Ideal   The "ordinary norm" of life in the various traditions of Indian religiousness can be summarized as life lived according to *dharma*. Although *dharma* has many meanings, its most common is similar to that of the Vedic Aryan concept of *Rta* (see Chapter 1). In this sense, it means "the right (order of things)," "moral law," "right conduct," or even "duty." It includes the cosmic order (compare the Chinese *Dao*) as well as the right conduct of political, commercial, social, and religious affairs and individual moral responsibility. For most people—those we might call the laity, as distinguished from monks and ascetics—life according to *dharma* is the life of moral action that will lead to a better birth in the next round of existence.

Life according to *dharma* has several implications. First, it accepts action in the world of *samsara* as necessary and legitimate. Second, it demands acceptance of the responsibilities appropriate to one's sex, class and caste group, stage in life, and other circumstances. Third, it allows for legitimate self-interest: One's duty is to do things that acquire merit for one's eternal *atman* and to avoid those that bring evil consequences. Fourth, rebirth in heaven, in paradise, is the highest goal attainable through the life of *dharma*. However (fifth), all

achievement in the world of *dharma* (which is also the world of *samsara*), even the attainment of heaven, is ultimately subject to change. (See Document, "The 'Turning of the Wheel of the Dharma': Basic Teachings of the Buddha.")

Ascetic Discipline: *Moksha* as Ideal   For those who abandon the world of ordinary life to gain freedom from *samsara*, the implications for living are in direct contrast to those of the ordinary norm. First, any action, good or bad, is at least counterproductive, for action produces only more action, more *karma*, more rebirth. Second, nonaction is achieved only by withdrawal from "normal" existence. The person seeking release from *samsara* has to move beyond the usual responsibilities of family and society. Most often, this involves becoming a "renouncer" (*sannyasi*)—whether a Hindu hermit, yogi, or wanderer, or a Jain or Buddhist monk. Third, this renunciation of the world and its goals demands selflessness, absence of ego. One must give up the desires and attachments that the self normally needs to function in the world. Fourth, the highest goal is not rebirth in heaven, but liberation (*moksha*) from all rebirth and redeath. Finally, this *moksha* is permanent. Its realization means no more becoming, no more suffering in the realm of *samsara*. Permanence, eternity, transcendence, and freedom from suffering are its attributes.

Seekers of the Extraordinary Norm   The ideas that led individuals to seek the extraordinary norm were first fully elaborated in the Upanishads. These ideas appealed to an increasing number of persons who abandoned both the ritualistic religious practices and the society of class distinctions and material concerns around them. Many of these seekers were of warrior-noble (*Kshatriya*), not Brahmanic, birth. They took up the wandering or hermit existence of the ascetic, seeking spiritual powers in yogic meditation and self-denial or even self-torture. Such seekers wanted to transcend bodily existence to realize the Absolute.

In the sixth century B.C.E., teachers of new ideas appeared, especially in the lower Ganges basin, in the area of Magadha (modern Bihar). Most of them rejected traditional religious practices as well as the authority of the Vedas in favor of ascetic discipline as the true spiritual path. The ideas and practices of two of these teachers became the foundations of new and lasting traditions of piety and faith, those of the Jains and the Buddhists.

MAHAVIRA AND THE JAIN TRADITION

The **Jains** are an Indian community that traces its tradition to Vardhamana, known as Mahavira ("the great hero"), who is traditionally believed to have lived from about 540 to 468 B.C.E. The Jains consider Mahavira as the final *Jina* ("victor" over *samsara*) or *Tirthankara* ("ford maker," one who finds a way

CHRONOLOGY

India

ca. 800–500 B.C.E.	The Upanishads
540–ca. 468 B.C.E.	Mahavira, the Jina/Vardamana
ca. 566–ca. 486 B.C.E.	Siddhartha Gautama, the Buddha

across the waters of existence), in a line of twenty-four great teachers who have appeared in the latter, degenerative half of the present-world time cycle. The Jains (or *Jainas*, "adherents of the *Jina*") see in Mahavira not a god, but a human teacher who found and taught the way to extricate the self, or soul, from the bonds of the material world and its karmic accretions.

In the Jain view, there is no beginning or end to phenomenal existence, only innumerable, ceaseless cycles of generation and degeneration. The universe is alive from end to end with an infinite number of souls, all immortal, omniscient, and pure in their essence. But all are trapped in *samsara*, whether as animals, gods, humans, plants, or even inanimate stones or fire. *Karma* here takes on a quasi-material form: Any thought, word, or deed attracts karmic matter that clings to and encumbers the soul. The greatest amounts come from evil acts, especially those done out of hate, greed, or cruelty to any other being.

Mahavira's path to release focused on eliminating evil thoughts and acts, especially those harmful to others. His radical ascetic practice aimed at destroying karmic defilements and, ultimately, all actions leading to further karmic bondage. At the age of thirty, Mahavira began practicing the radical self-denial of a wandering ascetic, eventually even giving up clothing altogether. After twelve years of self-deprivation and yogic meditation, he attained enlightenment. Then, for some thirty years, he went about teaching his discipline to others. At the age of seventy-two he chose to fast to death to burn out the last karmic residues, an action that some of the most advanced Jain ascetics have emulated down to the present day.

It would, however, be wrong to think of the Jain tradition in terms only of the extreme ascetic practices of some Jain mendicants. Jain monks are bound basically by the five great vows they share with other monastic traditions like the Buddhist and the Christian: not to kill, steal, lie, engage in sexual activity, or own anything.

Most Jains are not monks. Today there is a thriving lay community of perhaps 3 million Jains, most in western India (Gujarat and Rajasthan). Laypersons have close ties to the monks and nuns, whom they support with gifts and food. Many Jain laypersons spend part of their lives in retreat with monks or nuns. They are vegetarians and regard *ahimsa* ("noninjury") to any being as paramount. Compassion is the great virtue for them, as for Buddhists. The merit of serving the extraordinary-norm seekers who adopt the mendicant life

▲ **Mahavira Celebrating His Celibacy, ca. 1450, Cambay, Gujarat.** This picture is from the uttaradhyana Sutra, which is believed by some Jains to contain the last teachings of Mahavira. Here he is depicted as motionless and serene as a statue and blissfully unaware of the whirl of female activity around him. Two young women try to engage him in a seductive dance, while in the scene below female musicians and a dancer provide lively accompaniment.

and of living a life according to the high standards of the community provides a goal even for those who as laypersons are following the ordinary norm.

THE BUDDHA'S MIDDLE PATH

It can be argued that India's greatest contribution to world civilization was the Buddhist tradition, which ultimately faded out in India. Yet there it was born, developed its basic contours, and left its mark on Hindu and Jain religion and culture. Like the two other great universalist traditions, Christianity and Islam, it traces its origins to a single figure who for centuries has loomed larger than life for the faithful.

This figure is Siddhartha Gautama, known as the "sage of the Shakya tribe (Shakyamuni)" and, above all, as the Buddha, or "Enlightened/Awakened One." A contemporary of Mahavira, Gautama was also born (ca. 566 B.C.E.) of a *Kshatriya* family in comfortable—if not, as legend has it, royal—circumstances. His people lived near the modern Nepalese border in the Himalayan foothills. The traditional story of how Gautama came to teach the Middle Path to liberation from *samsara* begins with his sheltered life of ease as a young married prince.

At the age of twenty-nine, Gautama first perceived the reality of aging, sickness, and death as the human lot. Revolted at his previous delight in sensual pleasures and even his wife and child, he abandoned his home and family to seek an answer to the dilemma of the endless cycle of mortal existence. After this Great Renunciation, he studied first with renowned teachers and then took up extreme ascetic disciplines of penance and self-mortification. Still unsatisfied, Gautama turned finally to intense yogic meditation under a pipal tree in the place near Varanasi (Banaras) known as Gaya. In one historic night, he moved through different levels of trance, during which he realized all of his past lives, the reality of the cycle of existence of all beings, and how to stop the karmic outflows that fuel suffering. Thus he became the Buddha; that is, he achieved full enlightenment—the omniscient consciousness of reality as it truly is. Having realized the truth of suffering existence, he pledged himself to achieving release for all beings.

From the time of the experience under the Bodh tree, or "Enlightenment Tree," Gautama devoted the last of his earthly lives before his final release to teaching others his Middle Path between asceticism and indulgence. This path has been the core of Buddhist faith and practice ever since. It begins with realizing the Four Noble Truths: (1) all life is *dukkha*, or suffering; (2) the source of suffering is desiring; (3) the cessation of desiring is the way to end suffering; and (4) the path to this end is eightfold: Right Understanding, Right Thought, Right Speech, Right Action, Right Livelihood, Right Effort, Right Mindfulness, and Right Concentration. The key idea of the Buddha's teaching, or *dharma*, is that everything in the world of existence is causally linked. The essential fact of existence is *dukkha*: For no

Fasting Buddha. Before Gautama arrived at the "Middle Path," he practiced severe austerities for six years. This fourth to second-century B.C.E. statue of a fasting Buddha from Gandhara (in present-day Pakistan) reflects the Greek influence on early Buddhist sculpture. Borromeo, EPA/Art Resource, N.Y.

pleasure—however great—is permanent (here we see the Buddhist variation on the central Indian theme of *samsara*).

Thus, Buddhist discipline focuses on the moral Eightfold Path, and the cardinal virtue of compassion for all beings, as the way to eliminate the selfish desiring that is the root of *samsara* and its unavoidable suffering. The Buddha himself had attained this goal; when he died (ca. 486 B.C.E.) after a life of teaching others how to master desiring, he passed from the round of existence forever. In Buddhist terminology, he attained nirvana, the extinguishing of karmic bondage. This attainment became the starting point for the growth and eventual spread of the Buddhist *Dharma*, which was to assume new and diverse forms in its long history.

The Buddhist movement, like the Jain, included not only those who were willing to renounce marriage and normal occupations to become part of the Buddha's communities of monks or nuns, but also laypersons who would strive to live by the high moral standards of the tradition and support

The Wheel of *Dharma*. An early carving showing the *chakra*, or wheel of *Dharma*, the Buddha's teaching, adored by humans and gods. Above the wheel is an umbrella of lordship.
Corbis-Bettmann

those who became mendicants in attaining full release. Buddhist tradition, again like that of the Jains, encompassed from the outset seekers of both the extraordinary and the ordinary norms in their present lives. This dual community has remained characteristic of all forms of Buddhism wherever it is practiced. Later we shall see how varied these forms have been historically. But however much the essentially a-theistic, a-ritualistic, and pragmatic tradition was later modified and expanded (so that popular Buddhism would cultivate even theistic devotion to a divinized Buddha and other enlightened beings), the fundamental vision persisted of a humanly attainable wisdom that leads to compassion and release.

The varying visions of Upanishadic, Jain, and Buddhist thought proved durable, albeit in different ways and degrees in India itself, as we have noted. The later emergence of "Hindu" tradition drew on all three of these revolutionary strands in Indian thought and integrated parts of their fundamental ideas about the universe, human life, morality, and society into the cultic and mythic strands of both Brahmanic and popular Indian practice.

The Religion of the Israelites

The ancient Near East was a **polytheistic** world; its people worshiped many gods. They worshiped local or regional gods and goddesses. Some of these deities were associated with natural phenomena such as mountains or animals, the sky or the earth. For example, Shamash in Mesopotamia and Re in Egypt were both sun gods. Others were tribal or local deities, such as Marduk in Babylonia or Atum, the patron god of the Egyptian city of On (Heliopolis). Still others represented elemental powers of this world or the next, as with Baal, the fertility god of the Canaanites, and Ishtar, whom the Assyrians worshiped as goddess of love and of war. Furthermore, from our perspective, the gods were represented largely as capricious, amoral beings who were no more affected by the actions of humans than were the natural forces that some of them represented.

If the gods were many and diverse, so too were the religious traditions of the ancient Near Eastern world. Even the major traditions of religious thought in Egypt and Mesopotamia did not offer comprehensive interpretations of human life that linked history and human destiny to a transcendent or eternal realm of meaning beyond this world—or at least no one interpretation was able to predominate in this pluralistic, religiously fragmented region.

Out of this polytheistic and pluralistic world came the great tradition of monotheistic faith represented historically in the Jewish, Christian, and Islamic communities. This tradition traces its origin not to any of the great imperial cultures of the ancient world, but to the small nation of the Israelites, or Hebrews. Although they were people from a tiny tribe people whose external fortunes were at the mercy of the ebb and flow of the great dynasties and empires of the second and first millennia B.C.E., their impact on world civilization was far greater than that of their giant neighbors. For all the glories of the major civilizations of the Fertile Crescent and Nile valley, it was the Israelites, not the Babylonians or Egyptians, who generated a tradition that significantly affected later history. This tradition was ethical monotheism.

Monotheism, faith in a single, all-powerful God as the sole Creator, Sustainer, and Ruler of the universe, may be older than the Hebrews, but its first clear historical manifestation was with them. It was among the Hebrew tribes that emphasis on the moral demands and responsibilities that the one God placed on individual and community was first definitively linked to human history itself, and that history to a divine plan. This historically based ethical and monotheistic tradition culminated in the Jewish, Christian, and Islamic religions, but its direction was set among the ancient Hebrews.

The path from the appearance of the Hebrews as a nomadic people in the northern Arabian Peninsula, sometime after 2000 B.C.E., to the full flowering of Judaic monotheism in the mid–first millennium B.C.E. was a long one. Before we turn to the monotheistic revolution itself, we need to look briefly at this history.

FROM HEBREW NOMADS TO THE ISRAELITE NATION

The history of the Hebrews, later known as Israelites, must be pieced together from various sources. The records of their ancient Near Eastern neighbors mention the Hebrews only rarely, so historians must rely on their own accounts as compiled in the Hebrew Bible (the Old Testament in Christian terminology). It was not intended as a history in the contemporary sense; rather, it is a complicated collection of historical narrative, wisdom literature, poetry, law, and religious witness. Scholars once tended to discard the Bible as a source for historians, but the trend today is to take it seriously while using it cautiously and critically. Although its earliest writings go back at most to the ninth century B.C.E. (it was fixed in its present form only in the second century C.E.), it contains much older oral materials that allow us at least some glimpses of the earliest history of the Hebrew people.

We need not reject the core reality of the tradition that the Hebrew Abraham came from Ur in southern Mesopotamia and wandered west with his Hebrew clan to tend his flocks in the land later known as Palestine. Such a movement would be in accord with what we know of a general westward migration of seminomadic tribes from Mesopotamia after about 1950 B.C.E. Any precise dating of the arrival of the Hebrews in Palestine is impossible, but it was likely between 1900 and 1600 B.C.E.

It is with Moses, at about the beginning of the thirteenth century B.C.E., that the Hebrews tread clearly upon the stage of history. Some of Abraham's people had settled in the Palestinian region, but others apparently wandered farther, into Egypt, perhaps with the Hyksos invaders (see Chapter 1). By about 1400 B.C.E., as the biblical narrative tells it, they had become a settled but subjected, even enslaved, people there. Under Moses, some of the Egyptian Israelites fled Egypt to find a new homeland to the east, from which Abraham's descendants had come. They may then have wandered in the Sinai Desert and elsewhere for several decades before reaching Canaan, the province of Palestine that is described in the Bible as their promised homeland. The Bible presents this experience as the key event in Israel's history: the forging of the covenant, or mutual pact, between God, or Yahweh, and his people. We interpret this Exodus as the time when the Israelites emerged as a nation, a people with a sense of community and common faith.

By about 1200 B.C.E., they had displaced the Canaanite inhabitants of ancient Palestine. After perhaps two centuries of consolidation as a loose federation of tribes, the now settled nation reached its peak as a kingdom under David (r. ca. 1000–961 B.C.E.) and Solomon (r. ca. 961–922 B.C.E.). But in the ninth century B.C.E., the kingdom split into two parts: Israel in the north and Judah, with its capital at Jerusalem, in the south (see Map 2–1).

The rise of great empires around them brought disaster to the Israelites. The Northern Kingdom fell to the Assyrians in 722 B.C.E.; its people were scattered and, according to tradition, lost forever—the so-called ten lost tribes. Only the kingdom of Judah, with its seat at Jerusalem, remained, and after that we

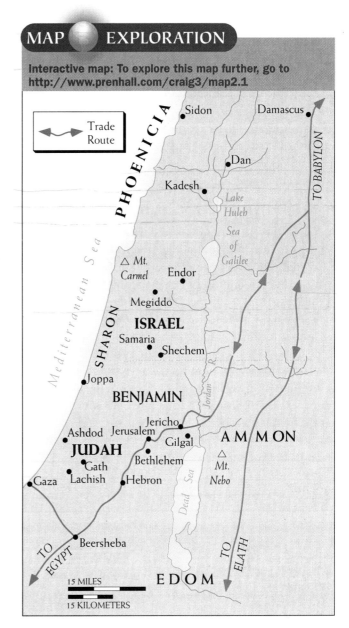

MAP EXPLORATION

Interactive map: To explore this map further, go to http://www.prenhall.com/craig3/map2.1

MAP 2–1 Ancient Palestine.   The Hebrews established a unified kingdom under Kings David and Solomon in the 10th century B.C.E. After Solomon, the kingdom was divided into Israel in the north and Judah, with its capital, Jerusalem, in the south. North of Israel were the great commercial cities of Phoenicia.

may call the Israelites Jews. In 586 B.C.E., Judah was defeated by the Neo-Babylonian king Nebuchadnezzar II (d. 562 B.C.E.). He destroyed the Jewish cult center, the great Temple built by Solomon, and carried off the cream of the Jewish nation as exiles to be resettled in Babylon. There, in the "Babylonian captivity" of the Exile, without a temple, the Jews clung to their traditions and faith. After the new Persian dynasty of the Achaemenids defeated the Babylonians in 539 B.C.E., the Jews were allowed to return and resettle in their homeland. Many, but not all, of the exiles did return, and by about 516 B.C.E., they erected a second temple in a restored Jerusalem.

The new Judaic state continued for centuries to be dominated by foreign peoples but was able to maintain its religious and national identity and occasionally to assert itself. However, it was again destroyed and its people dispersed after the Romans' destruction of Jerusalem, in 70 C.E. and again in 132 C.E. By this era, however, the Jews had developed a religious worldview that would long outlive any Judaic national state.

THE MONOTHEISTIC REVOLUTION

The fate of this small nation would be of little interest were it not for its unique religious achievement. It developed a tradition of faith that amounted to a revolution in ways of thinking about the human condition, the meaning of life and history, and the nature of the Divine. It was not the overt history of the Judaic state down to its catastrophic end in 132 C.E. that was to have lasting historical importance, but what the Jews made of that history—how they interpreted it and built upon it a lasting Jewish culture and identity. The revolutionary character of this interpretation lay in its uniquely moralistic understanding of human life and history and the uncompromising monotheism on which it was based.

At the root of this monotheistic tradition stands the figure of Abraham. Not only Jews but also Christians and Muslims look to him as the symbolic founder of their monotheistic faith. The Hebrews in Abraham's time were probably much like other primitive tribal peoples in their religious attitudes. For them, the world must have been alive with supernatural powers: ancestral spirits, personifications of the forces of nature, and deities of local places. Abraham probably conceived of his Lord simply as his chosen deity among the many divinities who might be worshiped. Yet for the strength of his faith in his God, the biblical account recognizes him as the "Father of the Faithful," the first of the Hebrew patriarchs to make a covenant with the God who would become unique and supreme. In this, Abraham promised to serve only him, and his God promised to bless his descendants and guide them as his special people.

After Abraham, the next major step came with Moses. As with Abraham's faith, it is difficult to say how much the Mosaic covenant at Sinai actually marked the achievement of an exclusively monotheistic faith. A notion of the supremacy of Yahweh is reflected in the biblical emphasis on the Israelites' rejection of all other gods after Sinai—and on their subsequent victory, through Yahweh's might, over the Canaanites. Certainly, the covenant event was decisive in uniting the Israelites as a people with a special relationship to God. At Sinai, they received both God's holy Law (the Torah) and his promise of protection and guidance as long as they kept the Law. This was the pivotal moment in the monotheistic revolution that came

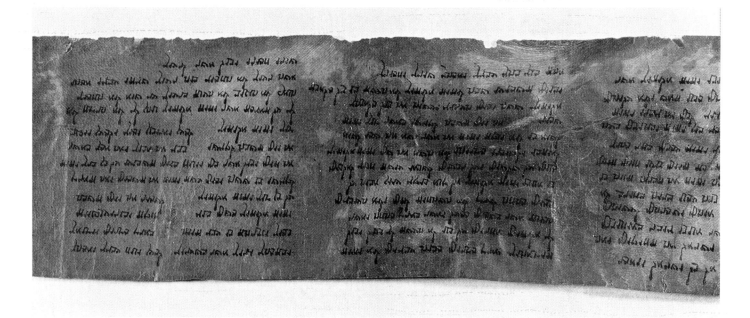

⚊ **Scroll from the Dead Sea.** This photograph shows part of one of the ancient scrolls found by Bedouins, beginning in 1947, in a remote cave at Khirbat near the Dead Sea in Jordan. The passage from the Hebrew Bible contains part of the Ten Commandments in the Book of Deuteronomy. The scrolls were written sometime between 200 B.C.E. and 68 C.E. They contain documents that suggest they belonged to a monastic sect of Jews called Essenes whose beliefs bear some similarity to those of John the Baptist and Jesus.
ASAP/David Harris.

Exile of the Israelites. In 722 B.C.E. the northern part of Jewish Palestine, the kingdom of Israel, was conquered by the Assyrians. Its people were driven from their homeland and exiled all over the vast Assyrian Empire. This wall carving in low relief comes from the palace of the Assyrian king Sennacherib at Nineveh. It shows the Jews with their cattle and baggage going into exile.
Erich Lessing/Art Resource, N.Y.

to full fruition only several hundred years later. But from the later perspective of the biblical redactors at least, from Sinai forward the Israelites saw themselves as God's chosen people among the nations and their history as the history of the mighty acts of the one God.

The monotheistic revolution might thus be said to have begun with Abraham or Moses. Historically, we can trace it primarily from the bipartite division of the Israelite kingdom in 922 B.C.E. After this, men and women known as the *prophets* arose. These inspired messengers of God were sent to call their people back from worship of false gods to faith in the one true God, and from immorality to obedience to God's commandments.

The important point in the colorful history of the great and lesser prophets is that their activity was closely linked to the saga of Israelite national success, exile, and return in the mid–first millennium B.C.E. In the biblical interpretation of these events, we can see the progressive consolidation of Judaic religion. This consolidation, even amidst the political demise of the Israelite kingdom, was largely the work of the prophets. Their concern with purifying Jewish faith, and with morality, focused in particular on two ideas that proved central to Judaic monotheism.

The first seminal idea for the Jews was the significance of history in the divine plan. Calling on the Jews' awareness of the Sinai covenant, the prophets saw in Israel's past and present troubles God's punishment for failing in their covenant duties. Their prophecies of coming disaster from their enemies were based on the conviction that unless Israel changed its ways, more punishment would follow. But they were not only prophets of doom. When the predicted disasters arrived, their vision extended to seeing Israel as the "suffering servant" among the nations, the people who, by their trials, would purify other nations and bring them ultimately to God. Here the nationalistic, particularistic focus of previous Israelite religion gave way to a more complete, universalist monotheism: Yahweh was now God of all, even the Babylonians or Assyrians.

The second central idea emphasized the nature of Yahweh. The prophets saw in him the transcendent ideal of justice and goodness. From this view followed naturally the demand for justice and goodness, individually and collectively, among his worshipers. God was a righteous God who expected righteousness from human beings. (See Document, "God's Purpose with Israel.") No longer could he be only the object of a sacrificial cult: he was a moral God who demanded goodness, not blood offerings or empty prayers. A corollary of God's goodness was his love for his people, as the prophet Hosea (late eighth century B.C.E.) emphasized. However much he might have to punish them for their sins, God would finally lead them back to his favor.

The crux of the breakthrough to ethical monotheism lay in linking the Lord of the Universe to history and morality. The Almighty Creator was seen as actively concerned with the actions

DOCUMENT | God's Purpose with Israel

According to Jewish tradition, the Ten Commandments that Moses received from God for the Israelites are given in two different places in the Torah, with slightly different wording in each. The Exodus passage is one of these; the other is in Deuteronomy 5, the chapter immediately followed by the second passage cited here, Deuteronomy 6:1–9. This latter passage contains the fundamental statement of Judaic faith (verses 4–5), known as the Shema ("Hear," the word that begins this divine command).

◆ How do these passages exemplify the moral consciousness and utter faith in God that Jewish monotheism is built upon?

And God spoke all these words, saying,

"I am the Lord your God, who brought you out of the land of Egypt, out of the house of bondage.

"You shall have no other gods before me.

"You shall not make for yourself a graven image, or any likeness of anything that is in heaven above, or that is in the earth beneath, or that is in the water under the earth; you shall not bow down to them or serve them; for I the Lord your God am a jealous God, visiting the iniquity of the fathers upon the children to the third and the fourth generation of those who hate me, but showing steadfast love to thousands of those who love me and keep my commandments.

"You shall not take the name of the Lord your God in vain; for the Lord will not hold him guiltless who takes his name in vain.

"Remember the sabbath day, to keep it holy. Six days you shall labor, and do all your work; but the seventh day is a sabbath to the Lord your God; in it you shall not do any work, you, or your son, or your daughter, your manservant, or your maidservant, or your cattle, or the sojourner who is within your gates; for in six days the Lord made heaven and earth, the sea, and all that is in them and rested the seventh day; therefore the Lord blessed the sabbath day and hallowed it.

"Honor your father and your mother, that your days may be long in the land which the Lord your God gives you.

"You shall not kill.

"You shall not commit adultery.

"You shall not steal.

"You shall not bear false witness against your neighbor.

"You shall not covet your neighbor's house; you shall not covet your neighbor's wife, or his manservant, or his maidservant, or his ox, or his ass, or anything that is your neighbor's."

—*Exodus 20:1–17*

"Now this is the commandment, the statutes and the ordinances which the Lord your God commanded me to teach you, that you may do them in the land to which you are going over, to possess it; that you may fear the Lord your God, you and your son and your son's son, by keeping all his statutes and his commandments, which I command you, all the days of your life; and that your days may be prolonged. Hear therefore, O Israel, and be careful to do them; that it may go well with you, and that you may multiply greatly, as the Lord, the God of your fathers, has promised you, in a land flowing with milk and honey.

"Hear, O Israel: The Lord our God is one Lord, and you shall love the Lord your God with all your heart, and with all your soul, and with all your might. And these words which I command you this day shall be upon your heart; and you shall teach them diligently to your children, and shall talk of them when you sit in your house, and when you walk by the way, and when you lie down, and when you rise. And you shall bind them as a sign upon your hand, and they shall be as frontlets between your eyes. And you shall write them on the doorposts of your house and on your gates.

—*Deuteronomy 6:1–9*

and fates of his human creatures as exemplified in Israel. This concern was reflected in God's involvement in history, which thus took on transcendent meaning. God had created humankind for an ultimately good purpose; they were called to be just and good like their Creator, for they were involved in the fulfillment of his divine purpose. This fulfillment would come in the restoration of Israel as a people purified of their sins: "I will put my law within them, and I will write it upon their hearts; and I will be their God, and they shall be my people" (Jeremiah 31:33).

Even after the exile, however, the realization of the prophesied days of peace and blessedness under God's rule clearly still had not come. Jews were scattered from Egypt to Babylonia, and their homeland was controlled by foreign powers. This context brought forth the late prophetic concept that history's culmination would come in a future Messianic age. Faith and morality were tied to human destiny, even without the still later Jewish idea that a Day of Judgment would cap the golden age of the **Messiah**, the redeemer who Jews believed would establish the kingdom of God on earth. The significance of these ideas, some of which might have come from the Jews' encounter with Zoroastrian traditions during the exile, did not stop with Judaic religion. They played a key role in similar Christian and Muslim ideas of a Messianic deliverer, resurrection of the body, and a life after death.

The Temple Mount, Seen from the West. The traditional site of the Jerusalem Temple (the Herodian western wailing wall is in the center), the Temple Mount is a holy site especially to Muslims, as well as to Jews and Christians. The dome in the center is the Muslim Dome of the Rock sanctuary (692 C.E.).
Bernard Boutrit / Woodfin Camp & Associates.

Alongside the prophets, the other key element in the monotheistic revolution of the Jews was the Law itself. The Law is embodied in the five books of Torah (the Pentateuch, or "five books": Genesis, Exodus, Leviticus, Numbers, and Deuteronomy). The central place of the Law in Jewish life was reestablished, after a period of decline, by King Josiah of Judah (ca. 649–609 B.C.E.) shortly before the fall of Jerusalem and the exile. Its presence and importance in Judaic faith enabled the Jews in exile to survive the loss of the Temple and its priestly cult, thereby fixing the Torah even over Jerusalem as the ultimate earthly focus of faith in God. Its centrality for the Judaic nation was reaffirmed after the reestablishment of the Temple by the prophets Ezra and Nehemiah in the fifth century B.C.E.

In the second century B.C.E., the enduring role of Torah was ensured by its physical compilation, together with the books of the prophets and other writings, into the Holy Scriptures, or Bible (from the Greek *bibloi*, "books"). The Torah has not only the Law itself, but also the record of the Jews' journey to the recognition of God's law for his people. A holy, authoritative, divinely revealed scripture as an element of Judaic monotheism had revolutionary conse-

quences, not only for Jews, but also for Christians and Muslims. It put the seal on the monotheistic revolution that had made the sovereignty and righteousness of God the focal points of faith.

The evolution of Judaic monotheistic faith was the beginning of one of the major traditions of world religion. For the first time, a nation defined itself not primarily by dynastic, linguistic, or geographic considerations, but by shared religious faith and practice. This was something new in human history. It was later to have still greater effects when not only Judaic but also Christian and Muslim traditions would change the face of much of the world.

Greek Philosophy

Greek thought offered different approaches and answers to many of the same concerns as those of the original monotheists. Calling attention to some of those differences will help to identify the distinctive outlook of the Greeks and of the later cultures of Western civilization that have drawn heavily on it.

Greek ideas had much in common with those of earlier peoples. The Greek gods had most of the characteristics of the Mesopotamian deities; magic and incantations played a part in Greek lives; and their law was usually connected with divinity. Many, if not most, Greeks in the ancient world must have lived with notions similar to those held by other peoples. But surprisingly, some Greeks developed ideas that were strikingly different and, in so doing, set a part of humankind on an entirely new path. As early as the sixth century B.C.E., Greeks living in the Ionian cities of Asia Minor raised questions and suggested answers about nature that produced an intellectual revolution. In speculating about the nature of the world and its origin, they made guesses that were completely naturalistic and included no reference to supernat-

---

OVERVIEW Four Great Systems of Thought and Religion

Between 800 B.C.E. and 300 B.C.E., four philosophical or religious revolutions occurred that shaped the subsequent history of the world. These revolutions, which were attempts to answer universal questions about the human condition, established cultural patterns that have endured to the present day.

Chinese Philosophy Three principal schools: Confucianism, Daoism, Legalism. Each school was concerned with social and political issues, how individuals interact with each other and the state, and the question of how to lead an ethical life that was in harmony with nature and the cosmos.

Indian Religion Hinduism, Jains, Buddhism. Indian religion saw existence as an endless cycle of birth and rebirth (*samsara*). *Karma*, the concept that every action has good or evil effects, was the key to resolving the dilemma of *samsara*. Good actions could result in a person's being reborn in a higher state, even as a god. Complete withdrawal from the world could lead to escape from *samsara* into nonexistence.

Hebrew Monotheism The Hebrews, or Israelites, were the first people in history to base their identity as a nation in faith in a single, all-powerful God who made ethical demands and placed responsibilities on them as individuals and as a community. History, itself, was the unfolding of a divine plan for human beings. Through the Christian and Muslim traditions, Hebrew monotheism would profoundly influence much of the world.

Greek Philosophy Beginning in the sixth century B.C.E., Greek thinkers were the first to try to explain the natural world without reference to supernatural powers. Later Greek thinkers used rational analysis to investigate ethical, political, and social problems: how human beings should govern themselves, live in society, and act toward each other. The Greek tradition of rational inquiry lies at the root of all subsequent Western science and philosophy.

---

ural powers. One historian of Greek thought, discussing the views of Thales (624–545 B.C.E.), the first Greek philosopher, put the case particularly well:

> In one of the Babylonian legends it says: "All the lands were sea. Marduk bound a rush mat upon the face of the waters, he made dirt and piled it beside the rush mat." What Thales did was to leave Marduk out. He, too, said that everything was once water. But he thought that earth and everything else had been formed out of water by a natural process, like the silting up of the Delta of the Nile. It is an admirable beginning, the whole point of which is that it gathers together into a coherent picture a number of observed facts without letting Marduk in.[3]

By putting the question of the world's origin in a naturalistic form, Thales may have initiated the unreservedly rational investigation of the universe, and in so doing, initiated both Western philosophy and Western science.

The same relentlessly rational approach was applied even to the gods themselves. In the same century as Thales, Xenophanes of Colophon expressed the opinion that humans think of the gods as resembling themselves, that like themselves they were born, that they wear clothes like theirs, and that they have voices and bodies like theirs. If oxen, horses, and lions had hands and could paint like humans, Xenophanes argued, they would paint gods in their own image; the oxen would draw gods like oxen and the horses like horses. Thus Africans believed in flat-nosed, black-faced gods, and the Thracians in gods with blue eyes and red hair.[4] In the fifth century B.C.E. Protagoras of Abdera (ca. 490–420 B.C.E.) went so far in the direction of agnosticism as to say, "About the gods I can have no knowledge either that they are or that they are not or what is their nature."[5]

This rationalistic, skeptical way of thinking carried over into practical matters as well. The school of medicine led by Hippocrates of Cos (ca. 400 B.C.E.) attempted to understand, diagnose, and cure disease without recourse to supernatural forces or beings. One of the Hippocrates wrote of the mysterious disease epilepsy:

> It seems to me that the disease is no more divine than any other. It has a natural cause, just as other diseases have. Men think it divine merely because they do not understand it. But if they called everything divine which they do not understand, why, there would be no end of divine things.[6]

[3]Benjamin Farrington, *Greek Science* (London: Penguin Books, 1953), p. 37.

[4]Frankfort et al., *Before Philosophy* (1949), pp. 14–16.
[5]Hermann Diels, *Fragmente der Vorsokratiker*, 5th ed., ed. by Walther Kranz (Berlin: Weidmann, 1934–1938), Frg. 4.
[6]Ibid., Frgs. 14–16.

By the fifth century B.C.E., it was possible for the historian Thucydides (ca. 460–400 B.C.E.) to analyze and explain the behavior of humans in society completely in terms of human nature and chance, leaving no place for the gods or supernatural forces.

The relative unimportance of divine or super-natural forces also characterized Greek views of law and justice. Most Greeks, of course, liked to think that law came ultimately from the gods. In practice, however, and especially in the demo-cratic states, they understood that laws were made by humans and should be obeyed because they repre-sented the expressed consent of the citizens. Law, accord-ing to the fourth-century B.C.E. statesman Demos-thenes (384–322 B.C.E.), was "a general covenant of the whole State, in accordance with which all men in that State ought to regulate their lives."[7]

These ideas, so different from any that came before the Greeks, open the discussion of most of the issues that appear in the long history of civilization and that remain major concerns in the modern world: What is the nature of the universe and how can it be controlled? Are there divine powers, and if so, what is human-ity's relationship to them? Are law and justice human, divine, or both? What is the place in human society of freedom, obe-dience, and reverence? The Greeks confronted and intensi-fied these and many other problems.

REASON AND THE SCIENTIFIC SPIRIT

The rational spirit characteristic of Greek culture blossomed in the sixth century B.C.E. into the intellectual examination of the physical world and the place of humankind in it that we call philosophy. It is not surprising that the first steps along this path were taken in Ionia on the coast of Asia Minor, which was on the fringe of the Greek world and therefore in touch with foreign ideas and the learning of the East. The Ionians were among the first to recognize that the Greek account of how the world was created and maintained and of the place of humans in it was not universally accepted. Perhaps this real-ization helped spark the first attempts at disciplined philo-sophical inquiry.

We have already met Thales of Miletus. He believed that the earth floated on water and that water was the primary sub-

Thales of Miletus, the First Greek Philosopher. His explanation for the origin of the world was based on reason and the observation of nature without any need for the supernatural. Corbis-Bettmann.

stance. This idea was not new; what was new was the absence of any magical or myth-ical elements in the explanation. Thales observed, as any person can, that water has many forms: liquid, solid, and gaseous. He saw that it could "create" land by alluvial deposit and that it was necessary for all life. These ob-servations he organized by rea-son into a single explanation that accounted for many phe-nomena without any need for the supernatural. The first philosopher thus set the tone for future investiga-tions. Greek philosophers assumed that the world was know-able, rational, and simple.

The search for fundamental rational explanations of phe-nomena was carried forward by another Milesian, Anaximan-der (ca. 611–546 B.C.E.). He imagined that the basic element was something undefined, "unlimited." The world emerged from this basic element as the result of an interaction of op-posite forces—wet and dry, hot and cold. Anaximander pic-tured the universe in eternal motion, with all sensible things emerging from the "unlimited," then decaying and returning to it. He also argued that human beings originated in water and had evolved to the present state through several stages, in-cluding that of a fish.

Anaximenes, another Milesian who flourished about 546 B.C.E., believed air was primary. It took different forms as a result of the purely physical processes of rarefaction and condensation.

Heraclitus of Ephesus, who lived near the end of the sixth century B.C.E., carried the dialogue further. His famous saying, "All is motion," raised important problems. If all is constantly in motion, nothing ever really exists. Yet Heraclitus believed that the world order was governed by a guiding principle, the *Logos*, and that though phenomena changed, the *Logos* did not. *Logos* has several meanings, among them "word," "lan-guage," "speech," and "reason." So when Heraclitus said that the physical world was governed by *Logos*, he implied that it could be explained by reason. Speculations about the physical

[7]*Against Aristogeiton*, p. 16.

DOCUMENT · The Atomists' Account of the Origin of the World Order

Leucippus and Democritus were Greek thinkers of the fifth century B.C.E. who originated the theory that the world is entirely material, made up of atoms and the void, moving through space without external guidance. As these selections show, they provided a fundamental explanation of things that was purely natural, without divine or mythical intervention. Their view was passed on and later influenced such Renaissance scientists as Galileo.

◆ Compare the atomists' explanation of the origins of the world with that presented in the box entitled "Hymn to Indra" in Chapter 1. How do these explanations of the nature of things and how they got that way differ from those offered by different civilizations and by the Greeks before the sixth century B.C.E.? What are the consequences and significance of this new way of looking at the universe?

1.

The world-orders arise in this way. Many bodies of all sorts of shapes "split off" from the infinite into a great void where, being gathered together, they give rise to a single vortex, in which, colliding and circling in all sorts of ways, they begin to separate apart, like to like. Being unable to circle in equilibrium any longer because of their congestion, the light bodies go off into the outer void like chaff, while the rest "remain together" and, becoming entangled, unite their motions and produce first a spherical structure. This stands apart like a "membrane," containing in itself all sorts of bodies; and, because of the resistance of the middle, as these revolve the surrounding membrane becomes thin as contiguous bodies continually flow together because of contact with the vortex. And in this way the earth arose, the bodies which were carried to the middle remaining together. Again, the surrounding membrane increases because of the acquisition of bodies from without; and as it moves with the vortex, whatever it touches it adds to itself. Certain of these, becoming entangled, form a structure at first very watery and muddy; but afterward they dry out, being carried about with the rotation of the whole, and ignite to form the substance of the heavenly bodies.

2.

Certainly the atoms did not arrange themselves in order by design or intelligence, nor did they propound what movements each should make. But rather myriad atoms, swept along through infinite time or myriad paths by blows and their own weight, have come together in every possible way and tried out every combination that they could possibly create. So it happens that, after roaming the world for aeons of time in making trial of every combination and movement, at length they come together—those atoms whose sudden coincidence often becomes the origin of mighty things: of earth and sea and sky and the species of living things.

The first selection is from Diogenes Laertius 9.31; the second is from Lucretius, *De Rerum Naturae* 5.419–431. Both selections from John Mansley Robinson, *An Introduction to Early Greek Philosophy.* Copyright © 1968 by John Mansley Robinson. Used with permission of the author.

world, what we would call natural science, thus soon led the way toward even more difficult philosophical speculations about language, about the manner of human thought, and about knowledge itself.

In opposition to Heraclitus, the fifth-century B.C.E. philosopher Parmenides of Elea and his pupil Zeno argued that change was only an illusion of the senses. Reason and reflection showed that reality was fixed and unchanging because it seemed evident that nothing could be created out of nothingness. Such fundamental speculations were carried forward by Empedocles of Acragas (fl. ca. 450 B.C.E.), who spoke of four basic elements: fire, water, earth, and air. Like Parmenides, he thought that reality was permanent but not immobile, for the four elements were moved by two primary forces, Love and Strife, or, as we might be inclined to say, attraction and repulsion.

This theory was clearly a step on the road to the atomic theory of Leucippus of Miletus (fl. fifth century B.C.E.) and Democritus of Abdera (ca. 460–370 B.C.E.). They believed that the world consisted of innumerable tiny, solid particles (atoms) that could not be divided or modified and that moved about in the void. The size of the atoms and the arrangement in which they were joined with others produced the secondary qualities that the senses could perceive, such as color and shape. These qualities—unlike the atoms themselves, which were natural—were merely conventional. Anaxagoras of Clazomenae (ca. 500–428 B.C.E.) had previously spoken of tiny fundamental particles called *seeds* that were put together on a rational basis by a force called *nous*, or "mind." Thus, Anaxagoras suggested a distinction between matter and mind. But the **atomists** regarded "soul," or "mind," as material and believed that everything was guided by purely physical laws. In the arguments of Anaxagoras and the atomists, we have the beginning of the philosophical debate between materialism and idealism that has continued through the ages. (See Document, "The Atomists' Account of the Origin of the World Order.")

These discussions interested few; indeed, most Greeks were suspicious of such speculations. A far more influential debate was begun by a group of professional teachers who emerged in the mid-fifth century B.C.E. Called **Sophists**, they traveled about and received pay for teaching practical techniques of persuasion, such as rhetoric, which were highly valued in democracies like Athens. Some claimed to teach wisdom and even virtue. (See Document, "The Sophists: From Rational Inquiry to Skepticism.") They did not speculate about the physical universe but applied reasoned analysis to human beliefs and institutions. This human focus was characteristic of fifth-century B.C.E. thought, as was the central problem that the Sophists considered: They discovered the tension and even the contradiction between nature and custom, or law. The more traditional among them argued that law itself was in accord with nature, and this view fortified the traditional beliefs about the **polis**, the Greek city-state (see Chapter 3).

Others argued that laws were merely conventional and not in accord with nature. The law was not of divine origin but merely the result of an agreement among people. It could not pretend to be a positive moral force but merely had the negative function of preventing people from harming each other. The most extreme Sophists argued that law was contrary to nature, a trick whereby the weak controlled the strong. Critias (ca. 460–403 B.C.E.) went so far as to say that the gods themselves had been invented by some clever man to deter people from doing what they wished. Such ideas attacked the theoretical foundations of the *polis* and helped provoke the philosophical responses of Plato and Aristotle in the next century.

POLITICAL AND MORAL PHILOSOPHY

Like thinkers in other parts of the world around the middle of the first millennium B.C.E., some Greeks were vitally concerned with the formulation of moral principles for the governance of the state and the regulation of individual life, as well as with more abstract problems of the nature of existence and transcendence. Nowhere is the Greek concern with ethical, political, and religious issues clearer than in the philosophical tradition that began with Socrates in the latter half of the fifth century B.C.E. That tradition continued with Socrates' pupil Plato and with Plato's pupil Aristotle. Aristotle also had great interest in and made great contributions to the scientific understanding of the physical world, but he is perhaps more important for his impact on later Western and Islamic metaphysics.

The three philosophical giants of Hellenic political and moral philosophy were Socrates, Plato, and Aristotle. The starting point for all three was the social and political reality of the Greek city-state, or *polis*. The greatest crisis for the *polis* was the Great Peloponnesian War (435–404 B.C.E.), which is discussed in Chapter 3. Probably the most complicated response to this crisis may be found in the life and teachings of Socrates (469–399 B.C.E.). Because he wrote nothing, our knowledge of

him comes chiefly from his disciples Plato and Xenophon (ca. 435–354 B.C.E.) and from later tradition. Although as a young man Socrates was interested in speculations about the physical world, he later turned to the investigation of ethics and morality. As the Roman writer and statesman Cicero (106–43 B.C.E.) put it, he brought philosophy down from the heavens.

Socrates was committed to the search for truth and for the knowledge about human affairs that he believed reason could reveal. His method was to go among men, particularly those reputed to know something, like craftsmen, poets, and politicians, to question and cross-examine them. The result was always the same: Those he questioned might have technical information and skills but seldom had any knowledge of the fundamental principles of human behavior. It is understandable that Athenians so exposed should become angry with their examiner, and it is not surprising that they thought Socrates was undermining the beliefs and values of the *polis*. Socrates' unconcealed contempt for democracy, which seemingly relied on ignorant amateurs to make important political decisions without any certain knowledge, created further hostility. Moreover, his insistence on the primacy of his own individualism and his determination to pursue philosophy even against the wishes of his fellow citizens reinforced this hostility and the prejudice that went with it.

Unlike the Sophists, Socrates did not accept pay for his teaching; he professed ignorance and denied that he taught at all. His individualism, moreover, was unlike the worldly hedonism of some of the Sophists. It was not wealth or pleasure or power that he urged people to seek, but "the greatest improvement of the soul." He differed also from the more radical Sophists in denying that the *polis* and its laws were merely conventional. He thought, on the contrary, that they had a legitimate claim on the citizen, and he proved it in the most convincing fashion. In 399 B.C.E., he was condemned to death by an Athenian jury on the charges of bringing new gods into the city and of corrupting its youth. His dialectical inquiries had angered many important people, and his criticism of democracy must have been viewed with suspicion. He was given a chance to escape, but in Plato's *Crito* we are told of his refusal to do so because of his veneration of the laws.

Socrates' career set the stage for later responses to the travail of the *polis*; he recognized its difficulties and criticized its shortcomings. Although he turned away from an active political life, he did not abandon the idea of the *polis*. He fought as a soldier in its defense, obeyed its laws, and sought to use reason to put its values on a sound foundation.

The Cynics   One branch of Socratic thought—the concern with personal morality and one's own soul, the disdain for worldly pleasure and wealth, and the withdrawal from political life—was developed and then distorted almost beyond recog-

DOCUMENT | The Sophists: From Rational Inquiry to Skepticism

The rational spirit inherent in Greek thought was carried to remarkable and dangerous extremes by the Sophists in the fifth century B.C.E. As these three selections suggest, they questioned even the nature, the existence, and the origin of the gods, subjecting these matters to rational analysis.

◆ What was new in the thinking of the Sophists? How was it similar to the thought of the atomists (Democritus and Leucippus)? How was it different? In what ways were Sophist ideas threatening to the Greek way of life?

1.

Concerning the gods, I do not know whether they exist or not. For many are the obstacles to knowledge: the obscurity of the subject and the brevity of human life.

2.

Prodicus says that the ancients worshiped as gods the sun, the moon, rivers, springs, and all things useful to human life, simply because of their usefulness—just as the Egyptians deify the Nile. For this reason bread is worshiped as Demeter, wine as Dionysus, water as Poseidon, fire as Hephaestus, and so on for each of the things that are useful to men.

3.

There was a time when the life of man was disorderly and bestial and subject to brute force; when there was no reward for the good and no punishment for the bad. At that time, I think, men enacted laws in order that justice might be absolute ruler and have arrogance as its slave; and if anyone did wrong he was punished.

Then, when the laws prohibited them from doing deeds of violence, they began to do them secretly. Then, I think, some shrewd and wise man invented fear of the gods for mortals, so that there might be some deterrent to the wicked even if they did or said or thought something in secret. Therefore he introduced the divine, saying that there is a god, flourishing with immortal life, hearing and seeing with his mind, thinking of all things and watching over them and having a divine nature; who will hear everything that is said among mortals and will be able to see all that is done. And if you plan any evil in secret it will not escape the notice of the gods, for they are of surpassing intelligence. In speaking thus he introduced the prettiest of teachings, concealing the truth under a false account. And in order that he might better strike fear into the hearts of men he told them that the gods dwell in that place which he knew to be a source of fears to mortals—and of benefits too—namely, the upper periphery where they saw lightnings and heard the dreaded rumblings of thunder and saw the starry body of the heaven, the beauteous embroidery of that wise craftsman Time, where the bright glowing mass of the sun moves and whence dark rains descend to earth. With such fears did he surround men, and by means of them he established the deity securely in a place befitting his dignity, and quenched lawlessness. Thus, I think, did some man first persuade mortals to believe in a race of gods.

The first selection is from Diogenes Laertius 9.51; the next two are from Sextus Empiricus, *Against the Schoolmasters* 9.18, 9.54. From John Mansley Robinson, *An Introduction to Early Greek Philosophy*. Copyright © 1968 by John Mansley Robinson. Used with permission of the author.

nition by the Cynic school. Antisthenes (ca. 455–360 B.C.E.), a follower of Socrates, is said to have been its founder, but its most famous exemplar was Diogenes of Sinope (ca. 400–325 B.C.E.). Socrates disparaged wealth and worldly comfort, so Diogenes wore rags and lived in a tub. He performed shameful acts in public and made his living by begging to show his rejection of convention. He believed that happiness lay in satisfying natural needs in the simplest and most direct way. Because actions to this end, being natural, could not be indecent, they could and should be done publicly.

Socrates questioned the theoretical basis for popular religious beliefs; the Cynics ridiculed all religious observances. As Plato said, Diogenes was Socrates gone mad. Beyond that, the way of the Cynics contradicted important Socratic beliefs. Socrates believed that virtue was not a matter of birth but of knowledge, and that people did wrong only through ignorance of what is virtuous. The Cynics, on the contrary, believed that virtue was an affair of deeds and did not need a store of words and learning. Wisdom and happiness came from pursuing the proper style of life, not from philosophy. The Cynics moved even further from Socrates by abandoning the concept of the *polis* entirely. When Diogenes was asked about his citizenship, he answered that he was *kosmopolites*, a citizen of the world. The Cynics plainly had turned away from the past, and their views anticipated those of the Hellenistic Age (see Chapter 3).

Plato   Plato (429–347 B.C.E.) was the most important of Socrates' associates and is a perfect example of the pupil who becomes greater than his master. He was the first systematic philosopher and therefore the first to place political ideas in their full philosophical context. He was also a writer of genius, leaving us twenty-six philosophical discussions. (See Document, "Plato on the Role of Women in His Utopian Republic.") Almost all are in the form of dialogues, which dramatize the examination of difficult and complicated philosophical problems and make them somewhat entertaining.

Born of a noble Athenian family, Plato looked forward to an active political career until he was discouraged by the excesses of Athenian politics and the execution of Socrates. Twice he went to Sicily in the hope of producing a model state at Syracuse under that city's rulers, but without success. In 386 B.C.E., Plato founded the Academy, a center of philosophical investigation and a school for training statesmen and citizens that had a powerful impact on Greek thought and endured until it was closed in the sixth century C.E.

Like Socrates, Plato firmly believed in the *polis* and its values. Its virtues were order, harmony, and justice, and one of its main objects was to produce good people. Like his master, and unlike the radical Sophists, Plato thought that the *polis* was in accord with nature. He accepted Socrates' doctrine of the identity of virtue and knowledge and made it plain what that knowledge was: *episteme*, science, a body of true and unchanging wisdom open to only a few philosophers whose training, character, and intellect allowed them to see reality. Only such people were qualified to rule; they themselves would prefer the life of pure contemplation but would accept their responsibility and take their turn as philosopher-kings. The training of such men required a specialization of function and a subordination of the individual to the community. This specialization would lead to Plato's definition of justice: that each man should do only that one thing to which his nature was best suited.

Plato understood that the *polis* of his day suffered from terrible internal stress, class struggle, and factional divisions. His solution, however, was not that of some Greeks—that is, conquest and resulting economic prosperity. For Plato the answer was in moral and political reform. The way to harmony was to destroy the causes of strife: private property, the family—anything, in short, that stood between the individual citizen and devotion to the *polis*.

The concern for the redemption of the *polis* was at the heart of Plato's system of philosophy. He began by asking the traditional questions: What is a good man, and how is he made? The goodness of a human being was a theme that belonged to moral philosophy, and when it became a function of the state, the question became part of political philosophy. Because goodness depended on knowledge of the good, it required a

theory of knowledge and an investigation of what the knowledge was that was required for goodness. The answer must be metaphysical and so required a full examination of metaphysics. Even when the philosopher knew the good, however, the question remained of how the state could bring its citizens to the necessary comprehension of that knowledge. The answer required a theory of education. Even purely logical and metaphysical questions, therefore, were subordinate to the overriding political questions. Plato's need to find a satisfactory foundation for the beleaguered *polis* thus contributed to the birth of systematic philosophy.

Aristotle Aristotle (384–322 B.C.E.) was a pupil of Plato and owed much to the thought of his master, but his different experience and cast of mind led him in new directions. He was born in northern Greece, the son of the court doctor of neighboring Macedon. As a young man, he came to study at the Academy, where he stayed until Plato's death. Then he joined a Platonic colony at Assos in Asia Minor, and from there, he moved to Mytilene. In both places, he carried on research in marine biology, and biological interests played a large part in all his thoughts. In 342 B.C.E., Philip, the king of Macedon, appointed him tutor to his son, the young Alexander (see Chapter 3). In 336 he returned to Athens, where he founded his own school, the Lyceum (or the Peripatos, as it was also called, based on the covered walk within it). In later years, its members were called Peripatetics. On the death of Alexander in 323 B.C.E., the Athenians rebelled against Macedonian rule, and Aristotle found it wise to leave Athens. He died the following year.

The Lyceum was different from the Academy. Its members took little interest in mathematics and were concerned with gathering, ordering, and analyzing all human knowledge. Aristotle wrote dialogues on the Platonic model, but none have survived. He and his students also prepared many collections of information to serve as the basis for scientific works, but of them only one remains, the *Constitution of the Athenians*, one of 158 constitu-

DOCUMENT   Plato on the Role of Women in His Utopian Republic

The Greek invention of reasoned intellectual analysis of all things led the philosopher Plato to consider the problem of justice, which is the subject of his most famous dialogue, the Republic. This inquiry leads him to sketch out a utopian state in which justice may be found and where the most radical arrangements may be necessary. These include the equality of the sexes and the destruction of the family in favor of the practice of men having wives and children in common. In the following excerpts he argues for the fundamental equality of men and women and that women are no less appropriate than men as Guardians, leaders of the state.

◆ What are Plato's reasons for treating men and women the same? What objections could be raised to that practice? Would that policy, even if appropriate in Plato's utopia, also be suitable to conditions in the real world of classical Athens? In the world of today?

"If, then, we use the women for the same things as the men, they must also be taught the same things."

"Yes."

"Now music and gymnastics were given to the men."

"Yes."

"Then these two arts, and what has to do with war, must be assigned to the women also, and they must be used in the same ways."

"On the basis of what you say," he said, "it's likely."

"Perhaps," I said, "compared to what is habitual, many of the things now being said would look ridiculous if they were to be done as is said."

"Indeed they would," he said.

"Well," I said, "since we've started to speak, we mustn't be afraid of all the jokes—of whatever kind—the wits might make if such a change took place in gymnastic, in music and, not the least, in the bearing of arms and the riding of horses."

"Then," I said, "if either the class of men or that of women shows its superiority in some art or other practice then we'll say that that art must be assigned to it. But if they look as though they differ in this alone, that the female bears and the male mounts, we'll assert that it has not thereby yet been proved that a woman differs from a man with respect to what we're talking about; rather, we'll still suppose that our Guardians and their women must practice the same things."

"And rightly," he said.

"Therefore, my friend, there is no practice of a city's governors which belongs to woman because she's woman, or to man because he's man; but the natures are scattered alike among both animals; and woman participates according to nature in all practices, and man in all, but in all of them woman is weaker than man."

"Certainly."

"So, shall we assign all of them to men and none to women?"

"How could we?"

"For I suppose there is, as we shall assert, one woman apt at medicine and another not, one woman apt at music and another unmusical by nature."

"Of course."

"And isn't there then also one apt at gymnastic and at war, and another unwarlike and no lover of gymnastic?"

"I suppose so."

"And what about this? Is there a lover of wisdom and a hater of wisdom? And one who is spirited and another without spirit?"

"Yes, there are these too."

"There is, therefore, one woman fit for guarding and another not, or wasn't it a nature of this sort we also selected for the men fit for guarding?"

"Certainly, that was it."

From *The Republic of Plato*, 2nd ed., trans. by Allan Bloom. Copyright © 1968 by Allan Bloom. Preface to paperback edition, © 1991 by Allan Bloom. pp. 130–134. Reprinted by permission of Basic Books, a member of Perseus Books, L.L.C.

---

tional treatises. Almost all we possess of his work is in the form of philosophical and scientific studies, whose loose organization and style suggest that they were lecture notes. The range of treated subjects is astonishing, including logic, physics, astronomy, biology, ethics, rhetoric, literary criticism, and politics.

In each field, the method was the same. Aristotle began with observation of the empirical evidence, which in some cases was physical and in others was common opinion. To this body of information he applied reason and discovered inconsistencies or difficulties. To deal with these, he introduced metaphysical principles to explain the problems or to reconcile the inconsistencies. His view on all subjects, like Plato's, was teleological; that is, he recognized purposes apart from

and greater than the will of the individual human being. Plato's purposes, however, were contained in the Ideas, or Forms—transcendental concepts outside the experience of most people. For Aristotle, the purposes of most things were easily inferred by observing their behavior in the world.

Aristotle's most striking characteristics are his moderation and common sense. His epistemology finds room for both reason and experience; his metaphysics gives meaning and reality to both mind and body; his ethics aims at the good life, which is the contemplative life, but recognizes the necessity for moderate wealth, comfort, and pleasure.

All these qualities are evident in Aristotle's political thought. Like Plato, he opposed the Sophists' assertion that the *polis* was contrary to nature and the result of mere convention. His response was to apply to politics the teleology that he saw in all nature. In his view, matter existed to achieve an end, and it developed until it achieved its form, which was its end. There was constant development from matter to form, from potential to actual. Therefore, human primitive instincts could be seen as the matter out of which the human's potential as a political being could be realized. The *polis* made individuals self-sufficient and allowed the full realization of their potentiality. It was therefore natural. It was also the highest point in the evolution of the social institutions that serve the human need to continue the species: marriage, household, village, and finally, *polis*. For Aristotle, the purpose of the *polis* was neither economic nor military, but moral: "The end of the state is the good life," the life lived "for the sake of noble actions," a life of virtue and morality.[8]

Characteristically, Aristotle was less interested in the best state—the utopia that required philosophers to rule it—than in the best state practically possible, one that would combine justice with stability. The constitution for that state he called *politeia*, not the best constitution, but the next best, the one most suited to and most possible for most states. Its quality was moderation, and it naturally gave power to neither the rich nor the poor but to the middle class, which also had to be the most numerous. The middle class possessed many virtues: Because of its moderate wealth, it was free of the arrogance of the rich and the malice of the poor. For this reason, it was the most stable class. The stability of the constitution also came from being a mixed constitution, blending in some way the laws of democracy and those of oligarchy. Aristotle's scheme was unique because of its realism and the breadth of its vision.

All the political thinkers of the fourth century B.C.E. recognized that the *polis* was in danger and hoped to save it. All recognized the economic and social troubles that threatened it. Isocrates (436–338 B.C.E.), a contemporary of Plato and Aristotle, urged a program of imperial conquest as a cure for poverty and revolution. Plato saw the folly of solving a political and moral problem by purely economic means and resorted to the creation of utopias. Aristotle combined the practical analy-

[8]Aristotle, *Politics*, 1280b, 1281a.

CHRONOLOGY

Major Greek Philosophers

469–399 B.C.E.	Socrates
429–347 B.C.E.	Plato
384–322 B.C.E.	Aristotle

sis of political and economic realities with the moral and political purposes of the traditional defenders of the *polis*. The result was a passionate confidence in the virtues of moderation and of the middle class, and the proposal of a constitution that would give it power. It is ironic that the ablest defense of the *polis* came soon before its demise.

The concern with an understanding of nature in a purely rational, scientific way remained strong through the fifth century B.C.E., culminating in the work of the formulators of the atomic theory, Democritus and Leucippus, and in that of the medical school founded by Hippocrates of Cos. In the mid–fifth century B.C.E., however, men like the Sophists and Socrates turned their attention to humankind and to ethical, political, and religious questions. This latter tradition of inquiry led, by way of Plato, Aristotle (in his metaphysical thought), and the Stoics, to Christianity; it had, as well, a substantial impact on Judaic and Islamic thought. The former tradition of thought, following a line from the natural philosophers, the Sophists, Aristotle (in his scientific thought), and the Epicureans, had to wait until the Renaissance in Western Europe to exert an influence. Since the eighteenth century, this line of Greek thought has been the more influential force in Western civilization. It may not be too much to say that since the Enlightenment of that century, the Western world has been engaged in a debate between the two strands of the Greek intellectual tradition. As Western influence has spread over the world in recent times, that debate has become of universal importance, for other societies have not separated the religious and philosophical from the scientific and physical realms as radically as has the modern West.

Late Zhou Dynasty Bronze Bell.

Summary

The Four Great Philosophical and Religious Revolutions   Between 800 and 300 B.C.E., four philosophical and religious revolutions arose that were to shape the subsequent history of the world. These were Chinese philosophy, Indian religion, Hebrew monotheism, and Greek philosophy.

Chinese Philosophy   Traditional Chinese philosophical thought, which took shape with the teachings of Confucius in the sixth century B.C.E., remained dominant in China until the early twentieth century. It was concerned with social and political issues and sought to teach human beings how to live harmoniously and ethically under Heaven by prescribing the correct relationships between ruler and subject, father and son, older and younger brother, husband and wife, and friend and friend. Confucianism became the official philosophy of China in the second century B.C.E. Other Chinese philosophies were Daoism, a mystical way of thought that offered a refuge from social responsibilities, and Legalism, which taught that a good society requires a strong state that enforces the law and punishes wrongdoers.

Indian Religion   Hinduism, the dominant Indian religious tradition, took shape by 400 B.C.E. In Indian religion, existence was an endless alteration between life and death (*samsara*). The escape from this dilemma lay in the concept of *karma*, the idea that good actions (*dharma*) could lead to rebirth as a higher being, even a god, or to escape the cycle entirely and cease to exist entirely (*moksha*).

Another Indian religious tradition, the Jains, sought to liberate the soul from the bonds of the material world by eliminating evil acts. Although there are few Indian Buddhists today, Buddhism traces its origins to the teachings of an Indian, Siddhartha Gautama (b. ca. 566 B.C.E.). Buddhism holds that escape from *samsara* lies in following a moral path of right understanding and actions and in having compassion for all beings.

Hebrew Monotheism   Monotheism is the faith in a single, all-powerful God as the sole creator, sustainer, and ruler of the universe. The Hebrews were the first people to emphasize the moral demands that the one God, Yahweh, placed on individual and community and to see history as the unfolding of a divine plan. The Hebrews, or Jews, were the first people in history to be defined by shared religious faith and practice. Through the Christian and Muslim traditions, Judaic monotheism would change the face of much of the world.

Greek Philosophy   The Greeks were the first to initiate the unreservedly rational investigation of the universe. They thus became the forerunners of Western philosophy and science. In the sixth and fifth centuries B.C.E., Greek thinkers, such as Thales of Miletus and Heraclitus, sought to explain natural phenomena without recourse to divine intervention. In the later fifth century and the fourth century B.C.E., philosophers, such as Socrates, Plato, and Aristotle, applied the same rational, inquisitive approach to the study of moral and political issues in the life of the Greek city state, or *polis*.

Review Questions

1. Is your outlook on life closer to Confucianism, Daoism, or Legalism? What specifically makes you favor one over the others?

2. Which fundamental assumptions about the world, the individual, and reality do the Jain, Hindu, and Buddhist traditions share? How do these assumptions compare with those that underlie Chinese philosophy, Jewish religious thought, and Greek philosophy?

3. How did the monotheism of the Hebrews differ from that of Egypt's Akhenaten (Chapter 1)? To what extent did their faith bind the Jews politically? Why was the concept of monotheism so radical for Near Eastern civilization?

4. In what ways did the ideas of the Greeks differ from those of other ancient peoples? How do Aristotle's political and ethical ideas compare with those of Confucius? What were Socrates' contributions to the development of philosophy?

Key Terms

atman-Brahman   (p. 57)

Atomists   (p. 70)

Brahmanas   (p. 56)

dharma   (p. 59)

Daoism   (p. 53)

Hindu   (p. 56)

Jains   (p. 59)

junzi   (p. 52)

karma   (p. 58)

Legalism   (p. 54)

Messiah   (p. 66)

monotheism   (p. 62)

polis   (p. 71)

polytheism   (p. 62)

samsara   (p. 58)

Sophists   (p. 71)

Documents CD-ROM

The Fertile Crescent
1.9 Hebrew Scriptures

Early Civilization in East Asia
2.4 Confucius: Analects
2.5 Mencius: the Counterattack on Legalism
2.6 Taoism

Early Civilization in South Asia
3.2 Bhagavad Gita: Hinduism

3.3 The Foundation of the Kingdom of Righteousness
3.4 Dhammapada: Buddhism
3.5 Mahavira: The "Great Hero" of the Jain Religion

Greece and the Hellenistic World
4.8a Against Communism
4.8b Virtue and Moderation: The Doctrine of the Mean

NOTE: *To learn more about the topics in this chapter, see the Suggested Readings at the end of the book.*

RELIGIONS OF THE WORLD

JUDAISM

Monotheism, the belief in a unique God who is the Creator of the universe and its all-powerful Ruler, first became a central and lasting element in religion among the Hebrews, later called Israelites and also Jews. Their religion, more than the many forms of polytheistic worship that characterized the ancient world, demanded moral rectitude and placed ethical responsibilities both on individuals and on the community as a whole. Their God had a divine plan for human history, which was linked to the behavior of his chosen people. This vision of the exclusive worship of the true God, obedience to the laws governing the community that derive from him, and a strong ethical responsibility was connected to humanity's historical experience in this world. Ultimately it gave rise to three great religions: Judaism, Christianity, and Islam.

At the beginning of this tradition stands Abraham, whom all three religions recognize as the founder. According to the Torah (the first five books of the Hebrew Bible; the Christian Old Testament), Abraham entered into a covenant with God in which he promised to worship only this God, who in turn promised to make Abraham's descendants his own chosen people—chosen to worship him, to obey his Laws, and to undertake a special set of moral responsibilities. God renewed the covenant with Moses at Mount Sinai when he freed the Israelites from Egyptian bondage. He promised

them the land of Canaan (later called Palestine and part of which is now the state of Israel) and gave them the Law (the Torah), including the Ten Commandments, by which they were to guide their lives. As long as they lived by his Law God would give them his guidance and protection.

In time the Israelites formed themselves into a kingdom which remained unified from about 1000 to 922 B.C.E. In the period after its division, prophets emerged. Thought to be inspired by God, they chastised the Israelites for their lapses into idolatry and immorality. Even as the kingdom was disintegrating and the Israelites falling under the control of alien empires, the prophets preached social reform and a return to God's laws. The prophets saw Israel's misfortune as punishment for failing to keep the covenant and predicted disaster if the Israelites did not change their ways. When disasters came—the Jewish kingdoms captured, the people enslaved and exiled—the prophets interpreted Israel's status as a chosen people to mean that their sufferings would make them "a light unto the nations," leading other nations to the true worship of one God.

The prophets also preached that God was righteous and demanded righteousness from his people. But he was also a God of justice; although he might need to punish his people for their sins, he would one day reward them with divine favor. Traditional Jewish belief expects that the Messiah, or Anointed One, will someday come and establish God's kingdom on earth. He will introduce an age of universal brotherhood in which all nations will acknowledge the one true God.

The Jews are people of the Book, and foremost among their sacred writings is the Hebrew Bible, consisting of the Five Books of Moses (the Torah), the books of the prophets, and other writings. The Torah is the source of Jewish Law. Over the centuries new experiences required new interpretation of the Law, which was accomplished by the oral Law, no less sacred than the written Law. Compilations of interpretation and commentary by rabbis (wise and learned teachers) were brought together to form the Talmud.

The destruction of their temple in Jerusalem by the Romans in 70 C.E. hastened the scattering of the Jews throughout the empire. Thereafter almost all Jews lived in the Diaspora (dispersion), without a homeland, a political community, or a national or religious center. In the fifth and sixth centuries the decline of the Sassanid Empire in Iran and the collapse of the Western Roman Empire

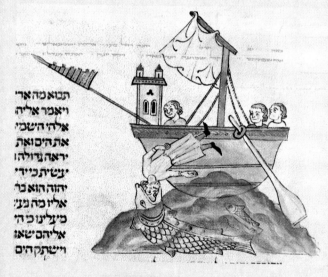

תבוא מהארי
ויאמר אליה
אלהי השמי
את היסואת
יראה גדולה
יעשת כיידי
יהוה הוא כר
אליה מה מני
כי עלינו כי הי
אליהם שאו
וישתקהים

Jonah Eaten by the Whale, from a Hebrew Bible, 1299. Like the Christian illuminated manuscripts they closely resembled, Jewish medieval manuscripts were filled with images of scenes from the Torah and Jewish history. Hebrew writing also developed into an elaborately beautiful calligraphy. Many of these Jewish medieval illuminated manuscripts were, like their Christian counterparts, commissioned by wealthy and influential leaders of Jewish communities in Europe.
Instituto da Biblioteca Nacional, Lisbon, Portugal/Bridgeman Art Library

Russian Persecution of the Jews. This 1900 painting, *After the Pogrom*, by the Polish painter Maurycy Minkowski (oil on canvas laid on board, 98.8 x 148.8 cm), shows a group of women and children in the aftermath of a pogrom, an organized persecution of Jews that often became a massacre. Encouraged by the Russian government, pogroms were especially brutal in the late 19th and early 20th centuries.

Gift of Mr. and Mrs. Lester Klein/Jewish Museum/Art Resource, N.Y.

undermined the institutions in which the Jews had found a stable way of life. In the seventh and eighth centuries the missionary zeal of the Christian church also brought hard times for the Jews in Western Europe and in the Byzantine East. In the West, their condition improved in the ninth century under Charlemagne and his successors.

Under Islam, Jews, like Christians, were tolerated as people of the Book. Jewish settlements flourished throughout the Islamic world. After the Islamic conquest of Spain in 711, the Jews there enjoyed an almost three-hundred-year-long golden age. During this period of extraordinary intellectual and cultural accomplishment, Jews practiced their religion openly and flourished economically.

The beginning of the Crusades in the eleventh century brought renewed persecution of the Jews in both the Christian and Islamic worlds. In the wake of the Christian reconquest of Spain, Jews were persecuted, killed, forced to convert, and finally expelled in 1492.

By the Middle Ages, Jews had divided into two distinct branches: those who lived in Christian Europe, called *Ashkenazim*, and those in the Muslim world, particularly Spain, called *Sephardim*. The Sephardim, with greater opportunities, developed a more secular life. Their language, Ladino, combined Hebrew and Spanish elements. The Ashkenazim, scattered in tiny communities, were forced to turn inward. Centered in German lands, they developed Yiddish, a combination of Hebrew and German. In time Yiddish became the language of most Jews in northern Europe, although the Torah was always read and studied in Hebrew.

Two of the dominant influences on modern Judaism have been Zionism—the effort to found a Jewish nation—and the death of some 6 million Jews in the Holocaust of World War II. Bolstered by the determination of Jews never again to find themselves victimized by the forces of anti-Semitism, the Zionist movement culminated in the founding of the state of Israel in 1948.

The adherents of Judaism are divided into several groups—Reform, Reconstruction, Conservative, and Orthodox—each holding significantly different views about the place of tradition and the traditional law in the modern world. All, however, would give assent to the saying of Hillel, the great Talmudic teacher of the first century B.C.E.: "What is distasteful to you do not to your fellow man. This is the Law, all the rest is commentary. Now go and study."

◆ In what ways did Judaism differ from the polytheistic religions?

◆ What elements of the religion helped it persist through the ages?

PART 2

EMPIRES AND CULTURES OF THE ANCIENT WORLD

The last five hundred years before the beginning of the common era and the two centuries that followed saw the appearance of great empires in Iran, India, and China, and of the Roman Empire in the Mediterranean. Although each arose in response to local conditions, they shared common features: centralized monarchies, large armies, well-organized bureaucracies, efficient taxation, and organized religions.

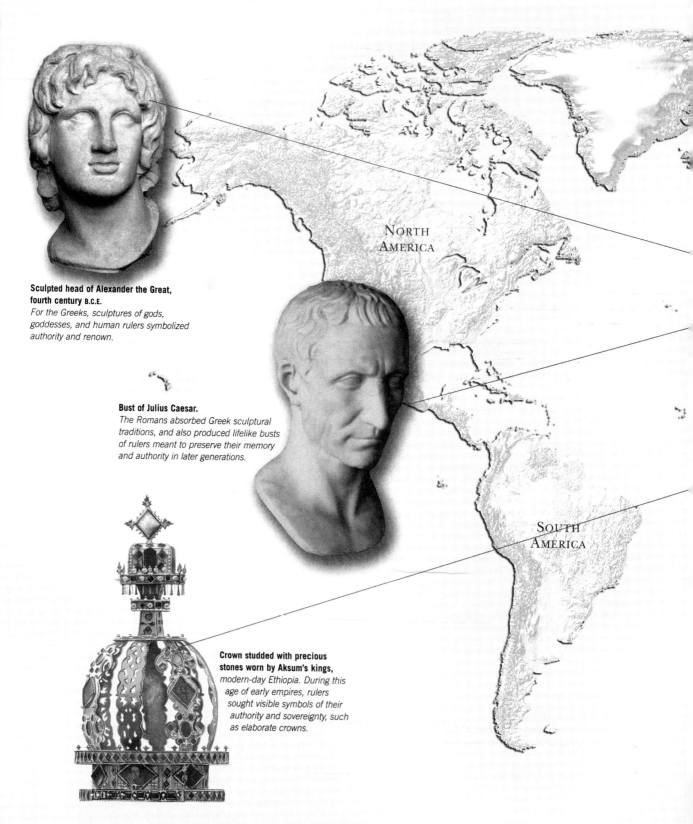

Sculpted head of Alexander the Great, fourth century B.C.E.
For the Greeks, sculptures of gods, goddesses, and human rulers symbolized authority and renown.

Bust of Julius Caesar.
The Romans absorbed Greek sculptural traditions, and also produced lifelike busts of rulers meant to preserve their memory and authority in later generations.

Crown studded with precious stones worn by Aksum's kings,
modern-day Ethiopia. During this age of early empires, rulers sought visible symbols of their authority and sovereignty, such as elaborate crowns.

NORTH AMERICA

SOUTH AMERICA

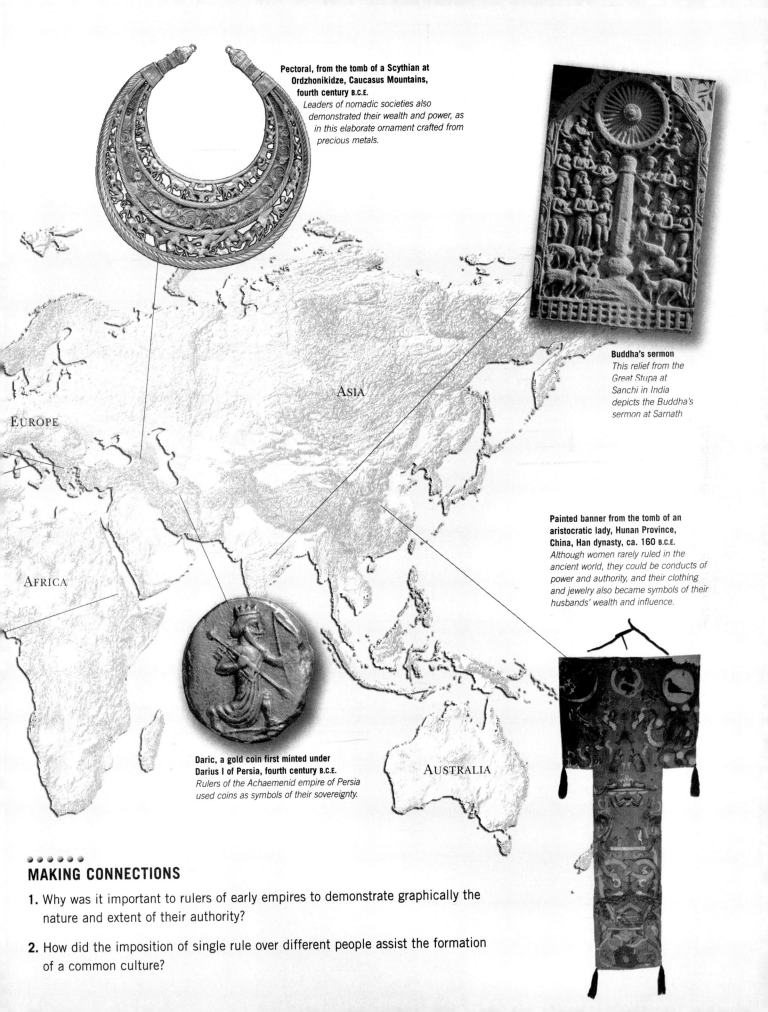

Pectoral, from the tomb of a Scythian at Ordzhonikidze, Caucasus Mountains, fourth century B.C.E.
Leaders of nomadic societies also demonstrated their wealth and power, as in this elaborate ornament crafted from precious metals.

Buddha's sermon
This relief from the Great Stupa at Sanchi in India depicts the Buddha's sermon at Sarnath

EUROPE

ASIA

AFRICA

Painted banner from the tomb of an aristocratic lady, Hunan Province, China, Han dynasty, ca. 160 B.C.E.
Although women rarely ruled in the ancient world, they could be conducts of power and authority, and their clothing and jewelry also became symbols of their husbands' wealth and influence.

Daric, a gold coin first minted under Darius I of Persia, fourth century B.C.E.
Rulers of the Achaemenid empire of Persia used coins as symbols of their sovereignty.

AUSTRALIA

●●●●●●
MAKING CONNECTIONS

1. Why was it important to rulers of early empires to demonstrate graphically the nature and extent of their authority?

2. How did the imposition of single rule over different people assist the formation of a common culture?

EUROPE

| ca. 2500–1100 | Minoan civilization on Crete |
| ca. 1600–1100 | Mycenaean civilization on Greek mainland |

ca. 1100–800	Greek "dark ages"
800	Etruscan civilization begins in Italy
ca. 750–550	Rise of the *polis*
594	Solon's legislation at Athens
509	Foundation of the Roman Republic
508	Democracy established in Athens

Sixth-century B.C.E. Attic jar ▶

NEAR EAST / INDIA

ca. 3500–3000	Emergence of Sumerian city–states
ca. 3000	Emergence of civilization along the Nile River
ca. 2300	Emergence of Harappan civilization in Indus valley
2276–2221	Sargon of Akkad creates the first Mesopotamian Empire
ca. 2000	*Epic of Gilgamesh*
1750	Hammurabi's code

ca. 1500	Aryan peoples migrate into northwestern India
960–933	Rule of Hebrew king Solomon
ca. 628–551	Traditional dates of Zarathushtra
ca. 537–486	Siddhartha Gautama
559–529	Cyrus the Great creates the Persian Empire

◀ *Ruins of pyramids in Ancient Kingdom of Kush-Sudan*

EAST ASIA

1027–771	Western Zhou dynasty, China
771–256	Eastern Zhou dynasty in China
ca. 771	Iron Age territorial states in China
551–479	Confucius in China

ca. 4000	Neolithic cultures in China
ca. 8000–300	Jōmon culture in Japan
ca. 1766–1050	Shang dynasty in China with city–states and writing

◀ *Homo habilis skull*

AFRICA

ca. 3000	Practice of agriculture spreads from Nile river valley to the Sudan
ca. 2000	Ivory and gold trade between Kush (Nubia) and Egypt
ca. 1500	Practice of agriculture spreads from the Sudan to Abyssinia and the savanna region

750	Kushite king Kashta conquers Upper Egypt; founds 25th Egyptian dynasty
ca. 720	Kushite king Piankhy completes conquest of Egypt and reigns as king of Kush and Egypt
ca. 600	Meroitic period of Kushan civilization begins

THE AMERICAS

| ca. 4000 | Maize already domesticated in Mexico |

| ca. 1500–800 | Olmec civilization in Mesoamerica |
| ca. 800–200 | Chavín (Early) Horizon in Andean South America |

◀ *Olmec monument, La Venta*

480–479 Persian invasion of Greece	**264** Rome rules all of Italy	**96–180** The good emperors rule Rome
478 Foundation of Delian League/Athenian Empire	**146** Rome destroys Carthage; rules all of western Mediterranean	**180–284** Breakdown of the *Pax Romana*
431–404 Peloponnesian Wars	**44–31** Civil wars destroy Roman Republic	**306–337** Constantine regins
338 Battle of Chaeronia; Macedonian conquest of Greece	**31** Rome rules Mediterranean	**313** Edict of Milan
336–323 Career of Alexander the Great	**31 B.C.E.–14 C.E.** Principate of Augustus	**325** Council of Nicaea

391 Theodosius makes Christianity the official imperial religion

▲ *Arch of Constantine*

ca. 400–500 The Germanic invasions

426 *The City of God,* by Augustine

476 The last Western emperor is deposed

◄ *The Charioteer of Delphi,* ca. 470 B.C.E.

540–468 Vardhamana Mahavira, founder of Jain tradition	**ca. 300** Foundation of Seleucid dynasty in Anatolia, Syria, and Mesopotamia; Ptolemaic Dynasty in Egypt	**30** Crucifixion of Jesus
334 Alexander begins conquest of the Near East; invades India in 327	**269–232** Mauryan emperor Ashoka patronizes Buddhism	**70** Romans destroy the Temple at Jerusalem
321–181 Mauryan Empire in India	**247 B.C.E.–224 C.E.** Parthian dynasty controls Persia	**216–277** Mani

180 B.C.E.–320 C.E. India politically divided

ca. 224 Fall of Parthians, rise of Sasanids, in Persia

ca. 320–500 Gupta Dynasty in India

ca. 400 Chandra Gupta (r. 375–415) conquers western India; increases trade with Near East and China

ca. 450 The Huns invade India

▲ *The Lion Capital of Sarnath*

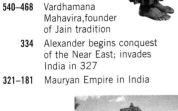

◄ *The Great Stupa at Sanchi*

500–200 Rise of Mohist, Daoist, and Legalist schools of thought in China	**256–206** Qin dynasty in China	
401–256 Period of the Warring States in China	**221** Qin emperor unites all of China	
ca. 300 Old Stone Age Jōmon culture in Japan replaced by Yayoi culture	**206 B.C.E.–8 C.E.** Former Han dynasty in China	

179–104 Han philosopher Tung Chung-shu

145–90 Han historian Ssu-ma Chien

141–187 Emperor Wu Ti of China reigns

Han dynasty ► *sculpture*

25–220 The Later Han dynasty, China

ca. 220–590 Spread of Buddhism in China

220–589 Six Dynasties period in China

ca. 300–500 Barbarian invasions of China

ca. 300–680 Archaic Yamato state in Japan

Standing attendant, ► *Han dynasty*

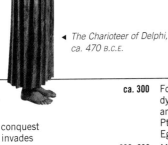

ra-cotta head ► *e Nok culture*

25 Romans sack Kushite capital of Napata

100 B.C.E.–1 C.E. Probable first Indonesian migrations to east African coast

ca. 200 Camel first used for trans-Saharan transport

ca. 200–900 Expansion of Bantu people

ca. 250 Aksum (Ethiopia) controls the Red Sea trade

ca. 300–400 Rise of kingdom of Ghana

ca. 350 Kush ceases to exist

---

ca. 200–600 Early Intermediate period in Andean South America; Moche and Nazca cultures

ca. 150–900 Classic period. Dominance of Teotihuacán in central Mexico, Tikal in southern Yucatán

. 500–200 Founding of Monte Alban

Greek and Hellenistic Civilization

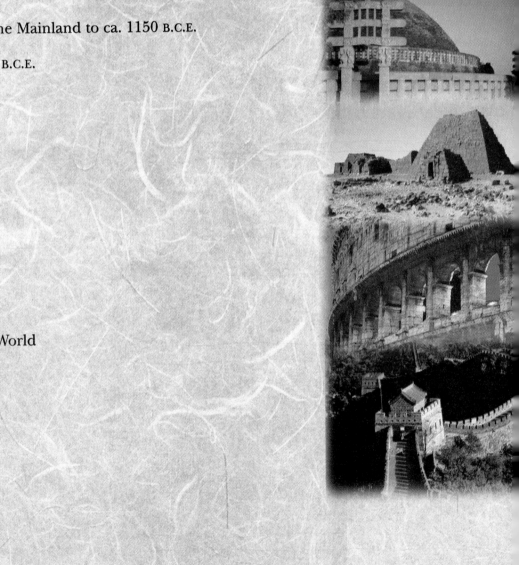

The god Dionysus dances with two female followers. The vase was painted in the sixth century B.C.E.
Bibliothèque Nationale de France, Paris

The Achievement of Greek and Hellenistic Civilization

Hellenic civilization lies at the root of Western civilization, and it has powerfully influenced the modern world. It emerged from the collapse of the Bronze Age Mycenaean civilization. However, it had little in common with Mycenaean civilization and the Bronze Age civilization of Crete or with other early civilizations—in Mesopotamia, Palestine-Syria, China, India, and elsewhere. These civilizations were characterized by strong, centralized monarchical governments ruling through tightly organized, large bureaucracies; hierarchical social systems; professional standing armies; and a regular system of taxation to support it all. To varying degrees, they all tended to cultural stability and uniformity. Hellenic civilization departed sharply from this pattern of development.

The crucial unit of the Greek way of life—forged in poverty and isolation following the Mycenaean collapse—was the *polis*, the Hellenic city-state. There were hundreds of *poleis*, ranging in size from a few thousand inhabitants to hundreds of thousands. Each evoked a kind of loyalty and attachment in its citizens that made it unthinkable for them to allow it to be part of a larger political unit. The result was a dynamic, many-faceted, competitive, sometimes chaotic society in which rivalry for excellence and victory had the highest value. This competitiveness led to almost constant warfare, but it also inspired the Greeks' extraordinary achievements in literature and art.

The classical Age, which followed in the wake of the Greeks' heroic defense of their homeland against the armies of the powerful Persian Empire in the early sixth century B.C.E., was a period of unparalleled achievement. While the rest of the world's civilizations remained monarchical, hierarchical, command societies, Athens, the seat of an Aegean empire, developed democratic government to an extent not seen again until modern times. Athenian citizenship—although limited to adult males of native parentage—granted full and active participation in every decision of the state without regard to wealth or class.

Despite the unique aspects of its culture, however, Greece was also deeply influenced by its neighbors, especially in its earliest stages. The influences of Egyptian art, for example, on early Greek sculpture are evident in the style and stance of stat-ues, jewelry, and figurines. The Greeks adopted the Phoenician alphabet as the basis for their own. These influences are not surprising, as the Minoans and Mycenaeans, whose legacies were of great importance to the evolution of classical Greek culture, were deeply enmeshed in Mediterranean trade. Seafaring and trade were equally fundamental to archaic and classical Greek society. Nonetheless, as in the case of political development and the unique *polis*-centered way of life, the Greeks adapted and made uniquely their own the artistic styles, alphabet, and intellectual ideas they borrowed from their neighbors.

Even more significant, however, was the influence of Greek culture in world history. The culture of democratic yet imperial Athens gave rise to the greatest artistic, literary, and philosophical achievements of the Greek classical period, achievements that became integral to Roman culture and, via the Greco-Roman cultural synthesis, a pillar of European civilization. The conquests of Alexander and the Hellenistic states that followed in their wake spread Greek culture over a remarkably wide area and made a significant and lasting impression on the conquered societies and their neighbors. The Seleucid dynasty ruled some parts of the Persian Empire for almost two centuries. As we will see in Chapter 4, a group of Greeks who broke away from the Seleucids carried Hellenistic culture even farther east, to the Indus valley in northwest India, creating the Indo-Greek Bactrian society. In art, Hellenistic influence reached even as far away as China. In the West, of course, the legacy of Hellenism was more substantial and enduring, powerfully shaping the culture of the Roman Empire that ultimately dominated the entire Mediterranean world.

THINK AHEAD

- Why are the achievements of Greek culture so fundamental to the development of Western civilization?

- In what ways was Greece influenced by neighboring civilizations? Which civilizations had the most influence on Greek culture, and why?

- How did the Hellenistic era differ from the Hellenic? What made Hellenistic culture more cosmopolitan than Hellenic culture?

ABOUT 2000 B.C.E., GREEK-SPEAKING PEOPLES SETTLED the lands surrounding the Aegean Sea at the eastern end of the Mediterranean, where they came in touch with the more advanced and earlier civilizations of the Near East, including the rich cultures of Egypt, Asia Minor, the Syria-Palestine region, and Mesopotamia. Adapting from these predecessors, the Greeks forged their own way of life, forming a set of ideas, values, and institutions that would spread far beyond their homeland. The foundation of this way of life was the independent city-state, or *polis* (plural *poleis*). In the eighth century B.C.E. the Greeks began to expand beyond the Aegean, establishing *poleis* on the shores of the Mediterranean Sea and, pushing on through the Dardanelles, placing many settlements on the coasts of the Black Sea in southern Russia and as far east as the approaches to the Caucasus Mountains. The center of Greek life, however, remained the Aegean Sea and the lands in and around it.

Early in the fifth century B.C.E., the great Persian Empire (see Chapter 4) threatened to extinguish Greek independence. The Greeks, however, led by the city-states of Sparta and Athens, won a remarkable victory over the Persians, securing for themselves a period of freedom and autonomy during which they realized their greatest political and cultural achievements. In Athens, especially, the victory produced a great sense of confidence and ambition. Sparta withdrew from active leadership against the Persians, leaving the Delian League—an alliance of Greek cities led by Athens—to fill the vacuum. The Delian League soon turned into the Athenian Empire.

At the same time that it tightened its hold over the Greek cities in and around the Aegean Sea, Athens developed an extraordinarily democratic constitution at home. Fears and jealousies of this new kind of state and empire created a split in the Greek world that led to a series of major wars.

These wars impoverished Greece and left it vulnerable to conquest. In 338 B.C.E. Philip of Macedon conquered the Greek states, ending the age of the *polis*. The conquests of Philip's son, Alexander, however, spread Greek culture far from its homeland, to Egypt and into Asia. Preserved and adapted by the Romans, Greek culture powerfully influenced the society of Western Europe in the Middle Ages and dominated the Byzantine Empire in the same period. The civilization emerging from the Greek and Roman experience spread across Europe and in time crossed the Atlantic to the Western Hemisphere.

Bronze Age on Crete and on the Mainland to ca. 1150 B.C.E.

One source of Greek civilization was the culture of the large island of Crete in the Mediterranean. With Greece to the north, Egypt to the south, and Asia to the east, Crete was a cultural bridge between the older civilizations and the new one of the Greeks.

THE MINOANS

In the third and second millennia B.C.E., a Bronze Age civilization arose on Crete that powerfully influenced the islands of the Aegean and the mainland of Greece (see Map 3–1). This civilization is called **Minoan**, after Minos, the legendary king of Crete. Scholars have divided Minoan history into three major periods—Early, Middle, and Late Minoan—with some

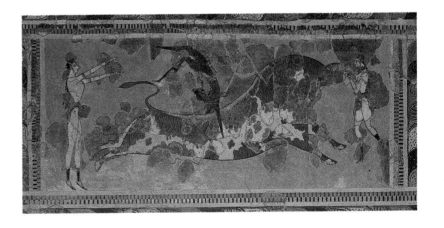

A Minoan fresco. Acrobats leaping over a charging bull, from ➤ the east wing of the Minoan-period palace at Cnossus on the island of Crete. It is not known whether such acrobatic displays were for entertainment or were part of some religious ritual.
Scala/Art Resource, N.Y.

MAP 3–1 The Aegean Area in the Bronze Age. The Bronze Age in the Aegean area lasted from ca. 1900 to ca. 1100 B.C.E. Its culture on Crete is called Minoan and was at its height about 1900–1400 B.C.E. Bronze Age Helladic culture on the mainland flourished from ca. 1600 to 1200 B.C.E.

subdivisions. Dates for Bronze Age settlements on the Greek mainland, for which the term *Helladic* is used, are derived from the same chronological scheme.

The civilization of the Middle and Late Minoan periods in eastern and central Crete centered around several great palaces, including those at Phaestus, Haghia Triada, and, most important, Cnossus. The distinctive and striking art and architecture of these palaces reflect the influence of Syria, Asia Minor, and Egypt but have a uniquely Cretan style and quality. Minoan cities lacked strong defensive walls, suggesting that they were not built for defense.

Along with palaces, paintings, pottery, jewelry, and other valuable objects, excavations at Minoan sites have revealed clay writing tablets like those found in Mesopotamia. Tablets found at the royal palace at Cnossus, accidentally preserved when a great fire that destroyed the palace hardened them, have three distinct kinds of writing on them. One has proved to be an early form of Greek. The contents of the tablets, primarily inventories, reveal an organization centered on the palace and ruled by a king who was supported by an extensive bureaucracy that kept remarkably detailed records. This sort of organization is typical of early civilizations in the Near East but, as we shall see, is nothing like that of the Greeks after the Bronze Age. Yet some of the inventories were written in a form of Greek. Why should Minoans, who were not Greek, write in a language not their own? This question raises the larger one of what the relationship was between Crete and the Greek mainland during the Bronze Age, leading us to an examination of mainland, or Helladic, culture.

THE MYCENAEANS

In the third millennium B.C.E., most of the Greek mainland, including many of the sites of later Greek cities, was settled by people who used metal, built some impressive houses, and traded with Crete and the islands of the Aegean. The names they gave to places—names that were sometimes preserved by later invaders—make it clear that they were not Greeks and that they spoke a language that was not Indo-European (the language family to which Greek belongs).

Not long after 2000 B.C.E., many of the Early Helladic sites were destroyed by fire, some were abandoned, and still others appear to have yielded peacefully to an invading people. These signs of invasion, which mark the beginning of the Middle Helladic period, probably signal the arrival of the Greeks.

The shaft graves cut into the rock at the royal palace-fortress of Mycenae show that by the Late Helladic the conquerors had prospered and sometimes became very rich. At Mycenae the richest finds come from the period after 1600 B.C.E. The city's wealth and power reached their peak during this time, and the culture of the whole mainland during the Late Helladic period goes by the name **Mycenaean**. Greek invaders also established themselves in a still flourishing Crete, and there is good reason to believe that at the height of Mycenaean power (1400–1200 B.C.E.) Crete was part of the Mycenaean world.

Excavations at Mycenae, Pylos, and other Mycenaean sites reveal a culture influenced by, but very different from, Minoan culture. Mycenae and Pylos, like Cnossus, were built some distance from the sea. Defense against attack, however, was plainly foremost in the minds of the founders of the Mycenaean cities. Both were built on hills in positions commanding the neighboring territory. The Mycenaean people were warriors, as their art, architecture, and weapons reveal. All available evidence suggests that they were led by strong kings who, with their retainers, lived in palaces protected by defensive walls while most of the population lived outside the walls. Like the palaces of Crete, Mycenaean palaces were adorned with murals, but instead of the peaceful scenery and games depicted on the Cretan murals, the Mycenaean murals depicted scenes of war and boar hunting.

About 1500 B.C.E. *tholos* tombs—large, beehivelike chambers cut into hillsides—replaced the earlier, already impressive, shaft graves. The *tholos* tombs, built of enormous, well-cut, fitted stones, were approached through an unroofed passage cut horizontally into the side of the hill. The lintel block alone of one of these tombs weighs over a hundred tons. Only a strong king whose wealth was great, whose power was unquestioned, and who commanded the labor of many could undertake such a project. His wealth probably came from plundering raids, piracy, and trade. Some of this trade went westward to Italy and Sicily, but most of it was with the islands of the Aegean, the coastal towns of Asia Minor, and the cities of Syria, Egypt, and Crete. The Mycenaeans exchanged pottery, olive oil, and animal hides for jewels and other luxuries.

Further evidence that the Mycenaean world was made up of a number of independent, powerful, and well-organized monarchies comes from the many clay tablets with Mycenaean writing found throughout the mainland, and in particular from a large collection of tablets found at Pylos. These reveal a society similar to that of Cnossus on Crete. A king whose title was *wanax* held a royal domain, appointed officials, commanded servants, and kept a close record of what he owned and what was owed to him.

The Fall of Mycenaean Power   At the height of their power (1400–1200 B.C.E.), the Mycenaeans were prosperous and active. They enlarged their cities, expanded their trade, and even established commercial colonies in the east. They are mentioned in the archives of the Hittite kings of Asia Minor. They are named as marauders of the Nile Delta in Egyptian records. Sometime about 1250 B.C.E. they probably sacked Troy, on the coast of northwestern Asia Minor, giving rise to the epic poems of Homer, the *Iliad* and the *Odyssey* (see Map 3–1). Around the year 1200 B.C.E., however, the Mycenaean world showed signs of great trouble; by 1100 B.C.E. it was gone: Its palaces were destroyed; many of its cities abandoned; and its art, its pattern of life, its system of writing buried and forgotten.

The reasons for the collapse of Mycenaean civilization are not known for certain. Greek legends attribute it to a new wave of Greek invaders, the Dorians, into the Greek mainland from the north. The legends identify the Dorians as a rude people who spoke a Greek dialect different from that of the Mycenaean peoples. The legend of "The Return of the Heraclidae," for example, recounts how the Dorians joined one of the Greek tribes, the Heraclidae, in an attack on the southern Greek peninsula of Peloponnesus, which was repulsed. A hundred years later they returned and gained full control.

Greek "Middle Age" to ca. 750 B.C.E.

The immediate effects of the Mycenaean collapse were disastrous. Palaces were destroyed, the kings and bureaucrats who managed them were swept away, and the wealth and organization that had supported artists and merchants evaporated. Greece entered a dark "middle age" about which little is known. Many villages were abandoned and never resettled. Some of their inhabitants probably turned to a nomadic life, and many undoubtedly perished.

Another result of the turmoil surrounding the Mycenaean collapse was the spread of the Greek people eastward from the mainland to the Aegean islands and the coast of Asia Minor. The Dorians, after occupying most of the Peloponnesus, swept across the Aegean to occupy the southern islands and the southern part of the Anatolian coast. Another group, known as the Ionians, spread from Attica and Euboea to the Cyclades and the central Anatolian coast, which came to be called Ionia.

These migrations made the Aegean a Greek lake. Trade with the old civilizations of the Near East, however, was virtually ended by the fall of the advanced Minoan and Mycenaean civilizations; nor was there much internal trade among the different parts of Greece. The Greeks were forced to turn inward, and each community was left largely to its own devices. The Near East was also in disarray at this time, and no great power arose to impose its ways and its will on the helpless people who lived about the Aegean. The Greeks were allowed time to recover from their disaster and to create their unique style of life.

AGE OF HOMER

For a picture of society in these dark ages, the best source is Homer. His epic poems the *Iliad* and the *Odyssey* emerged from a tradition of oral poetry whose roots extend into the Mycenaean Age. Through the centuries bards had sung tales of the heroes who had fought at Troy, using verse arranged in rhythmic formulas to aid the memory. In this way some very old material was preserved into the eighth century B.C.E., when the poems attributed to Homer were finally writ-

ten down. Although the poems tell of the deeds of Mycenaean heroes, the world they describe seems to be that of the tenth and ninth centuries B.C.E. rather than the earlier Mycenaean. Homer's heroes are not buried in *tholos* tombs but are cremated; they worship gods in temples, whereas the Mycenaeans had no temples; and although they have chariots, like the Mycenaeans, they do not know their proper use in warfare.

Government   In the Homeric poems the power of the kings is much less than that of the Mycenaean rulers. Homeric kings were limited in their ability to make important decisions by the need to consult a council of nobles. The nobles felt free to discuss matters in vigorous language and in opposition to the king's wishes. In the *Iliad*, Achilles does not hesitate to address Agamemnon, the "most kingly" commander of the Trojan expedition, in these words: "you with a dog's face and a deer's heart." Such language may have been impolite, but it was not treasonous. The king could ignore the council's advice, but it was risky for him to do so.

The right to speak in council was limited to noblemen, but the common people could not be ignored. If a king planned a war or a major change of policy during a campaign, he would not fail to call the common soldiers to an assembly; they could listen and express their feelings by acclamation, though they could not take part in the debate. Homer shows that even in these early times the Greeks, unlike their predecessors and contemporaries, practiced some forms of limited constitutional government.

◀ **The Trojan Horse, depicted on a seventh-century B.C.E. Greek vase.** According to legend, the Greeks finally defeated Troy by pretending to abandon their siege of the city, leaving behind a giant wooden horse. Soldiers hidden in the horse opened the gates of the city to their compatriots after the Trojans had brought it within their walls. Note the wheels on the horse and the Greek soldiers who are hiding inside it holding weapons and armor.
Deutsches Archäologisches Institut, Athens: Mycon 70.

Society   Despite the accommodation for noblemen and commoners, Homeric society was sharply divided into classes, the most important division being the one between nobles and everyone else. We do not know the origin of this distinction, but we cannot doubt that at this time Greek society was aristocratic. Birth determined noble status, and wealth usually accompanied it. Below the nobles were two other classes: *thetes* and slaves. *Thetes* worked the land, but we do not know whether they owned outright the land they worked (and so were free to sell it) or worked a hereditary plot that belonged to their clan (and was therefore not theirs to dispose of as they chose).

Those *thetes* who were landless laborers endured the worst condition in Homeric society. Slaves, at least, were attached to family households and so were protected and fed. In a world where membership in a settled group gave the only security, free laborers were desperately vulnerable. Slaves were few in number and were mostly women who served as maids and concubines. Some male slaves worked as shepherds. Few, if any, worked in agriculture, which depended chiefly on free labor throughout Greek history.

Homeric Values   The Homeric poems reflect an aristocratic code of values that powerfully influenced all future Greek thought. Homer was the schoolbook of the Greeks. They memorized his texts, settled diplomatic disputes by citing passages in them, and emulated the behavior and cherished the values they found in them. Those values were physical prowess; courage; and fierce protection of one's family, friends, and property, and above all, one's personal honor and reputation. Speed of foot, strength, and, most of all, excellence at fighting make a man great, and all these attributes serve to promote personal honor. The great hero of the *Iliad*, Achilles, refuses to fight in battle, allowing his fellow Greeks to be slain and almost defeated, because Agamemnon has wounded his honor by taking away his battle prize. He returns to the army not out of a sense of duty but to avenge the death of his dear friend Patroclus. Odysseus, the hero of the *Odyssey*, returning home after his wanderings, ruthlessly kills the many suitors who had, in his long absence, sought to marry his wife, Penelope; they had dishonored him by consuming his wealth, wooing Penelope, and scorning his son.

The highest virtue in Homeric society was *arete*—manliness, courage in the most general sense, and the excellence proper to a hero. This quality was best revealed in a contest, or *agon*. Homeric battles are not primarily group combats, but a series of individual contests between great champions. One of the prime forms of entertainment is the athletic contest, and the funeral of Patroclus is celebrated by such a contest.

The central ethical idea in Homer can be found in the instructions that the father of Achilles gives to his son when he

▲ **Attic Wine Cup.**   Painted ca. 490 B.C.E., this cup depicts a scene from Homer's *Iliad*: Priam, King of Troy, begs the Greek hero Achilles to return the body of the old man's son, Hector, the great Trojan warrior.

Vase Painting. Classical Greek 5th B.C.E. Brygos Painter. Troyan King Priamus begs Achilles to give him the body of Hector, his slain son, Hector's body lies under Achilles bed. Red-figured Attic skyphos from Caere, around 490 B.C.E. H: 25 cm. Inv. IV 3710. Kunsthistorisches Museum, Vienna, Austria. Erich Lessing/Art Resouce, N.Y.

sends him off to fight at Troy: "Always be the best and distinguished above others." The father of another Homeric hero has given his son exactly the same orders and has added to them the injunction: "Do not bring shame on the family of your fathers who were by far the best in Ephyre and in wide Lycia." Here in a nutshell are the chief values of the aristocrats of Homer's world: to vie for individual supremacy in *arete* and to defend and increase the honor of the family. These would remain prominent aristocratic values long after Homeric society was only a memory. (See Document, "Husband and Wife in Homer's Troy.")

The Polis

The characteristic Greek institution was the *polis*. The common translation of that word as "city-state" is misleading, for it says both too much and too little. All Greek *poleis* began as little more than agricultural villages or towns, and many stayed that way, so the word *city* is inappropriate. All of them were states, in the sense of being independent political units, but they were much more than that. The *polis* was thought of as a community of relatives; all its citizens, who were theoretically descended from a common ancestor, belonged to subgroups such as fighting brotherhoods (*phratries*), clans, and tribes. They worshiped the gods in common ceremonies.

DOCUMENT | Husband and Wife in Homer's Troy

Homer's poems provide a picture of early Greek ideas and institutions. In the Iliad, the poet tells of the return from battle of the Trojan hero Hector. He is greeted by his loving, "warm, generous wife," Andromache, who is carrying their baby son. Hector reaches for the boy, who is frightened to tears by the plume on his father's helmet. The father removes the helmet and prays that his son will grow up to be called "a better man than his father … a joy to his mother's heart." The rest of the scene reveals the character of their marriage and the division of responsibility between men and women in their world.

♦ How does Homer depict the feelings of husband and wife toward one another? What are the tasks of the aristocratic woman revealed in this passage? What can be learned about the attitude towards death and duty?

So Hector prayed and placed his son in the arms of his loving wife. Andromache pressed the child to her scented breast, smiling through her tears. Her husband noticed, and filled with pity now, Hector stroked her gently, trying to reassure her, repeating her name: "Andromache, dear one; why so desperate? Why so much grief for me? No man will hurl me down to Death, against my fate. And fate? No one alive has ever escaped it, neither brave man nor coward, I tell you—it's born with us the day that we are born. So please go home and tend to your own tasks, the distaff and the loom, and keep the women working hard as well. As for the fighting, men will see to that, all who were born in Troy but I most of all."

Hector aflash in arms took up his horsehair-crested helmet once again. And his loving wife went home, turning, glancing back again and again and weeping live warm tears. She quickly reached the sturdy house of Hector, man-killing Hector, and found her women gathered there inside and stirred them all to a high pitch of mourning. So in his house they raised the dirges for the dead, for Hector still alive, his people were so convinced that never again would he come home from battle, never escape the Argives' rage and bloody hands.

From The *Iliad* by Homer, translated by Robert Fagles, copyright © 1990 by Robert Fagles. Used by permission of Viking Penguin, a division of Penguin Putnam Inc.

Aristotle (see Chapter 2) argued that the *polis* was a natural growth and that the human being is by nature "an animal who lives in a *polis*." Humans alone have the power of speech and from it derive the ability to distinguish good from bad and right from wrong, "and the sharing of these things is what makes a household and a *polis*." Therefore, humans who are incapable of sharing these things or who are so self-sufficient that they have no need of them are not humans at all, but either wild beasts or gods. Without law and justice humans are the worst and most dangerous of the animals. With them they can be the best, and justice exists only in the *polis*. These high claims were made in the fourth century B.C.E., hundreds of years after the *polis* came into existence, but they accurately reflect an attitude that was present from the first.

DEVELOPMENT OF THE *POLIS*

Originally the word *polis* referred only to a citadel, an elevated, defensible rock to which the farmers of the neighboring area could retreat in case of attack. The **Acropolis** in Athens and the hill called Acrocorinth in Corinth are examples. For some time such high places and the adjacent farms made up the *polis*. The towns grew gradually and without planning, as their narrow, winding, and disorderly streets show. For centuries they had no walls. Unlike the city-states of the Near East, they were not placed for commercial convenience on rivers or the sea. Nor did they grow up around a temple to serve the needs of priests and to benefit from the needs of worshipers. The availability of farmland and of a natural fortress determined their location. They were placed either well inland or far enough away from the sea to avoid piratical raids. Only later and gradually did the *agora*—a marketplace and civic center—appear within the *polis*. The *agora* was to become the heart of the Greeks' remarkable social life, distinguished by conversation and argument carried on in the open air.

Some *poleis* probably came into existence early in the eighth century B.C.E. The institution was certainly common by the middle of that century, for all the colonies that were established by the Greeks in the years after 750 B.C.E. took the form of the *polis*. Once the new institution had been fully established, true monarchy disappeared. In some places kings survived, but they were almost always only ceremonial figures without power. The original form of the *polis* was an aristocratic republic dominated by the nobility through its council of nobles and its monopoly of the magistracies.

THE HOPLITE PHALANX

Crucial to the development of the *polis* was a new military strategy. In earlier times the brunt of fighting had been carried on by small troops of cavalry and individual "champions" who first threw their spears and then came to close quarters with swords. Toward the end of the eighth century B.C.E., however, the **hoplite phalanx** came into being and remained the basis of Greek warfare thereafter.

The hoplite was a heavily armed infantryman who fought with a spear and a large shield. These soldiers were arrayed in close order, usually at least eight ranks deep, to form a phalanx. As long as the hoplites fought bravely and held their ground, there would be few casualties and no defeat, but if they gave way, the result was usually a rout. All depended on the discipline, strength, and courage of the individual soldier. At its best, the phalanx could withstand cavalry charges and defeat infantries not as well protected or disciplined. Until defeated by the Roman legion, it was the dominant military force in the eastern Mediterranean.

The usual hoplite battle in Greece was between the armies of two *poleis* quarreling over a piece of land. One army invaded the territory of the other when its crops were almost ready for harvest. The defending army had no choice but to protect the fields. If the defenders were beaten, the fields were captured or destroyed and the people of the *polis* might starve. This style of fighting produced a single decisive battle that reduced the time lost in fighting other kinds of warfare; it spared the houses, livestock, and other capital of the farmer-soldiers who made up the phalanx, and it minimized casualties. It perfectly suited the farmer-soldier-citizen who was the backbone of the *polis* and, by keeping wars short and limiting their destructiveness and expense, it helped the *polis* prosper.

The phalanx and the *polis* arose together, and both heralded the decline of kings. The immediate beneficiaries of the royal decline were aristocrats, but because the phalanx, and with it the *polis*, depended on farmers working small holdings as well as aristocrats, the wishes of the small farmers could not for long be wholly ignored. The rise of the hoplite phalanx created a bond between aristocrats and family farmers who fought in it side by side, and this bond helps explain why class conflicts were muted for some time in Greece. It also guaranteed, however, that the aristocrats, who dominated the *poleis* at first, would not always be unchallenged.

Expansion of the Greek World

From the middle of the eighth century B.C.E. until well into the sixth, the Greeks vastly expanded the territory they controlled, their wealth, and their contacts with other peoples. A burst of colonizing activity placed *poleis* from Spain to the Black Sea. A century earlier a few Greeks had established trading posts in Syria. There they had learned new techniques in art and crafts and much more from the older civilizations of the Near East. About 750 B.C.E. they borrowed a writing system from one of the Semitic scripts and added vowels to create the first true alphabet. The new Greek alphabet was easier to learn than any earlier writing system and made possible a widely literate society.

GREEK COLONIES

Syria and its neighboring territory were too strong to penetrate, so the Greeks settled the sparsely populated southern coast of Macedonia and the Chalcidian peninsula (see Map 3–2). Southern Italy and eastern Sicily were even more inviting areas. Before long, there were so many Greek colonies in Italy and Sicily that the Romans called the whole region *Magna Graecia* ("Great Greece"). The Greeks also put colonies in Spain and southern France. In the seventh century B.C.E. Greek colonists settled the coasts of the northeastern Mediterranean, the Black Sea, and the straits connecting them. At about the same time they established settlements on the eastern part of the north African coast. The Greeks now had outposts throughout the Mediterranean world. Most colonies, although independent, were friendly with their mother cities. Each might ask the other for aid in time of trouble and expect to receive a friendly hearing, although neither was obliged to help.

Colonization had a powerful influence on Greek life. By relieving the pressure and land hunger of a growing population, it provided a safety valve that allowed the *poleis* to escape civil wars. By confronting them with the differences between themselves and the new peoples they met, colonization gave the Greeks a sense of cultural identity and fostered a **Panhellenic** ("all-Greek") spirit that led to the establishment of a number of common religious festivals. The most important of these were at Olympia, Delphi, Corinth, and Nemea.

Colonization also encouraged trade and industry. The influx of new wealth from abroad and the increased demand for goods from the homeland stimulated a more intensive use of the land and an emphasis on crops for export, chiefly the olive and the wine grape. The manufacture of pottery, tools, weapons, and fine metalwork as well as perfumed oil, the soap of the ancient Mediterranean world, was likewise encouraged. New opportunities allowed some men, sometimes outside the nobility, to become wealthy and important. These newly enriched became a troublesome element in the aristocratic *poleis*, for, although increasingly important in the life of their states, they were barred from political power, religious privileges, and social acceptance by the ruling aristocrats. These conditions soon created a crisis in many states.

THE TYRANTS (CA. 700–500 B.C.E.)

In some cities, perhaps only a small percentage of the more than one thousand Greek *poleis*, the crisis produced by new economic and social conditions led to or intensified factional divisions within the ruling aristocracy. In the years between 700 and 500 B.C.E., the result was often the establishment of a tyranny.

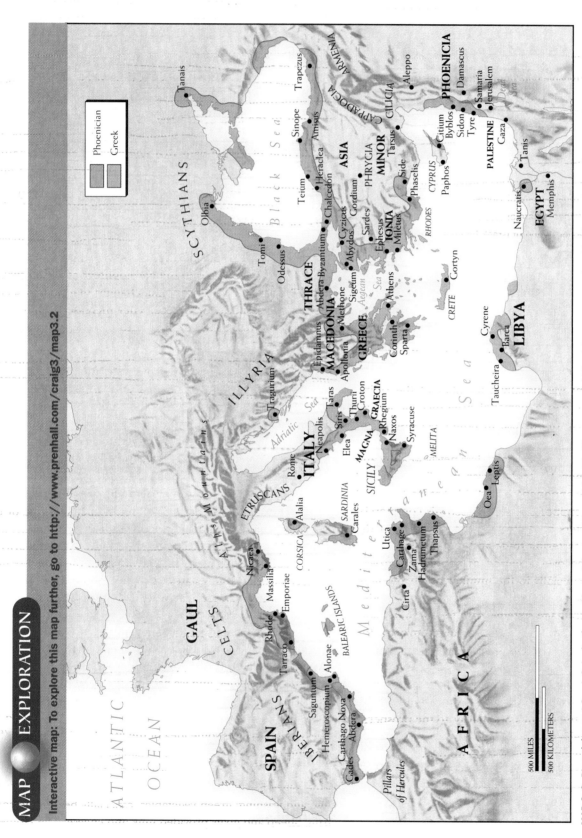

MAP 3-2 Phoenician and Greek Colonization. Most of the coastline of the Mediterranean and Black Seas was populated by Greek or Phoenician colonies. The Phoenicians were a commercial people who planted their colonies in North Africa, Spain, Sicily, and Sardinia, chiefly in the ninth century B.C.E. The height of Greek colonization came later, between ca. 750 and 550 B.C.E.

CHRONOLOGY

Rise of Greece

ca. 2900–1150 B.C.E.	Minoan period
ca. 1900 B.C.E.	Probable date of the arrival of the Greeks on the mainland
ca. 1600–1150 B.C.E.	Mycenaean period
ca. 1250 B.C.E.	Sack of Troy (?)
ca. 1200–1150 B.C.E.	Destruction of Mycenaean centers in Greece
ca. 1100–750 B.C.E.	Dark ages
ca. 750–500 B.C.E.	Major period of Greek colonization
ca. 725 B.C.E.	Probable date of Homer
ca. 700 B.C.E.	Probable date of Hesiod
ca. 700–500 B.C.E.	Major period of Greek tyranny

The Rise of Tyranny A tyrant was a monarch who had gained power in an unorthodox but not necessarily wicked way and who exercised a strong one-man rule that might well be beneficent and popular.

The founding tyrant was usually a member of the ruling aristocracy who either had a personal grievance or led an unsuccessful faction. He often rose to power because of his military ability and support from the hoplites. He generally had the support of the politically powerless newly wealthy and the poor farmers. When he took power he often expelled many of his aristocratic opponents and divided at least some of their land among his supporters. He pleased his commercial and industrial supporters by destroying the privileges of the old aristocracy and by fostering trade and colonization.

The tyrants presided over a period of population growth that saw an increase especially in the number of city dwellers. They responded with a program of public works that included the improvement of drainage systems, care for the water supply, the construction and organization of marketplaces, the building and strengthening of city walls, and the erection of temples. They introduced new local festivals and elaborated the old ones. They were active in the patronage of the arts, supporting poets and artisans with gratifying results. All this activity contributed to the tyrant's popularity, to the prosperity of his city, and to his self-esteem.

In most cases the tyrant's rule was secured by a personal bodyguard and mercenary soldiers. An armed citizenry, necessary for an aggressive foreign policy, would have been dangerous, so the tyrants usually pursued a program of peaceful alliances with other tyrants abroad and avoided war.

The End of the Tyrants By the end of the sixth century B.C.E., tyranny had disappeared from the Greek states and did not return in the same form or for the same reasons. The last tyrants were universally hated for their cruelty and repressiveness. They left bitter memories in their own states and became objects of fear and hatred everywhere.

Besides the outrages committed by individual tyrants, there was something about the very concept of tyranny that was inimical to the idea of the *polis*. The notion of the *polis* as a community to which every member must be responsible, the connection of justice with that community, and the natural aristocratic hatred of monarchy all made tyranny seem alien and offensive. The rule of a tyrant, however beneficent, was arbitrary and unpredictable. Tyranny came into being in defiance of tradition and law, and the tyrant governed without either. He was not answerable in any way to his fellow citizens.

From a longer perspective, however, the tyrants made important contributions to the development of Greek civilization. They encouraged economic changes that helped secure the future prosperity of Greece. They increased communication with the rest of the Mediterranean world and cultivated the crafts and technology, as well as the arts and literature. Most important of all, they broke the grip of the aristocracy and put the productive powers of the most active and talented of its citizens fully at the service of the *polis*.

Life in Archaic Greece

SOCIETY

As the dark ages came to an end, the features that would distinguish Greek society thereafter took shape. The role of the artisan and the merchant grew more important as contact with the non-Greek world became easier, but the great majority of people continued to make their living from the land. Wealthy aristocrats with large estates, powerful households, families, and clans, however, led very different lives from those of the poorer peasants and the independent farmers who had smaller and less fertile fields.

Farmers Ordinary country people rarely leave a record of their thoughts or activities, and we have no such record from ancient Greece. The poet Hesiod (ca. 700 B.C.E.), however, was certainly no aristocrat. He presented himself as a small farmer, and his *Works and Days* gives some idea of the life of such a farmer. (See Document, "Hesiod's Farmer's Almanac.") The crops included grain, chiefly barley but also wheat; grapes for the making of wine; olives for food, but mainly for oil, used for cooking, lighting, and washing; green vegetables, especially beans; and some fruit. Sheep and goats provided milk and cheese. The Homeric heroes had great herds of cattle and ate lots of meat, but by Hesiod's time land fertile enough to provide fodder for cattle was needed to grow grain. He and small farmers like him tasted meat chiefly from sacrificial animals at festivals.

These farmers worked hard to make a living. Although Hesiod had the help of oxen and mules and one or two hired helpers for occasional labor, his life was one of continual toil. The hardest work came in October, at the start of the rainy season, the time for the first plowing. The plow was light and easily broken, and the work of forcing the iron tip into the earth was backbreaking, even with the help of a team of oxen. For the less fortunate farmer, the cry of the crane that announced the time of year to plow "bites the heart of the man without oxen." Autumn and winter were the time for cutting wood, building wagons, and making tools. Late winter was the time to tend to the vines, May the time to harvest the grain, July to winnow and store it. Only at the height of summer's heat did Hesiod allow for rest, but when September came it was time to harvest the grapes. No sooner was that task done than the cycle started again. The work went on under the burning sun and in the freezing cold.

Hesiod wrote nothing of pleasure or entertainment, but less austere farmers than he gathered at the blacksmith's shop for warmth and companionship in winter, and even he must have taken part in religious rites and festivals that were accompanied by some kind of entertainment. Nonetheless, the lives of ordinary farmers were certainly hard and their pleasures few.

Aristocrats Most aristocrats were rich enough to employ many hired laborers, sometimes sharecroppers and sometimes even slaves, to work their extensive lands and were therefore able to enjoy leisure for other activities. The center of aristocratic social life was the drinking party, or *symposion*. This activity was not a mere drinking bout meant to remove inhibitions and produce oblivion. The Greeks, in fact, almost always mixed their wine with water, and one of the goals of the participants was to drink as much as the others without becoming drunk.

The *symposion* was a carefully organized occasion, with a "king" chosen to set the order of events and to determine that night's mixture of wine and water. Only men took part, and they ate and drank as they reclined on couches along the walls of the room. The sessions began with prayers and libations to the gods. Usually there were games, such as dice or *kottabos*, in which wine was flicked from the cups at different targets. Sometimes danc-

◀ **Attic jar.** From late in the sixth century B.C.E. this jar shows how olives, one of Athens's most important crops, were harvested. Courtesy of the Trustees of the British Museum.

ing girls or flute girls offered entertainment. Frequently the participants provided their own amusements with songs, poetry, or even philosophical disputes. Characteristically, these took the form of contests, with some kind of prize for the winner, for aristocratic values continued to emphasize competition and the need to excel, whatever the arena.

This aspect of aristocratic life appears in the athletic contests that became widespread early in the sixth century B.C.E. The games included running events; the long jump; the discus and javelin throws; the *pentathlon*, which included all of these; boxing; wrestling; and the chariot race. Only the rich could afford to raise, train, and race horses, so the chariot race was a special preserve of aristocracy. Wrestling was also especially favored by the nobility, and the *palaestra* where they practiced became an important social center for the aristocracy. The contrast between the hard, drab life of the peasants and the leisured and lively one of the aristocrats could hardly be greater.

RELIGION

Like most ancient peoples, the Greeks were polytheists, and religion played an important part in their lives. A great part of Greek art and literature was closely connected with religion, as was the life of the *polis* in general.

The Greek pantheon consisted of the twelve gods who lived on Mount Olympus. These were

- Zeus, the father of the gods
- Hera, his wife
- Zeus's siblings:
  Poseidon, his brother, god of the seas and earthquakes
  Hestia, his sister, goddess of the hearth
  Demeter, his sister, goddess of agriculture and marriage
- Zeus's children:
  Aphrodite, goddess of love and beauty
  Apollo, god of the sun, music, poetry, and prophecy
  Ares, god of war
  Artemis, goddess of the moon and the hunt
  Athena, goddess of wisdom and the arts
  Hephaestus, god of fire and metallurgy

DOCUMENT	Hesiod's Farmer's Almanac

Hesiod was a farmer and poet who lived in a village in Greece about 700 B.C.E. His poem Works and Days *contains wisdom on several subjects, but its final section amounts to a farmer's almanac, taking readers through the year and advising them on just when each activity is demanded. Hesiod painted a picture of a very hard life for Greek farmers. In the following passage he talks about one of the few times when the farmer is free from toil, during the hottest part of summer.*

> ◆ What might be Hesiod's purposes in writing this poem? What can be learned from this passage about the character of Greek farming? How did it differ from other modes of agriculture? What are the major virtues Hesiod associates with farming? How do they compare with the virtues celebrated by Homer?

But when House-on-Back, the snail, crawls from the
    ground up
the plants, escaping the Pleiades, it's no longer time for
    vine-digging;
time rather to put an edge to your sickles, and rout out
    your helpers.
Keep away from sitting in the shade or lying in bed till
    the sun's up
in the time of the harvest, when the sunshine scorches
    your skin dry.
This is the season to push work and bring home your
    harvest;
get up with the first light so you'll have enough to live on.
Dawn takes away from work a third part of the work's
    measure.
Dawn sets a man well along on his journey, in his work also,

dawn, who when she shows, has numerous people going
    their ways; dawn who puts the yoke upon many oxen.
But when the artichoke is in flower, and the clamorous
    cricket
sitting in his tree lets go his vociferous singing, that
    issues
from the beating of his wings, in the exhausting season
    of summer,
then is when goats are at their fattest, when the wine
    tastes best,
women are most lascivious, but the men's strength fails
    them
most, for the star Seirios shrivels them, knees and heads
    alike,
and the skin is all dried out in the heat; then, at that
    season,
one might have the shadow under the rock, and the
    wine of Biblis,
a curd cake, and all the milk that the goats can give you,
the meat of a heifer, bred in the woods, who has never
    borne a calf,
and of baby kids also. Then, too, one can sit in the
    shadow
and drink the bright-shining wine, his heart satiated
    with eating
and face turned in the direction where Zephyros blows
    briskly,
make three libations of water from a spring that keeps
    running forever
and has no mud in it; and pour wine for the fourth libation.

Hesiod, *Works and Days*, trans. by Richmond Lattimore. Copyright © 1959, University of Michigan Press, Ann Arbor, MI, pp. 87, 89. Reprinted by permission.

◆ Hermes, messenger of the gods, connected with commerce and cunning

The gods were seen as behaving very much as mortal humans behaved, with all the human foibles, except that they were superhuman in these as well as in their strength and immortality. On the other hand, Zeus, at least, was seen as a source of human justice, and even the Olympians were understood to be subordinate to the Fates. Each *polis* had one of the Olympians as its guardian deity and worshiped that god in its own special way, but all the gods were Panhellenic. In the eighth and seventh centuries B.C.E. common shrines were established at Olympia and at Nemea for the worship of Zeus, at Delphi for Apollo, and at the Isthmus of Corinth for Poseidon. Each held athletic contests in honor of its deity, to which all Greeks were invited and for which a sacred truce was declared.

The worship of these deities did not involve great emotion. Worshipers offered a god prayer, libations, and gifts in hopes of protection and favors. Greek religion offered no hope of immortality for the average human and little moral teaching. Most Greeks seem to have held to the commonsense notion that justice lay in paying one's debts. They thought that civic virtue consisted of worshiping the state deities in the traditional way, performing required public services, and fighting in defense of the state. To them, private morality meant to do good to one's friends and harm to one's enemies.

In the sixth century B.C.E., the influence of the cult of Apollo at Delphi and of his oracle there became very great. The oracle was the most important of several that helped satisfy human craving for a clue to the future. The priests of Apollo preached moderation; their advice was exemplified in the two famous sayings

The Charioteer of Delphi, ca. 470. B.C.E. This freestanding statue, the *Charioteer of Delphi*, is one of the few full-scale bronze sculptures that survive from the fifth century B.C.E. Polyzalus, the tyrant of the Greek city of Gela in Sicily, dedicated it after winning a victory in the chariot race in the Pythian games, either in 478 or 474. The games were held at the sacred shrine of the god Apollo at Delphi, and the statue was placed within the god's sanctuary, not far from Apollo's temple.

Greek (Classical). Bronze, H: 180 cm. Archaelogical museum, Delphi, Greece. Photograph © Nimatallah/Art Resource, NY.

identified with Apollo: "Know thyself" and "Nothing in excess." Humans need self-control (*sophrosyne*). Its opposite is arrogance (*hubris*), which is brought on by excessive wealth or good fortune. *Hubris* leads to moral blindness and finally to divine vengeance. This theme of moderation and the dire consequences of its absence was central to Greek popular morality and appears frequently in Greek literature.

The somewhat cold religion of the Olympian gods and of the cult of Apollo did little to assuage human fears, hopes, and passions. For these needs, the Greeks turned to other deities and rites. Of them, the most popular was Dionysus, a god of nature and fertility, of the grapevine and drunkenness and sexual abandon. In some of his rites the god was followed by maenads, female devotees who cavorted by night, ate raw flesh, and were reputed to tear to pieces any creature they came across.

POETRY

The great changes sweeping through the Greek world were also reflected in the poetry of the sixth century B.C.E. The lyric style, whether sung by a chorus or one singer, predominated. Sappho of Lesbos, Anacreon of Teos, and Simonides of Cous composed personal poetry, often speaking of the pleasure and agony of love. Alcaeus of Mytilene, an aristocrat driven from his city by a tyrant, wrote bitter invective.

Perhaps the most interesting poet of the century from a political point of view was Theognis of Megara. An aristocrat who lived through a tyranny, an unusually chaotic and violent democracy, and an oligarchy that restored order but ended the rule of the old aristocracy, Theognis was the spokesman for the old, defeated aristocracy of birth. He divided everyone into two classes, the noble and the base; the former were good, the latter bad. Those nobly born must associate only with others like themselves if they were to preserve their virtue; if they mingled with the base, they became base. Those born base, on the other hand, could never become noble. Only nobles could aspire to virtue, and only nobles possessed the critical moral and intellectual qualities: respect (or honor) and judgment. These qualities could not be taught; they were innate. Even so, nobles had to guard themselves against corruption by wealth or by mingling with the base. Intermarriage between the noble and the base was especially condemned. These were the ideas of the unreconstructed nobility, whose power had been destroyed or reduced in most Greek states by this time. They remained alive in aristocratic hearts throughout the next century and greatly influenced later thinkers, including Plato.

Major City-States

Generalization about the *polis* becomes difficult not long after its appearance, for although the states had much in common, some of them developed in unique ways. Sparta and Athens, which became the two most powerful Greek states, had especially unusual histories.

SPARTA

Sparta (see Map 3–3) began to assume its special character about 725 B.C.E., when population pressure and land hunger led the Spartans to conquer their western neighbor Messenia in the First Messenian War. The Spartans now had as much land as they would ever need, and because they reduced the Messenians to **Helots**, or serfs, they no longer had to work this land themselves. When the Helots—assisted by Argos and some other Peloponnesian cities—rebelled in the Second Messenian War in about 650 B.C.E., the Spartans faced a turning point. The long and bitter war, which at one point threatened their city's existence, made it clear to the Spartans that they could not expect to keep down the Helots, who outnumbered them perhaps ten to one, and maintain the free-and-easy habits typical of most Greeks. They thus chose to introduce fundamental reforms that turned their city forever after into a military academy and camp.

Society The new system, which emerged late in the sixth century B.C.E., exerted control over each Spartan from birth, when officials of the state decided which infants, male and female, were physically fit to survive. At age seven, the Spartan boy was

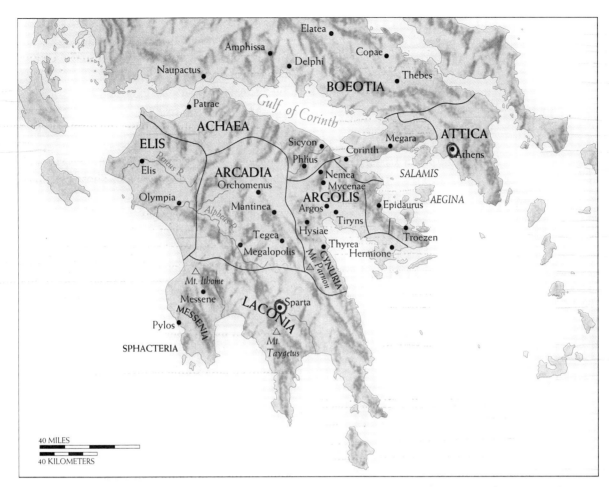

MAP 3–3 The Peloponnesus.   Sparta's region, Laconia, was in the Peloponnesus. Nearby states were members of the Peloponnesian League under Sparta's leadership.

taken from his mother and turned over to young instructors who trained him in athletics and the military arts and taught him to endure privation, to bear physical pain, and to live off the country, by theft if necessary. The Spartan youth was enrolled in the army at twenty and lived in barracks with his companions until he was thirty. He could marry but could visit his wife only infrequently and by stealth. At thirty he became a full citizen, an "equal," and was allowed to live in his own house with his wife, although he took his meals at a public mess in the company of fifteen comrades. His food, a simple diet without much meat or wine, was provided by his own plot of land, which was worked by Helots. Only when he reached sixty could the Spartan retire from military service to his home and family.

Spartan girls did not receive military training, but they were given gymnastic training and were permitted greater freedom than among other Greeks. Like boys, they too were indoctrinated with the idea of service to Sparta. The entire system was designed to change the natural feelings of devotion to family into a more powerful commitment to the *polis*. Privacy, luxury, and even comfort were sacrificed to the purpose of producing soldiers whose physical prowess, training, and discipline made them the best in the world. Nothing that might turn the mind away from duty was permitted. The very use of coins was forbidden for its potential to corrupt. Neither family nor money was allowed to interfere with the only ambition permitted to a Spartan male: to win glory and respect by bravery in war.

Government   In a mixture of monarchy, oligarchy, and democracy, Sparta was governed by two kings, a council of elders, and an assembly. The power of the kings was limited by law and by the rivalry that usually prevailed between them. The council of elders—twenty-eight men over sixty who were elected for life—had important judicial functions, sitting as a court in cases involving the kings. It was also consulted before any proposal was put before the assembly. In a traditional society like Sparta's, it must have had considerable influence. The assembly, which consisted of all males over thirty, was theoretically the final authority. In practice, however, it served only to ratify the decisions of magistrates, elders, and kings, or to decide between the positions of these leading figures.

Sparta also had another, unique, governmental institution, the board of ephors. This consisted of five men elected annually by the assembly. Apparently originally intended to check the power of the kings, the ephors gradually acquired other important functions. They controlled foreign policy, oversaw the generalship of the kings on campaign, presided at the assembly, and guarded against rebellion by the Helots.

Suppression of the Helots required all the effort and energy the Spartans had. They could not expand their borders, but at the same time they could not allow unruly independent neighbors to sow unrest among the Helots. Thus when the Spartans defeated Tegea, their northern neighbor, they imposed an unusual peace, allowing the Tegeans to keep their land and their freedom in exchange for following Sparta's lead in foreign affairs and supplying Sparta with a fixed number of troops on demand. As Sparta imposed this model on other neighbors, it emerged as the leader of an alliance—known to scholars today as the Peloponnesian League—that included every Peloponnesian state except Argos. This alliance provided the Spartans with the security they needed, and made Sparta the most powerful *polis* in Greece. Thanks to Sparta and the league, by 500 B.C.E. the Greeks had a force capable of facing mighty threats from abroad.

ATHENS

In the seventh century B.C.E. Athens and the region of Attica (see Map 3–4) constituted a typical aristocratic *polis*. Aristocrats held the most and best land and dominated religious and political life. There was no written law. The state was governed by the **Areopagus**, a council of nobles deriving its name from the hill where it held its sessions. Annually the council elected nine magistrates, called *archons*, who joined the Areopagus after their year in office. The Areopagus, however, not the archons, was the true master of the state. A broad-based citizens' assembly, which had little power, represented the four tribes into which Attica's inhabitants were traditionally divided.

Pressure for Change

In the seventh century B.C.E., quarrels within the nobility and the beginnings of an agrarian crisis disturbed the peaceful life of Athens. Many Athenians made their living from family farms, apparently planting wheat, the staple crop, year after year without rotating fields or using enough fertilizer. A shift to more intensive agricultural techniques and the cultivation of trees and vines, which required capital, forced some of the less successful farmers to borrow from wealthy neighbors. As their troubles grew, debtors pledged their wives, their children, and themselves as surety for new loans. Inevitably, many defaulted and were enslaved. Some were even sold abroad. Revolutionary pressures grew among the poor, who began to demand the abolition of debt and a redistribution of the land.

Reforms of Solon

In the year 594 B.C.E., as tradition has it, the Athenians elected Solon (ca. 639–559 B.C.E.) as the only archon, with extraordinary powers to legislate and revise Athens's governing institutions. In a program called the "shaking off of burdens," Solon immediately canceled current debts and forbade future loans secured by the person of the borrower. He helped bring back many Athenians enslaved abroad and freed those in Athens enslaved for debt. Solon did not redistribute land and failed in the short run to end Athens's economic crisis. Some of his actions, however, were profoundly successful in the long run. He encouraged commerce and turned Athens in the direction that would lead it to great prosperity in the fifth century. He forbade the export of wheat, initially making wheat more available in Attica, but he also encouraged the export of olive oil and wine. As a result, by the fifth century B.C.E. much Athenian land was diverted from grain production to the cultivation of olive trees and vines as cash crops, making Athens dependent on imported wheat. Solon also encouraged industry by offering citizenship to foreign artisans, stimulating the development of outstanding pottery in Attica in the sixth century.

Solon also significantly changed the way Athens was governed. He expanded citizenship—previously limited to adult males whose fathers were citizens—to include immigrant artisans and merchants, and divided the citizenry into four classes on the basis of wealth. Only men of the wealthiest two classes could be archons and sit on the Areopagus. Men of the third class could serve as hoplites and on a council of four hundred chosen by the assembly of all male citizens. The fourth class, the *thetes*, voted in the assembly and also sat on a new court of appeals that would hear almost all cases in Athens by the fifth century B.C.E.

Pisistratus the Tyrant

Despite Solon's reforms, Athens succumbed to factional strife that ended when the leader of one faction, Pisistratus (605?–527 B.C.E.), a nobleman and military hero, seized power firmly in 546 B.C.E. with the help of mercenary soldiers and made himself the city's first tyrant.

Pisistratus sought to increase the power of the central government at the expense of the nobles. To undermine their authority in the countryside, he sent out circuit judges to hear local cases. To fix attention on the capital, he engaged in great programs of public works, urban improvement, and religious piety. He built temples, expanded and improved religious centers, introduced new religious festivals, and increased the public appeal of traditional festivals. His reconstruction of Athens' Agora (marketplace) helped transform it into the center of public life. To add cultural luster to his court he supported poets and artists. Throughout his rule, Pisistratus made no formal change in the institutions of government. Assembly, councils, and courts met; magistrates and councils were elected; Pisistratus merely saw to it that his supporters filled key offices. The intended effect was to blunt the sharp edge of tyranny with the

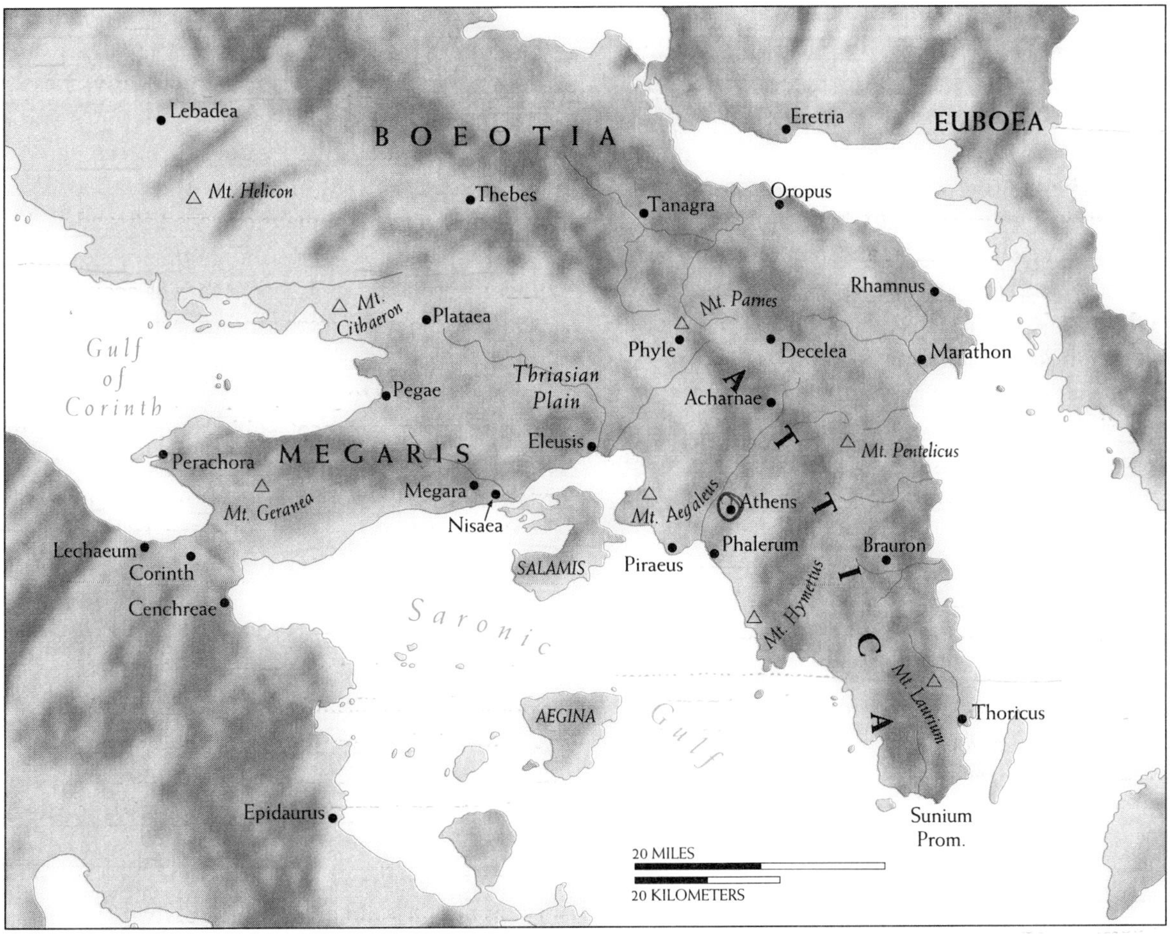

MAP 3–4 Attica and Vicinity.   Citizens of all towns in Attica were also citizens of Athens.

appearance of constitutional government, and it worked. The rule of Pisistratus was remembered as popular and mild. The unintended effect was to give the Athenians more experience in the procedures of self-government and a growing taste for it.

Invasion by Sparta   Pisistratus was succeeded by his oldest son, Hippias (r. 527–510 B.C.E.), whose rule became increasingly nervous, suspicious, and harsh after his brother Hipparchus was murdered in 514 B.C.E. Hippias was deposed and driven into exile in 510 B.C.E. when Sparta invaded Athens with the cooperation of a noble family that Hippias had exiled. The tyranny was over.

After the withdrawal of the Spartan army, some factions in the Athenian aristocracy, led by Isagoras, tried to restore the aristocracy to the position of dominance it held before Solon. Isagoras purged the citizen lists, removing those who had been enfranchised by Solon or Pisistratus and any others thought to have a doubtful claim. Isagoras, however, faced competitors, chief among them Clisthenes, of a rival aristocratic clan. In a challenge to Isagoras, Clisthenes took an unprecedented action—he turned to the people for political support and won it with a program of great popular appeal. In response, Isagoras called in the Spartans again, who expelled Clisthenes and many of his supporters. But the fire of Athenian political consciousness, ignited by Solon and kept alive under Pisistratus, had been fanned into flames by the popular appeal of Clisthenes. The people refused to tolerate an aristocratic restoration and drove out the Spartans and Isagoras with them. Clisthenes and his allies returned, ready to put their program into effect.

Clisthenes, the Founder of Democracy   A central aim of Clisthenes' reforms was to diminish the influence of traditional localities and regions in Athenian life, for they were an important source of power for the nobility and of factions in the state. Clisthenes immediately enrolled the disenfranchised who had supported him in the struggle with Isagoras. He also replaced Attica's traditional four tribes with ten new tribes organized to guarantee that no region would dominate any of them. Because members of a tribe had common religious activities and fought together in regimental units, the new organization increased devotion to the *polis*, weakening regional loyalties.

Clisthenes replaced Solon's council of four hundred with a new council of five hundred, but he vested final authority in all things in the assembly of all adult male Athenian citizens. Debate in the assembly was free and open; any Athenian could submit legislation, offer amendments, or argue the merits of any question. Although Clisthenes did not alter Solon's property qualifications for officeholders, his enlargement of the citizen rolls, his diminution of the power of the aristocrats, and his elevation of the role of the assembly with its effective and manageable council all give him a firm claim to the title of father of Athenian democracy.

Solon, Pisistratus, and Clisthenes put Athens well on the way to prosperity and democracy by the beginning of the fifth century B.C.E. It was much more centralized and united than it had been and was ready to take its place among the major states that would lead the defense of Greece against the dangers that lay ahead.

The Persian Wars

The Greeks' period of fortunate isolation and freedom ended in the sixth century B.C.E., when the Greek cities on the coast of Asia Minor came under the control first of King Croesus of Lydia (r. ca. 560–546 B.C.E.), and then in 546 B.C.E. of the powerful Persian Empire (see Chapter 4).

IONIAN REBELLION

Initially the cities of Ionia (those on the central part of the west coast of Asia Minor and nearby islands) prospered under Persian rule and remained obedient. The private troubles of Aristagoras, the ambitious tyrant of Miletus, however, ended this calm and set in motion events that would threaten the independence of all the Greeks. Aristagoras had urged a Persian expedition against the island of Naxos; when it failed, he feared the consequences and organized a rebellion in Ionia in 499 B.C.E. To gain support, he overthrew the tyrannies the Per-

CHRONOLOGY

Key Events in the Early History of Sparta and Athens

ca. 725–710 B.C.E.	First Messenian War
ca. 650–625 B.C.E.	Second Messenian War
ca. 600–590 B.C.E.	Solon initiates reforms at Athens
ca. 560–550 B.C.E.	Sparta defeats Tegea: beginning of Peloponnesian League
546–527 B.C.E.	Pisistratus reigns as tyrant at Athens (main period)
510 B.C.E.	Hippias, son of Pisistratus, deposed as tyrant of Athens
ca. 508–501 B.C.E.	Clisthenes institutes reforms at Athens

sians had installed and proclaimed democratic constitutions. Next he turned for help to the mainland Greeks, first petitioning Sparta, which refused him, and then Athens. The Athenians, who were related to the Ionians and had close ties of religion and tradition with them, agreed to send a fleet of twenty ships to help the rebels. This expedition was strengthened by five ships from Eretria in Euboea.

In 498 B.C.E., the Athenians and their allies made a swift march and a surprise attack on Sardis, the old capital of Lydia and now the seat of the Persian governor, and burned it. The revolt spread throughout the Greek cities of Asia Minor outside Ionia, but the Athenians withdrew and the Persians gradually reimposed their will. In 495 B.C.E. they defeated the Ionian fleet at Lade, and in the next year they wiped out Miletus, killing many of the city's men, transporting others to the Persian Gulf, and enslaving its women and children. The Ionian rebellion was over.

THE WAR IN GREECE

In 490 B.C.E. the Persian king Darius (r. 521–486 B.C.E.) sent an expedition to punish Athens, to restore Hippias, and to gain control of the Aegean Sea. Miltiades (d. 489 B.C.E.), an Athenian who had fled from Persian service, led the city's army to a confrontation with the invaders at Marathon. A Persian victory at Marathon would have destroyed Athenian freedom and led to the conquest of all the mainland Greeks. The greatest achievements of Greek culture, most of which lay in the future, would never have occurred. But the Athenians won a decisive victory, instilling them with a sense of confidence and pride in their *polis*, their unique form of government, and themselves.

The Great Invasion   For the Persians, Marathon was only a small and temporary defeat. In 481 B.C.E. Darius's successor, Xerxes (r. 486–465 B.C.E.), gathered an army of at least 150,000 men and a navy of more than 600 ships for the conquest of Greece. In Athens, Themistocles (ca. 525–462 B.C.E.), who favored making Athens into a naval power, had become the leading politician. During his archonship in 493 B.C.E., Athens had already taken the first step in that direction by building a fortified port at Piraeus. A decade later the Athenians came upon a rich vein of silver in the state mines, and Themistocles persuaded them to use the profits to increase their fleet. By 480 B.C.E. Athens had more than 200 ships, the backbone of a navy that was to defeat the Persians.

Of the hundreds of Greek states, only thirty-one—led by Sparta, Athens, Corinth, and Aegina—were willing to fight as the Persian army gathered south of the Hellespont. In the spring of 480 B.C.E. Xerxes launched his invasion. The Persian strategy was to march into Greece, destroy Athens, defeat the Greek army, and add the Greeks to the number of Persian subjects. The huge Persian army needed to keep in touch with the fleet for supplies. If the Greeks could defeat the Persian navy, the army could not remain in Greece long. Themistocles knew that the Aegean was subject to sudden devastating storms. His strategy was to delay the Persian army and then to bring on the kind of naval battle he might hope to win.

The Greeks chose Sparta to lead them and first confronted the Persians at Thermopylae on land and off Artemisium at sea. The opening between the mountains and the sea at Thermopylae is so narrow that it might be held by a smaller army against a much larger one. Severe storms wrecked many Persian ships while the Greek fleet waited safely in a protected harbor. Then Xerxes attacked Thermopylae, and for two days the Greeks butchered his best troops without serious loss to themselves. On the third day, however, a traitor showed the Persians a mountain trail that permitted them to come on the Greeks from behind. Many allies escaped, but Sparta's King Leonidas and the three hundred Spartans with him all died fighting. Although the naval battle at Artemisium was indecisive, the defeat at Thermopylae forced the Greek navy to withdraw. The Persian army then moved into Attica and burned Athens.

The fate of Greece was decided in a sea battle in the narrow straits to the east of the island of Salamis to which the Greek fleet withdrew after the battle of Artemisium. There the Greeks destroyed more than half the Persian fleet, forcing the rest to retreat to Asia with a good part of the Persian army.

The danger, however, was not over yet. The Persian general Mardonius spent the winter in central Greece, and in the spring he unsuccessfully tried to win the Athenians away from the Greek League. The Spartan regent, Pausanias (d. ca. 470 B.C.E.), then led the largest Greek army yet assembled to confront Mardonius in Boeotia. At Plataea, in the summer of 479 B.C.E., Mardonius died in battle, and his army fled toward home. Meanwhile, the Ionian Greeks urged King Leotychidas, the Spartan commander of the fleet, to fight the Persian fleet at Samos. At Mycale, on the nearby coast, Leotychidas destroyed the Persian camp and its fleet offshore. The Persians fled the Aegean and Ionia. For the moment, at least, the Persian threat was gone.

Classical Greece

The repulse of the Persians marks the beginning of the classical period in Greece, 150 years of intense cultural achievement that has rarely if ever been matched anywhere since (see Map 3–5). The classical period was also a time of destructive conflicts among the *poleis* that in the end left them weakened and vulnerable.

◄ A Greek Hoplite Attacks a Persian Soldier.
The contrast between the Greek's metal body armor, large shield, and long spear, and the Persian's cloth and leather garments indicates one reason the Greeks won.
Greek. Vase, Red-figured. Attic. ca. 480-470 B.C. Neck amphora, Nolan type. SIDE 1: "Greek warrior attacking a Persian." Said to be from Rhodes. Terracotta. H. 13-11/16 in. The Metropolitan Museum of Art, Rogers Fund, 1906 (Acc. # 06.1021.117) Photograph © The Metropolitan Museum of Art.

THE DELIAN LEAGUE

Within two years of the Persian retreat, Greek unity, strained even during the life-and-death struggle with Persia, gave way to division. Two spheres of influence emerged—one dominated by Sparta, the other by Athens. The reasons for the split lay in the Ionian Greeks' ongoing need for protection against the Persians and the desire of many Greeks for revenge and reparations. Sparta was ill suited to lead the Greeks under these conditions, which required a long-term commitment and continual naval action. It fell to Athens, the leading naval power in Greece, to lead the effort to drive the Persians from the Aegean and the Hellespont.

In the winter of 478–477 B.C.E. the islanders, the Greeks from the coast of Asia Minor, and some from other Greek cities on the Aegean met with the Athenians on the sacred island of Delos. Swearing themselves to a permanent alliance, they vowed to free Greeks under Persian rule, to protect all against a Persian return, and to obtain compensation from the Persians by attacking their lands and taking booty. Athens was clearly designated leader. Known as the **Delian League**, the alliance was remarkably successful, driving the Persians from Europe and the Hellespont and clearing the Aegean of pirates. A great Greek victory at the Eurymedon River in Asia Minor in 467 B.C.E. routed the Persians and added several cities to the league. Believing it necessary for their common safety, the members forced some states into the league and prevented others from leaving.

Leading Athens and the Delian League in this succession of victories was the statesman and soldier Cimon (d. 449 B.C.E.). Themistocles, the architect of the Greek victory in 480 B.C.E., was ostracized and driven from power soon after the Persian War by a coalition of his enemies, ironically ending his days at the court of the Persian king. Cimon dominated Athenian politics for almost two decades, pursuing a policy of aggressive attacks on Persia and friendly relations with Sparta. In domestic affairs, Cimon was conservative. He accepted the democratic constitution of Clisthenes, which appears to have become somewhat more limited when the aristocratic Areopagus

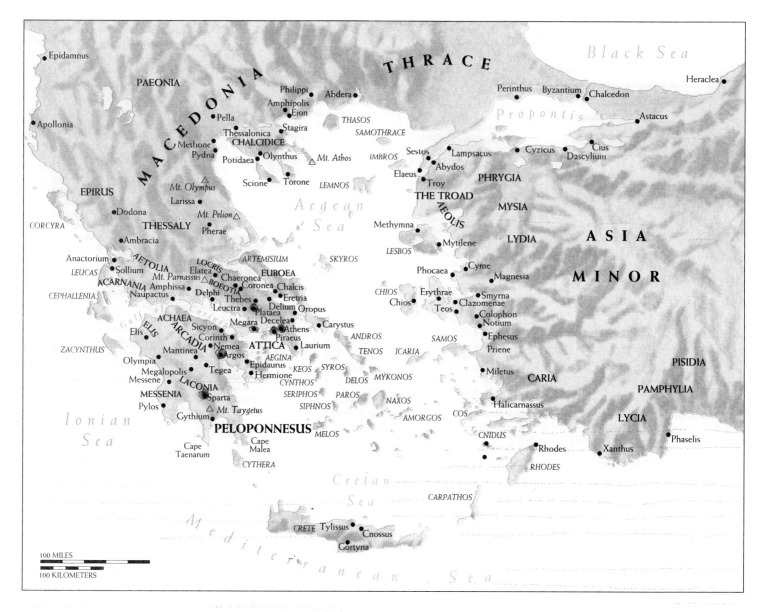

MAP 3–5 Classical Greece. Greece in the classical period (ca. 480–338 B.C.E.) centered on the Aegean Sea. Although there were important Greek settlements in Italy, Sicily, and all around the Black Sea, the area shown in this general reference map embraced the vast majority of Greek states.

usurped many powers from the council of five hundred, the assembly, and the popular courts after the Persian War.

THE FIRST PELOPONNESIAN WAR

The Fall of Cimon In 465 B.C.E., the island of Thasos rebelled against the league. Cimon's suppression of this rebellion after a siege of more than two years marked the first time Athenian interests alone determined league policy and was thus a significant step in the evolution of the league into an Athenian empire. Despite his success, Cimon faced a challenge at home from a faction led by Ephialtes (d. 462 B.C.E.), whose chief supporter was Pericles (ca. 495–429 B.C.E.), a member of a distinguished Athenian family. This faction wanted to reduce the power of the conservative Areopagus and increase the power of ordinary people in Athens and abroad to break with Sparta and contest its claim to leadership.

When the Thasians began their rebellion they asked Sparta to invade Athens, and the Spartans agreed. However, an earthquake, accompanied by a rebellion of the Helots that threatened the survival of Sparta, prevented the invasion. The Spartans asked for help from their allies, including the Athenians, and Cimon persuaded the Athenians, over the objections of Ephialtes, to send it. The results were disastrous for Cimon. While he was in the Peloponnesus helping the Spartans, Ephialtes stripped the Areopagus of almost all its power. Meanwhile, the Spartans, fearing "the bold-

CHRONOLOGY

Greek Wars Against Persia

ca. 560–546 B.C.E.	Greek cities of Asia Minor conquered by Croesus of Lydia
546 B.C.E.	Cyrus of Persia conquers Lydia and gains control of Greek cities
499–494 B.C.E.	Greek cities rebel (Ionian rebellion)
490 B.C.E.	Battle of Marathon
480–479 B.C.E.	Xerxes' invasion of Greece
480 B.C.E.	Battles of Thermopylae, Artemisium, and Salamis
479 B.C.E.	Battles of Plataea and Mycale

ness and revolutionary spirit of the Athenians," ultimately sent them home. In 461 B.C.E. Cimon was exiled, and Athens made an alliance with Argos, Sparta's traditional enemy. Almost overnight, Cimon's domestic and foreign policies had been overturned.

Outbreak of War   The policies of the confident and ambitious new regime at Athens helped bring on a conflict with Sparta known as the First **Peloponnesian War.** The war began after Megara, getting the worst of a border dispute with Corinth, withdrew from the Spartan-led Peloponnesian League and allied itself with Athens. Megara barred the way from the Peloponnesus to Athens, giving Athens a strategic advantage. The Athenians made great gains during the war's early years, conquering Aegina and gaining control of Boeotia. They appeared supreme and invulnerable, controlling neighboring states and dominating the sea.

The tide turned in 454 B.C.E.. The Athenian fleet, dispatched to help an Egyptian rebellion against Persia, suffered a disastrous defeat. Rebellions broke out within the Delian League, forcing Athens to make a truce in Greece to subdue its allies in the Aegean. In 449 B.C.E. Athens ended the war against Persia. In 446 B.C.E. the war on the Greek mainland broke out again. Rebellions in Boeotia and Megara opened Athens to a Spartan invasion. Rather than fight, Pericles, the commander of the Athenian army, agreed to a peace of thirty years, abandoning all Athenian possessions on the mainland in return for Spartan recognition of Athenian control of the Aegean. Greece was now divided into two blocs: Sparta and its alliance on the mainland, and Athens and what had become the Athenian Empire in the Aegean.

THE ATHENIAN EMPIRE

After the Egyptian disaster, the Athenians moved the Delian League's treasury to Athens and began to keep one sixtieth of the league's annual revenues for themselves. Athens was clearly becoming the master and its allies mere subjects (see Map 3–6). By 445 B.C.E. only Chios, Lesbos, and Samos were autonomous and provided ships. All the other states paid tribute.

The change from alliance to empire resulted largely from the pressure of war and rebellion and the unwillingness of the allies to see to their own defenses. Within the subject states, many democratic politicians and people in the lower classes supported the empire, but it nevertheless came to be seen more and more as a tyranny. For the Athenians, however, the empire recognized by the Thirty Years' Peace of 445 B.C.E. had become the key to prosperity and security, and they were determined to defend it at any cost.

ATHENIAN DEMOCRACY

Even as the Athenians were tightening their control over their empire, they were expanding democracy at home. Under the leadership of Pericles they evolved the freest government the world had yet seen. The hoplite class was made eligible for the archonship; in theory, no adult male was thereafter barred from that office on the basis of property class. Pericles proposed a law introducing pay for jury service, opening that important duty to the poor. Circuit judges were reintroduced, making swift impartial justice available even to the poorest residents in the countryside.

The benefits of this legislation were limited to citizens, and citizenship was sharply restricted. Pericles himself introduced a bill limiting it to those who had two citizen parents. In Greek terms this was quite natural. Democracy was the privilege of citizenship, making citizenship a valuable commodity. Limiting it would have increased its value and must have won a large majority. Participation in government in all the Greek states was also denied to slaves, resident aliens, and women. (See Document, "Athenian Democracy: An Unfriendly View.")

Among citizens, however, the extent of the democracy was remarkable. Every decision of the state had to be approved by the popular assembly—a collection of the people, not their representatives. Every judicial decision was subject to appeal to a popular court of not fewer than fifty-one citizens, chosen from an annual panel of jurors representative of the Athenian male population. Most officials were selected by lot, without regard to class. The main elected officials, such as the generals and the imperial treasurers, were generally nobles and almost always rich men, but the people were free to choose others. All public officials were subject to scrutiny before taking office, could be called to account and removed from office during their tenure, and were held to a compulsory examination and accounting at the end of their terms. There was no standing army; no police force, open or secret; and no way to coerce the people.

Pericles was elected to the generalship (a military office with important political influence) fifteen years in a row and thirty times in all—not because he was a dictator but because he was a persuasive speaker, a skillful politician, a respected general, an acknowledged patriot, and patently incorruptible. When he lost the people's confidence, they did not hesitate to depose

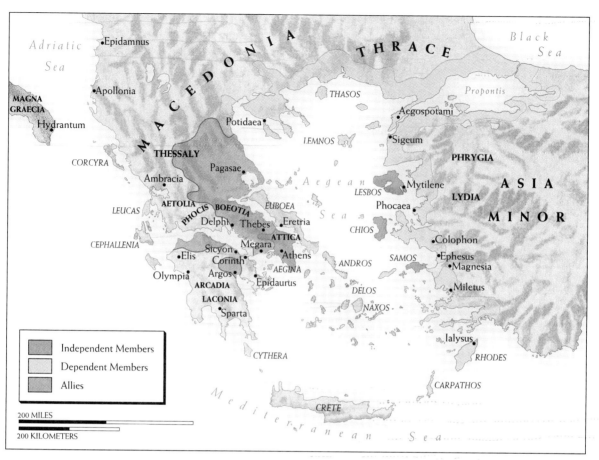

MAP 3–6 The Athenian Empire ca. 450 B.C.E.   The empire at its fullest extent. We see Athens and the independent states that provided manned ships for the imperial fleet but paid no tribute, the dependent states that paid tribute, and the states allied to but not actually in the empire.

him from office. In 443 B.C.E., however, he stood at the height of his power. The defeat of the Athenian fleet in the Egyptian campaign and the failure of Athens' continental campaigns persuaded him to favor a conservative policy, seeking to retain the empire in the Aegean and live at peace with the Spartans. It was in this direction that he led Athens's imperial democracy in the years after the First Peloponnesian War.

WOMEN OF ATHENS

Greek society, like most other societies all over the world throughout history, was dominated by men. This was true of the democratic Athens in the great days of Pericles in the fifth century B.C.E. no less than of other Greek cities. The actual position of women in classical Athens, however, has been the subject of much controversy.

Subjection   The bulk of the evidence, coming from the law, from philosophical and moral writings, and from information about the conditions of daily life and the organization of society, shows that Athenian women were excluded from most aspects of public life. Unlike Athenian men, they could not vote, take part in political assemblies, hold public office, or take any direct part at all in politics.

In private life, women were always under the control of a male guardian—a father, husband, or other appropriate male relative. Women married young, usually between the ages of twelve and eighteen; typically, their husbands were over thirty, making the relationship of a woman to her spouse similar to that of a daughter to her father. Marriages were arranged; the woman normally had no choice of husband, and her dowry was controlled by a male relative. Divorce was difficult for a woman to obtain, for she needed the approval of a male relative who had to be willing to serve as her guardian after the dissolution of the marriage. In case of divorce, the dowry returned with the woman but was controlled by her father or the appropriate male relative.

The main function and responsibility of a respectable Athenian woman of a citizen family was to produce male heirs for the household (*oikos*) of her husband. If, however, her father's *oikos* lacked a male heir, the daughter became an *epikleros*, the "heiress" to the family property. In that case she was required by law to marry a relative on her father's side in order to produce

The Acropolis. It was both the religious and civic center of Athens. In its final form it is the work of Pericles and his successors in the late fifth century B.C.E. This photograph shows the Parthenon and, to its left, the Erechtheum.

Meredith Pillon, Greek National Tourism Organization.

the desired male offspring. In the Athenian way of thinking, women were "lent" by one household to another for bearing and raising a male heir to continue the existence of the *oikos*.

Because the pure and legitimate lineage of the offspring was important, women were carefully segregated from men outside the family and were confined to the women's quarters in the house. Men might seek sexual gratification outside the house

with prostitutes of high or low style, frequently recruited from abroad. Respectable women stayed home to raise the children, cook, weave cloth, and oversee the management of the household. The only public function of women—an important one— was in the various rituals and festivals of the state religion. Apart from these activities, Athenian women were expected to remain at home out of sight, quiet and unnoticed. Pericles told the widows and mothers of the Athenian men who died in the first year of the Peloponnesian War only this: "Your great glory is not to fall short of your natural character, and the greatest glory of women is to be least talked about by men, whether for good or bad."

Power Evidence from mythology, from pictorial art, and from the tragedies and comedies by the great Athenian dramatists portrays women in a different light. These often show women as central characters and powerful figures in both the public and the private spheres, suggesting that the role played by Athenian women may have been more complex than their legal status suggests. For example, in Aeschylus's tragedy *Agamemnon*, Clytemnestra arranges the murder of her royal husband and establishes the tyranny of her lover, whom she dominates.

As a famous speech in Euripides' tragedy *Medea* makes clear, we are left with an apparent contradiction. In this speech, Medea paints a bleak picture of the subjugation of women as dictated by their legal status. Yet Medea, as depicted by Euripides, is herself a powerful and terrifying figure who negotiates with kings. She is the central figure in a tragedy bearing her name, produced at state expense before most of the Athenian population, and written by one of Athens' greatest poets and dramatists. She is a cause of terror to the audience and, at the same time, an object

CHRONOLOGY

Key Events in Athenian History Between the Persian War and the Great Peloponnesian War

478–477 B.C.E.	Delian League founded
ca. 474–462 B.C.E.	Cimon leading politician
467 B.C.E.	Victory over Persians at Eurymedon River
465–463 B.C.E.	Rebellion of Thasos
462 B.C.E.	Ephialtes murdered; Pericles rises to leadership
461 B.C.E.	Cimon ostracized
461 B.C.E.	Reform of Areopagus
ca. 460 B.C.E.	First Peloponnesian War begins
454 B.C.E.	Athens defeated in Egypt; crisis in the Delian League
449 B.C.E.	Peace with Persia
445 B.C.E.	Thirty Years' Peace ends First Peloponnesian War

DOCUMENT | Athenian Democracy: An Unfriendly View

The following selection comes from an anonymous pamphlet thought to have been written in late fifth century B.C.E. The obviously antidemocratic views of its author were common among members of the upper classes in Athens late in the fifth century and thereafter.

> ◆ What are the author's objections to democracy? Does he describe accurately the workings of the Athenian democracy? How would a defender of the Athenian constitution and way of life meet his complaints? Is there any merit in his criticisms? For other perspectives on law, leadership, and government, see "Legalism" (Chapter 2), "The Edicts of Ashoka" (Chapter 4), and "Machiavelli Discusses the Most Important Trait for a Ruler" (Chapter 16).

Now, in discussing the Athenian constitution, I cannot commend their present method of running the state, because in choosing it they preferred that the masses should do better than the respectable citizens; this, then, is my reason for not commending it. Since, however, they have made this choice, I will demonstrate how well they preserve their constitution and handle the other affairs for which the rest of the Greeks criticise them.

Again, some people are surprised at the fact that in all fields they give more power to the masses, the poor and the common people than they do to the respectable elements of society, but it will become clear that they preserve the democracy by doing precisely this. When the poor, the ordinary people and the lower classes flourish and increase in numbers, then the power of the democracy will be increased; if, however, the rich and the respectable flourish, the democrats increase the strength of their opponents. Throughout the world the aristocracy are opposed to democracy, for they are naturally least liable to loss of self control and injustice and most meticulous in their regard for what is respectable, whereas the masses display extreme ignorance, indiscipline and wickedness, for poverty gives them a tendency towards the ignoble, and in some cases lack of money leads to their being uneducated and ignorant.

It may be objected that they ought not to grant each and every man the right of speaking in the Ekklesia and serving on the Boule, but only the ablest and best of them; however, in this also they are acting in their own best interests by allowing the mob also a voice. If none but the respectable spoke in the Ekklesia and the Boule, the result would benefit that class and harm the masses; as it is, anyone who wishes rises and speaks, and as a member of the mob he discovers what is to his own advantage and that of those like him.

But someone may say: "How could such a man find out what was advantageous to himself and the common people?" The Athenians realise that this man, despite his ignorance and badness, brings them more advantage because he is well disposed to them than the ill-disposed respectable man would, despite his virtue and wisdom. Such practices do not produce the best city, but they are the best way of preserving democracy. For the common people do not wish to be deprived of their rights in an admirably governed city, but to be free and to rule the city; they are not disturbed by inferior laws, for the common people get their strength and freedom from what you define as inferior laws.

of their pity and sympathy as a victim of injustice. She is certainly not "least talked about by men, whether for good or for bad."

THE GREAT PELOPONNESIAN WAR

The Thirty Years' Peace of 445 B.C.E. endured little more than ten years. About 435 B.C.E. a dispute flared in a remote and unimportant part of the Greek world that ensnared Athens and Sparta, plunging them back into conflict. This new war was long and disastrous, shaking the foundations of Greek civilization.

The Spartan strategy was traditional: to invade the enemy's country and threaten the crops, forcing the enemy to defend them in a hoplite battle. Such a battle the Spartans were sure to win, because they had the better army and they and their allies outnumbered the Athenians at least two to one. Any ordinary polis would have yielded or fought and lost, but Athens had an enormous navy, annual income from its empire, a vast reserve fund, and long walls that connected the fortified city with the fortified port of Piraeus.

The Athenian strategy was to allow the devastation of their own land to prove that Spartan invasions could not hurt Athens. At the same time, the Athenians launched seaborne raids on the Peloponnesian coast to show that Sparta's allies could be hurt. Pericles expected that within a year or two, three at most, the Peloponnesians would become discouraged and make peace. A conflict of longer than four or five years would strain Athenian resources.

△ **An Athenian silver four-drachma coin (tetradrachm).** From the fifth century B.C.E. (440–430 B.C.E.), on the front (a) is the profile of Athena and on the back (b) is her symbol of wisdom, the owl. The silver from which the coins were struck came chiefly from the state mines at Sunium in southern Attica.
Hirmer Foto Archive.

The Athenian plan required restraint and the leadership that only Pericles could provide, but Pericles died in 429 B.C.E. Ten years of war ended in stalemate. In 421 B.C.E. Athens and Sparta agreed to the Peace of Nicias, which was supposed to last for fifty years but proved far more tenuous. Neither side carried out all the commitments of the peace, and several of Sparta's allies refused to ratify it.

In 415 B.C.E. Alcibiades (ca. 450–404 B.C.E.), a young and ambitious leader, persuaded the Athenians to attack Sicily to bring it under their control. In 413 B.C.E., the entire expedition was destroyed. The Athenians lost some 200 ships, about 4,500 of their own men, and almost ten times as many allies. It was a disaster that shook Athenian prestige, reduced the power of Athens, provoked rebellions, and brought Persia into the war on Sparta's side.

Remarkably, the Athenians were able to continue fighting in spite of the disaster. They survived a brief oligarchic coup in 411 B.C.E. and won several important victories at sea as the war shifted to the Aegean. As their allies rebelled, however, and were sustained by fleets paid for by Persia, the Athenians saw their financial resources shrink and finally disappear. When their fleet was caught napping and was destroyed at Aegospotami in 405 B.C.E., they could not build another. The Spartans, under Lysander (d. 395 B.C.E.), a clever and ambitious general who was responsible for obtaining Persian support, cut off the food supply to Athens, starving the city into submission. In 404 B.C.E. Athens surrendered unconditionally. Its walls were dismantled, its empire was gone, and it was forbidden from rebuilding its fleet. The Great Peloponnesian War was over (See Document, "Lysistrata Ends the War.")

STRUGGLE FOR GREEK LEADERSHIP

The Hegemony of Sparta   The collapse of the Athenian Empire created a vacuum of power in the Aegean and opened the way for Spartan leadership, or hegemony. Fulfilling the contract that had brought them the funds to win the war, the Spartans handed the Greek cities of Asia Minor back to Persia. Under the leadership of Lysander, the Spartans stepped into the imperial role Athens had lost. Making a mockery of the Spartan promise to free the Greeks, Lysander installed a board of ten local oligarchs loyal to him and supported by a Spartan garrison in most of the cities along the European coast and the islands of the Aegean. These tributaries brought Sparta almost as much revenue as the Athenians had collected.

Limited manpower, the Helot problem, and traditional conservatism all made Sparta less than an ideal state to rule a maritime empire. Some of Sparta's allies, especially Thebes and Corinth, were alienated by Sparta's increasingly arrogant policies. In 404 B.C.E. Lysander installed an oligarchic government in Athens whose outrageous behavior earned it the title "Thirty Tyrants." Democratic exiles took refuge in Thebes and Corinth and created an army to challenge the oligarchy. Sparta's conservative king, Pausanias, replaced Lysander, arranging a peaceful settlement and ultimately the restoration of democracy. Thereafter, Athenian foreign policy remained under Spartan control, but otherwise Athens was free.

In 405 B.C.E. Greek mercenaries recruited with Spartan help intervened in Persia on behalf of Cyrus the Younger, who was contesting the accession to the Persian throne of his brother Artaxerxes II (r. 404–358 B.C.E.) The Greeks marched inland to Mesopotamia, defeating the Persians at Cunaxa (see Map 3–7) in 401 B.C.E. Cyrus was killed, however, and the Greeks marched back to the Black Sea and safety. Their success revealed the potential weakness of the Persian Empire.

The Greeks of Asia Minor had supported Cyrus and were now

◁ **Red-figure kalyx krater, or wine bowl.** This was painted by the Dokimasia painter ca. 470–465 B.C.E. It shows the murder of King Agamemnon, on his return from the sack of Troy, by his wife Clytemnestra and her lover Aegisthus. In red-figure painting, the red color of the fired clay is used for the foreground (figure) and a black pigment for the background.
Carlyx, Krater, Greece, Attica, Athens, about 460 B.C.; Attributed to the Dokimasia Painter Ceramic, Red Figure; H: 51 cm (20 1/8 in.) Diam.: 51 (20 1/8 diam. in) William Francis Warden Fund, 63.1246. Courtesy, Museum of Fine Arts, Boston. Reproduced with permission. © 1999 Museum of Fine Arts, Boston. All rights Reserved.

DOCUMENT | Lysistrata Ends the War

Aristophanes, the greatest of the Athenian comic poets, presented the play Lysistrata in 411 B.C.E. two decades into the Great Peloponnesian War. The central idea of the plot is that the women of Athens, led by Lysistrata, tired of the privations imposed by the war, decide to take matters into their own hands and bring the war to an end. The device they employ is to get the women on both sides to deny their marital favors to their husbands, a kind of sexual strike that quickly achieves its purpose. Before the following passage, Lysistrata has set the terms the Spartans must accept. Next she turns to the Athenians. The play is a masterful example of Athenian Old Comedy, which was almost always full of contemporary and historical political satirical references and sexual and erotic puns and jokes. The references to "Peace" in the stage directions are to an actor playing to goddess Peace.

> ◆ To what historic event does the passage concerning "the Tyrant's days" refer? To what does the "Promontory of Pylos" refer? What was the real role of women in Athenian political life, and what does the play tell us about it? What is the relationship between humor and reality in this play?

LYSISTRATA

(*Turning to the Athenians*)
—Men of Athens, do you think I'll let you off?
Have you forgotten the Tyrant's days, when you wore
the smock of slavery, when the Spartans turned to the spear,
cut down the pride of Thessaly, despatched the friends
of tyranny, and dispossessed your oppressors?

Recall:
On that great day, your only allies were Spartans;
your liberty came at their hands, which stripped away
your servile garb and clothed you again in Freedom!

SPARTAN

(*Indicating Lysistrata*)
Hain't never seed no higher type of woman.

KINESIAS

(*Indicating Peace*)
Never saw one I wanted so much to top.

LYSISTRATA

(*Oblivious to the byplay, addressing both groups*)
With such a history of mutual benefits conferred
and received, why are you fighting? Stop this wickedness!
Come to terms with each other! What prevents you?

SPARTAN

We'd a heap sight druther make Peace, if we was indemnified
with a plumb strategic location.
(*Pointing at Peace's rear*)

We'll take thet butte.

LYSISTRATA

Butte?

SPARTAN

The Promontory of Pylos—Sparta's Back Door.
We've missed it fer a turrible spell.
(*Reaching*)

Hev to keep our hand in.

---

afraid of Artaxerxes' revenge. The Spartans accepted their request for aid and sent an army into Asia, attracted by the prospect of prestige, power, and money. In 396 B.C.E. the command of this army was given to Sparta's new king, Agesilaus (444–360 B.C.E.), whose aggressive policy was to dominate Sparta until his death.

The Persians responded to Agesilaus's plundering army by seeking assistance among Greek states disaffected with Spartan domination, offering them money and other support. Thebes forged an alliance with Argos, Corinth, and Athens and engaged Sparta in the Corinthian War (395–387 B.C.E.), ending Sparta's Asian adventure. In 394 B.C.E. the Persian fleet destroyed Sparta's maritime empire. Athens, meanwhile, had rebuilt its walls, resurrected its navy, and recovered some of its lost empire. The Persians, who dictated the terms of the peace that ended the Corinthian War to the exhausted Greeks, were alarmed by this Athenian recovery and turned the management of Greece over to Sparta.

CHRONOLOGY

● ●

The Great Peloponnesian War

435 B.C.E.	Civil war at Epidamnus
432 B.C.E.	Sparta declares war on Athens
431 B.C.E.	Peloponnesian invasion of Athens
421 B.C.E.	Peace of Nicias
415–413 B.C.E.	Athenian invasion of Sicily
405 B.C.E.	Battle of Aegospotami
404 B.C.E.	Athens surrenders

KINESIAS
(*Pushing him away*)
The price is too high—you'll never take that!

LYSISTRATA
Oh, let them have it.

KINESIAS
What room will we have left for maneuvers?

LYSISTRATA
Demand another spot in exchange.

KINESIAS
(*Surveying Peace like a map as he addresses the Spartan*)
Then you hand over to us—uh, let me see—let's try Thessaly—
(*Indicating the relevant portions of Peace*)
First of all, Easy Mountain …
then the Maniac Gulf behind it …
and down to Megara for the legs …

SPARTAN
You cain't take all of thet! Yore plumb
out of yore mind!

LYSISTRATA
(*To Kinesias*)
Don't argue. Let the legs go.
(*Kinesias nods. A pause, general smiles of agreement*)

KINESIAS
(*Doffing his cloak*)
I feel an urgent desire to plow a few furrows.

SPARTAN
(*Doffing his cloak*)
Hit's time to work a few loads of fertilizer in.

LYSISTRATA
Conclude the treaty and the simple life is yours.
If such is your decision, convene your councils,
and then deliberate the matter with your allies.

KINESIAS
Deliberate? Allies?
We're over-extended already!
Wouldn't every ally approve of our position—
Union Now?

SPARTAN
I know I kin speak for ourn.

KINESIAS
And I for ours.
They're just a bunch of gigolos.

LYSISTRATA
I heartily approve.
Now first attend to your purification,
then we, the women, will welcome you to the Citadel
and treat you to all the delights of a home-cooked banquet.
Then you'll exchange your oaths and pledge your faith,
and every man of you will take his wife
and depart for home.

Aristophanes, *Lysistrata* trans. by Douglass Parker in *Four Comedies by Aristophanes,* ed. by W. Arrowsmith (Ann Arbor: University of Michigan Press, 1969), pp. 79–81. Reprinted by permission of the University of Michigan Press.

Sparta's actions grew increasingly arrogant and lawless. Agesilaus broke up all alliances except the Peloponnesian League and put friends in power in several Greek cities. In 382 B.C.E. Sparta seized Thebes during peacetime without warning or pretext. In 379 B.C.E. a Spartan army made a similar attempt on Athens. That action persuaded the Athenians to join with Thebes, which had rebelled from Sparta a few months earlier. In 371 B.C.E. the Thebans defeated the Spartans at Leuctra (see Map 3–5). They then encouraged the Arcadian cities of the central Peloponnesus to form a federal league and freed the Helots, helping them found a city of their own. Sparta's population had been shrinking so that it could field an army of fewer than two thousand men at Leuctra. Now, hemmed in by hostile neighbors, deprived of much of its farmland and of the slaves who had worked it, Sparta ceased to be a first-rank power. Its aggressive policies had led to ruin.

Theban Hegemony   Thebes' power after its victory lay in its democratic constitution, its control over Boeotia, and the two outstanding and popular generals—Pelopidas (d. 364 B.C.E.) and Epaminondas (d. 362 B.C.E.)—who led its forces at Leuctra. Under their leadership Thebes gained dominance over the Corinthian gulf and all Greece north of Athens, challenging the reborn Athenian Empire in the Aegean. This success provoked resistance, however, and by 362 B.C.E. Thebes faced a Peloponnesian coalition as well as Athens. Epaminondas, who was once again leading a Boeotian army into the Peloponnesus, confronted this coalition at Mantinea. His army was victorious, but Epaminondas was killed, ending Theban dominance.

The Second Athenian Empire   In 378 B.C.E. Athens organized a second confederation aimed at resisting Spartan aggression in the Aegean. Its constitution was careful to avoid the abuses of

OVERVIEW   Greek Civilization

Historians divide ancient Greek civilization into periods marked by different forms of social and political organizations and by significant cultural achievements.

Minoan	Based on the island of Crete, ca. 2900–1150 B.C.E., sea-based power, probably ruled by kings. Palace architecture, vivid frescoes.
Mycenaean	Mainland Greece, ca. 1600–1150 B.C.E., city-states ruled by powerful kings assisted by an elaborate bureaucracy. Monumental architecture, gold and bronzework.
Archaic	Colonization from Greece to Asia Minor, southern Italy, and the coasts of the Black Sea, 700–500 B.C.E. Characteristic form of government was the *polis*, a city-state dominated by land-holding aristocrats or ruled by tyrants. Lyric poetry, natural philosophy.
Classical	Golden age of Athenian civilization, fifth century B.C.E. Athens and other *poleis* became much more democratic. Drama, sculpture in marble and bronze, architecture (the Acropolis), philosophy, history.
Hellenistic	Conquests of Alexander the Great (356–323 B.C.E.) spread Greek culture to Egypt and as far east as the Indus Valley. Decline of the *polis*. Domination of the Greek world by large monarchical states. Stoic and Epicurean philosophy, realistic sculpture, advances in mathematics and science.

the Delian League, but the Athenians soon began to repeat them anyway. This time, however, they lacked the power to suppress resistance. When the collapse of Sparta and Thebes and the restraint of Persia removed any reason for voluntary membership, Athens' allies revolted. By 355 B.C.E. Athens had to abandon most of the empire. After two centuries of almost continual warfare, the Greeks returned to the chaotic disorganization that characterized the time before the founding of the Peloponnesian League.

Culture of Classical Greece   The term *classical* often suggests calm and serenity, but ironically the word that best describes the common element in Greek life, thought, art, and literature during the classical period is tension. Among the great achievements of this era were the philosophical works of Socrates (469–399 B.C.E.), Plato (427?–347 B.C.E.), and Aristotle (384–322 B.C.E.) (see Chapter 2). The arts of the time were animated by the same concern with the nature, capacities, limits, and place in the universe of human beings that animated those works.

FIFTH CENTURY B.C.E.

Two sources of tension contributed to the artistic outpouring of fifth-century B.C.E. Greece. One arose from the conflict between the Greeks' pride in their accomplishments and their

concern that overreaching would bring retribution. The victory over the Persians brought a sense of exultation in the capacity of humans to accomplish great things, and a sense of confidence in the divine justice that had subdued the arrogant pride of Xerxes. But the Greeks recognized that the fate that had met Xerxes awaited all those who reached too far, creating a sense of unease. The second source of tension was the conflict between the soaring hopes and achievements of individuals and the claims and limits put on them by their fellow citizens in the *polis*. These tensions were felt throughout Greece. They had the most spectacular consequences, however, in Athens in its golden age, the time between the Persian and the Peloponnesian Wars.

Attic Tragedy   These concerns are best reflected in Attic (Athenian) tragedy, which emerged as a major form of Greek poetry in the fifth century B.C.E. The tragedies were selected in a contest and presented as part of public religious observations in honor of the god Dionysus.

Poets who wished to compete submitted their works to the archon. Each offered three tragedies, which might or might not have a common subject, and a satyr play (a comic choral dialogue with Dionysus) to close. The three best competitors were each awarded three actors and a chorus. The actors were paid by the state, and the chorus was provided by a wealthy cit-

Vase from ca. 470 B.C.E. It shows instruction in grammar and music in an Attic school. For the Greeks, music was always connected with literature, drama, and dance. Along with physical exercise, it was the backbone of Greek education.
Art Resource/Bildarchiv Preussischer Kulturbesitz.

izen selected by the state to perform this service as *chorego*. Most of the tragedies were performed in the theater of Dionysus on the south side of the Acropolis, where as many as thirty thousand Athenians could attend. Prizes and honors were awarded to the author, the actor, and the *choregos* voted best by a jury of Athenians chosen by lot.

Attic tragedy served as a forum for poets to raise vital issues. Until late in the century the tragedies, drawing mostly on mythological subjects, dealt solemnly with difficult questions of religion, politics, ethics, or morality. The plays of the dramatists Aeschylus (525–456 B.C.E.) and Sophocles (ca. 496–406 B.C.E.) follow this pattern. The plays of Euripides (ca. 480–406 B.C.E.) are less solemn and more concerned with individual psychology.

Old Comedy Comedy was introduced into the Dionysian festival early in the fifth century B.C.E. The great master of the genre called Old Comedy, Aristophanes (ca. 450–385 B.C.E.), the only one from whom we have complete plays, wrote political comedies filled with scathing invective and satire against such contemporary figures as Pericles, Socrates, and Euripides.

Architecture and Sculpture The great architectural achievements of Periclean Athens, like Athenian tragedy, reflect the tension generated by the union of individual genius with religious and civic responsibility. Beginning in 448 B.C.E. and continuing to the outbreak of the Great Peloponnesian War, Pericles undertook a great building program on the Acropolis with funds from the income of the empire. The new buildings included temples to honor the city's gods and a fitting gateway to the temples. They visually projected Athenian greatness, emphasizing the city's intellectual and artistic achievements

rather than its military power and providing tangible proof of Pericles' claim that Athens was "the school of Hellas,"[1] the intellectual center of all Greece.

History The first prose history ever written was an account of the Persian War by Herodotus (484?–425? B.C.E.). "The father of history," as he has deservedly been called, was born shortly before the outbreak of the war. His account goes far beyond all previous chronicles, genealogies, and geographical studies and attempts to explain human actions and to draw instruction from them.

Herodotus accepted the evidence of legends and oracles, although not uncritically, and often explained human events in terms of divine intervention. Yet his *History*, typical of its time, also celebrates the crucial influence of human intelligence on events, as exemplified by Miltiades at Marathon and Themistocles at Salamis. Herodotus also recognized the importance of institutions, pointing with pride to the way the Greek *polis* inspired discipline and a voluntary obedience to the law in its citizen soldiers, in contrast to the fear of punishment that motivated the Persians.

Thucydides, the historian of the Peloponnesian War, was born about 460 B.C.E. and died about 400, a few years after the end of the Great Peloponnesian War. His work, which was influenced by the secular, human-centered, skeptical rationalism of the Sophists (see Chapter 2), also reflects the scientific approach to medicine pioneered by his contemporary, Hippocrates of Cos (ca. 460–ca. 370 B.C.E.). The Hippocratic approach to the understanding, diagnosis, and treatment of disease combined careful observation with reason. Thucydides similarly took great pains to achieve factual accuracy and tried to use his evidence to discover

---

[1] Thucydides, *The Peloponnesian War*, trans. by Richard Crawley (New York: Modern Library, 1982), p. 110.

CHRONOLOGY

Spartan and Theban Hegemonies

404–403 B.C.E.	Thirty Tyrants rule at Athens
401 B.C.E.	Expedition of Cyrus, rebellious prince of Persia; Battle of Cunaxa
400–387 B.C.E.	Spartan War against Persia
398–360 B.C.E.	Reign of Agesilaus at Sparta
395–387 B.C.E.	Corinthian War
382 B.C.E.	Sparta seizes Thebes
378 B.C.E.	Second Athenian Confederation founded
371 B.C.E.	Thebans defeat Sparta at Leuctra; end of Spartan hegemony
362 B.C.E.	Battle of Mantinea; end of Theban hegemony

meaningful patterns of human behavior. He believed that human nature was essentially unchanging, so that a wise person equipped with an understanding of history might accurately foresee events and help guide them. He believed, however, that only a few were equipped to understand history and to put its lessons to good use, and that even the wisest could be foiled by the intervention of chance in human affairs. Thucydides focused on politics, and in that area his assumptions about human nature do not seem unwarranted.

FOURTH CENTURY B.C.E

Historians often call the Great Peloponnesian War the crisis of the *polis* and the fourth century B.C.E. the period of its decline. But the Greeks of the fourth century B.C.E. did not know that their traditional way of life was on the verge of destruction. Some looked to the past for ways to shore up the weakened structure of the polis; others tended toward despair and looked for new solutions; and still others averted their gaze from the public arena altogether. All of these responses are apparent in the literature, philosophy, and art of the period.

Drama The tendency of some to turn away from the life of the *polis* and inward to everyday life, the family, and the self is apparent in the poetry of the fourth century B.C.E. A new genre, called Middle Comedy, replaced the political subjects and personal invective of the Old Comedy with comic-realistic depictions of daily life, plots of intrigue, and mild domestic satire. Significantly, the role of the chorus, which in some ways represented the *polis*, was much diminished. These trends continued, resulting in New Comedy, whose leading exponent, Menander (342–291 B.C.E.), completely abandoned mythological subjects in favor of domestic tragicomedy. Menander's gentle satire of the foibles of ordinary people and his tales of lovers temporarily thwarted before a happy ending would be familiar to viewers of modern situation comedies.

Tragedy faded as a robust and original form in the fourth century B.C.E., but the great tragedies of the previous century were commonly revived. The plays of Euripides, which rarely won first prize when originally produced, became increasingly popular in the fourth century and after. Euripides was less interested in cosmic confrontations of conflicting principles than in the psychology and behavior of individual human beings. Some of his late plays, in fact, are less like the tragedies of Aeschylus and Sophocles than forerunners of later forms such as the New Comedy. Plays like *Helena, Andromeda,* and *Iphigenia in Tauris* are more like fairy tales, tales of adventure, or love stories than tragedies.

Sculpture Fourth-century sculpture reflects the same movement away from the grand, the ideal, and the general and toward the ordinary, the real, and the individual.

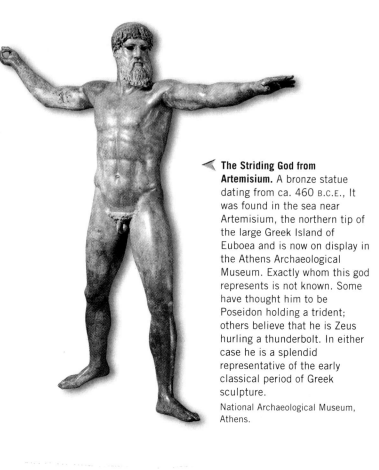

◀ **The Striding God from Artemisium.** A bronze statue dating from ca. 460 B.C.E., It was found in the sea near Artemisium, the northern tip of the large Greek Island of Euboea and is now on display in the Athens Archaeological Museum. Exactly whom this god represents is not known. Some have thought him to be Poseidon holding a trident; others believe that he is Zeus hurling a thunderbolt. In either case he is a splendid representative of the early classical period of Greek sculpture.
National Archaeological Museum, Athens.

Emergence of the Hellenistic World

The term *Hellenistic* was coined in the nineteenth century to describe a period of three centuries during which Greek culture spread from its homeland to Egypt and far into Asia. The result was a new civilization that combined Greek and Asian elements. The Hellenistic world was larger than the world of classical Greece, and its major political units were much larger than the *poleis*, although these endured in modified forms. Hellenistic civilization had its roots in the rise to power of a dynasty in Macedonia whose armies conquered Greece and the Persian Empire in the space of two generations.

MACEDONIAN CONQUEST

The kingdom of Macedon, north of Thessaly, had long served unknowingly as a buffer between the Greek states to the south and barbarian tribes farther to the north. The Macedonians were of the same stock as the Greeks and spoke a Greek dialect, and Macedonian nobles, at least, thought of themselves as Greeks. Macedon's kings, who claimed descent from Heracles and the royal house of Argos, sought to bring Greek culture into their court. By Greek standards, however, Macedon, although allowed to participate in the Olympic games, was backward and semibarbaric. It had no *poleis* and was ruled loosely by a king in a rather Homeric fashion. The king was chosen partly on the basis of descent, but gained legitimacy only with the acclamation of the army gathered in assembly. Quarrels between pretenders to the throne and even murder to secure it were not uncommon. A council of nobles checked the royal power and could reject a weak or incompetent king. Plagued by constant war with the barbarians, internal strife, loose organization, and lack of money, Macedon played no great part in Greek affairs up to the fourth century B.C.E. Once unified under a strong king, however, it was destined to play a great part in Greek affairs.

Philip of Macedon   That strong king was Philip II (r. 359–336 B.C.E.), who, while still under thirty, took advantage of his appointment as regent to overthrow his infant nephew and make himself king. Like many of his predecessors, he admired Greek culture. Between 367 and 364 B.C.E. he had been a hostage in Thebes, where he learned about Greek politics and warfare from Epaminondas. His natural talents for war and diplomacy and his boundless ambition made him the ablest king in Macedonian history. After first securing his hold on the throne and pacifying the tribes on his frontiers, he began to undermine Athenian control of the northern Aegean. Gaining control of a lucrative gold and silver mining region, he began to found new cities, to bribe foreign politicians, and to reorganize his army into the finest fighting force in the world.

Invasion of Greece   So armed, Philip turned south toward central Greece, threatening the vital interest of Athens. Although it still had a formidable fleet of three hundred ships, the Athens of 350 B.C.E. was not the Athens of Pericles. It had neither imperial revenue nor allies to share the burden of war, and its population was smaller than it had been in the fifth century B.C.E. The Athenians, therefore, were reluctant to go on expeditions themselves or even to send out mercenary armies under Athenian generals, for mercenaries had to be paid from Athenian coffers.

The leading critic of this cautious policy was Demosthenes (384–322 B.C.E.), one of the greatest orators in Greek history. Convinced that Philip was a dangerous enemy, Demosthenes spent most of his career urging the Athenians to resist him. Demosthenes was right. Beginning in 349 B.C.E. Philip attacked several cities in northern and central Greece, firmly establishing Macedonian power in those regions. The king of "barbarian" Macedon was elected president of the Pythian games at Delphi, and the Athenians were forced to concur in the election.

The years between 346 and 340 B.C.E. were spent in diplomatic maneuvering, each side trying to win strategically useful allies. In 340 B.C.E. Philip besieged Perinthus and Byzantium (see Map 3–5), the lifeline of Athenian commerce, and declared war. The Athenian fleet saved both cities, so in the following year

Philip marched into Greece. Demosthenes rallied the Athenians and won Thebes over to the Athenian side. In 338 B.C.E., however, Philip defeated the allied forces at Chaeronea in Boeotia. The decisive blow in this great battle was a cavalry charge led by Philip's eighteen-year-old son, Alexander.

Macedonian Government of Greece   Macedonian rule was not as harsh as many had feared, although in some cities Philip's supporters took power and killed or exiled their enemies. Demosthenes remained free to engage in politics. Athens was spared from attack on the condition that it give up what was left of its empire and follow the lead of Macedon. The rest of Greece was arranged in such a way as to remove all dangers to Philip's rule. To guarantee his security, Philip placed garrisons at Thebes, Chalcis, and Corinth.

In 338 B.C.E. Philip organized the Greek states into the Federal League of Corinth. The league's constitution provided its constituent states autonomy and freedom from tribute and garrisons, and called for the suppression of piracy and civil war. League delegates would make foreign policy, in theory without consulting their home governments or Philip. All this was a façade; not only was Philip of Macedon president of the league, he was also its ruler. The defeat at Chaeronea ended Greek freedom and autonomy. Although it maintained its form and internal life for some time, the *polis* had lost control of its own affairs and the special conditions that had made it unique.

Philip's choice of Corinth as the seat of his new confederacy was deliberate. It was at Corinth that the Greeks had gathered to resist a Persian invasion almost 150 years earlier, and it was there in 337 B.C.E. that Philip announced his intention to invade Persia as leader of the new league. In the spring of 336 B.C.E., however, as he prepared to begin the campaign, Philip was assassinated.

In 1977 excavations of a mound at the Macedonian village of Vergina revealed structures with extraordinarily rich associated artifacts that many scholars believe to be the royal tomb of Philip II. Philip certainly deserved so distinguished a resting place. He found Macedon a disunited kingdom of semibarbarians, despised and exploited by the Greeks. He left it a united kingdom, master and leader of the Greeks, rich, powerful, and ready to undertake the invasion of Asia.

ALEXANDER THE GREAT AND HIS SUCCESSORS

Philip's first son, Alexander III (356–323 B.C.E.), later called Alexander the Great, succeeded his father at the age of twenty. Along with his throne, the young king inherited his father's daring plans for the conquest of Persia.

The Conquest of Persia   The usurper Cyrus and his Greek mercenaries had shown the vast and wealthy Persian Empire to be vulnerable when they penetrated deep into its interior early in

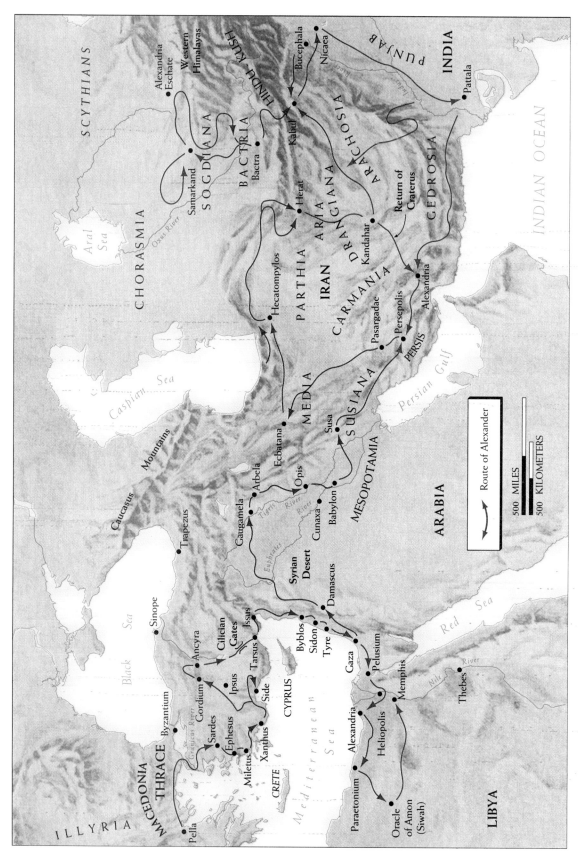

MAP 3–7 Alexander's Campaigns. The route taken by Alexander the Great in his conquest of the Persian Empire, 334–323 B.C.E. Starting from the Macedonian capital at Pella, he reached the Indus valley before being turned back by his own restive troops. He died of fever in Mesopotamia.

the fourth century B.C.E. In 334 B.C.E. Alexander crossed the Hellespont into Asia. His army consisted of about thirty thousand infantry and five thousand cavalry; he had no navy and little money. Consequently he sought quick and decisive battles to gain money and supplies from the conquered territory. To neutralize the Persian navy he moved along the coast, depriving it of ports.

Alexander met the Persian forces of Asia Minor at the Granicus River (see Map 3–7), where he won a smashing victory in characteristic style: He led a cavalry charge across the river into the teeth of the enemy on the opposite bank, almost losing his life in the process and winning the devotion of his soldiers. The coast of Asia Minor now open, Alexander captured the coastal cities, denying them to the Persian fleet.

In 333 B.C.E. Alexander marched inland to Syria, meeting the main Persian army under King Darius III (r. 336–330 B.C.E.) at Issus. Alexander himself led the cavalry charge that broke the Persian line and sent Darius fleeing to the east. He continued along the coast and captured previously impregnable Tyre after a long and ingenious siege, putting an end to the threat of the Persian navy. He took Egypt with little trouble and was greeted as liberator, pharaoh, and son of the Egyptian god Re. While Alexander was at Tyre, Darius offered him his daughter and his entire empire west of the Euphrates River in exchange for an alliance and an end to the invasion. But Alexander wanted the whole empire and probably whatever lay beyond that.

In the spring of 331 B.C.E. Alexander marched into Mesopotamia. At Gaugamela, near the ancient Assyrian city of Nineveh, he met Darius, ready for a last stand. Once again, Alexander's tactical genius and personal leadership carried the day. The Persians were broken and Darius fled once more. Alexander entered Babylon, again hailed as liberator and king. In January of 330 B.C.E. he came to Persepolis, the Persian capital, which held splendid palaces and the royal treasury. This bonanza ended his financial troubles and put a vast sum of money into circulation, with economic consequences that lasted for centuries. After a stay of several months, Alexander burned Persepolis to dramatize the destruction of the native Persian dynasty and the completion of Hellenic revenge for the earlier Persian invasion of Greece.

Setting off after Darius, Alexander found him, dead, just south of the Caspian Sea. He had been murdered and replaced by his relative Bessus, with the support of the Persian nobility. Alexander soon captured Bessus. This pursuit, and his own great curiosity and desire to see the most distant places, took him to the frontier of India.

Near Samarkand, in the land of the Scythians, he founded the city of Alexandria Eschate ("Furthest Alexandria"), one of the many cities bearing his name that he founded as he traveled. As a part of his grand scheme of amalgamation and con-

CHRONOLOGY

Rise of Macedon

359–336 B.C.E.	Reign of Philip II
338 B.C.E.	Battle of Chaeronea; Philip conquers Greece; founding of League of Corinth
336–323 B.C.E.	Reign of Alexander III, the Great
334 B.C.E.	Alexander Invades Asia
333 B.C.E.	Battle of Issus
331 B.C.E.	Battle of Gaugamela
330 B.C.E.	Fall of Persepolis
327 B.C.E.	Alexander reaches Indus valley
323 B.C.E.	Death of Alexander

quest, he married the Bactrian princess Roxane and enrolled thirty thousand young Bactrians to be trained for his army.

In 327 B.C.E. Alexander took his army through the Khyber Pass to conquer the lands around the Indus River (modern Pakistan). Reducing the region's king, Porus, to vassalage, he pushed on in the hope of reaching the river called Ocean that the Greeks believed encircled the world. Finally his weary men refused to go on. By the spring of 324 B.C.E. the army was back at the Persian Gulf, celebrating Macedonian style with a wild spree of drinking.

DEATH OF ALEXANDER

Alexander was filled with plans for the future: for the consolidation and organization of his empire; for geographic exploration; for new cities, roads, and harbors; perhaps even for further conquests in the West. There is even some evidence that he asked to be deified and worshiped as a god, although we cannot be sure if he really did so or what he had in mind if he did. In June of 323 B.C.E. he was overcome by a fever and died in Babylon at the age of thirty-three. His memory has never faded, and he soon became the subject of myth, legend, and romance. Some have seen in him a man of vision who transcended Greek and Macedonian ethnocentrism and sought to forge human solidarity in a great world state. Others have seen him as a calculating despot, given to drunken brawls, brutality, and murder. The truth is probably in between. Alexander was one of the greatest generals the world has seen; he never lost a battle or failed in a siege, and with a modest army, he conquered a vast empire. He had rare organizational talents, and his plan for creating a multinational empire was the only intelligent way to consolidate his conquests. He established many new cities—seventy, according to tradition—mostly along trade routes. These cities promoted commerce and prosperity and introduced Hellenic civilization into new areas. It is hard to know if even Alexander could have held together the vast new empire he had created, but his death proved that only he had a chance to succeed.

ALEXANDER'S SUCCESSORS

Alexander's sudden death left his enormous empire with no clear, strong heir. His able and loyal Macedonian generals, at first hoping to preserve the empire for the Macedonian royal house, appointed themselves governors of the various provinces of the empire. The conflicting ambitions of these strong-willed men, however, soon led to prolonged warfare among them in which three of the generals were killed and all of the direct members of the Macedonian royal house were either executed or murdered. The murder of Roxane and her son in 310 B.C.E. left the empire with no focus, and in 306 and 305 B.C.E. the surviving governors proclaimed themselves kings of their various holdings. Three of these generals founded dynasties of significance in the spread of Hellenistic culture:

◆ Ptolemy I, 367?–283 B.C.E.; founder of the Thirty-first dynasty in Egypt, the Ptolemies, of whom Cleopatra, who died in 30 B.C.E., was the last

◆ Seleucus I, 358?–280 B.C.E.; founder of the Seleucid dynasty in Mesopotamia

◆ Antigonus I, 382–301 B.C.E.; founder of the Antigonid dynasty in Asia Minor and Macedon

For the first seventy-five years or so after the death of Alexander, the world ruled by his successors enjoyed considerable prosperity. The vast sums of money he and they had put into circulation greatly increased economic activity. Opportunities for service and profit in the East attracted many Greeks and relieved their native cities of some of the pressure of the poor. The opening of vast new territories to Greek trade, the increased demand for Greek products, and the new availability of things Greeks wanted, as well as the conscious policies of the Hellenistic kings, all helped stimulate commerce. The new prosperity, however, was not evenly distributed. The urban Greeks, the Macedonians, and the Hellenized natives who made up the upper and middle classes lived lives of comfort and even luxury, but native peasants did not.

Prosperity initially tempered these distinctions. After a while, however, war, inflation, and a gradual lessening of the positive effects of the introduction of Persian wealth led to economic crisis. The kings bore down heavily on the middle classes, who were skilled in avoiding their responsibilities. The pressure on peasants and city laborers also increased, and they responded by slowing work and even by striking. In Greece, economic pressures brought clashes between rich and poor, demands for the abolition of debt and the redistribution of land, and, on occasion, civil war.

Ongoing warfare and these internal divisions made the Hellenistic kingdoms vulnerable to outside attack, and by the middle of the second century B.C.E. the expanding empire of Rome had absorbed all except Egypt. The two centuries of Hellenistic rule had great and lasting importance, however. They saw the entire eastern Mediterranean coast, Greece, Egypt, Mesopotamia, and the old Persian Empire formed into a single political, economic, and cultural unit.

Hellenistic Culture

Alexander's conquests and the establishment of the successor kingdoms, by ending the central role of the *polis* in Greek life and thought, marked a significant turning point in Greek literature, philosophy, religion, and art.

Deprived of control of their foreign affairs, their important internal arrangements determined by a foreign monarch, the postclassical cities lost the kind of political freedom that was basic to the old outlook. They were cities, perhaps—in a sense, even city-states—but not *poleis*. As time passed they lost their sovereignty, becoming municipalities within military empires. For the most part, the Greeks after Alexander turned inward, away from politics, to address their hopes and fears. The confident, sometimes arrogant, humanism of the fifth century B.C.E. gave way to a kind of resignation to fate, a recognition of helplessness before forces too great for humans to manage.

Philosophy   These developments are noticeable in the changes that overtook the established schools of philosophy as well as in the emergence of two new and influential groups of philosophers, the Epicureans and the Stoics.

Plato's Academy and Aristotle's Lyceum (see Chapter 2) continued to operate, reinforcing Athens' position as the center of philosophical studies. The Lyceum turned gradually away from Aristotle's universal investigations, even from his scientific interests, to become a center chiefly of literary and historical studies. The Academy turned even further from its founder's tradition, adopting the philosophical approach known as skepticism, established by Pyrrho of Elis (ca. 365–275 B.C.E.). The Skeptics thought that nothing could be known and so consoled themselves and their followers by suggesting that nothing mattered. It was easy for them, therefore, to accept conventional morality and the world as it was. The Cynics continued to denounce convention and to advocate a crude life in accordance with nature, which some of them practiced publicly, to the shock and outrage of respectable citizens. Neither of these views had much appeal to the middle-class city dweller of the third century B.C.E., who sought some basis for choosing a way of life now that the *polis* no longer provided one ready-made.

Epicureans Epicurus of Athens (342–271 B.C.E.), who founded a school in that city in 306 B.C.E., formulated a philosophy in keeping with the new mood. The goal of this philosophy was not knowledge but happiness, which Epicurus believed could be achieved through a life based on reason.

Accepting the description of the physical universe proposed by the atomists Democritus and Leucippus (see Chapter 2), the **Epicureans** took sense perception to be the basis of all human knowledge. According to Epicurus, atoms were continually falling through the void and giving off images in direct contact with the senses. These falling atoms could swerve in an arbitrary, unpredictable way to produce the combinations seen in the world. When a person died, the atoms that composed the body dispersed so that the person had no further existence or perception and therefore nothing to fear after death. The gods, according to Epicurus, took no interest in human affairs. This belief amounted to a practical atheism, and the Epicureans were often thought to be atheists.

The purpose of Epicurean physics was to liberate people from the fear of death, the gods, and the supernatural. Epicurean ethics were hedonistic, identifying happiness with pleasure. But *pleasure* for Epicurus was chiefly negative: the absence of pain and trouble. The goal of the Epicureans was *ataraxia*, the condition of being undisturbed, without trouble, pain, or responsibility. To achieve it, one should ideally have sufficient means to withdraw from worldly affairs; Epicurus even advised against marriage and children. He preached a life of genteel, restrained selfishness, which might appeal to intellectuals of means but was not calculated to be widely attractive.

Stoics The Stoic school, established by Zeno of Citium (335–263 B.C.E.) soon after Epicurus began teaching, took its name from the Stoa Poikile, or Painted Portico, in the Athenian Agora, where Zeno and his disciples met.

Like the Epicureans, the **Stoics** sought the happiness of the individual; but unlike Epicurean philosophy, Stoic philosophy was almost indistinguishable from religion. The Stoics believed that god and nature are the same and that humans must live in harmony within themselves and with nature. The guiding principle in nature is divine reason (*logos*), or fire. Every human has a spark of this divinity, and after death it returns to the eternal Divine Spirit. From time to time the world is destroyed by fire, from the ashes of which a new world arises.

Human happiness, according to the Stoics, lies in the virtuous life, lived in accordance with natural law, in which "all actions promote the harmony of the spirit dwelling in the individual man with the will of him who orders the universe."[2]

---

[2] Diogenes Laertius, *Lives of Eminent Philosophers (Zeno)* (Cambridge, MA: Harvard University Press, 1931–1938).

Only the wise—who know what is good, what is evil, and what is "indifferent"—can live such a life. Good and evil are dispositions of the mind or soul. Thus prudence, justice, courage, and temperance are good, whereas folly, injustice, and cowardice are evil. Life, health, pleasure, beauty, strength, wealth, and so on are neutral—morally "indifferent." The source of misery is passion, a disease of the soul and an irrational mental contraction that arises from morally indifferent things. The goal of the wise is apatheia, or freedom from passion.

The Stoics viewed the world as a single large *polis* and all people as children of god. Although they did not forbid political activity, and many Stoics were politically active, they believed the usual subjects of political argument to be indifferent. With their striving for inner harmony and a life lived in accordance with the Divine Will, their fatalistic attitude, and their goal a form of apathy, the Stoics fit the post-Alexandrian world well. The spread of Stoicism eased the creation of a new political system that relied on the docile submission, not the active participation, of the governed.

LITERATURE

The literary center of the Hellenistic world in the third and second centuries B.C.E. was Alexandria, Egypt. There, Egypt's Hellenistic rulers, the Ptolemies, had founded the museum—a great research institute where royal funds supported scientists and scholars—and a library with almost half a million books. The library housed much of the great body of past Greek literature, most of which has since been lost. Alexandrian scholars had what they judged to be the best works copied, editing and criticizing them from the point of view of language, form, and content, and writing biographies of the authors. It is to this work that we owe the preservation of most of what remains to us of ancient literature.

The scholarly atmosphere of Alexandria stimulated the study of history and its ancillary discipline, chronology. Eratosthenes (ca. 275–195 B.C.E.) developed a chronology of important events since the Trojan War, and others undertook similar tasks. Contemporaries of Alexander, such as Ptolemy I (d. 284 B.C.E.), Aristobulus, and Nearchus, wrote apparently sober, factual accounts of his career. The fragments we have of the work of most Hellenistic historians suggest that they emphasized sensational and biographical detail over the rigorous, impersonal analysis characteristic of Thucydides.

ARCHITECTURE AND SCULPTURE

The Hellenistic monarchies greatly increased the opportunities open to architects and sculptors. Money was plentiful, rulers sought outlets for conspicuous display, new cities needed to be built and beautified, and the well-to-do created an increasing demand for objects of art. New cities were

One of the masterpieces of Hellenistic sculpture, the *Laocoön*. This is a Roman copy. According to legend, Laocoön was a priest who warned the Trojans not to take the Greeks' wooden horse within their city. This sculpture depicts his punishment. Great serpents sent by the goddess Athena, who was on the side of the Greeks, devoured Laocoön and his sons before the horrified people of Troy.

Direzione Generale Musei Vaticani

usually laid out on the grid plan introduced in the fifth century B.C.E. by Hippodamus of Miletus. Temples were built on the classical model, and the covered portico, or *stoa*, became a very popular addition to Hellenistic agoras.

Reflecting the cosmopolitan nature of the Hellenistic world, leading sculptors accepted commissions wherever they were attractive. The result was a certain uniformity, although Alexandria, Rhodes, and the kingdom of Pergamum in Asia Minor developed distinctive styles. In general, Hellenistic sculpture continued the trend that emerged in the fourth century B.C.E. toward the sentimental, emotional, and realistic and away from the balanced tension and idealism of the fifth century B.C.E. The characteristics of Hellenistic sculpture are readily apparent in the *Laocoön*, carved at Rhodes in the second century B.C.E.

MATHEMATICS AND SCIENCE

Among the most spectacular intellectual accomplishments of the Hellenistic Age were those in mathematics and science. Indeed, Alexandrian scholars were responsible for most of the scientific

knowledge available to the West until the scientific revolution of the sixteenth and seventeenth centuries C.E. (See Document, "Plutarch Cites Archimedes and Hellenistic Science.")

Euclid's *Elements* (written early in the third century B.C.E.) is still the foundation for courses in plane and solid geometry. Archimedes of Syracuse (ca. 287–212 B.C.E.), who also made advances in geometry, established the theory of the lever in mechanics and invented hydrostatics.

Advances in mathematics, when applied to Babylonian astronomical tables available to Hellenistic scholars, spurred great progress in astronomy. As early as the fourth century Heraclides of Pontus (ca. 390–310 B.C.E.) had argued that Mercury and Venus circulate around the sun and not the Earth. He appears to have made other suggestions leading in the

A page from *On Floating Bodies*. Archimedes' work was covered over by a 10th century manuscript, but ultraviolet radiation reveals the original text and drawings underneath.

©2004 Christie's Images, Inc.

DOCUMENT   Plutarch Cites Archimedes and Hellenistic Science

Archimedes (ca. 287–212 B.C.E. was one of the great mathematicians and physicists of antiquity. He was a native of Syracuse in Sicily and a friend of its king. Plutarch discusses him in the following selection and reveals much about the ancient attitude toward applied science.

> ◆ What does this account reveal about the Greek attitude toward the mechanical arts? Why would Archimedes consider intellectual speculation to be superior to practical knowledge? Do you think Plutarch shared this view?

Archimedes, however, in writing to King Hiero, whose friend and near relation he was, had stated that given the force, any given weight might be moved, and even boasted, we are told, relying on the strength of demonstration, that if there were another earth, by going into it he could remove this. Hiero being struck with amazement at this, and entreating him to make good this problem by actual experiment, and show some great weight moved by a small engine, he fixed accordingly upon a ship of burden out of the king's arsenal, which could not be drawn out of the dock without great labour and many men; and, loading her with many passengers and a full freight, sitting himself the while far off, with no great endeavour, but only holding the head of the pulley in his hand and drawing the cords by degrees [he lifted the ship] … Yet Archimedes possessed so high a spirit, so profound a soul, and such treasures of scientific knowledge, that though these inventions had now obtained him the renown of more than human sagacity, he yet would not deign to leave behind him any commentary or writing on such subjects; but, repudiating as sordid and ignoble the whole trade of engineering, and every sort of art that lends itself to mere use and profit, he placed his whole affection and ambition in those purer speculations where there can be no reference to the vulgar needs of life. …

From Plutarch, "Marcellus," in *Lives of the Noble Grecians and Romans*, trans. by John Dryden, rev. by A. H. Clough (New York: Random House, n.d.), pp. 376–378.

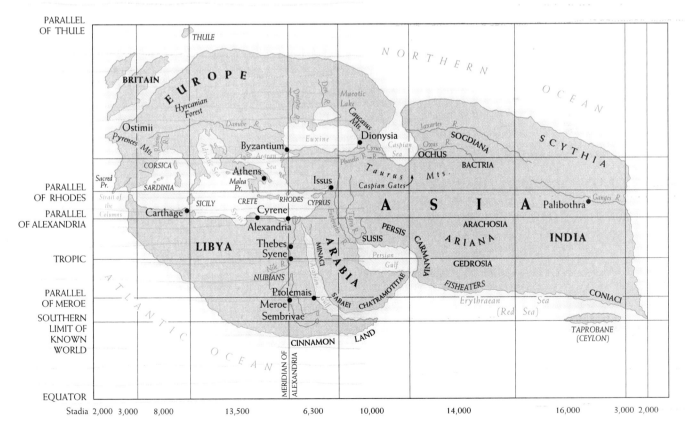

MAP 3–8 The World According to Eratosthenes.   Eratosthenes of Alexandria (ca. 275–195 B.C.E.) was a Hellenistic geographer. His map, reconstructed here, was remarkably accurate for its time. The world was divided by lines of "latitude" and "longitude," thus anticipating our global divisions.

direction of a **heliocentric theory** of the universe. It was Aristarchus of Samos (ca. 310–230 B.C.E.), however, who asserted that the sun, along with the other fixed stars, did not move and that the Earth revolved around the sun in a circular orbit and rotated on its axis while doing so. The heliocentric theory, however, did not take hold. It ran contrary not only to the traditional view codified by Aristotle, but also to what seemed to be common sense. And, of course, planetary orbits are not circular. Hipparchus of Nicaea (b. ca. 190 B.C.E.) constructed an ingenious and complicated geocentric model of the universe that did a good job of accounting for the move-

ments of the sun, the moon, and the planets. Ptolemy of Alexandria (second century C.E.) adopted Hipparchus's system with a few improvements, and it remained dominant until the work of Copernicus, in the sixteenth century C.E.

Hellenistic scientists made progress in mapping the Earth as well as the sky. Eratosthenes of Cyrene (ca. 275–195 B.C.E.) accurately calculated the circumference of the Earth and wrote a treatise on geography based on mathematical and physical reasoning and the reports of travelers. Eratosthenes' map (see Map 3–8) was in many ways more accurate than a later one, created by Ptolemy, which became standard during the Middle Ages.

Summary

The Parthenon.

Early Greece   Greek civilization is divided into several periods. In the Minoan and Mycenaean ages, the Greek states were ruled by powerful kings supported by elaborate bureaucracies. Invaders from the north destroyed Mycenaean civilization around 1150 B.C.E. By 750 B.C.E., during the archaic period, Greek society took its characteristic form: the *polis* (plural *poleis*), a self-governing city-state. The most important *poleis* were Athens and Sparta. At first governed by land-owning aristocrats, then by tyrants, many *poleis* evolved more democratic forms of government by 500 B.C.E. In an effort to avoid the pressures of overpopulation and land hunger, the Greeks established colonies around the shores of the Mediterranean and Black Seas.

Classical Greece   After defeating two Persian attempts to conquer them in the early fifth century B.C.E., the Greeks entered their golden age. The greatest achievements in art, literature, and philosophy of Classical Greece took place in Athens, where the government was the most democratic seen until modern times. Among the accomplishments of Greek artists, writers, and thinkers were naturalistic sculpture, tragedy and comedy, secular history, and systematic logic, all of which still influence Western art and thought.

Hellenistic Greece   The *polis* went into political and cultural decline after Sparta defeated Athens in the Great Peloponnesian War (435–404 B.C.E.). Macedon under Philip II (r. 359–336 B.C.E.) and Alexander the Great (r. 336–323 B.C.E.) came to dominate first Greece and then all the Near East from Asia Minor to northern India. Alexander's conquest of the Persian Empire spread Greek culture over a wide area and ushered in the Hellenistic era. Hellenistic Greek culture, which was fostered by the kingdoms that succeeded Alexander's empire, was more accessible to outsiders than that of classical Greece. Hellenistic scholars made Greek literature and science available to many different peoples who adopted it as their own. The Romans were particularly impressed. They spread Hellenistic culture across the Mediterranean world and transmitted it to later generations in the West.

Review Questions

1. Describe the Minoan civilization of Crete. How did the later Bronze Age Mycenaean civilization differ from the Minoan civilization in political organization, art motifs, and military posture? How valuable are the Homeric epics as sources of early Greek history?

2. Define the concept of *polis*. What role did geography play in its development, and why did the Greeks consider it a unique and valuable institution?

3. Compare the fundamental political, social, and economic institutions of Athens and Sparta about 500 B.C.E. Why did Sparta develop its unique form of government? What were the main stages in the transformation of Athens from an aristocratic state to a democracy between 600 and 500 B.C.E.?

4. Why did the Greeks and Persians go to war in 490 and 480 B.C.E.? What benefit could the Persians have derived from conquering Greece? Why were the Greeks able to defeat the Persians, and how did they benefit from the victory?

5. How was the Delian League transformed into the Athenian Empire during the fifth century B.C.E.? Did the empire offer any advantages to its subjects? Why was there such resis-tance to Athenian efforts to unify the Greek world in the fifth and fourth centuries B.C.E.?

6. Why did Athens and Sparta come to blows in the Great Peloponnesian War? What was each side's strategy for victory? Why did Sparta win the war?

7. Using examples from art, literature, and philosophy, explain the tension that characterized Greek life and thought in the classical period. How does Hellenistic art differ from that of the classical period?

8. Between 431 and 362 B.C.E. Athens, Sparta, and Thebes each tried to impose hegemony over the city-states of Greece, but none succeeded except for short periods of time. Why did each state fail? How was Philip II of Macedon able to conquer Greece? Where does more of the credit for Philip's success lie: in Macedon's strength, or in the weakness of the Greek city-states? What does your analysis reveal about the components of successful rule?

9. What were the major consequences of Alexander's death? Assess the achievements of Alexander. Was he a conscious promoter of Greek civilization, or just an egomaniac drunk with a lust for conquest?

Key Terms

Acropolis   (p. 92)

agora   (p. 92)

Areopagus   (p. 100)

Delian League   (p. 103)

Epicureans   (p. 119)

heliocentric theory   (p. 122)

Helots   (p. 98)

hoplite phalanx   (p. 93)

The *Iliad* and the *Odyssey*   (p. 89)

logos   (p. 119)

Magna Graecia   (p. 93)

Minoan   (p. 87)

Mycenaean   (p. 89)

Panhellenic   (p. 93)

Peloponnesian War   (p. 105)

Stoics   (p. 119)

symposion   (p. 96)

Documents CD-ROM

Greece and the Hellenistic World

4.1 Homer: The Iliad

4.2 Empires and Military Glory: Herodotus Relates the Story of Thermopylae

4.3 Thucydides

4.4 From Confederacy to Empire: Thucydides

4.5 The City-State of Sparta

4.6 The First Philippic: A Great Orator Warns of Macedonian Imperialsm

4.7 The figure of Alexander

NOTE: *To learn more about the topics in this chapter, see the Suggested Readings at the end of the book.*

4

Iran, India, and Inner Asia to 200 C.E.

 Polychrome glazed brick frieze depicting archers of the royal bodyguard from the palace of the Achaemenid king Darius at Susa (522–486 B.C.E.). The sumptuous palace was built by craftsmen from Egypt, Babylon, Greece, and Asia Minor.
Corbis–N.Y.

GLOBAL PERSPECTIVE

The Indo-Iranian World in Antiquity

By the second century C.E., the Indo-Iranian world had developed imperial governments with power and influence far surpassing those of any before them. In and of themselves, such empires do not necessarily equate with what we call "civilizations"—that is, societies characterized by cities, literate culture, technological sophistication, specialized division of labor, and complex social and political structures. Yet they mark the security and wealth that are necessary for civilization. This was clearly the case in the empires of the Achaemenids and Mauryans, which are discussed in this chapter. Developments in these empires paralleled those in other regions with which the Indo-Iranian world was in contact via trade. There Greek, Hellenistic, and Roman Empires, like the Han dynasty of China, provided contexts in which civilization could flourish and spread. Moreover, centralized governments like those of the Achaemenids and Mauryans were able to build the infra-

structures and secure the peace necessary for contacts among civilizations. For example, the Mauryans constructed an excellent road system that subsequently became the route for Buddhism's diffusion to East and Central Asia at the same time that it was declining in India.

In Asia this was also an era in which influential, lasting religious traditions came of age. Some spread to and took root in cultures far from their regions of origin—the Christian, Buddhist, Confucian, and even Judaic and Hindu traditions, for example. Others, such as Zoroastrianism, never attracted a wide following in many areas outside of their homelands. Nonetheless, Zoroastrianism was a religion especially attractive to merchants, who carried it throughout Central Asia in their travels along the old Silk Road. It won some converts among other merchants from elsewhere in Asia and, more importantly, it influenced in subtle ways other religions developing in Asia and Middle East, including Christianity, Islam and Buddhism.

In this period, another important development for the history of civilizations was an increase in cross-cultural contact,

epitomized by the Hellenizing conquests of Alexander the Great. The network of roads that spanned Inner Asia made this region a cradle of syncretism in which travelers from east and west met and exchanged ideas as well as trade goods.

The Central Asian periphery of Iran and India especially provided the great meeting ground of languages, customs, ideas, arts, and religious practices among settled peoples inhabitants of the steppe. In later centuries, Iranian and Indian cultures continued to develop distinctive, largely independent forms, and Central Asia remained a fragmented but fertile cultural melting pot. Yet developments in antiquity set in motion cross-cultural exchanges that continued apace in later centuries. In this period Rome, Iran, and India (less so China) experienced increased contact with other cultures and increased influence from abroad. These contacts and influences were manifested in new, governmental structures, technological innovations, specialized skills and arts, and religious ideas.

THINK AHEAD

◆ In what ways did the imperial governments that developed in Iran and India during this period contribute to civilization in these regions?

◆ Why did this period see a significant increase in cross-cultural contacts? How were these contacts manifested?

FROM THE MEDITERRANEAN TO CHINA, IN THE PERIOD from about 600 B.C.E. to 200 C.E., centralized empires flourished on an unprecedented scale—a development in which Iran and India preceded both China and the Roman West. Well before the Qin unification (221–207 B.C.E.) or the Han dynasty (202 B.C.E.–9 C.E.) in China, and long before *imperium* replaced the republic in Rome, imperial states developed in Iran. First the Elamites, in the third and the second millennia B.C.E., built regional empires centered on their homeland of Susa (modern Khuzistan) in lowland southwestern Iran. Then the Achaemenids (ca. 539–330 B.C.E.), an Aryan dynasty from southwestern Iran, created the greatest empire yet seen, based in Babylonia and Iran. Two centuries later the Mauryans, a northeast Indian dynasty centered in the Ganges basin, founded the first great Indian empire (ca. 321–185 B.C.E.). Both of these empires, like their later Chinese and Roman counterparts, built sophisticated bureaucracies, professional armies, and strong communication systems. They also contributed to new cultural, political, and religious developments in their domains.

Three characteristics mark this period. First, the era saw sustained contact among the major centers of culture from the Mediterranean to China. Large-scale empires created new markets for diverse goods, both material and human (such as slaves, soldiers, and artisans); more secure trade routes; new impetus for both diplomacy and conquest; and a wider interest in the world.

Alexander the Great's conquest (334–323 B.C.E.) of the Persian Empire and the regions eastward to North India provided the impetus for the era's second characteristic—dramatic increased contact among diverse cultures, races, and religious traditions. Although Alexander's empire was ephemeral, his conquests ended the Achaemenid dynasty and allowed the rising Mauryan power to extend across North India. The Hellenes and steppe peoples of northeastern Iran and Central (Inner) Asia, who ruled first post-Alexandrine Iran and then post-Mauryan India down to the third century C.E., inherited a much wider world than those of their original homelands.

A third characteristic of this period was the rise of major religious traditions that would influence history from Africa to China. The evolution of Judaism in the Second Temple (rebuilt 520–515 B.C.E.) and early Diaspora (second century C.E.) periods, and the rise and spread of Christianity and diverse Hellenistic cults profoundly affected the history of the Mediterranean and western Asia (see Chapters 2, 3, and 6). This period saw in China the rise of Han Confucianism and classical Daoist thought (see Chapters 2 and 7); in Iran the growth of the Zoroastrian tradition; in India, the emergence of an identifiable Hindu tradition and growth of the Buddhist movement; and in East Asia generally, the spread of Buddhist traditions, especially into Southeast Asia and China.

IRAN

"Iran" designates the vast expanse of southwest Asia bounded by the Caspian Sea and Jaxartes (Syr Darya) River to the north and northeast, the Indus valley to the southeast, the Arabian Sea and Gulf to the south, the Tigris-Euphrates basin to the west, and Armenia and the Caucasus to the northwest (see Map 4–1). The heart of this region is the vast Iranian plateau, bounded on all sides by mountain ranges, notably the Hindu Kush, the Sulaiman chain, the Zagros, and the Elburz. In its central reaches, the plateau contains two large, uninhabitable salt deserts whose desolation is a barrier to travel even more formidable than most of the great mountain ranges.

Early (and later) peoples in Iran clustered wherever rainfall or ground water was plentiful and communication easiest. The key areas were the slopes and lowlands between the Zagros, Persis, Media, Hyrcania, and Parthia. The great Asian trade routes put Iran at the heart of east-west interchange (see Map 4–3).

Ancient History

THE ELAMITES

The Elamites, a non-Semitic-speaking people, built a flourishing civilization in the southwestern lowlands and adjacent highlands of Susa (Elam, later Ahwaz or Khuzistan) and the neighboring regions between the Zagros and the Gulf. Even though we have tablets, monumental inscriptions, and brick imprints from Elamite remains, scholars have not determined to which language group Elamite belongs. It did, however, long outlive the Elamite state, since it was still recognized as one of three official languages in the Persian Empire of the Achaemenids. The Elamites were repeatedly at war with the great Mesopotamian dynasties of the Sumerians, Babylonians, and Assyrians from around 2700 B.C.E. until the end of the second millennium B.C.E. Their apogee came in the so-called "middle Elamite" period in the twelfth century B.C.E. While we know of Elamite attempts to contest the Assyrian power of the latter seventh and early sixth centuries, Assyrian armies set upon the Neo-Elamite rulers of the day from 692 until their complete destruction by Asshurbanipal's troops in 639, when their cities were ransacked and even their soil sown with salt.

THE IRANIANS

The forefathers of the Iranian dynasts who would eventually build cities and palaces again at Susa as well in the Assyrian heartlands were Aryans. The oldest texts in ancient Persian dialects show that Aryan peoples settled on the Iranian plateau around 1100 B.C.E. Like their Vedic or Indo-Aryan relations in North India, these peoples were pastoralists—horse breeders—from the Eurasian or Central Asian steppes. The most prominent of these ancient Iranians were the Medes and the Persians. By the eighth century B.C.E., they had spread around the deserts of the plateau to settle and control its western and southwestern reaches, to which they gave their names, Media and Persis (later Fars).

The Medes developed a tribal confederacy in western Iran. By 612 B.C.E., they and the Neo-Babylonians had defeated the mighty Assyrians and broken their hold on the Fertile Crescent. The rise of Persian power under the Achaemenid clan from the seventh century B.C.E. led to the end of Median supremacy on the Iranian plateau by the time of the Achaemenid ruler Cyrus the Great around 550 B.C.E. Many of the institutions that developed in the ensuing empire were apparently based on Median practices, which the Medes in turn had often drawn from Babylonian and Assyrian models. Part of the genius of the Achaemenids' unparalleled imperial success lay in their ability to use existing institutions to build their own state and administer far-flung dominions well.

ANCIENT IRANIAN RELIGION

We know more about religious traditions of ancient Iran than about other aspects of its culture because our only pre-Achaemenid texts are religious. They suggest that old Iranian culture and religion were similar to those of the Vedic Aryans. The importance of water, fire, sacrifice, and the cow, as well as the names and traits of major divine beings and religious concepts, all have counterparts in Vedic texts. The emphasis was on moral order, or the "Right"—that is, *asha* or *arta* (equivalent to the Vedic *rta*; see Chapter 1). The supreme heavenly deity was Ahura (the equivalent of the Vedic Varuna) Mazda,

◁ **A Fifth-Century** B.C.E. **Achaemenid Amphora.** This one from southwestern Iran has double tube-handles.
Gisela Croon/Bildarchiv Preussischer Kulturbesitz.

the "Wise Lord." However, ancient Iranian religion in the early second millennium was far from monolithic. Regional cultural variations were substantial.

ZOROASTER AND THE ZOROASTRIAN TRADITION

The first person who stands out in Iranian history was not Cyrus, the famous founder of the Achaemenid Empire, but the great prophet-reformer of Iranian religion, Zarathushtra, commonly known in the West by the Greek version of his name, Zoroaster. Until recently, the consensus was that Zoroaster lived in northeastern Iran from 628 to 551 B.C.E., but today most scholars accept a revised dating for him of no later than 1000 B.C.E. Whatever his dates, it is clear from his hymns that, not unlike the Hebrew prophets, the Buddha, and Confucius, Zoroaster presented a message of moral reform in an age of materialism, political opportunism, and ethical indifference. (See Document, "A Hymn of Zoroaster About the Two Spirits of Good and Evil.") While he is said to have gained the protection of an eastern Iranian tribal leader, his preaching probably did not become an official "state" creed during his lifetime.

Zoroaster was evidently trained as a priest in the old Iranian tradition, but his hymns, or *Gathas*, reflect his new religious vision. In these hymns we glimpse the values of a peasant-pastoralist society that was growing up alongside early urban trade centers in northeastern Iran. These values—for example, the sacralization of cow and ox or honest dealings in trade—contrasted with those of the nomadic warrior peoples of the steppes. Zoroaster's personal experience of Ahura Mazda as the supreme deity led him to reinterpret the old sacrificial fire as Ahura's symbol. He called on people to abandon worship of all lesser deities, or *daevas*, whom he identified as demons, not gods. He exhorted his people to turn from the "Lie" (*druj*) to the "Truth" (*asha*). He warned of a "final reckoning," when the good would be rewarded with "future glory" but the wicked with "long-lasting darkness, ill food, and wailing."

DOCUMENT   A Hymn of Zoroaster About the Two Spirits of Good and Evil

The focus of Zoroaster's reform was the supremacy of Ahura Mazda (the "Wise Lord") over all the deities of the Iranian pantheon. He is pictured in the hymns, or Gathas, as the greatest of the ahuras, the divinities associated with the good. The world is seen in terms of a moral dualism of good and evil, which is represented on the divine plane in the twin spirits created by Ahura Mazda, both of whom are given the freedom to choose the Truth or the Lie. The "Very Holy [Spirit]" chose Truth ("Righteousness"), and the "Evil [spirit]" (Angra Mainyu, or Ahriman), chose the evil of "the Lie." Similarly, humans can choose the side with which they will ally themselves—the good spirit and the ahuras, *or the evil spirit and the* daevas *("the false gods"). This selection is from a gatha in Yasna ("Worship"), section 45 of the main Zoroastrian holy book, the Avesta.*

◆ What lesson or values does this passage teach? Is there a conflict between the seeming omnipotence ascribed to Ahura Mazda and the existence of Ahriman, the Evil Spirit? How does the sharp choice offered here compare to the Buddha's Middle Path (see "The 'Turning of the Wheel of *Dharma*': Basic Teachings of the Buddha," in Chapter 2)?

(1) Then shall I speak, now give ear and hearken, both you who seek from near and you from far ... (2) Then shall I speak of the two primal Spirits of existence, of whom the Very Holy thus spoke to the Evil One: 'Neither our thoughts nor teachings nor wills, neither our choices nor words nor acts, not our inner selves nor our souls agree.' (3) Then shall I speak of the foremost (doctrine) of this existence, which Mazda the Lord, He with knowledge, declared to me. Those of you who do not act upon this manthra, even as I shall think and speak it, for them there shall be woe at the end of life. (4) Then shall I speak of the best things of this existence. I know Mazda who created it in accord with truth to be the Father of active Good Purpose. And his daughter is Devotion of good action. The all-seeing Lord is not to be deceived. (5) Then shall I speak of what the Most Holy One told me, the word to be listened to as best for men. Those who shall give for me hearkening and heed to Him, shall attain wholeness and immortality. Mazda is Lord through acts of the Good Spirit ... (8) Him shall I seek to turn to us by praises of reverence, for truly I have now seen with my eyes (the House) of Good Purpose, and of good act and deed, having known through Truth Him who is Lord Mazda. Then let us lay up supplications to Him in the House of Song. (9) Him shall I seek to requite for us with good purpose, Him who left to our will (the choice between) holy and unholy. May Lord Mazda by His power make us active for prospering our cattle and men, through the fair affinity of good purpose with truth. (10) Him shall I seek to glorify for us with sacrifices of devotion, Him who is known in the soul as Lord Mazda; for He has promised by His truth and good purpose that there shall be wholeness and immortality within His kingdom (khshathra), strength and perpetuity within His house.

From Mary Boyce, ed. and trans., *Textual Sources for the Study of Zoroastrianism* (Manchester, U.K.: Manchester University Press, 1984), p. 36.

By the mid-fourth century B.C.E., the Zoroastrian reform had spread into western as well as eastern Iran. The quasi-monotheistic worship of Ahura Mazda, the Wise Lord, was rapidly accommodated to the veneration of older Iranian gods by the interpretation of these deities as secondary gods or even manifestations of the Wise Lord himself. The old Iranian priestly clan of the *Magi* may have integrated Zoroastrian ideas and texts into their older, polytheistic tradition, thus becoming architects of a reformed tradition. Certainly the name "magi" was later used for the priests of the tradition that we call "Zoroastrian."

Zoroastrianism probably influenced not only Jewish, Christian, and Muslim ideas of angels, devils, the messiah, the last judgment, and afterlife, but also Buddhist concepts as well. Zoroastrianism was wiped out as a major force in Iran by the spread of Islam in the seventh and eighth centuries C.E. and later. However, its tradition continues in the faith and practice of the Parsis, a community today of perhaps 100,000 people, most of whom live in western India.

The First Iranian Empire (550–330 B.C.E.)

THE ACHAEMENIDS

In October 1971 C.E., the Iranian monarch Muhammad Reza Shah (r. 1941–1979) hosted a lavish pageant amid the ruins of the ancient Persian capital of Persepolis to commemorate the 2,500-year anniversary of the beginning, under Cyrus the Great, of "the imperial glory of Iran." The shah felt his modern secularist regime had re-created this traditional Iranian glory since the 1950s. Although the Iranian revolution of 1978 ended his heavy-handed attempts to kindle a secular Iranian nationalism, modern Iran does have a dual heritage: that of the rich Iranian Islamic culture and that of the far older, Indo-Iranian, Zoroastrian, and imperial culture of pre-Islamic Iran.

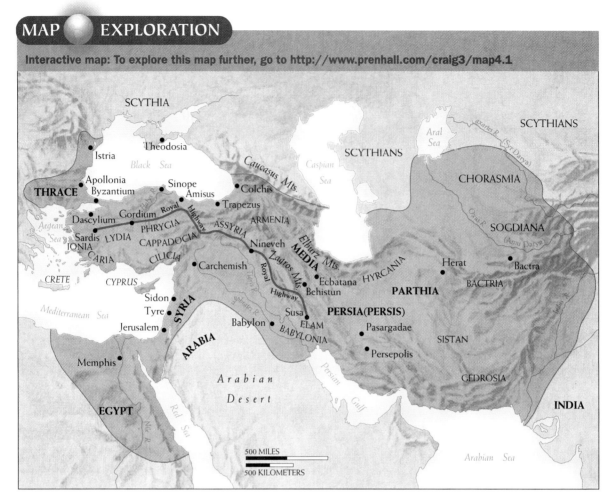

Interactive map: To explore this map further, go to http://www.prenhall.com/craig3/map4.1

MAP 4–1 The Achaemenid Persian Empire.   The empire created by Cyrus had reached its fullest extent under Darius when Persia attacked Greece in 490 B.C.E. It extended from India to the Aegean, and even into Europe, encompassing the lands formerly ruled by Egyptians, Hittites, Babylonians, and Assyrians.

The latter began with the Persian dynasty of the Achaemenids.

Achaemenid regional power in southwestern Iran (Persis) went back at least to Cyrus I (d. 600 B.C.E.), but the rise of Iran as a major civilization and empire is usually dated from the reign of his famous grandson, Cyrus the Great (559–530 B.C.E.). The empire Cyrus the Great founded was anticipated in many ways by the loosely controlled empire of his predecessors, the Medes, in Anatolia (Asia Minor) and western Iran (and the Elamites to the southwest, in and beyond the Zagros). Cyrus defeated the last Median king about 550 B.C.E. He then subdued northern Assyria, Cilicia, and the kingdom of Lydia, near the Aegean coast of Asia Minor. Next, Cyrus swiftly defeated the last Babylonian king.

This event, in 539 B.C.E., symbolizes the beginning of the Achaemenid Empire, for it joined Mesopotamia and Iran for the first time under one rule—a unity that would last for centuries (see Map 4–1). One of its results was the end of the Babylonian Exile of the Jews, for Cyrus allowed the Jews to return to their Holy Land and rebuild their temple in Jerusalem (see Chapter 2). Cyrus subsequently extended Achaemenid rule in the east before he was killed fighting steppe tribes there. His most notable legacy to his heirs was not only his ability to conquer, but also his readiness to rule through local elites and institutions rather than impose new political superstructures.

Early in his career, Cyrus had moved his capital from Susa to the old Median capital of Ecbatana (later Hamadan). He and his successors, in what was really a tribal confederation, adopted Median administrative practice, and many Medes served the new state. Thus the Bible and other sources refer to the Achaemenid rulers as the "Medes and Persians." What the Medes had set in motion, Cyrus and his heirs consolidated and expanded, so that the new Iranian Empire became the most extensive the world had ever seen.

Cyrus's successor, Cambyses (r. 529–522 B.C.E.) added Egypt to the Achaemenid dominions. His brief reign was followed by a suc-

Persepolis. The ruins of the famous royal complex at Persepolis, begun ca. 518 B.C.E. The foundation of the treasury is in the foreground; part of the recently restored women's quarters is visible on the left; and the tall pillars of the main audience hall stand in the rear.
Giraudon/Art Resource, N.Y.

cession struggle and civil war from Babylonia to the Hindu Kush. The winner, Darius I (r. 521–486 B.C.E.), enjoyed a prosperous reign in which the Achaemenid Empire reached its greatest extent—from Egypt northeast to southern Russia and Sogdiana (Transoxiana) and east to the Indus valley. Susa and Persepolis were Darius's principal capitals. (See Document, "Inscription of Darius I: Building the Royal Palace at Susa.")

The next five rulers (486–359 B.C.E.) fared less well, and after 478 B.C.E., the Persians found themselves militarily inferior to the Greeks. Although they kept the divided Greeks at bay by clever diplomacy, Greek cultural influence grew in Asia Minor. Egyptian rebellions, succession struggles, conflict with Scythian steppe tribes, and poor leadership now plagued Achaemenid rule. Much might have been recouped by the able, energetic Artaxerxes III (r. 359–338 B.C.E.), but he was poisoned in a palace coup just as Philip of Macedon was unifying the Greeks. Philip's son Alexander was to end Achaemenid rule.

THE ACHAEMENID STATE

Perhaps the greatest achievement of the Achaemenids was the relative stability of their rule. To justify their sovereignty—and the title of **Shahanshah**, "king of kings"—they claimed that Ahura Mazda had entrusted them with universal sovereignty. An inscription of Darius reads: "… I am king by the will of Ahuramazda."[1] Other inscriptions reflect the sense—underscored by court ceremony and impressive architecture—that a ruler earned Ahura Mazda's trust through justice and uprightness. The ruler acted as priest and sacrificer in the court rituals; a special royal fire that burned throughout his reign symbolized his role as cosmic ruler. The talents and success of the early Achaemenids strengthened their claim to divinely sanctioned royal status.

The Achaemenids, however, were tolerant of other cultural and religious traditions in ways earlier empires had not been. In part, the sheer size of their realms demanded it, but the

contrast to later Roman imperial practice is striking. Even Darius's emphasis on Zoroastrian ritual and theology did not bring forced conformity or conversion to the "state cult," as his lenient treatment of the Jews shows (see Chapter 2).

The Achaemenids built a powerful army, but much of their success lay in their administrative abilities and willingness to borrow from predecessors like the Medes or Babylonians. Most of their leaders were adept at conciliation and worked to establish what has been termed a *pax Achaemenica*.[2] They were able to maintain continuity as their state evolved from a tribal confederation into a sophisticated monarchy. The state of Cyrus, with its largely Iranian troops and tribute system of revenue, was replaced by a monarchy supported by a noble class, professional armies (led by loyal Persian elite troops), an administrative system of provinces ruled by governors called **satraps**, and fixed-yield levies of revenue.

---

[1] William W. Malandra, trans., *An Introduction to Ancient Iranian Religion* (Minneapolis: University of Minnesota Press, 1983), p. 50.

[2] Richard N. Frye, *The Heritage of Persia* (New York: New American Library, 1966), p. 110.

DOCUMENT | Inscription of Darius I: Building the Royal Palace at Susa

The Achaemenids, like other ancient rulers before them, used public inscriptions to underscore their accomplishments. These portions of an inscription of Darius were unearthed from the remains of Susa, the first of the two great palace-residences that he built (the second was Persepolis). They tell of his building accomplishments there and show also the extent of Achaemenid power and dominion in its heyday.

◆ Why did Darius build the palace? For what does he want to be remembered? From how large an area did Darius draw the materials for his palace? What political purpose might he have had for using builders and artisans from the diverse nations and peoples that made up his empire?

… This is the palace which I built at Susa. From afar its ornamentation was brought. Downward the earth was dug, until I reached rock in the earth. When the excavation has been made, then rubble was packed down … On that rubble the palace was constructed. And that the earth was dug downward, and that the rubble was packed down, and that the sun dried brick was moulded, the Babylonian people, it did [these tasks]. The cedar timber, this—a mountain by name Lebanon—from there was brought; the Assyrian people … brought it to Babylon; from Babylon the Carians and the Ionians brought it to Susa.

The yak timber was brought from Gandara and from Carmania. The gold was brought from Sardis and from Bactria, which here was wrought. The precious stone lapis-lazuli and carnelian which was wrought here, this was brought from Sogdiana. The precious stone turquois, this was brought from Chorasmia, which was wrought here. The silver and the ebony were brought from Egypt. The ornamentation with which the wall was adorned, that from Ionia was brought. The ivory which was wrought here, was brought from Ethiopia and from Sind and from Arachosia. The stone columns which were here wrought—a village by name Abiradus, in Elam—from there were brought. The stone cutters who wrought stone, these were Ionians and Sardians. The goldsmiths who wrought the gold, these were Medes and Egyptians. The men who wrought the wood, these were Sardians and Egyptians. The men who wrought the baked brick, these were Babylonians. The men who adorned the wall, these were Medes and Egyptians. Saith Darius the king: At Susa a very excellent [work] was [brought to completion]. Me may Ahuramazda protect, and Hystaspes, my father, and my country.

The excellence of Achaemenid administration can also be seen in their communication and propaganda systems. Couriers linked imperial outposts with the heartlands over well-kept highways, which also facilitated rapid troop deployment. Herodotus called the greatest of these highways, from Sardis to Susa, "the King's Road." A network of observers and royal inspectors kept the court abreast of activities outside the capital. An efficient chancery with large archives and numerous scribes served administrative needs. The Achaemenid bureaucracy's adoption of Aramaic, which had become the common language of the Near East under the Assyrians, helped link East and West. Royal proclamations were rapidly and widely distributed, often in several languages. Achaemenid inscriptions reflect a strong emphasis on universal justice through the rule of law.

Strategic capitals in western Iran, such as Ekbatana and Susa, were important to central imperial control. The Achaemenids never had a single fixed capital; they moved the court as needed from one to another of their palaces, whether in Babylon or the Iranian highlands. The *satrapy* divisions usually reflected the borders of former states incorporated into the empire. Although *satraps* were powerful princes in their own right, the power of the "king of kings" held together the diverse provinces and tribute-paying states.

THE ACHAEMENID ECONOMY

Economic life from Greece to India received a substantial boost from Achaemenid success. Although Croesus had introduced a true coin-based monetary system in Lydia (sixth century B.C.E.), the Achaemenids greatly expanded on this system. Coinage was used to pay part of the workers' wages in the construction of Persepolis and displaced in-kind payment altogether under Darius. Coinage stimulated banking operations, which had declined since the heyday of Mesopotamian rule in the previous millennium. Private banking houses arose: Deposits were taken; loans made; checks accepted; leases sold; monopolies secured; and capital invested in property, shipping, canals, and commodities. The Achaemenids taxed diverse sources of income—estates, livestock, mines, trade, and production. They regulated wages and established money-goods equivalences (thus a sheep might be set at three shekels).

Agriculture remained the basic industry and normal occupation of free men. Serfs and slaves formed most of the labor

OVERVIEW   Iranian and Indian Empires

From 600 B.C.E. to 200 C.E. a series of centralized empires arose on the Iranian plateau and in India. These states built sophisticated bureaucracies, professional armies, and effective communication systems. They also contributed to new cultural, religious, and social developments.

Achaemenid Empire, 539–330 B.C.E.	Founded by Cyrus the Great (r. 559–530 B.C.E.), it was based in Iran and ran from Egypt to northern India. Provided a tolerant, stable, and prosperous cosmopolitan environment that paved the way for the eventual Hellenization of western Asia under Alexander the Great and his successors.
Mauryan Empire, 321–185 B.C.E.	The first Indian empire, it stretched from northern India to the Deccan. Its greatest ruler was Ashoka (r. ca. 272–232 B.C.E.), who converted to Buddhism. The Mauryans helped spread Buddhism, developed strong administrative and communications systems that helped give India a sense of unity, established contact with the West, and fostered the growth of cities and the flourishing of art and literature.
Seleucid Empire, 312–125 B.C.E.	A successor state to Alexander's Empire. The Seleucids controlled much of the Near East from the Mediterranean to northern India for much of this period. By fusing Greek with Persian cultural and political elements, the Seleucids did much to spread Hellenistic culture throughout western Asia.

force. Work animals were bred, bees colonized, and grapes, wheat, barley, and olives cultivated widely. Where water was scarce, the government dug irrigation canals. Rulers such as Darius mandated the transfer of fruit trees and other plants to different parts of the empire; thus from the east pistachio cultivation came to Aleppo, rice to Mesopotamia, and sesame to Egypt.

Fishing, timbering, and mining were key elements in the economy. Some industries, such as those for producing cloth-ing, shoes, and furniture, developed alongside the older luxury crafts for the wealthy. The unprecedented volume of trade in Achaemenid times included large quantities of everyday household products that were now widely exchanged where earlier only luxury goods had been traded over long distances. Goods from India crossed paths with those of the Rhine valley; it was a prosperous era, marked by expanding markets—into southern Europe especially—and increased foreign travel, exploration, and investment (see Map 4–3).

The empire's overall stability for over two centuries testifies to the quality of the *pax Achaemenica*. This stable environment laid the cosmopolitan basis for the coming Hellenization of western Asia in the wake of Alexander's conquests.

CHRONOLOGY

Iran to the Third Century C.E.

ca. 2000–1000 B.C.E.	Indo-Iranian (Aryan) tribes move south into the Punjab of India and the Iranian plateau
ca. 628–551 B.C.E. (or before 1000 B.C.E.?)	Traditional dating of the life of Zoroaster, probably in eastern/northeastern Iran (perhaps originally in Herat?)
559–530 B.C.E.	Reign of Cyrus the Great, Persian Achaemenid ruler
539–330 B.C.E.	Achaemenid Empire
331–330 B.C.E.	Alexander (d. 323 B.C.E.) conquers Achaemenid Empire
312–ca. 125 B.C.E.	Seleucid rule in part of Achaemenid realm
ca. 248 B.C.E.– 224 C.E.	Parthian Empire of the Arsacids in Iran, Babylonia

INDIA

Large-scale imperial expansion came much later to the South Asian, or Indian, subcontinent than to Iran. A cultural and religious heritage going back to the Aryan invaders of North India left its mark on the subsequent history of the vast and diverse subcontinent, despite the many languages and regional traditions that have persisted there. Only rarely, however, has the subcontinent seen political unity among even a bare majority of its inhabitants. Today's division into India, Pakistan, and Bangladesh is just the most recent. Only four times has much of the whole come under one rule: in the Mauryan, Gupta, Mughal, and British imperial epochs. We look now at the first of these.

The First Indian Empire (321–185 B.C.E.)

Alexander the Great conquered the Achaemenids' northwest Indian provinces of Gandhara and the Indus valley in 327 B.C.E. The conquest had little or no impact on the Indian subcontinent except in Gandhara, where his passage opened the way for the increased Greek and Indian cultural interpenetration that developed under the Mauryan emperors of India. Only with the Mauryans was much of North India incorporated into the first true Indian empire.

POLITICAL BACKGROUND

The basis for empire in North India was the rise of regional states and commercial towns between the seventh and fourth centuries B.C.E. The most powerful of these were the monarchies of the Ganges plains. North and northwest of the plains, in the Himalayan foothills and in the Punjab and beyond, tribal republics were more common. The Buddha and Mahavira came from two of these republics (see Chapter 2), although both spent much of their lives in the two most powerful Gangetic monarchies, Kosala and Magadha. In their lifetimes, Magadha emerged as the strongest Indian state under King Bimbisara (d. 493 B.C.E.).

Bimbisara was, as far as we know, the first king to build (possibly on the Achaemenid model) a centralized state strong enough for imperial expansion. He emphasized good roads, able administrators, and fair agricultural taxes. His son annexed Kosala, giving Magadha control of the Ganges trade. Consequently, Magadha remained preeminent in the Ganges basin, even under less competent successors. A new dynasty, the Nandas, replaced the last of these on the Magadhan throne in the mid–fourth century B.C.E., but the rise of the Mauryan clan soon dashed their imperial hopes.

THE MAURYANS

Chandragupta Maurya (r. ca. 321–297 B.C.E.), an adventurer who seized Magadha and the Ganges basin in about 324 B.C.E., established the first true Indian empire and made Pataliputra (modern Patna) his capital (see Map 4–2). He next marched westward into the vacuum created by Alexander's departure (326 B.C.E.) and brought the Indus region and much of west-central India under his control. A treaty with the invading Seleucus (ca. 358–280 B.C.E.), Alexander's successor in Bactria, added Gandhara and Arachosia to his empire. The Greek sources say the treaty (303 B.C.E.) included a marriage alliance, possibly of a Seleucid woman to Chandragupta. Whether or not such a marriage occurred, there was much Seleucid–Mauryan contact thereafter.

Chandragupta's fame as the first Indian empire builder is rivaled by that of his Brahman minister, Kautilya. Known as the "Indian Machiavelli," Kautilya may have been the actual architect of Mauryan rule. However, he probably did not write the most famous Indian treatise on the art of government, the *Arthashastra*, even though it is ascribed to him.

Chandragupta's son and successor, Bindusara (r. ca. 297–272 B.C.E.), conquered the Deccan, the great plateau that covers central India and divides the far south (Tamilnad) from North India. Like his father, he had substantial contact with the Seleucid Greeks, including Antiochus I (r. 297–261 B.C.E.) of Syria, from whom he is said to have requested wine, figs, and a court philosopher.

Ashoka   The third and greatest Mauryan, Ashoka (r. ca. 272–232 B.C.E.), left us numerous rock inscriptions—the first significant Indian written sources after the (still undeciphered) Indus seals. From Ashoka's edicts, we can piece together much of his reign and glimpse his character. In his first years as king, he conquered

◄ **The Lion Capital of Sarnath.** This famous Ashokan column capital was taken by India as its state seal after independence in 1947. It reflects both Persian and Greek influences. Originally the capital stood atop a mighty pillar some 50 feet high; the lions supported a huge stone chakra, the Buddhist "Wheel of the *Dharma*," the symbol of universal law.
Bridgeman-Giraudon/Art Resource, N.Y.

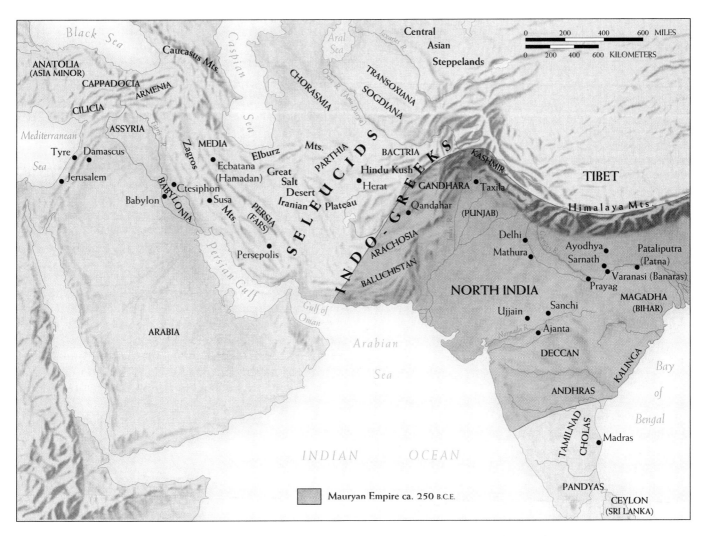

MAP 4–2 Southwest Asia and India ca. 250 b.c.e.   This map shows not only the major cities and regions of greater Iran and the Indian subcontinent, but also the neighboring eastern Mediterranean world. Although the Mediterranean was closely tied to Iran from Achaemenid times onward, its contacts with India in the wake of the conquests of Alexander the Great were many and varied.

Kalinga, the last independent kingdom in North India and the Deccan. He thus extended Mauryan control over the whole subcontinent except the far south.

Apparently revolted by the bloody Kalinga war, Ashoka underwent a religious conversion. Thereafter he pursued the Buddhist Middle Path as his ideal in both personal and state relations. Accordingly, he forsook hunting and meat eating and championed nonviolence (*ahimsa*). He did not abandon all warfare, but he did eschew aggression in favor of "conquest by righteousness" (*dharma*). He sought by moral example to win over others to humanitarian values. In the words of one edict, he looked on his subjects as his "children." His edicts show that he pursued the laity's norm of the Buddhist *dharma*, striving to attain heaven by the merit of good actions. While stressing tolerance for all traditions, he sent envoys abroad to spread the Buddhist teaching. Among his efforts to raise stan-

dards of morality in his realm was the appointment of "*dharma* officials" to investigate public welfare and foster just government. (See Document, "The Edicts of Ashoka.")

Ashoka evidently did ease some burdens imposed on the populace by earlier governments, and he instituted many beneficial public works. However, by the end of his reign, the empire's size hampered effective administration, and under his successors, Mauryan rule disintegrated. Neither Ashoka's Buddhism nor his rejection of aggression was the cause of decline; more likely factors were economic strains and increased bureaucratic corruption, as well as his heirs' inability to claim the personal allegiances he had maintained. After his death local dynasties seized power in many areas.

Ashoka provided the model of the ideal king for later Hindu and Buddhist thought—the *chakravartin*, or universal monarch who rules with righteousness, justice, and wisdom.

In the first of the two following excerpts from Ashokan edicts, the monarch explains his change of heart and conversion to nonviolence after the Kalinga war and states his determination to follow dharma. "The Beloved of the Gods" was the common royal epithet Ashoka used for himself. The second excerpt is from the end of Ashoka's reign and speaks of his efforts to better his and other people's lives by rule according to the dictates of dharma.

◆ What does Ashoka suggest is the role of the monarch? What is his concept of "conquest"? What does he think of those of other faiths and what does he want for them? What reforms does Ashoka propose, and why? Can you reconcile his expressed abhorrence of killing with his words to the forest tribes? How do these edicts compare to other approaches to law, leadership, and government? See, for example, "Hammurabi Creates a Code of Law in Mesopotamia" (Chapter 1), "Legalism" (Chapter 2), "Athenian Democracy: An Unfriendly View" (Chapter 3), and "Machiavelli on Why the Princes of Italy Lose Their States" (Chapter 16).

From the Thirteenth Rock Edict

When the king, Beloved of the Gods and of Gracious Mien, had been consecrated eight years Kalinga was conquered, 150,000 people were deported, 100,000 were killed, and many times that number died. But after the conquest of Kalinga, the Beloved of the Gods began to follow Righteousness [*dharma*], to love Righteousness, and to give instruction in Righteousness. Now the Beloved of the Gods regrets the conquest of Kalinga, for when an independent country is conquered people are killed, they die, or are deported, and that the Beloved of the Gods finds very painful and grievous … The Beloved of the Gods will forgive as far as he can, and he even conciliates the forest tribes of his dominions; but he warns them that there is power even in the remorse of the Beloved of the Gods, and he tells them to reform, lest they be killed.

For all beings the Beloved of the Gods desires security, self-control, calm of mind, and gentleness. The Beloved of the Gods considers that the greatest victory is the victory of Righteousness; and this he has won here [in India] and even five hundred leagues beyond his frontiers in the realm of the Greek king Antiochus, and beyond Antiochus among the four kings Ptolemy, Antigonus, Magas, and Alexander. Even where the envoys of the Beloved of the Gods have not been sent men hear of the way in which he follows and teaches Righteousness, and they too follow it and will follow it. Thus he achieves a universal conquest, and conquest always gives a feeling of pleasure; yet it is but a slight pleasure, for the Beloved of the Gods only looks on that which concerns the next life as of great importance ….

From the Seventh Pillar Edict

In the past kings sought to make the people progress in Righteousness, but they did not progress … And I asked myself how I might uplift them through progress in Righteousness … Thus I decided to have them instructed in Righteousness, and to issue ordinances of Righteousness, so that by hearing them the people might conform, advance in the progress of Righteousness, and themselves make great progress … For that purpose many officials are employed among the people to instruct them in Righteousness and to explain it to them. …

Moreover I have had banyan trees planted on the roads to give shade to man and beast; I have planted mango groves, and I have had ponds dug and shelters erected along the roads at every eight kos. Everywhere I have had wells dug for the benefit of man and beast. But this benefit is but small, for in many ways the kings of olden time have worked for the welfare of the world; but what I have done has been done that men may conform to Righteousness ….

I have enforced the law against killing certain animals and many others, but the greatest progress of Righteousness among men comes from exhortation in favor of non-injury to life and abstention from killing living beings.

I have done this that it may endure as long as the moon and sun, and that my sons and my great-grandsons may support it; for by supporting it they will gain both this world and the next.

From *Sources of Indian Tradition* by William Theodore de Bary. Copyright © 1988 by Columbia University Press. Reprinted with permission of the publisher.

He is a symbol of enlightened rule with few if any equals in the history of East or West.

The Mauryan State   Mauryan bureaucracy was marked by centralization, standardization, and efficiency in long-distance communications; civil and military organization; tax collection; and information gathering (by a secret service). The fundamental unit of government, as before and ever after, was the village, with its headman and council. Groups of villages formed districts within the larger provincial unit. Governors sent from the capital controlled most provinces although some local rulers were confirmed in these positions also, much as under the Achaemenids (who were probably a model for Mauryan imperialism).

The administration of the empire depended primarily on the king himself, who had an advisory council to assist him. Still, it was the king who commanded full allegiance of all subjects. Each of the three great Mauryan kings was associated with one of the "new" religious movements of the age: Chandragupta with the Jains (see Chapter 2), his son with the ascetic Ajivikas, and Ashoka with the Buddhists. Such links must have strengthened Mauryan claims to righteous leadership. The reputed ceremonialism of the Mauryan court probably also enhanced royal authority.

Revenues in the Mauryan empire came primarily from taxing the produce of the land, which was regarded as the king's property. Urban trade and production were also taxed heavily. The Mauryan economic system also involved slavery, although most of it was domestic labor, often a kind of temporary indentured service.

The Mauryan Legacy   An imperial ideal, a strengthened Buddhist movement, and strong central administration were among the Mauryans' gifts to Indian culture. They also left behind new cosmopolitan traditions of external relations and internal communication that encouraged cultural development and discouraged provincialism. Their many contacts with the West reflect their international perspective, as do the Ashokan edicts, which were executed in various languages and scripts. The edicts suggest that writing and reading must have been common by this time (perhaps because of Buddhist monastic schooling?). The Mauryans' excellent road system facilitated unprecedented internal and external contacts, above all west to Herat and northwest to Bactria. These roads would later be the routes for Buddhism's spread to Central Asia and China, as well as corridors for successive invaders of the subcontinent moving in the opposite direction.

This era also saw the flourishing of cities across the empire: Pataliputra, Varanasi (Banaras), Ayodhya, Prayag (modern Allahabad), Ujjain, Taxila, and Qandahar. They were centers for arts, crafts, industry, literature, and education. The architecture of the Mauryan capital, Pataliputra, has not survived because of its wood-and-brick construction. But Greek travelers such as Megasthenes (who was active around 300 B.C.E.) reported that its glories surpassed those of the Achaemenid palaces. Certainly the stone buildings and sculpture of the Ashokan period reflect sophisticated aesthetics and technique, as well as strong Persian and Greek influence.

Consolidation of Indian Civilization (ca. 200 B.C.E.–300 C.E.)

In the post-Mauryan period, the history of North India was dominated by the influx of various foreign peoples whom we shall consider shortly. In the rest of the subcontinent, indigenous Indian dynasties held sway, often controlling regional empires that became centers for developing Indian cultural styles. In this period a general pattern of regional and local political autonomy arose that would be broken only by the empire built much later by the Guptas (320 C.E.–ca. 550; see Chapter 10). However, religiously and culturally, the centuries between the Mauryans and the Guptas still saw the consolidation of transregional patterns and styles that helped shape permanently Indian and, through the diffusion of Buddhism, Asian civilization.

THE ECONOMIC BASE

Although agriculture remained the basis of the post-Mauryan economy, India's merchant classes prospered, as their patronage of Buddhist and Jain buildings shows. The fine Mauryan road system facilitated trade throughout India. India became a center of world trade, largely because of Chinese and Roman demand for Indian luxury goods—jewels, semiprecious stones, sandalwood, teak, spices, cotton and silk textiles, exotic animals, and slaves (see Map. 4–3). Considerable wealth flowed in, as evidenced by archaeological finds of Roman gold-coin hoards and remains of Roman trading communities in the Tamil south. Within India, guild organizations flourished and provided technical education in skilled crafts. Kings as well as the merchant classes invested in guilds. Coin minting increased after Mauryan times, and banking flourished.[3]

HIGH CULTURE

In the arts, the great achievements of the post-Mauryan era were primarily Buddhist in inspiration. Northwestern India saw the rise of the Gandharan school of Buddhist art, named

---

CHRONOLOGY

India from the Sixth Century B.C.E. to the End of Mauryan Rule

ca. 600–400 B.C.E.	Late Upanishadic age: local/regional kingdoms and tribal republics along the Ganges and in Himalayan foothills, the Punjab, and northwestern India
ca. 540–ca. 468 B.C.E.	Vardhamana Mahavira, Jain founder
ca. 537–ca. 486 B.C.E.	Siddhartha Gautama, the Buddha
ca. 550–324 B.C.E.	Regional empire of Maghadan kings
330–325 B.C.E.	Alexander campaigns in Indus valley, Soghdiana, Bactria, and Punjab
324–ca. 185 B.C.E.	Mauryan Empire controls most of northern India and the Deccan
ca. 272–232 B.C.E.	Reign of the Mauryan emperor Ashoka

---

[3] Romila Thapar, *A History of India*, vol. 1 (Harmondsworth, U. K.: Penguin Books, 1966), pp. 105–118.

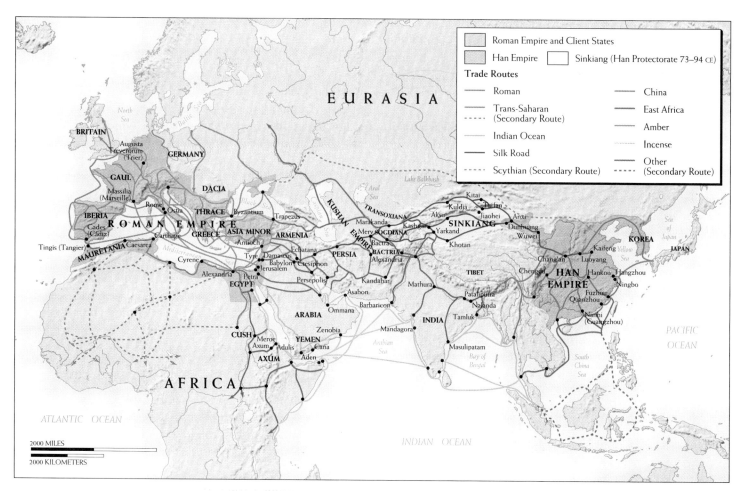

MAP 4–3   Eurasian Trade Routes ca. 100 C.E.   An extensive network of overland and sea routes connected Eurasia from the Mediterranean to China. The central position of Iran, Inner Asia, and India in this vast trading zone provided them with great wealth and influence, though Africa and Southeast Asia formed important links as well.

after the province that covered today's Pakistani Punjab and eastern Afghanistan. In Gandharan sculpture, Hellenistic naturalism of form joined with the more recent Indian tradition of Buddha images to produce sculptural figures with flowing draped garments through which the muscular lines of the human body are discernible. In central India as early as the first century B.C.E., artists were producing stone-relief sculpture with the naturalistic, yet flowing, plastic human and animal forms that would become earmarks of the "classical" style of Indian art. The finest surviving examples are at the great Buddhist *stupas* (shrines) of Bharhut and Sanchi.

Language and literature during this period rested on the sophisticated Sanskrit grammar of Panini (ca. 300 B.C.E.?), which remains standard even today. Two masterpieces of Sanskrit culture, the epics of the *Mahabharata* and the *Ramayana*, probably took shape by 200 C.E. The first is a composite work concerned largely with the nature of *dharma* (the moral and cosmic Law, see Chapter 2). Included in its earlier, narrative portions are systematic treatments of

dharma, such as the Bhagavad Gita, or "Song of the Blessed Lord," the most influential of all Indian religious texts. Evidence of the rise of devotional cults is seen in the importance of Krishna in the *Mahabharata* (especially in the Gita) and Rama in the *Ramayana*. Both are major incarnations, or *avataras*, of the god Vishnu.

RELIGION AND SOCIETY

The post-Mauryan period saw Buddhist monasticism and lay devotionalism thrive across the subcontinent. However, the Brahmans continued to dominate Vedic learning and ritual. It was also an era of diffusion of popular devotional cults of particular gods, above all Shiva and Vishnu. These traditions were to be the mainstays of all later "Hindu" religious life. The parallel development in Buddhist tradition was the rise, along with Mahayana thought (see Chapter 10), of a cult of the person of the Buddha. It focused on pilgrimages to sites where his relics were deposited or to places associated with his life.

The Great Stupa at Sanchi. This is an outstanding example of early Buddhist relic mounds. The mound, seated on an Ashokan foundation, was added to over the centuries. Magnificent carvings adorn its stone railing and gateways, one of which is shown in the left foreground. Sanchi is located in north-central India.

Dale Williams

Toward the end of this age, Buddhism in its Mahayana form began to spread from India over the trade routes to Central Asia and eventually to China and Japan.

Hindu Tradition   What we now call Hinduism emerged in this era. The major developments shaping a Hindu tradition were (1) the consolidation of the caste system, Brahman ascendancy, and the "high" culture of Sanskrit learning; (2) the increasing dominance of theistic devotionalism (especially the cults of Vishnu and Shiva); and (3) the intellectual reconciliation of these developments with the older ascetic and speculative traditions deriving from the Upanishadic age. These social and religious developments would continue and solidify in the Gupta era and beyond.

Buddhist Tradition   Indian Buddhist monastic communities prospered under mercantile and royal patronage, especially in or near urban centers—a trait they shared with the Jains. Merchants found both traditions attractive and strongly supported Jain and Buddhist monasteries, presumably for the merit to be gained.

Buddhist lay devotion figured prominently in Indian religious life, especially in the Ganges basin. It was, however, a different tradition from the Buddhism of the theological texts, which focuses on the quest for *nirvana* and the "extraordinary norm" (see Chapter 2). The Buddha and Buddhist saints were naturally identified with popular Indian deities, and Buddhist worship easily assimilated to

common Indian patterns of theistic piety. Thus popular Buddhist practice was indistinguishable from countless other devotional cults that began to dominate the Indian scene. One reason that Buddhist tradition remained only one among many Indian religious paths was its absorption into the religious variety that then and now typifies the Hindu religious scene.

Greek and Asian Dynasties
SELEUCIDS

We have seen that Alexander's successors in Achaemenid lands, the Greek general Seleucus and his heirs, soon lost Arachosia and Gandhara to the Mauryans. They did, however, rule most of the former Achaemenid realm from about 312 to 246 B.C.E. and lesser portions until about 125 B.C.E. Alexander's policies of Graeco-Persian fusion—the appointment of Iranians and Greeks as *satraps*, as well as large-scale Greek and Persian intermarriage—helped make viable the Seleucid rule of many eastern areas. The new "cities"—more accurately, military colonies—that Alexander left behind were bases for Seleucid control. As a foreign minority, the Seleucids had to maintain control with mercenary troops. However, the leaders of their own troops and satrapies gradually whittled away at Seleucid rule. Always at war, neither Seleucus (r. 311–281 B.C.E.; see Chapter 3) nor the greatest of his successors, Antiochus the Great (r. 223–187 B.C.E.), ever equaled the scale of Achaemenid rule.

Parthian Warrior. The Parthians were superb fighters and were particularly noted for the "parthian shot," firing arrows backward while mounted as a galloping horse. It is not difficult to imagine the fear that must have gripped sedentary peoples upon the sight of such swift and mobile cavalry men.
Werner Forman Archive.

In the end, Alexander's policy of linking Hellenes with Iranians in political power, marriage, and culture bore fruit more lasting than empire. The Seleucid emphasis on building Greek-style cities stimulated the Hellenization process. During the second century B.C.E., Hellenistic culture and law became new ideals among the Seleucid elites. The Seleucids welcomed into the ruling classes those non-Hellenes willing to become Hellenized. Aramaic, although declining in eastern Iran, remained the common tongue from Syria to the Hindu Kush. Greek culture penetrated but did not displace local sociocultural forms.

Zoroastrian religious tradition declined with the loss of its imperial-cult status. The many syncretic cults of the Mediterranean Hellenistic world made inroads even in the East in Seleucid and Parthian times. The later Parthians probably laid the groundwork for the subsequent revival of Zoroastrian tradition. Mystery and savior cults were becoming more popular in East and West. The new Hellenistic urban centers may have provided an environment in which the individual was less rooted in established traditions of culture and religious life. This enhanced the attractiveness of the focus on individual salvation common to many lesser Hellenistic cults and to emerging traditions like the Christian, Mahayana Buddhist, Manichaean, and Hindu devotionalist that came to dominate Eurasia over the next few centuries.

INDO-GREEKS

The farthest reach of Hellenization in the East came with the **Indo-Greeks** of Bactria.[4] About 246 B.C.E., Bactria's Greek satrap broke away from the Seleucids. His successor, Euthydemus (r. ca. 235–ca. 200 B.C.E.), extended his sway north and southwest and withstood a Seleucid attempt at reconquest by Antiochus the Great in 208 B.C.E. His son Demetrius exploited the growing Mauryan weakness and by 175 B.C.E. had crossed the Hindu Kush to conquer Arachosia. He then moved up the Indus valley to take Gandhara. Demetrius made Taxila his capital and controlled other parts of northern India. Most of the Indo-Greeks were Indian in language, culture, and religion, as their coins and inscriptions show.

Before their demise at the hands of invading steppe peoples (ca. 130–100 B.C.E.), these Indo-Greeks left their mark on civilization in all the areas around their Bactrian center. Bactria was a major source of the later Graeco-Buddhist art of Gandhara, one of history's remarkable examples of cross-cultural influence. The Indo-Greeks also probably helped spread Buddhism from India to Central Asia. The most famous of the Bactrian rulers, Menander, or Milinda (r. ca. 155–130 B.C.E.?), successor to Demetrius, is depicted as a Buddhist convert in a later Buddhist text, *The Questions of King Milinda*.

STEPPE PEOPLES

In considering the Parthian Arsacid dynasty, which succeeded the Seleucids in Iran, and the steppe dynasties that followed the Indo-Greeks in Bactria and North India, separation of Iranian from Indian history is misleading. The history of North India and the Iranian plateau was dominated from about 250 B.C.E. to 300 C.E. by incursions of Iranian tribal peoples originally from the Central Asian steppes. These were neither the first nor the last such invasions from the steppe. Although commonly ignored, these nomadic **steppe peoples** have been a major force in Eurasian history.

Parthians The Parni, said to be related to the Scythians, were probably the major group of Iranian steppe peoples who first settled the area south of the Aral Sea and Oxus. In late Achaemenid times, they moved south into Parthia and eventually adopted its dialect. Thenceforward we can call them Parthians. The independent control of Parthia by the dynastic family of the Arsacids dates from about 247 B.C.E. Shortly thereafter, the Parthians began to extend their dominion onto the Iranian plateau. Under Mithradates I (ca. 171–138 B.C.E.) they emerged as a new Eurasian imperial force, the true Achaemenid successors.

[4] In *The Indo-Greeks* (Oxford: Oxford University Press, 1957), A. K. Narian argues for "Indo-Greeks" as the appropriate term for these kings, who are usually called "Graeco-Bactrians" or "Euthydemids."

Facing weak Seleucid and Indo-Greek opposition, Mithradates by about 140 B.C.E., secured a sizable empire that stretched across the Iranian plateau from Mesopotamia to Arachosia. Its center was Mithradates's new winter capital of Ctesiphon, on the Tigris. The Parthians' imperial borders varied, but from their victory over the Romans at Carrhae in 53 B.C.E. (see Chapter 6) until their fall in 233 C.E., they were the major Eurasian power alongside Rome. Eventually the constant Roman wars of their last century and the pressure of the Kushan Empire in the east weakened them sufficiently for a new Persian dynasty to replace them.

It is not easy to measure Parthian rule in Iran, despite its duration and successes, because of the scarcity and bias of available sources. For much of their long reign, the Parthians were under pressure on all fronts—in Armenia, in Mesopotamia, and along their Indian and Central Asian frontiers. Yet during their rule, trade in and around their domains apparently increased, especially north over the Caucasus, on the "Silk Road" to China, and along the Indian Ocean coast (the ancient Arabs' "monsoon route," used for the spice trade with the Indies).

Culturally, the Parthians were oriented toward the Hellenistic world of their Seleucid predecessors until the mid–first century C.E., after which they seem to have experienced a kind of Iranian revival. They replaced Greek on their coins with Parthian and Aramaic, and their cities reverted to their older Iranian names. Their formerly Hellenic tastes in art turned to Iranian motifs like the hunt, the battle, and the feast. In late Parthian times, the Iranian national epic took its lasting shape. Similarly, the Magi preserved the worship of Ahura Mazda despite the success of other eastern and western cults and the common assimilation of Greek gods to Iranian ones. Still, the Parthians seem to have tolerated religious plurality. In their era, a huge variety of religious cults and cultural traditions rubbed shoulders with one another and vied for supremacy in different regions.

Sakas and Kushans The successors of the Indo-Greeks were steppe peoples even closer to their nomadic past than the Parthians. These peoples played a major political and cultural role in Asia for centuries, especially in the Indo-Iranian region. They reflect the cosmopolitan nature of the world of Central Asia, eastern Iran, and northwestern India at this time.

Beginning about 130 B.C.E., Scythian (Saka) tribes from beyond the Jaxartes (Syr Darya) overran northeastern Iran, taking Sogdiana's Hellenic cities and then Bactria. Thus ended the Indo-Greek heyday, although the last Greek petty ruler lasted in the upper Indus valley until about 50 B.C.E. One group of Sakas extended their domain from Bactria into North India, as far as Mathura. Another went southwest into Herat and Sistan, where they encroached on the Parthians. In

▲ **Parthian Marble Head of a Woman.** Note the Hellenistic style of her facial features.
Trudy Kawami.

CHRONOLOGY

Indo-Greek, Iranian, Indian, and Steppe Dynasties after Alexander

312–ca. 125 B.C.E.	Seleucid rule in part of the old Achaemenid realm
ca. 248 B.C.E.–224 C.E.	Parthian empire of the Arsacids in Iran, Babylonia
246–ca. 50 B.C.E.	Indo-Greek ("Graeco-Bactrian," "Euthydemid") rulers of region from modern Afghanistan to Oxus
ca. 171–138 B.C.E.	Reign of Arsacid king Mithradates I
ca. 140 B.C.E.– ca. 100 C.E.	Movements west and south of Yüeh Chih (including Kushans) and Sythians (Sakas) into Sogdiana, then Bactria, then northwestern India
ca. 50 C.E.– ca. 250 C.E.	Height of Kushan power in Oxus to Ganges region
ca. 105 C.E.	Accession of King Kanishka to Kushan throne in Taxila (ruled about 28 years)

The Buddha's Nirvana. This late second- or third-century C.E. Gandharan school relief has much in common with the style of contemporary Roman stone carvings. In this case the Indian-Buddhist concept does not mesh well with the realistic Roman style and craftsmanship (see Chapter 6). Note the emotions of the bystanders at their loss of the Lord Buddha; such depictions of emotion do not appear in native Indian carvings.
Bridgeman-Giraudon/Art Resource, N.Y.

northwestern India the Sakas were defeated by invading Iranians known as the Pahlavas, who went on to rule in northwestern India in the first century C.E.,[5] though Saka dynasties continued to rule in parts of northwestern and western India through the fourth century C.E.

The Sakas had been displaced earlier in Sogdiana by another steppe people, known from Chinese sources as the Yüeh Chih. The building of the Great Wall (ca. 215 B.C.E.) or drought in the steppes may have driven them from western China. These peoples, led by the Kushan tribe, drove the Sakas out of Bactria in the mid–first century B.C.E. About 100 years later, they swept over the mountains into northwestern India. Here they ended Pahlava rule and founded a long-lived Indian Kushan dynasty that controlled a relatively stable empire from the upper Oxus regions through Bactria, Gandhara, Arachosia, the Punjab, and over the Ganges plains as far as Varanasi (Banaras).

The Kushan kingdom of India was—along with Rome, China, and the weakened Parthian Empire of Iran—one of four major centers of civilization in Eurasia around 100 C.E. Its greatest ruler, Kanishka, reigned around either 100 or possibly 150 C.E. He was the greatest patron of Buddhism since Ashoka. In its heyday (the first to third centuries C.E.), Kushan power in Central Asia facilitated the missionary activity that carried Buddhism across the steppes into China. A lasting Kushan contribution was the school of Graeco-Buddhist art fostered in Gandhara by Kanishka and his successors and supported by a later Kushan dynasty for another five hundred years.

---

[5] Tradition gives one of their rulers, Gondophares, the role of host to Saint Thomas, who is said to have brought Christianity to India. But because Gondophares probably ruled in the early to mid–first century C.E., it may be a confused report. Even if traditions of Thomas's mission to India are correct, some connect him instead with southern India.

Summary

Indo-Iranian Empires   Between 600 B.C.E. and 200 C.E. imperial governments arose in the Indo-Iranian world whose power and influence surpassed that of any before them. The Achaemenid Empire based in Iran, the Mauryan Empire in India, and the Hellenistic empire of the Seleucids provided the security and wealth that permitted trade and culture to flourish from the Mediterranean to India. The Achaemenid Empire established two centuries of tolerant, stable, prosperous rule from Egypt to the borders of India. The Mauryans created the first Indian empire, while Seleucid rule fostered the spread of Greek culture in Western Asia.

The Great Stupa at Sanchi.

Cross-cultural Contacts   In Asia these empires enabled widely influential, lasting religious traditions to come of age and spread—Zoroastrianism, Buddhism, Hinduism. The empires also fostered increased cross-cultural contact, especially in Central Asia where Greek, Iranian, Indian, and steppe languages, ideas, arts, customs, and religious practices intermingled. These contacts and influences were manifested in new peoples, structures of government, technological innovations, specialized skills and arts, and ethical and religious ideas.

⋮ Review Questions

1. Why was the Achaemenid Empire successful for so long? What was the political basis for Achaemenid power?

2. How was the Mauryan Empire created? What role did Greeks play in its creation? How did Ashoka develop Mauryan power and prestige?

3. How did the role of religion in the Achaemenid Empire compare to its role in the Mauryan Empire?

4. Compare the Achaemenid and Mauryan Empires. What was their respective historical importance? How did each affect the world beyond its borders? How does each compare to the empires of Rome and China in the same centuries?

5. Compare the major features of the Hindu and Buddhist traditions. Why do you think Buddhism spread to Southeast and East Asia whereas Hinduism did not?

6. How did the Kushans, Sakas, and other inner Asian groups play important roles in world history?

⋮ Key Terms

Indo-Greeks   (p. 140)

satraps   (p. 131)

Shahanshah   (p. 131)

Steppe peoples   (p. 140)

Zoroastrianism   (p. 129)

⋮ Documents CD-ROM

Early Civilization in South Asia
3.6 Asoka: How a Life Was Turned Around

3.7 "King Milinda": The Greek World's Incursion Into India

NOTE: *To learn more about the topics in this chapter, see the Suggested Readings at the end of the book.*

HINDUISM

The term *Hinduism* is our modern word for the whole of the diverse religious traditions of India. Until the word was coined in the nineteenth century, it (like *Buddhism*) was not even a concept in the West, let alone in India. In contemporary usage, it has become a catchall term for all the Indian religious communities that look upon the texts of the Vedas (see Chapter 1) as eternal, perfect truth.

The historical beginnings of the varied Hindu traditions can be traced to the ancient Aryan migrations into southern Asia in the second millennium B.C.E. During this era the Vedic hymns were composed. They describe a pantheon of gods not unlike that among the Greeks, the Romans, and other Indo-European peoples. Centered on a sacrificial cult of these gods, Vedic religion increasingly became the preserve of the Brahman priestly class of early Indian society. The Brahmans gradually elaborated a cult characterized by sacrificial rituals, purificatory rules, and fixed distinctions of birth on which India's later caste system was based. These developments are mirrored in the later Vedic, or Brahmanical, texts (ca. 1000–500 B.C.E.) that provide commentary on and instructions for ritual use of the Vedic hymns.

After about 700 B.C.E. new developments emerged. North India produced a series of religious reformers, some of whom broke with Vedic tradition and championed knowledge and ascetic discipline over purity and ritual action. Of these, the most famous were Siddhartha Gautama (the Buddha, b. ca. 563 B.C.E.) and Mahavira Vardhamana (founder of the Jain tradition, b. ca. 550 B.C.E.). Other religious leaders reinterpreted the older sacrifice as an inner activity and deepened its spiritual dimensions. Their thinking is represented especially in the Upanishads, which many Hindus consider the most sublime philosophical texts in the Indian tradition.

Developed so long ago, such notions have been part of the complex vision of existence that lies behind the myriad forms of religious life known to us as Hinduism. In this vision the immortal part of each human being, the *atman*, is enmeshed in existence, but not ultimately of it. The nature of existence is *samsara* a ceaseless round of cause and effect determined by the inescapable consequences of *karma*, or "action." The doctrine of *karma* is a moral as well as physical economy in which every act has unavoidable results; so long as mental or physical action occurs, life and change go on repeatedly. Birth determines one's place and duties in the traditional Indian caste system. Caste is the most visible and concrete reminder of the pervasiveness of the Hindu concept of absolute causality that keeps us enmeshed in existence. The final goal is to transcend this cycle, or *samsara*, in which we are all caught. The only way out of this otherwise endless becoming and rebirth is *moksha*, which may be gained through knowledge, action, or devotion.

On the popular level, the period after about 500 B.C.E. is most notable in Indian religious life for two developments. Both took place alongside the ever deeper entrenchment in society of caste distinctions and a supporting ethic of obligations and privileges. The first was the elaboration of ascetic traditions of inner quest and self-realization, such as that of yoga. The second was the rise of devotional worship of specific gods and goddesses who were seen

This exquisitely crafted bronze figure of Shiva dating from the 11th century C.E. depicts him as Lord of the Dance. He is surrounded by a circle of fire, which symbolizes both death and rebirth.
The Cleveland Museum of Art, 2002, Purchase from the J.H. Wade Fund 1930.331.

worship one deity, but they do so in the awareness that faith in other deities can also lead one to the Ultimate.

The period between about 500 B.C.E. and 1000 C.E. saw the rise to special prominence of two gods, Vishnu and Shiva, as the primary forms in which the Supreme Lord was worshiped. Along with the mother-goddess figure, who takes various names and forms (Kali and Durga, for example), Vishnu and Shiva have remained the most important manifestations of the Divine in India. Their followers are known as Vaishnavas and Shaivas, respectively. A few recurring phenomena and ideas can suggest something of Indian religiousness in practice.

Hindu practice is characterized especially by temple worship (*puja*), in which *worshipers bring* offerings of flowers, food, and the like. They especially seek out temple images for the blessing that the sight of these images brings. Another important part of Hindu devotionalism is the recitation of sacred texts, many of which are vernacular hymns of praise to a particular deity. *Mantras*, or special recitative texts from the Vedas, are thought to have extraordinary power and are used by many Hindus in their original Sanskrit form. Pilgrimage to sacred sites, especially rivers, mountains, and famous shrines, is a prominent part of Hindu religious life. India's landscape is filled with sacred sites and sacred pilgrim routes, both local and national in reputation. A prominent feature of Hindu life is preoccupation with purity and pollution, most evident in the food taboos associated with caste groupings.

The ascetic tendency in India is also highly developed. Although only a tiny minority of Indians take up a life of full renunciation, they are influential. Ascetic worshipers do not settle in one place, acquire possessions, or perform regular worship. Rather, they wander about in search of teachers and devote themselves to meditation and self-realization. Even though most Hindus have families and work at their salvation through *puja* and moral living, the ascetic ideal has an important place in the overall Indian worldview. It stands as a constant reminder of the deeper reality beyond the everyday world and any individual, life.

▲ **Purification rituals in the waters of the holy Ganges.** Purification rituals are part of the obligatory daily rituals of all "twice-born" Hindus. The morning rituals performed by the women here in the Ganges include greeting the sun with recitation and prayer and purification by bathing.

Ian Berry/Magnum Photos, Inc.

by their worshipers as identical with the Ultimate—in other words, as supreme deities for those who served them. The latter development was of particular importance for popular religion in India. Evident in the famous and beloved Hindu devotional text, the Bhagavad Gita, it reached its highest level after 500 B.C.E. in the myriad movements of fervent, loving devotionalism, or *bhakti*, many of which remain important today. A striking aspect of Hindu piety has been its willingness to accommodate the focus on one "chosen deity" who is worshiped as supreme to a worldview that holds that the Divine can and does take many forms. Thus most Hindus

◆ Compared to other faiths that have expanded globally, such as Christianity and Islam, why has Hinduism been largely confined to India?

◆ How has Hinduism accomodated and absorbed different beliefs and value systems?

Africa

Early History to 1000 C.E.

◁ West African terra-cotta sculpture (36 cm high) from the Nok culture, which flourished in the Western Sudan from about 900 B.C.E. to about 200 C.E. The style of terra-cotta castings like this one suggests that they may have had wooden prototypes.

Nigeria, Nok head, 900 B.C.E.–200 A.D., Rafin Kura, Nok. prehistoric West African sculpture from the Nok Culture. Terracotta, 36 cms. high. © Werner Forman Archive, Art Resource, N.Y.

The Early History of Africa

The view that pre-Islamic Africa was a relatively isolated landmass that contributed little to political, cultural, and religious developments in antiquity and was little engaged on the world scene cannot withstand close scrutiny. The human species originated in Africa. In the ancient world, Pharaonic Egypt, the Kushite kingdoms of Napata and Meroe, and the Ethiopian state of Aksum were all major political-military powers with highly complex cultures in regular interchange with other civilizations, from Rome to India and beyond.

It is important to remember that Africa is an immensely large continent, and by no means a culturally homogenous one. Beginning with the Bantu expansion, considerable movement and mingling of quite different peoples and cultures took place within Africa, with the coastal peoples and Egypt often acting as cultural mediators between the peoples of the interior and the rest of the world.

Africa contributed to other cultures in many ways. Nilotic cultures had a strong influence on the Hellenistic world. Jewish scholars in Egyptian Alexandria produced the Greek biblical translation known as the Septuagint. Saint Augustine, a founding father of Christian theology, was an African, and bishop of the north African city of Hippo. Christian Abyssinia (Aksum) offered sanctuary to a part of Muhammad's fledgling Muslim community. Even Christian monasticism began in Egypt. Moreover, although during the New Kingdom Egypt's relationship with Nubia (Kush) farther up the Nile in the African interior was one of conquest and colonization, during the later, weaker Egyptian dynasties the tables were turned. By the Twenty-First Dynasty, the Upper Kingdom of Egypt fell under Nubian rule. Subsequently the Egyptians drove out the Nubian rulers, but a new Kushite state arose beyond the reach of Egyptian power—a state based on a profound syncretism of Egyptian and Nubian culture, religion, and concepts of kingship.

In addition, substantial evidence suggests that African products, ideas, and people reached distant lands during the first millennium C.E. Arab merchants sailed the trade circuits of the Indian Ocean and ventured across the Sahara and the Mediterranean into Europe and the Middle East. Medieval European and Persian paintings depict clear likenesses of Africans, showing that the artists had sufficient contact with Africans to render them in a recognizable manner. The settlement of Arabs in East African trading cities predates the coming of Islam and resulted in a society in which Arab and African people, culture, and even language mingled. Like Eurasia, Africa was home to numerous societies that varied greatly depending upon their adaptation to their local environments, and many of whom were in contact with each other and with the outside world. By 400 C.E., Takrur arose—the first in a series of trading states in West Africa that specialized in the exchange of North African goods and Saharan salt for gold and other products, including slaves from the interior. The middlemen and carriers of this trade were primarily Berbers, who like the Tuareg further to the east, specialized in plying the routes across the Sahara.

Thus, from a world perspective, Africa was engaged with lands far and near from at least the first millennium C.E.—in trade, in conflict and cooperation, and in religious and cultural life. Internal trade brought goods from the interior of the continent to the centers of external exchange. In Africa, however, as in much of Eurasia, the imminent coming of the last major world religious and cultural tradition—that of Islam—would redefine or even eliminate the overt presence of many previous centers of civilization.

THINK AHEAD

◆ Consider the migrations of peoples and ideas that took place within the African continent to 1000 C.E. Which regions of Africa were most in contact with the outside world?

◆ Why was Egypt an especially important mediator between other civilizations and the African interior? What role did geography play in this respect?

◆ What does the Bantu expansion tell us about the importance of internal migrations within the African continent?

W E NOW SHIFT OUR FOCUS FROM THE ANCIENT societies that emerged north and east of the Mediterranean—the Persian, Greek, and Hellenistic, worlds—to the world's second largest continent, Africa, beginning with the earliest archaeological record. Africa forms the southern frontier of the Mediterranean world and connects to Asia through the Arabian Peninsula and the Indian Ocean. The evidence suggests that the first humans emerged from eastern Africa to populate the rest of the world, and the continent's subsequent history is one of ongoing interaction, both internally across its many natural boundaries and externally with the rest of the world.

Problems of Interpretation and Sources

THE QUESTION OF "CIVILIZATION"

In Chapter 1 we defined "civilization" in terms of a cluster of attributes—among them writing, urban life, and metallurgy—that relate to social complexity and technological development. In that sense the term identifies some common characteristics of the ancient states that emerged in the Nile valley, Mesopotamia, the Indus and Ganges valleys, and China, and also of the larger, more complex societies developed since those ancient states. However, in a broader sense, the term civilization is associated with the sophistication of a people's intellectual, cultural, and artistic traditions. Too often we assume that societies that lack writing, cities, or a state bureaucracy are therefore "uncivilized." Once we move outside the Nile valley and the Ethiopian highlands, most African societies down to recent times—indeed, most societies anywhere for most of history—may not have been civilizations in the narrow sense, but they were hardly uncivilized in the broader sense. African history reveals important states with writing, cities, and technology, as well as many societies with rich, varied traditions that were not organized as bureaucratic states with literate, urban populations and new technologies.

THE SOURCE PROBLEM

African history has flourished in recent decades, but there is still much we do not know, largely because few sources are available for many regions and periods. This is especially acute for the small, local societies without writing, centralized governmental bureaucracies, or large urban centers that characterize much of sub-Saharan African history.

Stateless societies leave few historical records. Local oral traditions provide one valuable source of information. But even combined with reports of outside observers, oral traditions can give us access only to relatively recent history—no more than a few centuries. Another source for the history of Africa's states and its stateless societies is archaeological research. The tropical climate that prevails in much of sub-Saharan Africa unfortunately destroys many types of artifacts that survive in drier regions. Nonetheless, archaeological scholarship has brought to light many formerly unknown cultures. Some of this work indicates that ancient Africa may have had large and advanced societies and states that are still unknown. The Nok and Zimbabwean cultures, for example, left impressive but hard-to-decipher remains.

A third important source consists of reports of outside observers. It is only after about 950 C.E., however, that we get—from Islamic historians, geographers, and travelers, and still later, Europeans—real descriptions of life and peoples in the vast reaches of Africa beyond Egypt, Ethiopia, and North Africa. Before this, only a few brief Greek and Roman accounts are available. These outside records are of mixed value.

▲ **Excavation in Progress at Blombos Cave, South Africa.** The recent discovery of bone tools, decorated ochre blocks, and polished spear points that have been dated to about 70,000 years ago indicate that earliest evidence of tools and artwork come from Africa.
National Science Foundation.

Greek and Roman observers and, later, Islamic and European writers brought strong biases to their assessments of Africa and Africans; their commentaries did much to form the stereotypes with which many still view this vast, diverse continent.

Because relatively little is known about small African communities that left no written documents, monuments, or other decipherable artifacts, surveys therefore tend to focus on the larger societies, with known rulers, armies, and towns or cities, which left their own records or were documented by outsiders.

We shall try nonetheless to discuss both larger societies and states, for which we have more adequate evidence, and areas that have left us fewer sources.

Physical Description of the Continent

Africa (see Map 5–1) is three and a half times the size of the continental United States and second only to Asia in total area. Because its average elevation is 660 meters, Africa has few nat-

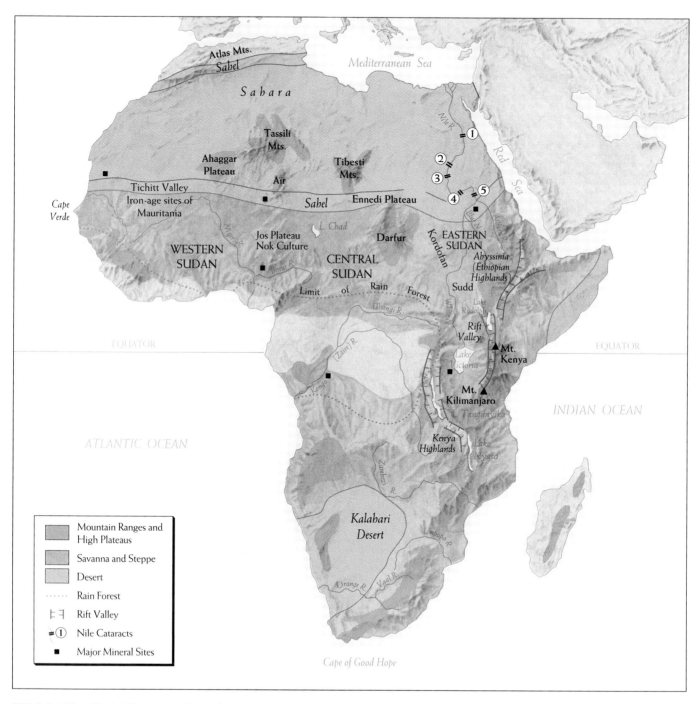

MAP 5–1 Africa: Physical Features and Early Sites. This map shows the major physical features of the continent and Iron Age sites of the western and central Sudan.

ural harbors and islands. Steep escarpments surmount most of its narrow coasts. This has made communication with its interior difficult. Of Africa's major rivers (the Niger, Kongo [Zaïre], Nile, Zambezi, and Orange), only the Nile has a relatively long navigable reach below its cataracts in upper Egypt. The vast size and sharp physical variations, from high mountains to swamplands, tropical forest, and deserts, have channeled long-distance communication and movement along certain corridors (such as the Rift Valley of East Africa, the coastal reaches of East or North Africa, the Niger or Zambezi river valley, or the Sahelian savannah lands bordering the great equatorial forest).

The special character of various regions is largely the result of Africa's position astride the equator. As a whole, its climate is unusually hot. North and south of the equator, dense rain forests dominate a west–east band of tropical woodland territory from the southern coasts of West Africa across the Kongo basin nearly to the Kenyan highlands. (However, tropical rain forests cover only about 5 percent of the continent.) North and south of this band (and in the Kenyan highlands), the lush rain forests give way to the **savanna**—open woodlands and grassy plains. This in turn passes into steppe and semidesert known as the **Sahel**, and finally into true desert as one moves farther from the equator. The **Sahara** ("the Desert"; Arabic *al-Sahrá*) is

OVERVIEW   The Geography of Africa

Geography has played a large role in the history and culture of Africa, limiting its contacts with non-African peoples and influencing patterns of trade and settlement. Africa is divided into a number of geographical zones and cultural regions.

North Africa	The region along the Mediterranean coast. It extends from Morocoo in the west to Egypt in the east. It has long had extensive contacts with Europe and the Near East and has been dominated by Islam since the seventh century C.E.
Sahara	The world's largest desert. It extends across Africa from the Atlantic to the eastern Sudan. Historically, the Sahara has hindered contact between the Mediterranean and sub-Saharan Africa.
Sahel	An area of steppe and semidesert that borders the Sahara.
Savannah	Areas of open woodlands and grassy plains that border the Sahel.
Rain forests	Large areas of dense vegetation along the equator and much of the West African coast.
Kalahari	A large desert in southwestern Africa that partially isolates southern Africa from the rest of the continent.
Nilotic Africa	The lands along the Nile River valley. It extends from the Mediterranean coast of Egypt south to include the modern Republic of Sudan and Ethiopia. Historically, it has been one of the African regions most open to outside cultural, religious, and economic influences.
Sudan	The broad belt of savannah and Sahel below the Sahara that extends east across the continent from the Atlantic.
West Africa	The woodland coastal regions, savannah, Sahel, and desert that extends as far east as the Lake Chad basin. Many of the slaves caught up in the Atlantic slave trade from the sixteenth to the nineteenth centuries came from this region.
East Africa	Extends from Eithiopia south over modern Kenya and Tanzania. Historically, East Africa has had extensive trade and cultural contacts with Arabia and east Asia.
Central Africa	Extends from the Chad basin across the Congo to Lake Tanganyika and the Zambezi River.
Southern Africa	Extends from the Kalahari desert and the Zambesi River south to the Cape of Good Hope.

the world's largest desert and has historically hindered contact between the Mediterranean world and sub-Saharan Africa. In southwestern Africa the desert of the **Kalahari** partially cuts off the southern plateau and coastal regions from central Africa.

Other natural factors are of importance to Africa's history. The soils of Africa are typically tropical in character, which means they lack much humus, or vegetable mold, and are easily leached of minerals and nutrients. Thus they are rapidly exhausted and not highly productive for long. Water is also scarce in most of Africa. Crop pests and insects such as the tsetse fly, mosquito, and locust have also hampered farming and pastoralism in Africa; the tsetse fly specifically has blocked the spread of cattle and horses to the forest regions. Still, abundant animal life has made hunting and fishing important means of survival from early times down to the present in most regions of Africa.

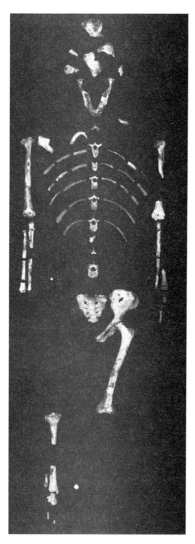

▲ **"Lucy."** One of the most famous fossils found in the north end of the Great Rift Valley, an area rich in fossils of species ancestral to humans, Lucy represents one of the earliest species to walk upright. Cleveland Museum of Natural History.

Africa has great mineral wealth. Salt, iron, copper, and gold were major trade goods from early times.

Finally, we should note that Africa is often discussed in terms of several major regions: *North Africa*—all the Mediterranean coastal regions from modern Morocco through modern Libya and the northern Sahara, including the Sahel that marks the transition from mountains to true desert; **Nilotic Africa** (i.e., the lands of the Nile), roughly the area of the modern states of Egypt and Sudan; *the Sudan*, the broad belt of Sahel and savannah below the Sahara, stretching from the Atlantic east across the entire continent; *West Africa*, including the woodland coastal regions from Cape Verde to Cameroon and the desert, Sahel, and savannah of the western Sudan as far east as the Lake Chad basin; *East Africa*, from the Ethiopian highlands (a high, fertile plateau cut off by steppe, Sahel, and desert to its north and south) south over modern Kenya and Tanzania, an area split north to south by the Great Rift Valley; *central Africa*, the region north of the Kalahari, from the Chad basin across the Zaire basin and southeast to Lake Tanganyika and south to the Zambezi (or, sometimes, the Limpopo) River; and *southern Africa*, from the Kalahari Desert and Zambezi (or Limpopo) south to the Cape of Good Hope.

African Peoples

AFRICA AND EARLY HUMAN CULTURE

Archaeological research indicates that our hominid ancestors evolved in the Great Rift Valley region of highland East Africa at least 1.5 to 1.8 million years ago. It was probably also here that, sometime before 100,000 B.C.E., modern humans—the species *Homo sapiens (sapiens)*—appeared and moved out to populate the world. In this sense, we are all African by descent.

The once popular view of sub-Saharan Africa as a vast region isolated from civilization until its "discovery" by Europeans distorts reality. Although its interior and southern reaches were isolated from direct contact with Eurasia until relatively recent centuries, African goods circulated for centuries through Indian Ocean as well as Mediterranean trade. Archaeological research is documenting the existence and substantial internal movements of peoples—and hence languages, cultures, and technologies—both north–south and east–west within the continent in ancient times. Commercial links between Africa and the outside date to earliest classical antiquity. Nilotic Egypt was always oriented to the Mediterranean and the Near East. Well before the common era, the peoples of the upper Nile, the Ethiopian highlands, and the coastal areas of East Africa below the Horn maintained contacts with Egypt, south Arabia, and probably India and Indonesia, via the Indian Ocean. Like Egypt, the North African coast engaged in Mediterranean trade throughout antiquity. Africa's Mediterranean littoral in particular was a place where Berber speakers mixed with other

Mediterraneans such as the Phoenicians. Here the powerful Carthaginian Punic state arose in the mid–first millennium, only to fall prey to Rome (see Chapter 6).

DIFFUSION OF LANGUAGES AND PEOPLES

Cultural and linguistic diffusion shows that, despite the continent's natural barriers, Africans have not been as internally compartmentalized as was once thought. Language is a particularly interesting phenomenon in Africa. Between 1,000 and 3,000 languages can be found there, depending on how one distinguishes languages from dialects. As a whole, they can be roughly divided into four major groups, plus two late colonial arrivals: the Indo-European family from Western Europe and the Malayo-Polynesian group (spoken only on Madagascar), which came with Southeast Asian colonists still earlier.

The four major groupings are the Afro-Asiatic, the Nilo-Saharan, the Niger-Kongo, and the "Khoisan." The first originated either in southwestern Asia and Arabia or in Africa, but in any case near the Red Sea. It is represented in the Semitic languages (which include Arabic, Hebrew, Aramaic, and Syriac) of southwestern Asia, as well as the ancient Egyptian, Berber, Chadic, Kushitic, and Omotic languages, all of which belong basically to North and northeastern Africa. The Nilo-Saharan family is spread over an area generally southwest of

⚐ **A Stone Age Saharan Rock Painting, the Fresco of Tassili n'Ajjer, Algeria.** One scholar believes this strikingly beautiful painting represents women gathering grain (represented by the dots, presumably). If so, it would have likely been wild grain unless cereal crops were cultivated very early here—something for which we have no evidence. Whether gathering grain or engaged in graceful dance, the figures here remind us of the ancient human presence in the once-green Saharan regions.

Henri Lhote Collection. Musee de l'Homme, Paris, France/© Erich Lessing/Art Resource, N.Y.

the Afro-Asiatic group, from the upper Nile across the central Sahara into the Rift highlands of Morocco. Niger-Kongo languages are found to the west and south of the Nilo-Saharan group, originally from the savannah and woodlands west of the Niger bend south and southeast to central and southern Africa. Finally, Khoisan is a collection of loosely related languages found today in southern Africa.[1]

Based on recent linguistic and archaeological investigations, the Africanist R. Oliver has attempted a plausible reconstruction of the diffusion of these language groups. He links the development of language families with a population growth that brought larger communities and extended movements of peoples. According to his interpretation, after about 8000 B.C.E., Afro-Asiatic languages from the Jordan and Nile valleys had spread to Arabia and across North Africa. Two southward extensions of these languages, from North Africa across the Sahara to the Chad basin, and from Egypt into the Ethiopian highlands and the Horn, likely occurred after 4000 B.C.E., possibly through the movement of sheep and cattle herders.

The Nilo-Saharan languages may have originated among fishing and cereal-growing societies in the Nubian region of the Nile and spread before about 5000 B.C.E. west into the Sahara. They were later largely displaced there by the southward extension of Afro-Asiatic languages into the Sahara with their pastoralist carriers. Isolated Nilo-Saharan tongues such as Zaghawa in the Tibesti, or Songhay above the Niger River, survived this influx. Nilo-Saharan languages must also have spread southeast with fisherman-farmers as far as the lakes region of the Great Rift Valley, where they were later partially displaced by Kushitic-speaking pastoralists or farmers.

The Niger-Kongo family had its homeland in the woodland savannah and equatorial forests of West and central Africa, perhaps near the Niger and Senegal headwaters west of the great bend of the Niger. Spoken by fisherfolk who may also have turned to farming, this group spread to the Atlantic coast from the Senegal River to the Cameroon mountains. Its largest subgroup, the Bantu speakers, later spread southward into the equatorial forestlands (largely as agriculturalists) and around the rain forests of central Africa (as herders and farmers) until they entered the eastern and southern savannahs.

The fourth language family, nowadays called Khoisan, apparently covered most of the southern half of the African continent by late Neolithic times but was largely displaced by the migration of Niger-Kongo Bantu speakers. The varied peoples who were the ancestors of today's Khoisan speakers were likely still primarily hunter-gatherers at this time. Eventually, most of these peoples adopted the languages of the immigrant Bantu-speaking agriculturalists and pastoralists, making Bantu tongues the most widely dispersed African languages and confining the diverse Khoisan tongues to smaller areas than they had once covered.

The development of the complex language map of present-day Africa can thus be seen in terms of ancient developments in food production and movement of peoples and ways of life within the continent. We shall return to several of these developments later in this chapter.

RACIAL DISTINCTIONS

Some interpreters have linked changes in African food production, development of local settled cultures, and even larger patterns of civilization to the apparent differences in appearance of African populations. In more recent times, lighter-skinned, Caucasoid African peoples have predominated in the Sahara, North Africa, and Egypt, whereas darker-skinned, Negroid peoples have been the majority in the rest of Africa.[2] (The Greeks called all the black peoples they were aware of in Africa *Ethiopians*, "those with burnt skins." The Arabs termed all of Africa south of the Sahara and Egypt *Bilad al-Sudan*, "the Land of the Blacks," and from this we get the term *Sudan*.) Other, yellowish-brown peoples occur in smaller numbers in sub-Saharan, especially southern, Africa, largely as herding or hunter-gatherer groups. These peoples are known as the Khoikhoi and San—the "Hottentots" and "Bushmen" of unfortunate traditional European usage—or today, collectively, the Khoisan; their greatest numbers are in the Kalahari and adjacent areas of southern Africa.

Some theories have attempted to relate color or racial differences to the development and spread of everything from language, agriculture, or cattle herding to ironworking or state building in Africa. However, none of these theories is tenable, if only because race itself is a problematic concept. In Africa, the various populations were so mixed that most Africans might best be considered to belong to one large race (or none), regardless of their color or other physical attributes.[3]

The Sahara and the Sudan to the Beginning of the Common Era
EARLY SAHARAN CULTURES

Since the second millennium B.C.E., the vast arid wilderness of the Sahara has separated the North African and Egyptian worlds from the Sudan and West and central Africa. What is hard for us to imagine, however, is that until about 2500 B.C.E. the Sahara was arable land with lakes and rivers, trees, grasses, and a rea-

---

[1] For the entire discussion of language here and later in the chapter, we rely on the summary and analysis of R. Oliver, *The African Experience* (1991), pp. 38–50.

[2] Note, however, that actual distribution of skin color in the past is hard to determine; there is even sharp disagreement as to whether the ancient Egyptians were more "white" or more "black." See the discussions in G. Mokhtar, ed., *Ancient Civilizations of Africa*, Vol. 2 of *UNESCO General History of Africa* (London: Heinemann, 1981), pp. 27–83; and W. MacGaffey, "Who Owns Ancient Egypt?" *Journal of African History* 32 (1991): 515–519.

[3] See Philip Curtin et al., *African History* (London, 1978), pp. 14–16.

sonable climate. During the so-called Wet Holocene period in Africa, from ca. 7500–2500 B.C.E., especially the southern half of the Sahara was positively well watered. The increased animal, fowl, reptile, and fish populations in these periods would have allowed riparian (river- and lakeside) communities of considerable size to live with ease off the land, and excavations near Khartoum in the Sudan support this likelihood.

Then, from about 2500 B.C.E., climatic changes caused the Sahara to undergo a relatively rapid dessication, and the riparian communities of this vast territory disappeared.[4]

By 1000 B.C.E., the dessication process progressed enough to make the Sahara an immense east–west expanse of largely uninhabitable desert separating most of Africa from the Mediterranean coastal rim and the Near Eastern centers of early civilization. Even then, however, regular contacts in ancient times between sub-Saharan Africa and the Mediterranean continued. Various north–south routes across the western and central Sahara were traversed by horses and carts or chariots and, most important, by migrating peoples long before the coming of the camel.

NEOLITHIC SUDANIC CULTURES

From the first millennium B.C.E., preliterate but complex agricultural communities of Neolithic and Early Iron Age culture dotted the central and western reaches of the great belt of the sub-Saharan Sudan. These peoples may have once been spread farther north, in the then-arable Saharan lands they would have shared with ancestors of the Berber-speaking peoples of contemporary west-Saharan and North Africa.

This hypothesis has been bolstered by the excavation of town cultures from the mid–fifth millennium B.C.E. in Mali and Mauritania. In inland Mauritania, remains of an ancient but later agricultural civilization with as many as 200 towns have also been found. These reflect the transition from a hunting and fishing to a herding and rudimentary agricultural society. The progressive dessication of the second millennium

◀ **A Terra-cotta Head.** This is from the Iron Age Nok culture, which occupied what is today northeastern Nigeria from about 900 B.C.E. to about 200 C.E.
© Werner Forman Archive/Art Resource, N.Y./Jos Museum, Nigeria.

B.C.E. may have forced these peoples farther south. Pottery found in the first-millennium settlements in places such as Jenne (in Mali) are clearly "offshoots of a Saharan pottery tradition."[5] These migrants carried with them both languages and techniques of settled agriculture, especially those based on cereal grains, as well as techniques of animal husbandry, because they kept to the savannah lands below the desert and Sahel. They also domesticated new crops using their old techniques. Assisted ultimately by knowledge of iron-working (probably passed on from North Africa or the Nilotic kingdom of Kush), they effected an agricultural revolution. This meant considerable population growth in the more fertile Sudanic regions, especially near the Niger and Senegal rivers and Lake Chad. (A similar spread of agricultural techniques and cattle and sheep raising seems to have occurred down the Rift Valley of the East African highlands.) This agricultural revolution, completed during the first millennium B.C.E., enabled new cultural centers in the sub-Saharan regions to develop.

Whatever their earlier history, we know that in the first millennium B.C.E. the Sudanic peoples developed and refined techniques of settled agriculture. They must have carried these together with their languages eastward through the savannahs and southward, largely along the rivers, into the tropical rain forests of central and West Africa. The result changed the face of sub-Saharan Africa, where before small groups of hunter-gatherers had predominated. With the advent of iron smelting, these settled peoples were able to develop larger and more complex societies than their predecessors.

THE EARLY IRON AGE AND THE NOK CULTURE

The common features of the oldest iron-smelting furnaces found in widely scattered sites across Africa from the seventh century B.C.E. to the fourth century C.E. suggest that smelting in Africa was invented within the continent, probably in Egypt and Nubia, or possibly in the central Saharan highlands of the Tibesti, Ahaggar, and Aïr. Thence it likely spread southward

---

[4] Oliver, pp. 31–37.

[5] S.J. and R.J. McIntosh, *Prehistoric Investigations at Jenne, Mali* (Oxford, U.K.: B.A.R., 1980), p. 436.

DOCUMENT | Kushite Conquest of Memphis

The following text comes from a granite pillar, a victory stele that the Kushite king Piankhi had erected near Napata to commemorate his conquest of Egypt in the decade before 750 B.C.E. It describes the siege and capture of Memphis.

> ◆ What elements in the description might be slight exaggerations or hyperbole rather than sober chronicling?

When day broke, at early morning, his majesty reached Memphis. When he had landed on the north of it, he found that the water had approached to the walls, the ships mooring at [the walls of] Memphis. Then his majesty saw that it was strong, and that the wall was raised by a new rampart, and battlements manned with mighty men. There was found no way of attacking it. Every man told his opinion among the army of his majesty, according to every rule of war. Every man said: "Let us besiege it—; lo, its troops are numerous." Others said: "Let a causeway be made against it; let us elevate the ground to its walls. Let us bind together a tower; let us erect masts and make the spars into a bridge to it. We will divide it on this [plan] on every side of it, on the high ground and on the north of it, in order to

elevate the ground at its walls, that we may find a way for our feet."

Then his majesty was enraged against it like a panther; he said: "I swear, as Re loves me, as my father, Amon (who fashioned me), favors me, this shall befall it, according to the command of Amon … I will take it like a flood of water. I have commanded …" Then he sent forth his fleet and his army to assault the harbor of Memphis; they brought to him every ferryboat, every (cargo) boat, every (transport), and the ships, as many as there were, which had moored in the harbor of Memphis, with the bow-rope fastened among its houses. [There was not] a citizen who wept, among all the soldiers of his majesty.

His majesty himself came to line up the ships, as many as there were. His majesty commanded his army: "Forward against it! Mount the walls! Penetrate the houses over the river. If one of you gets through upon the wall, let him not halt before it (so that) the (hostile) troops may not repulse you …"

Then Memphis was taken as (by) a flood of water, a multitude of people were slain therein, and brought as living captives to the place where his majesty was.

From J. H. Breasted, *Ancient Records of Egypt* (Chicago: University of Chicago Press, 1906), Vol. 4, pars. 861 ff. Reprinted in Basil Davidson, *The African Past* (New York: Grosset and Dunlap, 1967), pp. 51–52.

into western, central, and eastern parts of the continent. The western route lay between copper- and iron-rich southern Mauritania and both the great bend of the Niger River and the middle Senegal River farther west. The central route, to which we shall return, was from the Saharan mountains into northern Nigeria. In a route more to the east, iron appears to have spread indirectly from Meroe in Nubia (discussed below) through the Darfur or Ennedi highlands between the Chad basin and the Nile to the Bantu peoples in the northern Kongo basin, and thence to the lakelands of the East African Rift. The easternmost transmission route likely paralleled the East African coast from the Ethiopian highlands and Nubia south to the Zambezi and Limpopo.[6]

Some of the most significant Iron Age sites have been found in what is today northeastern Nigeria, on the Jos plateau. Here archaeological digs have yielded evidence of an Iron-Age people labeled the Nok culture (see Map 5–1). Excavations at Nok sites have yielded stone tools, iron implements, and highly artistic terra-cotta sculptures dating from about 900 B.C.E. to 200 C.E. Scholars date the introduction of iron smelting to about the sixth century B.C.E. The Nok people cleared sub-

stantial woodlands from the plateau, and combined agriculture with cattle herding.

The Nok people had the earliest Iron Age culture of West Africa. That they likely acquired this art before 500 B.C.E. by way of the Aïr Mountains to the north is further evidence of early contact among African cultures. Nok culture also produced extraordinary sculptural art, most vividly evident in magnificent burial or ritual masks. The apparent continuities of Nok sculptural traditions with those of other, later West African cultures to the south suggest that this culture influenced later West and central African life. These continuities indicate that sophisticated ancient communities laid a basis on which later, better-known Sudanic civilizations must have built.

Nilotic Africa and the Ethiopian Highlands

THE KINGDOM OF KUSH

If we move east across the Sudan to the upper Nile basin, just above the first cataract, we come to the lower Nubian land of Kush (see Map 5–2). There an Egyptianized segment of Nilo-Saharan-speaking Nubians built the earliest-known literate

[6] Oliver, pp. 64–76.

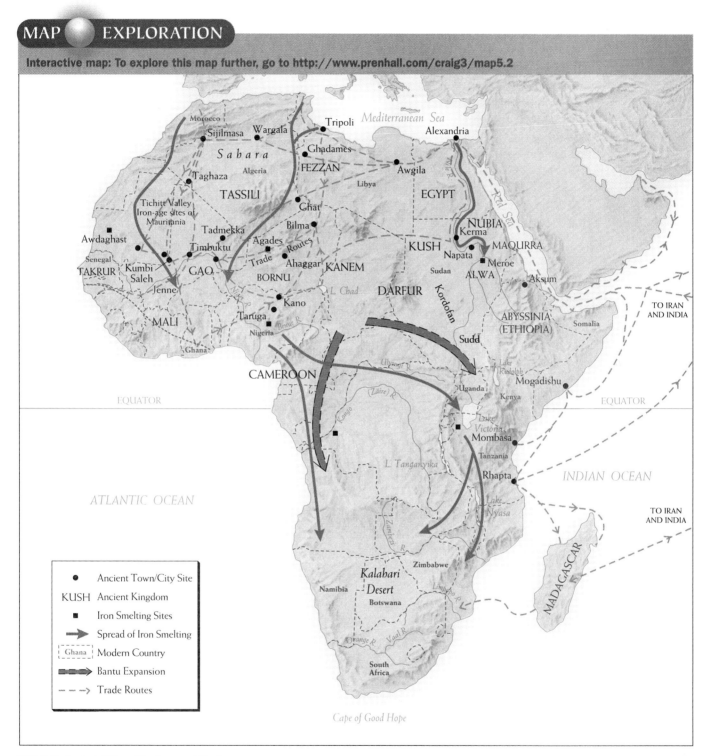

Interactive map: To explore this map further, go to http://www.prenhall.com/craig3/map5.2

MAP 5–2 Ancient African Kingdoms and Empires.

and politically unified civilization in Africa after Pharaonic Egypt. As early as the fourth millennium B.C.E., the Old Kingdom pharaohs had subjugated and colonized Nubia. In the early second millennium B.C.E., however, an independent kingdom arose in Kush in the broad floodplain just above the third cataract of the Nile. As early as 2000 B.C.E., its capital, Kerma, had been a major trading outpost for Middle Kingdom Egypt from which (and from neighboring settlements) a stream of building materials, ivory, slaves, mercenaries, and gold flowed north down the Nile.

The early Kushite kingdom reached its zenith between the Middle and New Kingdoms of Egypt, or about 1700–1500 B.C.E. Kush appears to have been a wealthy and prosperous kingdom. Finds in the royal palace fortress ruins and tombs suggest that these Nubian kings may have taken the gold mines of lower Nubia from the weakened Egyptian state in the Intermediate period. After the Hyksos invasions, with Egypt's recovery (from about 1500 B.C.E.) under the New Kingdom rulers, Kush came once more under Egyptian colonial rule and hence stronger Egyptian cultural influence. Then, sometime after 1000 B.C.E., as the New Kingdom floundered, a new Kushite state reasserted itself and by about 900 B.C.E. conquered lower as well as upper Nubia, regaining independence and the wealth from the Nubian gold mines.

THE NAPATAN EMPIRE

This new Kushite empire, centered first at Napata, just below the fourth Nile cataract, and then farther up the Nile at Meroe, was strong and lasting. (See Document, "Kushite Conquest of Memphis.") It survived from the tenth century B.C.E. until the fourth century C.E., when the Ethiopian Aksumites replaced Kush as the dominant power in northeastern Africa.

Napata, became the center of a new Nubian state and culture that flourished from the tenth to the seventh century B.C.E. as the true successor to pharaonic Egypt. The royal line that ruled at Napata saw themselves as Egyptian. They practiced the Pharaonic custom of marrying their own sisters, a practice known to many kingship institutions around the world. They buried their royalty embalmed in pyramids in traditional Egyptian style. They used Egyptian protocol and titles. In the eighth century B.C.E., they conquered Egypt and ruled it for about a century as the Twenty-fifth Pharaonic dynasty. This Kushite dynasty was driven out of Egypt proper by Assyria sometime around 650 B.C.E.

THE MEROITIC EMPIRE

Forced back above the lower cataracts of the Nile by the Assyrians and kept there by the Persians, the Napatan kingdom became increasingly isolated from Egypt and the Mediterranean and developed in its own distinctive ways. When an Egyptian army sacked Napata in 591 B.C.E., the capital was relocated farther south in the prosperous city of Meroe, bringing the seat of rule closer to the geographic center of the Kushite domains. By this time the Kushite kings had extended their sway westward into Kordofan, south above the confluence of the Blue and the White Nile, and southeast to the edges of the Abyssinian plateau. Meroe now became the kingdom's densely populated political and cultural capital. In the sixth century B.C.E. it was the center of a flourishing iron industry, from which iron smelting may first have spread west and south to the sub-Saharan world. The Meroitic state was built on a staggeringly wide network of internal African as well as intercontinental trade. (See Document, "Herodotus on Carthaginian Trade and the City of Meroe.") The empire lasted until it was defeated and divided in the fourth century C.E. by Nuba peoples from west of the upper Nile. The rival trading state of Aksum on the Abyssinian plateau then became the dominant regional power.

Culture and Economy   The heyday of Meroitic culture was from the mid–third century B.C.E. to the first century C.E. The kingdom was "middleman" for varied African goods in demand in the Mediterranean and Near East: animal skins, ebony and ivory, gold, oils and perfumes, and slaves. The Kushites traded

◄ **Ruins of the Great Amon Temple.** At Gebel (Mount) Barkal at the site of Napata, near Karima, Sudan, the Napatan kings were said to have been selected here by an oracle of the Egyptian god Amon, who was believed to reside inside the mountain.
Timothy Kendall.

with the Hellenistic-Roman world, southern Arabia, and India. They shipped quality iron to Aksum and the Red Sea, and the Kushite lands between the Nile and the Red Sea were a major source of gold for Egypt and the Mediterranean world. Cattle breeding and other animal husbandry and agriculture were their economic mainstays. Cotton cultivation in Kush preceded that of Egypt, and cotton may have been an early export of the kingdom.

This was an era of prosperity. Many monuments were built, including royal pyramids and the storied palace and walls of the capital. Fine pottery and jewelry were produced. Meroitic culture is especially renowned for its two kinds of pottery. The first, turned on wheels, was the product of an all-male industry attuned apparently to market demands; the second, made exclusively by hand by women, was largely for domestic use. This latter pottery seems to have come from an older tradition of African pottery craft found well outside the region of Kush—an indication of ancient traditions shared in varied regions of Africa and of the antiquity of African internal trade.

Rule and Administration   The political system of the Meroitic Empire, like the Pharaonic, endured for centuries. There were several features that distinguished it from its Egyptian models. The king seems to have ruled strictly by customary law, presumably as interpreted by whatever clerics served the state's needs. According to Greek accounts, firm taboos limited his actions; kings who violated those taboos could be forced to commit suicide. There was also a royal election system. The priests presented several candidates for king, from among whom the god would choose the new sacred king (how, we are not told). The priests apparently considered the king a living god, an idea found in both ancient Egypt and many other African societies.

A Kushite inscription tells us that King Aspelta (r. 593–568 B.C.E.) was elected to succeed his brother by twenty-four high officials and military leaders. Thus royal succession was within the royal family but not from father to son. Other inscriptions tell us that the succession was often through the maternal rather than the paternal line (matrilineal succession was widespread in ancient Africa). The role of the queen mother in the election appears to have been crucial—another parallel, if not a direct link, to African practices elsewhere. Indeed, the queen mother seems to have adopted formally her son's wife upon his succession. By the second century B.C.E. a woman had become sole monarch, initiating a long line of queens, or "Candaces" (*Kandake*, from the Meroitic word for "queen mother").

We know little of Meroitic administration. The empire seems to have been under the autocratic rule of the monarch, perhaps on the Egyptian

◄ **Meroitic Culture.** They produced many examples of fine pottery. This fired clay jar is decorated with giraffes and serpents.
University of Pennsylvania Museum of Archaelogy and Anthropology.

The Lion Temple and Kiosk at Naga. In the Butana Desert, about 60 miles northeast of Khartoum. Naga, founded in the early first century C.E., was a Meroitic caravanserai on the Red Sea trade routes. Initially, Kushite religion appears to have followed Egyptian tradition. By the third century B.C.E., however, gods who were unknown to Egypt rose in importance. Judging by the presence of many temples like this, the lion-headed god Apedemak was one of the most important of these gods.
Timothy Kendall.

model, who presided over a central administration run by numerous high officials: chiefs of the treasury, seal bearers, granary chiefs, army commanders, and chiefs of scribes and archives. The provinces were delegated to princes who must have enjoyed considerable autonomy, given the slow communications over the vast and difficult terrain of the upper Nile and eastern Sudanic region.

Society and Religion Because of the limited sources for Kushite history, we have to speculate about the social structure outside the palace circle—the ruling class of monarch and relatives, priests, courtiers and provincial nobility. We do find mention of slaves, both female domestics, and male laborers drawn largely from prisoners of war. Cattle breeders, farmers, traders, artisans, and minor government functionaries probably formed an intermediate class or classes between the slaves and the rulers.

We have no direct records of Kushite religious practices, but they clearly followed Egyptian traditions for centuries. To judge from the great temples dedicated to him, Amon was the highest god for the earlier kings, and his priests were influential. By the third century B.C.E., however, gods unknown to Egypt became prominent. Most notable was Apedemak, a warrior god with a lion's head. The many lion temples associated with him (forty-six have been identified) reflect his importance. Such gods likely represented local deities who gradually took their places alongside the highest Egyptian gods.

THE AKSUMITE EMPIRE

A highland people who had developed their own commercially powerful trading state to the south of Kush finished off the weakened Kushite empire, apparently about 330 c.e. This was the newly Christianized state of Aksum, which centered in the northern Ethiopian, or Abyssinian, highlands where the Blue Nile rises. With the ascendancy of Aksum, our sources lapse into relative silence concerning the Nubian regions of the Nile. Not until the rise of new Christian Nubian states in the mid–sixth century can we again find clear evidence of the inheritors of the land of Kush.

A Giant Stela at Aksum. Dating probably from the first century C.E., this giant carved monolith is the only one remaining of seven giant stelae—the tallest of which reached a height of 33 meters—that once stood in Aksum amidst numerous smaller monoliths. Although the exact purpose of the stelae is not known, the generally accepted explanation is that they were commemorative funerary monuments. Erecting them required engineering of great sophistication.
© Werner Former Archive/Art Resource, N.Y..

| DOCUMENT | Herodotus on Carthaginian Trade and on the City of Meroe |

Herodotus reports (in about 430 B.C.E. in the first passage below on what he has heard of the trading practices along the western or northwestern (Atlantic) coast of Africa ("Libya") as gleaned from the Carthaginian traders who passed beyond the Strait of Gibraltar ("Pillars of Hercules"). In the second passage he describes what he knows of the country, known to him as the land of the Ethiopians, above Elephantine (Aswan) on the Nile.

◆ What can we infer from the two passages about trade and interregional contacts in the fifth century B.C.E.?

The Carthaginians also tell us that they trade with a race of men who live in a part of Libya beyond the Pillars of Hercules. On reaching this country, they unload their goods, arrange them tidily along the beach, and then, returning to their boats, raise a smoke. Seeing the smoke, the natives come down to the beach, place on the ground a certain quantity of gold in exchange for the goods, and go off again to a distance. The Carthaginians then come ashore and take a look at the gold; and if they think it represents a fair price for their wares, they collect it and go away; if, on the other hand, it seems too little, they go back aboard and wait, and the natives come and add to the gold until they are satisfied. There is perfect honesty on both sides; the Carthaginians never touch the gold until it equals in value what they have offered for sale, and the natives never touch the goods until the gold has been taken.

I went as far as Elephantine to see what I could with my own eyes, but for the country still further south I had to be content with what I was told in answer to my questions. The most I could learn was that beyond Elephantine the country rises steeply; and in that part of the river boats have to be hauled along by the ropes—one rope on each side—much as one drags an ox. If the rope parts, the boat is gone in a moment, carried away by the force of the stream. These conditions last over a four days' journey, the river all the time winding greatly, like the Maeander, and the distance to be covered amounting to twelve *schoeni*. After this one reaches a level plain, where the river is divided by an island named Tachompso.

South of Elephantine the country is inhabited by Ethiopians who also possess half of Tachompso, the other half being occupied by Egyptians. Beyond the island is a great lake, and round its shores live nomadic tribes of Ethiopians. After crossing the lake one comes again to the stream of the Nile, which flows into it. At this point one must land and travel along the bank of the river for forty days, because sharp rocks, some showing above the water and many just awash, make the river impracticable for boats. After the forty days' journey on land one takes another boat and in twelve days reaches a big city named Meroë, said to be the capital city of the Ethiopians. The inhabitants worship Zeus and Dionysus alone of the Gods, holding them in great honor. There is an oracle of Zeus there, and they make war according to its pronouncements, taking from it both the occasion and the object of their various expeditions.

From the translation of *The Histories of Herodotus* by Aubrey de Selincourt, rev. by A. R. Burn (New York: Penguin Classics, 1954, revised 1972). Copyright © The estate of Aubrey de Selincourt, 1954, © A. R. Burn, 1972.

The peoples of Aksum were the product of a linguistic, cultural, and genetic mixing of African Kushitic speakers with Semitic speakers from Yemenite southern Arabia. This mixing occurred after southern Arabians infiltrated and settled on the Ethiopian plateau around 500 B.C.E., giving Aksum, and later Ethiopia, Semitic speech and script closely related to South Arabian. Greek and Roman sources tell of an Aksumite kingdom from at least the first century C.E. By this time the kingdom, through its chief port of Adulis, had already become the major ivory and elephant market of northeastern Africa. Adulis had been important in Ptolemaic times, when it was captured by Egypt and used as a conduit for Egyptian influence in the highlands. After Egypt fell to the Romans, Aksum and its major port became an important cosmopolitan commercial center.

In the first two centuries C.E., their Red Sea location gave the Aksumites a strategic seat astride the important Indian Ocean trade routes that linked India and the East Indies, Iran, Arabia, and the East African coast with the Roman Mediterranean. Aksum also controlled trade between the African interior and the extra-African world, from Rome to Southeast Asia—notably exports of ivory, but also of elephants, obsidian, slaves, gold dust, and other inland products. (See Document, "Seventh-Century Account of Aksumite Trade.")

By the third century C.E., Aksum was one of the most impressive states of its age. A work attributed to the prophet Mani, ca. 216–277 C.E., describes Aksum as one of the four greatest empires in the world. The Aksumites often held tributary territories across the Red Sea in southern Arabia. They also controlled northern Ethiopia and conquered Meroitic Kush. Thus they dominated some of the most fertile cultivated regions of the ancient world: their own plateau, the rich Yemenite highlands of southern Arabia, and much of the eastern Sudan across the upper Nile as far as the Sahara.

A king of kings in Aksum ruled this empire through tribute-paying vassal kings in the other subject states. By the sixth century

DOCUMENT | Seventh-Century Account of Aksumite Trade

The following document comes from a description of a trading voyage to Sri Lanka in 625 C.E. by a Greek-speaking monk and former merchant from Alexandria, known as Cosmas Indicopleustes. In the excerpt he describes what he had heard of the Aksum area and its products and resources.

◆ What does the passage tell us about ancient contact between northern East Africa and Arabia and beyond?

The region which produces frankincense is situated at the projecting parts of Ethiopia, and lies inland, but is washed by the ocean on the other side. Hence the inhabitants of Barbaria, being near at hand, go up into the interior and, engaging in traffic with the natives, bring back from them any kinds of spices, frankincense, cassia, calamus, and many other articles of merchandise, which they afterwards send by sea to Adule, to the country of the Homerites, to Further India, and to Persia. This very fact you will find mentioned in the Book of Kings, where it is recorded that the Queen of Sheba, that is, of the Homerite country, whom afterwards our Lord in the Gospels calls the Queen of the South, brought to Solomon spices from this very Barbaria, which lay near Sheba on the other side of the sea, together with bars of ebony, and apes and gold from Ethiopia, which, though separated from Sheba by the Arabian Gulf, lay in its vicinity. We can see again from the words of the Lord that he calls these places the ends of the earth, saying: *The Queen of the South shall rise up in judgment with this generation and shall condemn it, for she came from the ends of the earth to hear the wisdom of Solomon,* Matt. xii. 42. For the Homerites are not far distant from Barbaria, as the sea which lies between them can be crossed in a couple of days, and then beyond Barbaria is the ocean, which is there called Zingion. The country known as that of Sasu is itself near the ocean, just as the ocean is near the frankincense country, in which there are many gold mines. ...

From J. W. McCrindle, trans., *The Christian Topography of Cosmas, an Egyptian Monk* (London, 1897), as cited in G. S. P. Freeman-Grenville, ed., *The East African Coast,* 2nd ed. (London: Rex Collings, 1975), pp. 6–7.

---

the Aksumite king was even appointing southern Arabian kings himself. Aksum's coinage in gold, silver, and copper (it was the first tropical African state to mint these) coins symbolized both its political and economic power. The Aksumites enjoyed a long-lived economic prosperity. Goods of the Roman-Byzantine world and India and Sri Lanka, as well as of neighboring Meroe, flowed into Aksum. Vast herds and good agricultural produce also bolstered Aksumite prosperity.

In religion, the pre-Christian paganism of Aksum resembled the pre-Islamic paganism of southern Arabia, with various gods and goddesses closely tied to natural phenomena such as the sun, moon, and stars and worshiped with animal sacrifices. Jewish, Meroitic, and even Buddhist minorities lived in the major cities of Aksum—an index of the cosmopolitanism of the society and its involvement with the larger worlds beyond the Red Sea.

In an inscription of the powerful fourth-century ruler King Ezana, we read of his conversion to Christianity, which led to the Christianizing of the kingdom as a whole. The conversion of Ezana and his realm was the work of Frumentius, a Syrian bishop of Aksum who served as secretary and treasurer to the king. Subsequently, under Alexandrian influence, the Ethiopian church became Monophysite (that is, it adhered to the dogma of the single, unitary nature of Christ). Yet this did not end Aksumite trade with Byzantium, however much Constantinople persecuted Monophysites at home. In the fifth century C.E., the native Semitic language, Ge'ez, began to replace Greek in the liturgy, which proved a major step in the unique development of the Ethiopic or Abyssinian Christian church over the succeeding centuries.

CHRONOLOGY

●●●

Early African Civilizations

ca. 7500–2500 B.C.E.	"Wet Holocene" period
ca. 2500 B.C.E.	Rapid dessication of Saharan region begins
ca. 2000–1000 B.C.E.	Increasing Egyptian influence in Nubia
ca. 1000–900 B.C.E.	Kushite kingdom with capital at Napata becomes independent of Egypt
751–663 B.C.E.	Kushite kings Piankhi and Taharqa rule all Egypt
ca. 600–500 B.C.E.	Meroe becomes new Kushite capital
ca. 500 B.C.E.–330 C.E.	Meroitic kingdom of Kush (height of Meroitic Kushite power ca. 250 B.C.E.–50 C.E.)
ca. 500 B.C.E.–500 C.E.?	Nok culture flourishes on Jos plateau in western Sudan (modern central Nigeria)
First century C.E.	Rise of Aksum as trading power on Ethiopian (Abyssinian) plateau
ca. 330 C.E.	Aksumite conquest of Kush

ISOLATION OF CHRISTIAN ETHIOPIA

Aksumite trade continued to thrive through the sixth century, despite the decay of Rome. Strong enough at times to extend to the Yemen, Aksumite power was eclipsed in the end by Arab Islamic power. Nevertheless, the Aksumite state continued to exist. Having sheltered a refugee group of Muhammad's earliest Meccan converts, the Aksumites enjoyed relatively cordial relations with the new Islamic domains across the Red Sea and to the north in Egypt. But Aksum became increasingly isolated. Its center of gravity shifted south from the coast to the more rugged parts of the plateau. Here a Monophysite Christian, Ge'ez-speaking culture emerged in the region of modern Ethiopia and lasted in relative isolation until modern times, surrounded largely by Muslim peoples and states.

Ethiopia's northern neighbors, the Christian states of Maqurra and Alwa, also survived for centuries in the former Meroitic lands of the Nilotic Sudan under treaty relations with Muslim Egypt. However, incursions of the Muslim Mamluk rulers of Egypt in the fourteenth and fifteenth centuries and Arab migration from about 1300 led ultimately to the Islamization of the whole Nubian region. This left Ethiopia the sole predominantly Christian state in Africa.

The Western and Central Sudan
AGRICULTURE, TRADE, AND THE RISE OF URBAN CENTERS

Earlier we noted the presumed movements of Neolithic peoples southward from the Saharan regions into the western and central Sudan and ultimately into the equatorial forests. The rain forests were inhospitable to cows and horses, largely because of the animals' inability to survive the sleeping sickness (*trypanosomiasis*) carried by the tsetse fly. But the agriculturalists who brought their cereal grains and stone tools south found particularly good conditions in the savannah just north of the West African forests. By the first or second century C.E., settled agriculture, augmented by iron tools, had become the way of life of most inhabitants of the western Sudan; it had even progressed in the forest regions farther south. The savannah areas seem to have experienced a population explosion in the first few centuries C.E., especially around the Senegal River, the great northern bend of the Niger River, and Lake Chad. Villages, and chiefdoms of several villages, were the largest political units. As time went on, their growth provided the basis (and need) for larger towns and political units in the western Sudan to develop.

Trade also promoted or at least accompanied the eventual rise of larger political entities in the western and central Sudan. Regional and interregional trade networks in the western and central Sudan date to ancient times; as we saw earlier,

▲ **A Camel Caravan Crossing the Sahara.** The use of the camel as a beast of burden from the first century C.E. onward greatly increased trans-Saharan trade.
© Michael S. Lewis/Corbis.

contacts between the Sudanic regions and the Mediterranean were maintained throughout the first millennium B.C.E. over trans-Saharan trading routes. Extensive east–west trade connected the western Sahel to Egypt and the Nilotic Sudan. From the western Sahel this trade connected to Saharan routes and sites to the north (see Map 5–3).

By the latter first millennium B.C.E., urban settlements—such as Gao, Kumbi (or Kumbi Saleh), and Jenne—emerged in the western Sahel. Excavations at Jenne, in the upper Niger (the so-called Inland Delta) indicate that it dates from 250 B.C.E. and had a population of more than 10,000 by the late first millennium C.E.[7]

We have already noted even earlier evidence of urbanism farther west and north, in the southern Mauritanian desert. In addition, to the east, south of Lake Chad, 600 densely populated towns of the Sao, a Chadic-speaking people, can be dated to the early first millennium C.E.

All of these early urbanized areas combined farming with fishing and hunting, and all developed in oasis or river regions rich enough to support dense populations and trade. The existence of relatively autonomous settlements made possible loose confederations or even imperial networks as time went on (and much earlier than scholars used to think).

---

[7] S. J. and R. J. McIntosh, pp. 41–59, 434–461; and R. Oliver, p. 90. The ensuing discussion of West African urban settlement is also taken primarily from Oliver's excellent summary of current knowledge about this subject, ibid., pp. 90–101.

MAP 5–3 Africa: Early Trade Routes and Early States of the Western and Central Sudan. This map shows some of the major routes of north–south trans-Saharan caravan trade and their links with Egypt and with Sudanic and forest regions of West Africa.

The introduction of the domesticated camel (the one-humped Arabian camel, or dromedary) from the east around the beginning of the common era increased trans-Saharan trade. By the early Christian centuries the West African settled communities had developed important trading centers on their northern peripheries, in the Sahel near the edge of the true desert. The salt of the desert, so badly needed in the settled savannah, and the gold of West Africa, coveted in the north, were the prime

trade commodities. However, many other items were also traded, including cola nuts, slaves, dates, and gum from West Africa, and horses, cattle, millet, leather, cloth, and weapons from the north.

Towns such as Awdaghast, Walata, Timbuktu, Gao, Tadmekka, and Agades were the most famous southern terminals for this trade. These centers allowed the largely Berber middlemen who plied the desert routes to cross the ever-dangerous Sahara via oasis stations en route to the North African coasts or even Egypt. Some of the main routes ran as follows: (1) from Awdaghast, Walata, and Timbuktu to the major desert salt-producing center of Taghaza and thence to Morocco; (2) from Timbuktu or Gao over the desert direct to Morocco; and (3) from Tadmekka and Agades to the desert market town of Ghat in the north-central Sahara and on to the coasts of Libyan North Africa. Other lines went north from the region of Lake Chad; one route stretched as far east as Egypt itself. This was not an easy means of transporting goods for a typical crossing could take two to three months.

FORMATION OF SUDANIC KINGDOMS IN THE FIRST MILLENNIUM

The growth of settled agricultural populations and the expansion of trade coincided with the rise of sizable states in the western and central Sudan, significantly in the Sahel and savannah border region near the great water sources below the Sahara. The most important states were located in Takrur on the Senegal River, from perhaps the fifth century, if not earlier; Ghana, between the northern bends of the Senegal and the Niger, from the fifth or sixth century; Gao, on the Niger southeast of the great bend, from before the eighth century; and Kanem, northeast of Lake Chad, from the eighth or ninth century. Although the origins and even the full extent of the major states in these areas are obscure, each represents only the first of a series of large political entities in its region. All continued to figure prominently in subsequent West African history (see Chapter 17).

The states developed by the Fulbe people of Takrur and the Soninke people of Ghana depended on their ability to draw gold for the Saharan trade with Morocco from the savannah region west of the upper Senegal. Of all the sub-Saharan kingdoms of the late first millennium, Ghana was the most famous outside of the region, largely because of its control of the gold trade. Its

people built a large regional empire centered at its capital of Kumbi (or Kumbi Saleh). Inheriting his throne by matrilineal descent, the ruler was treated as a semidivine personage whose interaction with his subjects was mediated by a hierarchy of government ministers. An eleventh-century Arabic chronicle describes him as commanding a sizable army, including horsemen and archers, and being buried with his retainers under a dome of earth and wood. In contrast to the Soninke of Ghana, the Songhai rulers of Gao had no gold trade until the fourteenth century. Gao was oriented in its forest trade toward the lower Niger basin and in its Saharan trade toward eastern Algeria.

All of these states were based on agriculture and settled populations. By contrast, the power of Kanem, on the northwestern side of Lake Chad, originated in the borderlands of

▲ **Excavations at Jenne-Jeno.** (Ancient Jenne), an early urban settlement in the western Sahel. Note the layer-cake stratification. This photograph shows work progressing in levels dating to the first centuries B.C.E. and the founding of the site by agriculturalists who came from the Saharan north.

Roderick.J. Macintosh, Rice University.

CHRONOLOGY

The Western and Central Sudan: Probable Dates for Founding of Regional Kingdoms

ca. 400 C.E.	Takrur (Senegal River valley) or earlier
400–600 C.E.	Ghana (in Sahel between great northern bends of the Senegal and Niger Rivers)
ca. 700–800 C.E.	Gao (on the Niger River or before southeast of great bend)
ca. 700–900 C.E.	Kanem (northeast of Lake Chad)

the central Sudan and southern Sahara with a nomadic federation of black tribal peoples that persisted long enough for the separate tribes to merge and form a single people, the Kanuri. They then moved south to take over the sedentary societies of Kanem proper, just east of Lake Chad, and later, Bornu, west of Lake Chad. By the thirteenth century the Kanuri had themselves become sedentary. Their kingdom controlled the southern terminus of perhaps the best trans-Saharan route—that running north via good watering stations to the oasis region of Fezzan in modern central Libya and thence to the Mediterranean. We shall return to Kanem and the western Sudanic states and their later development in Chapter 17.

Central, Southern, and East Africa

The African subcontinent is that part of central, southern, and East Africa that lies south of a line from roughly the Niger Delta and Cameroon across to southern Somalia on the east coast. The few sources make it difficult to reconstruct a detailed history of this region before 1000 C.E.

⚠ **Prehistoric San Rock Painting.** This is from southern Africa.
Christopher and Sally Gable© Dorling Kindersley.

THE KHOISAN PEOPLES

In southern Africa, as already noted, we find alongside the Bantu-speaking majority a minority who speak "Khoisan." The main two peoples that constitute the Khoisan speakers are the San and the Khoikhoi (the "Bushmen" and the "Hottentots," respectively, in archaic Western usage). The conventional view holds that the Khoikhoi and the San can be distinguished from each other largely by their livelihood.[8] The Khoikhoi have generally been tagged as herdsmen and the San as hunter-gatherers, but recent research has challenged this. Both groups have also typically been seen as surviving representatives of a "primitive" stage of cultural evolution, a view many anthropologists and historians now reject. These scholars argue that much of the common wisdom about these peoples, who have low social and economic status in the Namibia-Botswana-Zimbabwe-South Africa areas results from colonialist and postcolonialist prejudice.

The San are likely the descendants of the Neolithic and Early Iron Age peoples who created the striking prehistoric rock paintings of southern Africa. They have developed linguistically and culturally diverse subgroups across southern Africa. Today they survive most prominently in the Kalahari region. The more homogeneous Khoikhoi were generally sheep- and cattle-herding pastoralists scattered across the south, yet speaking closely related Khoisan tongues. Their ancestors probably originated in northern Botswana. They were hunters who relatively late—likely between 700 and 1000 C.E.—adopted animal herding from their Bantu-speaking southern African neighbors. Thus they became primarily pastoralists and soon expanded as far south as the Cape of Good Hope. Here they flourished as pastoralist clans, until their tragic encounter with the invading Dutch colonists in the mid–seventeenth century, which resulted in their demise as a distinct people.

BANTU EXPANSION AND DIFFUSION

In the southern subcontinent, most people speak one of more than 400 languages that belong to a single language group known as *Bantu*. All of these languages are as closely related as are the Germanic or Romance tongues of Europe. The proto-Bantu language probably arose south of the Benue River, in eastern Nigeria and modern Cameroon. Thence, during the later centuries B.C.E.. and the first millennium C.E., migrations of Bantu-speaking peoples must have carried their languages in two basic directions: (1) south into the lower Zaïre (Kongo) basin and ultimately to the southern edge of the equatorial forest in present-day northern Katanga; and (2) east around the equatorial forests into the lakes of highland East Africa.

[8] On the vexing problem of distinguishing San and Khoikhoi, see Richard Elphick, *Kraal and Castle: Khoikhoi and the Founding of White South Africa* (New Haven: Yale University Press, 1977), pp. xxi–xxii, 3–42; on the "construction" of their respective identities and for a summary of recent research on their antiquity and history, see E. N. Wilmsen, *Land Filled with Flies* (Chicago: University of Chicago Press, 1989).

| **A Tenth-Century Arab Description of the East African Coast**

This selection is from the famous Baghdadi scholar al-Mas'udi, who died in Cairo about 956 C.E. It treats the country of the Zanj, by which he means the coastal region of East Africa from the Horn down to Mozambique, a region that he himself visited on a voyage from Oman.

◆ In what ways does this Muslim observer seem to be critical, and in what ways laudatory, of the East Africans?

The sea of the Zanj reaches down to the country of Sofala and of the Wak-Wak which produces gold in abundance and other marvels; its climate is warm and its soil fertile. It is there that the Zanj built their capital; then they elected a king whom they called *Waklimi* ....

The *Waklimi* has under him all the other Zanj kings, and commands three hundred thousand men. The Zanj use the ox as a beast of burden, for their country has no horses or mules or camels and they do not even know these animals. Snow and hail are unknown to them as to all the Abyssinians. Some of their tribes have sharpened teeth and are cannibals. The territory of the Zanj begins at the canal which flows from the Upper Nile and goes down as far as the country of Sofala and the Wak-Wak. Their settlements extend over an area of about seven hundred parasangs in length and in breadth; this country is divided by valleys, mountains and stony deserts; it abounds in wild elephants but there is not so much as a single tame elephant ....

Although constantly employed in hunting elephants and gathering ivory, the Zanj make no use of ivory for their own domestic purposes. They wear iron instead of gold and silver ....

... *Waklimi* ... means supreme lord; they give this title to their sovereign because he has been chosen to govern them with equity. But once he becomes tyrannical and departs from the rules of justice, they cause him to die and exclude his posterity from succession to the throne, for they claim that in thus conducting himself he ceases to be the son of the Master, that is to say of the king of heaven and earth. They call God by the name of Maklandjalu, which means supreme Master. ...

The Zanj speak elegantly, and they have orators in their own language ... These peoples have no code of religion; their kings follow custom, and conform in their government to a few political rules. ... Each worships what he pleases, a plant, an animal, a mineral.

They possess a great number of islands where the coconut grows, a fruit that is eaten by all the peoples of the Zanj. One of these islands, placed one or two days' journey from the coast, has a Muslim population who provide the royal family....

Translated from the French version of de Meynard and de Courteille (1864) by Basil Davidson, *The African Past* (New York: Grosset and Dunlap, 1967), pp. 108–109.

In all these regions, Bantu tongues developed and multiplied in contact with other languages. Likewise, Bantu speakers intermixed and adapted in diverse ways, as the wide variety of physical types among Bantu peoples today demonstrates. Further migrations, some as early as the fourth century C.E. and others as late as the twelfth or thirteenth century, dispersed Bantu peoples even more widely, into south-central Africa, coastal East Africa, and southern Africa. This dispersion led to the early civilization of "Great Zimbabwe" and Mapungubwe in the upper Limpopo region (treated in Chapter 17). The notion, however, that the Bantu and the Khoikhoi arrived in southern Africa at about the same time as the first European settlers was a fabrication to justify apartheid (see Chapter 34).

How the Bantu peoples managed to impose their languages on the earlier cultures of these regions remains unexplained. The proto-Bantu had apparently been fishermen and hunters who also cultivated yams, date palms, and cereals. They raised goats and possibly sheep and cattle, but they did not bring cattle with them in their migrations. Most of the migrating Bantus seem to have been mainly cereal farmers whose basic political and social unit was the village. Perhaps they had unusually strong social cohesion, which allowed them to absorb other peoples; they were apparently not military conquerors. Possibly they simply had sufficient numbers to become dominant, or they may have brought diseases with them against which the aboriginals of the forests and southern savannah had no immunities.

Bantu cultures became in time so fully interwoven with those of the peoples among whom they settled that these questions may never be answered. Bantu-Arab mixing on the eastern coasts produced the Swahili culture (see Chapter 17).

EAST AFRICA

The history of East Africa along the coast before Islam differed from that of the inland highlands. Long-distance travel was easy and common along the seashore but less so inland. The coast had had maritime contact with India, Arabia, and the Mediterranean via the Indian Ocean and Red Sea trade routes from at least the second century B.C.E. By contrast, we know little about the long-distance contacts of inland regions with the coastal areas until after 1000 C.E. Nonetheless, both regional inland and coastal trade must also be ancient. Both coastal and overseas trade remained important and interdependent over the centuries, because the Indian Ocean trade depended on the monsoon winds and could use only the northernmost coastal trading

CHRONOLOGY

Movement and Contact of Peoples in Central, Southern, and East Africa

ca. 1300–1000 B.C.E.	Kushitic-speaking peoples migrate from Ethiopian plateau south along Rift Valley
ca. 400 B.C.E.–1000 C.E.	Probable era of major Bantu migrations into central, East, and southeastern Africa
200–100 B.C.E.	East African coast becomes involved in Indian Ocean trade
ca. 100 B.C.E.	Probable time of first Indonesian immigration to East African coast
ca. 100–1500 C.E.	Nilotic-speaking peoples spread over upper Nile valley; Nilotic peoples spread over Rift Valley region

harbors of East Africa for round-trip voyages in the same year. The monsoon winds blow from the northeast from December to March and thus can carry sailing ships south from Iran, Arabia, and India only during those months; they blow from the southwest from April to August, so ships can sail from Africa northeast during those months. Local coastal shipping thus had to haul cargoes from south of Zanzibar and then transfer them to other ships for the annual round-trip voyages to Arabia and beyond.

Long-distance trade came into its own in Islamic times—about the ninth century—as an Arab monopoly. However, long before the coming of Islam, trade was apparently largely in the hands of Arabs, many of whom had settled in the East African coastal towns and in Iran and India to handle this international commerce. We can document Graeco-Roman contact with these East African centers of Red Sea and Indian Ocean trade from as early as the first century C.E. Most of the coastal trading towns apparently were independent, although Rhapta, the one town mentioned in the earliest Greek source, *The Periplus* (ca. 89 C.E.), was a dependency of a southern Arabian state.

The overseas trade was, however, evidently even more international than the earliest sources indicate. Today, Malagasy, the imported Malayo-Polynesian language of Madagascar, points to the antiquity of contact with the East Indies via the coastal trading routes of Asia's ancient southern rim. Even before the beginning of our era, bananas, coconut palms, and other crops indigenous to Southeast Asia had spread across Africa as staple foods. Further, as a result of the early regular commercial ties to distant lands of Asia, extra-African ethnic and cultural mixing has long been the rule for the East African coast; even today, its linguistic and cultural traditions are rich and varied (see Chapter 17). (See Document, "A Tenth-Century Arab Description of the East African Coast.")

East Africa also imported such items as Persian Gulf pottery, Chinese porcelain, and cotton cloth. The major African export

good around which the east-coast trade revolved was ivory, which was in perennial demand from Greece to India and even China. The slave trade was another major business. Slaves were procured, often inland, in East Africa and exported to the Arab and Persian world, as well as to India or China. Gold became important in external trade only in Islamic times, from about the tenth century onward, as we shall see in Chapter 17. Wood and cereals must also have been shipped abroad.

The history of inland East Africa south of Ethiopia is much more difficult to trace than that of the coast, again because of the absence of written sources and the immense difficulty of access. However, linguistic clues and other evidence indicate some key developments in the eastern highlands. These regions had seen an early diffusion of peoples from the north, and over the centuries small groups continued to move into new areas. Of the early migrants from the north, first came peoples speaking Kushitic languages of the Afro-Asiatic family, likely cattle herders and grain cultivators. Perhaps as early as 2000 B.C.E., they pushed from their homeland on the Ethiopian plateau south down the Rift Valley as far as the southern end of Lake Tanganyika. They apparently displaced Neolithic hunter-gatherers who may have been related to the Khoisan minorities of modern East and southern Africa. Although Kushitic languages are spoken from east of Lake Rudolph northward in abundance, farther south only isolated remnants of Kushitic speakers remain today, largely in the Rift Valley in Tanzania.

Later, Nilotic-Saharan speakers moved from the southwestern side of the Ethiopian plateau west over the upper Nile valley by about 1000 C.E. Then they pushed east and south, following older Kushite paths, to spread over the Rift Valley area by the fifteenth century and subsequently much of the East African highlands of modern-day Uganda, Kenya, and Tanzania, where they supplanted their Kushite predecessors. Two of these Nilotic peoples were the Lwo and the Maasai. The Lwo spread over a 900-mile-long swath of modern Uganda and parts of southern Sudan and western Kenya, absorbing new cultural elements and adapting to new situations wherever they went. The Maasai, on the other hand, were and still are cattle pastoralists proud of their separate language, way of life, and cultural traditions. These features have distinguished them from the farming or hunting peoples whose settlements abutted their pasturages at the top of the southern Rift Valley in modern Kenya and Tanzania. Here the Maasai have concentrated and remained.

These migrations and those of the Bantu peoples, who entered the eastern highlands over many centuries, have made the highlands a melting pot of Kushitic, Nilotic, Bantu, and Khoisan groups. Their characteristics are visible in today's populations, possessing an immense diversity of languages and cultures. Here as well as anywhere we can see the radical diversity of peoples and cultures of the entire African continent mirrored in a single region.

Summary

Geography and History   The human species, *homo sapiens* (*sapiens*) probably originated in Africa. Africa's geography and climate, however, limited Africans' contact with peoples outside the continent. Nonetheless, Africa cannot be considered a dark continent without a history. Within Africa itself, archaeology reveals that there were extensive migrations of peoples across the continent from the earliest days of African history with widespread cross-cultural influences.

Meroe.

Contact with Other Cultures   In three parts of Africa, there was considerable contact with non-African civilizations. In the Nile River valley, Egypt had extensive interaction with the Nubian peoples to its south. Nubian kingdoms—Kush, Napata, Meroe, and Aksum (Ethiopia)—adopted many features of Egyptian civilization and sometimes dominated Egypt itself. Aksum adopted Christianity in the fourth century C.E.

On the coast of East Africa, trade across the Red Sea and the Indian Ocean with Arabia and east Asia fostered a distinct and sophisticated culture. Extensive trade across the Sahara between North Africa and the western and central Sudan enabled products and ideas from the Mediterranean to reach the African interior in exchange for African products, such as gold, ivory, and salt.

Review Questions

1. Do early African societies lack true "civilization"? Explain your answer.

2. What are the primary sources for study of Africa to 1000 C.E.? Assess their advantages and drawbacks as reliable sources for early African history.

3. What does the diffusion of peoples and languages in Africa tell us about early African history?

4. How does the political system of the Meroitic Empire compare to that of Egypt?

5. How did Aksum become a Christian state?

6. What were the most important goods for African internal trade? Which products were traded abroad? What can we learn from these trade patterns?

7. How did geography "control" early African history? What about the specific case of Ghana? Of North Africa? Of the East African littoral? Of southern Africa?

Key Terms

Kalahari   (p. 152)

Nilotic Africa   (p. 152)

Sahara   (p. 151)

Sahel   (p. 151)

savannah   (p. 151)

Documents CD-ROM

Eurasian Connections before European Expansion
11.2 The Cities of the Zanj and The Indian Ocean Trade

NOTE: *To learn more about the topics in this chapter, see the Suggested Readings at the end of the book.*

Republican and Imperial Rome

◄ Imperial Procession" from the frieze of the Ara Pacis, Augustan
Rome, 9 B.C.E.

Museum of the Ara Pacis, Rome/Nimatallah/Art Resource, N.Y.

Republican and Imperial Rome

Despite the nearly continuous warfare that marked Roman history, including a long-lasting rivalry with the Sassanid Empire, it was primarily through trade that Romans came into contact with peoples beyond the borders of their empire. Strong, centralized empires in the West (Rome), in China (Han), and in India (Mauryan), were able to provide law and order to their citizens, protection to travelers, and an infrastructure that included decent roads and coinage. Likewise, merchants and missionaries found it possible to transport themselves and their goods in greater safety than ever before throughout much of Eurasia. As a result, a tenuous but continuous network of routes by land (the first Silk Road) and sea (the Arabian "monsoon route" across the Indian Ocean) linked the Roman world to China and allowed a thin but continuous stream of people, cargo, and ideas to cross Asia from east to west and from north to south. As yet the fruits of this exchange were small compared to the significance of the later, medieval Silk Road with Central Asia, whose merchants and towns were the vital intermediaries of trade and benefited the most. However, there is no doubt that Roman objects and with them some knowledge of Rome, reached China and India, and vice versa.

Nonetheless, most Romans focused their energies on internal Roman territory, which expanded considerably during the late republic and the early empire to include much of the former Hellenistic kingdoms. This is not surprising given that, despite the expansion of trade in this period, agriculture was still the primary occupation and source of income of most people in the empire. But Rome was a multicultural empire, encompassing territory and cultures in Africa and the Middle East, as well as northern and central Europe. Rome profited enormously from the territories it conquered in terms of material wealth, including foodstuffs, as Egypt quickly became the "breadbasket" of the empire. It also realized cultural benefits, especially that blending of Greek and Asian culture that characterized the Hellenistic world. But the infusion of new ideas caused tension among Romans, as many conservative Romans objected to what they viewed as corrupting Asian influences from even the much admired, and copied, Greeks which threatened to undermine traditional Roman values and strengths.

The conquest of a vast empire had moved the Romans away from their unusual historical traditions toward the more familiar path of empire trodden by rulers in Egypt, Mesopotamia, China, India, and Iran. It is especially instructive to look at Rome from the perspective of historians who discern a "dynastic cycle" in China (see Chapter 7). The development of the Roman Empire, although by no means the same as the Chinese, fits the same pattern fairly well. Like the Former Han dynasty in China, the Roman Empire in the West fell, leaving in its wake disunity, insecurity, disorder, and poverty. Like other similar empires in the ancient world, it had been unable to sustain its "immoderate greatness."

THINK AHEAD

- Why might we describe the Roman Empire as "multicultural"? What cultures most influenced Roman culture, and why?

- What was it about the period from the second century B.C.E. through the third century C.E. that allowed the opening of new routes by land and sea linking Europe to Central Asia, India, and China?

- Why did the Roman Empire decline in the West? Which of the problems that Rome faced were internal, and which were external? How were the two connected?

THE ANCIENT ROMANS WERE RESPONSIBLE FOR one of the most remarkable achievements in history. From their city in central Italy, which began as a small village, they conquered all of Italy, then the entire Mediterranean coastline, and finally most of the Near East and much of continental Europe. Their unifying government brought centuries of peace and prosperity to this vast region, which has never been unified again and has only rarely since enjoyed prolonged peace and stability.

When it began its expansion, Rome had a nonmonarchical, republican government. Few nonmonarchical governments have lasted for more than a relatively short time, and the Roman Republic, which endured for almost five hundred years and came to control a vast empire, has no parallel. The eventual fall of the republic and the imposition of an imperial monarchy under Augustus, Rome's first emperor, ended this unusual chapter in history. The transition was difficult. Romans continued to think in republican terms for generations, and many longed for the republic's restoration. Augustus skillfully maintained the appearance of republican institutions, helping to mask the monarchical reality. The passage of time made such deception less necessary. Hard times and chaos in the third century C.E. revealed the military foundation of the emperors' increasingly autocratic rule. Beginning in the first century C.E. emperors were declared divine after death; by the second century they were worshiped as gods while alive, like the rulers of ancient Egypt and other early empires.

Rome's legacy was not just of military prowess and superb political organization. The Romans also adopted and transformed the intellectual and cultural achievements of the Greeks, creating the Graeco-Roman tradition in literature, philosophy, and art. This tradition formed the core of learning during the Middle Ages and inspired the new intellectual paths taken during the Renaissance. It remains the heart of Western civilization.

Prehistoric Italy

About 1000 B.C.E. bands of warlike peoples speaking a set of closely related languages we call Italic began to infiltrate Italy. By 800 B.C.E. they had occupied the highland pastures of the Apennines and soon challenged the earlier settlers for control of the tempting western plains. The Romans would emerge from among the descendants of these tough mountain people. Others who shaped the future of Italy included the Etruscans, the Greeks who colonized Sicily and southern Italy, and the Celts, who established themselves in the north around 400 B.C.E.

The Etruscans

Etruscan civilization, which was to have a powerful influence on the Romans, arose about 800 B.C.E. (see Map 6–1). The Etruscans lived in self-governing, fortified city-states. They constituted a military ruling class, dominating the native people they had dispossessed and exploiting them to work their lands and fight in their infantry. The Etruscan states were first ruled by kings and later by an agrarian aristocracy that governed through a council and annually elected magistrates. This aristocracy accumulated considerable wealth through agriculture, industry, piracy, and commerce with the Carthaginians of North Africa and the Greeks.

In the seventh and sixth centuries B.C.E. the Etruscans conquered Latium (which included Rome) and Campania, where they became neighbors of the Greeks of Naples. But after 500 B.C.E. Etruscan power rapidly declined. The Celts drove them from the Po valley about 400 B.C.E., and soon thereafter they lost control of their Etrurian heartland to an expanding Rome.

Sarcophages of Etruscan Couple. Much of what we know of the Etruscans comes from their funerary art. This sculpture of an Etruscan couple is part of a sarcophagus.
© Erich Lessing/Art Resource, N.Y.

MAP 6–1 Ancient Italy.   This map of ancient Italy and its neighbors before the expansion of Rome shows the major cities and towns as well as a number of geographical regions and the locations of some of the Italic and non-Italic peoples.

Royal Rome

In the sixth century B.C.E. the town of Rome in Latium came under Etruscan control. Although it had been of little importance, it was a natural center for communication and trade. Led by Etruscan kings, the Roman army conquered most of Latium. Rome's effective political and social organization, which gave extraordinary power to its rulers, made this success possible.

GOVERNMENT

Roman kings had the awesome power of *imperium*, the right to issue commands and to enforce them by fines, arrests, and physical punishment, including execution. Although it tended to remain in families, kingship was elective. The Roman Senate approved the candidate for the office, and the Roman people, voting in assembly, formally granted the *imperium*. This procedure—the granting of great power to executive officers contingent on the approval of the Senate and ultimately the people—would remain a basic characteristic of Roman government.

The king was the commander of the army, the chief priest, and the supreme judge. He conducted foreign affairs, commanded the army, and disciplined his troops, all by virtue of his *imperium*. In practice the royal power was much more limited.

The Senate, the second branch of the early Roman government, ostensibly had neither executive nor legislative power; it met only when summoned by the king and then only to advise him. In reality its authority was great, for the senators, like the king, served for life. The Senate, therefore, had continuity and experience, and it was composed of the most powerful men in the state. It could not be ignored.

The third branch of government, the curiate assembly, was made up of all citizens and divided into thirty groups. The assembly also met only when summoned by the king. Usually, the assembly was called to listen and approve. Voting was not by head but by group; a majority within each group determined its vote, and the decisions were made by majority vote of the groups. Group voting would be typical of all future forms of Roman assembly.

FAMILY

The center of Roman life was the family. At its head stood the father, whose power and authority resembled those of the king within the state. Over his children he held broad powers analogous to *imperium*; he could sell his children into slavery and might even kill them. Over his wife he had less power; he could not sell or kill her. In practice his power to dispose of his children was limited by other family members, by public opinion, and, most of all, by tradition. A wife could be divorced only for serious offenses, and only after she had been convicted by a court made up of her male blood relatives. The Roman woman had a respected position and the main responsibility for managing the household. The father was the chief priest of the family, leading it in daily prayers to the dead that reflected the ancestor worship central to the Roman family and state.

CLIENTAGE

Clientage was one of Rome's most important institutions. The client was "an inferior entrusted, by custom or by himself, to the protection of a stranger more powerful than he, and rendering certain services and observances in return for this protection."[1] The client was said to be in the *fides*, or trust, of his patron, giving the relationship a moral dimension. The patron provided his client with physical and legal protection and economic support. In return the client would fight for his patron, work his land, and support him politically. These mutual obligations were enforced by public opinion and tradition. When early custom was codified in the mid–fifth century B.C.E., one of the twelve tablets of laws announced: "Let the patron who has defrauded his client be accursed."[2]

In early Rome patrons were rich and powerful, whereas clients were poor and weak, but in time, rich and powerful members of the upper classes increasingly became clients of even more powerful men. Because the client-patron relationship was hereditary and was sanctioned by religion and custom, it played an important part in the life of the Roman Republic.

PATRICIANS AND PLEBEIANS

In the royal period Roman society was divided into two classes based on birth. The wealthy **patrician** upper class held a monopoly of power and influence. Its members alone could conduct state religious ceremonies, sit in the Senate, or hold office. They formed a closed caste by forbidding marriage outside their own group.

The **plebeian** lower class must have consisted originally of poor, dependent small farmers, laborers, and artisans, the clients of the nobility. As Rome grew, nonpatrician families acquired wealth. From early times, therefore, there were rich plebeians and patrician families that fell into poverty from incompetence or bad luck. The line between the classes and the monopoly of privileges nevertheless remained firm.

The Republic

According to Roman tradition, the outrageous behavior of the last kings provoked the noble families to revolt in 509 B.C.E., leading to the creation of the republic.

CONSTITUTION

The Roman constitution was an unwritten accumulation of laws and customs.

Consuls   The Romans were never willing to deprive their chief magistrates of the great powers their kings had exercised. They elected two patricians to the office of consul and endowed them with *imperium*. Assisting the consuls were financial officials called *quaestors*. Like the kings, the consuls led the army,

had religious duties, and served as judges. Consular power, however, was limited legally, institutionally, and by custom.

The power of the consulship was granted for a year only. Each consul could overrule the other, and they shared their religious powers with others. Even the *imperium* was limited. Although the consuls had full powers of life and death while leading an army, within the sacred boundary of the city of Rome, citizens could appeal to the popular assembly all cases involving capital punishment. Besides, after their year in office, the consuls would spend the rest of their lives as members of the Senate, so only a reckless consul would ignore its advice.

The many checks on consular action tended to prevent initiative, swift action, and change, but this was just what a conservative, traditional, aristocratic republic wanted. Only in military matters did these limitations create problems. In serious crises, the consuls could, with the advice of the Senate, appoint a dictator, who would have *imperium* not subject to appeal both inside and outside the city for six months. These devices sufficed in the early republic, when Rome's battles were near home, but longer wars and more sophisticated opponents required significant changes.

In 325 B.C.E. the Romans created the office of proconsul, which permitted a consul in the field to retain command during a long campaign. Another new office, that of praetor, was primarily judicial, but praetors also had *imperium* and served as generals. They too could have their one-year term of office extended for long campaigns. Eventually there were eight praetors.

After the middle of the fifth century B.C.E. the job of identifying citizens and classifying them according to age and property was delegated to a new office, that of **censor**. The Senate elected two censors every five years. They conducted a census and drew up the citizen rolls. Because the classification fixed taxation and status, the censors had to be men of reputation, former consuls. They soon acquired additional powers and by the fourth century B.C.E. had the authority to exclude senators from the Senate on moral as well as financial grounds. As the prestige of the office grew, it came to be considered the ultimate prize of a political career.

Senate and Assembly   The end of the monarchy increased the power of the Senate. Composed of leading patricians, often clan leaders and patrons with many clients, it became the only ongoing deliberative body in the Roman state and soon controlled finances and foreign policy.

The *centuriate assemble*, the early republic's most important popular assembly, was, in a sense, the Roman army acting in a political capacity. Its basic unit was the century, theoretically one hundred fighting men who fought with the same kind of equipment. Because each man equipped himself, this organization divided the assembly into classes according to wealth.

---

[1] E. Badian, *Foreign Clientelae (264–70 B.C.E.)* (Oxford: Oxford University Press, 1958), p. 1.

[2] *Roman Civilization: Selected Readings*, Vol. 1, ed. by Naphtali Lewis and Meyer Reinhold (New York: Columbia University Press, 1963).

Lictors. Pictured here, lictors attended the chief Roman magistrates when they appeared in public. The ax carried by one of the lictors and the bound bundle of staffs carried by the others symbolize both the power of Roman magistrates to inflict corporal punishment on Roman citizens and the limits on that power. The bound staffs symbolize the right of citizens within the city of Rome not to be punished without a trial. The ax symbolizes the power of the magistrates, as commanders of the army, to put anyone to death without a trial outside the city walls.
Alinari/Art Resource, N.Y.

Struggle of the Orders   Patricians monopolized power in the early republic. Plebeians were barred from all political and religious offices. In response, the plebeians launched the "struggle of the orders," a fight for political, legal, and social equality that lasted two hundred years.

Plebeians made up much of the Roman army, giving them great political leverage. They formed the plebeian tribal assembly, and elected **tribunes**, officials with the power to protect plebeians from abuse by patrician magistrates. In effect, a tribune could veto any action of a magistrate or any bill in a Roman assembly or the Senate.

In 450 B.C.E. the Twelve Tables were published, the first attempt to codify Rome's harsh customs. In 445 B.C.E. plebeians won the right to marry patricians. It was not until 367 B.C.E. that one of the consuls was allowed to be of plebeian rank. Gradually other offices, including the dictatorship and the censorship, opened to them. In 300 B.C.E. they were admitted to the most important priesthoods. In 287 B.C.E. the plebeians secured the passage of a law making the decisions of the plebeian assembly binding on all Romans without the approval of the Senate.

The victory of the plebeians allowed wealthy plebeian families to enter politics and share the privileges of the patrician aristocracy. The *nobiles*—a relatively small group of wealthy and powerful families, both patrician and plebeian—dominated the increasingly powerful Senate and controlled the highest offices of the state.

The end of the struggle of the orders brought domestic peace under a republican constitution dominated by a capable, if narrow, senatorial aristocracy. Most Romans accepted this leadership, which secured them a growing empire and many benefits.

CONQUEST OF ITALY

Initial Expansion and Gallic Invasion   By the beginning of the fourth century B.C.E. the Romans were the chief power in central Italy, but in 387 B.C.E. the Gauls, marching south from the Po valley, captured, looted, and burned Rome. Rome appeared finished, but by about 350 B.C.E. it had reclaimed the leadership of central Italy.

In 340 B.C.E. the city's Latin neighbors, the Latin League, sought to curtail Rome's expansion. In 338 B.C.E. the Romans defeated the league and dissolved it. The terms they imposed provided a model for the way they were to treat opponents as they incorporated the rest of Italy.

Roman Policy Toward the Conquered   The Romans did not destroy any of the Latin cities nor did they treat them all alike. To some near Rome they granted full citizenship. To others farther away they granted municipal status, which included the right to local self-government and the right to trade and intermarry with Romans, but not to take part in Roman politics unless they moved to Rome and applied for citizenship. These states followed Rome's foreign policy and supplied soldiers for Rome's legions. Still other states became allies of Rome on the basis of treaties that differed from city to city. All the allies supplied troops to fight in auxiliary battalions under Roman officers, but they did not pay taxes to Rome.

The Romans established permanent colonies of veteran soldiers in conquered lands. The colonists remained Roman citizens and deterred rebellion. A network of durable roads—some still in use—connected the colonies to Rome, permitting troops to be moved swiftly to any trouble spot.

Rome divided its enemies and extended its influence through military force and diplomatic skill. Rebels were punished harshly and swiftly. But Rome was also generous to those who submitted. The status of a newly conquered city was not permanent. Loyal allies could improve their prospects, even gaining full Roman citizenship. This policy gave allies a stake in Rome's future and a sense of being colleagues rather than subjects. As a result, most remained loyal even when put to the severest test.

A Roman Warship. Rome became a naval power late in its history, in the course of the First Punic War. Roman sailors initially lacked the skill and experience in sea warfare of their Carthaginian opponents, who could maneuver their oared ships to ram the enemy. To compensate for this disadvantage, the Romans sought to make a sea battle more like an encounter on land by devising ways to grapple enemy ships and board them with armed troops. In time they also mastered the skillful use of the ram. This picture shows a Roman ship, propelled by oars, with both ram and soldiers, ready for either kind of fight.

Direzione Generale Musei Vaticani.

ROME AND CARTHAGE

Late in the ninth century B.C.E. the Phoenician city of Tyre had planted a colony on the North African coast, calling it the New City, or Carthage (see Map 6–2). In the sixth century B.C.E. Carthage became independent and free to take advantage of its defensible position, excellent harbor, and rich countryside. The Carthaginians expanded along the coast of North Africa west beyond the Straits of Gibraltar and east into Libya. They also gained control of southern Spain, Sardinia, Corsica, Malta, the Balearic Islands, and western Sicily. The people of these territories became Carthaginian subjects, paying tribute and serving in the Carthaginian military. Carthage claimed an absolute monopoly on trade in the western Mediterranean.

First Punic War (264–241 B.C.E.) Sicily was strategically important to both Carthage and Rome. It was there, in 264 B.C.E., that the two expanding powers first came to blows. Because the Romans called the Carthaginians Poeni or Puni (meaning "Phoenician"), the conflicts between them are called the **Punic Wars.**

Neither side made any progress against the other until the Romans built a fleet to blockade the Carthaginian ports at the western end of Sicily. Carthage capitulated in 241 B.C.E., giving up Sicily and the islands between Italy and Sicily and agreeing to pay a war indemnity, to keep its ships out of Italian waters, and not to recruit mercenaries in Italy. Neither side was to attack the allies of the other.

The terms of the peace were fair, but Rome broke them almost immediately, setting the stage for more conflict. In 238 B.C.E., while Carthage struggled to put down a revolt of unpaid mercenaries, Rome seized Sardinia and Corsica and demanded an additional indemnity. This cynical action provoked the Carthaginians without preventing them from recovering their strength to seek vengeance in the future.

Second Punic War (218–202 B.C.E.) After 241 B.C.E., Carthage recovered strength by building a rich empire in Spain while Rome looked on with concern. In 221 B.C.E. Hannibal (247–182 B.C.E.) took command of Carthaginian forces in Spain. A few years earlier Rome had received an offer from the Spanish town of Saguntum to become the friends of Rome. The Romans accepted, thereby taking on the responsibilities of friendship with a foreign state. At first Hannibal was careful to respect Saguntum, but the Saguntines, confident of Rome's protection, began to interfere with Spanish tribes allied with Hannibal. The Romans warned Hannibal to let Saguntum alone, but he ignored Rome's warning, besieged Saguntum, and captured it.

Rome declared war in 218 B.C.E. Starting in Spain, Hannibal launched a swift and daring invasion of Italy. By September of 218 B.C.E. he was across the Alps. His army was weary, bedraggled, and greatly reduced, but he was in Italy. Hannibal defeated the Romans in three consecutive battles, but his chances of prevailing would depend ultimately on Rome's ability to retain the loyalty of its allies.

In 216 B.C.E., at Cannae in Apulia, Hannibal destroyed a Roman army of some 80,000 men. It was the worst defeat in Roman history; Rome's prestige was shattered, and many of its allies went over to Hannibal. In 215 B.C.E. Philip V (r. 221–179 B.C.E.), king of Macedon, made an alliance with Hannibal and launched a war to recover his influence on the Adriatic. For more than a decade no Roman army would dare face Hannibal in the open field, and he was free to roam over all Italy and do as he pleased.

But crucial allies remained loyal to Rome, preventing Hannibal's victory. He had neither the numbers nor the supplies to besiege Rome or the cities of its major allies, nor did he have the equipment to take them by assault. The Romans

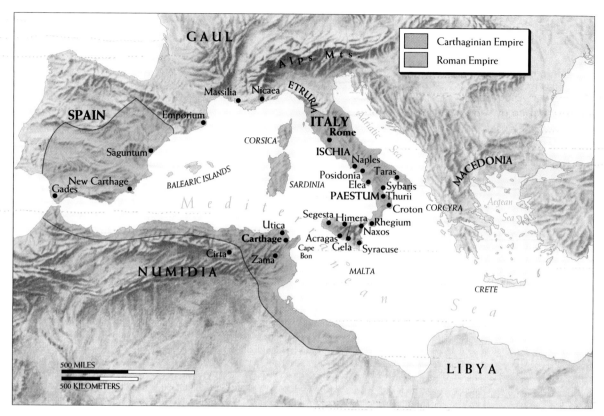

MAP 6–2 The Western Mediterranean Area During the Rise of Rome. This map covers the theater of the conflict between the growing Roman dominions and those of Carthage in the third century B.C.E. The Carthaginian Empire stretched westward from Carthage along the North African coast and into southern Spain.

appointed Publius Cornelius Scipio (237–183 B.C.E.), later called Scipio Africanus, to the command in Spain with proconsular *imperium*. He was a general almost as talented as Hannibal. Within a few years Scipio had conquered all Spain and had deprived Hannibal of hope of help from that region.

In 204 B.C.E. Scipio landed in Africa and forced the Carthaginians to accept a peace whose main clause was the withdrawal of Hannibal and his army from Italy. Hannibal had

CHRONOLOGY

The Punic Wars

264–241 B.C.E.	First Punic War
238 B.C.E.	Rome seizes Sardinia and Corsica
221 B.C.E.	Hannibal takes command of Punic army in Spain
218–202 B.C.E.	Second Punic War
216 B.C.E.	Battle of Cannae
202 B.C.E.	Battle of Zama
149–146 B.C.E.	Third Punic War
146 B.C.E.	Destruction of Carthage

won every battle but lost the war. His return inspired Carthage to risk all in battle. In 202 B.C.E. Scipio and Hannibal faced each other at Zama. Rome won and the new peace terms reduced Carthage to the status of a dependent ally of Rome. Carthage was no longer a great power. Rome ruled the seas and the entire Mediterranean coast from Italy westward.

The New Imperial System The Roman conquest of overseas territory presented a new problem. Instead of following the policy they had pursued in Italy, the Romans made Sicily, Sardinia, and Corsica provinces. It became common to extend the term of the governors of these provinces beyond a year. The governors were unchecked by colleagues and exercised full *imperium*. New magistracies, in effect, were thus created free of the limits put on the power of officials in Rome. The new populations were subjects who paid tribute instead of serving in the army. The old practice of extending citizenship, and with it loyalty to Rome, stopped at the borders of Italy. Rome collected the new taxes by "farming them out" at auction to the highest bidder. The tax collectors became powerful and wealthy by squeezing the provincials hard. These innovations were the basis for Rome's imperial organization; in time they so strained the constitution and traditions of Rome that the existence of the republic was threatened.

THE REPUBLIC'S CONQUEST OF THE HELLENISTIC WORLD

The East   By the middle of the third century B.C.E. the eastern Mediterranean had reached a stable balance of power. That equilibrium was threatened by two aggressive monarchs, Philip V of Macedon and the Seleucid Antiochus III (223–187 B.C.E.). Philip and Antiochus moved swiftly, the latter against Syria and Palestine, the former against Greek cities.

The threat that a more powerful Macedon might pose to Rome's friends, and perhaps even to Italy, persuaded the Romans to intervene. In 200 B.C.E. the Romans ordered Philip not to attack any Greek city and to pay reparations to the kingdom of Pergamum in Asia Minor. Philip refused. Two years later the Romans demanded that Philip withdraw from Greece entirely. In 197 B.C.E., with Greek support, they defeated Philip in Thessaly. The Greek cities taken from Philip were made autonomous and the freedom of the Greeks was proclaimed.

Soon after, the Romans came into conflict with Antiochus. On the pretext of freeing the Greeks from Roman domination, he landed an army on the Greek mainland. The Romans quickly drove him from Greece, and in 189 B.C.E. they crushed his army at Magnesia in Asia Minor. The peace of Apamia in the next year deprived Antiochus of his elephants and his navy and imposed a huge indemnity on him. Once again the Romans took no territory for themselves and left Greek cities in Asia free. They continued to regard Greece, and now Asia Minor, as a kind of protectorate in which they could intervene as they chose.

In 179 B.C.E. Perseus (r. 179–168 B.C.E.) succeeded Philip V as king of Macedon. He tried to gain popularity in Greece by favoring the democratic and revolutionary forces in the cities. The Romans, troubled by this threat to stability, defeated him in 168 B.C.E. and divided Macedon into four separate republics whose citizens were forbidden to intermarry or even to do business across the new national boundaries.

The new policy reflected the stern and businesslike approach favored by the conservative censor Cato (234–149 B.C.E.). The new harshness was applied to allies and bystanders as well as to defeated opponents. Leaders of anti-Roman factions in the Greek cities were punished severely. In 146 B.C.E., for instance, the ancient and wealthy commercial city of Corinth was completely destroyed.

The public treasury benefited to such a degree from these wars that the direct property tax on Roman citizens was abolished. Part of the booty went to the victorious general and part to their soldiers. New motives were thereby introduced into Roman foreign policy, or, perhaps, old motives were given new prominence. Foreign campaigns could bring profit to the state, rewards to the army, and wealth, fame, honor, and political power to the general.

The West   Harsh as the Romans had become toward the Greeks, they treated the Spaniards, whom they considered barbarians, even worse. The Romans committed dreadful atrocities; they lied, cheated, and broke treaties in their effort to exploit and pacify the natives, who fought back fiercely in guerrilla style. From 154 to 133 B.C.E. the fighting waxed, and it became hard to recruit Roman soldiers for the increasingly ugly war. At last, in 134 B.C.E., Scipio Aemilianus (185–129 B.C.E.) took the key city of Numantia by siege and put an end to the war in Spain.

Roman treatment of Carthage was no better. Although Carthage posed no threat, some Romans refused to abandon their hatred and fear of the traditional enemy. Cato is said to have ended all his speeches in the Senate with the same sentence, "*Ceterum censeo delendam esse Carthaginem*" ("Besides, I think that Carthage must be destroyed"). At last the Romans took advantage of a technical breach of the peace to destroy Carthage. In 146 B.C.E. Scipio Aemilianus took the city, plowed up its land, and put salt in the furrows as a symbol of the permanent abandonment of the site. The Romans incorporated Carthage as the province of Africa.

Civilization in the Early Roman Republic: Greek Influence

Among the most important changes wrought by Roman expansion overseas were those in the Roman style of life and thought brought about by close and continued association with the Greeks of the Hellenistic world. Attitudes toward the Greeks themselves ranged from admiration for their culture and history to contempt for their constant squabbling, their commercial practices, and their weakness. Such Roman aristocrats as the Scipios surrounded themselves with Greek intellectuals, like the historian Polybius (ca. 203–ca. 123 B.C.E.) and the philosopher Panaetius (ca. 185–ca. 110 B.C.E.). Conservatives, such as Cato, might speak contemptuously of the Greeks as "Greeklings" (Graeculi), but even he learned Greek and absorbed Greek culture.

RELIGION

Roman religion was influenced by the Greeks almost from the beginning; the Romans identified their own gods with Greek equivalents and incorporated Greek mythology into their own. For the most part, however, Roman religious practice remained simple and Italian, until the third century B.C.E. brought important new influences from the east. In 205 B.C.E. the Senate approved the public worship of Cybele, the Great Mother goddess from Asia Minor. Hers was a fertility cult accompanied by ecstatic, frenzied, and sensual rites that so shocked and outraged conservative Romans that they soon banned the cult to Romans. Similarly, the Senate banned the worship of Dionysus, or Bacchus, in 186 B.C.E. In the second century B.C.E. interest in Babylonian astrology also grew, and the Senate's attempt in 139 B.C.E. to expel the "Chaldaeans," as the astrologers were called, did not prevent the continued influence of their superstition.

EDUCATION

Education was entirely the responsibility of the Roman family, the fathers teaching their own sons at home. It is not clear whether girls received any education in early Rome, although they certainly did later on. The boys learned to read, write, and calculate, as well as how to farm. They memorized the Twelve Tables, Rome's earliest code of law; learned how to perform religious rites; heard stories of the great deeds of early Roman history, particularly those of their ancestors; and engaged in the physical training appropriate for potential soldiers. This course of study was practical, vocational, and moral. It aimed at making the boys moral, pious, patriotic, law-abiding, and respectful of tradition.

Contact with the Greeks of southern Italy produced momentous changes. Greek teachers came to Rome and introduced the study of language, literature, and philosophy, as well as the idea of a liberal education, or what the Romans called *humanitas*, the root of our concept of the humanities. This education emphasized broad intellectual training, critical thinking, an interest in ideas, and the development of a well-rounded person.

The first need was to learn Greek, for Rome did not yet have a literature of its own. Schools were established in which the teacher, called a *grammaticus*, taught his students the Greek language and its literature, particularly the works of Homer. Thereafter, educated Romans were expected to be bilingual. Roman boys of the upper classes then studied rhetoric—the art of speaking and writing well—with Greeks who were expert in it. The Greeks considered rhetoric less important than philosophy. But the more practical Romans took to it avidly, for it was of great use in legal disputes and was becoming ever more valuable in political life.

Some Romans, however, felt that the new learning would weaken Roman moral fiber. They were able to pass laws expelling philosophers and teachers of rhetoric. But these reactionary attempts failed. The new education suited the needs of the Romans of the second century B.C.E., who found themselves changing from a rural to an urban society and who were being thrust into the sophisticated world of the Hellenistic Greeks.

By the last century of the Roman republic the new Hellenized education had become dominant. Latin literature had come into being along with Latin translations of Greek poets, which formed part of the course of study. The Greek language and literature were still central to the curriculum. Many schools were established, and the number of educated people grew, extending beyond the senatorial class and outside Rome to the cities of Italy.

Girls of the upper classes were educated similarly to boys, at least through the earlier stages. They were probably taught by tutors at home rather than going to school. Young women did not study with philosophers and rhetoricians, for they were usually married by the age when the men were pursuing their higher education. Still, some women found ways to continue their education. Some became prose writers or poets. By the first century C.E. there were apparently enough learned women to provoke the complaints of a crotchety and conservative satirist:

A Master Among His Students. This carved relief from the second century C.E. shows a schoolmaster and his pupils. The one at the right is arriving late.

Rheinisches Landesmuseum, Triern, Germany/Alinari/Art Resource, N.Y.

Still more exasperating is the woman who begs as soon as she sits down to dinner, to discourse on poets and poetry, comparing Virgil with Homer; professors, critics, lawyers, auctioneers—even another woman—can't get a word in. She rattles on at such a rate that you'd think that all the pots and pans in the kitchen were crashing to the floor or that every bell in town was clanging. All by herself she makes as much noise as some primitive tribe chasing away an eclipse. She should learn the philosopher's lesson: "moderation is necessary even for intellectuals." And, if she still wants to appear educated and eloquent, let her dress as a man, sacrifice to men's gods and bathe in the men's baths. Wives shouldn't try to be public speakers; they shouldn't use rhetorical devices; they shouldn't read all the classics—there should be some things women don't understand. I myself cannot understand a woman who can quote the rules of grammar and never make a mistake and cites obscure, long-forgotten poets—as if men cared about such things. If she has to correct somebody let her correct her girl friends and leave her husband alone.[3]

A rich and ambitious Roman could support a Greek philosopher in his own home, so that his son could acquire through conversation the learning and polished thought necessary for the fully cultured gentleman. Some, like the great orator Cicero (106–43 B.C.E.), traveled to Greece to study with great teachers of rhetoric and philosophy. This style of education broadened the Romans' understanding and made them a part of the older and wider culture of the Hellenistic world, a world they had come to dominate and needed to understand.

Roman Imperialism

Rome's expansion in Italy and overseas was accomplished without a grand general plan. The new territories were acquired as a result of wars that the Romans believed were either defensive or preventive. Their foreign policy was aimed at providing security for Rome on Rome's terms, but these terms were often unacceptable to other nations and led to continued conflict. Whether intended or not, Rome's expansion brought the Romans an empire, and with it, power, wealth, and responsibilities (see Map 6–3).

---

[3] Juvenal. *Satires* 6.434–456. trans. by Roger Killian, Richard Lynch, Robert J. Rowland, and John Sims. cited by Sarah B. Pomeroy in *Goddesses, Whores, Wives, and Slaves* (New York: Schocken. 1975), p. 172.

▲ **Lady Playing the Cithara.** This wall painting from the first century B.C.E. comes from the villa of Publius Fannius Synistor at Pompeii and shows a woman playing a cithara.

Roman. Paintings. Pompeian, Boscoreale. 1st Century B.C. "Lady playing the cithara." Wall painting from the east wall of large room in the villa of Publius Fannius Synistor. Fresco on lime plaster. H. 6 ft. 1 1/2 in. (187 × 187 cm.) The Metropolitan Museum of Art, Rogers Fund, 1903. (03.14.5) Photograph © 1986 The Metropolitan Museum of Art.

AFTERMATH OF CONQUEST

War and expansion changed the economic, social, and political life of Italy. Before the Punic Wars most Italians owned their own farms, which provided most of the family's needs. The Second Punic War did terrible damage to Italian farmland. Many veterans found it impossible or unprofitable to go back to their farms. Some moved to Rome to work as occasional laborers, but most stayed in the country as tenant farmers or hired hands. No longer landowners, they were also no longer eligible for the army. Often the land they abandoned was acquired by the wealthy who converted these farms, later called *latifundia*, into large plantations for growing cash crops—grain, olives, and grapes for wine—or into cattle ranches.

The upper classes had plenty of capital to stock and operate these estates as a result of profits from the war and from exploiting the provinces. Land was cheap, and slaves conquered in war provided cheap labor. By fair means and foul, large landholders obtained sizable quantities of public land and forced small farmers

MAP EXPLORATION

Interactive map: To explore this map further, go to http://www.prenhall.com/craig3/map6.3

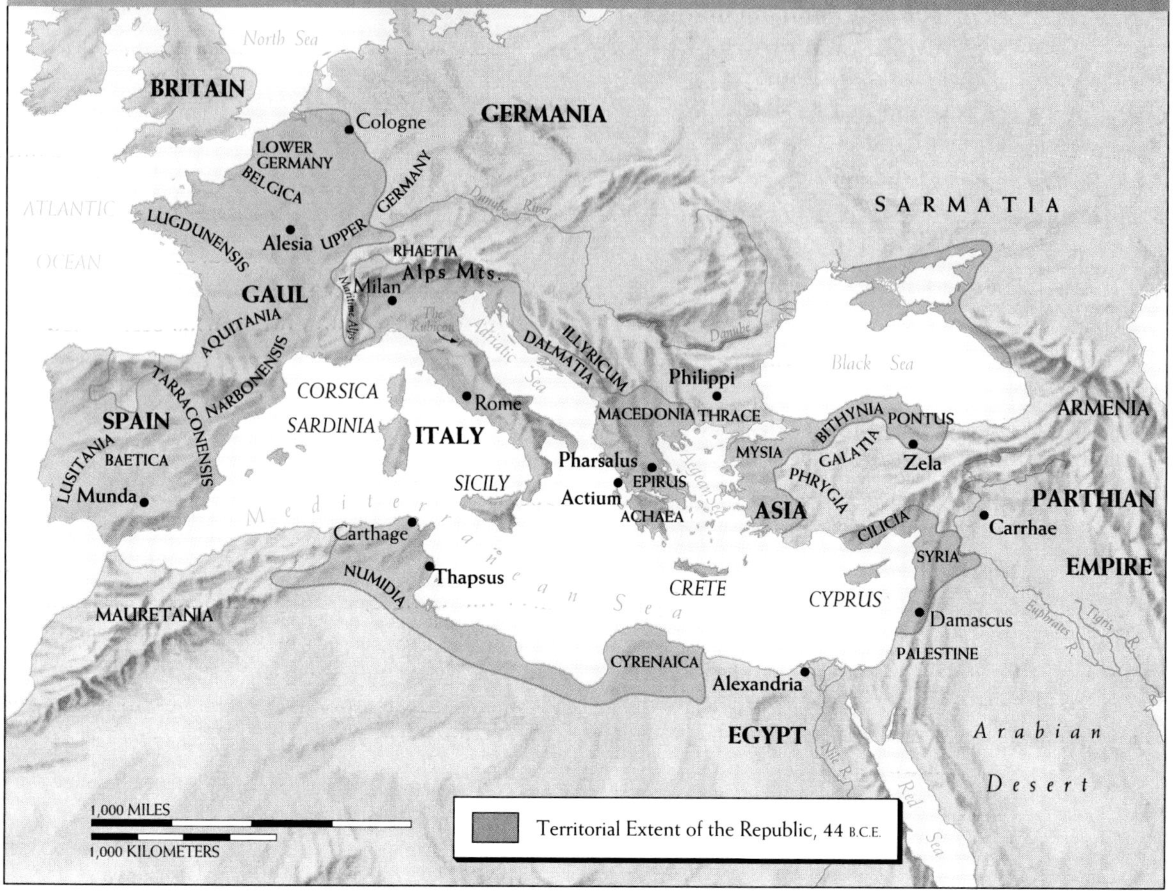

MAP 6–3 Roman Dominions of the Late Republic. This map shows the extent of the territory controlled by Rome at the time of Caesar's death in 44 B.C.E.

off it. These changes separated the people of Rome and Italy more sharply into rich and poor, landed and landless, privileged and deprived. The result was political, social, and ultimately constitutional conflict that threatened the republic.

The Gracchi

By the middle of the second century B.C.E. the problems caused by Rome's rapid expansion troubled perceptive Roman nobles. The fall in status of the peasant farmers made it harder to recruit soldiers and came to present a political threat as well. The patron's traditional control over his clients was weakened by their flight from their land. Even those former landowners who worked on the land of their patrons as tenants or hired hands were less reliable. The introduction of the secret ballot in the 130s B.C.E. made them even more independent.

Tiberius Gracchus (168–133 B.C.E.) tried to solve these problems. He became tribune in 133 B.C.E. on a program of land reform. The program aroused great hostility. When Tiberius put it before the tribal assembly, another tribune interposed his veto. Unwilling to give up, Tiberius put his bill before the tribal assembly again. Again it was vetoed, so Tiberius, strongly supported by the people, had the offending tribune removed from office, thereby violating the constitution.

Tiberius then proposed a second bill, harsher than the first and more appealing to the people, for he had despaired of conciliating the Senate. There could be no compromise: Either Tiberius or the Roman constitution must go under.

Tiberius understood the danger he would face if he stepped down from the tribunate, so he announced his candidacy for a second successive term, another blow at tradition. At the elections a riot broke out, and a mob of senators and their clients killed Tiberius and some 300 of his followers and threw their bodies into the Tiber River. The Senate had put down the threat to its rule, but at the price of the first internal bloodshed in Roman political history.

The tribunate of Tiberius Gracchus permanently changed Roman politics. Heretofore, politics had generally involved struggles for honor and reputation between great families or coalitions of such families. Fundamental issues were rarely at stake. The revolutionary proposals of Tiberius, however, and the senatorial resort to bloodshed created a new situation.

From then on Romans could pursue a political career that was not based solely on influence within the aristocracy; pressure from the people might be an effective substitute. In the last century of the republic such politicians were called *populares*, whereas those who supported the traditional role of the Senate were called *optimates* ("the best men").

The tribunate of Gaius Gracchus (ca. 159–121 B.C.E.), brother of Tiberius, was much more dangerous to the Senate than that of Tiberius because all the tribunes of 123 B.C.E. were Gaius's supporters. There could be no veto, and tribunes could now be reelected. Gaius appealed to a variety of groups. He proposed to establish new colonies for landless veterans: two in Italy and one on the old site of Carthage. Among other popular acts, he put through a law stabilizing the price of grain in Rome.

Gaius also appealed to the equestrian order in his struggle against the Senate. The **equestrians** were rich men who could qualify to serve in the Roman cavalry, the most expensive form of military service. Many supplied goods and services to the Roman state and collected its taxes in the provinces. These wealthy men usually had the same outlook as the Senate; generally they used their profits to purchase land and to try to reach senatorial rank themselves. Still, they had a special interest in Roman expansion and in the exploitation of the provinces. When Pergamum became the Roman province of Asia in 129 B.C.E. Gaius gave them the right to collect taxes there.

Gaius easily won reelection as tribune for 122 B.C.E. He aimed at giving citizenship to the Italians, both to resolve their dissatisfaction and to add them to his political coalition. But the common people did not want to share the advantages of Roman citizenship, and the Senate seized on this proposal to drive a wedge between Gaius and his supporters.

The Romans did not reelect Gaius in 121 B.C.E., and a hostile consul provoked an incident that led to violence. The Senate established martial law. Gaius was hunted down and killed, and some 3,000 of his followers were put to death without trial.

MARIUS AND SULLA

Before long the senatorial oligarchy faced more serious dangers arising from troubles abroad. Jugurtha (d. 104 B.C.E.) became king of Numidia, a client kingdom of Rome near Carthage, and his massacre of Roman and Italian businessmen in Numidia gained Roman attention. Pressure from the eques-

trians and the people forced the declaration of what became known as the Jugurthine War in 111 B.C.E.

The war dragged on until the people elected Gaius Marius (157–86 B.C.E.) to the consulship for 107 B.C.E., and the assembly, usurping the role of the Senate, assigned him to the province of Numidia. Marius was a *novus homo*, a "new man"—that is, the first in the history of his family to reach the consulship. He was outside the closed circle of the old Roman aristocracy and a political maverick.

Marius quickly defeated Jugurtha, but Jugurtha escaped and guerrilla warfare continued. Finally, Marius's subordinate, Lucius Cornelius Sulla (138–78 B.C.E.), trapped Jugurtha and brought the war to an end. Marius celebrated the victory, but Sulla, an ambitious but impoverished descendant of an old Roman family, resented being cheated of the credit. The seeds were planted for a personal rivalry that would last until Marius's death (See Document, "Sallust on Factions and the Decline of the Republic.")

While the Romans were fighting Jugurtha, a far greater danger from barbarians threatened Rome from the north. To meet the danger, the Romans elected Marius to his second consulship when these tribes threatened again. He served five consecutive terms from 104 B.C.E. until 100 B.C.E.

Marius made important changes in the army. He began using volunteers, mostly the dispossessed farmers and rural proletarians whose problems had not been solved by the Gracchi. They enlisted for a long term of service and looked on the army as an opportunity and a career. They became semiprofessional clients of their general and sought guaranteed food, clothing, shelter, and booty from victories. They came to expect land as a form of mustering-out pay or veteran's bonus when they retired. Volunteers were most likely to join a man who was a capable soldier and influential enough to obtain what they wanted. They looked to him rather than to the state for their rewards. He on the other hand, had to obtain grants from the Senate if he was to maintain his power and reputation.

Marius's innovation created both the opportunity and the necessity for military leaders to gain enough power to challenge civilian authority. The promise of rewards won these leaders the personal loyalty of their troops that allowed them to frighten the Senate into granting their demands.

WAR AGAINST THE ITALIAN ALLIES (90–88 B.C.E.)

For a decade Rome ignored Italian discontent. In frustration, the Italians revolted and established a separate confederation with its own capital and its own coinage.

Employing the traditional device of divide and conquer, the Romans immediately offered citizenship to those cities that remained loyal and soon made the same offer to the rebels if they laid down their arms. By 88 B.C.E. the war against the allies

DOCUMENT | Sallust on Factions and the Decline of the Republic

Sallust (86–35 B.C.E.) was a supporter of Julius Caesar and of the political faction called populares, translated here as "the democratic party," opponents of the optimates, translated here as "the nobility." In this selection from his monograph on the Jugurthine War, Sallust tries to explain Rome's troubles in the period after the destruction of Carthage in 146 B.C.E.

◆ Why did Sallust think the destruction of Carthage marked the beginning of the decline of the Roman Republic? Does his account of events seem fair and dispassionate? How would a member of "the nobility" have evaluated the same events? Is the existence of factions or "parties" inevitably harmful to a republic?

The division of the Roman state into warring factions, with all its attendant vices, had originated some years before, as a result of peace and of that material prosperity which men regard as the greatest blessing. Down to the destruction of Carthage, the people and Senate shared the government peaceably and with due restraint, and the citizens did not compete for glory or power; fear of its enemies preserved the good morals of the state. But when the people were relieved of this fear, the favourite vices of prosperity—licence and pride—appeared as a natural consequence. Thus the peace and quiet which they had longed for in time of adversity proved, when they obtained it, to be even more grievous and bitter than the adversity. For the nobles started to use their position, and the people their liberty, to gratify their selfish passions, every man snatching and seizing what he could for himself. So the whole community was split into parties, and the Republic, which hitherto had been the common interest of all, was torn asunder. The nobility had the advantage of being a close-knit body, whereas the democratic party was weakened by its loose organization, its supporters being dispersed among a huge multitude. One small group of oligarchs had everything in its control alike in peace and war—the treasury, the provinces, public offices, all distinctions and triumphs. The people were burdened with military services and poverty, while the spoils of war were snatched by the generals and shared with a handful of friends. Meantime, the soldiers' parents or young children, if they happened to have a powerful neighbour, might well be driven from their homes. Thus the possession of power gave unlimited scope to ruthless greed, which violated and plundered everything, respecting nothing and holding nothing sacred, till finally it brought about its own downfall. For the day came when noblemen rose to power who preferred true glory to unjust dominion: then the state was shaken to its foundations by civil strife, as by an earthquake.

Excerpt from Sallust, *The Jugurthine War: The Conspiracy of Catiline*, trans. by S. A. Hanford (London: Penguin Classics, 1963). Copyright © S. A. Hanford, 1963.

---

was over. All the Italians became Roman citizens with the protections that citizenship offered, but they retained local self-government and a dedication to their own municipalities that made Italy flourish. The passage of time blurred the distinction between Romans and Italians and forged them into a single nation.

SULLA'S DICTATORSHIP

Sulla had performed well during the war against the allies, and he was elected consul for 88 B.C.E. A champion of senatorial control, he won a civil war against Marius and his friends. He now held all power and had himself appointed dictator to reconstitute the state. He had enough power to make himself the permanent ruler of Rome. Yet he was traditional enough to want to restore senatorial government, reformed to prevent the misfortunes of the past.

Sulla retired to a life of ease and luxury in 79 B.C.E. He could not, however, undo the effect of his own example: a general using the loyalty of his own troops to take power and massacre his opponents, as well as innocent people. These actions proved to be far more significant than his constitutional arrangements.

The Fall of the Republic
POMPEY, CRASSUS, AND CAESAR

Within a year of Sulla's death, his constitution came under assault. Marcus Licinius Crassus (115–53 B.C.E.) and Cnaeus Pompey (106–48 B.C.E.) were ambitious men whom the Senate feared. Both demanded special honors and election to the consulship for the year 70 B.C.E. They both won election and repealed most of Sulla's constitution. This led to further attacks on senatorial control and to collaboration between ambitious generals and demagogic tribunes.

In 67 B.C.E. a special law gave Pompey *imperium* for three years over the entire Mediterranean and fifty miles in from the coast. He also was given the power to raise great quantities of troops and money to rid the area of pirates. His power was then extended to fight a war that had broken out in Asia Minor. When he returned to Rome in 62 B.C.E. he had more power, prestige, and popular support than any Roman in history. The Senate and his personal enemies feared that he might emulate Sulla and establish his own rule.

Crassus had the most reason to fear Pompey's return. Although rich and influential, he did not have the confidence of the Senate, a firm political base of his own, or the kind of military glory needed to rival Pompey. During the 60s B.C.E., therefore, he allied himself with various popular leaders. The ablest of these men was Gaius Julius Caesar (100–44 B.C.E.), a descendant of an old but politically obscure patrician family.

FIRST TRIUMVIRATE

To general surprise, Pompey disbanded his army, celebrated a great triumph, and returned to private life. He had achieved amazing things for Rome and simply wanted the Senate to approve his excellent arrangements in the east and to give land to his veterans. But the jealous and fearful Senate refused. Pompey was thus driven to an alliance with his natural enemies, Crassus and Caesar. So was born the First Triumvirate, an informal agreement among three Roman politicians, each seeking his private goals, that further undermined the future of the republic.

DICTATORSHIP OF JULIUS CAESAR

Caesar was rewarded with election to the consulship for 59 B.C.E. The Triumvirate's program was quickly enacted, and Caesar got the extraordinary command that would give him a chance to earn the glory and power with which to rival Pompey: the governorship of Illyricum and Gaul for five years.

Caesar was now free in Gaul to seek the military success he craved. By the time he was ready to return, after conquering the province and consolidating his gains, the Triumvirate had dissolved and a crisis was at hand. At Carrhae in 53 B.C.E. Crassus died trying to conquer the Parthians. Pompey joined the Senate in opposing Caesar.

Early in January 49 B.C.E. the more extreme faction in the Senate ordered Pompey to defend the state and Caesar to lay down his command. For Caesar this meant exile or death, so he ordered his legions to cross the Rubicon River, the boundary of his province. This action was the first act of a civil war that ended in 45 B.C.E., when Caesar defeated the last of the enemy forces under Pompey's sons at Munda in Spain. As dictator Caesar, in Shakespeare's words, bestrode "the narrow world like a Colossus."

Caesar's innovations generally sought to make rational and orderly what was traditional and chaotic. His reforms also tended to elevate Italians and even provincials at the expense of the old Roman families, most of whom were his political enemies.

Caesar made few changes in the government of Rome, but his monopoly of military power made the whole structure a sham. He treated the Senate as his creature, sometimes with

disdain. His enemies were quick to accuse him of aiming at monarchy and conspired against him. On March 15, 44 B.C.E., Caesar was stabbed to death in the Senate. The assassins regarded themselves as heroic "tyrannicides" and had no clear plan of action. No doubt they simply expected the republic to be restored in the old way, but things had gone too far for that. Instead thirteen years more of civil war ensued, at the end of which the republic received its final burial.

SECOND TRIUMVIRATE AND THE EMERGENCE OF OCTAVIAN

Caesar's heir was his grandnephew, Octavian (63 B.C.E.–14 C.E.), a youth of eighteen. He joined Marcus Antonius (Mark Antony, ca. 83–30 B.C.E.) and Lepidus (d. 13 B.C.E.), two of Caesar's officers, in the Second Triumvirate to fight the assassins. The new triumvirs defeated the enemy at Philippi in 42 B.C.E., but they soon quarreled among themselves. Octavian gained control of the western part of the empire. Antonius, together with Cleopatra (r. 51–30 B.C.E.), queen of Egypt, ruled the east. In 31 B.C.E. the forces of Octavian crushed the fleet and army of Antony and Cleopatra at Actium, resolving the conflict.

The civil wars were over, and at the age of thirty-two Octavian was absolute master of the Mediterranean world. His power was enormous, but so was the task before him. He had to restore peace, prosperity, and confidence, all of which required a constitution that would reflect the new realities without offending unduly the traditional republican prejudices that still had so firm a grip on Rome and Italy.

CHRONOLOGY

The Fall of the Roman Republic

133 B.C.E.	Tribunate of Tiberius Gracchus
123–122 B.C.E.	Tribunate of Gaius Gracchus
111–105 B.C.E.	Jugurthine War
104–100 B.C.E.	Consecutive consulships of Marius
90–88 B.C.E.	War against the Italian allies
70 B.C.E.	Consulship of Crassus and Pompey
60 B.C.E.	Formation of First Triumvirate
58–50 B.C.E.	Caesar in Gaul
53 B.C.E.	Crassus killed in Battle of Carrhae
49 B.C.E.	Caesar crosses Rubicon; civil war begins
46–44 B.C.E.	Caesar's dictatorship
45 B.C.E.	End of civil war
43 B.C.E.	Formation of Second Triumvirate
42 B.C.E.	Battle of Philippi
31 B.C.E.	Octavian defeats Antony at Actium

The Augustan Principate

If the problems facing Octavian after the Battle of Actium were great, so too were his resources for addressing them. He was the master of a vast military force, the only one in the Roman world, and he had loyal and capable assistants. Yet the memory of Julius Caesar's fate was still clear in Octavian's mind; it was dangerous to flaunt unprecedented powers and to disregard all republican traditions.

Octavian's constitutional solution proved to be successful and lasting, subtle and effective. Behind the republican trappings and the apparent sharing of authority with the Senate, the government of Octavian, like that of his successors, was a monarchy. All real power—both civil and military—lay with the ruler, whether he was called by the unofficial title of "first citizen" (*princeps*) like Octavian, who was the founder of the regime, or "emperor" (*imperator*) like those who followed.

On January 13, 27 B.C.E., he put forward a new plan in dramatic style, coming before the Senate to give up all his powers and provinces. In what was surely a rehearsed response, the Senate begged him to reconsider, and at last he agreed to accept the provinces of Spain, Gaul, and Syria with proconsular power for military command and to retain the consulship in Rome. The Senate would govern the other provinces as before. Because his provinces contained twenty of the twenty-six legions, his true power was undiminished, but the Senate responded with almost hysterical gratitude, voting him many honors. Among them was the semireligious title "**Augustus**," which connoted veneration, majesty, and holiness. Historians thus speak of Rome's first emperor as Augustus and of his regime as the Principate. This would have pleased him, for it helps conceal the novel, unrepublican nature of the regime and the naked power on which it rested.

ADMINISTRATION

Augustus made important changes in the government of Rome, Italy, and the provinces, intending to reduce inefficiency and corruption, eliminate the threat to peace and order by ambitious individuals, and reduce the distinction between Romans and Italians, senators and equestrians. Augustus controlled the elections and saw to it that promising young men, whatever their origin, served the state as administrators and provincial governors. Thus, many equestrians and Italians who had no connection with the Roman aristocracy entered the Senate, which Augustus was always careful to treat with respect and honor.

The Augustan period was one of great prosperity, based on the wealth that Augustus had brought in by the conquest of Egypt, on the great increase in commerce and industry made possible by general peace and a vast program of public works, and on a revival of successful small farming by Augustus's resettled veterans.

The union of political and military power in the hands of the princeps enabled him to install rational, efficient, and stable government in the provinces for the first time.

THE ARMY AND DEFENSE

Under Augustus, members of the armed forces became true professionals. Enlistment, chiefly by Italians, was for twenty years, but the pay was relatively good, and there were occasional bonuses and the promise of a pension on retirement in the form of money or land. Together with the auxiliaries from the provinces, these forces formed a frontier army of about 300,000 men. This was barely enough to hold the line. The Roman army permanently based in the provinces brought Roman culture to the natives. The soldiers spread their language

Emperor Augustus (r. 27 B.C.E.–14 C.E.). This statue, now in the Vatican, stood in the villa of Augustus's wife Livia. The figures on the elaborate breastplate are all of symbolic significance. At the top, for example, Dawn in her chariot brings in a new day under the protective mantle of the sky god; in the center, Tiberius, Augustus's successor, accepts the return of captured Roman army standards from a barbarian prince; and at the bottom, Mother Earth offers a horn of plenty.

Charitable Foundation, Gemeinnutzige Stiftung Leonard von Matt.

and customs, often marrying local women and settling down there. They attracted merchants, who often became the nuclei of new towns and cities that became centers of Roman civilization. As time passed, the provincials on the frontiers became Roman citizens and helped strengthen Rome's defenses against the barbarians outside.

RELIGION AND MORALITY

A century of political strife and civil war had undermined the foundations of traditional Roman society. Augustus undertook to preserve and restore the traditional values of the family and religion in Rome and Italy. He curbed adultery and divorce and encouraged early marriage and the procreation of legitimate children.

Augustus also worked to restore the dignity of formal Roman religion, building many temples, reviving old cults, and reorganizing and invigorating the priestly colleges; he also banned the worship of newly introduced foreign gods. During his lifetime he did not accept divine honors, although he was deified after his death; as with Julius Caesar, a state cult was dedicated to his worship.

Civilization of the Ciceronian and Augustan Ages

The high point of Roman culture came in the last century of the republic and during the Principate of Augustus. While Greek rhetoric, philosophy, and literature served as the models for Roman writers and artists, the art and writing of both periods show uniquely Roman qualities in spirit and sometimes in form.

THE LATE REPUBLIC

Cicero (106–43 B.C.E.)   The towering literary figure of the late republic was Cicero. He is most famous for his orations delivered in the law courts and the Senate. Together with many of his private letters, the speeches give us a clearer and fuller insight into his mind than the works of any other figure in antiquity. We see the political life of his period largely through his eyes. He also wrote treatises on rhetoric, ethics, and politics that put Greek philosophical ideas into Latin terminology and also changed them to suit Roman conditions and values.

Cicero believed in a world governed by divine and natural law that human reason could perceive and human institutions reflect. He looked to law, custom, and tradition to produce both stability and liberty. His literary style, as well as his values and ideas, was an important legacy for the Middle Ages and, reinterpreted, for the Renaissance.

Law   The period from the Gracchi to the fall of the Republic was important in the development of Roman law. Before that time Roman law was essentially national and had developed chiefly by means of juridical decisions, case by case, but contact with foreign peoples and the influence of Greek ideas forced a change. From the last century of the republic on, the edicts of the *praetors*, which interpreted and even changed and added to existing law, had increasing importance in developing the Roman legal code. Quite early the edicts of the magistrates who dealt with foreigners developed the idea of the *jus gentium*, or "law of peoples," as opposed to that arising strictly from the experience of the Romans. In the first century B.C.E. the influence of Greek thought made the idea of *jus gentium* identical to that of the *jus naturale*, or "natural law," taught by the Stoics. It was this view of a world ruled by divine reason that Cicero enshrined in his treatise on the laws, *De Legibus*.

Poetry   This was also the period of two of Rome's greatest poets, Lucretius and Catullus, each representing a different aspect of Rome's poetic tradition. The Hellenistic poets and literary theorists saw two functions for the poet: as entertainer and as teacher. They thought the best poet combined both roles, and the Romans adopted the same view. Lucretius (ca. 99–55 B.C.E.) pursued this path in his epic poem *De Rerum Natura* (On the Nature of Things). In it, he set forth the scientific and philosophical ideas of Epicurus and Democritus with the zeal of a missionary trying to save society from fear and superstition. He knew that his doctrine might be bitter medicine to the reader: "That is why I have tried to administer it to you in the dulcet strains of poesy, coated with the sweet honey of the Muses."[4]

Catullus (ca. 84–54 B.C.E.) was thoroughly different. His poems were personal, even autobiographical. He wrote of the joys and pains of love, he hurled invective at important contemporaries like Julius Caesar, and he amused himself in witty poetic exchanges. He offered no moral lessons and was not interested in Rome's glorious history and in contemporary politics. In a sense, he is an example of the proud, independent, pleasure-seeking nobleman who characterized part of the aristocracy at the end of the republic.

THE AGE OF AUGUSTUS

The spirit of the Augustan Age, the golden age of Roman literature, reflected the new conditions of society (see Document, "An Ideal Roman Woman").

The old aristocratic order, with its system of independent nobles following their own particular interests, was gone. So was the world of poets of the lower orders, receiving patronage from individual aristocrats. Augustus replaced the complexity of republican patronage with a simple scheme in which all

---

[4] Lucretius. *De Rerum Natura*, lines 931 ff. (New York: Oxford University Press. 1922).

DOCUMENT An Ideal Roman Woman

Just after the fall of the Roman republic, late in the first century B.C.E. *the poet Propertius wrote an elegy in honor of a woman of the Roman nobility, Cornelia, the stepdaughter of Augustus, the ruler of the newly established Principate. She was married to the aristocrat Paullus and was the mother of three children. Propertius presents her as defending herself before the last judgment of Hades, king of the underworld. Her words were written by a man, but they seem to be an accurate representation of the values of the upper classes of Rome of both sexes.*

◆ In what achievements, associations, and qualities did she take pride? What might a person of our time find absent? What limits are implied by what is missing?

I was born to this, and when the wreath of marriage
Caught up my hair, and I was a woman grown, it was
your bed, my Paullus, that I came to and now have left.
The carving on the stone says she wed but once. O fathers long respected victors in Africa, be my defense ...
I asked no favours when Paullus was made censor: no
evil found its way within our walls.
I do not think I have disgraced my fathers:
I set a decent pattern in these halls.

Days had a quiet rhythm: no scandal touched us from
the wedding torch to the torch beside my bier.
A certain integrity is proof of breeding: the love of
virtue should not be born of fear.
Whatever the judge, whatever the lot fate gives me, no
woman needs to blush who sits at my side—...
For my children I wore the mother's robe of honor;
It was no empty house I left behind.
Lepidus, Paullus, still you bring me comfort you closed
my eyes when death had made me blind.
Twice in the curule chair I have seen my brother; they
cheered him as a consul the day before I died.
And you, my daughter, think of your censor-father,
choose one husband and live content at his side.
Our clan will rest on the children that you give it,
Secure in their promise I board the boat and rejoice.
Mine is the final triumph of any woman, that her spirit
earns the praise of a living voice.

From Propertius, *Elegies*, 4.11, trans. by Constance Carrier, *The Poems of Propertius*, Indiana University Press, copyright © 1963, pp. 191–192. Reprinted by permission of Indiana University Press.

---

patronage flowed from the princeps, usually through his chief cultural adviser, Maecenas (d. 8 B.C.E.).

Two of the major poets of this time, Virgil and Horace, had lost their property during the civil wars. The patronage of the *princeps* allowed them the leisure and the security to write poetry and also made them dependent on him and limited their freedom of expression. They wrote on subjects that were useful for his policies and that glorified him and his family, but they were not mere propagandists. For the most part, they were persuaded of the virtues of Augustus and his reign and sincerely sang its praises. Because they were poets of genius, they were also able to maintain some independence in their work.

Virgil   Virgil (70–19 B.C.E.) was the most important of the Augustan poets. His greatest work is the *Aeneid*, a long national epic that placed the history of Rome in the great tradition of the Greeks and the Trojan War. Its hero, the Trojan Aeneas, personifies the ideal Roman qualities of duty, responsibility, serious purpose, and patriotism. As the Romans' equivalent to Homer, Virgil glorified not the personal honor and excellence of the Greek epic heroes, but the civic greatness represented by Augustus and the peace and prosperity that he and the Julian family had given to imperial Rome.

Horace   Horace (65–8 B.C.E.) was won over to the Augustan cause by the patronage of Maecenas and by the attractions of the Augustan reforms. His great skills as a lyric poet are best revealed in his *Odes*, which are ingenious in their adaptation of Greek meters to the requirements of Latin verse. Two of the odes are directly in praise of Augustus, and many of them glorify the new Augustan order, the imperial family, and the empire.

Ovid   The darker side of Augustan influence on the arts is revealed by the career of Ovid (43 B.C.E.–18 C.E.). He wrote light and entertaining love elegies that reveal the sophistication and the loose sexual code of a notorious sector of the Roman aristocracy. Their values and way of life were contrary to the seriousness and family-centered life that Augustus was trying to foster. Ovid's *Ars Amatoria*, a poetic textbook on the art of seduction, angered Augustus and was partly responsible for the poet's exile in 8 C.E. His most popular work is *Metamorphoses*, a kind of mythological epic that turns Greek myths into charming stories in a graceful and lively style. Ovid's fate was an effective warning to later poets.

History   The most important and influential prose writer of the time was Livy (59 B.C.E.–17 C.E.). His *History of Rome* treated the period from the legendary origins of Rome until 9 B.C.E.

Only one fourth of his work survives; of the rest we have only pitifully brief summaries. He based his history on earlier accounts and made no effort at original research. His great achievement was to tell the story of Rome in a continuous and impressive narrative. Its purpose was moral—setting up historical models as examples of good and bad behavior—and, above all, patriotic. He glorified Rome's greatness and connected it with Rome's past, just as Augustus tried to do.

Architecture and Sculpture   Augustus was the great patron of the visual arts, as he was of literature. He embarked on a building program that beautified Rome, glorified his reign, and contributed to the general prosperity and his own popularity. Most of the building was influenced by the Greek classical style, which aimed at serenity and the ideal type. The greatest monument of the age is the Altar of Peace (*Ara Pacis*), dedicated in 9 B.C.E. Its walls show a procession in which Augustus and his family appear to move forward, followed by the magistrates, the Senate, and the people of Rome. There is no better symbol of the new order.

PEACE AND PROSPERITY: IMPERIAL ROME (14–180 C.E.)

Augustus tried to cloak the monarchical nature of his government, but his successors soon abandoned all pretense. The rulers came to be called *imperator*—from which comes our word *emperor*—as well as *Caesar*. The latter title signified connection with the imperial house, and the former indicated the

▲ **A Panel from the Ara Pacis (Altar of Peace).**   The altar was dedicated in 9 B.C.E. It was part of a propaganda campaign—involving poetry, architecture, myth, and history—that Augustus undertook to promote himself as the savior of Rome and the restorer of peace. This panel shows the goddess Earth and her children with cattle, sheep, and other symbols of agricultural wealth.

Saturnia, Tellus, Goddess of Earth, Air and Water. Panel from the Ara Pacis. 13–9 B.C.E. Museum of the Ara Pacis, Rome. Nimatallah/Art Resource, N.Y.

military power on which their authority was based. Because Augustus was ostensibly only the "first citizen" of a restored republic and his powers were theoretically voted him by the Senate and the people, he could not legally name his successor. In fact, he plainly designated his heirs by favors lavished on them and by giving them a share in the imperial power and responsibility (see Map 6–4).

Tiberius (r. 14–37 C.E.), his immediate successor, was at first embarrassed by the ambiguity of his new role, but soon the monarchical and hereditary nature of the regime became patent. Gaius (Caligula, r. 37–41 C.E.), Claudius (r. 41–54 C.E.), and Nero (r. 54–68 C.E.) were all descended from Augustus's family. The year 69, however, saw four different emperors assume power in quick succession as different Roman armies took turns placing their commanders on the throne.

Vespasian (r. 69–79 C.E.) emerged victorious from the chaos, and his sons, Titus (r. 79–81 C.E.) and Domitian (r. 81–96 C.E.), carried forward his line, the Flavian dynasty. Vespasian was the first emperor who did not come from the old Roman nobility.

The Flavian dynasty ended with the assassination of Domitian. Because Domitian had no close relative who had been designated as successor, the Senate put Nerva (r. 96–98 C.E.) on the throne to avoid chaos. He was the first of the five "good emperors," who included Trajan (r. 98–117 C.E.), Hadrian (r. 117–138 C.E.), Antoninus Pius (r. 138–161 C.E.), and Marcus Aurelius (r. 61–180 C.E.). Until Marcus Aurelius, none of these emperors had sons, so they each followed the example set by Nerva of adopting an able senator and establishing him as successor. The result was almost a century of peaceful succession

CHRONOLOGY

● ●

Rulers of the Early Empire

27 B.C.E.–14 C.E.	Augustus
The Julio-Claudian Dynasty	
14–37 C.E.	Tiberius
37–41 C.E.	Gaius (Caligula)
41–54 C.E.	Claudius
54–68 C.E.	Nero
69 C.E.	Year of the four emperors
The Flavian Dynasty	
69–79 C.E.	Vespasian
79–81 C.E.	Titus
81–96 C.E.	Domitian
The "Good Emperors"	
96–98 C.E.	Nerva
98–117 C.E.	Trajan
117–138 C.E.	Hadrian
138–161 C.E.	Antoninus Pius
161–180 C.E.	Marcus Aurelius

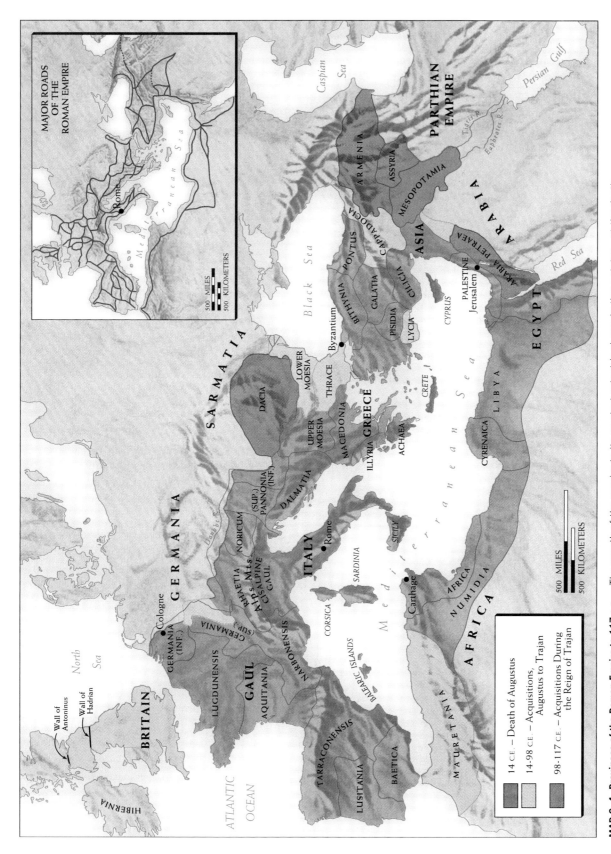

MAP 6–4 Provinces of the Roman Empire to 117 C.E.   The growth of the empire to its greatest extent is shown in three states—at the death of Augustus in 14 B.C.E., at the death of Nerva in 98 C.E., and at the death of Trajan in 117 C.E. The division into provinces is also indicated. The inset outlines the main roads that tied together the far-flung empire.

MAJOR ROADS OF THE ROMAN EMPIRE

Rome

500 MILES
500 KILOMETERS

Caspian Sea

Persian Gulf

PARTHIAN EMPIRE

ARMENIA

ASSYRIA

MESOPOTAMIA

Euphrates R.

Tigris R.

CAPPADOCIA

ASIA

ARABIA

ARABIA PETRAEA

PONTUS

BITHYNIA

GALATIA

CILICIA

PISIDIA

LYCIA

CYPRUS

PALESTINE

Jerusalem

Red Sea

EGYPT

Byzantium

THRACE

LOWER MOESIA

UPPER MOESIA

MACEDONIA

GREECE

ILLYRIA

ACHAEA

CRETE

LIBYA

CYRENAICA

Black Sea

SARMATIA

DACIA

PANNONIA (SUP.)

PANNONIA (INF.)

DALMATIA

NORICUM

RHAETIA

ALPS Mts.

CISALPINE GAUL

ITALY

Rome

SICILY

SARDINIA

CORSICA

Mediterranean Sea

GERMANIA

Cologne

GERMANIA (INF.)

GERMANIA (SUP.)

Danube

LUGDUNENSIS

GAUL

NARBONENSIS

AQUITANIA

BALEARIC ISLANDS

TARRACONENSIS

LUSITANIA

BAETICA

Carthage

AFRICA

NUMIDIA

MAURETANIA

AFRICA

BRITAIN

Wall of Antoninus

Wall of Hadrian

North Sea

ATLANTIC OCEAN

HIBERNIA

500 MILES
500 KILOMETERS

14 CE. – Death of Augustus

14-98 CE. – Acquisitions, Augustus to Trajan

98-117 CE. – Acquisitions During the Reign of Trajan

and competent rule, which ended when Marcus Aurelius allowed his incompetent son, Commodus (r. 180–192 C.E.), to succeed him, with unfortunate results.

There was, of course, opposition to imperial rule. Plots and the suspicion of plots led to repression, the use of spies and paid informers, book burning, and executions. The opposition consisted chiefly of senators who looked back to republican liberty for their class. Plots and repression were most common under Nero and Domitian. From Nerva to Marcus Aurelius, however, the emperors, without yielding any power, enlisted the cooperation of the upper class by courteous and modest deportment.

ADMINISTRATION OF THE EMPIRE

From an administrative and cultural standpoint, the empire was a collection of cities and towns. Roman policy during the Principate was to raise urban centers to the status of Roman municipalities with the rights and privileges attached to them. The Romans enlisted the upper classes of the provinces in their own government, spread Roman law and culture, and won the loyalty of the influential people.

Unlike most conquered peoples the Jews found accommodation to Roman rule difficult. Their first rebellion was crushed by Vespasian's son, the future emperor Titus, in 70 C.E. At that time the Temple in Jerusalem was destroyed. A second revolt was put down in 117 C.E. Finally, when Hadrian ordered a Roman colony placed on the site of Jerusalem, Simon, who was called Bar Kochba, or "Son of the Star," led a last uprising from 132 to 135 which was brutally suppressed.

As the bureaucracy became more efficient, so did the number and scope of its functions and therefore its size. The impor-tance and autonomy of the municipalities shrank as the central administration took a greater part in local affairs. The price paid for the increased efficiency offered by centralized control was the loss of the vitality of the cities throughout the empire.

Augustus's successors accepted his conservative and defensive foreign policy. Trajan was the first emperor to take the offensive in a sustained way. Between 101 and 106 C.E. he established the new province of Dacia between the Danube and the Carpathian Mountains. He was tempted, no doubt, by its important gold mines, but he was probably also pursuing a new general strategy: to defend the empire more aggressively by driving wedges into enemy territory. The same strategy dictated the invasion of the Parthian Empire in the east (113–117 C.E.). Trajan's early success there was astonishing, but his lines were overextended. Rebellions sprang up, and the campaign crumbled. Trajan was forced to retreat and died before returning to Rome.

Hadrian kept Dacia but abandoned Trajan's eastern conquests. Under Hadrian the Roman defense became rigid, and initiative passed to the barbarians. Marcus Aurelius spent most of his reign resisting dangerous attacks in the east and on the Danube frontier, and these attacks put enormous pressure on the empire's resources.

CULTURE OF THE EARLY EMPIRE

Literature   In Latin literature, the years between the death of Augustus and the time of Marcus Aurelius are known as the silver age; as the name implies, work of high quality—although probably inferior to that of the Augustan era—was produced. The writers of the silver age were gloomy, negative, and pessimistic. Criticism and satire lurk everywhere in their work.

Relief from Arch of Titus. Spoils from the Temple in Jerusalem were carried in triumphal procession by Roman troops. This relief from Titus's Arch of Victory in the Roman Forum celebrates his capture of Jerusalem in 70 C.E. after a two-year siege. The Jews found it difficult to reconcile their religion with Roman rule and frequently rebelled.
Scala/Art Resource, N.Y.

On the walls of the houses of Pompeii, buried and preserved by the eruption of Mount Vesuvius in 79 C.E. are many scribblings that give us an idea of what the life of ordinary people was like.

> ⬥ How do these graffiti differ from those one sees in a modern American city? What do they reveal about the similarities and differences between the ordinary people of ancient Rome and the people of today? How would you account for the differences?

I

Twenty pairs of gladiators of Decimus Lucretius Satrius Valens, lifetime flamen of Nero son of Caesar Augustus, and ten pairs of gladiators of Decimus Lucretius Valens, his son, will fight at Pompeii on April 8, 9, 10, 11, 12. There will be a full card of wild beast combats, and awnings [for the spectators]. Aemilius Celer [painted this sign], all alone in the moonlight.

II

Market days: Saturday in Pompeii, Sunday in Nuceria, Monday in Atella, Tuesday in Nola, Wednesday in Cumae, Thursday in Puteoli, Friday in Rome.

III

Pleasure says: "You can get a drink here for an as [a few cents], a better drink for two, Falernian for four."

IV

A copper pot is missing from this shop. 65 sesterces reward if anybody brings it back, 20 sesterces if he reveals the thief so we can get our property back.

V

The weaver Successus loves the innkeeper's slave girl, Iris by name. She doesn't care for him, but he begs her to take pity on him. Written by his rival. So long.

[Answer by the rival:] Just because you're bursting with envy, don't pick on a handsomer man, a lady-killer and a gallant.

[Answer by the first writer:] There's nothing more to say or write. You love Iris, who doesn't care for you.

VI

Take your lewd looks and flirting eyes off another man's wife, and show some decency on your face!

VII

Anybody in love, come here. I want to break Venus' ribs with a club and cripple the goddess' loins. If she can pierce my tender breast, why can't I break her head with a club?

VIII

I write at Love's dictation and Cupid's instruction; But damn it! I don't want to be a god without you.

IX

[A prostitute's sign:] I am yours for 2 asses cash.

From *Roman Civilization*, ed. by Naphtali Lewis and Meyer Reinhold. Copyright © 1955 by Columbia University Press. Reprinted with permission of the publisher.

Some of the most important writers of the silver age in the first century C.E. reflected the Stoic opposition's hostility to the growing power and personal excesses of the emperors.

The writers of the second century C.E. appear to have turned away from contemporary affairs and even recent history. Historical writing was about remote periods, so there was less danger of irritating imperial sensibilities. Scholarship was encouraged, but we hear little of poetry, especially about any dealing with dangerous subjects.

During the third century C.E. romances written in Greek became popular as an escape from contemporary realities.

Architecture The prosperity and relative stability of the first two centuries of imperial Rome allowed the full development of Roman architecture. To the fundamental styles of buildings developed by the Greeks, the Romans added little; the great public bath and a new, free-standing amphitheater were their main innovations.

The main contribution of the Romans lay in the size of the structures they could build and in the advances in engineering that made these large structures possible. To the basic post-and-lintel construction used by the Greeks, the Romans added the semicircular arch, borrowed from the Etruscans. They also made good use of concrete, a building material first used by the Hellenistic Greeks and fully developed by the Romans. The arch combined with the post and lintel produced the great Colosseum built by the Flavian emperors. When used

⚠ **Pompeiian Woman.** The Roman provincial city of Pompeii, near the Bay of Naples, was buried by an eruption of Mount Vesuvius in 79 C.E. As a result, the town, together with its private houses and their contents, was remarkably well preserved until recovery in the eighteenth century. Among the discoveries were a number of works of art, including pictorial mosaics and paintings. This depiction of a young woman, on a round panel from a house in Pompeii, is part of a larger painting that includes her husband holding a volume of Plato's writings. The woman is holding a stylus and a booklet of wax tables and is evidently in the process of writing. Her gold earrings and hair net show that she is a fashionable person of some means. Late first century C.E. Diameter 14 ⁵/₈ inches.

Sappho, idealized portrait of a girl poising as a poetess. Fresco from Pompeii, Insula occidentale. Museo Archeologico Nazionale, Naples, Italy, © Erich Lessing/Art Resource, N.Y.

internally in the form of vaults and domes, the arch permitted great buildings like the baths.

One of Rome's most famous buildings, the Pantheon, begun by Augustus's friend Agrippa (63–12 B.C.E.) and rebuilt by Hadrian, combines all these elements. Its portico of Corinthian columns is of Greek origin, but its rotunda of brick-faced concrete with its domed ceiling and relieving arches is thoroughly Roman. The new engineering also made possible the construction of more mundane but more useful structures like bridges and aqueducts.

Society   Seen from the harsh perspective of human history, the first two centuries of the Roman Empire deserve their reputation as a golden age, but by the second century C.E. troubles had arisen—troubles that foreshadowed the difficult times ahead. The literary efforts of the time reveal a flight from the present and from reality and the public realm to the past, to romance,

and to private pursuits. (See Document, "Daily Life in a Roman Provincial Town: Graffiti from Pompeii.") Some of the same aspects may be seen in the more prosaic world of everyday life, especially in the decline of vitality in local government.

In the first century C.E. the upper classes vied for election to municipal office and for the honor of serving their communities. By the second century much of their zeal had disappeared, and the emperors had to correct abuses in local affairs and even force unwilling members of the ruling classes to accept public office. The reluctance to serve was caused largely by the imperial practice of holding magistrates and councilmen personally and collectively responsible for revenues that were due. Some magistrates even fled to avoid their office, a practice that eventually became widespread.

All of these difficulties reflected more basic problems. The prosperity brought by the end of civil war and the influx of wealth from the east, especially Egypt, could not sustain itself beyond the first half of the second century C.E. For reasons that remain mysterious the population also seems to have declined. The cost of government kept rising as the emperors were required to maintain an expensive standing army, to keep the people in Rome happy with "bread and circuses," to pay for an increasingly large bureaucracy, and to defend the frontiers against dangerous and determined enemies.

The ever-increasing need for money compelled the emperors to raise taxes, to press hard on their subjects, and to cause inflation by debasing the coinage. These elements were to bring on the desperate crises that ultimately destroyed the empire.

LIFE IN IMPERIAL ROME: THE APARTMENT HOUSE

The civilization of the Roman Empire depended on the vitality of its cities. While the typical city had about 20,000 inhabitants, Rome had more than 500,000, and some scholars think it may have had more than a million. Newcomers found Rome overwhelming and were either thrilled or horrified by its size, bustle, and noise.

The mass of its inhabitants were squeezed into increasingly tall multiple dwellings. Most Romans during the imperial period lived in apartment buildings called *insulae* ("islands") that rose to five or six stories and sometimes even more. The apartments were cramped and uncomfortable, hot in summer, cold in winter, and stuffy and smoky when the stoves were lit. These buildings were also dangerous. They were lightly built of concrete and brick, far too high for their foundations, and so they often collapsed. Even more serious was the threat of fire. The floors were supported by wooden beams, and the rooms were lit by torches, candles, and oil lamps and heated by braziers. Fires broke out easily but, without running water, were not easily put out; once started, they usually led to disaster.

When we compare these apartments to the attractive public places in the city, we can easily understand why the people of Rome spent most of their time outdoors.

The Rise of Christianity

The story of how Christianity emerged, spread, survived, and ultimately conquered the Roman Empire is one of the most remarkable in history. Its origin among poor people from an unimportant and remote province of the empire gave little promise of what was to come. Christianity faced the hostility of the established religious institutions of its native Judaea and had to compete not only against the official cults of Rome and the highly sophisticated philosophies of the educated classes, but also against **"mystery religions"** like the cults of Mithras, Isis, and Osiris. The Christians also faced the opposition of the imperial government and suffered formal persecution, yet Christianity finally became the official religion of the empire.

JESUS OF NAZARETH

An attempt to understand this amazing outcome must begin with a discussion of Jesus of Nazareth. The most important evidence of his life and teachings is in the Gospel accounts. Their authors believed that Jesus was the Son of God and that he came into the world to redeem humanity and to bring immortality to those who believed in him and followed his way; to the Gospel writers, Jesus' resurrection was striking proof of his teachings. The Gospels also regard Jesus as a figure in history, and they recount events in his life as well as his sayings.

There is no reason to doubt that Jesus was born in the province of Judaea in the time of Augustus and that he was a most effective teacher in the tradition of the Jewish prophets.

This tradition promised the coming of a Messiah (in Greek, *christos*—so *Jesus Christ* means "Jesus the Messiah"), the Redeemer who would make Israel triumph over its enemies and establish the Kingdom of God on earth. In fact, Jesus seems to have insisted that the Messiah would not establish an earthly kingdom but, at the Day of Judgment, would bring an end to the world as human beings knew it. On that day God would reward the righteous and condemn the wicked. Until that day, which his followers believed would come soon, Jesus taught the faithful to abandon sin and worldly concerns; to follow the moral code described in the Sermon on the Mount, which preached love, charity, and humility; and to believe in him and his divine mission.

Jesus won a considerable following, especially among the poor. This success caused great suspicion among the upper classes and provoked the hostility of the religious establishment in Jerusalem. They convinced the Roman governor that Jesus and his followers might be dangerous revolutionaries. He was put to death in Jerusalem by the cruel and degrading device of crucifixion, probably in 30 C.E. His followers believed that he was resurrected on the third day after his death, and that belief became a critical element in their religion. (See Document, "Mark Describes the Resurrection of Jesus.")

Although the new belief spread quickly to the Jewish communities of Syria and Asia Minor, without the conversion and career of Saint Paul it might have had only a short life as a despised Jewish heresy.

PAUL OF TARSUS

Paul (?5–67 C.E.) was born Saul, a citizen of the city of Tarsus in Asia Minor. Even though he was trained in Hellenistic culture and was a Roman citizen, he was a zealous member

DOCUMENT | Mark Describes the Resurrection of Jesus

Belief that Jesus rose from the dead after his crucifixion (about 30 C.E.) was and is central to traditional Christian doctrine. The record of the resurrection in the Gospel of Mark, written a generation later (toward 70 C.E.), is the earliest we have. The significance to most Christian groups revolves about the assurance given them that death and the grave are not final and that, instead, salvation for a future life is possible. The appeal of these views was to be nearly universal in the West during the Middle Ages. The church was commonly thought to be the means of implementing the promise of salvation; hence the enormous importance of the church's sacramental system, its rules, and its clergy.

◆ Why are the stories of miracles such as the one described here important for the growth of Christianity? What is special and important about this miracle? Why is it important in the story that days passed between the death of Jesus and the opening of the tomb? Why might the early Christians believe this story? Why was belief in the resurrection important for Christianity in the centuries immediately after the life of Jesus? Is it still important today?

And when evening had come, since it was the day of Preparation, that is, the day before the sabbath, Joseph of Arimathea, a respected member of the council, who was also himself looking for the kingdom of God, took courage and went to Pilate, and asked for the body of Jesus. And Pilate wondered if he were already dead; and summoning the centurion, he asked him whether he was already dead. And when he learned from the centurion that he was dead, he granted the body to Joseph. And he bought a linen shroud, and taking him down, wrapped him in the linen shroud, and laid him in a tomb which had been hewn out of the rock; and he rolled a stone against the door of the tomb. Mary Magdalene and Mary the mother of Jesus saw where he was laid.

And when the sabbath was past, Mary Magdalene, and Mary the mother of James, and Salome, bought spices, so that they might go and anoint him. And very early on the first day of the week they went to the tomb when the sun had risen. And they were saying to one another, "Who will roll away the stone for us from the door of the tomb?" And looking up, they saw that the stone was rolled back; for it was very large. And entering the tomb, they saw a young man sitting on the right side, dressed in a white robe; and they were amazed. And he said to them, "Do not be amazed; you seek Jesus of Nazareth, who was crucified. He has risen, he is not here, see the place where they laid him. But go, tell his disciples and Peter that he is going before you to Galilee; there you will see him, as he told you." And they went out and fled from the tomb; for trembling and astonishment had come upon them; and they said nothing to any one, for they were afraid.

From the Gospel of Mark 15:42–47; 16:1–8, Revised Standard Version of the Bible (New York: Thomas Nelson and Sons, 1946, 1952).

---

of the Jewish sect known as the **Pharisees**, who were the strictest adherents of the Jewish law. He took a vigorous part in the persecution of the early Christians until his own conversion outside Damascus in about 35 C.E. The great problem facing the early Christians was their relationship to Judaism. If the new faith was a version of Judaism, then it must adhere to the Jewish law and seek converts only among Jews. James, called the brother of Jesus, held that view, whereas Hellenist Jews tended to see Christianity as a new and universal religion.

Paul, converted and with his new name, supported the position of the Hellenists and soon won many converts among the Gentiles. Paul believed it important that the followers of Jesus be evangelists ("messengers"), to spread the gospel ("good news") of God's gracious gift. He taught that Jesus would soon return for the Day of Judgment, and that all should believe in him and accept his way. Faith in Jesus as the Christ was necessary but not sufficient for salvation, nor could good deeds alone achieve it. That final blessing of salvation was a gift of God's grace.

ORGANIZATION

The new religion spread throughout the Roman Empire and even beyond its borders. It had its greatest success in the cities and among the poor and uneducated. The rites of the early communities appear to have been simple and few. Baptism by water removed original sin and permitted participation in the community and its activities. The central ritual was a common meal called the *agape* ("love feast"), followed by the ceremony of the *Eucharist* ("thanksgiving"), a celebration of the Lord's Supper in which unleavened bread was eaten and unfermented wine drunk. There were also prayers, hymns, and readings from the Gospels.

At first the churches had little formal organization. Soon, it appears, affairs were placed in the hands of boards of *presbyters* ("elders") and *deacons* ("those who serve"). By the second century C.E., as their numbers grew, the Christians of each city tended to accept the authority and leadership of bishops (*episkopoi*, or "overseers"), who were elected by the congregation. As time passed, bishops extended their authority over the Christian communities in outlying towns and the countryside. The power and almost monarchical authority of the bishops were soon enhanced by the doctrine of Apostolic Succession, which asserted that the powers Jesus had given his original disciples were passed on from bishop to bishop by the rite of ordination.

The bishops kept in touch with one another, maintained communications between different Christian communities, and prevented doctrinal and sectarian splintering, which would have destroyed Christian unity. They kept internal discipline and dealt with the civil authorities. In time they began coming together in councils to settle difficult questions, to establish orthodox opinion, and even to expel as heretics those who would not accept it. Christianity could probably not have survived without such strong internal organization and government.

PERSECUTION OF CHRISTIANS

The new faith soon incurred the distrust of the pagan world and of the imperial government. The Christians' refusal to worship the emperor was considered treason. The privacy and secrecy of Christian life and worship ran counter to a traditional Roman dislike of any private association, especially any of a religious nature, and the Christians thus earned the reputation of being "haters of humanity." By the end of the first century "the name alone"—that is, simple membership in the Christian community—was a crime.

Most persecutions during this period, however, were instituted not by the government but by mobs. But even this adversity had its benefits. It weeded out the weaklings among the Christians,

brought greater unity to those who remained faithful, and provided martyrs who inspired still greater devotion and dedication.

EMERGENCE OF CATHOLICISM

Most Christians held to what even then were traditional, simple, conservative beliefs. This body of majority opinion and the church that enshrined it came to be called **Catholic**, which means "universal." Its doctrines were deemed **orthodox**; those holding contrary opinions were **heretics**.

The need to combat heretics, however, compelled the orthodox to formulate their own views more clearly and firmly. By the end of the second century an Orthodox canon had been shaped that included the Old Testament, the Gospels, and the Epistles of Paul, among other writings. The process was not completed for at least two more centuries, but a vitally important start had been made. The Orthodox declared the church itself to be the depository of Christian teaching and the bishops to be its receivers. They also drew up creeds, brief statements of faith to which true Christians should adhere. In the first century all that was required of one to be a Christian was to be baptized, to partake of the Eucharist, and to call Jesus the Lord. By the end of the second century an Orthodox Christian—that is, a member of the Catholic Church—had to accept its creed, its canon of holy writings, and the authority of the bishops. The loose structure of the apostolic church had given way to an organized body with recognized leaders able to define its faith and to exclude those who did not accept it.

◀ **Christ's Arrest.** This Early Christian art shows Christ arrested by soldiers on the night before his crucifixion. Note that Christ is portrayed clean-shaven and dressed in the toga of a Roman aristocrat.

Hirmer Fotoarchiv, Munich.

ROME AS A CENTER OF THE EARLY CHURCH

During this same period the church in the city of Rome came to have special prominence. Besides having the largest single congregation of Christians, Rome also benefited from the tradition that both Jesus' apostles Peter and Paul were martyred there. Peter, moreover, was thought to be the first bishop of Rome, and the Gospel of Matthew (16:18) reported Jesus' statement to Peter: "Thou art Peter [in Greek, *Petros*] and upon this rock [in Greek, *petra*] I will build my church." As a result, later bishops of Rome were to claim supremacy in the Catholic Church.

The Crisis of the Third Century

The pressure on Rome's frontiers reached massive proportions in the third century C.E. In the east, by 224 C.E. a new Iranian dynasty, the Sassanids, reinvigorated Persia (see Chapter 10). They soon recovered Mesopotamia and raided deep into Roman territory.

BARBARIAN INVASIONS

On the western and northern frontiers the threat came from German tribes. The most aggressive in the third century C.E. were the Goths. In the 220s and 230s they began to put pressure on the Danube frontier, and by about 250 C.E. they overran the Balkan provinces. The need to meet these threats made the Romans weaken their western frontiers, and other Germanic peoples broke through there. There was a considerable danger that Rome would be unable to meet this challenge.

Septimius Severus (r. 193–211 C.E.) and his successors transformed the character of the Roman army. Septimius was a military usurper who owed everything to the support of his soldiers. He was prepared to make Rome into an undisguised military monarchy. Septimius drew recruits for the army increasingly from peasants of the less civilized provinces, and the result was a barbarization of Rome's military forces.

ECONOMIC DIFFICULTIES

Inflation had forced Commodus (r. 180–192 C.E.) to raise the soldiers' pay, but the Severan emperors had to double it to keep up with prices, which increased the imperial budget by as much as 25 percent. The emperors invented new taxes, debased the coinage, and even sold the palace furniture to raise money. Even then it was hard to recruit troops, and the new style of military life introduced by Septimius—with its laxer discipline, more pleasant duties, and greater opportunity for advancement, not only in the army but also in Roman society—was needed to attract men into the army. The policy proved effective for a short time but could not prevent the chaos of the late third century.

The same forces that caused problems for the army hurt society at large. The shortage of workers reduced agricultural production. As external threats distracted the emperors, they were less able to preserve domestic peace. Piracy, brigandage, and the neglect of roads and harbors hampered trade. So, too, did the debasement of the coinage and the resulting inflation. Imperial exactions and confiscations of the property of the rich removed badly needed capital from productive use.

The government now had to demand services that had once been gladly volunteered. Because the empire lived on a hand-to-mouth basis, with no significant reserve fund and no system of credit financing, the emperors had to compel the people to provide food, supplies, money and labor. The upper classes in the cities were made to serve as administrators without pay and to meet deficits in revenue out of their own pockets. There were provincial rebellions, and peasants and even town administrators fled to escape their burdens. These difficulties weakened Rome's economic strength when it was most needed.

THE SOCIAL ORDER

The new conditions caused important changes in the social order. The Senate and the traditional ruling class were decimated by direct attacks from hostile emperors and by economic losses. Their ranks were filled by military men. The whole state began to take on an increasingly military appearance. Distinctions among the classes by dress had been traditional since the republic, but in the third and fourth centuries C.E. people's everyday clothing became a kind of uniform that precisely revealed their status. Titles were assigned to ranks in society as to ranks in the army. The most important distinction was the one formally established by Septimius Severus, which drew a sharp line between the *honestiores* (senators, equestrians, the municipal aristocracy, and the soldiers) and the lower classes, or *humiliores*. Septimius gave the *honestiores* a privileged position before the law. They were given lighter punishments, could not be tortured, and alone had the right of appeal to the emperor.

It became more difficult to move from the lower order to the higher, another example of the growing rigidity of the late Roman Empire. Farmers were tied to their lands, artisans to their crafts, soldiers to the army, merchants and shipowners to the needs of the state, and citizens of the municipal upper class to the collection and payment of increasingly burdensome taxes. Freedom and private initiative yielded to the needs of the state and its ever expanding control of its citizens.

CIVIL DISORDER

By the mid–third century the empire seemed on the point of collapse, but two able soldiers, Claudius II Gothicus (r. 268–270 C.E.) and Aurelian (r. 270–275 C.E.), drove back the barbarians and stamped out disorder. The emperors who followed Aurelian on the throne were good fighters and changed Rome's system of defense. They built walls around Rome and other cities to resist barbarian attack. They drew back their best troops from the frontiers, relying chiefly on a newly organized heavy cavalry and a mobile army near the emperor's own residence. Hereafter, the army was composed largely of Germanic mercenaries whose officers gave personal loyalty to the emperor rather than to the empire. These officers became a foreign, hereditary caste of aristocrats who increasingly supplied high administrators and even emperors. In effect, the Roman people hired an army of mercenaries, only technically Roman, to protect them.

The Late Empire

THE FOURTH CENTURY AND IMPERIAL REORGANIZATION

The period from Diocletian (r. 284–305 C.E.) to Constantine (r. 306–337 C.E.) was one of reconstruction and reorganization.

Diocletian   The emperor Diocletian was a man of undistinguished birth who rose to the throne through the army. He knew that he was not a great general and that the job of defending and governing the entire empire was too great for one man. He therefore decreed the introduction of the **tetrarchy**, the rule of the empire by four men with power divided on a territorial basis (see Map 6–5). This system seemed to promise orderly, peaceful transitions instead of assassinations, chaos, and civil war.

Constantine   In 305 Diocletian retired and compelled his co-emperor to do the same. But his plan for a smooth succession failed completely. In 310 there were five competing emperors. Out of this chaos Constantine produced order. In 324 he defeated his last opponent and made himself sole emperor, uniting the empire once again; he reigned until 337.

The emperor had now become a remote figure surrounded by carefully chosen high officials. He lived in a great palace and was almost unapproachable. Those admitted to his presence had to prostrate themselves before him and kiss the hem of his robe, which was purple and had golden threads going through it. The emperor was addressed as *dominus* ("lord"), and his right to rule was not derived from the Roman people but from God. This remoteness and ceremony enhanced the dignity of the emperor and safeguarded him against assassination.

Constantine erected the new city of Constantinople on the site of ancient Byzantium on the Bosporus, which leads to both the Aegean and the Black Seas, and made it the new capital of the empire. Its strategic location was excellent for protecting the eastern and Danubian frontiers, and, surrounded on three sides by water, it was easily defended.

Administration and Finance   The autocratic rule of the emperors was carried out by a civilian bureaucracy, which was carefully separated from the military service to reduce the chances of rebellion. The entire system was supervised by a network of spies and secret police, without whom the increasingly rigid

authoritarian organization could not be trusted to perform. Despite these efforts, the system was corrupt and inefficient.

The cost of maintaining a 400,000-man army as well as the vast civilian bureaucracy, the expensive imperial court, and the imperial taste for splendid buildings strained an already weak economy. Diocletian's attempts to establish a uniform and reliable currency merely increased inflation. To deal with it he resorted to price control with his Edict of Maximum Prices in 301. For each product and each kind of labor a maximum price was set, and violations were punishable by death. The edict failed, despite its harsh provisions.

Peasants unable to pay their taxes and officials unable to collect them tried to escape, and Diocletian resorted to stern regimentation to keep all in their places and at the service of the government. The terror of the third century had turned many peasants into tenant farmers who fled for protection to the country estates of powerful landowners. They were tied to the land, as were their descendants, as the caste system hardened.

Division of the Empire   The peace and unity established by Constantine did not last. His death was followed by a struggle for succession that was won by Constantius II (r. 337–361). His death left the empire to his young cousin Julian (r. 361–363), called by the Christians "the Apostate" as a result of his attempt to restore paganism. Julian was killed in a campaign against the Persians. His death ended the pagan revival.

The Germans in the West attacked along the Rhine, but even greater trouble was brewing along the Danube (see Map 6–6) where the Visigoths had been driven from their home in the Ukraine by the fierce Huns, a nomadic people from Central Asia. The Emperor Valentinian (r. 364–375) saw that he could not defend the empire alone and appointed his brother Valens (r. 364–378) as co-ruler. Valentinian made his own headquarters at Milan and spent the rest of his life fighting barbarians in the West. Valens was given control of the East. The empire was once again divided in two. The two emperors maintained their own courts, and the two halves of the empire became increasingly separate and different. Latin was the language of the West and Greek of the East.

In 376 the hard-pressed Visigoths received permission to enter the empire to escape the Huns. When the Goths began to plunder the Balkan provinces, Valens attacked them and died, along with most of his army, at Adrianople in Thrace in 378. Theodosius (r. 379–395), an able and experienced general, was named co-ruler in the East. He tried to unify the empire again, but his death in 395 left it divided and weak.

Thereafter, the two parts of the empire went their separate and different ways. The West became increasingly rural as barbarian invasions grew. The villa, a fortified country estate, became the basic unit of life. There, *coloni* (tenant farmers) gave their services to the local magnate in return for economic assistance and protection from both barbarians and imperial

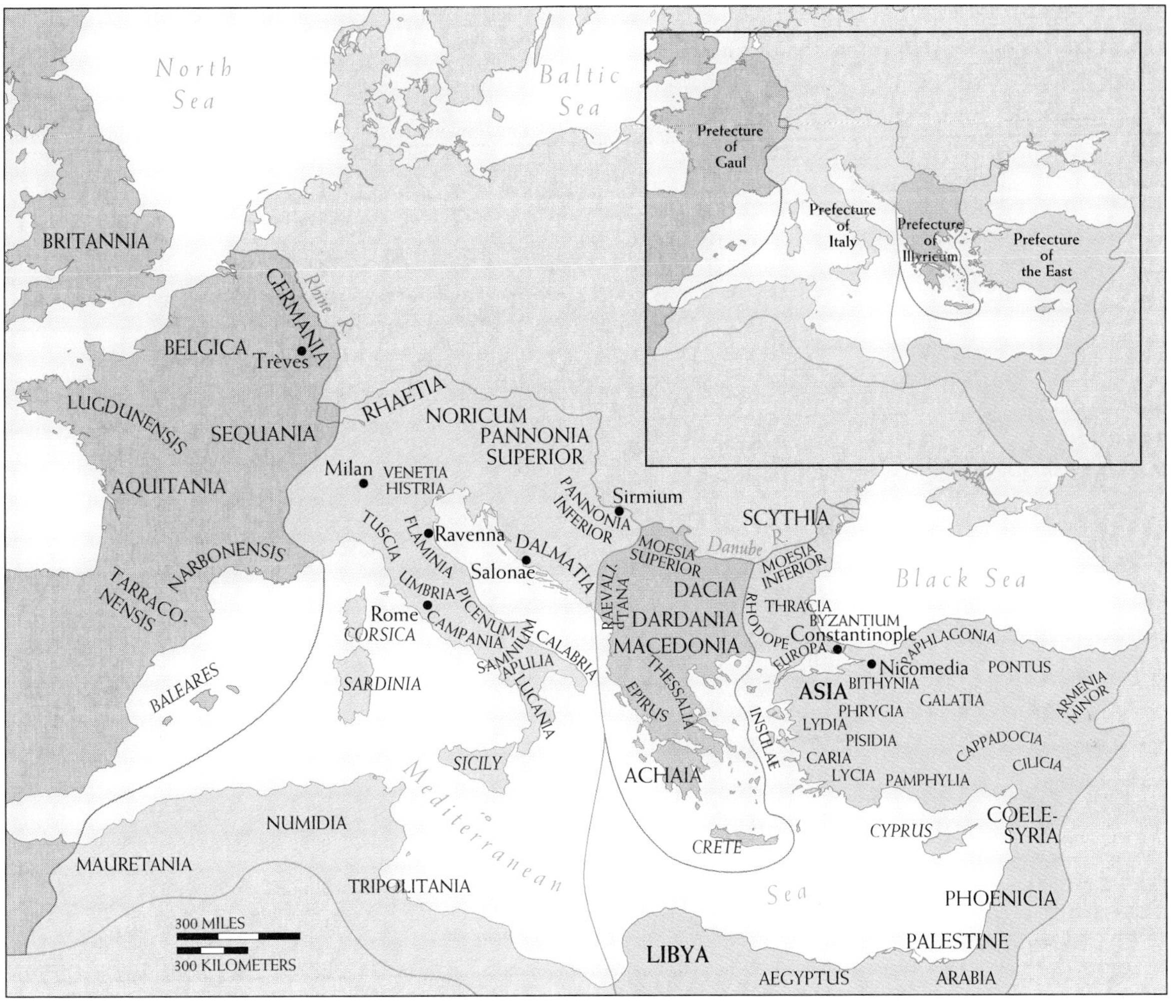

MAP 6–5 Divisions of the Roman Empire under Diocletian.   Diocletian divided the sprawling empire into four prefectures for more effective government and defense. The inset map shows their boundaries and the large map gives some details of regions and provinces. The major division between East and West was along the line running from north to south between Pannonia and Moesia.

officials. Many cities shrank to tiny walled fortresses ruled by military commanders and bishops. The upper classes moved to the country and asserted ever greater independence of imperial authority. The failure of the central authority to maintain the roads and the constant danger from robber bands sharply curtailed trade and communications, forcing greater self-reliance and a more primitive style of life. By the fifth century the West was increasingly made up of isolated units of rural aristocrats and their dependent laborers. The only unifying institution was the Christian church. The pattern for the early Middle Ages in the West was already formed.

The East was different. Constantinople became the center of a vital and flourishing culture that we call *Byzantine* and that lasted until the fifteenth century. Due to its defensible location, the skill of its emperors, and the firmness and strength of its base in Asia Minor, it was able to deflect and repulse barbarian attacks. A strong navy allowed commerce to flourish in the eastern Mediterranean and, in good times, far beyond it. Cities continued to pros-

per, and the emperors controlled the nobility. Byzantine civilization was a unique combination of classical culture, the Christian religion, Roman law, and Eastern artistic influences. While the West was being overrun by barbarians, the Roman Empire, in altered form, persisted in the East. While Rome shrank to an insignificant ecclesiastical town, Constantinople flourished as the seat of empire, the "New Rome," and the Byzantines called themselves "Romans." When we contemplate the decline and fall of the Roman Empire in the fourth and fifth centuries, we are speaking only of the West. A form of classical culture persisted in the Byzantine East for another thousand years.

TRIUMPH OF CHRISTIANITY

Religious Currents in the Empire   In the troubled fourth and fifth centuries people sought powerful, personal deities who would bring them safety and prosperity in this world and immortality in the next. Paganism was open and tolerant, and it

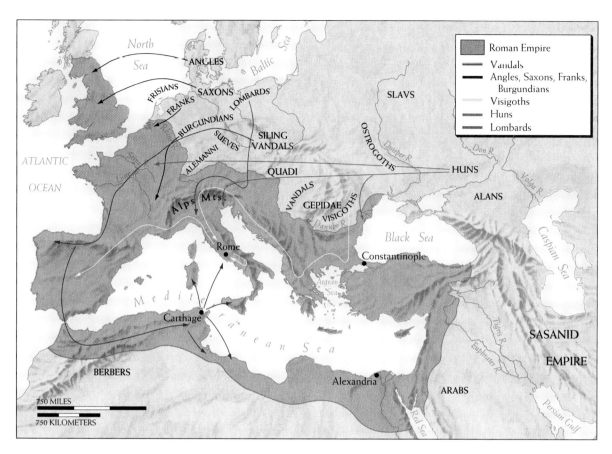

MAP 6–6 The Empire's Neighbors. In the fourth century the Roman Empire was nearly surrounded by ever more threatening neighbors. The map shows where these so-called barbarians lived and the invasion routes many of them took in fourth and fifth centuries.

was by no means unusual for people to worship new deities alongside the old and even to intertwine elements of several gods to form a new amalgam by the device called **syncretism**.

Christianity's success owed something to the same causes of the popularity of other cults, which are often spoken of as its rivals. None of them, however, attained Christianity's universality, and none appears to have given the early Christians and their leaders as much competition as the ancient philosophies or the state religion (see Map 6–7).

Imperial Persecution By the third century Christianity had taken firm hold in the Eastern provinces and Italy. As times became bad and the Christians became more numerous and visible, popular opinion blamed disasters, natural and military, on the Christians. About 250 the emperor Decius (r. 249–251) required that all citizens worship the state gods publicly. True Christians could not obey, and Decius instituted a major persecution. Valerian (r. 253–260) resumed the persecutions, partly to confiscate the wealth of rich Christians. His successors, however, let persecution lapse until the end of the century.

In 303 Diocletian launched the most serious persecution inflicted on the Christians in the Roman Empire. Because the

martyrs often aroused pity and sympathy, and because large ancient states were unable to carry out a program of terror with the thoroughness of modern totalitarian governments, the Christians and their church survived to enjoy what they must have considered a miraculous change of fortune. In 311 Galerius (r. 305–311), who had been one of the most vigorous persecutors, was influenced, perhaps by his Christian wife, to issue an edict of toleration permitting Christian worship.

The victory of Constantine and his emergence as sole ruler of the empire transformed Christianity from a precariously tolerated sect to the religion favored by the emperor. In 394 Theodosius forbade the celebration of pagan cults and abolished the pagan religious calendar. At his death Christianity was the official religion of the Roman Empire.

The favored position of the church attracted opportunistic converts and diluted the moral excellence and spiritual fervor of its adherents. The relationship between church and state presented the possibility that religion would become subordinate to the state, as it had traditionally been. In the East, that largely happened. In the West, the weakness of the emperors permitted church leaders to exercise remarkable independence. In 390 Ambrose (ca. 339–397), bishop of Milan, excommunicated

Emperor Theodosius, and the emperor did humble penance. This act provided an important precedent for future assertions of the church's autonomy and authority, but it did not stop secular interference and influence in the church by any means.

Arianism and the Council of Nicaea   Internal divisions within the church proved to be even more troubling as new heresies emerged. The most important and the most threatening was **Arianism**, founded by a priest named Arius of Alexandria (ca. 280–336) in the fourth century. Arius's view that Jesus was not co-equal and co-eternal with God the Father did away with the mysterious concept of the Trinity, the difficult doctrine that holds that God is three persons (the Father, the Son, and the Holy Spirit) but also one in substance and essence.

Athanasius (ca. 293–373), later bishop of Alexandria, saw the Arian view as an impediment to salvation. Only if Jesus were both fully human and fully God could the transformation of humanity to divinity have taken place in him and be transmitted by him to his disciples. "Christ was made man," he said, "that we might be made divine."

To deal with the growing controversy, Constantine called a council of Christian bishops at Nicaea, not far from Constantinople, in 325. For the emperor, the question was essentially political, but for the disputants, salvation was at stake. At the Council of Nicaea the view expounded by Athanasius won out, became orthodox, and was embodied in the **Nicene Creed**. The Christian emperors hoped to unify their increasingly decentralized realms by imposing a single religion, and it did prove to be a unifying force, but it also introduced new divisions where none had previously existed.

Arts and Letters in the Late Empire

The art and literature of the late empire reflect both the confluence of pagan and Christian ideas and traditions and the conflict between them. Much of the literature is polemical, and much of the art is propaganda.

The empire was saved from the chaos of the third century by a military revolution based on and led by provincials of lower class origins. They brought with them the fresh winds of cultural change, which blew out not only the dust of classical culture but much of its substance as well. Yet the new ruling class thought of itself as effecting

MAP 6–7 The Spread of Christianity.   Christianity grew swiftly in the third, fourth, fifth, and sixth centuries—especially after the conversion of the emperors in the fourth century. By 600, on the eve of the birth of the new religion of Islam, Christianity was dominant throughout the Mediterranean world and most of Western Europe.

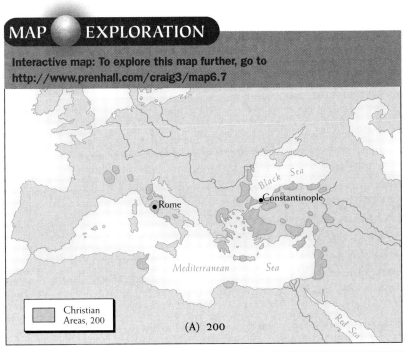

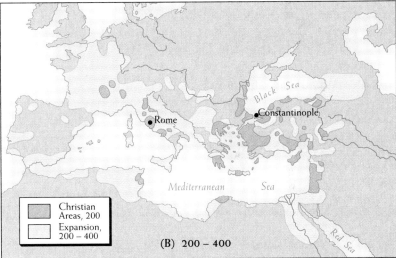

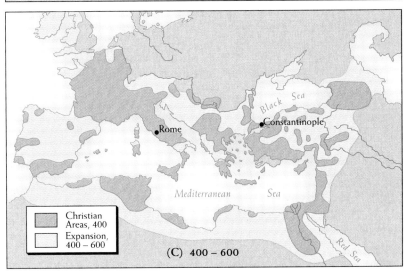

a great restoration rather than a revolution and sought to restore classical culture and absorb it. The confusion and uncertainty of the times were tempered in part, of course, by the comfort of Christianity, but the new aristocracy sought order and stability—ethical, literary, and artistic—in the classical tradition as well.

PRESERVATION OF CLASSICAL CULTURE

One of the main needs and accomplishments of this period was to preserve classical culture and make it available and useful to the new elite. The great classical authors were reproduced in many copies, and their works were transferred from perishable and inconvenient papyrus rolls to sturdier codices, bound volumes that were as easy to use as modern books. Scholars also digested long works like Livy's *History of Rome* into shorter versions and wrote learned commentaries and compiled grammars. Original works by pagan writers of the late empire were neither numerous nor especially distinguished.

CHRISTIAN WRITERS

Of Christian writings, on the other hand, the late empire saw a great outpouring: Christian apologetics in poetry and prose, as well as sermons, hymns, and biblical commentaries. Christianity could also boast important scholars. Jerome (348–420), thoroughly trained in classical Latin literature and rhetoric, produced a revised version of the Bible in Latin, commonly called the Vulgate, which became the Bible used by the Catholic Church.

Probably the most important Eastern scholar was Eusebius of Caesarea (ca. 260–340). His most important contribution was his *Ecclesiastical History*, an attempt to set forth the Christian view of history. He saw history as the working out of God's will. All of history, therefore, had a purpose and a direction, and Constantine's victory and the subsequent unity of empire and church were its culmination.

The closeness and complexity of the relationship between classical pagan culture and the Christianity of the late empire are nowhere better displayed than in the career and writings of Augustine (354–430), bishop of Hippo in North Africa. He was born at Carthage and was trained as a teacher of rhetoric. He passed through a number of intellectual way stations before his conversion to Christianity. His skill in pagan rhetoric and philosophy made him peerless among his contemporaries as a defender of Christianity and a theologian. His greatest works are his *Confessions*, an autobiography describing the road to his conversion, and *The City of God*. The latter was a response to the pagan charge that Rome's sack by the Goths in 410 was caused by the abandonment of the old gods and the advent of Christianity. The optimistic view held by some Christians that God's will worked its way in history and was easily comprehensible needed further support in the face of this disaster.

Augustine sought to separate the fate of Christianity from that of the Roman Empire. He contrasted the secular world—the city of man—with the spiritual—the City of God. Augustine argued that history was moving forward, in the spiritual sense, to the Day

---

OVERVIEW   The Fall of the Roman Empire in the West

For centuries historians and social scientists have speculated why the ancient world collapsed. By contrast, the great English historian Edward Gibbon (1737–1794) wrote in his classic work, *The Decline and Fall of the Roman Empire* that we should really ask not why Rome fell but why so vast an empire survived for so long. The following are some of the causes and explanations scholars have proposed for the fall of Rome. They range from the plausible to the ridiculous.

CAUSE	EXPLANATION
Climate change	A gradual drying and cooling climate destroyed the productivity of ancient agriculture on which the empire depended.
Soil exhaustion	Depleted soil around the Mediterranean no longer produced enough food to feed the population, which weakened and declined.
Lead poisoning	The use of lead pipes for drinking and cooking water led to widespread lead poisoning and sterility, especially among the upper classes who had most access to running water.
Racial pollution	Eastern immigrants to Rome—Syrians, Greeks, and Jews—sapped the vitality of the Romans and destroyed their ability to rule and defend themselves.
Slavery	The prevalence of slavery made the Romans lazy and undercut free labor.
Intellectual stagnation	The failure to make advances in science and technology—to achieve a scientific revolution—led the empire to an intellectual and economic dead end.
Social disorder	The destruction of the middle class through civil war, invasion, and over taxation wiped out the most productive and culturally aware part of the Roman population. Third-century emperors encouraged the rural poor to plunder the middle and upper classes.
Excessive government	Government exactions and regulations destroyed the operation of a market economy, which was the basis for prosperity.
Christianity	The adoption of Christianity as the official religion of the empire in the fourth century weakened the Roman state, diverted scarce resources to building and staffing churches and monasteries, and led large segments of the population to embrace pacifism.
Immorality	Gluttony, sloth, and sexual depravity replaced the old Roman virtues that had enabled Rome to conquer its empire.

CHRONOLOGY

The Triumph of Christianity

ca. 4 B.C.E.	Jesus of Nazareth born
ca. 30 C.E.	Crucifixion of Jesus
64 C.E.	Fire at Rome: persecution by Nero
ca. 70–100 C.E.	Gospels written
ca. 250–260 C.E.	Major persecutions by Decius and Valerian
303 C.E.	Persecution by Diocletian
311 C.E.	Galerius issues Edict of Toleration
312 C.E.	Battle of Milvian Bridge; conversion of Constantine to Christianity
325 C.E.	Council of Nicaea
ca. 330 C.E.	Georgia and Armenia become first Christian kingdoms
395 C.E.	Christianity becomes official religion of Roman Empire

Nag Hammadi Manuscripts. Found in Upper Egypt, in 1945 they were buried about 400 C.E. by members of the Gnostic Community of Christians. They contain copies and translations of early Christian texts condemned as heretical by the Church.
Institute for Antiquity and Christianity, Claremont, California.

of Judgment, but that there was no reason to expect improvement before then in the secular sphere. The fall of Rome was neither surprising nor important, for all states were part of the city of man and therefore corrupt and mortal. Only the City of God was immortal, and it was untouched by earthly calamities.

Augustine believed that faith is essential and primary but not a substitute for reason. Instead, faith is the starting point for the liberation of human reason the means by which people can understand what is revealed by faith. His writings constantly reveal the presence of both Christian faith and pagan reason and the tension between them, a legacy he left to the Middle Ages.

The Arch of Constantine. Built in 315 C.E., it represents a transition between classical and medieval, pagan and Christian. Many of the sculptures incorporated in it were taken from earlier works dating to the first and second centuries. Others, contemporary with the arch, reflect a new, less refined style.
Scala/Art Resource, N.Y.

The Problem of the Decline and Fall of the Empire in the West

Whether important to Augustine or not, the massive barbarian invasions of the fifth century ended effective imperial government in the West. For centuries people have speculated about why the ancient world collapsed. Soil exhaustion, plague, climatic change, and even poisoning from lead water pipes have been suggested as reasons for Rome's decline in population, vigor, and the capacity to defend itself. Some blame slavery and the failure to make advances in science and technology; others blame excessive government interference in the economic life; others, the destruction of the urban middle class.

Perhaps a more simple and obvious explanation can be found. The growth of so mighty an empire as Rome's was by no means inevitable. Rome's greatness had come from conquests that provided the Romans with the means to expand still further, until there were not enough Romans to conquer and govern any more peoples and territory. When pressure from outsiders grew, the Romans lacked the resources to advance and defeat the enemy as in the past. Still, the tenacity and success of their resistance were remarkable. Without new conquests to provide the immense wealth needed to defend and maintain internal prosperity, the Romans finally yielded to unprecedented onslaughts by fierce and numerous attackers.

To blame the ancients and slavery for the failure to produce an industrial and economic revolution like that of the later Western world, one capable of producing wealth without taking it from another, is to stand the problem on its head. No one yet has a satisfactory explanation for those revolutions, so it is improper to blame any institution or society for not achieving what has been achieved only once in human history, in what are still mysterious circumstances.

We may do well to think of the decline of Rome as the historian Edward Gibbon did:

> The decline of Rome was the natural and inevitable effect of immoderate greatness. Prosperity ripened the principle of decay; the cause of the destruction multiplied with the extent of conquest; and, as soon as time or accident had removed the artificial supports, the stupendous fabric yielded to the pressure of its own weight. The story of the ruin is simple and obvious; and instead of inquiring why the Roman Empire was destroyed, we should rather be surprised that it had subsisted so long.[5]

This explanation allows us to see the Roman Empire as one among several great empires around the world that had similar experiences.

[5] Edward Gibbon. *Decline and Fall of the Roman Empire*, ed. by J. B. Bury, 2nd ed., Vol. 4 (London: J. Murray, 1909), pp. 173–174.

Roman Colosseum.

Summary

Republican Rome   Rome began as a small settlement in Latium in central Italy ruled by Etruscan kings; Rome became a republic in 509 B.C.E. The Roman constitution divided power between elected magistrates, the chief of whom were two consuls; an appointed Senate, whose members served for life; and popular assemblies. During the third century B.C.E., the aristocratic patricians were forced to share power with the common people, the plebians. The institution of clientage by which clients pledged their loyalty to powerful patrons in return for legal and political protection was an important part of Roman political life.

Roman Expansion   By the early fourth century, Rome had expanded to control all of Italy through a policy of conquest, alliances, colonies of Roman veterans, and generosity to foes who submitted. Between 264 and 146 B.C.E., Rome fought three wars with Carthage for control of the western Mediterranean. These Punic Wars ended with the destruction of Carthage, but led to resolve social and political disorder in Italy. Many small farmers lost their land, and efforts by the Gracchi brothers to resolve the problems ended in their murders.

In the third century B.C.E., Rome turned to the east and defeated the Hellenistic monarchies that had succeeded Alexander's empire. Macedon and Greece fell under Roman rule. This led to the adoption of Greek culture by the Roman aristocracy and the rapid Hellenization of Roman culture. By the first century B.C.E., Rome controlled most of the Mediterranean world.

The Empire and Rise of Christianity   The Roman Republic was destroyed by social unrest and rivalry among ambitious generals and politicians, the most successful of whom was Julius Caesar. After a civil war that followed Caesar's assassination in 44 B.C.E., his nephew Octavian emerged as the most powerful man in Rome. Under the title of Augustus, he set up a system that preserved the façade of republican institutions but was in fact a monarchy.

The Roman Empire stretched from Scotland to Iraq. Rome fostered the growth of cities, developed the rule of law, built a vast network of roads and other public works, and established two centuries of peace and stability. Christianity, which arose in the Roman province of Judaea in the first century C.E., spread throughout the empire despite occasional persecutions by the Roman state, which itself became Christian in the late fourth century.

Decline and Fall   In the third century C.E., the Roman peace collapsed under the pressure of invasions by barbarians in the West and the Sassanids in the East. Rival generals murdered emperors and usurped the throne. The economy declined. The state exacted more and more taxes and resources from its citizens. The emperors Diocletian and Constantine managed to halt the decline, but in the fifth century C.E. Roman authority in the West collapsed. In the East, however, a Christian Roman empire based in the city of Constantinople survived and evolved into the Byzantine empire that did much to preserve the Greek and Roman heritage for another 1,000 years.

Review Questions

1. How did the institutions of family and clientage and the establishment of patrician and plebeian classes contribute to the stability of the early Roman Republic? How important was education to the success of the republic?

2. Discuss Rome's expansion to 265 B.C.E. How was Rome able to conquer and control Italy? In their relations with Greece and Asia Minor in the second century B.C.E., were the Romans looking for security? Wealth? Power? Fame?

3. Explain the clash between the Romans and the Carthaginians in the First and Second Punic Wars. Could the wars have been avoided? How did Rome benefit from its victory over Carthage? What problems were created by this victory?

4. What were the problems that plagued the Roman Republic in the last century? What caused these problems and how did the Romans try to solve them? To what extent was the republic destroyed by ambitious generals who loved power more than Rome itself?

5. Discuss the Augustan constitution and government. What solutions did Augustus provide for the problems that had plagued the Roman Republic? Why was the Roman population willing to accept Augustus as head of the state?

6. Despite unpromising beginnings, Christianity was enormously popular by the fourth century C.E. Why were Christians persecuted by Roman authorities? What were the more important reasons for Christianity's success?

7. Consider three theories that scholars have advanced to explain the decline and fall of the Roman Empire. What are the difficulties involved in explaining the fall? What explanation would you give?

Key Terms

agape   (p. 195)

Arianism   (p. 201)

Augustus   (p. 186)

Catholic   (p. 196)

censor   (p. 175)

equestrians   (p. 183)

Eucharist   (p. 195)

heretics   (p. 196)

humanitas   (p. 180)

imperator   (p. 186)

imperium   (p. 174)

latifundia   (p. 181)

"mystery religions"   (p. 194)

Nicene Creed   (p. 201)

orthodox   (p. 196)

patrician   (p. 175)

Pharisees   (p. 195)

plebeian   (p. 175)

populares   (p. 183)

Punic Wars   (p. 177)

syncretism   (p. 200)

tetrarchy   (p. 198)

tribunes   (p. 176)

Documents CD-ROM

Rome

5.1 A Hero Under Fire: Livy Relates the Trials and Tribulations of Scipio Africanus

5.2 "The War with Catiline": Sallust's Insights Into the Roman Republic's Decline

5.3 The Transition from Republic to Principate: Tacitus

5.4 "All Roads Lead to Rome!": Strabo

5.5 Gladiatorial Combat: Seneca

5.6 The Stoic Philosophy

5.7 Sidonius Appolinaris: Rome's Decay, and a Glimpse of the New Order

The Rise of Christianity

6.1 The Acts of the Apostles

6.2 Pliny the Younger on the Vesuvius Eruption and the Christian "Controversy"

6.3 Julian Imperator: The Ultimate Pagan

6.4 Bishop Synesius of Cyrene: A Lukewarm Churchman

6.6 St. Augustine of Hippo, The Just War

6.7 Paulus Orosius, History Against the Pagans

NOTE: *To learn more about the topics in this chapter, see the Suggested Readings at the end of the book.*

7

China's First Empire
221 B.C.E.–589 C.E.

- Qin Unification of China

- Former Han Dynasty (206 B.C.E.–8 C.E.)

- Later Han (25–220 C.E.) and Its Aftermath

- Han Thought and Religion

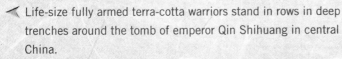

◄ Life-size fully armed terra-cotta warriors stand in rows in deep
trenches around the tomb of emperor Qin Shihuang in central
China.

National Geographic Image Collection.

GLOBAL PERSPECTIVE

China's First Empire

Were there world-historical forces that produced at roughly the same time great empires in China, India, and the Mediterranean? Certainly these empires had similar features. All three came after revolutions in thought. The Han built on Zhou thought (it would be hard to imagine the Han bureaucratic state without Legalism and Confucianism), just as Rome used Greek thought, and the Mauryan Empire, Buddhist thought. In each case, the conception of universal political authority sustaining the empire derived from earlier philosophies. All three were Iron Age empires, joining their respective technologies with new organizational techniques to create superb military forces. All three had to weld together diverse regions into a single polity. All three created legacies which continued long after the empire had disappeared.

The differences between the empires are also instructive. Consider China and Rome. In China the pervasive culture—the only higher culture in the area—was Chinese, even before the first empire arose. This culture had been slowly spreading for centuries and in places outran the polity. Even the Ch'u people south of the Yangzi, while viewed as "semibarbarian" by northern Chinese, had only a variation of the same common culture. Thus cultural unity had paved the way for political unity. In contrast, the polyglot empire of Rome encompassed quite different peoples, including older civilizations. The genius of Rome, in fact, was to fashion a government and a set of laws that could contain and reconcile its diverse cultures.

Geographically, however, Rome had an easier time of it, for the Mediterranean offered direct access to most parts of the empire and was a thoroughfare for commerce. In contrast, China was largely landlocked. It was composed of several regional economic units, each of which, located in a segment of a river basin separated from the others by natural barriers, looked inward. It was the genius of Chinese administration to overcome physical and spatial barriers and integrate the country politically.

A second difference was that government in Han China was more orderly, more complex, and more competent than that of Rome. For example, civil officials controlled the Chinese military almost until the end, whereas in later Roman times, emperor after emperor was set on the throne by the army or the Praetorian Guard. The Roman Empire was not a Chinese-type, single-family dynasty.

A third difference was in the military dynamics of the two empires. Roman power was built over centuries. Its history is the story of one state growing in power by steady increments, imposing its will on others, and gradually piecing together an empire. Not until the early centuries C.E. was the whole empire in place. China, in contrast, remained a multistate system right up to 232 B.C.E. and then, in a sudden surge, was unified by one state in eleven years. The greater dynamism of China during the first empire can be explained, perhaps, by the greater military challenge it faced across its northern border: an immense Hunnish (or Xiongnu) nomadic empire. Because the threat was more serious than that any European barbarian enemy posed to Rome, the Chinese response was correspondingly massive. (Some historians say that Chinese expansion to the north and northwest drove the Huns westward, displacing Germanic tribes that flooded into Europe and pressed against Roman frontiers.)

THINK AHEAD

◆ What challenges did the Roman, Han, and Mauryan Empires face in conquering and integrating new territories? How did they meet these challenges?

◆ Compare and contrast the Roman and Han Empires? What qualities did they have in common? How did they differ?

◆ Do you agree or disagree with the statement that there were "world-historical forces that produced at roughly the same time great empires in China, India, and the Mediterranean"?

ONE HALLMARK OF CHINESE HISTORY IS ITS striking continuity of culture, language, and geography. The Shang and Zhou dynasties were centered in north China along the Yellow River or its tributary, the Wei. The capitals of China's first empire were in exactly the same areas, and north China would remain China's political center through history to the present. If Western civilization had experienced similar continuity, it would have progressed from Thebes in the valley of the Nile to Athens on the Nile; Rome on the Nile; and then, in time, to Paris, London, and Berlin on the Nile; and each of these centers of civilization would have spoken Egyptian and written in Egyptian hieroglyphics.

The many continuities in its history did not mean, however, that China was unchanging. One key turning point came in the third century B.C.E., when the old, quasi-feudal, multistate Zhou system gave way to a centralized bureaucratic government. The new centralized state built an empire stretching from the steppe in the north to Vietnam in the south.

The history of the first empire is composed of three segments: the Qin dynasty, the Former Han dynasty, and the Later Han dynasty. The English word *China* is derived from the name of the first dynasty. The Qin overthrew the previous Zhou dynasty in 256 B.C.E. and went on to unify China in 221 B.C.E. In reshaping China, the Qin developed such momentum that it became overextended and collapsed a single generation after the unification. The succeeding Han dynasties each lasted about 200 years, the Early Han from 206 B.C.E. to 8 C.E., the Later Han (founded by a descendant of the Former Han rulers) from 25 to 220 C.E. Historians usually treat each of the Han dynasties as a separate period of rule, although they were almost back to back and shared many institutions and cultural traits. So deep was the impression left by these two dynasties on the Chinese that even today they call themselves the "Han people"—in contrast to Mongols, Manchus, Tibetans, and other minorities—and they call their ideographs, "Han writing."

Qin Unification of China

Of the territorial states of the Late Zhou era, none was more innovative and ruthless than Qin. Its location on the Wei River in northwest China—the same area from which the Zhou had launched their expansion a millennium earlier—gave it strategic advantages: It controlled the passes leading out onto the Yellow River plain and so was easy to defend and was a secure base from which to attack other states. From the late fourth century B.C.E., the Qin conquered a part of Sichuan and thus controlled two of the most fertile regions of ancient China. It welcomed Legalist administrators, who developed policies for enriching the country and strengthening its military. Despite its harsh laws, farmers moved to Qin from other areas, attracted by the order and stability of its society. Its armies had been forged by centuries of warfare against the nomadic raiders by whose lands it was half encircled. To counter these raiders, its armies adopted nomadic skills, developing cavalry in the fourth century. Other states regarded the Qin as tough, crude, and brutal but recognized its formidable strengths.

In 246 B.C.E. the man who would unify China succeeded to the Qin throne at the age of thirteen. He grew to be vigorous, ambitious, intelligent, and decisive. He is famous as a Legalist autocrat, but he was also well liked by his ministers, whose advice he usually followed. (See Chapter 2 for a description of Legalism.)

In 232 B.C.E., at the age of twenty-seven, he began the campaigns that destroyed the six remaining territorial states. On completing his conquests in 221 B.C.E., and to raise himself above the kings of the former territorial states, he adopted the glorious title that we translate as "emperor"—a combination of ideographs hitherto used only for gods or mythic heroes. Then, aided by officials of great talent, this First Qin Emperor set about applying to all of China the reforms that had been tried and found effective in his own realm. His accomplishments in the eleven years before his death, in 210 B.C.E., were stupendous.

Having conquered the civilized world of north China and the Yangzi River basin, the First Emperor sent his armies to conquer new lands. They reached the northern edge of the Red River basin in what is now Vietnam. They occupied China's southeastern coast and the area about the present-day city of Guangzhou (see Map 7–1). In the north and the northwest, the emperor's armies fought against the Xiongnu, Altaic-speaking Hunnish nomads. During the previous age, northern border states had built long walls to protect settled lands from incursions by horse-riding raiders. The Qin emperor had them joined into a single Great Wall that extended 1400 miles from the Pacific Ocean into Central Asia. (By comparison, Hadrian's Wall in England was 73 miles long.) Construction of the Great Wall cost the lives of vast numbers of conscripted laborers—by some accounts, 100,000; by others, as many as 1 million.

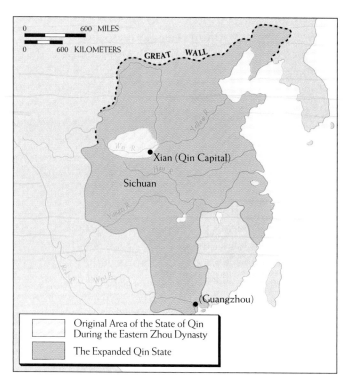

MAP 7–1 The Unification of China by the Qin State.   Between 232 and 221 B.C.E. the Qin state expanded and unified China.

The most significant reform, carried out by the Legalist minister Li Si, extended the Qin system of bureaucratic government to the entire empire. Li Si divided China into forty prefectures, which were further subdivided into counties. The county heads were responsible to prefects, who, in turn, were responsible to the central government. Officials were chosen by ability. Bureaucratic administration was impersonal, based on laws to which all were subject. No one, for example, escaped taxation. This kind of bureaucratic centralism broke sharply with the old Zhou pattern of establishing dependent principalities for members of a ruler's family. Furthermore, to ensure the smooth functioning of local government offices, former aristocrats of the territorial states were removed from their lands and resettled in the capital, near present-day Xian. They were housed in mansions on one side of the river, from which they could gaze across at the enormous palace of the First Emperor.

Other reforms further unified the First Emperor's vast domain. Roads were built radiating out from the capital city. The emperor decreed a system of uniform weights and measures. He unified the Chinese writing system, establishing standard ideographs to replace the great variety that had hitherto prevailed. He established uniform axle lengths for carts. Even ideas did not escape the drive toward uniformity. Following the precepts of Legalism, the emperor and his advisers launched a campaign for which they have subsequently been denounced throughout Chinese history. They collected and burned the books of Confucianism and other schools, and were said to have buried alive several hundred scholars opposed to the Legalist philosophy. Only useful books on agriculture, medicine, or Legalist teachings were spared.

But the Qin had changed too much too quickly. To pay for the roads, canals, and the Great Wall, burdensome taxes were levied on the people. Commoners hated conscription and

◀ **The Great Wall of China.** It was originally built during the Qin dynasty (256–206 B.C.E.), but what we see today is the wall as it was completely rebuilt during the Ming dynasty (1368–1644 C.E.).
Paolo Koch/Photo Researchers, Inc.

labor service, and nobles resented their loss of status. Merchants were exploited; scholars, except for Legalists, were oppressed. A Chinese historian wrote afterward: "The condemned were an innumerable multitude; those who had been tortured and mutilated formed a long procession on the roads. From the princes and ministers down to the humblest people everyone was terrified and in fear of their lives."[1] After the First Emperor died, in 210 B.C.E., intrigues broke out at court and rebellions arose in the land. At the end, the short-lived dynasty was destroyed by the domino effect of its own legal codes. When the generals sent to quell a rebellion were defeated, they joined the rebellion rather than return to the capital and incur the severe punishment decreed for failure. The Qin collapsed in 206 B.C.E.

In 1974 a farmer near Xian discovered the army of 8,000 life-size terra-cotta horses and soldiers that guarded the tomb of the First Emperor. The historical record tells us that in the tomb itself, under a mountain of earth, are a replica of his capital; a relief model of the Chinese world with quicksilver rivers; other warriors with chariots of bronze; and the remains of horses, noblemen, and criminals sacrificed to accompany in death the emperor whose dynasty was to have lasted for 10,000 generations.

Former Han Dynasty (206 b.c.e.–8 c.e.)
THE DYNASTIC CYCLE

Confucian historians have seen a pattern in every dynasty of long duration. They call it the **dynastic cycle**. The stages of the cycle are interpreted in terms of the "Mandate of Heaven." The cycle begins with internal wars that eventually lead to the military unification of China. Unification is proof that heaven has given the unifier the mandate to rule. Strong and vigorous, the first ruler, in the process of consolidating his political power, restores peace and order to China. Economic growth follows, almost automatically. The peak of the cycle is marked by public works, further energetic reforms, and aggressive military expansion. During this phase, China appears invincible. But then the cycle turns downward. The costs of expansion, coupled with increasing opulence at the court, place a heavy burden on tax revenues just as they are beginning to decline. The vigor of the monarchs wanes. Intrigues develop at court. Central controls loosen, and provincial governors and military commanders gain autonomy. Finally, public works fall into disrepair, floods and pestilence occur, rebellions break out, and the dynasty collapses. For Confucian historians, the last emperors in a cycle are not only politically weak, but morally culpable.

▲ **Terra-cotta Soldiers of the Qin Army.** Three of the over 7,000 life-size terra-cotta soldiers found in the tomb of the first emperor of the Qin dynasty (256–206 B.C.E.).
Adam Crowley/Getty Images, Inc./PhotoDisc, Inc.

EARLY YEARS OF THE FORMER HAN DYNASTY

The first sixty years of the Han may be thought of as the early phase of its dynastic cycle. After the collapse of the Qin, one rebel general gained control of the Wei basin and went on to unify China. He became the first emperor of the Han dynasty and is known by his posthumous title of Gaozu (r. 206–195 B.C.E.). He rose from plebeian origins to become emperor, which would happen only once again in Chinese history. Gaozu built his capital at Chang'an, not far from the capitals of the previous dynasties. It took the emperor and his immediate successors many years to consolidate their power because they consciously avoided actions that would remind the populace of the hated Qin despotism. They made punishments less severe and reduced taxes. Good government prevailed, the economy rebounded, granaries were filled, and the government accumulated vast cash reserves. Later historians often singled out the early Han rulers as model sage-emperors.

HAN WUDI

The second phase of the dynastic cycle began with the rule of Wudi (the "martial emperor"), who came to the throne in 141 B.C.E. at the age of sixteen and remained there for fifty-four years (141–87 B.C.E.). Wudi was daring, vigorous, and intelligent but also superstitious, suspicious, and vengeful. He wielded tremendous personal authority.

Building on the prosperity achieved by his predecessors, Wudi initiated new economic policies. He had a canal built from the Yellow River to the capital in northwest China, linking the two major economic regions of north China. He established "ever-level granaries" throughout the country so that the surplus from bumper crops could be bought and then

[1] C. P. Fitzgerald, *China, A Short Cultural History* (New York: Praeger, 1935), p. 147.

resold in time of scarcity. To increase revenues, he levied taxes on merchants, debased the currency, and sold some offices. Wudi also moved against merchants who had built fortunes in untaxed commodities by reestablishing government monopolies—a practice of the Qin—on copper coins, salt, iron, and liquor. For fear of Wudi, no one spoke out against the monopolies, but a few years after his death, a famous debate was held at the court.

Known after the title of the chronicle as the "Salt and Iron Debate," it was frequently cited thereafter in China, and in Japan and Korea as well. On one side, quasi-Legalist officials argued that the state should enjoy the profits from the sale of salt and iron. On the other side, Confucians argued that these resources should be left in private hands, for the moral purity of officials would be sullied by dealings with merchants. The Confucian scholars who compiled the chronicle made themselves the winner in the debate; but state monopolies became a regular part of Chinese government finance.

Wudi also aggressively expanded Chinese borders—a policy that would characterize every strong dynasty. His armies swept south into what is today northern Vietnam and northeast across Manchuria to establish a military outpost in northern Korea that would last until 313 C.E.

THE XIONGNU

The principal threat to the Han was from the Xiongnu, a nomadic **pastoral** people who lived to the north. Their mounted archers could raid China and flee before an army could be sent against them. To combat them, Wudi employed the entire repertoire of policies that would become standard thereafter. When possible he "used the barbarian to control the barbarian," making allies of border nomads against more distant tribes. Allies were permitted to trade with Chinese merchants; they were awarded titles and honors; and their kings were sent Chinese princesses as brides. Poems capture the pathos of their lives on grassy steppes far from China. (See Document, "Chinese Women Among the Nomads.") When trade and titles did not work, he used force. Between 129 and 119 B.C.E. he sent several armies of more than 100,000 troops into the steppe, destroying Xiongnu power south of the Gobi Desert in southern Mongolia. To establish a strategic line of defense aimed at the heart of the Xiongnu empire further to the west, Wudi then sent 700,000 Chinese colonists to the arid Kansu panhandle and extended the Great Wall to the Yumen (Jade Gate) outpost at the eastern end

of the Tarim basin. From this outpost, Chinese influence was extended over the rim oases of Central Asia, establishing the **Silk Road** that linked Chang'an with Rome (see Map 7–2)

GOVERNMENT DURING THE FORMER HAN

To demonstrate how different they were from the Qin, early Han emperors set up some Zhou-like principalities, small, semiautonomous states with independent lords. But this was a token gesture. The principalities were closely superintended and then curtailed after several generations. Basically, despite its repudiation of the Qin and all its works, the Han continued the Qin form of centralized bureaucratic administration. Officials were organized by grades and were paid salaries in grain, plus cash or silk. They were recruited by sponsorship or recommendation: Provincial officials had the duty of recommending promising candidates. A school established at Chang'an was said to have 30,000 students by the Later Han. Bureaucracy grew until, by the first century B.C.E., there were more than 130,000 officials—perhaps not too many for a population that, by that time, had reached 60 million.

During the Han dynasty, this "Legalist" structure of government became partially Confucianized. It did not happen overnight. The first Han emperor despised Confucians as bookish pedants—he once urinated in the hat of a scholar. But Confucian ideas proved useful. The mandate of heaven provided an ethical justification for dynastic rule. A respect for old records and the written word fit in well with the vast bookkeeping the empire entailed. Gradually the Confucian classics were accepted as the standard for education. Confucianism was seen as shaping moral men who would be upright officials, even in the absence of external constraints. For Confucius had taught the transformation of self through ethical cultivation and had presented a vision of benevolent government by men who were virtuous as well as talented. No one attempted to replace laws with a code of etiquette, but increasingly laws were interpreted and applied by men with a Confucian education.

The court during the Han dynasty exhibited features that would appear in later dynasties as well. All authority centered on the emperor, the all-powerful "son of heaven." The will of a strong adult emperor was paramount. When the emperor was

Tomb Figure of Standing Attendant. This is from the Former Han dynasty, second century B.C.E. The Asia Society, N. Y.: Mr. and Mrs. John D. Rockefeller 3rd Collection.

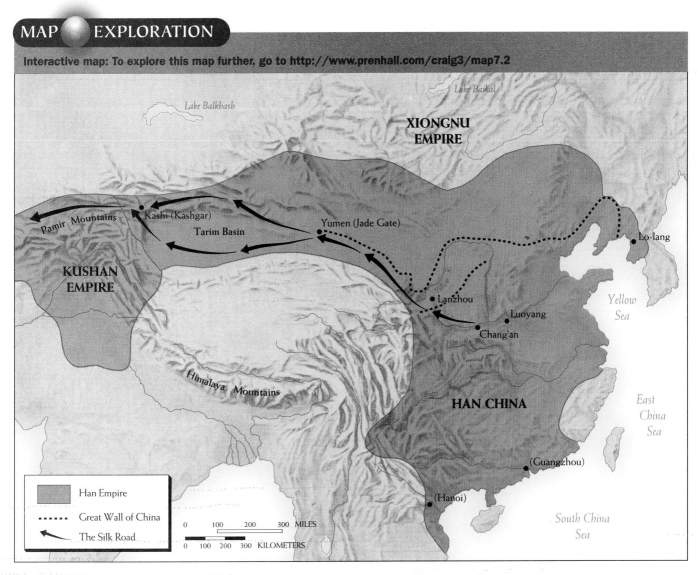

MAP EXPLORATION

Interactive map: To explore this map further, go to http://www.prenhall.com/craig3/map7.2

MAP 7–2 The Han Empire 206 B.C.E.–220 C.E.   At the peak of Han expansion, Han armies advanced far out into the steppe north of the Great Wall and west into Central Asia. The Silk Road to Rome passed through the Tarim basin to the Kushan Empire, and on to western Asia and the Middle East.

weak, however, or ascended to the throne when still a child, others competed to rule in his name. Four contenders for this surrogate role appeared and reappeared through Chinese history: court officials, the empress dowager, court eunuchs, and military commanders.

Court officials were selected for their ability to govern: They staffed the apparatus of government and advised the emperor directly. Apart from the emperor himself, they were usually the most powerful men in China, yet their position was often precarious. Few officials escaped being removed from office or banished once or twice during their careers. Of the seven prime ministers who served Wudi, five were executed by his order.

Of the emperor's many wives, the empress dowager was the one whose child had been named as the heir to the throne.

Her influence sometimes continued even after her child became an adult emperor. But she was most powerful as a regent for a child emperor. On Gaozu's death in 195 B.C.E., for example, the Empress Lu became the regent for her child, the new emperor. Aided by her relatives, she seized control of the court and murdered a rival, and when her son was about to come of age, she had him killed and a younger son made the heir to continue her rule as regent. When she died in 180 B.C.E., loyal adherents of the imperial family who had opposed her rule massacred her relatives.

Court eunuchs came mostly from families of low social status. They were brought to the court as boys, castrated, and assigned to work as servants in the emperor's harem. They were thus in contact with the future emperor from the day he was born, became

DOCUMENT | Chinese Women Among the Nomads

The first of these selections is the lament of Xijun, a Chinese lady sent by Wudi in about 105 B.C.E. to be the wife of a nomad king of the Wusun people of Central Asia. Once there, she found her husband to be old and decrepit. He saw her only once or twice a year, when they drank a cup of wine together. They could not converse, as they had no language in common. The second selection, written centuries later, is by the Tang poet Du Fu, who visited the village of another woman sent to be the wife of a nomad king.

> What does the fate of the women in these poems suggest about the foreign policy of the rulers of ancient China?

1.

My people have married me
In a far corner of Earth;
Sent me away to a strange land,
To the king of the Wu-sun.
A tent is my house,
Of felt are my walls;
Raw flesh my food
With mare's milk to drink.
Always thinking of my own country,
My heart sad within.

Would I were a yellow stork
And could fly to my old home!

2.

Ten thousand ranges and valleys approach the Ching
　　Gate
And the village in which the Lady of Light was born and
　　bred.
She went out from the purple palace into the desert-
　　land;
She has now become a green grave in the yellow dusk.
Her face!—Can you picture a wind of the spring?
Her spirit by moonlight returns with a tinkling
Telling her eternal sorrow.

1. From *Chinese Poems* by Arthur Waley. Copyright © 1946 by George Allen and Unwin Ltd., an imprint of HarperCollins Publishers Ltd. Reprinted by permission of the Arthur Waley Estate.

2. From *The Jade Mountain: A Chinese Anthology* trans. by Witter Bynner. Copyright © 1929 and renewed 1957 by Alfred A. Knopf, a division of Random House, Inc. Used by permission of Alfred A. Knopf, a division of Random House. Reprinted by permission of the publisher.

his childhood confidants, and often continued to advise him after he had gained the throne. Emperors found eunuchs useful as counterweights to officials. But to the scholars who wrote China's history, the eunuchs were greedy half-men, given to evil intrigues.

Military leaders, whether generals or rebels, were the usual founders of dynasties. In the later phase of most dynasties, regional military commanders often became semi-independent rulers. A few even usurped the throne. Yet they were less powerful at the Chinese court than they were, for example, in imperial Rome, partly because the military constituted a separate category, lower in prestige than the better-educated civil officials. It was also partly because the court took great pains to prevent its generals from establishing a base of personal power. Appointments to command a Han army were given only for specific campaigns, and commanders were appointed in pairs so that each would check the other.

Another characteristic of government during the Han and subsequent dynasties was that its functions were limited. It collected taxes, maintained military forces, administered laws, supported the imperial household, and carried out public works that were beyond the powers of local jurisdictions. But government in a district that remained orderly and paid its taxes was left largely in the hands of local notables and large landowners. This pattern was not, to be sure, unique to China. Most premodern governments, even those that were bureaucratic, floated on top of their local societies and only rarely reached down and interfered in the everyday lives of their subjects.

THE SILK ROAD

Roman ladies loved, and Roman moralists inveighed against, diaphanous gowns of Chinese silk. Wealthy Chinese coveted Roman glass and gold. Yet no camel train traveled from Chang'an all the way to Rome. Precious cargoes, moving more easily than persons, were passed across empires, like batons in relay races, from one network of merchants to another.

During the Han and later dynasties, the route began with a network of Chinese or Central Asian traders that stretched from the Chinese capital to Lanzhou in northeastern China, through the Gansu corridor to Yumen or later Dunhuang. It then crossed the inhospitable Tarim basin, intermittently under Chinese military control, from oasis to oasis, to Kashi (Kashgar). From Kashi, the route continued in a northerly sweep to Tashkent, Samarkand, and Bukhara or in a southerly sweep to Teheran, Bagdad, and Damascus, and finally on to the Mediterranean ports of Tyre,

Antioch, and Byzantium (Constantinople)—which traded with Rome. (See Map 7–2 and Map 4–3.) Of the goods that departed Chang'an, only a minute portion reached Rome—which was not a destination as much as the center of the westernmost trade net. Of goods consigned to Roman commerce, only the thinnest trickle reached China.

The Silk Road, and the alternate, more distant, and equally perilous oceanic route, points up China's isolation from other high centers of civilization. The "trip" took more than half a year; the distance was measured in thousands of miles; camel caravans at times traveled as little as fifteen miles a day. The route was hazardous, the climate extreme. Crossing deserts and mountain passes, travelers experienced cold, hunger, sand-storms, and bandits.

Most Chinese foreign trade was with their immediate steppe neighbors. The Chinese exported silk, lacquer, metalwork, and later jewels, musk and rhubarb (as a digestive for nomadic stomachs). They imported horses for their army, cattle, sheep, donkeys, and jade from Khotan and also woolens, medicines, indigo, and the occasional exotic animal. Only the most precious goods made their way to distant empires. Silk—light, compact, and valuable—was ideal. The Romans and Chinese had only the vaguest idea of where the other was located and knew nothing of the other's civilization. Romans thought silk came from a plant.

Exotic goods hawked in distant bazaars lend an aura of romance to the "Silk Road," but its true significance was as a transmission belt. In an early age China may have borrowed the chariot, compound bow, wheat, domesticated horses and the stirrup from western Asia. Even the idea of mold-casting bronze may have come from beyond China's frontiers. Chinese technologies of paper making, iron casting, water-powered mills, and shoulder collars for draft animals, and then the compass and gunpowder, spread slowly from China to the West, sometimes over centuries. Seeds of trees and plants went in both directions, as did germs. During the late Han (in the second century C.E.), the Roman Empire lost a quarter of its population to an epidemic that, some say, appeared in China forty years later with equally dire results. During the fourteenth century,

Chinese Galloping Horse. China traded with steppe merchants to obtain the horses needed to equip its armies against Steppe warriors. Especially desired by the Chinese Court were the fable "blood sweating" horses of far off Ferghana (present-day Tajikistan).
The New York Public Library for the Performing Arts/Art Resource

bubonic plague may have spread through the Mongol empire from southwestern China to central Asia to the Middle East, and then on to Europe as the Black Death. Missionary religions traveled the Silk Road east: Buddhism toward the end of the Han dynasty and Islam centuries later.

DECLINE AND USURPATION

During the last decade of Wudi's rule in the early first century B.C.E., military expenses ran ahead of revenues. His successor cut back on military costs, eased economic controls, and reduced taxes. But over the next several generations, large landowners began to use their growing influence in provincial politics to avoid paying taxes. State revenues declined. The tax burden on smaller landowners and free peasants grew heavier. In 22 B.C.E., rebellions broke out in several parts of the empire. At the court, too, a decline set in. There was a succession of weak emperors. Intrigues, nepotism, and factional struggles grew apace. Even officials began to sense that the dynasty no longer had the approval of heaven. The dynastic cycle approached its end.

Many at the court urged Wang Mang, the regent for the infant emperor and the nephew of an empress, to become the emperor and begin a new dynasty. Wang Mang refused several times—to demonstrate his lack of eagerness—and then accepted in 8 C.E. He drew up a program of sweeping reforms based on ancient texts. He was a Confucian, yet relied on new institutional arrangements rather than moral reform to improve society. He revived ancient titles, expanded state monopolies, abolished private slavery (about 1 percent of the population), made loans to poor peasants, and then moved to confiscate large private estates.

These reforms alienated many. Merchants disliked the monopolies. Large landowners resisted the expropriation of their lands. Nature also conspired to bring down Wang Mang: The Yellow River overflowed its banks and changed its course, destroying the northern Chinese irrigation system. Several years of poor harvests produced famines. The Xiongnu overran China's northern borders. In 18 C.E., a secret peasant society rose in rebellion. In 23 C.E., rebels attacked Chang'an, and Wang Mang was killed and eaten by rebel troops. He had tried to found a new dynasty from within a decrepit court without an independent military base. The attempt was futile. Internal wars continued in China for two more years until a large landowner, who had become the leader of a rebel army, emerged triumphant in 25 C.E. Because he was from a branch of the imperial family, his new dynasty was viewed as a restoration of the Han.

Later Han (25–220 C.E.) and Its Aftermath

FIRST CENTURY

The founder of the Later Han moved his capital east to Luoyang. Under the first emperor and his two successors, there was a return to strong central government and a laissez-faire economy. Agriculture and population recovered. By the end of the first century C.E., China was as prosperous as it had been during the good years of the Former Han. The shift from pacification and recuperation to military expansion came earlier than it had during the previous dynasty. During the reign of the first emperor, south China and Vietnam were retaken. Dissension among the Xiongnu enabled the Chinese to secure an alliance with some of the southern tribes in 50 C.E., and in 89 C.E. Chinese armies crossed the Gobi Desert and defeated the northern Xiongnu. This defeat sparked the migrations, some historians say, that brought those nomadic warriors to the southern Russian steppes and then, in the fifth century C.E., to Europe, where they were known as the Huns of Attila. In 97 C.E. a Chinese general led an army to the shores of the Caspian Sea. The Chinese expansion in inner Asia, coupled with more lenient government policies toward merchants, facilitated the camel caravans that carried Chinese silk across the Tarim basin and, ultimately, to merchants in Iran, Palestine, and Rome. (See Document, "Ban Zhao's Admonitions for Women.")

DECLINE DURING THE SECOND CENTURY

Until 88 C.E. the emperors of the Later Han were vigorous; afterward they were ineffective and short-lived. Empresses plotted to advance the fortunes of their families. Emperors turned for help to palace eunuchs, whose power at times surpassed that of officials. In 159 C.E. a conspiracy of eunuchs in the service of an emperor slaughtered the family of a scheming empress dowager and ruled at the court. When officials and students protested against the eunuch dictatorship, over 100 were killed and over 1,000 were tortured or imprisoned. In another incident in 190 C.E., a general deposed one emperor, installed another, killed the empress dowager, and massacred most of the eunuchs at the court.

In the countryside, large landowners who had been powerful from the start of the dynasty grew more so. They harbored private armies. Farmers on the estates of the mighty were reduced to serfs.

▲ A green glazed pottery model of a Later Han dynasty watchtower (87.6 × 35.6 × 38.1 cm). Note the resemblance to later Chinese Buddhist pagodas.
The Nelson-Atkins Museum of Art, Kansas City, Missouri (Purchase: Nelson Trust) © The Nelson Gallery Foundation, The Nelson-Atkins Museum of Art.

The landowners used their influence to avoid taxes. Great numbers of free farmers fled south for the same purpose. The remaining freeholders paid ever heavier taxes and labor services. Many peasants turned to neo-Daoist religious movements that provided the ideology and organization to channel their discontent into action. In 184 C.E. rebellions organized by members of the religious movements broke out against the government. Han generals suppressed the rebellions but stayed on to rule in the provinces they had pacified. In 220 C.E. they deposed the last Han emperor.

AFTERMATH OF EMPIRE

For more than three and a half centuries after the fall of the Han, China was disunited. For several generations it was divided into three kingdoms, whose heroic warriors and scheming statesmen were made famous by wandering storytellers. These figures later peopled the *Tale of the Three Kingdoms*, a great romantic epic of Chinese literature.

DOCUMENT | Ban Zhao's *Admonitions for Women*

Ban Zhao (45–116) was the sister of the famous historian Ban Gu. Her guide to morality, Admonitions for Woman, *was widely used during the Han dynasty. Humility is one of the seven womanly virtues about which she wrote; the others are resignation, subservience, self-abasement, obedience, cleanliness, and industry.*

◆ Given the range of female personalities in Chinese society, what are some of the likely responses to this sort of moral education? Are self-control and self-discipline more likely to be associated with weakness or with strength of character?

Humility

In ancient times, on the third day after a girl was born, people placed her at the base of the bed, gave her a pot shard to play with, and made a sacrifice to announce her birth. She was put below the bed to show that she was lowly and weak and should concentrate on humbling herself before others. Playing with a shard showed that she should get accustomed to hard work and concentrate on being diligent. Announcing her birth to the ancestors showed that she should focus on continuing the sacrifices. These three customs convey the unchanging path for women and the ritual traditions.

Humility means yielding and acting respectful, putting others first and oneself last, never mentioning one's own good deeds or denying one's own faults, enduring insults and bearing with mistreatment, all with due trepidation. Industriousness means going to bed late, getting up early, never shirking work morning or night, never refusing to take on domestic work, and completing everything that needs to be done neatly and carefully. Continuing the sacrifices means serving one's husband-master with appropriate demeanor, keeping oneself clean and pure, never joking or laughing, and preparing pure wine and food to offer to the ancestors.

There has never been a woman who had these three traits and yet ruined her reputation or fell into disgrace. If a woman loses these three traits, she will have no name to preserve and will not be able to avoid shame.

Chinese history during the post-Han centuries had two characteristics. The first was the dominant role played by the great aristocratic landowning families. With vast estates, huge numbers of serfs, fortified manor houses, and private armies, they were beyond the control of most governments. Because they took over many of the functions of local government, some historians describe post-Han China as having reverted to the quasi feudalism of the Zhou. The second characteristic of these centuries was that northern and southern China developed in different ways.

In the south, there followed a succession of ever weaker dynasties with capitals at Nanjing. Although these six southern states were called dynasties—and the entire period of Chinese history from 220 B.C.E. to 589 C.E. is called the Six Dynasties era after them—they were in fact short-lived kingdoms, plagued by intrigues, usurpations, and coups d'état; frequently at war with northern states; and in constant fear of their own generals. The main developments in the south were (1) continuing economic growth and the emergence of Nanjing as a thriving center of commerce; (2) the ongoing absorption of tribal peoples into Chinese society and culture; (3) large-scale immigrations of Chinese fleeing the north; and (4) the spread of Buddhism and its penetration to the heart of Chinese culture.

In the north, state formation depended on the interaction of nomads and Chinese. During the Han dynasty, Chinese invasions of the steppe had led to the incorporation of semi-Sinicized Xiongnu as the northernmost tier of the Chinese defense system—just as Germanic tribes had acted as the teeth and claws of the late Roman Empire. But as the Chinese state weakened, the highly mobile nomads broke loose, joined with other tribes, and began to invade China. The short-lived states that they formed are usually referred to as the "Sixteen Kingdoms." One kingdom was founded by invaders of Tibetan stock. Most spoke Altaic languages: the Xianbi (proto-Mongols), the Tuoba (proto-Turks), and the Ruan Ruan (who would later appear in eastern Europe as the Avars). But differences of language and stock were less important than these tribes' similarities:

1. All began as steppe nomads with a way of life different from that of agricultural China.

2. After forming states, all became at least partially Sinicized. Chinese from great families, which had preserved Han traditions, served as their tutors and administrators.

3. All were involved in wars—among themselves, against southern dynasties, or against conservative steppe tribes that resisted Sinicization.

4. Buddhism was as powerful in the north as in the south. As a universal religion, it acted as a bridge between "barbarians" and Chinese—just as Christianity was a unifying force

in post-Roman Europe. The barbarian rulers of the north were especially attracted to its magical side. Usually Buddhism was made the state religion. Of the northern states, the most durable was the Northern Wei (386–534 C.E.), famed for its Buddhist sculpture.

Han Thought and Religion

Poems describe the splendor of Chang'an and Luoyang: broad boulevards, tiled gateways, open courtyards, watchtowers, and imposing walls. Most splendid of all were the palaces of emperors, with their audience halls, vast chambers, harem quarters, and parks containing artificial lakes and rare animals and birds. But today little remains of the grandeur of the Han. Whereas Roman ruins abound in Italy and circle the Mediterranean, in China nothing remains above ground. Only the items buried in tombs—pottery, bronzes, musical instruments, gold and silver jewelry, lacquerware, and clay figurines—give a glimpse of the rich material culture of the Han period. And only paintings on the walls of tombs tell us of its art.

But a wealth of written records conveys the sophistication and depth of Han culture. Perhaps the two most important areas were philosophy and history.

HAN CONFUCIANISM

A major accomplishment of the early Han was the recovery of texts that had been lost during the Qin persecution of scholars. Some were retrieved from the walls of houses where they had been hidden; others were reproduced from memory by scholars. Debate arose regarding the relative authenticity of the old and new texts—a controversy that has continued until modern times. In 51 B.C.E. and again in 79 C.E. councils were held to determine the true meaning of the Confucian classics. In 175 C.E. an approved, official version of the texts was inscribed on stone tablets.

In about 100 C.E. the first dictionary was compiled. Containing about 9,000 characters, it helped promote a uniform system of writing. In Han times, as today, Chinese from the north could not converse with Chinese from the southeastern coast, but a common written language bridged differences of pronunciation, contributing to Chinese unity.

It was also in Han times that scholars began writing commentaries on the classics, a major scholarly activity throughout Chinese history. Scholars learned the classics by heart and used classical allusions in their writing.

Han philosophers also extended Zhou Confucianism by adding to it the teachings of cosmological naturalism. Zhou Confucianists had assumed that the moral force of a virtuous emperor would not only order society but also harmonize nature. Han Confucianists explained why. Dong Zhongshu (ca. 179–104 B.C.E.), for example, held that all nature was a single, interrelated system. Just as summer always follows spring, so does one color, one virtue, one planet, one element, one number, and one officer of the court always take precedence over another. All reflect the systematic workings of yang and yin and the five elements. And just as one dresses appropriately to the season, so was it important for the emperor to choose policies appropriate to the sequences inherent in nature. If he was moral, if he acted in accord with Heaven's natural system, then all would go well. But if he acted inappropriately, then Heaven would send a portent as a warning—a blue dog, a rat holding its tail in its mouth, an eclipse, or a comet. If the portent was not heeded, wonders and then misfortunes would follow. It was the Confucian scholars, of course, who claimed to understand nature's messages and advised the emperor.

It is easy to criticize Han philosophy as a pseudoscientific or mechanistic view of nature, but it represented a new effort by the Chinese to encompass and comprehend the interrelationships of the natural world. This effort led to inventions like the seismograph and to advances in astronomy, music, and medicine. It was also during the Han that the Chinese invented

◀ **Han Dynasty Tomb Painting.** Court figures painted on ceramic tile in a Han dynasty tomb (Gray earthenware; hollow tiles painted in ink and colors on a whitewashed wound 73.8 × 204.7 cm).

"Lintel & Pediment of a Tomb". China, Western Han dynasty, 1st century B.C. Gray earthenware; hollow tiles painted in ink & colors on a whitewashed ground. 73.8 × 204.7 cm. Denman Waldo Ross Collection, & Gift of C.T. Loo. Courtesy Museum of Fine Arts, Boston.

DOCUMENT | Sima Qian on the Wealthy

More than half of the chapters in Sima Qian's Historical Records *(early first century B.C.E. were biographies of extraordinary men and women. He wrote of scholars, wandering knights, diviners, harsh officials and reasonable officials, wits and humorists, doctors, and moneymakers. The following is his description of the vibrant economic life of Han cities and his judgments regarding the wealthy.*

> ◆ What economic "principles" can you derive from this passage? Can you detect an echo of Sima Qian's perspectives in present day debates on economic policy?

Anyone who in the market towns or great cities manages in the course of a year to sell the following items: a thousand brewings of liquor; a thousand jars of pickles and sauces; a thousand jars of sirups; a thousand slaughtered cattle, sheep, and swine; a thousand chung of grain; a thousand cartloads or a thousand boat-lengths of firewood and stubble for fuel; a thousand logs of timber; ten thousand bamboo poles; a hundred horse carriages; a thousand two-wheeled ox carts; a thousand lacquered wooden vessels; brass utensils weighing thirty thousand catties; a thousand piculs of plain wooden vessels, iron vessels, or gardenia and madder dyes; two hundred horses; five hundred cattle; two thousand sheep or swine; a hundred male or female slaves; a thousand catties of tendons, horns, or cinnabar; thirty thousand catties of silken fabric, raw silk, or other fine fabrics; a thousand rolls of embroidered or patterned silk; a thousand piculs of fabrics made of vegetable fiber or raw or tanned hides; a thousand pecks of lacquer; a thousand jars of leaven or salted bean relish; a thousand catties of globefish or mullet; a thousand piculs of dried fish; thirty thousand catties of salted fish; three thousand piculs of jujubes or chestnuts; a thousand skins of fox or sable; a thousand piculs of lamb or sheep skins; a thousand felt mats; or a thousand chung of fruits or vegetables—such a man may live as well as the master of an estate of a thousand chariots. The same applies for anyone who has a thousand strings of cash [i.e., a million in cash] to lend out on interest. Such loans are made through a money-lender, but a greedy merchant who is too anxious for a quick return will only manage to revolve his working capital three times while a less avaricious merchant has revolved his five times. These are the principal ways of making money. There are various other occupations which bring in less than twenty percent profit, but they are not what I would call sources of wealth.

Thrift and hard work are without doubt the proper way to gain a livelihood. And yet it will be found that rich men have invariably employed some unusual scheme or method to get to the top. Plowing the fields is a rather crude way to make a living, and yet Ch'in Yang did so well at it that he became the richest man in his province. Robbing graves is a criminal offense, but T'ien Shu got his start by doing it. Gambling is a wicked pastime, but Huan Fa used it to acquire a fortune. Most fine young men would despise the thought of traveling around peddling goods, yet Yung Lo-ch'eng got rich that way. Many people would consider trading in fats a disgraceful line of business, but Yung Po made a thousand catties of gold at it. Vending sirups is a petty occupation, but the Chang family acquired ten million cash that way. It takes little skill to sharpen knives, but because the Chih family didn't mind doing it, they could eat the best of everything. Dealing in dried sheep stomachs seems like an insignificant enough trade, but thanks to it the Cho family went around with a mounted retinue. The calling of a horse doctor is a rather ignominious profession, but it enabled Chang Li to own a house so large that he had to strike a bell to summon the servants. All of these men got where they did because of their devotion and singleness of purpose.

From this we may see that there is no fixed road to wealth, and money has no permanent master. It finds its way to the man of ability like the spokes of a wheel converging upon the hub, and from the hands of the worthless it falls like shattered tiles. A family with a thousand catties of gold may stand side by side with the lord of a city; the man with a hundred million cash may enjoy the pleasures of a king. Rich men such as these deserve to be called the "untitled nobility," do they not?

From *Records of the Grand Historian of China* trans. by Burton Watson. Copyright © 1961 by Columbia University Press. Reprinted by permission of the publisher.

paper, the wheelbarrow, the stern-post rudder, and the compass (known as the "south-pointing chariot").

HISTORY

The Chinese were the greatest historians of the premodern world. They wrote more history than anyone else, and what they wrote was usually more accurate. Apart from the *Spring and Autumn Annals* and the scholarship of Confucius himself, history writing in China began during the Han dynasty. Why the Chinese were so history-minded has been variously explained: Because the Chinese tradition is this-worldly; because Confucianists were scholarly and their veneration for the classics carried over to the written word; because history was seen as a lesson book (the Chinese called it a mirror) for statesmen, and thus a necessity for the literate men who operated the centralized Chinese state.

The practice of using actual documents and firsthand accounts of events began with Sima Qian (d. 85 B.C.E.), who set out to write a history of the known world from the most ancient times down to the age of the emperor Wudi. His *Historical Records* consisted of 130 substantial chapters (with a total of over 700,000 characters) divided into "Basic Annals"; "Chronological Tables"; "Treatises" on rites, music, astronomy, the calendar, and so on; "Hereditary Houses"; and seventy chapters of "Biographies," including descriptions of foreign peoples. (See Document, "Sima Qian on the Wealthy.") A second great work, *The Book of the Han*, was written by Ban Gu (d. 92 C.E.). It applied the analytical schema of Sima Qian to a single dynasty, the Former Han, and established the pattern by which each dynasty wrote the history of its predecessor.

NEO-DAOISM

As the Han dynasty waned, the effort to realize the Confucian ethic in the sociopolitical order became increasingly difficult. Some scholars abandoned Confucianism altogether in favor of **Neo-Daoism**, or "mysterious learning," as it was sometimes called. A few wrote commentaries on the classical Daoist texts that had been handed down from the Zhou. The *Zhuangzi* was especially popular. Other scholars, defining the natural as the

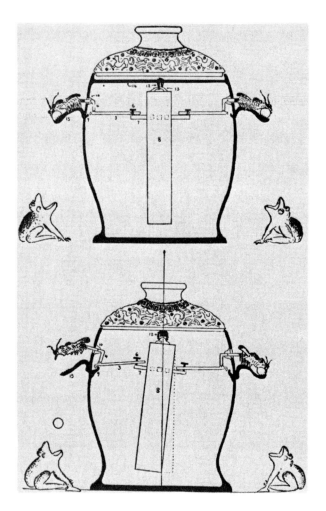

▲ **A Chinese Seismograph.** The suspended weight swings in the direction of the earthquake. This moves a lever and a dragon drops a ball into the mouth of one of the four waiting ceramic frogs.
National Archives and Records Administration.

pleasurable, withdrew from society to engage in witty "pure conversations." They discussed poetry and philosophy, played the lute, and drank wine. The most famous were the Seven Sages of the Bamboo Grove of the third century C.E.. One sage was always accompanied by a servant carrying a jug of wine and a spade—the one for his pleasure, the other to dig his grave should he die. Another wore no clothes at home. When criticized, he replied that the cosmos was his home, and his house his clothes. "Why are you in my pants?" he asked a discomfited visitor. Still another took a boat to visit a friend on a snowy night, but on arriving at his friend's door, turned around and went home. When pressed for an explanation, he said that it had been his pleasure to go, and that when the impulse died, it was his pleasure to return. This story reveals a scorn for convention coupled with an admiration for an inner spontaneity, however eccentric.

Another concern of what is called Neo-Daoism was immortality. Some sought it in dietary restrictions and Yoga-like meditation, some in sexual abstinence or orgies. Others, seeking elixirs to prolong life, dabbled in alchemy, and although no magical elixir was ever found, the schools of alchemy to which the search gave rise are credited with the discovery of medicines, dyes, glazes, and gunpowder.

Meanwhile, among the common people, there arose popular religious cults that, because they included the Daoist classics among their sacred texts, are also called Neo-Daoist. Like most folk religions, they contained an amalgam of beliefs, practices, and superstitions. They had a pantheon of gods and immortals and taught that the good or evil done in this life would be rewarded or punished in the innumerable heavens or hells of an afterlife. These cults had priests, shamans who practiced faith healing, seers, and sorceresses. For a time, they also had hierarchical church organizations, but these were smashed at the end of the second century C.E. Local Daoist temples and monasteries, however, continued until modern times. With many Buddhist accretions, they furnished the religious beliefs of the bulk of the Chinese population. Even in recent decades, these sects flourished in Taiwan and Chinese communities in Southeast Asia. They were suppressed in China in the Maoist era but revived during the 1990s.

BUDDHISM

Central Asian missionaries, following the trade routes East, brought Buddhism to China in the first century C.E. It was at first viewed as a new Daoist sect, which is not surprising because early translators used Daoist terms to render Buddhist concepts. **Nirvana**, for example, was translated as "not doing" *(wuwei)*. In the second century C.E., confusion about the two religions led to the very Chinese view that Laozi had gone to India, where the Buddha had become his disciple, and that Buddhism was the Indian form of Daoism.

Then, as the Han sociopolitical order collapsed in the third century C.E., Buddhism spread rapidly. We are reminded of the spread

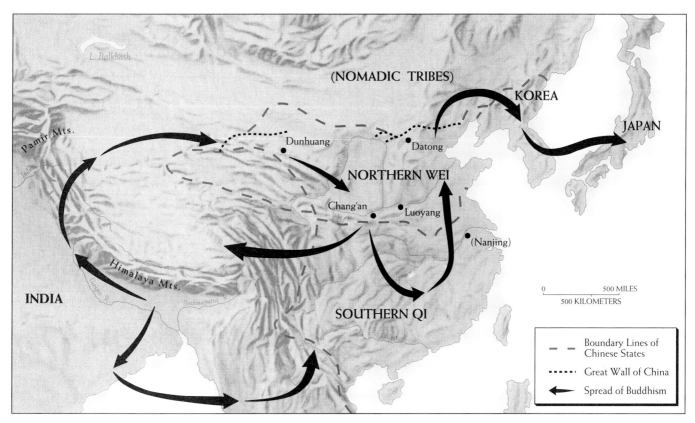

MAP 7–3 The Spread of Buddhism and Chinese States in 500 C.E.   Buddhism originated in a Himalayan state in northwest India. It spread in one wave south to India and on to Southeast Asia as far as Java. But it also spread into northwest India, Afghanistan, Central Asia, and then to China, Korea, and Japan.

of Christianity at the end of the Roman Empire. Although an alien religion in China, Buddhism had some advantages over Daoism:

1. It was a doctrine of personal salvation, offering several routes to that goal.

2. It upheld high standards of personal ethics.

3. It had systematic philosophies, and during its early centuries in China, it continued to receive inspiration from India.

4. It drew on the Indian tradition of meditative practices and psychologies, which were the most sophisticated in the world.

By the fifth century C.E. Buddhism had spread over all of China (see Map 7–3). Occasionally it was persecuted by Daoist emperors—in the north between 446 and 452 C.E., and again between 574 and 578 C.E. But most courts supported Buddhism. The "Bodhisattva Emperor" Wu of the southern Liang dynasty three times gave himself to a monastery and had to be ransomed back by his disgusted courtiers. Temples and monasteries abounded in both the north and the south. There were communities of women as well as of men. Chinese artists produced Buddhist painting and sculpture of surpassing beauty, and thousands of monk-scholars labored to translate sutras and philosophical treatises. Chinese monks went on pilgrimages to India. The record left by Fa Xian, who traveled to India overland and back by sea between 399 and

413 C.E., became a prime source of Indian history. The T'ang monk Xuanzang went to India from 629 until 645. Several centuries later, his pilgrimage was novelized as *Journey to the West*. The novel joins faith, magic, and adventure.

Buddha. A giant statue of the Buddha dwarfs visitors to the Yungang Grotto in Datong, China. Note the little Buddhas in the walls of the grotto.
China Tourism Press/Chan, Yat Nin/Getty Images, Inc.

DOCUMENT | The Peach Blossom Spring

The poet Tao Qian wrote in 380 C.E. of a lost village without taxes and untouched by the barbarian invasions and wars of the post-Han era. The simplicity and naturalness of his utopian vision were in accord, perhaps, with certain strains of Neo-Daoist thought. It struck a chord in the hearts of Chinese, and then Koreans and Japanese, inspiring a spate of paintings, poetry, and essays.

◆ Utopias are often based on religion, but this one is not. What does this suggest regarding the Chinese view of human nature?

During the T'ai-yuan period of the Ch'in [Qin] dynasty a fisherman of Wuling once rowed upstream, unmindful of the distance he had gone, when he suddenly came to a grove of peach trees in bloom. For several hundred paces on both banks of the stream there was no other kind of tree. The wild flowers growing under them were fresh and lovely, and fallen petals covered the ground—it made a great impression on the fisherman. He went on for a way with the idea of finding out how far the grove extended. It came to an end at the foot of a mountain whence issued the spring that supplied the stream. There was a small opening in the mountain and it seemed as though light was coming through it. The fisherman left his boat and entered the cave, which at first was extremely narrow, barely admitting his body; after a few dozen steps it suddenly opened out onto a broad and level plain where well-built houses were surrounded by rich fields and pretty ponds. Mulberry, bamboo and other trees and plants grew there, and criss-cross paths skirted the fields. The sounds of cocks crowing and dogs barking could be heard from one courtyard to the next. Men and women were coming and going about their work in the fields. The clothes they wore were like those of ordinary people. Old men and boys were carefree and happy.

When they caught sight of the fisherman, they asked in surprise how he had got there. The fisherman told the whole story, and was invited to go to their house, where he was served wine while they killed a chicken for a feast. When the other villagers heard about the fisherman's arrival they all came to pay him a visit. They told him that their ancestors had fled the disorders of Ch'in [Qin] times and, having taken refuge here with wives and children and neighbors, had never ventured out again; consequently they had lost all contact with the outside world. They asked what the present ruling dynasty was, for they had never heard of the Han, let alone the Wei and the Ch'in [Qin]. They sighed unhappily as the fisherman enumerated the dynasties one by one and recounted the vicissitudes of each. The visitors all asked him to come to their houses in turn, and at every house he had wine and food. He stayed several days. As he was about to go away, the people said, "There's no need to mention our existence to outsiders." After the fisherman had gone out and recovered his boat, he carefully marked the route. On reaching the city, he reported what he had found to the magistrate, who at once sent a man to follow him back to the place. They proceeded according to the marks he had made, but went astray and were unable to find the cave again.

From *The Poetry of Ta'o Ch'ien* by J. R. Hightower. Copyright © 1970 Clarendon Press. pp. 254–255. Reprinted by permission of Oxford University Press.

A comparison of Indian and Chinese Buddhism highlights some distinctive features of its spread. Buddhism in India had begun as a reform movement. Forget speculative philosophies and elaborate metaphysics, taught the Buddha, and concentrate on simple truths: Life is suffering, the cause of suffering is desire, death does not stop the endless cycle of birth and rebirth; only the attainment of *nirvana* releases one from the "wheel of *karma*." Thus, in this most otherworldly of the world's religions, all of the cosmic drama of salvation was compressed into the single figure of the Buddha meditating under the Bodhi tree. Over the centuries, however, Indian Buddhism developed contending philosophies and conflicting sects and, having become virtually indistinguishable from Hinduism, was largely reabsorbed after 1000 C.E.

In China, there were a number of sects with different doctrinal positions, but the Chinese genius was more syncretic. It took in the sutras and meditative practices of early Buddhism. It took in the Mahayana philosophies that depicted a succession of Buddhas, cosmic and historical, past and future, all embodying a single ultimate reality. It also took in the sutras and practices of Buddhist devotional sects. Finally, in the Tiantai sect, the Chinese joined together these various elements as different levels of a single truth. Thus the monastic routine of a Tiantai monk would include reading sutras, sitting in meditation, and also practicing devotional exercises.

Socially, too, Buddhism adapted to China. Ancestor worship demanded heirs to perform the sacrifices. Without progeny, ancestors might become "hungry ghosts." Hence, the first son would be expected to marry and have children, whereas the second son, if he were so inclined, might become a monk. The practice also arose of holding Buddhist masses for dead ancestors. Still another difference between China and India was the more extensive regulation of Buddhism by the state in China. Just as Buddhism was not to threaten the integrity of the family, so Buddhism was not to reduce the taxes paid on land. As a result, limits were placed on the number of monasteries, nunneries, and monastic lands, and the state had to give its permission before men or women abandoned the world to enter a religious establishment. The regulations, to be sure, were not always enforced.

Summary

Unification of China. The state of Qin unified China in 21 B.C.E. To the north it built the Great Wall to prevent incursions by the nomadic Xiongnu peoples. It ruled through a centralized bureaucracy, in line with its Legalist philosophy. But the pace of its reform was so frenetic and its legal punishments were so harsh that it alienated its people. The Qin collapsed after the death of the First Emperor.

The Two Han. The Former Han and Later Han, back to back dynasties, ruled China for more than four centuries (206 B.C.E.–220 C.E.). Under emperors, a pattern of centralized rule by officials educated in the Confucian classics was established. During long periods of peace and good government, literature, art, and history-writing flourished. Buddism entered China in the first century. Ever since this period, the core Chinese population has referred to itself as the "Han people."

The Great Wall of China.

Review Questions

1. How did Legalism help the Qin unify China? What other factors played a part? What were the main features of Qin administration? Why did the Qin collapse?

2. What was the "dynastic cycle"? In what sense was it a Confucian moral rationalization? Was a cycle of administrative and military decline especially true of Chinese government, or can we see the same pattern elsewhere?

3. Who were the players who sought power at the Han court? Did the means they used reflect the difference in their positions?

4. Did Buddhism "triumph" in China in the same sense in which Christianity triumphed in the Roman world? Compare China to the Roman Empire. What problems did both empires face and how did they try to resolve them?

Key Terms

dynastic cycle   (p. 211)

Neo-Daoism   (p. 220)

Nirvana   (p. 220)

pastorals   (p. 212)

Silk Road   (p. 212)

Documents CD-ROM

Early Civilization in East Asia
2.7 Sima Qian: The Historian's Historian Writes About the Builder of Great Wall

2.8 Shi Huang Ti of Qin: A Study in Absolutism

NOTE: *To learn more about the topics in this chapter, see the Suggested Readings at the end of the book.*

Between 500 and 1500, the major civilizations of the world shaped themselves politically and culturally in new and lasting ways. The rise of world religions like Buddhism, Christianity, and Islam supported the political power of new states and empires.

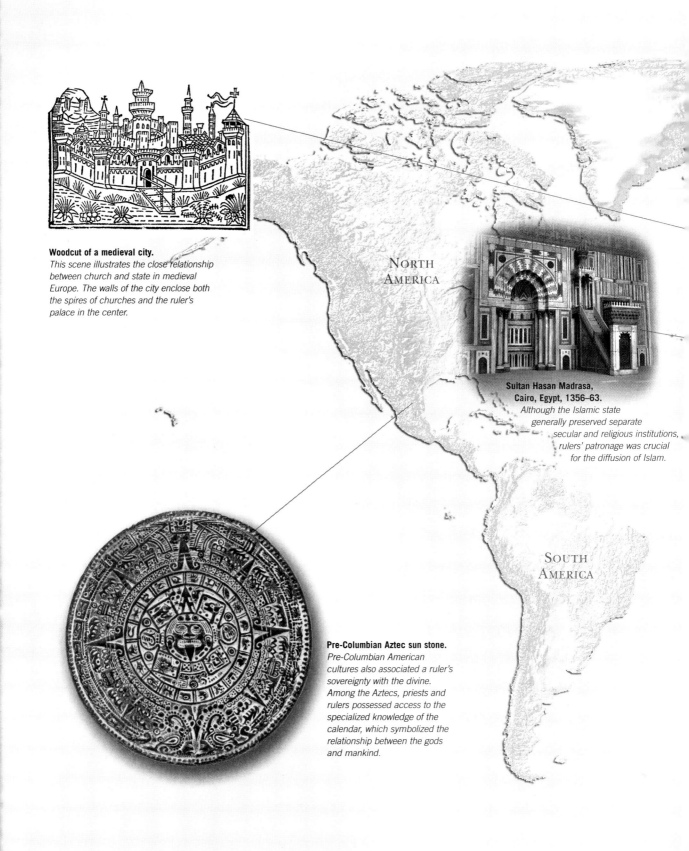

Woodcut of a medieval city.
This scene illustrates the close relationship between church and state in medieval Europe. The walls of the city enclose both the spires of churches and the ruler's palace in the center.

NORTH AMERICA

Sultan Hasan Madrasa, Cairo, Egypt, 1356–63.
Although the Islamic state generally preserved separate secular and religious institutions, rulers' patronage was crucial for the diffusion of Islam.

SOUTH AMERICA

Pre-Columbian Aztec sun stone.
Pre-Columbian American cultures also associated a ruler's sovereignty with the divine. Among the Aztecs, priests and rulers possessed access to the specialized knowledge of the calendar, which symbolized the relationship between the gods and mankind.

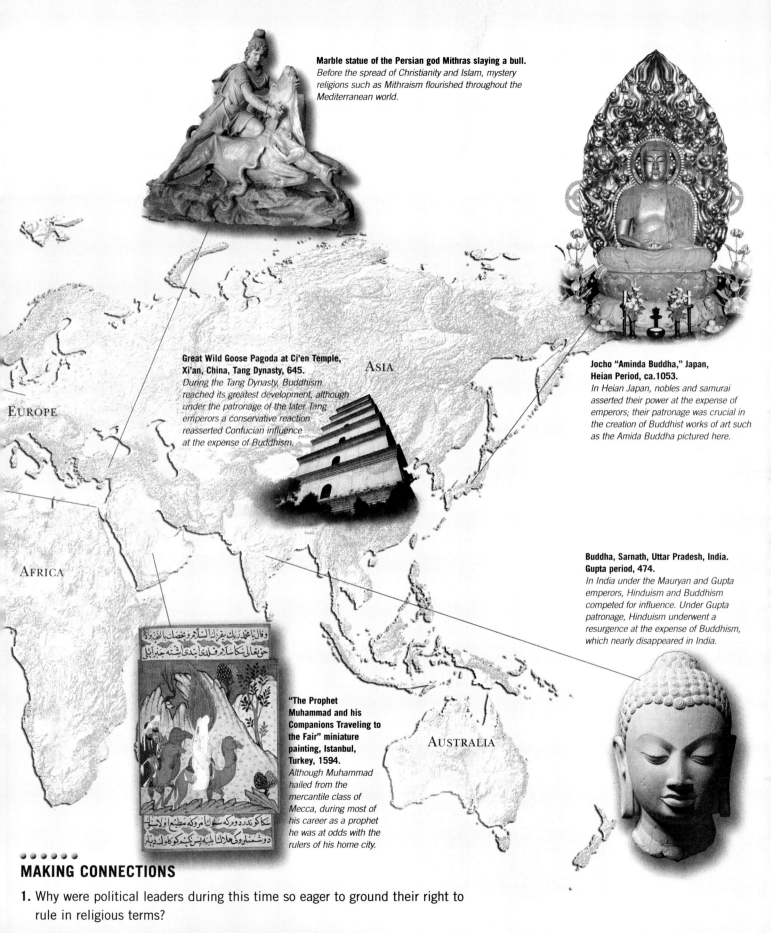

Marble statue of the Persian god Mithras slaying a bull.
Before the spread of Christianity and Islam, mystery religions such as Mithraism flourished throughout the Mediterranean world.

Great Wild Goose Pagoda at Ci'en Temple, Xi'an, China, Tang Dynasty, 645.
During the Tang Dynasty, Buddhism reached its greatest development, although under the patronage of the later Tang emperors a conservative reaction reasserted Confucian influence at the expense of Buddhism.

Jocho "Aminda Buddha," Japan, Heian Period, ca.1053.
In Heian Japan, nobles and samurai asserted their power at the expense of emperors; their patronage was crucial in the creation of Buddhist works of art such as the Amida Buddha pictured here.

Buddha, Sarnath, Uttar Pradesh, India. Gupta period, 474.
In India under the Mauryan and Gupta emperors, Hinduism and Buddhism competed for influence. Under Gupta patronage, Hinduism underwent a resurgence at the expense of Buddhism, which nearly disappeared in India.

"The Prophet Muhammad and his Companions Traveling to the Fair" miniature painting, Istanbul, Turkey, 1594.
Although Muhammad hailed from the mercantile class of Mecca, during most of his career as a prophet he was at odds with the rulers of his home city.

EUROPE

AFRICA

ASIA

AUSTRALIA

MAKING CONNECTIONS

1. Why were political leaders during this time so eager to ground their right to rule in religious terms?

2. How did the spread of world religions create larger, global communities?

PART 3

CONSOLIDATON AND INTERACTION OF WORLD CIVILIZATIONS

EUROPE

511	Death of Clovis, Frankish ruler of Gaul
529	Benedict of Nursia founds Benedictine Order
590–604	Pontificate of Gregory I, "the Great"
768–814	Charles the Great (Charlemagne)

◀ *Crown of the Holy Roman Emperor*
Kunsthistorisches Museum, Vienna

▲ *Charlemagne*

ca. 800–1000	Invasions of England and the Carolingian Empire (Vikings, Magyars, and Muslims)
843	Treaty of Verdun divides Carolingian Empire
910	Cluny Monastery founded
1019–1054	Yaroslav the Wise reigns; peak of Kievan Russia
1054	Schism between Latin and Greek churches
1066	Norman Conquest of England
1073–1085	Investiture controversy
1096–1270	The Crusades

▲ *Battle of Hastings*

NEAR EAST/INDIA

527–565	Justinian's reign
531–579	Reign of Chosroes Anosharvian in Iran
ca. 570–632	Muhammad
622	The Hijra
616–657	Reign of Harsha; neo-Gupta revival in India
651	Death of last Sasanid ruler
661–750	Umayyad dynasty
680	Death of Al-Husayn at Karbala; second civil war begins
ca. 710	First Muslim invasion of India
750–1258	Abbasid dynasty
786–809	Caliph Harun Al-Rashid reigns

800–1200	Period of feudal" overlordship in India
900–1100	Golden age of Muslim learning
909–1171	Fatimids in North Africa and Egypt
945–1055	Buyid rule in Baghdad
994–1186	Ghaznavid rule in northwestern India, Afghanistan, and Iran
1055–1194	Seljuk rule in Baghdad
1071	Seljuk Turks capture Jerusalem
1081–1118	Byzantine emperor Alexius Comnenus reigns
ca. 1000–1300	Turko-Afghan raids into India

Manichaean book ▶

EAST ASIA

589–618	Sui dynasty reunifies China
607	Japan begins embassies to China
618–907	Tang dynasty in China
701–762	Li Bo, Tang poet
710–784	Nara court, Japan's first permanent capital
712	*Records of Ancient Matters,* in Japan
713–756	Emperor Hsuan Tsung reigns in China
755	An Lushan rebellion in China
794–1185	Heian (Kyoto) court in Japan

◀ *Song dynasty wine pot*

856–1086	Fujiwara dominate Heian court
960–1279	Song dynasty in China
ca. 1000	*Pillow Book* by Sei Shōnagon and *Tale of Genji* by Murasaki Shikibu
1037–1101	Su Dungpo, Song poet

AFRICA

ca. 500	States of Takrur and Ghana founded
ca. 500–700	Political and commercial ascendancy of Aksum (Ethiopia)
ca. 600–1500	Extensive slave trade from sub-Saharan Africa to Mediterranean
ca. 700–800	Ghanians begin to supply gold to Mediterranean
ca. 700–900	States of Gao and Kanem
ca. 800	Appearance of the Kanuri people around Lake Chad

ca. 800–900	Decline of Aksum
ca. 900–1100	Kingdom of Ghana; capital city, Kumbi Saleh
ca. 1000–1100	Islam penetrates sub-Saharan Africa
1000–1500	"Great Zimbabwe" center of Bantu Kingdom in southeastern Africa

THE AMERICAS

ca. 150–900	Classic period. Dominance of Teotihuacán in central Mexico, Tikal in southern Yucatán

◀ *Stela at Aksum*

ca. 600–1000	Middle (Huari/Tiwanaku) Horizon in Andean South America

Ruins of Tikal ▶

1154–1158	Frederick Barbarosa invades Italy
1182–1226	St. Francis of Assisi
1198–1216	Pontificate of Innocent III
a. 1100–1300	Growth of trade and towns
1215	Magna Carta granted
a. 1225–1274	St. Thomas Aquinas
1265–1321	Dante Alighieri

1337	Hundred Years' War begins
ca. 1340–1400	Geoffrey Chaucer
1347–1349	The Black Death
1375–1527	The Italian Renaissance
1485	Battle of Bosworth Field; accession of Henry Tudor to the throne of England
1492	Columbus's first voyage to the New World

Book of Hours ▶
(15th century)

1174–1193	Saladin reigns
1192	Muslim conquerors end Buddhism in India
1206–1526	Delhi Sultanate in India; Indian culture divided into Hindu and Muslim
ca. 1220	Mongol invasions of Iran, Iraq, Georgia, Armenia, Syria, India
1258	Hulagu Khan, Mongol leader, conquers Baghdad
1260–1335	Il-Khans rule Iran

1250–1517	Mamluk rule in Egypt
1366–1405	Timur (Tameriane) reigns
1405–1494	Timurids rule in Transoxiana and Iran
1453	Byzantine Empire falls to the Ottoman Turks, with capture of Constantinople

◀ *Bronze Shiva*

1130–1200	Zhu Xi, Song philosopher
1167–1227	Genghis Khan, founder of Mongol Empire
1185–1333	Kamakura shogunate in Japan
1274–1281	Mongol invasions of Japan
1279–1368	Mongol (Yuan) dynasty in China

1336–1467	Ashikaga shogunate in Kyoto
1368–1644	Ming dynasty in China
1405–1433	Voyages of Cheng Ho to India and Africa
1467–1568	Warring States era in Japan
1472–1529	Wang Yang-ming, Ming philosopher

◀ *Genghis Khan*

▲ *Sesshū painting of a market day in Japan*

1100–1897	Kingdom of Benin in tropical rain forest region
1194–1221	Kanem Empire achieves greatest expansion
1203	Kingdom of Ghana falls to Sosso people
1230–1255	King Sundiata, first ruler of Mali Empire; Walata and Timbuktu become centers of trade and culture
1230–1450	Kingdom of Mali Empire

1307–1332	Mansa Musa, greatest king of Mali
1490s	Europeans establish trading posts on western African coast
mid–1400s	Decline of Mali Empire; creation of Songhai Empire
1468	Sonni Ali captures Timbuktu
1476–1507	Reign of King Mai Ali of Bornu in central Sudan
1493–1528	Songhai ruler Askia Muhammed reigns; consolidates Songhai Empire

▲ *Fatimid ceramic bowl*

| a. 800–1400 | Chimu Empire on north coast of Peru |

1325	Founding of Aztec capital of Tenochtitlán
1428–1519	Period of Aztec expansion
1492	European encounter with America
1519	Cortes conquers Aztec Empire
ca. 1350–1533	Inca Empire in Peru
1533	Pizarro executes Inca ruler Atahualpa

Relief carving ▶
of Aztec goddess
Coylxauhqui

Imperial China
589–1368

- Re-establishment of Empire: Sui (589–618) and Tang (618–907) Dynasties

- Transition to Late Imperial China: The Song Dynasty (960–1279)

- China in the Mongol World Empire: The Yuan Dynasty (1279–1368)

◄ Detail from Song Hand-Scroll of the Five Dynasties Period.
Suspicious of the licentious behavior of a court minister, the
emperor sent a painter to spy on him. Subsequently, the painter
produced this scene of wild revelry in which the minister listens
to five female flutists.
Werner Forman/Art Resource, N.Y.

Imperial China

Rough parallels between China and Europe persisted until the sixth century C.E. Both saw the rise and fall of great empires. At first glance, the three and a half centuries that followed the Han dynasty appear remarkably similar to the comparable period after the collapse of the Roman Empire: Central authority broke down, private armies arose, and aristocratic estates were established. Barbarian tribes once allied to the empires invaded and pillaged large areas. Otherworldly religions entered to challenge earlier official worldviews. In China, Neo-Daoism and then Buddhism challenged Confucianism, just as Christianity challenged Roman conceptions of the sociopolitical order.

But from the late sixth century C.E., a fundamental divergence occurred. Europe tailed off into centuries of feudal disunity and backwardness. A ghost of empire lingered in the European memory. But the reality, even after centuries had passed, was that tiny areas like France (one seventeenth the size of China), Italy (one thirty second), or Germany (one twenty seventh) found it difficult to establish an internal unity, much less re-create a pan-European or pan-Mediterranean empire. In contrast, China, which is about the size of Europe and geographically no more natural a political unit, put a unified empire back together again, attaining new wealth, power, and culture, and unified rule that has continued until the present. What explains the difference?

One reason the empire was reconstituted in China was that the victory of Buddhism in China was less complete than that of Christianity in Europe. Confucianism, and its conception of a unified empire, survived within the aristocratic families and at the courts of the Six Dynasties. It is difficult even to think of Confucianism apart from the idea of a universal ruler, aided by men of virtue and ability, ruling "all under Heaven" according to Heaven's Mandate. In contrast, the Roman concept of political order was not maintained as an independent doctrine. Moreover, empire was not a vital element in Christian thought—except perhaps in Byzantium, where the empire lasted longer than it did in Western Europe. The notion of a "Christian king" did appear in the West, but basically, the kingdom sought by Jesus was not of this world.

A second consideration was China's greater cultural homogeneity. It had a common written language that was fairly close to all varieties of spoken Chinese. Minority peoples and even barbarian conquerors—apart from the Mongols—were rapidly Sinicized. In contrast, after Rome the Mediterranean fell apart into its component cultures. Latin became the universal language of the Western church, but for most Christians it was a foreign language, a part of the mystery of the Mass, and even in Italy it became an artificial language, separate from the living tongue. European languages and cultures were divisive forces.

A third and perhaps critical factor was China's population density, at least fifteen times greater than that of France, Europe's most populous state. Population density explains why the Chinese could absorb barbarian conquerors so much more quickly than could Europe. More cultivators provided a larger agricultural surplus to the northern kingdoms than that enjoyed by comparable kingdoms in Europe. Greater numbers of people also meant better communications and a better base for commerce. To be sure, the centuries that followed the Han saw a decline in commerce and cities. In some areas barter or the use of silk as currency replaced money, but the economic level remained higher than in early medieval Europe. Several of the factors that explain the Sui-Tang regeneration of a unified empire apply equally well or better to the Song and subsequent dynasties. Comparisons across continents are difficult, but it seems likely that Tang and Song China had longer stretches of good government than any other part of the contemporary world. Not until the nineteenth century did comparable bureaucracies of talent and virtue appear in the West.

THINK AHEAD

- In what ways did China and Europe parallel each other in their development until the sixth century C.E.? How did they diverge after that?

- Why did China witness the reunification of empire after the fall of the Han dynasty, whereas after the fall of Rome, Europe was never again united in a single empire?

- Why did Tang and Song China enjoy longer stretches of good government than anywhere else in the contemporary world during the same time period?

IF CHINESE DYNASTIES FROM THE LATE SIXTH TO THE mid–fourteenth centuries were given numbers like those of ancient Egypt, the Sui and Tang dynasties would be called the Second Empire; the Song, the Third; and the Yuan, the Fourth. Numbers would not convey the distinct personalities of these dynasties, however. The Tang (618–907) is everyone's favorite dynasty: open, cosmopolitan, expansionist, exuberant, and creative. It was the example of Tang China that decisively influenced the formation of states and high cultures in Japan, Korea, and Vietnam. Poetry during the Tang attained a peak that has not been equaled since. The Song (960–1279) rivaled the Tang in the arts; it was China's great age of painting and the most significant period for philosophy since the Zhou, when Chinese philosophy began. Although not militarily strong, the Song dynasty also witnessed an important commercial revolution. The Yuan (1279–1368) was a short-lived dynasty of rule by Mongols during which China became the most important unit in the largest empire the world has yet seen.

Re-establishment of Empire: Sui (589–618) and Tang (618–907) Dynasties

In the period corresponding to the European early Middle Ages, the most notable feature of Chinese history was the reunification of China, the re-creation of a centralized bureaucratic empire consciously modeled on the earlier Han dynasty (206 B.C.E.–220 C.E.). Reunification, as usual, began in the north. The first steps were taken by the Northern Wei (386–534), the most enduring of the northern Sino-Turkic states. It moved its court south to Luoyang, made Chinese the language of the court, and adopted Chinese dress and surnames. It also used the leverage of its nomadic cavalry to impose a new land tax, mobilizing resources for state use. The Northern Wei was followed by several short-lived kingdoms. Because the emperors, officials, and military commanders of these kingdoms came from the same aristocratic stratum, the social distance between them was small, and the throne was often usurped.

THE SUI DYNASTY

The general of mixed Chinese-Turkic ancestry, Sui Wendi (d. 605), who came to power in 581 and began the Sui dynasty (589–618), was no exception to this rule. But he displayed great talent, unified the north, restored the tax base, reestablished a centralized bureaucratic government, and went on to conquer southern China and unify the country. During his reign, all went well. Huge palaces arose in his Wei valley capital. The Great Wall was rebuilt. The Grand Canal was constructed, linking the Yellow and Yangzi Rivers. This canal enabled the northern conquerors to tap the wealth of central and southern China. Peace was maintained with the Turkic tribes along China's northern borders. Eastern Turkic khans (chiefs) were sent Chinese princesses as brides.

The early years of the second Sui emperor were also constructive, but then, Chinese attempts to meddle in steppe politics led to hostilities and wars. The hardships and casualties in campaigns against Korea and along China's northern border produced rising discontent. Natural disasters occurred. The court became bankrupt and demoralized. Rebellions broke out, and once again, there was a free-for-all among the armies of aristocratic military commanders. The winner, and the founder of the Tang dynasty, was a relative of the Sui empress and a Sino-barbarian aristocrat of the same social background as those who had ruled before him.

Chinese historians often compare the short-lived Sui dynasty with that of the Qin (256–206 B.C.E.). Each brought all of China under a single government after centuries of disunity. Each did too much, fell, and was replaced by a long-lasting dynasty. The Tang built on the foundations that had been laid by the Sui, just as the Han had built on those of the Qin.

THE TANG DYNASTY

The first Tang emperor took over the Sui capital, renamed it Chang'an, and made it his own. Within a decade or so the new dynasty had extended its authority over all of China; tax revenues were adequate for government needs; and Chinese armies had begun the campaigns that would push Chinese borders out further than ever (see Map 8–1). Confucian scholars were employed at the court, Buddhist temples and monasteries flourished, and peace and order prevailed in the land. The years from 624 to 755 were the good years of the dynasty.

Government The first Tang emperor had been a provincial governor before he became a rebel general. Many of those whom he appointed to posts in his new administration were

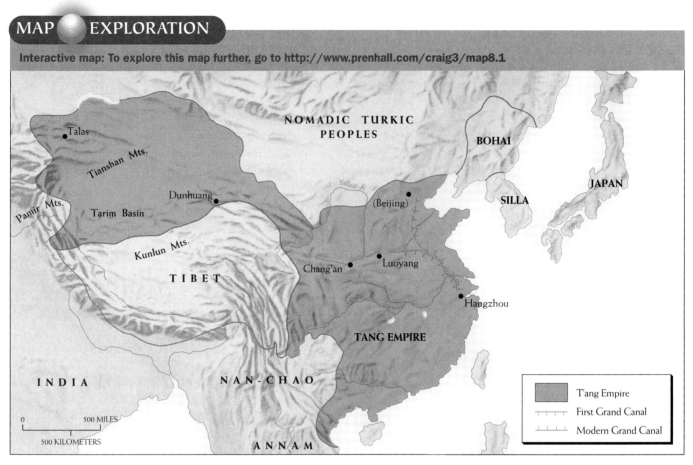

MAP 8–1 The Tang Empire at its Peak During the Eighth Century.   The Tang expansion into Central Asia reopened trade routes to the Middle East and Europe. Students from Bohai, Silla (Korea), and Japan studied in the Tang capital of Chang'an, and then returned, carrying with them Tang books and technology.

former Sui officials who had served with him. In building the new administration, he and his successors had to reconcile two conflicting sets of interests. On the one hand, the emperor wanted a bureaucratic government in which authority was centralized in his own person. On the other hand, he had to make concessions to the aristocrats—the dominant elements in Chinese society in the Late Han—who staffed his government and continued to dominate Early Tang society.

The degree to which political authority was centralized was apparent in the formal organization of the bureaucracy. At the highest level were three organs: Military Affairs, the **Censorate**, and the Council of State. Military Affairs supervised the Tang armies, with the emperor, in effect, the commander-in-chief. The Censorate had watchdog functions: It reported instances of misgovernment directly to the emperor and could also remonstrate with the emperor when it considered his behavior improper. The Council of State was the most important body. It met daily with the emperor and was made up of the heads of the Secretariat, which drafted policies; the Chancellery, which reviewed them; and State Affairs, which carried them out. Beneath State Affairs were

the Six Ministries, which continued as the core of the central government down to the twentieth century; beneath them were the several levels of local administration.

Concessions to the interests of the aristocratic families were embodied in the tax system. All land was declared to be the property of the emperor and was then redistributed to able-bodied cultivators, who paid taxes in labor and grain. Because all able-bodied adult males received an equal allotment of land (women got less), the land-tax system was called the "equal field system." But the system was not egalitarian. Aristocrats enjoyed special exemptions and grants of "rank" and "office" lands that, in effect, confirmed their estate holdings.

Aristocrats were also favored in the recruiting of officials. Most officials either were recommended for posts or received posts because their fathers had been high officials. They were drawn almost exclusively from the aristocracy. Only a tiny percentage were recruited by examinations. Those who passed the examinations had the highest prestige and were more likely to have brilliant careers. But as only well-to-do families could afford the years of study needed to master the Confucian classics and pass the rigorous examinations, even the examination bureaucrats were usually the able among the noble. Entrance to government schools at Chang'an and the secondary capital at Luoyang was restricted to the sons of nobles and officials.

The Empress Wu   Women of the inner court continued to play a role in government. For example, Wu Zhao (626–ca. 706), a young concubine of the strong second emperor, had so entranced his weak heir by her charms that when he succeeded to the throne, she was recalled from the nunnery to which all the former wives of deceased emperors were routinely consigned and installed at the court. She poisoned or otherwise removed her rivals and became his empress. She also murdered or exiled the statesmen who opposed her. When the emperor suffered a stroke in 660, she completely dominated the court. After his death in 683 she ruled for seven years as regent and then, deposing her son, became emperor herself, the only woman in Chinese history to hold the title. She moved the court to Luoyang in her native area and proclaimed a new dynasty. A fervent Buddhist with an interest in magic, she saw herself as the incarnation of the messianic Buddha Maitreya and built temples throughout the land. She patronized the White Horse Monastery, appointing one of her favorites as its abbot. Her sexual appetites were said to have been prodigious. She ruled China until 705, when at the age of eighty she was deposed.

After Empress Wu, no woman would ever become emperor again; yet her machinations did not seriously weaken the court. So highly centralized was power during these early years of the dynasty that the ill effects of her intrigues could be absorbed without provinces breaking away or military commanders becoming autonomous. In fact, her struggle for power may have strengthened the central government, for, to overcome the old northwestern Chinese aristocrats, she turned not to members of her family but to the products of the examination system and to a group known as the Scholars of the North Gate. This policy broadened the base of government by bringing in aristocrats from other regions of China. The dynamism of a young dynasty may also explain why her rule coincided with the maximal geographical expansion of Tang military power.

The Chang'an of Emperor Xuan Zong   Only a few years after Empress Wu was deposed—years filled with tawdry intrigues—Xuan Zong came to the throne. In reaction to Empress Wu, he appointed government commissions headed by distinguished aristocrats to reform government finances. Examination bureaucrats lost ground during his reign. The Grand Canal was repaired and extended. A new census extended the tax rolls. Wealth and prosperity returned to the court. His reign (713–756) was also culturally brilliant. Years later, while in exile, the great poet Li Bo (701–762) wrote a verse in which

memories of youthful exhilaration merged with the glory of the capital of Xuan Zong:

> Long ago, among the flowers and willows,
> We sat drinking together at Chang'an.
> The Five Barons and Seven Grandees were of our company,
> But when some wild stroke was afoot
> It was we who led it, yet boisterous though we were
> In the arts and graces of life we could hold our own
> With any dandy in the town—
> In the days when there was youth in your cheeks
> And I was still not old.
> We galloped to the brothels, cracking our gilded whips,
> We sent in our writings to the palace of the Unicorn,
> Girls sang to us and danced hour by hour on tortoise-shell mats.
> We thought, you and I, that it would be always like this.
> How should we know the grasses would stir and dust rise on the wind?
> Suddenly foreign horsemen were at the Hsien-ku Pass
> Just when the blossom at the palace of Ch'in was opening on the sunny boughs.[1]

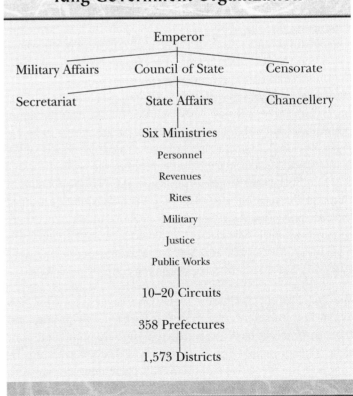

Tang Government Organization

	Emperor	
Military Affairs	Council of State	Censorate
Secretariat	State Affairs	Chancellery
	Six Ministries	
	Personnel	
	Revenues	
	Rites	
	Military	
	Justice	
	Public Works	
	10–20 Circuits	
	358 Prefectures	
	1,573 Districts	

[1] Arthur Waley, *The Poetry and Career of Li Po* © 1950, George Allen & Unwin Ltd, an imprint of HarperCollins Publishers, Ltd.

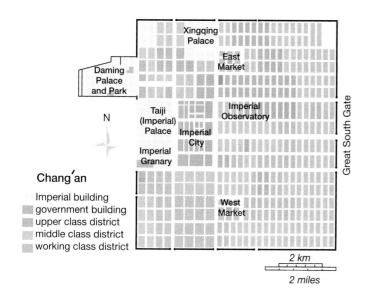

MAP 8–2 Chang'an   The great city of Chang'an had been a Chinese capital since the Han period. By the eighth century there were around a million people within the city walls, with the same number close by outside, making it the largest city in the world at the time. The rigorous grid structure accommodates a variety of districts, each with its own function.

Chang'an was an imperial city, an administrative center that lived on taxes (see Map 8–2). It was designed to exhibit the power of the emperor and the majesty of his court. At the far north of the city, the palace faced south. The placement was traditional: Confucius, speaking of Shun, said he had only "to hold himself in a respectful posture and to face due south." In front of the palace was a complex of government offices from which an imposing five-hundred-foot-wide avenue led to the main southern gate. The city was laid out on a north–south, east–west grid, which one Tang poet compared to a chessboard. Each block of the city was administered as a ward with interior streets and gates that were locked at night. Enclosed by great walls, the city covered thirty square miles. Its population was over 1 million: half within the walls, the other half in suburbs—the largest city in the world. (The population of China in the year 750 was about 50 million—about 4 percent of the country's present-day population.) Chang'an was also a trade center from which caravans set out across Central Asia. Merchants from India, Persia, Syria, and Arabia hawked the wares of the Near East and all of Asia in its two government-controlled markets.

The Tang Empire   A Chinese dynasty is like an accordion, first expanding into the territories of its barbarian neighbors and then contracting back to its original, densely populated core area. The principal threats to the Tang state were from Tibetans in the west, Turks in the northwest and north, and Khitan Mongols in Manchuria.

To protect their border, the Tang employed a four-tier policy. When nothing else would work, the Tang sent armies. But armies were expensive, and using them against nomads was like sweep-

ing back the waves with a broom. A victory might dissolve a tribal confederation, but a decade or two later it would reappear under a new leader. For example, in 630 Tang armies defeated the eastern Turks; in 648 they took the Tarim basin, opening trade routes to western Asia for almost a century; and in 657 they defeated the western Turks and extended Chinese influence across the Pamir Mountains to petty states near Samarkand. By 698, however, the Turks were back invading northeastern China, and between 711 and 736 they were in control of the steppe from the Oxus River to China's northern frontier.

Chinese efforts against Tibet were much the same. From 670 Tibet expanded and threatened China. In 679 it was defeated. In 714 it rose again; wars were fought from 727 to 729; and a settlement was reached in 730. But wars broke out anew. In 752 Tibet entered an alliance with the state of Nan Chao in Yunnan. In 763 Tibetan forces captured and looted Chang'an. They were driven out, but the point is that even during the good years of the Tang, no final victory was possible.

The human costs of sending armies far afield was detailed in a poem by Li Bo:

> Last year we were fighting at the source of the Sang-kan;
> This year we are fighting on the Onion River road.
> We have washed our swords in the surf of Parthian seas;
> We have pastured our horses among the snows of the T'ien Shan,
> The King's armies have grown grey and old
> Fighting ten thousand leagues away from home.
> The Huns have no trade but battle and carnage;
> They have no fields or ploughlands,
> But only wastes where white bones lie among yellow sands.
> Where the House of Ch'in built the great wall that was to keep away the Tartars.
> There, in its turn, the House of Han lit beacons of war.
> The beacons are always alight, fighting and marching never stop.
> Men die in the field, slashing sword to sword;
> The horses of the conquered neigh piteously to Heaven.
> Crows and hawks peck for human guts,
> Carry them in their beaks and hang them on the branches of withered trees.
> Captains and soldiers are smeared on the bushes and grass;
> The general schemed in vain.
> Know therefore that the sword is a cursed thing
> Which the wise man uses only if he must.[2]

The second tier of Chinese defenses was to use nomads against other nomads. The critical development for the Tang was the rise

[2] Waley, pp. 34–35.

OVERVIEW Chinese Policy Toward Barbarians

For much of the history of the Chinese Empire, nomadic peoples from the west and north, whom the Chinese considered to be barbarians, posed a recurrent threat. The imperial Chinese government adopted a variety of strategies for dealing with this threat.

Armies	When nothing else worked, the Chinese went on the offensive and sent armies against the nomads. But armies were expensive, and victories over nomads were transitory. Within a few years the tribes would regroup and menace China anew.
Nomads against nomads	A second strategy was to obtain allies from the nomads along China's borders and use them against more distant nomads. To win over neighboring tribes, a variety of bribes were employed.
Border Defense	In the north, an inner line of defense was the Great Wall. Also, late in dynasties, northern provinces were often placed under military governors.
Diplomacy	China sought to neutralize its neighbors by loosely attaching them to its empire. Nomadic tribes, Central Asian states, and Korea became "tributaries" of the emperor. Their rulers sent embassies bearing gifts ("tribute") to the imperial court, which fed and housed them, and sent them home with even costlier gifts and reports of China's power, wealth, splendor, and cultural achievements.

to power of the Uighur Turks. From 744 to 840, the Uighurs controlled Central Asia and were staunch allies of the Tang. Without their support, the Tang dynasty would have ended sooner.

A third tier was the defense along China's borders, including the Great Wall. At mid-dynasty, whole frontier provinces in the north and the northwest were put under military commanders, who in time came to control the provinces' civil governments as well. The bulk of the Tang military was in such frontier commands. At times their autonomy and potential as rebels were as much a threat to the Tang court as to the nomadic enemy.

Diplomacy is cheaper than war. The fourth line of defense was to bring the potential enemy into the empire as a tributary. The Tang defined the position of "tributary" with great elasticity. It included principalities truly dependent on China; Central Asian states conquered by China; enemy states, such as Tibet or the Thai state of Nan Chao in Yunnan, when they were not actually at war with China; the Korean state of Silla, which had unified the peninsula with Tang aid but had then fought Tang armies to a standstill when they attempted to impose Chinese hegemony; and wholly independent states, such as Japan. All sent embassies bearing gifts to the Tang court, which housed and fed them and sent back costly gifts in return.

For some countries these embassies had a special significance. As the only "developed nation" in eastern Asia, China was a model for countries still in the throes of forming a state. An embassy gained access to the entire range of Tang culture and technology: its philosophy and writing; governmental and land systems; Bud-dhism; and the arts, architecture, and medicine. In 640 there were 8,000 Koreans, mostly students, in Chang'an. Never again would China exert such an influence, for never again would its neighbors be at that formative stage of development.

Rebellion and Decline From the mid–eighth century, signs of decline began to appear. China's frontiers started to contract. Tribes in Manchuria became unruly. Tibetans threatened China's western border. In 751 an overextended Tang army led by a Korean general was defeated by Arabs near Samarkand in western Asia, shutting down China's caravan trade with the West for more than five centuries. Furthermore, in 755 a Sogdian general, An Lushan, who commanded three Chinese provinces on the northeastern frontier, led his 160,000 troops in a rebellion that swept across northern China, capturing Luoyang and then Chang'an. The emperor fled to Sichuan.

CHRONOLOGY

Imperial China

589–618	Sui dynasty
618–907	Tang dynasty
960–1279	Song dynasty
1279–1368	Yuan (Mongol) dynasty

The event contained an element of romance. Ten years earlier the emperor Xuan Zong had taken a young woman, Yang Guifei, from the harem of his son (he gave his son another beauty in exchange). So infatuated was he that he neglected not only the other "three thousand beauties of his inner chambers," but the business of government as well. For a while his neglect did not matter because he had an able chief minister, but when the minister died Xuan Zong appointed his concubine's second cousin to the post, initiating a train of events that resulted in rebellion. En route to Sichuan, his soldiers, blaming Yang Guifei for their plight, strangled her. The event was later immortalized in a poem that described her "snow-white skin," "flowery face," and "moth eyebrows," as well as the "eternal sorrow" of the emperor, who, in fact, was seventy-two at the time.

After a decade of wars and much devastation, a new emperor restored the dynasty with the help of the Uighur Turks, who looted Chang'an as part of their reward. The recovery and the century of relative peace and prosperity that followed illustrate the resilience of Tang institutions. China was smaller, but military governors maintained the diminished frontiers. Provincial governors were more autonomous, but taxes were still sent to the capital. Occasional rebellions were suppressed by imperial armies, sometimes led by eunuchs. Most of the emperors were weak, but three strong emperors appeared and reforms were carried out. Edwin O. Reischauer, after translating the diary of a Japanese monk who studied in China during the early ninth century, commented that the "picture of government in operation" that emerges "is amazing for the ninth century, even in China":

> The remarkable degree of centralized control still existing, the meticulous attention to written instructions from higher authorities, and the tremendous amount of paper work involved in even the smallest matters of administration are all the more striking just because this was a period of dynastic decline.[3]

Of the reforms of this era, none was more important than that of the land system. The official census, on which land allotments and taxes were based, showed a drop in population from 53 million before the An Lushan rebellion to 17 million afterward. Unable to put people back on the registers, the gov-

---

[3] E. O. Reischauer, *Ennin's Travels in T'ang China* (New York: Ronald Press, 1955), p. 7.

◀ **Tang Figurine.** During the Tang dynasty (618–907), well-to-do families placed glazed pottery figurines in the tombs of their dead. Perhaps they were intended to accompany and amuse the dead in the afterlife. Note the fancy chignon hairstyle of this female flutist, one figure in a musical ensemble. Today these figurines are sought by collectors around the world.
Werner Forman/Art Resource, N.Y.

ernment replaced the equal field system with a tax collected twice a year. The new system, begun in 780, lasted until the sixteenth century. Under it, a fixed quota of taxes was levied on each province. After the rebellion, government revenues from salt and iron surpassed those from land.

During the second half of the ninth century the government weakened further. Most provinces were autonomous, often under military commanders, and resisted central control. Wars were fought with the state of Nan Chao in the southwest. Bandits appeared. Droughts led to peasant uprisings. By the 880s warlords had carved all of China into independent kingdoms, and in 907 the Tang dynasty fell. But within half a century a new dynasty arose.

The fall of the Tang did not lead to the centuries of division that had followed the Han. Something had changed within China.

Tang Culture The creativity of the Tang period arose from the juxtaposition and interaction of cosmopolitan, medieval Buddhist, and secular elements. The rise of each of these cultural spheres was rooted in the wealth and the social order of the recreated empire.

Tang culture was cosmopolitan not just because of its broad contacts with other cultures and peoples but also because of its openness to them. Buddhist pilgrims to India and a flow of Indian art and philosophies to China were a part of it. The voluptuousness of Indian painting and sculpture, for example, helped shape the Tang representation of the *bodhisattva*. Commercial contacts were widespread. Foreign goods were vended in Chang'an marketplaces. Communities of central and western Asians were established in the capital, and Arab and Persian quarters grew up in the seaports of southeastern China. Merchants brought their religions with them. Nestorian Christianity, Zoroastrianism, Manichaeism, Judaism, and Islam entered China at this time. Most would be swept away in the persecutions of the ninth century, but Islam and small pockets of Judaism survived until the twentieth century.

Central Asian music and musical instruments became so popular they almost displaced the native tradition. Tang ladies

Relief of Tang Emperor's Horse.
A bearded "barbarian" groom tends the charger of the second Tang emperor (r. 626–649). This stone relief was found on the emperor's tomb. Note the stirrup, a Chinese invention of the fourth century C.E.

A Relief of Emperor T'ai T'sung's Horse, "Autumn Dew." University of Pennsylvania Museum, Philadelphia (NEG.# S8-62840).

adopted foreign hairstyles. Foreign dramas and acrobatic performances by western Asians could be seen in the streets of the capital. Even among the pottery figurines customarily placed in tombs there were representations of western Asian traders and Central Asian grooms, along with those of horses, camels, and court ladies that today may be seen in museums around the world. In Tang poetry, too, what was foreign was not shunned but judged on its own merits or even presented as exotically attractive. Of a gallant of Chang'an, Li Bo wrote:

> A young man of Five Barrows suburb east of the Golden Market,
> Silver saddle and white horse cross through wind of spring.
> When fallen flowers are trampled all under, where is it he will roam?
> With a laugh he enters the tavern of a lovely Turkish wench.[4]

Later in the dynasty, another poet, Li He, wrote of service on the frontier:

> A Tartar horn tugs at the north wind,
> Thistle Gate shines whiter than the stream.
> The sky swallows the road to Kokonor.
> On the Great Wall, a thousand miles of moonlight.[5]

The Tang dynasty, although slightly less an age of faith than the preceding Six Dynasties, was the golden age of Buddhism in China nonetheless. Patronized by emperors and aristocrats, the Buddhist establishment acquired vast landholdings and

[4] S. Owen, *The Great Age of Chinese Poetry: The High T'ang.* © 1980, New Haven, CT: Yale University Press, p. 130. Reprinted by permission
[5] A. C. Graham, *Poems of the Late T'ang* trans. by A. C. Graham (Penguin Classics, 1965). Copyright © 1965, A. C. Graham.

Caravaneer on a Camel. The animal's shaggy mane indicates that it is a Bactrian camel from Central Asia.
Réunion des Musées/Art Resource, N.Y.

Bodhisattva. Stone sculpture of bodhisattva reflecting the full-bodied, almost voluptuous, Tang ideal of beauty.
Corbis/Bettmann.

great wealth. Temples and monasteries were constructed throughout China. To gain even an inkling of the beauty and sophistication of the temple architecture, the wooden sculpture, or the paintings on the temple walls, one must see Hōryū ji or the ancient temples of Nara in Japan, for little of note has survived in China. The single exception is the Caves of the Thousand Buddhas at Dunhuang in China's far northwest, which were sealed during the eleventh century for protection from Tibetan raiders and not rediscovered until the twentieth century. They were found to contain stone sculptures, Buddhist frescoes, and thousands of manuscripts in Chinese and Central Asian languages.

Only during the Tang did China have a "church" establishment that was at all comparable to that of medieval Europe, and even then it was subservient to the far stronger Tang state. Buddhist wealth and learning brought with them secular functions. Temples served as schools, inns, or even bathhouses. They lent money. Priests performed funerals and dispensed medicines. Occasionally the state moved to recapture the revenues monopolized by temples. The severest persecution, which marked a turn in the fortunes of Buddhism in China, occurred from 841 to 845, when an ardent Daoist emperor confiscated millions of acres of tax-exempt lands, put back on the tax registers 260,000 monks and nuns, and destroyed 4,600 monasteries and 40,000 shrines.

During the early Tang, the principal Buddhist sect was the Tiantai, but after the mid-ninth-century suppression, other sects came to the fore:

1. One devotional sect focused on Maitreya, a Buddha of the future, who will appear and create a paradise on earth. Maitreya was a cosmic messiah, not a human figure. The messianic teachings of the sect often furnished the ideology for popular uprisings and rebellions like the White Lotus, which claimed that it was renewing the world in anticipation of Maitreya's coming.

2. Another devotional or faith sect worshiped the **Amitabha Buddha**, the Lord of the Western Paradise or Pure Land. This sect taught that in the early centuries after the death of the historical Buddha, his teachings had been transmitted properly and people could obtain enlightenment by their own efforts, but that at present the Buddha's teachings had become so distorted that only by reliance on Amitabha could humans obtain salvation. All who called on Amitabha with a pure heart and perfect faith would be saved. Developing a congregational form of worship, this sect became the largest in China and deeply influenced Chinese popular religion.

3. A third sect, and the most influential among the Chinese elites, was known in China, where it began, as Chan and is better known in the West by its Japanese name, **Zen**. Zen had no cosmic Buddhas. It taught that the historical Buddha was only a man and exhorted each person to attain enlightenment by his or her own efforts. Although its monks were often the most learned in China, Zen was anti-intellectual in its emphasis on direct intuition into one's own Buddha-nature. Enlightenment was to be obtained by a regimen of physical labor and meditation. To jolt the monk into enlightenment—after he had been readied by long hours of meditation—some Zen sects used little problems not answerable by normal ratiocination: "What was your face before you were conceived?" "If all things return to the One, what does the One return to?" "From the top of a hundred-foot pole, how do you step forward?" The psychological state of the adept attempting to deal with these problems is compared to that of "a rat pursued into a blocked pipe" or "a mosquito biting an iron ball." The discipline of meditation, combined with a Zen view of nature, profoundly influenced the arts in China and subsequently in Korea and Japan as well.

A third characteristic of Tang culture was the reappearance of secular scholarship and letters. The re-establishment of centralized bureaucratic government stimulated the tradition of learning that had been partially interrupted after the fall of the Han dynasty in the third century C.E. A scholarly bureau-

DOCUMENT | A Poem By Li Bo

The great Tang poet Li Bo reputedly wrote 20,000 poems, of which 1800 have survived.

◆ It has been said that concreteness of imagery is the genius of Chinese poetry. How does this poem support that contention?

The River Merchant's Wife: A Letter

While my hair was still cut straight across my forehead
I played about the front gate, pulling flowers.
You came by on bamboo stilts, playing horse,
You walked about my seat, playing with blue plums.
And we went on living in the village of Chokan:
Two small people, without dislike or suspicion.

At fourteen I married My Lord you.
I never laughed, being bashful.
Lowering my head, I looked at the wall.
Called to, a thousand times, I never looked back.

At fifteen I stopped scowling,
I desired my dust to be mingled with yours

Forever and forever and forever.
Why should I climb the look out?

At sixteen you departed,
You went into far Ku-to-yen, by the river of swirling
     eddies,
And you have been gone five months.
The monkeys make sorrowful noise overhead.

You dragged your feet when you went out.
By the gate now, the moss is grown, the different mosses,
Too deep to clear them away!
The leaves fall early this autumn, in wind.
The paired butterflies are already yellow with August
Over the grass in the West garden;
They hurt me. I grow older.
If you are coming down through the narrows of the
     river Kiang,
Please let me know beforehand,
And I will come out to meet you,
As far as Cho-fu-Sa.

---

cratic complex emerged. Most men of letters were also officials, and most high-ranking officials painted or wrote poems. An anthology of Tang poetry compiled during the Ming period (1368–1644) contained 48,900 poems by almost 2300 authors. This secular stream of Tang culture was not ideologically anti-Buddhist. Officials were often privately sympathetic to Buddhism, but as men involved themselves in the affairs of government, their values became increasingly this-worldly.

Court historians of the Tang revived the Han practice of writing an official history of the previous dynasty. For the first time scholars wrote comprehensive institutional histories and regional and local gazetteers. They compiled dictionaries and wrote commentaries on the Confucian classics. Other scholars wrote ghost stories or tales of adventure, using the literary language. (Buddhist sermons, in contrast, were often written in the vernacular.) More paintings were Buddhist than secular, but Chinese landscape painting had its origins during the Tang. Nowhere, however, was the growth of a secular culture more evident than in poetry, the greatest achievement of Tang letters.

Whether Li Bo (701–762) can be called wholly secular is questionable. He might better be called Daoist. But he clearly was not Buddhist. Born in Sichuan, he was exceptional among Tang poets in never having sat for the civil service examinations, although he briefly held an official post at Chang'an,

given in recognition of his poetry. Large and muscular, he was a swordsman and a carouser. Of the 20,000 poems he is said to have composed, 1800 have survived, and a fair number have titles like "Bring on the Wine" or "Drinking Alone in the Moonlight." According to legend, he drowned while drunkenly attempting to embrace the reflection of the moon in a lake. His poetry is clear, powerful, passionate, and always sensitive to beauty. (See Document, "A Poem by Li Bo.") It also contains a sense of fantasy, as when he climbed a mountain and saw a star-goddess, "stepping in emptiness, pacing pure ether, her rainbow robes trailed broad sashes." Li Bo, nearer to heaven than to earth, looked down below where

Far and wide Tartar troops were speeding,
And flowing blood mired the wild grasses
Where wolves and jackals all wore officials' caps.[6]

According to Li Bo, life is brief and the universe is large, but this view did not lead him to renounce the world. His Daoism was not of the quietistic strain close to Buddhism. Rather, he exulted, identifying with the primal flux of yin and yang:

I'll wrap this Mighty Mudball of a world all up in a bag
And be wild and free like Chaos itself![7]

[6] Owen, p. 134.
[7] Owen, p. 125.

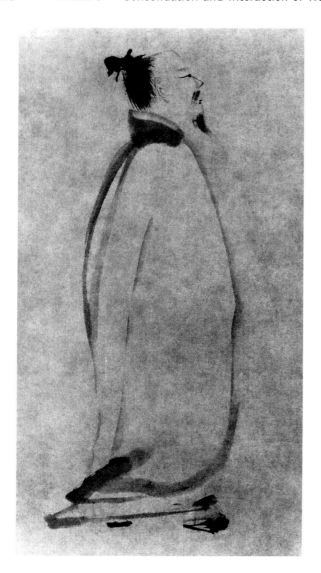

The Tang Poet Li Bo. As imagined by the great Song artist Liang Kai. Tokyo National Museum/DNP Archives.Com Co., Ltd.

Du Fu (712–770), an equally famous Tang poet, was from a literary family. He failed the metropolitan examination at the age of twenty-three and spent years in wandering and poverty. At thirty-nine he received an official appointment after presenting his poetry to the court. Four years later he was appointed to a military post. He fell into rebel hands during the An Lushan rebellion, escaped, and was reappointed to a civil post. But he was then dismissed and suffered further hardships. His poetry is less lyrical and more allusive than Li Bo's. It also reflects more compassion for human suffering: for the mother whose sons have been conscripted and sent to war; for brothers scattered by war; for his own family, to whom he returned after having been given up for dead. Like Li Bo, he felt that humans are short-lived and that nature

endures. Visiting the ruins of the palace of the second Tang emperor, he saw "Grey rats scuttling over ancient tiles" and "in its shadowed chambers ghost fires green." "Its lovely ladies are the brown soil" and only "tomb horses of stone remain." But his response to this sad scene was to

> Sing wildly, let the tears cover your open hands.
> Then go ever onward and on the road of your travels,
> Meet none who prolong their fated years.[8]

His response was unlike that of Li Bo. It was close to Stoicism but equally un-Buddhist.

Transition to Late Imperial China: The Song Dynasty (960–1279)

Most traditional Chinese history was written in terms of the dynastic cycle, and for good reason: The pattern of rise and fall, of expansion and contraction, within each dynasty cannot be denied. Certainly the Song can be viewed from this perspective. It reunified China in 960, establishing its capital at Kaifeng on the Yellow River (see Map 8–3). Mobilizing its resources effectively, it ruled for 170 years; this period is called the Northern Song. Then it weakened. In 1127 it lost the north but for another 150 years continued to rule the south from a new capital at Hangzhou in east-central China. The Southern Song fell before the Mongol onslaught in 1279.

But there is more to Chinese history than the inner logic of the dynastic cycle. Longer term changes that cut across dynastic lines were ultimately more important. One such set of changes began during the late Tang period and continued on into the Song period, affecting its economy, society, state, and culture. Taken together, these changes help to explain why China after the Tang did not relapse into centuries of disunity as it had after the Han, and why China would never again experience more than brief intervals of disunity. In this section we will skip over emperors and empresses, eunuchs and generals, and focus instead on more fundamental transformations.

AGRICULTURAL REVOLUTION OF THE SONG: FROM SERFS TO FREE FARMERS

Landed aristocrats had dominated local society in China during the Sui and Tang periods. The tillers of their lands were little more than serfs. Labor service was the heaviest tax, and whether performed on the office or rank lands of aristocrats or on other government lands, it created conditions of social subordination.

[8] Owen, pp. 223–224.

The aristocracy weakened, however, under the Tang and after its fall. Estates were divided among male children at each change of generation. Drawn to the capital, the aristocracy became less a landed, and more a metropolitan, elite. After the fall of the Tang, the aristocratic estates were often seized by warlords. As the aristocracy declined, the claims of those who worked the soil grew stronger, aided by changes in the land and tax systems. With the collapse of the equal field system (described earlier), farmers could buy and sell land. The ownership of land as private property gave the cultivators greater independence. They could now move about as they pleased. Taxes paid in grain gave way during the Song to taxes in money. The commutation of the labor tax to a money tax gave the farmers more control over their own time. Conscription, the cruelest and heaviest labor tax of all, disappeared as the conscript armies of the early and middle Tang gave way to professional armies.

Changes in technology also benefited the cultivator. New strains of an early-ripening rice permitted double cropping. In the Yangzi region, extensive water-control projects were carried out, and more fertilizers were used. New commercial crops were developed. Tea, which had been introduced during the Six Dynasties as a medicine and had been drunk by monks during the Tang, became widely cultivated; cotton also became a common crop. Because taxes paid in money tended to become fixed, much of the increased productivity accrued to the cultivator. Of course, not all benefited equally; there were landlords and landless tenants as well as independent small farmers.

The disappearance of the aristocrats also increased the authority of the district magistrate, who no longer had to contend with their interference in local affairs. The Song magistrate became the sole representative of imperial authority in local society. But there were too many villages in his district for him to be involved regularly in their internal governance. As long as taxes were paid and order maintained, affairs were left in the hands of the village elites, so the Song farmer enjoyed not only a rising income and more freedom, but also substantial self-government.

One other development that began during the Song—and became vastly more important later—was the appearance of a scholar-gentry class. The typical gentry family contained at least one member who had passed the provincial civil service examination and lived in a district seat or market town. Socially and culturally, these gentry were closer to magistrates than to villagers. But they usually owned land in the villages and thus shared some interests with the local landholders. Although much less powerful than the former aristocrats, they took a hand in local affairs and at times functioned as a buffer between the village and the magistrate's office.

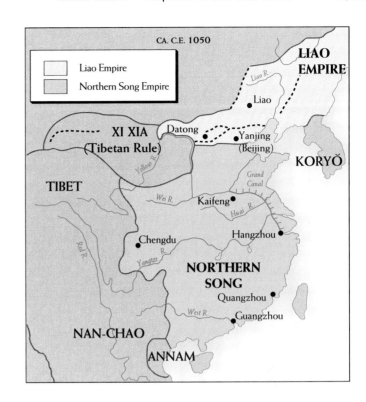

MAP 8–3 The Northern Song and Liao Empires (Top) and the Southern Song and Jin Empires (Bottom).   During the Northern Song, the Mongol Liao dynasty ruled only the extreme northern edge of China. During the Southern Song, in contrast, the Manchurian Jin dynasty ruled half of China.

Irrigation Methods on a Farm in the Yangzi Valley. A farmer and his wife use their legs and feet to work the square-pallet chain pump, a boy drives a water buffalo to turn a water-pumping device, and another boy fishes.
© Photograph by Wan-go Weng/Collection of H. C. Weng.

COMMERCIAL REVOLUTION OF THE SONG

Stimulated by changes in the countryside, and contributing to them as well, were demographic shifts, innovative technologies, the growth of cities, the spread of money, and rising trade. These developments varied by region, but overall the Song economy reached new prosperity.

Emergence of the Yangzi Basin Until late in the Tang, the north had been China's most populous and productive region. But from the late ninth century the center of gravity of China's population, agricultural production, and culture shifted to the lower and eastern Yangzi region. Between 800 and 1100 the population of the region tripled as China's total population increased to about 100 million. Its rice paddies yielded more per acre than the wheat or millet fields of the north, making rice the tax base of the empire. Its wealth led to the establishment of so many schools that the government set regional quotas for the examination system to prevent the Yangzi region from dominating all of China. The Northern Song capital itself was kept in the north for strategic reasons, but it was situated at Kaifeng, further east than Luoyang, at the point where the Grand Canal, which carried tax rice from the south, joined the Yellow River.

New Technology During the Northern Song a coal and iron-smelting industry developed in north China that provided China with better tools and weapons. Using coke and bellows to heat furnaces to the temperatures required for carbonized steel, it was the most advanced in the world.

Printing began in China with the use of carved seals. The earliest woodblock texts, mostly on Buddhist subjects, appeared in the seventh century. By the tenth century a complete edition of the classics had been published, and by the mid-Song books printed with movable type were fairly common.

Other advances during the Song were the abacus, the use of gunpowder in grenades and projectiles, and improvements in textiles and porcelains.

Rise of a Money Economy Exchange during the Tang had been based on silk. Coins had been issued, but their circulation was limited. During the Northern Song large amounts of copper cash were coined, but the demand rose more rapidly than the supply. Coins were made with holes in the center, and 1,000 on a string constituted the usual unit for large transactions. Beginning in the Southern Song, silver was minted to complement copper cash, ten times as much silver in the late twelfth century as in the early eleventh century. Letters of credit were used by merchants, and various kinds of paper money were also issued. The penetration of money into the village economy was such that by 1065 tax receipts paid in money had risen to 38 million strings of cash—in comparison with a mere 2 million in mid-Tang.

Trade The growth of trade spurred the demand for money. One may distinguish among trade within economic regions, trade between regions, and foreign trade. During the Tang most cities had been administrative, supported by taxes from the countryside. Official salaries and government expenditures created a demand for services and commercial products, making the cities into islands of commerce in a noncommercial hinterland. In most of China's seven or eight economic regions this pattern continued during the Song, but in the capital, and especially in the economically advanced regions along the Yangzi, cities became the hubs of regional commercial networks, with district seats or market towns serving as secondary centers for the local markets beneath them.

As this transition occurred, cities with more than 100,000 households almost quadrupled in number. The Northern Song capital at Kaifeng is recorded as having had 260,000 households—probably more than 1 million inhabitants—and the Southern Song capital at Hangzhou had 391,000 households. Compare these capitals to those of backward Europe: London during the Northern Song had a population of about 18,000; Rome during the Southern Song had 35,000; and Paris even a century later had fewer than 60,000.

DOCUMENT | "Chaste Woman" Shi

Hong Mai (1123–1202 C.E.) was a collector of stories—fantastic, folkloric, and factual. Unlike the usual Confucian homilies on the proper virtues of women, his stories, and those told by other Song storytellers, contained broader perspectives. They reflected the actual diversity of Chinese society. In this story the Chinese belief in ghosts enables the wronged Ning to have a hand in the villain's downfall.

◆ Is the moral of this tale simply that justice ultimately prevails? Can a more complex interpretation be made? What does it say about the dynamics of Song society?

Ning Six of South Meadow village, in the southern suburbs of Jianchang, was a simple-minded man who concentrated on his farming. His younger brother's wife, Miss Shi, was a little sleeker than her peers. She was also ruthless and licentious, and had an adulterous affair with a youth who lived there. Whenever Ning looked askance at her she would scold him and there was not much he could do.

Once Miss Shi took a chicken, wanting to cook it. When Ning learned of it, he went into her room, demanded that she give it to him, then left with it. Miss Shi quickly cut her arm with a knife, then went to the neighbors screaming, "Because my husband is not home, brother-in-law offered me a chicken and tried to force me to have sex with him. I resisted, threatening to kill myself with the knife I was holding, and so just managed to escape."

Ning at that time had no wife, so the neighbors thought she might be telling the truth. They took them to the village headman, then the county jail. The clerks at the jail reviewed the evidence and demanded 10,000 cash to set things right. Ning was poor and stingy, and moreover, knew himself to be in the right, so stubbornly refused. The clerks sent up the dossier to the prefect Dai Qi. Dai was unable to examine it but noted that it involved an ordinary village wife who was able to protect her virtue and her body and not be violated. The administrative supervisor, Zhao Shiqing, concurred with Qi, and they sent up the case making Ning look guilty. Ning received the death penalty and Miss Shi was granted 100,000 cash, regular visits from the local officials, and a banner honoring her for her chastity. From this, she acquired a reputation as a chaste wife. The local people all realized Ning had been wronged and resented how overboard she had gone.

In the end Miss Shi had an affair with a monk at the nearby Lintian temple. Charges were brought and she received a beating and soon became ill. She saw Ning as a vengeful demon and then died. The date was the sixth month of 1177.

Furthermore, these Song capitals, unlike Chang'an with its walled wards that closed at night, were open within and spread beyond their outer walls. As in present-day Chinese cities, their main avenues were lined with shops. Merchant guilds replaced government officials as the managers of marketplaces. Growing wealth also led to a taste for luxury and an increasingly secular lifestyle. Restaurants, theaters, wine shops, and brothels abounded. Entertainment quarters with fortunetellers, jugglers, chess masters, acrobats, and puppeteers sprang up. Such activity had been present in Chang'an, but the numbers increased, and now they catered to traders and rich merchants as well as to officials.

Trade between regions during the Song was limited mainly to luxury goods like silk, lacquerware, medicinal herbs, and porcelains. Only where transport was cheap—along rivers, canals, or the coast—was interregional trade in bulk commodities economical, and even then it was usually carried on only to make up for specific shortages.

Foreign trade also reached new heights during the Song. In the north, Chinese traders bought horses from Tibetan, Turkic, and Mongol border states and sold silks and tea. Along the coast, Chinese merchants took over the port trade that during the Tang had been in the hands of Korean, Arab, and Persian merchants. The new hegemony of Chinese merchants was based on improved ships using both sail and oars and equipped with watertight compartments and better rudders. Chinese captains, navigating with the aid of the compass, came to dominate the sea routes from Japan in the north to Sumatra in the south. The content of the overseas trade reflected China's advanced economy: It imported raw materials and exported finished goods. Porcelains were sent to Southeast Asia and then were carried by Arab ships to medieval trading centers on the Persian Gulf and down the coast of East Africa as far south as Zanzibar.

GOVERNMENT: FROM ARISTOCRACY TO AUTOCRACY

The millennium of late imperial China after the Tang is often spoken of as the age of autocracy or as China's age of absolute monarchy. Earlier emperors, as we have noted, were often personally powerful, but beginning with the Song, changes occurred that made it easier for emperors to be autocrats.

One change was that Song emperors had direct personal control over more offices than their Tang predecessors. For example, the Board of Academicians, an advisory office, presented the emperor with policy options separate from those presented by the Secretariat-Chancellery. The emperor could thus use the one against the other and prevent bureaucrats in the Secretariat-Chancellery from dominating the government.

A second change was that the central government was better funded than it had been previously. Revenues in 1100 were three times the peak revenues of the Tang, partly because of the growth of population and agricultural wealth, and partly because of the establishment of government monopolies on salt, wine, and tea and various duties, fees, and taxes levied on domestic and foreign trade. During the Northern Song these commercial revenues rivaled the land tax; during the Southern Song they surpassed it. Confucian officials would continue to stress the primacy of land, but throughout late imperial China, commerce became a vital source of revenues.

A third change that strengthened the emperors was the disappearance of the aristocracy. During the Tang the emperor had come from the same Sino-Turkic aristocracy of northwestern China as most of his principal ministers, and he was essentially the organ of a state that ruled on behalf of this aristocracy. Aristocrats monopolized the high posts of government. They married among themselves and with the imperial family. They called the emperor the Son of Heaven, but they knew he was one of them. During the Song, in contrast, government officials were commoners, mostly products of the examination system. They were separated from the emperor by an enormous social gulf and saw him as a person apart.

The Song examination system was larger than that of the Tang, though smaller than under later dynasties. Whereas only 10 percent of officials had been recruited by examination during the Tang, the Song figure rose to over 50 percent and included the most important officials. The first examination was given at regional centers. The applicant took the examination in a walled cubicle under close supervision. To ensure impartiality, his answers were recopied by clerks and his name was replaced by a number before his examination was sent to the officials who would grade it. Of those who sat for the examination, only a tiny percentage passed. The second hurdle was the metropolitan examination at the national capital, where the precautions were equally elaborate. Only one in five, or about two hundred a year, passed. The average successful applicant was in his midthirties. The final hurdle was the palace examination, which rejected a few and assigned a ranking to the others.

To pass the examinations, the candidate had to memorize the Confucian classics, interpret selected passages, write in the literary style, compose poems on themes given by the examiners, and propose solutions to contemporary problems in terms of Confucian philosophy. The quality of the officials produced by the Song system was impressive. A parallel might be drawn with nineteenth-century Britain, where students in the classics at Oxford and Cambridge went on to become generalist bureaucrats. The Chinese examination system that flourished during the Song continued, with some interruptions, into the twentieth century. The continuity of Chinese government during this millennium rested on the examination elite, with its common culture and values.

The social base for this examination meritocracy was triangular, consisting of land, education, and office. Landed wealth paid the costs of education. A poor peasant or city dweller could not afford the years of study needed to pass the examinations. Without passing the examinations, official position was out of reach. And without office, family wealth could not be preserved. The Chinese pattern of inheritance, as noted earlier, led to the division of property at each change of generation. Some families passed the civil service examinations for several generations running. More often, the sons of well-to-do officials did not study as hard as those with bare means. The adage "shirt sleeves to shirt sleeves in three generations" is not inappropriate to the Song and later dynasties. As China had an extended-family or clan system, a wealthy official often provided education for the bright children of poor relations.

How the merchants related to this system is less clear. They had wealth but were despised by scholar-officials as grubby profit seekers and were barred from taking the examinations. Some merchants avoided the system altogether—a thorough education in the Confucian classics did little to fit a merchant's son for a career in commerce. Others bought land for status and security, and their sons or grandsons became eligible to take the exams. Similarly, a small peasant might build up his holdings, become a landlord, and educate a son or grandson. The system was steeply hierarchical, but it was not closed nor did it produce a new, self-perpetuating aristocracy.

SONG CULTURE

As society and government changed during the Tang-Song transition, so too did culture. Song culture retained some of the energy of the Tang while becoming more intensely and perhaps more narrowly Chinese. The preconditions for the rich Song culture were a rising economy, an increase in the number of schools and higher literacy, and the spread of printing. Song culture was less aristocratic, less cosmopolitan, and more closely associated with the officials and the scholar-gentry, who were both its practitioners and its patrons. It also was less Buddhist than the Tang had been. Only the Zen (Chan) sect kept its vitality, and many Confucians were out-

An Elegant Song Dynasty Wine Pot with green celadon glaze (24.8 cm high). Ewer with carved flower sprays. Porcelain with molded and carved low-relief decoration in grayish-green glaze approx. 1000–12000. Northern Song Dynasty (960–1127) H. 9 5/8 in × W. 5 1/4 in × D. 7 3/4 in, H. 24.5 cm × W. 13.4 cm × D. 19.7 cm. China; Shaanxi province. © Gift of The Asian Art Museum Foundation.

spokenly anti-Buddhist and anti-Daoist. In sum, the secular culture of officials that had been a sidestream in the Tang broadened and became the mainstream during the Song.

Chinese consider the Song dynasty as the peak of their traditional culture. It was, for example, China's greatest age of pottery and porcelains. High-firing techniques were developed, and kilns were established in every area. There was a rich variety of beautiful glazes. The shapes were restrained and harmonious. Song pottery, like nothing produced in the world before it, made ceramics a major art form in East Asia. It was also an age of great historians. Sima Guang (1019–1086) wrote *A Comprehensive Mirror for Aid in Government*, which treated not a single dynasty but all Chinese history. His work was more sophisticated than previous histories in that it included a discussion of documentary sources and an explanation of why he chose to rely on one source rather than another. The greatest achievements of the Song, however, were in philosophy, poetry, and painting. (See Document, "Chaste Woman" Shi.")

Philosophy   The Song was second only to the Zhou as a creative age in philosophy. A series of original thinkers culminated in the towering figure of Zhu Xi (1130–1200). Zhu Xi studied Daoism and Buddhism in his youth, along with Confucianism. A brilliant student, he passed the metropolitan examination at the age of eighteen. During his thirties he focused his attention on Confucianism, deepening and making more systematic its social and political ethics by joining to it certain Buddhist and native metaphysical elements. As a consequence, the new Confucianism became a viable alternative to Buddhism for Chinese intellectuals. Zhu Xi became famous as a teacher at the White Deer Grotto Academy, and his writings were widely distributed. Before the end of the Song, his Confucianism had become the standard interpretation used in the civil service examinations, and it remained so until the twentieth century.

If we search for comparable figures in other traditions, we might pick Saint Thomas Aquinas (1224–1274) of medieval Europe or the Islamic theologian al-Ghazali (1058–1111), each of whom produced a new synthesis or worldview that lasted for centuries. Aquinas combined Aristotle and Latin theology just as Zhu Xi combined Confucian philosophy and metaphysical notions from other sources. Because Zhu Xi used terms such as the "great ultimate" and because he emphasized a Zen-like meditation called "quiet sitting," some contemporary critics said his Neo-Confucian philosophy was a Buddhist wolf in the clothing of a Confucian sheep. This was unfair. Whereas Aquinas would make philosophy serve religion, Zhu Xi made religion or metaphysics serve philosophy. In his hands, the great ultimate (also known as "principle" or *li*) lost its otherworldly character and became a constituent of all things in the universe. Perhaps the Zhu Xi philosophy may be characterized as innerworldly.

Later critics often argued that Zhu Xi's teachings encouraged metaphysical speculation at the expense of practical ethics. Zhu Xi's followers replied that, on the contrary, his teachings gave practical ethics a systematic underpinning and positively contributed to individual moral responsibility. What was discovered within by Neo-Confucian quiet sitting was just those positive ethical truths enunciated by Confucius over 1,000 years earlier. The new metaphysics did not change the Confucian social philosophy.

Zhu Xi himself advocated the selection of scholar-officials through schools, rather than by examinations. It is ironic that his teachings became a new orthodoxy that was maintained by the channelizing effect of the civil service examinations. Historians argue, probably correctly, that Zhu Xi's teachings were one source of stability in late imperial China. Like the examination system, the imperial institution, the scholar-gentry class, and the land system, his interpretation of Confucianism contributed to continuity and impeded change. Some historians go further and say that the emergence of the Zhu Xi orthodoxy stifled intellectual creativity during later dynasties, which probably is an overstatement. There were always contending schools.

Poetry   Song poets were in awe of those of the Tang, yet Song poets were also among China's best. A Japanese authority on Chinese literature wrote:

宋徽國朱文公遺像

Song Dynasty Philosopher Zhu Xi (1130–1200). His Neo-Confucian ideas remained central down to the twentieth century.
Collection of the National Palace Museum, Taiwan, R.O.C.

Tang poetry could be likened to wine, and Song poetry to tea. Wine has great power to stimulate, but one cannot drink it constantly. Tea is less stimulating, bringing to the drinker a quieter pleasure, but one which can be enjoyed more continuously.[9]

The most famous poet of the Northern Song was Su Dungpo (1037–1101), a man who participated in the full range of the culture of his age: He was a painter and a calligrapher, particularly knowledgeable about inks; he practiced Zen and wrote commentaries on the Confucian classics; he superintended engineering projects; and he was a connoisseur of cooking and wine. His life was shaped by politics. He was a conservative, believing in a limited role for government and social control through morality. (The other faction in the Song bureaucracy was the reformers, who stressed law and an expanded governmental role.)

Passing the metropolitan examination, Su rose through a succession of posts to become the governor of a province—a position of immense power. While considering death sentences, which could not be carried over into the new year, he wrote:

New Year's Eve—you'd think I could go home early
But official business keeps me.
I hold the brush and face them with tears:
Pitiful convicts in chains,
Little men who tried to fill their bellies,
Fell into the law's net, don't understand disgrace.
And I? In love with a meager stipend
I hold on to my job and miss the chance to retire.
Do not ask who is foolish or wise;
All of us alike scheme for a meal.
The ancients would have freed them a while at New Year's—Would
I dare do likewise? I am silent with shame.[10]

Eight years later, when the reformers came to power, Su himself was arrested and spent 100 days in prison, awaiting execution on a charge of slandering the emperor. Instead, he was released and exiled. He wrote, "Out the gate, I do a dance, wind blows in my face; our galloping horses race along as magpies cheer."[11] Arriving at his place of exile, he reflected:

Between heaven and earth I live,
One ant on a giant grindstone,
Trying in my petty way to walk to the right
While the turning of the mill wheel takes me endlessly left.
Though I go the way of benevolence and duty,
I can't escape from hunger and cold.[12]

But exile was soon turned to art. He farmed a plot of land at the "eastern slope" from which he took his literary name, Dungpo. Of his work there, he wrote:

A good farmer hates to wear out the land;
I'm lucky this plot was ten years fallow.
It's too soon to count on mulberries;
My best bet is a crop of wheat.
I planted seed and within the month
Dirt on the rows was showing green.
An old farmer warned me,
Don't let seedlings shoot up too fast!
If you want plenty of dumpling flour
Turn a cow or sheep in here to graze.
Good advice—I bowed my thanks;
I won't forget you when my belly's full.[13]

After 1086 the conservatives regained control of the government, and Su resumed his official career. In 1094 another shift occurred, and Su was again exiled to the distant southern

---

[9] Kojiro Yoshikawa, *An Introduction to Sung Poetry*, trans. by Burton Watson (Cambridge: Harvard University Press, Harvard-Yenching Institute Monograph Series, 1967), p. 37.

[10] Yoshikawa, p. 119.
[11] Yoshikawa, p. 117.
[12] Yoshikawa, p. 105.
[13] Yoshikawa, pp. 119–120.

DOCUMENT **Su Dungpo Imagined on a Wet Day, Wearing a Rain Hat and Clogs**

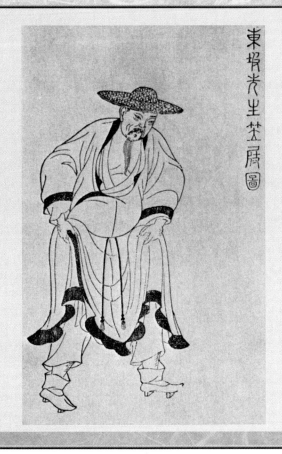

After Su's death, a disciple wrote these lines.

◆ How does the sentiment in this poem relate to the Confucian humanism encountered in the document in Chapter 2?

When with tall hat and firm baton he stood in council,
The crowds were awed at the dignity of the statesman in
    him.
But when in cloth cap he strolled with cane and sandals,
He greeted little children with gentle smiles.

From *An Introduction to Sung Poetry*, by Kojiro Yoshikawa, trans. by Burton Watson (Cambridge, MA: Harvard University Press). Copyright © 1967 by the Harvard-Yenching Institute, Monograph Series, poem, p. 122, illustration located on unnumbered page opposite p. 65. Reprinted by permission of Harvard-Yenching Institute.

island of Hainan. After still another shift, Su was on his way back to the capital when he died, in 1101. (See Document, "Su Dungpo Imagined on a Wet Day, Wearing a Rain Hat and Clogs.")

Painting In the West, penmanship and painting are quite separate, one merely a skill and the other esteemed as an art. In China, calligraphy and painting were equally appreciated and were seen as related. A scholar spent his life with brush in hand. The same qualities of line, balance, and strength needed for calligraphy carried over to painting. Chinese calligraphy is immensely pleasing even to the untutored Western eye, and it is not difficult to distinguish between the elegant strokes of Huineng, the last emperor of the Northern Song, and the powerful brushwork of the Zen monk Zhang Jizhi.

Song painting was varied—of birds or flowers; of fish or insects; of horses, monkeys, or water buffalo; of scholars, emperors, Buddhas, or Daoist immortals. But its crowning achievement was landscapes. Song landscapes are different from those of the West. Each stroke of the brush on silk or paper was final. Mistakes could not be covered up. Each element of a painting was presented in its most pleasing aspect; the painting was not constrained by single-point perspective. Paintings had no single source of illumination with light and shadow but contained an overall diffusion of light. Space was an integral part of the painting. A typical painting might have craggy rocks or twisted pine trees in the foreground, then mist or clouds or rain to create distance, and in the background the outlines of mountains or cliffs fading into space. If the painting contained human figures at all, they were small in a natural universe that was very large. Chinese painting thus reflected the same worldview as Chinese philosophy or poetry. The painter sought to grasp the inner reality of the scene and not be bound up in surface details.

In paintings by monks or masters of the Zen school, the presentation of an intuitive vision of an inner reality became even more pronounced. Paintings of Bodhidharma, the legendary founder of the Zen sect, are often dominated by a single powerful downstroke of the brush, defining the edge of his robe. Paintings of patriarchs tearing up sutras or sweeping dust with a broom from the mirror of the mind are almost as calligraphic as paintings of bamboo. A Yuan dynasty painting in the style of Shi Ke shows the figure of a monk or sage who is dozing or meditating. A Zen "broken ink" landscape might contain rocks, water, mountains, and clouds, each represented by a few explosive strokes of the brush.

China in the Mongol World Empire: The Yuan Dynasty (1279–1368)

The Mongols created the greatest empire in the history of the world. It extended from the Caspian Sea to the Pacific Ocean; from Russia, Siberia, and Korea in the north to Persia and Burma in the south. Invasion fleets were even sent to Java and Japan, although without success. Mongol rule in China is one chapter of this larger story.

RISE OF THE MONGOL EMPIRE

The Mongols, a nomadic people, lived to the north of China on grasslands where they raised horses and herded sheep. They lived in felt tents called yurts—they sometimes called themselves "the people of the felt tents." Women performed much of the work and were freer and more easygoing than women in China. Families belonged to clans and related clans to tribes. Tribes would gather during the annual migration from the summer plains to winter pasturage. Chiefs were elected, most often from noble lineages, for their courage, military prowess, judgment, and leadership. Like Manchu or Turkic, the Mongol tongue was Altaic.

The Mongols believed in nature deities and in the sky god above all others. Sky blue was their sacred color. They communicated with their gods through religious specialists called *shamans.* Politically divided, they traded and warred among themselves and with settled peoples on the borders of their vast grassland domains.

The founder of the Mongol Empire, Temujin, was born in 1167, the son of a tribal chief. While Temujin was still a child, his father was poisoned. He fled and after wandering for some years, returned to the tribe, avenged his father, and in time became chief himself. Through his shrewd policy of alliances and remarkable survival qualities, by the time he was forty, he had united all Mongol tribes and had been elected their great khan, or ruler. It is by the title *Genghis* (also spelled *Jenghiz* or *Chinggis) Khan* that he is known to history. Genghis possessed an extraordinary charisma, and his sons and grandsons also became wise and talented leaders. Why the Mongol tribes, almost untouched by the higher civilizations of the world, should have produced such leaders at this point in history is difficult to explain.

A second conundrum is how the Mongols, who numbered only about 1.5 million, created the army that conquered vastly denser populations. Part of the answer is institutional. Genghis

organized his armies into "myriads" of 10,000 troops, with decimal subdivisions of 1,000, 100, and 10. Elaborate signals were devised so that in battle, even large units could be manipulated like the fingers of a hand. Mongol tactics were superb: Units would retreat, turn, flank, and destroy their enemies. The historical record makes amply clear that Genghis's nomadic cavalry had a paralytic effect on the peoples they encountered. The Mongols were peerless horsemen, and their most dreaded weapon was the compound bow, short enough to be used from the saddle yet more powerful than the English longbow.

They were astonishingly mobile. Each man carried his own supplies. Trailing remounts, they covered vast distances quickly. In 1241, for example, a Mongol army had reached Hungary, Poland, and the shore of the Adriatic and was poised for a further advance into Western Europe. But when word arrived of the death of the great khan, the army turned and galloped back to Mongolia to help choose his successor.

When this army encountered walled cities, it learned the use of siege weapons from the enemies it had conquered. Chinese engineers were used in campaigns in Persia. The Mongols also used terror as a weapon. Inhabitants of cities that refused to surrender in the Near East and China were put to the sword. Large areas in north China and Sichuan were devastated and depopulated. Descriptions of the Mongols by those whom they conquered dwell on their physical toughness and pitiless cruelty.

But the Mongols had strengths that went beyond the strictly military. Genghis opened his armies to recruits from the Uighur Turks, the Manchus, and other nomadic peoples. As long as they complied with the military discipline demanded of his forces, they could participate in his triumphs. In 1206 Genghis promulgated laws designed to prevent the normal wrangling and warring between tribes that would undermine his empire. Genghis also obtained thousands of pledges of personal loyalty from his followers, and he appointed these "vassals" to command his armies and staff his government. This policy gave his forces an inner coherence that countered the divisive effect of tribal loyalties.

The Mongol conquests were all the more impressive in that, unlike the earlier Arab expansion, they lacked the unifying force of religious zeal. To be sure, at an assembly of chiefs in 1206, an influential shaman revealed that it was the sky god's will that Genghis conquer the world. Yet other unabashedly frank words attributed to Genghis may reveal a truer image of what lay behind the Mongol drive to conquest: "Man's highest joy is in victory: to conquer one's enemies, to pursue them, to deprive them of their possessions, to make their beloved weep, to ride on their horses, and to embrace their wives and daughters." [14]

[14] J. K. Fairbank, E. O. Reischauer, and A. M. Craig, *East Asia, Tradition and Transformation* (Boston: Houghton Mifflin, 1973), p. 164.

⚑ **Kublai Khan.** Wearing ermine coat, the Mongol emperor sits on a
horse amongst Mongol warriors at the hunt.
National Palace Museum, Taiwan, R.O.C.

Genghis divided his far-flung empire among his four sons.
Trade and communications were maintained between the
parts, but over several generations, each of the four khanates
became independent. The khanate of Chagatai was in Central
Asia and remained purely nomadic. A second khanate of the
Golden Horde ruled Russia from the lower Volga. The third
was in Persia, and the fourth, led by those who succeeded
Genghis as great khans, centered first in Mongolia and then in
China (see Map 8–4).

MONGOL RULE IN CHINA

The standard theory used in explaining Chinese history is the
dynastic cycle. A second theory explains Chinese history in terms
of the interaction between the settled peoples of China and
nomads of the steppe. When strong states emerged in China,
their wealth and population enabled them to expand militarily
onto the steppe. But when China was weak, as was more often the
case, the steppe peoples overran China. To review briefly:

1. During the Han dynasty (206 B.C.E.–220 C.E.), the most
   pressing problem in foreign relations was the Xiongnu
   Empire to the north.

2. During the centuries that followed the Han, various nomadic peoples invaded and ruled northern China.

3. The energy and institutions of these Sino-Turkic rulers of
   the northern dynasties shaped China's reunification during the Sui (589–618) and Tang (618–907) dynasties. The
   Uighur Turks also played a major role in Tang defense
   policy.

4. Northern border states became even more important during the Song. The Northern Song (960–1126) bought
   peace with payments of gold and silver to the Liao. The
   Southern Song (1126–1279), for all its cultural brilliance,
   was little more than a tributary state of the Jin dynasty,
   which had expanded into northern China.

From the start of the Mongol pursuit of world hegemony,
the riches of China were a target, but Genghis proceeded cautiously, determined to leave no enemy at his back. He first disposed of the Tibetan state to the northwest of China and then
the Manchu state of Jin that ruled north China. Mongol forces
took Beijing in 1227, the year Genghis died. They went on to
take Luoyang and the southern reaches of the Yellow River in
1234, and all of north China by 1241. During this time, the
Mongols were interested mainly in loot. Only later did Chinese
advisers persuade them that more wealth could be obtained by
taxation.

Kublai, a grandson of Genghis, was chosen as the great
khan in 1260. In 1264 he moved his capital from Karakorum
in Mongolia to Beijing. It was only in 1271 that he adopted a
Chinese dynastic name, the Yuan, and, as a Chinese ruler, went
to war with the Southern Song. Once the decision was made,
the Mongols swept across southern China. The last Song
stronghold fell in 1279.

Kublai Khan's rule in Beijing reflected the mixture of cultural elements in Mongol China. From Beijing, Kublai could
rule as a Chinese emperor, which would not have been possible in Karakorum. He adopted the Chinese custom of
hereditary succession. He rebuilt Beijing as a walled city in
the Chinese style. But Beijing was far to the north of any previous Chinese capital, away from centers of wealth and population; to provision it, the Grand Canal had to be extended.
From Beijing, Kublai could look out onto Manchuria and
Mongolia and maintain ties with the other khanates. The city
proper was for the Mongols. It was known to the West as
Cambulac, "the city (baliq) of the khan." Chinese were segregated in an adjoining walled city. The palace of the khan
was designed by an Arab architect; its rooms were Central
Asian in style. Kublai also maintained a summer palace at
Shangdu (the "Xanadu" of Samuel Taylor Coleridge's poem)
in Inner Mongolia, where he could hawk and ride and hunt
in Mongol style.

Early Mongol rule in northern China was rapacious and
exploitative, but it later shifted toward Chinese forms of government and taxation, especially in the south and at the local

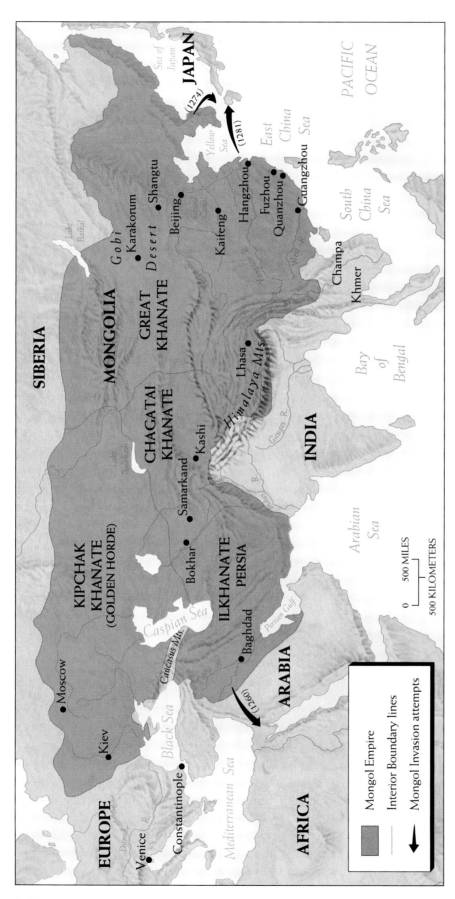

MAP 8–4 The Mongol Empire in the Late 13th Century. Note the four khanates: the Golden Horde in Russia, the Ilkhanate in Persia, Chagatai in Central Asia, and the Great Khanate extending from Mongolia to southern China.

The Journey of Marco Polo. Marco Polo and companions en route to China on the Silk Road.
Getty Images, Inc/Hulton Archive Photos.

level. Because it was a foreign military occupation, civil administration was highly centralized. Under the emperor was a Central Secretariat, and beneath it were ten "Moving Secretariats," which became the provinces of later dynasties. These highly centralized institutions and the arbitrary style of Mongol decision making accelerated the trend toward absolutism that had started during the previous dynasty.

About 400,000 Mongols lived in China during the Yuan period. For such a tiny minority to control the Chinese majority, it had to stay separate. One measure was to make military service a monopoly of Mongols and their nomadic allies. Garrisons were established throughout China, with a strategic reserve on the steppe. Military officers were always regarded as more important than civil officials. A second measure was to use ethnic classifications in appointing civil officials. The highest category was the Mongols, who held the top civil and military posts. The second category included Persians, Turks, and other non-Chinese, who were given high civil posts. The third category was the northern Chinese, including Manchus and other border peoples, and the fourth was the southern Chinese. Even when the examination system was sporadically revived after 1315, the Mongols and their allies took an easier examination; their quota was as large as that for Chinese, and they were appointed to higher offices.

The net result was an uneasy symbiosis. Chinese officials directly governed the Chinese populace, collecting taxes, settling disputes, and maintaining the local order. Few of these officials ever learned to speak Mongolian, yet without their positive cooperation, Mongol rule in China would have been impossible. The Mongols, concentrated in Beijing, large cities, and in garrisons, spoke Mongolian among themselves and usually did not bother to learn Chinese. A few exceptions wrote poetry in Chinese and painted in the Chinese style. Communication was through interpreters. When a Chinese district magistrate sent a query to the court, the ruling was made in Mongolian. (The Mongols had borrowed the alphabet of the Uighurs to transcribe their tongue.) A word-for-word translation in Chinese was written below the Mongolian and passed back down to the magistrate. As the two languages are syntactically very different, the resulting Chinese was grotesque.

FOREIGN CONTACTS AND CHINESE CULTURE

Diplomacy and trade within the greater Mongol Empire brought China into contact with other higher civilizations for the first time since the Tang period. Persia and the Arab world were especially important. Merchants, missionaries, and diplomats voyaged from the Persian Gulf and across the Indian Ocean to seaports in southeastern China. The Arab communities in Guangzhou and other ports were larger than they had been during the Song. Camel caravans carrying silks and ceramics left Beijing to pass through the Central Asian oases and on to Baghdad. Although the Mongols did not favor Chinese merchants and most trade was in other hands, Chinese trade also expanded. Chinese communities became established in Tabriz, the center of trading in western Asia, and in Moscow and Novgorod. It was during this period that knowledge of printing, gunpowder, and Chinese medicine spread to western Asia. Chinese ceramics influenced those of Persia as Chinese painting influenced Persian miniatures.

In Europe, knowledge of China was transmitted by the Venetian trader Marco Polo, who said he had served Kublai as an official between 1275 and 1292. His book, *A Description of the World*, was translated into most European languages. (See Document, "Marco Polo Describes the City of Hangzhou.") Many readers doubted that a land of such wealth and culture could exist so far from Europe, but the book excited an interest in

DOCUMENT | Marco Polo Describes the City of Hangzhou

Marco Polo was a Venetian. In 1300 Venice had a population of more than 100,000 and was the wealthiest Mediterranean city-state. But Polo was nonetheless unprepared for what he saw in China. Commenting on Hangzhou, China's capital during the Southern Song, he first noted its size (ten or twelve times larger than Venice), then its many canals and bridges, its streets "paved with stones and bricks," and its location between "a lake of fresh and very clear water" and "a river of great magnitude." He spoke of "the prodigious concourse of people" frequenting its ten great marketplaces and of its "capacious warehouses built of stone for the accommodation of merchants who arrive from India and other parts." He then described the life of its people.

♦ Europeans who read Marco Polo's account of China thought it was too good to be true. Would you agree?

Each of the ten market-squares is surrounded with high dwelling-houses, in the lower part of which are shops, where every kind of manufacture is carried on, and every article of trade is sold; such, amongst others, as spices, drugs, trinkets, and pearls. In certain shops nothing is vended but the wine of the country, which they are continually brewing, and serve out fresh to their customers at a moderate price. The streets connected with the market-squares are numerous, and in some of them are many cold baths, attended by servants of both sexes, to perform the offices of ablution for the men and women who frequent them, and who from their childhood have been accustomed at all times to wash in cold water, which they reckon highly conducive to health. At these bathing places, however, they have apartments provided with warm water, for the use of strangers, who from not being habituated to it, cannot bear the shock of the cold. All are in the daily practice of washing their persons, and especially before their meals.

In other streets are the habitations of the courtesans, who are here in such numbers as I dare not venture to report; and not only near the squares, which is the situation usually appropriated for their residence, but in every part of the city they are to be found, adorned with much finery, highly perfumed, occupying well-furnished houses, and attended by many female domestics. These women are accomplished, and are perfect in the arts of blandishment and dalliance, which they accompany with expres-sions adapted to every description of person, insomuch that strangers who have once become so enchanted by their meretricious arts, that they can never divest themselves of the impression. Thus intoxicated with sensual pleasures, when they return to their homes they report that they have been in Kin-sai [Hangzhou], or the celestial city, and pant for the time when they may be enabled to revisit paradise.

The inhabitants of the city are idolaters, and they use paper money as currency. The men as well as the women have fair complexions, and are handsome. The greater part of them are always clothed in silk, in consequence of the vast quantity of that material produced in the territory of Kin-sai, exclusively of what the merchants import from other provinces. Amongst the handicraft trades exercised in the place, there are twelve considered to be superior to the rest, as being more generally useful; for each of which there are a thousand workshops, and each shop furnishes employment for ten, fifteen, or twenty workmen, and in a few instances as many as forty; under their respective masters. The natural disposition of the native inhabitants of Kin-sai is pacific, and by the example of their former kings, who were themselves unwarlike, they have been accustomed to habits of tranquility. The management of arms is unknown to them, nor do they keep any in their houses. Contentious broils are never heard among them. They conduct their mercantile and manufacturing concerns with perfect candour and probity. They are friendly towards each other, and persons who inhabit the same street, both men and women, from the mere circumstance of neighbourhood, appear like one family. In their domestic manners they are free from jealousy or suspicion of their wives, to whom great respect is shown, and any man would be accounted infamous who should presume to use indecent expressions to a married woman. To strangers also, who visit their city in the way of commerce, they give proofs of cordiality, inviting them freely to their houses, showing them hospitable attention, and furnishing them with the best advice and assistance in their mercantile transactions. On the other hand, they dislike the sight of soldiery, not excepting the guards of the grand khan, as they preserve the recollection that by them they were deprived of the government of their native kings and rulers.

Excerpt from *The Travels of Marco Polo*, 1908, from Everyman's Library. Reprinted by permission of David Campbell Publishers, London, pp. 290–301.

geography. When Christopher Columbus set sail in 1492, his goal was to reach Polo's Zipangu (Japan).

The greatest of all Muslim travelers, the Moroccan Ibn Battuta (1304–c. 1370) traveled throughout much of the Mongol world in the fourteenth century. His observations are a rich source of information about the societies he visited. Ever curious, he had a sharp eye for detail: "The Chinese infidels eat the flesh of swine and dogs, and sell it in their markets. They are wealthy folk and well-to-do, but they make no display either in their food or their clothes."

Other cultural contacts were fostered by the Mongol toleration or encouragement of religion. Nestorian Christianity, spreading from Persia to Central Asia, reentered China during the Mongol era. Churches were built in main cities. The mother of Kublai Khan was a Nestorian Christian. Also, several papal missions were sent from Rome to the Mongol court. An archbishopric was established in Beijing; a church was built, sermons were preached in Turkish or Mongolian, and choirboys sang hymns. Kublai sent Marco Polo's father and uncle with a letter to the pope asking for 100 intelligent men acquainted with the seven arts.

Tibetan Buddhism with its magical doctrines and elaborate rites was the religion most favored by the Mongols, but Chinese Buddhism also flourished. Priests and monks of all religions were given tax exemptions. It is estimated that half a million Chinese became Buddhist monks during the Mongol century. The foreign religion that made the greatest gains was Islam, which became permanently established in Central Asia and western China. Mosques were built in the Islamic areas, in Beijing, and in southeastern port cities. Even Confucianism was regarded as a religion by the Mongols, and its teachers were exempted from taxes. But as the scholar-gentry rarely obtained important offices, they saw the Mongol era as a time of hardship.

Despite these wide contacts with other peoples and religions, the high culture of China appears to have been influenced almost not at all—partly because China had little to learn from other areas, and partly because the centers of Chinese culture were in the south, the last area to be conquered and the area least affected by Mongol rule. Also, in reaction to the Mongol conquest, Chinese culture became conservative and turned in on itself. Scholars wrote poetry in the style of the Song. New schools of painting developed, but the developments were from within the Chinese tradition, and the greatest Yuan paintings continued the style of the Song. Yuan historians wrote the official history of the dynasties that preceded it. The head of the court bureau of historiography was a Mongol, but the histories produced by his Chinese staff were in the traditional mold. As the dynasty waned, unemployed scholars wrote essays expressing loyalty toward the Song and satirizing the Mongols. Their writings were not censored: The Mongols either could not read them, did not read them, or did not care.

The major contribution to Chinese arts during the Yuan was by dramatists, who combined poetic arias with vaudeville theater to produce a new operatic drama. Performed by traveling troupes, the operas used few stage props. They relied for effect on makeup, costumes, pantomime, and stylized gestures. The women's roles were usually played by men. Except for the arias—the highlights of the performance—the dramas used vernacular Chinese, appealing to a popular audience. The unemployed scholars who wrote the scripts drew on the entire repertoire of the Song storyteller. Among the stock figures in the operas were a Robin Hood–like bandit; a famous detective-judge; the Tang monk who traveled to India; warriors and statesmen of the Three Kingdoms; and romantic heroes, villains, and ghosts. Justice always triumphed, and the dramas usually ended happily. In several famous plays the hero gets the girl, despite objections by her parents and seemingly insurmountable obstacles, by passing the civil service examinations in first place. As the examinations were not in effect during most of the Yuan, this resolution of the hero's predicament is one that looked back to the Song pattern of government. Yuan drama continued almost unchanged in later dynasties, and during the nineteenth century it merged with a form of southern Chinese theater to become today's Beijing Opera.

LAST YEARS OF THE YUAN

Despite the Mongol military domination of China and the highly centralized institutions of the Mongol court, the Yuan was the shortest of China's major dynasties. Little more than a century elapsed between Kublai's move to Beijing in 1264 and the dynasty's collapse in 1368. The rule of Kublai and his successor had been effective, but thereafter a decline set in. By then, the Mongol Empire as a whole no longer lent strength to its parts. The khanates became separated by religion and culture as well as by distance. Even tribesmen in Mongolia rebelled now and then against the great khans in Beijing, who, in their eyes, had become too Chinese. The court at Beijing, too, had never really gained legitimacy. Some Chinese officials served it loyally to the end, but most Chinese saw the government as carpetbaggers and Mongol rule as a military occupation. When succession disputes, bureaucratic factionalism, and pitched battles between Mongol generals broke out, Chinese showed little inclination to rally in support of the dynasty.

Problems also arose in the countryside. Taxes were heavy, and some local officials were corrupt. The government issued excessive paper money and then refused to accept it in payment for taxes. The Yellow River changed its course, flooding the canals that carried grain to the capital. At great cost and suffering, a labor force of 150,000 workers and 20,000 soldiers rerouted the river to the south of the Shandung Peninsula. Further natural disasters during the 1350s led to popular uprisings. The White Lotus sect preached the coming of Maitreya. Regional military commanders, suppressing the rebellions, became independent of central control. Warlords arose. The warlord who ruled Sichuan was infamous for his cruelty. Important economic regions were devastated and in part depopulated by rebellions. At the end, a rebel army threatened Beijing, and the last Mongol emperor and his court fled on horses to Shangdu. When that fell, they fled still deeper into the plains of Mongolia.

Chinese Ladies Preparing Silk.

Summary

Sui and Tang Dynasties   The Sui and Tang dynasties (589–907) reunited China's empire. Under the Tang, China expanded into Central Asia, taking control of much of the lucrative Silk Road along which trade moved to the West. Chang'an, the Tang capital, became the largest city in the world. Tang culture was rich and cosmopolitan, much influenced by its contacts with other cultures and immensely influential on the cultures of Japan, Korea and Vietnam. The Tang dynasty was also the golden age of Buddhism in China, and a variety of Buddhist sects flourished.

Song Dynasty   Under the Song dynasty (960–1279), China experienced an agricultural revolution in which large aristocratic estates worked by serfs gave way to small land holdings owned by free farmers. Advances in technology led to the invention of printing and the development of a coal and iron-smelting industry. The growth of a moncy economy encouraged the expansion of trade, both within China and with foreign countries. Song culture was particularly rich in philosophy, poetry, and painting.

The Mongols   After their unification by Genghis Khan (1167–1227), the Mongols created the greatest empire in history. The highly mobile Mongol cavalry overwhelmed Chinese armies. By 1279 the Mongols ruled all of China. But Mongol rule in China was short-lived and enjoyed only shallow Chinese support. Mongol rule in China ended in 1368.

Review Questions

1. Why could China re-create its empire—just 400 years after the fall of the Han—when Rome could not? Are there similarities between the Qin-Han transition and that of the Sui-Tang? Between Han and Tang expansion and contraction?

2. How did the Chinese economy change from the Tang to the Northern Song to the Southern Song? How did the polity change? How did China's relationships to surrounding states change?

3. What do Chinese poetry and art tell us about Chinese society? About women? What position did poets occupy in Chinese society?

4. What drove the Mongols to conquer most of the known world? How could their military accomplish the task? Once they conquered China, how did they rule it? What was the Chinese response to Mongol rule?

Key Terms

Amitabha Buddha   (p. 238)   **Censorate**   (p. 232)   **Zen**   (p. 238)

Documents CD-ROM

NOTE: *To learn more about the topics in this chapter,*
see the Suggested Readings at the end of the book.

CHAPTER 9

Japan
Early History to 1467

- Japanese Origins and the Yayoi Revolution

- Nara and Heian Japan

- Aristocratic Culture and Buddhism

- Japan's Early Feudal Age

- Buddhism and Medieval Culture

◁ A 12th-century Japanese fan. Superimposed on a painting of a gorgeously clad nobleman and his lady in a palace setting are verses in Chinese from a Buddhist sutra. The aesthetic pairing of sacred and secular was a feature of life at the Heian court. Such a fan might have been used by a figure in Sei Shōnagon's *Pillow Book*.

Tokyo National Museum.

GLOBAL PERSPECTIVE

Early Japanese History

During the first millennium C.E. the major development in world history was the spread of the civilizations that had risen out of the earlier philosophical and religious revolutions. In the West the process began with the spread of civilization from Greece to Rome, continued with the rise of Christianity and its diffusion within the late Roman Empire, and entered a third phase when the countries of northern Europe became civilized by borrowing Mediterranean culture. The spread was slow because Rome was no longer a vital center. By contrast, in East Asia the spread of civilization from its Chinese heartland was more rapid because in the early seventh century a centralized empire had been reestablished—more vital, more exuberant, and more powerful than ever before. Within the East Asian culture zone, apart from China itself, major societies developed in three regions: Vietnam, Korea, and Japan.

The peoples of all three of these areas used Chinese writing, combined indigenous and Chinese elements to create distinctive cultures and national identities, and in the premodern era went on to build independent states.

The contrast between Japan, Korea, and Vietnam and Tibet, Mongolia, and Manchuria is instructive. Japan, Korea, and Vietnam assimilated Chinese culture, and used it to forge political identities that could resist Chinese domination—just as present-day third world nations borrow western ideas to build states that are anti-western.

In contrast, Tibet, Mongolia, and Manchuria (before the Qing dynasty) were unable to assimilate Chinese culture, lacked a strong political identity, and in the modern era were swallowed up by China.

For all their political independence and unique social institutions, Vietnam and Korea absorbed increasingly large amounts of Chinese culture as the centuries passed. By the eighteenth century Korea, some say, was more Confucian than China, itself, although this is open to question. Similarly, Vietnamese law codes were essentially Chinese codes with a few minor variations. Japan, too, was powerfully influenced by suc-

cessive waves of Chinese culture, but because it was bigger, more populous, and more distant, it became the major variant to the Chinese pattern within East Asian civilization. It reflected, often brilliantly, the potentials of East Asian culture in a non-Chinese milieu.

Of particular interest to Western students are the striking parallels between the feudalism of Japan and that of northwest Europe (see Chapter 10). Both had estates with peasant-cultivators, castles, mounted warriors who wore armor and fought in the service of their lords, cultures in which the glorifications of valor and military prowess conflicted with the gentler virtues of their religions, and merchant guilds and decentralized economies. These parallels should not be surprising because both Japan and northwest Europe began as backward tribal or post-tribal societies onto which heartland cultures were grafted during the first millennium C.E.

THINK AHEAD

◆ Why did Korea, Vietnam, and Japan follow a distinctive trajectory in their relationship with China compared to other regions of east and central Asia?

◆ Why was the influence of China on the development of East Asia in the first millennium C.E. more rapid than that of Rome on the rest of Europe in the same era?

◆ Why did Japanese and northwestern European society develop along similar lines in the premodern period?

Japanese History has Three Main Turning Points, each marked by a major influx of an outside culture and each followed by a massive restructuring of Japanese institutions. The first turning point was in the third century B.C.E., when an Old Stone Age Japan became an agricultural, metalworking society, similar to those on the Korean peninsula or in northeastern Asia. This era lasted until 600 C.E.. The second turning point came during the seventh and eighth centuries, when whole complexes of Chinese culture entered Japan directly. Absorbing these, archaic Japan made the leap to a higher historical civilization, associated with the writing system, technologies, and philosophies of China, and with Chinese forms of Buddhism. Japan would remain a vital part of this civilization until the third turning point, in the nineteenth century, when it encountered the West.

Japanese Origins and the Yayoi Revolution

Japanese hotly debate their origins. New archaeological finds are front-page news. Bookstores have rows of books, often popular works, asking, Who are we and where did we come from? During the ice ages, Japan was connected by land bridges to Asia. Woolly mammoths entered the northern island of Hokkaido, and elephants, saber-toothed tigers, giant elk, and other continental fauna entered the lower islands. Did humans enter as well? Because Japan's acidic volcanic soil eats up bones, there are no early skeletal remains. The earliest evidence of human habitation is finely shaped stone tools dating from about 30,000 B.C.E. Then, from about 10,000 B.C.E., there exists pottery, the oldest in the world, and from about 8000 B.C.E., Jōmon or "cord-pattern" pottery.

Archaeologists are baffled by the appearance of pottery in an Old Stone Age hunting, gathering and fishing society—when in all other early societies it developed along with agriculture as an aspect of New Stone Age culture.

After 8,000 years of Jōmon culture, a second phase of Japanese prehistory began about 300 B.C.E. It is called the Yayoi culture, after the area in Tokyo where its distinctive hard, pale orange pottery was first unearthed. There is no greater break in the entire Japanese record than between the Jōmon and the Yayoi. For at the beginning of the third century B.C.E. the agricultural revolution, the bronze revolution, and the iron revolution—which

in the Near East, India, and China had been separated by thousands of years, and each of which singly had wrought profound transformations—burst into Japan simultaneously.

The new technologies were brought to Japan by peoples moving across the Tsushima Straits from the Korean peninsula. It is uncertain whether these immigrants came as a trickle and were absorbed—the predominant view in Japan—or whether they came in sufficient numbers to push back the indigenous Jōmon people. Physical anthropologists say that skulls from early Yayoi sites differ from those of the Jōmon.

The early Yayoi migrants, using the same seacraft by which they had crossed from Korea, spread along the coasts of northern Kyushu and western Honshu. Yayoi culture rapidly replaced that of the Jōmon as far east in Japan as the present-day city of Nagoya. After that, the Yayoi culture diffused overland into eastern Japan more slowly and with greater difficulty. Conditions were less favorable for agriculture, and a mixed agricultural-hunting economy lasted longer. The early Yayoi "frontier settlements" were located next to their fields. Their agriculture was primitive. By the first century C.E., the Yayoi population had so

Jōmon Figurine. Along with the cord-patterned pots, the hunting and gathering Jōmon people produced mysterious figurines. Is this a female deity? Why are the eyes slitted like snow goggles? Earthenware with traces of pigment (Kamegaoka type); 24.8 cm high.
Asia Society, N.Y.: Mr. and Mrs. John D. Rockefeller 3rd Collection.

expanded that wars were fought for the best land. Excavations have found extensive stone-ax industries and skulls pierced by bronze and iron arrowheads. An early Chinese chronicle describes Japan as made up of "more than one hundred countries" with wars and conflicts raging on all sides. During these wars, villages were relocated to defensible positions on low hills away from the fields. From these wars emerged a more peaceful order of regional tribal confederations and a ruling class of aristocratic warriors. Late Yayoi excavations once again reveal villages alongside fields and far fewer stone axes.

During the third century C.E. a temporary hegemony was achieved over a number of such regional tribal confederations by a queen named Pimiko. In the Chinese chronicle Pimiko is described as a shaman who "occupied herself with magic and sorcery, bewitching the people." She was mature but unmarried. "After she became the ruler, there were few who saw her. She had one thousand women as attendants but only one man. He served her food and drink and acted as a medium of communication. She resided in a palace surrounded by towers and stockades with armed guards in a state of constant vigilance."[1]

After Pimiko, references to Japan disappeared from the Chinese dynastic histories for a century and a half.

TOMB CULTURE, THE YAMATO STATE, AND KOREA

Emerging directly from Yayoi culture was an era, 300–600 C.E., characterized by giant tomb mounds. Even today these dot the landscape of the Yamato plain near present-day Osaka. The early tombs—patterned on those in Korea—were circular mounds of earth built atop megalithic burial chambers. Later tombs were sometimes keyhole shaped. The tombs were surrounded by moats and adorned with clay cylinders and statues of warriors, scribes, musicians, houses, boats, and the like. Early tombs, like the Yayoi graves that preceded them, contained mirrors, jewels, and other ceremonial objects. From the fifth century C.E. these objects were replaced by armor, swords, spears, and military trappings, reflecting a new wave of continental influences. The flow of people and culture from the Korean peninsula into Japan that began with Yayoi was continuous into historical times.

Japan reappeared in the Chinese chronicles in the fifth century C.E. This period was also covered in the earliest Japanese accounts of their own history, the *Records of Ancient Matters [Kojiki]* and the *Records of Japan [Nihongi]*, compiled in 712 and 720. These records dovetail with the evidence of the tombs. The picture that emerges is of regional aristocracies under the loose hegemony of the Yamato "great kings." Historians use the geographic label "Yamato" because the courts of the great kings were located on the Yamato plain, the richest agricul-

▲ **Japanese Tomb Painting.** In 1972, Japanese archaeologists found this painting on the interior wall of a megalithic burial chamber at Takamatsuzuka in Nara Prefecture. The most sophisticated tomb painting found in Japan, it dates to the 300–680 era and resembles paintings found in Korean and Chinese tombs.

Art Resource/Bildarchiv Preussischer Kulturbesitz.

tural region of ancient Japan. The Yamato rulers also held lands and granaries throughout Japan. The tomb of the great king Nintoku is 486 meters long and 36 meters high, with twice the volume of the Great Pyramid of Egypt. By the fifth century C.E. the great kings possessed sufficient authority to commandeer laborers for such a project.

The great kings awarded Korean-type titles to court and regional aristocrats, titles that implied a national hierarchy

CHRONOLOGY	
Early Japanese History	
8000–300 B.C.E.	Jōmon culture
Early Continental Influences	
300 B.C.E.–300 C.E.	Yayoi culture
300–680 C.E.	Tomb culture and the Yamato state
680–850 C.E.	Chinese Tang pattern in Nara and Early Heian Japan

[1] L. C. Goodrich, ed., and R. Tsunoda, trans., *Japan in the Chinese Dynastic Histories* (South Pasadena, CA: Perkins Asiatic Monographs, 1951), p. 13.

centering on the Yamato court. That regional rulers had the same kind of political authority over their populations can be seen in the spread of tomb mounds throughout Japan.

The basic social unit of Yamato aristocratic society was the extended family (*uji*), closer in size to a Scottish clan than to a modern household. Attached to these aristocratic families were groups of specialist workers called *be*. This word was of Korean origin and was originally used to designate potters, scribes, or others with special skills who had immigrated from Korea. It was then extended to include similar groups of indigenous workers and groups of peasants. Yamato society had a small class of slaves, possibly captured in wars. Many peasants were neither slaves nor members of aristocratic clans or specialized workers' groups.

What little is known of Yamato politics suggests that the court was the scene of incessant struggles for power between aristocratic families. There were also continuing efforts by the court to control outlying regions. Although marriage alliances were established and titles awarded, rebellions were not infrequent during the fifth and sixth centuries. Finally, there were constant wars with "barbarian tribes" in southern Kyushu and eastern Honshu on the frontiers of "civilized" Japan.

During the era of the Yamato court, a three-cornered military balance had emerged on the Korean peninsula between the states of Paekche in the southwest, Silla in the east, and Koguryo in the north (see Map 9–1). Japan was an ally of Paekche and maintained extensive trade and military relations with the weak southern federation known as the Kaya States.

The Paekche connection enabled the Yamato court to expand its power within Japan. Imports of iron weapons and tools gave it military strength. The migration to Japan of Korean potters, weavers, scribes, metalworkers, and other artisans increased its wealth and influence. The great cultural significance of the immigrants from Korea can be gauged by the fact that many became established as noble families. Paekche also served as a conduit for the first elements of Chinese culture to enter Japan. Chinese writing was adopted for the transcription of Japanese names during the fifth or sixth century. Confucianism entered in 513, when Paekche sent a "scholar of the Five Classics." Buddhism arrived in 538 when a Paekche king sent a Buddha image, sutras, and possibly a priest.

Eventually the political balance on the peninsula shifted. In 532 Paekche turned against Japan and joined Silla in attacking and then gobbling up the Kaya States. In 660 Silla, always hostile to Japan, defeated Paekche and unified the peninsula. But the

Terra-cotta Tomb Figurine. A clay statue of a Japanese warrior in armor from an ancient tomb. Tokyo National Museum.

rupture of ties with Korea was less of a loss than it would have been earlier, for by this time Japan had established direct relations with China.

RELIGION IN EARLY JAPAN

The indigenous religion of the Yamato Japanese was an animistic worship of the forces of nature, later given the name of **Shintō**, or "the way of the gods," to distinguish it from Buddhism. Shinto probably entered Japan from the continent as part of Yayoi culture. The underlying forces of nature might be embodied in a waterfall, a twisted tree, a strangely shaped boulder, a mountain, or in a great leader who would be worshiped as a deity after his death. Mount Fuji was holy not as the abode of a god but because the mountain itself was an upwelling of a vital natural force. Even today in Japan, a gnarled tree trunk may be girdled with a straw rope and set aside as an object of veneration. The more potent forces of nature such as the sea, the sun, the moon, the wind, and thunder and lightning became personified as deities. The sensitivity to nature and natural beauty that pervades Japanese art and poetry owes much to Shintō. See Document, "Darkness and the Cave of High Heaven.")

Throughout Japan's premodern history most villages had shamans, religious specialists who, by entering a trance, could directly contact the inner forces of nature and gain the power to foretell the future or heal sickness. The queen Pimiko was such a shaman. The sorceress is also a stock figure in tales of ancient or medieval Japan. More often than not, women, receiving the command of a god, have founded the "new" religions in this tradition, even into the nineteenth and twentieth centuries.

A second aspect of early Shintō was its connection with the state and the ruling post-tribal aristocracy. Each clan, or extended family, had its own myth centering on a nature deity (*kami*) that it claimed as its original ancestor. The clan genealogy in which the line of descent was traced was a patent of nobility and a title to political authority. The head of a clan, who was also its chief priest, made sacrifices to its deity. When Japan was unified by the Yamato court, the myths of several clans were joined into a composite national myth. The deity of the Yamato great kings was the sun goddess, so she became the chief deity, while other gods assumed lesser positions appropriate to the status of their clan.

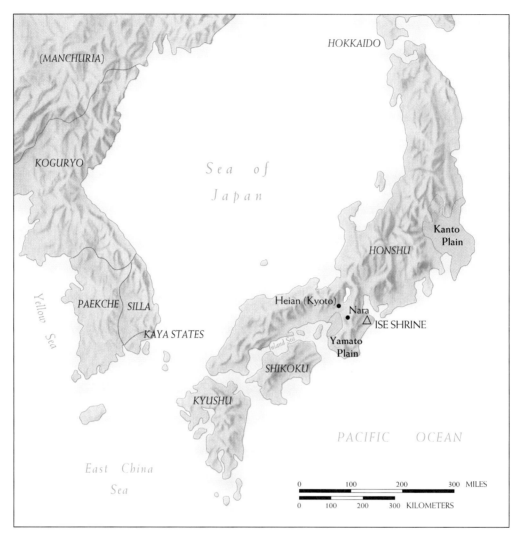

MAP 9–1 Yamato Japan and Korea (ca. 500 C.E.)   Paekche was Japan's ally on the Korean peninsula. Silla, Japan's enemy, was the state that would eventually unify Korea. (Note: Nara was founded in 710; Heian in 794.)

Had another clan won the struggle, its deity would have become paramount—perhaps a thunder god as in ancient Greece.

The *Records of Ancient Matters* and *Records of Japan* tell of the creation of Japan, of the deeds and misdeeds of gods on the "plain of high heaven," and of their occasional adventures on earth or in the underworld. In midvolume, the stories of the gods, interspersed with the genealogies of noble families, give way to stories of early emperors and early Japanese history. The Japanese emperors, today the oldest royal family in the world, were viewed as the lineal descendants of the sun goddess and as "living gods." The Great Shrine of the sun goddess at Ise has always been the most important in Japan.

Nara and Heian Japan

The second major turning point in Japanese history was its adoption of the higher civilization of China. This is a prime example of the worldwide process (described in Chapter 2) by which the heartland civilizations spread into outlying areas. In Japan the process occurred between the seventh and twelfth centuries and can best be understood in terms of three stages. During the seventh century Japanese studied China; during the eighth, they implanted Chinese institutions in Japan; after that, they adapted the institutions to meet Japanese needs. By the eleventh century the creative reworking of Chinese elements had led to distinctive Japanese forms, unlike those of China but equally unlike those of the earlier Yamato court.

COURT GOVERNMENT

The official embassies to the Tang court that began in 607 C.E. included traders, students, and Buddhist monks as well as representatives of the Yamato great kings. Like Third World students who study abroad today, Japanese who studied in China played key roles in their own government when they returned home. They brought back with them a quickening flow of technology, art, Buddhism, and knowledge of Tang legal and gov-

DOCUMENT   Darkness and the Cave of High Heaven

The younger brother of the sun goddess was a mischief-maker. Eventually the gods drove him out of heaven. On one occasion, he knocked a hole in the roof of a weaving hall and dropped in a dappled pony that he had skinned alive. One weaving maiden was so startled that she struck her genitals with the shuttle she was using and died.

◆ What does this myth suggest regarding the social relations of the Shinto gods? Entering a cave and then re-emerging signifies death and rebirth in the religions of many peoples. Compare this passage to "Mark Describes the Resurrection of Jesus" in Chapter 6.

The Sun Goddess, terrified at the sight, opened the door of the heavenly rock cave, and hid herself inside. Then the Plain of High Heaven was shrouded in darkness, as was the Central Land of Reed Plains [Japan]. An endless night prevailed. The cries of the myriad gods were like the buzzing of summer flies, and myriad calamities arose.

The eight hundred myriad gods assembled in the bed of the Quiet River of Heaven. They asked one god to think of a plan. They assembled the long-singing birds of eternal night and made them sing. They took hard rocks from the bed of the river and iron from the Heavenly Metal Mountain and called in a smith to make a mirror. They asked the Jewel Ancestor God to make a string of 500 curved jewels eight feet long. They asked other gods to remove the shoulder blade of a male deer and to obtain cherry wood from Mount Kagu, and to perform a divination. They uprooted a sacred tree, attached the string of curved jewels to its upper branches, hung the large mirror from its middle branches, and suspended offerings of white and blue cloth from its lower branches.

One god held these objects as grand offerings and another intoned sacred words. The Heavenly Hand-Strong-Male God stood hidden beside the door. A goddess bound up her sleeves with clubmoss from Mount Kagu, made a herb band from the spindle-tree, and bound together leaves of bamboōgrass to hold in her hands. Then she placed a wooden box facedown before the rock cave, stamped on it until it resounded, and, as if possessed, she exposed her breasts and pushed her skirt-band down to her genitals. The Plain of High Heaven shook as the myriad gods broke into laughter.

The Sun Goddess, thinking this strange, opened slightly the rock-cave door and said from within: "Since I have hidden myself, I thought that the Plain of Heaven and the Central Land of the Reed Plains would all be in darkness. Why is it that the goddess makes merry and the myriad gods all laugh?"

The goddess replied: "We rejoice and are glad because there is here a god greater than you." While she spoke two other gods brought out the mirror and held it up before the Sun Goddess.

The Sun Goddess, thinking this stranger and stranger, came out the door and peered into the mirror. Then the Hand-Strong-Male God seized her hand and pulled her out. Another god drew a rope behind her and said: "You may not go back further than this."

So when the Sun Goddess had come forth, the Plain of High Heaven and the Central Land of the Reed Plains once again naturally shone in brightness.

From the *Records of Ancient Matters (Kojiki)*, trans. by Albert Craig, with appreciation to Basil Hall Chamberlain and Donald L. Phillippi.

---

ernmental systems. But for Yamato Japanese, the difficulties of mastering Chinese and China's philosophical culture were enormous. Actual institutional changes using the Tang model began only in the 680s with the Emperor Temmu and his successor, the Empress Jito (r. 686–697).

Temmu's life illustrates the interplay between Japanese power politics and the adoption of Chinese institutions. He came to the throne by leading an alliance of eastern clans in rebellion against the previous great king, his nephew. The *Records of Japan* describes Temmu as "walking like a tiger through the eastern lands." He then used Chinese systems to consolidate his power. He rewarded his supporters with new court ranks and with positions in a new court government, both patterned after the Tang example. He extended the authority of the court and increased its revenues by a survey of agricultural lands and a census of their population. He promulgated a Chinese-type law code that greatly augmented the powers of the ruler. He styled himself as the "heavenly emperor," or *tennō*, which thereafter replaced the earlier title of "great king." In short, although Temmu must have admired immensely things Chinese, much of the borrowing was dictated by specific, immediate, and practical goals.

Until the eighth century the capital was usually moved each time an emperor died. Then, in 710 a new capital, intended to be permanent, was established at Nara. It was laid out on a checkerboard grid like the Chinese capital at Chang'an. But then it was moved again in 784—some say to escape the meddling in politics of powerful Buddhist temples. A final move occurred in 794 to Heian (later Kyoto) on the plain north of Nara. This site remained the capital until the move to Tokyo in 1869. Even today, Kyoto's regular geometry reflects Chinese city planning.

Prince Shōtoku (574–622). Shown here with two of his sons, he was a Buddhist and a reformer who began sending regular embassies to China in 607.
Corbis/Bettmann.

The superimposition of a Chinese-type capital on a still backward Japan produced as stark a contrast as any in history. In the villages, peasants—who worshiped the forces in mountains and trees—lived in pit dwellings and either planted in crude paddy fields or used slash-and-burn techniques of dryland farming. In the capital stood pillared palaces in which dwelt the emperor and nobles, descended from the gods on high. They drank wine, wore silk, and enjoyed the paintings, perfumes, and pottery of the Tang. Clustered about the capital were Buddhist temples, more numerous than in Nara, with soaring pagodas and sweeping tile roofs. With what awe must a peasant have viewed the city and its inhabitants!

Governments at the Nara and Heian courts were headed by emperors, who were at the same time Confucian rulers with the majesty accorded by Chinese law and Shintō rulers descended from the sun goddess. Protected by an aura of the sacred, their lineage was never usurped. It remained in place throughout the rest of Japanese history, though several emperors were killed and replaced by other family members.

Beneath the emperor, the same modified Chinese pattern prevailed. At the top was a Council of State, a powerful office from which leading clans sometimes manipulated the authority of an emperor who reigned but did not rule. Beneath the council were eight ministries—two more than in China. One of the extra ministries was a Secretariat and the other the Imperial Household Ministry. Size affected function. China had a population of 60 million; Nara Japan had 4 or 5 million. Since there were fewer people to govern in Japan and no external enemies, more of the business of court government was with the court itself. Of the 6,000 persons in the central ministries, more than 4,000 were concerned in one way or another with the care of the imperial house. The Imperial Household Ministry, for example, had an official staff of 1,296, whereas the Treasury had 305 and Military Affairs only 198.

Local government was handled by sixty-odd provinces, which were further subdivided into districts and villages. In pre-Nara times, the outlying areas had been governed in Yamato fashion by regional clans, but under the new system, provincial governors were sent out from the capital—leaving local aristocrats to occupy the lesser position of district magistrate. This substantially increased the power of the court.

In other respects, Japanese court government was unlike that of China. There were no eunuchs. There was little tension between the emperor and the bureaucracy—the main struggles were between clans. The Tang movement from aristocracy toward meritocracy was also absent in Japan. Apart from clerks and monastics, only aristocrats were educated, and only they were appointed to important official posts. Family counted for more than grades. A feeble attempt to establish an examination elite on the Chinese model failed completely.

Even during the Nara period the elaborate apparatus of Chinese government was too much. In the words of a Chinese proverb, it was like using an ax to carve a chicken. In the early Heian period the actual functions of government were taken over by three new offices outside the Chinese system:

1. *Audit officers.* A newly appointed provincial governor had to report on the accounts of his predecessor. Agreement was rare, so from the end of the Nara period audit officers were sent to examine the books. By early Heian times these auditors had come to superintend the collection of taxes and most other capital-province relationships. They tried to halt the erosion of tax revenues. But as the quota and estate systems developed, this office had less and less to do.

2. *Bureau of archivists.* This bureau was established in 810 to record and preserve imperial decrees. Eventually it took over the executive function at the Heian court, drafting imperial decrees and attending to all aspects of the emperor's life.

3. *Police commissioners.* Established in the second decade of the ninth century to enforce laws and prosecute criminals, the commissioners eventually became responsible for all law and order in the capital. They absorbed military functions as well as those of the Ministry of Justice and the Bureau of Impeachment.

Over the course of the Heian period, control of the court also shifted, though the emperor, with the power of appointments, remained the key figure.

1. Until the mid-ninth century, some emperors actually ruled or, more often, shared power with nobles of other leading clans.

2. From 856 the northern branch of the Fujiwara clan became preeminent, and from 986 to 1086 its stranglehold on the court was absolute. The private offices of the Fujiwara house were as powerful as those of the central government, and the Fujiwara family monopolized all key government posts. They controlled the court by marrying their daughters to the emperor, forcing the emperor to retire after a son was born, and then ruling as regents in place of the new infant emperor. At times they even ruled as regents for adult emperors. Fujiwara Michinaga's words were no empty boast when he said, "As for this world, I think it is mine, nor is there a flaw in the full moon." (See Document, Aristocratic Taste at the Fujiwara Court: Sei Shōnagon Records Her Likes and Dislikes.)

3. Fujiwara rule gave way, during the second half of the eleventh century, to rule by retired emperors. The imperial family and lesser noble houses had long resented Fujiwara domination. Disputes within the Fujiwara house itself enabled Emperor Shirakawa to regain control of the government. He reigned from 1072 to 1086 and then, abdicating at the age of thirty-three, ruled for forty-three years as retired emperor. After his death another retired emperor continued in the same pattern until 1156. Shirakawa set up offices in his quarters not unlike the private offices of the Fujiwara family. He appointed talented non-Fujiwara nobles to government posts and sought to reduce the number of tax-free estates by confiscating those of the Fujiwara. He failed in this and instead garnered huge estates for the imperial family. He also developed strong ties to regional military leaders and great temples. His sense of his own power was reflected in his words—more a lament than a boast: "The only things that do not submit to my will are the waters of the Kamo River, the roll of the dice, and the mountain-monks [of the Tendai temple on Mount Hiei to the northeast of Kyoto]." But Shirakawa's powers were exercised in a capital city that was increasingly isolated from the changes in outlying regions, and even the city itself was plagued by fires, banditry, and a sense of impending catastrophe.

LAND AND TAXES

The last embassy to China was in 839. By that time the frenetic borrowing of Chinese culture had slowed. The Japanese had taken in all they needed—or, perhaps, all they could handle—and were sufficiently self-confident to use Chinese ideas in innovative and flexible ways. The 350 years that followed until the end of the twelfth century were a time of assimilation and evolutionary change. Nowhere was this more evident than in the tax system.

In Nara and early Heian Japan, the economy was agricultural. The problem was to find labor to work the extensive landholdings of the government, imperial family, nobles, and temples. The solution—using the inappropriately named equal field system of China—was to distribute land to all ablebodied persons and collect from them three taxes: a light tax of grain, a light tax of cloth or other local products, and a heavy tax of labor service. But to tax persons meant knowing how many there were and where they were, and this necessitated elaborate population and land registers. Even in China, despite its sophisticated bureaucracy, the system broke down. In Japan, the marvel is that it could be carried out at all. Old registers and recent aerial photographs suggest that for a time it was, at least in western Japan. Its implementation speaks of the immense energy and ability of the early Japanese, who so quickly absorbed Chinese administrative techniques.

Whenever changes in a society are legislated or imposed from above, the results tend to be uniform. But when changes occur willy-nilly within a society, the results are usually messy and difficult to comprehend. The evolution of taxation in Heian Japan was of the second type.

One big change was from the equal field system to one of tax quotas payable in grain. Unable to maintain the elaborate records needed for the equal field system, court officials simply gave each governor a quota of taxes to collect from his province, and each governor, in turn, gave quotas to the district magistrates. Governors and magistrates, when they could, collected more than their quotas and pocketed the difference for themselves. By this means court nobles appointed as governors restored their family fortunes, while district magistrates, and the local notables and military families associated with them, transformed themselves into a new local ruling class.

CHRONOLOGY

Who Was in Charge at the Nara and Heian Courts

710–856	Emperors or combinations of nobles
856–1086	Fujiwara nobles
1086–1160	Retired emperors
1160–1180	Military house of Taira

A second change affecting about half the land in late Heian Japan was the conversion of tax-paying lands to tax-free estates. Court nobles and powerful temples did not like to pay taxes, so they used their influence at court to obtain immunities—exemptions from taxation for their lands. From the ninth century small landholders often commended their land to such nobles, figuring they would be better off as serfs on tax-free estates than as free farmers subject to taxation. The pattern of such commendations was random, resulting in estates composed of scattered parcels of land, unlike the unified estates of Europe. The noble owners of estates appointed stewards from among local notables to manage the land. The stewards took a small slice of the cultivators' surplus for themselves, and forwarded the rest to the noble or priestly owner in Kyoto. Since the stewards were from the same stratum of local society as the district magistrates, they shared an interest in upholding the local order.

Japanese Sword. From medieval times, Japanese artisans made the world's finest swords. They became a staple export to China. Worn only by samurai, they were also an emblem of class status, distinguishing them from commoners.

Philip Gatward © Dorling Kindersley.

RISE OF THE SAMURAI

During the Nara period, Japan experimented with a Chinese military system based on conscription. One third of all able-bodied men between the ages of twenty-one and sixty were taken. Conscript armies, however, proved inefficient, so in 792 the court abolished conscription and began a new system relying on local mounted warriors. Some were stationed in the capital and some in the provinces. They were official troops whose taxes were remitted in exchange for military service. The Japanese verb "to serve" is *samurau*, so those who served became **samurai**—the noun form of the verb. Then, in the mid-Heian period, the officially recruited local warriors were replaced by nonofficial private bands of local warriors. They constituted the military of Japan for the next half millennium or so, until the foot-soldier revolution of the fifteenth and sixteenth centuries.

Being a samurai was expensive. Horses, armor, and weapons were costly, and their use required long training. The primary weapon was the bow and arrow, used from the saddle. Most samurai were from well-to-do local families—district magistrates, notables, or the military families associated with them. Their initial function was to preserve local order and, possibly, to help with tax collection. But from early on they contributed at times to disorder. From the second half of the ninth century there are accounts of district magistrates leading local forces against provincial governors, doubtless in connection with tax disputes.

From the early tenth century regional military coalitions or confederations began to form. They first broke into history in 935–940, when a regional military leader, a descendant of an emperor, became involved in a tax dispute. He captured several provinces, called himself the new emperor, and appointed a government of civil and military officials. The Kyoto court responded by recruiting another military band as its champion. The rebellion was quelled and the rebel leader died in battle. That the Kyoto court could summon a military band points up the connections that enabled it to manipulate local military leaders and maintain its political control of Japan.

Other regional wars followed. Many were fought in eastern Japan—the "wild east" of those days. The east was more militarized because it was the headquarters for the periodic campaigns against the tribal peoples to the north. By the middle of the twelfth century there were regional military bands in every part of Japan.

In 1156 the rising countryside military forces intruded at the Heian court. The death of the ruling retired emperor precipitated a struggle for power between another retired emperor and the reigning emperor. Each called on a Fujiwara and a local military force for backing. The force led by Taira Kiyomori defeated the one led by a Minamoto, though it was challenged again in the Heiji War of 1159–1160. Taira Kiyomori had come to Kyoto to uphold an emperor, but finding himself in charge, he stayed to rule. His pattern of rule was not unlike that of the earlier Fujiwara: He married his daughter to the new emperor and, when a son was born, he forced the emperor to retire and ruled as the maternal grandfather. Otherwise, there were few changes: Court nobles kept their Chinese court offices. The reigning emperor, who had been supported by Kiyomori, retired and exercised control over the offices of the retired emperor and the estates of the imperial family. The head of the Fujiwara family kept the now meaningless post of regent. In short, the Taira ruled as a new stratum atop the many power centers of the old court.

Aristocratic Culture and Buddhism

If the parts of a culture could be put on a scale and weighed like sugar or flour, we would conclude that the culture of Nara and early Heian Japan was overwhelmingly one of Shintō religious practices and village folkways, an extension of the culture of the late Yamato period. The tiny aristocracy, about one tenth of 1 percent of Japan's population, was encapsulated in the routines of court life, as were Buddhist monks in the rounds of their monastic life. Most of the court culture had

In the Heiji War of 1159–1160, regional samurai bands became involved in Kyoto court politics. This is a scroll painting of the burning of the Sanjō Palace. Handscroll; ink and colors on paper, 41.3 × 699.7 cm.

"Scroll w/depictions of the Night attach on the Sanjō Palace" from Heiji monogatari emaki, 2nd half of the 13th c. Unknown. Japanese, Kamakura Period. Handscroll; ink & colors on paper .41.3 × 699.7 cm. Fenollosa-Weld C. Courtesy of Museum of Fine Arts, Boston.

only recently been imported from China. There had not been time for commoners to ape their betters or for the powerful force of indigenous culture to reshape that of the elite.

The resulting cultural gap helps to explain why the aristocrats, insofar as we can tell from literature, found commoners to be odd, incomprehensible, and, indeed, hardly human. The writings of courtiers reflect little sympathy for the suffering and hardships of the people—except in Chinese-style poetry, where such feelings were expected. When the fictional Prince Genji stoops in the novel *The Tale of Genji* to an affair with an impoverished woman, she is inevitably a princess. Sei Shō-nagon, who wrote the *Pillow Book*, was not atypical as a writer: She was offended by the vulgarity of mendicant nuns; laughed at an illiterate old man whose house had burned down; and found lacking in charm the eating habits of carpenters, who wolfed down their food a bowl at a time.

Heian high culture resembled a hothouse plant. It was protected by the political influence of the court. It was nourished by the flow of tax revenues and income from estates. Under these conditions, the aristocrats of the never-never land of Prince Genji indulged in a unique way of life and created canons of elegance and taste that are striking even today. The speed with which Tang culture was assimilated and reworked was amazing.

A few centuries after Mediterranean culture had been introduced into northwestern Europe, there appeared nothing even remotely comparable to *The Tale of Genji* or the *Pillow Book*.

CHINESE TRADITION IN JAPAN

Education at the Nara and Heian courts was largely a matter of reading Chinese books and acquiring the skills needed to compose poetry and prose in Chinese. These were daunting tasks, not only because there was no prior tradition of scholarship in Japan but also because the two languages were so dissimilar. To master written Chinese and use it for everyday written communications was as great a challenge to the Nara Japanese as it would have been to any European of the same century, but the challenge was met. From the Nara period until the nineteenth century, most philosophical and legal writings, as well as most of the histories, essays, and religious texts in Japan, were written in Chinese. From a Chinese perspective the writings may leave something to be desired. It would be astonishing if this were not the case, for the soul of language is the music of the spoken tongue. But the Japanese writers were competent, and the feelings they expressed were authentic—when not copybook exercises in the style of a Chinese master. In 883, when Sugawara Michizane wrote a poem on the death of his son, he naturally wrote it in Chinese. The poem began

Since Amaro died I cannot sleep at night;
if I do, I meet him in dreams and tears come coursing down.
Last summer he was over three feet tall;
this year he would have been seven years old.
He was diligent and wanted to know how to be a good son,
read his books and recited by heart the "Poem on the Capital."

The capital was Chang'an; the poem was one "used in Japan as a text for little boys learning to read Chinese."[2]

Japanese writings in Chinese and original Chinese works, too, shaped the Japanese cultural tradition. The late Tang poet Bo Zhuyi was widely read and appreciated, as were Du Fu and Li Bo. Despite the many differences between the two societies, Chinese history became the mirror in which Japan saw itself, its heroes and villains became the stock figures of the Japanese historical consciousness. Buddhist stories and the books of Confucianism were also consulted over the centuries for their wisdom and philosophy. The parallel might be the acceptance of such "foreign books" as the Bible and works of Plato and Aristotle in medieval and Renaissance England.

BIRTH OF JAPANESE LITERATURE

Stimulated by Chinese models, the Japanese began to compose poetry in their native tongue. The first major anthology was the *Collection of Ten Thousand Leaves (Man'yōshū)*, compiled in about 760. It contained 4,516 poems. The sentiments in the poems are fresh, sometimes simple and straightforward, but often sophisticated. They reveal a deep sensitivity to nature and strong human relationships between husband and wife, parents and children. They also display a love for the land of Japan and links to a Shintō past.

An early obstacle to the development of Japanese poetry was the difficulty of transcribing Japanese sounds. In the *Ten Thousand Leaves*, Chinese characters were used as phonetic symbols, but there was no standardization, and the transcription soon became unintelligible. In 951, when an empress wished to read it, a committee of poets deciphered the work and put it into *kana*, the new syllabic script that had developed during the ninth century. A second major anthology was the *Collection of Ancient and Modern Times*, compiled in 905. It was written entirely in *kana*.

The invention of *kana* opened the gate to the most brilliant developments of the Heian period. Most of the new works and certainly the greatest were by women, as most men were busy writing Chinese. One genre of writing was the diary or travel diary. An outstanding example was the *Izumi Shikibu Diary*, in

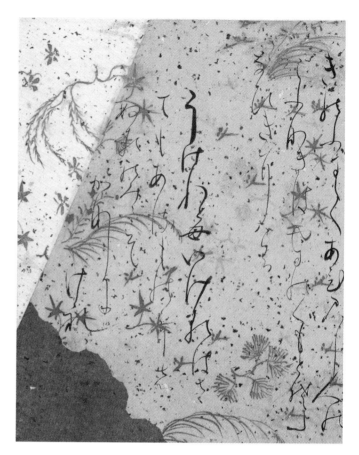

▲ **An album leaf from the Ishiyama-gire.** A (part) of a collection from the works of 36 poets compiled in the early 12th century. The poem is by Ki no Tsurayuki (868?–945?), who in the Preface to another anthology wrote: "The poetry of Japan has its roots in the human heart and flourishes in the countless leaves of words … Hearing the warbler sing among the blossoms and the frog in his fresh waters—is there any living being not given to song? It is poetry which, without exertion, moves heaven and earth, stirs the feelings of gods and spirits invisible to the eye, softens the relations between men and women, calms the hearts of fierce warriors." The calligraphy is by Fujiwara no Sadanobu (1088–1154). The poem is written on layered rice paper with gold and silver and foliage designs. Even to the untutored eye, the effect is elegant.

Calligraphy attributed to Fujiwara no Sadanobu. Album leaf from the "Ishiyama-gire." Heian, period, early 12th century. Ink with gold and silver on decorated and collaged paper, 8 × 6 3/8 in. (20.3 × 16.1 cm). Courtesy of The Freer Gallery of Art, Smithsonian Institution, Washington, D.C.

which Izumi Shikibu reveals her tempestuous loves through a record of poetic exchanges.

The greatest works of the period were by Sei Shōnagon and Murasaki Shikibu. Both were daughters of provincial officials serving at the Heian court. The *Pillow Book* of Sei Shōnagon contains sharp, satirical, amusing essays and literary jottings that reveal the demanding aristocratic taste of the early-eleventh-century Heian court, at which, as Sir George Sansom put it, "religion became an art and art a religion."[3]

---

[2] From *The Country of Eight Islands* by Hiroaki Sato and Burton Watson. Copyright © 1981 by Hiroaki Sato and Burton Watson. Used by permission of Doubleday, a division of Random House, Inc.

[3] G. Sansom, *Japan, A Short Cultural History* (New York: Appleton-Century-Crofts, 1962), p. 239.

OVERVIEW   Development of Japanese Writing

No two languages could be more different than Chinese and Japanese. Chinese is monosyllabic, uninflected, and tonal. Japanese is polysyllabic, highly inflected, and atonal. To adopt Chinese writing for use in Japanese was thus no easy task. What the Japanese did at first—when they were not simply learning to write in Chinese—was to use certain Chinese ideographs as a phonetic script. For example, in the *Man'yōshū*, the eighth-century poetic anthology, *shira-nami* (white wave) was written with 之 for shi, 良 for ra, 奈 for na, and 美 for mi. Over several centuries, these phonetic ideographs evolved into a unique Japanese phonetic script:

Original Chinese Ideograph	Simplified Ideograph	Phonetic Script (kana)
之	亨	し
良	戾	ら
奈	奈	な
美	乏	み

It is apparent in the above examples how the original ideograph was first simplified according to the rules of calligraphy and was then further simplified into a phonetic script known as *kana*. In modern Japanese, Chinese ideographs are used for nouns, verb stems, and adjectives, and the phonetic script is used for inflections and particles.

学生 は 図書館 へ 行きました Student/as for/library/to/went. (The student went to the library.)

In the above sentence, the Chinese ideographs are the forms with many strokes, and the phonetic script is shown in the simpler, cursive form.

The Tale of Genji, written by Murasaki Shikibu in about 1010, was the world's first novel. Emerging out of a short tradition of lesser works in which prose was a setting for poetry, *Genji* is a work of sensitivity, originality, and acute psychological delineation of character, for which there was no Chinese model. It tells of the life, loves, and sorrows of Prince Genji, the son of an imperial concubine, and, after his death, of his son Kaoru. The novel spans three quarters of a century and is quasi-historical in nature, although the court society it describes is more emperor-centered than was the Fujiwara age in which Murasaki lived. The book may be seen as having had a "definite and serious purpose." In one passage Genji twits a court lady whom he finds reading an extravagant romance. She is "hardly able to lift her eyes from the book in front of her." But then Genji relents and says,

> I think far better of this art than I have led you to suppose. Even its practical value is immense. Without it what should we know of how people lived in the past, from the Age of the Gods down to the present day? For history books such as the *Chronicles of Japan* show us only one small corner of life; whereas these diaries and romances, which I see piled around you contain, I am sure, the most minute information about all sorts of people's private affairs.[4]

[4] R. Tsunoda, W. T. deBary, and D. Keene, eds., *Sources of the Japanese Tradition* (New York: Columbia University Press, 1958), p. 181.

NARA AND HEIAN BUDDHISM

Buddhism came to Japan from China. The Six Sects of the Nara period each represented a separate doctrinal position within Mahayana Buddhism. Their monks trained as religious specialists in monastic communities set apart from the larger society. They studied, read sutras, copied texts, meditated, and participated in rituals. The typical monastery was a self-contained community with a Golden Hall for worship, a pagoda that housed a relic or sutra, a belfry that rang the hours of the monastic regimen, a lecture hall, a refectory, and dormitories with monks' cells.

As in China, monasteries and temples were involved with the state. In 741 the court established temples in every province to protect the state by reading sutras. Tax revenues were assigned for their support. Monks prayed for the health of the emperor and for rain in time of drought. The Temple of the Healing Buddha (Yakushiji) was built by an emperor when his consort fell ill. In China, to protect tax revenues and the family, laws limited the number of monks and nuns. In Nara Japan, where Buddhism spread only slowly outside the capital area, the same laws took on a prescriptive force: The figure that had been a limit in China became a goal in Japan. Thus the involvement of the state was patterned on that of China, but its role was more supportive.

Japan was also less culturally developed than China. Japanese came to Buddhism not from the philosophical perspectives of Confucianism or Daoism, but from the magic and mystery

DOCUMENT | Aristocratic Taste at the Fujiwara Court: Sei Shōnagon Records Her Likes and Dislikes

Here are some passages from the Pillow Book *of Sei Shōnagon, one of the masterpieces of Heian Japan.*

> ◆ In what sense can a literary work such as this also be considered a historical document? What kind of information does it provide about court life?

Elegant Things

A white coat worn over a violet waistcoat.
Duck eggs.
Shaved ice mixed with liana syrup and put in a new silver bowl.
A rosary of rock crystal.
Snow on wistaria or plum blossoms.
A pretty child eating strawberries.

Features That I Particularly Like

Someone has torn up a letter and thrown it away. Picking up the pieces, one finds that many of them can be fitted together.

A person in whose company one feels awkward asks one to supply the opening or closing line of a poem. If one happens to recall it, one is very pleased. Yet often on such occasions one completely forgets something that one would normally know.

Entering the Empress's room and finding that ladies-in-waiting are crowded round her in a tight group, I go next to a pillar which is some distance from where she is sitting. What a delight it is when Her Majesty summons me to her side so that all the others have to make way!

Hateful Things

A lover who is leaving at dawn announces that he has to find his fan and his paper. "I know I put them somewhere last night," he says. Since it is pitch dark, he gropes about the room, bumping into the furniture and muttering, "Strange! Where on earth can they be?" Finally he discovers the objects. He thrusts the paper into the breast of his robe with a great rustling sound; then he snaps open his fan and busily fans away with it. Only now is he ready to take his leave. What charmless behavior! "Hateful" is an understatement.

A good lover will behave as elegantly at dawn as at any other time. He drags himself out of bed with a look of dismay on his face. The lady urges him on: "Come, my friend, it's getting light. You don't want anyone to find you here." He gives a deep sigh, as if to say that the night has not been nearly long enough and that it is agony to leave. Once up, he does not instantly pull on his trousers. Instead he comes close to the lady and whispers what-

---

of Shintō. Its appeal, consequently, lay in its colorful and elaborate rituals, the beauty of its art, and the gods, demons, and angels of the Mahayana pantheon. The mastery of the philosophy took longer.

Another difference was in cultural identity. China's national self-consciousness had formed centuries earlier. Buddhism entered as a foreign cultural compound—China's only important borrowing from abroad prior to the nineteenth century. Though Buddhism became Sinicized and accepted, its Indian origins were understood, and the sense of it as somehow "alien" contributed to its occasional persecutions during the ninth century. In contrast, Japan's national self-awareness took shape during the Nara and early Heian periods just as the entire complex of Tang civilization—including Buddhism—entered. Buddhism was no more foreign to the Japanese than all the rest of their high culture. Consequently, there was no particular bias against it, no persecutions, and it retained its vitality longer. Not until the seventeenth or eighteenth century did a few Japanese scholars become so Confucian as to be anti-Buddhist.

During the Heian era the two great new Buddhist sects were Tendai and Shingon. The monk Saichō (767–822) had founded a temple on Mount Hiei to the northwest of Kyoto in 785, nine years before the Heian period began. He went to China as a student monk in 804 and returned the following year with the teachings of the Tendai sect (*Tiantai* in Chinese). He spread in Japan the doctrine that salvation was not solely for monastic specialists, but also for all persons who led lives of contemplation and moral purity. He instituted strict rules and a twelve-year training curriculum for novice monks at his mountain monastery. Over the next few centuries the sect grew until thousands of temples had been built on Mount Hiei. It remained a center of Japanese Buddhism until it was destroyed in the wars of the sixteenth century. Many later Japanese sects emerged from within the Tendai fold, stressing one or another doctrine of its syncretic teachings.

The Shingon sect was begun by Kūkai (774–835), who, as a youth, studied Confucianism, Taoism, and Buddhism at the court university. Deciding that Buddhism was superior, he became a monk at the age of eighteen, and in 804 he went to China with Saichō. He returned two years later bearing the Shingon doctrines and founded a monastery on Mount Koya to the south of the Nara plain and far from the new capital. Kūkai was an extraordinary figure: a bridge builder, poet, artist, and ever was left unsaid during the night. Even when he is dressed, he still lingers, vaguely pretending to be fastening his sash.

Presently he raises the lattice, and the two lovers stand together by the side door while he tells her how he dreads the coming day, which will keep them apart; then he slips away. The lady watches him go, and this moment of parting will remain among her most charming memories.

In Spring It Is the Dawn

In spring it is the dawn that is most beautiful. As the light creeps over the hills, their outlines are dyed a faint red and wisps of purplish cloud trail over them.

In summer the nights. Not only when the moon shines, but on dark nights too, as the fireflies flit to and fro, and even when it rains, how beautiful it is!

In autumn the evenings, when the glittering sun sinks close to the edge of the hills and the crows fly back to their nests in threes and fours and twos; more charming still is a file of wild geese, like specks in the distant sky. When the sun has set, one's heart is moved by the sound of the wind and the hum of the insects.

In winter the early mornings. It is beautiful indeed when snow has fallen during the night, but splendid too when the ground is white with frost; or even when there is no snow or frost, but it is simply very cold and the attendants hurry from room to room stir-

ring up the fires and bringing charcoal, how well this fits the season's mood! But as noon approaches and the cold wears off, no one bothers to keep the braziers alight, and soon nothing remains but piles of white ashes.

Things That Have Lost Their Power

A large tree that has been blown down in a gale and lies on its side with its roots in the air.

The retreating figure of a sumo wrestler who has been defeated in a match.

A woman, who is angry with her husband about some trifling matter, leaves home and goes somewhere to hide. She is certain that he will rush about looking for her; but he does nothing of the kind and shows the most infuriating indifference. Since she cannot stay away for ever, she swallows her pride and returns.

From *The Pillow Book of Sei Shōnagon*, trans. by Ivan Morris. Copyright © 1991 by Columbia University Press. Reprinted with permission of the publisher.

---

one of three great calligraphers of the period. He is sometimes credited with inventing the *kana* syllabary and with introducing tea into Japan. Shingon doctrines center on an eternal and cosmic Buddha, of whom all other Buddhas are manifestations. *Shingon* means "true word" or "mantra," a verbal formula with mystical powers. It is sometimes called esoteric Buddhism because it had secret teachings that were passed from master to disciple. In China, Shingon died out as a sect in the persecutions of the mid–ninth century, but it was tremendously successful in Japan. Its doctrines even spread to the Tendai center on Mount Hiei. Part of the appeal was its air of mystery and its complex rituals involving signs, the manipulation of religious objects, and mandalas—maps of the cosmic Buddhist universe.

During the later Heian period, Buddhism began to be assimilated. At the village level, the folk religion of Shinto took in Buddhist elements. In the high culture of the capital, Shinto was almost entirely absorbed by Buddhism. Shinto deities came to be seen as the local manifestations of universal Buddhas. The "Great Sun Buddha" of the Shingon sect, for example, was easily identified with the sun goddess. Often, great Buddhist temples had smaller Shinto shrines on their grounds. The Buddha watched over Japan and the cosmos; the

shrine deity guarded the temple itself. Not until the mid–nineteenth century was Shinto disentangled from Buddhism, and then for political ends.

Japan's Early Feudal Age

The late twelfth century marked another turning point in Japanese history. It began the shift toward rule by military houses. It saw the formation of the *bakufu* (tent government), a completely non-Chinese type of government. It saw the emergence of the *shōgun* as the *de facto* ruler of Japan—although in theory he remained a military official of the emperor. It initiated new cultural forms and changes in family and social organization.

THE KAMAKURA ERA

Taira Kiyomori's seizure of Kyoto in 1160 fell far short of being a national military hegemony, for other bands still flourished elsewhere in Japan. After Kiyomori's victory, the Taira embraced the elegant lifestyle of the Kyoto court while ties to their base area along the Inland Sea weakened. They assumed that their tutelage over the court would be as enduring as had been that of the Fujiwara. In the meantime, the Minamoto

▲ **The Hōryūji Temple.** Built by Prince Shōtoku in 607, it contains the oldest wooden buildings in the world. They are the best surviving examples of Chinese Buddhist architecture. Note the groups of visiting students in the foreground.
Susumu Takahashi/Reuters/Corbis-Bettmann.

were rebuilding their strength in eastern Japan. In 1180 Minamoto Yoritomo (1147–1199) responded to a call to arms by a disaffected prince, seized control of eastern Japan (the rich Kanto plain), and began the war that ended in 1185 with the downfall of the Taira.

Yoritomo's victory was national, for his armies had ranged over most of Japan. Afterwards, warriors from every area vied to become his vassals. Wary of the blandishments of Kyoto that had weakened the Taira, Yoritomo set up his headquarters at Kamakura, thirty miles south of present-day Tokyo, at the edge of his base of power in eastern Japan (see

Minamoto Yoritomo. Founder of the ➤ Kamakura Shogunate. He is depicted here in court robes as a statesman and official, though he was, above all, a warrior-general.
Seka Bunka Photo.

Map 9–2). He called his government the *bakufu* in contrast to the civil government in Kyoto. The offices he established were few and practical, and staffed by his vassals: one to deal with his samurai retainers, one to administer and execute his policies, and one to hear legal suits. The decisions of these offices, built up into a body of customary law, were codified in 1232 as the Jōei Code. Yoritomo also appointed military governors in each province and military stewards on the former estates of the Taira and others who had fought against him. These appointments carried the right to some income from the land. The remainder of the income, as earlier, went to Kyoto as taxes or as revenues to the owners of the estates.

When Yoritomo died in 1199, his widow and her Hōjō kinsmen moved to usurp the power of the Minamoto house. The widow, having taken holy orders after her husband's death, was

MAP ● EXPLORATION

Interactive map: To explore this map further, go to http://www.prenhall.com/craig3/map9.2

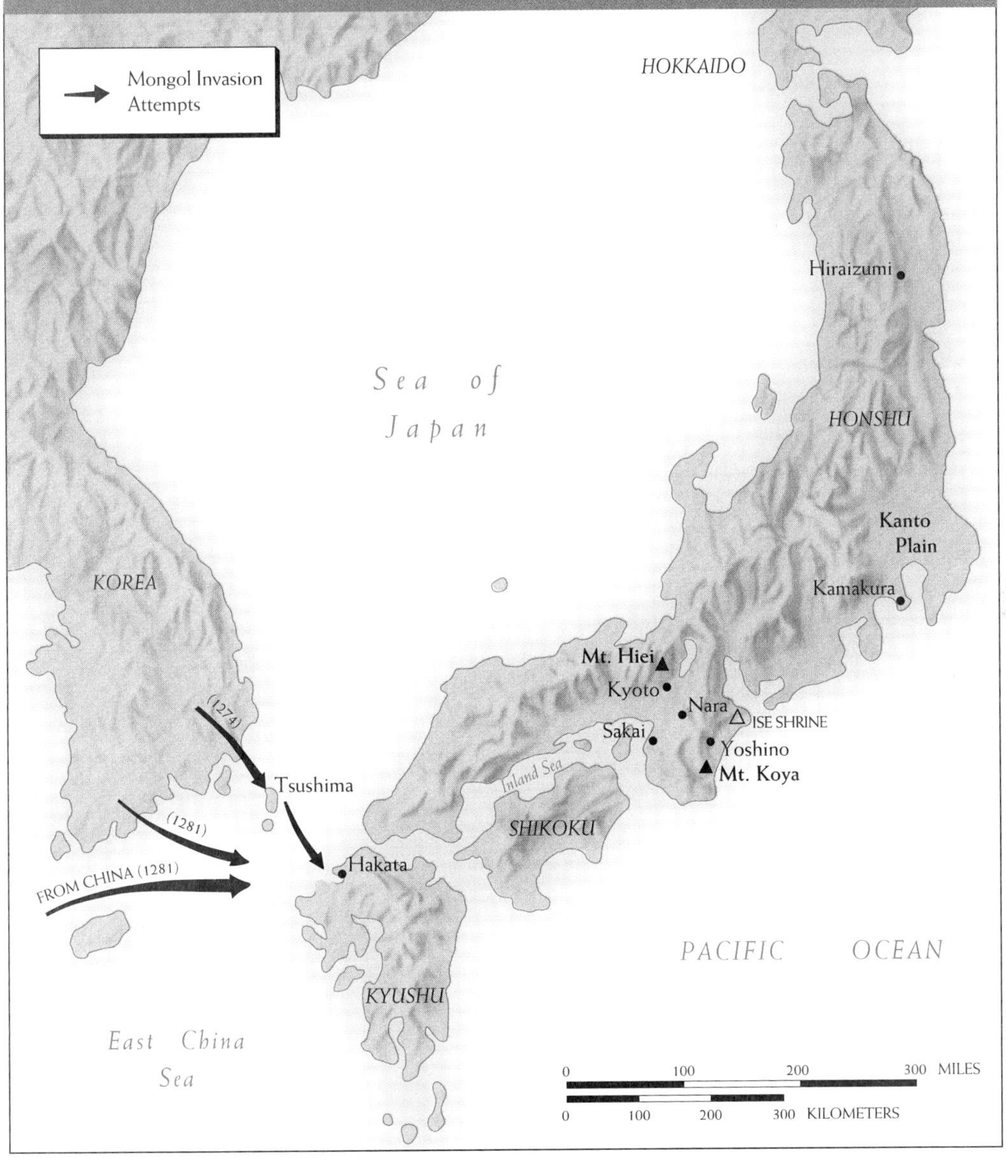

MAP 9–2 Medieval Japan and the Mongol Invasions.   The *bakufu* at Kamakura and the court at Kyoto were the two centers of power during the Kamakura period, 1185–1333. After 1336 the Ashikaga *bakufu* was established in Kyoto, absorbing the powers of the court.

known as the Nun Shōgun. One of her sons was pushed aside. The other became shōgun but was murdered in 1219. After that, the Hōjō ruled as regents for a puppet shōgun—just as the Fujiwara had been regents for figurehead emperors. The Kyoto court, trying to use the Hōjō usurpation, led an armed uprising against Kamakura in 1221, but it was quickly suppressed. New military stewards were then placed on the lands of those who had joined in the uprising.

Any society based on personal bonds faces the problem of how to transfer loyalty from one generation to another. That the Kamakura vassals fought for the Hōjō in 1221, despite the Hōjō usurpation of Minamoto rule, suggests that their loyalty had become institutional. They were loyal to the *bakufu*, which guaranteed their income from land. Their personal loyalty to the Minamoto had ended with the death of Yoritomo.

▲ **Japanese Scroll Painting.** Mongol invaders battling with an intrepid samurai horseman. Note the bomb bursting in the air at the upper right of this late 13th century Japanese scroll painting.
© Museum of Imperial Collections–Sannomaru Shozo Kan. Courtesy of the International Society for Educational Information, Inc.

The Mongols In 1266 Kublai Khan (see Chapter 8) sent envoys demanding that Japan submit to his rule. He had subjugated Korea in 1258, and his army looked outward across the Tsushima Straits. The Kyoto court was terrified, but the Hōjō at Kamakura refused to submit. The first Mongol invasion fleet arrived in 1274 with 30,000 troops, but withdrew after initial victories. The Mongols again sent envoys; this time, they were beheaded. A second invasion of 140,000 troops, an amphibious force on a scale unprecedented in world history, arrived in 1281, two years after Kublai had completed his conquest of southern China. With gunpowder bombs and phalanxes of archers protected by a forward wall of soldiers carrying overlapping shields, the Mongol forces were formidable.

The Japanese tactics of fierce individual combat were not appropriate to their foe. But a wall of stone had been erected along the curved shoreline of Hakata Bay in northwestern Kyushu, and the Mongols were held off for two months until again *kamikaze*, or "divine winds," sank a portion of their fleet and forced the rest to withdraw. Preparations for a third expedition ended with Kublai's death in 1294.

The burden of repelling the Mongols fell on Kamakura's vassals in Kyushu. Non-Kamakura warriors of Kyushu were also mobilized to fight under the command of military governors. But as no land was taken, unlike in 1221, there were few rewards for those who had fought, and dissatisfaction was rife. Even temples and shrines demanded rewards, claiming that their prayers had brought about the divine winds.

THE QUESTION OF FEUDALISM

Scholars often contend that Yoritomo's rule marks the start of feudalism in Japan. Feudalism may be defined in terms of three criteria: lord-vassal relationships, fiefs given in return for military service, and a warrior ethic. Do these apply to Kamakura Japan?

Certainly, the mounted warriors who made up the armies of Yoritomo were predominantly his vassals, not his kin. The Minamoto and Taira houses had originally been extended families, much like the Fujiwara or the earlier Yamato nobility. Yoritomo's brothers were among his generals. But after he came to power, he favored his vassals over his kin, and lateral blood ties gave way to vertical and political lord-vassal bonds. As for fiefs, the answer is ambiguous. Kamakura vassals received rights to income from land in exchange for military service, but the income was usually a slice of the surplus from the estates of Kyoto nonmilitary aristocrats. Fiefs, as such, did not appear until the late fifteenth century.

There is no ambiguity, however, regarding the warrior ethic, which had been developing among regional military bands for several centuries before 1185. The samurai prized martial qualities

CHRONOLOGY	
Government by Military Houses	
1160–1180	Taira rule in Kyoto
1185–1333	Kamakura *bakufu*
1185	Founded by Minamoto Yoritomo
1219	Usurped by Hōjō
1221	Armed uprising by Kyoto court
1232	Formation of Jōei Code
1274 and 1281	Invasion by Mongols
1336–1467	Ashikaga *bakufu*
1336	Begun by Ashikaga Takauji
1392	End of Southern Court
1467	Start of Warring States period

such as bravery, cunning, physical strength, and endurance. They gave their swords names. Their sports were hunting, hawking, and archery—loosing their arrows at the target while riding at full tilt. If military tales of the period are to be believed, their combat was often individual, and before engaging in battle warriors would call out their pedigrees. That is to say, warriors thought of themselves as a military aristocracy that practiced the "way of the bow and arrow," the "way of the bow and horse," the "way of the warriors," and so on. In the Buddhism-tinged *Tale of Heike*, a military romance recounting the struggle between the Taira and the Minamoto, a Taira general asks a vassal from eastern Japan,

> "Sanemori, in the eight eastern provinces are there many men who are as mighty archers as you are?"
>
> "Do you then consider me a mighty archer?" asked Sanemori with a scornful smile. "I can only draw an arrow thirteen handbreadths long. In the eastern provinces there are any number of warriors who can do so. There is one famed archer who never draws a shaft less than fifteen handbreadths long. So mighty is his bow that four or five ordinary men must pull together to bend it. When he shoots, his arrow can easily pierce two or three suits of armor at once. Even a warrior from a small estate has at least five hundred soldiers. They are bold horsemen who never fall, nor do they let their horses stumble on the roughest road. When they fight, they do not care if even their parents or children are killed; they ride on over their bodies and continue the battle.
>
> "The warriors of the western province are quite different. If their parents are killed, they retire from the battle and perform Buddhist rites to console the souls of the dead. Only after the mourning is over will they fight again. If their children are slain, their grief is so deep that they cease fighting altogether. When their rations have given out, they plant rice in the fields and go out to fight only after reaping it. They dislike the heat of summer. They grumble at the severe cold of winter. This is not the way of the soldiers of the eastern provinces."[5]

The Taira soldiers, according to the story, "heard his words and trembled."

The Kamakura military band thus pretty well fits our definition of feudalism. Nonetheless, qualifications are in order, as warrior bands were only a part of the whole society. One important qualification is that Kamakura Japan still had two political centers. The *bakufu* had military authority, but the Kyoto court continued the late Heian pattern of civil rule. It appointed civil governors, received tax revenues, and controlled the region about Kyoto. Noble families, retired emperors, and great Buddhist temples—in control of vast estates—also contributed to Kyoto's ongoing power. The court also remained the fount of rank and honors.

5 H. Kitagawa and B. Tsuchida, trans., *The Tale of Heike* (Tokyo: Tokyo University Press, 1975), p. 330.

After his victory in 1185, Yoritomo asked the emperor for the title of "barbarian-quelling generalissimo" (*Sei i tai shōgun*, conventionally shortened to *shōgun*). He was refused, and only after the retired emperor died in 1192 did Yoritomo get the title to match his power. Even then, the award of the title was justified because Yoritomo was a Minamoto offshoot of the imperial line.

The small size of Yoritomo's vassal band is an even more telling argument against viewing Japan as fully feudal at this time. Numbering perhaps 2,000 before 1221 and 3,000 thereafter, most of the band was concentrated in eastern Japan. But if as many as half were distributed about the rest of the country as military governors and stewards, there would have been only 100 in a region the size of Massachusetts—because Japan in 1180 was about fifteen times larger than that state. Given the difficulties of transportation and communications, how could so few have controlled such a large area? The answer is that they did not have to.

The local social order of the late Heian era continued into the Kamakura period. The Kyoto court, great temples, governors, district magistrates, and local notables—including many warriors who were not members of Yoritomo's band—functioned more or less as they had earlier. To influence the local scene, the newly appointed Kamakura vassals had to win the cooperation of the existing local power holders. In short, even if the Kamakura vassals themselves could be called feudal, they were only a thin skim on the surface of a society constructed according to older principles.

THE ASHIKAGA ERA

At times, formal political institutions seem rocklike in their stability, and history unfolds within the framework they provide. Then, almost as if a kaleidoscope had been shaken, the old institutions collapse and are swept away. In their place appear new institutions and new patterns of personal relations that, often enough, had begun to take shape within the confines of the old. It is not easy to explain the timing of such upheavals, but they are easy to recognize. One occurred in Japan between 1331 and 1336.

Various tensions had developed within late Kamakura society. The patrimony of a warrior was divided among his children. Over several generations vassals became poorer, often falling into debt. High-ranking vassals of Kamakura were dissatisfied with the Hōjō monopolization of key *bakufu* posts. In the meantime, the ties of vassals to Kamakura were weakening, while the ties to other warriors within their region were growing stronger. New regional bands were ready to emerge. The precipitating event was a revolt in 1331 by an emperor who thought emperors should actually rule. Kamakura sent Ashikaga Takauji (1305–1358), the head of a branch family of the Minamoto line, to put down the revolt. Instead he joined it, giving a clear signal to other regional lords, who threw off Kamakura's control and destroyed the Hōjō-controlled *bakufu*.

What emerged from the dust and confusion of the period from 1331 to 1336 was a new *bakufu* in Kyoto and a variety of semiautonomous regional states in the rest of Japan. Each regional state was governed by a lord, now called a *daimyo,* and a warrior band about the size of the band that had brought Yorimoto to power a century and a half earlier. The *bakufu* offices established by Ashikaga Takauji were simple and functional: a samurai office for police and military matters; an administrative office for financial matters; a documents office for land records; and a judicial board to settle disputes. They were staffed by Takauji's vassals, the most trusted vassals holding the highest posts and often holding concurrent appointments as military governors in the provinces surrounding Kyoto. The *bakufu* also appointed vassals to watch over its interests in the far north, in eastern Japan, and in Kyushu.

The pattern of rule in the outlying regions was diverse. Some lords held several provinces, some only one. Some had integrated most of the warriors in their areas into their bands. Others had several unassimilated military bands within their territories, forcing them to rely more on the authority of Kyoto. Formally, all regional lords or *daimyo* were the vassals of the shōgun. But the relationship was often nominal. Some regional lords lived on their lands; some lived in Kyoto.

The relationship between the *bakufu* and regional lords fluctuated from 1336 to 1467. At times, able lords made their regions into virtually independent states. At other times, the Kyoto *bakufu* became stronger. The third shōgun, for example, tightened his grip on the Kyoto court. He even relinquished the military post of shōgun—giving it to his son in 1394—in order to take the highest civil post of grand minister of state. He improved relations with the great Buddhist temples and Shintō shrines and established ties with Ming China. Most significant were his military campaigns, which dented the autonomy of regional lords outside of the inner Kyoto circle.

But even the third shōgun had to rely on his *daimyo* and their armies. To strengthen them for campaigns, he gave them the authority to levy taxes; unify in their own hands all judicial, administrative, and military matters in their regions; and take on unaffiliated warriors as their direct vassals. But in doing so, he left problems for his successors. As ties of personal loyalty wore thin, new local warrior bands began to form in the interstices of the Ashikaga regional states.

WOMEN IN WARRIOR SOCIETY

The Nun Shōgun was one of a long line of important women in Japan. Although historians no longer speak of an early matriarchal age, there is no denying that the central figure of Japanese mythology was the sun goddess, who ruled the Plain of High Heaven. In the late Yayoi age, the shaman ruler Pimiko was probably not an exceptional figure. She was followed by empresses during the Yamato and Nara courts, and

they in turn by great women writers in the Heian period. Under the Kamakura *bakufu,* there was only one Nun Shōgun, but daughters as well as sons of warrior families often trained in archery and other military arts. Women also occasionally inherited the position of military steward. As long as society was stable, women fared relatively well. But as fighting became more common in the fourteenth century, their position began to decline, and as warfare became endemic in the fifteenth, their status plummeted. The warrior's fief—his reward for serving his lord in battle and the lord's surety for his continuing service—had become all important. To protect it, multigeniture, in which daughters as well as sons inherited property, gave way to unigeniture, inheritance by the most able son.

AGRICULTURE, COMMERCE, AND MEDIEVAL GUILDS

Population figures for medieval Japan are rough estimates at best, but recent scholarship suggests 6 million for the year 1200 and 15 million for 1600. Much of the increase occurred during the late Kamakura and Ashikaga periods, when the country was fairly peaceful. The increase was brought about by land reclamation and improvements in agricultural technology. Iron-edged tools became available to all. New strains of rice were developed. Irrigation and diking improved. Double cropping began with vegetables planted during the fall and winter in dry fields, which were flooded and planted in rice during the spring and summer.

In the Nara and early Heian periods, the economy was almost exclusively agricultural. Japan had no money, no commerce, and no cities—apart from Nara, which developed into a temple town living on assigned revenues, and Kyoto, where taxes were consumed. Following the example of China, the government had established a mint, but little money actually circulated. Taxes were paid in labor or grain. Commerce consisted of barter transactions, with silk or grain as the medium of exchange. Artisans produced for the noble households or temples to which they were attached. Peasants were economically self-sufficient.

From the late Heian period, partly as a side effect of fixed tax quotas, more of the growing agricultural surplus stayed in local hands, though not in the hands of the cultivators. This trend accelerated during the Kamakura and Ashikaga periods, as warriors took ever larger slices of the income of estates. As this occurred, artisans detached themselves from noble households and began to produce for a wider market. Military equipment was an early staple of commerce, but gradually *sake,* lumber, paper, vegetable oils, salt, and products of the sea also became commercialized. A demand for copper coins appeared, and since they were no longer minted in Japan, huge quantities were imported from China.

During the Kamakura period, independent merchants appeared to handle the products of artisans. Some trade networks spread over all Japan. More often, artisan and merchant guilds, not unlike those of medieval Europe, paid a fee to obtain monopoly rights in a given area. Kyoto guilds paid fees to powerful nobles or temples, and later to the Ashikaga *bakufu*. In outlying areas guild privileges were obtained from the regional lords. From the Kamakura period onward, markets were held periodically in many parts of Japan, by a river or at a crossroads. Some place-names in Japan today reveal such an origin. Yokkaichi, today an industrial city, means "fourth-day market." It began as a place where markets were held on the fourth, fourteenth, and twenty-fourth days of each month. From the fifteenth century such markets were held with increasing frequency until, eventually, permanent towns were established.

Buddhism and Medieval Culture

The Nara and Heian periods are often referred to as Japan's classical age. The period that followed—say, from 1200 to 1600—is often called medieval. It was medieval in the root sense of the word in that it lay between the other two major spans of premodern Japanese history. It also shared some characteristics that we label medieval in Europe and China. However, there is one important difference. Medieval Japanese culture was a direct outgrowth of the classical age; one can even say that during the early Kamakura there was an overlap. In contrast, Europe was torn by barbarian invasions, and a millennium separated the classical culture of Rome from high medieval culture. Even to have a Charlemagne, Europe had to wait for almost half a millennium. In China, too, the era of political disunity and barbarian invasions lasted 400 years, and it was during these years that its medieval Buddhist culture blossomed.

The results of the historical continuity in Japan are visible in every branch of its culture. The earlier poetic tradition continued with great vigor. In 1205 the compilation of the *New Collection from Ancient and Modern Times (Shinkokinshū)* was ordered by the same emperor who began the 1221 rebellion against Kamakura. The flat *Yamato-e* style of painting that had reached a peak in the *Genji*

Kūja Invoking Buddha. The mid-Heian monk Kūya ➤ (903–972) preached Pure Land doctrines in Kyoto and throughout Japan. Little Buddhas emerge from his mouth.
PPS/Pacific Press Service.

Scrolls continued into the medieval era with scrolls on historical and religious themes or fairy-tale adventures. Artisanal production continued without a break. The same techniques of lacquerwork with inlaid mother-of-pearl that had been employed, say, to make a cosmetic box for a Heian court lady were now applied to produce saddles for Kamakura warriors. In short, just as Heian estates continued into the Kamakura era, and just as the authority of the court continued, so did Heian culture extend into medieval Japan.

Nonetheless, medieval Japanese culture had some distinctly new characteristics. First, as the leadership of society shifted from court aristocrats to military aristocrats, new forms of literature appeared. The medieval military tales were as different from the *Tale of Genji* as the armor of the mounted warrior was from the no less colorful silken robes of the court nobility. Second, a new wave of culture entered from China. If the Nara and Heian had been shaped by Tang culture, medieval Japan—although not its institutions—was shaped by Song culture. The link is immediately apparent in the ink paintings of medieval Japan. Third, and most important, the medieval centuries were Japan's age of Buddhist faith. A religious revolution occurred during the Kamakura period and deepened during the Ashikaga.

JAPANESE PIETISM: PURE LAND AND NICHIREN BUDDHISM

Among the doctrines of the Heian Tendai sect was the belief that the true teachings of the historical Buddha had been lost and that salvation could be had only by calling on the name of Amida, the Buddha who ruled over the Western Paradise, or **Pure Land**. During the tenth and eleventh centuries, itinerant preachers began to spread Pure Land doctrines and practices beyond the narrow circles of Kyoto. Kūya (903–972), the "saint of the marketplace," for example, preached not only in Kyoto and throughout the provinces, but also even to the aboriginal Ainu in northernmost Japan.

The doctrine that the world had fallen on evil times and that only faith would suffice was given credence by earthquakes, epidemics, fires, and banditry in the capital, as well as wars throughout the land. The deepening Buddhist coloration of the age can be read in the opening lines of the thirteenth-century *Tale of Heiki*, written just two centuries after the *Tale of Genji* and the *Pillow Book*.

The sound of the bell of Jetavana echoes the impermanence of all things. The hue of the flowers of the teak-tree declares that they who flourish must be brought low. Yea, the proud ones are but for a moment, like an evening dream in springtime. The mighty are destroyed at the last, they are but as the dust before the wind.[6]

Two early Kamakura figures stand out as religious geniuses who experienced the truth of Pure Land Buddhism within themselves. Hōnen (1133–1212) was perhaps the first to say that the invocation of the name of Amida alone was enough for salvation and that only faith, not works or rituals, counted. These claims brought Hōnen into conflict with the older Buddhist establishment and marked the emergence of Pure Land as a separate sect. After Hōnen came Shinran (1173–1262), who taught that even a single invocation in praise of Amida, if done with perfect faith, was sufficient for salvation. But perfect faith was a gift from Amida and could not be obtained by human effort. Shinran taught that pride was an obstacle to purity of heart. One of his most famous sayings is "If even a good man can be reborn in the Pure Land, how much more so a wicked man."[7] Shinran is saying that the wicked man is less inclined to assume that he is the source of his own salvation and therefore more apt to place his complete trust in Amida.

Shinran's emphasis on faith alone led him to break with many of the practices of earlier Buddhism. He ate meat, he married a nun—thereafter the Pure Land sect had a married clergy—and he taught that all occupations were equally "heavenly" if performed with a pure heart. Exiled from Kyoto, he traveled about Japan establishing "True Pure Land" congregations. (When the Jesuits arrived in Japan in the sixteenth century, they called this sect "the devil's Christianity.")

As a result of a line of distinguished teachers after Shinran, its doctrinal simplicity, and its reliance on piety, Pure Land Buddhism became the dominant form of Buddhism in Japan and remains so today. It was also the only sect in medieval Japan—apart from the Tendai sect on Mount Hiei—to develop political and military power. As a religion of faith, it developed a strong church as a protection for the saved while they were still in this world. As peasants became militarized during the fifteenth century, some Pure Land village congregations created self-defense forces. At times they rebelled against feudal lords. In one instance, Pure Land armies ruled the province of Kaga for over a century. These congregations were smashed during the late sixteenth century, and the sect depoliticized.

A second devotional sect was founded by Nichiren (1222–1282), who believed that the Lotus Sutra perfectly embodied the teachings of the Buddha. He instructed his adherents to chant, over and over, "Praise to the Lotus Sutra of the Wondrous Law," usually to the accompaniment of rapid drumbeats. Like the repetition of "Praise to the Amida Buddha" in the Pure Land sect or comparable verbal formulas in other religions around the world, the chanting optimally induced a state of religious rapture. The goal of an internal spiritual transformation was common to both the devotional and the meditative sects of Buddhism. Nichiren was remarkable for a Buddhist in being both intolerant and nationalistic. He blamed the ills of his age on rival sects and asserted that only his sect could protect Japan. He predicted the Mongol invasions, and his sect claimed credit for the "divine winds" that sank the Mongol fleets. Even his adopted Buddhist name, the Sun Lotus, combined the character for the rising sun of Japan with that of the flower that had become the symbol of Buddhism.

ZEN BUDDHISM

Meditation had long been a part of Japanese monastic practice. Zen teachings and meditation techniques were introduced by monks returning from study in Song China. Eisai (1141–1215) brought back the teachings of the Rinzai sect in 1191 and Dōgen (1200–1253) the Sōtō teachings in 1227. Eisai's sect was patronized by the Hojo rulers in Kamakura and the Ashikaga in Kyoto. Dōgen established his sect on Japan's western coast, far from centers of political power.

Zen was a religion of paradox. (See Document, Hakuin's Enlightenment.) Its monks were learned, yet it stressed a return to ignorance, to the uncluttered "original mind," attained in a flash of intuitive understanding. Zen was punctiliously traditional, the most Chinese of Japanese medieval sects. The authority of the Zen master over his pupil-monks was absolute. Yet Zen was also iconoclastic. Its sages were depicted in paintings as tearing up sutras to make the point that it is religious experience and not words that count. Within a rigidly structured monastic regimen, a vital give-and-take occurred as monks tested their understanding, gained through long hours of meditation, in encounters with their master. Buddhism stressed compassion for all sentient beings, yet in Japan the Zen sect included many samurai whose duty it was to kill the enemies of their lord. Some military leaders encouraged the practice of Zen among their retainers in the hope of reinforcing such a sense of duty; a handful of Hōjō and Ashikaga rulers even went so far as to practice Zen themselves.

Zen influenced the arts of medieval Japan. (See Document, The Arts and Zen Buddhism.) The most beautiful gardens were in Zen temples, many designed by Zen masters. The most famous, at Ryōanji, consists of fifteen rocks set in white sand. Others only slightly less austere contain moss, shrubs, trees, ponds, and streams. With these elements and within a small compass, rocks become cliffs, raked sand becomes rivers or the sea, and a little world of nature emerges. If a garden may be said to possess philosophic stillness, the Zen gardens of Daitokuji and other Kyoto temples have it.

Zen monks, such as Josetsu, Shūbun (ca. 1415), and Sesshū (1420–1506), number among the masters of ink painting in East

---

[6] A. L. Sadler, trans., *The Tenfoot Square Hut and Tales of the Heike* (Rutland, VT, and Tokyo: Charles E. Tuttle, 1972), p. 22.

[7] Tsunoda, deBary, and Keene, p. 217.

DOCUMENT   The Arts and Zen Buddhism

Zen Buddhism in Japan developed a theory of art that influenced every department of high medieval culture. Put simply, the theory is that intuitive action is better than conscious, purposive action. The best painter is one so skilled that he no longer needs to think of technique but paints as a natural act. Substitute a sword for a brush, and the same theory applies: A warrior who has to stop to consider his next move is at a disadvantage in battle. To this concern with direct, intuitive action is added the Zen distinction between the deluded mind and the "original mind." The latter is also referred to as the "no mind," or the mind in the enlightened state. The highest intuitive action proceeds from such a state of being. This theory was applied, in time, to the performance of the actor, the skill of the potter, archery, flower arrangement, and the tea ceremony. Compare the following two passages, one by Zeami (1363–1443), the author of many Nō plays, and the other by Takuan Sōhō (1573–1645), a famous Zen master of the early Tokugawa era (see Chapter 19).

♦ Could the same theory be applied to baseball or any other sport? If so, what effect would this have on how they are played?

1

Sometimes spectators of the Nō say, "The moments of 'no-action' are the most enjoyable." This is an art which the actor keeps secret. Dancing and singing, movements and the different types of miming are all acts performed by the body. Moments of "no-action" occur in between. When we examine why such moments without actions are enjoyable, we find that it is due to the underlying spiritual strength of the actor which unremittingly holds the attention. He does not relax the tension when the dancing or singing come to an end or at intervals between the dialogue and the different types of miming, but maintains an unwavering inner strength. This feeling of inner strength will faintly reveal itself and bring enjoyment. However, it is undesirable for the actor to permit this inner strength to become obvious to the audience. If it is obvious, it becomes an act, and is no longer "no-action." The actions before and after an interval of "no-action" must be linked by entering the state of mindlessness in which one conceals even from oneself one's intent. This, then, is the faculty of moving audiences, by linking all the artistic powers with one mind.

2

Where should a swordsman fix his mind? If he puts his mind on the physical movement of his opponent, it will be seized by the movement; if he places it on the sword of his opponent, it will be arrested by the sword; if he focuses his mind on the thought of striking his opponent, it will be carried away by the very thought; if the mind stays on his own sword, it will be captured by his sword; if he centers it on the thought of not being killed by his opponent, his mind will be overtaken by this very thought; if he keeps his mind firmly on his own or on his opponent's posture, likewise, it will be blocked by them. Thus the mind should not be fixed anywhere.

1. From *Sources of Japanese Tradition*, trans. by William Theodore de Bary. Copyright © 1958 by Columbia University. Reprinted with permission of the publisher.

2. From *The Buddhist Tradition* by William Theodore de Bary. Copyright © 1969 by William Theodore de Bary. Reprinted by permission of Random House Inc.

Asia. One painting by Josetsu shows a man trying to catch a catfish with a gourd. Like the sound of one hand clapping, the impossibility of catching a catfish with a gourd presents as art the kind of logical conundrum used to expound Zen teachings. Sesshū painted in both the broken-ink style, in which splashlike brush strokes represent an entire mountain landscape, and a more usual calligraphic style. Because the artist's creativity itself was seen as grounded in his experience of meditation, a painting of a waterfall or a crow on a leafless branch in late fall was viewed as no less religious than a painting of the mythic Zen founder Bodhidharma.

NŌ PLAYS

Another vital product of Ashikaga culture is the Nō play, a kind of mystery drama without parallels elsewhere in East Asia. The form has survived to the present day as the world's oldest living dramatic tradition. The play is performed on an almost square, bare wooden stage (usually outdoors) by male actors wearing robes of great beauty and carved, painted masks of enigmatic expressions. Many such masks and robes number among Japan's national treasures. The text is chanted by actors and a chorus to the accompaniment of flute and drums. The language is poetic. The action is slow and highly stylized: Circling about the stage can represent a journey, and a vertical motion of the hand, the reading of a letter. At a critical juncture in most plays, the protagonist is possessed by the spirit of another and performs a dance. (Spirit possession was commonplace in Japanese folk religion and also occurred in the *Tale of Genji*.) Several plays are shown in a single performance; comic skits called "Crazy Words" are usually interspersed between them to break the tension.

Nō plays reveal a medley of themes present in medieval culture. Some pivot on incidents in the struggle between the Taira and the Minamoto. Some are religious: A cormorant fisher is saved from the king of hell for having given lodging to a priest. Some dramatize incidents from the *Tale of Genji* or the Heian court: The famous Heian beauty and poet Ono no Komachi is possessed by the spirit of a lover she has spurned; their conflict is left to be resolved in a Buddhist afterlife. Buddhist ideas of impermanence, of this world as a place of suffering, and of the need to

DOCUMENT | Hakuin's Enlightenment

Hakuin (1686–1769) was a poet, painter, and Zen master. He wrote in colloquial Japanese as well as in Chinese. He illustrated the continuing power of the Zen tradition in postmedieval times. The following passages are from an autobiographical account of his spiritual quest. The first follows a recounting of his disappointments and failures and tells of his initial enlightenment. His teacher did not accept this as adequate, however. The second passage tells of his experience eight years later.

♦ Compare these passages to "The Bodhisattva Ideal" in Chapter 10.

1

In the spring of my twenty-fourth year, I was painfully struggling at the Eiganji in the province of Echigo. I slept neither day nor night, forgetting either to eat or sleep. A great doubt suddenly possessed me, and I felt as if frozen to death in the midst of an icy field extending thousands of *li*. A sense of an extraordinary purity permeated my bosom. I could not move. I was virtually senseless. What remained was only "*Mu.*" Although I heard the master's lectures in the Lecture Hall, it was as though I were listening to his disclosure from some sixty or seventy steps outside the Hall, or as if I were floating in the air. This condition lasted for several days until one night I heard the striking of a temple bell. All at once a transformation came over me, as though a layer of ice were smashed or a tower of jade pulled down. Instantly I came to my senses. Former doubts were completely dissolved, like ice which had melted away. "How marvelous! How marvelous!" I cried out aloud. There was no cycle of birth and death from which I had to escape, no enlightenment for which I had to seek.

2

At the age of thirty-two I settled in this dilapidated temple [Shoinji]. In a dream one night my mother handed me a purple silk robe. When I lifted it I felt great weights in both sleeves. Examining it, I found in each sleeve an old mirror about five or six inches in diameter. The reflection of the right-hand mirror penetrated deep into my heart. My own mind, as well as mountains and rivers, the entire earth, became serene and bottomless. The left-hand mirror had no luster on its entire surface. Its face was like that of a new iron pan not yet touched by fire. Suddenly I became aware that the luster on the left-hand mirror surpassed that of the right by a million times. After this incident, the vision of all things was like looking at my own face. For the first time I realized the meaning of the words, "The eyes of the Tatha-gata behold the Buddha-nature."

From *The Buddhist Tradition in India, China, and Japan* by William Theodore de Bary. Copyright © 1969 by William Theodore de Bary. Reprinted by permission of Modern Library, a division of Random House Inc.

relinquish worldly attachments, are found in many plays. Some plays are close to fairy tales: A fisherman takes the feather robe of an angel, but when she begins to sicken and grow wan, he returns the robe and she dances for him a dance that is performed only in heaven. Some plays are based on stories from China: A traveler dreams an entire lifetime on a magical pillow while waiting for a bowl of millet to cook. Another play reflects the constant Japanese ambivalence toward Chinese culture: Po Chūi, the Tang poet most esteemed in Japan, rows a boat over the seas and comes to the shores of Japan, where he is met by fishermen who turn him back in the name of Japanese poetry. One fisherman speaks:

You in China make your poems and odes out of the Scriptures of India; and we have made our "uta" out of the poems and odes of China. Since then our poetry is a blend of three lands, we have named it Yamato, the great blend, and all our songs "Yamato uta."[8]

At the end, the fisherman is transformed into the Shinto god of Japanese poetry and performs the "Sea Green Dance."

[8] A. Waley, trans., *The Nō Plays of Japan* (New York: Grove Press, 1957), p. 252.

Samurai Battle Scene.

Summary

Yamato Japan Early Japanese history has two main turning points. The first occurred in the third century B.C.E. when an Old Stone Age Japan became an agricultural, metal-working society. The new technologies came to Japan from Korea. By the fifth century C.E., the Yamato court ruled most of Japan. It was heavily influenced by Korea until the seventh century when, in the second main turning point of their history, the Japanese began to adopt and adapt many features of Chinese culture, including Buddhism and Chinese writing, literature, and political institutions.

Nara and Heian Japan In this period, Japan was ruled by a civil aristocracy under the emperor. An enormous gulf existed between aristocrats and commoners. Japanese government was heavily influenced by the Chinese imperial system. Japanese culture, however, was increasingly self-confident and was aristocratic in its tastes and forms of expression. Noblewomen wrote many of the great works of Japanese literature during this age. Buddhism became increasingly assimilated in Japan.

The Early Feudal Age In the eighth century mounted warriors called *samurai* began to dominate local society. By the late 1100s, power passed from the civil bureaucracy to military aristocrats. A series of *shōguns*, military officials, ruled in the emperor's name. The *shōguns'* power was based on their ability to command the loyalty of military vassals. Minamoto Yoritomo's seizure of power in 1185 marked the beginning of Japan's feudal age. He established the *bakufu*, or "tent government" in Kamakura. Some form of *bakufu* would endure in Japan until the mid-nineteenth century. In 1274 and 1281, the Japanese, with the help of storms that destroyed the Mongol fleet, managed to defeat Mongol invaders sent by Kublai Khan. In 1336, Ashitaga Takauji moved his *bakufu* to Kyoto.

Review Questions

1. In what sense was Yayoi society defined by its eastern frontier? What changes in this early frontier society led to the building of tombs and the emergence of the Yamato great kings?

2. Discuss Japan's cultural ties with China during the Nara and Heian periods. How did Chinese culture affect Japanese government and religion? How did the Japanese change what they borrowed? Was Japanese culture related to that of China like American culture to that of England (or more broadly, Europe)?

3. How did the Buddhism of the Nara and Heian periods differ from that of the early medieval era?

4. Trace the rise in Japan of a society dominated by military lords and their vassals. Do the late Heian, the Kamakura, and the Ashikaga represent different stages in the development of Japanese "feudalism"?

5. Contrast the Heian court culture with the "feudal" culture of the Kamakura and Ashikaga eras. Was the one not as aristocratic as the other? How did the role of women change over time?

Key Terms

bakufu (p. 271)

kamikaze (p. 274)

Pure Land Buddhism (p. 277)

samurai (p. 266)

Shintō (p. 261)

shō̄gun (p. 271)

tennō (p. 263)

Documents CD-ROM

Imperial China and the Diffusion of East Asian Civilization

9.3 Record of Ancient Matters: Futo NoYasumaro

9.4 Prince Shotoku's Seventeen Article Constitution

9.5 Pilgrimage to China (840): Ennin

NOTE: *To learn more about the topics in this chapter, see the Suggested Readings at the end of the book.*

RELIGIONS OF THE WORLD

BUDDHISM

Hinduism, Buddhism. and Jainism all arose out of the spiritual ferment of Vedic India after 700 B.C.E. Buddhism shares a kinship with these other religions much as Judaism, Christianity, and Islam have a relationship.

The founder of Buddhism, Siddhartha Gautama, was born about 563 B.C.E., a prince in a petty kingdom near what is now the border of India and Nepal. He was reared amid luxury and comforts, married at sixteen, and had a child. According to legend, at age twenty-nine he saw a decrepit old man, sick and suffering; and a corpse. He suddenly realized that all humans would suffer the same fate. Gautama renounced his wealth and family and entered the life of a wandering ascetic. He visited famous teachers, for almost six years practiced extremes of ascetic self-deprivation, and finally discovered the Middle Path between self-indulgence and self-mortification. At the age of thirty-five he attained *nirvana*, becoming the *Buddha*, or the Enlightened One. The rest of his eighty years the Buddha spent teaching others the truths he had learned.

Basic to the Buddha's understanding of the human condition were the "Four Noble Truths": (1) All life is suffering—an endless chain of births and rebirths (*karma*). (2) the cause of the suffering is desire—it is desire that binds humans to the wheel of *karma*; (3) escape from suffering and endless rebirths can come only by the cessation of desire and the attainment of *nirvana*; (4) the path to *nirvana* is eightfold, requiring right views, thought, speech, actions, living, efforts, mindfulness, and meditation. Buddhists say that *nirvana* cannot be described: It is the ground of all existence, ineffable, and beyond time and space—an ultimate reality that may be experienced, but not grasped intellectually.

The Buddha was a religious teacher, not a social reformer, yet his religious understanding led to ethical conclusions. He condemned the caste system that flourished in the India of his day. He denounced war, slavery, and the taking of life. He opposed appeals to miracles. He did not demand a blind faith in his doctrines: He told his followers to accept his teachings only after they had tested them against their own experience. He taught that poverty was a cause of immorality, and that it was futile to attempt to suppress crime with punishments. He identified with all humanity, saying, "He who attends on the sick attends on me."

Because the goal of Buddhism is for all humans to become Buddhas, some have called Buddhism the most contemplative and otherworldly of the great world religions. For the spiritually unprepared, and even for the historical Buddha, the way was not easy, and one lifetime was not enough.

Monks and nuns might practice the Eightfold Path, meditate for months and years, and experience an inner spiritual awakening, but only a few would gain enlightenment, the release from karmic causation. Most could only hope for a rebirth in a higher spiritual state—to begin again closer, to the goal.

For laypeople the emphasis of Buddhism was on ethical living in human society as a preparation for a more dedicated religious quest in a future life.

Two seated Buddhas. This fifth-to-sixth-century painting adorns a wall of a cave in Ajanta, India.
Borromeo/Art Resource, N.Y.

Buddhism spread rapidly along the Ganges River and through northern India. In the time of King Ashoka (272–232 B.C.E.) of the Mauryas, it spread to southern India, Ceylon, and beyond. This was its great missionary age. As it spread throughout India its influence on religious practice at the village level was enormous, and its meditative techniques helped reshape Hindu yogic exercises. Eventually, however Buddhism in India was re-Hinduized. It developed competing schools of metaphysics, a pantheon of gods and cosmic Buddhas, and devotional sects focusing on one or another of these cosmic figures. Its original character as a reform movement of Hinduism was lost, and between 500 and 1500 C.E. it was largely reabsorbed into Hinduism.

Beyond India, two major currents of Buddhism spread over Asia. One, known as the "Way of the Elders" (*Theravada*), swept through continental Southeast Asia and the islands that are today Indonesia. The Theravada teaching was close to early Indian Buddhism and, as it spread, it carried with it other strands of Indian culture as well.

Buddhism remains the predominant religion of Burma, Thailand, Cambodia, and Laos, although it must contend with more recent secular ideologies. In Thailand it remains the state religion: Thai kings rule as Buddhist monarchs; Thai boys spend short periods as Buddhist monks; and Thai temples (*wats*) continue as one center of village life. Before the spread of Islam, Buddhism also once flourished in Malaya, Sumatra, and Java.

The second major current, known as the "Greater Vehicle" (*Mahayana*), spread through northwest India to Afghanistan and Central Asia, and then to China, Tibet and Mongolia, Vietnam, Korea, and Japan. In each region the pattern that unfolded was different. In what is today Pakistan, Afghanistan, and Central Asia, Buddhism was overtaken and replaced by Islam. Mahayana doctrines entered Tibet during the sixth century C.E. and became firmly established several centuries later.

Today Tibetan Buddhism is the predominant religion of Tibet, Nepal, Sikkim, Bhutan, and Mongolia (although there it is severely curtailed by Chinese authorities). In China, and then spreading from China to Korea, Vietnam, and Japan, Mahayana Buddhism

saw its fullest development. One key doctrine in this current was the ideal of the *bodhisattva*, a being who had gone all the way to *nirvana*, but held back in order to help others attain salvation.

Another Mahayana doctrine, that of the Chan (in China) or Zen (in Japan) sect, stressed meditation and perhaps was closer to the teachings of the historical Buddha.

In China, the Tang dynasty (618–907) was the great Buddhist age, a time of unparalleled creativity in religious art, sculpture, and music. After that, although Buddhism continued to flourish at the village level, the governing scholar-gentry class shifted to the more worldly doctrines of Neo-Confucianism. In Vietnam, Korea, and Japan, the overall process replicated that of China, but the shift occurred later and with many local variations.

During modern times Buddhism—like all structures of faith—has struggled, with the secular doctrines of the scientific, and industrial, and communist revolutions exerting a powerful influence in the nineteenth and twentieth centuries. The future is unclear, but undoubtedly Buddhism will be powerfully affected by the ongoing transformations of Asian societies.

◆ In what way is Buddhism's relation to Hinduism parallel to Christianity's relation to Judaism?

◆ How can the teachings of a religion be tested against an individual's experience? If you were a Buddhist, how would you define a fair test?

Iran and India Before Islam

IRAN

- The Parthians

- The Sasanid Empire (224–651 C.E.)

INDIA

- Golden Age of the Guptas

- The Development of "Classical" Traditions in Indian Civilization (ca. 300–1000 C.E.)

◄ A SASSANIAN SHAHANSHAH (King of Kings), probably Bahram V, who ruled from 421 to 439, demonstrates his authority (and prowess as a lion hunter) on this magnificent silver dish.
The Granger Collection, New York.

GLOBAL PERSPECTIVE

Pre-Islamic Iran and India

From a Western perspective, the center of the world in the early centuries of the common era was the Roman-Byzantine world of late antiquity in the Mediterranean basin. However, in global perspective the loci of major political power, cultural creativity, and religious vitality throughout most of the early centuries C.E. also included Iran, India, and China.

Even in the Roman "West," by the third century C.E. "Roman" civilization remained a vital, living cultural force primarily in regions east and south of Rome itself, whereas in northwestern Europe Roman civilization endured more as a legacy still coexisting uneasily with the cultural traditions of the Germanic invaders. Roman imperial strength rapidly shifted east to Byzantium, where the influence of Africa and southwestern Asia were prominent both politically and culturally; Alexandria was the center of Hellenism for centuries; and the major Christian doctrinal councils were held in Asia. The perspective changes further when we consider other regions and cultures—the Sasanid imperial culture of Iran and its Zoroastrian revival, the Manichaean movement which spread throughout Central Asia, the completion of the *Mahabharata* and *Ramayana* epics, Gupta art and literature, Indian religious thought, and the diffusion of Mahayana Buddhism across Central Asia to China and thence to Japan.

Thus notions of a progressive "rise of the West" from classical antiquity to modern times do not hold for the first millennium C.E., especially when we consider the coming of Islam in the seventh century. To any impartial observer, the Western world in these centuries did not hold much promise as a future global center of political or cultural life. Instead, progressiveness and culture seemed best embodied either in Sasanid and Gupta culture in southwest and south Asia, or in China under the Han, Sui, and Tang dynasties and Japan in Nara and Heian times.

A revised perspective thus identifies important centers of cultural, religious, and political traditions around the globe—in South and East Asia, in the Mediterranean empire of Byzantium, and in Aksumite Ethiopia. Societies in each of these

regions, themselves the products of syncretistic blending of indigenous and imported cultural traditions, possessed sufficient dynamism to influence the development of neighboring peoples and in some cases exported their religions and cultures over great distances. Merchants and missionaries alike braved the hazards of travel by land and sea, carrying ideas as well as trade goods to remote regions. Wares and religions passed from hand to hand, and from mouth to mouth, on the journey from Byzantium to China, and Africa to India and beyond, as the centers of civilization in Africa and Asia waxed powerful. Hindu tradition and Indian culture were undergoing important internal developments, while Buddhism was finding new and rich fields for conversion in Central Asia, China, Japan, and Southeast Asia. Zoroastrian Iran appeared well on its way into a second millennium of imperial splendor under the Sasanids.

Yet with the imminent rise of the last major world religion, Islam, Iran would soon face cataclysmic changes—changes that would later overtake much of India and South Asia. In the time of Chosroes Anoshirvan in the sixth century C.E., who could have suspected that within a few hundred years Persian culture would be radically recast in Islamic forms?

I N THIS CHAPTER WE LOOK AT SOUTHWEST AND SOUTH ASIA before the spread of Islam. In Iran the Sasanids, a dynasty of Persian imperial rulers, reigned from the breakdown of Parthian rule in the early third century C.E. to the coming of Islam in the seventh. A small ruling nobility dominated the social and political system. During this time, the Silk Road, which connected China and the Middle East through Central Asia, developed into a thriving system of exchange between different cultures. Along with commerical merchandise and agricultural products, people exchanged ideas and influenced each other's culture, yet this was not merely a time of peace and prosperity. The Sasanid Empire was in constant competition with the Byzantine Empire. This competition finally exhausted both Sasanid and Byzantine resources. Both empires were defeated by the Arabs under the banner of Islam in the mid–seventh century.

In India the imperial Gupta kings presided over a cultural flowering of unprecedented magnificence until new incursions of steppe peoples from about 500 C.E. led to political fragmentation. Nevertheless, regional empires lasted until the thirteenth century, when Islamic power under the Delhi sultans began to forge new patterns of power and culture north and south.

The coming of Islamic civilization—with Muslim conquerors or, more often, with Muslim traders and religious brotherhoods—took place at different times. The process—sometimes peaceful and sometimes not—had differing consequences in Iran and India.

In Iran, Islam was prominent in government and public life from the early years of the Arab conquests in the mid–seventh century, although the populace in the regions of the traditional Iranian cultural sphere did not convert until much later.

In India, Arab armies penetrated the Indus region as early as 711, and Muslim rulers of Central Asian extraction controlled the Panjab from around 1000. The establishment of the so-called Delhi Sultanate in 1205 marked the entrenchment of Muslim ruling dynasties in the Indian heartlands. Similarly, Sufi brotherhoods made significant converts in India from about the thirteenth century onward. Even earlier, in trading communities on the coasts of Gujarat and South India, Muslim settlers and converts had already provided the nuclei of smaller, often scattered Muslim communities that grew up within the larger Hindu society.

IRAN
The Parthians

Parthian Arsacid rule (ca. 247 B.C.E.–223 C.E.) began in the eastern Iranian province of Parthia in Seleucid times and eventually dominated the Iranian heartlands of the Achaemenids (see Chapter 4). The Parthians even managed by 129 B.C.E. to extinguish Seleucid power east of the Euphrates. They also continued the Iranian imperial and cultural traditions of the Achaemenids. The relative Parthian tolerance of religious diversity was paralleled by the growth of regionalism in political and cultural affairs. A growing nobility built strong local power bases and became the backbone of Parthian military power. Aramaic, the common language of the empire, gradually lost ground to regional Iranian tongues after the second century B.C.E., although Greek was widely spoken.

Despite their general religious tolerance, the Parthians upheld such Zoroastrian traditions as maintenance of a royal sacred fire at a shrine in their Parthian homeland and included priestly advisers on the emperor's council. The last century or so of their rule saw increased emphasis on Iranian as opposed to foreign traditions in religious and cultural affairs, perhaps in reaction to the almost constant warfare with the Romans on their west flank and the Graeco-Bactrian Kushan threat to the east. By this time Christianity and Buddhism were making sufficient converts in border areas to threaten Zoroastrian tradition. These threats may have stimulated Parthian attempts to collect the largely oral Zoroastrian textual heritage. In such ways, Parthian rule laid the groundwork for the nationalistic emphases of subsequent centuries.

◀ **A cameo** depicts the capture of the Emperor Valerian by Shapur I, following the great Persian victory against the Romans near Edessa in 259 C.E. Bibliotheque Nationale. Paris, France.

DOCUMENT | A Report of Mani's Words About His Mission

The following excerpt is from The Cologne Mani Codex, *a Greek biographical work on Mani's early life that has only recently been discovered. The tiny parchment "pocketbook" on which it was written dates from around 400 C.E. within 150 years of Mani's death. In it, the Manichaean author cites one of Mani's "gospels."*

♦ What does Mani's proclamation suggest he shared with other Near Eastern traditions? What rank and role does he claim for himself? What seems to be his idea of scripture?

He wrote [thus again and] said in the Gospel of his most holy hope: "I, Mani, an apostle of Jesus Christ through the will of God, the Father of Truth, from whom I also was born, who lives and abides forever, existing before all and also abiding after all. All things which are and will be subsist through his power. For from this very one I was begotten; and I am from his will. From him all that is true was revealed to me; and I am from [his] truth. [The truth of ages which he revealed] I have seen, and [that] truth I have disclosed to my fellow travelers; peace I have announced to the children of peace, hope I have proclaimed to the immortal race. The Elect I have chosen and a path to the height I have shown to those who ascend according to this truth. Hope I have proclaimed and this revelation I have revealed. This immortal Gospel I have written, including in it these eminent mysteries, and disclosing in it the greatest works, the greatest and most august forms of the most eminently powerful works. These things which he [revealed], I have shown [to those who live from] the truest vision, which I have beheld, and the most glorious revelation revealed to me."

From *The Cologne Mani Codex*, trans. from the Greek by Ron Cameron and A. J. Dewey. Copyright © 1979, Scholars Press, p. 53. Reprinted by permission.

The Sasanid Empire (224–651 C.E.)

The Sasanids were a Persian dynasty and claimed to be the rightful Achaemenid heirs. They championed Iranian legitimacy and tried to brand the Parthians as outside invaders from the northeast who followed Greek and other foreign ways. The first Sasanid king, Ardashir (r. 224–ca. 239 C.E.), was a Persian warrior noble from a priestly family. The Sasanid name came from his grandfather, Sasan. Ardashir and his son, Shapur I (r. ca. 239–272), built a strong internal administration in Persia (Fars), extended their sway to Ctesiphon, and took Bactria from the Kushans. Under Shapur's long rule, the empire grew in the east, beyond the Caucasus, and into Syria, Armenia, and parts of Anatolia. Shapur defeated three Roman emperors, even capturing one of them, Valerian (r. 253–260). Thus he could justifiably claim to be a restorer of Iranian glory and a "king of kings," or *shahanshah*. He also centralized and rationalized taxation, the civil ministries, and the military, although neither he nor his successors could fully contain the growing power of the nobility.

With the shift of the Roman Empire east to Byzantium in the early fourth century C.E., the stage of imperial conflict was set for the next 350 years: Byzantium (Constantinople) on the Bosphorus and Ctesiphon on the Tigris were home to the two mightiest thrones of Eurasia until the coming of the Arabs. Each won victories over the other and championed a different religious orthodoxy, but neither could ever completely conquer the other. In the sixth century each produced its greatest emperor: the Byzantine Justinian (r. 527–565) and the Sasanid Chosroes Anosharvan ("Chosroes of the Immortal Soul," r. 531–579). Yet less than a century after their deaths, the new Arab power reduced one empire dramatically and destroyed the other. Byzantium survived with the loss of most of its territory for another 800 years, but the Sasanid imperial order was swept away in 651. Memory of the Sasanids did not, however, entirely die. Chosroes, for example, became a legendary model of greatness for Persians and a symbol of imperial splendor among the Arabs. The Pahlavi monarchy in twentieth-century Iran also utilized the historical memory of the Sasanid to legitimize their own rule and convince modern-day Iranians of their cultural distinctiveness.

SOCIETY AND ECONOMY

Sasanid society was largely like that of earlier times. The extended family was the basic social unit. Zoroastrian orthodoxy recognized four classes: priests, warriors, scribes, and peasants. However, a great divide separated the royal house, the priesthood, and the warrior nobility from the common people (artisans, traders, and the rural peasantry).

The basis of the economy remained agriculture, but land became increasingly concentrated in the hands of an ever-richer minority of the royalty, nobility, and priesthood. As in Roman domains, the growth of great estates was responsible for a growing imbalance between the rich few and the impoverished many. Many small farmers were reduced to serfdom.

The burden of land taxation, like that of conscript labor work and army duty, hit hardest those least able to afford it. This produced a popular reaction, as the Mazdakite movement, discussed below, shows.

The Sasanids also closely oversaw and heavily taxed the lucrative caravan and sea trade in their territory (see Map 10–1). Silk and glass production increased under government monopoly, and the state also controlled mining. The empire's many urban centers and its foreign trade relied on a money system. It was from Jewish bankers in Babylonia and their Persian counterparts that Europe and the rest of the world got the use of bills of exchange (the term *check* comes from a Pahlavi word).[1]

Sasanid aristocratic culture drew on diverse traditions, from Roman, Hellenistic, and Bactrian-Indian to Achaemenid and other native Iranian ones. Its heyday was the reign of Chosroes. Indian influences—not only religious ones, as in the case of Buddhist ideas, but also artistic and scientific ones—were especially strong. Indian medicine and mathematics were notably in demand. Hellenistic culture was also revived in the academy at Jundishapur in Khuzistan, where refugee scholars from Byzantium came to teach medicine and philosophy after Justinian closed the Greek academies in the West.

RELIGION

Zoroastrian Revival   The Sasanids institutionalized Zoroastrian ritual and theology as state orthodoxy. Although they were continuing the Arsacid patronage of Zoroastrian worship, the Sasanids claimed to be restoring the true faith after centuries of neglect. The initial architect of this propaganda and the Zoroastrian revival was the first chief priest (Mobad) of the empire, Tosar (or Tansar). Under Ardashir, Tosar instituted a state church and began to compile an authoritative, written canon of the Avesta, the scriptural texts that include the hymns of Zarathushtra (see Chapter 4). He may also have instituted a calendar reform and replaced all images in the temples with the sacred altar fires of Zoroastrian tradition.

The most influential figure in Sasanid religious history was Tosar's successor, Kartir (or Kirdir), who served as chief priest to Shapur I and three successors (ca. 239–293). Although his zealotry was initially restrained by the religiously tolerant Shapur, Kirdir gained greater power and influence after Shapur's death. He seems to have tried to convert not only pagans, but also Christians, Buddhists, and others. His chief opponents were the Manichaeans, whom he considered Zoroastrian heretics, much as Christian groups saw them as Christian heretics.

Manichaeism   Mani (216–277 C.E.) was born of a noble Parthian family but raised in Babylonia. A cosmopolitan who spoke Aramaic, Persian, and Greek and traveled to India, Mani preached a

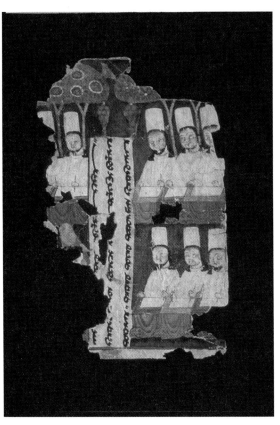

▲ **Manichaean Priests.** This leaf from a Manichaean book (ca. eighth–ninth century C.E.) shows priests in white robes and tall hats kneeling in front of low desks. Each has a sheet of white paper and some hold pens. Works such as this are an important source for our knowledge of Manichaean communities.

Aleaf from a Manchurian book, Roko, Templek (MIK III 6368), 8th-9th century, a manuscript painting 17.2 × 11.2 cm. Museum fur Indische Kunst, Staatliche Museen Preussischer Kulturbesitz, Berlin.

message both similar to and sharply divergent from its Zoroastrian, Judaic, and Christian forerunners. (See Document, "A Report of Mani's Words About His Mission.") *Manichaeism* centered on a radically dualistic and moralistic view of reality in which good and evil, spirit and matter, always warred. These ideas are now commonplace in the major monotheistic religions of today. He sought to convert others to his views which he presented as the culmination and restoration of the original unity of Zoroastrian, Christian, and Buddhist teachings. Mani may have been the first person in history consciously to "found" a new religious tradition or to seek to create a "scripture" for his followers. He called his new system "Justice," although outsiders called it *Manichaeism*. The popularity of Mani's movement probably contributed to Kirdir's and later attempts to establish a Zoroastrian "orthodoxy" and scriptural canon.[2]

Kirdir eventually had Mani executed as a heretic in 277, but Mani's movement had great consequences. It spread westward to challenge the Christian church (Saint Augustine was once a

---

[1] R. Girshman, *Iran* (Harmondsworth, U.K.: Penguin Books, 1954), pp. 341–346. "Pahlavi" is the name of the Middle Persian language that gradually replaced Aramaic as the Iranian common tongue in Sasanid times.

[2] W. C. Smith, *The Meaning and End of Religion* (New York: Harper & Row, 1962), pp. 92–98.

CHRONOLOGY

Sasanid Iran

223–224 C.E.	Ardashir (r. 224–ca. 239) defeats the last Arsacid ruler, becomes *shahanshah* of Iran
ca. 225–ca. 239	Tosar chief priest (Mobad) of realm
239–272	Reign of Shapur I; expansion of the empire east and west
ca. 239–293	Kirdir chief priest (Mobad) of the realm
216–277	Mani
ca. 307–379	Reign of Shapur II
488–531	Reign of Kavad I; height of Mazdakite movement
528	Mazdak and many of his followers massacred
531–579	Reign of Chosroes Anosharvan at Ctesiphon
651	Death of last Sasanid; Arabs conquer Persian Empire

Manichaean) and eastward along the Silk Road to Central Asia. Its ideas figured even centuries later in both Christian and Islamic heresies. Its adherents probably carried the Western planetary calendar to China, where in some areas it was used for centuries.

Zoroastrian Orthodoxy   Kartir had firmly grounded Zoroastrian orthodoxy despite the persistence of challenges to it, such as that of Mani. This orthodoxy became the backbone of Sasanid culture. Soon the Sasanids' Persian dialect, *Pahlavi*, became the official imperial language. Eventually the Zoroastrian sacred texts were set down in Pahlavi. Throughout Sasanid times, the priesthood increased its power as the jurists and legal interpreters as well as the liturgists and scholars of the land. With increasing endowments of new fire temples, the church establishment also eventually controlled much of Iran's wealth.

LATER SASANID DEVELOPMENTS

Despite the high Zoroastrian moral intent of many of their rulers, the Sasanid ideal of justice did not include equal distribution of the empire's bounty. The radical inequalities between the aristocracy and the masses erupted at least once in conflict with the Mazdakite movement at the end of the fifth century. Its leader, Mazdak, preached asceticism, pessimism about the evil state of the material world, the virtues of vegetarianism,

tolerance, and brotherly love—all ideas apparently drawn ultimately from *Manichaeism*—and the need for a more equal distribution of society's goods. This appealed to the oppressed classes, although even one Sasanid ruler, Kavad I (r. 488–531), was sympathetic for a time to Mazdak's ideas of social justice. However, in 528 Kavad's third son, the later Chosroes Anosharvan, massacred Mazdak and his most important followers. Although this finished the Mazdakites, the name was still used later, in Islamic times, for various Iranian popular revolts.

INDIA
Golden Age of the Guptas

Indians have always considered the Gupta era a high point of their civilization. Historians have seen in it the source of "classical" norms for Hindu religion and Indian culture—the symbolic equivalent of Periclean Athens, Augustan Rome, or Han China. The Guptas ruled when the various facets of Indian life took on the recognizable patterns of a single civilization that extended its influence over the whole subcontinent. A major factor in this development was the relative peace and stability that marked most of the Guptas' reign. (See Document, "A Chinese Traveler's Report on the Gupta Realm.")

GUPTA RULE

The first Gupta king was Chandragupta (r. 320–ca. 330 C.E.). He ruled first in Magadha and then became prominent in the whole Ganges basin after he married Princess Kumaradevi, daughter of a powerful tribal leader north of the Ganges. Although their reign inaugurated Gupta power, it was their son, Samudragupta (r. ca. 330–375), and especially their grandson, Chandragupta II (r. ca. 375–415), who turned kingdom into empire and presided over the Gupta "golden age."

The Gupta realm extended from the Panjab and Kashmir south to the Narbada River in the western Deccan and east to modern Assam (see Map 10–1), and their sphere of influence included some of the Kushan and

◁ **Gupta Sculpture.**   Fifth-century C.E. statue of Lokanatha from Sarnath, which despite damage, shows the fine sculptural work of the important school of Gupta artists at Sarnath and the influence on them of both Graeco-Roman antecedents and native Indian traditions and conventions.
Scala/Art Resource, N.Y.

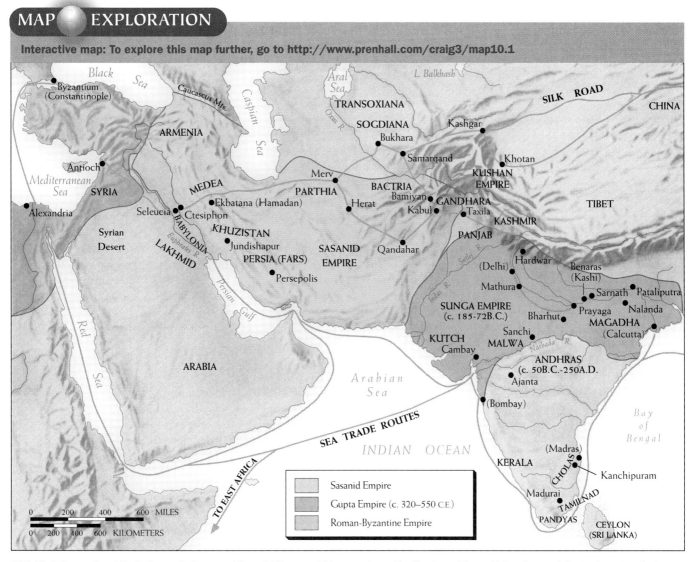

MAP EXPLORATION

Interactive map: To explore this map further, go to http://www.prenhall.com/craig3/map10.1

MAP 10–1 International Trade Routes in Gupta and Sasanid Times.   This map shows the Gupta and Sasanid Empires and the trade routes that linked them to each other and to other areas of the world.

Saka kingdoms of the northwest and much of the eastern coast of India and possibly Ceylon (Sri Lanka). Unlike the Mauryans, the Guptas usually accepted a defeated ruler as a vassal prince rather than rule his kingdom directly. Seated at the old Mauryan capital, Pataliputra, Gupta splendor and power had no rival. Under Chandragupta II, India was arguably the most civilized and peaceful country in the world.

Two further Gupta kings sustained this prosperity for another half century, despite invasions by a new wave of steppe nomads, the Huns, after about 440. By about 500 the Huns had overrun western India, and the Gupta Empire collapsed about 550. Harsha, a descendant of the Guptas through his grandmother, did revive a semblance of former Gupta splendor between 616 and 657. His loosely held dominions again spanned North India, but when he died without heirs the empire broke up again.

CHRONOLOGY

India from the Gupta Age to ca. 1000 C.E.

320 C.E.–ca. 467	Gupta period
320–330	Reign of Chandragupta, first Gupta king
376–454	Reigns of Chandragupta II and Kumaragupta: Kalidasa flourishes; heyday of Gupta culture
399–414	Chinese Buddhist monk, Fa-Hsien, travels in India
ca. 440	Beginning of Hun invasions from Central Asia
616–657	Reign of Harsha; revival of Gupta splendor and power
820	Death of Vedantin philosopher-theologian, Shankara
550–ca. 1000	Regional Indian kingdoms in north and south; major Puranas composed; age of first great Vaishnava and Shaivite devotional poets in southern India

DOCUMENT   A Chinese Traveler's Report on the Gupta Realm

Fa-Hsien, a Chinese Buddhist monk, was the first of several Chinese known for traveling to India to study and bring back Buddhist scriptures from the intellectual centers of Buddhist thought there. He wrote an account of his travels, first through Central Asia, then all over India, then through Ceylon and Indonesia again to China (399–414 C.E..

◆ What things about India seem most to surprise Fa-Hsien? Is his image of Indian rule a positive one? What do his remarks say about the prestige of the Buddhist tradition and its monks in the Indian state? What does he tell us about Indian society?

On the sides of the river, both right and left, are twenty san ghârâmas [monasteries], with perhaps 3000 priests. The law of the Buddha is progressing and flourishing. Beyond the deserts are the countries of Western India. The kings of these countries are all firm believers in the law of Buddha. They remove their caps of state when they make offerings to the priests. The members of the royal household and the chief ministers personally direct the food-giving; when the distribution of food is over, they spread a carpet on the ground opposite the chief seat (the president's seat) and sit down before it. They dare not sit on couches in the presence of the priests. The rules relating to the almsgiving of kings have been handed down from the time of Buddha till now. Southward from this is the so-called middle-country (Mâdhyade´sa). The climate of this country is warm and equable, without frost or snow. The people are very well off, without poll tax or official restrictions. Only those who till the royal lands return a portion of profit of the land. If they desire to go, they go; if they like to stop, they stop. The kings govern without corporal punishment; criminals are fined, according to circumstances, lightly or heavily. Even in cases of repeated rebellion they only cut off the right hand. The king's personal attendants, who guard him on the right and left, have fixed salaries. Throughout the country the people kill no living thing nor drink wine, nor do they eat garlic or onions, with the exception of Chandâlas [outcasts] only. The Chandâlas are named "evil men" and dwell apart from others; if they enter a town or market, they sound a piece of wood in order to separate themselves; then men, knowing who they are, avoid coming in contact with them. In this country they do not keep swine nor fowls, and do not deal in cattle; they have no shambles or wine-shops in their market places. In selling they use cowrie shells. The Chandâlas only hunt and sell flesh. Down from the time of Buddha's Nirvâna, the kings of these countries, the chief men and householders, have raised vihâras [monasteries] for the priests, and provided for their support by bestowing on them fields, houses, and gardens, with men and oxen. Engraved title-deeds were prepared and handed down from one reign to another; no one has ventured to withdraw them, so that till now there has been no interruption. All the resident priests having chambers (in these vihâras) have their beds, mats, food, drink, and clothes provided without stint; in all places this is the case. The priests ever engage themselves in doing meritorious works for the purpose of religious advancement (karma—building up their religious character), or in reciting the scriptures, or in meditation.

From "Buddhist Country Records," in Si-Yu-Ki, *Buddhist Records of the Western World*, trans. by Samuel Beal (London, 1884; reprint, Delhi: Oriental Books Reprint Corporation, 1969), pp. xxxvii–xxxviii. Reprinted by permission of Motilal Banarsidass Publishers Pvt. Ltd., Delhi, India.

The succeeding centuries before the arrival of Muslim invaders about 1000 C.E. saw several dynasties in North India share power, but no unified rule of any duration. Outside the north, several long-lived dynasties built regional empires in the western Deccan and Tamilnad (the extreme south) after Gupta times, and the main centers of Indian civilization shifted to those areas.

GUPTA CULTURE

With the decline of Rome in the West, Indian culture experienced little new outside influence from the Gupta era until Muslim times. India's chief contacts were now with Southeast Asia and China, and most of the cultural transmission was from India eastward, not vice versa (see Map 10–2).

The claim of the Gupta era to being India's golden age of culture could be sustained solely by its magnificent architecture and sculpture, the wall paintings of the Ajanta caves, and Kalidasa's matchless drama and verse. The "Shakespeare" of Sanskrit letters, Kalidasa flourished in the time of Chandragupta II and his successor.

We can see the depth of Gupta culture in the strong emphasis on education, whether in Jain and Buddhist monasteries or in Brahmanical schools. In addition to religious texts, typical subjects included rhetoric, prose and poetic composition, grammar, logic, medicine, and metaphysics. Using an older Indian number system that the Arabs transmitted to the West as "Arabic numerals," Gupta scholars cultivated mathematics especially.

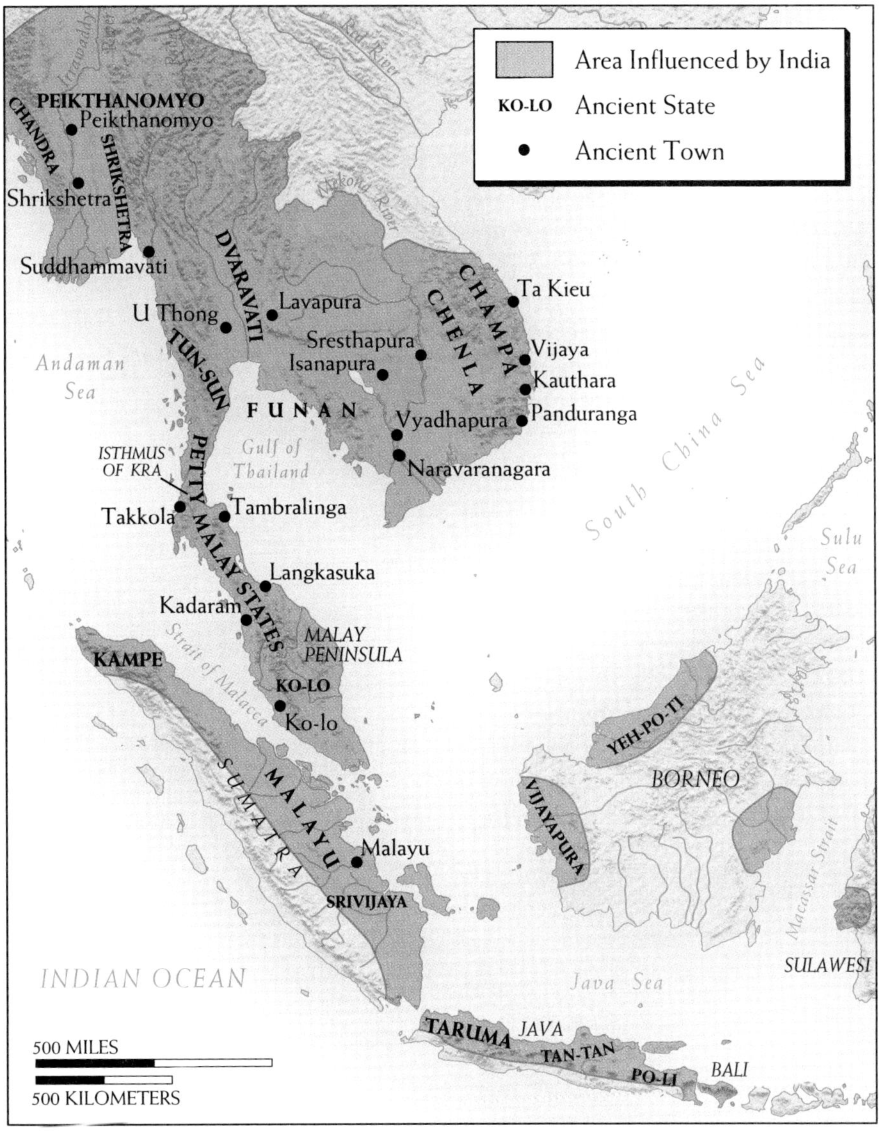

MAP 10–2 Indian influence in Southeast Asia, ca. 650 C.E.   By the middle of the 7th century C.E., Indian traditions, art, and music had a pervasive influence throughout Southeast Asia, even though the number of Indians who traded and migrated there was not great.

In sculpture, the monastic complex at Sarnath was a great center of activity. The superb technique and expressive serenity of Gupta style grew out of native Mathura and Graeco-Roman schools. Hindu, Jain, and Buddhist works all shared the same style and conventions. Even in handwork and luxury crafts, Gupta products achieved new levels of quality and were in great demand abroad: silks, muslin, linen, ivory and other carvings, bronze metalwork, gold and silver work, and cut stones, among others. In architecture, Gupta splendor is less evident, except in the culmination of cave-shrine (Chaitya-hall) development at Ajanta and in the earliest surviving free-standing temples in India. The Hindu temple underwent its important development in post-Gupta times, beginning in the eighth century.

The Development of "Classical" Traditions in Indian Civilization (ca. 300–1000 C.E.)

The Guptas' support of Brahmanic traditions and Vaishnava[3] devotionalism reflected the waning of Buddhist traditions in the mainstream of Indian religious life. In Gupta times and subsequently, down to the advent of Muslim rule, Indian civilization assumed its classical shape, its enduring "Hindu" forms of social, religious, and cultural life.

---

[3] *Vaishnava* or *Vaishnavite* means "related to Vishnu"; similarly, *Shaiva* or *Shaivite* refers to Shiva worship (compare with *Jaina/Jain* for devotees of the way of the *Jinas* such as Mahavira).

SOCIETY

In these centuries, the fundamentally hierarchical character of Hindu/Indian society solidified. The oldest manual of legal and ethical theory, the *Dharmashastra* of Manu, dates from about 200 C.E. Based on Vedic tradition, it treats the dharma appropriate to one's class and stage of life, rules for rites and study of the Veda, pollution and purification measures, dietary restrictions, royal duties and prerogatives, and other legal and moral questions.

In it we find the classic statement of the four-class theory of social hierarchy. This ideal construct rests on the basic principle that every person is born into a particular station in life (as a result of *karma* from earlier lives), and every station has its particular *dharma*, or appropriate duties and responsibilities, from the lowest servant to the highest prince or Brahman. The Brahmans' ancient division of Aryans into the four *varnas*, or classes, of *Brahman* (priest), *Kshatriya* (noble/warrior), *Vaishya* (tradesperson), and *Shudra* (servant) provides a schematic structure. These divisions reflect an attempt to fix the status and power of the upper three groups, especially the Brahmans, at the expense of the Shudras and the "fifth estate" of non-Aryan "outcasts," who performed the most polluting jobs in society. Although class distinctions had already hardened before 500 B.C.E., the classes were, in practice, somewhat fluid. If the traditional occupation of a varna was closed to a mem-

▲ **The Bodhisattva Avalokiteshvara.** Detail of a Buddhist wall painting from the cave shrines at Ajanta (Maharashtra, India), Gupta period, ca. 475 C.E. Avalokiteshvara (known in China as Kwan-yin and in Japan as Kannon) is the supreme figure of infinite mercy.
Art Resource, N.Y.

▲ **The Buddha Preaching His First Sermon.** This seated, high-relief figure of the Buddha, found in the ruins of Sarnath, is one of the finest pieces of Gupta sculpture. In Gupta times Sarnath was a thriving monastic center as well as one of the major schools for the best sculpture of the day.
The Granger Collection.

ber, he could often take up another, all theory to the contrary. When Brahmans, Vaishyas, or even Shudras gained political power as rulers (as was evidently the case with the Mauryas, for example), their family gradually became recognized as *Kshatriyas*, the appropriate class for princes.

Although the four classes, or **varnas**, are the theoretical basis for *caste* relations, much smaller and far more numerous subgroups, or **jatis**, are the units to which our English term caste best refers. (*Caste* comes from *casta*, the word the Portuguese used for *jati*.) These divisions (most representing occupational groups) were already the primary units of social distinction in Gupta times. *Jati* groupings are hereditary and distinguished essentially on principles of purity and pollution, which are expressed in three kinds of regulation: (1) commensality (one may take food only from or with persons of the same or a higher group); (2) endogamy (one may marry only within the group); and (3) trade or craft limitation (one must practice only the trade of one's group).[4]

The caste system has been the basis of Indian social organization for at least two millennia. It enabled Hindus to accommodate foreign cultural, racial, and religious communities within Indian society by treating them as new caste groups. It enabled everyone to tell by dress and other marks how to relate to

[4] A. L. Basham, *The Wonder That Was India* (New York: 1963), pp. 148–149.

DOCUMENT | Devoting Oneself to Krishna

The Bhagavad Gita is the most widely revered and often quoted of all Hindu religious texts. In these verses (Bhagavad Gita 9:22–34), Krishna (Vishnu) tells his friend and disciple, the young warrior Arjuna, of the highest path to salvation, which involves both renouncing one's attachment to the objects ("fruits") of one's actions and devoting oneself in pure faith to the Supreme Lord Krishna.

❖ How is the understanding of older Indian religious practices and ideals (about sacrifice, for example) transformed here? How does the Lord Krishna present himself in relation to other deities? Does the passage present a sharp dichotomy between faith and works? What are the social implications of the message here?

God and the Devotee

Those persons who, meditating on Me without any thought of another god, worship Me—to them, who constantly apply themselves [to that worship], I bring attainment [of what they do not have] and preservation [of what they have attained].

Even the devotees of other divinities, who worship them, being endowed with faith—they, too, O son of Kunti [actually] worship Me alone, though not according to the prescribed rites.

For I am the enjoyer, as also the lord of all sacrifices. But those people do not comprehend Me in My true nature and hence they fall.

Worshipers of the gods go to the gods; worshipers of the manes go to the manes; those who sacrifice to the spirits go to the spirits; and those who worship Me, come to Me.

A leaf, a flower, a fruit, or water, whoever offers to Me with devotion—that same, proffered in devotion by one whose soul is pure, I accept.

Whatever you do, whatever you eat, whatever you offer in sacrifice, whatever you give away, whatever penance you practice—that, O son of Kunti, do you dedicate to Me.

Thus will you be freed from the good or evil fruits which constitute the bondage of actions. With your mind firmly set on the way of renunciation [of fruits], you will, becoming free, come to Me.

Even-minded am I to all beings; none is hateful nor dear to Me. Those, however, who worship Me with devotion, they abide in Me, and I also in them.

Even if a person of extremely vile conduct worships Me being devoted to none else, he is to be reckoned as righteous, for he has engaged himself in action in the right spirit.

Quickly does he become of righteous soul and obtain eternal peace. O son of Kunti, know for certain that My devotee perishes not.

For those, O son of Prith,, who take refuge in Me, even though they be lowly born, women, vaishyas, as also shūdras—even they attain to the highest goal.

How much more, then, pious brōhmans, as also devout royal sages? Having come to this impermanent, blissless world, worship Me.

On Me fix your mind; become My devotee, My worshiper; render homage unto Me. Thus having attached yourself to Me, with Me as your goal, you shall come to Me….

From *Sources of Indian Tradition* by William Theodore de Bary. Copyright © 1988 by Columbia University Press. Reprinted with permission of the publisher.

---

another person or group, thus giving stability and security to the individual and to society. It represented also the logical extension of the doctrine of *karma* into society—whether as justification, result, or partial cause of the system itself (see Chapter 2).

RELIGION

Hindu Religious Life   Gupta and later times saw the growth of devotional cults of deities, preeminently Vishnu and Shiva, who were unknown or unimportant in Vedic religion. The temple worship of a particular deity has ever since been a basic form of Hindu piety. After Vishnu (especially in his form as the hero-savior Krishna) and Shiva (originally a fertility god), the chief focus of devotion came to be the Goddess in one of her many forms, such as Parvati, Shakti, Durga, or Kali. Vishnu and Shiva, like Parvati, have many forms and names and have always been easily identified with other deities, who are then worshiped as one form of the Supreme Lord or Goddess. Animal or nature deities were presumably part of popular piety from Indus Valley days forward. Indian reverence for all forms of life and stress on *ahimsa*, or "noninjury" to living beings (see Chapter 2), are most vivid in the sacredness of the cow, which has always been a mainstay of life in India.

In the development of Hindu piety and practice, a major strand was the tradition of ardent theism known as *bhakti*, or "loving devotion." *Bhakti* was already evident, at the latest by 200 C.E., in the Bhagavad Gita's treatment of Krishna. (See Document, "Devoting Onself to Krishna.") Gupta and later times saw the rise, especially in the Tamil-speaking south, of schools of bhakti poetry and worship. The central *bhakti* strand in Hindu life derives in good part from Tamil and other vernacular poets who first sang the praises of Shiva or Vishnu as Supreme Lord. Here, pre-Aryan religious sensibilities apparently reasserted themselves through the non-Aryan Dravidian peoples of the south. The great theologian of devotional Hinduism, Ramanuja (d. ca. 1137), would later come from this same Dravidian tradition. Of major importance also to devotional piety was the development in this era of the Puranas—epic, mythological, and devotional texts. They are still today the functional sacred scriptures of grass-roots Hindu religious life (the Vedic texts remaining the special preserve of the Brahmans).

Whatever god or goddess a Hindu worships, it is usual to also pay homage on proper occasions also to other appropriate deities. Most Hindus view one deity as Supreme Lord but see others as manifestations of the Ultimate at lower levels. Hindu polytheism is not "idolatry", but a vivid affirmation of the infinite forms that transcendence takes in this world. The sense of the presence of the Divine everywhere is evident in the importance attached to sacred places. India is the land of religious pilgrimage *par excellence*. Sacred mountains, rivers, trees, and groves are all *tirthas*, or "river fords" to the Divine.

The intellectual articulation of Hindu polytheism and relativism found its finest expression in post-Gupta formulations of Vedanta ("the end of the Veda"). The major Vedantin thinker, Shankara (d. 820), stressed a strict "nonduality" of the Ultimate, teaching that Brahman was the only Reality behind the "illusion" (*maya*) of the world of sense experience. Yet he accepted the worship of a lesser deity as appropriate for those who could not follow his

◄ A bronze statue of Hindu deity Vishnu from Thailand reflects the impact of Indian civilization on Southeast Asia.
Luca I. Tettoni/Corbis NY.

extraordinary norm—the intellectual realization of the formless Absolute beyond all "name and form."

Buddhist Religious Life   The major developments of these centuries were (1) the solidification of the two main strands of Buddhist tradition, the **Mahayana** and the **Theravada**, and (2) the spread of Buddhism abroad from its Indian homeland. The Mahayana ("Great Vehicle [of salvation]") arose in the first century B.C.E. Its proponents differentiated it sharply from the older, more conservative traditions of monk-oriented piety and thought, which they labeled the Hinayana ("Little Vehicle"). In Mahayana speculation Buddhas were seen as manifestations of a single principle of "Ultimate" Reality, and Siddhartha Gautama was held to be only one Buddha among many. The Mahayana stressed the model of the Buddha's infinite compassion for all beings. The highest goal was not a *nirvana* of "selfish" extinction but the status of a *bodhisattva*, or "Buddha-to-be," who postpones his own nirvana until he has helped all other beings become enlightened. (See Document, "The Bodhisattva Ideal.")

OVERVIEW   The Four Main Hindu Castes

Traditional Hindu/Indian society is fundamentally hierarchic in character. There are four main classes (*varnas*) into which a person is born according to how he or she lived in a previous life. Every class has its appropriate duties and responsibilities. In addition, there are numerous subgroups (*jatis*) based on a person's occupation. The English word "caste" is used to refer to all of these groups.

Brahman	Priest. This is the highest caste.
Kshatriya	Warrior or aristocrat. This is considered the appropriate caste for rulers.
Vaishya	Tradespeople and merchants.
Shudra	Servant. It includes peasants and manual laborers as well as domestic servants.

In addition, there is a fifth group of "outcastes" who performed the necessary but most polluting tasks in society, such as removing human waste. Persons in this category were considered "untouchable," and contact with them was considered morally and spiritually unclean.

The *bodhisattva* can offer this aid because his long career of self-sacrifice has gained him infinite merit. Salvation becomes possible not only through individual effort, but also through devotion to the Buddhas and *bodhisattvas*. At the popular level, this idea translated into devotional cults of transcendent Buddhas and *bodhisattvas* conceived of as cosmic beings. One of the most important events was that of the Buddha Amitabha, who personifies infinite compassion. Amitabha presides over a Western Paradise, or Pure Land, to which (through his infinite compassion) all who have faith in him have access. (See Chapter 9 for a discussion of Pure Land Buddhism in Japan.)

The older, more conservative "Way of the Elders" (Theravada) always focused on the monastic community but taught that service and gifts to the monks were a major source of merit for the laity. It emphasized gaining

Dancing Shiva. A magnificent South Indian bronze of Shiva. The fluid, balanced image depicts the so-called "dancing Shiva" engaged in his dance of simultaneous destruction and creation of the universe, an artistic-mythical rendering of the eternal flux of all worldly existence (13th century; bronze; 33.5 × 24.8 cm).
© The Nelson-Atkins Museum of Art, Kansas City, MO. (Purchase: Nelson Trust) 50-20.

merit for a better rebirth through high standards of conduct, lay devotion to the Buddha, and pilgrimage to his relics at various shrines, or **stupas.** The Mahayana also held up monastic life as the ideal, but some of its greatest attractions were its strong devotionalism and virtually polytheistic delight in divine Buddhas and *bodhisattvas* to whom one could pray for mercy, help, and rebirth in paradise. The basis of Theravada piety and practice was the scriptural collection of the traditional

DOCUMENT | The Bodhisattva Ideal

The following passages from two "perfection of wisdom" texts highlight the Mahayana doctrine of the Bodhisattva, who becomes a divine savior as well as an example for others. The Mahayana tradition sees all who enter the Buddhist path as bodhisattvas in the making, beings bound to become Buddhas. It sees its bodhisattva ideal as a higher one than that of the older ideal of the Enlightened Being (Arahant), or the pratyeka, or "private," Buddha of the Theravada tradition whose goal is to achieve nirvana for himself.

◆ The ideal of compassion for all beings is held up as the central one in the Mahayana. How is this developed in the first passage? How is it used in the second to polemicize against the ideals of the Theravada? What might be the appeal of the bodhisattva ideal as opposed to the older Buddhist ideal of the self-perfected Enlightened One, the Arahant?

1

The bodhisattva is endowed with wisdom of a kind whereby he looks on all beings as though victims going to the slaughter. And immense compassion grips him. His divine eye sees ... innumerable beings, and he is filled with great distress at what he sees, for many bear the burden of past deeds which will be punished in purgatory, others will have unfortunate rebirths which will divide

them from the Buddha and his teachings, others must soon be slain, others are caught in the net of false doctrine, others cannot find the path [of salvation], while others have gained a favorable rebirth only to lose it again.

So he pours out his love and compassion upon all those beings, and attends to them, thinking, "I shall become the savior of all beings, and set them free from their sufferings."

2

"What do you think, Shāriputra? Do any of the disciples and Private Buddhas ever think, 'After we have gained full enlightenment we will bring innumerable beings ... to complete Nirvāna'?"

"Certainly not, Lord!"

"But," said the Lord, "the bodhisattva (has this resolve). ... A firefly ... doesn't imagine that its glow will light up all India or shine all over it, and so the disciples and Private Buddhas don't think that they should lead all beings to Nirvāna ... after they have gained full enlightenment. But the disc of the sun, when it has risen, lights up all India and shines all over it. Similarly the bodhisattva,... when he has gained full enlightenment, brings countless beings to Nirvāna."

From *Sources of Indian Tradition* by William Theodore de Bary. Copyright © 1988 by Columbia University Press. Reprinted with permission of the publisher.

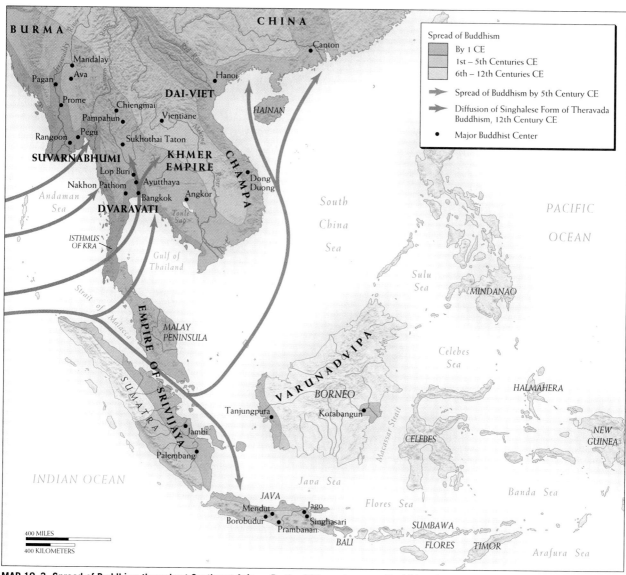

MAP 10–3 Spread of Buddhism throughout Southeast Asia.   By the 12th century C.E., Buddhism had taken root in many parts of Southeast Asia, often blending with local customs, as well as Hindu traditions that had been introduced earlier.

teachings ascribed to the Buddha, as reported by his disciples. Theravadins rejected the Mahayana claim that later texts (e.g., the Lotus Sutra) contained the highest teachings of the Buddha.

India gave Theravada Buddhism to Ceylon, Burma, and parts of Southeast Asia (see Map 10–3). Mahayana Buddhism predominated in Central Asia and China, from which it spread in the fifth to eighth centuries to Korea and Japan. Tantric Buddhism, an esoteric Mahayana tradition heavily influenced by Hinduism, entered Tibet from North India in the seventh century and became the dominant tradition there.

Summary

Iran   Under the Parthians (247 B.C.E.–223 C.E.) and the Sasanids (224–651 C.E.), Iran was a rival to Roman and Byzantine power in the Near East. The Sasanids, in particular, sought to restore the glory of the ancient Achaemenid Persian Empire and promoted native Persian culture. They also based their rule on orthodox Zoroastrianism and suppressed the Manichaeans as heretics. Although foreign trade flourished, the Parthian and Sasanid rulers favored the landed aristocracy at the expense of the peasantry, who were heavily taxed. The long wars with Rome and Byzantium ultimately sapped Sasanid strength and left the empire vulnerable to Islamic Arab invasion in the seventh century.

India   The Gupta period (320–467 C.E.) is considered one of the highlights of Indian civilization. Art, especially architecture and sculpture, flourished, and Indian civilization took on its enduring "Hindu" social, religious, and cultural shape. Indian contacts with Southeast Asia and China increased during this period. In society the fundamentally hierarchic nature of the caste system solidified. Hindu piety emphasized devotional cults to deities, especially Vishnu and Shiva. Indian Buddhism developed two main schools, the Mahayana and the Theravada, which spread to other parts of Asia.

Vishnu on the Serpent Sesa.

Review Questions

1. What are the key elements of Manichaean religion? How was it related to Christian and Zoroastrian traditions?

2. How did the Sasanid Empire develop after the fall of the Parthians? What were the principal economic bases of the Sasanid state?

3. What were the major religious issues in the Sasanid Empire? What role did Zoroastrian "orthodoxy" play in Sasanid affairs? What changes did Zoroastrianism undergo? Who were the main opponents of Zoroastrian tradition?

4. How did the Silk Road bring new religious ideas to Central Asia in these centuries?

5. In what sense can the high Gupta period (ca. 320–450) be considered a "golden age"? What was the extent of the empire? Why did it collapse? Where did the locus of Indian culture move after the fifth century and why?

6. What factors in Persia and India in the seventh century might have made the Arab invasions possible?

7. What major affinities do you see between the classical Buddhist and Hindu traditions that crystallized in the first half of the first millennium C.E.? What major differences?

Key Terms

bodhisattva   (p. 296)

jatis   (p. 294)

Mahayana   (p. 296)

Manichaeism   (p. 289)

stupa   (p. 297)

Theravada   (p. 296)

varnas   (p. 294)

Documents CD-ROM

Early Civilization in South Asia

3.8 Fa-Hsien: A Chinese Perspective on Gupta India

NOTE: *To learn more about the topics in this chapter, see the Suggested Readings at the end of the book.*

CHAPTER

11

The Formation of Islamic Civilization 622–945

- Origins and Early Development

- Women in Early Islamic Society

- Early Islamic Conquests

- The New Islamic Order

- The High Caliphate

- "Classical" Islamic Culture

◄ Page from an eighth- or ninth-century Qur'an in Kufic script (23.8 × 35.5 cm). The earliest Qur'ans were horizontal and written in the formal Kufic script (named for the city of Kufa in Iraq). Note the use of gold.

Courtesy of Freer Gallery of Art, Smithsonian Institution, Washington, D.C.

The Early Islamic World

The rise of Islam as both an international religious tradition and an international civilization is one of the great pivotal moments in world history. In its first three centuries, the Islamic polity was the most dynamic and expansive imperial state of its day. During the same centuries Chinese emperors of the Tang rebuilt and renovated the previous Han imperium; Charlemagne and the Carolingians struggled to hammer out a much smaller, more homogeneous empire in relatively backward Western Europe; Byzantium fought to survive against Islamic arms and turned inward to conserve its traditions; and post-Gupta India was divided into diverse regional kingdoms and still vulnerable to new forces (including those of Islam) moving into northwestern India.

Only China compared favorably with the Islamic world during this period in political and military power, cultural unity, creativity, and self-consciousness. The Tang and the Abbasids wielded commensurate power in their heydays, although the Chinese held together as a centralized state much better than the Islamic empire. Certainly they were the two greatest political and cultural units in the world at the time. They each had one cultural language, although Chinese was spoken by a greater percentage of Chinese than was Arabic by Islamic subjects. They also shared the military primacy of nomadic cavalry as well as the adaptive ability to incorporate new peoples into their larger culture—although Islamic cultures proved more flexible on this count. Indeed, the great elasticity and adaptability of Islam as a religious tradition and as a social order belie its current reputation in the West as an inherently inflexible system of values and practices.

Nevertheless, the bases of Islamic rule were clearly different, spread as the empire was over vastly more culturally heterogeneous and widely dispersed geographical areas than that of China. Conquest initially fueled the economy of the new Islamic state, but in the long run, trade and urban commercial centers became the backbone of Islamic prosperity, as well as the prime means of disseminating Muslim faith to new lands.

The Islamic achievement was unique in this period in that it resulted from an effort to build something new rather than to recapture old traditions, whether religious, social, or political. In later centuries the early Arab impact on Islamic culture and religion was tempered and changed by the vast numbers of Persian- and Turkish-speaking Muslims and also the many regional groups, from Swahili speakers in East Africa to the Malays and Indonesians of Southeast Asia. Nevertheless, Arabic went abroad with the holy Qur'an as the sacred medium of God's final revelation. Since Islam's emergence from the Arabian Peninsula, individual Muslims worldwide have always learned something of Arabic and the sacred book.

This achievement was a new historical phenomenon, at least in its scale. Although the Muslim faith can be seen as a reformation of Semitic monotheism, it was fundamentally an effort to do something new—not merely to reform, but to subsume older traditions of Jews or Christians in a more comprehensive vision of God's plan on earth. Muslims did build on previous traditions; they adopted and adapted the traditions of older Afro-Eurasian cultures. Yet as both a civilization and a religious tradition, Islam developed its own distinctive stamp that persisted wherever Muslims extended the *Umma*.

THINK AHEAD

◆ Why did only China compare favorably with the Muslim world during the first centuries after the birth of Islam? How were the two civilizations similar, and how were they different?

◆ What is unique about the Islamic achievement? In what ways was it built on the traditions of earlier religions?

Islamic civilization has been the last great world civilization to appear to date. On the one hand, its rise is the story of the creation of distinctive Islamic religious, social, and political institutions within an initially Arab-dominated empire. On the other, it is the story of how Islamic ideas and institutions evolved from their Arabian beginnings into a cosmopolitan array of other cultures. Each was a new creation of a particular place and particular circumstances, yet each was part of a larger, international Islamic civilization.

The basic ideas and ideals of the Islamic worldview derived from a single, prophetic-revelatory event, Muhammad's proclamation of the Qur'an.[1] This event galvanized the polytheist Arabs into a new kind of unity—that of the monotheist community of Muslims, or "submitters" to God. This community spread far beyond Arabia, and Persians, Indians, and others raised it to new heights. Arab military prowess and cultural pride joined with a new religious orientation to effect one of the most permanent revolutions in history, but the peoples of the older cultural heartlands sustained this revolution and built a new civilization upon it. Their acceptance of a new vision of society (and also of reality) as more compelling than any older vision—Jewish, Greek, Iranian, Christian, Buddhist—gave rise to Islamic civilization.

Origins and Early Development

The Setting

By 600 C.E., the dominant Eurasian political powers, Christian Byzantium and Zoroastrian, Sasanid Iran, or Persia, had confronted one another for over four centuries. This rivalry did not continue much longer. In the wake of one final, mutually exhausting conflict (608–627), a new Arab power broke in from the southern deserts to humble the one and destroy the other.

Pre-Islamic Arabia was not just a land of desert camel nomads. Byzantium and Iran had kept the nomads of the Syrian and northern Arabian steppe at bay by enlisting small Arab client kingdoms on the edge of the desert as buffer states. One of the biggest of these was Christian in faith. Arab kingdoms had long existed in the agriculturally rich highlands of southern Arabia, which had direct access to the international trade that moved along its coasts (see Chapter 4). Some of these kingdoms, including a Jewish one in the sixth century, had been independent; others had been under Persian or Abyssinian control. In the western Arabian highland of the Hijaz, astride its major trade route, the town of Mecca was a center of the caravan trade and a pilgrimage site because of its famous sanctuary, the **Ka'ba** (or Kaaba), where pagan Arab tribes enshrined gods. The settled Arabs of Mecca ran a merchant republic in which older tribal values were breaking down under the strains of urban and commercial life. But none of the settled Arabs were cut off from the nomads, who lived on herding and by raiding settlements and caravans.

The Arabic language, a Semitic tongue of the Afro-Asiatic family (see Chapter 4), defined and linked the Arab peoples, however divided they were by religion, blood feuds, rivalry, and conflict. From the Yemen north to Syria-Palestine and the Euphrates, the Arabs shared a highly developed poetic idiom.

Every tribe had a poet to exhort its warriors and insult its enemies before battle. Poetry contests were also held, often in conjunction with the annual trade fairs that brought tribes together under a general truce.

Islam is not a "religion of the desert." It began in a commercial center and first flourished in an agricultural oasis. Its first converts were Meccan townsfolk and date farmers of Yathrib (Medina). Before becoming Muslims, most of these Arabs were pagans, but some were Jews or Christians, or influenced by Jews or Christians. Caravans passed north and south through Mecca, and no merchant involved in this traffic, as Muhammad himself was, could have been ignorant of diverse cultures. Early Muslim leaders used the Arabs as warriors and looked to Arab culture for roots long after the locus of Islamic power had left Arabia. But the empire and civilization they built were centered in the heartlands of Eurasian urban culture and based on settled communal existence rather than desert tribal anarchy.

Muhammad and the Qur'an

Muhammad (ca. 570–632) was raised an orphan in one of the less well-to-do commercial families of the old Meccan tribe of Quraysh. Later, in the midst of a successful business career made possible by his marriage to Khadija (d. ca. 619), a wealthy Meccan widow and entrepreneur, he grew troubled by the idolatry, worldliness, and lack of social conscience around him. These traits would have equally offended sensitive Jewish or Christian morality, with which he was familiar. Yet these traditions remained foreign to most Arabs, even though some Arab tribes were Jewish or Christian.

[1] The common English transliteration of this Arabic word, *Koran*, is today being replaced by the more accurate *Qur'an*; similarly, *Muhammad* is preferable to *Mohammed*, *Muslim* to *Moslem*, *amir* to *emir*, and *ulama* to *ulema*.

▲ **The Ka'ba in Mecca.** The Ka'ba is viewed in Muslim tradition as the site of the first "house of God" built by Abraham and his son Ishmael at God's command. It is held to have fallen later into idolatrous use until Muhammad's victory over the Meccans and his cleansing of the holy cubical structure (*Ka'ba* means "cube"). The Ka'ba is the geographical point toward which all Muslims face when performing ritual prayer. It and the plain of Arafat outside Mecca are the two foci of the pilgrimage of Hajj that each Muslim aspires to make at least once in a lifetime.
Mehmet Biber/Photo Researchers, Inc.

When he was about forty years old, Muhammad felt himself called by the one true God to "rise and warn" his fellow Arabs about their frivolous disregard for morality and the worship due their Creator. On repeated occasions revelation came to him through a figure who was gradually identified as God's messenger angel, Gabriel. It took the form of a "reciting" (*qur'an*) of God's Word—now rendered in "clear Arabic" for the Arabs, just as it had been given to previous prophets in Hebrew or other languages for their peoples.

The message of the Qur'an was clear: The Prophet is to warn his people against worship of false gods and all immorality, especially injustice to the poor, orphans, widows, and women in general. At the end of time, on Judgment Day, every person will be bodily resurrected to face eternal punishment in hellfire or eternal joy in paradise, according to how he or she has lived. The way to paradise lies in gratitude to God for

the bounties of creation, his prophetic and revelatory guidance, and his readiness to forgive the penitent. Social justice and obedient worship of the one Lord are required of every person. Each is to recognize his or her creatureliness and God's transcendence. The proper response is "submission" (*islam*) to God's will, becoming *muslim* ("submissive" or "surrendering") in one's worship and morality. All of creation praises and serves God by nature except humans, who can choose to obey or to reject him. (See Document, The Qur'an, or "Recitation" of God's Word.)

In this Qur'anic message, the ethical monotheism of Judaic and Christian tradition (probably reinforced by Zoroastrian and Manichaean ideas) reached its logical conclusion in a radically theocentric vision; it demanded absolute obedience to the one Lord of the Universe. The Qur'anic revelations explicitly state that Muhammad is only the last in a long line of prophets chosen to bring God's word: Noah, Abraham, Moses, Jesus, and nonbiblical Arabian figures like Salih had been sent before on similar missions. The Qur'an is in fact filled with references and stories of earlier Biblical figures The person from the Bible who is mentioned most frequently in the Qur'an is the Virgin Mary. Because the communities of these earlier prophets had strayed from their scriptures' teachings or altered them, Muhammad was given one final iteration of God's message. Jews and Christians, like pagans, were summoned to respond to the moral imperatives of the Qur'an.

The Prophet's preaching fell largely on deaf ears in the first years after his calling. However, a few did follow the lead of his wife, Khadija, in recognizing him as a divinely chosen reformer of individual and communal life. Some prominent Meccans joined him, but the merchant aristocracy as a whole resisted. His preaching against their traditional gods and goddesses threatened both their ancestral ways and also the Meccan pilgrimage shrine and the lucrative trade it attracted. The Meccans began to persecute Muhammad's followers. After the deaths of Khadija and Muhammad's uncle and protector, Abu Talib, the situation worsened, and the Prophet even had to send a small band of Muslims to seek temporary refuge in Abyssinia. Then, as a result of his growing reputation as a moral and holy man, Muhammad was called to Yathrib (an agricultural oasis about 240 miles north of Mecca) to arbitrate among its five quarrelsome tribes, three of which were Jewish. Having sent his Meccan followers ahead, Muhammad fled Mecca in July 622 for Yathrib, afterward to be known as Medina (al-Madina, "the City [of the Prophet]"). Some dozen years later, this "emigration," or **Hegira**, became the starting point for the Islamic calendar, the event marking the creation of a distinctive Islamic community, or *Umma*.[2]

Muhammad quickly cemented ties between the Meccan emigrants and the Medinans, many of whom became converts. Raids on his Meccan enemies' caravans established his leadership. They reflect the economic dimension of the Medinan-Meccan struggle. The Arab Jews of Medina largely rejected his religious message and authority. They even made contact with his Meccan enemies, moving Muhammad to turn on them, kill or enslave some, banish others, and take their lands. Many of the continuing revelations of the Qur'an from this period pertain to communal order or to the Jews and Christians who rejected Islam.

The basic Muslim norms took shape in Medina: allegiance to the *Umma*; honesty in public and personal affairs; modesty in personal habits; abstention from alcohol and pork; fair divi-

sion of inheritances; improved treatment of women, especially as to property and other rights in marriage; careful regulation of marriage and divorce; ritual ablution before any act of worship, be it Qur'an reciting or prayer; three (later five) daily rites of worship, facing the Meccan shrine of the Ka'ba; payment of a kind of tithe to support less fortunate Muslims; daytime fasting for one month each year (Ramadan) and, eventually, pilgrimage to Mecca (*Hajj*) at least once in a lifetime, if one is able. Thus at the core of Islam are the so called Five Pillars: (1) *Shahada*, or the Muslim Creed ("There is no God but God and Muhammad is God's prophet"; (2) *Salat*, or prayer; (3) *Sawm*, fasting during ramadan; (4) *Zakat*, or alms; and finally (5) *Hajj* the pilgrimage.

Acceptance of Islamic political authority brought tolerance. A Jewish oasis yielded to Muhammad's authority and was allowed, unlike the resistant Medinan Jews, to keep its lands, practice its faith, and receive protection in return for paying a head tax. This practice was followed ever after for Jews, Christians, and other "people of Scripture" who accepted Islamic rule. After long conflict, the Meccans surrendered to Muhammad, and his generosity in accepting them into the *Umma* set the pattern for the later Islamic conquests. Following an age-old practice, Muhammad cemented many of his alliances with marriage (although as long as Khadija was alive, he did not take a second wife). In the last years of the Prophet's life, the once tiny band of Muslims became the heart of a pan-Arabian tribal confederation, bound together by personal allegiance to Muhammad, submission (*islam*) to God, and membership in the *Umma* of "submitters."

Women in Early Islamic Society

The *Umma* is a central concern in Islam and at the basis of the *umma* is the family. As a result, family law played a central role in the development of Islamic Law. It is in the context of Islamic family law that the rights of women and men are stipulated.

The Qur'an introduced into Arabian society radical new ideas that drastically improved the status of women. For example, it prohibited the common practice of female infanticide stating that all children regardless of sex should have the opportunity to live. The Qur'an recognizes a woman's right to contract her own marriage and that she, and not her male relatives, should receive the dowry from her husband. Legally speaking a woman entering marriage was not an object that was bought and sold but rather a party to a negotiated contract. A woman was also guaranteed the right to inherit, own, and manage property.

Women are therefore afforded many rights in the Qur'an. Yet the Qur'an does not assume full gender equality that is expected in modern societies in the twenty-first century. Islamic Law stipulates that the father or the senior male controls and

---

[2] The twelve-month Muslim lunar year is shorter than the Christian solar year by about eleven days, giving a difference of about three years per century. Muslim dates are reckoned from the month in 622 in which Muhammad began his Hegira (Arabic: *Hijra*). Thus Muslims celebrated the start of their lunar year 1401 in November 1980 (1979–1980 c.e. = a.h. [Anno Hegirae] 1400), whereas it was only 1,358 solar years from 622 to 1980.

Women mourning the death of martyrs in combat. Note the veils. Safavid fresco, 17th c. Imam zadeh Shah Zaid Isfahan, Iran.
Art Resource, N.Y.

guides the family unit. A male receives a larger share in inheritance, has fewer restrctions to initiate a divorce, and a man's eyewitness testimony is more valid in court than a woman's. Even though the Qur'an introduced many positive changes for women, it also legitimizes and presupposes a patriarchial society. The Qur'an did not outlaw particular customs that have both practically and symbolically prevented women to reach full equality.

Polygamy is a practice that is often closely identified with Islam. The Qur'an tolerates the practice but seeks to control it. It regulates the number of spouses that a man can have. It states that a man can have up to four wives provided he can treat them all equally and fairly (4:3). Some Muslims interpret that verse as essentially prohibiting the practice because it is impossible to guarantee that you treat and love two or more women "equally."

Another practice that is commonly associated with Muslim women is veiling. The veil is a generic term that applies to a variety ways of dress such as *hijab*, *chador*, and *burqa*. The veiling of women was a customary practice in pre-Islamic societies especially among upper-class women in the Byzantine and Sasanian Empires. It was, and still is, common in many parts of the Mediterranean.

Islam did not invent the veil. The Qur'an does not specifically stipulate veliling. On the contrary, it emphasizes that both men and women are resposible for their actions and should strive for the common good. However, the Qur'an stipulates that women should guard their modesty and that they "should draw their veils over their bosom and display their beauty only to their husbands and their fathers." (Q. 24:31). This call for modesty is also applicable to men.

As with the spirit of many religious dictums, the implementation of the letter of this imperative has proven problematic. Though the original intention of the veil was to protect women and their honor, the veil and the corrolary idea of seclusion, in effect largely barred women from public life up until the twentieth century. These verses along with other verses of the Qur'an have been used to justify patriarchy and militated against women utilizing the full rights which the Qur'an affords them. With more education in modern times, many Muslim women have turned to the Qur'an to interpret these verses anew to stipulate more actions and practices that are both Islamic and in concert with modern ideas of equality.

In early Islamic history, many women—such as the wives of Muhammad, Khadija, and A'isha—played influential roles in the development of Islam. They were instrumental in defining certain aspects of Islamic law and even commanded troops in warfare. In medieval times, however, women were not prominent in the public sphere. As in many other places around the world, women were cut off from the political, social, and educational activities. These negative effects are still visible today as women in the Middle East are increasingly negotiating their way into the public sphere.

Early Islamic Conquests

In 632 Muhammad died, leaving neither a son nor a designated successor. The new *Umma* faced its first major crisis. A political struggle between Meccan and Medinan factions ended in a pledge of allegiance to Abu Bakr, the most senior of the early Meccan converts. Following old Arabian patterns, many tribes renounced their allegiance to the Prophet at his death. Nevertheless, Abu Bakr's rule (632–634) as Muhammad's successor, or "caliph" (Arabic: *khalifa*), reestablished Medinan hegemony and at least nominal religious conformity for all Arabia. The Arabs were forced to recognize in the *Umma* a new kind of supratribal community that demanded more than allegiance to a particular leader.

COURSE OF CONQUEST

Under the next two caliphs, Umar (634–644) and Uthman (644–656), Arab armies burst out of the peninsula, intent on more than traditional Bedouin booty raids. In one of history's most astonishing military operations, by 643 they had conquered the Byzantine and Sasanid territories of the Fertile Crescent, Egypt, and most of Iran. For the first time in centuries the lands from Egypt to Iran came under one rule. Finally, Arab armies swept west over the Byzantine-controlled Libyan coast and, in the east, pushed to the Oxus, defeating the last Sasanid ruler by 651.

DOCUMENT | The Qur'an, or "Recitation," of God's Word

The Qur'an has many themes, from moral admonition, social justice, eternal punishment for the ungodly, and exemplary stories of past peoples and their prophets, to God's majesty and uniqueness, his bountiful natural world and compassion for humankind, and the joys of paradise.

> ◆ Can you identify at least four major Qur'anic themes in the selections below? To what end are the bounties of creation cited? What is the image of God conveyed in these selections? What can you infer about the Qur'anic conception of prophethood? Of the Judgment Day?

The revelation of the Book is from God who is mighty and wise. There are signs for men of faith, in the heavens and in the earth, in your being created and in God's scattered throng of creatures—signs for people with a grasp of truth.

There are signs, too—for those with a mind to understand—in the alternation of night and day, and in the gracious rain God sends from heaven to renew the face of the parched earth, and in the veering of the winds.

These are the signs of God which truly We recite to you. Having God and His signs, in what else after that will you believe as a message?

—*Sura 45:1–6*

Were you set to count up the mercies of God you would not be able to number them. God is truly forgiving and merciful.

—*Sura 16:18*

Such is God your Lord. There is no god but He, creator of all things. Then worship Him who is guardian over all there is. No human perception comprehends Him, while He comprehends all perception. He is beyond all conceiving, the One who is infinitely aware.

—*Sura 6:102–103*

To God belong the east and the west, and wheresoever you turn there is the face of God. Truly God is all-pervading, all-knowing.

—*Sura 2:115*

You people of the Book, why are you so argumentative about Abraham, seeing that the Torah and the Gospel were only sent down after his time? Will you not use your reason? You are people much given to disputing about things within your comprehension: why insist on disputing about things of which you have no knowledge? Knowledge belongs to God and you lack it!

Abraham was not a Jew, nor was he a Christian. He was a man of pure worship (a *hanif*) and a Muslim: he was not one of those pagan idolaters ....

—*Sura 3:65–67*

Yet you [people] deny the reality of the judgement. There are guardians keeping watch over you, noble beings keeping record, who know your every deed. The righteous will dwell in bliss. The evil-doers will be in *Jahim*, in the burning on Judgement Day, and there will be no absconding for them.

What can make you realize the Day of judgement as it is? ... the Day when there is no soul that can avail another soul. For the authority on that Day is God's alone.

Sura 82.1–5, 9, 19

Excerpt from *Readings in the Qur'an* by Kenneth Cragg. Copyright © 1988 by Kenneth Cragg. Reprinted by permission of HarperCollins, Inc

---

An interlude of civil war followed during the contested caliphate of Ali (656–661). Then the fifth caliph, Mu'awiya (661–680), directed further expansion and consolidated the new empire. In the Mediterranean, an Islamic fleet conquered Cyprus, plundered Sicily and Rhodes, and crippled Byzantine sea power. By 680 control of greater Iran was solidified by permanent Arab garrisoning of Khorasan, much of Anatolia was raided, Constantinople was besieged (but not taken), and Armenia was under Islamic rule.

Succeeding decades saw the eastern Berbers of Libyan North Africa defeated and converted to Islam in substantial numbers. With their help, "the West" (*al-Maghrib*, modern Morocco and Algeria) fell quickly. In 711 raids into Spain began (the name of the Berber Muslim leader of the first invaders, Tariq, lives on in *Gibraltar*, a corruption of *Jabal Tariq*, "Mount Tariq"). By 716 the disunited Spanish Visigoth kingdoms had fallen, and much of Iberia was under Islamic control. Pushing north into France, the Arabs were finally checked by a defeat at the hands of Charles Martel south of Tours (732). At the opposite end of the empire, buoyed by large-scale Arab immigration, Islamic forces consolidated their holdings as far as the Oxus River basin. In 710 Arab armies reached the Indus region. Islamic power was supreme from the Atlantic to central Asia (see Map 11–1).

FACTORS OF SUCCESS

The basic factor behind this rapid expansion was the weakened military and economic condition of the Byzantines and Sasanids—the result of their chronic warfare with one another. The new Islamic vision of society and life also united the Arabs and attracted others. Its corollary was the commitment among the Islamic leadership to extend "the abode of submission" (*Dar al-Islam*) abroad. However, too much has been made of Muslim zeal for martyrdom. Assurance of paradise

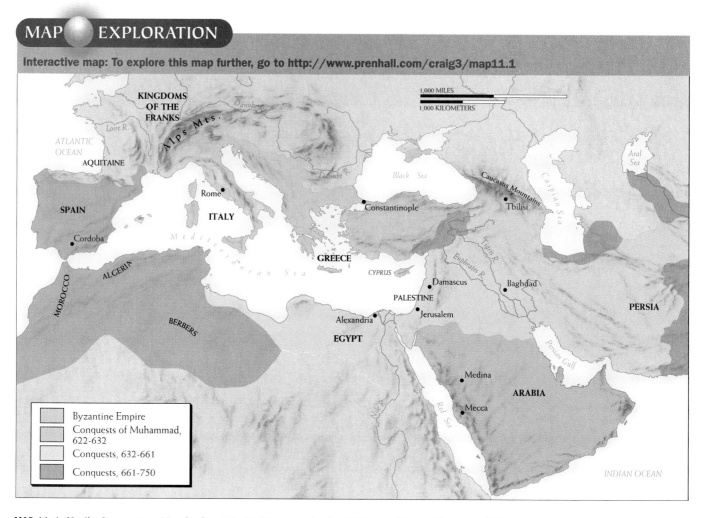

MAP 11–1 Muslim Conquests and Domination of the Mediterranean to about 750 C.E.   The rapid spread of Islam (both religion and political-military power) is shown here. Within 125 years of Muhammad's rise, Muslims came to dominate Spain and all areas south and east of the Mediterranean.

for those engaged in *jihad*, or "struggle (in the path of God)," is less likely to have motivated the average Arab tribesman—who, at least at the beginning, was usually only nominally a Muslim—as much as promise of booty. Life in the Arabian Peninsula was so hard that the hope of greater prosperity must have been compelling.

Still, religious zeal was important, especially as time went on. The early policy of sending Qur'an reciters among the Arab armies to teach essentials of Muslim faith and practice had its effects. Another major factor was the leadership of the first caliphs and field generals, which, combined with Byzantine and Iranian exhaustion, gave Arab armies a distinct advantage. Many subject populations also accepted, even welcomed, Islamic rule as a relief from Byzantine or Persian oppression. Crucial here was the Muslim willingness to allow Christian,

Jewish, and even Zoroastrian groups to continue as minorities (with their own legal systems and no military obligations) under protection of Islamic rule. In return, they had to recognize Islamic political authority, pay a non-Muslim head tax (*jizya*), and not proselytize or interfere with Muslim religious practice. (Ironically, as time went on, the head tax and other strictures on non-Muslims encouraged many Christians and Jews to convert.)

Finally, the astute policies of the early leaders helped give the conquests overall permanence: relatively little bloodshed, destruction, or disruption in conquest; adoption of existing administrative systems (and personnel) with minimal changes; adjustment of unequal taxation; appointment of capable governors; and strategic siting of new garrison towns like Basra, Kufa, and Fustat (later Cairo).

OVERVIEW   The Five Pillars of Islam

The five pillars of Islam constitute the basic ritual practices that are required of all Muslims. Muslims recognize that these rituals form the foundations of the faith. Yet not all Muslims observe them or do so only partially. As is common among adherents of other religions, the reality of practice is often far from the ideal.

The five pillars of Islam are

1. *Shahahda* ("Witnessing" or the Muslim creed)

2. *Salat* (the form of prayer or worship)

3. *sawm* (fasting)

4. *zakat* (alms giving)

5. *hajj* (pilgrimage to Mecca)

Some Muslims regard *jihad* (to struggle or strive for God; sometimes translated as "holy war") as the sixth pillar.

The *Shahahda* is the essence of Islamic theology and is the profession of faith: "There is no God but God and Muhammad is God's prophet." Stating this testimony makes a Muslim a Muslim and its affirmation constitutes the acceptance of Islam. The Shahahda emphasizes, like other monotheistic faiths, that there is only one God. The latter half of the creed, that is, that Muhammad is God's prophet, distinguishes Muslims from other faiths such as Christianity and Judaism.

Salat is the formal and ritualistic prayer or worship that Muslims are expected to perform five times a day: dawn, noon, midafternoon, sunset, and after dark. Muslims can pray by themselves or with others when possible, and the prayer can be performed basically anywhere. On Fridays, which is the Muslim Sabbath, Muslims tend to gather together for a communal worship around noontime. Before performing the prayer, a ritual purification called *wudu* is performed; this involves washing one's feet, hands, and face. Then facing Mecca, the worshiper follows a series of bodily motions which includes standing, sitting, and kneeling accompanied by prayers and verses from the Qur'an. The prayer affirms the relationship between humans and God.

Sawm is fasting during the month of Ramadan, which is the ninth month of the Islamic lunar calendar. Between sunrise and sunset, Muslims must abstain from all physical needs such as eating, drinking, smoking, or sexual intercourse. Those who are traveling, sick, or pregnant are not required to fast. Ramadan is the holiest month of the Islamic year and fasting is probably the pillar that is most commonly practiced. Abstinence from these bodily pleasures is supposed to remind Muslims of those less fortunate and is a time of spiritual enrichment and discipline. A time of self-reflection and denial, Ramadan is also a time of joy and communal solidarity. At sunset, when the fast is broken, there is a light meal (*iftar*) and people gather together to eat and drink, creating a festive atmosphere.

Zakat is the giving of charity. Typically people give a percentage of their wealth ranging from $2\frac{1}{2}$ percent to 10 percent. The purpose of *zakat* is to provide for the poor and thus constitutes a distribution of wealth throughout society. In modern society, the *zakat* is collected by the government in a form of a tax.

Hajj is the pilgrimage to Mecca in today's Saudi Arabia. Once in a lifetime a Muslim is expected to make this religious journey. The time for the *hajj* is about two months after Ramadan during the month of *Dhu al-Hijja*. During the hajj a reenactment of the prophet Muhammad's own pilgrimage to Mecca takes place. Before embarking on the *hajj*, the pilgrim must enter a state of ritual purity. Once in Mecca, all pilgrims wear the same simple dress to demonstrate that everyone is the same in the eyes of God regardless of race or class. The pilgrim begins the *hajj* by walking seven times around the Ka'ba, believed to have been built by Abraham, which is the focal point of the Islamic faith. Every mosque in the world has a *qibla* in the wall to signify the direction of the Ka'ba. Then the pilgrims slowly run seven times between the two hills of Safa and Marwa to commemorate Hagar's (the mother of Abraham's son Ishmael), search for water which was finally miraculously found at the well of Zamzam. Other rituals are performed but the pilgrimage ends with the pilgrims sacrificing animals (typically sheep or goats) to remember Abraham's willingness to sacrifice his son. The *hajj* is a powerful religious experience for the pilgrim, and the number of pilgrims who perform at the *hajj* every year, made so much easier by modern air travel, confirms the universal nature of Islam.

The New Islamic Order

Although they were quick to adopt and adapt existing traditions in the lands they conquered, the Muslims brought with them a new worldview that demanded a new political, social, and cultural reality, however long it might take to effect it. Beyond military and administrative problems loomed the more important question of the nature of Islamic society. Under the Prophet the new community of the *Umma* had replaced, at least in theory and basic organization, the tribal, blood-based sociopolitical order in Arabia. Yet once the Arabs (most of whom became Muslims) had to rule non-Arabs and non-Muslims, new problems tested the ideal of an Islamic polity. Chief among these were leadership and membership qualifications, social order, and religious and cultural identity.

THE CALIPHATE

Allegiance to Muhammad had rested on his authority as a divine spokesperson and gifted leader. His first successors were chosen much as were Arab *shaykhs* ("sheiks"), or tribal chieftains: by agreement of the leaders, or elders, of the new religious "tribe" of Muslims on the basis of superior personal qualities and the precedence in faith conferred by piety and association with the Prophet. The true line of succession to Muhammad was known as the **caliphate**, and the successors' titles were "successor" (*khalifa*, or caliph), "leader" (*imam*—literally, the one who stands in front to lead the ritual prayer), and "commander (*emir*) of the faithful." These names underscored religious and political authority, both of which most Muslims were willing to recognize in the caliphs Abu Bakr and

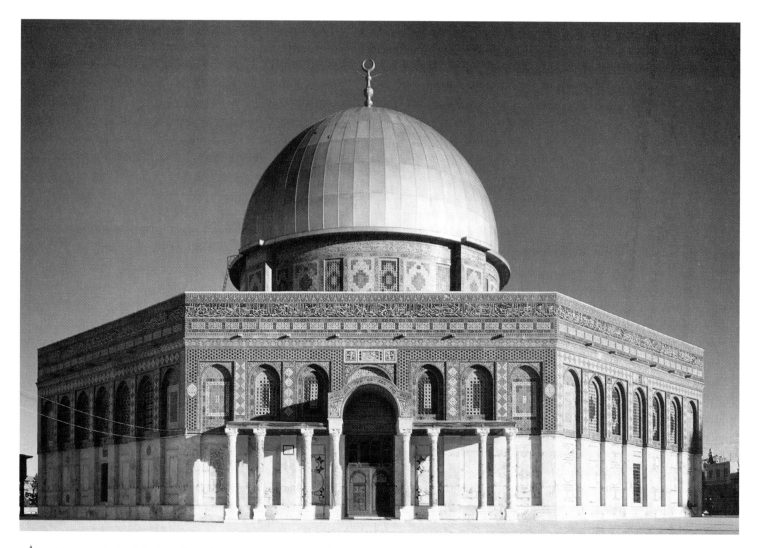

▲ **The Dome of the Rock, in Jerusalem.** An early example of Islamic architecture, it dates from the seventh century and the first wave of Arab expansion. It is built on the rock from which Muslims believe Muhammad ascended into heaven and on which Jews believe Abraham prepared to sacrifice Isaac. The Dome of the Rock has special symbolic significance for Muslims because the site is associated with the life and story of the Prophet. For a few years of Muhammad's time in Madina, Muslims faced Jerusalem when they prayed, before a new Qur'anic revelation changed the direction to Mecca.

Scala/Art Resource, N.Y.

Umar, and potentially in Uthman and Ali. Unfortunately, by the time of Uthman and Ali, dissension led to civil war. Yet the first four caliphs had all been close to Muhammad, and this closeness gave their reigns a nostalgic aura of pristine purity, especially as the later caliphal institution was based largely on sheer power legitimized by hereditary succession(see document, Al-Mawardi and al-Hilli).

The nature of Islamic leadership became an issue with the first civil war (656–661) and the recognition of Mu'awiya, a kinsman of Uthman, as caliph. He founded the first dynastic caliphate, that of his Meccan clan of Umayya (661–750). Umayyad descendants held power until they were ousted in 750 by the Abbasid clan, which based its legitimacy on descent from Abbas, an uncle of the Prophet. The Umayyads had the prestige of the office held by the first four, "rightly guided" caliphs. But many also deemed them to be worldly kings compared to the first four, who were seen as true Muslim successors to Muhammad.

The Abbasids won the caliphate by open rebellion in 750, aided by exploitation of pious dissatisfaction with Umayyad worldliness, non-Arab Muslim resentment of Arab preference (primarily in Iran), and dissension among Arab tribal factions in the garrison towns. For all their stress on the Muslim character of their caliphate, the Abbasids were scarcely less worldly and continued the hereditary rule begun by the Umayyads. This they did well enough to retain control of most of the far-flung Islamic territories until 945. Thereafter, although their line continued until 1258, the caliphate was primarily a titular office representing an Islamic unity that existed politically in name only.

THE *ULAMA*

Although the caliph could exert his power to influence religious matters, he was never "emperor and pope combined," as Western writers have claimed. Religious leadership in the *Umma* devolved instead on another group. The functional successors of the Prophet in society at large were those Muslims recognized for piety and learning and sought as informal or even formal (as with state-appointed judges) authorities. Initially, they were the "Companions" (male and female) of Muhammad with greatest stature in the old Medinan *Umma*—including the first four caliphs. This generation was replaced by those younger followers most concerned with preserving, interpreting, and applying the Qur'an and with maintaining the norms of the Prophet's original *Umma*. Because the Qur'an contained few actual legal prescriptions, they had to draw on precedents from Meccan and Medinan practice, as well as on oral traditions from and about the Prophet and Companions. They also had to develop and standardize grammatical rules for a common Arabic language based on the Qur'an and pre-Islamic poetry. Furthermore, they had to improve the phonetic, cursive Arabic script, a task done so well that the script was gradually applied as the standard writ-

ten medium for languages wherever Islamic religion and culture became dominant: among Iranians, Turks, Indians, Indonesians, Malays, East Africans, and others. Along with these and other religious, intellectual, and cultural achievements, they developed an enduring pattern of education based on study under those persons highest in the unbroken temporal chain of trustworthy Muslims linking the current age with that of the earliest *Umma*.

These scholars came to be known as **ulama** ("persons of right knowledge," the Anglicized Arabic plural of *alim*). Their personal legal opinions and collective discussions of issues, from theological doctrine to criminal punishments, established a basis for religious and social order. By the ninth century they had largely defined the understanding of the divine Law, or *Shari'a*, that Muslims ever after have held to be definitive for legal, social, commercial, political, ritual, and moral concerns. This understanding and the methods by which it was derived form the Muslim science of jurisprudence, the core discipline of Islamic learning.

The centers of *ulama* activity were Medina, Mecca, and especially Iraq (primarily Basra and Kufa, later Baghdad), then Khorasan, Syria, North Africa, Spain, and Egypt. In Umayyad times, the *ulama* had already become the guardians of the Muslim conscience, often criticizing caliphal rule when it strayed too far from Muslim norms. In time the *ulama* became a new elite, one eventually identified with the upper class of each regional society under Islamic rule. Caliphs and their governors regularly sought their advice, but often only for moral or legal (the two are, in Muslim view, the same) sanction of a contemplated (or accomplished) action. Some *ulama* gave dubious sanctions and compromised themselves. Yet incorruptible *ulama* were seldom persecuted for their opinions (except when they supported sectarian rebellions), mostly because of their status and influence among rank-and-file Muslims.

Thus, without building a formal clergy, Muslims developed a workable moral-legal system based on a formally trained if informally organized scholarly elite and a tradition of concern with religious ideals in matters of public affairs and social order. If the caliphs and their deputies were seldom paragons of piety and were often ruthless, they had at least to act with circumspection and support pious standards in public. Thus the *ulama* shared leadership in Muslim societies with the rulers, even if unequally—an enduring pattern in Islamic states.

THE *UMMA*

A strength of the Qur'anic message was its universalism. By the time of the first conquests, the new state was already so rooted in Muslim ideals that non-Arab converts had to be accepted, even if it meant loss of tax revenue. The social and political status of new converts was, however, clearly second to that of Arabs. Umar had organized the army register, or *diwan*, according to tribal precedence in conversion to, or (in the unique case of

Christian Arab tribes) fighting for, Islam. The *diwan* served as the basis for distributing and taxing the new wealth, which perpetuated Arab precedence. The new garrisons, which rapidly became urban centers of Islamic culture, kept the Arabs enough apart that they were not simply absorbed into the cultural patterns or traditions of the new lands. The dominance of the Arabic language was ensured by the centrality of the Qur'an in Muslim life and the notion of its perfect Arabic form, together with the increasing administrative use of Arabic to replace Aramaic, Greek, Middle Persian, or Coptic.

Non-Arab converts routinely attached themselves to Arab tribes as "clients," which assured protection and a place in the *diwan*. Still, this meant accepting a permanent second-class citizenship alongside the Arabs. Although many non-Arabs, especially Persians, mastered Arabic and prospered, dissatisfaction among client Muslims led to uprisings against caliphal authority. Persian-Arab tensions were especially strong in Umayyad and early Abbasid times. Nevertheless, a Persian cultural renaissance eventually raised the Islamicized modern Persian language to high status in Islamic culture. Consequently, it profoundly affected Islamic religion, art, and literature.

Caliphal administration joined with the evolution of legal theory and practice and the consolidation of religious norms to give stability to the emerging Islamic society. So powerful was the Muslim vision of society that, upon the demise of a caliph, or even a dynasty such as the Umayyads, the *Umma* and the caliphal office continued. There were, however, conflicting notions of that vision. In the first three Islamic centuries, two major interpretations crystallized that reflected idealistic interpretations of the *Umma*, its leadership, and membership. When neither proved practical, they became minority visions that continued to fire the imaginations of some but failed to win broad-based support. A third, "centrist," vision found favor with the majority because it spoke to a wide spectrum and accommodated inevitable compromises in the cause of Islamic unity.

The Kharijites   The most radical idealists traced their political origin to the first civil war (656–661). They were the Kharijites, or "seceders" from Ali's camp because, in their view, he compromised with his enemies. The Kharijites' position was that the Muslim polity must be based on strict Qur'anic principles. They espoused total equality of the faithful and held that the leader of the *Umma* should be the best Muslim, whoever that might be. They took a rigorist view of membership in the *Umma*: anyone who committed a major sin was no longer a Muslim. Extreme Kharijites called on true Muslims to rebel against the morally compromised reigning caliph. The extremist groups were constant rallying points for opposition to the Umayyads and the Abbasids.

More moderate Kharijites tolerated less-than-ideal Muslims and caliphs, yet they retained a strong sense of the moral imperatives of Muslim duty. Their ideals influenced wider Muslim pietism and even today moderate Kharijite groups survive in Oman and North Africa.

The Shi'a   A second position was defined largely in terms of leadership of the *Umma*. Muhammad had no surviving sons, and his son-in-law and cousin Ali claimed the caliphate in 656, partly on the basis of his blood tie to the Prophet. His claim was contested by Mu'awiya in the first Islamic civil war. When Mu'awiya took over after a Kharijite murdered Ali in 661, many of Ali's followers felt that Islamic affairs had gone awry. The roots of the "partisans of Ali" (*Shi'at Ali*, or simply the **Shi'a**, or *Shi'ites*), go back to Ali's murder and especially to that of his son Husayn at Karbala, in Iraq, at the hands of Umayyad troops (680).

While all Muslims esteem Ali for his closeness to Muhammad, Shi'ites believe him to be the Prophet's appointed suc-

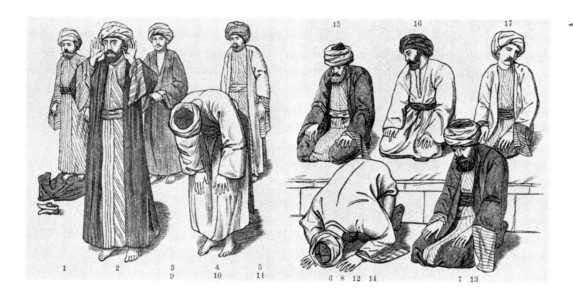

◄ **The Ritual Worship, or Prayer.** These illustrations show the sequence of movement prescribed for the ritual prayers that each Muslim should perform five times a day. Various words of praise, prayer, and recitation from the Qur'an accompany each position and movement. The ritual symbolizes the Muslim's complete obedience to God and recognition of God as the one, eternal, omnipotent Lord of the universe.
Library of Congress.

cessor. Ali's blood tie with Muhammad was augmented in Shi'ite thinking by belief in the Prophet's designation of him as the true *imam,* or Muslim leader, after him. Numerous rebellions in Umayyad times rallied around persons claiming to be such a true successor, whether as an Alid or merely a member of Muhammad's clan of Hashim. Even the Abbasids based their right to the caliphate on their Hashimite ancestry. The major Shi'ite pretenders who emerged in the ninth and tenth centuries based their claims on both the Prophet's designation and their descent from Ali and Fatima, Muhammad's daughter. They also stressed the idea of a divinely inspired knowledge passed on by Muhammad to his designated heirs. Thus the true Muslim was the faithful follower of the *imams,* who carried Muhammad's blood and spiritual authority.

Shi'ites saw Ali's assassination and the massacre of Husayn and his family as proofs of the evil nature of this world's rulers, and as rallying points for true Muslims. The martyrdom of Ali and Husayn was extended to a line of Alid *imams* that varied among different groups of Shi'ites. True Muslims, like their *imams,* must suffer. But they would be vindicated by a *mahdi,* or "guided one," who would usher in a messianic age and a judgment day that would see the faithful rewarded. (In the Sunni tradition, which we discuss next, similar "mahdist" movements arose throughout Islamic history.)

In later history Shi'ite rulers did head Islamic states, but only after 1500, in Iran, did Shi'ism prevail as the majority faith in a major Muslim state. The Shi'ite vision of the true *Umma* has not been able to dominate the larger Islamic world.

The Centrists   Most Muslims ultimately accepted a third, less sharply defined position on the nature of leadership and membership in the *Umma.* In some ways a compromise, it proved acceptable not only to lukewarm Muslims or pragmatists, but also to persons of intense piety. We may term the proponents of this position *centrists.* To emphasize the correctness of their views, they eventually called themselves *Sunnis*—followers of the tradition (*sunna*) established by the Prophet and the Qur'an. Sunnis encompass a wide range of reconcilable ideas and groups. They have made up the broad middle spectrum of Muslims who tend to put communal solidarity and maintenance of the Islamic polity above purist adherence to particular theological tenets. They have been inclusivist rather than exclusivist, a trait that has typified the Islamic (unlike the Jewish or Christian) community through most of its history.

The centrist position was the most workable framework for the new Islamic state. Its basic ideas were threefold. (1) The *Umma* is a theocratic entity, a state under divine authority; this translates into a nomocracy, or *Umma,* under the authority of God's Law, the Shari'a. The sources of guidance are, first, the Qur'an; second, Muhammad's precedent; and, third and fourth, the interpretive efforts and consensus of the Muslims (in practice, the *ulama*). (2) The caliph is the absolute temporal ruler, charged with administering and defending the Abode of Islam and protecting Muslim norms and practice; he possesses no greater authority than other Muslims in matters of faith. (3) A person who professes to be Muslim by witnessing that "There is no god but God, and Muhammad is his Messenger" should be considered a Muslim (because "only God knows what is in the heart"), and not even a mortal sin excludes such a person automatically from the *Umma.*

Under increasingly influential *ulama* leadership, these and other basic premises of Muslim community became the theological underpinnings of both the caliphal state and the international Islamic social order.

The High Caliphate

The consolidation of the caliphal institution began with the victory of the Umayyad caliph Abd al-Malik in 692 in the second civil war. The ensuing century and a half mark the era of the "high caliphate," the politically strong, culturally vibrant, wealthy, and centralized institution that flourished first under the Umayyads in Damascus and then in the Abbasid capital of Baghdad.[3] The height of caliphal power and splendor came in the first century of Abbasid rule, during the caliphates of the fabled Harun al-Rashid (786–809) and his son, al-Ma'mun (813–833).

CHRONOLOGY

Origins and Early Development of Islam

ca. 570	Birth of Muhammad
622	The Hegira ("emigration") of Muslims to Yathrib (henceforward *al-Madina,* "The City [of the Prophet]"); beginning of Muslim calendar
632	Death of Muhammad; Abu Bakr becomes first "successor" (*Khalifa,* caliph) to leadership, reigns 632–634
634–644	Caliphate of Umar; rapid conquests in Egypt and Iran
644–656	Caliphate of Uthman (member of Umayyad clan); more conquests; Qur'an text established; growth of sea power
656–661	Contested Caliphate of Ali; first civil war
661–680	Caliphate of Mu'awiya; founding of Umayyad dynasty (661–750); capital moved to Damascus; more expansion
680	Second civil war (680–692) begins with death of al-Hysayn at Karbala

---

[3] This periodization of early Islamic government follows that of M. G. S. Hodgson, *The Venture of Islam,* Vol. 1 (Chicago: University of Chicago Press, 1984), pp. 217–236.

THE ABBASID STATE

The Abbasids' revolution effectively ended Arab dominance as well as Umayyad ascendancy (except in Spain). The shift of the imperial capital from Damascus to the new "city of peace" built at Baghdad on the Tigris (762–766) symbolized the eastward shift in cultural and political orientation under the new regime. In line with this shift, more Persians entered the bureaucracy. The Abbasids' disavowal of Shi'ite hopes for a divinely inspired imamate reflected their determination to gain the support of a broad spectrum of Muslims, even if they still stressed their descent from al-Abbas (ca. 565–653), uncle of both Muhammad and Ali.

Whereas the Umayyads had relied on Syrian Arab forces, the Abbasids used Khorasanian Arabs and Iranians and, in the provinces, regional mercenaries for their main troops. Beginning in the ninth century, however, they enlisted slave soldiers (*mamluks*), mostly Turks from the northern steppes, as their personal troops. The officers of these forces, themselves *mamluks*, soon seized the positions of power in the central and provincial bureaucracies and the army. Eventually the caliphs were dominated by their *mamluk* officers. This domination led to increasing alienation of the Muslim populace from their own rulers. This was evident in Iraq itself, where unrest with his overbearing Turkish guard led the Abbasid caliph to remove the government from Baghdad to the new city of Samarra sixty miles up the Tigris, where it remained from 836 to 892 (see Map 11–2).

SOCIETY

The deep division between rulers and populace—the functionally secular state and its subjects—was ever after typical of most Islamic societies. However, even while the independence of provincial rulers reduced Abbasid central power after the mid–ninth century, such rulers generally recognized caliphal

▲ The Great Mosque of Samarra. Built in the middle of the ninth century by the Abbasid caliph al Mutawakkil, this Friday, or congregational Mosque has a prayer space larger than nine football fields, making it the largest enclosed such space in the Islamic world. The style of the Minaret recalls the ziggurats of ancient Babylon.
Aerofilms.

authority at least nominally. This gave them legitimacy as guardians of the Islamic socioreligious order, which meanwhile found its real cohesiveness in the Muslim ideals being standardized and propagated by the *ulama*.

However, full conversion of the populace of the Islamic empire lagged behind centralization of political power and development of Islamic socioreligious institutions. Iraq and Iran saw the fullest Islamization of local elites before the mid–twelfth century, followed by Spain, North Africa, and Syria. Conversion and fuller Islamization increased Muslim self-confidence and diminished the need for centralized caliphal power.[4]

DECLINE

The eclipse of the caliphal empire was foreshadowed at the outset of Abbasid rule, when one of the last Umayyads fled west to Spain where he founded a Spanish Islamic state (756–1030) that produced the spectacular Moorish culture of Spain. The Spanish Umayyads even claimed the title of caliph in 929, so strong were they and so weak the Abbasids by this

CHRONOLOGY	
Early Period of the High Caliphate	
680–694	Second civil war
685–705	Caliphate of Abd al-Malik; consolidation, Arabization of administration
705–715	Caliphate of al-Walïd; Morocco conquered, Spain invaded; Arab armies reach the Indus
ca. 750	Introduction of paper manufacture from China through Samarqand to Islamic world
750	Abbasids seize caliphate from Umayyads, begin new dynasty (750–1258)
756	Some Umayyads escape to Spain, found new dynasty (756–1030)
762–766	New Abbasid capital built at Baghdad

---

[4] Richard W. Bulliet, *Conversion to Islam in the Medieval Period* (Cambridge, MA: Harvard University Press, 1979), especially pp. 7–15, 128–138.

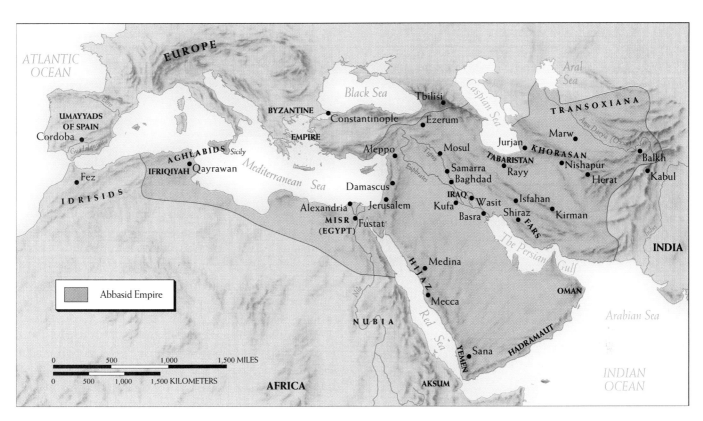

MAP 11–2 The Abbasid Empire, ca. 900 C.E.   A great diversity of peoples and nations were united by the abbasids. Their capital at Baghdad became the center of a trading network that linked India, Africa, and China.

time. In all the Abbasid provinces, regional governments were always potential independent states. In North Africa in 801 Harun al-Rashid's governor set up an independent state in modern Tunisia. In Egypt, the Fatimids set up Shi'ite rule in 969 and claimed to be the only true caliphate.

In the East, Iran grew ever harder for Baghdad to control. Beginning in 821 in Khorasan, Abbasid governors or rebels started independent dynasties repeatedly for two centuries, and the caliph had usually to recognize their sway. Among the longest lived of these Iranian dynasties were the Samanids who ruled at Bukhara as nominal Abbasid vassals from 875 until 999. They gave northeastern Iran a long period of economic and political security from Turkish steppe invaders. Under their aegis, Persian poetry and Arabic scientific studies began a Persian Islamic cultural renaissance and an influential scientific tradition.

Of greatest consequence for the Abbasid caliphate, however, was the rise in the mountains south of the Caspian of a Shi'ite clan, the Buyids, who took over Abbasid rule in 945. Henceforth the caliph and his descendants were largely puppets in the hands of a Buyid "commander" (*amirs* or *emirs*; later, *sultans*). In 1055 the Buyids were replaced by the more famous Seljuk *sultans*. Thus, the caliphal state broke up, even though Abbasid caliphs continued as figureheads of Muslim unity until the Mongols killed the last of them in 1258.

"Classical" Islamic Culture

The pomp and splendor of the Abbasid court were grand enough to become the stuff of Islamic legends, such as those preserved much later in *A Thousand and One Nights*. Their rich cultural legacy was made possible by a strong army and central government and vigorous internal and external trade, which may have been stimulated by the prosperous Tang Empire of China, with which the Islamic world had much overland and sea contact. Material factors, such as the introduction of paper manufacture (introduced from China through Samarkand about 750) or the flight of Byzantine scholars east to new Abbasid centers of learning, contributed also to making the early Abbasid era special.

INTELLECTUAL TRADITIONS

The Abbasid heyday was marked by sophisticated tastes and an insatiable thirst for knowledge—not simply religious knowledge, but *any* knowledge. An Arab historian called Baghdad "the market to which the wares of the sciences and arts were brought, where wisdom was sought as a man seeks after his stray camels, and whose judgment of values was accepted by the whole world."[5] Contacts (primarily among intellectuals)

[5] See Oleg Grabar, *The Formation of Islamic Art* (New Haven, CT: Yale University Press, 1973), especially pp. 1–103, 206–213.

◀ **An illustration from The Maqamat of al Hariri (d.1122),** one of the great masterpieces of Arabic literature of the later middle ages. It is a narrative written in rhymed prose for the purposes of entertainment.
Maquamat of Al Harira, Library in a mosque, Arab manuscript, 13th century (1237). Paris, France Bibliotheque Nationale (National Library), Photos 12.com-ARS.

between Muslims and Christian, Jewish, Zoroastrian, and other "protected" religious communities contributed to the cosmopolitanism of the age. Some older intellectual traditions experienced a revival in early Abbasid times, as in the case of Hellenistic learning. Philosophy, astronomy, mathematics, medicine, and other natural sciences enjoyed strong interest and patronage. In Islamic usage, philosophy and the sciences were subsumed under *falsafa* (from Greek *philosophia*). Islamic culture took over the tradition of rational inquiry from the Hellenistic world and developed and preserved it when Europe was a cultural backwater.

Arabic translations of Greek and Sanskrit works stimulated progress in astronomy and medicine. Translation reached its peak in al-Ma'mun's new academy headed by a Nestorian Christian, Hunayn ibn Ishaq (d. 873), noted for his medical and Greek learning. There were Arabic translations of everything from the Greek authors Galen, Ptolemy, Euclid, Aristotle, Plato, and the Neo-Platonists to the Indian Sanskrit fables

DOCUMENT | al-Mawardi and al-Hilli

After the death of the Prophet Muhammad, the Islamic community faced a serious political crisis. Muhammad did not provide his followers with specific instructions on who should rule the Muslim community and how it should be ruled. The question of political authority became a hotly contested issue and resulted in the split between Sunni and Shi'i Muslim that has prevailed to this day. Below are two early and important interpretations on political legitimacy by an influential Sunni official, al-Mawardi (974–1058) and al-Hilli (1250–1326), a leading Shi'i theologian.

◆ What are the essential characteristics of a ruler according to both thinkers?

◆ What do these thinkers have in common and what are their differences?

al-Mawardi

The *Imamate*: God, whose power be glorified, has instituted a chief of the Community as a successor to Prophethood and to protect the Community and assume the guidance of its affairs. Thus the *Imamate* is a principle on which stands the bases of the religious Community and by which its general welfare is regulated, so that the common good is assured by it. Hence rules pertaining to the Imamate take precedence over any other rules of government. ...

Thus the obligatory nature of the *Imamate* is established, and it is an obligation performed for all by a few, like fighting in a holy war, or the study of the religious sciences, and if no one is exercising it, then there emerge two groups. ...

As for those persons fitted for the *Imamate*, the conditions related to them are seven: ... Justice in all its characteristics. ... Knowledge requisite for independent judgment (*ijtihād*) about revealed and legal matters. ... Soundness of the senses in hearing, sight, and speech, in a degree to accord with their normal functioning. ... Soundness of the members from any defect that would prevent freedom of movement and agility. ... Judgment conducive to the governing of subjects and administering matters of general welfare. ... Courage and bravery to protect Muslim territory and wage the *jihād* against the enemy. ... Pedigree: he must be of the tribe of Quraysh, since there has come down an explicit statement on this, and the consensus has agreed. ...

He must maintain the Religion according to the principles established and agreed upon by the earliest Muslims (*salaf al-umma*), and if an innovator appears, or someone with dubious

Arabic astronomy in the middle ages attempted to correct Ptolemaic astronomy by means of direct observation and new calculations. As the following diagram from a 14th century Syrian astronomer indicates, they sought to demonstrate how the earth and the moon orbit the sun.
Bodleian Library, University of Oxford.

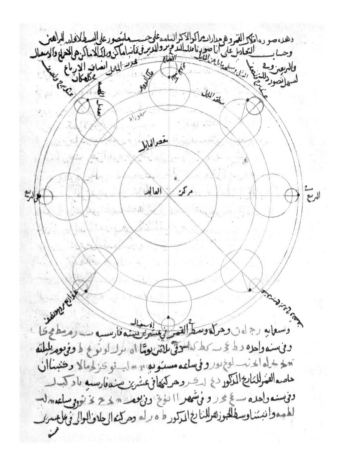

that had been translated into Middle Persian under the Sasanids. Such translations stimulated not only Arabic learning, but later also that of the less advanced European world, especially in the twelfth and thirteenth centuries.

LANGUAGE AND LITERATURE

Arabic language and literature developed greatly in the expanded cultural sphere of the new empire. There developed a significant genre of Arabic writing known as *adab*, or "manners" literature. It included essays and didactic literature influenced by earlier Persian letters. Poetry also flourished by building on the tradition of the Arabic ode, or *qasida*. Grammar was central to the interpretation of the Qur'an that occupied the ulama and undergirded an emerging curriculum of Muslim learning. Historical and biographical writings became major genres of Arabic writing. They owed much to the ancient Bedouin accounts of "the battle days of the Arabs" but arose primarily to record, first, the lives and times of the

---

opinions who deviates from those principles, then he must clarify matters by logical proofs, and show him the correct way, and finally apply the rules and punishments to which he is bound, that religion may be preserved from disorder, and the Community from stumbling. . . .

al-Hilli

He who is worthy of the *Imamate* is a person appointed and specified by God and His Prophet, not any chance person; it is not possible that there be more than one person at any one period who is worthy of it. . . . Hence the *Imamate* is *lutf* [what God does, directly or indirectly, to make it easier for people to obey the divine will]. . . .

It is necessary that the *Imam* be immune to sin [really, free from error, otherwise he would also need an *Imam*, or spiritual guide] and that is impossible. And also if he committed sin, he would lose his place in men's hearts, and the value of his appointment would be nullified. And because he is the guardian of the law, in which case he must be immune to sin . . . which no one perceives but God the most high. Hence . . . the *Imam* must be appointed by God, not by the people. Agreement has been reached that in appointing the

Imam the specification can be male by God and His Prophet, or by a previous *Imam* in an independent way (without the voice of the people). [There is disagreement over] whether or not his appointment can be in a way that is other than specification (by God and the Prophet). He who knows the unseen make[s] it known. And that comes about in two ways: (1) by making it known to someone immune to sin, such as the Prophet, and then he tells us of the *Imam*'s immunity to sin and of this appointment; (2) by the appearance of miracles wrought by his hand to prove his veracity in claiming the *Imamate*. Sunnis say that whenever the people [*umma*] acknowledge any person as chief, and [give the *baya* or allegiance, they] are convinced of his ability and his power increases, he becomes the *Imam*.

The *Imam* [must] be absolutely the best of the people of his age, because he takes precedence over all [or he is above everyone else]. And if there were among them one better than he then the worse would have to take precedence over the better, and that would be evil.

From *The Middle East and Islamic World Reader* by Marvin Gettlemen and Stuart Schar © 2003 by Marvin Gettlemen and Stuart Schar. Reprinted by permission of Grove Press.

Prophet and earliest companions, then those of subsequent generations of Muslims. This information was crucial to judging the reliability of the "chains" of transmitters included with each traditional report, or **hadith**. A *hadith* reports words or actions ascribed to Muhammad and the Companions; it became the chief source of Muslim legal and religious norms alongside the Qur'an, as well as the basic unit of most prose genres, from history to Qur'an exegesis. Collections of the *hadith* were mined by preachers and the schools of legal interpretation, whose crowning glory was the work of al-Shafi'i (d. 820) on legal reasoning. (See Document, "The Wit and Wisdom of Al-Jahiz.")

ART AND ARCHITECTURE

In art and architecture the Abbasid era saw the crystallization of a "classical" Islamic style by about 1000 C.E. Except for ceramics and Arabic calligraphy, most elements of Islamic art

Decorated Ceramic Bowl. A glazed ceramic bowl decorated with a gazelle or antelope, a symbolic figure of beauty and grace. From North Africa, Tunisian area, Fatimid (10th–12th centuries.)
Werner Forman/Art Resource, N.Y.

and architecture had clear antecedents in Graeco-Roman, Byzantine, or Iranian art. What was innovative was the use of older forms and motifs for new purposes and in new combinations, and the spread of such elements to new locales; generally from east (especially the Fertile Crescent) to west (Syria, Egypt, North Africa, and Spain). Sasanid stucco decoration techniques and designs turned up, for example, in Egypt and North Africa. Chronologically, urban Iraq developed an Islamic art first, then made its influence felt east and west, whether in Bukhara or in Syria and North Africa. Also new were the combination and elaboration of discrete forms, as in the case of the colonnade (or hypostyle) mosque or complex arabesque designs.

The Muslims had good reason to be self-confident about their faith and culture and to want to distinguish them from others. Most monuments of the age express the distinctiveness they felt. Particular formal items, such as calligraphic motifs and inscriptions on buildings, came to characterize Islamic architecture and define its functions. Most striking was the avoidance of pictures or icons in public art. This was, of course, in line with the Muslim aversion both to any hint of idolatry and to the strongly iconic Byzantine Christian art. Although this iconoclasm later diminished, it was a telling expression of the general thrust of Muslim faith and the culture it animated. Overall, the Muslims' artistic achievements before the year 1000 impress us with an identifiable quality that is both distinctively and "classically" Islamic, whatever the details of a particular example.[6]

CHRONOLOGY
"Classical" Period of the High Caliphate

786–809	Caliphate of Harun al-Rashid; apogee of caliphal power
813–833	Caliphate of al-Ma'mun; strong patronage of translations of Greek, Sanskrit, and other works into Arabic; first heavy reliance on slave soldiers (*mamluks*)
875	Rise of Samanid power at Bukhara; patronage of Persian poetry paves way for Persian literary renaissance
909	Rise of Shi'ite Fatimid dynasty in North Africa
945–1055	Buyid emirs rule the eastern empire at Baghdad; the Abbasid caliphs continue largely as figureheads
1055	Buyid emirs replaced by Seljuk sultans as effective rulers at Baghdad and custodians of the caliphate

[6] Grabar, *Formation of Islamic Art*, pp. 1–103, 206–213.

A

B

The Congregational Mosque. Two examples of the finest great mosques of the classical Islamic world. Such buildings were designed not only for worship; their large courtyards and pillared halls were also intended to hold the population of a given city and could be used for governmental purposes or for mustering troops in time of war. Their splendor also announced the power and wealth of Islamic rule. Figure A is the Great Mosque at Qayrawan in modern Tunisia, built between the 8th and 9th centuries. Figure B shows the Spanish Umayyad mosque in Cordoba, built and added to from the 8th to the 10th centuries, in a series of roofed extensions—unlike that in Qayrawan, which has only covered colonnades and one great hall (behind the photographer in this picture).

(A) Wemer Forman Archive, Art Resource, N.Y.; (B) Adam Lubroth, Art Resource, N.Y.

Summary

Muhammad Leading Muslims in Prayer.

Muhammad   The Prophet Muhammad (570–632) was the founder of Islam. Born in the Arabian commercial city of Mecca, he was influenced by contact with Arab Christians and with Jews. At about age 40, he had a religious experience during which, Muslims believe, God's messenger angel Gabriel repeatedly recited (*qur'an*) God's word to him. The message of the Qur'an was that social justice and worship of the one true God are required of every person. At the end of time, people will be resurrected and judged by God to be rewarded or punished according to how they lived. The proper response to God is submission (*islam*) to his will by becoming a Muslim (one who submits).

Islamic Conquest   By the time of Muhammad's death, his followers had conquered all of Arabia. Under his successors, the caliphs, Muslim Arab armies conquered most of the Near East, North Africa, Spain, Iran, and northwest India. Many of the peoples of these territories welcomed Islamic rule as liberation from Persian or Byzantine domination and eventually converted to Islam and became part of the *umma*, the community of Islamic believers. The status of women improved under Islam.

The High Caliphate   Under the Abbasid caliphs who ruled from the city of Baghdad, Islamic culture enjoyed its "classical" phase. Arabic translations of Greek and Sanskrit works stimulated progress in astronomy and medicine. Arabic literature and poetry flourished. As the sacred medium of God's final revelation, the Arabic language spread throughout the Islamic world. Arabic artists and architects built on Graeco-Roman, Byzantine, and Persian traditions, to develop a distinctive Islamic style in decoration, painting, and architecture. The *ulama*, Islamic religious and legal scholars, played a prominent part in Islamic society as interpreters of Islamic tradition and law.

Decline of the Caliphate   The Islamic empire began to splinter early. Disputes over the succession to the Prophet divided Muslims. Large parts of the Empire—Spain, North Africa, Iran—seceded. Military commanders (*amirs*) reduced the caliphs to mere figureheads. The last Abbasid caliph was killed by the Mongols when they sacked Baghdad in 1258.

Review Questions

1. Describe Arabian society before Islam. What were the prime targets of the Qur'anic message in that society?

2. What are the main features of the Islamic worldview? How do Islamic ideas about history, salvation, law, social justice, and other key issues compare to those of Christianity and Judaism?

3. What were the primary kinds of leadership in the early Islamic polities? To what extent were political and religious leadership separated in different offices and functions?

4. Discuss the conversion of subject populations in the early centuries of Islamic empire. What were incentives and obstacles to conversion?

5. Why were the initial Arab armies so successful? Why did the imperial caliphal state decline? What were some of the lasting accomplishments of the Umayyad and Abbasid Empires?

6. Discuss the "classical" culture of the high caliphate. What role did foreign traditions play in it? What were some of its prominent achievements?

⋮ Key Terms

caliphate   (p. 310)

emir   (p. 310)

hadith   (p. 318)

Hajj   (p. 305)

Hegira   (p. 305)

imam   (p. 310)

islam   (p. 304)

jihad   (p. 308)

Ka'ba   (p. 303)

qur'an   (p. 304)

Shi'a   (p. 312)

Sunna   (p. 313)

ulama   (p. 311)

Umma   (p. 305)

⋮ Documents CD-ROM

Islam

8.1 Muhammad: Koran

8.2 Al-Tabari: an Early biography of Islam's Prophet

8.3 Orations: The Words of the Prophet Through His Speeches

8.4 Islam in the Prophet's Absence: Continuation Under the Caliphate

8.5 Harun al-Rashid and the Zenith of the Caliphate

8.6 Al-Farabi: The Perfect State

8.7 Islamic Science and Mathematics

8.8 The Caliphate in Decline: Al-Matawwakil's Murder

8.9 Shiism and Caliph Ali: Controversy Over the Prophetic Succession

NOTE: *To learn more about the topics in this chapter, see the Suggested Readings at the end of the book.*

12

The Byzantine Empire and Western Europe to 1000

THE BIRTH OF EUROPE

⟨ One of the greatest achievements of Byzantine civilization, Hagia Sophia (the church of Holy wisdom) was completed in 537 by Anthemius of Tralles and Isidone of Miletus. Circled with numerous windows, the great dome floods the hall with light and, together with the church's many other windows, mosaics, and open spaces, gives the interior a remarkable airiness and luminosity. With the Turkish conquest of Constantinople in 1453, Hagia Sophia was transformed into a mosque.

Hagia Sophia, Istanbul.
Erich Lessing/Art Resource. N.Y.

GLOBAL PERSPECTIVE

The Early Middle Ages

In Western Europe, the centuries between 400 and 1000 witnessed both the decline of classical civilization and the birth of a new European civilization. Beginning with the fifth century, a series of barbarian invasions separated Western Europe culturally from its classical age. This prolonged separation was unique to Western Europe. Along with the invasions themselves and the new cultural traits they brought into Europe, it was pivotal to the development of European civilization. Although some important works and concepts survived from antiquity due largely to the Christian church, Western civilization labored for centuries to recover its rich classical past in "renaissances" stretching into the sixteenth century. Out of this mixture of barbarian and surviving (or recovered) classical culture, Western civilization was born. With the aid of a Christian church eager to restore order and centralized rule, the Carolingians created a new, albeit fragile, imperial tradition. But Western society remained highly fragmented politically and economically during the early Middle Ages. Meanwhile, many of the world's other great civilizations of the first millennium C.E. were peaking.

In China, particularly in the seventh and eighth centuries, Tang dynasty rulers also sought ways to secure their borders against foreign expansion, mainly pastoral nomads. China at this time was far more cosmopolitan and politically unified than Western Europe, and also centuries ahead in technology. By the tenth century, the Chinese were printing with movable type, an invention the West did not achieve until the fifteenth century, and then very likely borrowed in prototype from China. The effective authority of Chinese rulers extended far beyond their immediate centers of government. The Tang dynasty held sway over their empire in a way Carolingian rulers could only imagine.

In Japan, the Yamato court (300–680), much like the court of the Merovingians and Carolingians, struggled to unify and control the countryside. Shinto, a religion friendly to royalty, aided the Yamato. As in the West, a Japanese identity evolved through struggle and accommodation with outside cultures, especially with the Chinese, the dominant influence on Japan between the seventh and twelfth centuries. But foreign cultural influence, again as in the West, never managed to eradicate the

indigenous culture. By the ninth century a distinctive Sino-Japanese culture existed. But Japan, again like Western Europe, remained a fragmented land during these centuries, despite a certain allegiance and willingness to pay taxes to an imperial court. Throughout Japan, as in Western Europe, the basic unit of political control consisted of highly self-conscious and specially devoted armed retainers. A system of lordship and vassalage evolved around bands of local mounted warriors known as samurai. Through this system, local order was maintained in Japan until the fifteenth century. Like the Merovingian and Carolingian courts, the Japanese court had to tolerate strong and independent regional rulers.

While Western Europe struggled for political and social order in the fourth and fifth centuries, Indian civilization basked in a golden age under the reign of the Guptas (320–467). In this era of peace and stability, when a vocationally and socially limiting caste system neatly imposed order on Indian society from Brahmans to outcasts, culture, religion, and politics flourished.

In the seventh century, Islamic armies emerged from the Arabian Peninsula, conquered territory from India to Spain by 710, and gave birth to a powerful new international civilization. Cosmopolitan and culturally vibrant, this civilization flourished despite the breakdown of Islamic political unity beginning in the ninth and tenth centuries. Islamic cultural strides in this era overshadowed the modest cultural renaissance in the West under Charlemagne.

THINK AHEAD
- What caused the prolonged separation of Western European civilization from its classical past? What were the consequences of this separation for Western Europe?
- Which other society most resembled that of Western Europe during this period? Why?
- While Western Europe struggled to regain order, unity, and contact with its classical past, what was happening in the other great civilizations of the world?

THE EARLY MIDDLE AGES (OR EARLY MEDIEVAL period) marks the birth of Europe as a geographical entity. This period of recovery from the collapse of Roman civilization was also a time of forced experimentation with new ideas and institutions. Within what had been the northern and western provinces of the Roman Empire, Graeco-Roman culture combined with Germanic culture and an evolving Christianity to create distinctive political and cultural forms. In government, religion, and language, as well as geography, these regions grew separate from the eastern Byzantine world and an Islamic Arab world that extended across North Africa from Spain to the eastern Mediterranean. Yet as they did so they also drew vital knowledge and resources from both.

German tribes had been settling peacefully around the Roman Empire since the first century B.C.E., but in the fourth century C.E. they began to migrate directly into it from the north and east. During the fifth century they turned fiercely against their hosts, largely because the Romans, who regarded them as uncultured barbarians, treated them so cruelly. To the south, Arab dominance transformed the Mediterranean into an often inhospitable "Islamic lake," challenging Western trade with the East. Surrounded and assailed from north, east, and south, Western Europe became insular and even stagnant, its people losing touch with classical, especially Greek, learning and science. But forced to manage by themselves, they also learned to develop their native resources. The reign of Charlemagne saw a modest renaissance of antiquity aided by Byzantium and Arabia. And the peculiar social and political forms that emerged during this period—manorialism and feudalism—not only were successful at coping with unprecedented chaos on local levels but also proved to be fertile seedbeds for the growth of distinctively Western institutions.

OVERVIEW   Barbarian Invasions of the Western Roman Empire

The Germanic tribes—the barbarians—who overran the Western Roman Empire had coexisted with the Romans for centuries in a relationship marked more by the commingling of cultures and trade than by warfare. The arrival of the Huns from the east in the late fourth century, however, caused many of the tribes, beginning with the Visigoths in 376, to flee westward and seek refuge within the empire. They found the western half of the empire weakened by famine, disease, overtaxation, and an enfeebled military. The Romans lost control of their frontiers, and in the fifth century, the tribes overran the West and set up their own domains. The following is a list of the most important tribes and the areas they controlled by the year 500.

Tribes	Area of Control
Anglo-Saxons	Most of England
Franks	Northeast France
Burgundians	Eastern-central France
Alemanni	Switzerland
Visigoths	Most of Spain and southern France
Suevi	Northwest Spain
Vandals	North Africa
Ostrogoths	Italy, Austria, Croatia, Slovenia

The End of the Western Roman Empire

In the early fifth century, Italy and the "eternal city" of Rome suffered a series of devastating blows. In 410 the Visigoths, under Alaric (ca. 370–410), revolted and sacked Rome. In 452 the Huns, led by Attila—known to contemporaries as the "scourge of God"—invaded Italy. And in 455 Rome was overrun yet again, this time by the Vandals.

By the mid–fifth century, power in Western Europe had passed decisively from the hands of the Roman emperors to those of barbarian chieftains. In 476, the traditional date given for the fall of the Roman Empire, the barbarian Odovacer (ca. 434–493) deposed and replaced the Western emperor Romulus Augustulus. The Eastern emperor Zeno (r. 474–491) recognized Odovacer's authority in the West, and Odovacer acknowledged Zeno as sole emperor, contenting himself to serve as Zeno's Western viceroy . By the end of the fifth century the barbarians had thoroughly overrun the Western Empire. The Ostrogoths settled in Italy, the Franks in northern Gaul, the Burgundians in Provence, the Visigoths in southern Gaul and Spain, the Vandals in Africa and the western Mediterranean and the Angles and Saxons in England (see Map 12–1).

The barbarian military victories, however, did not result in a great defeat of Roman culture; Western Europe's new masters were willing to learn from the people they had conquered. They admired Roman culture and had no desire to destroy it. Except in Britain and northern Gaul, Roman law, Roman government, and Latin, the Roman language, coexisted with the new Germanic institutions. In Italy under Theodoric, tribal custom gradually gave way to Roman law. Only the Vandals and the Anglo-Saxons—and, after 466, the Visigoths—refused to profess at least titular obedience to the emperor in Constantinople.

The Visigoths, the Ostrogoths, and the Vandals entered the West as Christians, which helped them accommodate to Roman culture. They were, however, followers of the Arian creed, which had been condemned at the Council of Nicaea in 325 and was considered heretical in the West. Later, around 500, the Franks, who had settled in Gaul, would convert to the Orthodox, or "Catholic," form of Christianity supported by the bishops of Rome. As we will see, the Franks ultimately dominated most of Western Europe, helping convert the Goths and other barbarians to Roman Christianity.

All things considered, rapprochement and a gradual interpenetration of two strong cultures—a creative tension—marked the period of the Germanic migrations. The stronger culture was the Roman, and it became dominant in a later fusion. Despite Western military defeat, the Goths and the Franks became far more romanized than the Romans were germanized. Latin language, Nicene Christianity, and eventually Roman law and government were to triumph in the West during the Middle Ages.

THE BYZANTINE EMPIRE

As the Roman Empire in the West succumbed to Germanic and other barbarian invasions, imperial power shifted to the eastern part of the Roman Empire, whose center was the city of Byzantium (modern day Istanbul). Between 324 and 330, the emperor Constantine the Great rebuilt and renamed the city after himself: Constantinople. It remained the capital of both the old Roman and the new Byzantine Empire until the eighth century, when Charlemagne revived the Western Empire and reclaimed its imperial title. In its historical usage, the term Byzantine indicates the Greek, Hellenistic Roman, and Judaic monotheistic elements that distinguish the culture of the East from the Latin West.

MAP ◗ EXPLORATION

Interactive map: To explore this map further, go to http://www.prenhall.com/craig3/map12.1

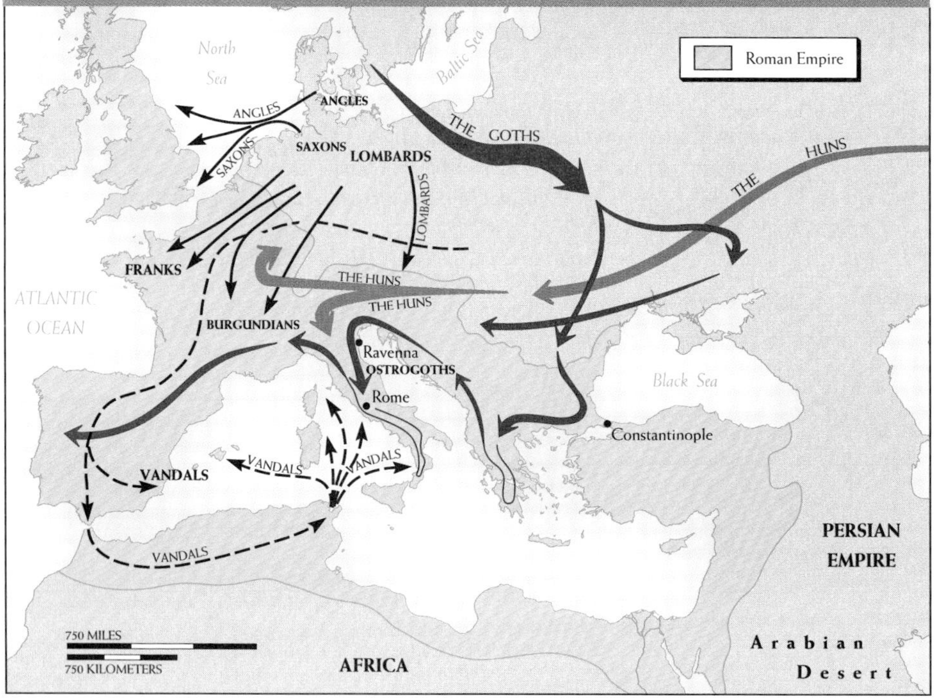

MAP 12–1 Barbarian Migrations into the West in the Fourth and Fifth Centuries. The forceful intrusion of Germanic and non-Germanic tribes into the empire from the last quarter of the fourth century through the fifth century made for a constantly changing pattern of movement and relations. The map shows the major routes taken by the usually unwelcome newcomers and the areas most deeply affected by the main groups.

Between 324 and 1453, the Byzantine Empire passed from an early period of expansion and splendor to a time of sustained contraction and splintering and finally catastrophic defeat. Historians divide its history into three distinct periods:

1. From the rebuilding of Byzantium as Constantinople in 324 to the beginning of the Arab expansion and the spread of Islam in 632

2. From 632 to the conquest of Asia Minor by the Seljuk Turks in 1071, or, as some prefer, to the fall of Constantinople to the Western Crusaders in 1204

3. From 1071, or 1204, to the fall of Constantinople to the Ottoman Turks in 1453, the end of the empire in the East.

THE REIGN OF JUSTINIAN

In terms of territory, political power, and cultural achievement, the first period of Byzantine history (324–632) was far the greater. (See Map 12–3.) Its pinnacle was the reign of Emperor Justinian (r. 527–565) and his like-minded wife, Empress Theodora (d. 548). (See Document, "The Character and 'Innovations' of Justinian and Theodora.") A strongman ruler who expected all his subjects, clergy and laity, high and low, to submit absolutely to his hierarchical control, Justinian spent, built, and destroyed on a grand scale. Theodora, the daughter of a circus bear trainer, had been an entertainer in her youth and, if Justinian's tell-all court historian, Procopius, is believed, a prostitute as well. Whatever the source, she possessed an intelligence and toughness that matched and might even have exceeded those of her husband. An influential counselor, Theodora was a true co-ruler. In 532, after massive tax riots—the so-called Nika Revolt—rocked the city threatening its destruction and the end of Justinian's brief rule, a panicked emperor contemplated abdication and flight. Theodora stiffened his resolve, insisting that he reestablish his authority unambiguously, which he thereafter did by ordering a bloodbath that left tens of thousands of protesters dead in the Hippodrome.

Cities   During Justinian's thirty-eight-year reign the empire's strength lay in its more than 1,500 cities. Constantinople, with perhaps 350,000 inhabitants, was the largest and the cultural crossroads of Asian and European civilizations. The large, dominant provincial cities had populations of 50,000. A fifth-century

DOCUMENT | The Character and "Innovations" of Justinian and Theodora

According to their court historian and biographer, Procopius, the emperor and his wife were tyrants, pure and simple. His Secret History *(sixth century), which some historians distrust as a source, had only criticism and condemnation for the two rulers. Procopius especially resented Theodora, and he did not believe that the rule of law was respected at the royal court.*

◆ Is Procopius being fair to Justinian and Theodora? Is the *Secret History* an ancient tabloid? How does one know when a source is biased and self-serving and when it is telling the truth? What does Procopius most dislike about the queen? Was Theodora the last woman ruler to receive such criticism?

Formerly, when the senate approached the Emperor, it paid homage in the following manner. Every patrician kissed him on the right breast; the Emperor [then] kissed the patrician on the head, and he was dismissed. Then the rest bent their right knee to the Emperor and withdrew. It was not customary to pay homage to the Queen.

But those who were admitted [in] to the presence of Justinian and Theodora, whether they were patricians or otherwise, fell on their faces on the floor, stretching their hands and feet out wide, kissed first one foot and then the other of the Augustus [i.e., the emperor], and then retired. Nor did Theodora refuse this honor; and she even received the ambassadors of the Persians and other barbarians and gave them presents, as if she were in command of the Roman Empire: a thing that had never happened in all previous time.

And formerly intimates of the Emperor called him Emperor and the Empress, Empress. … But if anybody addressed either of these two as Emperor or Empress without adding "Your Majesty" or "Your Highness," or forgot to call himself their slave, he was considered either ignorant or insolent, and was dismissed in disgrace as if he had done some awful crime or committed some unpardonable sin.

And [whereas] before, only a few were sometimes admitted to the palace … when these two came to power, the magistrates and everybody else had no trouble in fairly living in the palace. This was because the magistrates of old had administered justice and the laws according to their conscience … but these two, taking control of everything to the misfortune of their subjects, forced everyone to come to them and beg like slaves. And almost any day one could see the law courts nearly deserted, while in the hall of the Emperor there was a jostling and pushing crowd that resembled nothing so much as a mob of slaves.

From Procopius, *Secret History*, in *The Early Middle Ages 500–1000*, ed. by Robert Brentano (New York: Free Press, 1964), pp. 70–71.

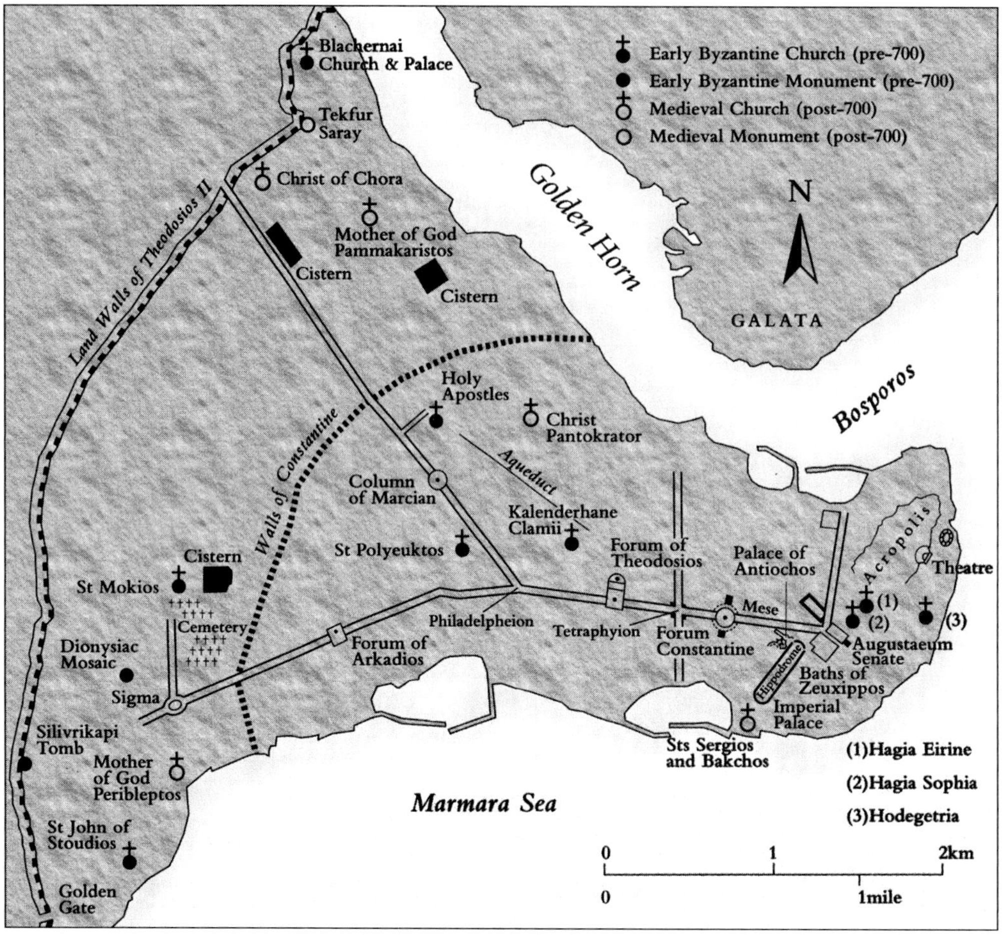

MAP 12–2 Constantinople.   This map indicates the location of major churches and monuments.

record suggests the size and splendor of Constantinople at its peak: 5 imperial and 9 princely palaces; 8 public and 153 private baths; 4 public forums; 5 granaries; 2 theaters; 1 hippodrome; 322 streets; 4,388 substantial houses; 52 porticoes; 20 public and 120 private bakeries; and 14 churches. The most popular entertainments were the races at the Hippodrome and the theater, where, according to clerical critics, nudity and immorality were on display. Many public taverns dotted the cities as well.

Between the fourth and fifth centuries, councils of roughly two hundred members, known as *Decurions,* all local, wealthy landowners, governed the cities. Being the intellectual and economic elite of the empire, they were heavily taxed, which did not make them the emperor's most docile or loyal servants. By the sixth century, fidelity had become the coin of the realm, and special governors, lay and clerical, chosen from the landholding classes, replaced the *decurion* councils as more reliable instruments of the emperor's sovereign will. As the sixth and seventh centuries saw the beginning of new barbarian invasions of the empire from the north and the east, such political tightening became imperative.

Law   The imperial goal reflected in Justinian's policy of "one God, one empire, one religion" was to centralize government by imposing legal and doctrinal conformity throughout. To this end, the emperor ordered a collation and revision of Roman law. Such a codification became a pressing matter because of the enormous number of legal decrees, often contradictory, that had been piling up since the mid–second century, as the empire grew ever more Christian and imperial rule increasingly autocratic. The goal: loyal and docile subjects guided by clear and enforceable laws.

The projected *Corpus Juris Civilis,* or "body of civil law," was a fourfold compilation undertaken by a committee of the most learned lawyers. The first compilation, known as the *Code,* appeared in 533, and revised imperial edicts issued since the reign of Hadrian (r. 117–138). A second compilation, the *Novellae,* or "new things," presented the decrees issued by Justinian and his immediate successors since 534. The third compilation, the *Digest,* gathered the major opinions of the old legal experts. And the goal of the fourth compilation, the *Institutes,* was to put in the hands of young scholars a practical

Emperor Justinian and His Attendants. Mosaic in the Church ➤
of San Vitale, Ravenna, Italy, ca 547.
Scala/Art Resource, N.Y.

textbook that drew its lessons from the *Code* and the *Digest*.
Although these various works had little immediate effect on
medieval common law, they became the foundation for most
subsequent European law between the Renaissance and the
nineteenth century. Because bringing subjects under the
authority of a single sovereign was the fundamental feature of
Roman Law, rulers aspiring to centralize their states especially
benefited from Justinian's legal legacy.

This strengthening of empire did not, however, enable Justinian to retrieve the Western imperial lands conquered and
occupied by barbarians in Italy, North Africa, and Spain. The
harder he tried to do so, the greater the price he paid.

Avars, Slavs, and Bulgars   In the sixth and seventh centuries, nomadic barbarian tribes of Avars, Slavs, and Bulgars invaded and
occupied the Eastern Empire, threatening a "dark age" there. Although initially fierce raiders, the Slavs later converted to Eastern
Orthodoxy or Byzantine Christianity. Hoping to build a cultural-
linguistic firewall against menacing Franks who were then
attempting to convert his people to Roman Catholicism in a language they did not understand (Latin), King Rastislav of Moravia
turned to Constantinople for help. In response, the Byzantine
emperor sent two learned missionaries to evangelize the Mora-
vians. They were the priests Constantine, later known as Cyril, and
Methodius, both of whom later become saints. In Moravia, the
two created a Greek-based alphabet for the Slavs, which allowed
them to develop a written language of their own. Through that
language the Christian gospels and Byzantine theology found a
lasting Slavic home. Later, after the Bulgars conquered and absorbed the Slavs, that same alphabet was elevated to a broader

script known as Cyrillic after the priest Cyril. Today known as Old
Church Slavonic, it has ever since been the international Slavic
language through which Byzantine Christianity penetrated eastern Europe: Bohemia, Bulgaria, Macedonia, Rumania, Serbia,
Ukraine, and Kievan Russia. In prior centuries, the Byzantines
had given Goths, Georgians, Armenians, and Syrians similar native tools for accessing Byzantine culture and religion.

Persians and Muslims   During the reign of Emperor Heraclius
(r. 610–641), the empire took a decidedly Eastern, as opposed
to a Roman, direction. Heraclius spoke only Greek, not Latin.
He spent his entire reign resisting Persian and Islamic invasions, the former successfully, the latter in vain. In 628 he defeated the Persian king Chosroes and took back one of Western
Christendom's great lost relics: a piece of Christ's Cross that
had been taken by Chosroes when he captured Jerusalem in
614. After 632, Islamic armies progressively overran the empire,
directly attacking Constantinople for the first time in the mid-
670s (see below). Not until the reign of Leo III of the Isaurian
dynasty (r. 717–740) did the Byzantines repel Arab armies and
regain at least most of Asia Minor, having lost forever its larger
Mediterranean empire. The setback was traumatic and forced
a major restructuring of the downsized empire. That was done
by creating locally governed and garrisoned provincial strongholds under the direct authority of imperially appointed generals. A major break with the old hierarchical governance of
the empire, the new system made possible a more disciplined
and flexible use of military power in time of crisis.

In the eleventh century, Byzantine fortunes rapidly reversed
as the Muslim Seljuk Turks overran vital Anatolia. A devastating

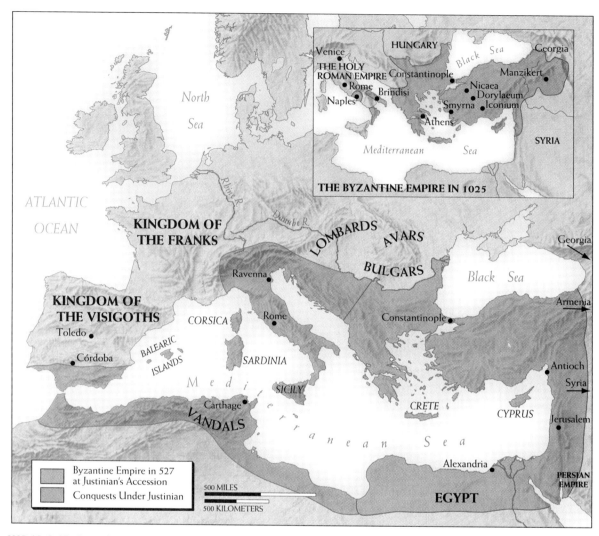

MAP 12–3 The Byzantine Empire at the Death of Justinian.   The inset shows the empire in 1025, before its losses to the Seljuq Turks.

defeat of the Byzantine army at Manzikert in 1071 signaled the end of the empire. That end—at the hands of the Seljuks' cousins, the Ottoman Turks—was still several centuries away. However, after two decades of steady Turkish advance, the Eastern emperor Alexius I Comnenus (r. 1081–1118) invoked Western aid in 1092. Three years later, the West launched the first Crusade. A century later (1204), the Fourth Crusade stopped in Constantinople en route to Jerusalem, not however to rescue the Eastern capital, but to inflict more damage on the holy city and Eastern Christendom than all previous non-Christian invaders had done. (See below.)

The Religious Diversity of Christendom   In both East and West, religious belief and controversy alternately served and undermined imperial political unity. Since the fifth century, the patriarch of Constantinople crowned Byzantine emperors in that city (the "second Rome"), attesting the close ties between rulers and the Eastern Church. In 391, Christianity became the official faith of the Eastern Empire, while all other religions and sects were deemed "demented and insane." Between the fourth and sixth centuries, the patriarchs of Constantinople, Alexandria, Antioch, and Jerusalem received generous endowments of land and gold from rich pious donors, empowering the church to act as the state's welfare agency. That great wealth and prestige swelled clerical ranks and bound the clergy tightly to state service.

While Orthodox Christianity was the religion that mattered most, it was not the only religion in the empire with a significant following. Nor did Byzantine rulers view religion as merely a political tool. From time to time, Christian heresies were also given imperial support. And beyond outright persecution, absorption into tolerated, popular forms of Christianity became a peaceful way for rulers to curtail pagan religious practices.

The empire was also home, albeit less hospitably, to large numbers of Jews. Non-Christian Romans viewed Jews as narrow, dogmatic, and intolerant by comparison with Christians. Under Roman law, Jews had legal protection as long as they did not proselytize among Christians, build new synagogues, or enter sensitive public offices and professions. Whereas the emperor most intent on religious conformity within the empire, Justinian, encouraged Jews to convert voluntarily, later emperors commanded them to be baptized and gave tax breaks to those who freely complied. However, neither persuasion nor coercion succeeded in converting the empire's Jews.

The differences between Eastern and Western Christianity became no less irreconcilable. One issue divided Justinian and Theodora lifelong. Whereas Justinian remained strictly orthodox in his Christian beliefs, Theodora supported a divisive Eastern teaching condemned as a heresy in the West in 451, namely, the teaching that Christ had a single, immortal nature and was not eternal God and mortal man in one and the same person. Still embraced by Coptic and Syrian Christians, the so-called Monophysite heresy exaggerated Orthodox Christianity's determination to protect the sovereignty of God, a concern apparent in Byzantine art, which portrays Christ, a self-same person with God, as impassive and transcendent, not as a suffering mortal man. In the sixth century, the Monophysites became a separate church in the East, particularly in Armenia.

A similar dispute appeared in Eastern debates over the relationship among the members of the Trinity, specifically whether the Holy Spirit proceeded "from the Son" (*filioque*) as well as from the Father in its generation. Again at issue was God's majesty, the theologians fearing a lost of divine unity and dignity if the Holy Spirit proceeded from both. Some perceive here a hidden political concern, important in the East. By protecting the unity and majesty of the Father, Eastern theology was safeguarding the unity and majesty of the emperor himself, from whom all power on earth was believed properly to flow. The idea of a divisible Godhead, no matter how abstract and subtle, suggested the divisibility of imperial power, particularly in an empeor who associated himself so closely with God.

Another major disagreement between the Christian East and West concerned the veneration of images in worship. In 726, Eastern emperor Leo III (717–714) forbade the use of images and icons throughout Christendom. As their veneration had been commonplace, the decree came as a shock, especially to the West. The change in policy may have been a pretext to close cloisters and secularize monastic lands. Or the emperor may have wished to accommodate Muslim sensitivities at a time when he was at war with the Arabs (Islam strictly forbade image worship). Regardless of the reason, the emperor's decree drove Western popes into the camp of the Franks, where they found in Charlemagne an effective protector against the Byzantine world. Although images were restored in the Eastern churches

Christ Pantocrator. Mosaic in the dome of the monastery Church at Daphni, Greece.
Erich Lessing/Art Resource, N.Y.

in the mid-ninth century, many masterpieces went missing during a century of theology- inspired iconoclasm.

A third difference between East and West was the Eastern emperor's pretension to absolute sovereignty, both secular and religious. Expressing his sense of sacred mission, he presented himself in the trappings of holiness and directly interfered in matters of church and religion, what is called Caesaropapism, or the emperor acting as if he were pope as well. To a degree unknown in the West, Eastern emperors appointed and managed the clergy, convening church councils and enforcing church decrees. By comparison, the West nurtured a separation of church and state that began to flower in the eleventh century.

The Eastern church rejected several disputed requirements of Roman Christianity. It denied the existence of Purgatory, permitted lay divorce and remarriage, allowed priests, but not bishops, to marry, and embraced vernacular liturgies in place of Greek and Latin. In these matters Eastern Christians gained opportunities and rights Christians in the West would not enjoy, and then only in part, until the Protestant Reformation in the sixteenth century.

Having accumulated over the centuries, these various differences resulted in a schism between the two churches in 1054. In that year a Western envoy of the pope, cardinal

Humbertus, visited the patriarch of Constantinople, Michael Cerularius, in the hope of overcoming the differences that divided Christendom. The patriarch was not welcoming, however. As he departed the scene, Humbertus left a bull of excommunication on the altar of Hagia Sophia. In response, the patriarch proclaimed Western popes to have been heretics since the sixth century! Nine hundred and eleven years would pass before that breach was repaired. In a belated ecumenical gesture in 1965, a Roman pope met with the patriarch of Constantinople to revoke the mutual condemnations of 1054.

⚠ Religious Diversity. A Muslim and a Christian play the *ud* or lute together, from a thirteenth-century *Book of Chants* in the Escorial Monastery of Madrid. Medieval Europe was deeply influenced by Arab-Islamic culture, transmitted particularly through Spain. In music some of the many works in Arabic on musical theory were translated into Latin and Hebrew, but the main influence came from the actual arts of singing and playing spread by minstrels.

A Moor and a Christian playing the lute, miniature in a book of music from the 'Cantigas' of Alfonso X 'the Wise' (1221–84). Thirteenth century (manuscript). Monastero de El Escorial, El Escorial, Spain/Index/Bridgeman Art Library.

The Impact of Islam on East and West

A new drama began to unfold in the sixth century with the rise of a rival far more dangerous to the West than the Germanic tribes: the new faith of Islam (see Chapter 11). During the lifetime of the Prophet Muhammad (570–632) and thereafter, invading Arab armies claimed the attention and resources of the emperors in Constantinople, who found themselves in a life-and-death struggle. Unlike the Germanic invaders, who absorbed and adopted the culture and religion of Rome, the Arabs, although generally tolerant of Christian and Jewish minorities, ultimately imposed their own culture and religion on the lands they conquered.

After an Arab-Berber army under Tariq ibn Ziyad (Gibralter, "mountain of Tariq," is named after him) conquered Visigothic Spain in 711, Muslims began a seven-hundred-year reign in what is today Andalusia. By the middle of the eighth century Arabs were masters of the southern and eastern Mediterranean coastline, territories today held, for the most part, by Islamic states. Muslim armies also pushed north and east through Mesopotamia and Persia, and beyond. The inhabitants of much of these territories, while Christian, were, like the Arabs, Semitic. Any religious unity they may have felt with the Byzantine Greeks appears to have been offset by their hatred of the Byzantine Greek occupation of their lands. The Christian community was in any case badly divided. Byzantine emperor Heraclius had tried to impose Greek "orthodox" beliefs on the churches of Egypt and Syria, creating enmity between Greek and Semitic Christians. As a result, many Egyptian and Syrian Christians, hoping for deliverance from Byzantine oppression, may have welcomed the Islamic conquerors.

The Muslim conquerors generally tolerated Christians and Jews, provided they paid taxes, kept their distance, and made no efforts to proselytize Muslim communities. Always anxious to maintain the purity of their religion and culture, the Arabs forbade mixed marriages and any conscious cultural interchange. Special taxes on conquered peoples encouraged them to convert to Islam.

Assaulted from East and West and everywhere challenged in the Mediterranean, Christian Europe developed a lasting fear and suspicion of the Muslims. In both the East and the West, the Muslim invasion was confronted and halted. Byzantine Emperor Leo III (r. 717–740) stopped Arab armies at Constantinople after a year's siege (717–718). In subsequent centuries the Byzantines further secured their borders and for a time expanded militarily and commercially into Muslim lands. In the West, the Franks under Charles Martel defeated a raiding party of Arabs on the western frontier of the Frankish kingdom near Tours (today in central France) in 732, ending the possibility of Arab expansion into the heart of Europe by way of Spain. To the extent that the Mediterranean remained something of a "Muslim lake" during the high Middle Ages, the center of the evolving West European civilization was shifted north, away from the Mediterranean. Yet, that did not mean the end of positive contact and influence between Muslim and Christian. Although carried on in keen awareness of a powerful Muslim presence in the Mediterranean, Western trade with the East continued to be of great importance to the Carolingians and pursued in these centuries.

THE WESTERN DEBT TO ISLAM

Arab invasions and presence in the Mediterranean area during a crucial part of the early Middle Ages contributed both directly and indirectly to the formation of Western Europe. They did so indirectly by driving West Europeans back onto their native tribal and inherited Judeo-Christian, Graeco-Roman, and Byzantine resources, from which they created a Western culture of their own. And by diverting the attention and energies of the Byzantine Empire during the formative centuries, the Arabs prevented it from expanding into and reconquering Western Europe. That allowed two Germanic peoples to gain ascendancy: first, the Franks and then the Lombards, who invaded Italy in the sixth century and settled in the Po valley.

Despite hostilities between the Christian West and the Muslim world, there was creative interchange between them, with the West having the most to gain. At this time, Arab civilizations were the more advanced, enjoying their golden age, and they had much to teach a toddling West. Between the eighth and tenth centuries, Moorish Cordoba was a model multicultural city embracing Arabs, Berbers, Spanish Christian converts to Islam, and native Jews. The Iberian Peninsula's largest city in the tenth century, it was a conduit for the finest Arabian tableware, leather, silks, dyes, aromatic ointments and perfumes into the West. The Arabs taught Western farmers how to irrigate fields and Western artisans how to tan leather and refine silk. The West also gained from its contacts with Arabic scholars. Thanks to the skills of Islamic philosophers and translators, ancient Greek works on astronomy, mathematics, and medicine became available in Latin translation to Western scholars. Down to the sixteenth century, the basic gynecological and child-care manuals guiding the work of Western midwives and physicians were compilations made by the Baghdad physician Al-Razi (Rhazes), the philosopher and physician Ibn-Sina (Avicenna) (980–1037), and Ibn Rushd (Averröes) (1126–1198), who was also Islam's greatest authority on Aristotle. Jewish scholars also throve amid the intellectual culture Islamic scholars created. The greatest of them all, Moses Maimonides (1135–1204), wrote in both Arabic and Hebrew. Also the great poets and philologists of the Middle Ages, the Arabs gave the West its most popular book—*The Arabian Nights*, poetic folk tales that are still read and imitated in the West.

The Developing Roman Church

Throughout the period of imperial decline, Germanic invasions, and Islamic expansion, one Western institution remained firmly entrenched and gained in strength: the Christian church. The church sought to organize itself according to the centralized, hierarchical administrative structure of the empire, with strategically placed "viceroys" (bishops) in European cities who looked for spiritual direction to their leader, the bishop of Rome (later pope). As the Western Empire crumbled, local bishops and cathedral chapters (ruling bodies of clergy) filled the resulting vacuum of authority. The local cathedral became the center of urban life and the local bishop the highest authority for those who remained in the cities. In Rome, on a larger and more fateful scale, the pope took control of the city as the Western emperors gradually departed and died out. Left to its own devices, Western Europe soon discovered that the Christian church was its best repository of Roman administrative skills and classical culture.

The Christian church had been graced with special privileges, great lands, and wealth by Emperor Constantine and his successors. In 313 Constantine issued the Edict of Milan, giving Christians legal standing and a favored status within the empire. In 380 Emperors Theodosius I (r. ca. 379–395) and Gratian I (r. 367–283), in a joint declaration, raised Christianity to the official religion of the empire. Both Theodosius and his predecessors acted as much for political effect as out of religious conviction; in 313 Christians composed about one fifth of the population of the empire, making Christianity the strongest among the empire's competing religions. Mithraism, a religion popular among army officers and restricted to males, was its main rival.

Challenged by Rome's decline to become a major political force, the church survived the period of Germanic and Arab invasions as a somewhat spiritually weakened and compromised institution. Yet it remained a potent civilizing and unifying force. It had a religious message of providential purpose and individual worth that could give solace and meaning to life at its worst. It had a ritual of baptism and a creedal confession that united people beyond the traditional barriers of social class, education, and gender. And alone in the West, the church retained an effective hierarchical administration, scattered throughout the old empire, staffed by the best-educated minds in Europe and centered in emperorless Rome.

MONASTIC CULTURE

The church also enjoyed the services of growing numbers of monks, who were not only loyal to its mission, but also objects of great popular respect. Monastic culture proved again and again to be the peculiar strength of the church during the Middle Ages.

▲ **Manual Labor at Monasteries.** The rule of Saint Benedict, followed by most medieval monasteries, required monks to spend one third of their day in manual labor. This served to make the monastery self-sufficient and self-contained. Here monks are shown doing a variety of agricultural tasks.
Courtesy of the Library of Congress.

The first monks were hermits who withdrew from society to pursue a more perfect way of life. They were inspired by the Christian ideal of a life of complete self-denial in imitation of Christ. The popularity of monasticism began to grow as Roman persecution of Christians waned and Christianity became the favored religion of the empire during the fourth century. Embracing the biblical "counsels of perfection" (chastity, poverty, and obedience), the monastic life became the purest form of religious practice.

Anthony of Egypt (ca. 251–356), the father of hermit monasticism, was inspired by Jesus' command to the rich young man: "If you will be perfect, sell all that you have, give it to the poor, and follow me" (Matthew 19:21). Anthony went into the desert to pray and work, setting an example followed by hundreds in Egypt, Syria, and Palestine in the fourth and fifth centuries. This hermit monasticism was soon joined by the development of communal monasticism. In the first quarter of the fourth century, Pachomius (ca. 286–346) organized monks in southern Egypt into a highly regimented community. Such monastic communities grew to contain 1,000 or more inhabitants. They were little "cities of God," trying to separate themselves from the collapsing Roman and the nominal Christian world. Basil the Great (329–379) popularized communal monasticism throughout the East, providing a rule that lessened the asceticism of Pachomius and directed monks beyond their segregated enclaves of perfection into such social services as caring for orphans, widows, and the infirm in surrounding communities.

Athanasius (ca. 293–373) and Martin of Tours (ca. 315–ca. 397) introduced monasticism into the West, where the teaching of John Cassian (ca. 360–435) and Jerome (ca. 340–420) helped shape its basic values and practices. The great organizer of Western monasticism was Benedict of Nursia (ca. 480–547). In 529 he established a monastery at Monte Cassino, in Italy, founding the form of monasticism—Benedictine—that bears his name and that quickly came to dominate in the West. Benedict also wrote a sophisticated *Rule for Monasteries*, a comprehensive plan that both regimented and enriched monastic life. Following the *Rule*, Benedictine monasteries were hierarchically organized and directed by an abbot, whose command was beyond question. Periods of study and religious devotion (about four hours each day of prayers and liturgical activities) alternated with manual labor—a program that permitted not a moment's idleness and carefully promoted the religious, intellectual, and physical well-being of the monks. During the early Middle Ages Benedictine missionaries Christianized both England and Germany. Their disciplined organization and devotion to hard work made the Benedictines an economic and political power as well as a spiritual force wherever they settled.

THE DOCTRINE OF PAPAL PRIMACY

Constantine and his successors, especially the Eastern emperors, ruled religious life with an iron hand and consistently looked on the church as little more than a department of the state. The bishops of Rome, however, never accepted such royal intervention and opposed it in every way they could. Taking advantage of imperial weakness and distraction, they developed for their own defense the doctrine of "papal primacy." This doctrine raised the bishop of Rome to an unassailable supremacy within the church when it came to defining church doctrine and maintaining clerical allegiance. As the "pope," he was both head of the Roman Catholic Church and Christ's vicar on earth continuing the line of Christ's apostles from St. Peter. The new title also put him in a position to claim power within the secular world, giving rise to repeated conflicts between church and state, pope and emperor, throughout the Middle Ages.

Pope Damasus I (r. 366–384) took the first step toward establishing the doctrine when he declared Rome's **apostolic primacy**. Pointing to Jesus' words to Peter in the Gospel of Matthew (16:18) ("Thou art Peter, and upon this rock I will build my church"), he claimed himself and all other popes to be Peter's direct successors as the unique "rock" on which the Christian church was built. Pope Leo I (r. 440–461) took still another step by assuming the title *pontifex maximus*—"supreme priest." He further proclaimed himself to be endowed with a "plenitude of power," thereby establishing the supremacy of the bishop of Rome over all other bishops in the church. During Leo's reign an imperial decree recognized his exclusive jurisdiction over the

Western church. At the end of the fifth century Pope Gelasius I (r. 492–496) proclaimed the authority of the clergy to be "more weighty" than the power of kings because priests had charge of divine affairs and the means of salvation.

DIVISION OF CHRISTENDOM

As these events suggest, the division of Christendom into Eastern (Byzantine) and Western (Roman Catholic) churches has its roots in the early Middle Ages. The division was due in part to linguistic and cultural differences between the Greek East and the Roman West. As in the West, Eastern church organization closely followed that of the secular state. A "patriarch" ruled over "metropolitans" and "archbishops" in the cities and provinces, who, in turn, ruled over bishops, who stood as authorities over the local clergy. A novel combination of Greek, Roman, and Asian elements shaped Byzantine culture, giving Eastern Christianity a stronger mystical dimension than Western Christianity, a difference in outlook that may have predisposed Eastern patriarchs to submit more passively than Western popes ever could to royal intervention in their affairs.

Contrary to the evolving Western tradition of universal clerical celibacy, which Western monastic culture encouraged, the Eastern church permitted the marriage of parish priests (but not monks), while strictly forbidding bishops to marry. The Eastern church also used leavened bread in the Eucharist, contrary to the Western custom of using unleavened bread. The Roman church also objected to the tendency of the Eastern church to compromise with the politically

---

CHRONOLOGY

•••

Major Political and Religious Developments of the Early Middle Ages

313	Emperor Constantine issues the Edict of Milan
325	Council of Nicaea defines Christian doctrine
410	Rome invaded by Visigoths under Alaric
413–426	Saint Augustine writes *The City of God*
451–453	Europe invaded by the Huns under Attila
476	Barbarian Odovacer deposes Western emperor and rules as king of the Romans
488	Theodoric establishes kingdom of Ostrogoths in Italy
529	Saint Benedict founds monastery at Monte Cassino
533	Justinian codifies Roman law
732	Charles Martel defeats Arabs at Tours
754	Pope Stephen II and Pepin III ally

---

powerful Arian Christians and the followers of another nonorthodox group, the Monophysite Christians (see the earlier section, "The Byzantine Empire"). Finally, the Eastern and Western churches both laid claim to jurisdiction over newly converted areas in the northern Balkans.

Beyond these issues, three major factors lay behind the religious break between East and West. The first revolved around questions of doctrinal authority. The Eastern church put more stress on the authority of the Bible and the ecumenical councils of the church in the definition of Christian doctrine than on the counsel and decrees of the bishop of Rome. The claims of Roman popes to a special primacy of authority on the basis of the Apostle Peter's commission from Jesus in the Gospel of Matthew were unacceptable to the East, where the independence and autonomy of regional churches held sway. This basic issue of authority in matters of faith lay behind the mutual excommunication of Pope Nicholas I and Patriarch Photius in the ninth century and that of Pope Leo IX (through his ambassador to Constantinople, Cardinal Humbert) and Patriarch Michael Cerularius in 1054.

A second major issue in the separation of the two churches, as explained above, was the Western addition of the *filioque* clause to the Nicene-Constantinopolitan Creed. According to this anti-Arian clause, the Holy Spirit proceeds "also from the Son" (*filioque*) as well as from the Father, making clear the Western belief that Christ was fully of one essence with God the Father and not a lesser being.

The third factor dividing the Eastern and Western churches was the iconoclastic controversy of the first half of the eighth century. As noted earlier, after 725 the Byzantine Emperor Leo III (r. 717–741) attempted to force Western popes to abolish the use of images in their churches. This stand met fierce official and popular resistance in the West, where images were greatly cherished, and in the East as well. To punish the West, Leo confiscated valuable papal lands. This direct challenge to the papacy coincided with a threat to Rome and the Western church from the Lombards of northern Italy. Assailed on two fronts, the Roman papacy seemed doomed. But there has not been a more resilient and enterprising institution in Western history than the papacy. Since the pontificate of Gregory the Great (590–604), who 150 years earlier had negotiated a treaty with the Lombards, popes had recognized the Franks of northern Gaul as Europe's ascendant power and seen in them their surest protectors. In 754 Pope Stephen II (r. 752–757), initiating the most fruitful political alliance of the Middle Ages, enlisted the Franks and their ruler, Pepin III, to defend the church against the Lombards and as a Western counterweight to the Eastern emperor. This marriage of religion and politics created a new Western church and empire; and determined much of the course of Western history thereafter.

The Kingdom of the Franks

MEROVINGIANS AND CAROLINGIANS: FROM CLOVIS TO CHARLEMAGNE

Clovis (ca. 466–511), a warrior chieftain who converted to Orthodox Christianity under the influence of his Christian wife around 496, founded the first Frankish dynasty, the Merovingians, named after Merovich, an early leader of one branch of the Franks. Clovis and his successors subdued the pagan Burgundians and the Arian Visigoths and established the kingdom of the Franks within ancient Gaul, making the Franks and the Merovingian kings a significant force in Western Europe. The Franks themselves occupied a broad belt of territory that extended through modern France, Belgium, the Netherlands, and western Germany, while their loyalties remained strictly tribal and local. In attempting to govern their sprawling kingdom, the Merovingians encountered what proved to be the most persistent problem of medieval political history—the competing claims of the "one" and the "many," with the king (the "one") struggling to impose centralized government and transregional loyalty on powerful local magnates (the "many"), determined to preserve their regional autonomy and traditions.

The Merovingian kings addressed this problem by making pacts with the landed nobility and by creating the royal office of count. The counts were men without possessions to whom the king gave great lands in the expectation that they would be, as the landed aristocrats often were not, loyal officers of the kingdom. But like local aristocrats, the Merovingian counts also let their immediate self-interests gain the upper hand. Once established in office for a period of time, they too became territorial rulers in their own right, with the result that the Frankish kingdom progressively fragmented into independent regions and tiny principalities. This centrifugal tendency was aggravated by the Frankish custom of dividing the kingdom equally among the king's legitimate male heirs.

Rather than purchase allegiance and unity within the kingdom, the Merovingian largess occasioned the rise of competing magnates and petty tyrants, who became laws unto themselves within their regions. By the seventh century, the Frankish king was king in title only, lacking effective executive power. Real power was concentrated in the office of the Mayor of the Palace, who was the spokesman at the king's court for the great landowners of the three regions into which the Frankish kingdom was divided: Neustria (roughly western France), Austrasia (roughly central Germany), and Burgundy. Through this office, the Carolingian dynasty rose to power.

The Carolingians, who took their name from the dynasty's greatest ruler, Carolus, later to be known as Charlemagne, controlled the office of the mayor of the palace from the ascent to that post of Pepin I of Austrasia (d. 639) until 751, when, with the enterprising connivance of the pope, they simply expropriated the Frankish crown. Pepin II (d. 714) ruled in fact, if not in title, over the Frankish kingdom. His illegitimate son, Charles Martel ("the Hammer," d. 741), created a great cavalry by bestowing lands known as *benefices* or **fiefs** on powerful nobles, who, in return, agreed to be ready to serve as the king's army. It was such an army that checked the Arab probings at Tours in 732.

The fiefs so generously bestowed by Charles Martel to create his army came in large part from landed property that he usurped from the church. His alliance with the landed aristocracy in this grand manner permitted the Carolingians to have some measure of political success where the Merovingians had failed. The Carolingians created counts almost entirely out of the landed nobility from which the Carolingians themselves had risen. The Merovingians, in contrast, had tried to compete directly with these great aristocrats by raising the landless to power. By playing to strength rather than challenging it, the Carolingians strengthened themselves, at least for the short term. The church, by this time dependent on the protection of the Franks against the Eastern emperor and the Lombards, had no choice but to tolerate the seizure of its lands. Later, although they never returned the lands, the Franks partially compensated the church for them.

Frankish Church The church played a large and enterprising role in the Frankish government. By Carolingian times, monasteries were a dominant force. Their intellectual achievements made them respected repositories of culture. Their religious teaching and example imposed order on surrounding populations. Their relics and rituals made them magical shrines to which pilgrims came in great numbers. Thanks to their donated lands and serf labor, many had become very profitable farms and landed estates, their abbots rich and powerful magnates. By Merovingian times, the higher clergy were already employed in tandem with counts as royal agents. It was the policy of the Carolingians, perfected by Charles Martel and his successor, Pepin III ("the Short," d. 768), to use the church to pacify conquered neighboring tribes—Frisians, Thuringians, Bavarians, and especially the Franks' archenemies, the Saxons.

Conversion to Nicene Christianity became an integral part of the successful annexation of conquered lands and people; the cavalry broke bodies, while the clergy won hearts and minds. The Anglo-Saxon missionary Saint Boniface (b. Wynfrith, ca. 680–754) was the most important of the German clergy who served Carolingian kings in this way. Christian bishops in missionary districts and elsewhere became lords, appointed by and subject to the king—an ominous integration of secular and religious policy in which lay the seeds of the later Investiture Controversy of the eleventh and twelfth centuries (see Chapter 15).

The church helped the Carolingians with more than territorial expansion. Pope Zacharias (r. 741–752) sanctioned Pepin the Short's termination of the vestigial Merovingian dynasty and the Carolingian accession to kingship of the Franks. With the pope's blessing, Pepin was proclaimed king by the nobility in council in 751. The last of the Merovingians, the puppet king Childeric III, was removed to a monastery and dynastic oblivion. According to legend, Saint Boniface annointed Pepin, thereby investing Frankish rule with a sacral character from the start.

Zacharias's successor, Pope Stephen II (r. 752–757), did not let Pepin forget the favor of his predecessor. Driven from Rome in 753 by the Lombards, Pope Stephen appealed directly to Pepin to cast out the invaders and to guarantee papal claims to central Italy, which was dominated at this time by the Eastern emperor. In 754 the Franks and the church formed an alliance against the Lombards and the Eastern emperor. Carolingian kings became the protectors of the Catholic Church and thereby "kings by the grace of God." Pepin gained the title *patricius Romanorum*, "father-protector of the Romans," a title heretofore borne only by the representative of the Eastern emperor. In 755 the Franks defeated the Lombards and gave the pope the lands surrounding Rome, creating what came to be known as the **Papal States**. In this period a fraudulent document appeared—the *Donation of Constantine*, written between 750 and 800—enterprisingly designed to remind the Franks of the church's importance as the heir of Rome. Many believed it to be genuine until fifteenth-century scholars exposed it as a forgery.

The papacy had looked to the Franks for an ally strong enough to protect it from the Eastern emperors. It is an irony of history that the church found in the Carolingian dynasty a Western imperial government that drew almost as slight a boundary between state and church, secular and religious policy, as did Eastern emperors. Although eminently preferable to Eastern domination, Carolingian patronage of the church proved to be no less constraining.

REIGN OF CHARLEMAGNE (768–814)

Charlemagne, the son of Pepin the Short, continued the role of his father as papal protector in Italy and his policy of territorial conquest in the north. After King Desiderius and the Lombards of northern Italy were decisively defeated in 774, Charlemagne took the title "King of the Lombards" in Pavia. He widened the frontiers of his kingdom further by subjugating surrounding pagan tribes, foremost among them the Saxons, whom the Franks brutally Christianized and dispersed in small groups throughout Frankish lands. The Danubian plains were brought into the Frankish orbit by the virtual annihilation of the Avars, a tribe related to the Huns. The Arabs were chased beyond the Pyrenees. By the time of his death on January 28, 814, Charlemagne's kingdom embraced modern France, Belgium, Holland, Switzerland, almost the whole of Germany, much of Italy, a portion of Spain, and the island of Corsica (see Map 12–4).

The New Empire Encouraged by his ambitious advisers, Charlemagne came to harbor imperial designs. He desired to be not only king of all the Franks but a universal emperor as well. He had his sacred palace city, Aachen (in French, Aix-la-Chapelle), constructed in conscious imitation of the courts of the ancient Roman and the contemporary Eastern emperors. Although he permitted the church its independence, he looked after it with a paternalism almost as great as that of any Eastern emperor. He used the church above all to promote social stability and hierarchical order throughout the kingdom—as an aid in the creation of a great Frankish Christian empire. Frankish Christians were ceremoniously baptized, professed the Nicene Creed (with the *filioque* clause), and learned in church to revere Charlemagne.

Charlemagne realized his imperial pretensions on Christmas Day 800, when Pope Leo III (795–816) crowned him emperor. This event created what would later be called the Holy Roman Empire, a revival, based after 870 in Germany, of the old Roman Empire in the West. If the coronation benefited the church, as it certainly did, it also served Charlemagne's designs. Before his coronation, Charlemagne had been a minor Western potentate in the eyes of Eastern emperors. After the coronation, Eastern emperors reluctantly recognized his new imperial dignity, and Charlemagne even found it necessary to disclaim ambitions to rule as emperor over the East.

The New Emperor Charlemagne stood six feet, three and one half inches tall—a fact confirmed when his tomb was opened and exact measurements of his remains were taken in 1861. He was restless, ever ready for a hunt. Informal and gregarious, he insisted on the presence of friends even when he bathed and was widely known for his practical jokes, lusty good humor, and warm hospitality. Aachen was a festive palace city to which people and gifts came from all over the world. In 802 Charlemagne even received from the caliph of Baghdad, Harun-al-Rashid, a white elephant, the transport of which across the Alps was as great a wonder as the creature itself.

Charlemagne had five official wives in succession, and many mistresses and concubines, and he sired numerous children. This connubial variety created problems. His oldest son by his first marriage, Pepin, jealous of the attention shown by his father to the sons of his second wife and fearing the loss of paternal favor, joined with noble enemies in a conspiracy against his father. He spent the rest of his life in confinement in a monastery after the plot was exposed.

Problems of Government Charlemagne governed his kingdom through counts, of whom there were perhaps as many as 250, strategically located within the administrative districts into which the kingdom was divided. In Carolingian practice, the count tended to be a local magnate, one who already had an armed following and the self-interest to enforce the will of a

MAP 12–4 The Empire of Charlemagne to 814. Building on the successes of his predecessors, Charlemagne greatly increased the Frankish domains. Such traditional enemies as the Saxons and the Lombards fell under his sway.

generous king. He had three main duties: to maintain a local army loyal to the king, to collect tribute and dues, and to administer justice throughout his district.

This last responsibility he undertook through a district law court known as the mallus, which heard testimony from the parties involved in a dispute or crime, passed judgment, and assessed a monetary compensation to be paid to the injured party. In very difficult cases, where guilt or innocence was unclear, recourse was often taken to judicial duels or "divine" tests and ordeals. Among these was the length of time a defendant's hand took to heal after immersion in boiling water. In another, the ordeal by water, a defendant was thrown with his hands and feet bound into a river or pond that a priest had

blessed. If he floated, he was pronounced guilty, because the pure water had obviously rejected him; if, however, the water received him and he sank, he was deemed innocent.

As in Merovingian times, many counts used their official position and new judicial powers to their own advantage, becoming little despots within their districts. As they grew stronger and more independent, they came to regard the land grants with which they were paid as hereditary positions rather than generous royal donations. This development signaled the impending fragmentation of Charlemagne's kingdom. Charlemagne tried to supervise his overseers and improve local justice by creating special royal envoys known as *missi dominici*, lay and clerical agents (counts, archbishops, and bishops) who made annual visits to districts other than their own. But their impact was marginal. In still another attempt to manage the counts and organize the outlying regions of his realm, the king appointed permanent provincial governors with titles like prefect, duke, or margrave. But as these governors became established in their areas, they proved as corruptible as the others.

Charlemagne never solved the problem of creating a loyal bureaucracy. Ecclesiastical agents proved no better than secular ones in this regard. Landowning bishops had not only the same responsibilities but also the same secular lifestyles and aspirations as the royal counts. Except for their attendance to the liturgy and to church prayers, they were largely indistinguishable from the lay nobility. Capitularies, or royal decrees, discouraged the more outrageous behavior of the clergy. But Charlemagne also sensed—rightly, as the Gregorian reform of the eleventh century would prove—that the emergence of a distinctive and reform-minded class of ecclesiastical landowners would be a danger to royal government. Charlemagne purposefully treated his bishops as he treated his counts, that is, as vassals who served at the king's pleasure.

Alcuin and the Carolingian Renaissance

Charlemagne used much of the great wealth his conquests brought him to attract Europe's best scholars to Aachen, where they developed court culture and education. By making scholarship materially as well as intellectually rewarding, Charlemagne attracted such scholars as Theodulf of Orleans (d. 821), Angilbert (d. 814), his own biographer Einhard (ca. 770–840), and the renowned Anglo-Saxon master Alcuin of York (735–804), who at almost fifty became director of the king's palace school in 782. Alcuin brought classical and Christian learning to Aachen and was handsomely rewarded for his efforts with several monastic estates, including that of Saint Martin of Tours, the wealthiest in the kingdom.

Although Charlemagne also appreciated learning for its own sake, his grand palace school was not created simply for love of antiquity. Charlemagne intended it to upgrade the administrative skills of the clerics and officials who staffed the royal bureaucracy. By preparing the sons of nobles to run the religious and secular offices of the realm, court scholarship served kingdom building. With its special concentration on grammar, logic,

Charlemagne. An equestrian figure of Charlemagne (or possibly one of his sons) from the early ninth century. Bronze equestrian statuette of Charlemagne, from Metz Cathedral, ninth-tenth century 3/4 view. Louvre, Paris, France. Copyright Bridgeman-Giraudon/Art Resource, NY.

rhetoric, and basic mathematics, the school provided training in the basic tools of bureaucracy: reading, writing, speaking, sound reasoning, and counting. Charlemagne's scholars also created a new, clear style of handwriting—Carolingian minuscule—and fostered the use of accurate Latin in official documents, developments that helped increase lay literacy. Through personal correspondence and visitations, Alcuin created a genuine, if limited, community of scholars and clerics at court and did much to infuse the highest administrative levels with a sense of comradeship and common purpose.

A modest renaissance, or rebirth, of antiquity occurred in the palace school as scholars collected and preserved ancient manuscripts for a more curious posterity. Alcuin worked on a correct text of the Bible and made editions of the works of Gregory the Great and the monastic *Rule* of Saint Benedict. These scholarly activities aimed at concrete reforms and served official efforts to bring uniformity to church law and liturgy, educate the clergy, and improve moral life within the monasteries.

The Manor and Serfdom The agrarian economy of the Middle Ages was organized and controlled through village farms known as **manors**. Here peasants labored as farmers in subordination to a lord, that is, a more powerful landowner who gave them land and a dwelling in exchange for their services and a portion of their crops. That part of the land farmed by the peasants for the lord was the **demesne**, on average about one quarter to one third of the arable land. All crops grown there were harvested for the lord.

Peasants were treated according to their social status and the size of their landholdings. A freeman—that is, a peasant with his own modest allodial, or hereditary, property (property free from the claims of an overlord)—became a **serf** by surrendering his property to a greater landowner—a lord—in exchange for protection and assistance. The freeman received

Plowing the Fields. The invention of the moldboard plow greatly improved farming. The heavy plow cut depply into the ground and furrowed it. This illustration from the Luttrell Psalter (ca. 1340) also shows that the traction harness, which lessened the strangulation effect of the yoke on the animals, had not yet been adopted. Indeed, one of the oxen seems to be on the verge of choking.

Picture Desk, Inc./Kobal Collection.

his land back from the lord with a clear definition of his economic and legal rights. Although the land was no longer his property, he had full possession and use of it and the number of services and amount of goods he was to supply to the lord were carefully spelled out. Peasants who entered the service of a lord with little real property to bargain with (perhaps only a few farm implements and animals) ended up as unfree serfs and were much more vulnerable to the lord's demands, often spending up to three days a week working the lord's fields. Truly impoverished peasants who lived and worked on the manor as serfs had the lowest status and were the least protected.

Serfs were subject to so-called dues in kind: firewood for cutting the lord's wood, sheep for grazing their sheep on the lord's land, and the like. Thus the lord, who for his part furnished shacks and small plots of land from his vast domain, had at his disposal an army of servants who provided him with everything from eggs to boots. That many serfs were discontented is reflected in the high number of recorded escapes. An astrological calendar from the period marks the days most favorable for escaping. Fugitive serfs roamed the land as beggars and vagabonds, searching for new and better masters.

By the time of Charlemagne, the moldboard plow, which was especially needed in northern Europe where the soil was heavy, and the three-field system of land cultivation were coming into use. These developments greatly improved agricultural productivity. Unlike the older "scratch" plow, which crisscrossed the field with only slight penetration, the moldboard cut deep into the soil and turned it to form a ridge, providing a natural drainage system for the field as well as permitting the deep planting of seeds. Unlike the earlier two-field system of crop rotation, which simply alternated fallow with planted fields each year, the **three-field system** increased the amount of cultivated land by leaving only one third fallow in a given year.

Religion and the Clergy As owners of the churches on their lands, the lords had the right to raise chosen serfs to the post of parish priest, placing them in charge of the churches on the lords' estates. Church law directed the lord to set a serf free before he entered the clergy, but lords were reluctant to do this and risk thereby a possible later challenge to their jurisdiction over the ecclesiastical property with which the serf, as priest, was invested. Lords preferred a "serf priest," one who not only said the Mass on Sundays and holidays but also continued to serve his lord during the week, waiting on the lord's table and tending his steeds. Like Charlemagne with his bishops, Frankish lords cultivated a docile parish clergy.

The ordinary people baptized themselves and their children, confessed the Creed Mass, tried to learn the Lord's Prayer, and received last rites from the priest when death approached. Local priests on the manors were no better educated than their congregations, and instruction in the meaning of Christian doctrine and practice remained at a bare minimum. People understandably became particularly attached in this period to the more tangible veneration of relics and saints.

Charlemagne shared many of the religious beliefs of his ordinary subjects. He collected and venerated relics, made pilgrimages to Rome, frequented the church of Saint Mary in

Aachen several times a day, and directed in his last will and testament that all but a fraction of his great treasure be spent to endow Masses and prayers for his departed soul.

BREAKUP OF THE CAROLINGIAN KINGDOM

In the last years of his life, an ailing Charlemagne knew that his empire was ungovernable. The seeds of dissolution lay in regionalism, that is, the determination of each locality, no matter how small, to look first—and often only—to its own self-interest. In medieval society, a direct relationship existed between physical proximity to authority and loyalty to authority. Local people obeyed local lords more readily than they obeyed a glorious but distant king. Charlemagne had been forced to recognize and even to enhance the power of regional magnates in order to win needed financial and military support.

Louis the Pious   The Carolingian kings did not give up easily, however. Charlemagne's only surviving son and successor, Louis the Pious (r. 814–840), had three sons by his first wife. According to Salic or Germanic law, a ruler partitioned his kingdom equally among his surviving sons. Louis recognized that a tripartite kingdom would hardly be an empire and acted early in his reign to break this legal tradition. This he did by making his eldest son, Lothar (d. 855), co-regent and sole imperial heir in 817. To Lothar's brothers he gave important but much lesser appanages, or assigned hereditary lands: Pepin (d. 838) became king of Aquitaine and Louis "the German" (d. 876) became king of Bavaria, over the eastern Franks.

In 823 Louis's second wife, Judith of Bavaria, bore him still a fourth son, Charles (d. 877). Determined that her son should receive more than just a nominal inheritance, the queen incited the brothers Pepin and Louis to war against Lothar and persuaded their father to divide the kingdom equally among his four living sons. As the bestower of crowns upon emperors, the pope had an important stake in the preservation of the revived Western Empire and the imperial title, both of which were threatened by Louis' belated agreement to an equal partition of his kingdom. The pope condemned Louis and restored Lothar to his original magnificent inheritance. But Lothar's regained imperial dignity only stirred anew the resentments of his brothers, including his half-brother, Charles, who joined in renewed war against him.

The Treaty of Verdun and its Aftermath   In 843, with the Treaty of Verdun, peace finally came to Louis' surviving heirs (Pepin had died in 838). The great Carolingian Empire was partitioned into three equal parts. Lothar received a middle section, which came to be known as Lotharingia and embraced roughly modern Holland, Belgium, Switzerland, Alsace-Lorraine, and Italy. Charles the Bald received the western part of the kingdom, or roughly

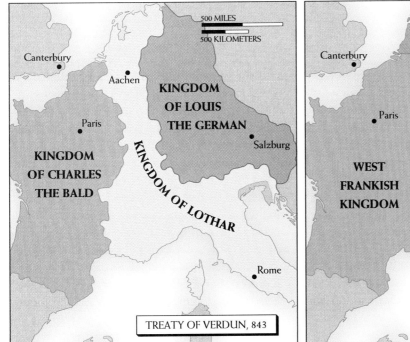

MAP 12–5 The Treaty of Verdun (843) and the Treaty of Mersen (870).   The Treaty of Verdun divided the kingdom of Louis the Pious among his three feuding children: Charles the Bald, Lothar, and Louis the German. After Lothar's death in 855, the middle kingdom was so weakened by division among his three sons that Charles the Bald and Louis the German divided it between themselves in the Treaty of Mersen.

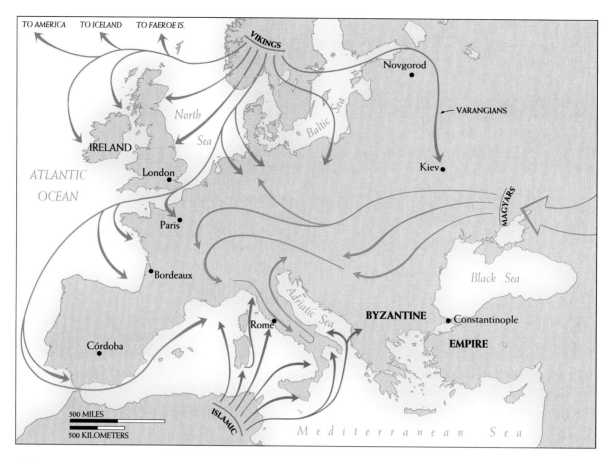

MAP 12–6 Viking, Muslim, and Magyar Invasions to the Eleventh Century.   Western Europe was sorely beset by new waves of outsiders from the ninth to the eleventh century. From north, east, and south, a stream of invading Vikings, Magyars, and Muslims brought the West at times to near collapse and of course gravely affected institutions within Europe.

modern France, and Louis the German came into the eastern part, or roughly modern Germany (see Map 12–5). Although Lothar retained the imperial title, the universal empire of Charlemagne and Louis the Pious now ceased to exist. Not until the sixteenth century, with the election in 1519 of Charles I of Spain as the Holy Roman Emperor Charles V, would the Western world again see a kingdom as vast as Charlemagne's.

The Treaty of Verdun proved to be only the beginning of Carolingian fragmentation. When Lothar died in 855 his kingdom was divided equally among his three surviving sons, leaving it much smaller and weaker than the kingdoms of Louis the German and Charles the Bald. Henceforth, Western Europe would be divided into an Eastern and a Western Frankish Kingdom—roughly Germany and France—at war over the fractionalized middle kingdom, a contest that has continued into modern times.

Vikings, Magyars, and Muslims The political breakdown of the Carolingian Empire coincided with new external threats. In the late ninth and tenth centuries, successive waves of Normans (North men), better known as Vikings, swept into Europe from

Scandinavia. Vikings was a catchall term for Scandinavian peoples who visited Europe alternately as gregarious traders and savage raiders, and their exploits have been preserved in sagas that reveal a cultural world filled with mythical gods and spirits. Taking to sea in ocean-going longboats of rugged, doubled-hulled construction, they terrified their neighbors to the south, invading and occupying English and European coastal and river towns. In the ninth century, the Danes briefly besieged Paris, while other Vikings turned York into a major trading post for their woolens, jewelry, and ornamental wares. Erik the Red made it to Greenland and his son, Leif Erikson wintered in Newfoundland and may even have walked on the shores of New England five hundred years before Columbus. In the eleventh century Christian conversions and English defeat of the Norwegians effectively restricted Vikings to their Scandinavian homelands.

Magyars, or Hungarians, who were great horsemen, also swept into Western Europe from the eastern plains, while Muslims made incursions across the Mediterranean from North Africa (see Map 12–6). The Franks built fortified towns and castles in strategic locations as refuges. When they could, they bought off the invaders with grants of land and payments of silver.

In the resulting turmoil, local populations became more dependent than ever on local strongmen for life, limb, and livelihood, creating the essential precondition for the maturation of feudal society.

Feudal Society

The Middle Ages were characterized by a chronic absence of effective central government and the constant threat of famine, disease, and foreign invasion. In this state of affairs the weaker sought the protection of the stronger, and the true lords and masters became those who could guarantee immediate protection from rapine and starvation. The term *feudal society* refers to the social, political, military, and economic system that emerged from these conditions.

A feudal society is a social order in which a regional prince or a local lord is dominant, and the highest virtues are those of mutual trust and fidelity. In a feudal society, what people require most is the firm assurance that others can be depended on in time of dire need. It is above all a system of mutual rights and responsibilities.

During the early Middle Ages, the landed nobility became great lords who ruled over their domains as miniature kingdoms. They maintained their own armies and courts, regulated

▲ **Lord and Vassal.** A seventh century portrayal of a vassal, who kneels before his lord and inserts his hands between those of his lord in a gesture of mutual loyalty: the vassal promising to obey and serve his lord, the lord promising to support and protect his vassal. Spanish school (seventh century). Lord and vassal, decorated page (vellum).
Archivo de la Corona de Aragon, Barcelona, Spain/Index/Bridgeman Art Library.

CHRONOLOGY	
Carolingian Dynasty (751–987)	
751	Pepin III "the Short" becomes king of the Franks
755	Franks drive Lombards out of central Italy; creation of Papal States
768–814	Charlemagne rules as king of the Franks
774	Charlemagne defeats Lombards in northern Italy
750–800	Fraudulent Donation of Constantine created in an effort to counter Frankish domination of church
800	Pope Leo III crowns Charlemagne
814–840	Louis the Pious succeeds Charlemagne as "Emperor"
843	Treaty of Verdun partitions the Carolingian Empire
870	Treaty of Mersen further divides Carolingian Empire
875–950	Invasions by Vikings, Muslims, and Magyars
962	Ottonian dynasty succeeds Carolingian in Germany
987	Capetian dynasty succeeds Carolingian in France

local tolls, and even minted their own coins. Large groups of warrior **vassals** were created by extensive bestowals of land, and these developed into a prominent professional military class with its own code of knightly conduct. In feudal society, most serfs docilely worked the land, the clergy prayed and gave counsel, and lords and knights maintained law and order.

ORIGINS

The origins of feudal government can be found in the divisions and conflicts of Merovingian society. In the sixth and seventh centuries, individual freemen began placing themselves under the protection of more powerful freemen. In this way, the latter built up armies and became local magnates, and the former solved the problem of simple survival. Freemen who so entrusted themselves to others were known as *ingenui in obsequio* (freemen in a contractual relation of dependence). Those who so gave themselves to the king were called *antrustiones*. All men of this type came to be described collectively as *vassi* ("those who serve"), from which evolved the term *vassalage*, meaning the placement of oneself in the personal service of another who promises protection in return.

Landed nobles, like kings, tried to acquire as many vassals as they could, because military strength in the early Middle Ages lay in numbers. Because it proved impossible to maintain these growing armies within the lord's own household, which was the original custom, or to support them by special monetary payments, the practice evolved of simply granting them land as a "tenement." Such land came to be known as a *benefice*, or a *fief*, and vassals were expected to dwell on it and maintain their horses and other accouterments of war in good order. Originally vassals, therefore, were little more than gangs-in-waiting.

VASSALAGE AND THE FIEF

Vassalage involved **fealty** to the lord. (See Document, "Bishop Fulbert Describes Obligations of Vassals and Lords.") To swear fealty was to promise to refrain from any action that might in any way threaten the lord's well-being and to perform personal services for him on his request. Chief among the expected services was military duty as a mounted knight. This could involve a variety of activities: a short or long military expedition, escort duty, standing castle guard, or the placement of one's own fortress at the lord's disposal, if the vassal was of such stature as to have one. Continuous bargaining and bickering occurred over the terms of service.

Limitations were placed on the number of days a lord could require services from a vassal. In France in the eleventh century, about forty days of service per year were considered sufficient. It also became possible for vassals to buy their way out of military service by a monetary payment known as *scutage*. The lord, in turn, applied this payment to the hiring of mercenaries, who often proved more efficient than contract-conscious vassals. Beyond his military duty, the vassal was also expected to give the lord advice when he requested it and to sit as a member of his court when it was in session.

The lord's obligations to his vassals were very specific. He was, first of all, obligated to protect the vassal from physical harm and to stand as his advocate in public court. After fealty was sworn and homage paid, the lord provided for the vassal's physical maintenance by the bestowal of a benefice, or fief. The fief was simply the physical or material wherewithal to meet the vassal's military and other obligations. It could take the form of liquid wealth as well as the more common grant of real property. There were so-called money fiefs, which empowered a vassal to receive regular payments from the lord's treasury. Such fiefs created potential conflicts because they made it possible for one country to acquire vassals among the nobil-

ity of another. Normally, the fief consisted of a landed estate of anywhere from a few to several thousand acres, but it could also take the form of a castle.

In Carolingian times, a benefice, or fief, varied in size from one or more small villas to several *mansi*, which were agricultural holdings of twenty-five to forty-eight acres. The king's vassals are known to have received benefices of at least 30 and as many as 200 such mansi, truly a vast estate. Royal vassalage with a benefice understandably came to be widely sought by the highest classes of Carolingian society. As a royal policy, however, it proved deadly to the king in the long run. Although Carolingian kings jealously guarded their rights over property granted in benefice to vassals, resident vassals were still free to dispose of their benefices as they pleased. Vassals of the king, strengthened by his donations, in turn created their own vassals. These vassals, in turn, created still further vassals of their own—vassals of vassals of vassals—in a reverse pyramiding effect that fragmented land and authority from the highest to the lowest levels by the late ninth century.

Beginning with the reign of Louis the Pious (r. 814–840), bishops and abbots swore fealty and received their offices from the king as a benefice. The king formally invested these clerics in their offices during a special ceremony in which he presented them with a ring and a staff, the symbols of high spiritual office. This presumptuous practice of lay investiture, like the Carolingian confiscation of church land mentioned earlier, was a sore point for the church. In the eleventh and twelfth centuries it would provoke a great confrontation between church and state as reform-minded clergy rebelled against what they believed to be involuntary clerical vassalage.

FRAGMENTATION AND DIVIDED LOYALTY

In addition to the fragmentation brought about by the multiplication of vassalage, effective occupation of the land led gradually to claims of hereditary possession. Hereditary possession became a legally recognized principle in the ninth century and laid the basis for claims to real ownership. Fiefs given as royal donations became hereditary possessions and, with the passage of time, in some instances even the real property of the possessor. Further, vassal engagements came to be multiplied in still another way as enterprising freemen sought to accumulate as much land as possible. One man could become a vassal to several different lords. This development led in the ninth century to the concept of a "liege lord"—one master whom the vassal must obey even to the harm of the others, should a direct conflict among them arise.

The problem of loyalty was reflected not only in the literature of the period, with its praise of the virtues of honor and fidelity, but also in the ceremonial development of the very act of "commendation" by which a freeman became a vassal. In the mid–eighth century, an "oath of fealty" highlighted the

DOCUMENT | Bishop Fulbert Describes Obligations of Vassals and Lords

Trust held the lord and vassal together. Their duties in this regard were carefully defined. Here are six general rules for vassal and lord, laid down by Bishop Fulbert of Chartres in a letter to William, Duke of Aquitaine, in 1020.

♦ What are the respective obligations of vassal and lord? Do they seem fair for each side? Why might a vassal have more responsibilities and a lord fewer?

He who swears fealty to his lord ought always to have these six things in memory: what is harmless, safe, honorable, useful, easy, practicable. Harmless, that is to say, that he should not injure his lord in his body; safe, that he should not injure him by betraying his secrets or the defenses upon which he relies for his safety; honorable, that he should not injure him in his possessions; easy and practicable, that that good which his lord is able to do easily he make not difficult, nor that which is practicable he make not impossible to him.

That the faithful vassal should avoid these injuries is certainly proper, but not for this alone does he deserve his holding; for it is not sufficient to abstain from evil, unless what is good is done also. It remains, therefore, that in the same six things mentioned above he should faithfully counsel and aid his lord, if he wishes to be looked upon as worthy of this benefice and to be safe concerning the fealty which he has sworn.

The lord also ought to act toward his faithful vassal reciprocally in all these things. And if he does not do this, he will be justly considered guilty of bad faith, just as the former, if he should be detected in avoiding or consenting to the avoidance of his duties, would be perfidious and perjured.

From James Harvey Robinson, ed., *Readings in European History,* Vol. 1 (Boston: Athenaeum, 1904), p. 184.

---

ceremony. A vassal reinforced his promise of fidelity to the lord by swearing a special oath with his hand on a sacred relic or the Bible. In the tenth and eleventh centuries, paying homage to the lord involved not only the swearing of such an oath, but also the placement of the vassal's hands between the lord's and the sealing of the ceremony with a kiss.

Despite their problems, feudal arrangements nonetheless provided stability throughout the early Middle Ages and aided the difficult process of political centralization during the high Middle Ages. The genius of feudal government lay in its adaptability. Contracts of different kinds could be made with almost anybody, as circumstances required. The process embraced a wide spectrum of people, from the king at the top to the lowliest vassal in the remotest part of the kingdom. The foundations of the modern nation-state would emerge in France and England from the fine-tuning of essentially feudal arrangements as kings sought to adapt their goal of centralized government to the reality of local power and control.

Summary

The Byzantine Empire   In the fifth century, Roman authority in the West collapsed under the impact of Germanic invasions. However, imperial power shifted to the Eastern part of the Roman Empire—known as the Byzantine Empire—with its capital at Constantinople. The Byzantine Empire would endure until the Ottoman Turks captured Constantinople in 1453. The peak of Byzantine power occurred during the reign of Justinian (527–565), one of whose major achievements was the *Corpus Juris Civilis,* a codification of Roman law on which most European law was based until the nineteenth century. The Byzantine Empire provided a model of civilized society to medieval Europe, helped protect it from Muslim invaders, and preserved much of classical learning.

The Emperor Justinian and His Court.

The Islamic world also acted as a conduit for classical learning to the West, particularly in medicine, astronomy, and mathematics.

The Roman Church   The church was the strongest and most prestigious institution in early medieval Europe where it filled the vacuum created by the collapse of Roman authority. Monastic culture was especially strong. The greatest organizer of Western monasticism was Saint Benedict of Nursia (480–547). Benedictine monasteries were an economic, political, and spiritual force throughout the West.

With the collapse of imperial authority in the West, the bishops of Rome, the popes, developed the doctrine of papal primacy by which they claimed supreme authority over church doctrine and the clergy. These claims were unacceptable in the East, where a separate Greek Orthodox Church developed under the control of the Byzantine emperors.

Charlemagne's Empire   The Frankish ruler Charlemagne (r. 768–814) sought to re-create a universal Western empire and was crowned emperor by the pope in 800. Charlemagne's realm embraced modern France, Belgium, Holland, and Switzerland, most of Germany, and parts of Italy and Spain. He formed a close alliance with the church and relied on churchmen as royal agents and administrators. His palace school at Aachen was the center of a modest renaissance of classical learning under scholars such as Alcuin of York (735–804).

Yet, despite his efforts at administrative control, Charlemagne's empire proved to be ungovernable. Charlemagne had increased the power of local lords whose support he needed to rule, but their power and wealth became so great that they were able to put their self-interest above royal authority. After Charlemagne's death, his empire dissolved amid quarrels among his heirs, the revolts of powerful nobles, and invasions by Vikings, Magyars, and Muslims.

Feudal Society   The Middle Ages were characterized by a chronic absence of central government and the constant threat of famine, disease, and invasion. Lords were those who could guarantee protection under these conditions. Feudal society was one in which a local lord was dominant and offered security in return for allegiance from his dependents or vassals. It was a system of mutual rights and responsibilities. Medieval vassals pledged fealty to their lord in return for a fief, or grant of land. They promised to support their "liege lord" with troops or money when he called upon them for aid.

The feudal economy was organized and controlled through agrarian villages known as manors, worked by free peasants, who had their own modest property and economic and legal rights, or by serfs, impoverished peasants who were bound to the land and obliged to provide their lords with an array of services, dues in kind, and products.

Review Questions

1. Trace the history of Christianity to the reign of the emperor Charlemagne. How did the church become a political power in the Western Roman Empire?

2. How did the Franks become the dominant force in Western Europe? What were the characteristics of Charlemagne's rule? Why did his empire break apart?

3. How and why was the history of the Eastern or Byzantine half of the Roman Empire so different from the Western half? What were the major political and religious differences? How would you compare Justinian to Charlemagne?

4. What were the tenets of Islam? How were the Muslims able to build an empire so suddenly? Compare and contrast the teaching of Islam, Roman Catholicism, and Byzantine or Orthodox Christianity. Are they irreconcilable?

5. What were the defining features of feudalism? Is a feudal society a "backward" society?

Key Terms

apostolic primacy   (p. 334)

demesne   (p. 339)

fealty   (p. 343)

feudal society   (p. 342)

fief   (p. 336)

Magyars   (p. 342)

manor   (p. 339)

Papal States   (p. 336)

serf   (p. 339)

three-field system   (p. 340)

vassal   (p. 342)

Documents CD-ROM

The Rise of Christianity

6.5 Leo I: The Man Who laid the Foundations for the Medieval Papacy

6.8 St. Benedict

Mediterranean Civilization after the Fall of Rome

7.1 Procopius, History of the Wars

7.2 Iconoclasm and Orthodoxy: The Second Council of Nicaea (787)

7.3 A Western Attitude Toward the Byzantine Greeks (1147): Odo of Deuil

7.4 Einhard

7.5 The Missi Dominici (802)

NOTE: *To learn more about the topics in this chapter, see the Suggested Readings at the end of the book.*

Islam in the Heartlands and Beyond, 1000–1600

◄ BUILDING THE CASTLE OF KHAWARNAQ, CA. 1494. This is one of the magnificent illustrations of the *Khamsa*, or "Five Poems," of Nizami, painted by Bihzad (d. ca. 1515), the head of the great art academy of Herat in present-day Afghanistan.
By permission of The British Library.

The Expansion of Islam, 1000–1600

In Islamic and other Asian territories, the period from 1000 to 1600 is difficult to characterize simply. The spread of Islam to new peoples or their ruling elites is a theme of this chapter. However, the history of Islam in India is hardly the history of India as a whole. The vast conquests and movements of the Mongols and Central Asian Turks across inner Asia were among the most striking developments in world history in this period. Their effects on the societies they conquered were often cataclysmic, whether in China, south Asia, west Asia, or eastern Europe. These conquests and migrations wiped out existing orders and forced many refugees to flee to new areas. After the initial conquests, however, the empires created by the nomadic peoples of Central Asia helped facilitate the movement across the Eurasian continent of people, merchandise, ideas, and, in the fourteenth century, disease. They also contributed, even if unintentionally, new and often significant human resources to existing civilizations, such as those of China and the Islamic heartlands.

In this era, Islam became a truly international tradition of religious, political, and social values and institutions. This achievement was largely because Islam was highly adaptable and open to "indigenization," or a syncretistic blending of cultural traits, in the seemingly hostile contexts of polytheistic Hindu and African societies. The ability to adapt while maintaining the core tenets of the Islamic religion explains the aptitude of Islam to take root in so many different regions of the globe. Also in this period, distinct traditions of art, language, and literature, for all their local or regional diversity, became part of a larger Muslim whole. Islamic civilization had none of the territorial contiguity or linguistic and cultural homogeneity of either Chinese or Japanese civilization. Nevertheless, the Islamic world was an international reality, a true *dar-al-Islam*, or "House of Islam," in which a Muslim could travel, encounter, and exchange ideas and goods with other Muslims of radically diverse backgrounds and have much in common with them.

Indian traditional culture was not bound up with an expanding missionary religious tradition like that of Islam, and the developing caste system closely associated with Hinduism was less adaptable, and thus less portable. Yet in this age Hindu kingdoms flourished in Indonesia, although these kingdoms mostly rejected the caste system and thus accommodated Hinduism and Indian culture to local conditions. Buddhism, another highly adaptable religion, was expanding across much of Central and eastern Asia, thereby solidifying its place as an international missionary tradition.

Christianity, by contrast, was not rapidly expanding in Africa, Asia, or Europe. The somewhat disastrous experience of the Crusades (see Chapter 15) brought Europeans into closer contact with the Islamic world than ever before but did little to attract converts to Christianity, or increase European power in the Middle East. By 1500, however, the Western European branch of Christianity was poised on the brink of internal revolution and international expansion. In the year 1000 Europe was almost a backwater of culture and power, compared to major Islamic or Hindu states, let alone China. By 1500, however, European civilization was riding the crest of a cultural renaissance, enjoying economic and political growth, and starting the global exploration that became a flood of imperial expansion and affected most of the rest of the globe. None of the world's other great civilizations saw their society and culture change as radically in this era as did that of Western Europe.

THINK AHEAD

◆ Describe the consequences of the invasions and conquests of the Mongol and Central Asian Turks.

◆ Why were Islam and Buddhism more successful than Hinduism and Christianity in expanding during this era? What does this suggest about the traits a religious tradition must have, besides ambition, to become a successful international missionary religion?

ENTRALIZED CALIPHAL POWER IN THE ISLAMIC world had broken down by the mid–tenth century. Regional Islamic states with distinctive political and cultural identities now dominated—a pattern that would endure to modern times (see Map 13–1). Yet the diverse Islamic lands remained part of a larger civilization. Muslims from Córdoba in Spain could (and did) travel to Bukhara in Transoxiana or Zanzibar on the East African coast and feel at home. Regionalism and cosmopolitanism, diversity and unity, have characterized Islamic civilization ever since.

The next 500 years saw the growth of a truly international Islamic community, united by shared norms of communal order represented and maintained by the Muslim religious scholars (*ulama*). Sufism, the strand of Islam that stressed piety and allegiance to a spiritual master, gained popularity, especially after 1200. The growth of Sufi affiliations or brotherhoods influenced Muslim life everywhere, often countering the more limiting and legalistic aspects of *ulama* conformity. Shi'ite ideas offered another alternative vision of

society. Movements loyal to Ali and his heirs challenged but failed to reverse centrist Sunni predominance in most of the Islamic world, even though Shi'ite dynasties ruled much of the Islamic heartlands in the tenth and eleventh centuries.

A cultural renaissance fueled the spread of Persian as the major language of Islam alongside Arabic. The Persian-dominated Iranian and Indian Islamic world became more distinct from the western Islamic lands where Arabic prevailed.

Two Asian steppe peoples, the Mongols and the Turks, came to rule much of the Islamic world in these centuries, but with different results. The spread of the Turks added a substantial Turkish element, especially where they became rulers, as happened with the Saljuqs in Iran and Anatolia, the Mamluks in Egypt, and the "slave-kings" in Delhi. The Mongols conquered much of the Islamic heartlands in the thirteenth century, but their culture and religion did not become dominant. In this age, Islam became the major new influence in the Indian subcontinent, Southeast Asia, and sub-Saharan Africa.

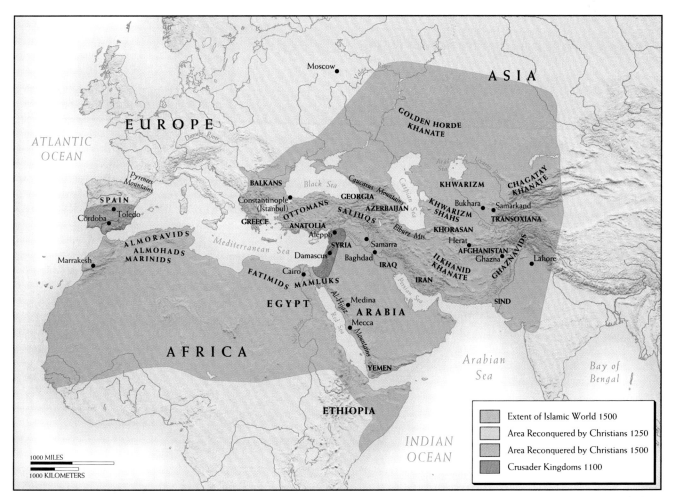

MAP 13–1 The Islamic World, 1000 ca. 1500.   Compare this map with map 11–1 on page 308. Though the Muslim world had expanded deep into Africa, India and Central Asia, it had also lost Spain to Christian reconquest.

THE ISLAMIC HEARTLANDS

Religion and Society

In this period Islamic society was shaped by the consolidation and institutionalization of Sunni legal and religious norms, Sufi traditions and personal piety, and Shi'ite legal and religious norms.

CONSOLIDATION OF SUNNI ORTHOPRAXY

The *ulama* (both Sunni and Shi'ite) gradually became entrenched religious, social, and political elites throughout the Islamic world, especially after the breakdown of centralized power in the tenth century. Their integration into local merchant, landowning, and bureaucratic classes led to stronger identification of these groups with Islam.

Beginning in the eleventh century, the *ulama*'s power and fixity as a class were expressed in the institution of the **madrasa**, or college of higher learning. On the one hand, the *madrasa* had grown up naturally as individual experts frequented a given mosque or private house and attracted students seeking to learn the Qur'an, the *Hadith* ("Tradition"), jurisprudence, Arabic grammar, and the like. On the other hand, rulers endowed the *madrasas* with buildings, scholarships, and salaried chairs, so that they could control the *ulama* by appointing teachers and influencing the curriculum. In theory, such control might combat unwelcome sectarianism. Unlike the university, with its corporate organization and institutional degrees, the *madrasa* was a support institution for individual teachers, who personally certified students' mastery of particular subjects. It gave an institutional base to Islam's long-developed system of students seeking out the best teachers and studying texts with them until they received the teachers' formal certification, or "permission" to transmit and teach those same texts themselves.

Largely outside *ulama* control, popular "unofficial" piety flourished in local pilgrimages to saints' tombs, in folk celebrations of Muhammad's birthday, in veneration of him in poetry, and in ecstatic chant and dance among Sufi groups. But the shared traditions that directed family and civil law, the daily worship rituals, fasting in the month of **Ramadan**, and the yearly Meccan pilgrimage united almost all Muslims, even most Kharijites or Shi'ites. In the Christian world, theological dogmas determined sectarian identity. In contrast, Muslims tended to define Islam in

▲ **The Sultan Hasan Madrasa and Tomb-Mosque.** This imposing Mamluk building (1356–1363) was built to house teachers and students studying all four of the major traditions or "schools" of Islamic law. Living and teaching spaces are combined here in a building with a mosque and the Sultan's tomb enclosure.

SuperStock, Inc.

terms of what Muslims do—by practice rather than by beliefs. The chief arbiters of "normative" Sunni and Shi'i Islam among the *ulama* were the *faqihs*, or legal scholars, not the theologians.

Basic Sunni **orthopraxy**, the correctness of religious practice, discouraged religious or social innovations. It was well established by the year 1000 as the dominant tradition, even though Shi'ite aspirations often made themselves felt either politically or theologically. The emergence of a conservative theological orientation tied to one of the four main Sunni legal schools, the Hanbalites (after Ibn Hanbal, d. 969), narrowed the scope, for creative doctrinal change. The Hanbalites relied on a literalist reading of the Qur'an and the *Hadith.* The *ulama* also became more socially conservative as they became integrated into social aristocracies. The *ulama* were often as committed to the status quo as the rulers.

SUFI PIETY AND ORGANIZATION

Sufi piety stresses the spiritual and mystical dimensions of Islam. The term *Sufi* apparently came from the Arabic *suf* ("wool"), based on the old ascetic practice of wearing only a coarse woolen garment. Sufi simplicity and humility had roots with the Prophet and the Companions but developed as a distinctive tendency when, after about 700 C.E., male and female pietists emphasized a godly life over and above mere observance of Muslim duties. Some stressed ascetic avoidance of temptations, others loving devotion to God. Sufi piety bridged the abyss between the human and the Divine that the exalted Muslim concept of the omnipotent God of creation implies. Socially, Sufi piety merged with folk piety in such popular practices as saint veneration, shrine pilgrimage, ecstatic worship, and seasonal festivals. Sufi writers collected stories of saints, wrote treatises on the Sufi path, and composed some of the world's finest mystical poetry. (See Document, "Jalaluddin Rumi: Who Is the Sufi?")

Some Sufis were revered as spiritual masters and saints. Their disciples formed brotherhoods with their own distinctive mystical teaching, Qur'anic interpretation, and devotional practice. These fraternal orders became the chief instruments of the spread of Muslim faith, as well as a locus of popular piety in almost all Islamic societies. Organized Sufism has always attracted members from the populace at large (in this, it differs from monasticism), as well as those dedicated to poverty or other radical disciplines. Indeed, Sufi orders became in this age one of the typical social institutions of everyday Muslim life. Whether Sunni or Shi'ite, many Muslims have ever since identified in some degree with a Sufi order.

CONSOLIDATION OF SHI'ITE TRADITIONS

Shi'ite traditions crystallized between the tenth and twelfth centuries. Many states now came under Shi'ite rulers, but only the Fatimids in Egypt established an important empire. A substantial Shi'ite populace developed only in Iran, Iraq, and the lower Indus (Sind).

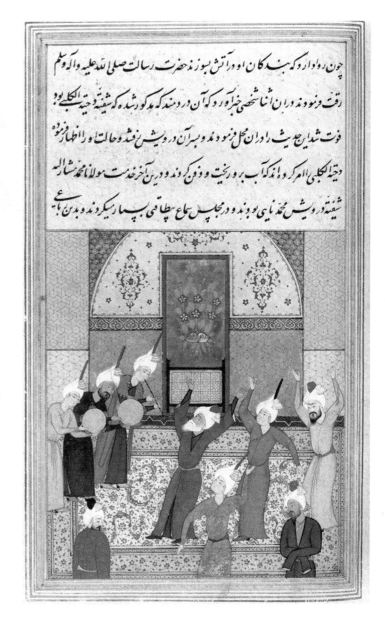

Dancing Dervishes. This image from a 1552 Persian manuscript depicts a Sufi master dancing with his disciples. Sufis often use music and bodily movement to induce a feeling of ecstasy which they feel brings them closer to God.
Bodleian Library, University of Oxford.

Two Shi'ite groups emerged as the most influential. The first were the "Seveners," or "Isma'ilis," who recognized Isma'il (d. ca. 760), first son of the sixth Alid *imam,* as the seventh *imam.* Their thought drew on Gnostic and Neo-Platonic philosophy, knowledge of which they reserved for a spiritual elite. Isma'ili groups were often revolutionary.

By the eleventh century, however, most Shi'ites accepted a line of twelve *imams,* the last of whom is said to have disappeared in Samarra (Iraq) in 873 into a cosmic concealment from which he will eventually emerge as the Mahdi, or "Guided One," to usher in the messianic age and final judgment. The "Twelvers," the

DOCUMENT   Jalaluddin Rumi: Who Is the Sufi?

Rumi (d. 1273) was one of the greatest and most influential mystics of Islamic history. Born in Mazar-e-Sharif (in a region that was once part of Khorasan), his family moved westward just before the Mongol invasion of Iran to settle finally in Seljuq Konya, in central Anatolia. Rumi succeeded his father as a madrasa professor and studied in Syria. The Mevlevi Sufi brotherhood considers him its founder. The following two selections come from Rumi's two longest works of mystical poetry.

◆ What qualities or attributes does the Sufi seem to have, or to seek to develop? What seems to be the Sufi's goal? What might be the aim of the remarks about the "patched mantle" (a common mark of Sufi initiation) and "lust perverse"? What does "Beauty" seem to refer to in the first poem?

What makes the sufi? Purity of heart;
Not the patched mantle and the lust perverse
Of those vile earth-bound men who steal his name.
He in all dregs discerns the essence pure:
In hardship ease, in tribulation joy.
The phantom sentries, who with batons drawn
Guard Beauty's palace gate and curtained bower,

Give way before him, unafraid he passes,
And showing the King's arrow, enters in.

—Mathnawi, p. 54

What to do, Muslims? For I do not recognize myself; not
    a Christian I nor Jew, Zoroastrian nor Muslim. ...
Not of India am I nor China, not Bulgar-land nor
    Turkistan; not the Kingdom of Both Iraqs nor the
    Land of Khurasan.
Not of this World am I nor the next, not of heaven or
    hell; not of Adam nor of Eve, not of Paradise nor
    Ridwan.
My place is no place, my trace has no trace; not body
    nor soul, for I belong to the soul of Love.
Duality have I put aside, I have seen both worlds as one.
    One I seek, One I know, One I see, One I call.
He is the first, He the last; he the Outward, He the
    inward.

—Diwan-i Shams-i Tabriz

Shi'ite majority, still focus on the martyrdom of the twelve *imams* and look for their intercession on the Day of Judgment. They have flourished best in Iran, the home of most Shi'ite thought. The Buyids who took control of the Abbasid caliphate in 945 were Twelvers. The Safavids of Iran made Twelver doctrine the "state religion" in the sixteenth century (see Chapter 23).

Regional Developments

After the tenth century the western half of the Islamic world developed two regional foci: (1) Spain (Al Andalus), Moroccan North Africa, and to a lesser extent, west Africa; and (2) Egypt, Syria-Palestine, Anatolia, along with Arabia and Libyan North Africa. The history of the eastern half of the Islamic world in the period between 1000 and 1500 was marked by the violent Mongol incursions of the thirteenth century.

THE ISLAMIC WEST: SPAIN AND NORTH AFRICA

The grandeur of Spanish Islamic ("Moorish") culture is visible still in Córdoba's Great Mosque and the remnants of the Alhambra castle. In European tradition, the *Chanson de Roland* preserves the echo of Charlemagne's retreat through the Pyrenees Mountains after failing to check the first Spanish Umayyad's growing power. That ruler, Abd al-Rahman I (r. 756–788), was the founder of the cosmopolitan tradition of Umayyad Spanish culture at Córdoba, which was the cultural center of the Western world for the next two centuries. Renowned for its medicine, science, literature, intellectual life, commercial activity, public baths and gardens, and courtly elegance, Córdoba reached its zenith under Abd al-Rahman III (r. 912–961), who took the title of caliph in 929. His absolutist, but benevolent, rule saw a largely unified, peaceful Islamic Spain. The mosque-university of Córdoba that he founded attracted students from Europe as well as the Islamic world.

A sad irony of this cosmopolitan world were recurring religious exclusivism and conflict among Muslims and Christians alike. Abroad, Abd al-Rahman III checked both the new Fatimid power in North Africa and the Christian kingdoms in northern Spain, making possible a golden era of Moorish power and culture. But after his death, fragmentation into warring Muslim principalities allowed a resurgence of Spain's Christian states between about 1000 and 1085, when the city of Toledo fell permanently into Christian hands.

⚑ **The Alhambra, Muqarnas Dome in the Hall of the Abencerrahes, Palace of the Lions.** Built in the 14th century, the Alhambra's serene, almost severe aspect belies its wealth of interior ornamentation. Considered one of the greatest examples of Islamic architecture and one of the most beautiful of all surviving medieval buildings, the Alhambra rises within its Curtain walls above Grenada, the last of the great Moorish cities of Andalusia. Getty Images Inc.-Stone Allstock.

Brief Islamic revivals in Spain and North Africa came under the African reform movements of the Almoravids and Almohads. The Almoravids originated as a religious-warrior brotherhood among Berber nomads in West Africa. Having subdued northwestern Africa, in 1086 they carried their zealotry from their new capital of Marrakesh into Spain and reunited its Islamic kingdoms. Under their rule, arabized Christians (Mozarabs) were persecuted as were some Moorish Jews. The subsequent wars began the last major phase of the Spanish "Reconquest" (*Reconquista*). These conflicts, in which Christian rulers sought to regain and Christianize the peninsula, are best known in the West for the exploits of El Cid (d. 1099), the mercenary adventurer who became the Spanish national hero.

The Almohads ended Almoravid rule in Morocco in 1147 and then conquered much of southern Spain. Before their demise (1225 in Spain; 1275 in Africa), they stimulated a brilliant revival of Moorish culture. During this era, paper manufacture reached Spain and then the rest of Western Europe. The long westward odyssey of Indian fable literature through Iran and the Arab world ended with Spanish and Latin translations in thirteenth-century Spain. The greatest lights of this Spanish Islamic intellectual world were the major philosopher and physician Ibn Rushd (Averroës, d. 1198); the great Muslim mystical thinker Ibn al-Arabi (d. 1240); and the famous Arab-Jewish philosopher Ibn Maymun, or Maimonides (d. 1204). (See Document, "A Muslim Biographer's Account of Maimonides.")

THE ISLAMIC WEST: EGYPT AND THE EASTERN MEDITERRANEAN WORLD

The Fatimids   The major Islamic presence in the Mediterranean from the tenth to the twelfth century was that of the Shi'ite Fatimids, who claimed descent from Muhammad's daughter, Fatima. They began as a Tunisian dynasty, then conquered Morocco, Sicily, and Egypt (969), where they built their new capital, Cairo (*al-Qahira*, "the Victorious"). Their rule as Shi'ite caliphs meant that, for a time, there were three "caliphates"—in Baghdad, Córdoba, and Cairo. The Fatimids were Isma'ilis (see above). Content to rule a Sunni majority in Egypt, they sought recognition as true imams by other Isma'ili groups and were able, for a time, to take western Arabia and most of Syria from the Buyid "guardians" of the Abbasid caliphate (see Chapter 11).

Fatimid rule spawned two splinter groups that have played visible, if minor, roles in history. The Druze of modern Lebanon and Syria originated around 1020 with a few members of the Fatimid court who professed belief in the divinity of one of the Fatimid caliphs. The tradition they founded is too far from Islam to be considered a Muslim sect. The Isma'ili Assassins, on the other hand, were a radical Muslim movement founded by a Fatimid defector in the Elburz mountains of Iran around 1100. The name "Assassins" comes not from the political assassinations that made them infamous, but from a European corruption of the Arabic *Hashishiyyin* ("users of hashish"). It was possibly connected with the story that their assassins were manipulated with drugs to undertake their usually suicidal missions. The Assassins were destroyed by the Mongols in the thirteenth century.

The Fatimids built the al-Azhar mosque in Cairo as a center of learning, a role it maintains today, although for Sunni, not (as then) Shi'ite, scholarship. Fatimid rulers treated Egypt's Coptic Christians generally as well as they did their Sunni majority and many Copts held high offices. Jews also usually fared well under the Fatimids.

After 1100 the Fatimids weakened, falling in 1171 to Salah al-Din (Saladin, 1137–1193), a field general and administrator under the Turkish ruler of Syria, Nur al-Din (1118–1174). Saladin, a Sunni Kurd, is well known in the West for his battles (including the retaking of Jerusalem in 1187) with the Crusaders. After Nur al-Din's death, Saladin added Syria-Palestine and Mesopotamia to his Egyptian dominions and founded the Ayyubid dynasty that, under his successors, controlled all three areas until Egypt fell to the Mamluks in 1250 and most of Syria and Mesopotamia to the Mongols by 1260.

Like Nur al-Din, and on the model of the Saljuqs (see Chapter 11), Saladin founded *madrasas* to teach and promote Sunni law. His and his Ayyubid successors' reigns in Egypt saw the entrenchment of a self-conscious Sunnism under a program of mutual recognition and teaching of all four Sunni schools of law. Henceforward Shi'ite Islam disappeared from Egypt.

The Mamluks The heirs of the Fatimids and Saladin in the eastern Mediterranean were the redoubtable **sultans** ("[those with] authority") of the Mamluk dynasty who were chiefly Cir-

◄ **Spanish Banner.** Made in southern Spain in the early thirteenth century, the banner of Las Navas de Tolosa, of silk tapestry with gold parchment (3.3 × 2.2 m), reflects the emphasis on architectural designs that emerged at this time among Spanish weavers. The central section of the banner, bordered with Qur'anic inscriptions, resembles a Spanish courtyard garden. The banner was captured in battle by Christians not long after it was made.

Banner of Las Navas de Tolosa, from southern Spain. First half of 13th century. Silk tapestry-weave w/gilt parchment, 10'9 7/8" x 7'2 5/8" (3.3 x 2.2 m) Museo de Telas Medievales, Monasterio de Santa Maria la Real de Las Huelgas, Burgos, Spain. Patrimonio Nacional. Arxiu Mas.

CHRONOLOGY

Western Islamic Lands

756–1021	Spanish Umayyad dynasty
912–961	Rule of Abd al-Rahman III; height of Umayyad power and civilization
969–1171	Fatimid Shi'ite dynasty in Egypt
ca. 1020	Origin of Druze community (Egypt/Syria)
1171	Fatimids fall to Salah al-Din (Saladin), Ayyubid lieutenant of the ruler of Aleppo
1056–1275	Almoravid and Almohad dynasties in North Africa, West Africa, and Spain
1096–1291	Major European Christian crusades into Islamic lands; some European presence in Syria-Palestine
1189	Death of Ibn Rushd (Averroës), philosopher
1204	Death of Musa ibn Maymun (Maimonides), philosopher and Jewish savant
1240	Death of Ibn al-Arabi, theosophical mystic
1250–1517	Mamluk sultanate in Egypt and (from late 1200s) Syria; claim laid to Abbasid caliphate
1260	Mamluk victory at Ain Jalut halts Mongol advance into Syria
ca. 1300	Rise of Ottoman state in western Anatolia
1406	Death of Ibn Khaldun, historian and social philosopher

cassians from the Caucasus, captured in childhood and trained as slave-bodyguards. The Mamluks were the only Islamic dynasty to withstand the Mongol invasions. Their victory at Ain Jalut in Palestine in 1260 marked the end of the Mongols' westward movement. The first Mamluk sultan, Aybak (r. 1250–1257), and his successors were elite Turkish and Mongol slave-officers drawn originally from the bodyguard of Saladin's dynasty. Whereas the early Mamluks were often succeeded by sons or brothers, succession after the 1390s was more often a survival of the fittest; no sultan reigned more than a few years. The Mamluk state was based on a military fief system and total control by the slave-officer elite.

The Mamluk sultan Baybars (r. 1260–1277), who took the last Crusader fortresses, is a larger-than-life figure in Arab legend. To legitimize his rule, he revived the Abbasid caliphate at least in name after its demise in the fall of Baghdad (1258; discussed later) by installing an uncle of Baghdad's last Abbasid as Caliph at Cairo. He made treaties with Constantinople and with European sovereigns, as well as with the newly converted Muslim ruler, or *khan*, of the Golden Horde—the Mongol

Tatars of southern Russia. His public works in Cairo were numerous. He also extended Mamluk rule south to Nubia and west among the Berbers.

As trade relations with the Mongol domains improved after 1300, the Mamluks enjoyed substantial prosperity and commanded a large empire. However, the Black Death epidemic of 1347–1348 in the Arab Middle East hurt the Mamluk and other regional states badly. Still the Mamluks survived even the Ottoman conquest of Egypt in 1517, since Mamluks continued to rule there as Ottoman governors into the nineteenth century.

Architecture, much of which still graces Cairo, remains the most magnificent Mamluk bequest to posterity. In addition, mosaics, calligraphy, and metalwork were among the arts and crafts of special note. The Mamluks were great patrons of scholars who excelled in history, biography, astronomy, mathematics, and medicine. The most important of these was Ibn Khaldun (d. 1406). Born of a Spanish Muslim family in Tunis, he settled in Cairo as an adult. He is still recognized as the greatest Muslim social historian and philosopher of history.

⋀ **Mamluk Trade.** Trade in spices and other precious commodities between the Mamuluks and western Europe was of great importance. In this painting from about 1500 we see Venetian ambassadors being received by the governor of Damascus, who sits on a low platform and wears a distinctively-shaped turban.

Erich Lessing/Art Resource, N.Y.

DOCUMENT | A Muslim Biographer's Account of Maimonides

The following are excerpts from the entry on Maimonides (Arabic: Musa ibn Maymun) in the biographical dictionary of learned men by Ibn al-Qifti (d. 1248). In one section (omitted here), Ibn al-Qifti describes how this most famous Spanish Jewish savant at first feigned conversion to Islam when a new Berber ruler demanded the expulsion of Christians and Jews from Spain in about 1133. He tells how Maimonides moved his family to the more tolerant Islamic world of Cairo, where he became the court physician. (Jews or Christians held high office under Muslim rulers.)

♦ Which Islamic dynasty forced Maimonides to leave Spain for Cairo? Why were the Fatimids in Cairo tolerant of Christians and Jews when their Berber co-religionists were not? From the Muslim biographer's treatment of his subject, what can you infer about Islamic societies and the intellectual atmosphere of the time?

Reading the Torah in a Spanish Synagogue. A picture from a Hebrew Haggada, Spain, 14th century. Until their expulsion by Christian rulers at the end of the 15th century, Jews formed a significant minority in Spain.

By permission of The British Library.

... This man was one of the people of Andalus, a Jew by religion. He studied philosophy in Andalus, was expert in mathematics, and devoted attention to some of the logical sciences. He studied medicine there and excelled in it. ...

... After assembling his possessions in the time that was needed for this, he left Andalus and went to Egypt, accompanied by his family. He settled in the town of Fustāt [part of greater Cairo], among its Jews, and practiced his religion openly. He lived in a district called al-Masīsa and made a living by trading in jewels and suchlike. Some people studied philosophy under him. ...

He married in Cairo the sister of a Jewish scribe called Abu'l-Ma'ālī, the secretary of the mother of Nūr al-Dīn 'Alī, known as al-Afdal, the son of Salāh al-Dīn Yūsuf ibn Ayyūb, and he had a son by her who today is a physician in Cairo after his father. ...

Mūsā, ibn Maymūn died in Cairo in the year 605 [1208-9].[1] He ordered his heirs to carry his body, when the smell had ceased, to Lake Tiberias and bury him there, seeking to be among the graves of the ancient Israelites and their great jurists, which are there. This was done.

He was learned in the law and secrets of the Jews and compiled a commentary on the Talmud, which is a commentary and explanation of the Torah; some of the Jews approve of it. Philosophic doctrines overcame him, and he compiled a treatise denying the canonical resurrection. The leaders of the Jews held this against him, so he concealed it except from those who shared his opinion in this. ...

In the latter part of his life he was troubled by a man from Andalus, a jurist called Abu'l-'Arab ibn Ma'īsha, who came to Fustāt and met him. He charged him with having been a Muslim in Andalus, accused him [of apostasy] and wanted to have him punished.[2] 'Abd al-Rahīm ibn 'Alī al-Fādil prevented this, and said to him, "If a man is converted by force, his Islam is not legally valid."

From *Islam: From the Prophet Muhammad to the Capture of Constantinople*, Vol. 2: *Religion and Society* by Bernard Lewis, ed. and trans. Copyright © 1987 by Bernard Lewis. Used by permission of Oxford University Press, Inc.

[1] In fact, he died in 1204.

[2] The penalty for apostasy was death.

THE ISLAMIC EAST: BEFORE THE MONGOL CONQUESTS

The Iranian dynasties of the Samanids at Bukhara (875–999) and the Buyids at Baghdad (945–1055) were the major usurpers of eastern Abbasid dominions. Their successes epitomized the rise of regional states that had begun to undermine the caliphate by the ninth century. Similarly, their demises reflected a second emerging pattern: the ascendancy of Turkish slave-rulers (like the Mamluks in the west) and of Oghuz Turkish peoples, known as Turkomans. With the Saljuqs, the process begun with use of Turkish slave troops in ninth-century Baghdad ended in the permanent presence in the Islamic world of Turkish ruling dynasties. As late converts, they became typically the most zealous of Sunni Muslims.

The Ghaznavids   The rule of the Samanids in Transoxiana was finally ended by a Turkoman group in 999, but they had already lost all of eastern Iran south of the Oxus in 994 to one of their own slave governors, Subuktigin (r. 976–997). He set up his own state in modern Afghanistan, at Ghazna, whence he and his son and successor, Mahmud of Ghazna (r. 998–1030), launched successful campaigns against his former masters. The Ghaznavids are notable for their patronage of Persian literature and culture and for their conquests in northwestern India, which began a lasting Muslim presence in India. Mahmud was their greatest ruler. He is still remembered for his booty raids and destruction of temples in western India. At its peak, his empire stretched from western Iran to the Oxus and to the Indus.

Mahmud attracted to Ghazna numerous scholars and artists, notably the great scientist and mathematician al-Biruni (d. 1048) and the epic poet Firdawsi (d. ca. 1020). Firdawsi's *Shahnama* ("The Book of Kings") is the masterpiece of Persian literature, an epic of sixty thousand verses that helped fix the New Persian language and revive the pre-Islamic Iranian cultural tradition. After Mahmud the empire began to break up, although Ghaznavids ruled at Lahore until 1186.

The Saljuqs   The Saljuqs were the first major Turkish dynasty of Islam. They were a steppe clan who settled in Transoxiana, became avid Sunnis, and extended their sway over Khorasan in the 1030s. In 1055 they took Baghdad. As the new guardian of

Mamluk Bottle. This elegant glass bottle was made in Mamluk workshops in Syria in the mid–14th century for the rulers of the Yemen in southern Arabia.
John Tsantes/Courtesy of the Freer Gallery of Art, Smithsonian Institution, Washington, D.C.

the caliphate and master of an Islamic empire, the Saljuq leader Tughril Beg (r. 1037–1063) took the title of *sultan* to signify his temporal power and control. He and his early successors made various Iranian cities their capitals instead of Baghdad.

As new Turkish tribes joined their ranks, the Saljuqs extended Islamic rule for the first time into the central Anatolian plateau at Byzantine expense, even capturing the Byzantine emperor in a victory in Armenia in 1071 (see Map 13–2). They also conquered much of Syria and wrested Mecca and Medina from the Shi'ite Fatimids. The first Turkish rule in Anatolia dates from 1077, when the Saljuq governor there formed a separate sultanate. Known as the Saljuqs of Rum ("Rome," i.e., Byzantium), these latter Saljuqs were only displaced after 1300 by the Ottomans, another Turkish dynasty, who would eventually conquer all of Anatolia and southeastern Europe (see Chapter 21).

The most notable figure of Saljuq rule was the vizier Nizam al-Mulk, the real power behind two sultans from 1063 to 1092. In his time new roads and inns (caravanserais) for trade and pilgrimage were built, canals were dug, mosques and other public buildings were founded (including the first great Sunni *madrasas*), and science and culture were patronized. He also founded in 1067 what some contend was the first Muslim "University," the legal-theological school, or *madrasah*, of the Nizamiyyah in Baghdad. He supported an accurate calendar reform and authored a major work on the art of governing, the *Siyasatnamah*. Before his murder by an Isma'ili assassin in 1092, he appointed as professor in his Baghdad *madrasa* Muhammad al-Ghazzali (d. 1111), probably the greatest Muslim religious thinker ever. He also patronized the mathematician and astronomer Umar Khayyam (d. 1123), whose Western fame rests on the poetry of his "Quatrains," or *Ruba'iyat.*

After declining fortunes in the early twelfth century, Iranian Saljuq rule crumbled and by 1194 was wholly wiped away by another Turkish slave dynasty from Khwarizm in the lower Oxus basin. By 1200 these Khwarizm Shahs had built a large,

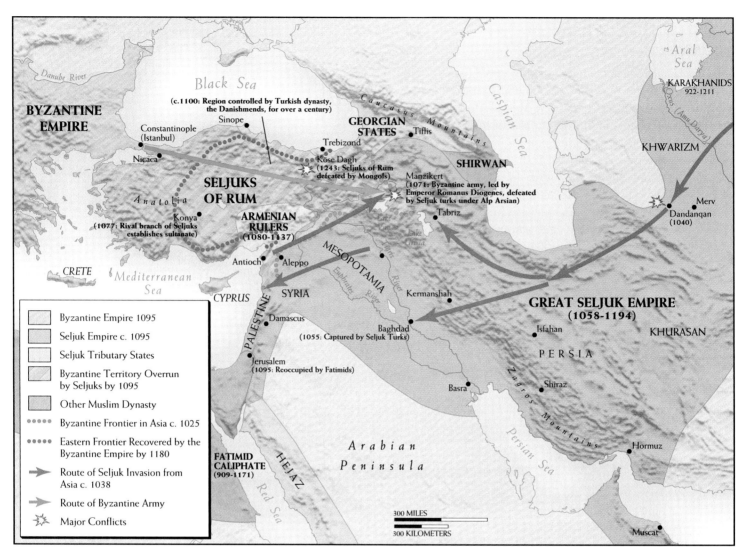

MAP 13–2 The Seljuk Empire, ca. 1095.   By the end of the eleventh century the Seljuks had conquered Persia, Mesopotamia, and Syria, and had inflicted a devasting blow against the Byzantine Empire at the battle of Manzikert in 1071, altering the balance of power in the eastern Mediterranean and the Near East.

if shaky, empire and sphere of influence covering Iran and Transoxiana. In the same era the Abbasid caliph at Baghdad, al-Nasir (r. 1180–1225), established an independent caliphal state in Iraq, but neither his heirs nor the Khwarizm Shahs were long to survive.

THE ISLAMIC EAST: THE MONGOL AGE

Mongols and Ilkhanids   The building of a vast Mongol empire spanning Asia from China to Poland in the thirteenth century proved momentous not only for eastern Europe and China (see Chapter 8), but also for Islamic Eurasia and India. A Khwarizm Shah massacre of Mongol ambassadors brought down the full wrath of the Great Khan, Genghis (ca. 1162–1227), on the Islamic east. He razed entire cities (1219–1222) from Transoxiana and Khorasan to the Indus. After his death, a division of his empire into four khanates under his four sons gave the Islamic world respite. Then in 1255 Hulagu Khan (r. 1256–1265), a

◀ **Genghis Khan.**
The Granger Collection, New York.

DOCUMENT | The Mongol Catastrophe

For the Muslim East, the sudden eruption of the Mongol hordes was an indescribable calamity. The shock and despair can be seen in the history of Ibn al-Athir (d. 1233). He writes here about the year 1220–1221, when the Mongols ("Tartars") burst in on the eastern lands.

◆ Is this a positive, negative, or neutral description of the Mongols? Why might the Mongols be compared to Alexander rather than, say, the Huns (see Chapter 6)?

I say, therefore, that this thing involves the description of the greatest catastrophe and the most dire calamity (of the like of which days and nights are innocent) which befell all men generally, and the Muslims in particular; so that, should one say that the world, since God Almighty created Adam until now, hath not been afflicted with the like thereof, he would but speak the truth. For indeed history doth not contain aught which approaches or comes nigh unto it. ...

Now this is a thing the like of which ear hath not heard; for Alexander, concerning whom historians agree that he conquered the world, did not do so with such swiftness, but only in the space of about ten years; neither did he slay, but was satisfied that men should be subject to him. But these Tartars conquered most of the habitable globe and the best, the most flourishing and most populous part thereof, and that whereof the inhabitants were the most advanced in character and conduct, in about [a] year; nor did any country escape their devastations which did not fearfully expect them and dread their arrival.

Moreover they need no commissariat, nor the conveyance of supplies, for they have with them sheep, cows, horses, and the like quadrupeds, the flesh of which they eat, [needing] naught else. As for their beasts which they ride, these dig into the earth with their hoofs and eat the roots of plants, knowing naught of barley. And so, when they alight anywhere, they have need of nothing from without. As for their religion, they worship the sun when it arises, and regard nothing as unlawful, for they eat all beasts, even dogs, pigs, and the like; nor do they recognise the marriage-tie, for several men are in marital relations with one woman, and if a child is born, it knows not who is its father.

Therefore Islâm and the Muslims have been afflicted during this period with calamities wherewith no people hath been visited. These Tartars (may God confound them!) came from the East, and wrought deeds which horrify all who hear of them, and which thou shalt, please God, see set forth in full detail in their proper connection. ...

From Edward C. Sachau, *Alberuni's Indian*, Vol. I (London: Kegan Paul, Trench, Truebner, 1910). pp. 17, 19, 20.

The House of Wisdom. A thirteenth century illustration of Aristotle teaching his pupils. Ancient Greek philosophy was a central concern for many Arab and Persian philosophers in the Middle Ages.
The Bridgeman Art Library International Ltd.

vented a Mongol advance into Egypt. A treaty in 1261 between the Mamluk sultan and Berke established a formal alliance that confirmed the breakup of Mongol unity and the autonomy of the four khanates: in China (the Yuan dynasty), in Iran (the Ilkhans), in Russia (the Golden Horde), and in Transoxiana (the Chagatays).

Hulagu and his heirs ruled the old Persian Empire from Azerbaijan for some seventy-five years as the Great Khan of China's viceroys (*Il-Khans*). Here, as elsewhere, the Mongols did not eradicate the society they inherited. Their native paganism and Buddhist and Christian leanings yielded to Muslim faith and practice, although they practiced religious tolerance. After 1335 Ilkhanid rule fell prey to the familiar pattern of a gradual breaking away of provinces, and for fifty years, Iran was again fragmented.

▲ **Tamerlane's Army.** A miniature painting of the Army of Tamerlane storming the walls of the Rajput city of Bhatnair in the year 1398. Bhatnair was one of the many North Indian cities and fortresses that fell to the relentless onslaught of Tamerlane's armies.
Art Resource/Bildarchiv Preussischer Kulturbesitz.

▲ **The Gur-i-mir, the tomb of timur in Samarkand.** Built from 1490 to 1501 by Timur's grandson, this tile-covered structure houses the tombs of Shahrukh, Ulug Beg, and other Timurids.
Giraudon/Art Resource, N.Y.

grandson of Genghis, led a massive army again across the Oxus. Adding Turkish troops to his forces (Mongol armies typically included many Turks), he went from victory to victory, destroying every Iranian state. In 1258, when the Abbasid caliph refused to surrender, Hulagu's troops plundered Baghdad, killing at least 80,000 inhabitants, including the caliph and his sons. (See Document, "The Mongol Catastrophe.")

Under the influence of his wife and many Nestorian Christians and Buddhists in his inner circle, Hulagu spared the Christians of Baghdad. He followed this policy in his other conquests, including the sack of Aleppo—which, like Baghdad, resisted. When Damascus surrendered, Western Christians had hopes of the impending fall of Mamluk Cairo and Islamic power, but Hulagu's drive west was slowed by rivalry with his kinsman Berke. A Muslim convert, Berke ruled the khanate of the Golden Horde, the Mongol state centered in southern Russia north of the Caucasus. He was in contact with the Mamluks, and some of his Mongol troops even helped them defeat Hulagu in Palestine (1260), which pre-

DOCUMENT | Ibn Khaldun "The Muqaddimah"

Abd al-Rahman Ibn Khaldun (1336–1406) of Tunisia was a brilliant thinker who has sometimes been called the first modern social scientist. He studied and held important positions in Granada, Cairo, and Fez. His most famous work, the Muqaddima, *or Introduction to Universal History was a major intellectual contribution. In this work, of which is a following selection he presented his philosophy of history. Like many Roman and Greek historians before him, he considered history to be cyclical. He considered culture, geography, climate, and economic trends to be the major forces behind historical changes. In the following chapter, Ibn Khaldun examines how dynasties rise and fall.*

♦ **What makes Ibn Khaldun a "modern" thinker? Does this description seem applicable today?**

We have stated that the life of a dynasty does not as a rule extend beyond three generations. The first generation retains the desert qualities, desert toughness, and desert savagery. (Its members are used to) privation and to sharing their glory (with each other); they are brave and rapacious. Therefore, the strength of group feeling continues to be preserved among them. They are sharp and greatly feared. People submit to them.

Under the influence of royal authority and a life of ease, the second generation changes from the desert attitude to sedentary culture, from privation to luxury and plenty, from a state in which everybody shared in the glory to one in which one man claims all the glory for himself while the others are too lazy to strive for glory, and from proud superiority to humble subservience. Thus, the vigour of group feeling is broken to some extent. People become used to lowliness and obedience. But many of the old virtues remain in them, because they had had direct personal contact with the first generation and its conditions, and had observed with their own eyes its prowess and striving for glory and its intention to protect and defend (itself). They cannot give all of it up at once, although a good deal of it may go. They live in hope that the conditions that existed in the first generation may come back, or they live under the illusion that those conditions still exist.

The third generation, then, has (completely) forgotten the period of desert life and toughness, as if it had never existed. They have lost (the taste for) the sweetness of fame and for group feeling, because they are dominated by force. Luxury reaches its peak among them, because they are so much given to a life of prosperity and ease. They become dependent on the dynasty and are like women and children who need to be defended. Group feeling disappears completely. People forget to protect and defend themselves and to press their claims. With their emblems, apparel, horseback-riding, and (fighting) skill, they deceive people and give them the wrong impression. For the most part, they are more cowardly than women upon their backs. When someone comes and demands something from them, they cannot repel him. The ruler, then, has need of other, brave people to support him. He takes many clients and followers. They help the dynasty to some degree, until God permits it to be destroyed, and it goes with everything it stands for.

As one can see, we have there three generations. In the course of these three generations, the dynasty grows senile and is worn out. Therefore, it is in the fourth generation that (ancestral) prestige is destroyed. . . .

In this way, the life span of a dynasty corresponds to the life span of an individual; it grows up and passes into an age of stagnation and thence into retrogression. Therefore, people commonly say that the life span of a dynasty is one hundred years. . . .

From Ibn Khaldun, *The Muqaddimah: An Introduction to History*, ed. N.J. Dawood, trans. Franz Rosenthal (Princeton NJ: Princeton University Press, 1967) pp. 137–138.

Timurids and Turkomans   This situation prepared the way for a new Turko-Mongol conquest from Transoxiana, under Timur-i Lang ("Timur the Lame," or "Tamerlane," 1336–1405). Even Genghis Khan's invasions could not match Timur's savage campaigns between 1379 and his death in 1405. These raids were not aimed at building a new empire, but at sheer conquest. In successive campaigns he swept everything before him in a wave of devastation: eastern Iran (1379–1385); western Iran, Armenia, the Caucasus, and upper Mesopotamia (1385–1387); southwestern Iran, Mesopotamia, and Syria (1391–1393); Central Asia from Transoxiana to the Volga and as far as Moscow (1391–1395); North India (1398); and northern Syria and Anatolia (1400–1402). Timur's sole positive contributions seem to have been the buildings he sponsored at Samarkand, his capital.

He left behind him ruins, death, disease, and political chaos across the entire eastern Islamic world, which did not soon recover. His was, however, the last great steppe invasion, for firearms soon destroyed the steppe horsemen's advantage.

Timur's sons ruled after him with varying results in Transoxiana and Iran (1405–1494). The most successful Timurid was Shahrukh (r. 1405–1447), who ruled a united Iran for a time. His capital, Herat, became an important center of Persian Islamic culture and Sunni piety. He patronized the famous Herat school of miniature painting as well as Persian literature and philosophy. The Timurids had to share Iran itself with Turkoman dynasties in western Iran, once even losing Herat to one of them. They and the Turkomans were the last Sunnis to rule Iran. Both were eclipsed at the end of the fifteenth century by the militant Shi'ite dynasty of the Safavids, who ushered in a new, Shi'ite era in the Iranian world (see Chapter 21).

The Spread of Islam Beyond the Heartlands

The period from roughly 1000 to 1500 saw the spread of Islam as a lasting religious, cultural, and political force into new areas (see Map 13–1). Not only Eurasia from the Caspian and Black Seas north to Moscow (under the Golden Horde), but also Greece and the Balkans, through the Ottoman Turks, came under the control of Islamic rulers (see Chapter 21). India, Malaysia, Indonesia, inland West Africa, and coastal East Africa all became major spheres of Islamic political or commercial power. In all these regions Sufi orders were most often responsible for converting people and spreading Islamic cultural influences. Merchants, too, were major agents of Islamization in these regions.

Conquest was a third (but demographically less important) means of conversion to Islam in these regions. Sometimes only ruling elites, sometimes wider circles, became Muslim, but in India, Southeast Asia, and sub-Saharan Africa much, often most, of the populace retained their inherited religious traditions. Nonetheless, in the most important of these regions, India, the coming of Islam signaled epochal changes.

INDIA AND SOUTHEAST ASIA

Islamic civilization in India (like earlier Indian civilization) was formed by creative interaction between invading foreigners and indigenous peoples. The early Arab and Turkish invaders were a foreign Muslim minority; their heirs were truly "Indian" as well as Muslim, adding a new dimension both to Indian and Islamic civilization. From then on, Indian civilization would both include and enrich Islamic traditions.

The Spread of Islam to South Asia

Well before the Ghaznavids came to the Punjab, Muslims were to be found even outside the original Arab conquest areas in Sind (see Map 13–3). Muslim merchants had settled in the port cities of Gujarat and southern India to profit from internal Indian trade as well as from trade with the Indies and China. Wherever Muslim traders went, converts to Islam were attracted by business advantages as well as by the straightforward ideology and practice of Islam and its officially egalitarian, "classless" ethic. Sufi orders had also gained a foothold in the south, giving today's south Indian Muslims old roots. Sufi piety also drew converts in

the north, especially when the Mongol devastation of Iran in the thirteenth century sent refugees into North India. These Muslim refugees strengthened Muslim life in the subcontinent.

Muslim-Hindu Encounter

From the outset Muslim leaders had to rule a country dominated by utterly different cultural and religious traditions. Much as early Muslim rulers in Iran had given Zoroastrians legal status as "people of Scripture" (like Christians and Jews; see Chapter 11), the first Arab conquerors in Sind (711) had treated Hindus similarly as "protected peoples" under Muslim sovereignty. These precedents gave Indian Muslim rulers a legal basis for coexistence with their Hindu subjects but did not remove Hindu resistance to Muslim rule.

▲ **The Qutub Minar (Victory Tower)** in Delhi in India is an example of classic Indo-Muslim art and architecture. Constructed in the twelfth century, this soaring tower made from red sandstone commemorated a recent Muslim military victory.
Getty Images, Inc.-Taxi.

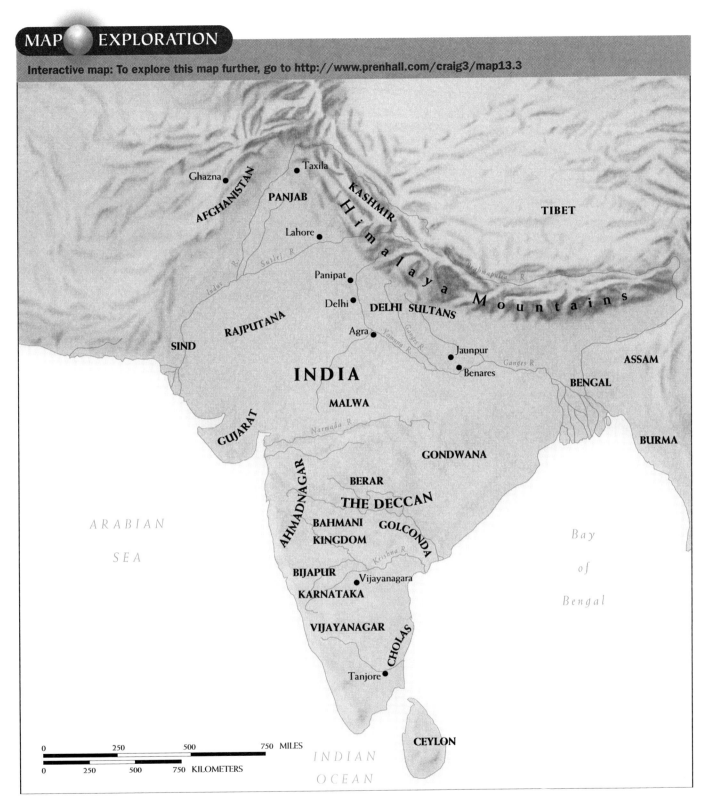

Interactive map: To explore this map further, go to http://www.prenhall.com/craig3/map13.3

MAP 13–3 The Indian Subcontinent, 1000–1500.   Shown are major kingdoms and regions.

The chief obstacle to Islamic expansion in India was the military prowess of the Hindu warrior class that emerged after the Hun and other Asian invasions of the fifth and sixth centuries. Apparently descended from such invaders and the native warrior (Kshatriya) class of Hindus, this class was known from about the mid–seventh century as *Rajputs.* The Rajputs were a large group of North Indian clans bound together by a fierce warrior ethic and strong Hindu cultural and religious traditionalism. They fought the Muslims with great tenacity, but their inability to unite brought them eventually under Muslim domination in the sixteenth century (see Chapter 21).

Islamic States and Dynasties

A series of Turkish-Afghan rulers known as the "Slave Sultans of Delhi" extended and maintained Islamic power over North India for nearly a century (1206–1290). Such slaves, or *mamluks*, figured prominently in the leadership and elites of the new regime. Five descendants of Iltutmish ruled after him until 1266. The most vigorous of these was his daughter Raziyya, who ruled as sultana from 1237 to 1241.

Four later Muslim dynasties—the Khaljis, Tughluqs, Sayyids, and Lodis—continued the Delhi sultanate through the fifteenth century. This run of Muslim dynasties was interrupted by the Mongol-Turkish invasion and sack of Delhi by Timur in 1398, from which the city took decades to recover. Even before this devastation, however—roughly from the mid-1300s—the sultanate's central authority began to dwindle. In the two centuries before the advent of the Mughals in the mid–sixteenth century, many regions became partially or wholly independent, smaller sultanates, Rajput kingdoms, or tiny Hindu or Muslim principalities. The sultanate was often only the most prominent among various kingdoms. Regional rule predominated across the subcontinent.

CHRONOLOGY

Eastern Islamic Lands

875–999	Samanid dynasty, centered at Bukhara
945–1055	Buyid Shi'ite dynasty in Baghdad, controls caliphs
994–1186	Ghaznavid dynasty in Ghazna (modern Afghanistan) and Lahore (modern Pakistan), founded by Subuktigin (r. 976–997) and his son, Mahmud of Ghazna (r. 998–1030)
1020	Death of Firdawsi, compiler of *Shahnama*
ca. 1050	Death of al-Biruni, scientist and polyglot
1055–1194	Saljuq rule in Baghdad
1063–1092	Viziership of Nizam al-Mulk
1067	Founding of the Madvasah Nizamiyyah in Bagdad by Nizam al-Mulk
1111	Death of al-Ghazzali, theologian and scholar
1219–1222	Genghis Khan plunders eastern Iran to Indus region
1258	Hulegu Khan conquers Baghdad
1261	Mamluk-Mongol treaty halts westward Mongol movement
1260–1335	Hulegu and his Il-Khanid successors rule Iran
1379–1405	Campaigns of Timur-i Lang (Tamerlane) devastate entire Islamic East
1405–1494	Timurids, successors of Tamerlane, rule in Transoxiana and Iran
1405–1447	Shahrukh, Timurid ruler at Herat; great patronage of the arts and philosophy

A Spice Market in the East Indies, ca. 1600.
Engraving by Theodore de Bry/The New York Public Library. Prints Division.

Southeast Asia

The most important independent Islamic state was that of the Bahmanids in the Deccan (1347–1527). These rulers were famous for their architecture and the intellectual life of their court, as well as for their role in containing the powerful South Indian Hindu state of Vijayanagar (1336–1565). (The first documented use of firearms in the subcontinent was in a Bahmani battle with the raja of Vijayanagar in 1366.) Most regional capitals fostered a rich cultural life. Jaunpur, to the north of Benares (Varanasi), for example, became an asylum for artists and intellectuals after Timur's sack of Delhi and boasted an impressive tradition of Islamic architecture. Kashmir, an independent sultanate from 1346 to 1589, was a center of literary activity where many Indian texts were translated into Persian.

Islam spread into Southeast Asia as a result of a natural extension from South Asia that subsequently took on unique charateristics of its own. Because of its geographic location, the islands in Southeast Asia connected India and China and thus became an important trade route by the fifteenth century. The spread of Islam in this region was not a steady, progressive development and was not dominated by one particular tradition. Rather the proliferation of Islam was idiosyncratic and a number of distinct Islamic traditions emerged centered largely around the five areas: Java, Samudra, Melaka, Acheh, and Moluccas (see Map 13–4).

In some of the areas, such as in the Moluccas, the traditional beliefs of Islam coexisted with worship and adulation of ancestors, sorcery, or magic. Various central Islamic rites

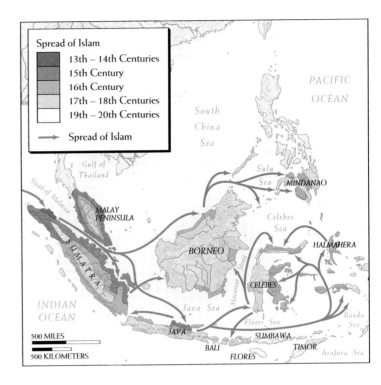

MAP 13–4 The Spread of Islam in Southeast Asia.

OVERVIEW   Major Islamic Dynasties, 1000–1500

The years between 1000 and 1500 were marked by political fragmentation in the Islamic world. While the Muslims eventually defeated the Crusader states in Palestine and Syria, in Spain the Christians gradually conquered every Islamic state. The Mongol invasions of the mid–thirteenth century and the campaigns of Timur-i Lang in the fourteenth century devastated much of the eastern Islamic world. Yet, despite these reverses and the rise and fall of dynasties, Islamic civilization endured, and the Muslim faith spread to new areas in Africa, India, and Southeast Asia.

Dynasty	Location	Dynasty	Location
Umayyads	Spain	Seljuks	Anatolia, Iraq
Almoravids	West Africa, North Africa, Spain	Abbasids	Iraq
Almohads	Morocco, Spain	Ghaznavids	Transoxiana, Pakistan
Fatimids	Tunisia, Egypt	Khwarzims	Iran
Ayyubids	Egypt, Syria	Ilkhanids	Iran
Mamluks	Egypt, Syria	Timurids	Transoxiana, Iran
Samanids	Transoxiana	Delhi Sultans	Northern India
Buyids	Iraq	Bahmanids	Deccan

such as the pilgrimage (*hajj*) were perceived to be an Arab custom and thus not required for "true" Muslims. Eventually, however, many political leaders adopted a more stringent Islamic practice largely for political reasons because Islam would allow for greater centralization and consolidation of power.

One of the greatest sources of tension and conflict in this area was not solely due to distinct religious views. Rather it was the struggle betweeen the center and the periphery. Before the arrival of the Dutch in the early seventeenth century, the various urban rulers, typically located in port cities, benefited from the new global economy. They sought to subsume under their control the hereditery chiefs, who had also converted to Islam, by invoking Islam and their vision of a perfect society. The local traditions proved to be durable, especially in the rural areas. Muslims in Southeast Asia therefore adapted Islam to their needs and customs rather than simply replacing the indigenous practices with the new universal and foreign religion.

Religious and Cultural Accommodation

Despite the enduring division of the subcontinent into multiple political and administrative units, the five centuries after Mahmud of Ghazna saw Islam become an enduring and influential element of Indian culture—especially in the north and the Deccan. The Delhi sultans were able, except for Timur's invasion, to fend off the Mongol danger, much as the Mamluks had in Egypt. They thereby provided a basic political and social framework within which Islam could take root. Although the ruling class remained a Muslim minority of Persianized Turks and Afghans ruling a Hindu majority, conversion went on at various levels of society. *Ghazis*, ("warriors") also carried Islam by force of arms to

---

DOCUMENT How the Hindus Differ from the Muslims

Al-Biruni (d. ca. 1050), the greatest scholar-scientist of medieval Islam, was born in northeastern Iran. He spent much of his life at the court of Mahmud of Ghazna, whom he accompanied on expeditions into northwestern India. Alongside his scientific work, he learned Sanskrit, studied India and the Hindus, and wrote a History of India. *The following selections from this work illustrate the reach and sophistication of his mind.*

♦ How does the emphasis on purity and the impurity of foreigners that Biruni imputes to the Hindus compare with the attitudes of Islam and other religions? Does this passage suggest why the Hindu tradition has remained largely an Indian one, while Islam became an international religion? At what might Biruni's comments about the relative absence of religous controversy among Hindus be aimed?

... The barriers which separate Muslims and Hindus rest on different causes.

First, they differ from us in everything which other nations have in common. And here we first mention the language, although the difference of language also exists between other nations. If you want to conquer this difficulty (i.e., to learn Sanskrit), you will not find it easy, because the language is of an enormous range, both in words and inflections, something like the Arabic, calling one and the same thing by various names, both original and derived, and using one and the same word for a variety of subjects, which, in order to be properly understood, must be distinguished from each other by various qualifying epithets. ...

Secondly, they totally differ from us in religion, as we believe in nothing in which they believe, and vice versa.

On the whole, there is very little disputing about theological topics among themselves; at the utmost, they fight with words, but they will never stake their soul or body or their property on religious controversy. On the contrary, all their fanaticism is directed against those who do not belong to them—against all foreigners. They call them *mleecha*, i.e., impure, and forbid having any connection with them, be it by intermarriage or any other kind of relationship, or by sitting, eating, and drinking with them, because thereby, they think, they would be polluted. They consider as impure anything which touches the fire and the water of a foreigner; and no household can exist without these two elements. Besides, they never desire that a thing which once has been polluted should be purified and thus recovered, as, under ordinary circumstances, if anybody or anything has become unclean, he or it would strive to regain the state of purity. They are not allowed to receive anybody who does not belong to them, even if he wished it, or was inclined to their religion. This, too, renders any connection with them quite impossible, and constitutes the widest gulf between us and them.

In the third place, in all manners and usages they differ from us to such a degree as to frighten their children with us, with our dress, and our ways and customs, and as to declare us to be devil's breed, and our doings as the very opposite of all that is good and proper. By the by, we must confess, in order to be just, that a similar depreciation of foreigners not only prevails among us and the Hindus, but is common to all nations towards each other.

From Edward C. Sachau, *Alberuni's India*, Vol. 1 (London: Kegan Paul. Trench, Truebner, 1910), pp. 17, 19, 20.

pagan groups in eastern Bengal and Assam. Some Hindu converts came from the ruling classes who served the Muslim overlords. Sufi orders converted many Hindus among the lower classes across the north. The Muslim aristocracy, at first mostly foreigners, was usually treated in Indian society as a separate caste group or groups. Lower class or other Hindu converts were assimilated into lower "Muslim castes," often identified by occupation. (See Document, "How the Hindus Differ from the Muslims.")

Sanskrit had long been the Indian scholarly and common language, but in this period regional languages, such as Tamil in the south, gained status as literary and administrative languages, and Persian became the language of intellectual and cultural life for the ruling elites of North India. However, the coming of substantial numbers of Muslims to the subcontinent led to the emergence of a new language, **Urdu-Hindi**, with both Perso-Arabic and indigenous Indian elements. It began to take shape not long after the initial Muslim influx in the eleventh century and developed in response to the increasing need of Hindus and Muslims for a shared language. It became the spoken idiom of the Delhi region and developed into a literary language of North Indian and Deccan Muslims in the seventeenth and eighteenth centuries. Indo-European in grammar, it used Perso-Arabic vocabulary and script and was at first called *Hindi* ("Indian") or *Dakani* ("southern"), then in British times *Hindustani*. Eventually *Urdu* came to serve as the name for the Muslim version of the language that continued to draw on its Perso-Arabic heritage, whereas *Hindi* was used for the version associated with Hindu culture and oriented in its further development toward its Hindu and Sanskritic heritage. Each became an official national language: Urdu for modern Pakistan and Hindi for modern India.

Indian Muslims were always susceptible to Hindu influence (in language, marriage customs, and caste consciousness). However, unlike earlier invaders, they were never utterly absorbed into the predominant Hindu culture but remained in some measure a group apart, conscious of their uniqueness in the Hindu world and proud to be distinct. The Muslim ruling classes saw themselves as the protectors and propagators of Islam in India, and most of the sultans of Delhi sought formal recognition for their rule from the nominal Abbasid caliphs in Baghdad or, in Mamluk times, in Cairo.

◄ **Krishna Dancing on the Head of the Serpent Kaliya.** This fifteenth-century bronze figure from Vijayanagar is based on a legend, according to which Kaliya was infesting the waters of the Jumna River until Krishna leaped in and emerged dancing on the vanquished snake.

Asian Art Museum of San Francisco. The Avery Brundage Collection B65B72.

Nevertheless, reciprocal influence of Muslims and Hindus was inevitable, especially in popular piety. Sufi devotion had an appeal similar to that of Hindu devotional, or *bhakti* movements (see Chapter 10), and each influenced the other. Some of India's most revered Sufi and *bhakti* saints date from the fourteenth and fifteenth centuries. During this period, various theistic mystics strove to transcend the mutual antagonism and exclusivism of Muslims and Hindus. They typically preached devotion to a God who saves his worshipers without regard either to Hindu caste obligations or to legalistic Muslim observance. The poet-saints Ramananda (d. after 1400) and Kabir (d. ca. 1518) were the two most famous such reformers.

Hindu and Other Indian Traditions

The history of India from 1000 to 1500 was also important for the other religious and cultural communities of India that as a whole vastly outnumbered the Muslims. The Jain tradition flourished, notably in Gujarat, Rajputana, and Karnataka. In the north the Muslim conquests effectively ended Indian Buddhism by the eleventh century. However, Buddhism had already been waning in Indian culture long before Islam arrived.

Hindu religion and culture flourished even under Muslim control, as the continuing social and religious importance of the Brahmans and the popularity of *bhakti* movements throughout India attest. This was an age of Brahmanic scholasticism that produced many commentaries and manuals but few seminal works. *Bhakti* creativity was much greater. The great Hindu Vaishnava Brahman Ramanuja (d. 1137) reconciled *bhakti* ideas with the classical Upanishadic Hindu worldview in the Vedantin tradition. *Bhakti* piety underlies the masterpiece of Hindu mystical love poetry, Jayadeva's *Gita Govinda* (twelfth century), which is devoted to Krishna, the most important of Vishnu's incarnations.

The south continued to be the center of Hindu cultural, political, and religious activity. The most important dynastic state in the south during this age was that of the Cholas which flourished from about 900–1300 and patronized a famous school of bronze sculpture at their capital of Tanjore. Their mightiest successor, the kingdom of Vijayanagar (1336–1565), subjugated the entire south in the fourteenth century and resisted its Muslim foes longer than any other kingdom. Vijayanagar itself was one of India's most lavishly developed cities and a center of the cult of Shiva before its destruction by the Bahmanid sultan of the Deccan.

CHRONOLOGY

India

ca. 900–1300	Chola dynasty in southern India
1137	Death of Ramanuja
1206–1290	Slave-kings of Delhi
1290–1320	Khalji sultans of Delhi
1320–1413	Tughluqid sultans of Delhi
1414–1526	Sayyid sultans of Delhi
1336–1565	Hindu dynasty of Vijayanagar
1347–1527	Muslim Bahmanid dynasty in the Deccan
1398	Timur's sack of Delhi

Sixteenth Century Persian Painting.

Summary

Religion Between 1000 and 1500, the most important developments for the shape of Islamic society were of Sunni and Shi'ite legal and religious norms and of Sufi traditions and personal piety. Sunnism was the dominant tradition across the Islamic world, but in both main branches of Islam, the *ulama* became the religious, social, and political elites and discouraged religious innovation. Shi'ism flourished in Iran under the Savafid rulers. Sufi piety stresses the spiritual and mystical dimensions of Islam. Sufi fraternal orders, whether Sunni or Shi'ite, became the chief instruments of the spread of Muslim faith in most Islamic societies.

Regional Developments Despite general religious tolerance and high cultural achievements, the Muslims were gradually pushed out of Spain by the Spanish Christian states between 1000 and 1492. In Egypt, the Shi'ite Fatamids established a separate caliphate from 969 to 1171. The Mamluks, whose rule in Egypt lasted from 1260 to 1517, were the only Muslim dynasty to withstand the Mongol invasions. The Seljuks, based in Anatolia and Iraq, were the first major Turkish dynasty of Islam. Other notable Islamic dynasties were the Ghaznavids in Transoxiana and the Khwarizam shahs in Iran.

Mongol Invasions In 1255 the Mongols invaded the Muslim world and swept all before them, conquering Transoxiana, Iran, and Iraq, where they captured Baghdad and killed the last Abbasid caliph in 1258, before being defeated by the Mamluks in Syria in 1260. Thereafter, the Mongols established the Ilkhanid dynasty in Iran and converted to Islam. Another wave of Turko-Mongol conquest under Timur-i Lang further devastated much of the Near East between 1379 and 1405.

India and Southeast Asia Muslim invaders and rulers spread Islam in India, where it became an enduring and influential part of Indian civilization. A new language, Urdu-Hindi, combined Persian-Arabic and indigenous Indian elements. There was reciprocal influence between Muslims and Hindus.

Buddhism all but disappeared from India during these years, but Hindu religion and culture flourished, even under Muslim control. Hindu devotional, or *Bhakti*, movements were especially creative.

In Southeast Asia, Islam was spread by Muslim merchants and traders, where it blended with local customs.

Review Questions

1. In 1000–1500, why did no Muslim leader build a large-scale Islamic empire of the extent of the early Abbasids?

2. How were the *ulama* educated? What was their relationship to political leadership? What social roles did they play?

3. What was the role and impact of religious sectarianism in this period? Of the institutionalization of Sufi piety and thought?

4. Discuss the cultural developments in Spain before 1500. Why was Córdoba such a model of civilized culture?

5. Why might Islam have been able to survive the successive invasions by steppe peoples (Turks and Mongols) from 945 on? What were the lasting results of these "invasions" for the Islamic world?

6. What were the primary obstacles to stable rule for India's Muslim invaders and immigrants? How did they deal with them?

Key Terms

bhakti (p. 369)

ghazis (p. 369)

madrasa (p. 352)

orthopraxy (p. 353)

Ramadan (p. 352)

Reconquista (p. 355)

Sufi (p. 353)

sultan (p. 356)

Urdu-Hindi (p. 369)

Documents CD-ROM

1. William of Rubruck: Impressions of the medieval Mongols

2. Farid al-Din Attari: The Conference of Birds

3. The Thousand and One Nights

4. Two Bhakti Poets: Ravidas and Mirabai

NOTE: *To learn more about the topics in this chapter, see the Suggested Readings at the end of the book.*

Ancient Civilizations of the Americas

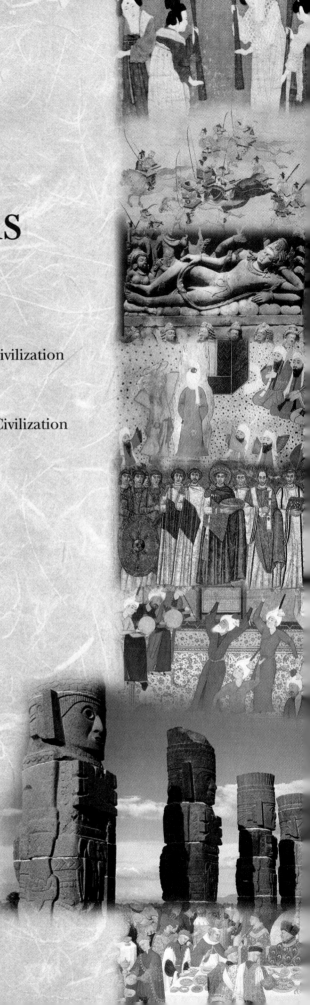

Ceramic images of shamans from the Bahia culture along the coast of Ecuador. The shamans would have been associated with healing or tribal religious rituals.
Neff Greenberg/AGE Fotostock America, Inc.

Ancient Civilizations of the Americas

Civilization in the Americas before 1492 developed independently of civilization in the Old World. As the kings of Egypt were erecting their pyramid tombs, the people of the desert coast of Peru were erecting temple platforms. While King Solomon ruled in Jerusalem, the Olmec were creating their monumental stone heads. As Rome reached its apogee and then declined, so did the great city of Teotihuacán in the Valley of Mexico. As Islam spread from its heartland, the rulers of Tikal brought their city to its greatest splendor before its abrupt collapse. Maya mathematics and astronomy rivaled those of any other peoples of the ancient world. And as the aggressive nation-states of Europe were emerging from their feudal past, the Aztecs and Incas were consolidating their great empires. The agriculture, engineering, and public works of these states, as exemplified by the famous Aztec drainage systems and floating gardens or *chiampas* of Lake Texcoco, and the Inca system of roads exquisitely demonstrate an ability to master the most challenging environments.

The encounter between Old World and New, however, proved devastating for American civilization. The technology that allowed Europeans to embark on the voyages of discovery and fight destructive wars among themselves caught the great native empires unprepared. More important, however, was what historian Alfred Crosby has called the "Columbian Exchange." The peoples of the New World exchanged trade goods, ideas, technology, and microbes among themselves, along north–south trade routes that linked the American Southeast and Southwest to Mesoamerica, and the peoples of the northern Andes to those of the central and southern regions, as well as east–west routes linking eastern North America with the Great Lakes region and beyond. Neither they nor their cultures were static or immobile; they were definitely not, in one historian's words, "a people without history," even if much of that history is lost to us because of the absence of written records. But overall, the Americas shared a single gene pool isolated from those of Sub-Saharan Africa and the Eurasian continent. Europeans, therefore, brought with them far more microbial invaders than they encountered in the New World, and it was epidemic disease, and the psychological edge it afforded the Europeans, that played a key role in the conquest of the peoples of the New World.

Equally important in understanding the ability of small numbers of Europeans to conquer these advanced civilizations, however, was the nature of the civilizations themselves. The European invaders succeeded most rapidly in toppling the most organized of the societies in the New World, the Aztecs and the Inca, precisely because these societies were organized, centralized, and hierarchical. It is important to remember that the history of New World civilizations, like that of any other civilization, was tightly linked to internal developments before the arrival of Europeans.

It is also important to recall that the Aztecs and Incas, in particular, ruled over different peoples, many of whom resented their subjugation and saw in the arrival of the Europeans an opportunity to assert their autonomy. Thus the Spanish in Mexico and, to a lesser extent, in Peru, found allies among the native peoples willing to do much of the fighting for them. When Cortés faced the Aztecs in the decisive battle for their capital city, Tenochtitlán, he did so with at least 30,000 native warriors by his side.

THINK AHEAD

◆ Why is it important to bear in mind that the civilizations of the New World had long and rich histories before the arrival of Europeans? Why it is so difficult to discover the details of the history of the peoples of the Americas? What are our major sources of information?

◆ What role did the environment play in the formation of American civilizations?

HUMANS FIRST SETTLED THE AMERICAN CONTINENTS between 12,000 and 40,000 years ago. At that time glaciers locked up much of the world's water, lowering the sea level and opening a bridge of dry land between Siberia and Alaska. The earliest undisputed evidence of humans in Tierra del Fuego, at the southern tip of South America, dates to 11,000 years ago, indicating that at least by then the immigrants and their descendants had spread over all of both North and South America. When the glaciers receded the oceans rose, flooding the Bering Straits and severing Asia from America. Despite some continued contact in the Arctic and perhaps sporadic contacts elsewhere, the inhabitants of the Americas were now isolated from the inhabitants of Africa and Eurasia and would remain so until overwhelmed by European invaders after 1492.

Although isolated from one another, the peoples of the Americas and the peoples of Africa and Eurasia experienced similar cultural changes at the end of the Paleolithic. In the Americas, as in the Eastern Hemisphere, people in some regions gradually shifted from hunting and gathering to a settled, agricultural way of life. And in some places civilization emerged as society grew increasingly stratified, villages coalesced into urban centers, monumental architecture appeared, and craft specialists developed sophisticated artistic traditions.

The two most prominent centers of civilization—and the focus of this chapter—were Mesoamerica, in what is today Mexico and Central America, and the Andean region of South America. Both regions have a long, rich history of civilization that reaches back thousands of years. At the time of the European conquest of the Americas in the sixteenth century both regions were dominated by powerful expansionist empires—the Aztecs, or Mexica, in Mesoamerica, and the Inca in the Andes. In both regions Spanish conquerors obliterated the native empires and nearly succeeded in obliterating native culture. But in both, Native American traditions have endured, overlaid and combined in complex ways with Hispanic culture, to provide clues to the pre-Hispanic past.

Problems in Reconstructing the History of Native American Civilization

Several difficulties confront scholars trying to understand the ancient civilizations of the Americas. One is simply the nature of the evidence. Andean civilizations never developed writing, and in Mesoamerica much of the written record was destroyed by time and conquest, and what remained was until recently undeciphered. The primary source of information has thus been archaeology, the study of the physical remains left by past cultures. Archaeologists have been successful at teasing out many details of the American past. Turning from the study of monumental remains in great urban centers to the study of the remains left by ordinary people in their everyday lives, they have been able to create an increasingly rich picture of the economic and social organization of ancient American civilizations. But archaeology alone cannot produce the kind of narrative history that thousands of years of written records have made possible for Eurasian civilization. For at least one ancient Mesoamerican people, however—the Maya—this situation is changing. Scholars have recently been able to decipher their writing and attach specific names, dates, and events to heretofore silent ruins.

We also have accounts of the history and culture of the Aztecs and Inca, the last great Native American civilizations, that were related to Spanish missionaries and officials in the wake of the conquest. Although these accounts are invaluable sources of information, it is almost impossible to know how much they are colored by the conquest and the needs and expectations of the conquerors. This dilemma raises another. The long physical separation of the peoples of the Americas from the peoples of Asia and Europe created a great cultural separation as well. Since the conquest, however, European culture has predominated. Both the Spanish conquerors seeking to make sense of the wonders they encountered and later scholars seeking to understand preconquest Native American civilization and reconstruct its history have had to rely on the language and categories of European thought to describe and analyze peoples and cultural experiences that had nothing to do with Europe. Cultural blinders and arrogance have exacerbated this gap—for example, the Spaniards, who sought to eradicate Native American religion and replace it with Christianity.

Again and again, European words, categories, and values have been used to describe the experience of America before it was America. Columbus and other early explorers (see Chapter 18), believing they had reached the East Indies,

OVERVIEW   The Periods of Mesoamerican and Andean Civilizations

Scholars divide the history of the Mesoamerican and Andean peoples into several distinct periods.

MESOAMERICA

Period	Civilization
Archaic, 8000–2000 B.C.E.	Agricultural villages; maize cultivation
Formative, 2000 B.C.E.–150 C.E.	Olmecs, Monte Alban; urban centers, writing, a calendar
Classic, 150–900 C.E.	Maya, Teotihuacán; sophisticated mathematics, astronomy, and calendar
Post-Classic, 900–1521 C.E.	Toltecs, Aztecs

ANDES

Period	Civilization
Preceramic and Initial, ca. 3000–800 B.C.E.	Coastal peoples; monumental architecture, pottery
Early Horizon, ca. 800–200 B.C.E.	Chavin; innovations in ceramics, weaving, and metallurgy
Early Intermediate, ca. 200 B.C.E.–600 C.E.	Nazca, Moche; political centralization, monumental earthworks, advanced pottery and metallurgy
Middle Horizon and Late Interemediate, ca. 600–1475 C.E.	Tiwanaku, Huari, Chimu; expansionist empires, sophisticated agriculture
Inca Empire, ca. 1475–1532	Extensive network of roads and bridges, sophisticated recordkeeping, advanced architecture

called the people they met in the Caribbean "Indians." This misnomer stuck, extending to all Native American peoples who, of course, have other names for themselves. The name *America* itself is European, taken from Amerigo Vespucci (1451–1512), a Florentine who explored the coast of Brazil in 1501 and 1502.

Mesoamerica

Mesoamerica (the name means "middle America") extends from central Mexico into Central America (see Map 14–7). This is a region of great physical diversity, ranging from lowland tropical rain forests to temperate highlands with fertile basins and valleys. Lowland regions include the Yucatán Peninsula and the Gulf and Pacific coasts. Highland regions include Mexico's central plateau, with the Valley of Mexico and the Oaxaca region, and the mountainous areas of Guatemala. Most of Mesoamerica's mineral resources are found in the highlands. The lowlands were the source of many important trading goods, including hardwoods, plant dyes, and the prized feathers of exotic birds.

Mesoamerica also designates a distinctive and enduring cultural tradition that emerged in this region between 1000 and 2000 B.C.E., manifested itself in a succession of impressive and powerful states until the coming of European conquerors in the sixteenth century, and continues to express itself in the lives of the region's Native American peoples. This is not to say that Mesoamerica was or is culturally homogeneous. The peoples of Mesoamerica were and are ethnically and linguistically diverse. There was no single Mesoamerican civilization, nor was there a single linear development of civilization in the region. Nonetheless, Mesoamerican civilizations shared many traits, including writing, a sophisticated calendrical system, many gods and religious ideas, a ritual ball game, and urban centers with religious and administrative buildings symmetrically arranged around large plazas.

Throughout its history the peoples of the region were linked by long-distance trade. Unlike the Andean region, where sophisticated metallurgy developed early, metallurgy came late to Mesoamerica. When it did come, it was used primarily for ceremonial objects rather than for weapons and tools. Instead, Mesoamericans made weapons and other tools from **obsidian**, a volcanic glass capable of holding a razor-sharp edge, and for that reason a valued trade commodity.

Mesoamerican history before the Spanish conquest is conventionally divided into four major periods: The term *Classic*, with its associations to ancient Greece and its connotations of "best" or "highest," derives from European historical frameworks. It reflects the view of many early Mesoamericanists that the Classic period, which corresponds more or less to the time during which the Maya civilizations of the southern Yucatán erected dated stone monuments, was the high point of Mesoamerican civilization. That view is no longer so prevalent, but the terminology has endured. The chronology continues to provide a useful framework for understanding Mesoamerican history.

The transition from hunting and gathering to settled village life occurred gradually in Mesoamerica during the Archaic period. The cornerstone of the process was the domestication of maize (corn) and other staple crops, including beans and squash. Other plants native to the Americas that were domesticated in this period include tomatoes, chili peppers, and avocado. Maize and beans were particularly important because together they provide a rich source of protein compared to the grains that were the basis of the Neolithic revolution in the ancient Near East and China. In those regions domesticated animals supplied the protein settled agriculturalists needed in their diet. Mesoamerica, however, was poor in sources of animal protein. It had only a few domesticated animals—among them dogs and turkeys—and no large herd animals like the cattle, sheep, and goats of the Old World.

The domestication of maize, beans, and other plants secured the people of Mesoamerica an adequate and dependable diet. Over time they devised myriad ways to prepare and store these staples. Maize has also been one of Mesoamerica's major contributions to the world. Since the conquest, maize cultivation has spread to many other parts of the world. Corn is now one of North America's most important crops, and it is used to feed livestock in both North and South America.

Probably because they had no large draft animals—no horses or oxen—the people of the Americas, including Mesoamerica, never developed the wheel, although they made wheeled toys. In Mesoamerica humans did all the carrying. And because there were no horses and chariots, warfare in Mesoamerica (and in Andean South America) was always between armies of foot soldiers.

Between 5000 and 2500 B.C.E. villages began to appear in both highland and lowland regions of Mesoamerica. By about 2000 B.C.E. settled agricultural life had taken hold in much of the region. As in the Old World when this happened, people began to make fired clay vessels, and ceramic technology appeared. Nomadic hunter-gatherers have little

need of storage, but farmers do, and clay vessels filled that need. Pottery is also a medium for artistic expression, and it played a role in religion and ritual observance throughout Mesoamerican history.

The Formative Period and the Emergence of Mesoamerican Civilization

By about 1500 B.C.E. Mesoamerica's agricultural villages were beginning to coalesce into more complicated societies, with towns and monumental architecture, the division of society into elite and commoner classes, long-distance trade among regions, and the emergence of sophisticated artistic traditions.

THE OLMEC

The most prominent of the Early Formative period cultures is that of the Olmec, centered on the lowlands of Mexico's Gulf coast. This is a densely vegetated region with slow, meandering streams bordered by areas of rich, alluvial soil. The Olmec were once thought of as Mesoamerica's "mother culture," but evidence is accumulating that similarly complex societies were emerging at about the same time throughout Mesoamerica.

Most of what is known about the Olmecs comes from the archaeological sites of San Lorenzo and La Venta. Other Olmec centers have not been as intensively studied. San Lorenzo was first occupied about 1500 B.C.E. and had developed into a prominent center by about 1200 B.C.E. It included public buildings, a drainage system linked to artificial ponds, and what was probably the earliest court for the Mesoamerican ball game. The center flourished until about 900 B.C.E. but then went into decline and had been abandoned by about 400 B.C.E. As San Lorenzo declined, La Venta rose to prominence, flourishing from about 900 to 400 B.C.E. La Venta's most conspicuous feature is a 110-foot, scalloped pyramid, known as the Great Pyramid, which stands at one end of a group of platforms and plazas aligned along a north–south axis. Archaeologists have recovered many caches of carved jade, serpentine, and granite artifacts that had been buried along the center line of this axis. Like San Lorenzo, La Venta also had an elaborate drainage system.

Probably the best known Olmec works of art are the massive stone heads, some weighing more than twenty tons, that have been found at both San Lorenzo and La Venta. Thought to be portraits of Olmec rulers, these were carved from basalt from quarries as much as sixty-five miles distant and transported, probably by raft, to the centers. The Olmec also carved other large basalt monuments, including altars and seated figures.

A **Olmec Monument.** A large carved monument from the Olmec site of La Venta with a naturalistically rendered human figure.
Robert and Linda Mitchell Photography.

The population of San Lorenzo and La Venta was never great, probably less than 1,000 people. The monumental architecture and sculpture at these sites nonetheless suggests that Olmec society was dominated by an elite class of ruler-priests able to command the labor of the rest of the population. The elite probably lived in the centers, supported by farmers who lived in villages of pole-and-thatch houses.

Among the most pervasive images in Olmec art is that of the were-jaguar, a half-human, half-feline creature. The were-jaguar may have been a divine ancestor figure, perhaps providing the elite with the justification for their authority. Similarities between the were-jaguar iconography and that of later Mesoamerican deities suggests some of the underlying continuities linking Mesoamerican societies over time.

The raw material for many Olmec artifacts, such as jade and obsidian, comes from other regions of Mesoamerica. Likewise, Olmec goods and Olmec iconography like the were-jaguar are found in other regions, all suggesting that from an early time the parts of Mesoamerica were linked in a web of trade. These contacts would have fostered the spread of ideas, contributing to the formation of common Mesoamerican traditions. Control of trade in high-status materials like jade and obsidian by the Olmec elite would also have contributed to their prestige and authority.

CHRONOLOGY

Major Periods in Ancient Mesoamerican Civilization

8000–2000 B.C.E.	Archaic
2000 B.C.E.–150 C.E.	Formative (or Pre-Classic)
150–900 C.E.	Classic
900–1521 C.E.	Post-Classic

THE VALLEY OF OAXACA AND THE RISE OF MONTE ALBAN

Olmec civilization faded after about 400 B.C.E. and had disappeared by about 200 B.C.E. Other regions, however, were rising to prominence. Some of the most significant developments in the Late Formative period occurred in the Valley of Oaxaca. The site of San José Mogote, located in one branch of the valley, had arisen at about the same time as San Lorenzo. By about 600 B.C.E. San José Mogote was a thriving center of perhaps 1,000 people. Around 500 B.C.E. a new center, Monte Alban, was built on a hill where three branches of the valley meet. Monte Alban's population soon grew to about 5,000, and it emerged as the capital of a state that dominated the Oaxaca region. Carved images of bound prisoners at Monte Alban suggest that warfare played a role in establishing its authority. They also suggest an early origin for the practice of ritual human sacrifice that characterized most Mesoamerican cultures. Monte Alban retained its authority in Oaxaca into the Classic period, maintaining its independence against the growing power of the greatest Classic city, Teotihuacán.

THE EMERGENCE OF WRITING AND THE MESOAMERICAN CALENDAR

The earliest evidence of writing and the Mesoamerican calendar have been found in the Valley of Oaxaca at San José Mogote and Monte Alban. The Mesoamerican calendar is based on two interlocking cycles, each with its own day and month names. One cycle, tied to the solar year, was of 365 days; the other was of 260 days. Combining the two cycles produced a "century" of fifty-two years, the amount of time required before a particular combination of days in each cycle would repeat itself. The hieroglyphs found in Oaxaca relate to the 260-day cycle.

At the time of the Spanish conquest, all the peoples of Mesoamerica used this fifty two-year calendrical system. As we will see, only the Maya developed a calendar based on a longer time period, anchored—like the Jewish, Christian, or Muslim calendars—to a fixed starting point in the past.

The Classic Period in Mesoamerica

The Classic period was a time of cultural florescence in Mesoamerica. In Central Mexico, it saw the rise of Teotihuacán, a great city that rivaled the largest cities of the world at the time. The Maya, who built densely populated cities in the seemingly inhospitable rain forests of the southern Yucatán, developed a sophisticated system of mathematics and Mesoamerica's most advanced hieroglyphic writing. Indeed, Classic urban life in Mesoamerica was richer and on a larger scale than in Europe north of the Alps at the same time.

Archaeologists and art historians have recently made enormous strides in understanding Classic civilization. Progress in deciphering Maya hieroglyphics has opened a window on the politics and statecraft of the Maya elite. Archaeological studies

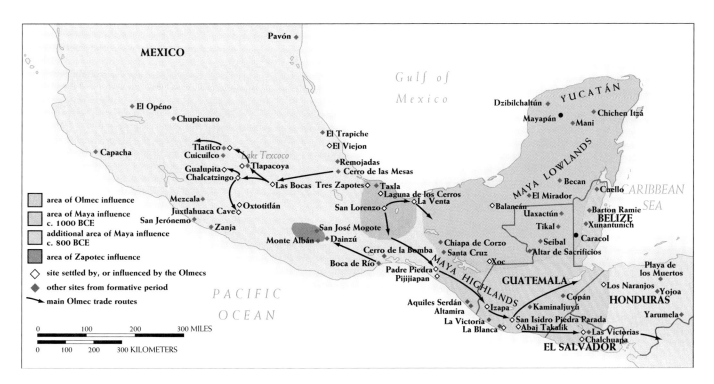

MAP 14–1 Mesoamerica in the Formative Periods.

have broadened our understanding of Teotihuacán and Maya cities, revealing their extent and structure and providing clues to the lives of the people who lived in them.

Classic cities, with their many temples, plazas, and administrative buildings, were religious and administrative centers whose rulers combined secular and religious authority. It was once thought that Classic society was composed of peaceful theocracies, without the chronic warfare characterizing Mesoamerica at the time of the Spanish conquest. It is now clear, however, that warfare was common during the Classic period and that Classic rulers did not hesitate to use force to expand their influence and maintain their authority. The ritual sacrifice of captive enemies was also a feature of Classic societies.

TEOTIHUACÁN

In the Late Formative period two centers competed for dominance over the rapidly growing population of the Valley of Mexico. One of these, Cuicuilco, was located at the southern end of the valley. The other, Teotihuacán, was located about thirty miles northeast of Mexico City. When a volcano destroyed Cuicuilco in the first century C.E., Teotihuacán was left unopposed and grew explosively into a great city, perhaps Mesoamerica's first true city-state, dominating central Mexico for many centuries and strongly influencing the rest of Mesoamerica.

Several natural advantages contributed to Teotihuacán's rise. The original source of its prestige may have been a network of caves recently discovered under its most prominent monument, the Pyramid of the Sun (the name by which the Aztecs knew it). These caves may have been considered an entrance to the underworld. Recent studies indicate that stone quarried from them was used to construct the city, creating a direct symbolic link between the city's buildings and its sacred origins. Teotihuacán is also located near an important source of obsidian, straddling a trade route to the Gulf coast and southern Mesoamerica. The quarrying of obsidian and the manufacture and trade of obsidian goods were apparently major sources of the city's wealth and influence. Finally, Teotihuacán is surrounded by fertile farmland susceptible to intensive cultivation with terracing and irrigation.

At its height in about 500 C.E. this remarkable city extended over almost nine square miles and had a popula-

▲ **The Pyramid of the Sun.** This monumental structure stands near the southern end of Teotihuacán's great central thoroughfare, the Avenue of the Dead.
Kal Muller/Woodfin Camp & Associates.

tion of more than 150,000, making it one of the largest cities in the world at the time. Its size and organization suggest that it was ruled by a powerful, centralized authority. It is laid out on a rigid grid plan dominated by a broad, three-mile-long thoroughfare known as the Avenue of the Dead. Religious and administrative structures and a market occupy the center of the city. At one end of the Avenue of the Dead is the so-called Pyramid of the Moon, and near it, to one side, is the 210-foot-high Pyramid of the Sun. More than 2,000 residential structures surround the city center. The most lavish of these, the homes of the city's elite, lie nearest the center. Most of the city's residents lived in walled apartment compounds farther from the center. These compounds were also centers of craft manufacture, with neighborhoods devoted to pottery, obsidian work, and other specialties. Some parts of the city were reserved for foreign traders. One neighborhood, for example, was home to people from Monte Alban and the Oaxaca region. Paintings and murals adorned the interiors of many buildings, including those of the common people as well as the elite. The humble dwellings of poor farmers occupied the city's periphery. As the city grew, local farmers had apparently been forced to abandon their villages and move to Teotihuacán, another indication of the power of the city's rulers.

Teotihuacán's influence extended throughout Mesoamerica. In the central highlands, dispersed settlements were consolidated into larger centers laid out similarly to Teotihuacán, suggesting conquest and direct control—a Teotihuacán empire. The city's influence in other, more distant regions may have reflected close trading ties rather than conquest. Buildings in Teotihuacán's distinctive architectural style at the site of Kaminaljuyu in the highlands of modern Guatemala, for example, may have been residences for Teotihuacano merchants. The city's obsidian and pottery were exchanged widely for items like the green feathers of the quetzal bird and jaguar skins, valued for ritual garments.

Many of the buildings in Teotihuacán were decorated with striking, skillfully made sculptures and murals of the city's gods and ritual practices. Among the deities of Teotihuacán are a storm god and his goddess counterpart, whose representation suggests a link to the Aztec's rain god, Tlaloc, and his consort, Chalchiuhtlicue. The people of Teotihuacán also worshiped a feathered serpent who is recognizably antecedent to the god the Aztecs worshiped as Quetzalcoatl and the Maya as Kukulcan. Murals also suggest that the Teotihuacán elite, like the Maya and later Mesoamerican peoples, drew their own blood as a form of sacrifice to the gods. A mass burial under one of the city's principal temples indicates that they also practiced human sacrifice.

After 500 C.E. Teotihuacán's influence began to wane, and some time in the eighth century, for reasons that are still poorly understood, its authority collapsed. A fire swept through the city, destroying the ritual center and the residences of the elite and hinting at an internal revolt. Although a substantial population lived on in the city, it never regained its former status. It retained its hold on the imagination of succeeding generations of Mesoamericans, however, much like the ruins of ancient Greece and Rome on the imaginations of later Europeans. The name by which we know it, Teotihuacán, is an Aztec word meaning "City of the Gods," and it was still a revered pilgrimage site at the time of the Spanish conquest.

THE MAYA

Maya civilization arose in southern Mesoamerica, which includes modern Guatemala, the Yucatán Peninsula, Belize, and parts of Honduras and El Salvador. Village life established itself in this region during the first millennium B.C.E., and thereafter the population began to rise steadily. The earliest distinctively Maya urban sites date to around 300 B.C.E. in the Late Formative period. During the Classic period, Maya civilization experienced a remarkable florescence in the lowland jungles of the southern Yucatán.

All the pre-Spanish societies of Mesoamerica were literate, recording historical and religious information on scrolled or screenfold books made with deerhide or bark paper. Only a handful of these books, four of them Mayan, have survived the ravages of time and the Spanish conquest. (Spanish priests, who viewed native religious texts as idolatrous, burned almost all of them.) The Maya of the Classic period, who developed Mesoamerica's most advanced writing system, were unique in the extent to which they inscribed writing and calendrical symbols in stone, pottery, and other imperishable materials.

Thanks to rapid advances in the decipherment of Maya writing and to intensive archaeological work at Maya cities, our understanding of the nature of Classic Maya civilization has changed radically in recent decades. According to earlier views, Maya cities were not really cities but empty ceremonial centers inhabited by scholar-priests. The inscriptions were thought to be concerned entirely with astronomical and calendrical observations tied to Maya ritual. Scattered farming communities were thought to have surrounded the centers, supporting the priestly elite. Relations between centers were thought to be peaceful. Contributing to this view was the belief that intensive agriculture capable of supporting dense populations was impossible in the tropical forests of the southern Yucatán where Classic Maya civilization developed.

Archaeologists have shown that Maya centers were indeed cities, and that the largest of them, Tikal, probably had a population of between 50,000 and 70,000 at its height. They have also found evidence of terracing, irrigation systems, and other agricultural technologies that would have increased yields

Mayan Mural. This reproduction of one of the remarkable murals found at the Maya site of Bonampak shows the presentation of captives to the city's ruler, Chan Muan.

enough to support dense populations. Powerful ruling families and their elite retainers dominated these cities, supported by a far larger class of farmer-commoners. The inscriptions are almost entirely devoted to recounting important events in the lives of these rulers. Cities competed for dominance, and warfare between them was chronic. As murals and sculptures show, captured prisoners were sacrificed to appease the gods and glorify the victorious ruler.

Religion deeply informed the social and political realm of the Maya. They believed that the world had gone through several cycles of creation before the present one. (See Document, "A Maya Myth of Creation.") They recognized no clear distinction between a natural and a supernatural world. As was probably true also of Teotihuacán, rulers and the elite combined religious and political authority, mediating between humans and gods through elaborate rituals in the temples and plazas of their cities. Rulers claimed association with the gods to justify their authority. They wore special regalia that symbolized their power, and they performed rituals to sustain the gods and the cosmic order. These rituals included bloodletting ceremonies, the sacrifice of captives, and ball games.

The significance of sacrifice and the ball game in Maya ideology is reflected in a Maya creation myth recorded in the *Popol Vuh*, a Maya book transcribed into European script by a

Maya noble in the sixteenth century. Imagery in Classic Maya art has been linked to this myth, which tells how the Hero Twins defeated the gods of the underworld in the ball game and returned to life after being sacrificed. One became the sun and the other Venus, and in their regular rising and setting reenact their descent into the underworld and their subsequent rebirth. All Maya cities had ball courts. The games played there were a symbolic reenactment of the confrontation between the Hero Twins and the lords of the underworld, and the losing team was sometimes sacrificed.[1]

The Classic Maya developed a sophisticated mathematics and were among the first peoples in the world to invent the concept of zero. In addition to the 52–year calendar round based on interlocking 260- and 365-day cycles they shared with other Mesoamerican societies, the Maya developed an absolute calendar, known as the **Long Count**, tied to a fixed point in the past. The calendar had great religious as well as practical significance for the Maya. They viewed the movements of the celestial bodies to which the calendar was tied—including the sun, moon, and Venus—as deities. The complexity and accuracy of their calendar reflect Maya skills in astronomical observation.

[1] Robert J. Sharer, *The Ancient Maya*, 5th ed. (Stanford, CA: Stanford University Press, 1994), p. 522.

DOCUMENT | A Maya Myth of Creation

This segment of the Maya creation myth is from The Popol Vuh, *a compendium of Maya mythology and history transcribed into European script by a Quiche Maya noble in the sixteenth century.*

◆ How does this myth describe the world before creation? Who are the beings that exist before creation and decide how it is to be carried out? What did they do to create the earth?

There was not yet one person, one animal, bird, fish, crab, tree, rock, hollow, canyon, meadow, forest. Only the sky alone is there; the face of the earth is not clear. Only the sea alone is pooled under all the sky; there is nothing whatever gathered together. It is at rest; not a single thing stirs. It is held back; kept at rest under the sky.

Whatever might be is simply not there; only murmurs, ripples, in the dark, in the night. Only the Maker, Modeler alone, Sovereign Plumed Serpent, the Bearers, Begetters are in the water, a glittering light ... .

So there were three of them, as Heart of Sky, who came to the Sovereign Plumed Serpent, when the dawn of life was conceived:

"How should it be sown, how should it dawn? Who is to be the provider, nurturer?"

"Let it be this way, think about it: this water should be removed, emptied out for the formation of the earth's own plate and platform, then comes the sowing, the dawning of the sky-earth. But there will be no high days and no bright praise for our work, our design, until the rise of the human work, the human design," they said.

And then the earth rose because of them; it was simply their word that brought it forth. For the forming of the earth, they said, "Earth." It arose suddenly, just like a cloud, like a mist, now forming, unfolding. Then the mountains were separated from the water, all at once the great mountains came forth. By their genius alone, by their cutting edge alone they carried out the conception of the mountain-plain, whose face grew instant groves of cypress and pine.

They adjusted their lunar calendar for the actual length of the lunar cycle (29.53 days) and may have had provisions like our leap years for the actual length of the solar year. They also made accurate observations of Venus and recognized before other peoples that it is both the morning and the evening star. The importance of the calendar, its association with divine forces, and the esoteric knowledge required to master it must have been an important source of prestige and power for its elite guardians.

Scholars have been able to correlate the Long Count calendar with the European calendar, and so can date Maya monuments with a precision unknown for other ancient Mesoamerican societies. The commemorative monuments erected by Classic Maya rulers to record their accomplishments almost always have Long Count dates. As a result, it is now possible to reconstruct the dynastic histories of many Maya cities in detail, keeping in mind, of course, that Maya rulers—like rulers everywhere throughout history—may have exaggerated their accomplishments to put themselves in a favorable light.

During the Classic period no single center dominated the Maya region. Rather, many independent units, each composed of a capital city and smaller subject towns and villages, alternately vied and cooperated with each other, rising and falling in relative prominence. Tikal, at its height the largest Classic Maya city, is also one of the most thoroughly studied. The res-

idential center covers more than fourteen square miles and has more than 3,000 structures. The city follows the uneven terrain of the rain forest and is not, like Teotihuacán, laid out on a grid. Monumental causeways link the major structures of the site.

Tikal emerged as an important center in the Late Formative, benefiting from its strategic position. The city is located near a source of flint, valued as a raw material for stone tools. It is also located near swamps that, with modification, might have been agriculturally productive. And it has access to river systems that lead both to the Gulf and the Caribbean coasts, giving it control of the trade between those regions.

A single dynasty of thirty-nine rulers reigned in Tikal from the Early Classic until the eighth century. The early rulers in this Jaguar Paw line were buried in a structure known as the North Acropolis, and the inscriptions associated with their tombs provide us with details about them, including in many cases their names, the dates of their rule, and the dates of major military victories. Monuments associated with the ruler Great Jaguar Paw, for example, suggests that in 378 C.E. he conquered the city of Uaxactún and installed a relative on its throne.

Late in the fourth century links developed between Tikal and Teotihuacán. One ruler, Curl Nose, who ascended to the throne in 379, may have married into the ruling family from

⬛ **Ruins of Tikal.** The structure on the right, towering above the jungle canopy, is known as Temple I or the Temple of the Giant Jaguar. It housed the tomb of Ah Cacao, who ruled Tikal from 682 to about 723.
Robert Frerk/Odyssey Productions.

the Teotihuacán-dominated city of Kaminaljuyu in the southern highlands.

For about 100 years beginning in the mid–sixth century, Tikal and most other lowland Maya sites experienced a hiatus during which there was little new construction. The city lost much of its influence and may have suffered a serious defeat at the hands of the city of Caracol. Then in 682 the ruler Ah Cacau (r. 682–723?) ascended the throne and initiated a new period of vigor and prosperity for Tikal, again expanding its influence through conquest and strategic marriage alliances. He and his two immediate successors, Yax Kin (r. 734–?) and Chitam (r. 769–?), began an ambitious building program, creating most of Tikal's surviving monumental structures, including the dramatic, soaring temples that dominate the site. Chitam was the last ruler in the Jaguar Paw dynasty. After he died Tikal again declined and, like other sites in the southern lowlands, it never recovered.

Similar dynastic histories have been emerging from research at other Classic Maya sites. Inscriptions in the shrine above the tomb of Lord Pacal (r. 615–683), the greatest ruler of the city of Palenque, located in the west of the Maya region in hills overlooking the Gulf coast plain, record the city's entire dynastic history back to mythic ancestors. Two of the rulers in this genealogy were women, one of them Pacal's mother, Lady Zac Kuk (r. 612–640), and another predecessor, Lady Kanal Ikal (r. 583–604). Palenque is also remarkable for its architectural innovations, which permitted its architects to build structures with thinner walls and larger rooms than at other Classic sites.

Between 800 and 900 c.e. Classic civilization collapsed in the southern lowlands. The ruling dynasties all came to an end, the construction of monumental architecture and sculpture with Long Count dates ceased, and the great cities were virtually abandoned. The cause of the collapse has long been a subject of intense speculation, and is still not known for sure. The factors that may have contributed to it, however, are becoming clearer. Among them are intensifying warfare, population growth, increased population concentration, and attempts to increase agricultural production that ultimately backfired. As the urban areas around the ceremonial centers grew, so did the demand for food. Ambitious building projects continued in the centers right up to the collapse, and some scholars believe that as a growing proportion of the population was employed in these projects, fewer were left to produce food. Overfarming may then have led to soil exhaustion. Some archaeologists also believe a major drought may have occurred. Clearly the Maya exceeded the capacities of their resources, but exactly why and how remain unknown.

After the abandonment of the Classic sites in the southern lowlands, the focus of Maya civilization shifted to the northern Yucatán. There the site of Chichén Itzá, located next to a sacred well, flourished from the ninth to the thirteenth centuries. Stylistic resemblances between Chichén Itzá and Tula, the capital of the Post-Classic Toltec Empire in central Mexico (see the next section) suggest ties between the two cities, but archaeologists are uncertain of their nature. Chichén Itzá had the largest ball court in the Maya area. After Chichén Itzá's fall, Mayapan became the main Maya center. By the time of the Spanish conquest it too had lost sway, and the Maya had divided into small, competing centers.

The Post-Classic Period

No new strong, centralized power arose immediately to replace Teotihuacán in the wake of its collapse in the eighth century. Warfare increased, and several smaller, militaristic states emerged, many centered around fortified hilltop cities. At the same time interregional trade and market systems became increasingly important, and secular and religious authority, closely linked during the Classic period, began to diverge.

THE TOLTECS

About 900 C.E. a people known as the Toltecs rose to prominence. Their capital, Tula, is located near the northern periphery of Mesoamerica. Like Teotihuacán, it lay close to an important source of obsidian. The Toltecs themselves were apparently descendants of one of many "barbarian" northern peoples (like the later Aztecs) who began migrating into Mesoamerica during the Late Classic.

Aztec mythology glorified the Toltecs, seeing them as the fount of civilization and attributing to them a vast and powerful empire to which the Aztecs were the legitimate heirs. Other Mesoamerican peoples at the time of the conquest also attributed legendary status to the Toltecs. The archaeological evidence for a Toltec empire, however, is ambiguous. Although a substantial city with a population of between 35,000 and

Tula Statuary. Tula, now Hidalgo, Mexico, was the capital of the Toltec civilization. These enormous statues, known as the Atlantes, stand atop the remains of the ancient Toltec pyramid raised in ancient Tula.
Sexto Sol/Getty Images, Inc.-Photodisc.

60,000 people, Tula was never as large or as organized as Teotihuacán. Toltec influence reached many regions of Mesoamerica—as already noted, there were many stylistic affinities between Tula and the Maya city of Chichén Itzá—but archaeologists are uncertain whether that influence translated into political control.

Toltec iconography, which stresses human sacrifice, death, blood, and military symbolism, supports their warlike reputation. Their deities are clearly antecedent to those worshiped by the Aztecs, including the feathered serpent Quetzalcoatl and the warlike trickster Tezcatlipoca.

Whatever the reality of Toltec power, it was short-lived. By about 1100 Tula was in decline and its influence gone.

THE AZTECS

The people commonly known as the Aztecs referred to themselves as the **Mexica**, a name that lives on as *Mexico*. At the time of the arrival of the Spanish in 1519 the Aztecs controlled a powerful empire that dominated much of Mesoamerica. Their capital city, Tenochtitlán, was the most populous yet seen in Mesoamerica. (See Document, "A Spaniard Describes the Glory of the Aztec Capital.") Built on islands and landfill in the southern part of Lake Texcoco in the Valley of Mexico, it was home to some 200,000 to 300,000 people. Its great temples and palaces gleamed in the sun. Bearing tribute to its rulers and goods to its great markets, canoes crowded the city's canals and people on foot thronged its streets and the great causeways linking it to the mainland. The city's traders brought precious goods from distant regions; vast wealth flowed in constantly from subject territories. Yet the people responsible for these accomplishments were relative newcomers, the foundation of their power being less than two hundred years old.

Because of the dramatic clash with Spanish adventurers that brought their empire to an end, we have more direct information about the Aztecs than any other preconquest Mesoamerican people. Many of the conquistadors recorded their experiences, and postconquest administrators and missionaries collected valuable information about their new subjects while at the same time seeking to extirpate their religion and culture. Although filtered through the bitterness of defeat for the Aztecs and the biases of the conquerors, these records nevertheless provide detailed information about Aztec society and Aztec history.

According to their own legends, the Aztecs were originally a nomadic people inhabiting the shores of a mythical Lake Aztlán somewhere to the northwest of the Valley of Mexico. At the urging of their patron god Huitzilopochtli, they began to migrate, arriving in the Valley of Mexico early in the thirteenth century. Scorned by the people of the cities and states already there, but prized and feared as mercenaries, they ended up in the marshy land on the shores of Lake Texcoco. They finally settled on the island that became Tenochtitlán in 1325 after seeing an eagle perched there on a prickly pear cactus, an omen Huitzilopochtli had said would identify the end of their wandering.

The Aztecs accepted a position as tributaries and mercenaries for Azcazpotzalco, then the most powerful state in the valley, but soon became trusted allies with their own tribute-paying territories. They further consolidated their position with marriage alliances to the ruling families of other cities. These alliances gave their own rulers claim to descent from the Toltecs. In 1428,

◀ **Codex Magliabecchiano.** Illustration from a colonial era manuscript volume, known as the Codex Magliabecchiano, presenting Aztec ritual sacrifice on a temple altar.
Scala/Art Resource.

Interactive map: To explore this map further, go to http://www.prenhall.com/craig3/map14.2

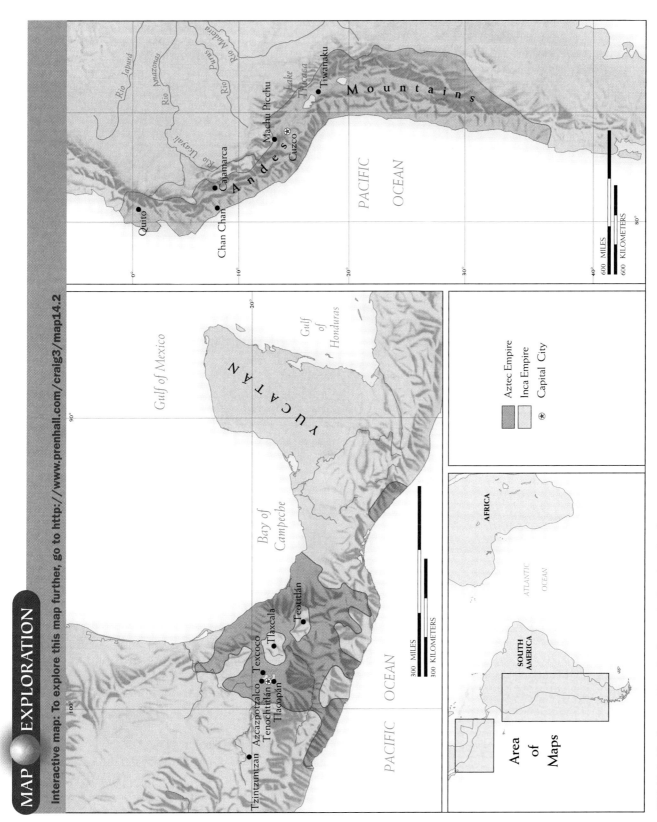

Aztec Empire
Inca Empire
⊛ Capital City

Area of Maps

MAP 14–2 The Aztec and Inca Empires on the Eve of the Spanish Conquest.

DOCUMENT | A Spaniard Describes the Glory of the Aztec Capital

On November 8, 1519, a group of approximately four hundred Spaniards under the command of Hernán Cortés entered the Aztec capital of Tenochtitlán. One of them was Bernal Díaz del Castillo (b. 1492) who later wrote The Conquest of New Spain, *a chronicle of his experience. This gives some sense of the magnificence of the Aztec capital.*

> ◆ Which elements of Aztec life especially astonished Díaz? What can one conclude about the social and political life of the Aztec elite from the manner in which Montezuma was attended? Which forms of wealth were most apparent?

Early next day we left Iztapalapa [where Cortés forces had been camped] with a large escort of these great Caciques [Aztec nobles], and followed the causeway, which is eight yards wide and goes so straight to the city of Mexico [Tenochtitlán] that I do not think it curves at all. Wide though it was, it was so crowded with people that there was hardly room for them all. Some were going to Mexico and others coming away, besides those who had come out to see us, and we could hardly get through the crowds that were there. For the towers and the cues [temples] were full, and they came in canoes from all parts of the lake. No wonder, since they had never seen horses or men like us before.

With such wonderful sights to gaze on we did not know what to say, or if this was real that we saw before our eyes. On the land side there were great cities, and on the lake many more. The lake was crowded with canoes. At intervals along the causeway there were many bridges, and before us was the great city of Mexico … .

We marched along our causeway to a point where another small causeway branches off to another city … and there, beside some towerlike buildings, which were their shrines, we were met by many more Caciques and dignitaries in very rich cloaks. The different chieftains wore different brilliant liveries, and the causeways were full of them ….

… When we came near to Mexico, at the place where there were some other small towers, the great Montezuma descended from his litter, and these other great Caciques supported him beneath a marvelously rich canopy of green feathers, decorated with gold work, silver, pearls … which hung from a sort of border. It was a marvelous sight. The great Montezuma was magnificently clad, in their fashion and wore sandals … the soles of which are of gold and the upper parts ornamented with precious stones. And the four lords who supported him were richly clad also in garments that seem to have been kept ready for them on the road so they could accompany their master … and many more lords … walked before the great Montezuma, sweeping the ground on which he was to tread, and laying down cloaks so that his feet should not touch the earth. Not one of these chieftains dared to look him in the face. All kept their eyes lowered most reverently except those four lords, his nephews, who were supporting him.

… Who could now count the multitude of men, women, and boys in the streets, on the roof-tops and in canoes on the waterways, who had come out to see us? …

They led us to our quarters, which were in some large houses capable of accommodating us all and had formerly belonged to the great Montezuma's father … . Here Montezuma now kept the great shrines of his gods, and a secret chamber containing gold bars and jewels. This was the treasure he had inherited from his father, which he never touched.

From *The Conquest of New Spain*, by Bernal Díaz, trans. by J. M. Cohen (New York: Penguin Books, 1963), copyright © J. M. Cohen, 1963, pp. 216–218.

---

under their fourth ruler, Itzcoatl (r. 1427–1440), the Aztecs formed a triple alliance with Texcoco and Tlacopan, turned against Azcazpotzalco, and became the dominant power in the Valley of Mexico. It was at this time, less than 100 years before the arrival of Cortés, that the Aztecs, as head of the Triple Alliance, began the aggressive expansion that brought them their vast tribute-paying empire (see Map 14–2).

Itzcoatl also laid the foundation of Aztec imperial ideology. He ordered the burning of all the ancient books in the valley, expunging any history that conflicted with Aztec pretensions, and restructured Aztec religion and ritual to support and justify Aztec preeminence. The Aztecs now presented themselves as the divinely ordained successors to the ancient Toltecs, and with each new conquest and the growing splendor of

Tenochtitlán, they seemed to ratify that claim. (See Document, "Nezahualcoyotl of Texcoco Sings of the Giver of Life.")

Aztec conquests ultimately included almost all of central Mexico. To the west, however, they were unable to conquer the rival Tarascan Empire with its capital of Tzintzuntzan. And within the Aztec realm several pockets, most prominently Tlaxcala, remained unsubdued but nonetheless locked into a pattern of ritual warfare with the Aztecs.

The Aztec Extractive Empire   The Aztec Empire was extractive. After a conquest, the Aztecs usually left the local elite intact and in power, imposing their rule indirectly. But they demanded heavy tribute in goods and labor. Tribute included goods of all kinds, including agricultural products, fine craft goods, gold and jade, textiles, and precious feathers. Tribute lists in Tenochtitlán, which the Spanish preserved because they, too, wished to exploit the empire they had conquered, indicate the immense quantity of goods that flowed into Tenochtitlán's coffers as a result. In a given year, for example, tribute included as much as 7,000 tons of maize and 2 million cotton cloaks. One nearby province alone was responsible for "12,800 cloaks …, 1600 loin cloths, 1600 women's tunics, 8 warriors' costumes …, 32,000 bundles of paper, 8000 bowls, and 4 bins of maize and beans."[2] It was this wealth that underwrote the grandeur of Tenochtitlán, making it, as one commentator has described it, "a beautiful parasite, feeding on the lives and labour of other peoples and casting its shadow over all their arrangements."[3]

Aztec Religion and Human Sacrifice   Aztec imperial exploitation did not end with food, cotton, and valued craft goods. Human sacrifice on a prodigious scale was central to Aztec ideology. The Aztecs believed that Huitzilopochtli, as sun god, required human blood to sustain him as he battled the moon and stars each night to rise again each day, and that it was their responsibility to provide the victims. The prime candidates for sacrifice were war captives, and the Aztecs often engaged in "flowery wars" with traditional enemies like Tlaxcala just to obtain captives. On major festivals, thousands of victims might perish. Led up the steps of the temple of Huitzilopochtli, a victim was thrown backward over a stone, his arms and legs pinned, while a priest cut out his heart. He would then be rolled down the steps of the temple, his head placed on a skull rack, and his limbs butchered and distributed to be eaten. Small children were sacrificed to the rain god Tlaloc, who, it was believed, was pleased by their tears.

Victims were also selected as god impersonators, stand-ins for particular gods who were sacrificed after a series of rituals. The rituals involved in the festivals honoring the powerful god Tezcatlipoca were particularly elaborate. A beautiful male youth was chosen to represent the god for an entire year, during which he was treated with reverence. He wandered through the city dressed as the god and playing the flute. A month before the end of his reign he was given four young women as wives. Twenty days before his death he was dressed as a warrior and for a few days he was virtually ruler of the city. Then he and his guardians left the city for an island in the lake. As he ascended the steps of the temple, there to be sacrificed, the new Tezcatlipoca began playing his flutes in Tenochtitlán.

As we have seen, human sacrifice had long been characteristic of Mesoamerican societies, but no other Mesoamerican people practiced it on the scale of the Aztecs. Whatever other reasons for it there might have been, one effect must certainly have been to intimidate subject peoples. It may also have had the effect of reducing the population of fighting-age men from conquered provinces, and with it the possibility of rebellion. Together with the heavy burden of tribute, human sacrifice may also have fed resentment and fear, explaining why so many subject peoples were willing to throw in their lot with Cortés when he challenged the Aztecs.

Tenochititlán   Three great causeways linked Tenochtitlán to the mainland. These met at the ceremonial core of the city, dominated by a double temple dedicated to Huitzilopochtli and the rain god Tlaloc. It was here that most of the Aztec's sacrificial victims met their fate. The palaces of the ruler and high nobles lay just outside the central precinct. The ruler's palace was the empire's administrative center, with government officials, artisans and laborers, gardens, and a zoo of exotic animals. The rest of the city was divided into four quarters, and these further divided into numerous wards (*calpulli*). Some *calpulli* were specialized, reserved for merchants (*pochteca*) or artisans. The city was laid out on a grid formed of streets and canals. Agricultural plots of great fertility known as *chinampas* bordered the canal and the lake shores. Aqueducts carried fresh water from springs on the lake shore into the city. A massive dike kept the briny water of the northern part of Lake Texcoco from contaminating the waters around Tenochtitlán. The neighboring city of Tlatelolco was noted for its great marketplace.

Society   Aztec society was hierarchical, authoritarian, and militaristic. It was divided into two broad classes, noble and commoner, with merchants and certain artisans forming an intermediate category. The nobility enjoyed great wealth and luxury. Laws and regulations relating to dress reinforced social divisions. Elaborate and brilliantly colored regalia distinguished nobles from commoners and rank within the nobility. Commoners were required to wear rough, simple garments.

The Aztecs were morally austere. They valued obedience, respectfulness, discipline, and moderation. Laws were strict and punishment severe. Standards for the nobility were higher than for commoners, and punishments for sexual and social offenses were more strictly enforced the higher one stood in the hierarchy. Drunkenness was frowned upon and harshly punished among the elite. Parents would even execute their own children for breaking moral laws and customs.

The highest rank in the nobility was that of *tlatoani* (plural *tlatoque*), or ruler of a major political unit. Of these, the highest were the rulers of the three cities of the Triple Alliance; of them, the highest was the *tlatoani* of Tenochtitlán. Below them were the *tetcutin*, lords of subordinate units. And below them were the *pipiltin*, who filled the bureaucracy and the priesthood.

[2] Frances F. Berdan. *The Aztecs of Central Mexico: An Imperial Society* (New York: Holt, Rinehart and Winston, 1982), p. 36.

[3] Inga Clendinnen, *Aztecs: An Interpretation* (Cambridge: Cambridge University Press, 1991). p. 8.

DOCUMENT | Nezahualcoyotl of Texcoco Sings of the Giver of Life

Nezahualcoyotl, ruler of Texcoco, lived from 1402 to 1472 and was admired as a philosopher-king. In this poem he sings of the presence of the Giver of Life who invents himself and of the ability of human beings to invoke this divinity, but at the same time he emphasizes the impossibility of achieving any close relationship with the divinity.

♦ In what ways does this song remind you of the thought and religious traditions of the early civilizations of China, India, Egypt, and Greece? What are the characteristics of "He Who invents Himself"? What kind of relationship can human beings achieve with this being? Why does the singer compare seeking the Giver of Life with seeking someone among flowers?

In no place can be the house of He Who invents
   Himself.
But in all places He is invoked,
in all places He is venerated,
His glory, His fame are sought on the earth.
It is He Who invents everything
He is Who invents Himself: God.
In all places He is invoked,
in all places He is venerated,
His glory, His fame are sought on the earth.
No one here is able,
no one is able to be intimate

with the Giver of Life;
only He is invoked, at His side,
near to Him,
one can live on the earth.
He who finds Him,
knows only one thing; He is invoked,
at His side, near to Him,
one can live on the earth.
In truth no one is intimate with You,
O Giver of Life!
Only as among the flowers,
we might seek someone,
thus we seek You,
we who live on the earth,
while we are at Your side.
Our hearts will be troubled,
only for a short time,
we will be near You and at Your side.
The Giver of Life enrages us,
He intoxicates us here.
No one can be perhaps at His side,
be famous, rule on the earth.
Only You change things
as our hearts know it:
No one can be perhaps at His side,
be famous, rule on the earth.

Excerpt (pp. 86–88) from *Fifteen Poets of the Aztec World* by Miguel León-Portilla. Copyright © 1992 by Miguel León-Portilla. Reprinted by permission of University of Oklahoma Press.

The bulk of the population were commoners. It was they who farmed the *chinampas*, harvested fish from the lake, and provided labor for public projects. All commoners belonged to a *calpulli*, each of which had its own temple. Children received training in ritual and ideology in the song houses attached to these temples. Young men received military training in the *telpochcalli*, or young men's house. *Calpulli* officials were responsible for assuring that the *calpulli* fulfilled its tribute obligations. Commoners unable to pay debts or their required tribute might become slaves. They might also become slaves for some criminal offenses. A class of serfs worked the estates of noblemen.

Professional traders and merchants—*pochteca*—were important figures in Aztec society. Their activities, backed by the threat of force from Aztec armies, were a key factor in spreading Aztec influence. Their far-reaching expeditions brought back precious luxury goods for the lords of Tenochtitlán. They organized their own guilds and established their own laws and customs for doing business. Their wealth put them in an ambiguous position in Aztec society. As a result,

they tended to be self-effacing and avoided ostentatious display. Artisans of luxury goods—including lapidaries, feather workers, and goldsmiths—also had their own *calpulli* and enjoyed a special status.

Markets were central to Aztec economic life. The great market at Tlatelolco impressed the Spaniards for its great size, orderliness, and the variety of goods traded there. More than 60,000 people went there daily. Market administrators, women as well as men, regulated transactions. Cacao beans and cotton cloaks served as mediums of exchange.

Above all else, Aztec society was organized for war. Although there was no standing army as such, the entire society stood on a war footing. All young men received military training, nobles in special schools reserved for them, commoners in their *calpulli* schools. Battles were fought to capture new territory, punish rebellious or recalcitrant tributaries, protect trading expeditions, and secure access to important natural resources. Some battles—the flowery wars—were fought just to secure sacrificial victims. Combat was a matter of individual contests, not the confrontation of massed infantry. A warrior's goal was to

CHRONOLOGY

Periods of Andean Civilization

ca. 3000–ca. 2000 B.C.E.	Preceramic
ca. 2000–ca. 800 B.C.E.	Initial
ca. 800–ca. 200 B.C.E.	Early Horizon
ca. 200 B.C.E.–ca. 600 C.E.	Early Intermediate
ca. 600 C.E.–ca. 800/1000 C.E.	Middle Horizon
ca. 800/1000–ca. 1475	Late Intermediate
ca. 1475–1532	Late Horizon (Inca Empire)

subdue and capture prisoners for sacrifice. Prowess in battle, as measured by the number of prisoners a warrior captured, was key to social advancement and rewards for both commoners and nobles. Failure in battle brought social disgrace.

Women in Aztec society could inherit and own property. They traded in the marketplace and served as market officials. With their craftwork they could provide their families with extra income. Girls and boys alike were educated in the song houses, and women had access to priestly roles, although they were barred from high religious positions. In general, however, the Aztec emphasis on warfare left women in a subordinate position, tending hearth and home and excluded from positions of high authority. As a man's primary role was to be a warrior, a woman's was to bear children, and childbirth was compared to battle. Death in childbirth, like death in battle, guaranteed rewards in the afterlife.

Andean South America

The Andean region of South America—primarily modern Peru and Bolivia—had, like Mesoamerica, a long history of indigenous civilization when Spanish conquerors arrived in the sixteenth century. This is a region of dramatic contrasts. From near the equator south, a narrow strip of desert, one of the driest in the world, lines the Pacific coast. Beyond this strip the Andes Mountains rise abruptly. Small river valleys descend the western face of the mountains, cutting the desert plain to create a series of oases from north to south. The cold waters of the Humboldt current sweep north along the coast from the Antarctic, carrying rich nutrients that support abundant sea life. Within the Andes are regions of high peaks and steep terrain, regions of grassland (*puna*), and deep, warm, fertile intermontane valleys. The eastern slopes of the mountains, covered with dense vegetation, descend into the great tropical rain forest of the Amazon basin.

From ancient times, the people of the coast lived by exploiting the marine resources of the Pacific and by cultivating maize, beans, squash, and cotton. They also engaged in long-distance trade by sea along the Pacific coast.

The people of the highlands domesticated several plants native to the Andean region, including the potato, other tubers, and a grain called quinoa. They cultivated (and still cultivate) these crops on the high slopes of the Andes. In the intermontane valleys they cultivated maize. And in the *puna* grasslands they kept herds of llamas and alpacas—the Andean camelids—using them for their fur, their meat, and as beasts of burden. Highland communities since ancient times have maintained access to the different resources available in different altitude zones, with holdings in each zone that can be far distant from each other. They share this adaptation, which anthropologists sometimes call *verticality*, with people in other mountainous regions, such as the Alps and the Himalayas.[4]

Andean civilization is conventionally divided into seven periods: The Early, Middle, and Late Horizons are periods in which a homogeneous art style spread over a wide area. The Intermediate periods are characterized by regional stylistic diversity.

The Preceramic and the Initial Period

The earliest monumental architecture in Peru dates to the early third millennium B.C.E., roughly contemporary with the Great Pyramids of Egypt. Located on the coast mostly near the shore, these earliest centers consist of ceremonial mounds and plazas and predate the introduction of pottery to Peru.

Coastal people at this time subsisted primarily on the bounties of the sea, supplementing their diets with squash, beans, and chili peppers cultivated in the floodplains of the coastal rivers. They also cultivated gourds—for use as containers and utensils—and cotton. The cotton fishing nets and other textiles of this period represent the beginning of the sophisticated Andean textile tradition.

The earliest public buildings in the highlands date to before 2500 B.C.E. These are typically stone-walled structures enclosing a sunken fire pit used to burn ritual offerings. The distribution of these structures, first identified at the site of Kotosh, suggests that highland people shared a set of religious beliefs that archaeologists have called the *Kotosh religious tradition*. Highland people were more dependent on agriculture than coastal people during the late preceramic, cultivating maize as well as potatoes and other highland tubers. Llamas and alpacas were fully domesticated by about 2500 B.C.E.

There is little evidence of social stratification for the late preceramic. The public structures of both the coast and the highlands appear to have been centers of community ritual for relatively egalitarian societies.

The introduction of pottery to Peru around 2000 B.C.E. marks the beginning of the Initial period and corresponds to a major shift in settlement and subsistence patterns on the

[4] Michael Mosley, *The Incas and Their Ancestors* (New York and London: Thames and Hudson, 1992), p. 42.

MAP 14–3 Pre-Inca Sites discussed in this chapter.

coast. People became increasingly dependent on agriculture as well as on maritime resources. They moved their settlements inland, built irrigation systems, began cultivating maize, and built large and impressive ceremonial centers. The form of these centers varied by region. On the central coast, for example, they consisted primarily of large U-shaped structures that faced inland, toward the mountains and the source of the water that nourished the coastal crops. On the north coast they consisted of large circular sunken courts and large platform structures. Centers were adorned with stone and adobe sculpture, and their façades were brightly painted. Population grew and society became gradually but increasingly stratified. Incised carvings of bodies with severed heads at Cerro Sechín and Sechín Alto in the Casma suggest growing conflict. Centers apparently remained independent of one another, however, with little evidence to suggest larger political groupings.

Chavín de Huantar and the Early Horizon

The large coastal centers of the Initial period declined early in the first millennium B.C.E. At about the same time, beginning around 800 B.C.E., a site in the highlands, Chavín de Huantar, was grow-

◀ **The Nazca Geoglyph** located in the Peruvian desert depicts a vast hummingbird. The lines were constructed by the Nazca people probably sometime between 250 C.E. and 600 C.E. They appear to have been sacred paths walked by Nazca people perhaps somewhat as a medieval Europeans walked a labyrinth. At the summer solstice the final parallel line points to the sun. The features of this and other geoglyphs can only be discerned from the air, and their exact purpose remains a matter of speculation.
Marilyn Bridges/Corbis Bettman.

ing in influence (see Map 14–3). Located on a trade route between the coast and the lowland tropical rain forest, Chavín was the center of a powerful religious cult with a population of perhaps 3,000 at its height. The architecture of its central temple complex, which includes U-shaped structures and a sunken circular courtyard, reflects coastal influence. Its artistic iconography draws on many tropical forest animals, including monkeys, serpents, and jaguars. The structure known as the Old Temple is honeycombed with passageways and drains. Archaeologists think that water could deliberately be channeled through these drains to produce a roaring sound. At the end of the central passageway is an imposing stela in the shape of a knife with the blade in the floor and the handle in the ceiling. Known as the Lanzon, this stela is carved in the image of a fanged deity that combines human and feline features. A small hole in the ceiling above the Lanzon suggests that it may have been an oracle whose "voice" was that of a priest in the gallery above.

Between about 400 and 200 B.C.E. Chavín influence spread widely throughout Peru, from the Nazca valley in the south to beyond Cajamarca in the north. This spread is seen in both the distribution of goods made at Chavín and in the incorporation of Chavín iconography into local traditions. Archaeologists believe Chavín influence reflects the prestige of its cult, not political or military expansion. The florescence of Chavín was also marked by important technological innovations in ceramics, weaving, and metallurgy.

Excavations at Chavín and other Early Horizon sites point to increasing social stratification. Examination of skeletal remains at Chavín, for example, suggests that people who lived closer to the ceremonial center ate better than people living on the margins of the site.

The Early Intermediate Period

Signs of increasing warfare accompany the collapse of the Chavín culture and the ideological unity it had brought to the Andes. The subsequent Early Intermediate period saw increasing regional diversity combined with increasing political centralization and the emergence of what were probably the first territorial states in the Andes. We will discuss briefly

Sipan Earspool. This magnificent earspool of gold, turquoise, quartz, and shell was found in the tomb of the Warrior Priest in the Moche site of Sipan, Peru, 300 C.E.
Courtesy of UCLA Fowler Museum of Cultural History/Susan Einstein/Christopher B. Donnan.

here only the two best-known cultures of this period, that of Nazca on the south coast of Peru, and of Moche on the north coast.

NAZCA

The Nazca culture, which flourished from about 100 B.C.E. to about 700 C.E., was centered in the Ica and Nazca valleys. The people of the Nazca valley built underground aqueducts to tap ground water in the middle of the valley and divert it into irrigation canals. Cahuachi, the largest Nazca site, was once thought to be a large, permanently occupied urban center. Recent research, however, indicates that it was empty most of the year, filling periodically with pilgrims during religious festivals. It may have been the capital of a Nazca confederation, with each of its many temple platforms representing a member unit.

The earlier Paracas culture on the south coast produced some of the world's finest and most intricate textiles. The Nazca too are renowned for their textiles as well as their fine polychrome pottery, elaborately decorated with images of Andean plants and animals. They may be most famous, however, for their colossal earthworks, or geoglyphs, the so-called Nazca lines. These were created by brushing away the dark gravel of the desert to reveal a lighter-colored surface. Some geoglyphs depict figures like hummingbirds, spiders, and killer whales that appear on Nazca pottery. These are usually located on hillsides visible to passers-by. Others, usually consisting of radiating lines and geometric forms, are drawn on the Nazca pampa flats and are only visible from the air.

MOCHE

The Moche culture flourished from about 200 to 700 C.E. on the north coast of Peru. At its height it dominated all the coastal river valleys from Piura in the north to Huarmey in the south, a distance of some 370 miles. The culture takes its name from the Moche valley, the location of its largest center next to

Cerro Blanco. Two huge structures, the Pyramid of the Sun and the Pyramid of the Moon, overlook this site. The cross-shaped Pyramid of the Sun, the largest adobe structure in the Americas, was some 1,200 feet long by 500 feet wide and rose in steps to a height of 60 feet. It was made with more than 143 million adobe bricks, each of which had a mark that probably identified the group that made it. Archaeologists think the marks enabled Moche lords to be sure that subject groups fulfilled their tribute obligations.

It was once thought that Cerro Blanco was the capital of a unified Moche empire. It appears now, however, that the Moche may not have been so centralized. Instead the Moche area may have been divided into northern and southern realms, and each valley ruled by Moche lords from its own center. Pampa Grande, a Moche site in the Lambayeque valley, was almost as large as Cerro Blanco.

The Moche were skilled potters, producing molded and painted vessels that reveal much about Moche life, religion, and warfare. Realistic portrait vessels may depict actual people. Other vessels provide evidence about the appearance of Moche architecture and the kind of regalia worn by the elite. The discovery in the late 1980s of the undisturbed tombs of Moche rulers at the site of Sipan in the Lambayeque valley and San José de Moro in the Jequetepeque valley suggests that a central theme in Moche iconography—the sacrifice ceremony—was an actual Moche ritual. Depictions of the sacrifice ceremony show elaborately dressed figures drinking the blood of sacrificed prisoners. Archaeologists have labeled one of the central figures the Warrior Priest and another the Priestess. The Moche lord in one of the tombs at Sipan was buried in the regalia of the Warrior Priest, and the occupant of one of the tombs at San José de Moro was buried in the regalia of the Priestess.

The Moche were also the most sophisticated smiths in the Andes. They developed innovative alloys, cast weapons and agricultural tools, and used the lost-wax process to create small, intricate works.

The Inca *Quipumayoc*. The grand treasurer, is shown holding a *quipu*, a device made of knotted strings, used to record administrative matters and sacred histories. Information was encoded in the colors of the strings and the style of the knots.
The Granger Collection.

The Middle Horizon Through the Late Intermediate Period

TIWANAKU AND HUARI

In the fifth century C.E., when the Germanic invasions were leading to the disintegration of the Roman Empire and as Teotihuacán was reaching its height in Mesoamerica, the first expansionist empires were emerging in the Andean highlands. One of these was centered at Tiwanaku in the Bolivian altiplano near the south shore of Lake Titicaca, and the other at Huari, in the south-central highlands of Peru. Although they differ in many ways, both are associated with productive new agricultural technologies, and both show evidence of a form of statecraft that reflects Andean verticality—the practice of sending out settlements to exploit the region's varied ecological zones—and that foreshadows the administrative practices of the later Inca Empire. The artistic symbolism of both also shares many features, suggesting a shared religious ideology. Archaeologists still do not have a firm grip on the chronology of Tiwanaku and Huari or the relationship between them.

Tiwanaku lies at more than 12,600 feet above sea level, making it the highest capital in the ancient world. Construction apparently began at the site about 200 C.E. It began its expansionist phase about 500–600 C.E. and collapsed some 500 years later in the eleventh century. The city occupied one to two square miles, and may have had a population of some 20,000–40,000 people at its height. Laid out on a grid, it is dominated by several large and impressive public structures and ceremonial gateways. The effort expended in transporting the stone for these monuments was enormous and indicates the power of the Tiwanaku's rulers over the labor of their subjects.

A system of raised-field agriculture on the shores of Lake Titicaca provided Tiwanaku with its economic base. This system involved farming on artificial platforms capped with rich topsoil and separated by basins of water. Experimental reconstructions have shown it to be extremely productive.

Tiwanaku dominated the Titicaca basin and neighboring regions. It probably exerted its influence through its religious prestige and by establishing colonies and religious-administrative structures in distant territories.

The Huari Empire flourished from about 600 to 800 C.E., dominating the highlands from near Cuzco in the south to Cajamarca in the north. For a brief period it also extended a fortified colony into Tiwanaku territory. The capital, Huari, covers about one and a half square miles. It consists of a sprawl of large, high-walled stone enclosures, and had a population of 20,000–30,000 people.

Huari is located in an intermontane valley and its rise is associated with the development of techniques for terracing and irrigating the slopes of the valley to increase their productivity. The spread of this beneficial technology may have facilitated the expansion of the Huari Empire, explaining its acceptance in most places without signs of overt military domination. Huari administrative centers were undefended and built in accessible places. Many archaeologists think they may have functioned like later Inca administrative centers, housing a small Huari elite that organized local labor for state projects. Again like the Inca, Huari administrators used *quipu* record-keeping devices made of string. Inca *quipu*, however, used knots, whereas Huari *quipu* used different colored string.

THE CHIMU EMPIRE

Although there is evidence of Huari influence on the Peruvian north coast, it is unlikely to have taken the form of direct political control. After the demise of Moche authority, two new states emerged on the north coast. One, named for the site of Sican, was centered in the Lambayeque valley. The central figure in Sican iconography, the Sican Lord, may have been a representation of a mythical founder figure named Nyamlap, mentioned in postconquest Spanish chronicles. Like their Moche predecessors in the Lambayeque valley, the Sican people were skilled smiths who produced sumptuous gold objects.

The other new north coast state, known as Chimu, was centered in the Moche valley. In two waves of expansion the Chimu built an empire that incorporated the Lambayeque Valley and stretched for 800 miles along the coast, from the border of Ecuador in the north to the Chillon valley in the south. The administrative capital of this empire, Chan Chan, in the Moche valley, was a vast city. Its walls enclosed eight square

miles and its central core covered over two square miles. The focus of the city are some ten immense adobe-walled enclosures known as *ciudadelas*. With their large open plazas, their administrative and storage facilities, and their large burial mounds, these probably housed the empire's ruling elite. Surrounding them were smaller compounds that probably housed the lesser nobility. And surrounding these were the homes and workshops of the artisans and workers who served the elite. Two areas were apparently transport centers, where llama caravans brought raw materials to the capital from the empire's territories. The total population of the city was between 30,000 and 40,000.

In about 1470, only sixty years before the arrival of the Spaniards, the Chimu Empire was swept away by a powerful new state from the southern highlands of Peru, the Inca Empire.

The Inca Empire

In 1532, when Francisco Pizarro and his companions happened on it, the Inca Empire was one of the largest states in the world, rivaling China and the Ottoman Empire in size. Its domains encompassed the area between the Pacific coast and the Amazon basin for some 2,600 miles, from Ecuador to northern Chile (see Map 14–2). Its ethnically and linguistically diverse population numbered in the millions.

The Inca themselves called their domain *Tawantinsuyu*, the Land of the Four Quarters. Their capital, Cuzco, lay at the intersection of these divisions. Home to the ruler (Inca) and the ruling elite, it was a city of great splendor and magnificence. Its principal temples, dedicated to the sun and moon, gleamed with gold and silver.

The origins of the Inca are obscure. According to their own traditions, Inca expansion began only in the fifteenth century in the wake of a revolt of the Chanca people that nearly destroyed Cuzco. Inca Yupanqui, son of the city's aging ruler, led a heroic resistance and crushed the revolt. Assuming the name Pachacuti, he laid the foundations of Inca statecraft; he and his successors expanded their domains to bring the blessings of civilization to the rest of the Andean world. There is clearly an element of imperial propaganda in this legend. The Inca did expand dramatically in the fifteenth century, but archaeological evidence suggests that they had been expanding their influence for decades and perhaps centuries before the Chanca revolt.

The Inca enlarged their empire through a combination of alliance and intimidation as well as conquest. They organized their realm into a hierarchical administrative structure and imposed a version of their language, **Quechua**, as the administrative language of the empire. As a result, Quechua is still widely spoken in the Peruvian Andes. (See Document, "The Incas Organize Their Empire.")

▲ **Machu Picchu.** The Inca city of Machu Picchu perches on a saddle between two peaks on the eastern slopes of the Andes.
Robert Frerk/Odyssey Productions.

Unlike the Aztecs, who extracted tribute from their subject peoples, the Inca relied on various forms of labor taxation. They divided agricultural lands into several categories, allowing local populations to retain some for their own support and reserving others for the state and the gods. In a system known as the *mita*, local people worked for the state on a regular basis, receiving in return gifts and lavish state-sponsored ritual entertainments. Men also served in the army and on public works projects, building cities and roads, for example, and terracing hillsides. In a policy that reflects the Andean practice of colonizing ecologically varied regions, the Inca also designated entire communities as *Mitimaqs*, moving them about, sometimes great distances, to best exploit the resources of their empire. They sometimes settled loyal people in hostile regions and moved hostile people to loyal regions.

The Inca employed several groups of people in what amounted to full-time state service. One of these, the *mamakuna*, consisted of women who lived privileged but celibate and carefully regulated lives in cities and towns throughout the empire. *Mamakuna* might also be given in marriage by Inca rulers to cement alliances. These so-called Virgins of the Sun played an important economic as well as religious role, weaving and brewing the maize beer known as *chicha* for the Inca elite. Textiles were highly prized in Andean society, and cloth was a form of wealth among the Incas. *Chicha* had great ritual importance and was consumed at state religious festivals. Another group of full-time state workers, the *yanakuna*, were men whose duties included tending the royal llama herds.

Cloth and clothing were not only a principal source of wealth and prestige in Inca society, they were also a means of

DOCUMENT | The Incas Organize Their Empire

The Incas were remarkable for their ability to organize a vast and diverse empire. One of their chief devices of government was the movement of large groups of people to new, unfamiliar provinces. The Incas were also very sensitive to the power of religion and religious rituals. Once they had moved a population, they required that the chief object of worship belonging to that people be moved to the Inca capital of Cuzco where it was attended by representatives of its original worshipers. This latter group was changed from time to time, allowing portions of the transferred population to become familiar with the language and customs of the court city of Cuzco. These processes of government are described in the following passage by Bernabé Cobo (1582–1657), a Jesuit, whose account is regarded as among the most complete and accurate discussions of Inca culture.

◆ To what extent did the Incas appear to be following a classic mode of rule by dividing and conquering? How did the Incas use one group to balance the threat to their rule from another group? How did they use religion and language to strengthen their authority?

The first thing that these kings did after conquering a province was to remove six or seven thousand families ... and to transfer these families to the quiet, peaceful provinces, assigning them to different towns. In their stead they introduced the same number of people, taken from the places to which the former families had been sent or from such other places as seemed convenient. ... In these transfers of population they saw to it that the migrants, both the newly conquered persons and the others, were moved to lands whose climate and conditions were the same as, or similar to, those which they had left behind them. ...

The Incas introduced these changes of domicile in order to maintain their rule with greater ease, quiet, and security. ... [T]hey ordered the majority of the *mitimaes* [the groups transferred] whom they sent to the recently conquered towns to make their homes in the provincial capitals, where they served as garrisons. ... As soldiers they received certain privileges to make them appear of nobler rank, and they were ordered always to obey the slightest commands of their captains and governors. Under this plan, if the natives revolted, the *mitimaes*, being devoted to the governors, soon reduced them to obedience to the Inca; and if the *mitimaes* rioted they were repressed and punished by the natives; thus, through this scheme of domiciling the majority of the people of some province in other parts, the king was made secure against revolts in his dominions. ... The Incas required everyone to absorb their language, laws, and religion with all the beliefs about these matters that were established at Cuzco. ... In order to introduce and establish these things more effectively, ... they would remove the principal idol from a conquered province and set it up in Cuzco with the same attendance and worship that it had formerly had; all this was seen to by persons who had come from that province. ... For this reason Indians from every province of the kingdom were at all times in residence in the capital and court, occupied in guarding and ministering to their own idols. Thus they learned the usages and customs of the court; and when they were replaced by others ... they taught their people what they had seen and learned in the court.

From *Historia del Nuevo Mundo* by Bernabé Cobe (Seville, 1890–1893), 3: 222–225; Benjamin Keen, trans., as reprinted in Benjamin Keen, ed., *Readings in Latin American Civilization 1492 to the Present* (Boston: Houghton Mifflin Company, 1955), pp. 29–30.

communication. Complex textile patterns served as insignia of social status, indicating a person's rank and ethnic affiliation. Textile production was among the forms of labor service required by the state, and Inca warehouses were filled with textiles as well as with food and other craft goods.

The Incas made their presence felt in their empire through regional administrative centers and warehouses linked by a remarkable system of roads. The centers served to organize, house, and feed people engaged in *mita* labor service and to impress upon them the power and beneficence of the state with feasting and ritual. The wealth of the empire, collected in storehouses, sustained the *mita* laborers, fed and clothed the army, and enriched the Inca elite. Although the Inca lacked writing, they kept detailed administrative records on string accounting devices called *quipu*.

To move their armies, administer their domains, and distribute the wealth of their empire efficiently, the Inca built more than 14,000 miles of road. These ranged from narrow paths to wide thoroughfares. Rope suspension bridges crossed gorges and rivers, and stairways eased the ascent of steep slopes. A system of relay runners sped messages to Cuzco from the far reaches of the empire.

Over their long history the people of the Andes developed an adaptation to their challenging environment that allowed them to prosper and grow, bringing more land under cultivation than today. Building on ancient Andean traditions, the Inca appear to have engineered a productive economy that brought its people a measure of well-being that would not survive the destruction of the empire by Spanish invaders.

Tula Statuary.

Summary

Mesoamerica Mesoamerica means "middle America." It extends from central Mexico to Central America. Although there was no single Mesoamerican civilization, the civilizations of the Olmecs, the peoples of Monte Alban and Teotihuacan, the Maya, the Toltecs, and the Aztecs shared many features: urban centers with monumental buildings arranged on large plazas, writing, a sophisticated calendrical system, religious ideas, including human sacrifice, and the cultivation of certain crops, especially maize and beans. Throughout its history, the cities of Mesoamerica were also linked by trade.

The Aztecs established the largest Mesoamerican state before the coming of the Spanish in the sixteenth century. The Aztec Empire depended on tribute from conquered peoples. Aztec society was organized for war and was divided into nobles and commoners, with merchants and certain artisans forming intermediate categories. The Aztecs practiced widescale human sacrifice. Most of the victims were captured warriors. Women could own property and participate in trade, but were subordinate to men and excluded from high authority.

Andean South America Monumental architecture and public buildings in Peru date from the third millennium B.C.E. Over the next 3,000 years, the Andean peoples developed pottery, urban centers, intricate cotton weaving, and sophisticated agriculture. The first expansionist empires emerged in the Andean highlands in the fifth century C.E.

The Incas built the most extensive Andean empire. It extended for 2,600 miles from Ecuador to Chile between the Pacific and the Amazon basin. Inca rule relied on conquest, intimidation, and alliances with other peoples. The Inca exacted taxation in terms of forced labor and constructed over 14,000 miles of roads and numerous rope bridges. Although the Inca lacked writing, they kept detailed accounts using knotted strings.

Review Questions

1. Describe the rise of civilization in Mesoamerica and Andean South America. What does it have in common with the rise of civilization in Africa and Eurasia? In what ways was it different?

2. The appearance of monumental architecture in the ancient world was often associated with hierarchical agricultural societies. Was this the case for the Peruvian coast?

3. What were some of the accomplishments of the Classic civilizations of Mesoamerica? How do they compare with contemporary civilizations elsewhere in the world?

4. How was the Aztec Empire organized? The Inca Empire? How do they compare to the early empires of the ancient world in the Near East, Europe, and Asia?

5. Both the Aztec and Inca Empires fell in the early sixteenth century when confronted with Spanish forces of a few hundred men. What factors might have contributed to their defeat?

Key Terms

calpulli (p. 389)

chicha (p. 397)

Long Count (p. 382)

Mexica (p. 386)

mita (p. 397)

Mitimaqs (p. 397)

mamakuna (p. 397)

obsidian (p. 377)

pipiltin (p. 389)

pochteca (p. 389)

quipu (p. 397)

Quechua (p. 397)

tlatoani (p. 389)

tetcutin (p. 389)

Documents CD-ROM

European Explorations and Expansion
14.6 Bernal Díaz de Castillo

NOTE: *To learn more about the topics in this chapter, see the Suggested Readings at the end of the book.*

15

Europe to the Early 1500s

Revival, Decline, and Renaissance

◄ The idealism of a devout Crusader is captured in this thirteenth-century drawing.
British Library, London. The Bridgeman Art Library Ltd..

The High Middle Ages in Western Europe

With its borders finally secured, Western Europe during the High Middle Ages was able to concentrate on its political institutions and cultural development which had been ignored during the early Middle Ages. For Western Europe, the High Middle Ages were a period of clearer self-definition during which individual lands gained much of the geographic shape we recognize today. Europe also began to escape its relative isolation from the rest of the world which had prevailed since the early Middle Ages. Two factors contributed to this increased engagement: the Crusades and renewed trade along the Silk Road linking China and Europe that the Mongol conquests in Asia made possible.

Under the Song dynasty (960–1279), before Mongol rule, China continued its technological advance. In addition to the printing press, the Chinese invented the abacus and gunpowder. They also enjoyed a money economy unknown in the West. But culturally, these centuries between 1000 and 1300 were closed and narrow by comparison with those of the Tang dynasty. Politically, the Song were far more autocratic. This was also an era of expansion for Chinese trade, and one of the few in Chinese history in which merchants as a group were able to advance in wealth and status. Although the imperial reach of the Song was limited, Chinese culture in this period was more open to outside influences than in any previous era.

In the late twelfth century Japan shifted from civilian to military rule; the Kamakura *bakufu* governed by mounted warriors who were paid with rights to income from land in exchange for their military services. This rise of a military aristocracy marked the beginning of Japan's "medieval," as distinct from its "classical," period. Three Mongol invasions in the thirteenth century also fostered a strong military to resist them. With a civilian court also in existence, Japan actually had a dual government (that is, two emperors and two courts) until the fourteenth century. However, this situation differed greatly from the deep and permanent national divisions developing at this time among the emerging states and autonomous principalities of Western Europe.

Within the many developing autonomous Islamic lands at this time, the teachings of Muhammad created an international culture. Religious identity enabled Muslims to transcend their new and often very deep regional divisions. Similarly, Christianity allowed Englishmen, Frenchmen, Germans, and Italians to think of themselves as one people and to unite in crusades to the Holy Land. As these Crusades got underway in the late eleventh century, Islam too was on the march, penetrating Anatolia and Afghanistan and impinging upon India, where it met a new challenge in Hinduism.

The legacy of the Crusades was mixed. They accomplished few of the goals that originally motivated the European Crusaders; the Holy Land remained under Islamic control, the Crusader kingdoms there collapsed within a few generations of their founding, and the animosity toward Christians fostered by the Crusades resonates even today in the Middle East. Still, the Crusades brought Europeans into more direct and frequent contact with the non-European world than they had known since the heyday of the Roman Empire. Crusaders sampled and sent home products from the Middle East, Asia, and North Africa, creating new tastes in food, art, and even fashion. The resulting growth in demand for these products impelled rising numbers of European merchants to seek these products beyond Europe. Eventually Europeans sought to bypass the Islamic world entirely and secure supplies of Eastern products, especially spices, by going directly to the sources in India and East Asia. By such development European isolation was ended.

THINK AHEAD

- How did the High Middle Ages in Europe differ from the Early Middle Ages?

- What was the legacy of the Crusades for Europe? In what ways did they signal the start of new relationships between Europe and the wider world?

THE HIGH MIDDLE AGES (FROM THE ELEVENTH through the thirteenth centuries) were a period of political expansion and consolidation and of intellectual flowering and synthesis. The Latin, or Western, church established itself as a spiritual authority independent of secular monarchies, which became more powerful and self-aggrandizing. The parliaments and popular assemblies that accompanied the rise of these monarchies laid the foundations of modern representative institutions.

The High Middle Ages saw a revolution in agriculture that increased food supplies and populations. Trade and commerce revived, towns expanded, protomodern forms of banking and credit developed, and a "new rich" merchant class became ascendant in Europe's cities. Universities sprouted. Contact with the Arab world made possible the discovery of antiquity in the writings of the ancient Greek philosophers. Those sources in turn stimulated the great expansion of Western education and culture during the late Middle Ages and the Renaissance.

The late Middle Ages and the Renaissance, roughly 1300–1500, were a time of both unprecedented calamity and bold new beginnings in Europe. France and England grappled with each other in a bitter conflict known as the Hundred Years' War (1337–1453). Bubonic plague, which contemporaries called Black Death, killed as much as one third of the population in many regions between 1348 and 1350. Thereafter a schism occurred in the church (1378–1417). If that were not calamity enough, in 1453 the Turks captured Constantinople and seemed to be taking dead aim at Western Europe.

The late Middle Ages also witnessed a rebirth that would continue into the seventeenth century. Scholars began to criticize medieval assumptions about the nature of God, humankind, and society. Italian and northern humanists made a full recovery of classical knowledge and languages and ignited new cultural fires that would burn bright throughout Europe. The "divine art" of printing was invented. The **vernacular**, the local language, took its place alongside Latin. In the independent nation-states of Europe, patriotism and incipient nationalism became major forces.

Revival of Empire, Church, and Towns

OTTO I AND THE REVIVAL OF THE EMPIRE

The fortunes of both the old empire and the papacy began to revive when the Saxon Henry I ("the Fowler"; d. 936) became the first non-Frankish king of Germany in 918. Henry rebuilt royal power and left his son and successor Otto I (r. 936–973) in a strong position. Otto maneuvered his own kin into power in Bavaria, Swabia, and Franconia and then invaded Italy and proclaimed himself its king in 951. In 955 he defeated the Hungarians at Lechfeld, securing German borders against new barbarian attacks and earning the title "the Great."

As part of a royal rebuilding program, Otto enlisted the strong hands of the church. Bishops and abbots, men who possessed a sense of universal empire, yet did not marry and found competitive dynasties, were made royal princes and agents of the king. On February 2, 962, Otto, who had long aspired to the imperial crown, gained it from Pope John XII (955–964) after having rescued the pope from his Italian enemies in the previous year. Thereafter, the church came more than ever under royal control and increasingly determined to be free of it.

▲ **Otto I and the Church.** Otto I presents the Magdeburg Cathedral to Christ, as the pope (holding the keys to the kingdom of heaven) watches, a testimony to Otto's guardianship of the Church.
"Christ Enthroned with Saints and Emperor Otto I" (r. 962-973). One from a series of 19 known as the Magdeburg Ivories. Ivory H 5" × W 4$\frac{1}{2}$" (12.7 × 11.4 cm).

THE REVIVING CATHOLIC CHURCH

With the royal focus shifted from Germany to Italy, Otto's successors, transfixed by their Italian possessions, allowed their German base to deteriorate. As the German empire began to crumble in the eleventh century, the church, long unhappy with imperial domination, declared its independence by embracing a reform movment that had erupted in a monastic order.

Cluny Reform Movement   In a great monastery at Cluny, founded in 910 in east-central France, a reform movement, aimed at freeing the church from secular political influence and control, was born. The reformers of Cluny were aided in their efforts by popular respect for the church that found expression in both religious fervor among laypersons and generous baronial patronage of religious houses. People admired clerics and monks because the church was medieval society's most open institution as far as lay participation was concerned. In the Middle Ages any man could theoretically become pope, since the pope was supposed to be elected by the people and the clergy of Rome. All people were candidates for the church's grace and salvation. The church promised a better life to come to the great mass of ordinary people, who found their present existence brutish and without hope.

The Cluny reformers condemned uncompromisingly the contemporary mixing of religious and secular institutions on the part of the state and the subservience of the clergy to royal authority. They taught that the pope in Rome alone commanded the clergy and demanded a clear demarcation between ecclesiastical and secular authority. They further denounced the transgression of ascetic piety by "secular" parish clergy, who lived openly with concubines in a relationship akin to marriage. Although in narrow religious guise, both the celibacy of the clergy and the separation of church and state found precedents in this powerful monastic reform movement. From Cluny, reformers were dispatched throughout France and Italy in the late eleventh century to save the clergy from wives and the church from the state. In both cases, the pope embraced their reforms.

◀ **Struggle Between Emperor and Pope.** A twelfth-century German manuscript portrays the struggle between Emperor Henry IV and Pope Gregory VII. In the top panel, Henry installs the puppet pope Clement III and drives Gregory from Rome. Below, Gregory dies in exile. The artist was a monk, whose sympathies were with Gregory, not Henry.

Thuringer Universities and Landesbibliothek, Jena: Bos. q. 6, Blatt 79r.

Investiture Struggle: Gregory VII and Henry IV   In 1075 Pope Gregory VII (r. 1073–1085), a fierce advocate of church reform, condemned under penalty of excommunication lay investiture of the clergy in their religious offices at any level. He had primarily in mind the emperor's well-established custom of installing favored bishops to administer his royal estates. This was done by presenting them with the ring and staff of episcopal office at the very same time they received their new secular titles and endowments. Henry IV considered Gregory's action a direct challenge to his ability to administer his realm, while Gregory believed the emperor was usurping the keys to his kingdom. Perceiving that such a measure would weaken royal power vis-à-vis their own, the German princes eagerly supported Gregory's edict.

The lines of battle were quickly drawn. Henry assembled his loyal German bishops at Worms in January 1076 and had them proclaim their independence from Gregory. Gregory promptly excommunicated Henry and absolved all Henry's subjects from loyalty to him. The German princes were delighted, and Henry now faced a general revolt. He had no choice but to come to terms with Gregory. In a famous scene, he prostrated himself outside the pope's castle retreat at Canossa in northern Italy on January 25, 1077. There he reportedly stood barefoot in the snow off and on for three days before the pope gave him absolution. Papal power had reached a pinnacle.

The Investiture Controversy was finally settled in 1122 with the Concordat of Worms. There, the new Emperor Henry V (r. 1106–1125) formally renounced his power to invest bishops with ring and staff. In exchange, the new Pope Calixtus II (r. 1119–1124) recognized the emperor's right to be present and to invest bishops with fiefs before or after their investment with ring and staff by the church. The emperor also effectively retained the right to nominate, or veto, candidates. Despite the continuing cooperation between church and state, which was desirable for both sides, distinctive spheres of ecclesiastical and secular authority had been stipulated to by both sides. In settling the Investiture Controversy in this way, pope and emperor had also set the stage for greater conflicts and division between church and state.

THE CRUSADES

If an index of popular piety and support for the pope in the High Middle Ages is needed, the **Crusades** amply provide it. What the Cluny reform was to the clergy, the Crusades to the Holy Land were to the laity: an outlet for the heightened religiosity of the late eleventh and twelfth centuries.

Late in the eleventh century, the Byzantine Empire was under severe pressure from the Seljuk Turks, and the Eastern emperor, Alexius I Comnenus, appealed for Western aid. At the Council of Clermont in 1095, Pope Urban II responded positively to that appeal, setting the First Crusade in motion. (See Document, "Pope Urban II (r. 1088–1099) Preaches the First Crusade.")

This event has puzzled some historians, because the First Crusade was a very risky venture. But the pope, the nobility, and Western society at large had much to gain by removing large numbers of nobility temporarily from Europe. Too many idle, restless noble youths spent too great a part of their lives feuding with each other and raiding other people's lands. The pope saw that peace and tranquility might more easily be gained at home by sending these factious aristocrats abroad, 100,000 of whom marched off with the First Crusade (see Map 15–1). The nobility, in turn, saw that fortunes could be made in foreign wars. That was especially true for the younger sons of noblemen, who, in an age of growing population and shrinking landed wealth, found in crusading the opportunity to become landowners. Pope Urban may well have also believed that the Crusade would reconcile and reunite Western and Eastern Christianity.

Religion was not the only motive inspiring the Crusaders; hot blood and greed were no less strong. But unlike the later Crusades, which were undertaken for mercenary reasons, the early Crusades were inspired by genuine religious piety and carefully orchestrated by a revived papacy. Popes promised the first Crusaders a plenary indulgence should they die in battle. That was a complete remission of the temporal punishment due them for unrepented mortal sins, and hence a release from suffering for them in purgatory. In addition to this spiritual reward, the prospect of Holy War against the Muslim infidel also propelled the Crusaders. The Crusade to the Holy Land was also a romantic pilgrimage. All these motives combined to make the First Crusade a Christian success.

En route the Crusaders began a general cleansing of Christendom that would intensify during the thirteenth-century papacy of Pope Innocent III. Accompanied by the new mendicant orders of Dominicans and Franciscans, Christian knights attempted to rid Europe of Jews as well as Muslims. Along the Crusaders' routes, especially in the Rhineland, Jewish communities were subjected to pogroms.

The First Victory   The Eastern emperor welcomed Western aid against advancing Islamic armies. However, the Crusaders had not assembled merely to defend Europe's outermost borders against Muslim aggression. Their goal was to rescue the holy city of Jerusalem, which had been in the hands of the Seljuk Turks since the seventh century. To this end, three great armies—tens of thousands of Crusaders—gathered in France, Germany, and Italy and taking different routes reassembled in Constantinople in 1097.

The convergence of these spirited soldiers on the Eastern capital was a cultural shock that deepened antipathy toward the West. The Eastern emperor suspected their motives, and the common people, whose villages they plundered and suppressed, did not consider them to be Christian brothers in a common cause. Nonetheless the Crusaders accomplished what

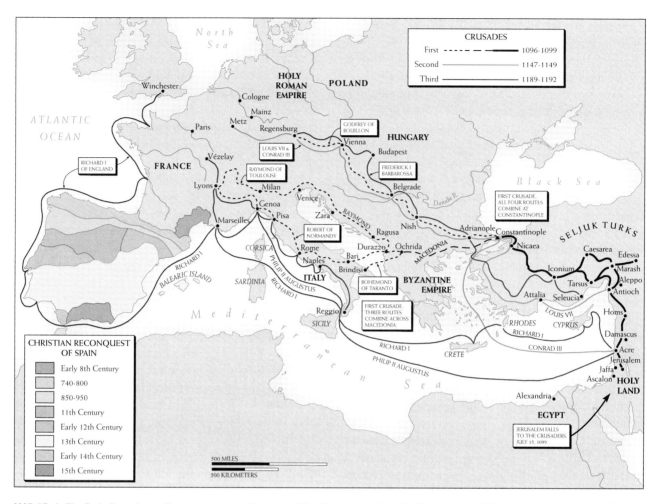

MAP 15–1 The Early Crusades.   Routes and several leaders of the Crusades during the first century of the movement are shown. The names on this map do not exhaust the list of great nobles who went on the First Crusade. The even showier array of monarchs of the Second and Third Crusades still left the Crusades, on balance, ineffective in achieving their goals.

no Byzantine army had been able to do. They soundly defeated one Seljuk army after another in a steady advance toward Jerusalem, which they captured on July 15, 1099. The Crusaders owed their victory to superior military discipline and weaponry and were also helped by the deep political divisions within the Islamic world that prevented a unified Muslim resistance.

The victorious Crusaders divided conquered territories into the feudal states of Jerusalem, Edessa, and Antioch, which were apportioned to them as fiefs from the pope. Godfrey of Bouillon, leader of the French-German army, and after him his brother Baldwin, ruled over the kingdom of Jerusalem. The Crusaders, however, remained small islands within a great sea of Muslims, who looked on the Western invaders as savages to be slain or driven out. Once settled in the Holy Land, the Crusaders found themselves increasingly on the defensive. Now an occupying rather than a conquering army, they became obsessed with fortification, building castles and forts throughout the Holy Land, the ruins of which can still be seen today.

Once secure within their new enclaves, the Crusaders ceased to live off the land as they had done since departing Europe and

Godfrey of Bouillon.
Bibliotheque Nationale, Paris, France.

increasingly relied on imports from home. As they developed the economic resources of their new possessions, the once fierce warriors were transformed into international traders and businessmen. The Knights Templar, originally a military-religious order, remade themselves into castle stewards and escorts for Western pilgrims going to and from the Holy Land. Through such endeavors, they became very rich, ending up as wealthy bankers and moneylenders.

The Second and Third Crusades   Native resistance broke the Crusaders' resolve around midcentury, and the forty-year plus Latin presence in the East began to crumble. Edessa fell to Islamic armies in 1144. A Second Crusade, preached by Christendom's most eminent religious leader, the Cistercian monk Bernard of Clairvaux (1091–1153), attempted a rescue but met with dismal failure. In October 1187, Saladin (r. 1138–1193), king of Egypt and Syria, reconquered Jerusalem. Save for a brief interlude in the thirteenth century, the holiest of cities remained thereafter in Islamic hands until the twentieth century.

A Third Crusade in the twelfth century (1189–1192) attempted yet another rescue, led by the most powerful Western rulers: Hohenstaufen emperor Frederick Barbarossa, Richard the Lion-Hearted, king of England, and Philip Augustus, king of France. It became instead a tragicomic commentary on the passing of the original crusading spirit. Frederick Barbarossa accidentally drowned while fording the Saleph River, a small stream, near the end of his journey across Asia Minor. Richard the Lion-Hearted and Philip Augustus reached the outskirts of Jerusalem, only to shatter the Crusaders' unity and chances of victory by their intense personal rivalry. Philip Augustus returned to France and

---

DOCUMENT | Pope Urban II (r. 1088–1099) Preaches the First Crusade

When Pope Urban II summoned the First Crusade in a sermon at the Council of Clermont on November 26, 1095, he painted a most savage picture of the Muslims who controlled Jerusalem. Urban also promised the Crusaders, who responded by the tens of thousands, remission of their unrepented sins and assurance of heaven. Robert the Monk is one of four witnesses who has left us a summary of the sermon.

◆ Is the pope engaging in a propaganda and smear campaign? What images of the enemy does he create and how accurate and fair are they? Did the Christian church have a greater claim to Jerusalem than the people then living there? Does a religious connection with the past entitle one group to confiscate the land of another?

From the confines of Jerusalem and the city of Constantinople a horrible tale has gone forth and very frequently has been brought to our ears, namely, that a race from the kingdom of the Persians [that is, the Seljuk Turks], an accursed race, a race utterly alienated from God, a generation forsooth which has not directed its heart and has not entrusted its spirit to God, has invaded the lands of those Christians and has depopulated them by the sword, pillage and fire; it has led away a part of the captives into its own country, and a part it has destroyed by cruel tortures; it has either entirely destroyed the churches of God or appropriated them for the rites of its own religion. They destroy the altars, after having defiled them with their uncleanness. They circumcise the Christians, and the blood of the circumcision they either spread upon the altars or pour into the vases of the baptismal font. When they wish to torture people by a base death, they perforate their navels, and dragging forth the extremity of the intestines, bind it to a stake; then with flogging they lead the victim around until the viscera having gushed forth the victim falls prostrate upon the ground. Others they bind to a post and pierce with arrows. Others they compel to extend their necks and then, attacking them with naked swords, attempt to cut through the neck with a single blow. What shall I say of the abominable rape of the women? The kingdom of the Greeks is now dismembered by them and deprived of territory so vast in extent that it can not be traversed in a march of two months. On whom therefore is the labor of avenging these wrongs and of recovering this territory incumbent, if not upon you? …

Jerusalem is the navel of the world; the land is fruitful above others, like another paradise of delights. This the Redeemer of the human race has made illustrious by His advent, has beautified by residence, has consecrated by suffering, has redeemed by death, has glorified by burial. This royal city, therefore, situated at the centre of the world, is now held captive by His enemies, and is in subjection to those who do not know God, to the worship of the heathens. She seeks therefore and desires to be liberated, and does not cease to implore you to come to her aid. From you especially she asks succor, because, as we have already said, God has conferred upon you above all nations great glory in arms.

Accordingly undertake this journey for the remission of your sins, with the assurance of the imperishable glory of the kingdom of heaven.

Translations and reprints from *Original Sources of European History*, Vol. 1 (Philadelphia: Department of History, University of Pennsylvania, 1910), pp. 5–7.

made war on Richard's continental territories. Richard, in turn, fell captive to the Emperor Henry VI while returning to England.

The English paid a handsome ransom for their adventurous king's release. Popular resentment of taxes levied for that ransom became part of the background of the revolt against the English monarchy that led to royal recognition of English freedoms in the Magna Carta of 1215.

The long-term results of the first three Crusades had little to do with their original purpose. Politically and religiously they were a failure. The Holy Land reverted as firmly as ever to Muslim hands. But the Crusades had been a safety valve for violence-prone Europeans. More importantly, they stimulated Western trade with the East, as Venetian, Pisan, and Genoan merchants followed the Crusaders across Byzantium to lucrative new markets. The need to resupply the Christian settlements in the Near East also created new trade routes and reopened old ones long closed by Islamic warships in the Mediterranean.

The Fourth Crusade   It is a commentary on both the degeneration of the original crusading ideal and the Crusaders' true historical importance that a Fourth Crusade transformed itself into a piratical commercial venture controlled by the Venetians. Launched in 1202, 30,000 crusaders arrived in Venice to set sail for Egypt. When they could not pay the price of transport, the Venetians negotiated an alternative venture: the conquest of Zara, a rival Christian port city on the Adriatic. As a shocked world watched, the Crusaders obliged the Venetians. Zara, however, proved to be only their first digression; in 1204, they besieged Constantinople itself.

This stunning event brought Venice new lands and maritime rights that assured its domination of the eastern Mediterranean. Constantinople was now the center for Western trade throughout the Near East. Although its capture embarrassed reigning Pope Innocent III, the papacy was soon sharing the spoils, gleeful at the prospect of extending Roman Christianity East. A confidant of the pope became patriarch of Constantinople and launched a mission to win the Greeks and the Slavs to the Roman Church. Western control of Constantinople continued until 1261, when Eastern emperor Michael Paleologus, helped by the Genoese, who envied their great rival's windfall in the East, finally recaptured the city. This fifty-year plus occupation of Contstantinople did nothing to heal the political and religious divisions between East and West.

TOWNS AND TOWNSPEOPLE

In the eleventh and twelfth centuries, most towns were small and held only about 5 percent of western Europe's population, but they contained the most creative segments of medieval society.

The Chartering of Towns   Towns were originally dominated by feudal lords, both lay and clerical, who granted charters to those who would agree to live and work within them. The charters guaranteed the towns' safety and gave their inhabitants an in-

CHRONOLOGY

The Crusades

1095	Pope Urban II launches the First Crusade
1099	The Crusaders take Jerusalem
1147–1149	The Second Crusade
1187	Jerusalem retaken by the Muslims
1189–1192	Third Crusade
1202–1204	Fourth Crusade

dependence unknown to peasants who worked the land. The purpose was originally to concentrate skilled laborers who could manufacture the finished goods desired by lords and bishops.

As towns grew and beckoned, many serfs took their skills to the new urban centers. There they found the freedom and profits that could lift an industrious craftsperson into higher social ranks. As this migration of serfs to the towns accelerated, the lords in the countryside offered serfs more favorable terms of tenure to keep them on the land. The growth of towns thus improved the lot of serfs generally.

The Rise of Merchants   Rural society not only gave the towns their craftspeople and day laborers, but the first merchants themselves may also have been enterprising serfs. Certainly, some of the long-distance traders were people who had nothing to lose and everything to gain from the enormous risks of foreign trade. They traveled together in armed caravans and convoys, buying goods and products as cheaply as possible at the source and selling them for all they could get in Western ports (see Map 15–2).

▲ **Foundry in Florence.** Skilled workers were an integral component of the commerce of medieval towns. This scene shows the manufacture of cannons in a foundry in Florence.

Scala/Art Resource, N.Y.

MAP **EXPLORATION**

Interactive map: To explore this map further, go to http://www.prenhall.com/craig3/map15.2

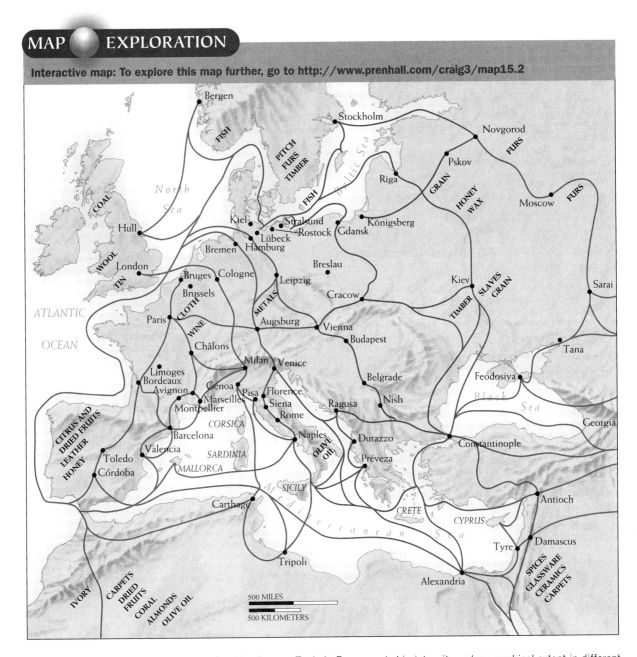

MAP 15–2 Medieval Trade Routes and Regional Products. Trade in Europe varied in intensity and geographical extent in different periods during the Middle Ages. The map shows some of the channels that came to be used in interregional commerce. Labels tell part of what was carried in that commerce.

At first the merchants were disliked because they were outside the traditional social groups of nobility, clergy, and peasantry. Over time, however, the powerful grew to respect the merchants, and the weak always tried to imitate them, because the merchants left a trail of wealth behind them wherever they went.

As the traders established themselves in towns, they grew in wealth and numbers, formed their own protective associations, and soon found themselves able to challenge traditional seigneurial authority. Merchants especially wanted to end the arbitrary tolls and tariffs regional magnates imposed over the surrounding countryside. Such regulations hampered the flow of commerce on which both merchant and craftsman in the growing urban export industries depended.

Townspeople needed simple and uniform laws and a government sympathetic to their new forms of business activity, not the fortress mentality of the lords of the countryside. The result was often a struggle with the old nobility within and outside the towns. This conflict led towns in the High and late Middle Ages to form their own independent communes and to ally themselves with kings against the nobility in the countryside, a development that would eventually rearrange the centers of power in medieval Europe and dissolve classic feudal government.

Because the merchants were the engine of the urban economy, small shopkeepers and artisans identified far more with them than with aloof lords and bishops, who had been medieval society's traditional masters. The lesser nobility (small knights) outside the towns also recognized the new mercantile economy as the wave of the future. During the eleventh and twelfth centuries, the burgher upper classes increased their economic strength and successfully challenged the old noble urban lords for control of the towns.

New Models of Government   With urban autonomy came new models of self-government. Around 1100 the old urban nobility and the new burgher upper class merged into an urban patriciate. It was a marriage between those wealthy by birth (inherited property) and those whose fortunes came from long-distance trade. From this new ruling class was born the aristocratic town council, which henceforth governed towns.

Enriching and complicating the situation, small artisans and craftspeople also slowly developed their own protective associations or **guilds** and began to gain a voice in government. The towns' opportunities for the "little person" had created the slogan "Town air brings freedom." Within town walls people thought of themselves as citizens with basic rights, not subjects at the mercy of their masters' whim.

Towns and Kings   By providing kings with the resources they needed to curb factious noblemen, towns became a major force in the transition from feudal societies to national governments. Towns were a ready source of educated bureaucrats and lawyers who knew Roman law, the tool for running the

state. Money was also to be found in the towns in great quantity, enabling kings to hire their own armies and free themselves from dependence on the nobility. In turn towns won royal political recognition and had their constitutions guaranteed. In France, towns became integrated early into royal government. In Germany, they fell under ever-tighter control by the princes. In Italy, uniquely, towns became genuine city-states during the Renaissance.

Jews in Christian Society   Towns also attracted Jews who plied trades in small businesses. Many became wealthy as moneylenders to kings, popes, and businesspeople. Jewish intellectual and religious culture both dazzled and threatened Christians. These various factors encouraged suspicion and distrust among Christians and led to an unprecedented surge in anti-Jewish sentiment in the late twelfth and early thirteenth centuries.

Schools and Universities   In the twelfth century, Byzantine and Spanish Islamic scholars made it possible for the philosophical works of Aristotle, the writings of Euclid and Ptolemy, the texts of Greek physicians and Arab mathematicians, and the corpus of Roman law to circulate among Western scholars. Islamic scholars wrote thought-provoking commentaries on Greek texts that were subsequently translated into Latin and made available to Western scholars and students. The resulting intellectual ferment gave rise to Western universities as we know them today. The first important one was established in 1158 in Bologna, which became the model for the universities of Spain, Italy, and southern France, and gained renown for the revival of Roman law. The University of Paris, became the model for northern European universities and the study of theology.

In the High Middle Ages the learning process was basic. People assumed that truth was already known and only needed to be properly organized, elucidated, and defended. Students wrote commentaries on authoritative texts, especially those of Aristotle and the church fathers. Teachers did not encourage students to strive independently for undiscovered truth beyond the received knowledge of the experts. Rather, students learned to organize and harmonize the accepted truths of tradition, which were drilled into them.

This method of study, was known as **Scholasticism**. Students summarized and compared the traditional authorities in their field, elaborated their arguments pro and con, and drew the logical conclusions. With

◀ **The University of Bologna** in central Italy was distinguished as the center for the revival of Roman law. This carving on the tomb of a Bolognese professor of law shows students attending one of his lectures.
Scala/Art Resource, N.Y.

OVERVIEW   Medieval Universities

In the twelfth century, Latin translations of ancient texts in law, astronomy, philosophy, and mathematics, and learned commentaries on them by Islamic and Byzantine scholars, reached the West. The resulting intellectual ferment gave rise to the medieval universities. The first university was established at Bologna in Italy in 1158. By 1500, there were almost fifty universities across Europe from Scotland to Poland. Universities helped bring wealth and prestige to towns; graduated professionals, such as lawyers, physicians, and theologians; and provided rulers with trained bureaucrats for their increasingly complex administrations. The following is a list of the medieval universities and the dates of their founding.

University	Country	Date of Founding	University	Country	Date of Founding
Bologna	Italy	1158	Erfurt	Germany	1379
Paris	France	ca. 1150–1160	Heidelberg	Germany	1385
Oxford	England	1167	Ferrara	Italy	1391
Vicenza	Italy	1204	Wurzburg	Germany	1402
Cambridge	England	1209	Leipzig	Germany	1409
Salamanca	Spain	1218	St. Andrews	Scotland	1411
Padua	Italy	1222	Turin	Italy	1412
Naples	Italy	1224	Louvain	Belgium	1426
Toulouse	France	1229	Poitiers	France	1431
Rome	Italy	1244	Caen	France	1437
Siena	Italy	1247	Bourdeaux	France	1441
Piacenza	Italy	1248	Barcelona	Spain	1450
Montpellier	France	1289	Trier	Germany	1450
Lisbon	Portugal	1290	Glasgow	Scotland	1451
Avignon	France	1303	Freiburg	Germany	1455
Orleans	France	1305	Ingolstadt	Germany	1459
Perugia	Italy	1308	Basel	Switzerland	1460
Coimbra	Portugal	1308	Nantes	France	1463
Grenoble	France	1339	Bourges	France	1465
Pisa	Italy	1343	Ofen	Germany	1475
Valladolid	Spain	1346	Tubingen	Germany	1477
Prague	Bohemia	1348	Uppsala	Sweden	1477
Pavia	Italy	1361	Copenhagen	Denmark	1479
Vienna	Austria	1364	Aberdeen	Scotland	1494
Cracow	Poland	1364			

the arrival of Aristotle's works in the West, logic and dialectic became the new tools for disciplining thought and knowledge. Dialectic was the art of discovering a truth by pondering the arguments against it. Together with aspiring philosophers, theologians, and lawyers, even medical students learned their vocation by debating the authoritative texts in their field, not by clinical medical practice.

Abelard   No one promoted the new Aristotelian learning more boldly and controversially than Peter Abelard (1079–1142), the leading philosopher and theologian of his time and the first European scholar to gain a large student audience. He ended up, however, not as an academic superstar, but as an obscure abbot of a monastery in Brittany. That was because his bold subjection of church teaching to Aristotelian logic and critical reasoning made him many powerful enemies at a time when there was no tenure to protect genius and free speech in schools and universities. Accused of multiple transgressions of church doctrine, he wrote an autobiography recounting the "calamities" that befell him over a lifetime. His critics especially condemned his subjective interpretations. He likened the trinitarian bonds among God the Father, the Son, and the Holy Spirit to those created among people by sworn documents and covenants. Rather than a God-begotten cosmic ransom of humankind from the Devil, Christ's crucifixion was said to redeem Christians by virtue of its impact on their hearts and minds when they heard and pondered the story. Abelard's ethical teaching stressed intent: The motives of the doer made an act good or evil, not the deed itself. Inner feelings were also said to be more important for receiving divine forgiveness than the sacrament of penance performed by the priest.

Between his native genius and youthful disrespect for seniority and tradition, Abelard gained powerful enemies in high places. He gave those enemies the opportunity to strike him down when, in Paris, where he was Master of Students at Notre Dame, he seduced the bright, seventeen-year-old niece of a powerful canon (her name was Heloise), who hired Abelard to be her tutor in his home. The passionate affair ended in public scandal, with Heloise pregnant. Unable to marry her officially (university teachers had to be single and celibate), they wed secretly. Intent on punishing Abelard and ending his career, the enraged uncle not only exposed their affair and secret marriage but also hired men to castrate Abelard.

Thereafter both entered cloisters in nearby Paris: Heloise at Argenteuil, Abelard at St. Denis. She continued to love Abelard and relive their passion in her mind, while Abelard became a self-condemning monk's monk, who assured Heloise in his letters that his "love" for her had only been wretched desire. The famous philosopher ended his life as a platitudinous monk. In 1121, a church synod ordered his writings burned. Another synod in 1140 condemned nineteen propositions from his works as heresy. Retracting his teaching, Abelard lived out the remaining two years of his life in the monastery of St. Denis. Heloise lived another twenty years and gained renown for her positive efforts to reform the rules for the cloistered life of women, under which she had suffered so much. Their story is a revelation of contemporary academic and religious life, the relationship of men and women, and the power of a reform-minded and controlling church.

Society

THE ORDER OF LIFE

In the art and literature of the Middle Ages, three basic social groups were represented: those who fought as mounted knights (the landed nobility), those who prayed (the clergy), and those who labored in fields and shops (the peasantry and village artisans). After the revival of towns in the eleventh century, a fourth social group emerged: the long-distance traders and merchants.

Nobles By the late Middle Ages, a distinguishable higher and lower nobility had evolved, living in both town and country. The higher were the great landowners and territorial magnates, long the dominant powers in their regions; the lower were petty landlords, the descendants of minor knights, newly rich merchants, or wealthy farmers.

Arms were the nobleman's profession, waging war his sole occupation. The nobility accordingly celebrated physical strength, courage, and the constant activity of warfare. Warring brought new riches and a chance to gain honor and glory, whereas peace meant boredom and economic stagnation. In the eighth century the adoption of stirrups by mounted knights gave armies the edge.

◀ **Dominicans (left) and Franciscans (right).** Unlike the other religious orders, the Dominicans and Franciscans did not live in cloisters but wandered about preaching and combating heresy. They depended for support on their own labor and the kindness of the laity.
Cliche Bibliothèque Nationale de France, Paris.

No medieval social group was absolutely uniform. Noblemen formed a broad spectrum—from minor vassals without subordinate vassals to mighty barons, the principal vassals of a king or prince, who had many vassals of their own. Dignity and status within the nobility were directly related to the exercise of authority over others; a chief with many vassals far excelled the small country nobleman who was lord over none but himself.

By the late Middle Ages, several factors forced the landed nobility into a steep economic and political decline from which it never recovered. Climatic changes and agricultural failures created large famines, while the great plague (see below) brought about unprecedented population losses. Changing military tactics occasioned by the use of infantry and heavy artillery during the Hundred Years' War made the noble cavalry nearly obsolete. And the alliance of wealthy towns with the king weakened the nobility within their own domains. After the fourteenth century, land and wealth counted for far more than lineage as qualification for entrance into the highest social class.

Clergy   Unlike the nobility and the peasantry, the clergy was an open estate: One was a cleric by religious training and ordination, not because of birth or military prowess.

There were two basic types of clerical vocation: regular and secular. The **regular clergy** comprised the orders of monks who lived according to a special ascetic rule (*regula*) in cloisters separated from the world. In the thirteenth century, two new orders—the Franciscans and the Dominicans—gained the sanction of the church. Their members went out into the world to preach the church's mission and to combat heresy.

The **secular clergy**, those who lived and worked directly among the laity in the world (*saeculum*), formed a vast hierarchy. At the top were the wealthy cardinals, archbishops, and bishops who were drawn almost exclusively from the nobility. Below them were the urban priests, the cathedral canons, and the court clerks. Finally, there was the great mass of poor parish priests, who were neither financially nor intellectually much above the common people they served.

During most of the Middle Ages, the clergy were the first estate, and theology was the queen of the sciences. How did the clergy attain such prominence? A lot of it was self-proclaimed. However, there were also popular respect and reverence for the clergy's role as mediator between God and humanity. The priest brought the Son of God down to earth when he celebrated the sacrament of the Eucharist; his absolution released penitents from punishment for sin. It was declared improper for mere laypeople to sit in judgment on such a priest.

Peasants   The largest and lowest social group in medieval society was one on whose labor the welfare of all others depended: the agrarian peasantry. Many peasants lived and worked on the manors of the nobility, the vital cells of rural social life. The lord of the manor required a certain amount of produce (grain, eggs, and the like) and services from the peasant families and held both judicial and police powers. He owned and operated the machines that processed crops into food and drink. The lord also had the right to subject his tenants to exactions known as *banalities*. He could, for example, force them to breed their cows with his bull, and to pay for the privilege; to grind their bread grains in his mill; to bake their bread in his oven; to make their wine in his wine press; to buy their beer from his brewery; and even to surrender to him the choice parts of all animals slaughtered on his lands. The lord also collected as an inheritance tax a serf's best animal. Without the lord's permission, a serf could neither travel nor marry outside the manor in which he served.

However, the serfs' status was not chattel slavery. It was to a lord's advantage to keep his serfs healthy and happy; his welfare, like theirs, depended on a successful harvest. Serfs had their own dwellings and modest strips of land, and they lived off the produce of their own labor and organization. They could also market for their own profit any surpluses that remained after the harvest. And serfs could pass their property (their dwellings and field strips) on to their children, along with their worldly goods.

Two basic changes occurred in the evolution of the manor from the early to the later Middle Ages. The first was the increasing importance of the single-family holding. As family farms replaced manorial units, land and property remained in the possession of a single family from generation to generation. Second was the conversion of the serf's dues into money payments, a change made possible by the revival of trade and the rise of the towns. This development, completed by the thirteenth century, permitted serfs to hold their land as rent-paying tenants and to overcome their servile status.

By the mid–fourteenth century, a declining nobility in England and France, faced with the ravages of the great plague and the Hundred Years' War, tried to turn back the historical clock by increasing taxes on the peasantry and restricting their migration to the cities. The response was armed revolt. The revolts of the agrarian peasantry, like those of the urban proletariat, were brutally crushed. They stand out at the end of the Middle Ages as violent testimony to the breakup of medieval society. As growing national sentiment would break its political unity and heretical movements end its nominal religious unity, the peasantry's revolts revealed the absence of medieval social unity.

MEDIEVAL WOMEN

The image and the reality of medieval women are two very different things. The image was strongly influenced by the views of male Christian clergy, whose ideal was the celibate life of chastity, poverty, and obedience. Drawing on both the Bible and classical medical, philosophical, and legal writings predating Christianity, Christian theologians depicted women as physically, mentally,

Virgin and Child, surrounded by angels, by Giovanni Cimabue (1240-1302).
SuperStock, Inc.

and morally weaker than men. On the basis of such assumptions, Christian clergy considered marriage a debased state by comparison with the religious life, and in their writings praised virgins and celibate widows over wives. In marriage, a woman's role was to be obedient to her husband, who, as the stronger, had a duty to protect and discipline her.

This image suggests that medieval women had two basic options in life: to become either a subjugated housewife or a confined nun. In reality, the vast majority of medieval women were neither.

Image and Status   Both within and outside the Church, this image of women is contradicted. Together with the cult of the Virgin Mary, the chivalric romances and courtly love literature of the twelfth and thirteenth centuries put women on pedestals and treated them as superior to men in purity. If the church harbored misogynist sentiments, it also condemned them, as in the case of the thirteenth-century *Romance of the Rose* and other popular bawdy literature.

The learned churchman Peter Lombard (1100–1169) asked why God created Eve from Adam's rib rather than taking her from his head or one of his feet? His answer: God took Eve

from Adam's side because woman was created neither to rule over man nor to be enslaved by him but rather to stand squarely at his side, as a companion and partner in mutual aid and trust. By such insistence on the spiritual equality of men and women and their shared responsibility to one another, the church also helped raise the dignity of women.

Germanic law treated women better than Roman law had done, recognizing basic rights that forbade their treatment as chattel. Unlike Roman women, who as teens married much older men, German women married husbands of similar age. Another practice unknown to the Romans was the groom's conveyance of a portion, or dowry (*dos*), to his bride which became her own in the event of his death. All major Germanic law codes recognized the economic freedom of women: their right to inherit, administer, dispose of, and confer property and wealth on their children. They could also press charges in court against men for bodily injury and rape, the latter receiving punishments ranging from fines, flogging, and banishment to blinding, castration, and death.

Life Choices   The nunnery was an option for single women from the higher social classes. Entrance required a dowry and could be almost as expensive as a wedding, although usually cheaper. Within the nunnery, a woman could rise to leadership as an abbess or a mother superior, exercising a degree of authority denied her in much of secular life. However, the nunneries of the established religious orders remained under male supervision, so that even abbesses had to answer to higher male authority.

In the ninth century, under the influence of Christianity, the Carolingians made monogamy official policy. Heretofore they had practiced polygamy and concubinage and permitted divorce. The result was both a boon and a burden to women. On one hand,

Medieval Marketplace. A fifteenth-century rendering of an 11th- or 12th-century marketplace. Medieval women were active in all trades, but especially in the food and clothing industries.
Scala/Art Resource, N.Y.

wives gained a greater dignity and legal security. On the other hand, a wife's labor as household manager and bearer of children greatly increased. And the Carolingian wife was now also the sole object of her husband's wrath and pleasure. Such demands clearly took their toll. The mortality rates of Frankish women increased and their longevity decreased after the ninth century.

Under such conditions, the cloister became an appealing refuge for women. However, the number of women in cloisters was never very large. In late medieval England no more than 3,500 women entered the cloister.

Working women The vast majority of medieval women were neither housewives nor nuns, but working women. The evidence suggests they were respected and loved by their husbands, perhaps because they worked shoulder by shoulder with them in running the household and often also home-based businesses. Between the ages of ten and fifteen, girls were apprenticed in a trade and learned to be skilled workers much like boys. If they married, they often continued their trade, operating their bake or dress shops next to their husbands' business, or becoming assistants and partners in the shops of their husbands. Women appeared in virtually every "blue-collar" trade, from butcher to goldsmith, but mostly worked in the food and clothing industries. Women belonged to guilds, just like men, and they became craftmasters. By the fifteenth century, townswomen increasingly had the opportunity to go to school and gain vernacular literacy.

Although women did not have as wide a range of vocations as men, their vocational destinies were just as fixed. Unlike men, however, women were excluded from the learned professions of scholarship, medicine, and law by reason of gender alone. Their freedom of movement within a profession was often more regulated than a man's and their wages for the same work were not as great. Still, women remained as prominent and as creative a part of workaday medieval society as men.

Growth of National Monarchies

ENGLAND AND FRANCE: HASTINGS (1066) TO BOUVINES (1214)

William the Conqueror The most important change in English political life was occasioned in 1066 by the death of the childless Anglo-Saxon ruler Edward the Confessor (r. 1042–1066), so named because of his reputation of piety. Edward's mother was a Norman princess, which gave Duke William of Normandy (d. 1087) a hereditary claim to the English throne. The Anglo-Saxon assembly, however, chose instead Harold Godwinsson (ca. 1022–1066). That defiant action brought the swift conquest of England by the powerful Normans. William's forces defeated Harold's army at Hastings on October 14, 1066, and William was crowned king of England in Westminster Abbey within weeks of the invasion.

Thereafter William established a strong monarchy but kept the Anglo-Saxon tax system, the practice of court writs (legal warnings) as a flexible form of central control over localities, and the Anglo-Saxon quasi-democratic tradition of frequent *parleying*—that is, the holding of conferences between the king and lesser powers who had vested interests in royal decisions. The result was a balancing of monarchical and parliamentary elements that remains true of English government today.

Popular Rebellion and Magna Carta William's grandson, Henry II (r. 1154–1189), brought to the throne greatly expanded French holdings through inheritance from his father (Maine, Touraine, and Anjou) and his marriage to Eleanor of Aquitaine (1122–1204), a union that created the so-called Angevin or English-French empire. As Henry II acquired new lands abroad, he became more autocratic at home. The result was strong political resistance from both the nobility and the clergy.

Battle of Hastings. William the Conqueror on horseback urging his troops into combat with the English at the Battle of Hastings (October 14, 1066). From the Bayeux Tapestry, about 1073–1083.
Giraudon/Art Resource, N.Y.

DOCUMENT | The English Nobility Imposes Restraints on King John

The gradual building of a sound English constitutional monarchy in the Middle Ages required the king's willingness to share power. He had to be strong but could not act as a despot or rule by fiat. The danger of despotism became acute in England under the rule of King John. In 1215 the English nobility forced him to recognize the Magna Carta, which reaffirmed traditional rights and personal liberties that are still enshrined in English law.

◆ Are the rights protected by the Magna Carta basic ones or special privileges? Do they suggest there was a sense of "fairness" in the past? Does the granting of such rights in any way weaken the king?

A free man shall not be fined for a small offense, except in proportion to the gravity of the offense; and for a great offense he shall be fined in proportion to the magnitude of the offense, saving his freehold [property]; and a merchant in the same way, saving his merchandise; and the villein [a free serf, bound only to his lord] shall be fined in the same way, saving his wainage [wagon], if he shall be at [the king's] mercy. And none of the above fines shall be imposed except by the oaths of honest men of the neighborhood. ...

No constable or other bailiff of [the king] shall take anyone's grain or other chattels without immediately paying for them in money, unless he is able to obtain a postponement at the good will of the seller.

No constable shall require any knight to give money in place of his ward of a castle [i.e., standing guard], if he is willing to furnish that ward in his own person, or through another honest man, if he himself is not able to do it for a reasonable cause; and if we shall lead or send him into the army, he shall be free from ward in proportion to the amount of time which he has been in the army through us.

No sheriff or bailiff of [the king], or any one else, shall take horses or wagons of any free man, for carrying purposes, except on the permission of that free man.

Neither we nor our bailiffs will take the wood of another man for castles, or for anything else which we are doing, except by the permission of him to whom the wood belongs. ...

No free man shall be taken, or imprisoned, or dispossessed, or outlawed, or banished, or in any way injured, nor will we go upon him, nor send upon him, except by the legal judgment of his peers, or by the law of the land.

To no one will we sell, to no one will we deny or delay, right or justice.

James Harvey Robinson, ed., *Readings in European History*, Vol. 1 (Boston: Athenaeum, 1904), pp. 236–237.

Under Henry's successors, the brothers Richard the Lion-Hearted (r. 1189–1199) and John (r. 1199–1216), burdensome taxation in support of foreign Crusades, and a failing war with France turned resistance into outright rebellion. With the full support of the clergy and the townspeople, English barons forced the king's grudging recognition of the **Magna Carta** ("Great Charter") in 1215. (See Document, "The English Nobility Imposes Restraints on King John.")

This famous cornerstone of modern English law put limits on royal power and secured the rights of the privileged to be represented at the highest levels of government in important matters like taxation. The Great Charter enabled the English to avoid both a dissolution of the monarchy by the nobility and the abridgment of the rights of the nobility by the monarchy.

Philip II Augustus Powerful feudal princes dominated France from the beginning of the Capetian dynasty (987) until the reign of Philip II Augustus (1180–1223). During this period the Capetian kings wisely concentrated their limited resources on securing the territory surrounding Paris known as the Île-de-France. By the time of Philip II, Paris had become the center of French government and culture, and the Capetian dynasty a secure hereditary monarchy. Thereafter, the kings of France were able to impose their will on the French nobles.

The Norman Conquest of England enabled the Capetian kings to establish a truly national monarchy. The Duke of Normandy, who after 1066 was master of England, was also a vassal of the French king in Paris. Capetian kings understandably watched with alarm as the power of their Norman vassal grew.

Philip Augustus faced both an internal and an international struggle, and he succeeded at both. His armies occupied all the English territories on the French coast except for Aquitaine. At Bouvines on July 27, 1214, the French won handily over the English and their German allies. The victory unified France around the monarchy and thereby laid the foundation for French ascendancy in the late Middle Ages.

FRANCE IN THE THIRTEENTH CENTURY: REIGN OF LOUIS IX

Louis IX (r. 1226–1270), the grandson of Philip Augustus, embodied the medieval view of the perfect ruler. He inherited a unified and secure kingdom.

▲ **Gothic Cathedral.** The portal of Reims Cathedral, where the kings of France were crowned. The cathedral was built in the Gothic style—emblematic of the High and late Middle Ages—that originated in France in the mid–twelfth century. The earlier Romanesque (Roman-like) style from which it evolved is characterized by fortresslike buildings with thick stone walls, rounded arches and vaults, and few windows. The Gothic style, in contrast, is characterized by soaring sturctures, their interiors flooded with colored light from vast expanses of stained glass. Distinctive features of the Gothic style include ribbed, crisscrossing vaulting; pointed rather than rounded arches; and prominent exteriror flying buttresses. The vaulting and the flying buttresses made possible the great height of Gothic buildings. By shifting structural weight from the walls, the buttresses also made possible the large, stained-glass-filled windows. The windows were used much as mosaics had been earlier, to show stories from the Bible, saints' lives, and local events.
Scala/Art Resource, N.Y.

Louis' greatest achievements lay at home. The efficient French bureaucracy became under him an instrument of order and fair play in local government. He sent forth royal commissioners to monitor the royal officials responsible for local governmental administration and ensure justice. These royal ambassadors were received as genuine tribunes of the people. Louis further abolished private wars and serfdom within his own royal domain, gave his subjects the right of

appeal from local to higher courts, and made the tax system more equitable. The French people came to associate their king with justice, and national feeling, the glue of nationhood, grew strong during his reign.

During Louis' reign, French society and culture became an example to all of Europe, a pattern that would continue into the modern period. Northern France became the showcase of monastic reform, chivalry, and Gothic art and architecture. Louis' reign also coincided with the golden age of Scholasticism, which saw the convergence of Europe's greatest thinkers on Paris, among them Saint Thomas Aquinas.

THE HOHENSTAUFEN EMPIRE (1152–1272)

While stable governments developed in both England and France during the Middle Ages, the Holy Roman Empire fragmented in disunity and blood feuding (see Map 15–3).

Frederick I Barbarossa   Frederick I Barbarossa (1152–1190), the first of the Hohenstaufens, reestablished imperial authority but also initiated a new phase in the contest between popes and emperors. Never have rulers and popes despised and persecuted one another more than they did during the Hohenstaufen dynasty. Frederick attempted to hold the empire together by stressing feudal bonds, but his reign ended with stalemate in Germany and defeat in Italy. In 1186 his son—the future Henry VI (r. 1190–1197)—married Constance, heiress to the kingdom of Sicily. That alliance became a fatal distraction for the Hohenstaufens. This union of the empire with Sicily left Rome encircled, thereby ensuring the undying hostility of a papacy already thoroughly distrustful of the emperor.

When Henry VI died in September 1197, chaos followed. Germany was thrown into anarchy and civil war. Meanwhile, Henry VI's four-year-old son, Frederick, who had a direct hereditary claim to the imperial crown, had for his own safety been made—fatefully, it would prove—a ward of Pope Innocent III (r. 1198–1215), who proclaimed and practiced as none before him the doctrine of the plenitude of papal power. Innocent had both the will and the means to challenge the Hohenstaufens.

Frederick II   Hohenstaufen support had meanwhile remained alive in Germany, where in December 1212 young Frederick, with papal support, became Emperor Frederick II. But Frederick soon disappointed papal hopes. He was Sicilian and only nine of his thirty-eight years as emperor were spent in Germany. To secure the imperial title for himself and his sons, he gave the German princes what they wanted. The German princes became undisputed lords over their territories, petty kings.

Frederick had an equally disastrous relationship with the papacy, which excommunicated him four times and led the German princes against him, launching the church into European politics on a massive scale. This transformation of the papacy into a formidable political and military power soon made the church highly vulnerable to criticism from religious reformers and royal apologists.

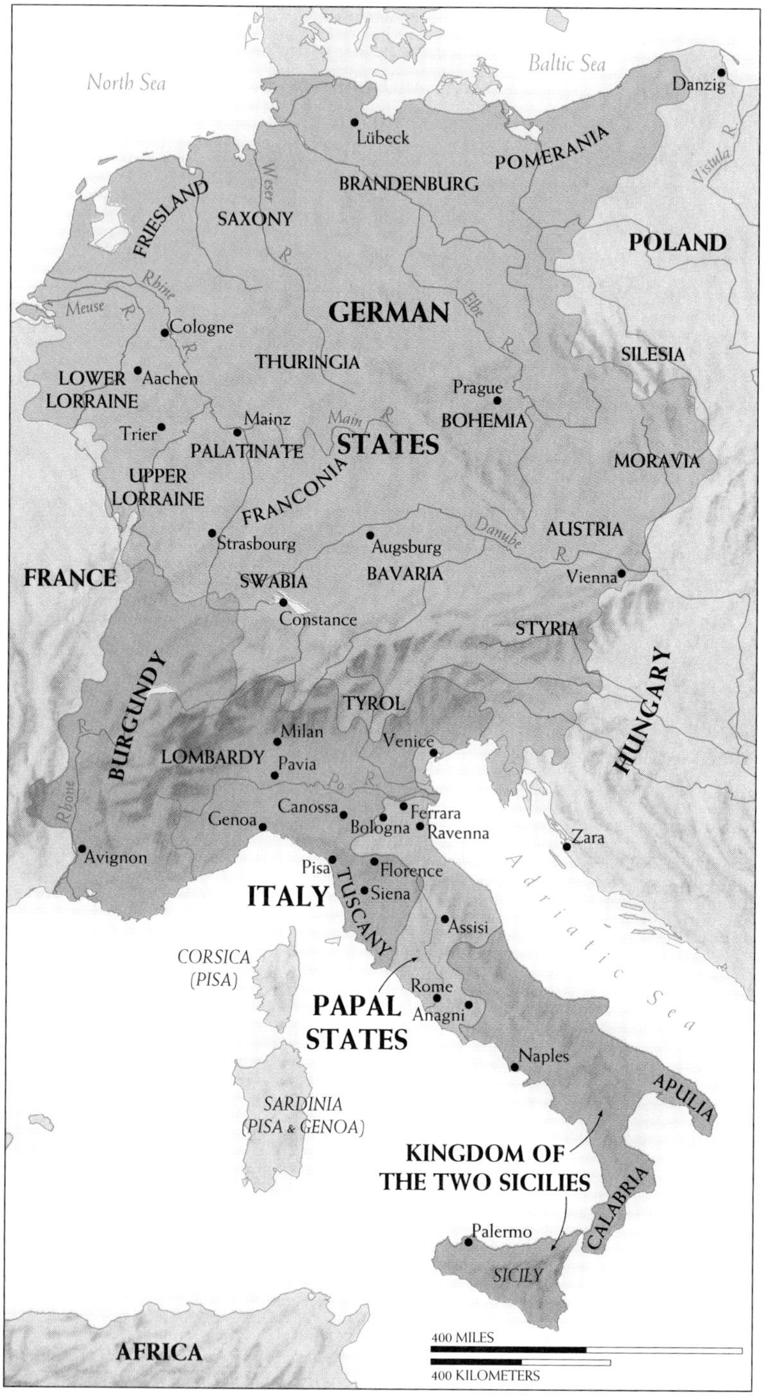

When Frederick died in 1250, the German monarchy died with him. The princes established an electoral college in 1257 to pick the emperor, and the "king of the Romans" became their puppet. Between 1250 and 1272 the Hohenstaufen dynasty slowly faded into oblivion.

Political and Social Breakdown

HUNDRED YEARS' WAR

The Causes of the War The Hundred Years' War, which began in May 1337 and lasted until October 1453, started when the English king Edward III (r. 1327–1377), the grandson of Philip the Fair of France (r. 1285–1314), claimed the French throne. But the war was more than a dynastic quarrel. England and France were territorial and economic rivals with a long history of prejudice and animosity between them. These factors made the Hundred Years' War a struggle for national identity.

Although France had three times the population of England, was far wealthier, and fought on its own soil, most of the major battles were stunning English victories. The primary reason for these French failures was internal disunity caused by endemic social conflicts. Unlike England, France was still struggling to make the transition from a fragmented feudal society to a centralized modern state.

France's defeats also resulted from incompetent leadership and English military superiority. The English infantry was more disciplined than the French, and English archers could fire six arrows a minute with enough force to pierce an inch of wood or the armor of a knight at 200 yards. Eventually, thanks in part to the inspiring leadership of Joan of Arc (1412–1431), and a sense of national identity and self-confidence, the French were able to expel the English from France. By 1453, all that remained to the English was their coastal enclave of Calais.

Charles forgot his liberator as quickly as he had embraced her. When the Burgundians captured Joan in May 1430, he could have secured her release but did not. The Burgundians and the English wanted her publicly discredited, believing this would demoralize French resistance. She was turned over to the Inquisition in English-held Rouen, where, after ten weeks of interrogation, she was executed on May 30, 1431.

The Hundred Years' War had lasting political and social consequences. It devastated France, but it also awakened French nationalism and hastened the country's transition from a feudal monarchy to a centralized state. In both France and England the burden of the war fell most heavily on the peasantry, who were forced to support it with taxes and services.

MAP 15–3 Germany and Italy in the Middle Ages. Medieval Germany and Italy were divided lands. The Holy Roman Empire (Germany) embraced hundreds of independent territories that the emperor ruled only in name. The papacy controlled the Rome area and tried to enforce its will in the Romagna. Under the Hohenstaufens (mid–twelfth to mid–thirteenth centuries), internal German divisions and papal conflict reached new heights; German rulers sought to extend their power to southern Italy and Sicily.

THE BLACK DEATH

Preconditions and Causes   In the fourteenth century, nine tenths of the population worked the land. The three-field system of crop production increased the amount of arable land and with it the food supply. But as that supply grew, so did the population. It is estimated that Europe's population doubled between the years 1000 and 1300 and began thereafter to outstrip food production. There were now more people than there was food to feed them or jobs to employ them, and the average European faced the probability of extreme hunger at least once during his or her expected thirty-five-year life span.

Between 1315 and 1317, crop failures produced the greatest famine of the Middle Ages. Densely populated urban areas such as the industrial towns of the Netherlands experienced great suffering. Decades of overpopulation, economic depression, famine, and bad health progressively weakened Europe's population and made it highly vulnerable to a virulent bubonic plague that struck with full force in 1348.

The **Black Death**, so called by contemporaries because of the way it discolored the body, was most likely introduced by rats from Black Sea areas, the epidemic following the trade routes from Asia into Europe. Appearing in Sicily in late 1347, it entered Europe through the port cities of Venice, Genoa, and Pisa in 1348, and from there it swept rapidly through Spain and southern France and into northern Europe. Areas that lay outside the major trade routes, like Bohemia, appear to have remained virtually unaffected. Bubonic plague made

ymago mortis

▲ **The Image of Death.**   The brevity and fragility of life were favorite themes of late medieval artists, who graphically depicted the horrors of death and death's power to sweep away all human pretensions to pomp and glory.
Corbis/Bettmann.

CHRONOLOGY

Church and Empire

910	Monastery of Cluny founded
918	Henry I becomes king of Germany
951	Otto I invades Italy
955	Otto I defeats the Hungarians at Lechfeld
962	Otto I crowned emperor by Pope John XII
1077	Gregory VII pardons Henry IV at Canossa
1122	Concordat of Worms settles the investiture controversy
1152–1190	Reign of Frederick Barbarossa
1198–1215	Reign of Innocent III
1214	Collapse of the claims of Otto IV
1220	Frederick II crowned emperor
1232	Frederick II devolves authority to the German princes
1257	The German monarchy becomes elective

numerous reappearances in succeeding decades. It is estimated that western Europe had lost as much as two fifths of its population by the early fifteenth century. (See Map 15–4.)

Popular Remedies   Transmitted by rat- or human-borne fleas, the plague often reached a victim's lungs during the course of the disease. From the lungs, it was spread from person to person by the victim's sneezing and wheezing. Contemporary physicians had little understanding of these processes, so the most rudimentary prophylaxis was lacking. Throughout much of Western Europe, the plague brought with it an obsession with death and dying, engendering a deep pessimism that endured for decades.

Popular wisdom held that a corruption in the atmosphere caused the disease. Some blamed poisonous fumes released by earthquakes. Many wore aromatic amulets as a remedy. According to the contemporary observations of Boccaccio, who recorded the reactions in the *Decameron* (1353), some sought a remedy in moderation and a temperate life, others gave themselves over entirely to their passions (sexual promiscuity ran high within the stricken areas), and still others, "the most sound, perhaps, in judgment," chose flight and seclusion as the best medicine.

One extreme reaction was processions of flagellants, religious fanatics who beat themselves in ritual penance, believing such action would bring divine intervention. The terror created by the flagellants, whose dirty bodies may have transported the disease, became so socially disruptive and threatening that the church finally outlawed such processions.

In some places, Jews were cast as scapegoats. Centuries of Christian propaganda had bred hatred toward Jews, as had their role as society's moneylenders. Pogroms occurred in several cities, sometimes incited by the flagellants.

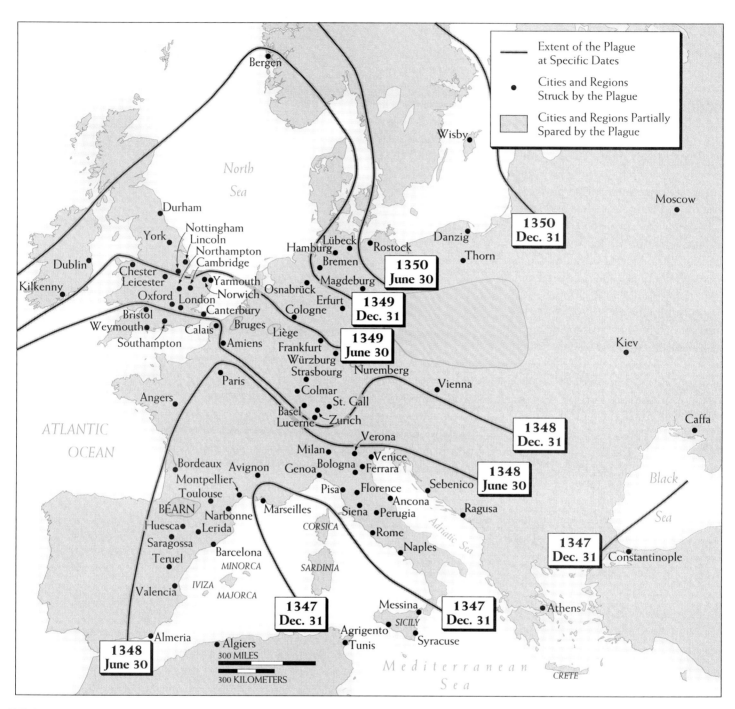

MAP 15–4 Spread of the Black Death.   Apparently introduced by sea-borne rats from areas around the Black Sea where plague-infested rodents have long been known, the Black Death had great human, social, and economic consequences. According to one of the lower estimates, it killed 25 million in Europe. The map charts the spread of the plague in the mid–14th century. Generally following trade routes, it reached Scandinavia by 1350, and some believe it then went on to Iceland and even Greenland. Areas off the main trade routes were largely spared.

Social and Economic Consequences   Whole villages vanished in the wake of the plague. Among the social and economic consequences of such high depopulation were a shrunken labor supply and a decline in the value of the estates of the nobility. As the number of farm laborers decreased, wages increased and those of skilled artisans soared. Many serfs chose to commute their labor services by money payments and pursue more interesting and rewarding jobs in skilled craft industries in the cities. Agricultural prices fell because of lowered demand, and the price of luxury and manufactured goods—the work of skilled artisans—rose. The noble landholders suffered the greatest decline in power. They were forced to pay more for finished products and for farm labor, while receiving a smaller return on their agricultural produce. Everywhere rents declined after the plague.

Peasants Revolt   To recoup their losses, some landowners converted arable land to sheep pasture, substituting more profitable wool production for labor-intensive grain crops. Others abandoned the farms leasing them to the highest bidder. Landowners also sought to reverse their misfortune by new repressive legislation that forced peasants to stay on their farms while freezing their wages at low levels. In 1351, the English Parliament passed a Statute of Laborers, which limited wages to preplague levels and restricted the ability of peasants to leave the land of their masters. Opposition to such legislation was also a prominent factor in the English peasants' revolt in 1381. In France the direct tax on the peasantry, the *taille*, was increased, and opposition to it helped ignite the French peasant uprising known as the Jacquerie.

Cities Rebound   Although the plague hit urban populations hard, the cities and their skilled industries came in time to prosper from its effects. Cities had always protected their interests, passing legislation as they grew to regulate competition from rural areas and to control immigration. After the plague, the reach of such laws extended beyond the cities to include the surrounding lands of nobles and landlords, many of whom now peacefully integrated into urban life.

The omnipresence of death also whetted the appetite for goods that only skilled industries could produce. Expensive cloths and jewelry, furs from the north, and silks from the south were in great demand in the decades after the plague. Initially this new demand could not be met. The basic unit of urban industry, the master and his apprentices (usually one or two), purposely kept its numbers low, jealously guarding its privileges. The first wave of plague turned this already restricted supply of skilled artisans into a shortage almost overnight. As a result, the prices of manufactured and luxury items rose to new heights, which in turn encouraged workers to migrate from the countryside to the city and learn the skills of artisans. Townspeople profited coming and going. As wealth poured into the cities and per capita income rose, agricultural products from the countryside, now less in demand, declined.

There was also gain and loss for the church. It suffered as a landholder and was politically weakened, yet at the same time, it received new revenues from the vastly increased demand for religious services for the dead and the dying, along with new gifts and bequests.

NEW CONFLICTS AND OPPORTUNITIES

By increasing the importance of skilled artisans, the plague contributed to new social conflicts within the cities. The economic and political power of local artisans and trade guilds grew steadily in the late Middle Ages, along with the demand for their goods and services. The merchant and patrician classes found it increasingly difficult to maintain their traditional dominance and grudgingly gave guild masters a voice in city government. As the guilds won political power, they encouraged restrictive legislation to protect local industries. The restrictions, in turn, caused conflict between master artisans, who wanted to keep their numbers low and expand their industries at a snail's pace, and the many journeymen, who were eager to rise to the rank of master. To the long-existing conflict between the guilds and the ruling urban patriciate was now added a conflict within the guilds themselves.

Also after 1350, the two traditional "containers" of monarchy—the landed nobility and the church—were put on the defensive as a consequence of the plague. Kings now exploited growing national sentiment in an effort to centralize their governments and economies. At the same time, the battles of the Hundred Years' War demonstrated the military superiority of paid professional armies over the traditional noble cavalry, thus bringing into question the latter's future role. The plague also killed many members of the clergy—perhaps one third of the German clergy fell victim as they dutifully ministered to the sick and dying. This reduction in clerical ranks occurred in the same century that saw the pope move from Rome to Avignon (1309–1377) and the Great Schism (1378–1417) divide the Church into warring factions.

Black Death. Men and women carrying plague victims in coffins to the burial ground in Tournai, Belgium, 1349.
The Granger Collection, New York.

Ecclesiastical Breakdown and Revival: The Late Medieval Church

BONIFACE VIII AND PHILIP THE FAIR

By the fourteenth century popes faced rulers far more powerful than the papacy. When Pope Boniface VIII (r. 1294–1303) issued a bull, *Clericis Laicos,* which forbade lay taxation of the clergy without prior papal approval, King Philip the Fair of France (r. 1285–1314) unleashed a ruthless antipapal campaign. Boniface made a last-ditch stand against state control of national churches on November 18, 1302, when he issued the bull *Unam Sanctam,* which declared that temporal authority was "subject" to the spiritual power of the church.

The French responded with force. Philip sent troops who beat the pope badly and might even have executed him had not an aroused populace liberated the pope and returned him safely to Rome.

There was no papal retaliation. No pope ever again so seriously threatened kings and emperors. Future relations between church and state would henceforth tilt toward state control of religion within particular monarchies.

THE GREAT SCHISM (1378–1417) AND THE CONCILIAR MOVEMENT TO 1449

After Boniface VIII's death, his successor, Clement V (r. 1305–1314), moved the papal court to Avignon on the southeastern border with France, where it remained until Pope Gregory XI (r. 1370–1378) reestablished the papacy in Rome in January 1377. His successor, Pope Urban VI (r. 1378–1389), proclaimed his intention to reform the papal government in the **Curia**. This announcement alarmed the cardinals, most of whom were French. Not wanting to surrender the benefits of a papacy under French influence, the French king, Charles V (r. 1364–1380), supported a schism in the church, known thereafter as the **Great Schism**. On September 20, 1378, thirteen cardinals, all but one of whom was French, elected a cousin of the French king as Pope Clement VII (r. 1378–1397). Clement returned to Avignon. Thereafter allegiance to the two papal courts divided along political lines: Acknowledging Urban VI were England and its allies—the **Holy Roman Empire** (based on the old Roman Empire, mostly

Papal Authority. Pope Boniface VIII (r. 1294–1303), who opposed the taxation of the clergy by the kings of France and England, issued one of the strongest declarations of papal authority, the bull *Unam Sanctam*. This statue is in the Museo Civico, Bologna, Italy.
Scala/Art Resource, N.Y.

Germany and Northern Italy), Hungary, Bohemia, and Poland. Supporting Clement VII were France and its orbit—Naples, Scotland, Castile, and Aragon. Only the Roman line of popes, however, is recognized as official by the church.

In 1409 a council at Pisa deposed both the Roman and the Avignon popes and elected its own new pope. But neither Rome nor Avignon accepted its action, so after 1409 there were three contending popes. This intolerable situation ended when the emperor Sigismund (r. 1410–1437) prevailed on the Pisan pope to summon a legal council of the church in Constance in 1414, a council also recognized by the reigning Roman pope Gregory XII (r. 1406–1415). After the three contending popes had either resigned or been deposed, the council elected a new pope, Martin V (r. 1417–1431), in November 1417, reuniting the church.

Under Pope Eugenius IV (r. 1431–1447), the papacy regained much of its prestige and authority, and in 1460 the papal bull *Execrabilis* condemned all appeals to councils as "completely null and void." But the conciliar movement had planted deep within the conscience of all Western peoples the conviction that the leader of an institution must be responsive to its members and not act against their best interests.

The Renaissance in Italy (1375–1527)

The **Renaissance** is the term used to described the fourteenth and fifteenth-century effort to revive ancient learning. Most scholars agree that it was a transition from the medieval to the modern world. Medieval Europe, especially before the twelfth century, had been a fragmented feudal society with an agricultural economy, its thought and culture dominated by the church. Renaissance Europe, especially after the fourteenth century, was characterized by growing national consciousness and political centralization, an urban economy based on organized commerce and capitalism, and ever greater lay and secular control of thought and culture.

The distinctive features and achievements of the Renaissance are most strikingly revealed in Italy from roughly 1375 to 1527, the year of the infamous sack of Rome by imperial soldiers. What was achieved in Italy during these centuries also deeply influenced northern Europe.

THE ITALIAN CITY-STATE: SOCIAL CONFLICT AND DESPOTISM

Renaissance society took distinctive shape within the cities of late medieval Italy. Italy was the natural gateway between East and West. Venice, Genoa, and Pisa traded uninterruptedly with the Near East throughout the Middle Ages and maintained vibrant urban societies. During the thirteenth and fourteenth centuries, the trade-rich Italian cities became powerful city-states, dominating the political and economic life of the surrounding countryside. By the fifteenth century, the great Italian cities had become the bankers for much of Europe. There were five such major, competitive states in Italy: the duchy of Milan, the republics of Florence and Venice, the Papal States, and the kingdom of Naples (see Map 15–5).

Social strife and competition for political power were so intense within the cities that for survival's sake, most had evolved into despotisms by the fifteenth century. Venice, ruled by a successful merchant oligarchy, was the notable exception. Elsewhere, the new social classes and divisions within society produced by rapid urban growth fueled chronic, near-anarchic conflict.

In Florence, these social divisions produced conflict at every level of society. True stability was not established until the ascent to power in 1434 of Cosimo de' Medici (1389–1464). The wealthiest Florentine and a most astute statesman, Cosimo controlled the city internally from behind the scenes, skillfully manipulating the constitution and influencing elections. His grandson Lorenzo the Magnificent (1449–1492, r. 1478–1492) ruled Florence in almost totalitarian fashion.

Despotism was less subtle elsewhere in Italy. To prevent internal social conflict and foreign intrigue from paralyzing their cities, the dominant groups in many cities cooperated in the hiring of a strongman, known as a *podesta*, to maintain law and order. Because these despots could not depend on the divided populace, they operated through mercenary armies.

Political turbulence and warfare also gave birth to diplomacy, through which the various city-states stayed abreast of foreign military developments and, if shrewd enough, gained power and advantage without actually going to war. Most city-states established resident embassies during the fifteenth century, their ambassadors watchful eyes and ears at rival courts. Renaissance culture was promoted as vigorously by despots as by republicans and by popes as enthusiastically as by humanists.

HUMANISM

Humanism was the scholarly study of the Latin and Greek classics and the ancient Church Fathers, both for their own sake and to promote a rebirth of ancient norms and values. Humanists advocated the *studia humanitatis*, a liberal arts program that embraced grammar, rhetoric, poetry, history, politics, and moral philosophy.

The first humanists were orators and poets. They wrote original literature in both the classical and the vernacular lan-

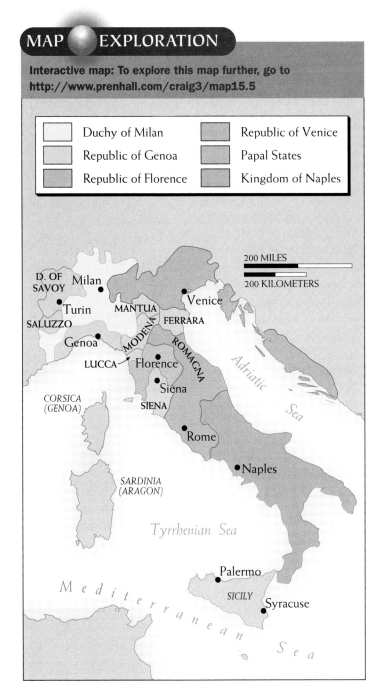

MAP EXPLORATION

Interactive map: To explore this map further, go to
http://www.prenhall.com/craig3/map15.5

☐ Duchy of Milan   ▨ Republic of Venice
☐ Republic of Genoa   ▨ Papal States
▨ Republic of Florence ▨ Kingdom of Naples

MAP 15–5 Renaissance Italy.   The city-states of Renaissance Italy were self-contained principalities whose internal strife was monitored by their despots and whose external aggression was long successfully controlled by treaty.

guages, inspired by the newly discovered works of the ancients, and they taught rhetoric within the universities. Their talents were sought as secretaries, speech writers, and diplomats in princely and papal courts.

Classical and Christian antiquity had been studied before the Italian Renaissance—during the Carolingian renaissance of the ninth century, for example. However, the Italian Renaissance of the late Middle Ages was more secular and lay dominated, had broader interests, recovered more manuscripts, and possessed far superior technical skills than earlier rebirths of antiquity.

Unlike their Scholastic rivals, humanists were not content only to summarize and compare the views of recognized authorities on a question but instead went directly to the original source and drew their own conclusions. Avidly searching out manuscript collections, Italian humanists made the full sources of Greek and Latin antiquity available to scholars during the fourteenth and fifteenth centuries. Mastery of Latin and Greek was their surgeon's tool. There is a kernel of truth—but only a kernel—in the arrogant boast of the humanists that the period between themselves and classical civilization was a "dark middle age."

Petrarch, Dante, and Boccaccio   Francesco Petrarch (1304–1374) was the father of humanism. He left the legal profession to pursue his love of letters and poetry. Petrarch celebrated ancient Rome in his writings and tirelessly collected ancient manuscripts; among his finds were letters by Cicero. His critical textual studies, elitism, and contempt for the allegedly useless learning of the Scholastics were shared by many later humanists.

Petrarch was far more secular in orientation than Dante Alighieri (1265–1321), whose *Vita Nuova* and *Divine Comedy*— together with Petrarch's sonnets—form the cornerstones of Italian vernacular literature. Also pioneering humanist studies was Petrarch's student and friend Giovanni Boccaccio (1313–1375), author of the *Decameron*, 100 bawdy tales told by three men and seven women in a country retreat from the plague that ravaged Florence in 1348. An avid collector of manuscripts, Boccaccio assembled an encyclopedia of Greek and Roman mythology.

Educational Reforms and Goals   The classical ideal of a useful education that produces well-rounded, effective people inspired far-reaching reforms in traditional education. The most influential Italian Renaissance tract on education, Pietro Paolo Vergerio's (1349–1420) *On the Morals That Befit a Free Man*, was written directly from classical models. Vittorino da Feltre (d. 1446) directed his students to a highly disciplined reading of ancient authors, together with vigorous physical exercise and games with intellectual pursuits.

Educated and cultured noblewomen also had a prominent place at Renaissance courts, among them Christine de Pisan (1363?–1434). She was an expert in classical, French, and Italian languages and literature and became a well-known woman of letters in the courts of Europe. Her most famous work, *The City of Ladies*, describes the accomplishments of the great women of history.

RENAISSANCE ART

In Renaissance Italy, as later in Reformation Europe, the values and interests of the laity were less subordinated to those of the clergy than previously. In education, culture, and religion,

Cosimo de' Medici (1389–1464). Florentine banker and statesman, in his lifetime the city's wealthiest man and most successful politician. This portrait is by Jacopo da Pontormo (1494–1556).

Jacopo Pontormo (1494–1556), "Cosimo de' Medici the Elder, Pater Patriae," (1389–1464). Oil on wood, 87 × 65 cm. Inv. 3574. Uffize, Florence. Photograph © Erich Lessing/Art Resource, N.Y.

medieval Christian values were adjusting to a more this-worldly spirit. Men and women began again to appreciate and even to glorify the secular world, secular learning, and purely human pursuits as ends in themselves.

This perspective on life is especially prominent in the painting and sculpture of the High Renaissance (late fifteenth and early sixteenth centuries), when Renaissance art reached its full maturity. In imitation of Greek and Roman art, painters and sculptors attempted to create harmonious, symmetrical, and properly proportioned figures, portraying the human form with a glorified realism. Whereas Byzantine and Gothic art had been religious and idealized in the extreme, Renaissance art, especially in the fifteenth century, realistically reproduced nature and human beings as a part of nature.

Renaissance artists took advantage of new technical skills and materials developed during the fifteenth century: the use of oil paints, using shading to enhance realism (**chiaroscuro**), and adjusting the size of figures to give the viewer a feeling of continuity with the painting (linear perspective). Compared with their flat Byzantine and Gothic counterparts, Renaissance paintings seem filled with energy and life and stand out from the canvas in three dimensions. The great masters of the High Renaissance included Leonardo da Vinci (1452–1519), Raphael (1483–1520), and Michelangelo Buonarroti (1475–1564).

Leonardo da Vinci   Leonardo personified the Renaissance ideal of the universal person, one who is not only a jack-of-all-trades, but also a master of many. (See Document, "Pico Della Mirandola States the Renaissance Image of Man.") A military engineer and advocate of scientific experimentation, he dissected corpses to learn anatomy and was a self-taught botanist. He foresaw such modern machines as airplanes and submarines. The variety of his interests tended to shorten his attention span, so that he constantly moved from one activity to another. As a painter, his great skill lay in conveying inner moods through complex facial features, such as that seen in the most famous of his paintings, the *Mona Lisa*.

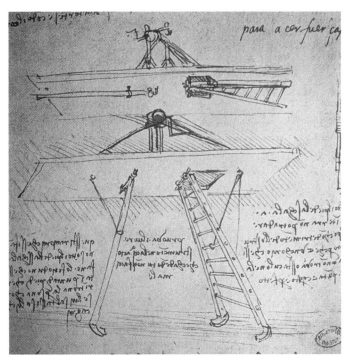

▲ **Aviation Drawings by Leonardo da Vinci (1452–1519).** He imagined a possible flying machine with a retractable ladder for boarding.
David Forbert/SuperStock, Inc.

DOCUMENT   Pico della Mirandola States the Renaissance Image of Man

One of the most eloquent Renaissance descriptions of the abilities of humankind comes from the Italian humanist Pico della Mirandola (1463–1494). In his famed Oration on the Dignity of Man *(ca. 1186), Pico described humans as free to become whatever they choose.*

◆ In what does the dignity of humankind consist? Does Pico reject the biblical description of Adam and Eve's fall? Does he exaggerate a person's ability to choose freely to be whatever he or she wishes? What inspired such seeming hubris during the Renaissance?

The best of artisans [God] ordained that that creature (man) to whom He [God] had been able to give nothing proper to himself should have joint possession of whatever had been peculiar to each of the different kinds of being. He therefore took man as a creature of indeterminate nature and, assigning him a place in the middle of the world, addressed him thus: "Neither a fixed abode nor a form that is thine alone or any function peculiar to thyself have we given thee, Adam, to the end that according to thy longing and according to thy judgment thou mayest have and possess what abode, what form, and what functions thou thyself shalt desire. The nature of all other beings is limited and constrained within the bounds of laws prescribed by Us. Thou, constrained by no limits, in accordance with thine own free will, in whose hand We have placed thee, shalt ordain for thyself the limits of thy nature. We have set thee at the world's center that thou mayest from thence more easily observe whatever is in the world. We have made thee neither of heaven nor of earth, neither mortal nor immortal, so that with freedom of choice and with honor, as though the maker and molder of thyself, thou mayest fashion thyself in whatever shape thou shalt prefer. Thou shalt have the power to degenerate into the lower forms of life, which are brutish. Thou shalt have the power, out of thy soul's judgment, to be reborn into the higher forms, which are divine." O supreme generosity of God the Father, O highest and most marvelous felicity of man! To him it is granted to have whatever he chooses, to be whatever he wills.

From Giovanni Pico della Mirandola, *Oration on the Dignity of Man*, in *The Renaissance Philosophy of Man*, ed. by E. Cassirer et al. Phoenix Books, 1961, pp. 224–225. Reprinted by permission of The University of Chicago Press.

▲ **Raphael's Portrait (ca. 1515) of Baldassare Castiglione (1478–1529)**
Now in the Louvre. Castiglione, author of the *Book of the Courtier*, was Raphael's close friend. The self-restraint and inner calm that he considered the chief qualities of the gentleman are also qualities of Raphael's art, reflected in the portrait's perfect balance and harmony. This painting greatly influenced Rembrandt, who later tried unsuccessfully to buy it.
Reunion des Musées Nationaux/Art Resource, N.Y.

Raphael Raphael, who died young (thirty-seven), is famous for his tender madonnas. Art historians also praise his fresco *The School of Athens*, which depicts Plato and Aristotle surrounded by philosophy and science, as one of the most perfect examples of Renaissance artistic theory and technique.

Michelangelo This melancholy genius also excelled in a variety of arts and crafts. His eighteen-foot godlike sculpture *David* is a perfect example of the Renaissance artist's devotion to harmony, symmetry, and proportion, as well as his extreme glorification of the human form. Four different popes commissioned works by Michelangelo, the best known of which are the frescoes for the Sistine Chapel, painted for Pope Julius II (r. 1503–1513).

His later works mark, artistically and philosophically, the passing of High Renaissance painting and the advent of a new, experimental style known as *mannerism*, which reached its peak in the late sixteenth and early seventeenth centuries. It derived its name from the fact that it permitted the artist to express his own individual perceptions and feelings to paint, compose, or write in a "mannered" or "affected" way. Tintoretto (d. 1594) and especially El Greco (d. 1614) became its supreme representatives.

ITALY'S POLITICAL DECLINE: THE FRENCH INVASIONS (1494–1527)

Autonomous city-states of Italy had always preserved their peace and safety from foreign invasion by cooperation with each other. However, in 1494 Naples, supported by Florence and the Borgia pope Alexander VI (1492–1503), prepared to attack Milan. At this point, the Milanese despot Ludovico il Moro (r. 1476–1499) invited the French to revive their dynastic claim to Naples. But France also had dynastic claims to Milan, and the French appetite for new territory became insatiable once French armies had crossed the Alps and reestablished themselves in Italy.

The French king Charles VIII (r. 1483–1498) responded rapidly to Ludovico's call. Within five months he had crossed the Alps (August 1495) and raced as conqueror through Florence and the Papal States into Naples.

Charles' lightning march through Italy alarmed Ferdinand of Aragon (r. 1479–1516), who was also king of Sicily, and helped to create a counteralliance: the League of Venice, which was able to force Charles to retreat.

The French returned to Italy under Charles's successor, Louis XII (r. 1498–1515), this time assisted by the Borgia pope Alexander VI (1492–1503). Alexander, probably the most corrupt pope in history, sought to secure a political base in Romagna, officially part of the Papal States, for his son Cesare.

Seeing that a French alliance could allow him to reestablish control over the region, Alexander agreed to abandon the League of Venice, which made the league too weak to resist a French reconquest of Milan. Louis successfully invaded Milan in August 1499. In 1500 he and Ferdinand of Aragon divided Naples between themselves, while the pope and Cesare Borgia conquered the Romagna without opposition.

In 1503 Cardinal Giuliano della Rovere became Pope Julius II (1503–1513). He suppressed the Borgias and placed their newly conquered lands in Romagna under papal jurisdiction. After fully securing the Papal States with French aid, Julius changed sides and sought to rid Italy of his former ally, the French invaders. Julius, Ferdinand of Aragon, and Venice formed a Holy League in October 1511, and soon Emperor Maximilian I (r. 1493–1519) and the Swiss joined them. By 1512 the French were in full retreat.

The French invaded Italy again under Louis's successor, Francis I (r. 1515–1547). French armies massacred Swiss soldiers of the Holy League at Marignano in September 1515. That victory won from the Medici pope Leo X (r. 1513–1521) an agreement known as the Concordat of Bologna (August 1516), which gave the French king control over the French clergy and the right to collect taxes from them, in exchange for French recognition of the pope's superiority over church councils. This helped keep France Catholic after the outbreak of the Protestant Reformation. But the new French entry into Italy also led to the first of four major wars with Spain in the first half of the sixteenth century: the Habsburg-Valois wars, none of which France won.

NICCOLÒ MACHIAVELLI

The foreign invasions made a shambles of Italy. One who watched as French, Spanish, and German armies wreaked havoc on his country was Niccolò Machiavelli (1469–1527). The more he saw, the more convinced he became that Italian political unity and independence were ends that justified any means. Machiavelli admired the heroic acts of ancient Roman rulers, what Renaissance people called their *Virtù*. Romanticizing the old Roman citizenry, he lamented the absence of heroism among his compatriots. Such a perspective caused his interpretation of both ancient and contemporary history to be exaggerated.

The juxtaposition of what Machiavelli believed the ancient Romans had been with the failure of contemporary Romans to realize such high ideals made him the famous cynic we know in the popular epithet *Machiavellian*. Only an unscrupulous strongman, he concluded, using duplicity and terror, could impose order on so divided and selfish a people. Machiavelli seems to have been in earnest when he advised rulers to discover the advantages of fraud and brutality. He apparently hoped to see a strong ruler emerge from the Medici family. The Medicis, however, were not destined to be Italy's deliverers. The second Medici pope, Clement VII (r. 1523–1534), watched helplessly as Rome was sacked by the army of Emperor Charles V (r. 1519–1556) in 1527, the year of Machiavelli's death.

Revival of Monarchy: Nation Building in the Fifteenth Century

With the emergence of sovereign rulers after 1450, unified national monarchies progressively replaced fragmented and divisive feudal governance, but the dynastic and chivalric ideals of feudalism did not disappear. Minor territorial princes survived, and representative assemblies even grew in influence in some regions. But by the late fifteenth and early sixteenth centuries, the old problem of the one and the many was being decided clearly in favor of monarchy.

In the feudal monarchy of the High Middle Ages, the basic powers of government were divided between the king and his semi-autonomous vassals. The nobility and the towns acted with varying degrees of unity and success through such evolving representative bodies as the English Parliament, the French Estates

▲ **Niccolò Machiavelli.** Santi di Tito's portrait of Machiavelli, perhaps the most famous Italian political theorist, who advised Renaissance princes to practice artful deception and inspire fear in their subjects if they wished to succeed.
Scala/Art Resource, N.Y.

General, and the Spanish Cortes to thwart the centralization of royal power. However, as a result of the Hundred Years' War and the schism in the church, the landed nobility and the clergy were in decline in the late Middle Ages. The increasingly important towns now began to ally with the king. Loyal, businesswise townspeople, not the nobility and the clergy, staffed the royal offices, becoming the king's lawyers, bookkeepers, military tacticians, and diplomats. This new alliance between king and town would slowly break the bonds of feudal society and make possible the rise of the modern sovereign state.

In a sovereign state, the powers of taxation, war making, and law enforcement are no longer the local right of semi-autonomous vassals but are concentrated in the monarch and exercised by his chosen agents. Taxes, wars, and laws become national rather than merely regional matters. Only as monarchs were able to act independently of the nobility and the representative assemblies could they overcome the decentralization that had been the basic obstacle to nation building.

Monarchies also began to create standing national armies in the fifteenth century. As the noble cavalry receded and the

CHRONOLOGY

Major Political Events of the Italian Renaissance (1375–1527)

1378–1382	Ciompi revolt in Florence
1434	Medici rule in Florence established by Cosimo de' Medici
1454–1455	Treaty of Lodi allies Milan, Naples, and Florence (in effect until 1494)
1494	Charles VIII of France invades Italy
1495	League of Venice unites Venice, Milan, the Papal States, the Holy Roman Empire, and Spain against France
1499	Louis XII invades Milan (the second French invasion of Italy)
1500	The Borgias conquer Romagna
1512–1513	The Holy League (Pope Julius II, Ferdinand of Aragon, Emperor Maximilian I, and Venice) defeat the French
1513	Machiavelli writes The Prince
1515	Francis I leads the third French invasion of Italy
1516	Concordat of Bologna between France and the papacy
1527	Sack of Rome by imperial soldiers

infantry and the artillery became the backbone of armies, mercenary soldiers were recruited from Switzerland and Germany to form the mainstay of the "king's army."

The growing cost of warfare increased the need to develop new national sources of royal income. The expansion of royal revenues was especially hampered by the stubborn belief among the highest classes that they were immune from government taxation. The nobility guarded their properties and traditional rights and despised taxation as an insult and a humiliation. Royal revenues accordingly grew at the expense of those least able to resist and least able to pay. Monarchs had several options. As feudal lords they could collect rents from their royal domain. They might also levy national taxes on basic food and clothing, such as the *gabelle* or salt tax in France and the *alcabala* or 10 percent sales tax on commercial transactions in Spain. Kings could also levy direct taxes on the peasantry and on commercial transactions in towns under royal protection. This they did through agreeable representative assemblies of the privileged classes in which the peasantry did not sit. The French *taille* was such a tax. Sale of public offices and the issuance of high-interest government bonds appeared in the fifteenth century as innovative fund-raising devices. But kings did not levy taxes on the powerful nobility. They turned for loans to rich nobles, as they did to the great bankers of Italy and Germany, bargaining with the privileged classes, who often remained as much the kings' creditors and competitors as their subjects.

MEDIEVAL RUSSIA

In the late tenth century Prince Vladimir of Kiev (r. 972–1015), then Russia's dominant city, received delegations of Muslims, Roman Catholics, Jews, and Greek Orthodox Christians, each group hoping to win the Russians to its religion. Prince Vladimir chose Greek Orthodoxy, which became the religion of Russia, adding a new cultural bond to the long-standing commercial ties the Russians had with the Byzantine Empire.

Vladimir's successor, Yaroslav the Wise (r. 1016–1054), developed Kiev into a magnificent political and cultural center, but after his death, rivalry among princes challenged Kiev's dominance, and it became just one of several national centers.

Mongol Rule (1243–1480)   Mongol (or Tatar) armies (see Chapters 8 and 13) invaded Russia in 1223, and Kiev fell in 1240. Russian cities became tribute-paying principalities of the segment of the Mongol Empire called the *Golden Horde*, which had its capital at Sarai, on the lower Volga.

Mongol rule further divided Russia from the West but left Russian political institutions and religion largely intact. Thanks to their far-flung trade, the Mongolians brought most Russians greater peace and prosperity than they had enjoyed before.

Russian Liberation   The princes of Moscow cooperated with the Mongols and grew wealthy. They then gradually expanded the principality through land purchases, colonization, and conquest.

In 1380 Grand Duke Dimitri of Moscow (1350–1389) defeated Tatar forces at Kulikov Meadow in a victory that marked the beginning of the decline of Mongolian hegemony. Another century would pass before Ivan III, called Ivan the Great (d. 1505), would bring all of northern Russia under Moscow's control and end Mongol rule in 1480. By the last

Exterior of a Russian Orthodox Church in Novgorod, Russia
UNESCO, Ann Ronan/ The Image Works.

quarter of the fifteenth century, Moscow had replaced Kiev as the political and religious center of Russia. In Russian eyes it was destined to become the "third Rome" after the fall of Constantinople to the Turks in 1453.

FRANCE

There were two cornerstones of French nation building in the fifteenth century. The first was the collapse of the English holdings in France following the Hundred Years' War. The second was the defeat of Charles the Bold (r. 1467–1477) and the duchy of Burgundy. Perhaps Europe's strongest political power in the mid–fifteenth century, Burgundy aspired to lead a dominant middle kingdom between France and the Holy Roman Empire. It might have succeeded had not the Continental powers joined together in opposition. When Charles the Bold was killed at Nancy in 1477, the dream of Burgundian empire died with him.

The dissolution of Burgundy ended its constant intrigue against the French king and left Louis XI (r. 1461–1483) free to secure the monarchy. The newly acquired Burgundian lands and his own Angevin inheritance permitted the king to double the size of his kingdom. Louis harnessed the nobility and expanded trade and industry.

A strong nation is a two-edged sword. It was because Louis' successors inherited such a secure and efficient government that France was able to pursue Italian conquests in the 1490s and to fight a long series of losing wars with the Habsburgs in the first half of the sixteenth century. By the mid–sixteenth century France was again a defeated nation and almost as divided internally as it had been during the Hundred Years' War.

SPAIN

Spain, too, became a strong country in the late fifteenth century. Both Castile and Aragon had been poorly ruled, divided kingdoms in the mid–fifteenth century. The marriage of Isabella of Castile (r. 1474–1504) and Ferdinand of Aragon (r. 1479–1516) changed that situation. The two future sovereigns married in 1469, despite strong protests from neighboring Portugal and France, both of which foresaw the formidable European power such a union would create. Castile was by far the richer and more populous of the two, having an estimated 5 million inhabitants to Aragon's population of under 1 million. Castile was also distinguished by its lucrative sheep-farming industry, which was run by a government-backed organization called the *Mesta*, another example of developing centralized economic planning. Although the two kingdoms were dynastically united by the marriage of Ferdinand and Isabella in 1469, each retained its own government agencies—separate laws, armies, coinage, and taxation—and cultural traditions.

Ferdinand and Isabella could do together what neither was able to accomplish alone, namely, subdue their realms, secure their borders, and venture abroad militarily. Townspeople

allied themselves with the crown and progressively replaced the nobility within the royal administration. The crown also extended its authority over the wealthy chivalric orders, a further circumscription of the power of the nobility.

Spain had long been remarkable as a place where three religions—Islam, Judaism, and Christianity—coexisted with a certain degree of toleration. This toleration ended dramatically under Ferdinand and Isabella, who made Spain the prime example of state-controlled religion. Ferdinand and Isabella exercised almost total control over the Spanish church as they placed religion in the service of national unity. They appointed the higher clergy and the officers of the Inquisition. The Inquisition, run by Tomás de Torquemada (d. 1498), Isabella's confessor, was a key national agency established in 1479 to monitor the activity of converted Jews (*conversos*) and Muslims (*Moriscos*) in Spain. In 1492 the Jews were exiled and their properties were confiscated. In 1502 nonconverting Moors in Granada were driven into exile. Spanish spiritual life remained largely uniform and regimented, a major reason for Spain's remaining a loyal Catholic country throughout the sixteenth century and providing a base of operation for the European Counter-Reformation.

Ferdinand and Isabella had wide horizons. They contracted anti-French marriage alliances that came to determine much of European history in the sixteenth century. In 1496 their eldest daughter, Joanna, later known as "the Mad" (1479–1555), married Archduke Philip (1478–1506), the son of Emperor Maximilian I (r. 1493–1519). Their son, Charles I, the first ruler over a united Spain, came by his inheritance and election as Emperor Charles V in 1519 to rule over a European kingdom almost equal in size to that of Charlemagne. A second daughter, Catherine of Aragon (1485–1536), married King Henry VIII of England. The failure of this latter marriage became the key factor in the emergence of the Anglican Church and the English Reformation.

The new Spanish power was also evident in Ferdinand and Isabella's promotion of overseas exploration. Their patronage of the Genoese adventurer Christopher Columbus (1451–1506), who discovered the islands of the Caribbean while sailing west in search of a shorter route to the spice markets of the Far East, led to the creation of the Spanish Empire in Mexico and Peru, whose gold and silver mines helped to make Spain Europe's dominant power in the sixteenth century.

ENGLAND

The last half of the fifteenth century was a period of especially difficult political trial for the English. Following the Hundred Years' War, a defeated England was subjected to internal warfare between two rival branches of the royal family, the House of York and the House of Lancaster. This conflict, known to us today as the Wars of the Roses (as York's symbol, according to legend, was a white rose, and Lancaster's a red rose), kept England in turmoil from 1455 to 1485.

The Lancastrian monarchy of Henry VI (r. 1422–1461) was consistently challenged by the Duke of York and his supporters in the prosperous southern towns. In 1461 Edward IV (r. 1461–1483), son of the Duke of York, seized power and, assisted by loyal and able ministers, effectively bent Parliament to his will. His brother and successor was Richard III (r. 1483–1485), whose reign saw the growth of support for the exiled Lancastrian Henry Tudor. Henry returned to England to defeat Richard on Bosworth Field in August 1485.

Henry Tudor ruled as Henry VII (r. 1485–1509), the first of the new Tudor dynasty that would endure until 1603. To bring the rival royal families together and to make the hereditary claim of his offspring to the throne uncontestable, Henry married Edward IV's daughter, Elizabeth of York. He succeeded in disciplining the English nobility through a special and much-feared instrument of the royal will known as the Court of Star Chamber. Henry shrewdly construed legal precedents to the advantage of the crown, using English law to further his own ends. He confiscated so much noble land and so many fortunes that he governed without dependence on Parliament for royal funds, always a cornerstone of strong monarchy. Henry thus began to shape a monarchy that became one of early modern Europe's most exemplary governments during the reign of his granddaughter, Elizabeth I (r. 1558–1603).

Tres Riches Heures du Duc de Berry.

Summary

Medieval Society In theory, medieval society was divided into three main groups: clergy (those who prayed), nobility (those who fought as mounted warriors), and laborers (peasants and artisans). The rise of merchants, self-governing towns, and universities helped break down this division. By supporting rulers against the nobility, towns gave kings the resources—money and university-trained bureaucrats and lawyers—to build national governments. Much of medieval history involved the struggle by rulers to assert their authority over powerful local lords and the church.

Church and State The medieval papacy sought to extend its power over both church and state. In the tenth century, the Cluny reform movement increased popular respect for the church and strengthened the papacy. In the Investiture Struggle, the papacy secured the independence of the clergy by enlisting the support of the German princes against the Holy Roman Emperors, thus weakening imperial power in Germany. The First Crusade further strengthened papal prestige. But, by the end of the thirteenth century, kings had become more powerful than popes, and the French king, Philip the Fair, was able to defy the papacy. In the fourteenth century, the Great Schism further weakened papal prestige. Although it was able to fend off a movement to make church councils superior to popes, the papacy never recovered its authority over national rulers.

The Renaissance The Renaissance, which began in the Italian city-states in the late fourteenth century, marks the transition from the medieval to the modern world. Humanism, the scholarly study of the Greek and Latin classics and the ancient Church fathers, promoted a rebirth of ancient norms and values and the classical ideal of an educated, well-rounded person. The growth of secular values led to a great burst of artistic activity by artists such as da Vinci, Raphael, and Michelangelo. The political weakness of the Italian states invited foreign intervention by France, Spain, and the Habsburgs. The sack of Rome by imperial forces in 1527 marks the end of the Renaissance.

Nation Building By the fifteenth century, England, France, and Spain had developed into strong national monarchies with centralized bureaucracies and professional armies. Although medieval institutions, such as the English Parliament, in theory limited royal power, in practice monarchs in these countries held unchallenged authority. The Great Schism, the Hundred Years' War, and the Black Death had weakened the church and the nobility, while townspeople supported the kings. A similar process was beginning in Russia where the rulers of Moscow were extending their authority after throwing off Mongol rule. In the Empire, however, regional lords had defeated the emperors' attempts to build a strong central state.

Review Questions

1. How do you account for the success of the Cluny reform movement? Can major features of the modern Catholic Church be found in the Cluny reforms?

2. Was the Investiture Controversy a political or a religious conflict? Summarize the respective arguments of Gregory VII and Henry IV. Is the conflict a precedent for the modern doctrine of the separation of church and state?

3. Why did Germany remain divided while France and England began to coalesce into reasonably strong states during the High Middle Ages?

4. How did the responsibilities of the nobility differ from those of the clergy and the peasantry during the High Middle Ages? How did each social class contribute to the stability of society?

5. Describe the circumstances that gave rise to towns. How did towns change traditional medieval society?

6. How did the Hundred Years' War, the Black Death, and the Great Schism in the church affect the course of history? Which had the most lasting effects on the institutions it touched?

7. Was the church an aggressor or a victim in the late Middle Ages and the Renaissance? How successful was it in its confrontations with Europe's emerging dynastic states?

8. What was "reborn" in the Renaissance? Were the humanists the forerunners of modern secular education and culture, or eloquent defenders of a still-medieval Christian view of the world against the church's secular and pagan critics?

9. Historians find features of modern states developing in Europe during the late Middle Ages and Renaissance. What modern features can you identify in the governments of the Italian city-states and the northern monarchies? In Russia?

Key Terms

Black Death   (p. 419)

chiaroscuro   (p. 425)

Crusades   (p. 405)

Curia   (p. 422)

Golden Horde   (p. 428)

Great Schism   (p. 422)

guilds   (p. 410)

Holy Roman Empire   (p. 422)

humanism   (p. 423)

Magna Carta   (p. 416)

mannerism   (p. 426)

regular clergy   (p. 413)

Renaissance   (p. 422)

Scholasticism   (p. 410)

secular clergy   (p. 413)

studia humanitatis   (p. 423)

taille   (p. 420)

vernacular   (p. 403)

Documents CD-ROM

Mediterranean Civilization after the Fall of Rome

7.6 Launching the Crusades (1095): "It is the Will of God!"

The Formation of European Civilization

10.1 St. Hidegard of Bingen, Know the Ways

10.2 St. Francis of Assisi, "The Rule of St. Francis"

10.3 The Goodman of Paris

10.4 The Love of God

10.5 St. Thomas Aquinas

10.6 Unam Sanctam (1302): Pope Boniface VIII

10.7 "A Most Terrible Plague": Giovanni Boccaccio

Renaissance and Reformation in Europe

13.1 Oration on the Dignity of Man (1486)

13.2 The Soul of Man (1474)

13.3 Castiglione's "Courtier": Prosperity Makes a Gentleman

Eurasian Connections before European Expansion

11.4 The Mongol Khan's Ultimatum to the Nations of Europe

11.5 Kuyuk Khan, Letter to Pope Innocent IV

NOTE: *To learn more about the topics in this chapter, see the Suggested Readings at the end of the book.*

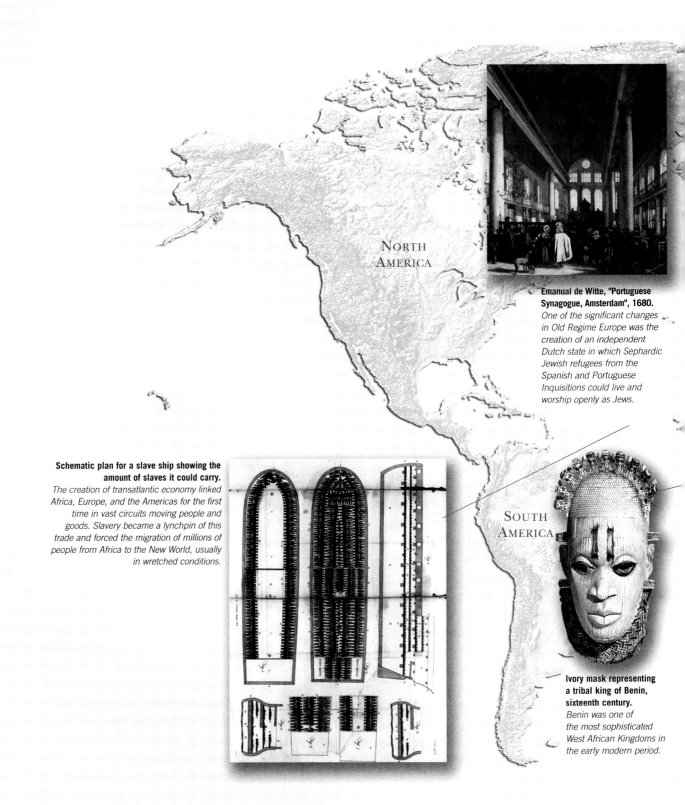

The sixteenth through the eighteenth centuries were a period of great transition in world history, both in terms of social change and in the expansion of trade and migration. The European voyages of discovery and subsequent colonization of the New World created a new transatlantic economy linking the world's oceans for the first time.

THE WORLD IN TRANSITION

NORTH AMERICA

SOUTH AMERICA

Emanual de Witte, "Portuguese Synagogue, Amsterdam", 1680.
One of the significant changes in Old Regime Europe was the creation of an independent Dutch state in which Sephardic Jewish refugees from the Spanish and Portuguese Inquisitions could live and worship openly as Jews.

Schematic plan for a slave ship showing the amount of slaves it could carry.
The creation of transatlantic economy linked Africa, Europe, and the Americas for the first time in vast circuits moving people and goods. Slavery became a lynchpin of this trade and forced the migration of millions of people from Africa to the New World, usually in wretched conditions.

Ivory mask representing a tribal king of Benin, sixteenth century.
Benin was one of the most sophisticated West African Kingdoms in the early modern period.

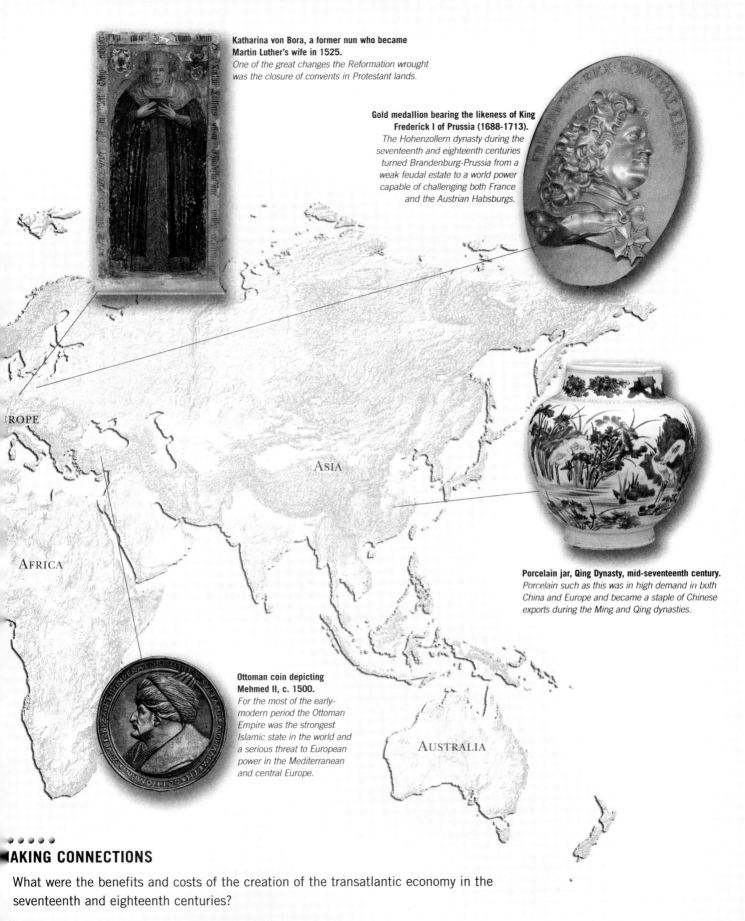

Katharina von Bora, a former nun who became Martin Luther's wife in 1525.
One of the great changes the Reformation wrought was the closure of convents in Protestant lands.

Gold medallion bearing the likeness of King Frederick I of Prussia (1688-1713).
The Hohenzollern dynasty during the seventeenth and eighteenth centuries turned Brandenburg-Prussia from a weak feudal estate to a world power capable of challenging both France and the Austrian Habsburgs.

EUROPE

ASIA

AFRICA

Porcelain jar, Qing Dynasty, mid-seventeenth century.
Porcelain such as this was in high demand in both China and Europe and became a staple of Chinese exports during the Ming and Qing dynasties.

Ottoman coin depicting Mehmed II, c. 1500.
For the most of the early-modern period the Ottoman Empire was the strongest Islamic state in the world and a serious threat to European power in the Mediterranean and central Europe.

AUSTRALIA

MAKING CONNECTIONS

What were the benefits and costs of the creation of the transatlantic economy in the seventeenth and eighteenth centuries?

How did shifts in the balance of power alter societies around the world between 1500 and 1800?

EUROPE

1517–1555	Protestant Reformation
1533–1584	Ivan the Terrible of Russia reigns
1540	Jesuit Order founded by Ignatius Loyola
1543–1727	Scientific Revolution
1556–1598	Philip II of Spain reigns
1558–1603	Elizabeth I of England reigns
1562–1598	French Wars of Religion
1581	The Netherlands declares its independence from the Spanish Habsburgs
1588	Defeat of the Spanish Armada
1589–1610	Henry IV, Navarre, founds Bourbon dynasty of France

▲ Queen Elizabeth I

NEAR EAST/ INDIA

1500–1722	Safavid Shi'ite rule in Iran
1512–1520	Ottoman ruler Selim I
1520–1566	Ottoman ruler Suleiman the Magnificent
1525–1527	Babur founds Mughal dynasty in India
1540	Hungary under Ottoman rule
1556–1605	Akbar the Great of India reigns
1571	Battle of Lepanto; Ottomans defeated
ca. 1571–1640	Safavid philosopher-writer Mullah Sadra
1588–1629	Shah Abbas I of Iran reigns

Leaf from "Divan" ▶
by the poet, Hafiz

EAST ASIA

1500–1800	Commercial revolution in Ming-Qing China; trade with Europe; flourishing of the novel
1543	Portuguese arrive in Japan
1568–1600	Era of unification follows end of Warring States Era in Japan
1587	Spanish arrive in Japan
1588	Hideyoshi's sword hunt in Japan
1592–1598	Ming troops battle Hideyoshi's army in Korea

Feluccas ▶
on the Nile

AFRICA

1506	East coast of Africa under Portuguese domination
1507	Mozambique founded by Portuguese
1517	Spanish crown authorizes slave trade to its South American colonies; rapid increase in importation of slaves to the New World
1554–1659	Sa'did Sultanate in Morocco
1575	Union of Bornu and Kanem by Idris Alawma (r. 1575–1610); Kanem-Bornu state the most fully Islamic in West Africa
1591	Moroccan army defeats Songhai army; Songhai Empire collapses

THE AMERICAS

1519	Conquest of the Aztecs by Cortes; Aztec ruler, Montezuma (r. 1502–1519) killed; Tenochtitlán destroyed
1529	Mexico City becomes capital of the viceroyalty of New Spain
1533	Pizarro begins his conquest of the Incas
1536	Spanish under Mendoza arrive in Argentina
1544	Lima becomes capital of the viceroyalty of Peru
1584	Sir Walter Raleigh sends expedition to Roanoke Island (North Carolina)

◀ Algonquin village of Secotton

▲ Aztec drawing of Spanish conquest of Mexico

◄ Louis XIV
of
France

1618–1648 Thirty Years' War

1640–1688 Frederick William, the Great Elector, reigns in Brandenburg-Prussia

1642–1646 Puritan Revolution in England

1643–1715 Louis XIV of France reigns

1682–1725 Peter the Great of Russia reigns

1688 Glorious Revolution in England

1690 "Second Treatise of Civil Government," by John Locke

1701 Act of Settlement provides for Protestant succession to English throne

1702–1713 War of Spanish Succession

1740–1748 War of Austrian Succession

1756–1763 Seven Years' War

ca. 1750 Industrial Revolution begins in England

1772 First partition of Poland

1789 First French Revolution

1793 and 1795 Last two partitions of Poland

▲ "Evening" by Francis Wheatley

1628–1657 Shah Jahan reigns; builds Taj Mahal as mausoleum for his beloved wife

1646 Founding of Maratha Empire

1648 Delhi becomes the capital of Mughal Empire

1658–1707 Shah Aurangzeb, the "World Conqueror," reigns in India; end of religious toleration toward Hindus; beginning Mughal decline

1669–1683 Last military expansion by Ottomans: 1669, seize Crete; 1670s, the Ukraine; 1683, Vienna

▲ The Taj Mahal

1700 Sikhs and Marathas bring down Mughal Imperial Power

1708 British East India Company and New East India Company merge

1722 Last Safavid ruler forced to abdicate

1724 Rise in the Deccan of the Islamic state of Hyderabad

1725 Nadir Shah of Afganhistan becomes ruler of Persia

1739 Persian invasion of northern India, by Nadir Shah

1748–1761 Ahmad Shah Durrani of Afghanistan invades India

1757 British victory at Plassey, in Bengal

1600 Tokugawa Ieyasu wins battle of Sekigahara, completes unification of Japan

1600–1868 Tokugawa shogunate in Edo

1630s Seclusion adopted as national policy in Japan

1644–1694 Bashō, Japanese poet

1644–1911 Qing (Manchu) dynasty in China

1661–1722 Kangxi reign in China

1673–1681 Revolt of southern generals in China

1699 British East India Company arrives in China

1701 Forty-seven rō-nin incident in Japan

1716–1733 Reforms of Tokugawa Yoshimune in Japan

1737–1795 Reign of Qianlong in China

1742 Christianity banned in China

1784 American traders arrive in China

1787–1793 Matsudaira Sadanobu's reforms in Japan

1798 White Lotus Rebellion in China

Manchu emperor ►
Qianlong

◄ "White Heron" castle in Jimeji

1600s English, Dutch, and French enter the slave trade; slaves imported to sugar plantations in the Caribbean

1619 First African slaves in North America land in Virginia

1652 First Cape Colony settlement of Dutch East India Company

1660–1856 Omani domination of East Africa; Omani state centered in Zanzibar; 1698, takes Mozambique from Portuguese

1702 Asiento Guinea Trade Company founded for slave trade between Africa and the Americas

1700s Transatlantic slave trade at its height

1741–1856 United Sultanate of Oman and Zanzibar

1754–1817 Usman Dan Fodio, founder of sultanate in northern and central Nigeria; the Fulani become the ruling class in the region

1762 End of Funj Sultanate in eastern Sudanic region

◄ The Friday Mosque at Shela

◄ Slave labor on sugar plantation in Brazil and the West Indies

1607 The London Company establishes Jamestown Colony (Virginia)

1608 Champlain founds Quebec

1619 Slave labor introduced at Jamestown (Virginia)

1733 Georgia founded as last English colony in North America

1739–1763 Era of trade wars in Americas between Great Britain and the French and Spanish

1763 Peace of Paris establishes British government in Canada

1776–1781 American Revolution

1783–1830 Simón Bolívar, Latin American soldier, statesman

1789 U.S. Constitution

1791 Negro slave revolt in French Santo Domingo

1791 Canada Constitution Act divides the country into Upper and Lower Canada

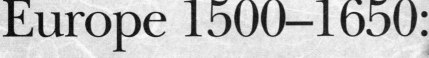

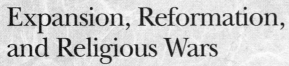

CHAPTER

16

Europe 1500–1650:

Expansion, Reformation, and Religious Wars

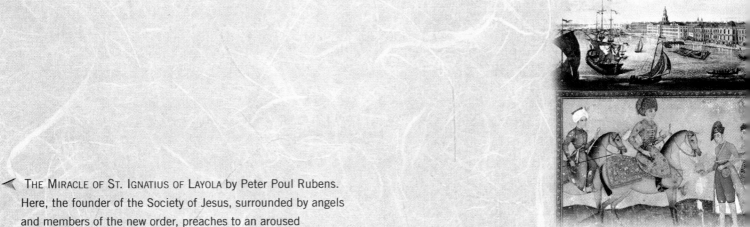

◄ THE MIRACLE OF ST. IGNATIUS OF LAYOLA by Peter Poul Rubens. Here, the founder of the Society of Jesus, surrounded by angels and members of the new order, preaches to an aroused assembly.
Erich Lessing/Art Resource, N.Y.

European Expansion

In the late fifteenth and the sixteenth centuries, Europeans sailed far from their own shores, reaching Africa, southern and eastern Asia, and the New World of the Americas. From Japan to Peru, they now directly confronted for the first time civilizations other than their own and that of Islam, with which they had already been in contact in the form of trade and, more often, military confrontation. A major motivation for the voyages, which began with a reconnaissance of the coast of West Africa, was to find a way to circumvent the monopoly Muslim merchants had over the movement of spices from the Indian Ocean into Europe, a grip that only strengthened with the rise of the Ottomans. A wealthier, more self-confident Europe, now recovered from the devastating plague-induced population decline of the fourteenth century, its taste for Asian spices long since whetted during the Crusades, was ready to go to the sources of those spices itself.

Voyages of exploration also set forth from Ming China, especially between 1405 and 1433, reaching India, the Arabian Gulf, and East Africa. If followed up, they might have prevented Europeans from establishing a presence in the Indian Ocean. The Chinese now faced both serious pressures on their northern and western borders and the problem of administrating a vast, multicultural empire stretching into Central Asia, where non-Chinese rivals had to be kept under control. Moreover, the dominant Neo-Confucian philosophy espoused by the scholar-bureaucrats in the imperial court disdained merchants and commerce, extolling instead a peasant agrarian economy.

These factors led the Chinese to turn inward and abandon overseas trade and exploration precisely at the moment when Europeans were exploring the coast of Africa on their way to the Indian Ocean. It was a fateful choice, because it meant that the Asian power best able to resist the establishment of European commercial and colonial empires in the Indian Ocean, had abdicated that role, leaving a vacuum of power for Europeans to fill. Still, Chinese merchants continued to ply ocean trade routes and settle as far from home as the Philippines and, in later centuries, the West Coasts of North and South America. Wherever there was commerce in Chinese goods, there were Chinese merchants, albeit now operating without support from their government.

Although parallels may be drawn between the court culture of the Forbidden Palace in Beijing and that of King Louis XIV in seventeenth-century France, the Chinese government with its philosophy of Confucianism remained more unified and patriarchal than its counterparts in the West. The Chinese, at first, readily tolerated other religions, warmly embracing Jesuit missionaries, doing so in part because political power in China was not bound to a particular religion. The Japanese were also admirers of the Jesuits, who arrived in Japan with the Portuguese in 1543. The admiration was mutual, leading to three hundred thousand Christian converts by 1600. Tolerance of Christianity did not last as long in Japan as in China. Hideyoshi, in his drive for internal unity, banned Christianity in the late sixteenth century. Nonetheless China and Japan, as well as many Islamic societies, including the Ottomans and the Mughals, demonstrated more tolerance for foreign religions, such as Christianity, than did the West for Islam, or Asian religious traditions.

THINK AHEAD

- Why did the Europeans launch voyages of exploration in the fifteenth and sixteenth centuries? What role did the Crusades and the rise of the Ottoman Empire play in this enterprise?

- Why did the Chinese voyages of exploration under the Ming come to a halt? What were the consequences for the history of the Indian Ocean?

- How did the Chinese and Japanese react to the introduction of Christianity?

I N THE SECOND DECADE OF THE SIXTEENTH CENTURY, a powerful religious movement began in Saxony in Germany and rapidly spread throughout northern Europe, deeply affecting society and politics as well as the spiritual lives of men and women. Attacking what they believed to be burdensome superstitions and corrupt practices that robbed people of both their money and their peace of mind, Protestant reformers led a revolt against the medieval church. In a short period of time, hundreds of thousands of people from all social classes set aside the beliefs of centuries and adopted a more simplified religious practice.

The Protestant Reformation challenged aspects of the Renaissance, especially its tendency to follow classical sources in glorifying human nature and its loyalty to traditional religion. Protestants were more impressed by the human potential for evil than by the inclination to do good, and encouraged parents, teachers, and magistrates to be firm disciplinarians. On the other hand, Protestants also embraced many Renaissance values, especially humanist educational reforms and in the study of ancient languages. Here they found tools to master Scripture and challenge the papacy.

Protestantism was not the only reform movement to grow out of the religious grievances and reforms of the late Middle Ages. Within the church itself a reform was emerging that would give birth to new religious orders, rebut Protestantism, and win back a great many of its converts.

As different groups identified their political and social goals with either Protestantism or Catholicism, a hundred years of bloody opposition between Protestants and Catholics darkened the second half of the sixteenth century and the first half of the seventeenth. The political conflict that had previously been confined to central Europe and a struggle for Lutheran rights and freedoms then shifted to Western Europe—to France, the Netherlands, England, and Scotland—and became a struggle for Calvinist recognition. In France Calvinists fought Catholic rulers for the right to form their own communities, practice their chosen religion openly, and exclude from their lands those they deemed heretical. During the Thirty Years' War (1618–1648), international armies of varying religious persuasions clashed in central and northern Europe. By 1649 English Puritans had overthrown the Stuart monarchy and the Anglican Church.

For Europe the late fifteenth and the sixteenth centuries were a period of unprecedented territorial expansion. Permanent colonies were established in the Americas and the exploitation of the New World's human and mineral resources begun. Imported American gold and silver spurred scientific invention and a new weapons industry. The new bullion helped create an international traffic in African slaves as rival tribes eagerly sold their captives to the Portuguese. Slaves came in ever-increasing numbers to work the mines and the plantations of the New World as replacements for faltering American natives.

The Discovery of a New World

The discovery of the Americas dramatically expanded the horizons of Europeans, both geographical and intellectual. Knowledge of the New World's inhabitants and exploitation of its mineral and human wealth set new cultural and economic forces in motion throughout Western Europe. Beginning with the successful voyages of the Portuguese and Spanish in the fifteenth century, commercial supremacy progressively shifted from the Mediterranean and Baltic Seas to the Atlantic seaboard, setting the stage for global expansion (see Map 16–1).

The Portuguese Chart the Course Seventy-seven years before Columbus, who sailed under the flag of Spain, set foot in the Americas, Prince Henry "the Navigator" (1394–1406), ruler of a stong and united Portugal, captured the West African Muslim city of Ceuta at the mouth of the Mediterranean Sea.

There began the Portuguese exploration of the African coast, first in search of Guinea gold and slaves, and by century's end a sea route to Asia's spice markets. Topping the list of spices were pepper and cloves as they both preserved and enhanced the dull diet of most Europeans. Initially the catch of raiders, African slaves were soon taken effortlessly by Portuguese traders in direct exchanges with tribal chiefs, who readily swapped their captured enemies for horses, corn, and finished goods (cloth and brassware). Over the second half of the fifteenth century, Portuguese ships delivered 150,000 slaves to Europe.

Before there was a sea route to the Orient, spices could only be obtained through the Venetians, who bought or bartered them from Eastern Muslim merchants. This was a powerful Venetian-Mameluke (Turkish) monopoly the Portuguese resolved to beat by going directly to the source by sea. Overland

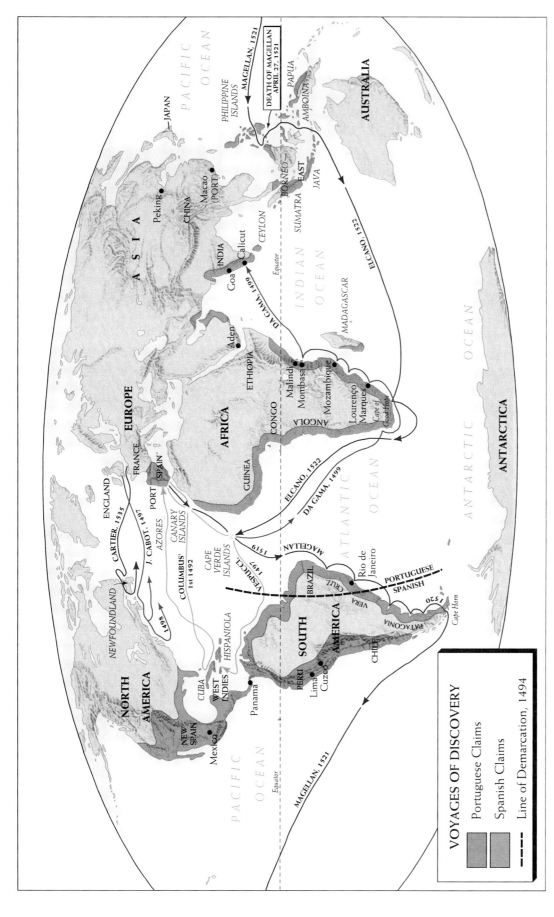

MAP 16–1 European Voyages of Discovery and the Colonial Claims of Spain and Portugal in the Fifteenth and Sixteenth Centuries. The map dramatizes Europe's global expansion in the fifteenth and sixteenth centuries.

routes to India and China had long existed, but their transit had become too difficult and unprofitable by the fifteenth century. The route by sea posed a different obstacle and risk: fear of the unknown, making the first voyages of exploration slow and tentative. Venturing down the African coast Portuguese square riggers were turned out into the deep ocean by cape after cape, and the farther out they sailed to round them, the greater the sailors' fear that they would not have the sail power to return home. Each cape successfully rounded became a victory and a lesson, allowing the crews to discover the rigging and the skills they would need to cross the oceans to the Americas and the Orient.

In addition to spice markets, the voyages of discovery also sought allies against Western Europe's archenemies, the Muslims.

In 1455, a very self-interested pope gave the Portuguese explorers virtual carte blanche from the coast of Guinea to the Indies, granting them all the spoils of war: land, goods, and slaves. The church expected mass conversions in the wake of conquest, a Christian coup as well as mercantile advantage. The explorers also kept an eye out for a reportedly friendly Eastern potentate known as Prester John. Rumored to be a potential Christian ally against the Muslim infidel, he was real enough for Vasco da Gama to carry a letter of introduction to him from the Portuguese king, when he sailed East in 1497.

Bartholomew Dias pioneered the eastern Portuguese Empire after safely rounding the Cape of Good Hope at the tip of Africa in 1487. A decade later, in 1498, Vasco da

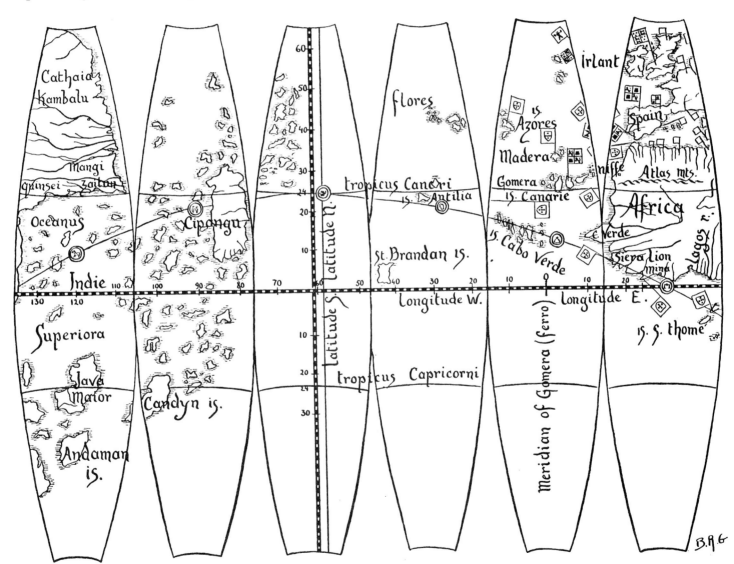

▲ **Martin Behaim's "Globe Apple."** What Columbus knew of the world in 1492 was contained in this map by Nuremberg geographer Martin Behaim (1440–1507), creator of the first spherical globe of the earth. The ocean section of Behaim's globe is reproduced here. Departing the Canary Islands (in the second section from the right), Columbus expected his first major landfall to be Japan, or what he calls Cipangu (in the second section from the left). When he landed at San Salvador, he thought he was on an outer island of Japan; after reaching Cuba, he believed it to be Japan. Only slowly did it dawn on him that these new lands had never before been seen by Europeans.

From Admiral of the Ocean Sea by Samuel Eliot Morison. Copyright 1942 © renewed 1970 by Samuel Eliot Morison. By permission of Little, Brown and Company, Boston, MA.

Gama stood on the shores of India. When he returned to Portugal, he carried a cargo worth sixty times the cost of the voyage. Later, the Portuguese established successful colonies in Goa and Calcutta, whence they successfully challenged the Arabs and the Venetians for control of the European spice trade.

The Portuguese had concentrated their explorations on the Indian Ocean. Initially following in their wake, the Spanish turned out into the Atlantic Ocean, believing they could find a shorter route to the East Indies by sailing due West. Rather than beating the Portuguese to Asia, Columbus instead discovered the Americas—although he did not know that on his first voyage.

The Spanish Voyages of Christopher Columbus Thirty-three days after departing the Canary Islands, on October 12, 1492, Columbus landed in San Salvador (Watlings Island) in the eastern Bahamas. Thinking he was in the East Indies, he mistook his first landfall as an outer island of Japan. The error was understandable given the information he relied on: Marco Polo's thirteenth-century account of his years in China and Nuremberg mapmaker Martin Behaim's spherical map of the presumed world. That map showed nothing but ocean between the west coast of Europe and the east coast of Asia, with Cipangu, or Japan, in between (see Map 16-2).

Naked and extremely friendly natives met Columbus and his crew on the beaches of the New World. They were Taino Indians, who spoke a variant of a language known as Arawak. Believing the island on which he landed to be the East Indies, Columbus called the native people who met him Indians, a name that stuck even after it was known that he had actually discovered a new continent. The natives' generosity amazed Columbus, as they freely gave his men all the corn and yams they desired, along with many sexual favors. "They never say no," Columbus marveled, as he observed how easily they could be enslaved by the Spanish.

On the heels of Columbus, Amerigo Vespucci (1451–1512), after whom America is named, and Ferdinand Magellan (1480–1521) carefully explored the coastline of South America. Their travels proved that the new lands discovered by Columbus were not the outermost territory of the Far East, but an entirely unknown continent that opened on the still greater Pacific Ocean. Magellan, who was continuing the search for a westward route to the Indies, made it all the way to the Philippines, where he died.

Impact on Europe and America Unknowingly to those who undertook and financed it, Columbus's first voyage marked the beginning of more than three centuries of Spanish conquest, exploitation, and administration of a vast American empire. What began as voyages of discovery became expeditions of conquest similar to the warfare Christian Aragon and Castile waged against Islamic Moors. Those wars had just ended in 1492, and their conclusion imbued the early Spanish explorers with a zeal for conquering and converting other non-Christian peoples.

The voyages to the New World had important consequences for the cultures of both Europe and America. Much to the benefit of Spain, they created Europe's largest and longest surviving trading bloc and spurred other European countries to undertake their own colonial ventures. The wealth extracted from its American possessions financed Spain's commanding role in the religious and political wars of the sixteenth century, while fueling a Europe-wide economic expansion.

European expansion also had a profound biological impact. Europeans introduced numerous species of fruits, vegetables, and animals from Europe, into the Americas, and vice versa. European expansion also led to a spread of European diseases. Vast numbers of indigenous American peoples died from measles and smallpox, which broke out in massive epidemics among populations with no natural or acquired immunity. Likewise, syphillis killed a million Europeans (see Map 16–2).

For the native peoples of America, the voyages began a long period of conquest during which native populations were devastated by warfare, new diseases, and slave labor. In both South and North America, Spanish rule left a lasting footprint of Roman Catholicism, economic dependency, and hierarchical social structure, all of which is still visible today (see Chapter 18).

▲ **Magellan's Global Circumnavigation.** An imaginative portrayal of Portuguese explorer Ferdinand Magellan's circumnavigation of the globe amid fires, monsters, mythological figures, guided by a naked angel with a harp and halo.
The Mariners' Museum, Newport News, VA.

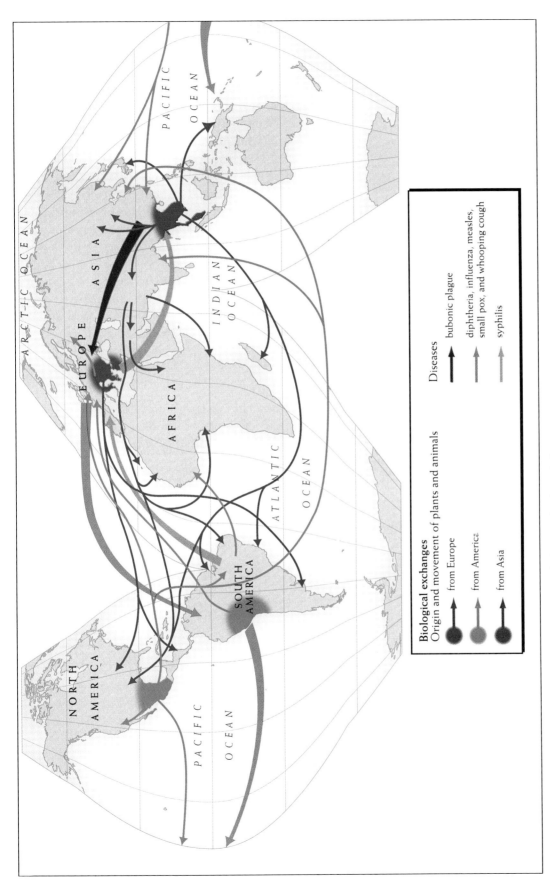

MAP 16–2   Biological Exchanges.   The world-wide movement of plants, animals, and diseases.

The Reformation

The **Reformation** was the sixteenth-century religious movement that sought to reform the Church and led to the establishment of Protestantism. It began in Germany.

Religion and Society   The Reformation broke out first in the free imperial cities of Germany and Switzerland. There were about sixty-five such cities, and each was in a sense a little kingdom unto itself. Most had Protestant movements, but with mixed success and duration. Some quickly turned Protestant and remained so. Some were Protestant only for a short time. Others developed mixed confessions, frowning on sectarianism and aggressive proselytizing, letting Catholics and Protestants coexist.

What seemed a life-and-death struggle with higher princely or royal authority was not the only conflict cities were experiencing. They also suffered deep internal social and political divisions. Certain groups favored the Reformation more than others. In many places, guilds like that of the printers, whose members were prospering both socially and economically and who had a history of conflict with local authority, were in the forefront of the Reformation. Evidence suggests that people who felt pushed around and bullied by either local or distant authority—a guild by an autocratic local government, a city or region by a prince or king—perceived in the Protestant movement an ally, at least initially.

Social and political experience thus coalesced with the larger religious issues in both town and countryside. When Martin Luther and his comrades wrote, preached, and sang about a priesthood of all believers, scorned the authority of ecclesiastical landlords, and ridiculed papal laws as arbitrary human inventions, they touched political as well as religious nerves in German and Swiss cities. This was also true in the villages, for the peasants on the land also heard in the Protestant sermon and pamphlet a promise of political liberation and even a degree of social betterment.

Popular Movements and Criticism of the Church   The Protestant Reformation could also not have occurred without the monumental crises of the late medieval church and the Renaissance papacy. For many people, the church had ceased to provide a viable foundation for religious piety. Laity and clerics alike began to seek a more heartfelt, idealistic, and often—in the eyes of the pope—increasingly heretical religious piety. The late Middle Ages were marked by independent lay and clerical efforts to reform local religious practice and by widespread experimentation with new religious forms that shared a common goal of religious simplicity in imitation of Christ.

A variety of factors contributed to the growth of lay criticism of the church. The laity in the cities were becoming increasingly knowledgeable about the world and those who controlled their lives. They traveled widely—as soldiers, pilgrims, explorers, and traders. New postal systems and the printing press increased the information at their disposal. The new age of books and libraries raised literacy and heightened curiosity. Laypersons were increasingly able to take the initiative in shaping the cultural life of their communities.

Secular Control over Religious Life   On the eve of the Reformation, Rome's international network of church offices began to fall apart in many areas, hurried along by a growing sense of regional identity—incipient nationalism—and local secular administrative competence. The late medieval church had permitted important ecclesiastical posts ("benefices") to be sold to the highest bidders and had not enforced residency requirements in parishes. Rare was the late medieval German town that did not have complaints about the maladministration, concubinage, or fiscalism of its clergy, especially the higher clergy (bishops, abbots, and prelates).

City governments also sought to restrict the growth of ecclesiastical properties and clerical privileges and to improve local religious life by bringing the clergy under the local tax code and by endowing new clerical positions for well-trained and conscientious preachers.

THE NORTHERN RENAISSANCE

The scholarly works of northern humanists created a climate favorable to religious and educational reforms. Northern humanism was initially stimulated by the importation of Italian learning through such varied intermediaries as students who had studied in Italy, merchants, and the Brothers of the Common Life. The northern humanists tended to come from more diverse social backgrounds and to be more devoted to reli-

Gutenberg Bible. The printing press made possible the diffusion of Renaissance learning. But no book stimulated thought more at this time than did the Bible. With Gutenberg's publication of a printed Bible in 1454, scholars gained access to a dependable, standardized text, so that Scripture could be discussed and debated as never before.
The Pierpont Morgan Library/Art Resource/N.Y.

gious reforms than were their Italian counterparts. They were also more willing to write for lay audiences.

The growth of schools and lay education combined with the invention of cheap paper to create a mass audience for printed books. In response, Johann Gutenberg (d. 1468) invented printing with movable type in the German city of Mainz around 1450. Thereafter, books were rapidly and handsomely produced on topics both profound and practical. By 1500, printing presses operated in at least 60 German cities and in more than 200 throughout Europe. A new medium now existed for politicians, humanists, and reformers alike.

The most famous of the northern humanists was Desiderius Erasmus (1466–1536), the "prince of the humanists." Idealistic and pacifistic, Erasmus gained fame as both an educational and a religious reformer. He aspired to unite the classical ideals of humanity and civic virtue with the Christian ideals of love and piety. He believed that disciplined study of the classics and the Bible, if begun early enough, was the best way to reform both individuals and society. He summarized his own beliefs with the phrase *philosophia Christi*, a simple, ethical piety in imitation of Christ. He set this ideal against what he believed to be the dogmatic, ceremonial, and factious religious practice of the late Middle Ages. To promote his own religious beliefs, Erasmus edited the works of the Church Fathers and made a Greek edition of the New Testament (1516), which became the basis for a new, more accurate Latin translation (1519). Martin Luther later used both these works as the basis for his famous German translation.

The best known of early English humanists was Sir Thomas More (1478–1535), a close friend of Erasmus. It was while visiting More that Erasmus wrote his most famous work, *The Praise of Folly* (1511), an amusing and profound exposé of human self-deception that was quickly translated from the original Latin into many vernacular languages. More's *Utopia* (1516), a criticism of contemporary society, depicts an imaginary society based on reason and tolerance that requires everyone to work and has rid itself of all social and political injustice. Although More would remain staunchly Catholic, humanism in England, as in Germany, paved the way for the English Reformation. A circle of English humanists, under the direction of Henry VIII's minister Thomas Cromwell, translated and disseminated late medieval criticisms of the papacy and many of Erasmus's satirical writings as well.

Whereas in Germany, England, and France, humanism helped the Protestants, in Spain it entered the service of the Catholic Church. Here the key figure was Francisco Jiménez de Cisneros (1437–1517), a confessor to Queen Isabella, and after 1508 Grand Inquisitor—a position from which he was able to enforce the strictest religious orthodoxy. Jiménez was a conduit for humanist scholarship and learning. He founded the University of Alcalá near Madrid in 1509, printed a Greek edition of the New Testament, and translated many religious

tracts that aided clerical reform and control of lay religious life. His greatest achievement, taking fifteen years to complete, was the Complutensian Polyglot Bible, a six-volume work that placed the Hebrew, Greek, and Latin versions of the Bible in parallel columns. Such scholarly projects and internal church reforms joined with the repressive measures of Ferdinand and Isabella to keep Spain strictly Catholic.

MARTIN LUTHER AND GERMAN REFORMATION TO 1525

Unlike France and England, late medieval Germany lacked the political unity to enforce "national" religious reforms during the late Middle Ages. There were no lasting Statutes of Provisors and Praemunire, as in England, nor a Pragmatic Sanction of Bourges, as in France, both limiting papal jurisdiction and taxation on a national scale. What happened on a unified national level in England and France occurred only locally and piecemeal within German territories and towns. As popular resentment of clerical immunities and ecclesiastical abuses, especially over the selling of indulgences, spread among German cities and towns, an unorganized "national" opposition to

▲ **John Tetzel.** A contemporary caricature depicts John Tetzel, the famous indulgence preacher. The last lines of the jingle read: "As soon as gold in the basin rings, right then the soul to heaven springs." It was Tetzel's preaching that spurred Luther to publish his ninety-five theses.
Courtesy Stiftung Luthergedenkstaten in Sachsen-Anhalt/Lutherhalle, Wittenberg.

Rome formed. German humanists had long given voice to such criticism, and by 1517 it was pervasive enough to provide a solid foundation for Martin Luther's reform.

Luther (1483–1546) was the son of a successful Thüringian miner. He was educated in Mansfeld, Magdeburg (where the Brothers of the Common Life were his teachers), and Eisenach. Between 1501 and 1505 he attended the University of Erfurt, where the nominalist teachings of William of Ockham and Gabriel Biel (d. 1495) prevailed. After receiving his master of arts degree in 1505, Luther registered with the law faculty, following his parents' wishes, but he never began the study of law. To the disappointment of his family, he instead entered the Order of the Hermits of Saint Augustine in Erfurt on July 17, 1505. This decision had apparently been building for some time and was resolved during a lightning storm in which Luther, terrified and crying out to Saint Anne for assistance (Saint Anne was the patron saint of travelers in distress), promised to enter a monastery if he escaped death.

Ordained in 1507, Luther pursued a traditional course of study. In 1510, he journeyed to Rome on the business of his order, finding there justification for the many criticisms of the church he had heard in Germany. In 1511, he moved to the Augustinian monastery in Wittenberg, where he earned his doctorate in theology in 1512. Thereafter, he became a leader within the monastery, the new university, and the spiritual life of the city.

Justification by Faith Alone Reformation theology grew out of a problem then common to many of the clergy and the laity: the failure of traditional medieval religion to provide either full personal or intellectual satisfaction. Luther was especially plagued by the disproportion between his own sense of sinfulness and the perfect righteousness that God required for salvation, according to medieval theology. Traditional church teaching and the sacrament of penance proved no consolation. Luther wrote that he came to despise the phrase "righteousness of God," for it seemed to demand of him a perfection he knew neither he nor any other human being could ever achieve. His insight into the meaning of "justification by faith alone" was a gradual process that extended between 1513 and 1518. The righteousness that God demands, he concluded, did not result from many religious works and ceremonies but was given in full measure to those who believe and trust in Jesus Christ, who alone is the perfect righteousness satisfying to God. To believe in Christ meant to stand before God clothed in Christ's sure righteousness.

The Attack on Indulgences An **indulgence** was a remission of the temporal penalty imposed by priests on penitents as a "work of satisfaction" for their mortal sins. According to medieval theology, after the priest absolved a penitent of guilt for the sins, the penitent remained under an eternal penalty, a punishment God justly imposed for sin. After absolution, however, this eternal penalty was said to be transformed into a temporal penalty, a manageable "work of satisfaction" that the penitent might perform here and now (for example, through prayers, fasting, almsgiving, retreats, and pilgrimages). Penitents who defaulted on such prescribed works of satisfaction could expect to suffer for them in purgatory.

At this point, indulgences, which had earlier been given to Crusaders who did not complete their penances because they had fallen in battle, became an aid to laity, made genuinely anxious by their belief in a future suffering in purgatory for neglected penances or unrepented sins. In 1343, Pope Clement VI (r. 1342–1352) had proclaimed the existence of a "treasury of merit," an infinite reservoir of good works in the church's possession that could be dispensed at the pope's discretion. On the basis of this declared treasury, the church sold "letters of indulgence," which covered the works of satisfaction owed by penitents. In 1476, Pope Sixtus IV (r. 1471–1484) extended indulgences also to cover purgatory.

Originally, indulgences had been given only for the true self-sacrifice of going on a Crusade to the Holy Land. By Luther's time, they were regularly dispensed for small cash payments (very modest sums that were regarded as a good work of almsgiving). They were presented to the laity as remitting not only their own future punishments, but also those of their dead relatives presumed to be suffering in purgatory.

In 1517, Pope Leo X (r. 1513–1521) revived a plenary Jubilee Indulgence that had first been issued by Pope Julius II (r. 1503–1513), whose proceeds were to be used to rebuild St. Peter's Basilica in Rome. Such an indulgence promised forgiveness of all outstanding unrepented sins upon the completion of certain acts. That kind of indulgence was subsequently preached on the borders of Saxony in the territories of the future Archbishop Albrecht of Mainz, who was much in need of revenues because of the large debts he had incurred in order to hold, contrary to church law, three ecclesiastical appointments. The selling of the indulgence was a joint venture by Albrecht, the Augsburg banking house of Fugger, and Pope Leo X, with half the proceeds going to the pope and half to Albrecht and his creditors. The famous indulgence preacher John Tetzel (d. 1519) was enlisted to preach the indulgence in Albrecht's territories because he was a seasoned professional who knew how to stir ordinary people to action. As he exhorted on one occasion:

> Don't you hear the voices of your dead parents and other relatives crying out, "Have mercy on us, for we suffer great punishment and pain. From this you could release us with a few alms. ... We have created you, fed you, cared for you, and left you our temporal goods. Why do you treat us so cruelly and leave us to suffer in the flames, when it takes only a little to save us?"[1]

---

[1] *Die Reformation in Augenzeugen Berichten*, ed. by Helmar Junghans (Dusseldorf: Karl Rauch Verlag, 1967), p. 44

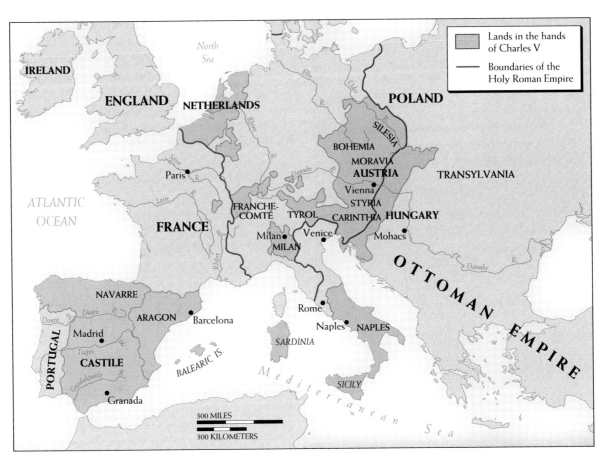

MAP 16–3 The Empire of Charles V.   Dynastic marriages and good luck concentrated into Charles's hands rule over the lands shown here, plus Spain's overseas possessions. Crowns and titles rained down on him; election in 1519 as emperor gave him new burdens and responsibilities.

When Luther, according to tradition, posted his ninety-five theses against indulgences on the door of Castle Church in Wittenberg, on October 31, 1517, he protested especially against the impression created by Tetzel that indulgences actually remitted sins and released the dead from punishment in purgatory. Luther believed these claims went far beyond the traditional practice and seemed to make salvation something that could be bought and sold.

Election of Charles V   Luther's **ninety-five theses** made him famous overnight. They were embraced by humanists and other proponents of reform, but they prompted official proceedings against him. In October, he was called before the general of the Dominican order in Augsburg. As sanctions were being prepared against Luther, however, Emperor Maximilian I died (January 12, 1519), and this event, fortunate for the Reformation, turned attention away from heresy in Saxony to the contest for a new emperor.

The pope backed the French king, Francis I. However, Charles I of Spain, a youth of nineteen, succeeded his grandfather and became Emperor Charles V. (See Map 16–3.) Charles was assisted by both a long tradition of Habsburg imperial rule and a massive Fugger campaign chest, which secured the votes of the seven electors. The electors, who traditionally enhanced their power at every opportunity, wrung new concessions from Charles for their votes. The emperor agreed to a revival of the Imperial Supreme Court and the Council of Regency and promised to consult with a diet of the empire on all major domestic and foreign affairs that affected the empire. These measures also helped the development of the Reformation by preventing unilateral imperial action against the Germans, something Luther could be thankful for in the early years of the Reformation.

Luther's Excommunication and the Diet of Worms   In the same month in which Charles was elected emperor, Luther entered a debate in Leipzig (June 27, 1519) with the Ingolstadt professor John Eck. During this contest, Luther challenged the infallibility of the pope and the inerrancy of church councils, appealing for the first time to the sovereign authority of Scripture alone. He burned all his bridges to the old church when he further defended certain teachings of John Huss that had been condemned by the Council of Constance.

▲ **A Catholic Portrayal of Martin Luther Tempting Jesus (1547).**
Reformation propaganda often portrayed the pope as the Antichrist or
the devil. Here Catholic propaganda turns the tables on the
Protestant reformers by portraying a figure of Martin Luther as the
devil (note the monstrous feet and tail under his academic robes).
Versuchung Christi, 1547, Gemälde, Bonn, Landschaftsverband Rheinland/Rheinisches
Landesmuseum, Bonn. Inv. Nr. 58.3.

In 1520, Luther described the pillars of his reform in three
pamphlets. The *Address to the Christian Nobility of the German
Nation* urged the German princes to force reforms on the
Roman church, especially to curtail its political and economic
power in Germany. The *Babylonian Captivity of the Church* examined the traditional seven sacraments of the church, arguing
that only two, baptism and the Eucharist, were biblical, and
exalted the authority of Scripture, church councils, and secular princes over that of the pope. The *Freedom of a Christian*
summarized the new theology for the laity, describing a "happy
union" between the soul and Christ by faith alone, in which
everything the soul had (sin, death, and damnation) became
Christ's and everything Christ had (purity, life, and heaven)
became the believer's.

In April 1521, Luther defended his religious teaching
before the imperial **Diet of Worms**, over which newly elected

Emperor Charles V presided. Ordered to recant, Luther
declared that he could not act against Scripture, reason, and
his own conscience. On May 26, 1521, he was placed under the
imperial ban and thereafter became an "outlaw" to secular as
well as religious authority. For his own protection, friends hid
him in a secluded castle, where he spent almost a year, from
April 1521 to March 1522. During his stay, he translated the
New Testament into German, using Erasmus's new Greek text
and Latin translation, and he attempted, by correspondence,
to oversee the first stages of the Reformation in Wittenberg.

Imperial Distractions: France and the Turks The Reformation
was greatly helped in these early years by the emperor's war
with France and the advance of the Ottoman Turks into eastern Europe. Against both adversaries Charles V, who also remained a Spanish king with dynastic responsibilities outside
the empire, needed German troops, and to that end he promoted friendly relations with the German princes. Between
1521 and 1559, Spain (the Habsburg dynasty) and France (the
Valois dynasty) fought four major wars over disputed territories in Italy and along their borders. In 1526, the Turks overran Hungary at the Battle of Mohacs; in Western Europe the
French-led League of Cognac formed against Charles for the
second Habsburg-Valois war.

Thus preoccupied, the emperor agreed through his representatives at the German Diet of Speyer in 1526 that each German territory was free to enforce the Edict of Worms (1521)
against Luther "so as to be able to answer in good conscience
to God and the emperor." That concession, in effect, gave the
German princes territorial sovereignty in religious matters and
gave the Reformation time to put down deep roots. Later, in
1555, the Peace of Augsburg would enshrine such local
princely control over religion in imperial law.

How the Reformation Spread In the late 1520s and on into the
1530s, the Reformation passed from the hands of the theologians and pamphleteers into those of the magistrates and
princes. In many cities, the magistrates quickly followed the lead
of the Protestant preachers and their sizable congregations in
mandating the religious reforms they preached. In numerous
instances, magistrates had themselves worked for decades to
bring about basic church reforms and thus welcomed the
preachers as new allies. Reform now ceased to be merely slogans
and became laws that all townspeople had to obey.

The religious reform became a territorial political movement
as well led by the elector of Saxony and the prince of Hesse, the
two most powerful German Protestant rulers. Like the urban
magistrates, the German princes quickly recognized the political
and economic opportunities offered them by the demise of the
Roman Catholic Church in their regions. Soon they, too, were
pushing Protestant faith and politics onto their neighbors. By the

1530s, Protestant cities and lands formed powerful defensive alliances and prepared for war with the Catholic emperor.

The Peasants' Revolt In its first decade, the Protestant movement suffered more from internal division than from imperial interference. By 1525, Luther had become as much an object of protest within Germany as was the pope. Original allies, sympathizers, and fellow travelers declared their independence from him. Like the German humanists, the German peasantry also had at first believed Luther to be an ally. Since the late fifteenth century, the peasantry had been organized against efforts by territorial princes to override their traditional laws and customs and to subject them to new regulations and taxes. (See Document, "German Peasants Protest Rising Feudal Exactions.") Peasant leaders, several of whom were convinced Lutherans, saw in Luther's teaching about Christian freedom and his criticism of monastic landowners a point of view close to their own. They openly solicited Luther's support of their political and economic rights, including their revolutionary request for release from serfdom.

Lutheran pamphleteers made Karsthans, the burly, honest peasant who earned his bread by the sweat of his brow and sacrificed his comfort for the well-being of others, a symbol of the simple life God desired all people to live. Lutherans were not, however, social revolutionaries. Luther believed the freedom of the Christian to be an inner release from guilt and anxiety, not the right to create an egalitarian society by violent revolution. When the peasants revolted against their landlords in 1524–1525, Luther predictably condemned them as "un-Christian" and urged the princes to crush their revolt. An estimated 70,000 to 100,000 peasants may have died by the time the revolt was put down. Had Luther supported the peasants' revolt, not only would he have contradicted his own teaching, he would surely also have ended any chance of the survival of his reform beyond the 1520s.

Luther and the Jews Also controversial is Luther's stand toward the Jews. In 1523, as part of a heady program of civic reform, he published a pamphlet entitled, "Jesus Christ was Born a Jew." Therein, he urged Christians to be kinder and gentler to German Jews in the hope that "some" or "many" might assimilate to Christian society and eventually convert to the new reformed Christianity. By the late 1530s, Luther's Protestant reform was only one among many and even faltering, and some Christians in Bohemia and Moravia, he was told, were even converting to Judaism. He tells the story of three rabbis even coming to him in Wittenberg in the hope of "finding a new Jew in me." Was his kindness to Jews to be repaid by Jewish proselytization of the great reformer himself? From that suspicion on, he regretted his 1523 pamphlet and viewed the Jews as just another in a long history of foreign predators threatening German Christians. He took his anger at Jews out in several new pamphlets published in the late 1530s and early 1540, in which he urged German princes forcibly to remove nonconverting Jews to a land of their own as France, Spain, and Bohemia had already done. Although far short of making Judaism a capital crime, as imperial law had done with Anabaptism in 1529, Luther's proposals ran along a similar line: assimilation or exile. Fortunately, the shocked and disappointed Jews had a protector in Emperor Charles V, and Luther's colleagues had no heart to replace traditional Christian watchful waiting on the Jews with forced conversions and exile. In Hesse and Saxony around this time, rulers tightened traditional restrictions on Jews. Had Luther been willing, he might have softened these restrictions or prevented them altogether as expectant Jewish leaders had asked him to do.

ZWINGLI AND THE SWISS REFORMATION

Although Luther's was the first, Switzerland and France had their own independent reform movements almost simultaneously with Germany's. Switzerland was a loose confederacy of thirteen autonomous cantons or states and allied areas (see Map 16–4). Some became Protestant, some remained Catholic, and a few managed to effect a compromise. The two preconditions of the Swiss Reformation were the growth of national sentiment and a desire for church reform.

▲ **Execution of a Peasant Leader.** The punishment of a peasant leader in a village near Heilbronn. After the defeat of rebellious peasants in and around the city of Heilbronn, Jacob Rorbach, a well-to-do peasant leader from a nearby village, was tied to a stake and slowly roasted to death.
© Badische Landesbibliothek

The Reformation in Zurich Ulrich Zwingli (1484–1531), the leader of the Swiss Reformation, was widely known for opposition to the sale of indulgences and religious superstition. The people's priest in Zurich, he made the city his base for reform. Zwingli's reform guideline was simple and effective: whatever lacked literal support in Scripture was to be neither believed nor practiced. After a public disputation in January 1523, based on his Scripture test, Zurich became, to all intents and purposes, a Protestant city and the center of the Swiss Reformation. Its harsh discipline in pursuit of its religious ideals made it one of the first examples of a "puritanical" Protestant city.

The Marburg Colloquy Landgrave Philip of Hesse (1504–1567) sought to unite Swiss and German Protestants in a mutual defense pact, a potentially significant political alliance. His efforts were spoiled, however, by theological disagreements between Luther and Zwingli over the nature of Christ's presence in the Eucharist. Zwingli maintained a symbolic interpretation of Christ's words, "This is my body". Christ, he argued, was only spiritually, not bodily, present in the bread and wine of the Eucharist. Luther, to the contrary, insisted that Christ's human nature could share the properties of his divine nature; hence, where Christ was spiritually present, he could also be bodily present, for his was a special nature (*transubstantiation*).

Philip of Hesse brought the two Protestant leaders together in his castle in Marburg in early October 1529, but they were unable to work out their differences on this issue. Luther left thinking Zwingli a dangerous fanatic. The disagreement splintered the Protestant movement theologically and politically.

ANABAPTISTS AND RADICAL PROTESTANTS

The moderate pace and seemingly small ethical results of the Lutheran and Zwinglian reformations discontented many people, among them some of the original co-workers of Luther and Zwingli. Many desired a more rapid and thorough implementation of primitive Christianity and accused the major reformers of going only halfway. The most important of these radical groups were the Anabaptists, the sixteenth-century ancestors of the modern Mennonites and Amish. The Anabaptists were especially distinguished by their rejection of infant baptism and their insistence on only adult baptism (*Anabaptism* derives from the Greek word meaning "to rebaptize"), believing that baptism as a consenting adult conformed to Scripture and was more respectful of human freedom.

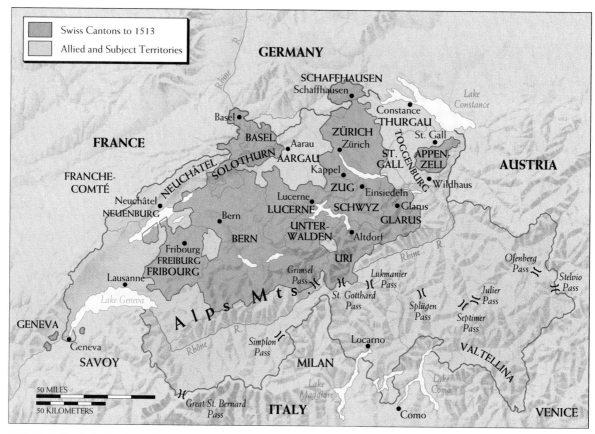

MAP 16–4 The Swiss Confederation. While nominally still a part of the Holy Roman Empire, Switzerland grew from a loose defensive union of the central "forest cantons" in the thirteenth century to a fiercely independent association of regions with different languages, histories, and religions in the sixteenth century.

| ## German Peasants Protest Rising Feudal Exactions

In the late fifteenth and early sixteenth centuries, German feudal lords, both secular and ecclesiastical, tried to increase the earnings from their lands by raising demands on their peasant tenants. As the lords restricted the traditional freedoms and property rights of peasants, massive revolts occurred in southern Germany in 1525. The following, representative statement of peasant grievances, summarized in twelve articles, came from the town of Memmingen.

◆ Are the peasants more interested in material than in spiritual freedom? Which of their demands are the most revolutionary, and which are the least problematic for their lords to grant? Why do some centuries exhibit greater social and political equality than others?

1. It is our humble petition and desire that in the future each community should choose and appoint a pastor, and that we should have the right to depose him should he conduct himself improperly ...

2. We are ready and willing to pay the fair tithe of grain ... The small tithes [of cattle], whether [to] ecclesiastical or lay lords, we will not pay at all, for the Lord God created cattle for the free use of man ...

3. We ... take it for granted that you will release us from serfdom as true Christians, unless it should be shown us from the Gospel that we are serfs.

4. It has been the custom heretofore that no poor man should be allowed to catch venison or wildfowl or fish in flowing water, which seems to us quite unseemly and unbrotherly as well as selfish and not agreeable to the Word of God ...

5. We are aggrieved in the matter of woodcutting, for the noblemen have appropriated all the woods to themselves ...

6. In regard to the excessive services demanded of us which are increased from day to day, we ask that this matter be properly looked into so that we shall not continue to be oppressed in this way ...

7. We will not hereafter allow ourselves to be further oppressed by our lords, but will let them demand only what is just and proper according to the word of the agreement between the lord and the peasant. The lord should no longer try to force more services or other dues from the peasant without payment ...

8. We are greatly burdened because our holdings cannot support the rent exacted from them ... We ask that the lords may appoint persons of honor to inspect these holdings and fix a rent in accordance with justice ...

9. We are burdened with a great evil in the constant making of new laws ... In our opinion we should be judged according to the old written law ...

10. We are aggrieved by the appropriation ... of meadows and fields which at one time belonged to a community as a whole. These we will take again into our own hands ...

11. We will entirely abolish the due called Todfall [that is, *heriot* or *death tax*, by which the lord received the best horse, cow, or garment of a family upon the death of a serf] and will no longer endure it, nor allow widows and orphans to be thus shamefully robbed against God's will, and in violation of justice and right ...

12. It is our conclusion and final resolution, that if any one or more of the articles here set forth should not be in agreement with the Word of God, as we think they are, such article we will willingly retract.

Translations and Reprints from the Original Sources of European History, Vol. 2 (Philadelphia: Department of History, University of Pennsylvania, 1897).

Anabaptists physically separated from society to form a more perfect community in imitation of what they believed to be the example of the first Christians. Due to the close connection between religious and civic life in this period, the political authorities viewed such separatism as a threat to basic social bonds.

At first Anabaptism drew its adherents from all social classes. But as Lutherans and Zwinglians joined with Catholics in opposition to it, a more rural, agrarian class came to make up the great majority of Anabaptists. In 1529 rebaptism became a capital offense throughout the Holy Roman Empire. It has been estimated that from 1525 to 1618, between one and five thousand men and women were executed for rebaptizing themselves as adults.

JOHN CALVIN AND THE GENEVAN REFORMATION

Calvinism was the religious ideology that inspired or accompanied massive political resistance in France, the Netherlands, and Scotland. Believing in both divine predestination and the individual's responsibility to create a godly society, Calvinists became zealous reformers. In a famous and controversial study, *The Protestant Ethic and the Spirit of Capitalism* (1904), the German sociologist Max Weber argued that this combination of religious confidence and self-disciplined activism produced an ethic congenial to emergent capitalism, bringing Calvinism and later Puritanism into close association with the development of modern capitalist societies.

Political Revolt and Religious Reform in Geneva Whereas in Saxony religious reform paved the way for a political revolution against the emperor, in Geneva a political revolution against the local prince-bishop laid the foundation for religious change. In late 1533 the Protestant city of Bern sent Protestant reformers to Geneva and by the summer of 1535, after much internal turmoil, the Protestants triumphed. On May 21, 1536, the city voted officially to adopt the Reformation: "to live according to the Gospel and the Word of God ... without ... any more masses, statues, idols, or other papal abuses."

John Calvin (1509–1564), a reform-minded humanist and lawyer, arrived in Geneva after these events, in July 1536. The local Protestant reformer persuaded him to stay and assist the Reformation. Before a year had passed, Calvin had drawn up articles for the governance of the new church, as well as a catechism to guide and discipline the people. As a result of the strong measures proposed to govern Geneva's moral life, many suspected the reformers of trying to create a "new papacy." In February 1538 they were exiled from the city.

Calvin went to Strasbourg, a model Protestant city, where he became pastor to the French exiles. During his two years in Strasbourg he wrote biblical commentaries and a second edition of his masterful *Institutes of the Christian Religion*, which many consider the definitive theological statement of the Protestant faith. He also married and participated in the ecumenical discussions urged on Protestants and Catholics by Charles V. Most important, he learned from the Strasbourg

reformer Martin Bucer (1491–1551) how to implement the Protestant Reformation successfully.

Calvin's Geneva In 1540 Geneva elected officials favorable to Calvin and he was invited to return. Within months of his arrival, new ecclesiastical ordinances were implemented that allowed the magistrates and the clergy to cooperate in matters of internal discipline.

Calvin and his followers were motivated above all by a desire to make society godly. The "elect," Calvin taught, should live a manifestly God-pleasing life, if they are truly God's elect. The majesty of God demanded nothing less. The consistory, a judicial body composed of clergy and laity, became his instrument of power. It enforced the strictest moral discipline, meting out punishments for a broad range of moral and religious transgressions, and became unpopular with many Genevans.

After 1555 the city's magistrates were all devout Calvinists, and Geneva became home to thousands of exiled Protestants who had been driven out of France, England, and Scotland. Refugees (more than five thousand), most of them utterly loyal to Calvin, came to make up over one third of the population of Geneva. From this time until his death in 1564, Calvin's position in the city was greatly strengthened and the magistrates were very cooperative.

POLITICAL CONSOLIDATION OF THE LUTHERAN REFORMATION

By 1530 the Reformation was in Europe to stay. It would, however, take several decades and major attempts to eradicate it before all would recognize this fact. With the political triumph of Lutheranism in the empire by the 1550s, Protestant movements elsewhere gained a new lease on life.

Expansion of the Reformation In the 1530s German Lutherans formed regional consistories, which oversaw and administered the new Protestant churches. These consistories replaced the old Catholic episcopates. Under the leadership of Philip Melanchthon (1497–1560), Luther's most admired colleague, educational reforms were enacted that provided for compulsory primary education, schools for girls, a humanist revision of the traditional curriculum, and catechetical instruction of the laity in the new religion.

The Reformation also dug in elsewhere. Introduced into Denmark by Christian II (r. 1513–1523), Lutheranism became the state religion under Christian III (r. 1536–1559). In Sweden, Gustavus Vasa (r. 1523–1560), supported by a nobility greedy for church lands, confiscated church property and subjected the clergy to royal authority at the Diet of Vesteras (1527). In politically splintered Poland, Lutherans, Calvinists, and others found room to practice their beliefs. The absence of a central political authority made Poland a model of religious pluralism and toleration in the second half of the sixteenth century.

▲ **A Portrait of the Young John Calvin.**
Bibliotheque Publique et Universitaire, Geneva.

Reaction Against Protestants: The "Interim"   Charles V made abortive efforts in 1540–1541 to enforce a compromise agreement between Protestants and Catholics. As these and other conciliar efforts failed, he turned to a military solution. In 1547 imperial armies crushed the Protestant Schmalkaldic League.

The emperor established puppet rulers in Saxony and Hesse and issued as imperial law the Augsburg Interim, a new order that Protestants everywhere must readopt Catholic beliefs and practices. But the Reformation was too entrenched by 1547 to be ended even by brute force. Confronted by fierce Protestant resistance and weary from three decades of war, the emperor was forced to relent.

The Peace of Augsburg in September 1555 made the division of Christendom permanent. This agreement recognized in law what had already been well established in practice: *cuius regio, eius religio*, meaning that the ruler of a land would determine the religion of the land. Lutherans were permitted to retain all church lands forcibly seized before 1552. Those discontented with the religion of their region were permitted to migrate to another.

Calvinism was not recognized as a legal form of Christian belief and practice by the Peace of Augsburg. Calvinists remained determined not only to secure the right to worship publicly as they pleased, but also to shape society according to their own religious convictions. They organized to lead national revolutions throughout northern Europe.

THE ENGLISH REFORMATION TO 1553

Late medieval England had a well-earned reputation for defending the rights of the crown against the pope. It was, however, the unhappy marriage of King Henry VIII (r. 1509–1547) that ensured the success of the English protest against the church.

The King's Affair   Henry had married Catherine of Aragon (d. 1536), a daughter of Ferdinand and Isabella of Spain, and the aunt of Emperor Charles V. By 1527 the union had produced only one surviving child, a daughter, Mary Tudor. Henry was justifiably concerned about the political consequences of leaving only a female heir. People in this period believed it unnatural for women to rule over men. At best, a woman ruler meant a contested reign; at worst, turmoil and revolution. Henry even came to believe that his union with Catherine, who had had numerous miscarriages and stillbirths, had been cursed by God, because before their marriage Catherine had briefly been the wife of his late brother, Arthur.

By 1527 Henry, thoroughly enamored of Anne Boleyn (ca. 1504–1536), one of Catherine's ladies in waiting, decided to put Catherine aside and marry Anne. This he could not do in Catholic England without papal annulment of the marriage to Catherine. And therein lay a problem. In 1527 the reigning pope, Clement VII (r. 1523–1534), was a prisoner of Charles V, Catherine's nephew. Even if this had not been the case, it would have been virtually impossible for the pope to grant an annulment of the marriage. Not only had it survived for eighteen years, but it had also been made possible in the first place by a special papal dispensation required because Queen Catherine had previously been the wife of Henry's brother, Arthur.

After Cardinal Wolsey (1475–1530), Lord Chancellor of England since 1515, failed to secure the annulment, Thomas Cranmer (1489–1556) and Thomas Cromwell (1485–1540), both of whom harbored Lutheran sympathies, became the king's closest advisers. Finding the way to a papal annulment closed, Henry's new advisers struck a different course: Why not simply declare the king supreme in English spiritual affairs as he was in English temporal affairs? Then the king could settle his own affair.

Reformation Parliament   In 1529 Parliament convened for what would be a seven-year session that earned it the title of "Reformation Parliament." It passed a flood of legislation that harassed and finally placed royal reins on the clergy. In January 1531 the clergy publicly recognized Henry as head of the church in England "as far as the law of Christ allows." In 1533 Parliament passed the Submission of the Clergy, effectively placing canon law under royal control and thereby the clergy under royal jurisdiction.

CHRONOLOGY

Progress of Protestant Reformation on the Continent

1517	Luther posts ninety-five theses against indulgences
1519	Charles I of Spain elected Holy Roman emperor (as Charles V)
1519	Luther challenges infallibility of pope and inerrancy of church councils at Leipzig Debate
1521	Papal bull excommunicates Luther for heresy
1521	Diet of Worms condemns Luther
1521–1522	Luther translates the New Testament into German
1524–1525	Peasants' Revolt in Germany
1529	Marburg Colloquy between Luther and Zwingli
1530	Diet of Augsburg fails to settle religious differences
1531	Formation of Protestant Schmalkaldic League
1536	Calvin arrives in Geneva
1540	Jesuits, founded by Ignatius of Loyola, recognized as order by pope
1546	Luther dies
1547	Armies of Charles V crush Schmalkaldic League
1555	Peace of Augsburg recognizes rights of Lutherans to worship as they please
1545–1563	Council of Trent institutes reforms and responds to the Reformation

Tudor Succession. An allegorical depiction of the Tudor succession by the painter Lucas de Heere (1534–1584). On Henry VIII's right stands his Catholic daughter Mary (1533–1558) and her husband Philip II of Spain. They are accompanied by Mars, the god of war. Henry's son, Edward VI (r. 1547–1553), kneels at the king's left. Elizabeth I (1558–1603) is shown standing in the foreground attended by Peace and Plenty, allegorical figures of what her reign brought to England.

Sudeley Castle National Museums & Galleries of Wales.

CHRONOLOGY

Main Events of the English Reformation

1529	Reformation Parliament convenes
1532	Parliament passes the Submission of the Clergy, an act placing canon law and the English clergy under royal jurisdiction
1533	Henry VIII weds Anne Boleyn
1534	Act of Succession makes Anne Boleyn's children legitimate heirs to the English throne
1534	Act of Supremacy declares Henry VIII the only supreme head of the Church of England
1535	Thomas More executed for opposition to Acts of Succession and Supremacy
1535	Publication of Coverdale Bible
1539	Henry VIII imposes the Six Articles, condemning Protestantism and reasserting traditional doctrine
1547	Edward VI succeeds to the throne
1549	First Act of Uniformity imposes Book of Common Prayer on English churches
1553–1558	Mary Tudor restores Catholic doctrine
1558–1603	Elizabeth I fashions an Anglican religious settlement

In January 1533 Henry wed the pregnant Anne Boleyn, with Thomas Cranmer officiating. In 1534 Parliament ended all payments by the English clergy and laity to Rome and gave Henry sole jurisdiction over high ecclesiastical appointments. The Act of Succession in the same year made Anne Boleyn's children legitimate heirs to the throne, and the Act of Supremacy declared Henry "the only supreme head in earth of the church of England."

The Protestant Reformation Under Edward VI Despite his political break with Rome, Henry remained decidedly conservative in his religious beliefs, and Catholic doctrine remained prominent in a country seething with Protestant sentiment. Henry forbade the English clergy to marry and threatened to execute clergy caught twice in concubinage. The Six Articles of 1539 reaffirmed transubstantiation, denied the Eucharistic cup to the laity, declared celibate vows inviolable, provided for private Masses, and ordered the continuation of auricular confession.

Edward VI (r. 1547–1553), Henry's son by his third wife, Jane Seymour, became king at age ten. Under his regents, England enacted much of the Protestant Reformation. Henry's Six Articles and laws against heresy were repealed, and clerical marriage and Communion with the cup were sanctioned. An Act of Uniformity imposed Thomas Cranmer's Book of Common Prayer on all English churches, which were stripped of their images and altars. His forty-two-article confession of faith set forth a moderate Protestant doctrine.

These changes were short-lived because in 1553 Catherine of Aragon's daughter, Mary Tudor (d. 1558), succeeded to the throne and restored Catholic doctrine and practice with a single-mindedness that rivaled that of her father. It was not until the reign of Anne Boleyn's daughter, Elizabeth I (r. 1558–1603), that a lasting religious settlement was worked out in England.

CATHOLIC REFORM AND COUNTER-REFORMATION

The Protestant Reformation did not take the medieval church completely by surprise. There were many internal criticisms and efforts at reform before there was a **Counter-Reformation** in reaction to Protestant successes.

Sources of Catholic Reform   Before the Reformation began, ambitious proposals had been made for church reform. But sixteenth-century popes, mindful of how the Councils of Constance and Basel had stripped the pope of his traditional powers, quickly squelched such efforts to bring about basic changes in the laws and institutions of the church. Despite such papal foot-dragging, the church was not without its reformers. Many new religious orders sprang up in the sixteenth century to lead a broad revival of piety within the church.

Ignatius of Loyola and the Society of Jesus   Of the various reform groups, none was more instrumental in the success of the Counter-Reformation than the Society of Jesus, the new order of Jesuits. Organized by Ignatius of Loyola in the 1530s, it was officially recognized by the church in 1540. Within a century the society had more than fifteen thousand members scattered throughout the world, with thriving missions in India, Japan, and the Americas.

Ignatius of Loyola (1491–1556) was a heroic figure. A dashing courtier and caballero in his youth, he began his spiritual pilgrimage in 1521 after having been seriously wounded in the legs during a battle with the French. During a lengthy and painful convalescence, he read Christian classics. So impressed was he with the heroic self-sacrifice of the church's saints and their methods of overcoming mental anguish and pain that he underwent a profound religious conversion. Henceforth, he too would serve the church as a soldier of Christ.

After recuperating, Ignatius applied the lessons he had learned during his convalescence to a program of religious and moral self-discipline that came to be embodied in the *Spiritual Exercises.* This psychologically perceptive devotional guide contained mental and emotional exercises designed to teach one absolute spiritual self-mastery. A person could shape his or her own behavior, even create a new religious self, through disciplined study and regular practice.

Whereas in Jesuit eyes Protestants had distinguished themselves by disobedience to church authority and by religious innovation, the exercises of Ignatius were intended to teach

▲ **The Ecstasy of Saint Teresa of Avila** by Gianlorenzo Bernini (1598–1680). Catholic mystics like Saint Teresa and Saint John of the cross helped revive the traditional piety of medieval monasticism. © Scala/Art Resource, N.Y.

good Catholics to submit without question to higher church authority and spiritual direction. Perfect discipline and self-control were the essential conditions of such obedience. To these were added the enthusiasm of traditional spirituality and mysticism and uncompromising loyalty to the church's cause above all else. (See Document, "Ignatius of Loyola's 'Rules for Thinking with the Church.'") This potent combination helped counter the Reformation and win many Protestants back to the Catholic fold, especially in Austria and Germany.

The Council of Trent (1545–1563)   The broad success of the Reformation and the insistence of the emperor Charles V forced Pope Paul III (r. 1534–1549) to call a general council of the church to reassert church doctrine. The pope also appointed a

Ignatius of Loyola's "Rules for Thinking with the Church"

As leaders of the Counter-Reformation, the Jesuits attempted to live by and instill in others the strictest obedience to church authority. The following are some of the eighteen rules included by Ignatius in his Spiritual Exercises *to give Catholics positive direction. These rules also indicate the Catholic reformers' refusal to compromise with Protestants.*

◆ Would Protestants find any of Ignatius's "rules" acceptable? Might any of them be controversial among Catholic laity as well as among Protestant laity?

In order to have the proper attitude of mind in the Church Militant we should observe the following rules:

1. Putting aside all private judgment, we should keep our minds prepared and ready to obey promptly and in all things the true spouse of Christ our Lord, our Holy Mother, the hierarchical Church.
2. To praise sacramental confession and the reception of the Most Holy Sacrament once a year, and much better once a month, and better still every week. …
3. To praise the frequent hearing of Mass. …
4. To praise highly the religious life, virginity, and continence; and also matrimony, but not as highly. …
5. To praise the vows of religion, obedience, poverty, chastity, and other works of perfection and supererogation. …
6. To praise the relics of the saints … [and] the stations, pilgrimages, indulgences, jubilees, Crusade indulgences, and the lighting of candles in the churches.
7. To praise the precepts concerning fasts and abstinences … and acts of penance. …
8. To praise the adornments and buildings of churches as well as sacred images. …
9. To praise all the precepts of the church. …
10. To approve and praise the directions and recommendations of our superiors as well as their personal behaviour. …
11. To praise both the positive and scholastic theology. …
12. We must be on our guard against making comparisons between the living and those who have already gone to their reward, for it is no small error to say, for example: "This man knows more than St. Augustine"; "He is another Saint Francis, or even greater." …
13. If we wish to be sure that we are right in all things, we should always be ready to accept this principle: I will believe that the white that I see is black, if the hierarchical Church so defines it. For I believe that between … Christ our Lord and … His Church, there is but one spirit, which governs and directs us for the salvation of our souls.

From *The Spiritual Exercises of St. Ignatius*, trans. by Anthony Mottola. Copyright © 1964 by Doubleday, a division of Bantam, Doubleday, Dell Publishing Group, Inc., pp. 139–141. Used by permission of Doubleday, a division of Random House, Inc.

reform commission, whose report, presented in February 1537, bluntly criticized the fiscality and simony[2] of the papal Curia (court) as the primary source of the church's loss of esteem. The report was so critical that Pope Paul attempted unsuccessfully to suppress its publication, Protestants reprinted and circulated it widely.

The long-delayed council met in 1545 in the imperial city of Trent in northern Italy. There were three sessions, spread over eighteen years, with long interruptions due to war, plague, and politics. Unlike the general councils of the fifteenth century, Trent was strictly under the pope's control, with high Italian prelates prominent in the proceedings.

The council's most important reforms concerned internal church discipline. The selling of church offices and other religious goods was forbidden. Trent strengthened the authority of local bishops so they could effectively discipline popular religious

practice. Bishops who resided in Rome were forced to move to their appointed seats of authority. They had to preach regularly and conduct annual visitations. Parish priests were required to be neatly dressed, better educated, strictly celibate, and active among their parishioners. To train better priests, Trent also called for the establishment of a seminary in every diocese.

The Council did not make a single doctrinal concession to the Protestants, however. In the face of Protestant criticism, the Council of Trent reaffirmed the traditional scholastic education of the clergy; the role of good works in salvation; the authority of tradition; the seven sacraments; **transubstantiation**; the withholding of the Eucharistic cup from the laity; clerical celibacy; the reality of purgatory; the veneration of saints, relics, and sacred images; and the granting of letters of indulgence.

Rulers initially resisted Trent's reform decrees, fearing a revival of papal political power within their lands. But in time the new legislation took hold, and parish life revived under the guidance of a devout and better-trained clergy.

---

[2] The sin of selling of sacred or spiritual things, in this instance church offices.

The Reformation's Achievements

Although politically conservative, the Reformation brought about far-reaching changes in traditional religious practices and institutions in many lands. By the end of the sixteenth century, what had disappeared or was radically altered was often dramatic.

Religion in Fifteenth-Century Life   In the fifteenth century, on the streets of the great cities of central Europe that later turned Protestant (for example, Zurich, Strasbourg, Nuremberg, or Geneva), the clergy and the religious were everywhere. They made up 6 to 8 percent of the total urban population, and they exercised considerable political as well as spiritual power. They legislated and taxed; they tried cases in special church courts; and they enforced their laws with threats of excommunication.

The church calendar regulated daily life. About one third of the year was given over to some kind of religious observance or celebration. There were frequent periods of fasting. On almost a hundred days out of the year a pious Christian could not, without special dispensation, eat eggs, butter, fat, or meat.

Monasteries and especially nunneries were prominent and influential institutions. The children of society's most powerful citizens resided there. Local aristocrats were closely identified with particular churches and chapels, whose walls recorded their lineage and proclaimed their generosity. On the streets, friars from near and far begged alms from passersby. In the churches the Mass and liturgy were read entirely in Latin. Images of saints were regularly displayed, and on certain holidays their relics were paraded about and venerated.

There was a booming business at local religious shrines. Pilgrims gathered there by the hundreds, even thousands, many sick and dying, all in search of a cure or a miracle, but also for diversion and entertainment. Several times during the year special preachers arrived in the city to sell letters of indulgence.

Many clergy walked the streets with concubines and children, although they were sworn to celibacy and forbidden marriage. The church tolerated such relationships upon payment of penitential fines.

People everywhere could be heard complaining about the clergy's exemption from taxation and, in many instances, also from the civil criminal code. People also grumbled about having to support church offices whose occupants actually lived and worked elsewhere. Townspeople also expressed concern that the church had too much influence over education and culture.

Religion in Sixteenth-Century Life   In these same cities after the Reformation had firmly established itself, few changes in politics and society were evident. The same aristocratic families governed as before, and the rich generally got richer and the poor poorer. But overall numbers of clergy fell by two thirds and religious holidays shrunk by one third. Monasteries and

nunneries were nearly absent. Many were transformed into hospices for the sick and poor or into educational institutions, their endowments also turned over to these new purposes. A few cloisters remained for very devout old monks and nuns, who could not be pensioned off or who lacked families and friends to care for them. But these remaining cloisters died out with their inhabitants.

In the churches, which had also been reduced in number by at least a third, worship was conducted almost completely in the vernacular. In some, particularly those in Zwinglian cities, the walls were stripped bare and whitewashed to make sure the congregation meditated only on God's Word. The laity observed no obligatory fasts. Indulgence preachers no longer appeared. Local shrines were closed down, and anyone found openly venerating saints, relics, and images was subject to fine and punishment.

Copies of Luther's translation of the New Testament, or more often excerpts from it, could be found in private homes, and meditation on them was encouraged by the new clergy. The clergy could marry, and most did. They paid taxes and were punished for their crimes in civil courts. Domestic moral life was regulated by committees composed of roughly equal numbers of laity and clergy, over whose decisions secular magistrates had the last word.

Not all Protestant clergy remained enthusiastic about this new lay authority in religion. And the laity themselves were also ambivalent about certain aspects of the Reformation. Over half of the original converts returned to the Catholic fold before the end of the sixteenth century. Whereas half of Europe could be counted in the Protestant camp in the mid–sixteenth century, only a fifth would be there by the mid–seventeenth century.[3]

FAMILY LIFE IN EARLY MODERN EUROPE

Changes in the timing and duration of marriage, family size, and infant and child care suggest that family life was under a variety of social and economic pressures in the sixteenth and seventeenth centuries. The Reformation was only one factor in these changes and not the major one.

Later Marriages   Between 1500 and 1800, men and women in Western Europe and England married at later ages than they had in previous centuries: men in their mid- to late twenties, and women in their early to mid-twenties. The canonical, or church-sanctioned, age for marriage remained fourteen for men and twelve for women. The church also recognized as valid free, private exchanges of vows between a man and a woman otherwise qualified. After the Reformation, which condemned such clandestine unions, both Protestants and

3 Geoffrey Parker, *Europe in Crisis, 1598–1648* (Ithaca, NY: Cornell University Press, 1979), p. 50.

▲ **A Young Couple in Love** (ca. 1480) by an anonymous artist.
Bildarchiv Preussischer Kulturbesitz.

Catholics required parental consent and public vows in church before a marriage could be deemed fully licit.

Late marriage in the West reflected the difficulty couples had supporting themselves independently. It simply took the average couple a longer time than before to prepare themselves materially for marriage. In the sixteenth century, one in five women never married, and these, combined with the estimated 15 percent who were widows, constituted a large unmarried female population. A later marriage was a marriage of shorter duration, since couples who married in their thirties did not spend as much time together as couples who married in their twenties. And because women who bore children for the first time at advanced ages had higher mortality rates, late marriage meant more frequent remarriage for men. As evidenced by the rapid growth of orphanages and foundling homes between 1600 and 1800, delayed marriage also increased premarital sex and the number of illegitimate children.

Arranged Marriages   Marriage tended to be "arranged" in the sense that the parents met and discussed the terms of the marriage before the prospective bride and bridegroom became directly party to the preparations. But the wealth and social standing of the bride and the bridegroom were not the only things considered when youth married. By the fifteenth century, it was usual for the future bride and bridegroom to have known each other and to have had some prior relationship. Also, their emotional feeling for one another was respected by parents. Parents did not force total strangers to live together, and children had a legal right to protest and resist a coerced marriage, which was by definition invalid. The best marriage was one desired by the bride and groom and their families.

Family Size   The West European family was conjugal, or nuclear, consisting of a father and a mother and two to four children who survived into adulthood. This nuclear family lived within a larger household, including in-laws, servants, laborers, and boarders. The average husband and wife had six to seven children, a new birth about every two years. Of these, an estimated one third died by age five, and one half by their teens. Rare was the family, at any social level, that did not experience infant mortality and child death.

Birth Control   Artificial birth control (sponges, acidic ointments) has existed since antiquity. The church's condemnation of coitus interruptus (male withdrawal before ejaculation) during the thirteenth and fourteenth centuries suggests the existence of a contraceptive mentality, that is, a conscious, regular effort at birth control. Early birth control measures, when applied, were not very effective, and for both historical and moral reasons the church opposed them. According to Saint Thomas Aquinas, a moral act must aid and abet, never frustrate, nature's goal and the natural end of sex was the birth of children and their godly rearing within the bounds of holy matrimony and the community of the church.

Wet Nursing   The church allied with the physicians of early modern Europe on another intimate family matter. Both condemned women who hired wet nurses to suckle their newborn children. The practice was popular among upper-class women and a reflection of their social standing. The practice appears to have increased the risk of infant mortality by exposing infants to a strange and shared milk supply from women who were often not as healthy as the infants' own mothers and lived under less sanitary conditions. But nursing was distasteful to some upper-class women, whose husbands also preferred that they not do it. Among women, vanity and convenience appear to have been motives for hiring a wet nurse, while for husbands, even more was at stake. Because the church forbade sexual intercourse to lactating women, a nursing wife often became a reluctant lover. In addition, nursing had a contraceptive effect (about 75 percent effective). Some women prolonged nursing their children to delay a new pregnancy, and some husbands cooperated in this form of family planning. For other husbands, however, especially noblemen and royalty who desired an abundance of male heirs, nursing seemed to rob them of offspring and jeopardize their patrimony—hence their support of hired wet nurses.

Loving Families?   The traditional Western European family had features that seem cold and distant. Children between the ages of eight and thirteen were routinely sent from their homes into apprenticeships, school, or employment in the homes and businesses of relatives, friends, and occasionally strangers. The emotional ties between spouses also seem to have been as tenuous as those between parents and children. Widowers and widows often married again within a few months of their spouses' deaths, and marriages with extreme disparity in age between partners suggest limited affection.

In response to modern-day criticism, an early modern parent might well have asked, "What greater love can parents have for their children than to equip them well for a worldly vocation?" A well-apprenticed child was a self-supporting child, and hence a child with a future. In light of the comparatively primitive living conditions, contemporaries also appreciated the purely utilitarian and humane side of marriage and understood when widowers and widows quickly remarried. Marriages with extreme disparity in age, however, were no more the norm in early modern Europe than the practice of wet nursing, and they received just as much criticism and ridicule.

The Wars of Religion

After the Council of Trent adjourned in 1563, Catholics began a Jesuit-led counteroffensive against Protestants. At the time of John Calvin's death in 1564, Geneva had become both a refuge for Europe's persecuted Protestants and an international school for Protestant resistance, producing leaders fully equal to the new Catholic challenge.

Genevan Calvinism and the reformed Catholicism of the Council of Trent were two equally dogmatic, aggressive, and irreconcilable church systems. Calvinists may have looked like "new papists" to critics when they dominated cities like Geneva, but when as minorities they found their civil and religious rights denied in the empire and elsewhere, they became true firebrands and revolutionaries.

Calvinism adopted a presbyterian organization that magnified regional and local religious authority. Boards of presbyters, or elders, representing the many individual Calvinist congregations, directly shaped the policy of the church at large. By contrast, the Counter-Reformation sponsored a centralized episcopal church system, hierarchically arranged from pope to parish priest and stressing absolute obedience to the person at the top. The high clergy—the pope and his bishops—not the synods of local churches, ruled supreme. Calvinism attracted proponents of political decentralization who opposed totalitarian rulers, whereas Catholicism remained congenial to proponents of absolute monarchy determined to maintain "one king, one church, one law."

The wars of religion were both internal national conflicts and truly international wars. Catholic and Protestant subjects struggled to control France, the Netherlands, and England. The Catholic governments of France and Spain conspired and finally sent armies against Protestant regimes in England and the Netherlands. The outbreak of the Thirty Years' War in 1618 made the international dimensions of the religious conflict especially clear; before it ended in 1648, the war drew every major European nation directly or indirectly into its deadly net.

FRENCH WARS OF RELIGION (1562–1598)

When Henry II (r. 1547–1559) died accidentally during a tournament in 1559, his sickly fifteen-year-old son, Francis II (d. 1560), came to the throne under the regency of the queen mother, Catherine de Médicis (1519–1589). With the monarchy so weakened, three powerful families began to compete to control France. They were the Bourbons, whose power lay in the south and west; the Montmorency-Châtillons, who controlled the center of France; and the Guises, who were dominant in eastern France. The Guises were by far the strongest, and the name of *Guise* was interchangeable with militant, ultra-Catholicism. The Bourbon and Montmorency-Châtillon families, in contrast, developed strong Huguenot sympathies, largely for political reasons. (French Protestants were called **Huguenots** after Besançon Hughes, the leader of Geneva's political revolt against the Savoyards in the late 1520s.) The Bourbon Louis I, prince of Condé (d. 1569), and the Montmorency-Châtillon admiral Gaspard de Coligny (1519–1572) became the political leaders of the French Protestant resistance.

Often for quite different reasons, ambitious aristocrats and discontented townspeople joined Calvinist churches in opposition to the Guise-dominated French monarchy. In 1561 over two thousand Huguenot congregations existed throughout France. Although they made up only about a fifteenth of the population, Huguenots held important geographic areas and represented the more powerful segments of French society. Over two fifths of the French aristocracy became Huguenots. Many apparently hoped to establish within France a principle of territorial sovereignty akin to that secured within the Holy Roman Empire by the Peace of Augsburg (1555). Calvinism thus indirectly served the forces of political decentralization.

Catherine de Médicis and the Guises   Following Francis II's death in 1560, Catherine de Médicis continued as regent for her second son, Charles IX (r. 1560–1574). Fearing the Guises, Catherine, whose first concern was always to preserve the monarchy, sought allies among the Protestants. Early in 1562 she granted Protestants freedom to worship publicly outside towns—although only privately within them—and to hold synods, or church assemblies. In March of the same year this royal toleration ended when the Duke of Guise surprised a Protestant congregation worshiping illegally at Vassy in Champagne and proceeded to massacre several score—an event that marked the beginning of the French wars of religion. Perpetually caught between fanatical Huguenot and Guise extremes, Queen Catherine always sought to play the one side against the other. She wanted a Catholic France but not a Guise-dominated monarchy.

On August 22, 1572, four days after the Huguenot Henry of Navarre had married Charles IX's sister—another sign of growing Protestant power in the queen mother's eye—the Huguenot leader Coligny, who increasingly had the king's ear, was wounded by an assassin's bullet. Catherine had apparently been a part of this Guise plot to eliminate Coligny. After its failure, she feared both the king's reaction to her complicity and the Huguenot response under a recovered Coligny. Catherine convinced Charles that a Huguenot coup was afoot, inspired by Coligny, and that only the swift execution of Protestant leaders could save the crown from a Protestant attack on Paris. On the eve of Saint Bartholomew's Day, August 24, 1572, Coligny and three thousand fellow Huguenots were butchered in Paris. Within three days an estimated twenty thousand Huguenots were executed in coordinated attacks throughout France.

▲ **The St. Bartholemew's Day Massacre.** In this notorious event, here depicted by the contemporary Protestant painter François Dubois, three thousand Protestants were slaughtered in Paris and an estimated twenty thousand others died throughout France. The massacre transformed the religious struggle in France from a contest for political power into an all-out war between Protestants and Catholics.

Le Massacre de la St–Barthelemy, entre 1572 et 1584. Oil on wood, 94 × 154 cm. Musée Cantonal des Beaux Arts, Lausanne. Photo: J.–C. Ducret Musee Cantonal des Beaux–Arts, Lausanne.

This event changed the nature of the struggle between Protestants and Catholics both within and beyond the borders of France. It was thereafter no longer an internal contest between Guise and Bourbon factions for French political influence, nor was it simply a Huguenot campaign to win basic religious freedoms. Henceforth, in Protestant eyes, it became an international struggle to the death for sheer survival against an adversary whose cruelty justified any means of resistance.

The Rise to Power of Henry of Navarre   Henry III (r. 1574–1589), who was Henry II's third son and the last Valois king, found the monarchy wedged between a radical Catholic League, formed in 1576 by Henry of Guise, and vengeful Huguenots. Like the queen mother, Henry III sought to steer a middle course, and in this effort he received support from a growing body of neutral Catholics and Huguenots who put the political survival of France above its religious unity. Such *politiques*, as they were called, were prepared to compromise religious creeds to save the nation.

In the mid-1580s the Catholic League, supported by the Spanish, became completely dominant in Paris. Henry III failed to rout the league with a surprise attack in 1588 and had to flee Paris. Forced by his weakened position into guerrilla tactics, the king had both the Duke and the Cardinal of Guise assassinated. The Catholic League reacted with a fury that matched the earlier Huguenot response to the Massacre of Saint Bartholomew's Day. The king was now forced to strike an alliance with his Protestant cousin and heir, Henry of Navarre, in April 1589.

As the two Henrys prepared to attack Paris, however, a fanatical Dominican friar murdered Henry III. Thereupon the Bourbon Huguenot Henry of Navarre became Henry IV of France (r. 1589–1610).

Henry IV came to the throne as a *politique*, weary of religious strife and prepared to place political peace above absolute religious unity. He believed that a royal policy of tolerant Catholicism would be the best way to achieve such peace. On July 25, 1593, he publicly abjured the Protestant faith and embraced the traditional and majority religion of his country. "Paris is worth a Mass," he is reported to have said.

The Edict of Nantes   Five years later, on April 13, 1598, Henry IV's famous Edict of Nantes proclaimed a formal religious settlement. In 1591 he had already assured the Huguenots of at least qualified religious freedoms. The Edict of Nantes made good that promise. It recognized and sanctioned minority religious rights within what was to remain an officially Catholic country. This religious truce—and it was never more than that—granted the Huguenots, who by this time numbered well over a million, freedom of public worship, the right of assembly, admission to public offices and universities, and permission to maintain fortified towns. Most of the new freedoms, however,

were to be exercised within their own localities. Concession of the right to fortify towns reveals the continuing distrust between French Protestants and Catholics. The edict only transformed a long hot war between irreconcilable enemies into a long cold war. To its critics, it created a state within a state.

A Catholic fanatic assassinated Henry IV in May 1610. Although Henry is best remembered for the Edict of Nantes, the political and economic policies he put in place were equally important. They laid the foundations for the transformation of France into the absolutist state it would become in the seventeenth century. Ironically, in pursuit of the political and religious unity that had escaped Henry IV, his grandson Louis XIV (r. 1643–1715), calling for "one king, one church, one law," would later revoke the Edict of Nantes in 1685 (see Chapter 20). This action would force France and Europe to learn again by bitter experience the hard lessons of the wars of religion. Rare is the politician who learns from the lessons of history rather than repeat its mistakes.

IMPERIAL SPAIN AND THE REIGN OF PHILIP II (1556–1598)

Until the English defeated his mighty Armada in 1588, no one person stood larger in the second half of the sixteenth century than Philip II of Spain. During the first half of his reign, attention focused on the Mediterranean and Turkish expansion. On October 7, 1571, a Holy League of Spain, Venice, and the pope defeated the Turks at Lepanto in the largest naval battle of the sixteenth century. Before the engagement ended, thirty thousand Turks had died and over one third of the Turkish fleet was sunk or captured.

Revolt in the Netherlands   The spectacular Spanish military success in southern Europe was not repeated in northern Europe when Philip attempted to impose his will within the Netherlands and on England and France. The resistance of the Netherlands especially proved the undoing of Spanish dreams of world empire.

The Netherlands were the richest area in Europe (see Map 16–5). The merchant towns of the Netherlands were Europe's most independent, however; many, like magnificent Antwerp, were also Calvinist strongholds. A stubborn opposition to the Spanish overlords formed under William of Nassau, the Prince of Orange (r. 1533–1584). Like other successful rulers in this period, William of Orange was a *politique* who placed the Netherlands' political autonomy and well-being above religious creeds. He personally passed through successive Catholic, Lutheran, and Calvinist stages.

The year 1564 saw the first fusion of political and religious opposition to Spanish rule, the result of Philip II's unwise insistence that the decrees of the Council of Trent be enforced throughout the Netherlands. A national covenant was drawn

MAP 16–5 The Netherlands During the Reformation. The northern provinces of the Netherlands—the United Provinces—were mostly Protestant in the second half of the sixteenth century. The southern provinces—the Spanish Netherlands—made peace with Spain and remained largely Catholic.

up called the Compromise, a solemn pledge to resist the decrees of Trent and the Inquisition.

Philip dispatched the Duke of Alba (1508–1582) to suppress the revolt. His army of ten thousand men marched northward from Milan in 1567 in a show of combined Spanish and papal might. A special tribunal, known to the Spanish as the Council of Troubles and among the Netherlanders as the Council of Blood, reigned over the land. Several thousand suspected heretics were publicly executed before Alba's reign of terror ended.

William of Orange had been an exile in Germany during these turbulent years. He now emerged as the leader of a broad movement for the Netherlands' independence from Spain.

After a decade of persecution and warfare, the ten largely Catholic southern provinces (what is roughly modern Belgium) came together in 1576 with the seven largely Protestant northern provinces (what is roughly the modern Netherlands) in unified opposition to Spain. This union, known as the Pacification of Ghent, declared internal regional sovereignty in matters of religion. It was a Netherlands version of the Peace of Augsburg.

After more fighting, in January 1579 the southern provinces formed the Union of Arras and made peace with Spain. The northern provinces responded with the formation of the Union of Utrecht and continued the struggle. Spanish preoc-

The Milch Cow. This sixteenth-century satirical painting depicts the Netherlands as a land all the great powers of Europe wish to exploit. Elizabeth of England is feeding her (England had long-standing commerical ties with Flanders); Philip II of Spain is attempting to ride her (Spain was trying to reassert its control over the entire region); William of Orange is trying to milk her (he was the leader of the anti-Spanish rebellion); and the king of France holds her by the tail (France hoped to profit from the rebellion at Spain's expense).

The "Milch Cow." Rijksmuseum, Amsterdam.

cupation with France and England in the 1580s permitted the northern provinces to drive out all Spanish soldiers by 1593. In 1596 France and England formally recognized the independence of these provinces. However, the northern provinces did not formally conclude peace with Spain until 1609, when the Twelve Years' Truce concluded their virtual independence. But Spain did not fully recognize that independence until the Peace of Westphalia in 1648.

ENGLAND AND SPAIN (1558–1603)

Elizabeth I   Elizabeth I (r. 1558–1603), the daughter of Henry VIII and Anne Boleyn, was perhaps the most astute politician of the sixteenth century in both domestic and foreign policy. She repealed the anti-Protestant legislation of her predecessor Mary Tudor and guided a religious settlement through Parliament that prevented England from being torn asunder by religious differences in the sixteenth century, as the Continent was.

Catholic extremists hoped to replace Elizabeth with the Catholic Mary Stuart, Queen of Scots. But Elizabeth acted swiftly against Catholic assassination plots and rarely let emotion override her political instincts.

Elizabeth dealt cautiously with the Puritans, Protestants who sought to "purify" the national church of every vestige of "popery" and to make its Protestant doctrine more precise. The Puritans had two special grievances: (1) the retention of Catholic ceremony and vestments within the Church of England, and (2) the continuation of the episcopal system of church governance.

△ **Elizabeth I (1558–1603) Standing on a Map of England in 1592.** An astute, if sometimes erratic, politician in foreign and domestic policy, Elizabeth was one of the most successful rulers of the sixteenth century.

National Portrait Gallery, London/SuperStock.

Sixteenth-century Puritans were not separatists, however. They worked through Parliament to create an alternative national church of semi-autonomous congregations governed by representative presbyteries (hence, Presbyterians), following the model of Calvin and Geneva. The more extreme Puritans wanted every congregation to be autonomous, a law unto itself, with no higher control. They came to be known as Congregationalists. Elizabeth refused to tolerate this group, whose views she considered subversive.

Deterioration of Relations with Spain

A series of events led inexorably to war between England and Spain, despite the sincere desires of both Philip II and Elizabeth to avoid it. Following Spain's victory at Lepanto in 1571, England signed a mutual defense pact with France. Also in the 1570s, Elizabeth's famous seamen, John Hawkins (1532–1595) and Sir Francis Drake (?1545–1596), began to prey regularly on Spanish shipping in the Americas. Drake's circumnavigation of the globe between 1577 and 1580 was one in a series of dramatic demonstrations of English ascendancy on the high seas. In 1585 Elizabeth signed a treaty that committed English soldiers to the Netherlands. These events made a tinderbox of English-Spanish relations. The spark that finally touched it off was Elizabeth's reluctant execution of Mary, Queen of Scots (1542–1587) on February 18, 1587, for complicity in a plot to assassinate Elizabeth. Philip II ordered his Armada to make ready.

On May 30, 1588, a mighty fleet of 130 ships bearing 25,000 sailors and soldiers under the command of the Duke of Medina-Sidonia set sail for England. But the day belonged completely to the English. The barges that were to transport Spanish soldiers from the galleons onto English shores were prevented from leaving Calais and Dunkirk. The swifter English and Netherlands ships, assisted by an "English wind," dispersed the waiting Spanish fleet, over a third of which never returned to Spain. The Armada's defeat gave heart to Protestant resistance everywhere. Spain never fully recovered from it. By the time of Philip's death on September 13, 1598, his forces had been rebuffed by the French and the Dutch. His seventeenth-century successors were all inferior leaders who never knew responsibilities equal to Philip's; nor did Spain ever again know such imperial grandeur. The French soon dominated the Continent, while the Dutch and the English whittled away Spain's overseas empire.

Elizabeth died on March 23, 1603, leaving behind her a strong nation poised to expand into a global empire.

THE THIRTY YEARS' WAR (1618–1648)

The Thirty Years' War in the Holy Roman Empire was the last and most destructive of the wars of religion. Religious and political differences had long set Catholics against Protestants and Calvinists against Lutherans. What made the Thirty Years'

War so devastating was the now entrenched hatred of the various sides and their seeming determination to sacrifice all for their territorial sovereignty and religious beliefs. As the conflicts multiplied, virtually every major European land became involved either directly or indirectly. When the hostilities ended in 1648, the peace terms shaped much of the map of northern Europe as we know it today (see Map. 16–6).

Fragmented German

During the second half of the sixteenth century, Germany was an almost ungovernable land of 360 autonomous political entities. The Peace of Augsburg (1555) had given each a significant degree of sovereignty within its own borders. Each levied its own tolls and tariffs and coined its own money, practices that made land travel and trade between the various regions difficult, if not impossible. Many of these little "states" also had great power pretensions. Political decentralization and fragmentation characterized Germany as the seventeenth century opened; it was not a unified nation like Spain, England, or even strife-torn France.

Religious Division

Religious conflict accentuated the international and internal political divisions (see Map 16–6). The Holy Roman Empire was about equally divided between Catholics and Protestants, the latter having perhaps a slight numerical edge by 1600 (see Map 16–7). The terms of the Peace of Augsburg (1555) had attempted to freeze the territorial holdings of the Lutherans and the Catholics. In the intervening years, however, the Lutherans had gained political control in many Catholic areas, as had the Catholics in a few previously Lutheran areas. There was also religious strife between liberal and conservative Lutherans and between Lutherans and the growing numbers of Calvinists.

As elsewhere in Europe, Calvinism was the political and religious leaven within the Holy Roman Empire. Unrecognized as a legal religion by the Peace of Augsburg, Calvinism established a strong foothold within the empire when Elector Frederick III (r. 1559–1576), a devout convert to Calvinism, made it the official religion within the Palatinate in 1559. By 1609 Palatine Calvinists headed a Protestant defensive alliance supported by Spain's sixteenth-century enemies: England, France, and the Netherlands.

If the Calvinists were active within the Holy Roman Empire, so also were their Catholic counterparts, the Jesuits. Staunchly Catholic Bavaria, supported by Spain, became militarily and ideologically for the Counter-Reformation what the Palatinate was for Protestantism. From Bavaria, the Jesuits launched successful missions throughout the empire. In 1609 Maximilian, Duke of Bavaria (1573–1651), organized a Catholic League to counter a new Protestant alliance that had been formed by the Calvinist Elector Palatine, Frederick IV (r. 1583–1610). When the league fielded a great army under the command of Jean't Senclaes, Count of Tilly, (1559–1632), the stage was set, internally and internationally, for the Thirty

MAP 16–6 The Holy Roman Empire ca. 1618.   On the eve of the Thirty Years' War the empire was politically and religiously fragmented, as this somewhat simplified map reveals. Lutherans dominated the north and Catholics the south, while Calvinists controlled the United Provinces and the Palatinate and also had an important presence in Switzerland and Brandenburg.

Years' War, the worst European catastrophe since the Black Death of the fourteenth century.

The Treaty of Westphalia   In 1648 all hostilities within the Holy Roman Empire were brought to an end by the Treaty of Westphalia. It firmly reasserted the major feature of the religious settlement of the Peace of Augsburg (1555), as rulers were again permitted to determine the religion of their lands. The treaty also gave the Calvinists their long-sought legal recognition while still denying it to sectarians. The independence of the Swiss Confederacy and the United Provinces of Holland, long recognized in fact, now became law.

By confirming the territorial sovereignty of Germany's many political entities, the Treaty of Westphalia perpetuated German division and political weakness into the modern period. However, two German states attained international significance during the seventeenth century: Austria and Brandenburg-Prussia. The petty regionalism within the

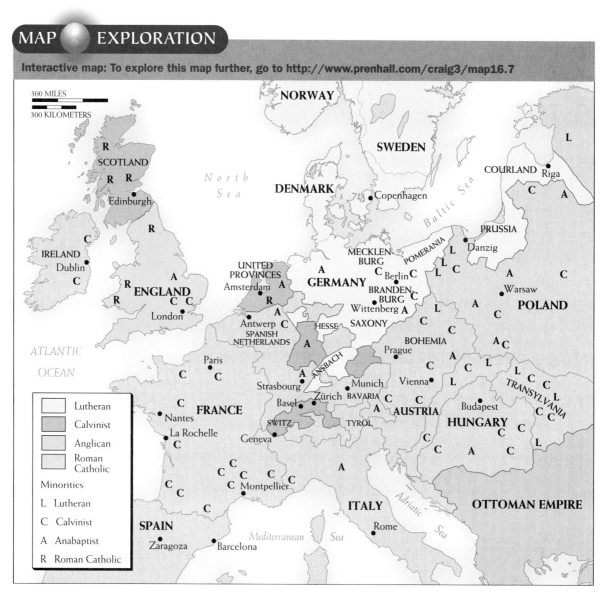

Interactive map: To explore this map further, go to http://www.prenhall.com/craig3/map16.7

MAP 16–7 Religious Division ca. 1600. By 1600 few could expect Christians to return to a uniform religious allegiance. In Spain and southern Italy Catholicism remained relatively unchallenged, but note the existence elsewhere of large religious minorities, both Catholic and Protestant.

empire also reflected on a small scale the drift of larger European politics. During the seventeenth century distinctive nation-states, each with its own political, cultural, and religious identity, reached maturity and firmly established the competitive nationalism of the modern world.

Superstition and Enlightenment: The Battle Within

Religious reform and warfare permanently changed religious institutions in major European lands. They also moved intellectuals to rethink human nature and society. One side of that

reconsideration was dark and cynical, perhaps because the peak years of religious warfare had also been those of the great European witch hunts. Another side, however, was brilliantly skeptical and constructive, reflecting the growing scientific movement of the years between 1500 and 1700.

WITCH HUNTS AND PANIC

Nowhere is the dark side of early modern thought and culture better seen than in the witch hunts and panics that erupted in almost every Western land. Between 1400 and 1700, courts sentenced an estimated 70,000 to 100,000 people to death for harmful magic (*maleficium*) and diabolical witchcraft. In addition to inflicting

OVERVIEW   The Religious Divisions of Europe

The Reformation permanently shattered the religious unity of Western Europe that had existed since the fifth century C.E. It also gave rise to more than a century of warfare, in which Catholics fought Protestants, and Protestants fought each other all in the name of faith. By 1648 when the Treaty of Westphalia ended the Thirty Years' War, Europe remained divided into regions that were mostly Catholic, those that were mostly Protestant, and those areas with large religious minorities. Most of these divisions have persisted to the present day.

Country	Religion
Scotland	Calvinist
England	Protestant (Anglicans, Calvinists, and Anabaptists); a declining Catholic minority
Ireland	Mostly Catholic but with a Protestant minority (Anglicans and Calvinists) mainly in the north
France	Catholic, but with substantial numbers of Calvinists
Belgium	Catholic
Netherlands	A Calvinist majority, but with a large Catholic minority
Spain	Catholic
Portugal	Catholic
Sandinavia	Lutheran
Switzerland	Almost evenly divided between Catholics and Protestants (both Calvinists and Lutherans)
Italy	Catholic
Austria	Catholic
Germany	The north was predominately Protestant (Lutheran, Calvinist, Anabaptist); the south and the Rhineland were mostly Catholic; but each area had religious minorities
Hungary	Mostly Catholic, but with a large Calvinist minority
Poland	Catholic
Lithuania	Catholic
Latvia	Lutheran
Estonia	Lutheran
Croatia	Catholic
Slovenia	Catholic
Bohemia (modern Czech Republic)	Catholic
Slovakia	Catholic

harm on their neighbors, witches were said to attend mass meetings known as *sabbats*, to which they were believed to fly. They were also accused of indulging in sexual orgies with the devil, who appeared in animal form, most often as a he-goat. Still other charges against them were cannibalism (especially the devouring of small Christian children) and a variety of ritual acts and practices, often sexual, that denied or perverted Christian beliefs.

Why did great witch panics occur in the second half of the sixteenth and early seventeenth centuries? The misfortune created by religious division and warfare were major factors. Some argue that the Reformation spurred the panics by ridiculing the traditional church defenses against the devil and demons, compelling people to protect themselves by searching out and executing witches. Political consolidation by secular governments

and the papacy probably played a greater role, with both aggressively conforming their realms and eliminating competition for the loyalty of their subjects.

Village Origins   The roots of witch beliefs are found in both popular and elite culture. In village societies, feared and respected "cunning folk" helped people cope with natural disasters and disabilities by magical means. For local people, these were important services that kept village life moving forward in times of calamity.

The possession of magical powers, for good or ill, made one an important person within village society. Claims to such powers were often made by those who were most in need of security and influence, particularly women, and especially old, impoverished single or widowed women. In village society witch beliefs may also have been a way to defy urban Christian society's attempts to impose its orthodox beliefs, laws, and institutions on the countryside. Under church persecution local fertility cults, whose customary semipagan practices were intended to ensure good harvests, acquired the features of diabolical witchcraft.

Influence of the Clergy   Popular belief in magic was the essential foundation of the witch hunts. Had ordinary people not believed that "gifted persons" could help or harm by magical means, and had they not been willing to make accusations against them, the hunts would never have occurred. The contribution of learned, Christian society was equally great. The Christian clergy also practiced magic, that of the holy sacraments, transforming bread and wine into the body and blood of Christ, and eternal punishments for sins into temporal ones. And they also exorcised demons.

In the late thirteenth century the church declared its magic the only legitimate magic. Since such power was not human, the theologians reasoned, it came either from God or from the devil.

That from God was properly exercised within and by the church. Any who practiced magic outside and against the church did so on behalf of the devil. From such reasoning grew allegations of "pacts" between non-Christian magicians and Satan. Attacking accused witches became a way for the church to extend its spiritual hegemony, especially in new areas being conformed by church and state to higher Christian society. As spiritual authorities revered and feared by villagers or townspeople, local cunning folk posed an obstacle to that mission. To accuse, try, and execute witches was a declaration of moral and political authority over a village or territory.

Why Women?   Roughly 80 percent of the victims of witch hunts were women, most single and between forty-five and sixty years of age. This suggests that misogyny fueled the witch hunts. Inspired by male hatred and sexual fear of women, and occurring at a time when women were also breaking out from under male control, witch hunts were simply a conspiracy of males against females.

Older single women claiming supernatural powers, may, however, have been vulnerable for more basic social reasons. As a dependent social group ever in need of public assistance, they were natural targets for the peculiar "social engineering" of the witch hunts. Because of their economic straits, more women than men laid claim to the supernatural powers that made them influential in village society. Such women thus found themselves on the front lines in disproportionate numbers when the church declared war against those who practiced magic without its special blessing. Also, many of these women were midwives an activity that which associated them with the deaths of beloved mothers and infants during childbirth; this misfortune made them targets of local resentment and accusations. Both the church and their neighbors were prepared to think and say the worst about them, a deadly combination.

End of the Witch Hunts   Many factors helped end the witch hunts. The emergence of a more scientific worldview made it difficult to believe in the powers of witches. In the seventeenth century mind and matter came to be viewed as two independent realities, making it harder to believe that words and thoughts could impact physical things. A witch's curse was merely words. With advances in medicine, the rise of insurance companies, and the availability of lawyers, people could protect themselves when physical affliction and natural calamity struck. Witch hunts also tended to get out of hand. Tortured witches sometimes alleged having seen leading townspeople at sabbats; even the judges themselves! At this point the trials ceased to serve the interests of those conducting them. They not only became dysfunctional but threatened anarchy as well.

WRITERS AND PHILOSOPHERS

By the end of the sixteenth century, many could no longer embrace either old Catholic or new Protestant absolutes. Intellectually as well as politically, the seventeenth century would be a period of transition, one already well prepared by the humanists and scientists of the Renaissance and post-Renaissance (see Chapter 22), who reacted strongly against medieval intellectual traditions.

The writers and philosophers of the late sixteenth and the seventeenth centuries were aware that they lived in a period of transition. Some embraced the emerging new science wholeheartedly (Hobbes and Locke), some tried to straddle the two ages (Cervantes and Shakespeare), and still others ignored or opposed the new developments that seemed mortally to threaten traditional values (Pascal).

Miguel de Cervantes Saavedra   Spanish literature of the sixteenth and seventeenth centuries was influenced by the peculiar religious and political history of Spain in this period. Spain was dominated by the Catholic Church, whose piety was strongly promoted by the state. The intertwining of Catholic piety and Spanish political power underlay literary preoccupation with medieval chivalric virtues—in particular, honor and loyalty.

Generally acknowledged to be the greatest Spanish writer of all time, Cervantes (1547–1616) was preoccupied in his work with the strengths and weaknesses of religious idealism. He was the son of a nomadic physician. Having received only a smattering of formal education, he educated himself by insatiable reading in vernacular literature and immersion in the school of life. As a young man, he worked in Rome for a Spanish cardinal. In 1570 he became a soldier and was decorated for gallantry at Lepanto (1571). He conceived and began to write his most famous work, *Don Quixote*, in 1603, while languishing in prison after conviction for theft.

The first part of *Don Quixote* appeared in 1605, and a second part in 1615. If, as many argue, the intent of this work was to satirize the chivalric romances so popular in Spain, Cervantes failed to conceal his deep affection for the character he had created as an object of ridicule, Don Quixote. Don Quixote, a none-too-stable middle-aged man, is driven mad by reading too many chivalric romances. He comes to believe that he is an aspirant to knighthood and must prove his worthiness. To this end, he acquires a rusty suit of armor, mounts an aged horse, and chooses for his inspiration a quite unworthy peasant girl whom he fancies to be a noble lady to whom he can, with honor, dedicate his life.

Don Quixote's foil in the story—Sancho Panza, a clever, worldly wise peasant who serves as his squire—watches with bemused skepticism, but also with genuine sympathy, as his lord does battle with a windmill (which he mistakes for a dragon) and repeatedly makes a fool of himself as he gallops across the countryside. The story ends tragically with Don Quixote's humiliating defeat by a well-meaning friend, who, disguised as a knight, bests Don Quixote in combat and forces him to renounce his quest for knighthood. The humiliated Don Quixote does not, however,

⋀ **Miguel de Cervantes Saavedra (1547–1616),** the author of Don Quixote, considered by many to be Spain's greatest writer. Art Resource, N.Y.

come to his senses as a result. He returns sadly to his village to die a shamed and broken-hearted old man.

Throughout *Don Quixote*, Cervantes juxtaposed the down-to-earth realism of Sancho Panza with the old-fashioned religious idealism of Don Quixote. Cervantes admired the one as much as the other. He wanted his readers to remember that to be truly happy, men and women need dreams, even impossible ones, just as much as a sense of reality.

William Shakespeare　There is much less factual knowledge about William Shakespeare (1564–1616), the greatest playwright in the English language, than one would expect of such an important figure. He apparently worked as a schoolteacher for a time and in this capacity acquired his broad knowledge of Renaissance learning and literature. His work shows none of the Puritan distress over worldliness. He took the new commercialism and the bawdy pleasures of the Elizabethan Age in stride and with amusement. In politics and religion, he was a man of his time and not inclined to offend his queen.

That Shakespeare was interested in politics is apparent from his history plays and the references to contemporary political events that fill all his plays. He seems to have viewed government simply, however, through the character of the individual ruler, whether Richard III or Elizabeth Tudor, not in terms of ideal systems or social goals. By modern standards he was a political conservative, accepting the social rankings and the power structure of his day and demonstrating unquestioned patriotism.

Shakespeare knew the theater as one who participated in every phase of its life. A member and principal dramatist of a famous company of actors known as the King's Men, he was a playwright, actor, and part owner of a theater. His work brought together in an original synthesis the best past and current achievements in the dramatic arts. He particularly mastered the psychology of human motivation and passion and had a unique talent for psychological penetration.

Shakespeare wrote histories, comedies, and tragedies. The tragedies are considered his unique achievement. Four of these were written within a three-year period: *Hamlet* (1603), *Othello* (1604), *King Lear* (1605), and *Macbeth* (1606). The most original of the tragedies, *Romeo and Juliet* (1597), transformed an old popular story into a moving drama of "star-cross'd lovers."

In his lifetime and ever since, Shakespeare has been immensely popular with both audiences and readers. As Ben Jonson (1572–1637), a contemporary classical dramatist who created his own school of poets, put it in a tribute affixed to the *First Folio* edition of Shakespeare's plays (1623): "He was not of an age, but for all time."

Blaise Pascal　Blaise Pascal (1623–1662) was a French mathematician and a physical scientist widely acclaimed by his contemporaries. Torn between the continuing dogmatism and the

new skepticism of the seventeenth century, he aspired to write a work that would refute two groups: the Jesuits, whose casuistry (i.e., confessional tactics designed to minimize and even excuse sinful acts) he considered a distortion of Christian teaching, and the skeptics, who either denied religion altogether (atheists) or accepted it only as it conformed to reason (deists). Pascal never realized such a definitive work, and his views on these matters exist only in piecemeal form. He wrote against the Jesuits in his *Provincial Letters* (1656–1657), and he left behind a provocative collection of reflections on humankind and religion that was published posthumously under the title *Pensées*.

Pascal was early influenced by the Jansenists, seventeenth-century Catholic opponents of the Jesuits. Although good Catholics, the Jansenists shared with the Calvinists Saint Augustine's belief in the total sinfulness of human beings, their eternal predestination by God, and their complete dependence on faith and grace for knowledge of God and salvation.

Pascal believed that reason and science, although attesting to human dignity, remained of no avail in religion. Here only the reasons of the heart and a "leap of faith" could prevail. Pascal saw two essential truths in the Christian religion: A loving God, worthy of human attainment, exists, and human beings, because they are corrupted in nature, are utterly unworthy of God. Pascal believed that the atheists and deists of the age had spurned the lesson of reason. For him, rational analysis of the human condition attested to humankind's utter mortality and corruption and exposed the weakness of reason itself in resolving the problems of human nature and destiny. Reason should rather drive those who truly heed it to faith and dependence on divine grace.

Pascal made a famous wager with the skeptics. It is a better bet, he argued, to believe that God exists and to stake everything on his promised mercy than not to do so; if God does exist, everything will be gained by the believer, whereas the loss incurred by having believed in God should he prove not to exist is, by comparison, very slight.

Pascal was convinced that belief in God measurably improved earthly life psychologically and disciplined it morally, regardless of whether God proved in the end to exist. He thought that great danger lay in the surrender of traditional religious values. Pascal urged his contemporaries to seek self-understanding by "learned ignorance" and to discover humankind's greatness by recognizing its misery. Thereby he hoped to counter what he believed to be the false optimism of the new rationalism and science.

Baruch Spinoza　The most controversial thinker of the seventeenth century was Baruch Spinoza (1632–1677), the son of a Jewish merchant of Amsterdam. Spinoza's philosophy caused his excommunication by his own synagogue in 1656. In 1670 he published his *Treatise on Religious and Political Philosophy*, a work that criticized the dogmatism of Dutch Calvinists and championed freedom of thought. During his lifetime, both Jews and Protestants attacked him as an atheist.

Spinoza's most influential writing, *Ethics*, appeared after his death in 1677. Religious leaders universally condemned it for its apparent espousal of pantheism. God and nature were so closely identified by Spinoza that little room seemed left either for divine revelation in Scripture or for the personal immortality of the soul, denials equally repugnant to Jews and to Christians.

The most controversial part of *Ethics* deals with the nature of substance and of God. According to Spinoza there is only one substance, which is self-caused, free, and infinite, and God is that substance. From this definition, it follows that everything that exists is in God and cannot even be conceived of apart from him. Such a doctrine is not literally pantheistic, because God is still seen to be more than the created world that he, as primal substance, embraces. Nonetheless, in Spinoza's view, statements about the natural world are also statements about divine nature. Mind and matter are seen to be extensions of the infinite substance of God; what transpires in the world of humankind and nature is a necessary outpouring of the Divine.

Such teaching clearly ran the danger of portraying the world as eternal and human actions as unfree and inevitable, the expression of a divine fatalism. Such points of view had been considered heresies by Jews and Christians because these views deny the creation of the world by God and destroy any voluntary basis for personal reward and punishment.

Thomas Hobbes   Thomas Hobbes (1588–1679) was the most original political philosopher of the seventeenth century. Although he never broke with the Church of England, he came to share basic Calvinist beliefs, especially the low view of human nature and the ideal of a commonwealth based on a covenant, both of which find eloquent expression in his political philosophy.

Hobbes was an urbane and much traveled man and one of the most enthusiastic supporters of the new scientific movement. During the 1630s he visited Paris, where he came to know Descartes; after the outbreak of the Puritan Revolution (see Chapter 20) in 1640, he lived as an exile in Paris until 1651. Hobbes also spent time with Galileo (see Chapter 22) in Italy and took a special interest in the works of William Harvey. Harvey was a physiologist famed for the discovery of how blood circulated through the body; his scientific writings influenced Hobbes's own tracts on bodily motions.

Hobbes was driven to the vocation of political philosophy by the English Civil War (see Chapter 20). In 1651 his *Leviathan* appeared. Its subject was the political consequences of human passions, and its originality lay in (1) its making natural law, rather than common law (i.e., custom or precedent), the basis of all positive law, and (2) its defense of a representative theory of absolute authority against the theory of the divine right of kings. Hobbes maintained that statute law found its justification only as an expression of the law of nature and that rulers derived their authority from the consent of the people.

Hobbes viewed humankind and society in a thoroughly materialistic and mechanical way. Human beings are defined as a collection of material particles in motion. All their psychological processes begin with and are derived from bare sensation, and all their motivations are egotistical, intended to increase pleasure and minimize pain.

Despite this seemingly low estimate of human beings, Hobbes believed much could be accomplished by the reasoned use of science. All was contingent, however, on the correct use of that greatest of all human powers, one compounded of the powers of most people: the commonwealth, in which people are united by their consent in one all-powerful person.

The key to Hobbes' political philosophy is a brilliant myth of the original state of humankind. According to this myth, human beings in the natural state are generally inclined to a "perpetual and restless desire of power after power that ceases only in death."[4] As all people desire—and in the state of nature have a natural right to—everything, their equality breeds enmity, competition, and diffidence, and the desire for glory begets perpetual quarreling—"a war of every man against every man."[5]

Whereas earlier and later philosophers saw the original human state as a paradise from which humankind had fallen, Hobbes saw it as a corruption from which only society had delivered people. Contrary to the views of Aristotle and of Christian thinkers like Thomas Aquinas, Hobbes saw human beings not as sociable, political animals, but as self-centered beasts, laws unto themselves, utterly without a master unless one is imposed by force.

According to Hobbes, people escape the impossible state of nature only by entering a social contract that creates a commonwealth tightly ruled by law and order. The social contract obliges every person, for the sake of peace and self-defense, to agree to set aside personal rights to all things. We should impose restrictions on the liberty of others only to the degree that we would allow others to restrict our own.

Because words and promises are insufficient to guarantee this state, the social contract also establishes the coercive force necessary to compel compliance with the covenant. Hobbes believed that the dangers of anarchy were far greater than those of tyranny, and he conceived of the ruler's power as absolute and unlimited. There is no room in Hobbes's political philosophy for political protest in the name of individual conscience, nor for resistance to legitimate authority by private individuals—features of *Leviathan* criticized by his contemporary Catholics and Puritans alike.

---

[4] *Leviathan*, Parts I and II, ed. by H. W. Schneider (Indianapolis, IN: Bobbs-Merrill, 1958), p. 86.
[5] Ibid., p. 106.

John Locke   John Locke (1632–1704) has proved to be the most influential political thinker of the seventeenth century.[6] His political philosophy came to be embodied in the so-called Glorious Revolution of 1688–1689 (Chapter 20). Although he was not as original as Hobbes, his political writings were a major source of the later Enlightenment criticism of absolutism, and they gave inspiration to both the American and French Revolutions.

Locke's two most famous works are the *Essay Concerning Human Understanding* (1690) (discussed in Chapter 22) and *Two Treatises of Government* (1690). Locke wrote *Two Treatises of Government* against the argument that rulers were absolute in their power. Rulers, Locke argued, remain bound to the law of nature, which is the voice of reason, teaching that "all mankind [are] equal and independent, [and] no one ought to harm another in his life, health, liberty, or possessions,"[7] inas-

[6] Locke's scientific writings are discussed in Chapter 24.

much as all human beings are the images and property of God. According to Locke, people enter social contracts, empowering legislatures and monarchs to "umpire" their disputes, precisely to preserve their natural rights, and not to give rulers an absolute power over them.

"Whenever that end [namely, the preservation of life, liberty, and property for which power is given to rulers by a commonwealth] is manifestly neglected or opposed, the trust must necessarily be forfeited and the power devolved into the hands of those that gave it, who may place it anew where they think best for their safety and security."[8] From Locke's point of view, absolute monarchy was "inconsistent" with civil society and could be "no form of civil government at all."[9]

[7] *The Second Treatise of Government*, ed. by T. P. Peardon (Indianapolis, IN: Bobbs-Merrill, 1952), chap. 2, sects. 4–6, pp. 4–6.
[8] Ibid., chap. 13, sect. 149, p. 84.
[9] Ibid.

Ships of a Portuguese Explorer.

Summary

Voyages of Discovery   In the late fifteenth century, Europe began to expand around the globe. Driven by both mercenary and religious motives, the Portuguese pioneered a sea route around Africa to India and the Far East, and the Spanish discovered the Americas. Social, political, and biological consequences were immense for Europeans, Native Americans, Africans, and Asians. In time, a truly global world would emerge.

The Reformation   The Reformation began in Germany with Martin Luther's attack on indulgences in 1517. Despite the opposition to the Reformation of Emperor Charles V, Luther had the support of many German princes. The Reformation shattered the religious unity of Europe. In Switzerland, Zwingli and Calvin launched their own versions of Protestantism. In England, Henry VIII repudiated papal authority when the pope refused to grant him a divorce. The different protestant sects were often as hostile to each other as they were to Catholicism. The Reformation also led to far-reaching changes in religious practices and social attitudes, including steps toward the advancement of women.

The Roman Catholic Church also acted to reform itself. The Council of Trent tightened church discipline and reaffirmed traditional doctrine. The Jesuits converted many Protestants back to Catholicism.

The Wars of Religion   The religious divisions of Europe led to more than a century of warfare from the 1520s to 1648. The chief battlegrounds were in France, the Netherlands, and Germany. When the Thirty Years' War ended in 1648, Europe was permanently divided into Catholic and Protestant areas.

Superstition and Enlightenment   The Reformation led to both dark and constructive views of human nature. Perhaps the darkest view was the witch crazes that erupted across Europe. Thousands of innocent people, mostly women, were persecuted and executed as witches between 1400 and 1700 by both Catholic and Protestant authorities.

In literature and philosophy, however, these years witnessed an outpouring of creative thinking. Among the greatest writers of the age were Cervantes, Shakespeare, Pascal, Spinoza, Hobbes, and Locke.

Review Questions

1. What impact did European expansion have on the societies of both the Old and New Worlds?

2. What were the main problems of the church that contributed to the Protestant Reformation? Why was the church unable to suppress dissent as it had earlier?

3. How did the theologies of Luther, Zwingli, and Calvin differ? Were their differences only religious, or did they have political consequences for the Reformation as well?

4. Why did the Reformation begin in Germany and not in France, Italy, England, or Spain?

5. What was the Catholic Reformation? Did the Council of Trent alter the character of traditional Catholicism?

6. Why did Henry VIII break with the Catholic Church? Was the "new" religion he established really Protestant?

7. Were the wars of religion really over religion? Explain.

8. Henry of Navarre (later Henry IV of France), Elizabeth I, and William of Orange have been called *politiques*. What does that term mean, and how might it apply to each?

9. Why was England more successful than other lands in resolving its internal political and religious divisions peacefully during the sixteenth and seventeenth centuries?

10. "The Thirty Years' War is the outstanding example in European history of meaningless conflict." Evaluate this statement and provide specific reasons.

Key Terms

Counter-Reformation   (p. 454)

Diet of Worms   (p. 447)

Huguenot   (p. 459)

indulgences   (p. 445)

ninety-five theses   (p. 446)

Reformation   (p. 443)

transubstantiation   (p. 450, 456)

Documents CD-ROM

Renaissance and Reformation in Europe

13.4 Martin Luther

13.5 Luther vs. Erasmus: A Reformer's Attack on Free Will

13.6 John Calvin and the Genevan Reformation

13.7 Council of Trent: The Catholic-Reformation

13.8 The Society of Jesus

European Explorations and Expansion

14.2 Vasco da Gama, Journey to India

14.4 "Cut Off Their Ears, Hands and Noses!": Gaspar Correa

14.5 Christopher Columbus

14.9 The Prospects of Christian Conversion: Saint Francis Xavier

From Old Regime to Revolution

18.1 "The Mortal God": Leviathan (1651)

NOTE: *To learn more about the topics in this chapter, see the Suggested Readings at the end of the book.*

CHRISTIANITY

Christianity is based on the teaching of Jesus of Nazareth, a Jew who lived in Palestine during the Roman occupation. His simple message of faith in God and self-sacrificial love of one's neighbor attracted many people. The Roman authorities, perceiving his large following as a threat, crucifed him. After Jesus' crucifixion, his followers proclaimed that he had been resurrected from the dead and that he would return in glory, to defeat sin, death, and the devil, and take all true believers with him to heaven—a radical vision of judgment and immortality that has driven Christianity's appeal since its inception. In the teachings of the early church, Jesus became the Christ, the son of God, the long-awaited Messiah of Jewish prophecy. His followers called themselves Christians.

Christianity proclaimed the very incarnation of God in a man, the visible presence of eternity in time. According to early Christian teaching, the power of God's incarnation in Jesus lived on in the preaching and sacraments of the church under the guidance of the Holy Spirit. According to the Christian message, in Jesus, eternity has made itself accessible to every person here and now and forevermore.

The new religion attracted both the poor and powerless and the socially rising and well-to-do. For some, the gospel of Jesus promised a better material life. For others, it imparted a sense of spiritual self-worth regardless of one's place or prospects in society.

In the late second century the Romans began persecuting Christians as "heretics" (because of their rejection of the traditional Roman gods) and as social revolutionaries (for their loyalty to a lord higher than the emperor of Rome). At the same time dissenting Christians, particularly sects claiming direct spiritual knowledge of God apart from Scripture, internally divided the young church, To meet these challenges the church established effective weapons against state terrorism and Christian heresy: an ordained clergy, a hierarchical church organization, orthodox creeds, and a biblical canon (the New Testament). Christianity not only gained legal status within the Roman Empire, but also, by the fourth century, most favored religious status thanks to Emperor Constantine's embrace of it.

After the fall of the Western Roman Empire in the fifth century C.E., Christianity became one of history's great success stories. Aided by the enterprise of its popes and the example of its monks, the church cultivated an appealing lay piety centered around the Lord's Prayer, the Apostles' Creed, veneration of the Virgin, and the sacrament of the Eucharist. Clergy became both royal teachers and bureaucrats within the kingdom of the Franks. Despite a growing schism between the Eastern (Byzantine) and Western churches, and a final split in 1054, by 1000 the church held real economic and political power. In the eleventh century reform-minded prelates put an end to presumptuous secular interference in its most intimate spiritual affairs by ending the lay investiture of clergy in their spiritual offices. For several centuries thereafter the church remained a formidable international force, able to challenge kings and emperors and inspire crusades to the Holy Land.

By the fifteenth century the new states of Europe had stripped the church of much of its political power. It was thereafter progressively confined to spiritual and moral authority. Christianity's

Pentecost. This exquisite enamel plaque, from the Mosan school that flourished in France in the eleventh and twelfth centuries, shows the descent of the Holy Spirit upon the apostles, fifty days after the resurrection of Jesus, on the ancient Jewish festival called the "feast of weeks," or Pentecost.
Courtesy Metropolitan Museum of ART.

Female Bishop. Women are entering the ministry and priesthood of many Christian denominations. The first woman bishop of the Episcopal Church of North America is here shown consecrating the Eucharist. The Church of England has also voted to admit women to the priesthood.
Ira Wyman/Corbis/Sygma.

greatest struggles ever since have been not with kings and emperors over political power, but with materialistic philosophies and worldly ideologies, matters of spiritual and moral hegemony within an increasingly pluralistic and secular world. Since the sixteenth century a succession of humanists, skeptics, Deists, Rationalists, Marxists, Freudians, Darwinians, and atheists have attempted to explain away some of traditional Christianity's most basic teachings. In addition, the church has endured major internal upheavals. After the Protestant Reformation (1517–1555) made the Bible widely available to the laity, the possibilities for internal criticism of Christianity multiplied geometrically. Beginning with the split between Lutherans and Zwinglians in the 1520s, Protestant Christianity has fragmented into hundreds of sects each claiming to have the true interpretation of Scripture. The Roman Catholic church, by contrast, has maintained its unity and ministry throughout perilous times, although present-day discontent with papal authority threatens the modern Catholic church almost as seriously as the Protestant Reformation once did.

Christianity has remained remarkably resilient. It possesses a simple, almost magically appealing gospel of faith and love in and through Jesus. In a present-day world whose religious needs and passions still run deep, evangelical Christianity has experienced a remarkable revival. The Roman Catholic church, still troubled by challenges to papal authority, has become more pluralistic than in earlier periods. The pope has become a world figure, traveling to all continents to represent the church and advance its position on issues of public and private morality. A major ecumenical movement emerging in the 1960s has promoted unprecedented cooperation among evangelical Christian denominations. Everywhere Christians of all stripes are politically active, spreading their divine, moral, and social messages. Meanwhile, old hot-button issues, such as the ordination of women, are being overtaken by new ones, particularly the marriage of gay men and women and the removal of clergy who do not maintain the moral discipline of their holy orders.

♦ Over the century what have been some of the chief factors attracting people to Christianity?

♦ What forces have led to disunity among Christians in the past; what factors cause tensions among modern Christians?

17

Africa
ca. 1000–1800

◄ HEAD OF A KING, FROM IFE. ca. thirteenth century C.E. The serene classicism of Ife art is equaled only by that of ancient Greece.

Head of a King, from Ife. c. thirteenth Century C.E. Brass, height $11^{7}/_{16}$" (29 cm).© Frank Willett.

Africa, 1000–1800

Developments in African history from 1000 to 1800 varied markedly by region. Because of trade, the North African coast and the Sahel, because of trade, were oriented toward the Mediterranean and the *dar-al-Islam*. The East African coast, also under Islamic influence was integrated into the Indian Ocean basin, while Sub-Saharan Africa was culturally diverse. It is important to remember that Africa, unlike China, India, or Japan, is a continent home to many societies with different histories, languages, religions, and cultures. Africa is also much larger than Europe, which some geographers view more as a peninsula of a vast Eurasian continent than as a continent in its own right, and more ethnically and culturally diverse.

Along the Mediterranean, the key new factor in African history at this time was the Ottomans' imperial expansion into Egypt and the Magrehb. Their long hegemony in the Mediterranean, altered the political configuration of the Mediterranean world. Merchants and missionaries carried Islam and Arabian cultural influences across the Sahara from North Africa and the Middle East to the Sudan, where Muslim conversion played a growing social and political role, especially among the ruling elites who profited most from brokering trade between their lands and the Islamic north. Islam provided a shared arena of expression for at least some classes and groups in societies over a vast area from Egypt to Senegambia. In Africa as elsewhere, the successful diffusion of Islam and Arabian culture depended upon their modification through a process of syncretism to create a distinctive African form of Islam faithful to tenets of the religion, but differing in its observances and customs from those of the Arabian cultural sphere, especially in attitudes toward women and relationships between the sexes.

At the same time, most Africans from the Sahara south clung to their older traditions. In central and southern Africa, except along the east coast, and in the West African forests, there was little or no evidence of Islam beyond individual Muslims involved in trade. On the east coast, however, Islam influenced the development of the Swahili culture and language, a

unique blend of African, Indian, and Arabian traditions, and Islamic traders linked the region to India, China, and the Indies. In sub-Saharan Africa, the spread of Islam took place almost entirely through peaceful means.

Along the Atlantic and Indian Ocean coasts of Africa, the key development of the fifteenth century was the appearance of ships from Christian Europe and the traders and missionaries they carried. First the Portuguese and later the Dutch, Spaniards, and other Europeans came by sea in search of commerce and eventually spheres of influence. The strength of African societies and the geographical and ecological dangers to Europeans venturing into the interior meant, however, that most of the trade between the African interior and Europeans on both the east and west coasts remained in the hands of Africans for generations after the first arrival of the Europeans. Even before Europeans themselves penetrated into the interior, however, the trade in slaves, weapons, and gold that they fostered disrupted traditional political and social structures and greatly altered African societies that had not yet even seen a European. The European voyages of discovery of the fifteenth and sixteenth centuries were especially important for Africa, therefore, presaging the continent's involvement in a new, expanding and, by the eighteenth century, European-dominated global trading system. This system generally exploited rather than bolstered African development, as the infamous Atlantic slave trade and the South African experience illustrate.

THINK AHEAD

- Which parts of Africa were most influenced by Islam?

- Where in Africa was Islam concentrated? How did Islam spread? What does this reveal about the relationship between commerce and cultural diffusion?

- What impact did the arrival of Europeans have on African societies?

THE HISTORY OF AFRICA IN THE FIRST HALF OF THE second millennium C.E. varied considerably for different parts of the continent. Many African regions were little influenced by outsiders; others were strongly influenced by Europe and the Islamic world.

The Atlantic slave trade was the major phenomenon that affected almost all of Africa between the fifteenth and nineteenth centuries and is treated in Chapter 18. However, in this chapter we cannot overlook its importance in disrupting and reconfiguring African economies, social organization, and political life

We begin with Africa above the equator, where the influence of Islam increased and where substantial empires and kingdoms developed. Then we discuss west, east, central, and southern Africa and the effects of first Arab-Islamic and then European influence in these regions.

North Africa and Egypt

As we saw in Chapter 13, Egypt and other North African societies played a central role in Islamic and Mediterranean history after 1000 C.E. From Tunisia to Egypt, Sunni religious and political leaders and their Shi'ite, especially Isma'ili, counterparts struggled for the minds of the masses. By the thirteenth century, however, the Shi'ites had become a small minority of the Muslim population of Mediterranean Africa. In Egypt a Sunni revival confirmed the Sunni character of Egyptian religiosity and legal interpretation: In general, a feisty regionalism characterized states, city-states, and tribal groups north of the Sahara and along the lower Nile. No single power controlled them for long. Regionalism persisted even after 1500, when most of North Africa came under the influence—and often direct control—of the Ottoman Empire centered in Istanbul and felt the pressure of Ottoman–European naval rivalry in the Mediterranean.

By 1800 the nominally Ottoman domains from Egypt to Algeria were effectively independent. In Egypt the Ottomans had established direct rule after their defeat of the Mamluks in 1517, but by the seventeenth and eighteenth centuries, power had passed to Egyptian governors descended from the former ruling Mamluks. These Mamluk governors survived until the rise of Muhammad Ali in the wake of the French invasion of 1800 (see Chapter 27). The Mediterranean coastlands between Egypt and Morocco were officially Ottoman provinces, or regencies. By the eighteenth century, however, Algiers was a separate, locally run principality with an economy based on piracy. Tripoli (in modern Libya) was ruled by a family of hereditary, effectively independent rulers, and Tunisia was virtually independent of its nominal Ottoman overlords.

Morocco, ruled by a succession of *Sharifs* (leaders claiming descent from the family of the Prophet Muhammad), was the only North African sultanate to remain fully independent after 1700. The most important *Sharifian* dynasty was that of the Sa'dis (1554–1659). One major reason for Morocco's independence was that its Arab and Berber populations united after 1500 to oppose the Portuguese and the Spaniards.

The Spread of Islam South of the Sahara

Islamic influence in sub-Saharan Africa began as early as the eighth century and by 1800 affected most of the Sudanic belt and the coast of East Africa as far south as modern Zimbabwe. The process was mostly peaceful, gradual, and partial. Islam

⚓ **Feluccas on the Nile.** These lateen-rigged sailing vessels are the traditional riverboats of Egypt and are still in use today.
Hisham F. Ibrahim/Getty Images, Inc.-Photodisc.

The Great Mosque in Timbuktu. This mud and wood building is typical of western Sudanese mosques. The distinctive tower of the mosque was a symbol of the presence of Islam, which came to places like Timbuktu in central and West Africa by way of overland trade routes. Werner Forman/Art Resource, N.Y.

rarely penetrated beyond the ruling or commercial classes and tended to coexist or blend with indigenous ideas and practices. Nevertheless, agents of Islam brought commercial and political changes as well as the Qur'an, new religious practices, and literate culture, which proved as important for subsequent history as any other development. Many innovations, from architecture and technology to intellectual life and administrative practice, depended on writing and literacy, two major bases for developing large-scale societies and cultures.

Comparison of the spread of Islam in West and central Africa with that in East Africa is instructive. In East Africa, Muslim traders moving down the coastline with the ancient monsoon trade routes had begun to "Islamize" ports and coastal regions even before 800 C.E. From the thirteenth century on, Islamic trading communities and city-states developed along the coast from Mogadishu to Kilwa.

By contrast, in the western and central parts of the continent, Islam penetrated south of the Sahara into the Sudan by overland routes, primarily from North Africa and the Nile valley. Yet as in East Africa, its agents were traders, chiefly Berbers who plied the desert routes (see Chapter 5) to trading towns such as Awdaghast on the edge of the Sahel, as early as the eighth century. From there Islam spread south to centers such as Kumbi and beyond, southeast across the Niger, and west

into Senegambia. Another source for the gradual spread of Islam into the central and western Sudan were Egypt and the Nilotic Sudan. Its agents were primarily emigrants from the east seeking new land; migrating Arab tribal groups in particular came west to settle in the central sub-Saharan Sahel.

Some Muslim conversion in the western and central Sudan came early, again virtually always through the agency of Muslim traders. The year 985 marks the first time a West Africa royal court—that of the kingdom of Gao, east of the Niger bend—officially became Muslim (see Chapter 5 and below). The Gao rulers did not, however, try to convert their subjects. By contrast, as we shall see later in the chapter, the rulers of the later kingdom of Ghana long maintained their indigenous traditions even though they traded with Muslims and had Muslim advisors.

From the 1030s zealous militants known as Almoravids (see Chapter 13) began an overt conversion campaign that extended to the western Sahel and Sahara. This movement eventually swept into Ghana's territory, taking first Awdaghast and finally Kumbi in 1076. Thereafter, the forcibly converted Soninke ruling group of Ghana spread Islam among their own populace and farther south in the savannah. Here they converted Mande-speaking traders, who brought Islam south into the forests. Farther west, the Fulbe rulers of Takrur along the Senegal became Muslim in the 1030s and propagated their new faith among their subjects. The Fulbe, or Fulani, remained important carriers of Islam over the next eight centuries as they migrated gradually into new regions as far east as Lake Chad, where some rulers were Muslim as early as 1100.

Major groups in West Africa strongly resisted Islamization, especially the Mossi kingdoms founded in the Volta region at Wagadugu around 1050 and Yatenga about 1170.

Sahelian Empires of the Western and Central Sudan

As we noted in Chapter 5, substantial states had risen in the first millennium C.E. in the Sahel regions just south of the Sahara proper.[1] From about 1000 to 1600, four of these developed into relatively long-lived empires: Ghana, Mali, and Songhai in the western Sudan, and Kanem-Bornu in the central Sudan.

GHANA

Ghana established the model for later empires of the Sahel region of the western Sudan. It was located well north of modern Ghana (and unrelated to it except by name) in the region between the inland Niger Delta and the upper Senegal to the

[1] S. K. and R. J. McIntosh, *Prehistoric Investigations at Jenne, Mali* (1980), pp. 41–59, 434–461; R. Oliver, *The African Experience* (New York: Harper-Collins, 1991), pp. 90–101.

DOCUMENT   **Ghana and Its People in the Mid–Eleventh Century**

The following excerpt is from the geographical work of the Spanish Muslim geographer al-Bakri (d. 1094). In it he describes customs of the ruler and people of the capital of Ghana as he carefully gleaned them from other Arabic sources and travelers (he never visited West Africa himself, it seems).

◆ How did the ruler of Ghana deal with the differing religious groups in his capital?

Ghana is a title given to their kings; the name of the region is Awkar, and their king today, namely in the year 460 [1067–8], is Tanka Manin. ... This Tanka Manin is powerful, rules an enormous kingdom, and possesses great authority.

The city of Ghana consists of two towns situated on a plain. One of these towns, which is inhabited by Muslims, is large and possesses twelve mosques, in one of which they assemble for the Friday prayer. There are salaried imams and muezzins, as well as jurists and scholars. In the environs are wells with sweet water, from which they drink and with which they grow vegetables. The king's town is six miles distant from this one and bears the name of Al-Ghaba. Between these two towns there are continuous habitations. The houses of the inhabitants are of stone and acacia (*sunt*) wood. The king has a palace and a number of domed dwellings all surrounded with an enclosure like a city wall (*sur*). In the king's town, and not far from his court of justice, is a mosque where the Muslims who arrive at his court ... pray. Around the king's town are domed buildings and groves and thickets where the sorcerers of these people, men in charge of the religious cult, live. In them too are their idols and the tombs of their kings. ...

All of them shave their beards, and women shave their heads. The king adorns himself like a woman [wearing necklaces] round his neck and [bracelets] on his forearms, and he puts on a high cap (*tartur*) decorated with gold and wrapped in a turban of fine cotton. He sits in audience or to hear grievances against officials (*mazalim*) in a domed pavilion around which stand ten horses covered with gold-embroidered materials. Behind the king stand ten pages holding shields and swords decorated with gold, and on his right are the sons of the [vassal] kings of his country wearing splendid garments and their hair plaited with gold. The governor of the city sits on the ground before the king and around him are ministers seated likewise. ... When the people who profess the same religion as the king approach him they fall on their knees and sprinkle dust on their heads, for this is their way of greeting him. As for the Muslims, they greet him only by clapping their hands.

Their religion is paganism and the worship of idols (*dakakir*). When their king dies they construct over the place where his tomb will be an enormous dome of saj wood. Then they bring him on a bed covered with a few carpets and cushions and place him beside the dome. At his side they place his ornaments, his weapons, and the vessels from which he used to eat and drink, filled with various kinds of food and beverages.

From J. F. P. Hopkins, trans.; N. Levtzion and J. F. P. Hopkins, eds., *Corpus of Early Arabic Sources for West African History*. Reprinted with permission of Cambridge University Press, pp. 79–80.

---

north. A Ghanaian kingdom originated as early as 400–600 C.E., but Ghana emerged as a regional power only near the end of the first millennium and flourished for about two centuries. Its capital, Kumbi (or Kumbi Saleh), on the desert's edge, was well sited for the Saharan and Sahelian trade networks. Ghana's major population group was the Soninke. (*Ghana* is the Soninke term for "ruler.")

The Ghanaian rulers were matrilineally descended (through the previous king's sister). They ruled through a council of ministers. The reports we have, especially from the eleventh-century Muslim writer al-Bakri (see Document, "Ghana and Its People in the Mid–Eleventh Century."), indicate that the king was supreme judge and held court regularly to hear grievances. The royal ceremonies reported to have been held in Kumbi Saleh were embellished with the full trappings of regal wealth and power appropriate to a king held to be divinely blessed if not semidivine himself.

Ghana's power rested on a solid economic base. Tribute from the empire's many chieftaincies and taxes on royal lands and crops supplemented duties levied on all incoming and outgoing trade. This trade, both north–south between the Sahara and the savannah and especially east–west through the Sahel between Senegambia and more easterly trading towns like Gao on the Niger Bend, involved a variety of goods— notably imported salt, cloth, and metal goods such as copper— probably in exchange for gold and perhaps kola nuts from the south. The regime apparently also controlled the gold (and, presumably, the slave) trade that originated in the savannah to the south and west, in the tributary regions of the Bambuk and Galam regions of the middle Senegal and its southern tributary, the Faleme, and in the Boure region of the upper Niger and its tributaries.

Although the king and court of Ghana did not convert to Islam, they made elaborate arrangements to accommodate

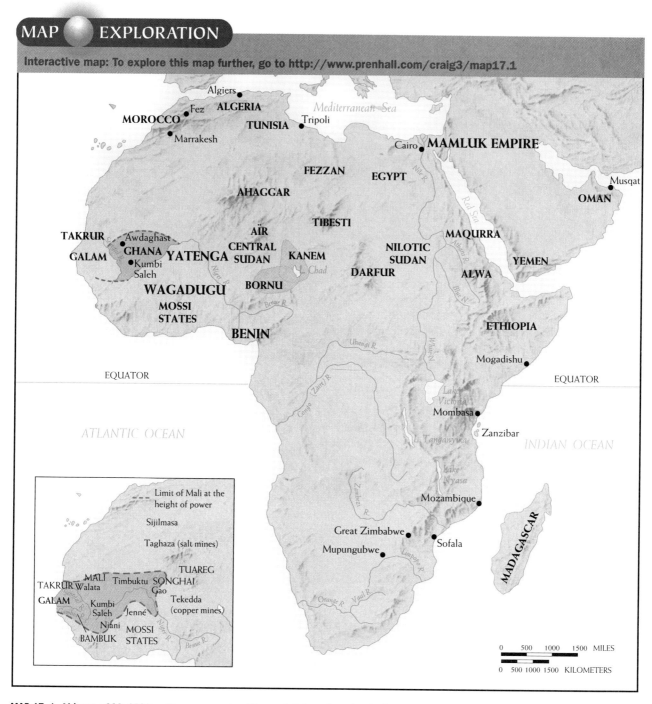

MAP 17–1 Africa ca. 900–1500.   Shown are major cities and states referred to in the text. The main map shows the region of West Africa occupied by the empire of Ghana from ca. 990 to ca. 1180. The inset shows the region occupied by Mali between 1230 and 1450.

Muslim traders and government servants in their own settlement a few miles from the royal preserve in Kumbi Saleh. Muslim traders were prominent in the court, literate Muslims administered the government, and Muslim legists advised the ruler. In Ghana's hierarchical society, slaves were at the bottom; farmers and draftsmen above them; merchants above them; and the king, his court, and the nobility on top.

A huge, well-trained army secured royal control and enabled the kings to extend their sway in the late tenth century to the Atlantic shore and to the south (see Map 17–1). Ghanaian troops captured Awdaghast, the important southern terminus of the trans-Saharan trade route to Morocco, from the Berbers in 992. The empire was, however, vulnerable to attack from the desert fringe, as Almoravid Berber forces proved in 1054 when they took Awdaghast in a single raid.

⚠ **The Great Mosque at Jenne.** Jenne was one of the important commercial centers controlled by the empire of Mali in the 13th and 14th centuries. Ann Stalcup.

Ghana's empire was probably destroyed in the late twelfth century by the anti-Muslim Soso people from the mountains southeast of Kumbi Saleh, a Malinke clan who had long been part of the Ghanaian Empire. Their brief ascendancy between 1180 and 1230 apparently spelled the end of the once great transregional power centered at Kumbi.[2]

MALI

With Ghana's collapse and the Almoravids' failure to build a new empire below the Sahara (largely because of their focus on North Africa), the western Sudan broke up into smaller kingdoms. The former Ghanaian provinces of Mande and Takrur were already independent before 1076, and in the early twelfth century Takrur's control of the Senegal valley and the gold-producing region of Galam made it briefly the strongest state in the western Sudan. Like Ghana, however, it was soon eclipsed, first by the brief Soso ascendancy and then by the rise of Mali.

In the mid–thirteenth century the Keita ruling clan of a Ghanaian successor kingdom, Mali, forged a new and lasting empire. This empire seems to have been built on the same economic base as that of Ghana and Takrur earlier: monopolization of the lucrative north–south gold trade. The Keita kings dominated enough of the Sahel to control the flow of West African gold from the Senegal regions and the forest lands south of the Niger to the trans-Saharan trade routes, and the influx of copper and salt in exchange. Because they were farther south, in the fertile land along the Niger, than their Ghanaian predecessors had been, they were better placed to control all trade on the upper Niger and to add to it the Gambia and Senegal trade to the west. They also used captives for plantation labor in the Niger inland delta to produce surplus food for trade.

Agriculture and cattle farming were the primary occupations of Mali's population and, together with the gold trade, the mainstays of the economy. Rice was grown in the river valleys and millet in the drier parts of the Sahel. Together with beans, yams, and other agricultural products, this made for a plentiful food supply. Fishing flourished along the Niger and elsewhere. Cattle, sheep, and goats were plentiful. The chief craft specialties were metalworking (iron and gold) and weaving of cotton grown within the empire.

[2] D. Conrad and H. Fisher, "The Conquest That Never Was: Ghana and the Almoravids, 1076," *History in Africa* 9 (1982): 1–59; 10 (1983): 53–78.

> **Mansa Musa, King of Mali.** The fourteenth century Catalan Atlas shows King Mansa Musa of Mali, seated on a throne. A rider on a camel approaches him.
> The Granger Collection.

The Malinke, a southern Mande-speaking people of the upper Niger region, formed the core population of the new state. They apparently lived in walled urban settlements typical of the western savannah region. Each walled town was surrounded by its own agricultural land, held perhaps 1,000 to 15,000 people, and presumably had enough arable land within its walls to deal with siege. Each was linked to neighboring cities by trade and possibly intermarriage.

The Keita dynasty had converted early to Islam (ca. 1100) and even claimed descent from Muhammad's famous muezzin (the person who calls the faithful to worship), Bilal, a former black slave from Abyssinia whose son was said to have settled in the Mande-speaking region. During Mali's heyday in the thirteenth and fourteenth centuries, its kings often made the pilgrimage to Mecca. From their travel in the central Islamic lands, they brought back with them not only military aids, such as large Barbary war horses, but also new ideas about political and military organization. Through Muslim traders' networks, Islam also connected Mali to other areas of Africa, especially those to the east.

Mali's imperial power was built largely by the Keita King Sundiata (or Sunjaata, r. 1230–1255). Sundiata and his successors exploited their agricultural resources, significant population growth, and Malinke commercial skills to build an empire even more powerful than that of Ghana. Sundiata extended his control west to the Atlantic coast and east beyond Timbuktu. By controlling the commercial entrepôts of Gao, Walata, and Jenne, he dominated the Saharan as well as the Niger trade. He built his capital, Niani, into a major city. Niani was located on a tributary of the Niger in the savannah at the edge of the forest in a gold- and iron-rich region. It had access to the forest trade products of gold, kola nuts, and palm oil; it

was easily defended by virtue of its surrounding hills; and it was readily reached by river.

The empire that Sundiata and his successors built ultimately encompassed three major regions and language groups of Sudanic West Africa: (1) the Senegal region (including Takrur), occupied by speakers of the West Atlantic Niger-Kongo language group (including Fulbe, Tukulor, Wolof, Serer); (2) the central Mande states between Senegal and Niger, occupied by the Niger-Kongo-speaking Soninke and Mandinke peoples; and (3) the peoples of the Niger in the Gao region who spoke Songhai, the only Nilo-Saharan language west of the Lake Chad basin. Mali was less a centralized bureaucratic state than the center of a vast sphere of influence that included provinces and tribute-paying kingdoms. Many individual chieftaincies were independent but recognized the sovereignty of the supreme, sacred *mansa*, or "emperor," of the Malian realms.

The greatest Keita king proved to be Mansa Musa (r. 1312–1337), whose pilgrimage through Mamluk Cairo to Mecca in 1324 became famous. He paid out or gave away so much gold in Cairo alone that he started massive inflation lasting over a decade. He returned with many Muslim scholars, artists, and architects. At home, he consolidated Mali's power, securing peace for most of his reign throughout his vast dominions. Musa's devoutness as a Muslim fostered the spread of Islam in the empire and beyond. Under his rule, Timbuktu became famous for its *madrasas* and libraries, and for its poets, scientists, and architects, making it the leading intellectual center of sub-Saharan Islam and a major trading city of the Sahel—roles it retained long after Mali's imperial sway ended.

Mali's dominance waned after Musa, evidently as the result of rivalries for the throne. Eventually the empire withered, and after 1450 a new Songhai power in Gao to the east ended Mali's imperial authority.

SONGHAI

Evidence suggests that as early as the eleventh or twelfth century there was a Songhai kingdom around Gao, on the eastern arc of the great bend of the Niger. In 1325 Mansa Musa brought this kingdom and the Gao region under the control of Mali and the Malinke. Mali's domination ended with the rise of a dynasty in Gao known as the Sunni or Sonni around 1375. The kingdom became an imperial power, under the greatest Sunni ruler, Sonni Ali (r. 1464–1492). Thereafter the Songhai Empire for more than a century was arguably the most powerful state in Africa (see Map 17–2). With a strong military built around a riverboat flotilla and cavalry, Sonni Ali took Jenne and Timbuktu. He pushed the Tuareg Berbers

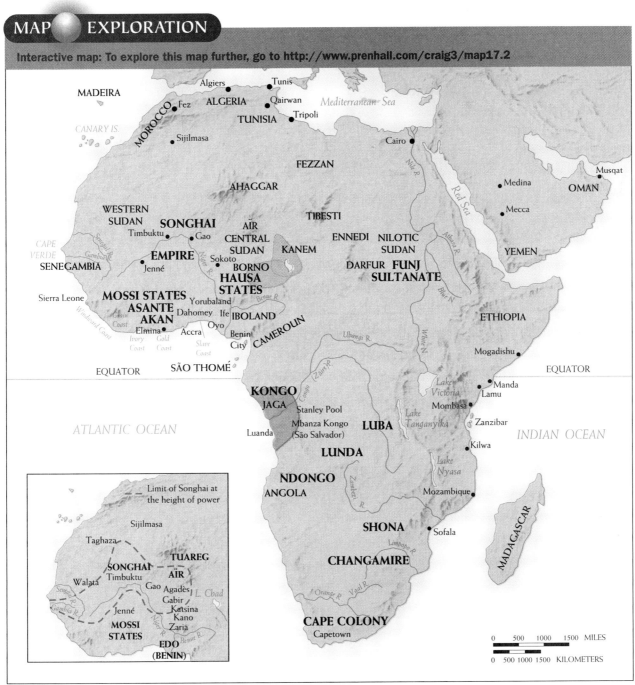

MAP 17–2 Africa ca. 1500–1800. Important towns, regions, peoples, and states. The inset shows the empire of Songhai at its greatest extent in the early 16th century.

back into the northern Sahel and Sahara and stifled threats from the southern forestland.

His successor Askia Muhammad al-Turi (r. 1493–1528) continued Sonni Ali's expansionist policies. Between them, Sonni Ali and Askia Muhammad built an empire that stretched west nearly to the Atlantic, northwest into the Sahara, and east into the central Sudan. Taking advantage of their control of access to the gold and other desirable commodities of West Africa, they emulated their Ghanaian predecessors in cultivating and expanding the ancient caravan trade across the Sahara to the North African coasts of Libya and Tunisia. This provided their major source of wealth.

Unlike Sonni Ali, who held to the traditional African religious faith of his people, Muhammad al-Turi was an enthusiastic Muslim. He built up the Songhai state after the model of the Islamic empire of Mali. (See Document, "Muslim Reform in Songhai.") In his reign, many Muslim scholars came to Gao, Timbuktu, and Jenne. He appointed Muslim judges (*qadis*) in towns throughout the empire and made Timbuktu a major intellectual and legal training center for the whole Sudan. He also replaced native Songhais with Arab Muslim immigrants as government officials to strengthen his centralized power. Like Mansa Musa before him, Muhammad made a triumphal pilgrimage to Mecca, where he was hailed as "Caliph of the western Sahara." From his vast royal treasury he supported the poor and the Sufi leaders, or *marabouts*, and built mosques throughout the realm. Nevertheless, he failed to Islamize the empire or to ensure a strong central state for his successors.

The last powerful Askia leader was Askia Dawud (r. 1549–1583), under whom Songhai economic prosperity and intellectual life achieved its apogee. The trans-Saharan trade reached new heights, and royal patronage of the arts rose to new levels. Still, difficulties mounted. The Askia battled the Mossi to the south and Berber forces from the north. Civil

CHRONOLOGY

Sahelian Empires of the Western Sudan

ca. 990–ca. 1180?	Empire of Ghana
1076	Ghana loses Awdaghast to Almoravids
1180–1230	Soso clan briefly controls the old Ghanaian territories
ca. 1230–1450	Empire of Mali, founded by Sundiata
1230–1255	Reign of Sundiata
1312–1337	Reign of Mansa Musa
1374	Independent Songhai state emerges in Gao after throwing off Malian rule
ca. 1450–1600	Songhai Empire at Gao
1464–1591	Askia dynasty
1464–1492	Reign of Sonni Ali
1493–1528	Reign of Askia Muhammad al-Turi
1549–1583	Reign of Askia Dawud
1590s	Collapse of the Songhai Empire

war broke out over succession to the throne in 1586, and the empire was divided. In 1591 an assay sent by the Sa'dis of Morocco used superior gunpowder weapons, and the aid of disaffected Songhai princes to defeat the last Askia of Gao at Tondibi, and the Gao Empire collapsed.

KANEM AND KANEM-BORNU

A fourth sizable Sahelian empire—in the central Sudan—arose after 1100. Called Kanem, it began as a southern Saharan confederation of the black nomadic tribes known as Zaghawah that were spread over much of the south-central and southeastern Sahara. By the twelfth century a Zaghawah group known as the Kanuri had apparently settled in Kanem,

◀ **Mosque Tomb.** A mosque tomb in Gao reputed to have been built for the Askia rulers of Songhai.

John O. Hunwick.

DOCUMENT | Muslim Reform in Songhai

Around 1500 Askia Muhammad al-Turi, the first Muslim among the rulers of Songhai, wrote to the North African Muslim theologian Muhammad al-Maghili (d. 1504) about proper Muslim practices. These excerpts are from the seventh question of al-Turi and the answers al-Maghili gave. One sees the zeal of the new convert to conform to traditional religious norms and the puritanical "official line" of the conservative Maliki ulama on "pagan" mores. Also evident is the king's desire for bettering social order and his concern for justice. It is also manifest that many of the more strongly Shari'a-minded ulama did not want to compromise at all, let alone allow syncretism to emerge among formerly pagan, newly converted groups.

◆ What are the problems and corresponding solutions listed in the letter? Which problem did al-Maghili find most serious? Why? Which do you think would have been most serious? Why?

From Al-Turi's Seventh Question

Among the people [of the Songhay Empire said Askia Muhammad], there are some who claim knowledge of the supernatural through sand divining and the like, or through the disposition of the stars ... [while] some assert that they can write (talismans) to bring good fortune ... or to ward off bad fortune. ... Some defraud in weights and measures. ...

One of their evil practices [continued Askia Muhammad] is the free mixing of men and women in the markets and streets and the failure of women to veil themselves ... [while] among the people of Djenné [Jenne] it is an established custom for a girl not to cover any part of her body as long as she remains a virgin ... and all the most beautiful girls walk about naked among people. ...

So give us legal ruling concerning these people and their ilk, and may God Most High reward you!

From Al-Maghili's Answer

The answer—and God it is who directs to the right course—is that everything you have mentioned concerning people's behavior in some parts of this country is gross error. It is the bounden duty of the commander of the Muslims and all other believers who have the power [replied al-Maghili] to change every one of these evil practices.

As for any who claims knowledge of the supernatural in the ways you have mentioned ... he is a liar and an unbeliever. ... Such people must be forced to renounce it by the sword. Then whoever renounces such deeds should be left in peace, but whoever persists should be killed with the sword as an unbeliever; his body should not be washed or shrouded, and he should not be buried in a Muslim graveyard. ...

As for defrauding in weights and measures [continued al-Maghili] it is forbidden (*haram*) according to the Qur'an, the Sunna and the consensus of opinion of the learned men of the Muslim community. It is the bounden duty of the commander of the Muslims to appoint a trustworthy man in charge of the markets, and to safeguard people's means of subsistence. He should standardize all the scales in each province. ... Similarly, all measures both large and small must be rectified so that they conform to a uniform standard. ...

Now, what you mentioned about the free mixing of men and women and leaving the pudenda uncovered is one of the greatest abominations. The commander of the Muslims must exert himself to prevent all these things. ... He should appoint trustworthy men to watch over this by day and night, in secret and in the open. This is not to be considered as spying on the Muslims; it is only a way of caring for them and curbing evildoers, especially when corruption becomes widespread in the land as it has done in Timbuktu and Djenné [Jenne] and so on.

From *The African Past*, trans. by J. O. Hunwick, reprinted in Basil Davidson (Grosset and Dunlap, The Universal Library), pp. 86–88. Reprinted by permission of Curtis Brown Ltd. Copyright © 1964 by Basil Davidson.

and from there they began a campaign of military expansion during the thirteenth century. Their key leader in this, Mai Dunama Dibbalemi (r. ca. 1221–1259), was a contemporary of Sundiata in Mali. Like Sundiata, Dibbalemi was a Muslim, and Islam appears to have entrenched itself among the Kanuri ruling class during his reign. Dibbalemi used it to sanction his rule, which otherwise had the familiar African trappings of sacred kingship. It also provided a rationale for expansion through *jihad*, or holy "struggle" against polytheists.

Dibbalemi and his successors expanded Kanuri power north into the desert to include the Fezzan in modern Libya and northeast along the Sahel-Sahara fringe toward Nilotic Africa. In both directions they controlled important trade routes—north to Libya and east to the Nile and Egypt. The next two centuries saw the mixing of Kanuri and local Kanembu peoples, primarily those known as the So. There was a corresponding transformation of the Kanuri leader from a nomadic *shaykh* to a Sudanic king and a shift of Kanem from a nomadic to a largely sedentary kingdom with quasi-feudal institutions. Like Mali to the west, Kanem's dominion was of two kinds: direct rule over and taxation of core territories and groups, and indirect control over and collection of tribute from a wider region of vassal chieftaincies. Islamic acculturation progressed most rapidly in the core territories under direct rule.

Civil strife, largely over the royal succession, weakened the Kanuri state in the later fourteenth and fifteenth centuries. After 1400 the locus of power shifted from Kanem proper westward, to the land of Bornu, southwest of Lake Chad. Here, at the end of the fifteenth century, a new Kanuri empire arose almost simultaneously with the collapse of the Askia dynasty of the Songhai Empire at Gao. Near the end of the sixteenth century firearms and Turkish military instructors enabled the Kanuri leader Idris Alawma (r. ca. 1575–1610) to unify Kanem and Bornu. He set up an avowedly Islamic state and extended his rule even into Hausaland, between Bornu and the Niger River. The center of trading activity as well as political power and security now shifted from the Niger Bend east to the territory under Kanuri control.

Deriving its prosperity from the trans-Saharan trade, Idris Alawma's regional empire survived for nearly a century. It was finally broken up by a long famine, repeated Tuareg attacks, lack of strong leadership, and loss of control over trade to smaller, better-organized Hausa states. The ruling dynasty held out until 1846, but by 1700 its power had been sharply reduced by the growing Hausa states to the west in what is now northern Nigeria. Their real power came only in the nineteenth century with their unification under the Fulani sultanate of Sokoto (see Chapter 27).

The Eastern Sudan

The Christian states of Maqurra and Alwa in the Nilotic Sudan, or Nubia, lasted for more than 600 years from their early-seventh-century beginnings and maintained political, religious and commercial contact with Egypt, the Red Sea world, and much of the Sudan.

After 1000 C.E. Maqurra and Alwa continued treaty relations with their more powerful northern Egyptian neighbors. However, the Mamluks intervened repeatedly in Nubian affairs, and Arab nomads constantly threatened the Nubian states.

CHRONOLOGY

Central Sudanic Empires

ca. 1100–1500	Kanuri empire of Kanem
ca. 1220s–1400	Height of empire of Kanem
1221–1259	Reign of Mai Dunama Dibbalemi
1575–1846	Kanuri empire of Kanem-Bornu
1575–1610	Reign of Idris Alawma, major architect of the state

From late Fatimid times onward, both Maqurra and Alwa were increasingly subject to immigrating Muslim Arab, tribesmen and to traders and growing Muslim minorities. The result was a long-term intermingling of Arabic and Nubian cultures and the creation of a new Nilotic Sudanese people and culture.

A significant factor in the gradual disappearance of Christianity in Nubia was its elite character there and its association with the foreign Egyptian world of Coptic Christianity. Maqurra became officially Muslim at the beginning of the fourteenth century, although Christianity survived until late in the same century. The Islamization of Alwa came somewhat later, most effectively under the long-lived Funj sultanate that replaced the Alwa state.

The Funj state flourished between the Blue and White Niles and to the north along the main Nile from just after 1500 until 1762. The Funj were originally cattle nomads who apparently adopted Islam soon after setting up their kingdom. During the late sixteenth and the seventeenth centuries, the Funj developed an Islamic society whose Arabized character was unique in sub-Saharan Africa. A much reduced Funj state held out until an Ottoman Egyptian invasion in 1821.

The Forestlands—Coastal West and Central Africa
WEST AFRICAN FOREST KINGDOMS: THE EXAMPLE OF BENIN

Many states, some with distinct political, religious, and cultural traditions, had developed in the southern and coastal regions of West Africa several centuries before the first Portuguese reports in 1485. Even those states like Asante or the Yoruba kingdoms of Oyo and Ife, which reached their height only after 1500, had much earlier origins. Benin, the best known of these forest kingdoms, reflects, especially in its art, the sophistication of West African culture before 1500.

Benin State and Society   The Edo speakers of Benin have occupied the southern Nigerian region between Yorubaland and the Ibo peoples east of the lower Niger for millennia. Traditional Edo society is organized according to a patrilineal system emphasizing primogeniture. The village is the fundamental political unit, and authority is built around the organization of males into age-grade units.[3]

According to archaeological evidence, the local traditions of the Edo culture of Benin were closely linked to those of Ife, one of the most prominent Yoruba states northwest of Benin. Some kind of distinct kingdom of Benin likely existed as early

---

[3] A. F. C. Ryder, *Benin and the Europeans, 1485–1897* (New York: Longman, 1969), p. 1. Ryder's work is a basic reference for the following brief summary about Benin.

as the twelfth century, and traditional accounts of both Ife and Edo agree that an Ife prince was sent to rule in Benin around 1300. There are indications that the power of the king, or **oba**, at this time was sharply limited by the Edo leaders who invited the foreign ruler. These leaders were known as the **uzama**, an order of hereditary indigenous chiefs. According to tradition, the fourth *oba* managed to wrest more control from these chiefs and instituted something of the ceremonial authority of absolute monarchy. However, only in the fifteenth century, with King Ewuare, did Benin become a royal autocracy and a large state of major regional importance.

Ewuare rebuilt the capital—known today as Benin City—and named it and his kingdom Edo. He apparently established a government in which he had sweeping authority, although he exercised it in light of the deliberations of a royal council. Ewuare formed this council not only from the palace *uzama*, but also from the townspeople. He gave each chief specific administrative responsibilities and rank in the government hierarchy. Ewuare and his successors developed a tradition of military kingship and engaged in major wars of expansion, both into Yorubaland to the west and Ibo country east across the Niger River. They also claimed for the office of *oba* an increasing ritual authority that presaged more radical developments in the king's role.

In the seventeenth century the *oba* was transformed from a military leader into a religious figure with supernatural powers. Human sacrifice, specifically of slaves, seems to have accompanied the cult of deceased kings and became even more frequent later, in the nineteenth century. The succession by primogeniture was discontinued, and the *uzama* chose *obas* from any branch of the royal family.

Benin Art   The lasting significance of Benin, however, lies in its court art, especially its famous brass sculptures. The splendid terra-cotta, ivory, and brass statuary sculpture of Ife-Benin are among the glories of human creativity. These magnificent sculptures seem to be wholly indigenous African products, and some scholars trace their artistic and technical lineage to the sculptures of the Nok culture of ancient West Africa (see Chapter 5).

The best sculptures before the sixteenth century and the coming of the Portuguese are cast bronze plaques depicting legendary and historical scenes. These were mounted in the royal palace in Benin City. There are also brass heads, apparently of royalty, that resemble the many life-size terra-cotta and brass heads found at Ife. The heads at Ife are held to represent the Oni, or religious chief of ancient Ife, or particular ancestors, who are thereby reverently remembered by their descendants.

Similar sculptures have been found both to the north and in the Niger Delta. Recent excavations east of the Niger at Igbo-Ukwu have unearthed stunning terra cottas and bronzes

▲ **Benin Plaque.** Some of the world's finest works of art were made by the artists of Benin and Ife, though much is still unknown about them. Rarely found elsewhere in Africa, bronze panels like the plaque shown here, possibly inspired by European illustrated books, adorned the royal palace, and are considered examples of "court art." The figures are typical of the Benin style in their proportions of head to body—about one to four—perhaps emphasizing the head's importance as a symbol of life and behavior.

Benin Plaque. Brass. Lost wax W. Africa 16th-17th C.A.D. Hillel Burger/Peabody Museum, Harvard University © President and Fellows of Harvard College. All rights reserved.

that belong to the same general artistic culture, which is dated as early as the ninth century. These artifacts testify to the high cultural level attained in traditional African societies that had little or no contact with the extra-African world.

EUROPEAN ARRIVALS ON THE COASTLANDS

Along the coasts of West and central Africa, many important changes occurred between 1500 and 1800. Those wrought by the burgeoning Atlantic slave trade are the most famous (see Chapter 18). Of comparable importance are changes connected with trade in West African gold and other commodities and the effects associated with the importation and spread in West and central Africa of food crops, such as maize, peanuts, squash, sweet potatoes, cocoa, and cassava (manioc) from the Americas. The gradual involvement of Africa in the emerging global economic system paved the way for eventual colonial domination of the continent, especially its coastal regions, by the Europeans. The European names for segments of the coastline—the Grain (or Pepper) Coast, the Ivory Coast, the Gold Coast, and the Slave Coast—identify the main exports that could be extracted by ship.

Senegambia In West Africa, Senegambia—which takes its name from the Senegal and Gambia Rivers—was one of the earliest regions affected by European trade. Its interior had long been involved in both trans-Saharan trade and east–west trade in the Sahel and the savannah, especially in the heydays of the empires of Ghana, Mali, and Songhai. Senegambia's maritime trade with European powers, like the older overland trade, was primarily in gold and products such as salt, cotton goods, hides, and copper. For roughly a century Senegambian states also provided slaves for European purchase; indeed, perhaps a third of all African slaves exported during the sixteenth century came from Senegambia. Thereafter, however, the focus of the slave trade shifted south and east along the coast (see Chapter 18). Over time, Portuguese-African mulattos and the British came to control the Gambia River trade, while the French won the Senegal River markets.

The Gold Coast The Gold Coast, like Senegambia, was one of the West African coastal districts most affected by the arrival of international maritime trade. The name derives from the region's

Benin Bronze Plaque. From the palace of the Obas of Benin it dates to the Edo period of Benin culture, 1575–1625. It depicts two Portuguese males, perhaps a father and son, holding hands. It is likely that they represent the traders or government officials who came to the African coasts in increasing numbers from the end of the 15th century on.

Werner Forman, Art Resource, N.Y.

importance after 1500 as the outlet for the more southern of West Africa's gold fields in the forestland of Akan. Here, beginning with the Portuguese at Elmina in 1481, but primarily after 1600, European states and companies built coastal forts to protect their trade and to serve as depots for inland goods. The trade in gold, kola nuts, and other commodities seems to have encouraged the growth of larger states in the region, perhaps because they could better handle and control the overland commerce.

The intensive contact of the Gold Coast with Europeans also led to the importation and spread of American crops, notably maize and cassava. The success of these crops in West and central Africa likely contributed to substantial population growth in the sixteenth and seventeenth centuries.

The Gold Coast escaped the ravages of the slave trade for some decades; it was even an importer of slaves until long after 1500. Slaves, however, became big business here in the late seventeenth century, especially in the Accra region. The economy was so disrupted by the slave trade that gold mining declined sharply. Eventually more gold came into the Gold Coast from the sale of slaves than went out from its mines (see Chapter 18).

CENTRAL AFRICA

The vast center of the subcontinent is bounded by swamps in the north, coastal rain forests to the west, highlands to the east, and deserts in the south. Before 1500 these natural barriers impeded international contact and trade with the interior. They also shaped the two-pronged route by which Bantu peoples and languages moved, over many centuries, from western and west-central Africa south into the Zaire basin and east around the equatorial forest into the lakes of highland East Africa. In the tropical central area, regional interaction in

CHRONOLOGY	
Benin	
ca. 1100–1897	Benin state
ca. 1300	First Ife king of Benin state
1440–1475	Reign of Ewuare

movements of peoples and in trade and culture had always been the norm. Here as elsewhere in Africa, however, large as well as small political, economic, and social units could be found. Peoples such as the Lunda and the Luba, for example, on the southern savannah below the rain forest, carved out sizable kingdoms by the fifteenth century and expanded their control over neighboring areas into the eighteenth century.

The Portuguese came to the western coastal regions looking for gold and silver but found none. Ultimately, their main export was slaves. These slaves were taken, first for gang labor to the Portuguese sugar plantations on Sao Thomé island in the Gulf of Guinea and then, in vast numbers to perform similar plantation labor in Brazil. In the 1640s the Dutch briefly succeeded the Portuguese as the major suppliers of African slaves to English and French plantations in the Caribbean.

The Kongo Kingdom   Kongo was the major state with which the Portuguese dealt after coming to central Africa in 1483. Dating from probably the fourteenth century, the Kongo kingdom was located on a fertile, well-watered plateau south of the lower Zaïre River valley, between the coast and the Kwango River in the east. Here, astride the border between forest and grassland, the Kongo kings had built a central government based on a pyramid structure of tax or tribute collection. The king's, authority was tied to acceptance of him as a kind of spiritual spokesman of the gods or ancestors. By 1600 Kongo was half the size of England and boasted a high state of specialization in weaving and pottery, salt production, fishing, and metalworking.

The Portuguese brought Mediterranean goods, preeminently luxury textiles from North Africa, to trade for African goods. Such luxuries augmented the prestige and wealth of the ruler and his elites. However, slaves became the primary export that could be used to obtain foreign luxuries. Meanwhile, imports such as fine clothing, tobacco, and alcohol did nothing to replace the labor pool lost to slavery.

At first the Portuguese put time and effort into education and Christian proselytizing, but the need for more slaves eventually outweighed these concerns. Regional rulers sought to procure slaves from neighboring kingdoms, as did Portuguese traders who went inland themselves. As the demand grew,

local rulers increasingly attacked neighbors to garner slaves for Portuguese traders (see Chapter 18 .).

The Kongo ruler Affonso I (r. ca. 1506–1543), a Christian convert, at first welcomed Jesuit missionaries and supported conversion. But in time he broke with the Jesuits and encouraged traditional practices, even though he himself remained a Christian. Affonso had constant difficulty curbing the more exploitative slaving practices and independent-minded provincial governors, who often dealt directly with the Portuguese, undermining royal authority. (See Document, "Affonso I Writes to the King of Portugal.") Affonso's successor finally restricted Portuguese activity to Mpinda harbor and the Kongo capital of Mbanza Kongo (São Salvador). A few years later, Portuguese attempts to name the Kongo royal successor caused a bloody uprising against them that led in turn to a Portuguese boycott on trade with the kingdom.

Thereafter, disastrous internal wars shattered the Kongo state. Slavery apparently contributed significantly to provincial unrest. Independent Portuguese traders and adventurers soon did their business outside of government channels and tried to manipulate the Kongo kings.

Kongo, however, enjoyed renewed vigor in the seventeenth century. The Kongo kings, all descended from Affonso, ruled as divine-right monarchs at the apex of a complex sociopolitical pyramid that rose from district headmen through provincial governors to the court nobility and king. Royal power came to depend on a guard of musket-armed hired soldiers. The financial base of the kingdom rested on tribute from officials and taxes and tolls on commerce. Christianity, the state religion, was accommodated to the traditional ancestor cult, magic, and sorcery. Sculpture, iron and copper technology, and dance and music flourished.

Angola   To the south, in Portuguese Angola, the experience was even worse than in Kongo. The Ndongo kingdom flourished among the Mbundu people during the sixteenth century, though the Portuguese tried and failed to make Angola a proprietary colony (the first white colonial enterprise in black Africa). By the end of the 1500s Angola was exporting thousands of slaves yearly through the port of Luanda. In less than a century the hinterland had been depopulated. New internal trade in salt and the spread of American food crops such as maize and cassava (which became part of the staple diet of the populace) produced some positive changes in the interior, but in the coastal region the Portuguese brought catastrophe.

East Africa
Swahili Culture and Commerce

The participation of East African port towns in the lucrative South Seas trade was ancient. Arabs, Indonesians, and even some Indians had trafficked there for centuries. Many had

CHRONOLOGY

Central Africa

1300s	Kongo kingdom founded
1483	Portuguese come to central African coast
ca. 1506–1543	Reign of Affonso I as king of Kongo
1571	Angola becomes Portuguese proprietary colony

DOCUMENT | Affonso I of Kongo Writes to the King of Portugal

In 1526 Affonso, the Christian African king of Kongo, wrote to the Portuguese monarch ostensibly to complain about the effects of slaving on the Kongo people and economy. But the real issue was that the Portuguese were circumventing his own royal monopoly on the inland slave trade. One of the insidious effects of the massive demand of the Atlantic trade for slaves was the ever-increasing engagement in it of African monarchs, chieftains, and merchants.

◆ How had the introduction of Portuguese merchants and European goods upset the social and political situation in Kongo? How had these goods tempted Affonso's subjects into the slave trade? How did Affonso wish to change the relationship of his people to Portugal? Was the king more worried about human rights or his economic losses?

Sir, Your Highness [of Portugal] should know how our Kingdom is being lost in so many ways that it is convenient to provide for the necessary remedy, since this is caused by the excessive freedom given by your factors and officials to the men and merchants who are allowed to come to this Kingdom to set up shops with goods and many things which have been prohibited by us, and which they spread throughout our Kingdoms and Domains in such an abundance that many of our vassals, whom we had in obedience, do not comply because they have the things in greater abundance than we ourselves; and it was with these things that we had them content and subjected under our vassalage and jurisdiction, so it is doing a great harm not only to the service of God, but the security and peace of our Kingdoms and State as well.

And we cannot reckon how great the damage is, since the mentioned merchants are taking every day our natives, sons of the land and the sons of our noblemen and vassals and our relatives, because the thieves and men of bad conscience grab them wishing to have the things and wares of this Kingdom which they are ambitious of; they grab them and get them to be sold; and so great, Sir, is the corruption and licentiousness that our country is being completely depopulated, and Your Highness should not agree with this nor accept it as in your service. And to avoid it we need from those [your] Kingdoms no more than some priests and a few people to teach in schools, and no other goods except wine and flour for the holy sacrament. That is why we beg of Your Highness to help and assist us in this matter, commanding your factors that they should not send here either merchants or wares, because it is *our will that in these Kingdoms there should not be any trade of slaves nor outlet for them.**

Concerning what is referred above, again we beg of Your Highness to agree with it, since otherwise we cannot ... remedy such an obvious damage. Pray Our Lord in His mercy to have Your Highness under His guard and let you do for ever the things of His service. I kiss your hands many times. ...

From *The African Past*, trans. by J. O. Hunwick, reprinted in Basil Davidson (Grosset and Dunlap, The Universal Library), pp. 191–193. Reprinted by permission of Curtis Brown Ltd. Copyright © 1964 by Basil Davidson.

*Emphasis in the original

---

been absorbed into what had become, during the first millennium C.E., from Somalia south, a predominantly Bantu-speaking population. From the eighth century onward Islam traveled with Arab and Persian sailors and merchants to these southerly trading centers of what the Arabs called the land of the *Zanj*, or "Blacks" (hence "Zanzibar"). Conversion to Islam, however, occurred only along the coast. In the thirteenth century Muslim traders from Arabia and Iran began to dominate the coastal cities from Mogadishu to Kilwa. By 1331 the traveler Ibn Battuta writes of Mogadishu as a thoroughly Islamic port and of the ruler and inhabitants of Kilwa as Muslims. He also notes that towns there had mosques for the faithful.[4] (See Document, "Visiting Mogadishu and Kilwa [1331].")

By this time a common language called **Swahili**, or *Kiswahili*, from the Arabic *sawahil*, "coastlands," had developed from the interaction of Bantu and Arabic speakers along the coast. Its structure is Bantu, its vocabulary has a strong admixture of Arabic, and it is written in Arabic script.

Current theory suggests that, like the language, Swahili culture is basically African with a large contribution by Arab, Persian, and other extra-African elements. This admixture created a new consciousness and identity. Today, the many coastal peoples who share Swahili language join African to Persian, Indian, Arab, and other ancestry.

Swahili language and culture probably developed first in the northern towns of Manda, Lamu, and Mombasa, then farther south along the coast to Kilwa. They remained localized largely along the coast until recently. Likewise, the spread of Islam was largely limited to the coastal civilization, with the

[4] *Travels in Asia and Africa, 1325–1354*, trans. and selected by H. A. R. Gibb (New York: Robert M. McBride, 1929), pp. 110–113.

possible exception of the Zambezi valley, where Muslim traders penetrated upriver. This contrasts with the Horn of Africa, where Islamic kingdoms developed both in the Somali hinterland and on the coast.

Swahili civilization reached its apogee in the fourteenth and fifteenth centuries. The harbor trading towns were the administrative centers of the local Swahili states, and most of them were sited on coastal islands or easily defended peninsulas. To these ports came merchants from abroad and from the African hinterlands. These towns were impressive. Stone mosques, fortress-palaces, harbor fortifications, fancy residences, and commercial buildings have their own distinctive cast, which combines African and Arabo-Persian elements.

The Swahili states' ruling dynasties were probably African in origin, with an admixture of Arab or Persian blood. Swahili coastal centers boasted an advanced, cosmopolitan culture; by comparison, most of the populace in the small villages lived in mud and sometimes stone houses and earned their living by farming or fishing. Society seems to have consisted of three principal groups: the local nobility, the commoners, and resident foreigners engaged in commerce. Slaves constituted a fourth class, although their local extent (as opposed to their sale) is disputed.

The flourishing trade of the coastal centers was fed mainly by export of inland ivory. Other exports included gold, slaves, turtle shells, ambergris, leopard skins, pearls, fish, sandalwood, ebony, and cotton cloth. The chief imports were cloth, porcelain, glassware, glass beads, and glazed pottery. Certain exports tended to dominate particular ports: cloth, sandalwood, ebony, and ivory at Mogadishu, ivory at Manda, and gold at Kilwa (brought up the coast from Sofala, still farther south). Cowrie shells were a common currency in the inland trade, but coins minted at Mogadishu and Kilwa from the fourteenth century on were increasingly used in the major trading centers.

THE PORTUGUESE AND THE OMANIS OF ZANZIBAR

The original Swahili civilization declined in the sixteenth century primarily because the trade that had originally made everything possible waned with the arrival of the Portuguese and their destruction of both the old oceanic trade (in particular, the Islamic commercial monopoly) and the main Islamic city-states along the eastern coast. Decreases in rainfall or invasions of Zimba peoples from inland regions may also have contributed to the decline.

Nevertheless, the Portuguese undoubtedly intended to gain control of the South-Seas trade (see Chapter 18). In Africa, as everywhere, they saw the **Moors** (the Spanish and Portuguese term for Muslims) as their implacable enemies and viewed the struggle to wrest the commerce and the parts of Africa and Asia from Islamic control as a Christian crusade.

Swahili Mosque. The Friday Mosque at Shela on the southeastern coast of Lamu Island, Kenya. This fine example of Late Swahili architecture dates to the early 19th century. It is the only surviving pre-20th-century mosque in the region with a minaret. Swahili settlements on Lamu Island date to about the 15th century and enjoyed a period of substantial wealth that reached its zenith in the nineteenth century.

Embassy of Kenya.

The initial Portuguese victories along the African coast led to the submission of many small Islamic ports and states. Still, there was no concerted effort to spread Christianity beyond the fortified settlements established in places like Sofala, Zanzibar, Mozambique, and Mombasa. Thus the long-term cultural and religious consequences of the Portuguese presence were slight.

The Portuguese did, however, cause widespread economic decline on the east coast. When the inland Africans refused to cooperate with them, the formerly heavy gold trade up the Zambezi from Sofala dried up. The militant Portuguese presence also sharply reduced Muslim coastal shipping from India and Arabia. Ottoman efforts in the late sixteenth century failed to defeat the Portuguese, but after 1660 the strong eastern Arabian state of Oman raided the African coast with impunity. In 1698 the Omanis took Mombasa and ejected the Portuguese everywhere north of Mozambique.

Under the Omanis, Zanzibar became a new and major power center in East Africa. Their control of the coastal ivory

DOCUMENT · Visiting Mogadishu and Kilwa (1331)

Ibn Battuta (d. 1369 or 1377), a native of Tangier, became one of history's most famous travelers through his voluminous and entertaining writings about his years of journeying from West and East Africa to India and China. In the following two excerpts from his description of his trip down the East African coast in 1331, he describes first the daily proceedings at the grievance and petitions court presided over by the Sultan of Mogadishu, then the generosity of the Sultan of Kilwa. The East Africans referred to their Sultan as "Shaikh" (a term used also for any religiously learned man). A qadi *is a judge; a* faqih, *a jurisconsult or legal scholar; a* wazir, *a government minister; an* amir, *a military commander; and a* sharif, *a descendant of the Prophet Muhammad (which carries special social status).*

♦ What Muslim values and practices do the two reports seem to describe? Does Ibn Battuta as a Muslim, but also as an Arab outsider to the African Muslim societies he is visiting, seem to approve or disapprove of what he reports?

Mogadishu

When it is Saturday, the people come to the door of the shaikh (the local term for the Sultan), and they sit in covered halls outside the house. The *qadi*, the *faqihs*, the *sharifs*, the men of piety, the shaikhs and the men who have performed the pilgrimage enter the second council room. They sit on wooden platforms prepared for the purpose. The *qadi* is on a platform by himself and each group on a platform reserved for them which nobody shares with them. Then the shaikh sits in his council and sends for the *qadi* who sits on his left. Then enter the *faqihs* and their leaders sit in front of him while the rest of them salute and go away. Then the *sharifs* enter, their leaders sit before him, the rest of them salute and go away. If they are guests, they sit on his right. Then enter the shaikhs and those who have performed the pilgrimage, and their great ones sit and the rest salute and go away. Then enter the *wazirs* and *amirs*; the heads of the soldiers, rank upon rank, they salute and go. Food is brought and the *qadi*, the

sharifs and whoever is sitting in that session eat with the shaikh and the shaikh eats with them. If he wishes to honour one of the leaders of his *amirs*, he sends for him that he should eat with them. The rest of the people eat in the dining hall and their eating is according to precedence in the manner of their entrance before the shaikh. Then the shaikh goes into his house and the *qadi*, the *wazirs*, the private secretary, and four of the leading *amirs* sit for hearing litigation between the members of the public and hearing the cases of people with complaints. In a matter connected with the rules of the *shari'a* [religious law] the *qadi* passes judgement; in a matter other than that, the members of the council pass judgement, that is, the ministers and the *amirs*. In a matter where there is need of consultation with the sultan, they write about it to him and he sends out the reply to them immediately on the back of the note in accordance with his view. And such is always their custom.

The Sultan of Kilwa

When I arrived, the Sultan was Abu al-Muzaffar Hasan surnamed Abu al-Mawahib [the Father of Gifts] on account of his numerous charitable gifts. He frequently makes raids into the Zanj country, attacks them and carries off booty, of which he reserves a fifth, using it in the manner prescribed by the Koran. That reserved for the kinsfolk of the Prophet is kept separate in the Treasury, and, when *sharifs* come to visit him, he gives it them. They come to him from Iraq, the Hijaz, and other countries. I found several *sharifs* from the Hijaz at his court, among them Muhammad ibn Jammaz, Mansur ibn Labida ibn Abi Nami and Muhamma ibn Shumaila ibn Abi Nami. At Mogadishu I saw Tabl ibn Kubaish ibn Jammaz, who also wished to visit him. This Sultan is very humble: he sits and eats with beggars, and venerates holy men and descendants of the Prophet.

From Said Hamdun and Noël King, ed. and trans., *Ibn Battuta in Black Africa*, (Princeton, NJ: Markus Wiener, rev. ed., 1994), pp. 20–21. Reprinted by permission of Markus Wiener Publishers, Inc.

---

and slave trade seems to have fueled a substantial recovery of prosperity by the later eighteenth century. Zanzibar itself benefited from the introduction of clove cultivation in the 1830s; cloves became its staple export thereafter. (The clove plantations became also the chief market for a new, devastating internal slave trade, which flourished in East Africa into the late nineteenth century even as the external trade in slaves was crushed.) Omani African sultans dominated the east coast until 1856. Thereafter, Zanzibar and its coastal holdings became independent under a branch of the same family that ruled in Oman. Zanzibar passed eventually to the British when they, the

Germans, and the Italians divided East Africa in the late 1880s. Still, the Islamic imprint on the whole coast survives today.

Southern Africa
SOUTHEASTERN AFRICA: "GREAT ZIMBABWE"

At about the same time that the east-coast trading centers were beginning to flourish, a different kind of civilization was enjoying its heyday farther south, in the rocky, savannah-woodland watershed between the Limpopo and Zambezi Rivers, in modern

⚊ **Great Zimbabwe.** The most impressive of 300 such stone ruins in modern Zimbabwe and neighboring countries. These sites give clear evidence of the advanced Iron Age mining and cattle-raising culture that flourished in this region between about 1000 and 1500 c.e. The people, thought to have been of Bantu origins, apparently had a highly developed trade in gold and copper with outsiders, including Arabs on the east coast. As yet, all too little is known about this impressive society.
Werner Forman/Art Resource, N.Y.

southern Zimbabwe. This civilization was a purely African one sited far enough inland never to have felt the impact of Islam. It was founded in the tenth or eleventh century by Bantu-speaking Shona people, who still inhabit the same general area today. It seems to have become a large and prosperous state between the late thirteenth and the late fifteenth centuries. We know it only through the archaeological remains of an estimated 150 settlements in the Zambezi-Limpopo region.

The most impressive of these ruins, and the apparent capital of this ancient Shona state, is known today as "Great Zimbabwe"—a huge, sixty-odd-acre site encompassing two major building complexes. One—the so-called acropolis—is a series of stone enclosures on a high hill. It overlooks another, much larger enclosure that contains many ruins and a circular tower, all surrounded by a massive wall some thirty-two feet high and up to seventeen feet thick. The acropolis complex may have contained a shrine, whereas the larger enclosure was appar-

ently the royal palace and fort. The stonework reflects a wealthy and sophisticated society. Artifacts from the site include gold and copper ornaments, soapstone carvings, and imported beads, as well as glass and porcelain of Chinese, Syrian, and Persian origins.

The state itself seems to have had partial control of the increasing gold trade between inland areas and the east-coast port of Sofala. Its territory lay east and south of substantial gold-mining enterprises. We can speculate that this large settlement was the capital city of a prosperous empire and the residence of a ruling elite. Its wider domain was made up mostly of smaller settlements whose inhabitants lived by subsistence agriculture and cattle raising and whose culture was different from that of the capital.

We are not sure why Great Zimbabwe civilization flourished. The evidence suggests first general population growth and increasing economic prosperity in the Zambezi-Limpopo region before 1500 C.E. Even earlier Iron Age sites farther south suggest that other large state entities may have preceded the heyday of Great Zimbabwe proper. The specific impetus for Great Zimbabwe may have been a significant immigration around 1000 C.E. of Late Iron Age Shona speakers who brought with them mining techniques and farming innovations, along with their ancestor cults. Improved farming and animal husbandry could have led to substantial population growth. The gold trade between the inland gold mining areas and Sofala may also have expanded. Great Zimbabwe may have been the chief beneficiary of this trade. This hypothesis links the flourishing of Zimbabwe to that of the East African coast from about the thirteenth century.

However, without new sources, we may never know why this impressive civilization developed and dominated its region for nearly 200 years. The reasons for its demise are also obscure. It appears that the northern and southern sectors of the state split up, and people moved away from Great Zimbabwe, probably because the farming and grazing land there was exhausted. The southern successor kingdom was known as Changamire, which became powerful from the late 1600s until about 1830. The northern successor state, stretched along the middle and lower course of the Zambezi, was known to the first Portuguese sources as the kingdom ruled by the Mwene Mutapa, or "Master Pillager," the title of its sixteenth-century ruler, Mutota, and his successors.

THE PORTUGUESE IN SOUTHEASTERN AFRICA

The Portuguese destroyed Swahili control of both the inland gold trade and the multifaceted overseas trade. Their chief object was to obtain gold from the Zambezi region of the interior. However, because the gold production of the entire region

◄ **Carving from Great Zimbabwe.** This carving (steatite, 40.5 cm high) is thought to represent a mythical eagle that carries messages from man to the gods. It dates to ca. 1200–1400 C.E.
Werner Forman Archive/Art Resource, N.Y.

was small and because they encountered repeated difficulties trying to control it, the Portuguese derived little lasting profit from the enterprise. When they had problems sustaining the Zambezi gold trade by trying simply to supplant the Swahili merchants on the coast, they established fortified posts up the Zambezi and meddled in the regional politics of the Shona who controlled the region. This tactic led to ongoing strife between the invaders and the Shona kingdoms. In the 1690s the Changamire Shona dynasty conquered the northern Shona territory and pushed the Portuguese out of gold country.

All along the Zambezi, however, a lasting and destabilizing consequence of Portuguese intrusion was the creation of quasi-tribal chiefdoms. These were led by mixed-blood Portuguese landholders, or *prazeros*, descended from the first Portuguese estate holders along the Zambezi, who had built up huge estates. Their descendants eventually formed a few clanlike groups of mixed-blood members (from unions with Africans, Indian immigrants, or other estate families). By the end of the eighteenth century, they controlled vast land holdings, commanded armies (often made up largely of slaves), and were a disruptive force in the region because they were too strong for either the Portuguese or the regional African rulers to control. They remind us of how diverse the peoples of modern Africa are.

SOUTH AFRICA: THE CAPE COLONY

In South Africa the Dutch planted the first European colonials almost inadvertently, yet the consequences of their action were to be ultimately as grave and far-reaching as any European incursion onto African soil. The first Cape settlement was built in 1652 by the Dutch East India Company as a resupply point and way station for Dutch vessels on their way back and forth between the Netherlands and the East Indies. The support station grew gradually into what became by century's end a large settler community (the population of the colony in 1662, including slaves, was 392; by 1714 it had reached 3,878).[5] These settlers were the forebears of the Afrikaners of modern South Africa.

[5] R. Elphick and H. Giliomee, *The Shaping of South African Society, 1652–1820* (Cape Town: Longman, 1979), p. 4.

CHRONOLOGY

East and Southeast Africa

900–1500	"Great Zimbabwe" civilization
ca. 1200–1400	Development of Bantu Kiswahili language
ca. 1300–1600	Height of Swahili culture
1698	Omani forces take Mombasa, oust Portuguese from East Africa north of the port of Mozambique
1741–1856	United sultanate of Oman and Zanzibar

Cape Town, with European Ships in its harbor. The colony relied on shipping for commercial links with the outside world.
National Archives of South Africa.

CHRONOLOGY

Southern Africa

1652	First Cape Colony settlement of Dutch East India Company
1795	British replace Dutch as masters of Cape Colony

The colony also imported slaves from all along the southern-seas trade routes, including India, East Africa, and Madagascar. Slavery set the tone for relations between the emergent, and ostensibly "white," Afrikaner population and the "coloreds" of other races. Free or not, the latter were eventually all too easily identified with slave peoples.

After the first settlers spread out around the Company station, nomadic white livestock farmers, or *Trekboers*, moved more widely afield, leaving the richer, but limited, farming lands of the coast for the drier interior tableland. There they contested still wider groups of Khoikhoi cattle herders for the best grazing lands. To this end, they developed military techniques—notably the "commando," a collective civilian punitive raid—to secure their way of life by force where necessary. Again the Khoikhoi were the losers. By 1700 they were stripped almost completely of their own pasturages, and their way of life was destroyed. More and more Khoikhoi took up employment in the colonial economy, among the Trekboers as well as the settled colonists. Others moved north to join with other refugees from Cape society (slaves, mixed bloods, and some freedmen) to form raiding bands operating along the frontiers of Trekboer territory close to the Orange River. The disintegration of Khoikhoi society continued in the eighteenth century, accelerated sharply by smallpox—a European import against which this previously isolated group had no immunity.

Many of the less powerful Khoikhoi people of the region were gradually incorporated into the new colonial economy. The local Khoikhoi (see Chapter 5) were almost exclusively pastoralists; they had neither traditions of strong political organization nor an economic base beyond their herds. At first they bartered livestock freely to Dutch ships and then to the Company settlement for iron, copper, and tobacco. However, when settlers began to displace the Khoikhoi in the southwestern Cape, conflicts ensued. The results were the consolidation of European landholdings and a breakdown of Khoikhoi society. Dutch military success led to even greater Dutch control of the Khoikhoi by the 1670s. Treated as free persons, they became the chief source of colonial wage labor—labor in ever-greater demand as the colony grew.

OVERVIEW   Major African States, 1000–1800

North Africa	Sahel	Eastern Sudan	West and Central Africa	East Africa	Southern Africa
Morocco	Ghana	Maqurra	Benin	Zanzibar	"Great Zimbabwe"
Algiers	Mali	Alwa	Kongo		
Tunis	Songhai	Funj			
Tripoli	Kanem				
Egypt					

The Cape society in this period was thus a diverse one. The Dutch Company officials (including Dutch Reformed ministers), the emerging Afrikaners (both settled colonists and Trekboers), the Khoikhoi, and the slaves played differing roles in the emerging new society radiating from Capetown. Intermarriage and cohabitation of masters and slaves added to the social complexity, despite laws designed to check such mixing.

Accommodation of nonwhite minority groups within Cape society went on apace; the slow emergence of *Afrikaans*, a new vernacular language of the colonials, shows that the Dutch immigrants themselves were also subject to acculturation processes. By the time of English domination after 1795, the sociopolitical foundations—and the bases of *apartheid*—of modern South Africa were firmly laid.

Feluccas on the Nile at Luxor.

Summary

North Africa   Developments in African history from 1000 to 1800 varied from region to region. In North Africa, the key new factor was the imperial expansion of the Ottoman Empire as far west as Morocco. But regionalism soon rendered Ottoman authority in North Africa purely nominal.

Empires of the Sudan   Several substantial states arose south of the Sahara: Ghana, Mali, Songhai, and Kanem. The ruling elites of these states converted to or were heavily influenced by Islam, although most of their populations clung to their older traditions. Much of the wealth of these states was tied to their control of the trans-Saharan trade routes. Farther south, in the coastal forestlands of Central Africa, another substantial kingdom arose in Benin, famous for its brass sculptures.

East Africa   On the east coast, Islam influenced the development of the distinctive Swahili culture and language, and Islamic traders linked the region to India and East Asia.

The Coming of the Europeans   The key development of the fifteenth century was the arrival of European traders, missionaries, and warships. The Portuguese and later Europeans came in search of commerce, converts to Christianity, and spheres of influence. Their arrival disrupted indigenous African culture and political relations and presaged Africa's involvement in and exploitation by a new, expanding global trading system dominated by Europeans.

⦂ Review Questions

1. Why did Islam succeed in sub-Saharan and East Africa? What role did warfare play in its success? What role did trade have in it?

2. What was the importance of the empires of Ghana, Mali, and Songhai to world history? Why was the control of the trans-Saharan trade so important to these kingdoms? What was the importance of Islamic culture to them? Why did each of these empires break up?

3. What was the impact of the Portuguese on East Africa? On Central Africa? How did European coastal activities affect the African interior?

4. Why did Ottoman influence decline in northern Africa in the eighteenth century?

5. How did the Portuguese and Dutch differ from or resemble the Arabs, Persians, and other Muslims who came as outsiders to sub-Saharan Africa?

6. Discuss the diversity of Cape society in South Africa before 1800. Who were the Trekboers and what was their conflict with the Khoikhoi? How was the basis for apartheid formed in this period?

Key Terms

Afrikaans (p. 498)

apartheid (p. 498)

Moors (p. 493)

oba (p. 489)

Swahili (p. 492)

Trekboers (p. 497)

uzama (p. 489)

Documents CD-ROM

Eurasian Connections before European Expansion

11.1 Mansa Musa: The "King Who Sits on a Mountain of Gold"

11.3 Ibn Battuta in Mali

NOTE: To learn more about the topics in this chapter, see the Suggested Readings at the end of the book.

European Explorations and Expansion

14.1 Kilwa, Mombasa, and the Portuguese: Realities of Empire

14.3 The Portuguese in Africa and India: Duarte Barbosa

18

Conquest and Exploitation

The Development of the Transatlantic Economy

- Periods of European Overseas Expansion

- Mercantilist Theory of Economic Exploitation

- Establishment of the Spanish Empire in America

- Economies of Exploitation in the Spanish Empire

- Colonial Brazil and Slavery

- French and British Colonies in North America

- Slavery in the Americas

- Africa and the Transatlantic Slave Trade

◁ JOHN SINGLETON COPLEY, AMERICAN, 1738–1815. *WATSON AND THE SHARK*, 1778. In several respects, this painting illustrates the interconnectedness of the eighteenth-century transatlantic world. Copley is an American artist working in London. The action occurs in a Spanish colony during a commercial venture. The person being rescued is an English subject who will become a rich merchant. The boat holds a cross section of races and cultures from Africa, Europe, and the Americas that characterized the world of the plantation economies.

Oil on canvas, $72^1/_4 \times 90^3/_8$ in. Gift of Mrs. George von Lengerke Meyer. Courtesy, Museum of Fine Arts, Boston. Reproduced with permission © Museum of Fine Arts, Boston. All Rights Reserved.

The Atlantic World

The contact between the native peoples of the American continent and the European explorers of the fifteenth and sixteenth centuries transformed world history. In the Americas, the native peoples—whose ancestors had migrated from Asia millennia before—had established a wide variety of civilizations. Some of their most remarkable architectural monuments and cities were constructed during the very centuries when European civilizations were reeling from the collapse of Roman power. Until European exploration, the civilizations of the Americas and the civilizations of Eurasia and Africa had had no significant contact with each other.

Within half a century of the landing of Columbus, millions of America's native peoples in Florida, the Caribbean islands, Mesoamerica, and South America had encountered Europeans intent on conquest, exploitation, and religious conversion. The Europeans' rapid conquest was the result of several factors—their advanced weapons and navies; the new diseases they brought with them; and internal divisions among the Native Americans. Thereafter, Spain and Portugal dominated Latin America, and England, France, and Holland set out to settle North America. The Europeans imported their own food crops, such as wheat and apples, while also taking advantage of American plants, such as potatoes, corn, and tobacco.

In both North and South America, Europeans established economies of exploitation. They were generally determined to do little labor themselves. In Latin America, they developed various institutions to extract native labor. They established a long corridor of slave-labor plantation systems from the Mid-Atlantic English colonies through the Caribbean and into Brazil. Except for tobacco, the crops grown derived largely from the Old World. So did the slaves, forcibly imported from Africa and sold in America to plantation owners who preferred them to less easily controlled white indentured servants and less hardy indigenous laborers who lacked the Africans' immunity to European diseases. The slave trade corroded the political and social structures of African societies while drawing the economies and peoples of Europe, Africa, and the Americas into a vast worldwide web of production based on slave labor

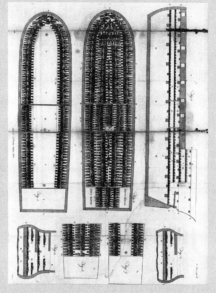

that some historians have suggested in its efficient organization and use of labor set the stage for the Industrial Revolution.

The impact of slavery in the Americas was not limited to the lives of the black slaves. Whites in the New World numbered about 12 million in 1820, compared to some 6 million blacks. However, up to that time only about 2 million whites had migrated there, compared to some 11 million or more Africans forcibly imported as slaves. Such numbers reveal the effects of brutal slave working conditions and the high mortality and sharply reduced birthrates of the slave population relative to those of the free white population.

None of the statistics, however, enables us to assess adequately the role of slavery in the history of the Americas or, more particularly, the United States. The United States actually imported only slightly more than a quarter as many slaves as did Brazil or the British and French Caribbean regions together, yet the consequences of the forced migration of just over half a million Africans have been and remain massive. Consider just the American Civil War and the endurance of societal racism and inequality or, more positively, the African contribution to American industrial development, language, music, literature, and artistic culture. The impact of the Atlantic slave trade has been and continues to be felt at both ends of the original "trade."

THINK AHEAD

◆ Why was the Spanish Empire an empire based on economies of exploitation? How was the labor of non-European peoples drawn into the economy of this empire?

◆ How and why did the plantation economy develop? Why did it rely on African slaves for its labor? What were the consequences of the slave trade for Africa? What were the consequences for Africans forced to migrate and their descendants in the Americas?

◆ Why do we think of the plantation economy as a global, rather than regional system of production? Why was it the "engine" of Atlantic basin trade?

THE LATE-FIFTEENTH-CENTURY EUROPEAN encounter with the American continents changed the world. The more than two and a half centuries of European domination and government that followed the encounter made the Americas a region where European languages, legal and political institutions, trade, and religion prevail. These developments in the Americas gave Europe more influence over other world cultures and civilizations than it would otherwise have achieved.

Within decades of the European voyages of discovery, Native Americans, Europeans, and Africans began to interact in a manner unprecedented in human history. The Native Americans of North and South America encountered bands of European conquerors and European Roman Catholic missionaries. Technological and military superiority as well as political divisions among the Native Americans allowed the Europeans to realize their material and religious ambitions. By the middle of the sixteenth century Europeans had begun to import black Africans into the American continents as chattel slaves, converting them to Christianity in the process. Consequently, by the close of the sixteenth-century Europe, the Americas, and Africa had become linked in a vast transatlantic economy that extracted material and agricultural wealth from the American continents largely on the basis of the nonfree labor of impressed Native Americans and imported African slaves.

The next century would see English and French colonists settling in North America and the Caribbean, introducing different political values and, through the English, Protestantism. These North American colonists would also become part of the transatlantic economy, and many would become economically involved directly or indirectly with African slavery. They too would interact with the Native Americans of North America, sometimes destroying their cultures, sometimes converting them to Christianity, and always drawing them into the transatlantic economy as they exploited the American wilderness.

Beginning in the sixteenth century the importation of African slaves and the use of slave labor were fundamental to the plantation economy that eventually extended from Maryland to Brazil. The slave trade intimately connected the economy of certain sections of Africa to the transatlantic economy. The slave trade had a devastating effect on the African people and cultures involved in it, but it also enriched the Americas with African culture and religion.

Periods of European Overseas Expansion

It may be useful to see the establishment of this vast new transatlantic economy in the larger context of European overseas expansion. That expansion loosed the forces that created the transatlantic economy.

Since the late fifteenth century, European contacts with the rest of the world have gone through four distinct stages. The first was that of the European discovery, exploration, initial conquest, and settlement of the Americas and commercial expansion elsewhere in the world. By the close of the seventeenth century Spain governed South America, except for Portuguese-ruled Brazil. French and British colonies had been established in North America. France, Britain, the Netherlands, and Spain controlled various islands in the Caribbean. The French, British, and Dutch held outposts in Asia.

The second era was one of colonial trade rivalry among Spain, France, and Great Britain. The Anglo-French side of the contest has often been compared to a second Hundred Years' War. During this second period both the British colonies of the North American seaboard and the Spanish colonies of Mexico and Central and South America emancipated themselves from European control. This era may be said to have closed during the 1820s (see Chapter 23).

The third stage of European contact with the non-European world occurred in the nineteenth century when European governments carved new formal empires in Africa and Asia. Those nineteenth-century empires also included new areas of European settlement such as Australia, New Zealand, and South Africa. The bases of these empires were trade, national honor, racial theories, religious expansion, and military superiority (see Chapter 25).

The last period of European empire occurred during the mid–twentieth century with the decolonization of peoples who had previously been under European colonial rule (see Chapters 32 and 33).

During the four and a half centuries before decolonization, Europeans exerted political dominance over much of the rest of the world that was out of all proportion to Europe's size or population. Europeans frequently treated other peoples as social, intellectual, and economic inferiors. They ravaged existing cultures because of greed, religious zeal, or political ambition. These actions significantly affect the contemporary relationship between Europe and its former colonies. What allowed the Europeans to exert such influence and domination for so long

Batavia. The Dutch established a major trading ▶ base at Batavia in the East Indies in the seventeenth century. Its geographical position allowed the Dutch to dominate the spice trade. Batavia is now Djakarta, capital of modern-day Indonesia.
Bildarchiv Preussicher Kulturbesitz.

over so much of the world was not any innate cultural superiority, but a technological supremacy related to naval power and gunpowder. Ships and guns allowed the Europeans to exercise their will almost wherever they chose.

Mercantilist Theory of Economic Exploitation

The early modern European empires of the sixteenth through the eighteenth centuries—empires based on commerce—existed primarily to enrich trade. Extensive trade rivalries sprang up around the world. The protection of these empires required naval power. Spain dominated the largest of these empires and constructed elaborate naval, commercial, and political structures to exploit and govern it. Finally, these empires depended largely on slave labor. Indeed, the Atlantic slave trade was a major way in which European merchants enriched themselves. That trade in turn forcibly brought the peoples of Africa into the life and culture of the New World.

To the extent that any formal economic theory lay behind the conduct of these empires, it was mercantilism, that practical creed of hard-headed business people. The terms *mercantilism* and *mercantile system* (coined by later opponents) designate a system in which governments heavily regulate trade and commerce in hope of increasing individual national wealth. Economic writers of the time believed that a nation had to gain a favorable trade balance of gold and silver bullion. A nation was truly wealthy only if it amassed more bullion than its rivals.

From beginning to end, the economic well-being of the home country was the primary concern of mercantilist writers. Colonies existed to provide markets and natural resources for the indus-

◢ As this painting of the Custom House Quay in London suggests, trade form European empires and the tariffs imposed on it were expected to generate revenue for the home country. But behind many of the goods carried in the great sailing ships in the harbor and landed on these docks lay the labor of African slaves working on the plantations of North and South America.
Samuel Scott, "Old Custom House Quay" Collection. V&A Images, the Victoria and Albert Museum. London.

DOCUMENT   Buccaneers Prowl the High Seas

Piracy was a major problem for transatlantic trade. There was often a fine line between freewheeling, buccaneering pirates operating for their own gain and privateers who in effect worked for various European governments who wanted to penetrate the commercial monopoly of the Spanish Empire. Alexander Exquemelin was a ship's surgeon who for a time plied his trade on board a pirate ship and then later settled in Holland. He wrote an account of those days in which he emphasizes the careful code of conduct among the pirates themselves and the harshness of their behavior to both wealthy ships they captured and poor farmers and fishermen whom they robbed and virtually enslaved.

◆ How did the restrictive commercial policy of the Spanish Empire encourage piracy and privateering? Was there a code of honor among the pirates? What kinds of people may have suffered most from piracy? To what extent did pirates have any respect for individual freedom? How romantic was the real world of pirates?

When a buccaneer is going to sea he sends word to all who wish to sail with him. When all are ready, they go on board, each bringing what he needs in the way of weapons, powder and shot.

On the ship, they first discuss where to go and get food supplies. … The meat is either [salted] pork or turtle … Sometimes they go and plunder the Spaniards' *corrales*, which are pens where they keep perhaps a thousand head of tame hogs. The rovers … find the house of the farmer … [whom] unless he gives them as many hogs as they demand, they hang … without mercy. …

When a ship has been captured, the men decide whether the captain should keep it or not: if the prize is better than their own vessel, they take it and set fire to the other. When a ship is robbed, nobody must plunder and keep the loot to himself. Everything taken … must be shared …, without any man enjoying a penny more than his faire share. To prevent deceit, before the booty is distributed everyone has to swear an oath on the Bible that he has not kept for himself so much as the value of six-pence … And should any man be found to have made a false oath, he would be banished from the rovers, and never be allowed in their company. …

When they have captured a ship, the buccaneers set the prisoners on shore as soon as possible, apart from two or three whom they keep to do the cooking and other work they themselves do not care for, releasing these men after two or three years.

The rovers frequently put in for fresh supplies at some island or other, often … lying off the south coast of Cuba. … Everyone goes ashore and sets up his tent, and they take turns to go on marauding expedition in their canoes. They take prisoner … poor men who catch and set turtles for a living, to provide for their wives and children. Once captured, these men have to catch turtle for the rovers as long as they remain on the island. Should the rovers intend to cruise along a coast where turtle is abound, they take the fishermen along with them. The poor fellows may be compelled to stay away from their wives and families four or five years, with no news whether they are alive or dead.

From John Exquemelin, *The Buccaneers of America*, Alexis Brown, trans. Penguin Books © 1969. pp. 70–72.

tries of the home country. In turn, the home country furnished military security and political administration for the colonies. For decades both sides assumed that the colonies were the inferior partner in the relationship. The mercantilist statesmen and traders regarded the world as an arena of scarce resources and economic limitation. They assumed that one national economy could grow only at the expense of others. The home country and its colonies were to trade exclusively with each other. To that end, they tried to forge trade-tight systems of national commerce through navigation laws, tariffs, bounties to encourage production, and prohibitions against trading with the subjects of other monarchs. National monopoly was the ruling principle.

Mercantilist ideas were always neater on paper than in practice. By the early eighteenth century, mercantilist assumptions were far removed from the economic realities of the colonies. The colonial and home markets simply did not mesh. Spain could not produce enough goods for South

America. Economic production in the British North American colonies challenged English manufacturing and led to British attempts to limit certain colonial industries, such as iron and hat making.

Colonists of different countries wished to trade with each other. English colonists could buy sugar more cheaply from the French West Indies than from English suppliers. The traders and merchants of one nation always hoped to break the monopoly of another. For all these reasons, the eighteenth century became the "golden age of smugglers."[1] The governments could not control the activities of all their subjects. Clashes among colonists could and did lead to war between governments. Consequently, the problems associated with the European mercantile empires led to conflicts around the world. (See Document, "Buccaneers Prowl the High Seas.")

[1] Walter Dorn, *Competition for Empire, 1740–1763* (New York: Harper, 1940), p. 266.

This brief overview of the periods of the European empire and of mercantile theory should provide a clearer context for understanding the character of the conquest of America and the establishment of the transatlantic economy.

Establishment of the Spanish Empire in America

CONQUEST OF THE AZTECS AND THE INCAS

Within twenty years of the arrival of Columbus (1451–1506), Spanish explorers in search of gold had claimed the major islands of the Caribbean and brutally suppressed the native peoples. These actions presaged what was to occur on the continent. The Caribbean islands became the staging areas for the further exploration and conquest of other parts of the Americas.

In 1519 Hernán Cortés (1485–1547) landed in Mexico with about 500 men and a few horses. He opened communication with nearby communities and then with Moctezuma II (1466–1520), the Aztec emperor. Moctezuma may initially have believed Cortés to be the god Quetzalcoatl, who, according to legend, had been driven away centuries earlier but had promised to return. Whatever the reason, Moctezuma hesitated to confront Cortés, attempting at first to appease him with gifts of gold that only whetted Spanish appetites. Cortés succeeded in forging alliances with some subject peoples and, most importantly, with Tlaxcala, an independent state and traditional enemy of the Aztecs. His forces then marched on the

Aztec capital of Tenochtitlán (modern Mexico City), where Moctezuma welcomed him. Cortés soon seized Moctezuma, making him a prisoner in his own capital. Moctezuma died in unexplained circumstances, and the Aztecs' wary acceptance of the Spaniards turned to open hostility. The Spaniards were driven from Tenochtitlán and nearly wiped out, but they ultimately returned and laid siege to the city. The Aztecs, under their last ruler, Cuauhtemoc (ca. 1495–1525), resisted fiercely but were finally defeated in late 1521. Cortés razed Tenochtitlán, building his own capital over its ruins, and proclaimed the Aztec Empire to be New Spain.

In 1532, largely inspired by Cortés's example in Mexico, Francisco Pizarro (ca. 1478–1541) landed on the western coast of South America to take on the Inca Empire, about which he knew almost nothing. His force included about 200 men armed with guns, swords, and horses, the military power of which the Incas did not understand. Pizarro lured the Inca ruler Atahualpa (ca. 1500–1533) into a conference and then seized him. The imprisoned Atahualpa tried to ransom himself with a hoard of gold, but instead of releasing him Pizarro treacherously had him garroted in 1533. The Spaniards fought their way to Cuzco, the Inca capital, and captured it, effectively ending the Inca Empire. The Spanish faced insurrections, however, and fought among themselves for decades. Effective royal control was not established until the late 1560s.

The conquests of Mexico and Peru are among the most dramatic and brutal events in modern world history. Small military forces armed with advanced weapons and in alliance with indigenous enemies of the ruling Aztecs and Incas subdued, in a remarkably brief time, thise two advanced, powerful peoples. The spread of European diseases, especially smallpox, among the Native Americans also aided the conquest. The native populations had long lived in isolation, and many of them succumbed to the new diseases. But beyond the drama and bloodshed, these conquests, as well as those of other Native American peoples, marked a fundamental turning point. Whole civilizations with long histories and a record of enormous social, architectural, and technological achievement were effectively destroyed. Native American cultures endured, accommodating to European dominance, but there was never any doubt about which culture had the upper hand.

THE ROMAN CATHOLIC CHURCH IN SPANISH AMERICA

The Spanish conquest of the West Indies, Mexico, and the South American continent opened that vast region to the Roman Catholic faith. Roman Catholic priests followed in the steps of the explorers and conquerors. As it had in the Castilian reconquest of the Iberian Peninsula from the Moors, religion played a central role in the conquest of the New World. In this respect the crusade against Islamic civilization in Spain and

Ⱥ **Spanish Conquest of Mexico.** A sixteenth-century Aztec drawing depicts a battle during the Spanish conquest of Mexico.
Corbis–Bettmann. Archivo Iconografico. S. A./Corbis.

OVERVIEW   The Columbian Exchange

The same ships that that carried Europeans and Africans to the Americas also transported animals, plants, and diseases that had never before appeared in the New World. There was a similar transport back to Europe and Africa. Historians call this cross-continental flow "the Columbian exchange." The overall result was an ecological transformation that continues to shape the world.

To the Americas

Animals	pigs, cattle, horses, goats, sheep, chickens
Plants	apples, peaches, pears, apricots, plums, oranges, mangos, lemons, olives, melons, almonds, grapes, bananas, cherries, sugar cane, rice, wheat, oats, barley, onions, radishes, okra, dandelions, cabbage, and other green vegetables
Diseases	smallpox, influenza, bubonic plague, typhoid, typhus, measles, chicken pox, malaria, and diphtheria

From the Americas

Animals	turkeys
Plants	maize, tomatoes, sweet peppers, chilis, potatoes, sweet potatoes, squash, pumpkins, manioc (tapioca), beans, cocoa, peanuts, pecans, pineapples, guavas, avocados, blueberries, and tobacco
Diseases	syphilis

the crusade against the indigenous religions of the Americas were closely related. In both cases the Castilian monarchy received approval from church authorities for a policy of military conquest on the grounds of converting non-Christians to the Christian faith and eradicating their indigenous religious practices. The mission of conversion justified military conquest and the extension of political control and dominance. As a consequence of this policy, the Roman Catholic Church in the New World was always a conservative force working to protect the political power and prestige of the conquerors and the interests of the Spanish authorities.

The relationship between political authority and the propagation of religious doctrine was even closer in the New World than on the Iberian Peninsula. The papacy recognized that it could not from its own resources support so extensive a missionary effort, the full requirements for which became clear only after the conquests of Mexico and Peru. The papacy therefore turned over much of the control of the church in the New World directly to the Spanish monarchy. There was thus always a close relationship between the political and economic goals of the monarchy and the role of the church. The zeal of both increased early in the sixteenth century as the papacy and the Habsburg monarchy fought the new enemy of Protestantism, which they were determined should have no foothold in America. As a consequence, the Roman Catholicism that spread throughout the Spanish domains of America

took the form of the increasingly zealous faith associated with the Counter-Reformation.

During the sixteenth century the Roman Catholic Church, represented more often than not by the mendicant orders such as the Franciscans and Dominicans, and later by the newly formed Jesuits, sought to convert the Native Americans. In the early decades these conversions often occurred shortly before the Spanish exterminated Native Americans or after they had conquered them. The conversion effort also involved attempts to eradicate surviving Indian religious practices. The Roman Catholic authorities tended to tolerate some residual Indian ceremonies in the sixteenth century but worked to prohibit them during the seventeenth century. Thus religious conversion represented, among other things, an attempt to destroy still another part of the Native American culture. Furthermore, conversion did not bring acceptance; even until late in the eighteenth century, there were few Native American Christian priests.

Real tension, however, existed between the early Spanish conquerors and the mendicant friars who sought to minister to the Native Americans. Without conquest the church could not convert the Native Americans, but the priests often deplored the harsh conditions imposed on the native peoples. By far the most effective and outspoken clerical critic of the Spanish conquerors was Bartolomé de Las Casas (1474–1566), a Dominican. He contended that conquest was not necessary for conversion. One result of his campaign was new royal regulations after 1550.

DOCUMENT | A Contemporary Describes Forced Indian Labor at Potosí

The Potosí range in Bolivia was the site of the great silver-mining industry in the Spanish Empire. The vast wealth of the region became legendary almost as soon as mining commenced there in the 1540s. Native Americans, most of whom were forced laborers working under the mita *system of conscription, did virtually all of the work underground. This description, written by a Spanish friar in the early seventeenth century, portrays both the large size of the enterprise and the harsh conditions that the Native Americans endured. At any one time only one third of the 13,300 conscripted Native Americans were employed. The labor force was changed every four months.*

◆ How efficient does the description suggest the mines were? What would have been the likely effects of working so long underground surrounded by burning candles?

According to His Majesty's warrant, the mine owners on this massive range have a right to the *mita* [conscripted labor] of 13,300 Indians in the working and exploitation of the mines, both those which have been discovered, those now discovered, and those which shall be discovered. It is the duty of the Corregidor [municipal governor] of Potosí to have them rounded up and to see that they come in from all the provinces between Cuzco over the whole of El Collao and as far as the frontiers of Tarija and Tomina. ...

The *mita* Indians go up every Monday morning to the locality of Guayna Potosí which is at the foot of the range; the Corregidor arrives with all the provincial captains or chiefs who have charge of the Indians assigned them, and he there checks off and reports to each mine and smelter owner the number of Indians assigned him for his mine or smelter; that keeps him busy till 1 P.M., by which time the Indians are already turned over to these mine and smelter owners.

After each has eaten his ration, they climb up the hill, each to his mine, and go in, staying there from that hour until Saturday evening without coming out of the mine; their wives bring them food, but they stay constantly underground, excavating and carrying out the ore from which they get the silver. They all have tallow candles, lighted day and night; that is the light they work with, for as they are underground, they have need of it all the time. ...

These Indians have different functions in the handling of the silver ore; some break it up with bar or pick, and dig down in, following the vein in the mine; others bring it up; others up above keep separating the good and the poor in piles; others are occupied in taking it down from the range to the mills on herds of llamas; every day they bring up more than 8,000 of these native beasts of burden for this task. These teamsters who carry the metal do not belong to the *mita*, but are mingados—hired.

From Antonio Vázquez de Espinosa, *Compendium and Description of the Indies* (ca. 1620), trans. by Charles Upson Clark (Washington, DC: Smithsonian Institution Press, 1968), p. 62, quoted in Helen Delpar, ed., *The Borzoi Reader in Latin American History* (New York: Alfred A. Knopf, 1972), pp. 92–93.

Another result of Las Casas's criticism was the emergence of the "**Black Legend**," according to which all Spanish treatment of the Native Americans was unprincipled and inhumane. Those who created this view of Spanish behavior drew heavily on Las Casas's writings. Although substantially true, the "Black Legend" nonetheless exaggerated the case against Spain. Certainly the rulers of the native empires—as the Aztec demands for sacrificial victims attest—had often themselves been exceedingly cruel to their subject peoples.

By the end of the sixteenth century the church in Spanish America had become largely an institution upholding the colonial status quo. Although individual priests did defend the communal rights of Indian tribes, the colonial church prospered as the Spanish elite prospered through its exploitation of the resources and peoples of the New World. The church became a great landowner through crown grants and through bequests from Catholics who died in the New World. The monasteries took on an economic as well as a spiritual life of their own. Whatever its concern for the spiritual welfare of the Native Americans, the church remained one of the indications

that Spanish America was a conquered world. Those who spoke for the church did not challenge Spanish domination or any but the most extreme modes of Spanish economic exploitation. The church at best only modestly moderated the forces exploiting human labor and material wealth. By the end of the colonial era in the late eighteenth century, the Roman Catholic Church had become one of the single most conservative forces in Latin America and would continue to be so for at least the next century and a half.

Economies of Exploitation in the Spanish Empire

The colonial economy of Spanish America was an economy of exploitation in two senses. First, the organization of labor within the Spanish Empire in one situation after another involved structures of highly dependent servitude or slavery. Second, the resources of the continent were exploited in mercantilist fashion for the economic advantage of Spain.

VARIETIES OF ECONOMIC ACTIVITY

The early *conquistadores* ("conquerors") had primarily been interested in gold, but by the middle of the sixteenth century silver mining provided the chief source of metallic wealth. The great silver mining centers were Potosí in present-day Bolivia and smaller sites in northern Mexico. The Spanish crown was particularly interested in mining because it received one fifth (the *quinto*) of all mining revenues. The crown thus maintained a monopoly over the production and sale of mercury, which was required for separating silver from the other impurities in the ore. Silver mining was a flourishing source of wealth for the Spanish until the early seventeenth century, when the industry underwent a recession because of lack of new investment and the increasing costs involved in deeper mines. Nonetheless, silver predominated during the colonial era and experienced a major boom, especially in Mexico, during the eighteenth century. Its production for the benefit of Spaniards and the Spanish crown epitomized the wholly extractive economy on which Latin American colonial life was based.

The activities associated with this extractive economy—mining the ore, smelting it, harvesting wood to feed the smelters' fires—required labor. From the initial contact with America, there were too few Spanish colonists to provide the needed labor. Furthermore, the social status and expectations of those colonists who did come to the Americas made them unlikely to provide wage labor. Consequently, the Spaniards looked first to the native Indian population and then to black African slaves. Indian labor dominated on the continent and African labor in the Caribbean. (See Document, "A Contemporary Describes Forced Indian Labor at Potosi.")

Encomienda   The Spanish devised a series of institutions to exploit Native American labor. The first was the *encomienda*, a formal grant by the crown of the right to the labor of a specific number of Native Americans for a particular time. An *encomienda* usually involved a few hundred Native Americans but might grant the right to the labor of several thousand. The *encomienda* was first used on Hispaniola but spread to the continent as the conquest took place. *Encomienda* as an institution persisted in some parts of Latin America well into the eighteenth century but had generally declined by the middle of the sixteenth. Some Native Americans substituted payments in kind or cash for labor.

The Spanish crown disliked the *encomienda* system. The monarchy was distressed by reports from concerned clergy that the Native Americans were being mistreated under the system and feared that *encomienda* holders were attempting to transform themselves into a powerful independent nobility in the New World.

Repartimiento   The passing of the *encomienda* led to another arrangement of labor servitude, the *repartimiento*, which was largely copied from the draft labor practices of the Incas. *Repartimiento*, in an adaptation of the Incan *mita*, required adult male Native Americans to devote a set number of days of labor annually to Spanish economic enterprises. In the mines of Potosí, the *repartimiento* was known as the *mita*. The time limitation on *repartimiento* led some Spanish managers to use their workers in an extremely harsh manner, under the assumption that more fresh workers would soon be appearing on the scene. Native Americans sometimes did not survive their days of labor rotation.

The Cruelties Used by the Spaniards on the Indians, from a 1599 English edition of *The Destruction of the Indies* by Bartolomé de las Casas. These scenes were copied from a series of engravings produced by Theodore de Bry that accompanied an earlier edition. British Library.

The Hacienda Outside the mines, the major institution using dependent labor in the Spanish colonies was the *hacienda*. This institution, which dominated rural and agricultural life in Spanish colonies on the continent, developed when the crown, partly to counter the extension of the *encomienda*, made available grants of land. These grants led to the establishment of large landed estates owned by **peninsulares**, whites born in Spain, or Creoles, whites born in America. The crown thus continued to use the resources of the New World for patronage without directly impinging on the Native Americans because the grazing that occurred on the *haciendas* required far less labor than did the mines. The establishment of *haciendas* represented the transfer of the principle of the large unit of privately owned land, which was characteristic of Europe and especially of Spain, to the New World. Such estates would become one of the most important features of Latin American life. Laborers on the *hacienda* usually stood in some relation of formal servitude to the owner. Furthermore, they were usually required to buy goods for everyday living on credit from the owner. They were rarely able to repay the resulting debts and thus could not move to work for new landowners. This system was known as **debt peonage**. There were two major products of the *hacienda* economy: foodstuffs for mining areas and urban centers, and leather goods used in vast quantities on mining machinery. Both farming and ranching were thus subordinate to the mine economy.

THE DECLINE OF THE NATIVE AMERICAN POPULATION

The conquest and the economy of exploitation and forced labor (and the introduction of European diseases) produced extraordinary demographic consequences for the Indian population. Beginning in the sixteenth century Native Americans had begun to die off in huge numbers. The pre-Columbian population of America is a matter of great controversy, but conservative estimates put the Indian population at the time of Columbus's discovery at well over 50 million. In New Spain (Mexico) alone, the population probably declined from approximately 25 million to fewer than 2 million within the first century after the conquest. Similar depopulation of native peoples appears to have occurred elsewhere in Spanish America during approximately the same period. Thereafter the Indian population began to expand slowly. Whatever the exact figures, the precipitous drop eliminated the *conquistadores'* easy supply of exploitable labor.

COMMERCIAL REGULATION AND THE FLOTA SYSTEM

Because Queen Isabella of Castile (r. 1474–1504) had commissioned Columbus, the technical legal link between the New World and Spain was the crown of Castile. Its powers both at home and in America were subject to few limitations.

Smallpox. Introduced by Europeans to the Americas, ▶ smallpox had a devastating effect on Native American populations. It swept through the Aztec capital of Tenochtitlán soon after the Spaniards arrived, contributing to the fall of the city. This illustration of the effect of the plague in the Aztec capital is from a postconquest history known as the Florentine Codex compiled for Spanish church authorities by Aztec survivors.

Sixteenth century drawing of smallpox victims. Atzec original codex Florentino. Courtesy President and Fellows of Harvard College. Courtesy Peabody Museum of Archeology and Ethnology, Harvard University, photograph by Hillel Burger.

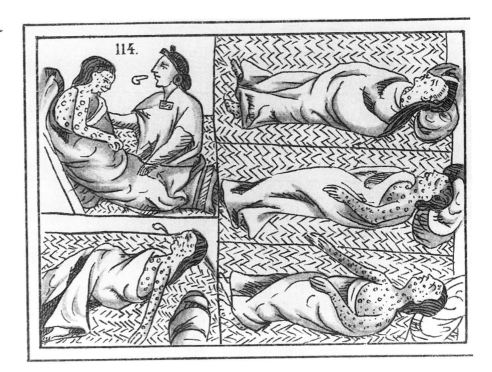

Government of America was assigned to the Council of the Indies, which, in conjunction with the monarch, nominated the viceroys of New Spain and Peru. These viceroys were the chief executives in the New World and carried out the laws promulgated by the Council of the Indies. Each of the viceroyalties included subordinate judicial councils known as *audiencias*. There were also a variety of local officers, the most important of which were the *corregidores*, who presided over municipal councils. These offices provided the monarchy with a vast array of opportunities for patronage, usually bestowed on persons born in Spain. Virtually all political power flowed from the top of this political structure downward; in effect, there was little or no local initiative or self-government (see Map 18–1).

The colonial political structures existed largely to support the commercial goals of Spain. Spanish control of its American empire involved a system of monopolistic trade regulation that was more rigid in appearance than in practice. The trade monopoly was often breached. The Casa de Contratación (House of Trade) in Seville regulated all trade with the New World. Cádiz was the only Spanish port to be used for the American trade. In America there were similarly specific ports for trade both to Spain and with non-Spanish merchants. The latter trade was highly restricted. The Casa de Contratación was the single most influential institution of the Spanish Empire, and its members worked closely with the Consulado (Merchant Guild) of Seville and other groups involved with the American commerce in Cádiz. The entire organization was geared to benefit the Spanish monarchy and these privileged merchant groups.

A complicated system of trade and bullion fleets administered from Seville provided the key for maintaining the trade monopoly. Each year a fleet of commercial vessels (the *flota*) controlled by Seville merchants, escorted by warships, carried merchandise from Spain to a few specified ports in America. These included Portobello, Veracruz, and Cartagena. There were no authorized ports on the Pacific coast. Areas far to the south, such as Buenos Aires, received goods only after the shipments had been unloaded at one of the authorized ports. After selling their wares, the ships were loaded with silver and gold bullion, usually wintered in heavily fortified Caribbean ports, and then sailed back to Spain. The flota system always worked imperfectly, but trade outside it was illegal. Regulations prohibited the Spanish colonists within the American empire from trading directly with each other and from building their own shipping and commercial industry. Foreign merchants were also forbidden to breach the Spanish monopoly.

Colonial Brazil and Slavery

Spain and Portugal originally had rival claims to the Americas. In 1494, by the Treaty of Tordesillas, the pope divided the seaborne empires of Spain and Portugal by drawing a line west of the Cape Verde Islands. In 1500 a Portuguese explorer landed on the coast of what is present-day Brazil, which extended east of the papal line of division, and thus Portugal gained a major hold on the South American continent.

Portugal had fewer human and material resources to devote to its New World empire than did Spain. The crown granted captaincies to private persons that permitted them to attempt

MAP 18–1 Viceroyalties in Latin America in 1870. Spain organized its vast holdings in the New World into Viceroyalties, each of which had its own governor and other administrative officials.

to exploit the region. The native people in the lands that Portugal governed lived for the most part in small, nomadic groups. In this they differed from the native peoples of Spanish America, with their centralized empires, cities, and organized political structures. As a result, labor practices in the two regions were also different. The Portuguese imported Africans as slaves rather than using the Native Indian population, as did the Spanish in most areas.

By the mid–sixteenth century, sugar production had gained preeminence in the Brazilian economy, although some minerals were discovered and some cattle raised. Because sugar cane was grown on large estates (*fazendas*) with African slave labor, the dominance of sugar meant also the dominance of slavery.

Toward the close of the seventeenth century, sugar prices declined and the economy suffered. In the early eighteenth century, however, significant deposits of gold were discovered in southern Brazil. Immigrants from Portugal joined the ensuing gold rush, and economic activity moved suddenly toward the south. This shift, however, did not reduce Brazil's reliance on slave labor. In fact, the expansion of gold mining also led to the increased importation of African slaves. Nowhere, except perhaps in the West Indies, was slavery as important as it was in Brazil, where it persisted until 1888.

The taxation and administration associated with gold mining brought new, unexpected wealth to the eighteenth-century Portuguese monarchy, allowing it to rule without recourse to the Cortés or traditional parliament for taxation. Through transatlantic trade the new wealth generated from Brazilian gold also filtered into all the major trading nations, which could sell their goods to Portugal as well as profit from the slave trade.

As in the Spanish Empire, the Portuguese crown attempted to establish a strong network of regulation around Brazilian trade. Brazil, however, required less direct control by the Portuguese than the Spanish Empire required from Spain, and as a result, Brazil's colonial settlers may have felt less resentment toward the Portuguese government than the settlers of the Spanish Empire felt toward the Spanish administrators. In Brazil, where the basic unit of production was the plantation, there were fewer large cities than in Spanish America. The crown's determination in Spanish America to have precious metals sent to Spain required a vast colonial administration. The sugar plantations of Brazil, in contrast, did not require such direct administration. Consequently, the Portuguese were willing to allow more local autonomy than was Spain. More local officials were allowed to serve in the government in Brazil than in Spanish America, where the administration was dominated by officials born in Spain. In Spanish America the use of Indian labor, which was important to the colonial economy, required government supervision. Brazil, less dependent on Indian labor, felt no such constraints. Indeed, the Portuguese government condoned policies whereby Indian tribes were driven into the back country or exterminated. Throughout the eighteenth century the Portuguese government also favored the continued importation of slaves.

Sugar plantations of Brazil and the West Indies were a major source of the demand for slave labor. Slaves are here shown grinding sugar cane and refining sugar, which was then exported to the consumer markets in Europe.
© Hulton-Deutsch Collection/Corbis.

Native Americans in the Saint Lawrence region of North America were drawn into the transatlantic economy through interaction with French fur traders in the early 17th century. This illustration shows Samuel de Champlain, the founder of New France, assisting his Huron allies in an attack on the Iroquois in part of an ongoing struggle for control of valuable fur grounds. The palm trees in the background suggest that the artist was unfamiliar with the region.

Samuel de Champlain "Voyages…," Paris, 1613. Illustration opp. pg. 322. Early battle with the Iroquois. Rare Books Division, the New York Public Library, Astor Lenox and Tilden Foundation.

French and British Colonies in North America

French explorers had pressed down the St. Lawrence river valley in Canada during the seventeenth century. French fur traders and Roman Catholic Jesuit missionaries had followed in their wake, with the French government supporting the missionary effort. By the end of the seventeenth century a significant but sparsely populated French presence existed in Canada. Trade rather than extensive settlements characterized the French effort. The largest settlement was Quebec, founded in 1608. Some French settlers married Native American women; the absence of a drive to permanently claim land reduced conflict between the French and the Native Americans. It was primarily through the fur trade that French Canada functioned as part of the early transatlantic economy.

For most readers of this volume, the story of the founding of the English-speaking colonies along the Atlantic seaboard is relatively familiar, but it needs to be set in the larger world context. Beginning with the first successful settlement in Jamestown, Virginia, in 1607 and ending with the establishment of Georgia in 1733, the eastern seaboard of the United States became populated by a series of English colonies. Other nations, including the Dutch and Swedes, had founded settlements, but all of them were eventually taken over during the seventeenth century by the English.

A wide variety of reasons led to the founding of the English colonies. Settlement for enrichment from farming and trade accounted for some settlements, such as Virginia and New Amsterdam (after 1664, New York). Others, such as the Carolinas, were developed by royal favorites who were given vast

land tracts. James Oglethorpe founded Georgia as a refuge for English debtors. But the pursuit of religious liberty constituted the major driving force of the Pilgrim and Puritan founders of Massachusetts, the Baptist Roger Williams in Rhode Island, the Quaker William Penn in Pennsylvania, and the Roman Catholic Lord Baltimore in Maryland.

With the exception of Maryland, these colonies were Protestant. The Church of England dominated the southern colonies. In New England, varieties of Protestantism associated with or derived from Calvinism were in the ascendancy. In their religious affiliations, the English-speaking colonies manifested two important traits derived from the English experience. First, much of their religious life was organized around self-governing congregations. Second, their religious outlook derived from those forms of Protestantism that were suspicious of central political authority and especially of potentially despotic monarchs. In this regard, their cultural and political outlook differed sharply from the cultural and political outlook associated with the Roman Catholicism of the Spanish Empire. In a sense the values of the extreme Reformation and Counter-Reformation confronted each other on the two American continents.

The English colonists had complex interactions with the Native American populations. Unlike the Spanish to the south or the French to the north, they had only modest interest in missionary enterprise. As in South America, new diseases imported from Europe took a high death toll among the native population. Unlike Mexico and Peru, however, North America had no large Native American cities. The Native American populations were far more dispersed, and intertribal animosity was intense. The English often encountered well-organized resistance, as from the Powhatan conspiracy in Virginia and the Pequots in New England. The most powerful of the Native American groups was the Iroquois Nation, organized in the early eighteenth century in New York. The Iroquois battled successfully against other tribes and long negotiated successfully with both the Dutch and the English. The English also often used one tribe against another, and the Native Americans also tried to use the English or the French in their own conflicts. The outcome of these struggles between the English settlers and the Native Americans was rarely full victory for either side, but rather mutual exhaustion, with the Native Americans temporarily retreating beyond the reach of English settlements and the English temporarily restraining their initial claims. From the late seventeenth century through the American Revolution, however, the Native Americans of North America were drawn into the Anglo-French Wars that were fought in North America as well as Europe. Indeed, Native American alliances became important for the Anglo-French conflict on the Continent, which was intimately related to their rivalry over transatlantic trade (see Chapter 20).

The largest economic activity throughout the English-speaking colonies was agriculture. From New England through the Middle Atlantic states there were mostly small farms tilled by free white labor; from Virginia southward it was the plantation economy, dependent on slavery. During the early eighteenth century the chief products raised on these plantations were tobacco, indigo, rice, and sugar. Although slavery was a dominant institution in the South, all of the colonies included slaves. The principal port cities along the seaboard—Boston, Newport, New York, Philadelphia, Baltimore, and Charleston—resembled small provincial English cities. They were primarily trading centers through which goods moved back and forth between the colonies and England and the West Indies. The commercial economies of these cities were all related to the transatlantic slave trade.

Until the 1760s the political values of the Americans resembled those of their English counterparts. The colonials were thoroughly familiar with events in England. They sent many of their children there to be educated. They were monarchists but, like their English counterparts, suspicious of monarchical power. Their politics involved vast amounts of patronage and individual favors. Their society was clearly hierarchical, with an elite that functioned like a colonial aristocracy and many ordinary people who were dependent on that aristocracy. Throughout the colonies during the eighteenth century, the Anglican Church grew in influence and membership. The prosperity of the colonies might eventually have led them to separate from England, but in 1750 few people thought that would occur.

Both England and France had important sugar islands in the Caribbean. England held Jamaica and Barbados, and France held Saint Domingue (Haiti), Guadeloupe, and Martinique. The plantations on these islands were worked by African slaves, and the trade and commerce of the northern British colonies were closely related to meeting the needs of these islands.

Roanoke. The first successful English colonies in North America in the 17th century were preceded by two failed efforts on Roanoke Island in what is now North Carolina in the late 16th century. John White accompanied both attempts, the second as governor. White was a perceptive and sensitive observer whose watercolor paintings provide invaluable information about Native American life in the coastal Carolina region at the time of contact. This painting shows the Algonquian village of Secoton. The houses were bark covered. In the lower left is a mortuary temple. The dancers in the lower right are performing a fertility ceremony. The man sitting in the platform in the upper right is keeping birds away from the corn crop.

The Bridgeman Art Library International Ltd.

Slavery in the Americas

Black slavery was the final mode of forced or subservient labor in the New World. Unlike the labor exploitation of Native Americans discussed earlier in this chapter, black slavery extended throughout not only the Spanish Empire but also Portuguese Brazil and the English-speaking colonies of North America.

ESTABLISHMENT OF SLAVERY

As the numbers of Native Americans in South America declined due to disease and exploitation, the Spanish and the Portuguese turned to the labor of imported African slaves.

By the late sixteenth century, in the islands of the West Indies and the major cities of South America, black slaves equaled or surpassed the white European population.

On much of the South American continent dominated by Spain, the number of slaves declined during the late seventeenth century, and the institution became less fundamental there than elsewhere. Slavery continued to prosper, however,

Slave Auction Notice. Africans who survived the voyage across the Atlantic were immediately sold into slavery in the Americas. This slave-auction notice relates to a group of slaves whose ship had stopped at Charleston, South Carolina, and then landed elsewhere in the region to auction its human cargo. Notice the concern to assure potential buyers that the slaves were healthy.
Corbis-Bettmann.

in Brazil and in the Caribbean. Later, starting with the importation of slaves to Jamestown in 1619, slavery spread into the British North American colonies and became a fundamental institution there.

One of the forces that led to the spread of slavery in Brazil and the West Indies was the cultivation of sugar. Sugar cane required a large investment in land and equipment, and only slave labor could provide enough workers for the extremely profitable sugar plantations. As the production of sugar expanded, so did the demand for slaves, and more slaves were imported.

By the close of the seventeenth century the Caribbean islands were the world center for sugar production. As the European appetite for sugar continued to grow, the slave population continued to expand. By 1725 black slaves may have constituted almost 90 percent of the population of Jamaica. The situation was similar throughout the West Indies. There and elsewhere, in Brazil and the southern British colonies, prosperity and slavery went hand in hand. The wealthiest and most prized of the colonies were those that raised consumer staples, such as sugar, rice, tobacco, or cotton, by slave labor.

THE PLANTATION ECONOMY AND TRANSATLANTIC TRADE

The **plantation economy** was comprised of plantations that stretched from Maryland through the West Indies and into Brazil. They formed a vast corridor of slave societies in which social and economic subordination was based on both involuntary servitude and race. This kind of society, in its total dependence on slave labor and racial differences, was something novel in world history; it had not existed before the European discovery and exploitation of the Americas. The social and economic influence of plantation slavery touched not only the plantation societies themselves, but also West Africa, western Europe, and New England. It persisted from the sixteenth century through the second half of the nineteenth century, ending with the British effort to outlaw the slave trade during the first half of the nineteenth century, the Latin American Wars of Independence, the Emancipation Proclamation of 1862 in the United States, and the Brazilian emancipation of 1888. Every society in which it existed still contends with its long-term effects.

The slave trade was part of the larger system of transatlantic trade that linked Europe, Africa, and the European colonies in South America, the Caribbean, and North America. In this system the Americas supplied labor-intensive raw materials like tobacco, sugar, coffee, precious metals, cotton, and indigo. Europe supplied manufactured goods like textiles, liquor, guns, metal wares, and beads, not to mention various forms of cash, including even gold. And Africa supplied gold, ivory, wood, palm oil, gum, and other products, as well as the slaves who provided the labor to create the American products. By the eighteenth century slaves were the predominant African export.

SLAVERY ON THE PLANTATIONS

The plantations in the Americas to which the African slaves eventually arrived were always in a fairly isolated rural setting. Their products, however, were agricultural goods produced for an external overseas market that was part of a larger integrated transatlantic economy. The plantation might raise food for its owners and their slaves, but the main production—whether sugar, tobacco, or, later, cotton and coffee—was intended for export. In turn, plantation owners imported from other parts of the world virtually all the finished or manufactured goods they used or consumed.

The life conditions of plantation slaves differed from colony to colony. Most owners possessed relatively few slaves, and vast slaveholdings were the exception. Black slaves living in Portuguese areas had the fewest legal protections. In the Spanish colonies the church attempted to provide some small protection for black slaves but devoted much more effort toward protecting the Native Americans. Slave codes were developed in the British and the French colonies during the seventeenth century, but they provided only the most limited protection. Virtually all slave owners feared a slave revolt; slave-related legislation and other regulations were intended to prevent such an event. Slave laws favored the master rather than the slave. Masters were permitted to punish slaves by whipping and other harsh corporal punishment. Furthermore, slaves were often forbidden to gather in large groups lest they plan a revolt. In most slave-owning societies, the marriages of slaves were not recognized by law. The children of slaves continued to be slaves and were owned by the owner of the parents. Slave families could be separated by the owner or after the owner's death.

The daily life of most slaves during these centuries was one of hard agricultural labor, poor diet and clothing, and inadequate housing. The death rate among slaves was high. Their welfare and their lives were sacrificed to the ongoing expansion of the plantations that made their owners wealthy and that produced goods demanded by consumers in Europe. Scholars have argued that slaves in one area or another had a better existence than others, but it is generally accepted that slaves in all plantation societies suffered under difficult conditions. The specifics of those conditions may have varied, but they were not significantly better in one place than another.

The African slaves who were transported to the Americas were, like the Native Americans, converted to Christianity: in the Spanish domains to Roman Catholicism, and in the English colonies to various forms of Protestantism. In both cases, they became largely separated from African religious outlooks. Although some African practices survived in muted forms, and slaves did manage to mix Christianity with African religion, the conversion of Africans to Christianity nonetheless represented another example of the crushing of a set of non-European cultural values in the context of the New World economies and social structures.

The European settlers in the Americas and the slave traders were also prejudiced against black Africans. Many Europeans thought Africans were savage or less than civilized. Others looked down on them simply because they were slaves. These attitudes had been shared by both Christians and Muslims in the Mediterranean world, where slavery had long existed. Furthermore, many European languages and European cultures attached negative connotations to the idea and image of blackness. In virtually all plantation societies, race was an important element in keeping black slaves subservient. Although racial thinking in regard to slavery became more important in the nineteenth century, the fact that slaves were differentiated from the rest of the population by race as well as by their status as chattel property was fundamental to the system.

Africa and the Transatlantic Slave Trade

It was the establishment of plantations demanding the use of slave labor that drew Africa and its peoples into the heart of the transatlantic economy. As Native American peoples were decimated by conquest and European diseases or proved unsatisfactory as plantation laborers, colonial entrepreneurs began to look elsewhere for people to work their plantations. First the Portuguese, and then the Spanish, Dutch, French, and English (others would follow, including Americans) turned to west, central, and, to a lesser degree, southeastern Africa for an ample supply of slaves. Thus the Atlantic slave trade was not overtly the result of racist principles, but of the economic needs of the colonial powers and their willingness to exploit weaker peoples to satisfy them. However, this willingness was based on the tacit racist assumption that non-European, nonwhite tribal peoples were subhuman and could be enslaved for European purposes.

The Portuguese, who were the principal carriers throughout most of the history of the trade, had a virtual monopoly until the Dutch broke it in the 1640s and briefly became the chief carriers. The French and the English came into the trade only in the late seventeenth century, yet during the eighteenth century, which saw the greatest shipments, they carried almost half the total traffic. Americans, too, were latecomers but avid slavers who managed to make considerable profits before and even after Britain and the United States outlawed slaving in 1807.

If gold and the search for a sea route to Asia brought the first European ships to Africa, slaves were the main commodity for which they returned for a long time. Slaving was an important part of the massive new overseas trade that financed much European and American economic development that so dramatically changed the West during the nineteenth century. The success of this trade, bought at the price of immense human suffering, helped propel Europe and some of its colonial offshoots in the Americas into world dominance.

THE BACKGROUND OF SLAVERY

Slavery seems to have been one of the tragic facts of human societies as far back as we can trace its history. Although linked to warfare and the age-old practice of taking captives, it cannot be fully explained by military or economic necessity.

Virtually every premodern state around the globe depended on slavery to some extent (see Map 18–2). The Mediterranean and African worlds were no exception, in both the pre-Islamic and the Islamic periods. Slave institutions in sub-Saharan Africa were ancient and included traffic with the Mediterranean world. The Islamic states of southwestern Asia and North Africa continued and even increased this traffic, importing slaves from both the Sudan and Horn of Africa as well as the East African coast,

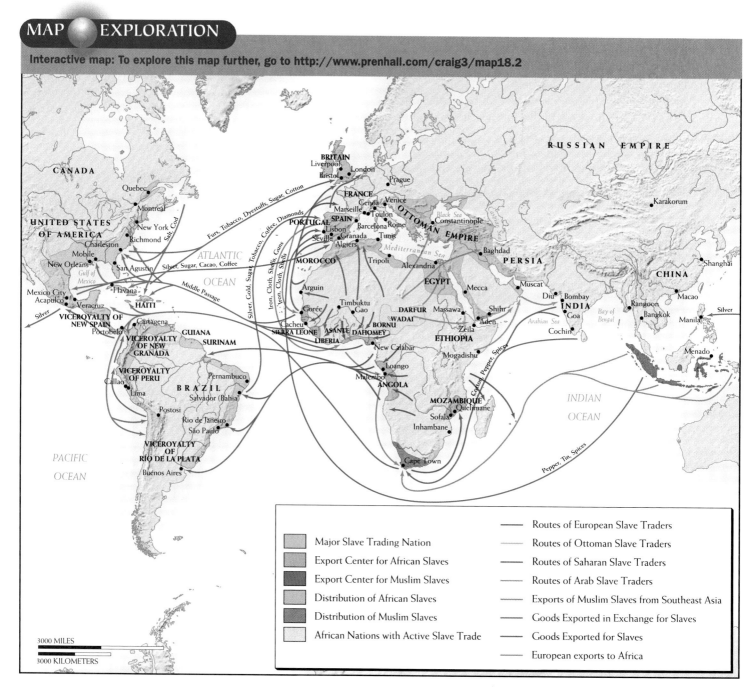

MAP EXPLORATION

Interactive map: To explore this map further, go to http://www.prenhall.com/craig3/map18.2

MAP 18–2 The Slave Trade, 1400–1860. Slavery is an ancient institution and complex slave-trading routes were in existence in Africa, the Middle East, and Asia for centuries, but it was the need to supply labor for the plantations of the Americas that led to the greatest movement of peoples across the face of the earth.

although they took fewer slaves from Africa than from eastern Europe and Central Asia. Central Asia, for example, was the source of most of the (largely Turkish) slave-soldier dynasties that came to rule many Islamic states from India to North Africa. (Hence it is not surprising that the word *slave* is derived ultimately from *Slav*.) Both Mediterranean Christian and Islamic peoples were using slaves—mostly Greeks, Bulgarians, Turkish prisoners of war, and Black Sea Tartars, but also Africans—well before the voyages of discovery opened sub-Saharan sources of slaves for the new European colonies overseas.

Not all forms of slavery were as dehumanizing as the chattel slavery that came to predominate (with the sanction of Christian authorities) during the colonization of the Americas. Islamic law, for example, although permitting slavery, also ameliorated it. All slavery, however, involved the forceful exploitation and degradation of some human beings for the profit of others, the denial of basic freedoms, and sometimes the sundering, often violently, of even the closest family ties.

Africa suffered immense social devastation when it was the chief supplier of slaves to the world. The societies that were built to a great extent on the exploitation of African slavery also suffered enduring consequences, not the least of which, many believe, is racism.

SLAVERY AND SLAVING IN AFRICA

The trade that long before the fifteenth century supplied African slaves to the Islamic lands of the Mediterranean and to southwestern and southern Asia has conventionally been termed the "Oriental" slave trade. The savannahs of the Sudan and the Horn of Africa were the two prime sources of slaves for this trade. The trade managed by Europeans, conventionally called the "Occidental" slave trade, can be traced at least to the thirteenth century, when Europeans established sugar cane plantations on Cyprus soon after Muslim forces had driven them out of the Holy Land. In Cypress, as later in Brazil and the Caribbean islands, slaves proved an especially profitable workforce for the labor-intensive process of sugar production. This industry subsequently spread westward to Crete and Sicily and, in the fifteenth century, to the Portuguese Atlantic islands of Madeira and São Thomé.

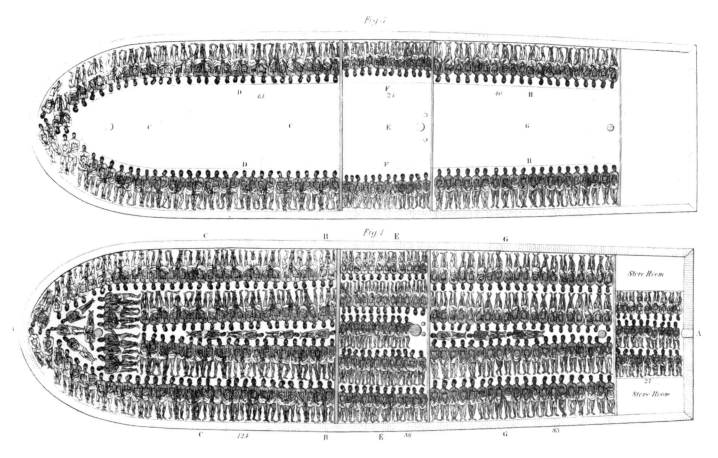

Slave Ship.   Loading plan for the main decks of the 320-ton slave ship *Brookes*. The *Brookes* was only 25 feet wide and 100 feet long, but as many as 609 slaves were crammed on board for the nightmarish passage to the Americas. The average space allowed each person was only about 78 inches by 16 inches.
Photographs and Prints Division, Schomburg Center for Research in Black Culture, The New York Public Library, Astor, Lenox, and Tilden Foundations.

<King Alfonzo I** of the Congo holds an audience with
European ambassadors who kneel before him.
Courtesy of the Library of Congress.

The Portuguese in particular developed the plantation system of slave labor as they began their expansion into the Atlantic and beyond. Although the savannah and Horn regions were the earliest sources for this trade, voyages beginning in the fifteenth century by first the Portuguese and then other Europeans opened the western coasts of Africa as far south as Angola, making them the prime slaving areas. A third but less important source region for both Occidental and Oriental trades was the eastern coast of Africa below the Horn.

Before the full development of the transatlantic slave trade by about 1650, slavery and slave trading had been no more significant in Africa than anywhere else in the world.[2] Indigenous African slavery resembled that of other premodern societies. It was apparently most common, if still limited, in the areas of the savannah and Horn, presumably because these areas were involved in external slave trading. In the western and central Sudan, slavery came largely to be regulated by Islamic norms, but in the Horn, specifically in Ethiopia, slavery was practiced in both Christian and Muslim communities. Estimates suggest that about 10,000 slaves per year, most of them female, were taken from sub-Saharan Africa through the Oriental trade.

By about 1650 the newer Occidental slave trade of the Europeans had become as large as the Oriental trade and for the ensuing two centuries far surpassed it. It affected adversely all of Africa, disrupting especially western and central African society. As a result of the demand for young male slaves on the plantations of the Americas, West Africa experienced a sharp

drain on its productive male population. Between 1640 and 1690, although the price of a slave at the coast remained constant, the number of slaves sold to European carriers doubled, indicating the increasing participation of Africans in the expanding trade. With the growing demand for slaves came an increase in internal warfare in western and central Africa. Moreover, as the external trade destroyed the regional male-female population balance, an internal market for female slaves in particular arose.

These developments accelerated during the eighteenth century—at the height of the Occidental trade. It was also during this period that African states and slave traders were most heavily involved as regulators and suppliers of the trade. Slave prices at times accelerated accordingly. Owing to population depletion and regional migrations, however, the actual number of sold slaves declined in some areas. The population declined sharply in the coastal and inland areas hardest hit by the ravages of the trade in the later eighteenth century and continued to decline in places even until 1850.

As European nations, followed by nations in the Americas, slowly began to outlaw slaving and slavery in the nineteenth century, occidental demand slowed and prices for slaves sank. The result was that the oriental and internal trades increased. Slave exports from East Africa and the Sudan and Horn increased significantly after about 1780, and indigenous African slavery, predominantly of women, also expanded. Indeed, by about 1850 the internal African trade surpassed the combined oriental and (now outlawed and decreasing) occidental trade. This traffic was dominated by the same figures— merchants, warlords, and rulers—who had previously profited from external trade.

---

[2] The summary follows closely that of P. Manning, *Slavery and African Life: Occidental, Oriental, and African Slave Trades* (Cambridge: Cambridge University Press, 1990), pp. 127–140.

Slave dealing in the streets of Zanzibar. ➤
Slaving was a part of East African trade
for centuries.
Corbis-Bettmann.

Indigenous African slavery began a real decline only at the end of the nineteenth century, in part because of the dominance of European colonial regimes and in part because of internal changes. The formal end of African indigenous slavery occurred over a long period, beginning in 1874 in the Gold Coast and ending only in 1928 in Sierra Leone.

THE AFRICAN SIDE OF THE TRANSATLANTIC TRADE

Africans were actively involved in the transatlantic slave trade. Except for the Portuguese in central Africa, European slave traders generally obtained their human cargoes from private or government-sponsored African middlemen at coastal forts or simply at anchorages along the coast. A system of forts built by Europeans mostly between 1640 and 1750, for example, dominated the Gold Coast. This situation was the result of both the desire and ability of Africans to control inland trade and the vulnerability of Europeans to tropical disease (a new European arrival stood a less than 50 percent chance of surviving a year on the tropical African coast). Thus it was largely African middlemen who undertook the actual capture or procurement of slaves and the difficult, dangerous task of marching them to the coast. These middlemen were generally either wealthy merchants who could mount slaving expeditions inland or the agents of African chieftaincies or kingdoms who sought to profit from the trade. (See Document, "A Slave Trader Describes the Atlantic Passage.")

The media of exchange were varied. At first they usually involved mixed barter for goods that ranged from gold dust or firearms to beads and alcohol. As time went on they came increasingly to involve some form of monetary payment. This exchange drained productive resources (human beings) in return for nonproductive wealth.

The chief western and central African slaving regions provided different numbers of slaves at different times, and the total number of exported slaves varied sharply between periods. When one area was unable to produce sufficient numbers to meet demand (whether as a result of depopulation of choice areas, local warfare, or changing state policies), the European traders shifted their buying to other points. Thus, between 1526 and 1550 the major sources of the slaves for the Atlantic trade were the Kongo-Angola region (34 percent), the Guinea coast of Cape Verde (25.6 percent), and Senegambia (23.5 percent).[3] By contrast, between 1761 and 1810 the French drew some 52 percent of their slaves from Angola and 24 percent from the Bight of Benin, but only 4.8 percent from Senegambia, whereas the British relied most heavily on the Bight of Biafra and central Africa.[4] Traders naturally went where population density and the presence of active African merchant or state suppliers promised the best numbers and prices, although prices do not seem to have varied radically in a given period.

THE EXTENT OF THE SLAVE TRADE

The slave trade varied sharply in extent from period to period. Only about 3 percent of the total Occidental trade occurred before 1600, and only about 14 percent between 1600 and 1700. The period of greatest activity, 1701–1810, accounted for

[3] Philip Curtin, *The Atlantic Slave Trade: A Census* (Madison: University of Wisconsin Press, 1969), p. 101.
[4] Curtin, *The Atlantic Slave Trade*, pp. 101, 129; James A. Rawley, *The Transatlantic Slave Trade: A History* (New York: W. W. Norton, 1981), p. 129.

DOCUMENT | A Slave Trader Describes the Atlantic Passage

During 1693 and 1694 Captain Thomas Phillips carried slaves from Africa to Barbados on the ship Hannibal. *The financial backer of the voyage was the Royal African Company of London, which held an English crown monopoly on slave trading. Phillips sailed to the west coast of Africa, where he purchased the Africans who were sold into slavery by an African king. Then he set sail westward.*

◆ Who are the various people described in this document who in one way or another were involved in or profited from the slave trade? What dangers did the Africans face on the voyage? What contemporary attitudes could have led this ship captain to treat and think of his human cargo simply as goods to be transported? What are the grounds of his self-pity for the difficulties he met?

Having bought my complement of 700 slaves, 480 men and 220 women, and finish'd all my business at Whidaw [on the Gold Coast of Africa], I took my leave of the old king and his cappasheirs [attendants], and parted, with many affectionate expressions on both sides, being forced to promise him that I would return again the next year, with several things he desired me to bring from England. ... I set sail the 27th of July in the morning, accompany'd with the East-India Merchant, who had bought 650 slaves, for the Island of St. Thomas ... from which we took our departure on August 25th and set sail for Barbadoes.

We spent in our passage from St. Thomas to Barbadoes two months eleven days, from the 25th of August to the 4th of November following: in which time there happened such sickness and mortality among my poor men and Negroes. Of the first we buried 14, and of the last 320, which was a great detriment to our voyage, the Royal African Company losing ten pounds by every slave that died, and the owners of the ship ten pounds ten shillings, being the freight agreed on to be paid by the charter-party for every Negro delivered alive ashore to the African Company's agents at Barbadoes. ... The loss in all amounted to near 6500 pounds sterling.

The distemper which my men as well as the blacks mostly died of was the white flux, which was so violent and inveterate that no medicine would in the least check it, so that when any of our men were seized with it, we esteemed him a dead man, as he generally proved. ...

The Negroes are so incident to the small pox that few ships that carry them escape without it, and sometimes it makes vast havock and destruction among them. But tho' we had 100 at a time sick of it, and that it went thro' the ship, yet we lost not above a dozen by it. All the assistance we gave the diseased was only as much water as they desir'd to drink, and some palm-oil to annoint their sores, and they would generally recover without any other helps but what kind nature gave them. ...

But what the small pox spar'd, the flux swept off, to our great regret, after all our pains and care to give them their messes in due order and season, keeping their lodgings as clean and sweet as possible, and enduring so much misery and stench so long among a parcel of creatures nastier than swine, and after all our expectations to be defeated by their mortality. ...

No gold-finders can endure so much noisome slavery as they do who carry Negroes; for those have some respite and satisfaction, but we endure twice the misery; and yet by their mortality our voyages are ruin'd, and we pine and fret ourselves to death, and take so much pains to so little purpose.

From Thomas Phillips, *"Journal," A Collection of Voyages and Travels*, Vol. VI, ed. by Awnsham and John Churchill (London, 1746), as quoted in Thomas Howard, ed., *Black Voyage: Eyewitness Accounts of the Atlantic Slave Trade* (Boston: Little, Brown and Company, 1971), pp. 85–87.

over 60 percent of the total, and even the final half century of slaving until 1870 accounted for over 20 percent of the total. Despite moves by European nations to abolish slaving in the early 1800s, the Portuguese still transported more than a million slaves to Brazil between 1811 and 1870. In fact, more slaves landed in the Americas in these final years of the trade than during the entire seventeenth century.[5] We would do well to remember how long it actually took the "modern" occidental world to abolish the trade in African slaves.

The overall number of African slaves exported during the occidental trade—effectively, between 1451 and 1870—is still debated and must be seen in the larger context of all types of slaving in Africa in the same period. A major unknown—for both the occidental and the oriental trades—is the number of slaves who died under the brutal conditions to which they were subjected when captured and transported overland and by sea. The most reliable estimates pertain only to those slaves who actually landed abroad, and these estimates are more reliable for the occidental trade than for the older, smaller, and more dispersed oriental trade. Those who actually reached an American or Old World destination in the occidental trade totaled more than 11 million souls.

Recent scholarship estimates that at a minimum Africa lost some 13 million people to the Atlantic trade alone during its four centuries of existence. Another 5 million or

[5] Rawley, *The Transatlantic Slave Trade*, p. 429; Curtin, *Atlantic Slave Trade*, p. 268.

LANGUAGE	Estimated Slave Imports into the Americas and Old World by Region, 1451–1870				
British North America	523,000	French Caribbean	1,655,000	Brazil (Portuguese)	4,190,000
Spanish America	1,687,000	Dutch Caribbean	500,000	Old World	297,000
British Caribbean	2,443,000	Danish Caribbean	50,000	**Total**	**11,345,000**

Figures as calculated by James A. Rawley, *The Transatlantic Slave Trade: A History* (New York: W. W. Norton, 1981), p. 428, based on his and other more recent revisions of the careful but older estimates of Philip D. Curtin, *The Atlantic Slave Trade: A Census* (Madison: University of Wisconsin Press, 1969), especially pp. 266, 268.

more were lost to the oriental trade. Finally, the occidental trade spurred an apparently huge increase in internal slavery, and according to the estimate of one expert, an additional 15 million people were enslaved within African societies themselves.[6]

CONSEQUENCES OF THE SLAVE TRADE FOR AFRICA

The statistics in the previous section hint at the massive impact slave trading had on African life and history. Still, the question of the actual effects remains difficult and disputed. Modern scholarship has tended to emphasize the importance for African history of the coming of the maritime European powers in general and the Atlantic slave trade in particular. Regarding the slave trade, it is safe to say that the impact was considerable, however much that general conclusion must be qualified in the light of particular cases. (See Document, "Olaudah Equiano Recalls His Experience at the Slave Market in Barbados.") Consider some examples.

We do not know for certain if the Atlantic trade brought net population loss or gain to specific areas of West Africa. The wide and rapid spread of maize and cassava cultivation in forest regions after these plants had been imported from the Americas may have fueled African population increases that offset regional human loss through slaving. We know, however, that slaving took away many of the strongest young men in many areas and, in the oriental trade zones, most of the young women.

Similarly, we do not know if more slaves were captured as byproducts of local wars or from pure slave raiding, but we do know they were captured and removed from their societies.

Nor do we know if slaving always inhibited development of trade or perhaps sometimes stimulated it because com-

Slave Coffle. This 18th-century print shows bound African captives being forced to a slaving port. It was largely African middlemen who captured slaves in the interior and marched them to the coast. North Wind Picture Archives.

merce in a range of African products—from ivory to wood and hides—often accompanied that in slaves. Still, we do know that in general, the exchange of productive human beings for money or goods that were generally not used to build a productive economy was a great loss for African society as a whole.

Finally, because we do not yet have accurate estimates of the total population of Africa at different times over the four centuries of the Atlantic slave trade, we cannot determine with certainty its demographic impact. We can, however, make some educated guesses. If, for example, tropical Africa had possibly 50 million inhabitants in 1600, it would then have had 30 percent of the combined population of the Americas, the Middle East, Europe, and Africa. If in 1900, after the depredations of the slave trade, it had 70 million inhabitants, its population would have dropped to only slightly more than 10 percent of the combined population of the same world regions. Accordingly, current best estimates indicate that overall

---

[6] Manning, *Slavery African and Life*, pp. 37, 170–171.

Job ben Solomon. Captured by Mandingo enemies and sold to a Maryland tobacco planter, Job ben Solomon accomplished the nearly impossible feat of returning to Africa as a freeman. By demonstrating his talents as a Muslim scholar, including his ability to write the entire Qur'an from memory, he astonished his owners and eventually convinced them to let him go home.

"The Fortunate Slave," An Illustration of African Slavery in the early 18th century by Douglas Grant (1968). From "Some Memoirs of the Life of Job," by Thomas Bluett 1734. Photo by Robert D. Rubic/Precision Chromes, Inc., Rare Books Division, the New York Public Library/Art Resource, NY, Lenox and Tilden Foundations.

African population growth suffered significantly as a result of the devastating numbers of people lost to enslavement or to the increased warfare and decreased birthrate tied to the slave trade. Figures like these also give some idea of slavery's probable impact on Africa's ability to keep up with the modern industrializing world.[7]

It is important to remember that even in West and central Africa, which bore the brunt of the Atlantic trade, its impact and the response to it were so varied in different places and times that even accurate overall statistics could be misleading for particular cases. In a few cases, kingdoms such as Dahomey

(the present Republic of Benin) seem to have sought and derived immense economic profit for a time by making slaving a state monopoly. Other kingdoms, such as Benin, sought to stay almost completely out of slaving and derived no gain from it. In many instances, including the rise of Asante power or the fall of the Yoruba Oyo Empire, it now appears that increased slaving was in part a result as well as a cause of regional instability and change. Increased warfare meant increased prisoners to be enslaved and a surplus to be sold off; however, whether slaving gave good cause for war is still a major question in each regional context.

Similarly, if one can establish, as seems evident, a major increase in indigenous slavery as a result of the external trade to occident and orient during the centuries in question, we have to assume major social consequences for African society as a whole, but the specific consequences would differ according to the specifics of regional situations. For example, in West Africa relatively more men were taken as slaves than women, whereas in the Sahelian Sudanic regions relatively more women than men were taken. In the west the loss of so many men increased the pressures for polygamy and possibly the regional use of women slaves as well, whereas in the Sahelian Sudanic regions the loss of women may have stimulated polyandry and reduced the birthrate significantly.

CHRONOLOGY

Conquest of the Americas and the Transatlantic Slave Trade

1494	The Treaty of Tordesillas divides the seaborne empires of Spain and Portugal
1500	The Portuguese arrive in Brazil
1519–1521	Hernan Cortés conquers the Aztec Empire
1531–1533	Francisco Pizarro conquers the Inca Empire
1607	Jamestown, Virginia, first permanent English settlement in North America founded
1608	The French found Quebec
1619	First African slaves brought to British North America
1650	Transatlantic slave trade becomes bigger than the older oriental slave trade
1700s	Over 6 million slaves imported from Africa to the Americas
1807	Slavery abolished in British domains
1808	The importation of slaves abolished in the United States
1874–1928	Indigenous African slavery abolished
1888	Slavery abolished in Brazil

---

[7] On all of the preceding points regarding probable impact of the trade, see Manning, *Slavery and African Life*, pp. 126–148, 168–176.

DOCUMENT | Olaudah Equiano Recalls His Experience at the Slave Market in Barbados

Olaudah Equiano composed one of the most popular and influential slave narratives of the late eighteenth and early nineteenth centuries. He had led a remarkable life. Born in West Africa in what is today Nigeria, he spent his early life among the Ibo. He was captured and sold into slavery, making the dreaded Atlantic crossing described in the previous document. In the passage that follows, he recounts his arrival in Barbados and the experience of cultural disorientation, sale into slavery, and seeing Africans separated from their families. Equiano's life did not end in slavery, the most destructive aspects of which he also described in vivid detail. He achieved his freedom and then led an adventuresome life on various commercial and military ships plying the Caribbean, the Atlantic, and the Mediterranean. He also made a trip to the Arctic Ocean. Equiano's account consequently describes not only the life of a person taken from Africa and sold into American slavery, but also the life of a person who, once free, explored the entire transatlantic world. His autobiographical narrative, which first appeared in 1789 and displayed Equiano's wide reading, served two purposes for the antislavery campaign that commenced in the second half of the eighteenth century. First, it provided a firsthand report of the slave experience in crossing from Africa to America. Second, his powerful rhetoric and clear arguments demonstrated that, if free, Africans could achieve real personal independence. Many defenders of slavery had denied that Africans possessed the character and intelligence to be free persons.

♦ What were the fears of the Africans on the slave ship as they approached the port? How were older slaves in Barbados used to calm their fears? How did the sale of slaves proceed? What happened to African families in the process of the sale?

At last, we came in sight ... of Barbados, ... and we soon anchored ... off Bridgetown. Many merchants and planters now came on board. ... They put us in separate parcels, and examined us attentively. They also made us jump, and pointed to the land, signifying we were to go there. We thought by this we should be eaten by these ugly men, as they appeared to us; and when, soon after we were all put down under the deck again, there was much dread and trembling among us, and nothing but bitter cries to be heard all the night from these apprehension, insomuch that at last the white people got some old slaves from the land to pacify us. They told us we were not to be eaten, but to work, and were soon to go on land, where we should see many of our country people. This report eased us much.... We were conducted immediately to the merchant's yard, where we were all pent up together like so many sheep in a fold, without regard to sex or age. As every object was new to me, everything filled me with surprise ... and indeed I thought these people were full of nothing but magical arts. ... We were not many days in the merchant's custody before we were sold after their usual manner which was this: On a signal given (as the beat of a drum), the buyers rush at once into the yard where the slaves are confined, and make choice of that parcel they like best. The noise and clamour with which this is attended, and the eagerness visible in the countenances of the buyers, serve not a little to increase the apprehension of the terrified Africans, who may well be supposed to consider them as the ministers of that destruction to which they think themselves devoted. In this manner, without scruple, relations and friends separate, most of them never to see each other again. I remember in the vessel in which I was brought over, in the men's apartment, there were several brothers who, in the sale, were sold in different lots; and it was very moving on this occasion to see and hear their cries at parting.... Surely this is a new refinement in cruelty, which, while it has no advantage to atone for it, thus aggravates distress, and adds fresh horrors even to the wretchedness of slavery.

From *The Interesting Narrative of the Life of Olaudah Equiano or Gustavus Vassa, The African, Written by Himself* (first published 1789), as quoted in Henry Louis Gates Jr., and William L. Andrews, eds., *Pioneers of the Black Atlantic: Five Slave Narratives from the Enlightenment, 1772–1815* (Washington, DC: Counterpoint, 1998), pp. 221–223.

Even though slavery existed previously in Africa, the scale of the Atlantic trade was unprecedented and hence had an unprecedented impact on indigenous social, political, and economic realities. In general, the slave trade measurably changed patterns of life and balances of power in the main affected areas, whether by stimulating trade or warfare (or at least raiding for new supplies), by disrupting previous market and political structures, by substantially increasing slavery inside Africa, or by disturbing the male-female ratio (and hence the workforce balance and birthrate patterns) and consequently the basic social institution of monogamous marriage.

If the overseas slave trade did not substantially and irrevocably change every region it touched, at the least it siphoned indigenous energy into ultimately counterproductive or destructive directions. This, in turn, meant the inhibition of true economic development, especially in central and coastal West Africa. The Atlantic slave trade must by any standard be described as one of the most tragic aspects of European involvement in Africa.

Slave Ship.

Summary

European Conquest of the New World   The contact between the native peoples of the American continents and the European explorers of the fifteenth and sixteenth centuries transformed world history. In the Americas, the native peoples had established a wide variety of civilizations. Some of their most remarkable architectural monuments and cities were constructed during the centuries when European civilizations were feeble in comparison. Until the European explorations, the civilizations of the Americas, and Eurasia, and Africa had had no significant contact with each other.

Within half a century of the landing of Columbus, millions of America's native peoples had encountered Europeans intent on conquest, exploitation, and religious conversion. Because of their advanced weapons, navies, and the new diseases they brought with them, as well as internal divisions among the Native Americans, the Europeans achieved a rapid conquest.

The Transatlantic Economy   In both North and South America, economies of exploitation were established. In Latin America, various institutions were developed to extract native labor. From the Mid-Atlantic English colonies through the Caribbean and into Brazil, slave-labor plantation systems were established. The slaves were forcibly imported from Africa and sold in America to plantation owners. The economies and peoples of Europe, Africa, and the Americas were thus drawn into a vast worldwide web of production based on slave labor.

Slavery   The impact of slavery in the Americas was not limited to the life of the black slaves. Whites in the New World numbered about 12 million in 1820, compared to some 6 million blacks. However, only about 2 million whites had migrated there, compared to some 11 million or more Africans forcibly imported as slaves. Such numbers reveal the effects of brutal slave conditions and the high mortality and low birthrates of slave populations.

None of these statistics, however, enables us to assess the role that slavery has played in the Americas or, in particular, the United States. The United States actually received only a bit more than a quarter as many slaves as did Brazil alone or the British and French Caribbean regions together, yet the forced migration of Africans as slaves into the United States had profound consequences. Consider just the American Civil War and the endurance of racism and inequality or, more positively, the African contribution to American industrial development, language, music, literature, and artistic culture. The Atlantic slave trade's impact continues to be felt at both ends of the original "trade."

Review Questions

1. How were small groups of Spaniards able to conquer the Aztec and Inca Empires?

2. What was the basis of the mercantilist theory of economics? What was the relationship between the colonial economies and those of the homelands?

3. Describe the economies of Spanish America and Brazil. What were the similarities and differences between them and the British and French colonies in the Caribbean and North America? What role did the various colonies play in the transatlantic economy?

4. Why did forced labor and slavery develop in tropical colonies? How was slavery in the Americas different from slavery in earlier societies?

5. What was the effect of the transatlantic slave trade on West African societies? On East Africa? What role did Africans themselves play in the slave trade?

Key Terms

Black Legend   (p. 508)

conquistadores   (p. 509)

debt peonage   (p. 510)

encomienda   (p. 509)

hacienda   (p. 510)

mercantilism   (p. 504)

peninsulares   (p. 510)

plantation economy   (p. 516)

repartimiento   (p. 509)

Documents CD-ROM

European Explorations and Expansion
14.7 Bartolomé de las Casas: Persecutor Turns Protector
14.8 The British Encounter Maoris: A Sailor's Impressions

Trade and Exploitation Across the Atlantic
15.1 The "Black Legend" of Spain: Bartolomé de las Casas

15.2 "Our Kingdom Is Being Lost": Nzinga Mbemba (Afonso I)
15.3 Olaudah Equiano, The Life of Olaudah Equiano, or Gustavus Vassa, The African
15.4 Commerce, Slavery, and Religion in North Africa
15.5 Thomas Nelson, Slavery and the Slave of Brazil

NOTE: *To learn more about the topics in this chapter, see the Suggested Readings at the end of the book.*

Glossary

absolutism Term applied to strong centralized continental monarchies that attempted to make royal power dominant over aristocracies and other regional authorities.

Acropolis The religious and civic center of Athens. It is the site of the Parthenon.

Afrikaans The new language, derived from Dutch, that evolved in the seventeenth-and eighteenth-century Cape Colony.

agape Meaning "love feast." A common meal that was part of the central ritual of early Christian worship.

agora The Greek marketplace and civic center. It was the heart of the social life of the polis.

agricultural revolution The innovations in farm production that began in the eighteenth century and led to a scientific and mechanized agriculture.

amir/emir An Islamic military commander.

Amitabha Buddha The Buddhist Lord of the Western Paradise, or Pure Land.

Annam The Chinese term for Vietnam.

Anschluss Meaning "union." The annexation of Austria by Germany in March 1938.

anti-Semitism Prejudice, hostility, or legal discrimination against Jews.

apartheid "Apartness," the term referring to racist policies enforced by the white-dominated regime that existed in South Africa from 1948 to 1992.

apostolic primacy The doctrine that the popes are the direct successors to the Apostle Peter and as such heads of the church.

appeasement The Anglo-French policy of making concessions to Germany in the 1930s to avoid a crisis that would lead to war. It assumed that Germany had real grievances and Hitler's aims were limited and ultimately acceptable.

Areopagus The governing council of Athens, originally open only to the nobility. It was named after the hill on which it met.

Arianism The belief formulated by Arius of Alexandria (ca. 280–336 C.E.) that Jesus was a created being, neither fully man nor fully God, but something in between.

aristocratic resurgence Eighteenth-century aristocratic efforts to resist the expanding power of European monarchies.

Aryans The Indo-European speakers who invaded India and Iran in the second and first millenia B.C.E.

assignats Government bonds based on the value of confiscated church lands issued during the early French Revolution.

Atman-Brahman The unchanging, infinite principle of reality in Indian religion.

Atomists School of ancient Greek philosophy founded in the fifth century B.C.E. by Leucippus of Miletus and Democritus of Abdera. It held that the world consists of innumerable, tiny, solid, indivisible, and unchangeable particles called atoms.

Augustus The title given to Octavian in 27 B.C.E. and borne there–after by all Roman emperors.

Ausgleich Meaning "compromise." The agreement between the Habsburg Emperor and the Hungarians to give Hungary considerable administrative autonomy in 1867. It created the Dual Monarchy, or Austria-Hungary.

Axis The alliance between Nazi Germany and fascist Italy. Also called the Pact of Steel.

ayan Ottoman notables.

ayatollah A major Shi'ite religious leader.

bakufu "Tent government." The military regime that governed Japan under the shōguns.

bazaari The Iranian commercial middle class.

bhakti Hindu devotional movements.

bishop Originally a person elected by early Christian congregations to lead them in worship and supervise their funds. In time, bishops became the religious and even political authorities for Christian communities within large geographical areas.

Black Death The bubonic plague that killed millions of Europeans in the fourteenth century.

Black Legend The argument that Spanish treatment of native Americans was uniquely inhumane.

blitzkrieg Meaning "lightning war." The German tactic early in World War II of employing fast-moving, massed armored columns supported by airpower to overwhelm the enemy.

bodhisattva A "Buddha to be" who postpones his own nirvana until he has helped all other beings become enlightened.

Bolsheviks Meaning the "majority." Term Lenin applied to his faction of the Russian Social Democratic Party. It became the Communist Party of the Soviet Union after the Russian Revolution.

Boxers A nationalistic Chinese religious society that attacked foreigners and their encroachments on China in the late nineteenth century.

boyars The Russian nobility.

Brahmanas Texts dealing with the ritual application of the Vedas.

brainwashing The Communist practice of forced indoctrination of individuals in Marxist thought followed by confession of errors, repentance, and reacceptance by society. It was particularly favored in China under Mao.

Bronze Age The name given to the earliest civilized era, c. 4000 to 1000 B.C.E. The term reflects the importance of the metal bronze, a mixture of tin and copper, for the peoples of this age for use as weapons and tools.

caliphate The true line of succession to Muhammad.

calpulli The wards into which the Aztec capital, Tenochtitlan, was divided.

cantonments The segregation of areas in which Europeans lived in British-ruled India from those areas inhabited by native Indians.

Catholic Emancipation The grant of full political rights to Roman Catholics in Britain in 1829.

catholic Meaning "universal." The body of belief held by most Christians enshrined within the church.

caudillo Latin American strongman, or dictator, usually with strong ties to the military.

censor Official of the Roman republic charged with conducting the census and compiling the lists of citizens and members of the Senate.

Censorate The branch of the imperial Chinese government that acted a watchdog, reporting instances of misgovernment directly to the emperor and remonstrating when it considered the emperor's behavior improper.

Chartism The first large-scale European working-class political movement. It sought political reforms that would favor the interests of skilled British workers in the 1830s and 1840s.

chiaroscuro The use of shading to enhance naturalness in painting and drawing.

chicha A maize beer brewed by the *mamakuna* for the Inca elite.

civilization A form of human culture marked by urbanism, metallurgy, and writing.

clash of civilizations   Political theory, most often identified with Harvard political scientist Samuel P. Huntington, which contends that conflict between the world's religio-cultural traditions or "civilizations" increasingly dominates world affairs.

Cold War   The ideological and geographical struggle between the United States and its allies and the USSR and its allies that began after World War II and lasted until the dissolution of the USSR in 1989.

collectivization   The bedrock of Stalinist agriculture, which forced Russian peasants to give up their private farms and work as members of collectives, large agricultural units controlled by the state.

conquistadores   Meaning "conquerors." The Spanish conquerors of the New World.

Consulate   French government dominated by Napoleon from 1799 to 1804.

Convention   French radical legislative body from 1792 to 1794.

corvée   A French labor tax requiring peasants to work on roads, bridges, and canals.

Counter-Reformation   The sixteenth-century reform movement in the Roman Catholic Church in reaction to the Protestant Reformation.

Creoles   Persons of European descent who were born in the Spanish colonies.

Crusades   Religious wars directed by the church against infidels and heretics.

Cultural Revolution   A movement launched by Mao between 1965 and 1976 against the Soviet-style bureaucracy that had taken hold in China. It involved widespread disorder and violence.

culture   The ways of living built up by a group and passed on from one generation to another.

cuneiform   A writing system invented by the Sumerians that used a wedge-shaped stylus, or pointed tool, to write on wet clay tablets that were then baked or dried (*cuneus* means "wedge" in Latin). The writing was also cut into stone.

Curia   The papal government.

daimyo   Japanese territorial lord.

Daoism   A Chinese philosophy that teaches that wisdom lies in becoming one with the *Tao*, the "way," which is the creative principle of the universe.

debt peonage   A system that forces agricultural laborers (peons) to work and live on large estates (haciendas) until they have repaid their debts to the estate's owner.

deism   A belief in a rational God who had created the universe, but then allowed it to function without his interference according to the mechanisms of nature and a belief in rewards and punishments after death for human action.

Delian League   An alliance of Greek states under the leadership of Athens that was formed in 478–477 B.C.E. to resist the Persians.

demesne   The part of a manor that was cultivated directly for the lord of the manor.

dependency theory   Theory that contends that after the states of Latin America achieved independence in the early-mid nineteenth century they remained economically and culturally dependent on Europe, and later, the United States.

devshirme   The system under the Ottoman Empire that required each province to furnish a levy of Christian boys who were raised as Muslims and became soldiers in the Ottoman army.

dharma   Moral law or duty.

diaspora   Dispersion of an originally homogeneous people or culture. Among the many diasporas in world history, some of the most famous are the Jewish, the Chinese, the African, the Irish, and the Armenian.

Diet   The bicameral Japanese parliament.

Diet of Worms   The meeting of the representative (diet) of the Holy Roman Empire presided over by the Emperor Charles V at the Germain city of Worms in 1521 at which Martin Luther was ordered to recant his ninety-five theses. Luther refused and was declared outlaw although he was protected by the Elector of Saxony and other German princes.

diffusion   The spread of ideas, objects, or traits from one culture to another.

divine right of kings   The theory that monarchs are appointed by and answerable only to God.

domestic or putting-out system of textile production   Method of producing textiles in which agents furnished raw materials to households whose members spun them into thread and then wove cloth, which the agents then sold as finished products.

Duce   Meaning "leader." Mussolini's title as head of the Fascist Party.

Duma   The Russian parliament, after the revolution of 1905.

dynastic cycle   The term used to describe the rise, decline, and fall of China's imperial dynasties.

ego   According to Freudian theory, the part of the mind that mediates between the impulses of the id and the asceticism of the superego and allows the personality to cope with the inner and outer demands of its existence.

empiricism   The use of experiment and observation derived from sensory evidence to construct scientific theory or philosophy of knowledge.

enclosures   The consolidation or fencing in of common lands by British landlords to increase production and achieve greater commercial profits. It also involved the reclamation of waste land and the consolidation of strips into block fields.

encomienda   The grant by the Spanish crown to a colonist of the labor of a specific number of Indians for a set period of time.

Enlightenment   The eighteenth-century movement led by the *philosophes* that held that change and reform were both desirable through the application of reason and science.

Epicureans   School of philosophy founded by Epicurus of Athens (342–271 B.C.E.). It sought to liberate people from fear of death and the supernatural by teaching that the gods took no interest in human affairs and that true happiness consisted in pleasure, which was defined as the absence of pain.

equestrians   Literally "cavalrymen" or "knights." In the earliest years of the Roman Republic, those who could afford to serve as mounted warriors.

Estado Novo   The "new state" based on political stability and economic and social progress supposedly established by the dictator Getulio Vargas after 1937.

Etruscans   A people of central Italy who exerted the most powerful external influence on the early Romans.

Eucharist   Meaning "thanksgiving." The celebration of the Lord's Supper. Considered the central ritual of worship by most Christians. Also called Holy Communion.

euro   The common currency created by the EEC in the late 1990s.

European Economic Community (EEC)   The economic association formed by France, Germany, Italy, Belgium, the Netherlands, and Luxembourg in 1957. Also known as the Common Market.

European Union   The new name given to the EEC in 1993. It included most of the states of Western Europe.

Fabians   British socialists in the late nineteenth and early twentieth century who sought to achieve socialism through gradual, peaceful, and democratic means.

family economy   The basic structure of production and consumption in preindustrial Europe.

fascism Political movements that tend to be antidemocratic, anti-Marxist, antiparliamentary, and often anti-Semitic. Fascists were invariably nationalists and exhalted the nation over the individual. They supported the interests of the middle class and rejected the ideas of the French Revolution and nineteenth-century liberalism. The first fascist regime was founded by Benito Mussolini (1883–1945) in Italy in the 1920s.

fealty An oath of loyalty by a vassal to a lord, promising to perform specified services.

feudal society The social, political, military, and economic system that prevailed in the Middle Ages and beyond in some parts of Europe.

fief Land granted to a vassal in exchange for services, usually military.

Fourteen Points President Woodrow Wilson's (1856–1924) idealistic war aims.

Führer Meaning "leader." The title taken by Hitler when he became dictator of Germany.

gentry In China, a largely urban, landowning class that represented local interests and functioned as quasi-bureaucrats under the magistrates.

ghazis Warriors who carried Islam by force of arms to pagan groups.

ghettos Separate communities in which Jews were required by law to live.

glasnost Meaning "openness." The policy initiated by Mikhail Gorbachev in the 1980s of permitting open criticism of the policies of the Soviet Communist Party.

globalization Term used to describe the increasing economic and cultural interdependence of societies around the world.

Glorious Revolution The largely peaceful replacement of James II by William and Mary as English monarchs in 1688. It marked the beginning of constitutional monarchy in Britain.

Golden Horde Name given to the Mongol rulers of Russia from 1240 to 1480.

Grand Mufti The chief religious authority of the Ottoman Empire. Also called "the Shaykh of Islam."

Great Depression A prolonged worldwide economic downturn that began in 1929 with the collapse of the New York Stock Exchange.

Great Leap Forward Mao's disastrous attempt to modernize the Chinese economy in 1958.

Great Purges The imprisonment and execution of millions of Soviet citizens by Stalin between 1934 and 1939.

Great Reform Bill (1832) A limited reform of the British House of Commons and an expansion of the electorate to include a wider variety of the propertied classes. It laid the groundwork for further orderly reforms within the British constitutional system.

Great Schism The appearance of two and at times three rival popes between 1378 and 1415.

Great Trek The migration between 1835 and 1847 of Boer pioneers (called *voortrekkers*) north from British-ruled Cape Colony to establish their own independent republics.

guild An association of merchants or craftsmen that offered protection to its members and set rules for their work and products.

Guomingdang (GMD) China's Nationalist Party, founded by Sun Yat-sen.

hacienda Large landed estates in Spanish America.

hadith A saying or action ascribed to Muhammad.

Hajj The pilgrimage to Mecca that all Muslims are enjoined to perform at least once in their lifetime.

Harappan Term used to describe the first civilization of the Indus Valley.

harem The wives, concubines, female relatives, and servants in a Muslim household – usually confined to a section of a house or palace.

Hegira The flight of Muhammad and his followers from Mecca to Medina in 622 C.E. It marks the beginning of the Islamic calendar.

heliocentric theory The theory, now universally accepted, that the earth and the other planets revolve around the sun. First proposed by Aristarchos of Samos (310–230 B.C.E.).

Helots Hereditary Spartan serfs.

heretics People who publicly dissent from officially accepted dogma.

hieroglyphics The complicated writing script of ancient Egypt. It combined picture writing with pictographs and sound signs. Hieroglyph means "sacred carvings" in Greek.

Hindu Term applied to the diverse social, racial, linguistic, and religious groups of India.

Holocaust The Nazi extermination of millions of European Jews between 1940 and 1945. Also called the "final solution to the Jewish problem."

Holy Roman Empire The revival of the old Roman Empire, based mainly in Germany and northern Italy, that endured from 870 to 1806.

home rule The advocacy of a large measure of administrative autonomy for Ireland within the British Empire between the 1880s and 1914.

hoplite phalanx The basic unit of Greek warfare in which infantrymen fought in close order, shield to shield, usually eight ranks deep.

Huguenots French Calvinists.

humanism The study of the Latin and Greek classics and of the Church Fathers both for their own sake and to promote a rebirth of ancient norms and values.

humanitas The Roman name for a liberal arts education.

id According to Freudian psychoanalysis, the part of the mind that consists of amoral, irrational, driving instincts for sexual gratification, aggression, and physical and sensual pleasure.

The Iliad and the Odyssey, The Epic poems by Homer about the "Dark Age" heroes of Greece who fought at Troy. The poems were written down in the eighth century B.C.E. after centuries of being sung by bards.

imams Islamic prayer leader.

impact of modernity The effect of western political, economic, and social ideas and institutions on traditional societies.

imperator Under the Roman Republic, it was the title given to a victorious general. Under Augustus and his successors, it became the title of the ruler of Rome, meaning "emperor."

imperium In ancient Rome, the right to issue commands and to enforce them by fines, arrests, and even corporal and capital punishment.

import substitution The replacement of imported goods with those manufactured domestically.

Indo-European A widely distributed language group that includes most of the languages spoken in Europe, Persian, Sanskrit, and their derivatives.

Indo-Greeks Bactrian rulers who broke away from the Seleucid Empire to found a state that combined elements of Greek and Indian civilizations.

indulgences Remission of the temporal penalty of punishment in purgatory that remained after sins had been forgiven.

Industrial Revolution Mechanization of the European economy that began in Britain in the second half of the eighteenth century.

intifadah Literally, "shaking." Uprisings by the Palestinians against Israeli occupation.

Islam Meaning "submission." The religion founded by the prophet Muhammad.

Islamic fundamentalism A movement among many Muslims to return to the "fundamentals" of Islamic faith, life, and society.

Italia Irredenta Meaning "unredeemed Italy." Italian-speaking areas that had been left under Austrian rule at the time of the unification of Italy.

jacobins The radical republican party during the French Revolution that displaced the Girondins.

Jains An Indian religious community that teaches compassion for all beings.

Janissaries Elite Ottoman troops who were recruited through the *devshirme.*

jatis The many subgroups that make up the Hindu caste system.

jihad "Struggle in the path of God." Although not necessarily implying violence, it is often interpreted to mean holy war in the name of Islam.

July Monarchy The French regime set up after the overthrow of the Bourbons in July 1830.

Junkers The noble landlords of Prussia.

junzi The Confucian term for a person who behaves ethically, in harmony with the cosmic order.

Ka'ba A black meteorite in the city of Mecca that became Islam's holiest shrine.

Kabuki A realistic form of Japanese theater similar to English Elizabethan drama.

Kalahari A large desert in southwestern Africa that partially isolates southern Africa from the rest of he continent.

kamikaze "Divine winds" which sank a portion of the invading Mongol fleet in Japan in 1281.

karma The Indian belief that every action has an inevitable effect. Good deeds bring good results; evil deeds have evil consequences.

Khmer Rouge Meaning "Red Cambodia." The radical Communist movement that ruled Cambodia from 1975 to 1978.

kleindeutsch Meaning "small German." The argument that the German-speaking portions of the Habsburg Empire should be excluded from a united Germany.

Kristallnacht Meaning "crystal night" because of the broken glass that littered German streets after the looting and destruction of Jewish homes, businesses, and synagogues across Germany on the orders of the Nazi Party in November 1938.

La Reforma the nineteenth-century Mexican liberal reform movement that opposed Santa Ana's dictatorship and sought to foster economic progress, civilian rule, and political stability. It was strongly anti-clerical.

laissez-faire French phrase meaning "allow to do." In economics, the doctrine of minimal government interference in the working of the economy.

latifundia Large plantations for growing cash crops owned by wealthy Romans.

LDP The Liberal Democratic Party. A conservative party that has dominated postwar Japanese politics.

League of Nations The association of sovereign states set up after World War I to pursue common policies and avert international aggression.

Lebensraum Meaning "living space," The Nazi plan to colonize and exploit Eastern Europe.

Legalism The Chinese philosophical school that argued that a strong state was necessary in order to have a good society.

levée en masse The French revolutionary conscription (1792) of all males into the army and the harnessing of the economy for war production.

liberalism In the nineteenth century, support for representative government dominated by the propertied classes and minimal government interference in the economy.

liberation theology The effort by certain Roman Catholic theologians to combine Marxism with traditional Christian concern for the poor.

Logos Divine reason, or fire, which according to the Stoics, was the guiding principle in nature.

Long Count A Mayan calendar that dated from a fixed point in the past.

Long March The flight of the Chinese communists from their Nationalist foes to northwest China in 1934.

Luftwaffe The German air force in World War II.

madrasa An Islamic college of higher learning.

Magna Carta The "Great Charter" limiting royal power that the English nobility forced King John to sign in 1215.

Magna Graecia Meaning "Great Greece" in Latin, it was the name given by the Romans to southern Italy and Sicily because there were so many Greek colonies in the region.

Magyars The majority ethnic group in Hungary.

Mahabharata and *Ramayana* The two classical Indian epics.

Mahayana The "Great Vehicle" for salvation in Buddhism. It emphasized the Buddha's infinite compassion for all beings.

manakuna Inca women who lived privileged but celibate lives and had important economic and cultural roles.

Mandate of Heaven The Chinese belief that Heaven entrusts or withdraws a ruler's or a dynasty's right to govern.

Manichaeism A dualistic and moralistic view of reality in which good and evil, spirit and matter warred with each other.

mannerism A style of art in the mid to late sixteenth century that permitted artists to express their own "manner" or feelings in contrast to the symmetry and simplicity of the art of the High Renaissance.

manor Village farms owned by a lord.

Marshall Plan The U.S. program, named after Secretary of State George C. Marshall, that provided economic aid to Europe after World War II.

Marxism The theory of Karl Marx (1818–1883) and Friedrich Engels (1820–1895) that history is the result of class conflict, which will end in the inevitable triumph of the industrial proletariat over the bourgeoisie and the abolition of private property and social class.

Meiji restoration The overthrow of the Tokugawa *bakufu* in Japan in 1868 and the transfer, or "restoration," of power to the imperial government under the Emperor Meiji.

Mein Kampf Meaning "My Struggle." Hitler's statement of his political program, published in 1924.

Mensheviks Meaning the "minority." Term Lenin applied to the majority moderate faction of the Russian Social Democratic Party opposed to him and the Bolsheviks.

mercantilism Term used to describe close government control of the economy that sought to maximize exports and accumulate as much precious metals as possible to enable the state to defend its economic and political interests.

Mesoamerica The part of North America that extends from the central part of modern Mexico to Central America.

Mesopotamia Modern Iraq. The land between the Tigris and Euphrates Rivers where the first civilization appeared around 3000 B.C.E.

Messiah The redeemer whose coming Jews believed would establish the kingdom of God on earth. Christians considered Jesus to be the Messiah (Christ means Messiah in Greek).

mestizos Persons of mixed Native American and European descent.

Mexica The Aztecs name for themselves.

mfecane A period of widespread warfare and chaos among Bantu peoples in east-central Africa during the early nineteenth century.

millets Within the Ottoman Empire, ethnic communities that administered their own educational, charitable, and judicial affairs.

Minoan The Bronze Age civilization that arose in Crete in the third and second millennia B.C.E.

mita The Inca system of forced labor in return for gifts and ritual entertainments.

Mitimaqs Communities whom the Incas forced to settle in designated regions for strategic purposes.

mobilization The placing of a country's military forces on a war footing.

monotheism The worship of one universal God.

Moors The Spanish and Portuguese term for Muslims.

Mughals Descendants of the Mongols who established an Islamic empire in India in the sixteenth century with its capital at Delhi.

mujtahid A Shi'ite religious-legal scholar.

mulattos Persons of mixed African and European descent.

Mycenaean The Bronze Age civilization of mainland Greece that was centered at Mycenae.

mystery religions The cults of Isis, Mithras, and Osiris, which promised salvation to those initiated into the secret or "mystery" of their rites.

nacionalismo A right-wing Argentine nationalist movement that arose in the 1930s and resembled European fascism.

National Studies A Japanese intellectual tradition that emphasized native Japanese culture and institutions and rejected the influence of Chinese Confucianism.

nationalism The belief that one is part of a nation, defined as a community with its own language, traditions, customs, and history that distinguish it from other nations and make it the primary focus of a person's loyalty and sense of identity.

natural selection According to Darwin, the process in nature by which only the organisms best adapted to their environment tend to survive and transmit their genes, while those less adapted tend to be eliminated.

Nazis The German Nationalist Socialist Party.

neocolonial economy An economic relationship between a former colonial state and countries with more developed economies in which the former colony exports raw materials to and imports manufactured goods from the more developed nations.

Neo-Daoism A revival of Taoist "mysterious learning" that flourished as a reaction against Confucianism during the Han dynasty.

Neolithic Revolution The shift beginning 10,000 years ago from hunter-gatherer societies to settled communities of farmers and artisans. Also called the Age of Agriculture, it witnessed the invention of farming, the domestication of plants and animals, and the development of technologies such as pottery and weaving. "Neolithic" comes from the Greek words for "new stone."

New Economic Policy (NEP) A limited revival of capitalism, especially in light industry and agriculture, introduced by Lenin in 1921 to repair the damage inflicted on the Russian economy by the Civil War and War Communism.

New Imperialism The extension in the late nineteenth and early twentieth centuries of Western political and economic dominance to Asia, the Middle East, and Africa.

Nicene Creed A statement of Christian belief, formulated by the council of Christian bishops at Nicaea in 324 C.E., that rejected Arianism in favor of the doctrine that Christ is both fully human and fully divine.

Nilotic Africa The lands along the Nile River.

ninety-five theses Document posted on the door of Castle Church in Wittenberg, Germany on October 31, 1517 by Martin Luther protesting, among other things, the selling of indulgences.

Nirvana In Buddhism the attainment of release from the wheel of *karma.*

Nō play A highly stylized form of Japanese drama in which the chorus provides the narrative line as in classical Greek plays.

oba Title of the king of Benin.

obsidian A hard volcanic glass that was widely used in Mesoamerica.

occupied territories Land occupied by Israel as a result of wars with its Arab neighbors in 1948-1949, 1967, and 1973.

Old Regime Term applied to the pattern of social, political, and economic relationships and institutions that existed in Europe before the French Revolution.

orthodox Meaning "holding the right opinions." Applied to the doctrines of the Catholic Church.

orthopraxy The correct practice of a religion.

Ottoman Empire The imperial Turkish state centered in Constantinople that ruled large parts of the Balkans, North Africa, and the Middle East until 1918.

padishah Meaning "emperor." One of the titles of the Ottoman monarchs.

Paleolithic Age The earliest period when stone tools were used, from about 1,000,000 to 10,000 B.C.E. From the Greek meaning "old stone."

Panhellenic ("all-Greek") The sense of cultural identity that all Greeks felt in common with each other.

pan-Islamism The movement that advocates that the entire Muslim world should form a unified political and cultural entity.

Pan-Slavic movement The movement to create a nation or federation that would embrace all the Slavic peoples of Eastern Europe.

Papal States Territory in central Italy ruled by the pope until 1870.

parlement French regional court dominated by hereditary nobility. The most important was the Parlement of Paris, which claimed the right to register royal decrees before they could become law.

parliamentary monarchy A state headed by a monarch but whose power is shared with a national representative body.

pastoralists People whose way of life centers on the raising and herding of livestock; nomads.

patricians The hereditary upper class of early Republican Rome.

peace process Efforts, chiefly by the United States, to broker a peace between the State of Israel and the PLO.

Peloponnesian Wars The protracted struggle between Athens and Sparta to dominate Greece between 465 and Athens' final defeat in 404 B.C.E.

peninsulares Native-born Spaniards who immigrated from Spain to settle in the Spanish colonies.

perestroika Meaning "restructuring." The attempt in the 1980s to reform the Soviet government and economy.

Perónism An authoritarian, nationalist movement founded in Argentina in the 1940s by the dictatore Juan Perón.

pharaoh The god-kings of ancient Egypt. The term originally meant "great house" or palace.

Pharisees The group that was most strict in its adherence to Jewish law.

philosophes The eighteenth-century writers and critics who forged the new attitudes favorable to change. They sought to apply reason and common sense to the institutions and societies of their day.

Phoenicians The ancient inhabitants of modern Lebanon. A trading people, they established colonies throughout the Mediterranean.

pipiltin Aztec bureaucrats and priests.

pirs   Shi'ite holy men.

plantation economy   The economic system stretching between Chesapeake Bay and Brazil that produced crops, especially sugar, cotton, and tobacco, using slave labor on large estates.

plebeians   The hereditary lower class of early Republican Rome.

plenitude of power   The teaching that the popes have power over all other bishops of the church.

pochteca   Aztec merchants.

pogroms   Organized riots against Jews in the Russian Empire.

polis   The basic Greek political unit. Usually, but incompletely, translated as "city-state," the Greeks thought of the *polis* as a community of citizens theoretically descended from a common ancestor.

political Islamism   Political movement that seeks to return to the fundamentals of Islamic life through rejuvenation of Muslim faith and society and the rejection of Western, Materialist, and secularist values and norms.

polytheism   The worship of many gods.

Popular Front   A government of all left-wing parties that took power in France in 1936 to enact social and economic reforms.

populares   Roman politicians who sought to pursue a political career based on the support of the people rather than just the aristocracy.

positivism   the philosophy of Auguste Comte that science is the final, or positive, stage of human intellectual development because it involves exact descriptions of phenomena, without recourse to unobservable operative principles, such as gods or spirits.

Pragmatic Sanction   The legal basis negotiated by the Emperor Charles VI (r. 1711–1740) for the Habsburg succession through his daughter Maria Theresa (r. 1740–1780).

PRI   The Institutional Revolutionary Party, which emerged from the Mexican revolution of 1911 and governed Mexico until the end of the twentieth century.

Proletarianization   The process whereby independent artisans and factory workers lose control of the means of production and of the conduct of their own trades to the owners of capital.

Ptolemaic system   The pre-Copernican explanation of the universe, which placed the Earth at the center of the universe.

Punic Wars   Three wars between Rome and Carthage for dominance of the western Mediterranean that were fought from 264 B.C.E. to 146 B.C.E.

Pure Land Buddhism   A variety of Japanese Buddhism that maintained that only faith was necessary for salvation.

puritans   English Protestants who sought to "purify" the Church of England of any vestiges of Catholicism.

Qanun   Ottoman administrative law.

Quechua   The Inca language.

quipu   Knotted string used by Andean peoples for recordkeeping.

Qur'an   Meaning "a reciting." The Islamic bible, which Muslims believe God revealed to the prophet Muhammad.

racism   The pseudoscientific theory that biological features of race determine human character and worth.

raj   The years from 1858 to 1947 during which India was governed directly by the British Crown.

raja   An Indian King.

Ramadan   The month each year when Muslims must fast during daylight hours.

Reconquista   The Christian reconquest of Spain from the Muslims from 1000 to 1492.

Reformation   The sixteenth-century religious movement that sought to reform the Roman Catholic Church and led to the establishment of Protestantism.

regular clergy   Monks and nuns who belong to religious orders.

Reichstag   The German parliament, which existed in various forms, until 1945.

Reign of Terror   The period between the summer of 1793 and the end of July 1794 when the French revolutionary state used extensive executions and violence to defend the Revolution and suppress its alleged internal enemies.

relativity   Theory of physics, first expounded by Albert Einstein in 1905, in which time and space exist not separately, but rather as a combined continuum.

Renaissance   The revival of ancient learning and the supplanting of traditional religious beliefs by new secular and scientific values that began in Italy in the fourteenth and fifteenth centuries.

reparations   The requirement incorporated into the Versailles Treaty that Germany should pay for the cost of World War I.

repartimiento   A labor tax in Spanish America that required adult male native Americans devote a set number of days a year to Spanish economic enterprises.

revisionism   The advocacy among nineteenth-century German socialists of achieving a humane socialist society through the evolution of democratic institutions, not revolution.

SA   The Nazi parliamentary forces, or stormtroopers.

Sahara   The world's largest desert. It extends across Africa from the Atlantic to the eastern Sudan. Historically, the Sahara has hindered contact between the Mediterranean and sub-Saharan Africa.

Sahel   An area of steppe and semidesert that borders the Sahara.

samsara   The endless cycle of existence, of birth and rebirth.

samurai   Professional Japanese warriors.

Sandinistas   The Marxist guerrilla force that overthrew the Somoza dictatorship in Nicaragua in 1979.

sans-culottes   Meaning "without breeches." The lower-middle classes and artisans of Paris during the French Revolution.

satraps   Governors of provinces in the Persian Empire.

savannah   An area of open woodlands and grassy plains.

Schlieffen Plan   Germany's plan for achieving a quick victory in the West at the outbreak of World War I by invading France through Belgium and Luxembourg.

Scholasticism   Method of study based on logic and dialectic that dominated the medieval schools. It assumed that truth already existed; students had only to organize, elucidate, and defend knowledge learned from authoritative texts, especially those of Aristotle and the Church Fathers.

Scientific Revolution   The sweeping change in the scientific view of the universe that occurred in the West in the sixteenth and seventeenth centuries.

scramble for Africa   The late nineteenth-century takeover of most of Africa by European powers.

secular clergy   Parish clergy who did not belong to a religious order.

serfs   Peasants tied to the land they tilled.

Shahanshah   "King of kings," the title of the Persian ruler.

Shari'a   Islamic religious law.

Shi-a   The minority of Muslims who trace their beliefs from the caliph Ali who was assassinated in 661 C.E.

Shintō   "The way of the gods." The animistic worship of the forces of nature that is the indigenous religion of Japan.

Shōgun   A military official who was the actual ruler of Japan in the emperor's name from the late 1100s until the mid-nineteenth century.

Silk Road   Trade route from China to the West that stretched across Central Asia.

Sophists   Professional teachers who emerged in Greece in the mid-fifth century B.C.E. who were paid to teach techniques of rhetoric, dialectic, and argumentation.

soviets Workers' and soldiers' councils formed in Russia during the Revolution.

spinning jenny A machine invented in England by James Hargreaves around 1765 to mass-produce thread.

SS The chief security units of the Nazi state.

Steppe peoples Nomadic tribespeople who dwelled on the Eurasian plains from eastern Europe to the borders of China and Iran. They frequently traded with or invaded more settled cultures.

Stoics A philosophical school founded by Zeno of Citium (335–263 B.C.E.) that taught that humans could only be happy with natural law.

streltsy Professional troops who made up the Moscow garrison. They were suppressed by Peter the Great.

studia humanitatis During the Renaissance, a liberal arts program of study that embraced grammar, rhetoric, poetry, history, philosophy, and politics.

stupa A Buddhist shrine.

suffragettes British women who lobbied and agitated for the right to vote in the early twentieth century.

Sufi A movement within Islam that emphasizes the spiritual and mystical.

sultan A Muslim royal title that means "authority."

Sunna Meaning "tradition." The dominant Islamic group whose followers are called Sunnis.

superego According to Freud, the part of the mind that embodies the external moral imperatives and expectations imposed on the personality by society and culture.

Swahili A language and culture that developed from the interaction of native Africans and Arabs along the East African coast.

symposion The carefully organized drinking party that was the center of Greek aristocratic social life. It featured games, songs, poetry, and even philosophical disputation.

syncretism Blending or fusion of different systems of religious or philosophical beliefs.

Table of Ranks An official hierarchy established by Peter the Great in imperial Russia that equated a person's social position and privileges with his rank in the state bureaucracy or army.

taille The direct tax on the French peasantry.

Taiping rebellion A nineteenth-century revolt against China's Manchu dynasty that was inspired by quasi-Christian ideas and that led to enormous suffering and destruction before its collapse in 1868.

Tennō "Heavenly emperor." The official title of the emperor of Japan.

tetcutin Subordinate Aztec lords.

tetrarchy Diocletian's (r. 306–337 C.E.) system for ruling the Roman Empire by four men with power divided territorially.

theocracy A state ruled by religious leaders who claim to govern by divine authority.

Theravada The "Way of the Elders." A school of Buddhism that emphasized the monastic ideal.

Thermidorean Reaction The reaction against the radicalism of the French Revolution that began in July 1794. Associated with the end of terror and establishment of the Directory.

Third Estate The branch of the French Estates General representing all of the kingdom outside the nobility and the clergy.

three-field system A medieval innovation that increased the amount of land under cultivation by leaving only one-third fallow in a given year.

tlatoani An Aztec ruler.

transubstantiation The doctrine that the entire substances of the bread and wine are changed in the Eucharist into the body and blood of Christ.

treaty ports Chinese ports ruled by foreign consuls where foreigners enjoyed commercial privileges and immunity from Chinese laws.

Trekboers White livestock farmers in Cape Colony.

tribunes Roman officials who had to be plebeians and were elected by the plebeian assembly to protect plebeians from the arbitrary power of the magistrates.

Tripartite Pact The alliance between Japan and Nazi Germany and Fascist Italy that was signed in 1940.

ulama "Persons with correct knowledge." The Islamic scholarly elite who served a social function similar to the Christian clergy.

Umma The Islamic community.

"unequal treaties" Agreements imposed on China in the nineteenth century by European powers, the United States, and Japan that granted their citizens special legal and economic privileges on Chinese soil.

Upanishads Vedic texts most concerned with speculation about the universe.

Urdu-Hindi A language that combines Persian-Arabic and native Indian elements. Urdu is the Muslim version of the language. Hindi is the Hindu version.

uzama An order of hereditary chiefs in Benin.

varnas The four main classes that form the basis for Hindu caste relations.

vassal A person granted an estate or cash payments in return for accepting the obligation to render services to a lord.

Vedas The sacred texts of the ancient Aryan invaders of India. The Rig Vedas are the oldest materials in the Vedas.

vernacular The everyday language spoken by the people as opposed to Latin.

Viet Minh The Communist-dominated popular front organization formed by Ho Chi Minh to establish an independent Vietnamese republic.

Wahhabis Followers of Ibn Abd al-Wahhab (1703-1792) who sought to combat the excesses of popular and Sufi piety in Islam and looked to the Qur'an and the traditions of the Prophet as the sole authoritative guidance in religion.

War Communism The economic policy adopted by the Bolsheviks during the Russian Civil War to seize the banks, heavy industry, railroads, and grain.

war guilt clause Clause of the Versailles Treaty, which assigned responsibility for World War I solely to Germany.

water frame A water-powered device invented by Richard Arkwright to produce a more durable cotton fabric. It led to the shift in the production of cotton textiles from households to factories.

Weimar Republic The German democratic regime that existed between the end of World War I and Hitler's coming to power in 1933.

White Russians Those Russians who opposed the Bolsheviks (the "Reds") in the Russian Civil War of 1918–1921.

Works Progress Administration (WPA) New Deal program created by the Roosevelt administration in 1935 that provided relief for the unemployed in the industrial sector during the Great Depression in the United States.

yangban Elite Korean families of the Choson period.

zaibatsu Large industrial combines that came to dominate Japanese industry in the late nineteenth century.

Zen A form of Buddhism, which taught that Buddha was only a man and exhorted each person to attain enlightenment by his or her own efforts.

Zionism The movement to create a Jewish state in Palestine (the Biblical Zion).

Zoroastrianism A quasi-monotheistic Iranian religion founded by Zoroaster (ca. 628–551 B.C.E.) who preached a message of moral reform and exhorted his followers to worship only Ahura Mazda, the Wise Lord.

Suggested Readings

CHAPTER 1

General Prehistory

P. BOGUCKI, *The Origins of Human Society* (1999). An excellent summary of recent scholarship on the earliest origins of human societies.

F. BRAY, *The Rice Economies: Technology and Development in Asian Societies* (1986). Still the best authority on the origins of rice cultivation and its effect on the develepment of ancient Asia.

M. EHRENBERG, *Women in Prehistory* (1989). An account of the role of women in early times.

C. FREEMAN, *Egypt, Greece and Rome: Civilizations of the Ancient Mediterranean* (2004). Good comparative study of Egypt with Greece and Rome.

D. C. JOHNSON and M. R. EDEY, *Lucy: The Beginning of Mankind* (1981). An account of the African origins of humans.

S. M. NELSON, ed., *Ancient Queens: Archaeological Explorations* (2003). Reassesses women rulers and female power in the ancient world.

S. M. NELSON and M. ROSEN-AYALON, *In Pursuit of Gender: Worldwide Archaeological Approaches* (2002). Essays on gender and the archaeology of the ancient world.

D. L. NICHOLS and T. H. CHARLTON, eds., *The Archaeology of CityStates: Cross-cultural Approaches* (1997). One of a growing body of books and essay collections employing cross-cultural and comparative approaches to world history and archaeology.

M. OLIPHANT, *The Atlas of the Ancient World: Charting the Great Civilizations of the Past* (1992). An excellent comprehensive atlas of the ancient world.

P. L. SHINNIE, *Ancient Nubia* (1996). A study of the African state most influenced by Egyptian culture.

Near East

M. E. AUBER, *The Phoenicians and the West* (1996). A new study of an important sea-going people who served as a conduit between East and West.

BEN-TOR, ed., *The Archaeology of Ancient Israel* (1992). A useful and up-to-date survey.

J. BOTTÉRO, *Everyday Life in Ancient Mesopotamia* (2001). Interesting vignettes of ancient Mesopotamian life.

H. CRAWFORD, *Sumer and the Sumerians* (1991). A discussion of the oldest Mesopotamian civilization.

I. FINKELSTEIN and N. A. SILBERMAN, *The Bible Unearthed: Archaeology's New Vision of Ancient Israel and the Origin of its Sacred Texts* (2001). An interesting discussion of the insights of recent archaeological finds on the history of the Bible and ancient Israel.

G. LEICK, *Mesopotamia: The Invention of the City* (2002). Good discussion of the urban history of ancient Mesopotamia.

J. N. POSTGATE, *Early Mesopotamia* (1992). An excellent study of Mesopotamian economy and society from the earliest times to about 1500 B.C.E., helpfully illustrated with drawings, photos, and translated documents.

D. B. REDFORD, *Akhenaten* (1987). A study of the controversial religious reformer.

W. F. SAGGS, *The Might That Was Assyria* (1984). A history of the northern Mesopotamian Empire and a worthy companion to the author's account of the Babylonian Empire in the south.

M. VAN DE MIEROOP, *A History of the Ancient Near East, ca. 3000–323 B.C.* (2004). An up-to-date comprehensive survey of ancient Near Eastern history.

India

D. P. AGRAWAL, *The Archaeology of India* (1982). A fine survey of the problems and data. Detailed, but with excellent summaries and brief discussions of major issues.

C. CHAKRABORTY, *Common Life in the Rigveda and Atharvaveda—An Account of the Folklore in the Vedic Period* (1977). An interesting attempt to reconstruct everyday life in the Vedic period from the principal Vedic texts.

J. R. MCINTOSH, *A Peaceful Realm: The Rise and Fall of the Indus Civilization* (2002). Discusses what archaeologists have managed to unearth so far regarding Harrapan civilization.

W. D. O'FLAHERTY, *The Rig Veda: An Anthology* (1981). An excellent selection of Vedic texts in prosaic but very careful translation, with helpful notes on the texts.

J. E. SCHWARTZBERG, ed., *A Historical Atlas of South Asia* (1978). The definitive reference work for historical geography. Includes chronological tables and substantive essays.

R. THAPAR, *Early India: From the Origins to A.D. 1300* (2003). A comprehensive introduction to the early history of India.

China

M. LOEWE and E. SHAUGHNESSY eds., *The Cambridge History of Ancient China: From the Origins of Civilization to 221 B.C.* (1999). A comprehensive and authoritative history of ancient China.

K. C. CHANG, *The Archeology of Ancient China*, 4th ed. (1986). The standard work on the subject.

K. C. CHANG, *Art, Myth, and Ritual, The Path to Political Authority in Ancient China* (1984). A study of the relation between shamans, gods, agricultural production, and political authority during the Shang and Zhou dynasties.

N. DI COSMO, *Ancient China and its Enemies: The Rise of Nomadic Power in East Asian History* (2002). An excellent study of the relationship between China and nomadic peoples that was a powerful force in shaping Chinese and Central Asian history.

C. Y. HSU, *Western Chou Civilization* (1988).

D. N. KEIGHTLEY, *The Origins of Chinese Civilization* (1983).

M. E. LEWIS, *Sanctioned Violence in Early China* (1990).

X. Q. LI, *Eastern Zhou and Qin Civilizations* (1986). This work includes fresh interpretations based on archaeological finds.

Americas

R. L. BURGER, *Chavín and the Origins of Andean Civilization* (1992). A lucid and detailed account of the rise of civilization in the Andes.

M. D. COE and R. KOONTZ, *Mexico: From the Olmecs to the Aztecs* (2002). Good survey of ancient Mexico.

D. DREW, *The Lost Chronicles of the Maya Kings* (1999). Fine introduction to the history of Maya civilization.

V. W. FITZHUGH and A. CROWELL, *Crossroads of Continents: Cultures of Siberia and Alaska* (1988). Covers the area where the immigration from Eurasia to the Americas began.

R. FORD, ed., *Prehistoric Food Production in North America* (1985). Examines the origins of agriculture in the Americas.

P. D. HUNT, *Indian Agriculture in America: Prehistory to the Present* (1987). Includes a discussion of preconquest agriculture.

A. KNIGHT, *Mexico: From the Beginning to the Spanish Conquest* (2002). First of a three-volume comprehensive history of Mexico.

C. MORRIS and A. VON HAGEN, *The Inka Empire and Its Andean Origins* (1993). An overview of Andean civilization with excellent illustrations.

M. MOSELEY, *The Incas and Their Ancestors: The Archaeology of Ancient Peru* (1992). An overview of Peruvian archaeology.

J. A. SABLOFF, *The New Archaeology and the Ancient Maya* (1990). A lively account of recent research in Maya archaeology.

I. SILVERBLATT, *Moon, Sun, and Witches: Gender Ideologies and Class in Inca and Colonial Peru* (1987). A controversial but thought-provoking discussion of Incan ideas about gender.

CHAPTER 2

China

R. BERSTEIN, *Ultimate Journey: Retracing the Path of an Ancient Buddhist Monk who Crossed Asia in Search of Enlightenment* (2001). Discusses the diffusion of Buddhism from India to China.

H. G. CREEL, *What Is Taoism? And Other Studies in Chinese Cultural History* (1970).

W. T. DE BARY et al., *Sources of Chinese Tradition* (1960). A reader in China's philosophical and historical literature. It should be consulted for the later periods as well as for the Zhou.

H. FINGARETE, *Confucius—The Secular as Sacred* (1998).

Y. L. FUNG, *A Short History of Chinese Philosophy*, ed. by D. Bodde (1948). A survey of Chinese philosophy from its origins down to recent times.

A. GRAHAM, *Disputers of the Tao* (1989).

D. HAWKES, *Ch'u Tz'u: The Songs of the South* (1985).

D. C. LAU, trans., *Lao-tzu, Tao Te Ching* (1963).

D. C. LAU, trans., *Confucius, The Analects* (1979).

C. LI, ED., *The Sage and the Second Sex: Confucianism, Ethics, and Gender* (2000). A good introduction to gender and ethics in Confucian thought.

B. I. SCHWARTZ, *The World of Thought in Ancient China* (1985).

A. WALEY, *Three Ways of Thought in Ancient China* (1956). An easy yet sound introduction to Confucianism, Daoism, and Legalism.

A. WALEY, *The Book of Songs* (1960).

B. WATSON, trans., *Basic Writings of Mo Tzu, Hsun Tzu, and Han Fei Tzu* (1963).

B. WATSON, trans., *The Complete Works of Chuang Tzu* (1968).

H. WELCH, *Taoism, The Parting of the Way* (1967).

India

A. L. BASHAM, *The Wonder That Was India*, rev. ed. (1963). Still unsurpassed by more recent works. Chapter VII, "Religion," is a superb introduction to the Vedic Aryan, Brahmanic, Hindu, Jain, and Buddhist traditions of thought.

W. N. BROWN, *Man in the Universe: Some Continuities in Indian Thought* (1970). A penetrating yet brief reflective summary of major patterns in Indian thinking.

W. T. DE BARY ET AL., *Sources of Indian Tradition* (1958). 2 vols. Vol. I, *From the Beginning to 1800*, ed. and rev. by Ainslie T. Embree (1988). Excellent selections from a variety of Indian texts, with good introductions to chapters and individual selections.

P. HARVEY, *An Introduction to Buddhism* (1990). Chapters 1–3 provide an excellent historical introduction.

T. J. HOPKINS, *The Hindu Religious Tradition* (1971). A first-rate, thoughtful introduction to Hindu religious ideas and practice.

K. KLOSTERMAIER, *Hinduism: A Short History* (2000). A relatively compact survey of the history of Hinduism.

J. M. KOLLER, *The Indian Way* (1982). A useful, wide-ranging handbook of Indian thought and religion.

R. H. ROBINSON and W. L. JOHNSON, *The Buddhist Religion*, 3rd ed. (1982). An excellent first text on the Buddhist tradition, its thought and development.

R. C. ZAEHNER, *Hinduism* (1966). One of the best general introductions to central Indian religious and philosophical ideas.

Israel

A. BACH, ed., *Women in the Hebrew Bible: A Reader* (1999). Excellent introduction to the ways in which biblical scholars are exploring the role of women in the Bible.

BRIGHT, *A History of Israel* (1968), 2nd ed. (1972). One of the standard scholarly introductions to biblical history and literature.

W. D. DAVIES and L. FINKELSTEIN, eds., *The Cambridge History of Judaism*. Vol. I, *Introduction: The Persian Period* (1984). Excellent essays on diverse aspects of the exilic period and later.

J. NEUSNER, *The Way of Torah: An Introduction to Judaism* (1979). A sensitive introduction to the Judaic tradition and faith.

The Oxford History of the Biblical World, M. D. Coogan, ed. (1998).

Greece

The Cambridge Companion to Greek and Roman Philosophy, D. SEDLEY ed., (2003).

G. B. KERFERD, *The Sophistic Movement* (1981). An excellent description and analysis.

J. LEAR, *Aristotle: The Desire to Understand* (1988). A brilliant yet comprehensible introduction to the work of the philosopher.

T. E. RIHIL, *Greek Science* (1999). Good survey of Greek science incorporating recent reseach on the topic.

J. M. ROBINSON, *An Introduction to Early Greek Philosophy* (1968). A valuable collection of the main fragments and ancient testimony to the works of the early philosophers, with excellent commentary.

G. VLASTOS, *The Philosophy of Socrates* (1971). A splendid collection of essays illuminating the problems presented by this remarkable man.

G. VLASTOS, *Platonic Studies*, 2nd ed. (1981). A similar collection on the philosophy of Plato.

G. VLASTOS, *Socrates, Ironist and Moral Philosopher* (1991). The results of a lifetime of study by the leading interpreter of Socrates in our time.

Comparative Studies

(Increasingly world historians are looking at ancient civilizations in relationship to each other rather than as isolated entities to try to understand commonalities and differences in social and cultural development.)

W. DONIGER, *Splitting the Difference: Gender and Myth in Ancient Greece and India* (1999).

G. E. R. LLOYD, *The Ambitions of Curiosity: Understanding the World in Ancient Greece and China* (2002).

G. E. R. LLOYD, *The Way and the Word: Science and Medicine in Early China and Greece* (2002).

T. MCEVILLEY, *The Shape of Ancient Thought: Comparative Studies of Greek and Indian Philosopies* (2002).

CHAPTER 3

The Rise of Greek Civilization

P. CARTLEDGE, *The Spartans* (2003). A readable account of this enigmatic people.

J. CHADWICK, *The Mycenaean World* (1976). A readable account by a man who helped decipher Mycenaean writing.

R. DREWS, *The Coming of the Greeks* (1988). A fine discussion of the Greeks' arrival as part of the movements of the Indo-European peoples.

J. V. FINE, *The Ancient Greeks* (1983). An excellent survey that discusses historical problems and the evidence that gives rise to them.

M. I. FINLEY, *World of Odysseus*, rev. ed. (1965). A fascinating attempt to reconstruct Homeric society.

P. GREEN, *Xerxes at Salamis* (1970). A lively and stimulating history of the Persian War.

D. HAMEL, *Trying Neaira* (2003). A lively account of the events surrounding a famous jury trial that sheds interesting light on Athenian society in the fourth century B.C.E.

V. D. HANSON, *The Western Way of War* (1989). A brilliant and lively discussion of the rise and character of the hoplite phalanx and its influence on Greek society.

V. D. HANSON, *The Other Greeks* (1995). A revolutionary account of the Greek invention of the family farm and its centrality for the shaping of the *polis*.

D. KAGAN, *The Great Dialogue: A History of Greek Political Thought from Homer to Polybius* (1965). A discussion of the relationship between the Greek historical experience and political theory.

W. K. LACEY, *The Family in Ancient Greece* (1984).

J. F. LAZENBY, *The Defense of Greece, 490–479 B.C.* (1993). A new and valuable study of the Persian Wars.

J. F. MCGLEW, *Tyranny and Political Culture in Ancient Greece* (1993). A recent account of political developments in the Archaic period.

O. MURRAY, *Early Greece* (1980). A lively and imaginative account of the early history of Greece to the end of the Persian War.

A. M. SNODGRASS, *The Dark Age of Greece* (1972). A good examination of the archaeological evidence.

B. S. STRAUSS, *The Battle of Salamis: The Naval Encounter That Saved Greece and Western Civilization* (2004). A lively account of the major naval battle of the Persian Wars and its setting.

A. G. WOODHEAD, *Greeks in the West* (1962). An account of the Greek settlements in Italy and Sicily.

W. J. WOODHOUSE, *Solon the Liberator* (1965). A discussion of the great Athenian reformer.

S. G. MILLER, *Ancient Greek Athletics* (2004). The most complete and most useful account of the subject.

Classical and Hellenistic Greece

W. BURKERT, *Greek Religion* (1987). An excellent study by an outstanding student of the subject.

J. R. LANE FOX, *Alexander the Great* (1973). An imaginative account that does more than the usual justice to the Persian side of the problem.

Y. GARLAN, *Slavery in Ancient Greece* (1988). An up-to-date survey.

P. GREEN, *Alexander to Actium: The Historical Evolution of the Hellenistic Age* (1990). A remarkable synthesis of political and cultural history.

C. D. HAMILTON, *Agesilaus and the Failure of Spartan Hegemony* (1991). An excellent biography of the king who was the central figure in Sparta during its domination in the fourth century B.C.E.

N. G. L. HAMMOND, *Philip of Macedon* (1994). A new biography of the founder of the Macedonian Empire.

N. G. L. HAMMOND AND G. T. GRIFFITH, *A History of Macedonia*, Vol. 2, *550–336 B.C.* (1979). A thorough account of Macedonian history that focuses on the careers of Philip and Alexander.

R. JUST, *Women in Athenian Law and Life* (1988). An account of women's place in Athenian society.

D. KAGAN, *The Peloponnesian War* (2003). A narrative history of the war.

B. M. W. KNOX, *The Heroic Temper: Studies in Sophoclean Tragedy* (1964). A brilliant analysis of tragic heroism.

D. M. LEWIS, *Sparta and Persia* (1977). A valuable discussion of relations between Sparta and Persia in the fifth and fourth centuries B.C.E.

A. A. LONG, *Hellenistic Philosophy: Stoics, Epicureans, Sceptics* (1974). An account of Greek science in the Hellenistic and Roman periods.

R. MEIGGS, *The Athenian Empire* (1972). A fine study of the rise and fall of the empire, making excellent use of inscriptions.

J. J. POLLITT, *Art and Experience in Classical Greece* (1972). A scholarly and entertaining study of the relationship between art and history in classical Greece, with excellent illustrations.

J. J. POLLITT, *Art in the Hellenistic Age* (1986). An extraordinary analysis that places the art in its historical and intellectual context.

E. W. ROBINSON, *Ancient Greek Democracy* (2004). A stimulating collection of ancient sources and modern interpretations.

D. M. SCHAPS, *Economic Rights of Women in Ancient Greece* (1981).

B. S. STRAUSS, *Athens After the Peloponnesian War* (1987). An excellent discussion of Athens' recovery and of the nature of Athenian society and politics in the fourth century B.C.E.

B. S. STRAUSS, *Fathers and Sons in Athens* (1993). An unusual synthesis of social, political, and intellectual history.

V. TCHERIKOVER, *Hellenistic Civilization and the Jews* (1970). A fine study of the impact of Hellenism on the Jews.

G. VLASTOS, *Socrates, Ironist and Moral Philosopher* (1991). The results of a lifetime of study by the leading interpreter of Socrates in our time.

CHAPTER 4

Iran

M. BOYCE, *Zoroastrians: Their Religious Beliefs and Practices* (1979). The most recent survey, organized historically and based on extensive research.

M. BOYCE, ed. and trans., *Textual Sources for the Study of Zoroastrianism* (1984). Well-translated selections from a broad range of ancient Iranian materials.

J. M. COOK, *The Persian Empire* (1983). Survey of the Achaemenid period.

J. CURTIS, *Ancient Persia* (1989). Excellent portfolio of photographs of artifacts and sites, with a clear historical survey of the arts and culture of ancient Iran.

W. D. DAVIES AND L. FINKLESTEIN, ed., *The Cambridge History of Judaism*, Vol. 1, Introduction; "The Persian Period". Good articles on Iran and Iranian religion as well as Judaism.

J. DUCHESNE-GUILLEMIN, trans., *The Hymns of Zarathushtra*, trans. by M. Henning (1952, 1963). The best short introduction to the original texts of the Zoroastrian hymns.

R. N. FRYE, *The Heritage of Persia* (1963, 1966). A first-rate survey of Iranian history to Islamic times: readable but scholarly.

R. GHIRSHMAN, *Iran* (1954). Good material on culture, society, and economy as well as politics and history.

W. W. MALANDRA, trans. and ed., *An Introduction to Ancient Iranian Religion: Readings from the Avesta and Achaemenid Inscriptions* (1983). Helpful especially for texts of inscriptions relevant to religion.

India

A. L. BASHAM, *The Wonder That Was India*, rev. ed. (1963). Excellent material on Mauryan religion, society, culture, and history.

A. L. BASHAM, ed., *A Cultural History of India* (1975). A fine collection of historical-survey essays by a variety of scholars. See Part I, "The Ancient Heritage" (Chapters 2–16).

N. N. BHATTACHARYYA, *Ancient Indian History and Civilization: Trends and Perspectives* (1988). Covers Mauryan and Gupta times as well as earlier periods, with chapters on political systems, cities and villages, ideology and religion, and art.

W. T. DE BARY et al., COMP., *Sources of Indian Tradition*, 2nd ed. (1958). Vol. I: *From the Beginning to 1800*, ed. and rev. by Ainslie T. Embree (1988). Excellent selections from a wide variety of Indian texts, with good introductions to chapters and selections.

B. ROWLAND, *The Art and Architecture of India: Buddhist/Hindu/Jain*, 3rd rev. ed. (1970). The standard work, lucid and easy to read. Note Part Three, "Romano-Indian Art in North-West India and Central Asia."

V. A. SMITH, ed., *The Oxford History of India*, 4th rev. ed. by Percival Spear et al. (1981), pp. 71–163. A dry, occasionally dated historical survey. Includes useful reference chronologies.

R. THAPAR, *Ashoka and the Decline of the Mauryans* (1973). The standard treatment of Ashoka's reign.

R. THAPAR, *A History of India, Part I* (1966), pp. 50–108. Three chapters that provide a basic survey of the period.

S. WOLPERT, *A New History of India*, 2nd ed. (1982). A basic survey history. Chapters 5 and 6 cover the Mauryans, Guptas, and Kushans.

Greek and Asian Dynasties

A. K. NARAIN, *The Indo-Greeks* (1957. Reprinted with corrections, 1962). The most comprehensive account of the complex history of the various kings and kingdoms.

F. E. PETERS, *The Harvest of Hellenism* (1970), pp. 222–308. Helpful chapters on Greek rulers of the Eastern world from Seleucus to the last Indo-Greeks.

J. W. SEDLAR, *India and the Greek World: A Study in the Transmission of Culture* (1980). A basic work that provides a good overview.

D. SINOR, ed., *The Cambridge History of Early Inner Asia* (1990). See especially Chapters 6 and 7.

CHAPTER 5

P. BOHANNAN AND P. CURTIN, *Africa and Africans*, rev. ed. (1971). An enjoyable and enlightening discussion of African history and prehistory and of major African institutions (e.g., arts, family life, religion).

R. BULLIET, *The Camel and the Wheel* (1990). Explains why the camel was chosen over the wheel as a means of transport in the Sahara.

P. CURTIN, S. FEIERMANN, L. THOMPSON, AND J. VANSINA, *African History* (1978). Probably the best survey history. The relevant portions are chapters 1, 2, 4, 8, and 9.

T. R. H. DAVENPORT, *South Africa: A Modern History*, 3rd rev. ed. (1987). Chapter 1 gives excellent summary coverage of prehistoric southern Africa, the Khoisan peoples, and the Bantu migrations.

B. DAVIDSON, *The African Past* (1967). A combination of primary-source selections and brief secondary discussions trace sympathetically the history of the diverse parts of Africa.

P. GARLAKE, *The Kingdoms of Africa* (1978). A lavishly illustrated set of photographic essays that provide a helpful introduction to the various historically important areas of precolonial Africa.

E. GILBERT AND J. REYNOLDS, *Africa in World History* (2004). The best new survey of African history, placing it in a global context.

R. W. JULY, *Precolonial Africa: An Economic and Social History* (1975). A very readable, topically arranged study. See especially "The Savannah Farmer," "The Bantu," "Cattle-men," and "The Traders" chapters.

H. LOTH, *Woman in Ancient Africa*, trans. by S. Marnie (1987). An interesting survey of legal, familial, cultural, and other aspects of women's roles.

R. OLIVER, *The African Experience* (1991). A masterly, balanced, and engaging sweep through African history. The chapters on prehistory and early history are outstanding summaries of the results and implications of recent research.

I. VAN SERTIMA, *Black Women in Antiquity* (1984, 1988). Studies of queens, goddesses, matriarchy, and other aspects of the role and status of women in Egyptian, Ethiopian, and other African societies of the past.

CHAPTER 6

From Republic to Empire

R. BAUMANN, *Women and Politics in Ancient Rome* (1995). A Study of the role of women in roman public life.

A. H. BERNSTEIN, *Tiberius Sempronius Gracchus: Tradition and Apostasy* (1978). A new interpretation of Tiberius's place in Roman politics.

T. J. CORNELL, *The Beginnings of Rome: Italy and Rome from the Bronze Age to the Punic Wars, c. 1000–264 B.C.* (1995). A consideration of the royal and early republican periods of Roman history.

T. CORNELL AND J. MATTHEWS, *Atlas of the Roman World* (1982). Much more than the title indicates, this book presents a comprehensive view of the Roman world in its physical and cultural setting.

J-M. DAVID, *The Roman Conquest of Italy* (1997). A good analysis of how Rome united Italy.

A. GOLDSWORTHY, *Roman Warfare* (2002). A good military history of Rome.

A. Goldsworthy, *In the Name of Rome: The Men Who Won the Roman Empire* (2004). The story of Rome's greatest generals in the republican and imperial periods.

E. S. Gruen, *Diaspora: Jews Amidst Greeks and Romans* (2002). A fine study of Jews in the Hellenistic and Roman world.

E. S. Gruen, *The Hellenistic World and the Coming of Rome* (1984). A new interpretation of Rome's conquest of the eastern Mediterranean.

W. V. Harris, *War and Imperialism in Republican Rome, 327–70 B.C.* (1975). An analysis of Roman attitudes and intentions concerning imperial expansion and war.

A. Keaveney, *Rome and the Unification of Italy* (1988). The story of how Rome organized her defeated opponents.

S. Lancel, *Carthage, A History* (1995). Includes a good account of Rome's dealings with Carthage.

J. F. Lazenby, *Hannibal's War: A Military History of the Second Punic War* (1978). A careful and thorough account.

F.G.B. Millar, *The Crowd in Rome in the Late Republic* (1999). A challenge to the view that only aristocrats counted in the late republic.

M. Pallottino, *The Etruscans*, 6th ed. (1974). Makes especially good use of archaeological evidence.

H. H. Scullard, *A History of the Roman World 753–146 B.C.*, 4th ed. (1980). An unusually fine narrative history with useful critical notes.

G. Williams, *The Nature of Roman Poetry* (1970). An unusually graceful and perceptive literary study.

Imperial Rome

W. Ball, *Rome in the East: The Transformation of an Empire* (2001). A thorough account of the influence of the East on Roman history.

T. Barnes, *The New Empire of Diocletian and Constantine* (1982).

K. R. Bradley, *Slavery and Society at Rome* (1994). A study of the role of slaves in Roman life.

P. Brown, *The Rise of Western Christendom: Triumph and Diversity, 200–1000* (1996). A vivid picture of the spread of Christianity by a master of the field.

A. Ferrill, *The Fall of the Roman Empire, The Military Explanation* (1986). An interpretation that emphasizes the decline in the quality of the Roman army.

K. Galinsky, *Augustan Culture* (1996). A work that integrates art, literature, and politics.

A. H. M. Jones, *The Later Roman Empire*, 3 vols. (1964). A comprehensive study of the period.

D. Kagan, ed., *The End of the Roman Empire: Decline or Transformation?* 3rd ed. (1992). A collection of essays discussing the problem of the decline and fall of the Roman Empire.

J. E. Lendon, *Empire of Honor, The Art of Government in the Roman World* (1997). An original and path-breaking interpretation.

E. N. Luttwak, *The Grand Strategy of the Roman Empire* (1976). An original and fascinating analysis by a keen student of modern strategy.

R. MacMullen, *Roman Social Relations, 50 B.C. to A.D. 284* (1981).

R. MacMullen, *Corruption and the Decline of Rome* (1988). A study that examines the importance of changes in ethical ideas and behavior.

R. W. Mathison, *Roman Aristocrats in Barbarian Gaul: Strategies for Survival* (1993). An unusual slant on the late empire.

J.F. Matthews, *Laying Down the Law: A Study of the Theodosian Code* (2000). A study of the importance of Roman law as a source for the understanding of Roman history and civilization.

W. A. Meeks, *The Origins of Christian Morality: The First Two Centuries.* An account of the shaping of Christianity in the Roman Empire.

F. Millar, *The Emperor in the Roman World, 31 B.C.–A.D. 337* (1977). A study of Roman imperial government.

F. Millar, *The Roman Empire and Its Neighbors*, 2nd ed. (1981).

H. M. D. Parker, *A History of the Roman World from A.D. 138 to 337* (1969). A good survey.

M. I. Rostovtzeff, *Social and Economic History of the Roman Empire*, 2nd ed. (1957). A masterpiece whose main thesis has been much disputed.

V. Rudich, *Political Dissidence Under Nero, The Price of Dissimulation* (1993). A brilliant exposition of the lives and thoughts of political dissidents in the early empire.

E. T. Salmon, *A History of the Roman World, 30 B.C. to A.D. 138* (1968). A good survey.

R. Syme, *The Roman Revolution* (1960). A brilliant study of Augustus, his supporters, and their rise to power.

R. Syme, *The Augustan Aristocracy* (1985). An examination of the new ruling class shaped by Augustus.

L. A. Thompson, *Romans and Blacks* (1989).

Chapter 7

D. Bodde, *China's First Unifier* (1938). A study of the Qin unification of China, viewed through the Legalist philosopher and statesman LiSi.

T. T. Ch'u, *Law and Society in Traditional China* (1961). Treats the sweep of Chinese history from 202 B.C.E. to 1911 C.E.

T. T. Ch'u, *Han Social Structure* (1972).

A. Cotterell, *The First Emperor of China* (1981). A study of the first Qin emperor.

R. Coulborn, *Feudalism in History* (1965). One chapter interestingly compares the quasi feudalism of the Zhou with that of the Six Dynasties period.

J. K. Fairbank, E. O. Reischauer, and A. M. Craig, *East Asia: Tradition and Transformation* (1989). A fairly detailed single-volume history covering China, Japan, and other countries in East Asia from antiquity to recent times.

J. Gernet, *A History of Chinese Civilization* (1982). A survey of Chinese history.

D.A. Graff and R. Higham, *A Military History of China* (2002).

C. Y. Hsu, *Ancient China in Transition* (1965). On social mobility during the Eastern Zhou era.

C. Y. Hsu, *Han Agriculture* (1980). A study of the agrarian economy of China during the Han dynasty.

J. Levi, *The Chinese Emperor* (1987). A novel about the first Qin emperor based on scholarly sources.

M. Loewe, *Everyday Life in Early Imperial China* (1968). A social history of the Han dynasty.

J. Needham, *The Shorter Science and Civilization in China* (1978). An abridgment of the multivolume work on the same subject with the same title—minus Shorter—by the same author.

S. Owen, ed. and Trans., *An Anthology of Chinese Literature: Beginnings to 1911* (1996).

I. ROBINET, *Taoism: Growth of a Religion* (1987).

M. SULLIVAN, *The Arts of China* (1967). An excellent survey history of Chinese art.

D. TWITCHETT AND M. LOEWE, eds., *The Ch'in and Han Empires, 221 B.C.E.–C.E. 220* (1986). Vol. 1 of *The Cambridge History of China*.

Z. S. WANG, *Han Civilization* (1982).

B. WATSON, *Ssu-ma Ch'ien, Grand Historian of China* (1958). A study of China's premier historian.

B. WATSON, *Records of the Grand Historian of China*, Vols. 1 and 2 (1961). Selections from the *Shiji* by Sima Qian.

B. WATSON, *The Columbia Book of Chinese Poetry* (1986).

F. WOOD, *The Silk Road: Two Thousand Years in the Heart of Asia* (2003). A lively narrative combined with photographs and paintings.

A. WRIGHT, *Buddhism in Chinese History* (1959).

Y. S. YU, *Trade and Expansion in Han China* (1967). A study of economic relations between the Chinese and their neighbors.

CHAPTER 8

General

P. BOL, *This Culture of Ours* (1992). An insightful intellectual history of the Tang through the Song dynasties.

J. CAHILL, *Chinese Painting* (1960). An excellent survey.

J. K. FAIRBANK AND M. GOLDMAN, *China: A New History* (1998). The summation of a lifetime engagement with Chinese history.

F. A. KIERMAN JR., AND J. K. FAIRBANK, eds., *Chinese Ways in Warfare* (1974). Chapters by different authors on the Chinese military experience from the Zhou to the Ming.

Sui and Tang

P. B. EBREY, *The Aristocratic Families of Early Imperial China* (1978).

D. MCMULLEN, *State and Scholars in T'ang China* (1988).

S. OWEN, *The Great Age of Chinese Poetry: The High T'ang* (1980).

S. OWEN, trans. and ed., *An Anthology of Chinese Literature: Beginnings to 1911* (1996).

E. G. PULLEYBLANK, *The Background of the Rebellion of An Lu-shan* (1955). A study of the 755 rebellion that weakened the central authority of the Tang dynasty.

E. O. REISCHAUER, *Ennin's Travels in T'ang China* (1955). China as seen through the eyes of a ninth-century Japanese Marco Polo.

E. H. SCHAFER, *The Golden Peaches of Samarkand* (1963). A study of Tang imagery.

So. TEISER, *The Ghost Festival in Medieval China* (1988). On Tang popular religion.

D. TWITCHETT, ed., *The Cambridge History of China*, Vol. III: *Sui and T'ang China, 589–906 Part 1*, (1979).

G. W. WANG, *The Structure of Power in North China During the Five Dynasties* (1963). A study of the interim period between the Tang and the Song dynasties.

A. F. WRIGHT, *The Sui Dynasty* (1978).

Song

B. BIRGE, *Women, Property, and Confucian Reaction in Song and Yuan China (960–1366)* (2002). The rights of women to property—whether in the form of dowries or inheritances—were considerable during the Song but declined thereafter.

C. S. CHANG AND J. SMYTHE, *South China in the Twelfth Century* (1981). China as seen through the eyes of a twelfth-century Chinese poet, historian, and statesman.

E. L. DAVIS, *Society and the Supernatural in Song China* (2001).

J. W. HAEGER, ed., *Crisis and Prosperity in Song China* (1975).

R. HYMES, *Statesmen and Gentlemen* (1987). On the transformation of officials into a local gentry elite during the twelfth and thirteenth centuries.

R. HYMES, *Way and Byway: Taoism, Local Religion, and Models of Divinity in Sung and Modern China* (2002).

M. ROSSABI, *China Among Equals* (1983). A study of the Liao, Qin, and Song Empires and their relations.

W. M. TU, *Confucian Thought, Selfhood as Creative Transformation* (1985).

K. YOSHIKAWA, *An Introduction to Song Poetry*, trans. by B. Watson (1967).

Yuan

T. T. ALLSEN, *Mongol Imperialism* (1987).

J. W. DARDESS, *Conquerors and Confucians: Aspects of Political Change in Late Yuan China* (1973).

DE RACHEWILTZ, trans., *The Secret History of the Mongols: A Mongolian Epic Chronicle of the Thirteenth Century* (2003). A new translation of a key historical work on the life of Genghis.

H. FRANKE AND D. TWITCHETT, eds., *The Cambridge History of China*, Vol. VI: *Alien Regimes and Border States, 710–1368* (1994).

J. D. LANGLOIS, *China Under Mongol Rule* (1981).

R. LATHAM, trans., *Travels of Marco Polo* (1958).

H. D. MARTIN, *The Rise of Chingis Khan and His Conquest of North China* (1981).

D. MORGAN, *The Mongol Empire and its Legacy* (1999). Genghis, the several khanates, and the aftermath of empire.

P. RATCHNEVSKY, *Genghis Khan, His Life and Legacy* (1992). The rise to power of the Mongol leader, with a critical consideration of historical sources.

CHAPTER 9

M. ADOLPHSON, *The Gates of Power: Monks, Courtiers, and Warriors in Premodern Japan* (2000). A new interpretation stressing the importance of temples in the political life of Heian and Kamakura Japan.

B.L. BATTEN, *To the Ends of Japan: Premodern Frontiers, Boundaries, and Interactions.* (2003). An interesting treatment of Heian Japan, topic by topic.

C. BLACKER, *The Catalpa Bow* (1975). An insightful study of folk Shinto.

R. BORGEN, *Sugawara no Michizane and the Early Heian Court* (1986). A study of a famous courtier and poet.

D. M. BROWN, ed., *The Cambridge History of Japan: Ancient Japan* (1993). This series of six volumes sums up several decades of research on Japan.

D. BROWN AND E. ISHIDA, eds., *The Future and the Past* (1979). A translation of a history of Japan written in 1219.

The Cambridge History of Japan, D.M. BROWN, ed.; Vol. 1, *Ancient Japan*, W. McCullough and D. H. Shively eds; Vol. 2, *Heian Japan*, K. Yamamura, ed. Vol. 3, *Medieval Japan*. Fine multi-author works.

M. COLLCUTT, *Five Mountains* (1980). A study of the monastic organization of medieval Zen.

T.D. CONLON, *State of War: The Violent Order of Fourteenth Century Japan* (2003). Compare Conlon's account with those of Souyri and Friday.

P. DUUS, *Feudalism in Japan* (1969). An easy survey of the subject.

W. W. FARRIS, *Population, Disease, and Land in Early Japan, 645–900* (1985). An innovative reinterpretation of early history.

W. W. FARRIS, *Heavenly Warriors: The Evolution of Japan's Military, 500–1300* (1992).

W. W. FARRIS, *Sacred Texts and Buried Treasures* (1998). Studies of Japan's prehistory and early history, based on recent Japanese research.

K. F. FRIDAY, *Samurai, Warfare and the State in Early Medieval Japan* (2004). Weapons and warfare in Japan from the tenth to fourteenth centuries.

A. E. GOBLE, *Gō Daigo's Revolution* (1996). A provoking account of the 1331 revolt by an emperor who thought emperors should rule.

J. W. HALL, *Government and Local Power in Japan, 500–1700: A Study Based on Bizen Province* (1966). A splendid and insightful book.

J. W. HALL AND T. TOYODA, *Japan in the Muromachi Age* (1977). Another collection of essays.

D. KEENE, ed., *Anthology of Japanese Literature from the Earliest Era to the Mid-Nineteenth Century* (1955).

D. KEENE, ed., *Twenty Plays of the Nō Theatre* (1970).

T. LAMARRE, *Uncovering Heian Japan: An Archeology of Sensation and Inscription* (2000). The "archeology" in the title refers to digging into literature.

I. H. LEVY, *The Ten Thousand Leaves* (1981). A fine translation of Japan's earliest collection of poetry.

J. P. MASS AND W. HAUSER, eds., *The Bakufu in Japanese History* (1985). Topics in *bakufu* history from the twelfth to the nineteenth centuries.

I. MORRIS, trans., *The Pillow Book of Sei Shōnagon* (1967). Observations about the Heian court life by the Jane Austen of ancient Japan.

S. MURASAKI, *The Tale of Genji*, trans. by A. Waley (1952). A comparison of this translation with that of Seidensticker is instructive.

S. MURASAKI, *The Tale of Genji*, trans. by E. G. Seidensticker (1976). The world's first novel and the greatest work of Japanese fiction.

R. J. PEARSON et al., eds., *Windows on the Japanese Past: Studies in Archaeology and Prehistory* (1986).

D. L. PHILIPPI, trans., *Kojiki* (1968). Japan's ancient myths.

J. PIGGOT, *The Emergence of Japanese Kingship* (1997).

E. O. REISCHAUER, *Ennin's Diary, the Record of a Pilgrimage to China in Search of the Law and Ennin's Travels in T'ang China* (1955).

E. O. REISCHAUER AND A. M. CRAIG, *Japan: Tradition and Transformation* (1989). A more detailed work covering the sweep of Japanese history from the early beginnings through the 1980s.

H. SATO, *Legends of the Samurai* (1995). Excerpts from various tales and writings.

D. H. SHIVELY and W. H. MCCULLOUGH, eds., *The Cambridge History of Japan: Heian Japan* (1999).

D. T. SUZUKI, *Zen and Japanese Culture* (1959).

H. TONOMURA, *Community and Commerce in Late Medieval Japan* (1992).

R. TSUNODA, W. T. DE BARY, AND D. KEENE, comps., *Sources of the Japanese Tradition* (1958). A collection of original religious, political, and philosophical writings from each period of Japanese history. The best reader. A new edition should be out soon.

H. P. VARLEY, *Imperial Restoration in Medieval Japan* (1971). A study of the 1331 attempt by an emperor to restore imperial power.

A. WALEY, trans., *The Nō Plays of Japan* (1957). Medieval dramas.

K. YAMAMURA, ed., *Cambridge History of Japan: Medieval Japan* (1990).

CHAPTER 10

Iran

M. BOYCE, *Zoroastrians: Their Religious Beliefs and Practices* (1979). A detailed survey by the current authority on Zoroastrian religious history. See Chapters 7–9.

M. BOYCE, ed. and trans., *Textual Sources for the Study of Zoroastrianism* (1984). A valuable anthology with an important introduction that includes Boyce's arguments for a revision of the dates of Zoroaster's life (to between 1400 and 1200 B.C.E.).

R. N. FRYE, *The Heritage of Persia* (1963). Still one of the best surveys, Chapter 6 deals with the Sasanid era.

R. GHIRSHMAN, *Iran* (1954 [orig. ed. 1951]). An introductory survey of similar extent to Frye, but with differing material also.

R. GHIRSHMAN, *Persian Art: The Parthian and Sasanid Dynasties* (1962). Superb photographs, and a very helpful glossary of places and names. The text is minimal.

GEO WIDENGRAN, *Mani and Manichaeism* (1965). Still the standard introduction to Mani's life and the later spread and development of Manichaeism.

India

A. L. BASHAM, *The Wonder That Was India* (1963). The best survey of classical Indian religion, society, literature, art, and politics.

W. T. DE BARY et al., comp., *Sources of Indian Tradition*, 2nd ed. (1958), Vol. I, *From the Beginning to 1800*, ed. and rev. by Ainslie T. Embree (1988). Excellent selections from a wide variety of Indian texts, with good introductions to the text selections.

S. DUTT, *Buddhist Monks and Monasteries of India* (1962). The standard work. See especially Chapters 3 ("Bhakti") and 4 ("Monasteries Under the Gupta Kings").

D. G. MANDELBAUM, *Society in India* (1972). 2 vols. The first two chapters in Volume I of this study of caste, family, and village relations are a good introduction to the caste system.

B. ROWLAND, *The Art and Architecture of India: Buddhist/Hindu/Jain*, 3rd rev. ed. (1970). See the excellent chapters on Sungan, Andhran, and other early Buddhist art (6–8, 14), the Gupta period (15), and the Hindu Renaissance (17–19).

V. A. SMITH, *The Oxford History of India*, 4th rev. ed. (1981). See especially pages 164–229 (the Gupta period and following era to the Muslim invasions).

R. THAPAR, *A History of India, Part I* (1966), pp. 109–193. Three chapters covering the rise of mercantilism, the Gupta "classical pattern," and the southern dynasties to ca. 900 C.E..

P. YOUNGER, *Introduction to Indian Religious Thought* (1972). A sensitive attempt to delineate classical concerns of Indian religious thought and culture.

CHAPTER 11

O. GRABAR, *The Formation of Islamic Art* (1973). A critical and creative interpretation of major themes in the development of distinctively Islamic forms of art and architecture.

A. HOURANI, *A History of the Arab Peoples* (1991). A masterly survey of the Arabs down through the centuries and a clear picture of many aspects of Islamic history and culture that extend beyond the Arab world.

H. KENNEDY, *The Prophet and the Age of the Caliphates: The Islamic Near East from the Sixth to the Eleventh Century* (1986). The best survey of early Islamic history.

I. LAPIDUS, *A History of Islamic Societies* (1988). A comprehensive overview of the rise and development of Islam all over the world.

F. E. PETERS, *Muhammad and the Origins of Islam* (1994). A balanced analysis of the life of Muhammad.

F. RAHMAN, *Major Themes of the Qur'an* (1980). The best introduction to the basic ideas of the Qur'an and Islam, seen through the eyes of a perceptive Muslim modernist scholar.

F. SCHUON, *Understanding Islam* (1994). Compares the Islamic worldview with Catholic Christianity. A dense, but intellectually stimulating, discussion.

M. SELLS, *Approaching the Qur'an. The Early Revelations* (1999). A fine introduction and new translations of some of the more common earlier Qur'anic revelations.

B. STOWASSER, *Women in the Qur'an, Traditions and Interpretation* (1994). An outstanding systematic study of statements regarding women in the Qur'an.

CHAPTER 12

K. ARMSTRONG, *Muhammad: A Biography of the Prophet* (1992). Strong on religion.

R. BARTLETT, *The Making of Europe, 950–1350* (1992). A study of the way immigration and colonial conquest shaped the Europe we know.

M. BLOCH, *Feudal Society*, Vols. 1 and 2, trans. by L. A. Manyon (1971). A classic on the topic and as an example of historical study.

P. BROWN, *Augustine of Hippo: A Biography* (1967). Late antiquity seen through the biography of its greatest Christian thinker.

J. H. BURNS, *The Cambridge History of Medieval Political Thought c. 350–c. 1450* (1991). The best scan.

R. H. C. DAVIS, *A History of Medieval Europe: From Constantine to St. Louis* (1972). Unsurpassed in clarity.

R. FLETCHER, *The Barbarian Conversion: From Paganism to Christianity* (1998). Up-to-date survey.

J. B. GLUBB, *The Great Arab Conquests* (1995). Jihadists.

G. GUGLIELMO, ed., *The Byzantines* (1997). Updates key issues.

D. GUTAS, *Greek Thought, Arabic Culture* (1998). A comparative intellectual history.

G. HOLMES, Ed., *The Oxford History of Medieval Europe* (1992). Overviews of Roman and northern Europe during the "Dark Ages."

B. LEWIS, *The Middle East: A Brief History of the Last 2,000 Years* (1995)

C. MANGO, *Byzantium: The Empire of New Rome* (1980).

J. MARTIN, *Medieval Russia 980–1584* (1995). A concise narrative history.

R. MCKITTERICK, ed., *Carolingian Culture: Emulation and Innovation* (1994). Fresh essays.

J.J. NORWICH, *Byzantium: The Decline and Fall* (1995).

J.J. NORWICH, *Byzantium: The Apogee* (1997). The whole story in two volulmes.

R.I. PAGE, *Chronicles of the Vikings: Records, Memorials, and Myths* (1995). Sources galore.

F. ROBINSON, ed., *The Cambridge Illustrated History of the Islamic World* (1996). Spectacular.

S. RUNCIMAN, *Byzantine Civilization* (1970). Succinct, comprehensive account by a master.

P. SAWYER, *The Age of the Vikings* (1962). Old but solid account.

C. STEPHENSON, *Medieval Feudalism* (1969). Excellent short summary and introduction.

L. WHITE JR., *Medieval Technology and Social Change* (1962). Often fascinating account of how primitive technology changed life.

H. WOLFRAM, *The Roman Empire and Its Germanic Peoples* (1997). Challenging, but most rewarding.

CHAPTER 13

The Islamic Heartlands

L. AHMED, *Women and Gender in Islam. Historical Roots of a Modern Debate* (1992). A good historical survey of the status of women in Middle Eastern societies.

J. BERKEY, *The Formation of Islam. Religion and Society in the Near East 600–1800* (2002). An interesting new synthesis foducing on political and religious trends.

C. E. BOSWORTH, *The Islamic Dynasties: A Chronological and Genealogical Handbook* (1967). A handy reference work for dynasties and families important to Islamic history in all periods and places.

M. A. COOK, *Commanding Right and Forbidding Wrong in Islamic Thought* (2001). A masterful anaylsis of the development of Islamic law.

P. K. HITTI, *History of the Arabs*, 8th ed. (1964). Still a useful English resource, largely for factual detail. See especially Part IV, "The Arabs in Europe: Spain and Sicily."

A. HOURANI, *A History of the Arab Peoples* (1991). The newest survey history and the best, at least for the Arab Islamic world.

S. K. JAYYUSI, ed., *The Legacy of Muslim Spain*, 2 vols. (1994). A comprehensive survey of the arts, politics, literature, and society by experts in various fields.

B. LEWIS, ed., *Islam and the Arab World* (1976). A large-format, heavily illustrated volume with many excellent articles on diverse aspects of Islamic (not simply Arab, as the misleading title indicates) civilization through the premodern period.

D. MORGAN, *The Mongols* (1986). A recent and readable survey history.

J. J. SAUNDERS, *A History of Medieval Islam* (1965). A brief and simple, if sketchy, introductory survey of Islamic history to the Mongol invasions.

India

W. T. DE BARY et al., comp., *Sources of Indian Tradition*, 2nd ed. (1958), Vol. I, *From the Beginning to 1800*, ed. and rev. by Ainslie T. Embree (1988). Excellent selections from a wide variety of Indian texts, with good introductions to chapters and individual selections.

S. M. IKRAM, *Muslim Civilization in India* (1964). The best short survey history, covering the period 711 to 1857.

R. C. MAJUMDAR, gen. ed., *The History and Culture of the Indian People*, Vol. VI, *The Delhi Sultanate*, 3rd ed. (1980). A comprehensive political and cultural account of the period in India.

F. ROBINSON, ed., *The Cambridge History of India, Pakistan, Bangladesh, Sri Lanka, Nepal, Bhutan, and the Maldives* (1989). A very helpful quick reference source with brief but well-done survey essays on a wide range of topics relevant to South Asian history down to the present.

A. WINK, *Al-Hind: The Making of the Indo-Islamic World*, Vol. 1 (1991). The first of five promising volumes to be devoted to the Indo-Islamic world's history. This volume treats the seventh to eleventh centuries.

Southeast Asia

L. ANDAYA, *The World of Maluku: Eastern Indonesia in the Early Modern Period* (1993). A comprehensive view of the formation of what is now Indonesia.

B. W. ANDAYA AND L. ANDAYA, *A History of Malaysia* (1982). A good overiew of Indonesia's smaller but critical northern neighbor.

J. SIEGEL, *Shadow and Sound: The Historical Thought of a Sumatran People* (1979). An excellent analysis tracing the relation between foreign influences and local practice.

CHAPTER 14

B. S. BAUER, *The Development of the Inca State* (1992). An important new work that emphasizes archaeological evidence over the Spanish chronicles in accounting for the emergence of the Inca Empire.

F. F. BERDAN, *The Aztecs of Central Mexico: An Imperial Society* (1982). An excellent introduction to the Aztecs.

R. E. BLANTON, S. A. KOWALEWSKI, G. FEINMAN, AND J. APPEL, *Ancient Mesoamerica: A Comparison of Change in Three Regions* (1981). Concentrates on ancient Mexico.

K. O. BRUHNS, *Ancient South America* (1994). A clear discussion of the archaeology and civilization of the region with emphasis on the Andes.

R. L. BURGER, *Chavín and the Origins of Andean Civilization* (1992). A detailed study of early Andean prehistory by one of the leading authorities on Chavín.

R. M. CARMACK, J. GASCO, AND G. H. GOSSEN, *The Legacy of Mesoamerica: History and Culture of a Native American Civilization* (1996). A survey of Mesoamerica from its origins to the present.

I. CLENDINNEN, *Aztecs: An Interpretation* (1995). A fascinating attempt to reconstruct the Aztec world.

M. D. COE, *Breaking the Maya Code* (1992). The story of the remarkable achievement of deciphering the ancient Maya language.

M. D. COE, *The Maya* (1993). The best introduction.

M. D. COE, *Mexico from the Olmecs to the Aztecs* (1994). A wide-ranging introductory discussion.

G. CONRAD AND A. A. DEMAREST, *Religion and Empire: The Dynamics of Aztec and Inca Expansionism* (1984). An interesting comparative study.

S. D. GILLESPIE, *The Aztec Kings* (1989).

R. HASSIG, *Aztec Warfare.*

J. HYSLOP, *Inka Settlement Planning* (1990). A detailed study.

M. LEÓN-PORTILLA, *Fifteen Poets of the Aztec World* (1992). An anthology of translations of Aztec poetry.

M. E. MILLER, *The Art of Mesoamerica from Olmec to Aztec* (1986). A well-illustrated introduction.

C. MORRIS AND A. VON HAGEN, *The Inka Empire and Its Andean Origins* (1993). A clear overview of Andean prehistory by a leading authority. Beautifully illustrated.

M. E. MOSELY, *The Incas and Their Ancestors: The Archaeology of Peru* (1992). Readable and thorough.

J. A. SABLOFF, *The Cities of Ancient Mexico* (1989). Capsule summaries of ancient Mesoamerican cultures.

J. A. SABLOFF, *Archaeology and the Maya* (1990). A look at changing views of the ancient Maya.

L. SCHELE and M. E. MILLER, *The Blood of Kings* (1986). A rich and beautifully illustrated study of ancient Maya art and society.

R. S. SHARER, *The Ancient Maya*, 5th ed. (1994). A classic. Readable, authoritative, and thorough.

M. P. WEAVER, *The Aztecs, Maya, and Their Predecessors* (1993). A classic textbook.

CHAPTER 15

L. B. ALBERTI, *The Family in Renaissance Florence*, trans. by R. N. Watkins (1962). A contemporary humanist, who never married, explains how a family should behave.

E. AMT, ed., *Women's Lives in Medieval Europe: A Source-book* (1992). Outstanding collection of sources.

H. BARON, *The Crisis of the Early Italian Renaissance*, Vols. 1 and 2 (1996). New edition of an old, major work, setting forth the civic dimension of Italian humanism.

G. BARRACLOUGH, *The Origins of Modern Germany* (1963). Penetrating political narrative.

S. BRAMLY, *Discovering the Life of Leonardo da Vinci* (1991). The man and the genius.

G. BRUCKER, *Renaissance Florence* (1983). Still one of the best introductions.

G. BULL, *Michelangelo: A Biography* (1995). Recent life in full.

J. BURCKHARDT, *The Civilization of the Renaissance in Italy* (1867). The famous classic that still has as many defenders as detractors.

S. FLANAGAN, *Hildegard of Bingen, 1098–1179: A Visionary Life* (1995). A most interesting German woman.

E. HALLAM, ed., *Chronicles of the Crusades (1989).* All nine!

D. HERLIHY, *Medieval Households* (1985). Survey of Middle Ages that defends the medieval family against modern caricatures.

D. HERLIHY AND C. KLAPISCH-ZUBER, *Tuscans and Their Families* (1985). Important work based on unique demographic data that gives the reader an appreciation of quantitative history.

G. HOLMES, *Renaissance* (1996). An expert's take on the subject.

J. C. HOLT, *Magna Carta*, 2nd ed. (1992). The famous document and its interpretation by succeeding generations.

J. HUIZINGA, *The Waning of the Middle Ages: A Study of the Forms of Life, Thought, and Art in France and the Netherlands in the Dawn of the Renaissance* (1924). A classic study of "mentality" at the end of the Middle Ages.

L. JARDINE, *Worldly Goods: A New History of the Renaissance* (1996). The material side of the Renaissance.

M. KING, *Women of the Renaissance* (1991). Women's presence and creativity.

W. H. MCNEILL, *Plagues and Peoples* (1976). The Black Death in a broader context.

R. I. MOORE, *The Formation of a Persecuting Society: Power and Deviance in Western Europe, 950–1250* (1987). A sympathetic look at heresy and dissent.

T. Noonan, *Contraception: A History of Its Treatment by the Catholic Theologians and Canonists* (1967). A fascinating account of medieval theological attitudes toward sexuality and sex-related problems.

J. Riley-Smith, ed., *Oxford Illustrated History of the Crusades* (1995) Lucid, gorgeous, and up-to-date.

J. Weisheipl, *Friar Thomas* (1980). Biography of Saint Thomas Aquinas, both the man and the theologian.

CHAPTER 16

M. Brecht, *Martin Luther: His Road to Reformation, 1483–1521* (1985). Best on young Luther.

C. Brown, et al., *Rembrandt: The Master and His Workshop* (1991) A great master's art and influence.

R. Briggs, *Witches and Neighbors: A History of European Witchcraft* (1996). A readable introduction.

E. Duffy, *The Stripping of the Altars* (1992). Strongest argument yet that there was no deep reformation in England.

H. O. Evennett, *The Spirit of the Counter Reformation* (1968). The continuity and independence of Catholic reform.

Hans-Jürgen Goertz, *The Anabaptists* (1996). Best treatment of minority Protestants.

O. P. Grell and A. Cunningham, *Health Care and Poor Relief in Protestant Europe* (1997) The civic side of the Reformation.

M. Holt, *The French Wars of Religion, 1562–1629* (1995). Scholarly appreciation of religious side of the story.

J. C. Hutchison, *Albrecht Durer* (1990). The life behind the art.

H. Jedin, *A History of the Council of Trent*, Vols. 1, 2 (1957–1961). Comprehensive, detailed, and authoritative.

M. Kitchen, *The Cambridge Illustrated History of Germany* (1996). Comprehensive and accessible.

A. Kors and E. Peters, eds., *European Witchcraft, 1100–1700* (1972). Classics of witch belief.

W. Maccaffrey, *Elizabeth I* (1993). Magisterial study.

G. Mattingly, *The Armada* (1959). A masterpiece, novel-like in style.

D. Mcculloch, *The Reformation* (2004). No stone unturned, with English emphasis.

H. A. Oberman, *Luther: Man Between God and Devil* (1989). Authoritative biography

J. W. O'Malley, *The First Jesuits* (1993). Extremely detailed account of the creation of the Society of Jesus and its original purposes.

S. Ozment, *The Age of Reform 1250–1550: An Intellectual and Religious History of Late Medieval and Reformation Europe* (1980). Broad, lucid survey.

S. Ozment, *When Fathers Ruled: Family Life in Reformation Europe* (1983). Effort to portray the constructive side of Protestant thinking about family relationships.

S. Ozment, *The Bürgermeister's Daughter: Scandal in a Sixteenth Century German Town* (1996). What a woman could do at law in the sixteenth century.

G. Parker, *The Thirty Years' War* (1984). Large, lucid survey.

J. H. Parry, *The Age of Reconnaissance* (1964). A comprehensive account of explorations from 1450 to 1650.

W. Prinz, *Durer* (1998). Latest biography of Germany's greatest painter.

J. J. Scarisbrick, *Henry VIII* (1968). The best account of Henry's reign.

G. Strauss, ed. and trans., *Manifestations of Discontent in Germany on the Eve of the Reformation* (1971). A rich collection of sources for both rural and urban scenes.

H. Wunder, *He Is the Sun, She Is the Moon: Women in Early Modern Germany* (1998). Best study of early modern women.

CHAPTER 17

J. Abun-Nasr, *A History of the Maghrib in the Islamic Period* (1987). The most recent North African survey. Pages 59–247 are relevant to this chapter.

D. Birmingham, *Central Africa to 1870* (1981). Chapters from the *Cambridge History of Africa* that give a brief, lucid overview of developments in this region.

P. Bohannan and P. Curtin, *Africa and Africans*, rev. ed. (1971). Accessible, topical approach to African history, culture, society, politics, and economics.

P. D. Curtin, S. Feiermann, L. Thompson, and J. Vansina, *African History* (1978). An older, but masterly survey. The relevant portions are Chapters 6–9.

R. Elphick, *Kraal and Castle: Khoikhoi and the Founding of White South Africa* (1977). An incisive, informative interpretation of the history of the Khoikhoi and their fateful interaction with European colonization.

R. Elphick and H. Giliomee, *The Shaping of South African Society, 1652–1820* (1979). A superb, synthetic history of this crucial period.

J. D. Fage, *A History of Africa* (1978). Still a readable survey history.

M. Hiskett, *The Development of Islam in West Africa* (1984). The standard survey study of the subject. Of the relevant sections (Chapters 1–10, 12, 15), that on Hausaland, which is treated only in passing in this text, is noteworthy.

R. W. July, *Precolonial Africa: An Economic and Social History* (1975). Chapter 10 gives an interesting overall picture of slaving in African history.

R. W. July, *A History of the African People*, 3rd ed. (1980). Chapters 3–6 treat Africa before about 1800 area by area; Chapter 7 deals with "The Coming of Europe."

I. M. Lewis, Ed., *Islam in Tropical Africa* (1966), pp. 4–96. Lewis's introduction is one of the best brief summaries of the role of Islam in West Africa and the Sudan.

D. T. Niani, ed., *Africa from the Twelfth to the Sixteenth Century, UNESCO General History of Africa*, Vol. IV (1984). Many survey articles cover the various regions and major states of Africa in the centuries noted in the title.

R. Oliver, *The African Experience* (1991). A masterly, balanced, and engaging survey, with outstanding syntheses and summaries of recent research.

J. A. Rawley, *The Transatlantic Slave Trade: A History* (1981). Impressively documented, detailed, and well-presented survey history of the Atlantic trade; little focus on African dimensions.

A. F. C. Ryder, *Benin and the Europeans: 1485–1897* (1969). A basic study.

John K. Thornton, *The Kingdom of Kongo: Civil War and Transition, 1641–1718* (1983). A detailed and perceptive analysis for those who wish to delve into Kongo state and society in the seventeenth century.

M. Wilson and L. Thompson, eds., *The Oxford History of South Africa*, Vol. I., *South Africa to 1870* (1969). Relatively detailed, if occasionally dated, treatment.

Chapter 18

I. Berlin, *Many Thousands Gone: The First Two Centuries of Slavery in North America* (1998); *Generations of Captivity: A History of African American Slaves* (2003). Two volumes representing the most extensive and important recent treatment of slavery in North America.

R. Blackburn, *The Making of New World Slavery from the Baroque to the Modern 1492–1800* (1997). An extraordinary work.

B. Cobo, *History of the Inca Empire* (1979). A major discussion.

N. D. Cook, *Born to Die: Disease and New World Conquest, 1492–1650* (1998) A survey of the devastating impact of previously unknown diseases on the native populations of the Americas.

P. D. Curtin, *The Atlantic Slave Trade: A Census* (1969). Remains a basic work.

D. B. Davis, *The Problem of Slavery in Western Culture* (1966). A brilliant and far-ranging discussion.

H. L. Gates Jr. and W. L. Andrews, eds., *Pioneers of the Black Atlantic: Five Slave Narratives from the Enlightenment 1772–1815* (1998). An anthology of autobiographical accounts.

S. Gruzinski, *The Conquest of Mexico: The Incorporation of Indian Societies into the Western World, 16th–18th Centuries* (1993). Interprets the experience of Native Americans, from their own point of view, during the time of the Spanish conquest.

L. Hanke, *Bartolomé de Las Casas: An Interpretation of His Life and Writings* (1951). A classic work.

R. Harms, *The Diligent: A Voyage through the Worlds of the Slave Trade* (2002). A powerful narrative of the voyage of a French slave trader.

J. Hemming, *The Conquest of the Incas*, (1970). A lucid account of the conquest of the Inca Empire and its aftermath.

J. Hemming, *Red Gold: The Conquest of the Brazilian Native Americans, 1500–1760* (1978). A careful account with excellent bibliography.

H. Klein, *The Middle Passage: Comparative Studies in the African Slave Trade* (1978). A far-ranging overview of the movement of slaves from Africa to the Americas.

M. Leon-Portilla, ed., *The Broken Spears: The Aztec Account of the Conquest of Mexico* (1961). A collection of documents recounting the experience of the Aztecs from their own point of view.

P. Manning, *Slavery and African Life: Occidental, Oriental, and African Slave Trades* (1990). An admirably concise economic-historical synthesis of the evidence, with multiple tables and statistics to supplement the magisterial analysis.

A. Pagden, *Lords of All the World: Ideologies of Empire in Spain, Britain, and France* c. 1500–c. 1800 (1995). An effort to explain the imperial thinking of the major European powers.

S. B. Schwartz, *Sugar Plantations in the Formation of Brazilian Society: Bahia, 1550–1835* (1985). A broad-ranging study of the emergence of the plantation economy.

I. K. Steele, *The English Atlantic, 1675–1740s: An Exploration of Communication and Community* (1986). An exploration of culture and commerce in the transatlantic world.

S. J. Stein, *Peru's Indian Peoples and the Challenge of Spanish Conquest: Huamanga to 1640* (1983). A work that examines the impact of the conquest of the Inca empire over the scope of a century.

H. Thomas, *Conquest: Montezuma, Cortés, and the Fall of Old Mexico* (1993). A splendid modern narrative of the event with careful attention to the character of the participants.

H. Thomas, *The Slave Trade: The Story of the Atlantic Slave Trade: 1440–1870* (1999). A sweeping narrative overview.

J. Thornton, *Africa and Africans in the Making of the Atlantic World, 1400–1680* (1992). A discussion of the role of Africans in the emergence of the transatlantic economy.

N. Wachtel, *The Vision of the Vanquished: The Spanish Conquest of Peru Through Indian Eyes, 1530–1570* (1977). A presentation of Incan experience of conquest.

Chapter 19

China

D. Bodde and C. Morris, *Law in Imperial China* (1967). Focuses on the Qing dynasty (1644–1911).

T. Brook, *The Confusions of Pleasure: Commerce and Culture in Ming China* (1988).

C. S. Chang and S. L. H. Chang, *Crisis and Transformation in Seventeenth Century China: Society, Culture, and Modernity* (1992).

P. Crossley, *Translucent Mirror: History and Identity in Qing Imperial Ideology* (1999).

W. T. De Bary, *Learning for One's Self: Essays on the Individual in Neo-Confucian Thought* (1991). A useful corrective to the view that Confucianism is simply a social ideology.

M. C. Elliott, *The Manchu Way: The Eight Banners and Ethnic Identity in Late Imperial China* (2001). The latest word; compare to Crossley above.

M. Elvin, *The Pattern of the Chinese Past: A Social and Economic Interpretation* (1973). A controversial but stimulating interpretation of Chinese economic history in terms of technology. It brings in earlier periods as well as the Ming, Qing, and modern China.

J. K. Fairbank, ed., *The Chinese World Order: Traditional China's Foreign Relations* (1968). An examination of the Chinese tribute system and its varying applications.

H. L. Kahn, *Monarchy in the Emperor's Eyes: Image and Reality in the Ch'ien-lung Reign* (1971). A study of the Chinese court during the mid-Qing period.

P. Kuhn, *Soulstealers: The Chinese Sorcery Scare of 1768* (1990).

Li Yu, *The Carnal Prayer Mat*, trans. by P. Hanan (1990).

F. Mote and D. Twitchett, eds., *The Cambridge History of China: The Ming Dynasty 1368–1644*, Vols. VI (1988) and VII (1998).

S. Naquin, *Peking Temples and City Life, 1400–1900* (2000).

S. Naquin and E. S. Rawski, *Chinese Society in the Eighteenth Century* (1987).

J. B. Parsons, *The Peasant Rebellions of the Late Ming Dynasty* (1970).

P. C. Perdue, *Exhausting the Earth, State and Peasant in Hunan, 1500–1850* (1987).

D. H. Perkins, *Agricultural Development in China, 1368–1968* (1969).

E. Rawski, *The Last Emperors: A Social History of Qing Imperial Institutions* (1998).

M. Ricci, *China in the Sixteenth Century: The Journals of Matthew Ricci, 1583–1610* (1953).

W. Rowe, *Hankow* (1984). A study of a city in late imperial China.

G. W. Skinner, *The City in Late Imperial China* (1977).

J. D. Spence, *Ts'ao Yin and the K'ang-hsi Emperor: Bondservant and Master* (1966). An excellent study of the early Qing court.

J. D. Spence, *Emperor of China: A Self-Portrait of K'ang-hsi* (1974). The title of this readable book does not adequately convey the extent of the author's contribution to the study of the early Qing emperor.

J. D. Spence, *Treason by the Book* (2001). An account of the legal workings of the authoritarian Qing state that reads like a detective story.

L. A. Struve, trans. and ed., *Voices from the Ming-Qing Cataclysm* (1993). A reader with translations of Chinese sources.

F. Wakeman, *The Great Enterprise* (1985). On the founding of the Manchu dynasty.

Japan

M. E. Berry, *Hideyoshi* (1982). A study of the sixteenth-century unifier of Japan.

M. E. Berry, *The Culture of Civil War in Kyoto* (1994). On the Warring States era.

H. Bolitho, *Treasures Among Men: The Fudai Daimyo in Tokugawa Japan* (1974). A study in depth.

H. Bolitho, *Bereavement and Consolation: Testimonies from Tokugawa Japan* (2003). Instances of how Tokugawa Japanese handled the death of a child.

C. R. Boxer, *The Christian Century in Japan, 1549–1650* (1951).

The Cambridge History of Japan; Vol. 4 J.W. Hall (ed.), *Early Modern Japan* (1991). A multi-author work.

M. Chikamatsu, *Major Plays of Chikamatsu*, trans. by D. Keene (1961).

R. P. Dore, *Education in Tokugawa Japan* (1965).

G. S. Elison, *Deus Destroyed: The Image of Christianity in Early Modern Japan* (1973). A brilliant study of the persecutions of Christianity during the early Tokugawa period.

J. W. Hall and M. Jansen, eds., *Studies in the Institutional History of Early Modern Japan* (1968). A collection of articles on Tokugawa institutions.

J. W. Hall, K. Nagahara, and K. Yamamura, eds., *Japan Before Tokugawa* (1981).

S. Hanley, *Everyday Things in Premodern Japan: The Hidden Legacy of Material Culture* (1997).

H. S. Hibbett, *The Floating World in Japanese Fiction* (1959). An eminently readable study of early Tokugawa literature.

M. Jansen, ed., *The Nineteenth Century*, Vol. 5 in *The Cambridge History of Japan* (1989).

K. Katsu, *Musui's Story* (1988). The life and adventures of a boisterous, no-good samurai of the early nineteenth century. Eminently readable.

D. Keene, trans., *Chushingura, the Treasury of Loyal Retainers* (1971). The puppet play about the forty-seven rōnin who took revenge on the enemy of their former lord.

O.G. Lidin, *Tanegashima: The Arrival of Europe in Japan* (2002). The impact of the musket and Europeans on sixteenth-century Japan.

M. Maruyama, *Studies in the Intellectual History of Tokugawa Japan*, trans. by M. Hane (1974). A seminal work in this field by one of modern Japan's greatest scholars.

J.L. McClain, et. al., *Edo and Paris: Urban Life and the State in the Early Modern Era* (1994). Comparison of city life and government role in capitals of Tokugawa Japan and France.

K. W. Nakai, *Shogunal Politics* (1988). A brilliant study of Arai Hakuseki's conceptualization of Tokugawa government.

P. Nosco, ed., *Confucianism and Tokugawa Culture* (1984). A lively collection of essays.

H. Ooms, *Tokugawa Village Practice: Class, Status, Power, Law* (1996).

A. Ravina, *Land and Lordship in Early Modern Japan* (1999). A sociopolitical study of three Tokugawa domains.

I. Saikaku, *The Japanese Family Storehouse*, trans. by G. W. Sargent (1959). A lively novel about merchant life in seventeenth-century Japan.

G. B. Sansom, *The Western World and Japan* (1950).

J. A. Sawada, *Confucian Values and Popular Zen* (1993). A study of *Shingaku*, a popular Tokugawa religious sect.

C. D. Sheldon, *The Rise of the Merchant Class in Tokugawa Japan* (1958).

T. C. Smith, *The Agrarian Origins of Modern Japan* (1959). On the evolution of farming and rural social organization in Tokugawa Japan.

P. F. Souyri, *The World Turned Upside Down: Medieval Japanese Society* (2001). After a running start from the late Heian period, an analysis of the overthrow of lords by their vassals.

R. P. Toby, *State and Diplomacy in Early Modern Japan: Asia in the Development of the Tokugawa Bakufu* (1984).

C. Totman, *Tokugawa Ieyasu: Shōgun* (1983).

C. Totman, *Green Archipelago, Forestry in Preindustrial Japan* (1989).

H. P. Varley, *The Ō'nin War: History of Its Origins and Background with a Selective Translation of the Chronicle of Ō'nin* (1967).

K. Yamamura and S. B. Hanley, *Economic and Demographic Change in Preindustrial Japan, 1600–1868* (1977).

Korea

T. Hatada, *A History of Korea* (1969).

W. E. Henthorn, *A History of Korea* (1971).

Ki-Baik Lee, *A New History of Korea* (1984).

P. Lee, *Sourcebook of Korean Civilization*, Vol. I (1993).

Vietnam

J. Buttinger, *A Dragon Defiant, a Short History of Vietnam* (1972).

Nguyen Du, *The Tale of Kieu* (1983).

N. Tarling, ed., *The Cambridge History of Southeast Asia* (1992).

K. Taylor, *The Birth of Vietnam* (1983).

A. B. Woodside, *Vietnam and the Chinese Model* (1988).

CHAPTER 20

F. Anderson, *The Crucible of War: The Seven Years' War and the Fate of Empire in British North America, 1754–1766* (2000) A splendid narrative and analysis.

J. Blum, *Lord and Peasant in Russia from the Ninth to the Nineteenth Century* (1961). Remains a thorough and wide-ranging discussion.

P. Burke, *The Fabrication of Louis XIV* (1992). Examines the manner in which the public image of Louis XIV was forged in art.

P. Bushkovitch, *Peter the Great: The Struggle for Power, 1671–1725* (2001). Replaces previous studies.

L. Colley, *Britons: Forging the Nation, 1707–1837* (1992) A major study of the making of British nationhood.

P. Deane, *The First Industrial Revolution*, (1999). A well-balanced and systematic treatment.

J. De Vries, *European Urbanization 1500–1800* (1984). The most important and far-ranging of recent treatments of the subject.

W. Doyle, *The Old European Order, 1660–1800* (1992). The most thoughtful treatment of the subject.

R. J. W. Evans, *The Making of the Habsburg Monarchy, 1550–1700: An Interpretation* (1979). Places much emphasis on intellectual factors and the role of religion.

D. Fraser, *Frederick the Great: King of Prussia* (2001) Excellent on both Frederick and eighteenth-century Prussia.

E. Hobsbawm, *Industry and Empire: The Birth of the Industrial Revolution* (1999). A survey by a major historian of the subject.

K. Honeyman, *Women, Gender and Industrialization in England, 1700–1850* (2000). Emphasizes how certain work or economic roles became associated with either men or women.

O. H. Hufton, *The Poor of Eighteenth-Century France, 1750–1789* (1975). A brilliant study of poverty and the family economy.

L. Hughes, *Russia in the Age of Peter the Great* (1998). An excellent account.

D. I. Kertzer and M. Barbagli, *The History of the European Family: Family Life in Early Modern Times, 1500–1709* (2001). A series of broad-ranging essays covering the entire Continent.

S. King and G. Timmons, *Making Sense of the Industrial Revolution: English Economy and Society, 1700–1850* (2001). Examines the Industrial Revolution through the social institutions that brought it about and were changed by it.

M. Kishlansky, *A Monarchy Transformed: Britain 1603–1714* (1996) An excellent synthesis.

P. Langford, *A Polite and Commercial People: England 1717–1783* (1989). An excellent survey of mid-eighteenth-century Britain covering social history as well as politics, the overseas wars, and the American Revolution.

A. Lossky, *Louis XIV and the French Monarchy* (1994). The most recent major analysis.

F. E. Manuel, *The Broken Staff: Judaism Through Christian Eyes* (1992). An important discussion of Christian interpretations of Judaism.

M. A. Meyer, *The Origins of the Modern Jew: Jewish Identity and European Culture in Germany, 1749–1824* (1967). A general introduction organized around individual case studies.

D. Underdown, *Fire from Heaven: Life in an English Town in the Seventeenth Century* (1992). A lively account of how a single English town experienced the religious and political turmoil of the century.

D. Valenze, *The First Industrial Woman* (1995). An elegant work exploring the manner in which industrialization transformed the work of women.

J. West, *Gunpower, Government, and War in the Mid–Eighteenth Century* (1991). A study of how warfare touched much government of the day.

Chapter 21

S. S. Blair and J. Bloom, *The Art and Architecture of Islam, 1250–1800* (1994). A fine survey of the period for all parts of the Islamic world.

R. Canfield, ed., *Turko-Persia in Historical Perspctive* (1991). A good general collection of essays.

K. Chelebi, *The Balance of Truth* (1957). A marvelous volume of essays and reflections by probably the major intellectual of Ottoman times.

W. T. de Bary et al., comp., *Sources of Indian Tradition*, 2nd ed. (1958),Vol. I, *From the Beginning to 1800*, ed. and rev. by Ainslie T. Embree (1988). Excellent selections from a wide variety of Indian texts, with good introductions to chapters and individual selections.

S. Faroqi, *Towns and Townsmen of Ottoman Anatolia* (1984). Examines the changing balances of economic power between the urban and rural areas.

C. H. Fleischer, *Bureaucrat and Intellectual in the Ottoman Empire: The Historian Mustafa Ali (1541–1600)* (1986). A major study of Ottoman intellectual history.

G. Hambly, *Central Asia* (1966). Excellent survey chapters (9–13) on the Chaghatay and Uzbek (Shaybanid) Turks.

R. S. Hattox, *Coffee and Coffee-Houses: The Origins of a Social Beverage in the Medieval Near East* (1985). A fascinating piece of social history.

M. G. S. Hodgson, *The Gunpowder Empires and Modern Times*, Vol. 3 of *The Venture of Islam*, 3 vols. (1974). Less ample than Vols. 1 and 2 of Hodgson's monumental history, but a thoughtful survey of the great post-1500 empires.

S. M. Ikram, *Muslim Civilization in India* (1964). Still the best short survey history, covering the period from 711 to 1857.

H. Inalcik, *The Ottoman Empire: The Classical Age 1300–1600* (1973). An excellent, if dated, survey with solid treatment of Ottoman social, religious, and political institutions.

H. Inalcik, *An Economic and Social History of the Ottoman Empire, 1300–1914* (1994). A masterly survey by the dean of Ottoman studies today.

C. Kafadar, *Between Two Worlds: The Construction of the Ottoman State* (1995). A readable analysis of theories of Ottoman origins and early development.

N. R. Keddie, ed., *Scholars, Saints, and Sufis: Muslim Religious Institutions in the Middle East Since 1500* (1972). A collection of interesting articles well worth reading.

M. Mujeeb, *The Indian Muslims* (1967). The best cultural study of Islamic civilization in India as a whole, from its origins onward.

G. Necipoglu, *Architecture, Ceremonial, and Power: The Topkapi Palace in the Fifteenth and Sixteenth Centuries* (1991). A superb analysis of the symbolism of Ottoman power and authority.

L. Pierce, *The Imperial Harem: Women and Sex in the Ottoman Empire* (1993). Ground-breaking study on the role of women in the Ottoman Empire.

D. Quatarert, *An Economic and Social history of the Ottoman Empire 1300–1914* (1994). The authoritative account of Ottoman economy and society.

J. Richards, *The Mughal Empire*, Vol. 5 of *The New Cambridge History of India* (1993). A impressive synthesis of the varying interpretations of the Mughal India.

S. A. A. Rizvi, *The Wonder That Was India*, Vol. II (1987). A sequel to Basham's original *The Wonder That Was India*; treats Mughal life, culture, and history from 1200 to 1700.

F. Robinson, *Atlas of the Islamic World Since 1500* (1982). Brief, excellent historical essays, color illustrations with detailed accompanying text, and chronological tables, as well as precise maps, make this a refreshing general reference work.

R. Savory, *Iran Under the Safavids* (1980). A solid and readable survey.

S. J. Shaw, *Empire of the Gazis: The Rise and Decline of the Ottoman Empire, 1280–1808*, Vol. I of *History of the Ottoman Empire and Modern Turkey* (1976). A solid historical survey with excellent bibliographic essays for each chapter and a good index.

CHAPTER 22

D. BEALES, *Joseph II: In the Shadow of Maria Theresa, 1741–1780* (1987). The best treatment in English of the early political life of Joseph II.

M. BIAGIOLI, *Galileo Courtier: The Practice of Science in the Culture of Absolutism* (1993). A major revisionist work that emphasizes the role of the political setting on Galileo's career and thought.

D. D. BIEN, *The Calas Affair: Persecution, Toleration, and Heresy in Eighteenth-Century Toulouse* (1960). Classic treatment of the famous case.

T. C. W. BLANNING, *The Culture of Power and the Power of Culture: Old Regime Europe 1660–l789* (2002). The strongest treatment of the relationship of eighteenth-century cultural changes and politics.

R. DARNTON, *The Literary Underground of the Old Regime* (1982). Classic essays on the world of printers, publishers, and booksellers.

P. DEAR, *Revolutionizing the Sciences: European Knowledge and Its Ambitions, 1500–1700* (2001). A broad-ranging study of both the ideas and institutions of the new science.

I. DE MADARIAGA, *Catherine the Great: A Short History* (1990). A good brief biography.

S. GAUKROGER, *Francis Bacon and the Transformation of Early-Modern Philosophy* (2001). An excellent, accessible introduction.

J. GLEIXK, *Isaac Newton* (2003) The best brief biography.

D. GOODMAN, *The Republic of Letters: A Cultural History of the French Enlightenment* (1994). Concentrates on the role of salons.

I. HARRIS, *The Mind of John Locke: A Study of Political Theory in Its Intellectual Setting* (1994). The most comprehensive recent treatment.

J. L. HEILBRON, *The Sun in the Church: Cathedrals as Solar Observatories* (2000). A remarkable study of the manner in which Roman Catholic cathedrals were used to make astronomical observations and calculations.

K. J. HOWELL, *God's TwoBooks: Copernican Cosmology and Biblical Interpretqation in Early Modern Science* (2003) Best introduction to early modern issues of science and religion.

J. MELTON, *The Rise of the Public in Enlightenmen Europe* (2001). A superb overview of the emergence of new institutions which made the expression of a broad public opinion possible in Europe.

T. MUNCK, *The Enlightenment: A Comparative Social History 1721–1794* (2000). A clear introduction to the social background making possible the spread of Enlightenment thought.

S. MUTHU, *Enlightenment against Empire* (2003) A study of philosophes who criticized the European empires of their day.

D. OUTRAM, *The Enlightenment* (1995). An excellent brief introduction.

R. PORTER, *The Creation of the Modern World: The Untold Story of the British Enlightenment* (2001) A superb, lively overview.

P. RILEY, *The Cambridge Companion to Rousseau* (2001). Excellent accessible essays by major scholars.

E. ROTHCHILD, *Economic Sentiments: Adam Smith, Condorcet, and the Enlightenment* (2001). A sensitive account of Smith's thought and its relationship to the social questions of the day.

S. SHAPIN, *The Scientific Revolution* (1996). An important revisionist survey emphasizing social factors.

L. STEINBRÜGGE, *The Moral Sex: Woman's Nature in the French Enlightenment* (1995). Emphasizes the conservative nature of Enlightenment thought on women.

P. ZAGORIN, *How the Idea of Religious Toleration Came to the West* (2003) An excellent exploration of the rise of toleration.

CHAPTER 23

R. ANSTEY, *The Atlantic Slave Trade and British Abolition, 1760–1810* (1975). A standard overview that emphasizes the role of religious factors.

B. BAILYN, *The Ideological Origins of the American Revolution* (1967). An important work illustrating the role of English radical thought in the perceptions of the American colonists.

K. M. BAKER, *Inventing the French Revolution: Essays on French Political Culture in the Eighteenth Century* (1990). Important essays on political thought before and during the revolution.

K. M. BAKER AND C. LUCAS, eds., *The French Revolution and the Creation of Modern Political Culture*, 3 vols. (1987). A splendid collection of important original articles on all aspects of politics during the revolution.

R. J. BARMAN, *Brazil: The Forging of a Nation, 1798–1852* (1988). The best coverage of this period.

C. BECKER, *The Declaration of Independence: A Study in the History of Political Ideas* (1922). Remains an important examination of the political and imperial theory of the Declaration.

J. F. BERNARD, *Talleyrand: A Biography* (1973). A useful account.

L. BETHELL, *The Cambridge History of Latin America*, Vol. 3 (1985). Contains an extensive treatment of independence.

R. BLACKBURN, *The Overthrow of Colonial Slavery, 1776–1848* (1988). A major discussion quite skeptical of the humanitarian interpretation.

T. C. W. BLANNING, ed., *The Rise and Fall of the French Revolution* (1996). A wide-ranging collection of essays illustrating the debates over the French Revolution.

J. BROOKE, *King George III* (1972). The best biography.

R. COBB, *The People's Armies* (1987). The major treatment in English of the revolutionary army.

O. CONNELLY, *Napoleon's Satellite Kingdoms* (1965). The rule of Napoleon and his family in Europe.

E. V. DA COSTA, *The Brazilian Empire* (1985). Excellent coverage of the entire nineteenth-century experience of Brazil.

D. B. DAVIS, *The Problem of Slavery in the Age of Revolution, 1770–1823* (1975). A transatlantic perspective on the issue.

F. FEHÉR, *The French Revolution and the Birth of Modernity* (1990). A wide-ranging collection of essays on political and cultural facets of the revolution.

A. FORREST, *The French Revolution and the Poor* (1981). A study that expands consideration of the revolution beyond the standard social boundaries.

M. GLOVER, *The Peninsular War, 1807–1814: A Concise Military History* (1974). An interesting account of the military campaign that so drained Napoleon's resources in western Europe.

J. GODECHOT, *The Counter-Revolution: Doctrine and Action, 1789–1804* (1971). An examination of opposition to the revolution.

A. GOODWIN, *The Friends of Liberty: The English Democratic Movement in the Age of the French Revolution* (1979). A major work that explores the impact of the French Revolution on English radicalism.

L. HUNT, *Politics, Culture, and Class in the French Revolution* (1986). A series of essays that focus on the modes of expression of the revolutionary values and political ideas.

W. W. KAUFMANN, *British Policy and the Independence of Latin America, 1802–1828* (1951). A standard discussion of an important relationship.

E. KENNEDY, *A Cultural History of the French Revolution* (1989). An important examination of the role of the arts, schools, clubs, and intellectual institutions.

M. KENNEDY, *The Jacobin Clubs in the French Revolution: The First Years* (1982). A careful scrutiny of the organizations chiefly responsible for the radicalizing of the revolution.

M. KENNEDY, *The Jacobin Clubs in the French Revolution: The Middle Years* (1988). A continuation of the previously listed study.

H. KISSINGER, *A World Restored: Metternich, Castlereagh and the Problems of Peace, 1812–1822* (1957). A provocative study by an author who became an American secretary of state.

G. LEFEBVRE, *The Coming of the French Revolution* (trans. 1947). A classic examination of the crisis of the French monarchy and the events of 1789.

G. LEFEBVRE, *Napoleon*, 2 vols., trans. by H. Stockhold (1969). The fullest and finest biography.

J. LYNCH, *The Spanish American Revolutions, 1808–1826* (1986). An excellent one-volume treatment.

P. MAIER, *American Scripture: Making the Declaration of Independence* (1997). Stands as a major revision of our understanding of the Declaration.

G. MASUR, *Simón Bolívar* (1969). The standard biography in English.

S. E. MELZER AND L. W. RABINE, eds., *Rebel Daughters: Women and the French Revolution* (1992). A collection of essays exploring various aspects of the role and image of women in the French Revolution.

M. MORRIS, *The British Monarchy and the French Revolution* (1998). Explores the manner in which the British monarchy saved itself from possible revolution.

R. MUIR, *Tactics and the Experience of Battle in the Age of Napoleon* (1998). Examines the wars from the standpoint of the soldiers in combat.

H. NICOLSON, *The Congress of Vienna* (1946). A good, readable account.

T. O. OTT, *The Haitian Revolution, 1789–1804* (1973). An account that clearly relates the events in Haiti to those in France.

R. R. PALMER, *Twelve Who Ruled: The Committee of Public Safety During the Terror* (1941). A clear narrative and analysis of the policies and problems of the committee.

R. R. PALMER, *The Age of the Democratic Revolution: A Political History of Europe and America, 1760–1800*, 2 vols. (1959, 1964). An impressive survey of the political turmoil in the transatlantic world.

C. PROCTOR, *Women, Equality, and the French Revolution* (1990). An examination of how the ideas of the Enlightenment and the attitudes of revolutionaries affected the legal status of women.

A. J. RUSSELL-WOOD, ed., *From Colony to Nation: Essays on the Independence of Brazil* (1975). A series of important essays.

P. SCHROEDER, *The Transformation of European Politics, 1763–1848* (1994). A fundamental treatment of the diplomacy of the era.

T. E. SKIDMORE AND P. H. SMITH, *Modern Latin America*, 4th ed. (1997). A very useful survey.

A. SOBOUL, *The Parisian Sans-Culottes and the French Revolution, 1793–94* (1964). The best work on the subject.

A. SOBOUL, *The French Revolution* (trans. 1975). An important work by a Marxist scholar.

D. G. SUTHERLAND, *France, 1789–1825: Revolution and Counterrevolution* (1986). A major synthesis based on recent scholarship in social history.

T. TACKETT, *Religion, Revolution, and Regional Culture in Eighteenth-Century France: The Ecclesiastical Oath of 1791* (1986). The most important study of this topic.

T. TACKETT, *Becoming a Revolutionary: The Deputies of the French National Assembly and the Emergence of a Revolutionary Culture (1789–1790)* (1996). The best study of the early months of the revolution.

J. M. THOMPSON, *Robespierre*, 2 vols. (1935). The best biography.

D. K. VAN KEY, *The Religious Origins of the French Revolution: From Calvin to the Civil Constitution, 1560–1791* (1996). Examines the manner in which debates within French Catholicism influenced the coming of the revolution.

M. WALZER, ed., *Regicide and Revolution: Speeches at the Trial of Louis XVI* (1974). An important and exceedingly interesting collection of documents with a useful introduction.

I. WOLOCH, *The New Regime: Transformations of the French Civic Order, 1789–1820s* (1994). An important overview of just what had and had not changed in France after the quarter century of revolution and war.

G. WOOD, *The Radicalism of the American Revolution* (1991). A major interpretation.

CHAPTER 24

I. BERLIN, *Generations of Captivity: A History of African-American Slaves* (2003) A major work.

D. BLACKBOURN, *The Long Nineteenth Century: A History of Germany, 1780–1918* (1998). An outstanding survey.

D. G. CREIGHTON, *John A. MacDonald* (1952, 1955). A major biography of the first Canadian prime minister.

D. DONALD, *Lincoln* (1995). Now the standard biography.

R. B. EDGERTON, *Death or Glory: The Legacy of the Crimean War* (2000). Multifaceted study of a badly mismanaged war that transformed many aspects of European domestic politics.

M. HOLT, *The Rise and Fall of the American Whig Party: Jacksonian Politics and the Onset of the Civil War* (2003) An extensive survey of the Jacksonian era.

R. KEE, *The Green Flag: A History of Irish Nationalism* (2001). A vast survey.

W. LACQUER, *A History of Zionism* (1989). The most extensive one-volume treatment.

M. B. LEVINGER, *Enlightened Nationalism: The Transformation of Prussian Political Culture, 1806–1848* (2002). A major work based on the most recent scholarship.

J. M. MCPHERSON, *The Battle Cry of Freedom: The Civil War Era* (1988). An excellent one-volume treatment.

D. MORTON, *A Short History of Canada* (2001). Useful popular history.

J. P. PARRY, *The Rise and Fall of Liberal Government in Victorian Britain* (1994). An outstanding study.

A. PLESSIS, *The Rise and Fall of the Second Empire, 1852–1871* (1985). A useful survey of France under Napoleon III.

D. M. POTTER, *The Impending Crisis, 1848–1861* (1976) A penetrating study of the coming of the American Civil War.

A. SKED, *Decline and Fall of the Habsburg Empire 1815–1918* (2001). A major, accessible survey of a difficult subject.

D. M. SMITH, *Cavour* (1984). An excellent biography.

C. P. STACEY, *Canada and the Age of Conflict* (1977, 1981). A study of Canadian foreign relations.

D. Wetzel, *A Duel of Giants: Bismarck, Napoleon III, and the Origins of the Franco-Prussian War* (2001). Broad study based on most recent scholarship.

Chapter 25

M. Adas, *Machines as the Measure of Men: Science, Technology, and Ideologies of Western Dominance* (1989). The best single volume on racial thinking and technological advances as forming ideologies of European colonial dominance.

A. Ascher and P. A. Stolypin, *The Search for Stability in Late Imperial Russia* (2000). A broad-ranging biography based on extensive research.

I. Berlin, *Karl Marx: His Life and Environment*, 4th ed. (1996). A classics volume that remains an excellent introduction.

Janet Browne, *Charles Darwin*, 2 vols. (2002) An eloquent, accessible biography.

J. Burrow, *The Crisis of Reason: European Thought, 1848–1914* (2000). The best overview available.

A. D. Chandler Jr., *The Visible Hand: Managerial Revolution in American Business* (1977). Remains the best discussion of the innovative role of American business.

A. Clarke, *The Struggle for the Breeches: Gender and the Making of the British Working Class* (1995). An examination of the manner in which industrialization made problematical the relationships between men and women.

W. Cronin, *Nature's Metropolis: Chicago and the Great West, 1848–1893* (1991) The best examination of any major American nineteenth-century city.

P. Gay, *Freud: A Life for Our Time* (1988). The new standard biography.

R. F. Hamilton, *Marxism, Revisionism, and Leninism: Explication, Assessment, and Commentary* (2000). A contribution from the perspective of a historically minded sociologist.

S. Hahn, *A Nation under Our Feet: Black Political Struggles in the Rural South from Slavey to the Great Migration* (2003). A major synthesis.

A. Hourani, *Arab Thought in the Liberal Age 1789–1939* (1967). A classic account, clearly written and accessible to the nonspecialist.

D. I. Kertzer and M. Barbagli, eds., *Family Life in the Long Nineteenth Century, 1789–1913: The History of the European Family* (2002). Wide-ranging collection of essays.

J. T. Kloppenberg, *Uncertain Victory: Social Democracy and Progressivism in European and American Thought* (1986). An extremely important comparative study.

J. Köhler, *Zarathustra's Secret: The Interior Life of Friedrich Nietzsche* (2002). A controversial new biography.

L. Kolakowski, *Main Currents of Marxism: Its Rise, Growth, and Dissolution*, 3 vols. (1978). Especially good on the last years of the nineteenth century and the early years of the twentieth.

P. Krause, *The Battle for Homestead, 1880–1892* (1992). Examines labor relations in the steel industry.

D. Landes, *The Wealth and Poverty of Nations: Why Some Are So Rich and Some So Poor* (1998). A major international discussion of the subject.

M. McGerr, *A Fierce Discontent: The Rise and Fall of the Progressive Moevement in America l870–1920* (2003). The best recent synthesis.

E. Morris, *Theodore Rex* (2002). Major survey of Theodore Roosevelt's presidency and personality.

A. Pais, *Subtle Is the Lord: The Science and Life of Albert Einstein* (1983). Remains the most accessible scientific biography.

J. Rendall, *The Origins of Modern Feminism: Women in Britain, France and the United States, 1780–1860* (1985). A well-informed introduction.

R. Service, *Lenin: A Biography* (2002). Based on new sources and will no doubt become the standard biography.

R. M. Utley, *The Indian Frontier and the American West, 1846–1890* (1984). A broad survey of the pressures of white civilization against Native Americans.

D. Vital, *A People Apart: The Jews In Modern Europe, l789–1939* (1999). A deeply informed survey.

Chapter 26

S. Arrom, *The Women of Mexico City, 1790–1857* (1985). A pioneering study.

E. Berman, ed., *Women, Culture, and Politics in Latin America* (1990). Useful essays.

L. Bethell, ed., *The Cambridge History of Latin America*, 8 vols. (1992). The single most authoritative coverage, with extensive bibliographical essays.

V. Bulmer-Thomas, *The Economic History of Latin America Since Independence* (1994). A major study in every respect.

E. B. Burns, *The Poverty of Progress: Latin America in the Nineteenth Century* (1980). Argues that the elites suppressed alternative modes of cultural and economic development.

E. B. Burns, *A History of Brazil* (1993). The most useful one-volume treatment.

D. Bushnell and N. Macaulay, *The Emergence of Latin America in the Nineteenth Century* (1994). A survey that examines the internal development of Latin America during the period.

R. Conrad, *The Destruction of Brazilian Slavery, 1850–1889* (1971). A good survey of the most important problem in Brazil in the second half of the nineteenth century.

R. Conrad, *World of Sorrow: The African Slave Trade to Brazil* (1986). An excellent survey of the subject.

E. V. Da Costa, *The Brazilian Empire: Myths and Histories* (1985). Essays that provide a thorough introduction to Brazil during the period of empire.

H. S. Ferns, *Britain and Argentina in the Nineteenth Century* (1968). Explains clearly the intermeshing of the two economies.

M. Font, *Coffee, Contention, and Change in the Making of Modern Brazil* (1990). Extensive discussion of the problems of a single-commodity economy.

R. Graham, *Britain and the Onset of Modernization in Brazil* (1968). Another study of British economic dominance.

S. H. Haber, *Industry and Underdevelopment: The Industrialization of Mexico, 1890–1940* (1989). Examines the problem of industrialization before and after the revolution.

G. Hahner, *Emancipating the Female Sex: The Struggle for Women's Rights in Brazil, 1850–1940* (1990). An extensive examination of a relatively understudied issue in Latin America.

C. H. Haring, *Empire in Brazil: A New World Experiment with Monarchy* (1958). Remains a useful overview.

J. Hemming, *Amazon Frontier: The Defeat of the Brazilian Indians* (1987). A brilliant survey of the experience of Native Americans in modern Brazil.

R. A. HUMPHREYS, *Latin America and the Second World War*, 2 vols. (1981–1982). The standard work on the topic.

F. KATZ, ed., *Riot, Rebellion, and Revolution in Mexico: Social Base of Agrarian Violence, 1750–1940* (1988). Essays that put the violence of the revolution in a longer context.

A. KNIGHT, *The Mexican Revolution*, 2 vols. (1986). The best treatment of the subject.

S. MAINWARING, *The Catholic Church and Politics in Brazil, 1916–1985* (1986). An examination of a key institution in Brazilian life.

M. C. MEYER AND W. L. SHERMAN, *The Course of Mexican History* (1995). An excellent survey.

M. MORNER, *Adventurers and Proletarians: The Story of Migrants in Latin America* (1985). Examines immigration to Latin America and migration within it.

J. PAGE, *Perón: A Biography* (1983). The standard English treatment.

D. ROCK, *Politics in Argentina, 1890–1930: The Rise and Fall of Radicalism* (1975). The major discussion of the Argentine Radical Party.

D. ROCK, *Argentina, 1516–1987: From Spanish Colonization to Alfonsin* (1987). Now the standard survey.

D. ROCK, ed., *Latin America in the 1940s: War and Postwar Transitions* (1994). Essays examining a very difficult decade for the continent.

R. M. SCHNEIDER, *"Order and Progress": A Political History of Brazil* (1991). A straightforward narrative with helpful notes for further reading.

T. E. SKIDMORE, *Black into White: Race and Nationality in Brazilian Thought* (1993). Examines the role of racial theory in Brazil.

P. H. SMITH, *Argentina and the Failure of Democracy: Conflict Among Political Elites. 1904–1955* (1974). An examination of one of the major political puzzles of Latin American history.

S. J. STEIN AND B. H. STEIN, *The Colonial Heritage of Latin America: Essays on Economic Dependence in Perspective* (1970). A major statement of the dependence interpretation.

D. TAMARIN, *The Argentine Labor Movement, 1930–1945: A Study in the Origins of Perónism* (1985). A useful introduction to a complex subject.

H. J. WIARDA, *Politics and Social Change in Latin America: The Distinct Tradition* (1974). Excellent essays that stress the ongoing role of Iberian traditions.

J. D. WIRTH, ed., *Latin American Oil Companies and the Politics of Energy* (1985). A series of case studies.

J. WOLFE, *Working Women, Working Men: São Paulo and the Rise of Brazil's Industrial Working Class, 1900–1955* (1993). Pays particular attention to the role of women.

J. WOMACK, *Zapata and the Mexican Revolution* (1968). A classic study.

CHAPTER 27

General Works

S. COOK, *Colonial Encounters in the Age of High Imperialism* (1996). A good introduction to the imperial enterprise in Africa and Asia.

D. K. FIELDHOUSE, *The West and the Third World. Trade, Colonialism, Dependence and Development* (1999). Addresses whether colonialism was detrimental or beneficial to colonized peoples.

P. HOPKIRK, *The Great Game: The Struggle for Empire in Central Asia* (1992). Focuses on the political and economic rivalries of the imperial powers.

India

A. AHMAD, *Islamic Modernism in India and Pakistan, 1857–1964* (1967). The standard survey of Muslim thinkers and movements in India during the period.

C. A. BAYLY, *Indian Society and the Making of the British Empire*, The New Cambridge History of India, II. 1 (1988). One of several major contributions of this author to the ongoing revision of our picture of modern Indian history since the eighteenth century.

A. GHOSH, *In an Antique Land. History in the Guise of a Traveler's Tale* (1992). An anthropologist traces the footsteps of a premodern slave traveling with his master from North Africa to India. A gripping tale of premodern life in the India Ocean basin and also of contemporary Egypt.

R. GUHA, ed., *Subaltern Studies: Writings on South Asian History and Society* (1982). Essays on the colonial period that focus on the social, political, and economic history of "subaltern" groups and classes (hill tribes, peasants, etc.) rather than only the elites of India.

S. N. HAY, ed., "Modern India and Pakistan," Part VI of Wm. Theodore de Bary et al., eds., *Sources of Indian Tradition*, 2nd ed. (1988). A superb selection of primary-source documents with brief introductions and helpful notes.

F. ROBINSON, ed., *The Cambridge Encyclopedia of India, Pakistan, Bangladesh, Sri Lanka, Nepal, Bhutan, and the Maldives* (1989). A fine collection of survey articles by various scholars, organized into topical chapters ranging from "Economies" to "Cultures."

Central Islamic Lands

J. J. DONAHUE AND J. L. ESPOSITO, eds., *Islam in Transition: Muslim Perspectives* (1982). An interesting selection of primary-source materials on Islamic thinking in this century.

W. CLEVELAND, *A History of the Modern Middle East*, 3rd ed. (2004). A balanced and well-organized overview of modern Middle Eastern history.

A. DAWISHA, *Arab Nationalism in the Twentieth Century. From Triumph to Despair* (2003). A good overview of the development of Arab nationalism.

S. DERINGIL, *The Well-Protected Domains: Ideology and the Legitimation of Power in the Ottoman Empire, 1876–1909* (1998). An impressive study on nationalism and reform in the Ottoman Empire.

D. F. EICKELMAN, *Knowledge and Power in Morocco: The Education of a Twentieth-Century Notable* (1985). A fascinating study of traditional Islamic education and society in the twentieth century through a social biography of a Moroccan religious scholar and judge.

A. HOURANI, *Arabic Thought in the Liberal Age, 1798–1939* (1967). The standard work, by which all subsequent scholarship on the topic is to be judged.

N. R. KEDDIE, *An Islamic Response to Imperialism* (1968). A brief study of al-Afghani, the great Muslim reformer, with translations of a number of his writings.

B. LEWIS, *The Emergence of Modern Turkey*, 2nd ed. (1968). A concise but thorough history of the creation of the Turkish state, including nineteenth-century background.

J. O. VOLL, *Islam: Continuity and Change in the Modern World* (1982). Chapters 1–6. An interpretive survey of the Islamic world since the eighteenth century. Its emphasis on eighteenth-century reform movements is especially noteworthy.

Africa

A. A. BOAHEN, *Africa Under Colonial Domination, 1880–1935* (1985). Vol. VII of the *UNESCO General History of Africa*. Excellent chapters on various regions of Africa in the period. Chapters 3–10 detail African resistance to European colonial intrusion in diverse regions.

W. CARTEY AND M. KILSON, eds., *The Africa Reader: Colonial Africa* (1970). Original source materials give a vivid picture of African resistance to colonial powers, adaptation to foreign rule, and the emergence of the African masses as a political force.

P. CURTIN, S. FEIERMANN, L. THOMPSON, AND J. VANSINA, *African History* (1978). The relevant portions are Chapters 10–20.

B. DAVIDSON, *Modern Africa: A Social and Political History* (1989). A very useful survey of African history.

J. D. FAGE, *A History of Africa* (1978). The relevant chapters, which give a particularly clear overview of the colonial period, are 12–16.

B. FREUND, *The Making of Contemporary Africa: The Development of African Society Since 1800* (1984). A refreshingly direct synthetic discussion and survey that take an avowedly, but not reductive, materialist approach to interpretation.

T. PAKENHAM, *The Scramble for Africa* (1991). An excellent analysis of the imperialist age in Africa.

A. D. ROBERTS, ed., *The Colonial Moment in Africa: Essays on the Movement of Minds and Materials, 1900–1940* (1986). Chapters from *The Cambridge History of Africa* treating various aspects of the colonial period in Africa, including economics, politics, and religion.

CHAPTER 28

China

P. M. COBLE, *The Shanghai Capitalists and the Nationalist Government, 1927–1937* (1980).

L. E. EASTMAN, *The Abortive Revolution: China Under Nationalist Rule, 1927–1937* (1974).

L. E. EASTMAN, *Seeds of Destruction: Nationalist China in War and Revolution, 1937–1949* (1984).

M. ELVIN AND G. W. SKINNER, *The Chinese City Between Two Worlds* (1974). A study of the late Qing and Republican eras.

J. W. ESHERICK, *The Origins of the Boxer Rebellion* (1987).

S. ETŌ, *China's Republican Revolution* (1994).

J. K. FAIRBANK AND M. GOLDMAN, *China, a New History* (1998). A survey of the entire sweep of Chinese history; especially strong on the modern period.

J. K. FAIRBANK AND D. TWITCHETT, eds., *The Cambridge History of China*. Like the premodern volumes in the same series, the volumes on modern China represent a survey of what is known. Volumes 10–15, which cover the history from the late Qing to the People's Republic, have been published, and the others will be available soon. The series is substantial. Each volume contains a comprehensive bibliography.

J. FITZGERALD, *Awakening China: Politics, Culture, and Class in the Nationalist Revolution* (1996).

C. HAO, *Chinese Intellectuals in Crisis: Search for Order and Meaning, 1890–1911* (1987).

W. C. KIRBY, ed., *State and Economy in Republican China* (2001).

P. A. KUHN, *Rebellion and Its Enemies in Late Imperial China: Militarization and Social Structure, 1796–1864* (1980). A study of how the Confucian gentry saved the Manchu dynasty after the Taiping Rebellion.

P. KUHN, Origins of the Modern Chinese State (2002).

J. LEVENSON, *Liang Ch'i-ch'ao and the Mind of Modern China* (1953). A classic study of a major Chinese reformer and thinker.

LU XUN, *Selected Works* (1960). Novels, stories, and other writings by modern China's greatest writer.

S. NAQUIN, *Peking: Temples and City Life, 1400–1900* (2000).

E. O. REISCHAUER, J. K. FAIRBANK, AND A. M. CRAIG, *East Asia: Tradition and Transformation* (1989). A detailed text on East Asian history. Contains ample chapters on Japan and China and shorter chapters on Korea and Vietnam.

H. Z. SCHIFFRIN, *Sun Yat-sen, Reluctant Revolutionary* (1980). A biography.

B. I. SCHWARTZ, *Chinese Communism and the Rise of Mao* (1951). A classic study of Mao, his thought, and the Chinese Communist Party before 1949.

B. I. SCHWARTZ, *In Search of Wealth and Power: Yen Fu and the West* (1964). A fine study of a late-nineteenth-century thinker who introduced Western ideas into China.

J. D. SPENCE, *The Gate of Heavenly Peace: The Chinese and Their Revolution, 1895–1980* (1981). Historical reflections on twentieth-century China.

J. D. SPENCE, *The Search for Modern China* (1990). A thick text but well written.

M. SZONYI, *Practicing Kinship: Lineage and Descent in Late Imperial China* (2002).

S. Y. TENG AND J. K. FAIRBANK, *China's Response to the West* (1954). A superb collection of translations from Chinese thinkers and political figures, with commentaries.

T. H. WHITE AND A. JACOBY, *Thunder Out of China* (1946). A view of China during World War II by two who were there.

Japan

G. AKITA, *Foundations of Constitutional Government in Modern Japan* (1967). A study of Itō Hirobumi in the political process leading to the Meiji constitution.

G. C. ALLEN, *A Short Economic History of Modern Japan* (1958).

A. E. BARSHAY, *The Social Sciences in Modern Japan: the Marxian and Modernist Traditions* (2004). Different interpretations of history.

J. R. BARTHOLOMEW, *The Formation of Science in Japan* (1989). The pioneering English-language work on the subject.

W. G. BEASLEY, *Japanese Imperialism, 1894–1945* (1987). Excellent short book on subject.

G. M. BERGER, *Parties Out of Power in Japan, 1931–1941* (1977). An analysis of the condition of political parties during the militarist era.

G.L. BERNSTEIN, *Recreating Japanese Women, 1600–1945* (1991).

The Cambridge History of Japan, The Nineteenth Century, M.B. Jansen, ed. (1989); *The Twentieth Century*, P. Duus, ed. (1988). Multi-author works.

A. M. CRAIG, *Chōshū in the Meiji Restoration* (2000). A study of the Chōshū domain, a Prussia of Japan, during the period 1840–1868.

A. M. CRAIG AND D. H. SHIVELY, eds., *Personality in Japanese History* (1970). An attempt to gauge the role of individuals and their personalities as factors explaining history.

P. DUUS, *Party Rivalry and Political Change in Taisho Japan* (1968). A study of political change in Japan during the 1910s and 1920s.

P. DUUS, *The Abacus and the Sword, the Japanese Penetration of Korea, 1895–1910* (1995). A thoughtful analysis.

S. ERICSON, *The Sound of the Whistle: Railroads and the State in Meiji Japan* (1996). An economic and social history of railroads, an engine of growth and popular symbol.

Y. FUKUZAWA, *Autobiography* (1966). Japan's leading nineteenth-century thinker tells of his life and of the birth of modern Japan.

A. GARON, *The State and Labor in Modern Japan* (1987). A fine study of the subject.

C. N. GLUCK, *Japan's Modern Myths: Ideology in the Late Meiji Period* (1988). A brilliant study of the complex weave of late Meiji thought.

A. GORDON, *The Evolution of Labor Relations in Japan: Heavy Industry, 1853–1955* (1985). A seminal work.

B. R. HACKETT, *Yamagata Aritomo in the Rise of Modern Japan, 1932–1922* (1973). History as seen through the biography of a central figure.

I. HALL, *Mori Arinori* (1973). A biography of Japan's first minister of education.

T. R. H. HAVENS, *The Valley of Darkness: The Japanese People and World War II* (1978). Wartime society.

C. IRIYE, *After Imperialism: The Search for a New Order in the Far East, 1921–1931* (1965). (Also see other studies by this author.)

D. M. B. JANSEN AND G. ROZMAN, eds., *Japan in Transition from Tokugawa to Meiji* (1986). Contains fine essays.

W. JOHNSTON, *The Modern Epidemic: A History of Tuberculosis in Japan* (1995). A social history of a disease.

E. KEENE, Ed., *Modern Japanese Literature, An Anthology* (1960). A collection of modern Japanese short stories and excerpts from novels.

F. Y.T. MATSUSAKA, *The Making of Japanese Manchuria, 1904–1932* (2001). On railroad strategies in empire building.

J. W. MORLEY, ed., *The China Quagmire* (1983). A study of Japan's expansion on the continent between 1933 and 1941. (For diplomatic history, see also the many other works by this author.)

R. H. MYERS AND M. R. PEATTIE, eds., *The Japanese Colonial Empire, 1895–1945* (1984).

T. NAJITA, *Hara Kei in the Politics of Compromise, 1905–1915* (1967). A study of one of Japan's greatest party leaders.

K. OHKAWA AND H. ROSOVSKY, *Japanese Economic Growth: Trend Acceleration in the Twentieth Century* (1973).

M. RAVINA, *The Last Samurai: The Life and Battles of Saigo Takamori* (2004). Unlike the movie, this account of the Satsuma uprising is historical.

G. SHIBA, *Remembering Aizu* (1999). A stirring autobiographical account of a samurai youth whose domain lost in the Meiji Restoration.

K. SMITH, *A Time of Crisis: The Great Depression and Rural Revitalization* (2001). An intellectual history of village movements during the 1930s.

J. J. STEPHAN, *Hawaii Under the Rising Sun* (1984). Japan's plans for rule in Hawaii.

R. H. SPECTOR, *Eagle Against the Sun: The American War with Japan* (1985). A narrative of World War II in the Pacific.

E. P. TSURUMI, *Factory Girls: Women in the Thread Mills of Meiji Japan* (1990). A sympathetic analysis of the key component of the Meiji labor force.

W. WRAY, *Mitsubishi and the N. Y. K., 1870–1914* (1984). The growth of a shipping *zaibatsu*, with analysis of business strategies, the role of government and imperialist involvements.

CHAPTER 29

L. ALBERTINI, *The Origins of the War of 1914*, 3 vols. (1952, 1957). Discursive but invaluable.

V. R. BERGHAHN, *Germany and the Approach of War in 1914* (1973). A work similar in spirit to both of Fischer's (see below) but stressing the importance of Germany's naval program.

R. BOSWORTH, *Italy and the Approach of the First World War* (1983). A fine analysis of Italian policy.

S. B. FAY, *The Origins of the World War*, 2 vols. (1928). The most influential of the revisionist accounts.

F. FISCHER, *Germany's Aims in the First World War* (1967). An influential interpretation that stirred a great controversy in Germany and around the world by emphasizing Germany's role in bringing on the war.

F. FISCHER, *War of Illusions* (1975). A long and diffuse book that tries to connect German responsibility for the war with internal social, economic, and political developments.

D. FROMKIN, *Europe's Last Summer: Who Started the Great War in 1914?* (2004). A lively account that fixes on the final crisis in July 1914.

J. N. HORNE, *Labour at War: France and Britain, 1914–1918* (1991). An examination of a major issue on the home fronts.

J. JOLL, *The Origins of the First World War* (1984). A brief but thoughtful analysis.

P. KENNEDY, *The Rise of the Anglo-German Antagonism 1860–1914* (1980). An unusual and thorough analysis of the political, economic, and cultural roots of important diplomatic developments.

W. L. LANGER, *European Alliances and Alignments*, 2nd ed. (1966). A splendid diplomatic history of the years 1871–1890.

W. L. LANGER, *The Diplomacy of Imperialism* (1935). A continuation of the previous study for the years 1890–1902.

D. C. B. LIEVEN, *Russia and the Origins of the First World War* (1983). A good account of the forces that shaped Russian policy.

A. MOMBAUER, *The Origins of the First World War. Controversies and Consensus* (2002). A fascinating survey of the debate over the decades and the current state of the question.

R. PIPES, *A Concise History of the Russian Revolution* (1996). A one-volume version of a scholarly masterpiece.

Z. STEINER, *Britain and the Origins of the First World War* (1977). A perceptive and informed account of the way British foreign policy was made in the years before the war.

H. STRACHAN, *The First World War* (2004). A fine one-volume account of the war.

A. J. P. TAYLOR, *The Struggle for Mastery in Europe, 1848–1918* (1954). Clever but controversial.

S. R. WILLIAMSON, JR., *Austria-Hungary and the Origins of the First World War* (1991). A valuable study of a complex subject.

CHAPTER 30

W. S. ALLEN, *The Nazi Seizure of Power: The Experience of a Single German Town, 1930–1935*, rev. ed. (1984). A classic treatment of Nazism in a microcosmic setting.

J. BARNARD, *Walter Reuther and the Rise of the Auto Workers* (1983). A major introduction to the new American unions of the 1930s.

K. D. BRACHER, *The German Dictatorship* (1970). A comprehensive treatment of both the origins and the functioning of the Nazi movement and government.

A. BULLOCK, *Hitler: A Study in Tyranny*, rev. ed. (1964). The best biography.

M. BURLEIGH AND W. WIPPERMAN, *The Racial State: Germany 1933–1945* (1991). Emphasizes the manner in which racial theory influenced numerous areas of policy.

R. CONQUEST, *The Great Terror: Stalin's Purges of the Thirties* (1968). The best treatment of the subject to this date.

G. CRAIG, *Germany, 1866–1945* (1978). A major survey.

I. DEUTSCHER, *The Prophet Armed* (1954), *The Prophet Unarmed* (1959), and *The Prophet Outcast* (1963). Remains the major biography of Trotsky.

I. DEUTSCHER, *Stalin: A Political Biography*, 2nd ed. (1967). The best biography in English.

B. EICHENGREEN, *Golden Fetters: The Gold Standard and the Great Depression, 1919–1939* (1992). A remarkable study of the role of the gold standard in the economic policies of the interwar years.

E. EYCK, *A History of the Weimar Republic*, 2 vols. (trans. 1963). The story as narrated by a liberal.

M. S. FAUSOLD, *The Presidency of Herbert Hoover* (1985). An important treatment.

G. FELDMAN, *The Great Disorder: Politics, Economics, and Society in the German Inflation, 1914–1924* (1993). The best work on the subject.

S. FITZPATRICK, *Stalin's Peasants: Resistance and Survival in the Russian Village After Collectivization* (1994). A pioneering study.

P. FUSSELL, *The Great War and Modern Memory* (1975). A brilliant account of the literature arising from World War I during the 1920s.

J. K. GALBRAITH, *The Great Crash* (1979). A well-known account by a leading economist.

R. GELLATELY, *The Gestapo and German Society: Enforcing Racial Policy, 1933–1945* (1990). A discussion of how the police state supported Nazi racial policies.

H. J. GORDON, *Hitler and the Beer Hall Putsch* (1972). An excellent account of the event and the political situation in the early Weimar Republic.

R. HAMILTON, *Who Voted for Hitler?* (1982). An examination of voting patterns and sources of Nazi support.

J. HELD, ed., *The Columbia History of Eastern Europe in the Twentieth Century* (1992). Individual essays on each country.

P. KENEZ, *The Birth of the Propaganda State: Soviet Methods of Mass Mobilization, 1917–1929* (1985). An examination of the manner in which the Communist government inculcated popular support.

B. KENT, *The Spoils of War: The Politics, Economics, and Diplomacy of Reparations, 1918–1932* (1993). A comprehensive account of the intricacies of the reparations problem of the 1920s.

D. LANDES, *The Unbound Prometheus: Technological Change and Industrial Development in Western Europe from 1750 to the Present* (1969). Includes an excellent analysis of both the Great Depression and the few areas of economic growth.

B. LINCOLN, *Red Victory: A History of the Russian Civil War* (1989). An excellent narrative account.

M. MCAULEY, *Bread and Justice: State and Society in Petrograd, 1917–1922* (1991). A study that examines the impact of the Russian Revolution and Leninist policies on a major Russian city.

D. J. K. PEUKERT, *Inside Nazi Germany: Conformity, Opposition, and Racism in Everyday Life* (1987). An excellent discussion of life under Nazi rule.

R. PIPES, *The Unknown Lenin: From the Secret Archives* (1996). A collection of previously unpublished documents that indicated the repressive character of Lenin's government.

P. PULZER, *Jews and the German State: The Political History of a Minority, 1848–1933* (1992). A detailed history by a major historian of European minorities.

L. J. RUPP, *Mobilizing Women for War: German and America Propaganda, 1939–1945* (1978). Although concentrating on a later period, it includes an excellent discussion of general Nazi attitudes toward women.

A. M. SCHLESINGER, JR., *The Age of Roosevelt*, 3 vols. (1957–1960). The most important overview.

D. M. SMITH, *Mussolini's Roman Empire* (1976). A general description of the Fascist regime in Italy.

D. M. SMITH, *Italy and Its Monarchy* (1989). A major treatment of an important neglected subject.

A. SOLZHENITSYN, *The Gulag Archipelago*, 3 vols. (1974–1979). A major examination of the labor camps under Stalin by one of the most important contemporary Russian writers.

R. J. SONTAG, *A Broken World, 1919–1939* (1971). An exceptionally thoughtful and well-organized survey.

A. J. P. TAYLOR, *English History, 1914–1945* (1965). Lively and opinionated.

H. A. TURNER JR., *German Big Business and the Rise of Hitler* (1985). An important major study of the subject.

H. A. TURNER JR., *Hitler's Thirty Days to Power* (1996). A narrative of the events leading directly to the Nazi seizure of power.

L. YAHIL, *The Holocaust: The Fate of European Jewry, 1932–1945* (1990). A major study of this fundamental subject in twentieth-century history.

CHAPTER 31

A. ADAMTHWAITE, *France and the Coming of the Second World War, 1936–1939* (1977). A careful account making good use of the French archives.

E. R. BECK, *Under the Bombs: The German Home Front, 1942–1945* (1986). An interesting examination of a generally unstudied subject.

R. S. BOTWINICK, *A History of the Holocaust*, 2nd ed., 2002. A brief but broad and useful account of the causes, character and results of the Holocaust.

A. BULLOCK, *Hitler: A Study in Tyranny*, rev. ed. (1964). A brilliant biography.

W. S. CHURCHILL, *The Second World War*, 6 vols. (1948–1954). The memoirs of the great British leader.

A. CROZIER, *The Causes of the Second World War*, 1997. An examination of what brought on the war.

R. B. FRANK, *Downfall: The End of the Imperial Japanese Empire*, 1998. A thorough, well-documented account of the last months of the Japanese empire and the reasons for its surrender.

J. L. GADDIS, *We Now Know: Rethinking Cold War History* (1998). A fine account of the early years of the Cold War making use of new evidence emerging since the collapse of the Soviet Union.

J. L. GADDIS, P. H. GORDON, E. MAY, eds., *Cold War Statesmen Confront the Bomb: Nuclear diplomacy Since 1945* (1999). A collection of essays discussing the effect of atomic and nuclear weapons on diplomacy since WW II.

M. GILBERT, *The Holocaust: A History of the Jews of Europe During the Second World War* (1985). The best and most comprehensive treatment.

A. IRIYE, *Pearl Harbor and the Coming of the Pacific War* (1999). Essays on how the Pacific war came about, including a selection of documents.

J. KEEGAN, *The Second World War* (1990). A lively and penetrating account by a master military historian.

I. KERSHAW, *Hitler: 1889–1936: Hubris* (1999) and *Hitler: 1936–1945: Nemesis* (2001). An outstanding two-volume biography.

W. F. KIMBALL, *Forged in War: Roosevelt, Churchill, and the Second World War*, (1998). A study of the collaboration between the two great leaders of the West based on a thorough knowledge of their correspondence.

W. MURRAY AND A. R. MILLETT, *A War to be Won: Fighting the Second World War*, (2000). A splendid account of the military operations in the war.

R. OVERY, *Why the Allies Won* (1997). An anlysis of the reasons for the victory of the Allies with special emphasis on technology.

N. RICH, *Hitler War Aims*, 2 vols. (1973–1974). The best study of the subject in English.

H. THOMAS, *The Spanish Civil War*, 3rd ed. (1986). The best account in English.

P. WANDYCZ, *The Twilight of French Eastern Alliances, 1926–1936* (1988). A well-documented account of the diplomacy of central and eastern Europe in a crucial period.

G. L. WEINBERG, *A World at Arms: A Global History of World War II* (1994). A thorough and excellent narrative account.

CHAPTER 32

B. S. ANDERSON AND J. P. PINSSER, *A History of Their Own: Women in Europe from Prehistory to the Present*, Vol. 2 (1988). A broad-ranging survey.

R. BERNSTEIN, *Out of the Blue: The Story of September 11, 2001 from Jihad to Ground Zero* (2002). An excellent account by a gifted journalist.

A. BROWN, *The Gorbachev Factor* (1996). An important commentary by an English observer.

D. CALLEO, *Rethinking Europe's Future* (2003) A daring book by an experienced commentator.

J. L. GADDIS, *What We Know Now* (1997). Examines the Cold War in light of newly released documents.

D. J. GARROW, *Bearing the Cross: Martin Luther King, Jr. and the Southern Leadership Conference 1955–1968* (1986). The best work on the subject.

W. HITCHCOCK, *Struggle for Europe: The Turbulent History of a Divided Continent, 1945–2002* (2003). The best overall narrative now available

D. KEARNS, *Lyndon Johnson and the American Dream* (1976). A useful biography.

J. KEEP, *The Last of the Empires: A History of the Soviet Union, 1956–1991* (1995). A clear narrative.

M. MANDELBAUM, *The Ideas That Conquered the World: Peace, Democracy, and Free Markets* (2002). An important analysis by a major commentator on international affairs.

J. MANN, *The Rise of the Vulcans: The History of Bush's War Cabinet* (2004). An account of the major foreign policy advisors behind the invasion of Iraq.

R. MANN, *A Grand Delusion: America's Descent into Vietnam* (2001). The best recent narrative.

J. McCORMICK, *Understanding the European Union: A Concise Introduction* (2002) Outlines the major features.

N. NAIMARK, *Fires of Hatred: Ethnic Cleansing in Twentieth-Century Europe* (2002). A remarkably sensitive treatment of a tragic subject.

R. SAWKA AND ANNE STEVENS, eds., *Contemporary Europe* (2000). A collection of essays on major topics.

G. STOKES, ed., *From Stalinism to Pluralism: A Documentary History of Eastern Europe Since 1945* (1996). An important collection of documents that are not easily accessible elsewhere.

M. WALKER, *The Cold War and the Making of the Modern World* (1994). A major survey.

CHAPTER 33

China

R. BAUM, *Burying Mao: Chinese Politics in the Age of Deng Xiaoping* (1996).

A. CHAN, R. MADSEN, J. UNGER, *Chen Village under Mao and Deng* (1992).

J. CHANG, *Wild Swans: Three Daughters of China* (1991). An intimate look at recent Chinese society through three generations of women. Immensely readable.

J. FENG, *Ten Years of Madness: Oral Histories of China's Cultural Revolution* (1996).

J. FEWSMITH, *China Since Tiananmen: The Politics of Transition* (2001). Focus is on the rise to power of Jiang Zemin and Chinese politics during the nineties.

B. M. FROLIC, *Mao's People: Sixteen Portraits of Life in Revolutionary China* (1987).

T. GOLD, *State and Society in the Taiwan Miracle* (1986). The story of economic growth in postwar Taiwan.

M. GOLDMAN, *Sowing the Seeds of Democracy in China: Political Reform in the Deng Xiaoping Era* (1994).

A. IRIYE, *China and Japan in the Global Setting* (1992).

D. M. LAMPTON, *Same Bed, Different Dreams: Managing U.S.–China Relations, 1989–2000* (2001).

H. LIANG, *Son of the Revolution* (1983). An autobiographical account of a young man growing up in Mao's China.

K. LIEBERTHAL, *Governing China, from Revolution Through Reform* (2004).

B. LIU, *People or Monsters? and Other Stories and Reportage from China After Mao* (1983). Literary reflections on China.

R. MacFARQUHAR AND J. K. FAIRBANK, eds., *The Cambridge History of China*, Vol. 14, *Emergence of Revolutionary China* (1987), and Vol. 15, *Revolutions Within the Chinese Revolution, 1966–1982* (1991).

L. PAN, *Sons of the Yellow Emperor: A History of the Chinese Diaspora* (1990). A pioneer study that treats not only Southeast Asia but the rest of the world as well.

M. R. RISTAINO, *Port of Last Resort: The Diaspora Communities of Shanghai* (2001).

T. SAICH, *Governance and Politics of China* (2004).

H. WANG, *China's New Order* (2003). Translation of a work by a Qinghua University professor, a liberal within the boundaries of what is permissable in China.

G. WHITE, ed., *In Search of Civil Society: Market Reform and Social Change in Contemporary China* (1996).

M. WOLF, *Revolution Postponed: Women in Contemporary China* (1985).

ZHANG X. AND SANG Y., *Chinese Lives: An Oral History of Contemporary China* (1987).

Japan

G. L. BERNSTEIN, *Haruko's World: A Japanese Farm Woman and Her Community* (1983). A study of the changing life of a village woman in postwar Japan.

T. BESTOR, *Neighborhood Tokyo* (1989). A portrait of contemporary urban life in Japan.

G. L. CURTIS, *The Logic of Japanese Politics: Leaders, Institutions, and the Limits of Change* (1999).

G. L. CURTIS, *Policymaking in Japan: Defining the Role of Politicians* (2002).

M. H. CUSUMANO, *The Japanese Automobile Industry* (1985). A neat study of the postwar business strategies of Toyota and Nissan.

R. P. DORE, *City Life in Japan* (1999). A classic, reissued.

R. P. DORE, *Land Reform in Japan* (1959). Another classic.

S. GARON, *Molding Japanese Minds: The State in Everyday Life* (1997).

S. M. GARON, *The Evolution of Civil Society from Meiji to Heisei* (2002). That is to say, from the mid–nineteenth century to the present day.

A. GORDON, ed., *Postwar Japan as History* (1993).

H. HIBBETT, ed., *Contemporary Japanese Literature: An Anthology of Fiction, Film, and Other Writing Since 1945* (1977). Translations of postwar short stories.

Y. KAWABATA, *The Sound of the Mountain* (1970). Sensitive, moving novel by Nobel author.

J. NATHAN, *Sony, the Private Life* (1999). A lively account of the human side of growth in the Sony Corporation.

D. OKIMOTO, *Between MITI and the Market* (1989). A discussion of the respective roles of government and private enterprise in Japan's postwar growth.

S. PHARR, *Losing Face: Status Politics in Japan* (1996).

E. F. VOGEL, *Japan as Number One: Lessons for America* (1979). While dated and somewhat sanguine, this remains an insightful classic.

Korea and Vietnam

B. CUMINGS, *Korea, The Unknown War* (1988).

B. CUMINGS, *The Origins of the Korean War* (Vol. 1, 1981; Vol. 2, 1991).

B. CUMINGS, *The Two Koreas: On the Road to Reunification?* (1990).

C. J. ECKERT, *Korea Old and New, A History* (1990). The best short history of Korea, with extensive coverage of the postwar era.

C. J. ECKERT, *Offspring of Empire: The Koch'ang Kims and the Colonial Origins of Korean Capitalism, 1876–1945* (1991).

G. M. T. KAHIN, *Intervention: How America Became Involved in Vietnam* (1986).

S. KARNOW, *Vietnam: A History*. rev. ed. (1996).

L. KENDALL, *Shamans, Housewives, and Other Restless Spirits: Women in Korean Ritual and Life* (1985).

K. B. LEE, *A New History of Korea* (1984). A translation by E. Wagner and others of an outstanding Korean work covering the full sweep of Korean history.

T. LI, *Nguyen Cochinchina: South Vietnam in the Seventeenth and Eighteenth Centuries* (1998).

D. MARR, *Vietnam 1945: The Quest for Power* (1995).

C. W. SORENSEN, *Over the Mountains Are Mountains* (1988). How peasant households in Korea adapted to rapid industrialization.

A. WOODSIDE, *Vietnam and the Chinese Model* (1988). Provides the background for Vietnam's relationship to China.

CHAPTER 34

Latin America

P. BAKEWELL, *A History of Latin America: c. 1450 to the Present* (2003). An up-to-date survey.

A. CHOMSKY et al., *The Cuba Reader: History, Culture, Politics* (2004). Very useful, broad-ranging anthology.

J. DOMINGUEZ AND M. SHIFTER, *Contructing Democratic Governance in Latin America* (2003). Contains individual country studies.

G. JOSEPH et al. , *The Mexico Reader: History, Culture, Politics* (2003). Excellent introduction to major issues.

P. LOWDEN, *Moral Opposition to Authoritarian Rule in Chile* (1996). A discussion of Chilean politics from the standpoint of human rights.

J. PRESTON AND S. DILLON, *Opening Mexico: The Making of a Democracy* (2004). Excellent analysis of recent developments in Mexico.

H. WIRARDA, *Democracy and Its Discontents: Development, Interdependence, and U.S. Policy in Latin America* (1995). A useful overview.

Africa

B. DAVIDSON, *Let Freedom Come* (1978). Remains a thought commentary of African independence.

R. W. JULY, *A History of the African People*, 5th ed. (1995). Provides a careful and clear survey of post–World War I history and consideration of nationalism.

J. HERBST, *States and Power in Africa* (2000). Relates current issues of African state-building to those before to the colonial era.

J. H. LATHAM, *Africa, Asia, and South America Since 1800: A Bibliographic Guide* (1995). A valuable tool for finding materials on the topics in this chapter.

N. MANDELA, *Long Walk to Freedom: The Autobiography of Nelson Mandela* (1995). Autobiography of the African leader who transformed South Africa.

L. THOMPSON, *A History of South Africa* (2001). The best survey.

N. VAN DE WALLE, *African Economies and the Politics of Permanent Crisis, 1979–1999* (2001). Exploration of difficulties of African economic development.

India and Pakistan

O. B. JONES, *Pakistan: Eye of the Storm* (2003). Best recent introduction.

R. RASHID, *Taliban: Militant Islam, Oil and Fundamentalism in Central Asia* (2001). Analysis of radical Isalmist regime in Afghanistan.

R. W. STERN, *Changing India: Bourgeois Revolution on the Subcontinent* (2003). Overview of forces now changing Indian society.

S. WOLPERT, *A New History of India* (2003). The closing chapters of this fine survey history are particularly helpful in orienting the reader in postwar Indian history until the mid-1980s.

Islam and the Middle East

A. AHMED, *Discovering Islam. Making Sense of Muslim Hisotry and Society,* rev. ed. (2003). An excellent and readable overivew of Islamic–Western relations.

J. ESPOSITO, *The Islamic Threat: Myth or Reality,* 2nd ed. (1992). A useful corrective to some of the polemics against Islam and Muslims today.

J. J. ESPOSITO, ed., *The Oxford Encyclopedia of Islam* (1999). A thematic survey of Islamic history, particularly strong in the Modern Era.

D. FROMKIN, *A Peace to End All Peace: The Fall of the Ottoman Empire and the Creation of the Modern Middle East* (2001). Very good on the impact of World War I on the region.

G. FULLER, *The Future of Political Islam* (2003). A very good overview of Islamist ideology by a former CIA staff member.

J. KEAY, *Sowing the Wind: The Seeds of Conflict in theMiddle East* (2003). A balanced account.

N. R. KEDDIE, *Modern Iran. Roots and Results of Revolution* (2003). Chapters 6–12 focus on Iran from 1941 through the first years of the 1978 revolution and provide a solid overview of history in this era.

G. KEPEL, *Jihad: The Trail of Political Islam* (2002). An extensive treatment by a leading French scholar of the subject.

Credits

Chapter 13, page 349: Bodleian Library, University of Oxford.

Chapter 14, page 373: Getty Images, Inc. - Photodisc.

Chapter 15, page 401: Musee Conde, Chantilly.

Part 4, page 432, top to bottom, left to right: Emanuel de Witte, "Interior of the Portugese Synagogue on Amsterdam," 1680. Oil on canvas, 43-1/2 × 39″ (110.5 × 99.1 cm). © Rijksmuseum, Amsterdam; Library of Congress; The Granger Collection.

Part 4, page 433, top to bottom, left to right: Pawel Wojcik © Dorling Kindersley; Dorota and Mariusz Jarymowicz © Dorling Kindersley; Royal Ontario Museum/Corbis; Corbis/Bettmann.

Part 4 Timeline, page 434, top to bottom, left to right: Elizabeth I (1558-1603) standing on a map of England in 1592. An astute politician in both foreign and domestic policy, Elizabeth was perhaps the most successful ruler of the sixteenth century. By courtesy of the National Portrait Gallery, London; Sultan Muhammad (active ca. 1501-1545), "Allegory of Worldly and Otherworldly Drunkenness". Leaf from a manuscript of a "Divan" by Hafiz, folio 137r. Opaque watercolor, ink and gold on paper. 11 3/8 × 8 1/2 in. (28.9 × 21.6 cm). Promised Gift of Mr. and Mrs. Stuart Cary Welch, Jr. in honor of the students of Harvard University and Radcliffe College. Partially owned by The Metropolitan Museum of Art and The Arthur M. Sackler Museum, Harvard University, 1988. Copyright 1989, Metropolitan Museum of Art; Library of Congress; The Bridgeman Art Library International Ltd; © Archivo Iconografico, S. A./Corbis.

Part 4 Timeline, page 435, top to bottom, left to right: Bridgeman-Giraudon/Art Resource, NY; Francis Wheatley (RA) (1747-1801) "Evening", signed and dated 1799, oil on canvas, 17 1/2 × 21 1/2 in. (44.5 × 54.5 cm), Yale Center for British Art, Paul Mellon Collection/Bridgeman Art Library (B1977.14.118); Getty Images Inc. - Stone Allstock; Japan Airlines Photo; Unidentified Artist. The Emperor Ch'ien Lung (1736-1795) as a Young Man. Colors on silk. H. 63-1/2 in. W. 30-1/2 in. © The Metropolitan Museum of Art, Rogers Fund, 1942. (42.141.8). Photograph © 1980 The Metropolitan Museum of Art; Embassy of Kenya; © Hulton-Deutsch Collection/CORBIS.

Chapter 16, page 437: The Granger Collection.

Page 474 (top): Getty Images, Inc.- Photodisc.

Chapter 17, page 477: Max Alexander © Dorling Kindersley

Chapter 18, page 501: North Wind Picture Archives.

Chapter 19, page 529: Tai Chin, "Fisherman on an Autumn River", (1390-1460). Painting. Ink and color on paper. 18-1/8 × 291-1/4 in. (46 × 740 cm). Courtesy of the Freer Gallery of Art, Smithsonian Institution, Washington, D.C.

Chapter 20, page 571: The Granger Collection.

Chapter 21, page 609: Copyright The British Museum.

Part 5, page 632, top to bottom, left to right: © The Wallace Collection, London; © Dorling Kindersley, Courtesy of the Museu da Cidade, Lisbon.

Part 5, page 633, top to bottom, left to right: © James A. Sugar/CORBIS; © The Wallace Collection, London; Francisco de Goya, "Los fusilamientos del 3 de Mayo, 1808" 1814. Oil on canvas, 8′6″ × 11′4″. © Museo Nacional del Prado, Madrid; Antoine Jean Gros (1771-1835), "Napoleon in the Plague House at Jaffa". 1804. Oil on Canvas. Louvre, Paris, France. Reunion des Musees Nationaux/Art Resource, NY.

Part 5 Timeline, page 634, top to bottom, left to right: Anonymous, France, 18th century, "Seige of the Bastille, 14 July, 1789." Obligatory mention of the following: Musee de la Ville de Paris, Musee Carnavalet, Paris, France. Bridgeman-Giraudon/Art Resource, NY; Bildarchiv Preubischer Kulturbesitz; Corbis/Bettmann; Bettmann/Corbis; The Granger Collection, New York.

Part 5 timeline, page 635, top to bottom, left to right: "Col. James Todd on elephant Indian painting" ca. 1880. E.T. Archive, Victoria and Albert Museum; © Hulton-Deutsch Collection/CORBIS; © Christie's Images/Corbis.

Chapter 22, page 637: Réunion des Musées Nationaux/Art Resource, NY.

Chapter 23, page 665: Erich Lessing/Art Resource, NY.

Chapter 24, page 699: Museum of the City of New York/Hulton/Archive.

Part 6, page 732, top to bottom, left to right: Bridgeman Art Library, London/SuperStock; Linda Whitwam © Dorling Kindersley.

Part 6, page 733, top to bottom, left to right: © Dorling Kindersley, Courtesy of the Selimiye Barracks / Florence Nightingale Museum, Istanbul; Mita Arts Gallery, Tokyo; Ray Moller/Dorling Kindersley © Royal Pavilion Museum and Art Galleries, Brighton; Woodfin Camp & Associates.

Part 6 Timeline, page 734, top to bottom, left to right: Bildarchiv Preubischer Kulturbesitz; Bildarchiv Preubischer Kulturbesitz; Corbis/Bettmann; © Hulton-Deutsch Collection/CORBIS; Library of Congress.

Part 6 Timeline, page 735, top to bottom, left to right: Bildarchiv Preubischer Kulturbesitz; Shosai Ginko (Japanese, act. 1874-1897), View of the Issuance of the State Constitution in the State Chamber of the New Imperial Palace, March 2, 1889 (Meiji 22), Ink and color on paper, 14 1/8 × 28 3/8 in. The Metropolitan Museum of Art, Gift of Lincoln Kirstein, 1959 (JP3233-3235) Photograph © The Metropolitan Museum of Art; Corbis/Bettmann; The Granger Collection.

Chapter 25, page 737: Reunion des Musees Nationaux/Art Resource, NY.

Chapter 26, page 773: Diego Rivera (1866-1957), "The Flower Carrier (formerly "The Flower Vendor". 1935.Oil and tempera on Masonite. 48 in. × 47 3/4 in. (121.92 cm × 121.29 cm) San Francisco Museum of Modern Art. Albert M. Bender Collection, Gift of Albert M. Bender in memory of Caroline Walter. © Banco de Mexico Diego Rivera & Frida Kahlo Museums Trust. Av. Cinco de Mayo No. 2, Col. Centro, Del. Cuauhtemoc 06059, Mexico, D.F. Reproduction authorized by the Instituto Nacional de Bellas Artes y Literatura.

Chapter 27, page 799: Getty Images Inc. - Hulton Archive Photos.

Page 828 (top): © Werner Forman/Art Resource, NY.

Chapter 28, page 831: Courtesy United States Naval Academy Museum

Part 7, page 866, top to bottom, left to right: Peter Wilson © Dorling Kindersley; Corbis/Bettmann; Andy Crawford/Dorling Kindersley © Imperial War Museum, London.

Part 7, page 867, top to bottom, left to right: Andy Crawford / Dorling Kindersley © Imperial War Museum, London; Matthew Ward © Dorling Kindersley; Aurora & Quanta Productions Inc; Art Resource, N.Y.

Part 7 Timeline, page 868, top to bottom, left to right: The Granger Collection; Pablo Picasso , 'Guernica' 1937, Oil on canvas.

11′5 1/2 × 25′5 3/4. Museo Nacional Centro de Arte Reina Sofia/ © 2004 Estate of Pablo Picasso/Artists Rights Society (ARS), New York; Getty Images Inc. - Hulton Archive Photos; Corbis/Bettmann.

Part 7 Timeline, page 869, top to bottom, left to right: Corbis/Sygma; Corbis/Bettmann; Corbis/Bettmann; Getty Images Inc. - Hulton Archive Photos; AP/Wide World Photos.

Chapter 29, page 871: Corbis/Bettmann.

Chapter 30, page 901 Underwood & Underwood/Corbis.

Chapter 31, page 929: Corbis/Bettmann.

Chapter 32, page 959: Peter Arnold, Inc.

Chapter 33, page 993: Getty Images Inc. - Stone Allstock.

Chapter 34, page 1023: AP Wide World Photos.

Index

World History Documents CD-ROM

SINGLE PC LICENSE AGREEMENT AND LIMITED WARRANTY